For Students

MEANINGFUL HELP AND FEEDBACK

- Personalized interactive learning aids for point-of-use help and immediate feedback. These learning aids include:

  - "Help Me Solve This" walks students through solving an algorithmic version of the questions they are working, with additional detailed tutorial reminders. These informational cues assist the students and help them understand concepts and mechanics.

  - "Accounting Simplified" videos give students a 3- to 5-minute lesson on concepts. Our new videos are engaging whiteboard animations that help illustrate concepts for students.

  - eText links students directly to the concept covered in the problem they are working on.

  - Homework and practice exercises with additional algorithmically generated problems for further practice and mastery.

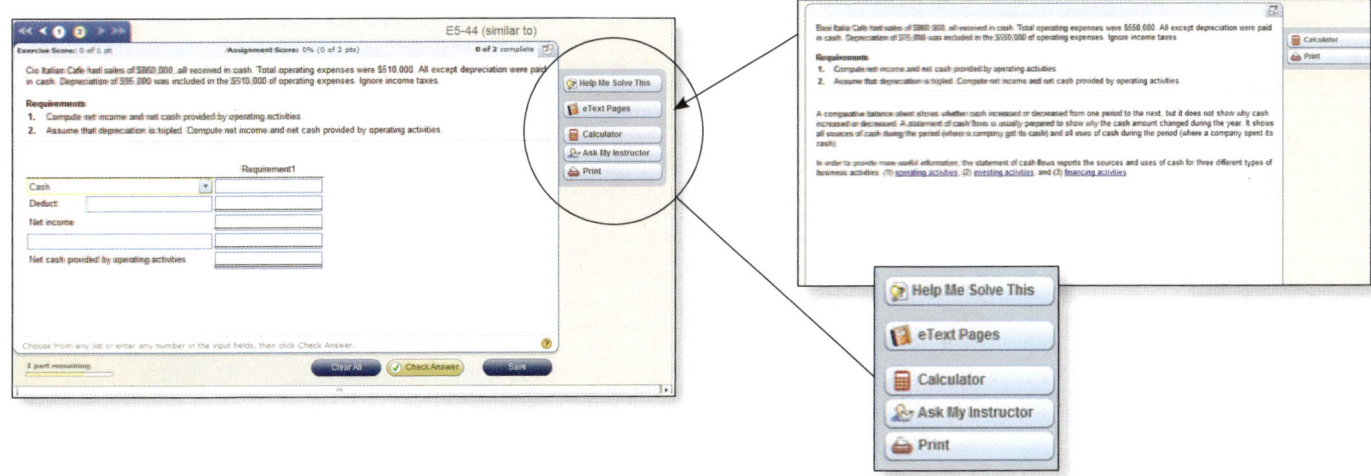

PERSONALIZED STUDY PATH

- Assists students in monitoring their own progress by offering them a customized study plan based on Homework, Quiz, and Test results.

- Includes regenerated exercises with unlimited practice and the opportunity to prove mastery through Quizzes on recommended learning objectives.

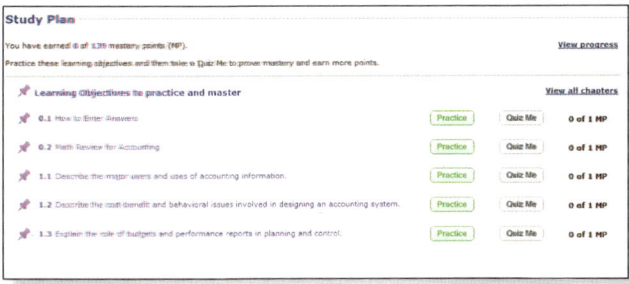

ELEVENTH EDITION

Introduction to

FINANCIAL ACCOUNTING

Charles T. Horngren
Stanford University

Gary L. Sundem
University of Washington

John A. Elliott
University of Connecticut

Donna R. Philbrick
Portland State University

Boston Columbus Indianapolis New York San Francisco Upper Saddle River
Amsterdam Cape Town Dubai London Madrid Milan Munich Paris Montréal Toronto
Delhi Mexico City São Paulo Sydney Hong Kong Seoul Singapore Taipei Tokyo

To Chuck Horngren whose contributions over many years have made this textbook what it is.

Editor in Chief: Donna Battista
Acquisitions Editor: Lacey Vitetta
Director of Editorial Services: Ashley Santora
Senior Editorial Project Manager: Karen Kirincich
Marketing Manager: Alison Haskins
Marketing Assistant: Kimberly Lovato
Senior Production Project Manager: Roberta Sherman

Manufacturing Buyer: Carol Melville
Art Director: Anthony Gemmellaro
Interior Design: Lisa Delgado/Emily Friel, Integra
Cover Design: Anthony Gemmellaro
Cover Photos: Ryan McVay/Stone/Getty Images; Mary Rice/Shutterstock
Art Studio: GEX Publishing Services
Compositor: GEX Publishing Services

Credits and acknowledgments borrowed from other sources and reproduced, with permission, in this textbook appear on appropriate page within text (or on page PC1).

Library of Congress Cataloging-in-Publication Data
Horngren, Charles T.
  Introduction to financial accounting / Charles T. Horngren, Gary L. Sundem, John A. Elliott,
Donna R. Philbrick. -- Eleventh edition.
    pages cm
  Includes index.
  ISBN 978-0-13-325103-6 (casebound)
1. Accounting. I. Title.
  HF5635.H813 2014
  657--dc23
                        2012047453

ISBN-13: 978-0-13-325103-6
ISBN-10: 0-13-325103-9

About the Authors

Charles T. Horngren passed away in the midst of this current revision of *Introduction to Financial Accounting*. He was the Edmund W. Littlefield professor of accounting emeritus at Stanford University. A graduate of Marquette University, he received his MBA from Harvard University and his PhD from the University of Chicago. He also received honorary doctorates from Marquette University and DePaul University.

A certified public accountant, Horngren served on the Accounting Principles Board, the Financial Accounting Standards Board Advisory Council, and the Council of the American Institute of Certified Public Accountants. In addition, he served as a trustee of the Financial Accounting Foundation, which oversees the Financial Accounting Standards Board and the Government Accounting Standards Board. He is a member of the Accounting Hall of Fame.

Horngren served the American Accounting Association as its president and its director of research. He received the association's first annual Outstanding Accounting Educator Award and also received its Lifetime Contribution to Management Accounting Award.

The California Certified Public Accountants Foundation gave Horngren its Faculty Excellence Award and its Distinguished Professor Award. He is the first person to have received both awards. The American Institute of Certified Public Accountants presented him with its first Outstanding Educator Award. He was also named Accountant of the Year, Education, by the national professional accounting fraternity, Beta Alpha Psi.

Professor Horngren was also a member of the Institute of Management Accountants, where he received its Distinguished Service Award. He was a member of the Institute's Board of Regents, which administers the Certified Management Accountant examinations.

Horngren is the author of other accounting books published by Pearson Education: *Cost Accounting: A Managerial Emphasis*, *Introduction to Management Accounting*, *Accounting*, and *Financial Accounting*. He was also the Consulting Editor for the Charles T. Horngren Series in Accounting.

Gary L. Sundem is professor of accounting emeritus at the Foster School of Business at the University of Washington, Seattle. He received his BA from Carleton College and his MBA and PhD from Stanford University.

Professor Sundem has served as President of the American Accounting Association, Executive Director of the Accounting Education Change Commission, and Editor of *The Accounting Review*. He is currently president of the International Association for Accounting Education and Research.

Sundem is a past president of the Seattle chapter of the IMA (formerly the Institute of Management Accountants). He has served on IMA's national board of directors and chaired its Academic Relations and Professional Development committees. He has chaired the AACSB's Accounting Accreditation Committee and currently serves on the Board of Trustees of Rainier Mutual Funds and the Board of Trustees of Carleton College, where he chairs the Audit Committee. He received the Carleton College Outstanding Alumni award in 2002.

Professor Sundem has numerous publications in accounting and finance journals including *Issues in Accounting Education*, *The Accounting Review*, *Journal of Accounting Research*, and *Journal of Finance*. He was selected as the Outstanding Accounting Educator by the American Accounting Association in 1998 and by the Washington Society of CPAs in 1987.

John A. Elliott is the dean of the School of Business at the University of Connecticut and the Auran J. Fox Chair in Business. Prior to joining the University of Connecticut, he served for 10 years as dean of the Zicklin School of Business at Baruch College, part of the City University of New York (CUNY). He was the Irwin and Arlene Ettinger professor of accountancy. He received his BS and MBA from the University of Maryland and his PhD from Cornell University. Prior to accepting the deanship at the Zicklin School, he spent 20 years on the faculty at Cornell University's Johnson Graduate School of Management, most recently as associate dean for academic affairs.

Dean Elliott is a certified public accountant with professional experience as an auditor and consultant for Arthur Andersen & Co. and in the controller's office of the Westinghouse Defense and Space Center. During his career he has taught at seven different institutions. His responsibilities have included financial accounting, intermediate accounting, financial statement analysis, taxation, and extensive executive teaching.

In 2004 his paper on earnings management (with Nelson and Tarpley) received the award from the American Accounting Association for Notable Contributions to Accounting Literature. His research is concentrated on the role of accounting information in financial analysis and contracts.

He serves on two corporate boards, NFP and Liquidnet, and chairs their audit committees. He has previously served on and chaired the boards for the Hangar Theatre, Cayuga Medical Center, and the Graduate Management Admissions Council.

Donna R. Philbrick is Professor of Accounting at Portland State University. She received her BS from the University of Oregon and her MBA and PhD from Cornell University.

Professor Philbrick is a certified public accountant (inactive) and worked as an auditor for Touche Ross (now Deloitte & Touche) and Price Waterhouse (now PricewaterhouseCoopers) prior to returning for her graduate degrees. Before joining the faculty at Portland State University, she taught at the University of Oregon and Duke University.

She currently teaches at both the graduate and undergraduate levels, focusing on financial accounting, intermediate accounting, and financial statement analysis. Professor Philbrick has taught for many years in the Oregon Executive MBA program and has experience teaching in numerous corporate programs.

Professor Philbrick's research has been published in accounting journals including *The Accounting Review*, *Journal of Accounting Research*, and *Journal of Accounting and Economics*. Most recently her research has focused on corporate governance issues. She has served on the Advisory Board and as an associate editor of *Accounting Horizons*.

Brief Contents

Contents

Preface

"You have to know what something is before you know how to use it."
Introduction to Financial Accounting, 11/E, describes the most widely accepted accounting theory and practice with an emphasis on using and analyzing the information in financial statements. It compares U.S. generally accepted accounting principles (U.S. GAAP) to International Financial Reporting Standards (IFRS) where appropriate.

IFA, 11/E, takes the view that business is an exciting process and that accounting is the perfect window through which to see how economic events affect businesses. Because we believe that accounting aids the understanding of economic events and that accounting builds on simple principles, this book introduces a number of concepts earlier than many other textbooks. We cover these early concepts at the most accessible level and illustrate them with carefully chosen examples from real companies. Our coverage addresses the choices that management makes when preparing financial statements and how these choices affect the way users interpret the information. We also discuss ethical issues throughout the book and in the assignment materials.

This is the eleventh edition of this text, and that is a testimonial to its effectiveness. But it also is a testimonial to our former colleagues, students, and adopters who, in each prior edition, have shared their thoughts and suggestions and driven us to change and adapt it to better meet the needs of today's students and adopting faculty.

Continuing strengths of this edition:

- Text coverage and problem material based on classic issues arising in the last 30 years
- Integration of ethics coverage throughout
- Coverage of U.S. GAAP and IFRS requirements where material differences exist
- Use of international-company examples, especially to illustrate differences in U.S. GAAP and IFRS

New to this edition:

- Totally updated text to include current examples from real companies
- Extensive revisions for clarity
- Revision of problem material to include examples from corporate outcomes in the last two years
- Coverage of the current status of FASB and IASB regulatory action
- Highlights of likely upcoming changes in accounting standards, including revenue recognition and leases
- Updated Business First Boxes

Our Philosophy

Introduce the simple concepts early, revisit concepts at more complex levels as students gain understanding, and provide appropriate real-company examples at every stage—that's our philosophy. Our goal is for students to be able to read and interpret a real company's financial statements: balance sheet, income statement, statement of cash flows, and statement of changes in stockholders' equity.

We want students to view accounting as a tool that enhances their understanding of economic events. Students should be asking questions such as "After this transaction, are we better or worse off?" and "What do these statements tell us about the company's financial position and performance?"

Students cannot understand financial statements in isolation. Rather, they must look at all the financial statements within the context of the company's business environment. They need to understand the accrual basis of accounting that underlies the balance sheet and income statement, but they must also understand the importance of cash as presented in the statement of cash flows. We present the balance sheet, income statement, statement of changes in stockholders' equity, and statement of cash flows in the first five chapters. By presenting the statement of cash flows in Chapter 5, immediately after the presentation of the basics of accrual accounting, students learn the importance of all the statements and the unique information each statement presents before encountering details about financial reporting practices in the later chapters.

One of our former colleagues often focuses on an economic event by asking, "Are you happy or are you sad?" We believe that accounting provides a way to understand what is happening and to answer that question. You might think of the basic financial statements as scorecards in the most fundamental economic contests. Each year the financial statements help you answer the most important questions: Are you happy or sad? Did you make or lose money? Are you prospering or just surviving? Will you have the cash you need for the next big step?

Who Should Use This Book?

Introduction to Financial Accounting, 11/E, presupposes no prior knowledge of accounting and is suitable for any undergraduate or MBA student enrolled in a financial accounting course. It is also appropriate for management education programs where the participants have little or no accounting background. It deals with important topics that all managers should know and all business students should study. We have aimed to present relevant subject matter and to present it clearly and accessibly.

This text is oriented to the user of financial statements but gives ample attention to the needs of potential accounting practitioners. *IFA*, 11/E, stresses underlying concepts yet makes them concrete with numerous illustrations, many taken from recent corporate annual reports. Moreover, accounting procedures such as transaction analysis, journalizing, and posting are given due consideration where appropriate. Managers and accountants can develop a better understanding of the economic consequences of a company's transactions by summarizing those transactions into journal entries and T-accounts. However, the ultimate objective is an understanding of financial position and prospects, which we achieve by a focus on the balance sheet equation.

Coverage of IFRS

- We cover critical differences between U.S. generally accepted accounting principles (U.S. GAAP) and International Financial Reporting Standards (IFRS) without unnecessary details.
- We include problem materials from companies reporting under IFRS as well as U.S. GAAP.

Emphasis on Understanding and Analyzing Financial Statements

- **Financial Statement Portfolio**, inserted in Chapter 2 and identified by a blue vertical bar on the page edges, provides a visual roadmap to financial statement analysis by highlighting key financial ratios and how to derive them from the financial statements. The Financial Statement Portfolio also refers students to appropriate chapters in the book for in-depth coverage of these ratios. It is included in Chapter 2 to focus students on the uses of accounting information early in the course.
- **Interpreting Financial Statements** sections within each chapter permit students to pause and ponder how to use the information they are learning to better understand the financial position and prospects of a company.

- **Analyzing and Interpreting Financial Statements problems at the end of each chapter** include financial statement research, analyses of Starbucks financial statements, and analysis of other companies' financial statements using the Internet.
- **Focus on Starbucks' Annual Report** is used to illustrate various methods for analyzing financial statements. There is a problem based on Starbucks in each chapter, allowing students to get a more complete picture of many financial reporting issues relating to one particular company.

Other Features

- **Extensive treatment of ethics**, with both text coverage and end-of-chapter problems focusing on this important topic in nearly every chapter.
- **Critical Thinking Exercises** in the assignment material of each chapter that ask students to consider conceptual issues that may have no right answer.
- **Business First Boxes** in each chapter, many new or completely revised. These boxes provide insights into operations at well-known domestic and international companies, accenting today's real-world issues.

Teaching and Learning Support: Because Resources Should Simplify, Not Overwhelm: A successful accounting course requires more than a well-written book. Today's classroom requires a dedicated teacher and a fully integrated teaching package. The following material supports this title.

Student Resources

www.myaccountinglab.com
MyAccountingLab is Web-based tutorial and assessment software for accounting that gives students more "I get it!" moments. MyAccountingLab provides students with a personalized interactive learning environment where they can complete their course assignments with immediate tutorial assistance, learn at their own pace, and measure their progress.

In addition to completing assignments and reviewing tutorial help, students have access to the following resources in MyAccountingLab:

- **Flash-based eText**
- **Study Guide**
- **Excel Templates**
- **PowerPoints**

Student Resource Website

www.pearsonhighered.com/horngren

- **Excel Templates**

Instructor Resources

www.myaccountinglab.com
MyAccountingLab provides instructors the flexibility to make technology an integral part of their course. And, because practice makes perfect, MyAccountingLab offers exactly the same end-of-chapter material found in the text with algorithmic options that instructors can assign for homework. MyAccountingLab also replicates the text's exercises and problems with journal entries and financial statements so that students are familiar and comfortable working with the material.

Solutions Manual

The Solutions Manual, written by the text authors, is available electronically. It contains the fully worked-through and accuracy-checked solutions for every question, exercise, and problem in the text. Special thanks to Carolyn Streuly for reviewing this material.

Instructor Resource Center

www.pearsonhighered.com/horngren

For your convenience, many of our instructor supplements are available for download from the textbook's catalog page or your MyAccountingLab account. Available resources include the following:

- **Test Item File:** The Test Item File includes multiple choice, true/false, exercises, comprehensive problems, short answer problems, critical thinking essay questions, and so on. Each test item is tied to the corresponding learning objective and has an assigned difficulty level.
- **TestGen:** This PC/MAC-compatible test generating software is powerful and easy to use. It is preloaded with all the questions from the new Test Item File and allows users to manually or randomly view test bank questions and drag and drop them to create a test. Add or modify questions using the built-in Question Editor, print up to 25 variations of a single test, and create and export tests that are compatible with commonly used course management systems.
- **Instructor's Resource Manual:** This manual contains the following elements for each chapter of the text: chapter overviews, chapter outlines organized by objectives, teaching tips, chapter quiz.
- **PowerPoint Slides:** Comprehensive slides designed to aid in presentation of key chapter concepts
- **Excel Templates and Solutions**
- **Solutions Manual**
- **Image Library**

Technical support is available at http://247pearsoned.custhelp.com.

Acknowledgements

Our appreciation extends to our present and former mentors, colleagues, and students. This book and our enthusiasm for accounting grew out of their collective contributions to our knowledge and experience.

A special thanks to Norbert Tschakert, University of the Virgin Islands, for his suggestions on IFRS. Thank you to the following people who provided valuable contributions on the supplements: Carolyn Streuly; Sheila Handy, East Stroudsburg University; and Victoria Kaskey, Ashland University.

We would also like to thank those who gave valuable feedback on previous editions: John E. Armstrong, Dominican College; Frances L. Ayers, University of Oklahoma; Karthik Balakrishnan, The Wharton School; Roderick S. Barclay, University of Texas at Dallas; Ronald S. Barden, Georgia State University; Mary Barth, Stanford University; Paul E. Bayes, East Tennessee State University; Martin J. Birr, Indiana University; Robert Bowen, University of San Diego; Marianne Bradford, The University of Tennessee; Nancy Cassidy, Texas A&M University; David T. Collins, Bellarmine College; Michele J. Daley, Rice University; Ray D. Dillon, Georgia State University; Patricia A. Doherty, Boston University; Philip D. Drake, Thunderbird, The American Graduate School of International Management; Allan R. Drebin, Northwestern University; Roland "Pete" Dukes, University of Washington; Robert Dunn, Georgia Institute of Technology; Thomas R. Dyckman, Cornell University; Alan H. Falcon, Loyola Marymount University; Anita Feller, University of Illinois; Catherine Finger-Podolsky, Saint Mary's College of California; Richard Frankel, University of Michigan; John D. Gould, Western Carolina University; D. Jacque Grinnell, University of Vermont; Leon J. Hanouille, Syracuse University; Al Hartgraves, Emory University; Suzanne Hartley, Franklin University; Robert E. Holtfreter, Central Washington University; Peter Huey, Collin County Community College; Yuji Ijiri, Carnegie Mellon University; M. Zafar Iqbal, California Polytechnic State University–San Luis Obispo; Jane Jollineau, University of San Diego; Gregory D. Kane, University of Delaware; Urooj Khan, Columbia Business School; Sungsoo Kim, Rutgers University; April Klein, New York University; Robert Libby, Cornell University; Joan Luft, Michigan State University; Maureen McNichols, Stanford University; Mark J. Myring, Ball State University; Brian M. Nagle, Duquesne University; John L. Norman Jr., Keller Graduate School of Management; Mohamed Onsi, Syracuse University; David M. Perkal, NYU–Stern School of Business; Elizabeth Plummer, Southern Methodist University; Patrick M. Premo, St. Bonaventure University; Renee A. Price, University of Nebraska; Leo A. Ruggle, Mankato State University; James A. Schweikart, Rhode Island College; Chandra Seethamraju, Washington University–St. Louis; Bill Shoemaker, University of Dallas; William Smith, Xavier University; Robert Swieringa, Cornell University; Daniel Taylor, University of Pennsylvania–The Wharton School; Katherene P. Terrell, University of Central Oklahoma; Michael G. Vasilou, DeVry Institute of Technology–Chicago; Deborah Welch, Tyler Junior College; William Wells, University of Washington; Christine Wiedman, University of Western Ontario; Patrick T. Wirtz, University of Detroit Mercy; and Peter D. Woodlock, Youngstown State University.

Finally, we'd like to thank the following people at Pearson Education: Lacey Vitetta, Donna Battista, Ashley Santora, Karen Kirincich, Roberta Sherman, and Jeff Holcomb.

Comments from users are welcome.

Charles T. Horngren
Gary L. Sundem
John A. Elliott
Donna R. Philbrick

Introduction to

FINANCIAL ACCOUNTING

1 Accounting: The Language of Business

ACCOUNTING IS THE LANGUAGE OF business. It is the method companies use to communicate financial information to their employees and to the public. Until recently, the accounting language, like spoken languages, differed country to country. Today only two main accounting languages have survived, one used in the United States and another used in Europe and most of the rest of the world. These are actually more like dialects of a single language because they are identical in most respects and are gradually converging into a single language. In this text we focus on the U.S. perspective but discuss the significant differences between the languages when they arise.

We also use real companies to illustrate the language of accounting in practice. Consider Starbucks Corporation, a U.S.-based company that uses the accounting language employed by all U.S. companies. You have probably purchased a latte in, or at least walked by, one of Starbucks' 18,000 coffee stores throughout the world. Did you know that you could also buy a share of Starbucks stock, making you a part owner of Starbucks? When you buy a latte, you want to know how it tastes. When you buy a share of stock, you want to know about the financial condition and prospects of Starbucks Corporation. You would want to own part of Starbucks only if you think it will be successful in the future. To learn this, you need to understand the accounting language used in Starbucks' financial reports. By the time you finish reading this book, you will be comfortable reading the financial reports of Starbucks and other companies and be able to use those reports to assess the financial health of these companies.

Starbucks was founded in 1985 and first issued shares of stock to the public in 1992. If you had purchased shares at that time, as of this writing your investment would be worth more than $60 for every $1 you invested. Will Starbucks be a good investment in the future? No one can predict with certainty Starbucks' financial prospects. However, the company's financial statements, which are available on Starbucks' Web site, can give you clues. But you need to understand accounting to make sense of this financial information.

LEARNING OBJECTIVES *After studying this chapter, you should be able to:*

1 Explain how accounting information assists in making decisions.

2 Describe the components of the balance sheet.

3 Analyze business transactions and relate them to changes in the balance sheet.

4 Prepare a balance sheet from transactions data.

5 Compare the features of sole proprietorships, partnerships, and corporations.

6 Identify how the owners' equity section in a corporate balance sheet differs from that in a sole proprietorship or a partnership.

7 Explain the regulation of financial reporting, including differences between U.S. GAAP and IFRS.

8 Describe auditing and how it enhances the value of financial information.

9 Evaluate the role of ethics in the accounting process.

10 Recognize career opportunities in accounting, and understand that accounting is important to both for-profit and nonprofit organizations.

Starbucks has established a worldwide reputation in a short time. It was #16 on *Fortune* magazine's list of Most Admired Companies in 2011. It has consistently been included among the Top 5 Global Brands of the Year as identified by Brandchannel.com's Readers' Choice survey and ranked among CR Magazine's 100 Best Corporate Citizens in 2011 for the 12th year in a row, one of only three companies to make the list all 12 years. It has also been on Ethisphere's list of the world's most ethical companies every year since the list started in 2007. Despite all these awards, potential investors want to know something about Starbucks' financial prospects. Let's look at a few financial facts. As you proceed through this book, you will develop a better understanding of how to interpret these facts.

In 2011, Starbucks reported total revenues—the amount the company received for all the items sold—of $11.7 billion, compared with only $700 million in 1996. Net income—the profit that Starbucks made—was $1,246 million, up from $42 million in 1996 and $946 million in 2010. Total assets—the recorded value of the items owned by Starbucks—grew from less than $900 million to almost $7.4 billion from 1996 to 2011. You can see that the amount of business done by Starbucks has grown quickly. However, there is much more to be learned from the details in Starbucks' financial statements. You will learn about revenues, income, assets, and other elements of accounting as you read this book. ●

As we embark on our journey into the world of accounting, we explore how a company such as Starbucks reports on its financial activities and how investors use this accounting information to better understand Starbucks. Keep this in mind: The same basic accounting framework that supported a small coffee company like Starbucks in 1985 supports the larger company today, and indeed it supports businesses (big and small, old and new) worldwide.

Accounting is a process of identifying, recording, and summarizing economic information and reporting it to decision makers. You are correct if you expect to learn a set of rules and procedures about how to record and report financial information. However,

Starbucks has more than 18,000 coffee shops throughout the world. Although a majority (71%) are in the Americas, fully 18% are in the China/Asia Pacific region.

accounting
The process of identifying, recording, and summarizing economic information and reporting it to decision makers.

understanding accounting reports goes beyond rules and procedures. To use your financial accounting education effectively, you must also understand the underlying business transactions that give rise to the economic information and why the information is helpful in making financial decisions.

We hope that you want to know how businesses work. When you understand that Starbucks' financial reports help its management make decisions about producing and selling products, as well as helping investors assess the performance and prospects of Starbucks, you will see why being able to read and interpret these reports is important. Both outside investors and internal managers need this information.

Our goal is to help you understand business transactions—to know how accounting information describes such transactions and how decision makers both inside the company (managers) and outside the company (investors) use that information in deciding how, when, and what to buy or sell. In the process, you will learn about some of the world's premier companies. You may wonder what it costs to open a new Starbucks store. Are new stores worth such a major investment? How many people visit each Starbucks store every year? Can Starbucks keep track of them all, and are there enough customers to make the stores profitable? If investors consider purchasing Starbucks stock, what do they need to know to decide whether the current price is a reasonable one? Accounting information cannot completely answer every such question, but it provides important insights into many of them. To illustrate how to use accounting information, we will often explore issues that arise in real companies.

In pursuing actual business examples, we consider details about many of the 30 companies in the Dow Jones Industrial Average (the DJIA), the most commonly reported stock market index in the world. Well-known companies, such as **Coca-Cola**, **Microsoft**, and **McDonald's**, are among these 30 companies, along with many other large but less familiar companies, such as **Alcoa**, **The Travelers Companies**, and **United Technologies Corporation**. Exhibit 1-1 lists the 30 Dow companies together with their ticker symbol—the common shorthand used by stockbrokers and investors to identify these companies. The Business First box on page 5 describes the DJIA. We also consider younger and faster-growing companies such as Starbucks, **Amazon.com**, **Apple**, and **Google** and international companies such as **Toyota**, **Nokia**, **Nestlé**, and **Volkswagen** to illustrate various accounting issues and practices. For now, we start with the basics, most of which are the same regardless of the accounting language a company uses.

EXHIBIT 1-1

Dow Industrials
Listed by Year Added to the Index

Company	Symbol	Year Added	Company	Symbol	Year Added
General Electric	GE	1907	Walt Disney	DIS	1991
ExxonMobil	XOM	1928	Hewlett-Packard	HPQ	1997
Procter & Gamble	PG	1932	Johnson & Johnson	JNJ	1997
DuPont	DD	1935	Wal-Mart	WMT	1997
United Technologies Corporation	UTX	1939	AT&T	T	1999
Alcoa	AA	1959	Home Depot	HD	1999
3M	MMM	1976	Intel	INTC	1999
IBM	IBM	1979	Microsoft	MSFT	1999
Merck	MRK	1979	Pfizer	PFE	2004
American Express	AXP	1982	Verizon Communications	VZ	2004
McDonald's	MCD	1985	Bank of America	BAC	2008
Boeing	BA	1987	Chevron Corporation	CVX	2008
Coca-Cola	KO	1987	Cisco Systems	CSCO	2009
Caterpillar	CAT	1991	The Travelers Companies	TRV	2009
JPMorgan Chase	JPM	1991	UnitedHealth Group	UNH	2012

BUSINESS FIRST

THE DOW JONES INDUSTRIAL AVERAGE

Why did the Dow Jones Industrial Average (DJIA) fall from over 14,000 in late 2007 to under 7,000 in 2009? Why did it rebound to over 13,000 by early 2012? What does this mean to investors? To explain this 50% drop followed by an 86% gain, you need to understand the DJIA. However, to fully understand the reasons for the drop and gain, you need to understand accounting—what the financial reports prepared by companies really tell you about their financial results and outlook.

The DJIA is one of many indices used to describe the performance of stock markets around the world. All indices provide a picture of what is happening on average to the value of securities owned by investors. The Dow began as the average value of an investment in one share of each of 12 stocks and was first published in 1896 by Charles Dow. To calculate it, he simply added the prices of the 12 stocks and divided by 12. It began at 40.94 but fell to an all-time low of 28.48 in August of that year. The calculation today is more complex, but the basic concept is unchanged. Since 1928, the number of stocks in the DJIA has been constant at 30, but there have been 41 changes in the composition of the average. These changes reflect the dynamic nature of American industry. The original DJIA had several auto and petroleum companies to capture the massive importance of these industries. Among the original 12 companies were U.S. Leather, U.S. Rubber, American Tobacco, Tennessee Coal & Iron, and Laclede Gas. Of these, only Laclede Gas, a Missouri utility, still exists—although it is not included in the Dow. Today, only General Electric remains from the original 12, and it was dropped from the index briefly in the early 1900s and reinstated in 1907. Just since 2004 there have been nine changes in the Dow. Pfizer, Verizon, and AIG replaced Eastman Kodak, AT&T, and International Paper in 2004; AT&T returned in 2005 because of its merger with SBC, which had been added in 1999; Bank of America, Chevron Corporation, and Kraft Foods replaced Altria Group, Honeywell, and AIG in 2008; and Cisco Systems and The Travelers Companies replaced Citicorp and General Motors in 2009. It is also interest-ing to note that the largest one-day Dow increase, 15%, was in October 1931. The largest drop was October 19, 1987, when the Dow fell 23%.

Although indices such as the DJIA give a picture of how stock prices have changed, they do not explain why those changes occurred. There is clear evidence that accounting results affect stock prices. Therefore, most financial analysts rely on companies' financial reports, along with other information, to explain movements in stock prices. For example, *BusinessWorld* focused on corporate earnings in a recent report: "Demand for a stock moves on the basis of changes in the market's perception of a stock's future earnings." Annual and quarterly financial reports provide much of the information investors use. They use this financial information to predict future financial positions and prospects of companies. In this way, they try to anticipate movements in stock prices. The classic advice to investors is to "buy low and sell high." Although this is never easy, accounting information can help investors approach this ideal. The DJIA falls when the economy weakens and companies' profits decline. It rebounds when companies' financial reports indicate that financial results are on the upswing.

The DJIA is not the only index that provides information on the general direction of movements in stock prices. In the United States, Standard and Poor's publishes the S&P 500, an index of 500 large companies traded in the United States, and NASDAQ publishes an index that tracks many smaller and high-tech firms. Similarly, in the international arena you will often see references to the FTSE, an index of UK companies listed on the London Stock Exchange, and the Nikkei, the most widely quoted index of stocks traded on the Tokyo Stock Exchange. Both are indices of general share-price movements in those markets. Investors worldwide closely follow all of these indices.

Sources: D. Somera, "Forces That Move Stock Prices," BusinessWorld, January 12, 2009, p. S4/2; Dow Jones Indexes (http://djaverages.com); Nikkei index (http://e.nikkei.com; FTSE index (http://www.ftse.com).

The Nature of Accounting

Accounting organizes and summarizes economic information so decision makers can use it. Accountants present this information in reports called financial statements. To prepare these statements, accountants analyze, record, quantify, accumulate, summarize, classify, report, and interpret economic events and their financial effects on an organization.

accounting system
The series of steps an organization uses to record financial data and convert them into informative financial statements.

An organization's **accounting system** is the series of steps it uses to record financial data and convert them into informative financial statements. Accountants analyze the information used by managers and other decision makers and create the accounting system that best meets their needs. Bookkeepers and computers then perform the routine tasks of collecting and compiling economic data. The real value of any accounting system lies in the information it provides to decision makers.

Consider a university's accounting system. It collects information about tuition charges and payments and tracks the status of each student. The university must be able to bill individuals with unpaid balances. It must be able to schedule courses and hire faculty to meet the course demands of students. It must ensure that tuition and other cash inflows are sufficient to pay the faculty and keep the buildings warm (or cool) and well lit. In the past, students often became frustrated with university accounting systems. Perhaps there were too many waiting lines at registration or too many complicated procedures in filing for financial aid. However, modern systems allow electronic registration for courses and electronic payments of tuition. The right information system can streamline your life.

Every business maintains an accounting system, from the store where you bought this book to the company that issued the credit card you used. MasterCard, Visa, and American Express maintain fast, complicated accounting systems. At any moment, thousands of credit card transactions occur around the globe, and accounting systems keep track of them all. When you use your charge card, a scanner reads it electronically and transmits the transaction amount to the card company's central computer. The computer verifies that your charges are within acceptable limits and approves or denies the transaction. At the same time, the computer also conducts security checks. For example, if stores in Chicago and London registered sales using your card within an hour of each other, the system might sense that something is wrong and require you to call a customer service representative before the credit card company approves the second charge. Without reliable accounting systems, credit cards simply could not exist.

Accounting as an Aid to Decision Making

▶▶ OBJECTIVE 1

Explain how accounting information assists in making decisions.

Accounting information is useful to anyone making decisions that have economic consequences. Such decision makers include managers, owners, investors, and politicians. Consider the following examples:

- When the engineering department of Apple Computer developed the iPad, accountants developed reports on the potential profitability of the product, including estimated sales and estimated production and selling costs. Managers used the reports to help decide whether to produce and market the product.
- When QBC Information Services, a small consulting firm with five employees, decides who to promote (and possibly who to fire), the managing partner produces reports on the productivity of each employee and compares productivity to the salary and other costs associated with the employee's work for the year.
- When portfolio managers at Vanguard Group consider buying stock in either Ford Motor Company or Volkswagen Group, they consult published accounting reports to compare the most recent financial results of the companies. They must be able to compare Ford's information reported in the accounting language of U.S. companies with that of Volkswagen reported in the accounting language of Europe. Understanding the information in the reports helps the managers decide which company would be the better investment choice.
- When Chase Bank considers a loan to a company that wants to expand, it examines the historical performance of the company and analyzes projections the company provides about how it will use the borrowed funds to produce new business.

Accounting helps decision making by showing where and when a company spends money and makes commitments. It also helps predict the future effects of decisions, and it helps direct attention to current problems, imperfections, and inefficiencies, as well as opportunities.

Consider some basic relationships in the decision-making process:

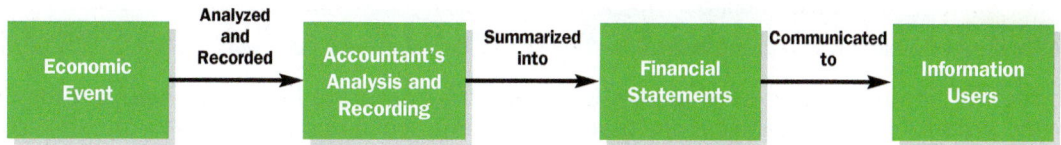

Accountants analyze and record economic events. Periodically, accountants summarize the results of the events into financial statements. Users then rely on the financial statements to make decisions. Our focus includes all four boxes. All financial accounting courses cover the analysis and recording of information and the preparation of financial statements. We pay more attention to the underlying business processes creating the events and to the way in which the financial reports help decision makers to take action.

Financial and Management Accounting

The financial statements we discuss in this book are common to all areas of accounting. Accountants often distinguish "financial accounting" from "management accounting" based on who uses the information. **Financial accounting** serves external decision makers, such as stockholders, suppliers, banks, and government agencies, and is the major focus of this book. In contrast, **management accounting** serves internal decision makers, such as top executives, department heads, college deans, hospital administrators, and people at other management levels within the organization.[1] The two fields of accounting share many of the same procedures for analyzing and recording the effects of individual transactions.

A common source of financial information used by investors and others outside the company is the **annual report**. The annual report is a document prepared by management and distributed to current and potential investors to inform them about the company's past performance and future prospects. Firms distribute their annual reports to stockholders automatically. Potential investors may request the report by calling the investor relations department of the company or by visiting the company's Web site to access the report. In addition to the financial statements, annual reports usually include the following:

1. A letter from corporate management
2. A discussion and analysis by management of recent economic events
3. Footnotes that explain many elements of the financial statements in more detail
4. The report of the independent registered public accounting firm (auditors)
5. Statements by both management and auditors on the company's internal controls
6. Other corporate information

Some large companies also use their annual reports to promote the company, using pleasing photographs extensively to communicate their message. You can find annual reports for most companies on their Web sites, as described in the Business First box on page 8.

Although all elements of the annual report are important, we concentrate on the principal financial statements and how accountants collect and report this information. You can also find U.S. companies' financial statements in their **Form 10-K** filed annually with the **Securities and Exchange Commission (SEC)**, the government agency responsible for regulating capital markets in the United States. U.S. Companies with **publicly traded stock**, that is, companies that sell shares in their ownership to the public, must file 10-Ks and many other forms with the SEC. The 10-K contains more than the basic financial statements, including detailed financial information beyond that included in most annual reports. A growing number of U.S. companies

financial accounting
The field of accounting that serves external decision makers, such as stockholders, suppliers, banks, and government agencies.

management accounting
The field of accounting that serves internal decision makers, such as top executives, department heads, college deans, hospital administrators, and people at other management levels within an organization.

annual report
A document prepared by management and distributed to current and potential investors to inform them about the company's past performance and future prospects.

Form 10-K
A document that U.S. companies file annually with the Securities and Exchange Commission. It contains the companies' financial statements.

Securities and Exchange Commission (SEC)
The government agency responsible for regulating capital markets in the United States.

publicly traded stock
Shares in the ownership of a company that are sold to the public.

---

[1]For a book-length presentation of management accounting, see C. Horngren, G. Sundem, D. Burgstahler, and J. Schatzberg, *Introduction to Management Accounting*, 16th ed. (Upper Saddle River, NJ: Prentice-Hall, 2013), the companion volume to this textbook.

BUSINESS FIRST

ANNUAL REPORTS AND THE INTERNET

Until the last decade, annual reports were generally glossy documents produced by companies more than 3 months after year-end. In addition to being a primary source of financial information about the company, annual reports also contained much other information (some might call it propaganda) about the company. However, the Internet has changed and continues to change the way investors get information about a company. Today, more information is available more quickly on the Web than on paper.

Most companies with publicly traded stock, and certainly the large ones, include their annual reports on their Web site. You can usually find a company's annual report in a segment of its site called *Investors* or *Investor Relations*. Often this comes under a heading *Corporate Information*, *About the Company*, or some such title included on the company's home page.

Most companies provide at least an indexed electronic version of their financial statements in PDF format. But many companies are providing files that are more flexible, mainly statements that users can download into Excel spreadsheets. This allows users to perform their own analyses of the data. There is even a competition for the best annual reports. The League of American Communications Professionals (LACP) rates annual reports based on how well they communicate their messages. The top 2010 annual reports by category, selected from more than 5,000 entries representing more than 24 countries, are as follows:

Category	Company	Country
Best Agency Report	National Savings Bank	Sri Lanka
Overall	Vossloh AG	Germany
Most Creative	RTL Group	Germany
Most Engaging	PT Adaro Energy Tbk	Indonesia
Most Improved	KOÇ Holding	Turkey
Best In-House Report	Daiwa House Industry Co., Ltd.	Japan
Best Shareholder Letter	Garanti Emeklilik	Turkey
Best Report Cover	Vossloh AG	Germany
Best Report Financials	Deufol AG	Germany
Best Report Narrative	U.S. Department of State	USA

Some executives use their company's annual report to educate investors. Warren Buffett, chairman and CEO of Berkshire Hathaway, always includes a long letter explaining his philosophies as well as his company's performance. In 2011, his letter contained 20 pages of insightful comments. For example, a few years ago he commented on the housing and credit crisis as one where "borrowers who shouldn't have borrowed [were] being financed by lenders who shouldn't have lent." One year he even compared financial reporting to his golf game.

Annual reports are venerable documents that have been useful to investors for many years. They are not likely to go away. However, their content and format are changing. Use of the Internet opens up possibilities for presenting financial information (as well as other information) to investors that were previously impossible. This should lead to better information for those making investment decisions and therefore better functioning capital markets.

Sources: LACP 2010 Annual Report Competition Results, http://www.lacp.com/2010vision/competition.htm; Berkshire Hathaway, 2008 and 2011 Annual Reports.

are eliminating their expensive and glossy annual reports and simply issuing the 10-K to investors and potential investors.

While decision makers are most interested in a company's future performance, the information in an annual report or 10-K is largely historical. However, past performance is an important input in predicting future success. Therefore, the annual report or 10-K enables decision makers to answer the following relevant questions:

What is the financial picture of the organization at a moment in time?

How well did the organization do during a period of time?

Accountants answer these questions with four major financial statements: the balance sheet, the income statement, the statement of cash flows, and the statement of stockholders' equity. The balance sheet focuses on the financial picture as of a given day. The income statement, cash flow statement, and statement of stockholders' equity focus on the performance over a period of time. Usually the period is a year or one quarter of the year and the balance sheet shows the company's status on the last day of the period. We discuss the balance sheet in this chapter, the income statement and statement of stockholders' equity in Chapter 2, and the statement of cash flows in Chapter 5. After introducing the balance sheet, this chapter also explores several topics that are important to understanding the environment in which a business operates.

The Balance Sheet

The **balance sheet**, also called the **statement of financial position**, shows the financial status of an organization at a particular instant in time. It is essentially a snapshot of the organization at a given date. It has two counterbalancing sections. One section lists the resources of the firm (everything the firm owns and controls—from cash to buildings, etc.). The other section lists the claims against the resources. The resources and claims form the **balance sheet equation**:

$$\text{Assets} = \text{Liabilities} + \text{Owners' equity}$$

Some accountants prefer the following (equivalent) form of the balance sheet equation:

$$\text{Assets} - \text{Liabilities} = \text{Owners' equity}$$

We define the terms in this equation as follows:

Assets are economic resources that the company expects to help generate future cash inflows or reduce or prevent future cash outflows. Examples are cash, inventories, and equipment.

Liabilities are economic obligations of the organization to outsiders, or claims against its assets by outsiders. An example is a debt to a bank. When a company takes out a bank loan, it generally signs a promissory note that states the terms of repayment. Accountants use the term **notes payable** to describe the existence of promissory notes.

Owners' equity (or owner's equity if there is only one owner) is the owners' claims on the organization's assets. Because debt holders have first claim on the assets, the owners' claim is equal to total assets less total liabilities.

To illustrate the balance sheet, suppose Hector Lopez, a salaried employee of a local bicycle company, quits his job and opens his own bicycle shop, Biwheels Company, on January 2, 20X2. Lopez invests $400,000 in the business. Then, acting for the business, he borrows $100,000 from a local bank. That gives Biwheels $500,000 in assets, all currently in the form of cash. The opening balance sheet of this new business enterprise follows:

Biwheels Company
Balance Sheet
January 2, 20X2

Assets		Liabilities and Owner's Equity	
Cash	$500,000	Liabilities (Note payable)	$100,000
		Lopez, capital	400,000
Total assets	$500,000	Total liabilities and owner's equity	$500,000

Because the balance sheet shows the financial status at a particular point in time, it always includes a specific date. The elements in this balance sheet show the financial status of the Biwheels Company as of January 2, 20X2. The Biwheels balance sheet lists the company's assets ($500,000) on the left. They are balanced on the right by an equal amount of liabilities

▶▶ OBJECTIVE 2
Describe the components of the balance sheet.

balance sheet (statement of financial position)
A financial statement that shows the financial status of an organization at a particular instant in time.

balance sheet equation
Assets = Liabilities + Owners' equity

assets
Economic resources that a company expects to help generate future cash inflows or help reduce future cash outflows.

liabilities
Economic obligations of the organization to outsiders, or claims against its assets by outsiders.

notes payable
Promissory notes that are evidence of a debt and state the terms of payment.

owners' equity
The owners' claims on an organization's assets, or total assets less total liabilities.

and owner's equity ($100,000 liability owed to the bank plus $400,000 paid in by Lopez). The double underscores (double ruling) under the column totals denote final numbers. Note that we always keep the left and right sides in balance.

When someone first starts a business, the owners' equity is equal to the total amount invested by the owner or owners. As illustrated by "Lopez, capital" in the Biwheels Company example, accountants often use the term capital instead of owners' equity to designate an owner's investment in the business. We can emphasize the residual, or "leftover," nature of owners' equity by expressing the balance sheet equation as follows:

$$\text{Owners' equity} = \text{Assets} - \text{Liabilities}$$

This shows that the owners' claims are the amount left over after deducting the liabilities from the assets. Accountants also use the term **net assets** to refer to assets less liabilities.

net assets
Assets less liabilities.

Balance Sheet Transactions

> ▶▶ **OBJECTIVE 3**
>
> Analyze business transactions and relate them to changes in the balance sheet.

Accountants record every transaction entered into by an entity. An **entity** is an organization or a section of an organization that stands apart from other organizations and individuals as a separate economic unit. For most of our examples the entity is a company. A **transaction** is any event that affects the financial position of an entity and that an accountant can reliably record in monetary terms. Every transaction affects the balance sheet. When accountants record a transaction, they make at least two entries so the total assets always equal the total liabilities plus owners' equity. That is, they must maintain the equality of the balance sheet equation for every transaction. If a balance sheet balances before a transaction, adding or subtracting a single amount would necessarily leave the balance sheet out of balance. Because single entries cannot maintain the balance in the balance sheet, we often call the system that records transactions a *double-entry* accounting system, as we explain further in Chapter 3.

entity
An organization or a section of an organization that stands apart from other organizations and individuals as a separate economic unit.

transaction
Any event that affects the financial position of an entity and that an accountant can reliably record in monetary terms.

Let's take a look at some transactions of Biwheels Company to see how typical transactions affect the balance sheet.

TRANSACTION 1, INITIAL INVESTMENT The first Biwheels transaction was the investment by the owner on January 2, 20X2. Lopez deposited $400,000 in a business bank account entitled Biwheels Company. The transaction affects the balance sheet equation as follows:

	Assets	=	Liabilities	+	Owner's Equity
	Cash				Lopez, Capital
(1)	+400,000	=			+400,000
					(Owner investment)

This transaction increases both the assets, specifically Cash, and the owner's equity, specifically Lopez, Capital. It does not affect liabilities. Why? Because Lopez's business has no obligation to an outside party because of this transaction. We use a parenthetical note, "Owner investment," to identify the reason for the transaction's effect on owner's equity. The total amounts on the left side of the equation are equal to the total amounts on the right side, as they should be.

TRANSACTION 2, LOAN FROM BANK On January 2, 20X2, Biwheels Company also borrows from Chase Bank, signing a promissory note for $100,000. The $100,000 increases Biwheels' cash. The effect of this loan transaction on the balance sheet equation is as follows:

	Assets	=	Liabilities	+	Owner's Equity
	Cash	=	Note Payable	+	Lopez, Capital
(1)	+400,000	=			+400,000
(2)	+100,000	=	+100,000		
Bal.	500,000	=	100,000		400,000
	500,000			500,000	

The loan increases the asset, Cash, and increases the liability, Note Payable, by the same amount, $100,000. After completing the transaction, Biwheels has assets of $500,000, liabilities of $100,000, and owner's equity of $400,000. As always, the sums of the individual account balances (abbreviated Bal.) on each side of the equation are equal.

TRANSACTION 3, ACQUIRE STORE EQUIPMENT FOR CASH On January 3, 20X2, Biwheels acquires miscellaneous store equipment—shelves, display cases, lighting, et cetera—for $15,000 cash. Store equipment is an example of a **long-lived asset**—an asset that a company expects to use for more than 1 year.

long-lived asset
An asset that a company expects to use for more than 1 year.

	Assets			=	Liabilities	+	Owner's Equity
	Cash	+	Store Equipment	=	Note Payable	+	Lopez, Capital
Bal.	500,000			=	100,000		400,000
(3)	−15,000		+15,000	=			
Bal.	485,000		15,000	=	100,000		400,000
		500,000				500,000	

This transaction increases one asset, Store Equipment, and decreases another asset, Cash, by the same amount. The form of the assets changes, but the total amount of assets remains the same. Moreover, the right-side items do not change.

Biwheels can prepare a balance sheet at any point in time. The balance sheet for January 3, after the first three transactions, would look like this:

Biwheels Company

Balance Sheet

January 3, 20X2

Assets		Liabilities and Owner's Equity	
Cash	$485,000	Liabilities (Note payable)	$100,000
Store equipment	15,000	Lopez, capital	400,000
Total assets	$500,000	Total liabilities and owner's equity	$500,000

Transaction Analysis

Accountants record transactions in an organization's accounts. An **account** is a summary record of the changes in a particular asset, liability, or owners' equity, and the account balance is the total of all entries to the account to date. For example, Biwheels' Cash account through January 3 shows increases of $400,000 and $100,000 and a decrease of $15,000, leaving an account balance of $485,000. The analysis of transactions is the heart of accounting. For each transaction, the accountant determines (1) which specific accounts the transaction affects, (2) whether it increases or decreases each account balance, and (3) the amount of the change in each account balance. After recording all the transactions for some period, the accountant will summarize these transactions into financial statements that managers, investors, and others use when making decisions.

account
A summary record of the changes in a particular asset, liability, or owners' equity.

Exhibit 1-2 shows how to analyze a series of transactions using the balance sheet equation. We number the transactions for easy reference. Examine the first three transactions in Exhibit 1-2, which summarize the transactions we have already discussed.

Next, consider how to analyze each of the following additional transactions:

4. January 4. Biwheels acquires bicycles from Trek for $120,000 cash.
5. January 5. Biwheels buys bicycle parts for $10,000 from Shimano. Biwheels will sell these parts in addition to the bicycles themselves. No cash changes hands on January 5. Rather, Shimano requires $4,000 by January 10 and the balance in 30 days.
6. January 6. Biwheels buys bicycles from Schwinn for $30,000. Schwinn requires a cash down payment of $10,000, and Biwheels must pay the remaining balance in 60 days.

EXHIBIT 1-2

Biwheels Company

Analysis of Transactions for January 2 to January 12, 20X2

Description of Transactions	Assets			=	Liabilities + Owner's Equity		
	Cash +	Merchandise Inventory +	Store Equipment =		Note Payable +	Accounts Payable +	Lopez, Capital
(1) Initial investment	+400,000			=			+400,000
(2) Loan from bank	+100,000			=	+100,000		
(3) Acquire store equipment for cash	−15,000		+15,000	=			
(4) Acquire inventory for cash	−120,000	+120,000		=			
(5) Acquire inventory on credit		+10,000		=		+10,000	
(6) Acquire inventory for cash plus credit	−10,000	+30,000		=		+20,000	
(7) Sale of equipment	+1,000		−1,000	=			
(8) Return of inventory acquired on January 6		−800		=		−800	
(9) Payment to creditor	−4,000			=		−4,000	
Balance, January 12, 20X2	352,000 +	159,200 +	14,000 =		100,000 +	25,200+	400,000
		525,200				525,200	

7. January 7. Biwheels sells a store display case to a business neighbor after Lopez decides he dislikes it. Its selling price, $1,000, happens to be exactly equal to its cost. The neighbor pays cash.
8. January 8. Biwheels returns four bicycles (which it had acquired for $200 each) to Schwinn for full credit (an $800 reduction of the amount that Biwheels owes Schwinn).
9. January 10. Biwheels pays $4,000 to Shimano.
10. January 12. Lopez remodels his home for $35,000, paying by check from his personal bank account.

Use the format in Exhibit 1-2 to analyze each transaction. Try to do your own analysis of each transaction before looking at the entries in the exhibit.

INTERPRETING FINANCIAL STATEMENTS

Transaction 10 does not appear in Exhibit 1-2. Why not?

Answer

Transaction 10 is a personal transaction by Lopez and does not involve Biwheels as a business. Lopez would record it in his personal accounts, but it does not belong in Biwheels' business accounts. It is important for readers of financial statements to identify the entity accounted for in the financial statements—which in our case is Biwheels, a business.

inventory

Goods held by a company for the purpose of sale to customers.

TRANSACTION 4, PURCHASE INVENTORY FOR CASH **Inventory** refers to goods held by the company for the purpose of sale to customers. The bicycles are inventory, or Merchandise Inventory, to Biwheels. Inventory increases by the amount paid for the bicycles, and cash decreases by the same amount.

	Assets			=	Liabilities + Owner's Equity	
	Cash	+	Merchandise Inventory	+ Store Equipment	=	Note Payable	+ Lopez, Capital

	Cash	Merchandise Inventory	Store Equipment	=	Note Payable	Lopez, Capital
Bal.	485,000		15,000	=	100,000	400,000
(4)	−120,000	+120,000		=		
Bal.	365,000	120,000	15,000	=	100,000	400,000

$$\underbrace{500,000}_{} \qquad \underbrace{500,000}_{}$$

TRANSACTION 5, PURCHASE INVENTORY ON CREDIT Companies throughout the world make most purchases on credit instead of for cash. An authorized signature of the buyer is usually good enough to ensure payment. We call this practice buying on **open account**. The buyer records the money owed on its balance sheet as an account payable. Thus, an **account payable** is a liability that results from a purchase of goods or services on open account. As Exhibit 1-2 shows for this transaction, the merchandise inventory (an asset account) of Biwheels increases, and we add an account payable to Shimano (a liability account) in the amount of $10,000 to keep the equation in balance. Both total assets and total liabilities and owner's equity increase to $510,000.

open account
Buying or selling on credit, usually by just an "authorized signature" of the buyer.

account payable
A liability that results from a purchase of goods or services on open account.

	Assets			=	Liabilities + Owner's Equity		
	Cash	+ Merchandise Inventory	+ Store Equipment	=	Note Payable	+ Accounts Payable	+ Lopez, Capital
Bal.	365,000	120,000	15,000	=	100,000		400,000
(5)		+10,000		=		+10,000	
Bal.	365,000	130,000	15,000	=	100,000	10,000	400,000

$$\underbrace{510,000}_{} \qquad \underbrace{510,000}_{}$$

TRANSACTION 6, PURCHASE INVENTORY FOR CASH PLUS CREDIT This transaction illustrates a **compound entry** because it affects more than two balance sheet accounts (two asset accounts and one liability account, in this case). Merchandise inventory increases by the full amount of its cost regardless of whether Biwheels makes its payment in full now, in full later, or partially now and partially later. Therefore, Biwheels' Merchandise Inventory (an asset account) increases by $30,000, Cash (an asset account) decreases by $10,000, and Accounts Payable (a liability account) increases by the difference, $20,000.

compound entry
A transaction that affects more than two accounts.

	Assets			=	Liabilities + Owner's Equity		
	Cash	+ Merchandise Inventory	+ Store Equipment	=	Note Payable	+ Accounts Payable	+ Lopez, Capital
Bal.	365,000	130,000	15,000	=	100,000	10,000	400,000
(6)	−10,000	+30,000		=		+20,000	
Bal.	355,000	160,000	15,000	=	100,000	30,000	400,000

$$\underbrace{530,000}_{} \qquad \underbrace{530,000}_{}$$

TRANSACTION 7, SALE OF ASSET FOR CASH This transaction increases Cash by $1,000 and decreases Store Equipment by $1,000. In this case, the transaction affects asset accounts only. One increases and one decreases, with no change in total assets. Liabilities and owner's equity do not change.

	Assets			=	Liabilities + Owner's Equity		
	Cash	+ Merchandise Inventory	+ Store Equipment	=	Note Payable +	Accounts Payable +	Lopez, Capital
Bal.	355,000	160,000	15,000	=	100,000	30,000	400,000
(7)	+1,000		−1,000	=			
Bal.	356,000	160,000	14,000	=	100,000	30,000	400,000
		530,000				530,000	

TRANSACTION 8, RETURN OF INVENTORY TO SUPPLIER When a company returns merchandise to its suppliers for credit, the transaction reduces its merchandise inventory account and reduces its liabilities. In this instance, the amount of the decrease on each side of the equation is $800.

	Assets			=	Liabilities + Owner's Equity		
	Cash	+ Merchandise Inventory	+ Store Equipment	=	Note Payable +	Accounts Payable +	Lopez, Capital
Bal.	356,000	160,000	14,000	=	100,000	30,000	400,000
(8)		−800		=		−800	
Bal.	356,000	159,200	14,000	=	100,000	29,200	400,000
		529,200				529,200	

creditor

A person or entity to whom a company owes money.

TRANSACTION 9, PAYMENT TO CREDITOR A **creditor** is a person or entity to whom the company owes money. For Biwheels, Shimano, who supplied the bicycle parts on credit, is a creditor. The payment to Shimano decreases both assets (Cash) and liabilities (Accounts Payable) by $4,000.

	Assets			=	Liabilities + Owner's Equity		
	Cash	+ Merchandise Inventory	+ Store Equipment	=	Note Payable +	Accounts Payable +	Lopez, Capital
Bal.	356,000	159,200	14,000	=	100,000	29,200	400,000
(9)	−4,000			=		−4,000	
Bal.	352,000	159,200	14,000	=	100,000	25,200	400,000
		525,200				525,200	

Preparing the Balance Sheet

▶▶ OBJECTIVE 4

Prepare a balance sheet from transactions data.

To prepare a balance sheet, we can compute a cumulative total for each account in Exhibit 1-2 at any date. The following balance sheet uses the totals at the bottom of Exhibit 1-2. Observe once again that a balance sheet represents the financial impact of all transactions up to a specific point in time, here January 12, 20X2.

Biwheels Company
Balance Sheet
January 12, 20X2

Assets		Liabilities and Owner's Equity	
Cash	$352,000	Note payable	$100,000
Merchandise inventory	159,200	Accounts payable	25,200
Store equipment	14,000	Total liabilities	$125,200
Total	$525,200	Lopez, capital	400,000
		Total	$525,200

Although Biwheels could prepare a new balance sheet after each transaction, companies usually produce balance sheets only when needed by managers and at the end of each quarter for reporting to the public.

Summary Problem for Your Review

PROBLEM

Analyze the following additional transactions of Biwheels Company. Begin with the balances shown for January 12, 20X2, in Exhibit 1-2 on page 12. Prepare a balance sheet for Biwheels Company on January 16, after recording these additional transactions.

i. Biwheels pays $10,000 on the bank loan (ignore interest).
ii. Lopez buys furniture for his home for $5,000, using his family's charge account at Macy's.
iii. Biwheels buys more bicycles for inventory from Cannondale for $50,000. Biwheels pays one-half the amount in cash and owes one-half on open account.
iv. Biwheels pays another $4,000 to Shimano.

SOLUTION

See Exhibits 1-3 and 1-4. Note that we ignored transaction ii because it is wholly personal. However, visualize how this transaction would affect Lopez's personal balance sheet. His assets, Home Furniture, would increase by $5,000, and his liabilities, Accounts Payable, would also increase by $5,000.

EXHIBIT 1-3

Biwheels Company

Analysis of Additional January Transactions (in $)

Description of Transaction	Cash	+	Merchandise Inventory	+	Store Equipment	=	Note Payable	+	Accounts Payable	+	Lopez, Capital
Balance, January 12, 20X2	352,000	+	159,200	+	14,000	=	100,000	+	25,200	+	400,000
(i) Payment on bank loan	−10,000					=	−10,000				
(ii) Personal; no effect											
(iii) Acquire inventory, half for cash, half on credit	−25,000		+50,000			=			+25,000		
(iv) Payment to supplier	−4,000					=			−4,000		
Balance, January 16, 20X2	313,000	+	209,200	+	14,000	=	90,000	+	46,200	+	400,000
			536,200			=			536,200		

Assets		Liabilities and Owner's Equity	
Cash	$313,000	Liabilities:	
Merchandise inventory	209,200	Note payable	$ 90,000
Store equipment	14,000	Accounts payable	46,200
Total	$536,200	Total liabilities	$136,200
		Lopez, capital	400,000
		Total	$536,200

EXHIBIT 1-4

Biwheels Company

Balance Sheet
January 16, 20X2

Examples of Actual Corporate Balance Sheets

To become more familiar with the balance sheet, consider the balance sheets for Starbucks and Jack in the Box for 2011, shown in Exhibit 1-5. (We have omitted many details present in the actual balance sheets to simplify and condense the examples.) Both Starbucks and Jack in the Box provide food services, but their strategies are different. Starbucks focuses on coffee, has

EXHIBIT 1-5

Comparative Consolidated Condensed Balance Sheets, October 2, 2011

($ in millions)

	Starbucks	Jack in the Box
Assets		
Cash and cash equivalents	$1,148.1	$ 11.4
Inventories	965.8	38.9
Prepaid expenses	161.5	18.7
Property, plant, and equipment	2,355.0	855.4
Other assets	2,730.0	507.9
Total assets	$7,360.4	$1,432.3
Liabilities and Owners' Equity		
Accounts payable	$ 540.0	$ 94.3
Long-term debt	549.5	447.3
Other liabilities	1,883.6	484.7
Total liabilities	2,973.1	1,026.3
Total owners' equity	4,387.3	406.0
Total liabilities and owners' equity	$7,360.4	$1,432.3

17,000 outlets, more than six times as many as Jack in the Box's 2,500, and has expanded internationally to 50 countries. Jack in the Box sells fast food and has outlets primarily in the western and southern United States.

From the companies' balance sheets, we learn that Starbucks has more than five times as many total assets as Jack in the Box, but it has less than three times more property, plant, and equipment. Starbucks has invested ($2,355,000,000 ÷ 17,000) = $138,529 in property, plant, and equipment for each coffee shop, while Jack in the Box has invested ($855,400,000 ÷ 2,500) = $342,160 per location, two-and-a half times as much. Just think about the investment required by a drive-in restaurant compared with that in a coffee shop—the difference is logical. We also see that Starbucks has much more cash, almost 23% more long-term debt, and more than ten times the owners' equity. Notice that on the balance sheets of both companies the total assets are equal to the total liabilities and owners' equity. Every balance sheet maintains this equality. Details about various items in the balance sheet will gradually become more understandable as each chapter explains the nature of the various major financial statements and examines their components.

Summary Problem for Your Review

PROBLEM

Exhibit 1-6 contains Starbucks' condensed balance sheets for 2010 and 2011. Respond to the following questions:

1. As of what date were the 2010 and 2011 balance sheets prepared? Are these points in time or spans of time?
2. What are total assets for each of the 2 years shown in the balance sheets? What balance sheet accounts changed the most over the 2 years?
3. Total assets increased by $974.5 million from October 3, 2010, to October 2, 2011. What was the change in total liabilities plus owners' equity over that same time period?
4. Of the following items on Starbucks' balance sheet, which are assets and which are liabilities: Property, Plant, and Equipment; Cash and Cash Equivalents; Long-Term Debt; Inventories; and Accounts Payable?

SOLUTION

1. Starbucks presents two balance sheets. The most recent is dated October 2, 2011, and the earlier one is dated October 3, 2010. These are both points in time; all balance sheets represent a single point in time.

Assets	October 2, 2011	October 3, 2010
Cash and cash equivalents	$1,148.1	$1,164.0
Inventories	965.8	543.3
Prepaid expenses	161.5	156.5
Property, plant, and equipment	2,355.0	2,416.5
Other assets	2,730.0	2,105.6
Total assets	$7,360.4	$6,385.9
Liabilities and Owners' Equity		
Accounts payable	$ 540.0	$ 282.6
Long-term debt	549.5	549.4
Other liabilities	1,883.6	1,871.6
Total liabilities	2,973.1	2,703.6
Total owners' equity	4,387.3	3,682.3
Total liabilities and owners' equity	$7,360.4	$6,385.9

EXHIBIT 1-6

Starbucks Corporation
Consolidated Balance Sheets ($ in millions)

2. Total assets increased by $974.5 million, from $6,385.9 million to $7,360.4 million. Most of the increase occurred in Inventory ($422.5 million) and Other Assets ($624.4 million). Property, plant, and equipment decreased by $61.5 million despite the increase in total assets.
3. Total Liabilities and Owners' Equity increased by the same amount as the increase in total assets: $974.5 million. The two increases must be the same to keep the balance sheet equation in balance.
4. Property, Plant, and Equipment, Cash and Cash Equivalents, and Inventories are assets. Long-term Debt and Accounts Payable are liabilities.

Types of Ownership

Although most accounting processes are the same for all types of companies, a few differences in accounting for owners' equity arise because of the legal structure of the company. We next look at three basic forms of ownership structures for business entities: sole proprietorships, partnerships, and corporations.

Sole Proprietorships

A **sole proprietorship** is a business with a single owner. Most often, the owner is also the manager. Therefore, sole proprietorships tend to be small businesses such as local stores and restaurants and professionals such as dentists or attorneys who operate alone. Biwheels started out as a sole proprietorship owned and operated by Hector Lopez. From an accounting viewpoint, a sole proprietorship is a separate entity that is distinct from the proprietor. Thus, the cash in a dentist's business account is an asset of the dental practice, whereas the cash in the dentist's personal account is not. Similarly, Lopez's remodeling of his home (see transaction 10, p. 12) was a personal transaction, not a business transaction.

Partnerships

A **partnership** is an organization that joins two or more individuals who act as co-owners. Many auto dealerships are partnerships, as are groups of physicians, attorneys, or accountants who group together to provide services. Partnerships can be gigantic. The largest international accounting firms have thousands of partners. Again, from an accounting viewpoint, each partnership is an individual entity that is separate from the personal activities of each partner.

Corporations

Most large businesses, including all 30 Dow companies listed in Exhibit 1-1 (p. 4), are corporations. **Corporations** are business organizations created under state laws in the United States. The owners of a corporation have **limited liability**, which means that corporate creditors (such

▸▸**OBJECTIVE 5**
Compare the features of sole proprietorships, partnerships, and corporations.

sole proprietorship
A business with a single owner.

partnership
A form of organization that joins two or more individuals together as co-owners.

corporation
A business organization that is created by individual state laws.

limited liability
A feature of the corporate form of organization whereby corporate creditors (such as banks or suppliers) ordinarily have claims against the corporate assets only, not against the personal assets of the owners.

as banks or suppliers) ordinarily have claims against the corporate assets only, not against the personal assets of the owners. In contrast, owners in sole proprietorships and partnerships are usually personally liable for any obligations of the business. (An exception is a partnership structured as a limited liability company [LLC], which limit the liability of partners.) Another difference is that the owners of proprietorships and partnerships are typically active managers of the business, whereas large corporations generally hire professional managers.

Ownership shares in most large corporations consist of publicly traded stock. This means that the company sells shares in its ownership to the public. Purchasers of the shares become shareholders (or stockholders). Large publicly traded corporations often have thousands of shareholders. In contrast, some corporations are **privately owned** by families, small groups of shareholders, or a single individual, with shares of ownership not sold to the public. These are also called **closely held** or **unlisted** corporations. Corporations in the United States often use one of the abbreviations Co., Corp., or Inc. in their names.

Internationally, organizational forms similar to corporations are common. In the United Kingdom, such companies frequently use the word "limited" (Ltd.) in their names. In Germany you will see AG or GmbH, while in Spain corporations use the initials S.A. Corporate laws vary in details across countries, but the basic characteristics of corporations are quite universal.

privately owned (closely held, unlisted)
A corporation owned by a family, a small group of shareholders, or a single individual, in which shares of ownership are not publicly sold.

Advantages and Disadvantages of the Corporate Form

The corporate form of organization has many advantages. We have already discussed limited liability. What are some other advantages? One is easy transfer of ownership. To sell shares in its ownership, the corporation usually issues **stock certificates** as formal evidence of ownership. Some shareholders may hold the physical certificates. However, the most common type of ownership is a brokerage account that electronically registers ownership shares. Owners of these shares, whether they hold them physically or electronically, can sell them to others. Numerous stock exchanges in the United States and worldwide facilitate buying and selling of shares. Investors buy and sell nearly 2 billion shares on an average day on the **New York Stock Exchange** (NYSE), the largest exchange in the world with about 2,300 listed companies valued at $12.4 trillion. Another U.S. exchange, **NASDAQ**, lists the stock of more than 2,700 companies with a total market value of $3.5 trillion. While the NASDAQ is composed primarily of smaller, tech-oriented companies, it also includes **Microsoft**, **Intel**, **Yahoo!**, **Ebay**, **Comcast**, and a few other large companies, mostly technology companies, among its listings. Other large exchanges include those in Tokyo, Hong Kong, Shanghai, Frankfurt, and London. Companies can be listed on more than one exchange. Many Japanese, German, and British firms have shares traded on the NYSE, and many U.S. companies list their shares abroad. The London Stock Exchange is one of the most international of the exchanges with listed companies from 70 countries. Exhibit 1-7 displays just a few of the international companies listed on the London exchange.

stock certificate
Formal evidence of ownership shares in a corporation.

Because owners can easily trade shares of stock, corporations have the advantage of raising ownership capital from hundreds or thousands of potential stockholders. For example, **General Electric** has millions of stockholders, owning a total of nearly 10 billion shares of stock. More than 60 million shares of General Electric trade hands on a typical day.

A corporation also has the advantage of continuity of existence. The life of a corporation is indefinite—it continues even if its ownership changes. In contrast, proprietorships

---

INTERPRETING FINANCIAL STATEMENTS

Biwheels is organized as a sole proprietorship. What would be the biggest advantage for Mr. Lopez in converting it to a corporation?

Answer
As a sole proprietorship, Mr. Lopez is personally liable for all the liabilities of Biwheels. If it were a corporation, his liability would

be limited to the investment he has already made. There may also be tax advantages, and Mr. Lopez would find it easier to sell part of the business by issuing shares if it is a corporation.

EXHIBIT 1-7

Sample of Companies Traded on the London Stock Exchange

Company	Country	Company	Country
Platinum Australia Ltd.	Australia	Kazkommertsbank JSC	Kazakhstan
Grupo Clarín SA	Argentina	Press Corp.	Malawi
Arab Insurance Group	Bahrain	Steppe Cement	Malaysia
Beximco Pharmaceuticals	Bangladesh	Go PLC	Malta
Worldsec	Bermuda	Royal Dutch Shell	Netherlands
Canadian Pacific Railways	Canada	Norsk Hydro ASA	Norway
Integra Group	Cayman Islands	MCB Bank	Pakistan
China Petroleum and Chemical Corp.	China	Telekomunikacja Polska	Poland
Hrvatski Telekom	Croatia	Qatar Telecom	Qatar
Komerčni Banka	Czech Republic	Bank of Ireland	Republic of Ireland
Suez Cement Company	Egypt	Gazprom OAO	Russia
Powerflute Oyj	Finland	Harmony Gold Mining Co.	South Africa
Groupe Eurotunnel SA	France	Hyundai Motor Co.	South Korea
Siemens AG	Germany	Telefónica SA	Spain
National Bank of Greece	Greece	XCounter	Sweden
Tisza Chemical Group	Hungary	IBC Financial Group	Switzerland
Amtek Auto	India	Sunplus Technology	Taiwan
Emblaze Systems	Israel	Boeing Co.	USA
Honda Motor Co.	Japan	Abbott Laboratories	USA
Sony Corp.	Japan	General Electric	USA

and partnerships in the United States officially terminate on the death or complete withdrawal of an owner.

Finally, tax laws may favor a corporation or a partnership or a proprietorship. This depends heavily on the personal tax situations of the owners and is beyond the scope of this book.

Although only 20% of U.S. businesses are corporations, they do 90% of the business. The 70% of businesses that are sole proprietorships generate only about 6% of the business activity. Because of the economic importance of corporations, this book emphasizes the corporate form of ownership.

Accounting Differences Between Proprietorships, Partnerships, and Corporations

All business entities account for assets and liabilities similarly. However, corporations account for owners' equity differently than do sole proprietorships and partnerships. The basic concepts that underlie the owners' equity section of the balance sheet are the same for all three forms of ownership—owners' equity always equals total assets less total liabilities. However, we often label the owners' equities for proprietorships and partnerships with the word capital. In contrast, we call owners' equity for a corporation **stockholders' equity** or **shareholders' equity**. Examine the possibilities for the Biwheels Company in Exhibit 1-8.

The accounts for the proprietorship and the partnership show owners' equity as straightforward records of the capital invested by the owners. (In the partnership example, we assume that Lopez has two partners, each with a 10% stake in Biwheels.) For a corporation, though, we call the total capital investment by owners, both at and subsequent to the inception of the business, **paid-in capital**. We record it in two parts: common stock (or capital stock) at par value and paid-in capital in excess of par value. Let's next explore what par value means.

> ▶▶ **OBJECTIVE 6**
> Identify how the owners' equity section in a corporate balance sheet differs from that in a sole proprietorship or a partnership.

stockholders' equity (shareholders' equity)
Owners' equity of a corporation. The excess of assets over liabilities of a corporation.

paid-in capital
The total capital investment in a corporation by its owners, both at and subsequent to the inception of the business.

EXHIBIT 1-8

Owners' Equity for Different Types of Organizations

OWNER'S EQUITY FOR A PROPRIETORSHIP	
(Assume Hector Lopez Is the Sole Owner)	
Hector Lopez, capital	$400,000
OWNERS' EQUITY FOR A PARTNERSHIP	
(Assume Lopez Has Two Partners)	
Hector Lopez, capital	$320,000
Alex Handl, capital	40,000
Susan Eastman, capital	40,000
Total partners' capital	$400,000
OWNERS' EQUITY FOR A CORPORATION	
(Assume Lopez Has Incorporated)	
Stockholder's equity:	
Paid-in capital:	
Capital stock, 10,000 shares issued at par value of $10 per share	$100,000
Paid-in capital in excess of par value	300,000
Total paid-in capital	$400,000

The Meaning of Par Value

par value (stated value)
The nominal dollar amount printed on stock certificates.

Many states require stock certificates to have some dollar amount printed on them. We call this amount **par value** or **stated value**. Typically, a company sells stock at a price that is higher than its par value. The excess of the total amount the company receives for the stock and the par value of the shares is called **paid-in capital in excess of par value** or **additional paid-in capital**. This distinction is of little economic importance, and we introduce it here only because you will frequently encounter it in actual financial statements.

paid-in capital in excess of par value (additional paid-in capital)
When issuing stock, the excess of the total amount the company receives for the stock over the par value of the shares.

Let's take a closer look at par value by altering our Biwheels example. We now assume that Biwheels is a corporation and that Lopez received 10,000 shares of stock for his $400,000 investment. Thus, he paid $40 per share. The par value is $10 per share, and the paid-in capital in excess of par value is $30 per share. The total ownership claim of $400,000 arising from the investment is split between two equity claims, one for $100,000 capital stock at par value and one for $300,000 paid-in capital in excess of par value:

$$\text{Total Paid-in Capital} = \text{Capital Stock at Par} + \begin{array}{c} \text{Paid-in Capital in} \\ \text{Excess of Par Value} \end{array}$$

$$\begin{array}{c} \text{(Average Issue Price per Share} \\ \times \text{Number of Shares Issued)} \end{array} = \begin{array}{c} \text{(Par Value per Share} \\ \times \text{Number of Shares Issued)} \end{array} + \begin{array}{c} \text{[(Average Issue Price per Share} \\ - \text{Par Value per Share)} \\ \times \text{Number of Shares Issued]} \end{array}$$

$$(\$40 \times 10,000) = (\$10 \times 10,000) + [(\$40 - \$10) \times 10,000]$$

$$\$400,000 = \$100,000 + \$300,000$$

common stock
Par value of the stock purchased by common shareholders of a corporation.

Exhibit 1-9 shows the paid-in capital for Starbucks as of October 2, 2011. Notice that Starbucks separates the par value from the capital in excess of par value. It uses the label **common stock** to describe the par value of the stock purchased by the common shareholders. Starbucks uses "other additional paid-in capital" to describe the amount paid-in above the par value. Some companies, such as General Motors, use a less descriptive term, capital surplus, for this amount. Although it would be nice to use only one phrase for each item in this textbook, the world is full of different words used for identical accounting items. One of our goals is to help you to prepare to read and understand actual financial statements and reports. Therefore, we use many of the synonyms you will encounter when reading financial statements.

EXHIBIT 1-9

Paid-in Capital for Starbucks

(in millions except per share amounts)

Starbucks
October 2, 2011

Common stock ($.001 par value)—authorized, 1,200.0 shares; issued and outstanding, 744.8 shares	$ 0.7
Other additional paid-in capital	40.5
Total paid-in capital	$41.2

The par value per share for Starbucks is only $0.001, much smaller than the amount investors paid Starbucks for the common shares. We know this because the capital in excess of par value is much larger than the common stock at par value. The extremely small amount of par value is common in practice and illustrates the insignificance of par value in today's business world. Some companies provide a single total for par value and additional paid-in capital on their balance sheets. This combined reporting is acceptable because readers of financial statements would learn little of significance from separating the two components. Just remember that the sum of common stock at par value and additional paid-in capital is the amount that owners actively contributed to the firm. These **common stockholders** have a "residual" ownership in the corporation, that is, they have a claim on whatever is left over after all other claimants have been paid at liquidation. This could be a large amount for a successful company or nothing for an unsuccessful one. Although these paid-in capital accounts identify the amount the stockholders contributed, this is not the amount they might receive now or in the future.

common stockholders
The owners who have a "residual" ownership in the corporation.

Common stockholders buy shares of stock as investments. Sometimes they purchase the stock from the company. In such a case, the company increases both its cash and its paid-in capital. However, the majority of stock transactions occur between stockholders. Often, a broker matches a buyer and seller using the services of one of the stock exchanges such as the NYSE or the NASDAQ. When Mary sells 100 shares of Starbucks stock to Carlos, the transaction does not affect Starbucks' balance sheet. Starbucks does not receive cash, and it issues no new shares. The only effect on Starbucks will be to replace Mary with Carlos on the corporate records as an owner of the 100 shares of stock.

Summary Problems for Your Review

PROBLEM

"If I purchase 100 shares of the outstanding stock of Google, I invest my money directly in that corporation. Google must record that event." Do you agree? Explain.

SOLUTION

Stockholders invest directly in a corporation only when the corporation originally issues the stock. For example, Google may issue 100,000 shares of stock at $30 per share, bringing in $3 million to the corporation. This is a transaction between the corporation and the stockholders. It affects the corporate financial position:

> Cash $3,000,000   Stockholders' equity $3,000,000

Subsequently, an original stockholder (Kyung Kim) may sell 100 shares of that stock to another individual (Jane Soliman) for $50 per share. This is a private transaction. The corporation receives no cash. Of course, the corporation records the fact that Soliman now owns the 100 shares originally owned by Kim, but the corporate financial position is unchanged. Accounting focuses on the business entity. Private stock trades of the owners have no effect on the financial position of the entity.

PROBLEM

"One individual can be an owner, an employee, and a creditor of a corporation." Do you agree? Explain.

SOLUTION

The corporation enters contracts, hires employees, buys buildings, and conducts other business. The president, the other officers, and all the workers are employees of the corporation. Thus, Bill Gates could own some of the capital stock of **Microsoft** and also be an employee. Because money owed to employees for salaries is a liability, he could be an owner, an employee, and a creditor. Similarly, Carmen Smith could be an employee of a cell phone company, a stockholder of the company, and also receive cell phone services from the same company. Suppose she has earned wages that the company has not yet paid and she has not yet paid her current cell phone bill. She is simultaneously an owner, employee, customer, creditor, and debtor of the company.

Stockholders and the Board of Directors

board of directors
A body elected by the shareholders to represent them. It is responsible for appointing and monitoring the managers, among other duties.

In sole proprietorships and partnerships, the owners are usually also managers. In contrast, corporate shareholders (that is, the owners) delegate responsibility for management of the company to professional managers. To oversee managers, the shareholders elect a **board of directors**. Among other duties, the board of directors is responsible for appointing and monitoring the managers, as shown in the following diagram:

chief executive officer (CEO)
The top manager in an organization.

Why is the separation of ownership and management in a corporation desirable? It allows stockholders to invest resources without needing to devote time to managing. In addition, the company can select managers for their managerial skills, not their ability to invest large sums of money in the firm. The board of directors is the link between stockholders and managers. The board's duty is to ensure that managers act in the best interests of shareholders. In some of the business scandals of the last decade, shareholders have accused boards of not fulfilling this responsibility and thereby causing shareholders to lose billions of dollars.

When boards of directors do their duty in monitoring management, the corporate form of organization has proved to be effective. When such monitoring fails, management may line its own pockets at the expense of shareholders. When management has too much influence on the election of board members, perhaps by nominating a slate of candidates beholden to management, such monitoring may fail. Additionally, in the United States it has been common for the top manager (**chief executive officer or CEO**) to also serve as chairman of the board. It is difficult for the chairman of the board to monitor the CEO when they are the same person. In the United Kingdom and much of the rest of Europe it is common for the chairman of the board to be an independent director rather than a member of management, and this practice is becoming more common in the United States. In the past, other top managers of the company, such as the president, financial vice president, and marketing vice president, have also been members of the board of directors. However, it is increasingly common for these company officers to attend board meetings as needed but not to serve as voting members of the board.

Independent members of a board often include CEOs and presidents of other corporations, university presidents and professors, attorneys, and community representatives. For example, the eleven-member board of **Starbucks** in 2012 included CEO and Board Chair Howard Schultz, three retired executives from companies other than Starbucks, three current executives of major companies that do not compete with Starbucks, an investment banker, a mutual fund president, a venture capitalist, and a foundation president. Although boards once often had 15–20 members, many companies are moving toward having smaller boards of directors that include fewer members of the company's management team.

Regulation of Financial Reporting

Financial statements are the result of a measurement process that rests on a set of principles. If every accountant used a different set of measurement rules, investors would find it difficult to use and compare financial statements. For example, consider the recording of an asset such as a machine on the balance sheet. If one accountant listed the purchase cost, another the amount for which the company could sell the used machine, and others listed various other amounts, the readers of financial statements would be confused. It would be as if each accountant were speaking a different language. Therefore, accountants have agreed to apply a common set of measurement principles—that is, a common language—to report information on financial statements.

▶▶ **OBJECTIVE 7**
Explain the regulation of financial reporting, including differences between U.S. GAAP and IFRS.

Generally Accepted Accounting Principles

Generally accepted accounting principles (GAAP) is the term that applies to all the broad concepts and detailed practices to be followed in preparing and distributing financial statements. There are two primary sets of GAAP. Companies reporting in more than 100 countries around the world, including all European Union countries, use **International Financial Reporting Standards (IFRS)**. U.S. companies use **Financial Accounting Standards**, usually referred to as **U.S. GAAP**. Each set of standards contains conventions, rules, and procedures that determine acceptable accounting practices. The standards are identical on most significant issues. However, there are a few conceptual differences and more differences in specific measurement details. Authorities are working to eliminate (or at least minimize) the differences in standards between IFRS and U.S. GAAP statements, but many differences are likely to remain in the near future.

Until recently, all companies with stock traded on U.S. stock exchanges had to report using U.S. GAAP or to prepare a report detailing the differences between their statements and statements prepared under U.S. GAAP. However, foreign companies listed on U.S. exchanges can now use IFRS for their financial statements. While companies based in the United States must still use U.S. GAAP, many accountants believe that U.S. regulators will allow all companies to use IFRS within a few years. Why? Because they believe that global capital markets will function more efficiently if all companies issue financial statements based on the same GAAP.

In this book we focus on reporting regulations under U.S. GAAP. Many of the differences between IFRS and U.S. GAAP are in relatively minor details that are beyond the scope of an introductory text. However, we do point out significant differences between U.S. GAAP and IFRS requirements. But before exploring the standards, let's look more closely at the bodies that set the standards.

Standard Setting Bodies

Until recently, most accounting standards were set country by country. However, forces ranging from the creation of the European Union to the emergence of global financial markets have resulted in most companies adopting one of the two main competing sets of standards—U.S. GAAP or IFRS.

The **Financial Accounting Standards Board (FASB)** has been responsible for establishing U.S. GAAP since 1973. The FASB is an independent entity within the private sector consisting of seven individuals who work full-time with a staff to support them. A mandatory fee assessed on all public companies and sales of publications provide the FASB's annual budget of about $32 million. Between 1973 and 2009 the FASB issued 168 Financial Accounting Standards, and in 2009 it compiled all standards and other elements of U.S. GAAP into a single searchable database, the **FASB Accounting Standards Codification**. The Codification classifies U.S. GAAP by topic to make it easy to research financial reporting issues. All changes in U.S. GAAP are now made via *Accounting Standards Updates*. These updates amend the Codification so that it will always be an up-to-date source of U.S. GAAP. As of early 2012 there were 55 such updates.

generally accepted accounting principles (GAAP)
The term that applies to all the broad concepts and detailed practices to be followed in preparing and distributing financial statements. It includes all the conventions, rules, and procedures that together comprise acceptable accounting practice.

International Financial Reporting Standards (IFRS)
The set of GAAP that applies to companies reporting in more than 100 countries around the world.

Financial Accounting Standards (U.S. GAAP)
The set of GAAP that applies to financial reporting in the United States.

Financial Accounting Standards Board (FASB)
The independent private sector body that is responsible for establishing GAAP in the United States.

FASB Accounting Standards Codification
A compilation of all standards and other elements of U.S. GAAP into a single searchable database that is organized by topic to make it easy to research financial reporting issues.

The U.S. Congress has charged the Securities and Exchange Commission (SEC) with the ultimate responsibility for specifying GAAP for companies with publicly traded stock. However, the SEC has formally delegated much rule-making power to the FASB. This public sector–private sector authority relationship can be sketched as follows:

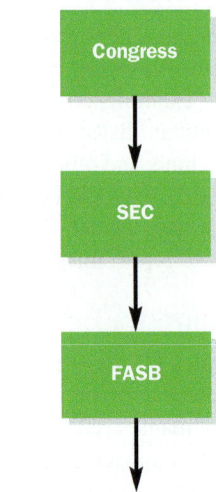

Issues pronouncements on various accounting topics. These pronouncements govern the preparation of typical financial statements.

Note that Congress can overrule both the SEC and the FASB, and the SEC can overrule the FASB. The FASB and the SEC work closely together and seldom have public disagreements. However, on occasion Congress has overruled FASB decisions. The accounting for stock options is an example of this political interplay. In the 1990s, Congress heeded the pleas of constituents and donors and threatened to overrule the FASB if it required companies to recognize stock options granted to managers as an expense of doing business. This caused the FASB to rescind such a proposed requirement and issue a standard that allowed companies flexibility in accounting for stock options. In 2001 and 2002, the FASB received much criticism for submitting to the wishes of Congress. In 2004, after the financial turmoil of the early 2000s and with support from the SEC, the FASB was able to assert its original plan and require companies to record an expense for stock options. Although you may not understand the accounting for stock options at this point, you can see from the example that the setting of accounting principles in the United States (and, indeed, globally) is a complex political process involving heavy interactions among the affected parties: public regulators (Congress and the SEC), private regulators (FASB), companies, those in the public accounting profession, representatives of investors, and other interested groups and lobbyists. GAAP is not a set of arcane rules of interest only to accountants. GAAP can affect many people and companies, and it is an important part of a country's public policy.

International Accounting Standards Board (IASB)
An international body established to develop, in the public interest, a single set of high-quality, understandable, and enforceable global accounting standards.

The **International Accounting Standards Board (IASB)**, which was established in 2001 (as successor to the International Accounting Standards Committee) "to develop, in the public interest, a single set of high quality, understandable and enforceable global accounting standards," sets International Financial Reporting Standards (IFRS). The IASB has 16 members who represent a diversity of geographic and professional backgrounds. Nearly 120 counties require or permit the use of IFRS. A significant step for international accounting standards was the required use of IFRS by companies in the European Union for financial statements prepared after 2005. Of the G20 countries—19 countries plus the European Union, which represent around 90% of global gross national product—all but one either require or permit IFRS or are converging their standards to IFRS.

The motivation for this conformity movement lies in the explosive growth of international commerce. Increasingly, investors commit their money worldwide either as individuals or through retirement accounts or mutual funds. Companies rely on international capital to finance their growth. Therefore, comparability of financial information across companies in different countries is important. Examples of major multinational firms that now publish their financial statements in conformity with IFRS are Allianz (Germany), Nestlé (Switzerland), Nokia (Finland), and Shanghai Petrochemical (China).

Credibility and the Role of Auditing

The separation of owners and managers in a corporation creates potential problems in getting truthful information about the performance of a company. Corporate managers have the best access to information about the company, but they may also have incentives to make the company's performance look better than it really is. Perhaps doing so will make it easier to raise money to open new stores, or perhaps it will lead to increases in managers' compensation. In addition, managers often believe that company conditions are better than they really are because managers are optimistic about the good decisions they have made and the plans they are implementing. The problem shareholders face is that they must rely on managers to tell the truth, because shareholders cannot personally see what is going on in the firm.

One way to solve this credibility problem is to introduce an honorable, expert third party. In the area of financial statements, this third party is an independent registered public accounting firm, commonly called the auditor. The **auditor** examines the information that managers use to prepare the financial statements and provides assurances about the credibility of those statements. Auditors do not provide a guarantee that everything on the financial statements is correct because they examine only a sample of the data underlying the financial statements. However, on seeing the auditor's assurance that the financial statements fairly present a company's economic circumstances, shareholders and potential shareholders can feel more comfortable about using the information to guide their investing activity.

The Certified Public Accountant and the Auditor's Opinion

The desire for third-party assurance about the credibility of financial statements gave rise to the profession of **public accountants**—accountants who offer services to the general public on a fee basis. Providing credibility requires individuals who have both the technical knowledge to assess financial statements and the integrity and independence to assure that they will honestly tell shareholders and other interested parties if management has not produced reliable statements. Such professionals are called certified public accountants (CPAs) in many countries, including the United States, and chartered accountants (CAs) in many others, including most British Commonwealth countries.

In the United States, each state has a Board of Accountancy that sets standards of both knowledge and integrity that public accountants must meet to be licensed as a **certified public accountant (CPA)**. Only CPAs have the right to issue official opinions on financial statements in the United States. To assess management's financial disclosures, CPAs conduct an **audit**—an examination of a company's transactions and the resulting financial statements. The **auditor's opinion** (also called an **independent opinion**) describes the scope and results of the audit. Companies include the opinion with the financial statements in their annual reports and 10-K filings. Auditors use a standard phrasing for their opinions, as illustrated by the opinion rendered by a large CPA firm, Deloitte & Touche LLP, for Starbucks Corporation that appears in Exhibit 1-10. Some phrases in this opinion may be unfamiliar now, but they will become more clear as you read further. For now, reflect on the fact that auditors do not prepare a company's financial statements. Instead, the auditor's opinion is the public accountant's judgment about whether the financial statements prepared by management fairly present economic reality.

The Accounting Profession

To understand auditors and auditors' opinions, you need to know something about the accounting profession. There are many ways to classify accountants, but the easiest and most common way is to divide them into public and private accountants. We already learned that public accountants offer services to the general public for a fee. All other accountants are **private accountants**. This category consists not only of those individuals who work for businesses, but also of those who work for government agencies, including the Internal Revenue Service (IRS), and other nonprofit organizations.

OBJECTIVE 8
Describe auditing and how it enhances the value of financial information.

auditor
A person or firm who examines the information used by managers to prepare the financial statements and attests to the credibility of those statements.

public accountants
Accountants who offer services to the general public on a fee basis.

certified public accountant (CPA)
In the United States, a person earns this designation by meeting standards of both knowledge and integrity set by a State Board of Accountancy. Only CPAs can issue official opinions on financial statements in the United States.

audit
An examination of a company's transactions and the resulting financial statements.

auditor's opinion (independent opinion)
A report describing the scope and results of an audit. Companies include the opinion with the financial statements in their annual reports.

private accountants
Accountants who work for businesses, government agencies, and other nonprofit organizations.

REPORT OF INDEPENDENT REGISTERED PUBLIC ACCOUNTING FIRM

To the Board of Directors and Shareholders of Starbucks Corporation
Seattle, Washington

We have audited the accompanying consolidated balance sheets of Starbucks Corporation and subsidiaries (the "Company") as of October 2, 2011 and October 3, 2010, and the related consolidated statements of earnings, shareholders' equity, and cash flows for each of the three years in the period ended October 2, 2011. These financial statements are the responsibility of the Company's management. Our responsibility is to express an opinion on these financial statements based on our audits.

We conducted our audits in accordance with the standards of the Public Company Accounting Oversight Board (United States). Those standards require that we plan and perform the audit to obtain reasonable assurance about whether the financial statements are free of material misstatement. An audit includes examining, on a test basis, evidence supporting the amounts and disclosures in the financial statements. An audit also includes assessing the accounting principles used and significant estimates made by management, as well as evaluating the overall financial statement presentation. We believe that our audits provide a reasonable basis for our opinion.

In our opinion, such consolidated financial statements present fairly, in all material respects, the financial position of Starbucks Corporation and subsidiaries as of October 2, 2011 and October 3, 2010, and the results of their operations and their cash flows for each of the three years in the period ended October 2, 2011, in conformity with accounting principles generally accepted in the United States of America.

We have also audited, in accordance with the standards of the Public Company Accounting Oversight Board (United States), the Company's internal control over financial reporting as of November 18, 2011, based on criteria established in Internal Control—Integrated Framework issued by the Committee of Sponsoring Organizations of the Treadway Commission and our report dated November 18, 2011, expressed an unqualified opinion on the Company's internal control over financial reporting.

/s/ DELOITTE & TOUCHE LLP
Seattle, Washington
November 18, 2011

Public Accounting Firms

Public accountants work for firms that vary in size and in the type of accounting services they perform. There are small sole proprietorships and partnerships that focus entirely on income tax reporting and bookkeeping services. Other small- to medium-sized firms provide some audit services, as well, and generally serve local, regional, or national clients. There are also a handful of large firms with more than 100,000 partners and offices located throughout the world. Such enormous firms are necessary because their clients also tend to be enormous. For instance, one large CPA firm reported that its annual audit of one client takes the equivalent of 72 accountants working a full year. Another client has 300 separate corporate entities in 40 countries that it must ultimately consolidate into one set of overall financial statements.

The four largest international public accounting firms are as follows:

- **Deloitte Touche Tohmatsu**
- **Ernst & Young**
- **KPMG**
- **PwC**

These four firms audit more than 95% of the companies listed on the NYSE. They have annual billings in excess of $22 billion each.

Audit Regulation

Until the last decade, the U.S. audit profession regulated itself through the **American Institute of Certified Public Accountants (AICPA)**, a professional association of CPAs. The AICPA has counterparts in other parts of the world, such as the Institute of Chartered Accountants in England and Wales (ICAEW) and the Association of Chartered Certified Accountants (ACCA).

The **International Auditing and Assurance Standards Board (IAASB)**, established by the International Federation of Accountants, is working to standardize audit regulation around the globe, but regulation of auditing continues to differ significantly across countries. We will focus on the situation in the United States.

Most government regulation of the accounting profession in the United States stems from the **Sarbanes-Oxley Act** passed in 2002. Among other things, the act (1) established the **Public Company Accounting Oversight Board (PCAOB)** with powers to regulate many aspects of public accounting and to set standards for audit procedures; (2) prohibited public accounting firms from providing to audit clients certain nonaudit services, such as financial information systems design and implementation and internal audit outsourcing services; and (3) required rotation every 5 years of the lead audit or coordinating partner and the reviewing partner on an audit. All accounting firms that audit companies with publicly traded stock in the United States must register with the PCAOB. These **registered public accounting firms** numbered nearly 2,400 in early 2012. The act also regulated corporate governance by requiring boards of publicly held companies to appoint an audit committee composed only of "independent" directors, requiring CEOs and chief financial officers (CFOs) to personally sign a statement taking responsibility for their companies' financial statements, and increasing the criminal penalties for knowingly misreporting financial information.

Despite the government's growing role, the AICPA remains a force in accounting regulation. It regulates entry to the accounting profession by requiring new accountants to (1) have adequate technical knowledge and know how to apply it, and (2) adhere to standards of integrity and independence. To ensure that CPAs have the necessary technical knowledge, the AICPA administers and grades a national examination. The 14-hour, 4-part, computer-based CPA examination covers auditing and attestation, financial accounting and reporting, regulation, and business environment and concepts. Each section of the exam generally has a pass rate of less than 50%, and less than 20% of the candidates pass all four parts in their first attempt.

To ensure proper application of a CPA's technical knowledge, the Public Company Accounting Oversight Board issues **generally accepted auditing standards (GAAS)**. These standards prescribe the minimum steps that an auditor must take in examining the transactions and financial statements and issuing an auditor's opinion. Following GAAS ensures a reasonable chance of discovering any errors or omissions, intentional or unintentional, in a company's financial statements. However, in several well-publicized cases in the last decade, auditors were accused of failure to discover some accounting irregularities in companies such as WorldCom, Tyco, Fannie Mae, Washington Mutual, and others.

Professional Ethics

Auditors have a professional obligation to truthfully report their findings to the public. This is why we call them *public* accountants. Meeting this obligation requires accountants to act with integrity and be independent of management's influence. To help achieve this, members of the AICPA (and many other such organizations globally) must abide by a code of professional conduct. Surveys of public attitudes toward CPAs have consistently ranked the accounting profession as having high ethical standards. However, the corporate scandals in the last decade have caused investors to question some auditors' integrity and, especially, their independence. This led to additional government regulation of auditor independence and a revision of the AICPA's independence and integrity standards. Exhibit 1-11 presents the major requirements of those standards.

The emphasis on ethics extends beyond public accounting. Various professional accounting organizations and state regulatory bodies have procedures for reviewing behavior alleged to violate codes of professional conduct and imposing appropriate penalties. For example, the Institute of Management Accountants (IMA) and the Association of Government Accountants (AGA) each has a code of ethics that its members must meet to retain their membership.

Beyond codes of ethics or codes of conduct, a major influence on the ethical decisions of employees is the "tone at the top." Complete integrity and outspoken support for ethical standards by senior managers is a great motivator of ethical behavior in any organization. Ultimately, ensuring ethical behavior begins with hiring employees who value ethical issues when making decisions.

International Auditing and Assurance Standards Board (IAASB)
A body established by the International Federation of Accountants that is working to standardize audit regulation around the globe.

Sarbanes-Oxley Act
The source of most government regulation of the accounting profession in the United States.

Public Company Accounting Oversight Board (PCAOB)
An agency that regulates many aspects of public accounting and sets standards for audit procedures in the United States.

registered public accounting firm
An accounting firm that registers with the PCAOB and therefore is allowed to audit companies with publicly traded stock in the United States.

generally accepted auditing standards (GAAS)
Standards issued by the Public Company Accounting Oversight Board that prescribe the minimum steps that an auditor must take in examining the transactions and financial statements and issuing an auditor's opinion.

▶▶ OBJECTIVE 9
Evaluate the role of ethics in the accounting process.

EXHIBIT 1-11

AICPA Code of Professional Conduct, Independence, Integrity, and Objectivity Standards: Excerpted and Paraphrased*

I. INDEPENDENCE: The standards indicate that independence will be impaired if

- During the period of the professional engagement a covered member (a) had or was committed to acquire any direct or material indirect financial interest in the client, (b) was a trustee of any trust or executor or administrator of any estate if such trust or estate had or was committed to acquire any direct or material indirect financial interest in the client, (c) had a joint, closely held investment that was material to the covered member, or (d) except as specifically permitted, had any loan to or from the client, any officer or director of the client, or any individual owning 10% or more of the client's outstanding equity securities or other ownership interests.
- During the period of the professional engagement, a partner or professional employee of the firm, his or her immediate family, or any group of such persons acting together owned more than 5% of a client's outstanding equity securities or other ownership interests.
- During the period covered by the financial statements or during the period of the professional engagement, a partner or professional employee of the firm was simultaneously associated with the client as a (a) director, officer, or employee, or in any capacity equivalent to that of a member of management; (b) promoter, underwriter, or voting trustee; or (c) trustee for any pension or profit-sharing trust of the client.

II. INTEGRITY AND OBJECTIVITY: The standards indicate that integrity will be impaired by

- *Knowing misrepresentations in the preparation of financial statements or records.* A member shall be considered to have knowingly misrepresented facts when he or she knowingly (a) makes, or permits or directs another to make, materially false and misleading entries in an entity's financial statements or records; or (b) fails to correct an entity's financial statements or records that are materially false and misleading when he or she has the authority to record an entry; or (c) signs, or permits or directs another to sign, a document containing materially false and misleading information.
- *Conflicts of interest.* A conflict of interest may occur if a member performs a professional service for a client or employer and the member or his or her firm has a relationship with another person, entity, product, or service that could, in the member's professional judgment, be viewed by the client, employer, or other appropriate parties as impairing the member's objectivity.
- *Subordination of judgment.* A member may not knowingly misrepresent facts or subordinate his or her judgment when performing professional services.

*For more details see http://www.aicpa.org/Research/Standards/CodeofConduct/Pages/sec100.aspx. Reprinted by permission of American Institute of CPAs.

High ethical standards by accountants and business executives are also important for a healthy economy. Even if only a few let power and greed drive them to ethically dubious actions, it affects the trust people put in companies. The recent great recession exposed mortgage frauds, investment schemes, and excessive executive compensation. While most companies maintained high ethical standards, enough violated them to create a distrust that negatively affected the entire world economy.

Some managers and accountants justify ethical lapses with statements such as "Everyone else is doing it, why shouldn't I?" However, the vast majority of successful accountants and managers recognize the ethical dimensions of their decisions and act with absolute integrity. Those who do not may get most of the publicity, but there has also been acclaim for those responsible for revealing dishonest accounting, as indicated in the Business First box on page 29.

Career Opportunities for Accountants

▸▸ **OBJECTIVE 10**

Recognize career opportunities in accounting, and understand that accounting is important to both for-profit and nonprofit organizations.

Most of you who read this book will not become accountants. You are or will be intelligent consumers of accounting information in your business and personal lives. Because accounting cuts across all management functions, including purchasing, manufacturing, wholesaling, retailing, and a variety of marketing and transportation activities, it provides an excellent background for almost any manager.

BUSINESS FIRST

ETHICS, ACCOUNTING, AND WHISTLE-BLOWERS

Companies often rely on accountants to safeguard the ethics of the company. Accountants have a special responsibility to ensure that managers act with integrity and that the information disclosed to customers, suppliers, regulators, and the public is accurate. If accountants do not take this responsibility seriously, or if the company ignores the accountants' reports, bad consequences can follow. Just ask WorldCom or Enron. In both companies, an accountant decided to be a whistle-blower, one who reports wrongdoings to his or her supervisor. The WorldCom and Enron whistle-blowers became Persons of the Year in *Time* magazine.

Cynthia Cooper, Vice President of Internal Audit for WorldCom, told the company's board of directors that fraudulent accounting entries had turned a $662 million loss into a $2.4 billion profit. This disclosure led to additional discoveries totaling $9 billion in erroneous accounting entries—the largest accounting fraud in history. Cooper was proud of WorldCom and highly committed to its success. Nevertheless, when she and her internal audit team discovered the unethical actions of superiors she admired, she did not hesitate to do the right thing. She saw no joy when CEO Bernie Ebbers and CFO Scott Sullivan were placed in handcuffs and led away. She simply applied what she had learned when she sat in the middle of the front row of seats in her accounting classes at Mississippi State University. Accountants ask hard questions, find the answers, and act with integrity. Being a whistle-blower has not been easy for Cooper. She is a hero to some, a villain to others. However, regardless of the reaction of others, Cooper knows that she just did what any good accountant should do—no matter how painful it is to tell the truth. To read more about Cooper and WorldCom, see her book *Extraordinary Circumstances: Journey of a Corporate Whistleblower*. The following quote is on Cooper's Web site (http://cynthiacooper.com/index.html): "At a time when corporate dishonesty is dominating public attention, … the tone set at the top is critical to fostering an ethical environment in the workplace."

At Enron, Sherron Watkins had a similar experience. An accounting major at the University of Texas at Austin, she started her career at Arthur Andersen. Then she went to work for Enron, eventually working directly for CFO Andrew Fastow. In her job she discovered the off-the-books liabilities that now have become famous. She first wrote a memo to CEO Kenneth Lay and had a personal meeting with him, explaining to him "an elaborate accounting hoax." Later she discovered that, rather than the hoax being investigated, her report had generated a memo from Enron's legal counsel titled "Confidential Employee Matter" that included the following: "… how to manage the case with the employee who made the sensitive report…. Texas law does not currently protect corporate whistle-blowers… ." In addition, her boss confiscated her hard drive and demoted her. She now regrets that she did not take the matter to higher levels, but she believed that Mr. Lay would take her allegations seriously. In the end, Watkins proved to be right. Although many at Enron knew what was happening, they ignored it. Watkins' accounting background made her both able to spot the irregularities and compelled to report them. Another Enron employee, Lynn Brewer, said that "hundreds, perhaps thousands, of people inside the company knew what was going on, and chose to look the other way." Watkins made the ethical decision and did not simply look the other way. As a result, she is a popular speaker on corporate governance, and Matt Lauer told her story on national television.

Sources: A. Ripley, "Whistle-Blower Cynthia Cooper," *Time.com*, February 4, 2008; J. Reingold, "The Women of Enron: The Best Revenge," *Fast Company*, December 19, 2007; "The Party Crasher," *Time*, Jan. 30, 2002 to Jan. 6, 2003, pp. 52–56; "The Night Detective," *Time*, Jan. 30, 2002 to Jan. 6, 2003, pp. 45–50; M. Flynn, "Enron Insider Shares Her Insights," *Puget Sound Business Journal*, March 7–13, 2003, p. 50; C. Cooper, *Extraordinary Circumstances: Journey of a Corporate Whistleblower*, Wiley, 2009.

Knowledge of accounting is especially important for finance professionals. After many of the problems in the economy, a *BusinessWeek* article indicated that "even professional money managers are scared that they don't know enough accounting." However, accounting's value is not restricted to financial managers. Managers who want to move up in the management structure of a company need to know accounting. Surveys have ranked accounting as the most important business school course for future managers. The Web site for the Agonist Learning Center reported that "[a] manager without accounting savvy is like a car driver without eyes. That is why more and more corporates are recruiting CPAs to senior management positions." Accounting is the language of business, and it is hard to succeed without speaking the language.

EXHIBIT 1-12

**Common Accounting
Career Paths**

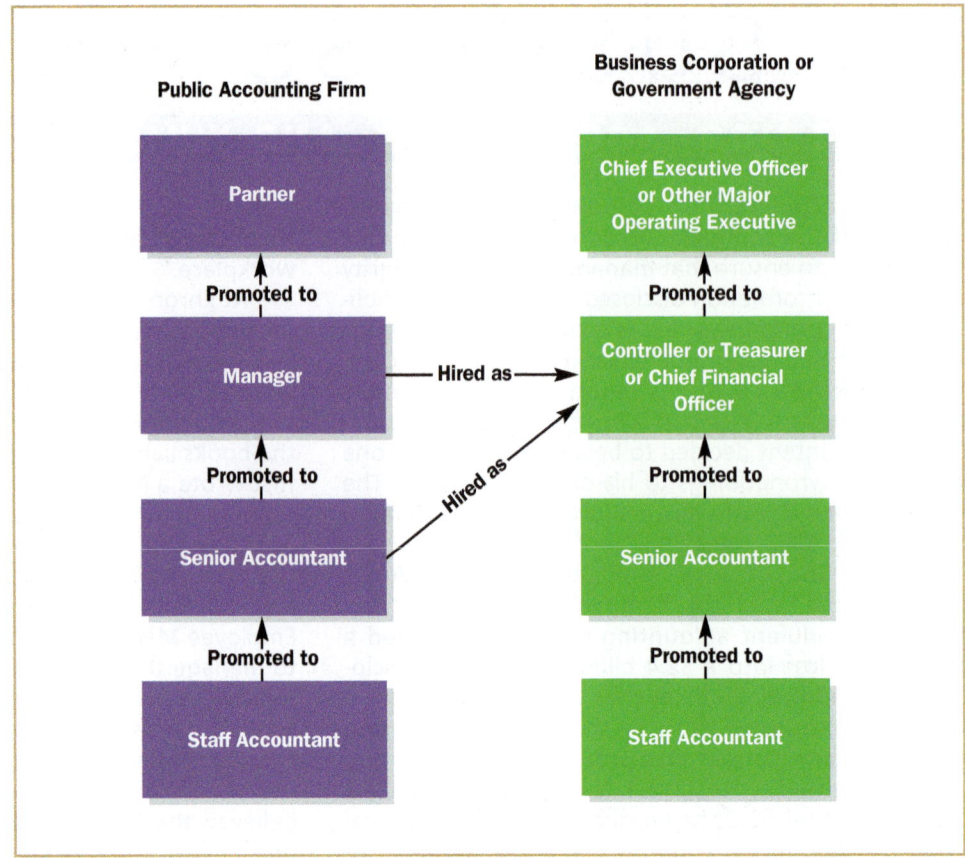

Accounting is an especially good entry position in a company. Because accountants are responsible for collecting and interpreting financial information about the entire company, they develop detailed knowledge about various parts of a company and form close relationships with key decision makers. Senior accountants or controllers in a corporation often become production or marketing executives. Why? Because they have acquired management skills through their dealings with a variety of managers. Others continue in the finance function to become vice presidents of finance or CFOs. Exhibit 1-12 shows various potential career paths for those hired into entry-level accounting positions. Some accountants join a public accounting firm and reach partner after a series of promotions. Others join a business corporation or government agency and proceed up the ladder of success. Many others start in public accounting, even if they do not intend to stay for their entire careers. After being promoted once or twice in public accounting, they shift to an executive position in government or industry.

Accounting provides exciting career opportunities. It is a great training ground for future managers and executives. Accountants in public accounting firms perform work for many clients and encounter many different work experiences. Accountants in private companies work with managers throughout the organization and gain a broad understanding of the various functional and product areas. In addition, accountants are well-rewarded. Beginning accountants in large public accounting firms earned between $52,000 and $62,000 a year in 2012—even more with overtime pay. Top partners in the international accounting firms and CFOs at some of the largest corporations earn more than $1 million annually.

A Note on Nonprofit Organizations

The major focus of this book is on profit-seeking organizations, such as business firms. However, the fundamental accounting principles also apply to nonprofit organizations. Managers and accountants in hospitals, universities, government agencies, and other nonprofit organizations use financial statements. After all, such organizations must raise and spend money, prepare budgets, and judge financial performance. Some nonprofit organizations, such as the Red Cross or Girl Scouts, are as big as large corporations. Others, such as Bainbridge Island Land Trust or Northwest Harvest Food Bank, serve a specific local interest. There is a growing pressure on nonprofit organizations to disclose financial information to the public. In the United States, the **Governmental Accounting Standards Board (GASB)** regulates disclosures for governmental organizations, and the FASB regulates financial reporting for other nonprofit organizations.

Governmental Accounting Standards Board (GASB)
The agency that regulates disclosures for governmental organizations in the United States.

Highlights to Remember

1 **Explain how accounting information assists in making decisions.** Financial statements provide information to help managers, creditors, and owners of all types of organizations make decisions. The balance sheet (or statement of financial position) provides a "snapshot" of the financial position of an organization at an instant in time. That is, it answers the basic question, "Where are we?"

2 **Describe the components of the balance sheet.** The balance sheet equation is Assets = Liabilities + Owners' Equity. This equation must always be in balance. The balance sheet presents the balances of the components of Assets, Liabilities, and Owners' Equity at a specific point in time. Assets are resources a company owns, liabilities are what it owes, and owners' equity is the owners' claims on assets less liabilities.

3 **Analyze business transactions and relate them to changes in the balance sheet.** Transaction analysis is the heart of accounting. A transaction is any event that both affects the financial position of an entity and can be reliably recorded in monetary terms. For each transaction, an accountant must determine what accounts the transaction affects and the amount to record.

4 **Prepare a balance sheet from transactions data.** Accountants can prepare a balance sheet at any time from the detailed transactions that affect the balance sheet equation. The balance sheet reflects the cumulative total of all past transactions. In other words, it is the sum of the beginning balance and the changes caused by the current period transactions for every balance sheet account. However, accountants generally prepare balance sheets only when needed by managers or at the end of each quarter for reporting to the public.

5 **Compare the features of sole proprietorships, partnerships, and corporations.** Sole proprietorships and partnerships usually have owners who also act as managers. In corporations, shareholders delegate management of the firm to professional managers. The shareholders elect a board of directors, which in turn appoints and monitors the managers. Owners of corporations have limited liability; their personal assets are not at risk. Corporations are the most important form of business ownership because corporations conduct a majority of the world's business.

6 **Identify how the owners' equity section in a corporate balance sheet differs from that in a sole proprietorship or a partnership.** For all three forms of ownership structure, owners' equity equals total assets less total liabilities. In sole proprietorships or partnerships we usually refer to owners' equity as capital. The ownership equity of a corporation is usually called stockholders' equity or shareholders' equity. It initially takes the form of common stock at par value (or stated value) plus additional paid-in capital.

7 **Explain the regulation of financial reporting, including differences between U.S. GAAP and IFRS.** Financial statements throughout the world must adhere to generally accepted accounting principles (GAAP). There are two primary sets of GAAP. Companies in most countries follow the GAAP defined by International Financial Reporting Standards (IFRS), which are set by the International Accounting Standards Board (IASB). In contrast, companies in the United States follow U.S. GAAP. The SEC is responsible for setting U.S. GAAP, and it has delegated this responsibility to the Financial Accounting Standards Board (FASB). The AICPA administers the CPA exam that ensures that professional accountants meet minimum qualification standards. In addition, the Public Company Accounting Oversight Board (PCAOB) regulates the accounting profession and sets auditing standards.

8 **Describe auditing and how it enhances the value of financial information.** Separation of ownership from management in corporations creates a demand for auditing, a third-party examination of the financial statements. Auditors evaluate a company's record-keeping system and test specific transactions and account balances to provide assurance that the balances fairly reflect the financial position and performance of the company.

9 **Evaluate the role of ethics in the accounting process.** Ethical behavior is critically important in all areas of accounting. If users cannot trust accounting numbers, financial statements will have little value. In public accounting, the value of an audit is directly linked to the credibility of the auditor as an ethical, independent professional who is qualified to evaluate the financial statements of the firm and is also reliably committed to disclosing problems or concerns uncovered in the evaluation.

10 **Recognize career opportunities in accounting, and understand that accounting is important to both for-profit and nonprofit organizations.** There are excellent career opportunities in accounting, but it is important for all managers, not just accountants, to understand accounting. Accountants and managers in for-profit, nonprofit, and governmental organizations all rely on knowledge of accounting principles in the performance of their duties.

Accounting Vocabulary

account, p. 11
account payable, p. 13
accounting, p. 3
accounting system, p. 6
additional paid-in capital, p. 20
American Institute of Certified Public Accountants (AICPA), p. 26
annual report, p. 7
assets, p. 9
audit, p. 25
auditor, p. 25
auditor's opinion, p. 25
balance sheet, p. 9
balance sheet equation, p. 9
board of directors, p. 22
certified public accountant (CPA), p. 25
chief executive officer (CEO), p. 22
closely held, p. 18
common stock, p. 20
common stockholders, p. 21
compound entry, p. 13
corporation, p. 17
creditor, p. 14
entity, p. 10
FASB Financial Standards Codification, p. 23

financial accounting, p. 7
Financial Accounting Standards (U.S. GAAP), p. 23
Financial Accounting Standards Board (FASB), p. 23
Form 10-K, p. 7
generally accepted accounting principles (GAAP), p. 23
generally accepted auditing standards (GAAS), p. 27
Governmental Accounting Standards Board (GASB), p. 31
independent opinion, p. 25
International Accounting Standards Board (IASB), p. 24
International Auditing and Assurance Standards Board (IAASB), p. 27
International Financial Reporting Standards (IFRS), p. 23
inventory, p. 12
liabilities, p. 9
limited liability, p. 17
long-lived asset, p. 11
management accounting, p. 7
net assets, p. 10

notes payable, p. 9
open account, p. 13
owners' equity, p. 9
paid-in capital, p. 19
paid-in capital in excess of par value, p. 20
par value, p. 20
partnership, p. 17
private accountants, p. 25
privately owned, p. 18
public accountants, p. 25
Public Company Accounting Oversight Board (PCAOB), p. 27
publicly traded stock, p. 7
registered public accounting firm, p. 27
Sarbanes-Oxley Act, p. 27
Securities and Exchange Commission (SEC), p. 7
shareholders' equity, p. 19
sole proprietorship, p. 17
stated value, p. 20
statement of financial position, p. 9
stock certificate, p. 18
stockholders' equity, p. 19
transaction, p. 10
unlisted, p. 18
U.S. GAAP, p. 23

Assignment Material

MyAccountingLab The assignment material for each chapter is divided into Questions, Critical Thinking Questions, Exercises, Problems, a Collaborative Learning Exercise, and three projects on Analyzing and Interpreting Financial Statements. In each chapter, one of these projects involves analyzing Starbucks' financial statements, allowing students to develop a more in-depth understanding of the financial reporting of this one company. The assignment material contains problems based on fictitious companies and problems based on real-life situations. We hope our use of actual companies and news events enhances your interest in accounting.

We identify problems based on real companies by highlighting the name in blue. These problems underscore a major objective of this book: to increase your ability to read, understand, and use published financial reports and news articles. In later chapters, these problems provide the principal means of reviewing not only the immediate chapter but also the previous chapters.

Questions

1-1 Describe accounting.

1-2 "It's easier to learn accounting if you avoid real-world examples." Do you agree? Explain.

1-3 Give three examples of decisions where the decision maker is likely to use financial statements.

1-4 Give three examples of users of financial statements.

1-5 Briefly distinguish between financial accounting and management accounting.

1-6 Describe the balance sheet equation.

1-7 "The balance sheet may be out of balance after some transactions, but it is never out of balance at the end of an accounting period." Do you agree? Explain.

1-8 "When a company buys inventory for cash, total assets do not change. However, when it buys inventory on open account, total assets increase." Explain.

1-9 Explain the difference between a note payable and an account payable.

1-10 "Balance sheets for companies in the same industry should look similar except for the overall size of the accounts. That is, if one company's property, plant, and equipment is 40% of total assets, you would expect other companies in the industry to also have property, plant, and equipment that totals about 40% of total assets." Do you agree? Explain.

1-11 List three differences between a corporation and a sole proprietorship or a partnership.

1-12 Explain the meaning of limited liability.

1-13 Why does this book emphasize the corporation instead of the proprietorship or the partnership?

1-14 "International companies with Ltd. or S.A. after their name are essentially the same in organizational form as U.S. companies with Corp. after their name." Do you agree? Explain.

1-15 "The idea of par value is insignificant." Explain.

1-16 Explain the relationship between the board of directors and top management of a company.

1-17 How is GAAP set in the United States? How is it set internationally?

1-18 "All companies with stock traded on U.S. stock exchanges must issue financial statements that conform to U.S. GAAP." Do you agree? Explain.

1-19 What gives value to an audit?

1-20 What is a CPA, and how does someone become one? What is a CA?

1-21 What are the most important ethical standards for accountants?

1-22 Why is understanding accounting important to nonaccountants?

1-23 "The accounting systems described in this book apply to corporations and are not appropriate for nonprofit organizations." Do you agree? Explain.

Critical Thinking Questions

1-24 Double-Entry Accounting

The accounting process in use today is typically called "double-entry" bookkeeping. Discuss the meaning and possible importance of this name.

▶▶ **OBJECTIVE 3**

1-25 Accountants as Historians

Critics sometimes refer to accountants as historians and do not mean it kindly. In what sense are accountants historians, and do you believe this is a compliment or a criticism?

▶▶ **OBJECTIVE 1**

1-26 The Corporation

Some historians were arguing over the most important innovation in the history of business. Most thought of things and processes such as the railroad, the automobile, the printing press, the telephone, television, or more recently, the computer chip, fiber-optic cable, or even the Internet. One person argued that the really important innovation was the corporation. How would this person argue for this idea? What role did accounting play in the rise of the corporation?

▶▶ **OBJECTIVE 5**

▶▶ OBJECTIVE 8

1-27 The Auditor's Opinion

In reviewing the annual report of a company in which you might invest, you noted that you did not recognize the name of the audit firm that signed the audit opinion. What questions would this raise in your mind, and how might you resolve them?

Exercises

▶▶ OBJECTIVE 2

1-28 The Balance Sheet Equation

Laredo Company reported total assets of $7 million and total liabilities of $4 million at the end of 20X0.

1. Construct the balance sheet equation for Laredo Company at the end of 20X0 and include the correct amount for owners' equity.
2. Suppose that during January 20X1 Laredo borrowed $2 million from Wells Fargo Bank. How would this affect Laredo's assets, liabilities, and owners' equity?

▶▶ OBJECTIVE 3

1-29 Describing Underlying Transactions

Radloff's Furniture Company, which was recently formed, is engaging in some preliminary transactions before beginning full-scale operations for retailing household furnishings. The balances of each item in the company's accounting equation are given next for May 1 and for each of the next 9 business days.

		Cash	Furniture Inventory	Store Fixtures	Accounts Payable	Owners' Equity
May	1	$ 5,000	$18,000	$2,000	$ 3,000	$22,000
	2	11,000	18,000	2,000	3,000	28,000
	3	11,000	18,000	6,000	3,000	32,000
	4	8,000	21,000	6,000	3,000	32,000
	5	8,000	27,000	6,000	9,000	32,000
	6	11,000	27,000	3,000	9,000	32,000
	7	6,000	27,000	9,000	10,000	32,000
	8	4,000	27,000	9,000	8,000	32,000
	9	4,000	26,600	9,000	7,600	32,000
	10	1,000	26,600	9,000	7,600	29,000

State briefly what you think took place on each of the 9 days beginning May 2, assuming that only one transaction occurred each day.

▶▶ OBJECTIVE 3

1-30 Describing Underlying Transactions

The balances of each item in Melbourne Company's accounting equation are given next for November 1 and for each of the next 7 business days.

		Cash	Computer Inventory	Store Fixtures	Accounts Payable	Owners' Equity
Nov.	1	$5,000	$ 8,000	$ 7,500	$5,500	$15,000
	2	5,000	8,000	10,000	8,000	15,000
	3	3,000	8,000	10,000	8,000	13,000
	4	3,000	3,000	10,000	3,000	13,000
	5	3,000	10,000	10,000	3,000	20,000
	8	2,500	10,000	10,000	2,500	20,000
	9	1,500	10,000	13,500	5,000	20,000
	10	1,500	10,000	13,000	4,500	20,000

State briefly what you think took place on each of the 7 days beginning November 2, assuming that only one transaction occurred each day.

1-31 Prepare Balance Sheet

▶▶ **OBJECTIVE 4**

Jacksonville Corporation's balance sheet at March 30, 20X1, contained only the following items (arranged here in random order):

Cash	$14,000	Accounts payable	$ 8,000
Notes payable	10,000	Furniture and fixtures	3,000
Merchandise inventory	40,000	Long-term debt	12,000
Paid-in capital	80,000	Building	24,000
Land	14,000	Machinery and equipment	15,000

On March 31, 20X1, these transactions and events took place:

1. Purchased merchandise on account, $3,000
2. Sold at cost for $1,000 cash some furniture that was not needed
3. Issued additional capital stock for machinery and equipment valued at $12,000
4. Purchased land for $25,000, of which $10,000 was paid in cash, the remaining being represented by a 5-year note (long-term debt)
5. The building was valued by professional appraisers at $43,000

Prepare in good form a balance sheet for March 31, 20X1, showing supporting computations for all new amounts.

1-32 Prepare Balance Sheet

▶▶ **OBJECTIVE 4**

Southampton Company's balance sheet at November 29, 20X1, contained only the following items (arranged here in random order):

Paid-in capital	£190,000	Machinery and equipment	£ 20,000
Notes payable	21,000	Furniture and fixtures	8,000
Cash	22,000	Land	41,000
Accounts payable	16,000	Building	241,000
Merchandise inventory	29,000	Long-term debt payable	134,000

On the following day, November 30, these transactions and events occurred:

1. Purchased machinery and equipment for £13,000, paying £4,000 in cash and signing a 90-day note for the balance
2. Paid £7,000 on accounts payable
3. Sold some land that was not needed for cash of £6,000, which was the Southampton Company's acquisition cost of the land
4. The remaining land was valued at £240,000 by professional appraisers
5. Issued capital stock as payment for £23,000 of the long-term debt, that is, debt due beyond 1 year

Prepare in good form a balance sheet for November 30, 20X1, showing supporting computations for all new amounts.

1-33 Balance Sheet

▶▶ **OBJECTIVE 2**

Costco is the third largest retail company in the United States with sales of nearly $90 billion. The company's balance sheet on August 28, 2011, had total assets of $26,271 million and stockholders' equity of $12,002 million.

1. Compute Costco's total liabilities on August 28, 2011.
2. As of August 28, 2011, Costco had issued 434,266,000 shares of common stock with a par value of $.005 per share. Compute the balance in the account, Common Stock, Par Value on Costco's balance sheet.

▶▶ OBJECTIVE 6

1-34 Sole Proprietorship and Corporation

The Mammal Center pet store is owned by Jon Wilson and has been a sole proprietorship with the following condensed balance sheet on June 30, 20X1:

Assets		Liabilities and Owner's Equity	
Cash	$15,000	Accounts payable	$14,000
Accounts receivable	13,000	Bank loan payable	9,000
Property, plant, and equipment	25,000	Capital—Jon Wilson	30,000
Total assets	$53,000	Total liabilities and owner's equity	$53,000

Mr. Wilson decides to incorporate his company on July 1, 20X1, by creating 2,000 shares of common stock, holding 1,000 shares himself, representing his current interest in the store, and selling 1,000 shares to the public for cash of $30 per share. Each share has a $1 par value.

Prepare a balance sheet for The Mammal Center immediately after incorporation.

MyAccountingLab

Problems

▶▶ OBJECTIVES 3, 4

1-35 Analysis of Transactions

Use the format of Exhibit 1-2 (p. 12) to analyze the following transactions for April of Marymount Services, Inc. Then prepare a balance sheet as of April 30, 20X1. Marymount Services was founded on April 1.

1. Issued 1,000 shares of common stock for cash, $60,000; use a single Paid-in-Capital account.
2. Issued 500 shares of common stock for equipment, $20,000
3. Borrowed cash, signing a note payable for $35,000
4. Purchased equipment for cash, $33,000
5. Purchased office furniture on account, $10,000
6. Disbursed cash on account (to reduce the account payable), $4,000
7. Sold equipment for cash, $8,000, an amount equal to its cost
8. Discovered that the most prominent competitor in the area was bankrupt and was closing its doors on April 30

▶▶ OBJECTIVES 3, 4

1-36 Analysis of Transactions

Consider the following January transactions:

1. On January 1, 20X1, three persons, James, Bosh, and Wade, formed JBW Corporation. JBW is a wholesale distributor of electronic equipment. The company issued 10,000 shares of common stock ($1 par value) to each of the three investors for $10 cash per share. Use two stockholders' equity accounts: Capital Stock (at par) and Additional Paid-in Capital.
2. JBW acquired merchandise inventory of $75,000 for cash.
3. JBW acquired merchandise inventory of $85,000 on open account.
4. JBW returned for full credit unsatisfactory merchandise that cost $11,000 in transaction 3.
5. JBW acquired equipment of $40,000 for a cash down payment of $10,000, plus a 3-month promissory note of $30,000.
6. As a favor, JBW sells equipment of $4,000 to a business neighbor for cash. The equipment had cost $4,000.
7. JBW pays $16,000 on the account described in transaction 3.
8. JBW buys merchandise inventory of $100,000. The company pays one-half of the amount in cash, and owes one-half on open account.
9. Wade sells one-half of his common stock to Nowitzki for $13 per share.

Required
1. By using a format similar to Exhibit 1-2, prepare an analysis showing the effects of the January transactions on the financial position of JBW Corporation.
2. Prepare a balance sheet as of January 31, 20X1.

1-37 Analysis of Transactions

Suppose you began a business as a wholesaler of auto parts in Lisbon. The following events have occurred (the symbol € represents the euro, the European currency):

▶▶ OBJECTIVES **3, 4**

1. On March 1, 20X1, you invested €80,000 cash in your new sole proprietorship, which you call Autopartes Lisbon.
2. You acquired €10,000 inventory for cash.
3. You acquired €8,000 inventory on open account.
4. You acquired equipment for €15,000 in exchange for a €5,000 cash down payment and a €10,000 promissory note.
5. A large retail store, which you had hoped would be a big customer, discontinued operations.
6. You take tires home for your family car. Autopartes Lisbon's inventory carried the tires at €600. (Regard this as taking part of your capital out of Autopartes Lisbon.)
7. Parts that cost €300 in transaction 2 were damaged in shipment. You returned them and obtained a full cash refund.
8. Parts that cost €800 in transaction 3 were the wrong size. You returned them and obtained parts of the correct size in exchange.
9. Parts that cost €500 in transaction 3 had an unacceptable quality. You returned them and obtained full credit on your account.
10. You paid €2,000 on the promissory note.
11. You use your personal cash savings of €5,000 to acquire some equipment for Autopartes Lisbon. You consider this to be an additional investment in your business.
12. You paid €3,000 on open account.
13. Two transmission manufacturers who are suppliers for Autopartes Lisbon announced a 7% rise in prices, effective in 60 days.
14. You use your personal cash savings of €1,000 to acquire a new TV set for your family.
15. You exchange equipment that cost €4,000 in transaction 4 with another wholesaler. However, the equipment received, which is almost new, is smaller and is worth only €1,500. Therefore, the other wholesaler also pays you €2,500 in cash. (You recognize no gain or loss on this transaction.)

Required

1. By using Exhibit 1-2 (p. 12) as a guide, prepare an analysis of Autopartes Lisbon's transactions for March. Confine your analysis to the effects on the financial position of Autopartes Lisbon.
2. Prepare a balance sheet for Autopartes Lisbon as of March 31, 20X1.

1-38 Analysis of Transactions

Leida Cruz, a recent law school graduate, was penniless on December 25, 20X0.

▶▶ OBJECTIVES **3, 4**

1. On December 26, Cruz inherited an enormous sum of money.
2. On December 27, she placed $60,000 in a business checking account for her unincorporated law practice.
3. On December 28, she purchased a home for a down payment of $120,000 plus a home mortgage payable of $230,000.
4. On December 28, Cruz agreed to rent a law office. She provided a $1,000 cash damage deposit (from her business cash), which will be fully refundable when she vacates the premises. This deposit is a business asset. She will make rental payments in advance on the first business day of each month. (The first payment of $700 is not to be made until January 2, 20X1.)
5. On December 28, Cruz purchased a computer for her law practice for $2,000 cash, plus a $3,000 promissory note due in 90 days.
6. On December 28, she purchased legal supplies for $1,000 on open account.
7. On December 28, Cruz purchased office furniture for her practice for $4,000 cash.
8. On December 29, Cruz hired a legal assistant receptionist for $380 per week. She was to report to work on January 2.
9. On December 30, Cruz's law practice lent $3,000 cash in return for a 1-year note from Sam Whitman, a local candy store owner. Whitman had indicated that he would spread the news about the new lawyer.

Required

1. Use the format demonstrated in Exhibit 1-2 (p. 12) to analyze the transactions of Leida Cruz, lawyer. To avoid crowding, put your numbers in thousands of dollars. Do not restrict yourself to the account titles in Exhibit 1-2.
2. Prepare a balance sheet as of December 31, 20X0.

▶▶ OBJECTIVES 3, 4

1-39 Analysis of Transactions

Walgreen Company is a well-known drugstore chain. A condensed balance sheet for August 31, 2011, follows ($ in millions):

Assets		Liabilities and Stockholders' Equity	
Cash	$ 1,556	Accounts payable	$ 4,810
Inventories	8,044	Other liabilities	7,797
Property and other assets	17,854	Stockholders' equity	14,847
Total	$27,454	Total	$27,454

Use a format similar to Exhibit 1-2 (p. 12) to analyze the following transactions for the first two days of September ($ amounts are in millions). Then prepare a balance sheet as of September 2.

1. Issued 1,000,000 shares of common stock to employees for cash, $30
2. Issued 1,500,000 shares of common stock for the acquisition of $42 of special equipment from a supplier
3. Borrowed cash, signing a note payable for $13
4. Purchased equipment for cash, $18
5. Purchased inventories on account, $89
6. Disbursed cash on account (to reduce the accounts payable), $35
7. Sold for $2 cash some display equipment at original cost of $2

▶▶ OBJECTIVES 3, 4

1-40 Analysis of Transactions

Nike, Inc., had the following condensed balance sheet on May 31, 2011 ($ in millions):

Assets		Liabilities and Stockholders' Equity	
Cash	$ 1,955	Total liabilities	$ 5,155
Inventories	2,715	Stockholders' equity	9,843
Property, plant, and equipment	2,115	Total liabilities and stockholders' equity	$14,998
Other assets	8,213		
Total assets	$14,998		

Suppose the following transactions occurred during the first 3 days of June ($ in millions):

1. Nike acquired inventories for cash, $28.
2. Nike acquired inventories on open account, $19.
3. Nike returned for full credit, $4, some unsatisfactory shoes that it acquired on open account in May.
4. Nike acquired $14 of equipment for a cash down payment of $5, plus a 2-year promissory note of $9.
5. To encourage wider displays, Nike sold some special store equipment to New York area stores for $40 cash. The equipment had cost $40 in the preceding month.
6. Clint Eastwood produced, directed, and starred in a movie. As a favor to a Nike executive, he agreed to display Nike shoes in a basketball scene. Nike paid no fee.
7. Nike disbursed cash to reduce accounts payable, $16.
8. Nike borrowed cash from a bank, $50.
9. Nike sold additional common stock for cash to new investors, $90.
10. The president of the company sold 5,000 shares of his personal holdings of Nike stock through his stockbroker.

Required

1. By using a format similar to Exhibit 1-2 (p. 12), prepare an analysis showing the effects of the June transactions on the financial position of Nike.
2. Prepare a balance sheet as of June 3.

1-41 Prepare Balance Sheet

▶▶ OBJECTIVE 4

Jennifer Grant is a realtor. She buys and sells properties on her own account, and she also earns commissions as a real estate agent for buyers and sellers. Her business was organized on November 24, 20X1, as a sole proprietorship. Grant also owns her own personal residence. Consider the following on November 30, 20X1:

1. Grant owes $85,000 on a mortgage on some undeveloped land, which her business acquired for a total price of $170,000.
2. Grant had spent $18,000 cash for a Century 21 real estate franchise. Century 21 is a national affiliation of independent real estate brokers. This franchise is an asset.
3. Grant owes $100,000 on a personal mortgage on her residence, which she acquired on November 20, 20X3, for a total price of $180,000.
4. Grant owes $3,800 on a personal charge account with Nordstrom's.
5. Grant acquired business furniture for $17,000 on November 25, for $6,000 on open account, plus $11,000 of business cash. On November 26, Grant sold a $1,000 business chair for $1,000 to her next-door business neighbor for cash.
6. On November 28, Grant hired her first employee, Aaron Rubenstein. He was to begin work on December 1. Grant was pleased because Rubenstein was one of the best real estate salesmen in the area. On November 29, Rubenstein was killed in an automobile accident.
7. Grant's balance at November 30 in her business checking account after all transactions was $6,000.

Prepare a balance sheet as of November 30, 20X1, for Jennifer Grant, realtor.

1-42 Bank Balance Sheet

▶▶ OBJECTIVE 2

Consider the following simplified balance sheet accounts of Wells Fargo & Company as of September 30, 2011 (in billions of $):

Assets		Liabilities and Stockholders' Equity	
Cash	$ 18	Deposits	$ 895
Investment securities	398	Other liabilities	271
Loans receivable	740	Total liabilities	1,166
Other assets	149	Stockholders' equity	139
Total assets	$1,305	Total liabilities and stockholders' equity	$1,305

This balance sheet illustrates how Wells Fargo gathers and uses money. More than 87% of the total assets are in the form of investments and loans, and more than 68% of the total liabilities and stockholders' equity are in the form of deposits, a major liability. That is, financial institutions such as Wells Fargo are in the business of raising funds from depositors and, in turn, lending those funds to businesses, homeowners, and others. The stockholders' equity is usually small in comparison with the deposits (less than 11% of total liabilities and stockholders' equity in this case).

1. What Wells Fargo accounts would be affected if you deposited $1,000?
2. Why are deposits listed as liabilities?
3. What accounts would be affected if the bank loaned Jens Olafson $75,000 for home renovations?
4. What accounts would be affected if Isabel Valdez withdrew $5,000 from her savings account?

1-43 Airline Balance Sheet

▶▶ OBJECTIVE 2

Air France-KLM S.A. is an international airline headquartered in France with stock traded in both Paris and Amsterdam. It has more than 400 aircraft and more than 100,000 employees. On September 30, 2011, Air France-KLM's noncash assets were €24,860 million. Total assets were €27,739 million, and total liabilities were €21,512 million. The symbol € represents the euro, the European currency.

1. Compute the following:
   a. Air France-KLM's cash on September 30, 2011.
   b. Air France-KLM's stockholders' equity on September 30, 2011.
2. Explain the easiest way to determine Air France-KLM's total liabilities and stockholders' equity from the information given in this problem.

1-44 Prepare Balance Sheet

United Technologies Corporation provides a broad range of high-technology products and support services to the building systems and aerospace industries. Those products include Pratt & Whitney aircraft engines, Carrier heating and air conditioning equipment, Otis elevators, and Sikorsky helicopters. United Technologies' September 30, 2011, balance sheet included the following items ($ in millions):

Fixed assets	$ 6,137
Accounts payable	5,597
Common stock	13,330
Cash	?
Total stockholders' equity	?
Long-term debt	9,501
Total assets	61,948
Inventories	8,617
Other assets	41,228
Other stockholders' equity	?
Other liabilities	22,935

Prepare a condensed balance sheet, including amounts for

1. Cash.
2. Total Stockholders' Equity.
3. Other Stockholders' Equity.

1-45 Prepare Balance Sheet

Macy's, Inc., headquartered in both Cincinnati and New York, operates more than 840 stores in 45 states under the Macy's and Bloomingdale's names. Its balance sheet on October 29, 2011, contained the following items ($ in millions):

Long-term debt	$ 6,151
Cash	?
Total liabilities	?
Shareholders' equity	?
Inventories	7,158
Merchandise accounts payable	3,576
Property, plant, and equipment	8,423
Other assets	5,585
Other liabilities	6,684
Total assets	22,263

Prepare a condensed balance sheet, including amounts for

1. Cash. What do you think of its relative size?
2. Total Liabilities.
3. Shareholders' Equity.

1-46 Partnership and Corporation

El-Hashem Partners is a partnership started by two brothers, Muhab and Ghassan El-Hashem. Each has an equal share of the total owners' equity of $90,000. There is only one asset, a rental house listed at \$350,000, and one liability, a mortgage loan of \$260,000. The date is June 15, 20X0. The El-Hashem brothers are considering changing their partnership to El-Hashem Corporation by issuing each brother 1,000 shares of common stock.

1. Prepare a balance sheet for the current partnership.
2. Prepare a balance sheet if the brothers form a corporation. The par value of each share of common stock is \$1.

1-47 Presenting Paid-in Capital

Consider excerpts from two balance sheets (amounts in millions):

▶▶ **OBJECTIVE 6**

Citigroup

Common stock (\$.01 par value; authorized shares: 60 billion), issued shares 29,224,016,234 at December 31, 2010	\$	292
Additional paid-in capital		101,024

IBM

Common stock, par value \$.20 per share and additional paid-in capital	\$ 45,418
Shares authorized: 4,687,500,000	
Shares issued: 2,161,800,054	

1. How would the presentation of Citigroup stockholders' equity accounts be affected if the company issued 500 million more shares for \$25 cash per share?
2. How would the presentation of IBM's stockholders' equity accounts be affected if the company issued 1 million more shares for \$180 cash per share? Be specific.

1-48 Presenting Paid-in Capital

Chevron, the petroleum exploration, production, refining, and marketing company, presented the following in its September 30, 2011, balance sheet.

▶▶ **OBJECTIVE 6**

Common stock—\$.75 par value, 2,442,676,580 shares issued	?
Capital in excess of par value	\$15,110,000,000

What amount should be shown on the common stock line? What was the average price per share paid by the original investors for the Chevron common stock? How do your answers compare with the \$100 market price of the stock in early 2012? Comment briefly.

1-49 Presenting Paid-in Capital

Honda Motor Company is the largest producer of motorcycles in the world, as well as a major auto manufacturer. Honda included the following items in its 2011 balance sheet (in millions of Japanese Yen, ¥):

▶▶ **OBJECTIVE 6**

Common stock—authorized 7,086,000,000 shares; issued 1,811,428,430 shares	¥ 86,067
Capital surplus*	172,529

*Honda uses the term "capital surplus" instead of the preferred terms, additional paid-in capital or capital in excess of par value.

1. What is the par value of Honda's common stock?
2. What was the average price per share paid by the original investors for the Honda common stock?
3. How do your answers compare with the ¥3,000 market price of the stock at the end of fiscal 2011? Comment briefly.

1-50 Audit Opinion and IFRS Versus U.S. GAAP

Carrefour, the French supermarket company, included the following paragraph from its auditor in its 2011 annual report:

> *In our opinion, the consolidated financial statements give a true and fair view of the assets and liabilities and of the financial position of the Group as of 31 December 2011 and of the results of its operations for the year then ended in accordance with the IFRS as adopted by the European Union.*

Safeway the U.S. supermarket chain had a similar paragraph in its 2011 annual report:

> *In our opinion, the consolidated financial statements referred to above present fairly, in all material respects, the financial position of Safeway Inc. and subsidiaries as of January 3, 2012, . . . and the results of their operations and their cash flows for [the year] ended January 3, 2012, in conformity with accounting principles generally accepted in the United States of America.*

Explain what is meant by "in accordance with the IFRS as adopted by the European Union" and "in conformity with accounting principles generally accepted in the United States of America."

OBJECTIVE 8

1-51 Board of Directors and Audit Committee

Examine the 2011 annual report of **General Mills**, maker of cereals such as Cheerios, Betty Crocker cake mixes, Progresso soups, and other foods (http://phx.corporate-ir.net/phoenix.zhtml?c=74271&p=irol-reportsannual). Turn to the listing of General Mills' Board of Directors on page 16 of the annual report.

1. How many board members does General Mills have? How many of them are General Mills executives?
2. How many of the nonexecutive directors are executives or retired executives of other companies? How many are academics? What other positions are represented on the board? How does the background of board members influence their ability to carry out the responsibilities of the board?
3. How many members of the General Mills' Board of Directors are on the audit committee? Are any audit committee members also General Mills executives? Why would investors want to know the composition of the audit committee?

OBJECTIVE 9

1-52 Accounting and Ethics

A 2009 survey by Clemson University researchers examined the ethics concerns of chief executive officers of 300 large- and mid-sized corporations in the United States. Their number one concern was improper accounting practices. Recognizing the importance of ethics in accounting, professional associations for both internal accountants and external auditors place much emphasis on their standards of ethical conduct. Discuss why maintaining a reputation for ethical conduct is important for (1) accountants within an organization, and (2) external auditors. What can accountants do to foster a reputation for high ethical standards and conduct?

Collaborative Learning Exercise

1-53 Understanding Transactions

Form groups of three to five students each. Each group should choose one of the companies included in the Dow Jones Industrial Average (Exhibit 1-1), and find its most recent balance sheet. (You might try the company's home page on the Internet or the SEC's EDGAR database at www.sec.gov/edgar.shtml.) Ignore much of the detail on the balance sheet, focusing on the following accounts: Cash, Inventory, Equipment, Notes Payable, Accounts Payable, and Total Stockholders' Equity. Exact names may vary slightly across companies.

Divide the following six assumed transactions among the members of the group:

1. Sold 1 million shares of common stock for a total of $9 million cash (ignore par value)
2. Bought inventory for cash of $3 million
3. Borrowed $5 million from the bank, receiving the $5 million in cash
4. Bought inventory for $7 million on open account
5. Paid $4 million to suppliers for inventory bought on open account
6. Bought equipment for $9 million cash

Required

1. The student responsible for each transaction should explain to the group how the transaction would affect the company's balance sheet, using the accounts listed earlier.
2. By using the most recent published balance sheet as a starting point, prepare a balance sheet for the company, assuming the preceding six transactions are the only transactions since the date of the latest balance sheet.

Analyzing and Interpreting Financial Statements

1-54 Financial Statement Research

Select the financial statements of any company, and focus on the balance sheet.

▶▶ **OBJECTIVE 2**

1. Identify the amount of cash (including cash equivalents, if any) shown on the most recent balance sheet.
2. What were the total assets shown on the most recent balance sheet, and the total liabilities plus stockholders' equity? How do these two amounts compare?
3. Identify (a) total liabilities, and (b) total stockholders' equity. (Assume that all items on the right side of the balance sheet that are not explicitly listed as stockholders' equity are liabilities.) Compare the size of the liabilities to stockholders' equity, and comment on the comparison. Write the company's accounting equation, as of the most recent balance sheet date, by filling in the dollar amounts.

1-55 Analyzing Starbucks' Financial Statements

This and similar problems in each succeeding chapter focus on the financial statements of Starbucks Corporation. Starbucks is a worldwide retailer of specialty coffees. As you solve each of these homework problems, you will gradually strengthen your understanding of Starbucks' complete financial statements. You can find these statements either on the investor relations page of Starbuck's Web site (http://investor.starbucks.com) or via the SEC's EDGAR database (www.sec.gov/edgar.shtml).

▶▶ **OBJECTIVE 2**

Refer to Starbucks' balance sheet and answer the following questions:

1. How much cash did Starbucks have on October 2, 2011? (Include cash equivalents as part of cash.)
2. List the account titles and amounts from Starbucks' balance sheet that are accounts that were discussed in this chapter.
3. Write the company's accounting equation as of October 2, 2011, by filling in the dollar amounts: Assets = Liabilities + Stockholders' equity.

1-56 Analyzing Financial Statements Using the Internet: Cisco

Locate the Cisco annual report. Do this by searching for "Cisco Systems," clicking Investor Relations under About Cisco, and opening Annual Reports under the Financial Reporting tab. Then click Open Printable Report in the box for the most recent annual report.

▶▶ **OBJECTIVES 2, 7**

Answer the following questions concerning Cisco:

1. Select Letter to Shareholders from the menu. Is the message optimistic?
2. Select Business – General from the menu. When was the company founded? What is its focus?
3. Now find Cisco's balance sheet under Part II – Financial Statements. What are Cisco's Total Assets, Total Liabilities, and Total Shareholders' Equity?
4. How much are Cisco's inventories? Have they increased or decreased in the last year? Do you think that change is good or bad?
5. Select the Report of Independent Registered Public Accounting Firm, which is also under the Financial Statements tab. Who is responsible for the preparation, integrity, and fair presentation of Cisco's financial statements? What is the auditor's responsibility?
6. Find Cisco's list of members of its board of directors near the end of the report. How many directors are there? How many are Cisco executives? How many are academics? How many directors are on the audit committee?

2

Measuring Income to Assess Performance

IT IS HARD TO MISS "Big G" cereals when you walk down the breakfast-food aisle in a grocery store. Both children and adults recognize Cheerios, Wheaties, Lucky Charms, and other Big G cereals, all made by General Mills. Cadwallander Washburn certainly did not envision today's General Mills when he built his first flour mill on the banks of the Mississippi River in Minneapolis in 1866. Little did he know that in 2013 his company's products would satisfy customers worldwide.

General Mills is not just a breakfast-food company. Its products include convenience foods such as Old El Paso Mexican foods, Progresso soups, Green Giant vegetables, and "helper" casseroles; baking supplies such as Betty Crocker cake mixes, Bisquick baking mixes, and Gold Medal flour; snack foods such as Fruit Roll-Ups, Pop Secret microwave popcorn, and Nature Valley granola bars; and refrigerated items such as Pillsbury frozen breakfast pastries, Pillsbury frozen waffles, and Totino's frozen pizza, not to mention Yoplait yogurt, Häagen-Dazs ice cream, and many more. In addition, General Mills is a leading supplier to the foodservice and commercial baking industries, so you may eat General Mills products when you dine away from home. For General Mills to have grown so large and to have so many products, management must have been successful. Although companies cannot measure success with any single metric, in this chapter we see one important measure of a company's success—its profitability.

How can we measure the overall performance of a company such as General Mills and its management? When owners and investors want to evaluate performance, they often use measures of profitability for the entire company as well as profitability measures related to segments of the company. The most common measure of profitability for a company is its net income—its sales less its expenses—which is the topic of this chapter. In 2011, General Mills had sales of almost $14.9 billion and expenses of about $13.1 billion, leaving income of approximately $1.8 billion or

▶▶ **LEARNING OBJECTIVES** *After studying this chapter, you should be able to:*

1 Explain how accountants measure income.

2 Determine when a company should record revenue from a sale.

3 Use the concept of matching to record the expenses for a period.

4 Prepare an income statement and show how it is related to a balance sheet.

5 Account for cash dividends and prepare a statement of stockholders' equity.

6 Compute and explain earnings per share, price-earnings ratio, dividend-yield ratio, and dividend-payout ratio.

7 Explain how the conceptual framework guides the standard setting process and how accounting regulators trade off relevance and faithful representation in setting accounting standards.

8 Explain how the following concepts affect financial statements: entity, going concern, materiality, stable monetary unit, periodicity, and reliability.

12.1% of sales. This means that, on average, when you buy a General Mills product for which the store paid $1.00, General Mills ends up with 12.1¢ of income. It takes a lot of boxes of cereal, bags of flour, cans of soup, and cartons of yogurt to add up to $14.9 billion in sales. To achieve this level of sales, General Mills sells its products in more than 100 countries around the world. In addition, General Mills pays a lot of employees and farmers, uses many buildings and machines, purchases much advertising and other promotion services, and incurs many other expenses—all of which add up to $13.1 billion of expenses. It takes skillful management to oversee such a large operation, and accounting reports are an important tool used by management. It also takes huge amounts of capital to support such operations, and General Mills has raised part of that capital by selling more than 750 million ownership shares to the public. These owners also want financial reports on General Mills' operations to help them evaluate their decision to invest in the firm.

Until now you may have thought of a trip to the grocery store as nothing more than a chance to replenish your food supply. However, from now on you can think about the accounting systems that record sales for the items you buy and identify the expenses required to bring these products to you. It might not make your trip more enjoyable, but it will make it more enlightening.

Investors in General Mills eagerly await reports about the company's annual income. Investors care about the price of their shares, and stock prices generally reflect investors' expectations about income. However, actual reported income often differs from what investors expected, and stock prices react to the difference between expectations and reported income. For example, on September 21, 2011, General Mills issued a press release reporting first quarter income of $.64 per share. This amount was identical to that reported a year earlier, but it beat analysts' expectations of $.62 per share. What happened to General Mills' stock price? After the announcement, General Mills' stock price jumped by 2.5%. Although other company, industry, or general economic news that day also influenced the stock price, the unexpectedly positive earnings announcement certainly contributed to the increased stock price. ●

Most people recognize General Mills for the "Big G" breakfast cereals such as those shown here. However, the company has many other products on the shelves of nearly every grocery store. General Mills' income statement, described in this chapter, summarizes the profits the company makes on cereals together with all its other products.

EXHIBIT 2-1

Relationship Between Stock Price and Net Income for General Mills Corporation

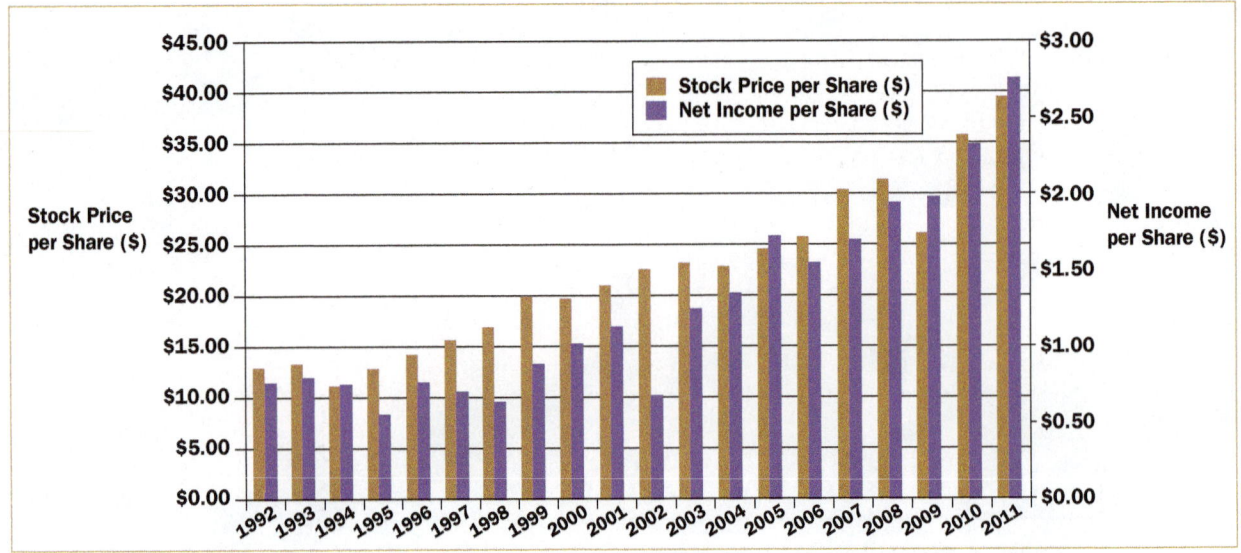

Although income and stock prices tend to move in the same direction, the relationship is not perfect. Look at Exhibit 2-1, which shows the income and stock price of **General Mills** for the last 20 years. The left vertical axis and the brown bars represent the stock price in dollars per share, and the right vertical axis and purple bars are the net income in dollars per share.

Overall, the company has experienced increasing trends in both net income per share and stock price per share. However, as is true for most companies, the correlation between net income and stock price for General Mills is not perfect. Company-specific, industry-specific, or general economic conditions can produce deviations in the trend. For example, note that in 2002, General Mills had a small increase in stock price over 2001 but the 2002 net income per share was significantly lower. In the annual report General Mills explained that the acquisition of Pillsbury on October 31, 2001, significantly affected the financial condition and results in fiscal 2002. Also notice that, in 2009, General Mills experienced a very modest increase in net income per share, while the stock price decreased substantially. This may be attributable to the overall market decline that was still evident at General Mills' May 31, 2009, fiscal year end. You can see that income—the topic of this chapter—is a key measure of performance and value.

Introduction to Income Measurement

▶▶ **OBJECTIVE 1**

Explain how accountants measure income.

Measuring income is important to everyone, from individuals to businesses, because we all need to know how well we are doing economically. Income is one metric we use to evaluate economic performance. We can think of income like the number on the scoreboard that tells how well a team is performing. However, measuring income is not as easy as measuring the number of runs scored in a baseball game. Most people regard income as a measure of the increase in the "wealth" of an entity over a period of time. However, companies can measure wealth and income in various ways. To allow decision makers and investors to compare the performance of one company with that of another, generally accepted accounting principles specify certain measurement rules that all companies must follow in measuring net income. While measurement details differ somewhat between the two sets of GAAP, IFRS and U.S. GAAP, the basic principles covered in this chapter apply to both. Let's begin by looking at the period over which accountants measure income.

Operating Cycle

The activities in most companies follow a repeating operating cycle. The **operating cycle**, also known as the **cash cycle**, begins with the acquisition of goods and services in exchange for cash. The company then sells products to customers, who in turn pay for their purchases with cash. This brings us back to the beginning of the cycle. Consider a retail company such as Wal-Mart:

operating cycle (cash cycle)
The time elapsing between the acquisition of goods and services in exchange for cash and the subsequent sale of products to customers, who in turn pay for their purchases with cash.

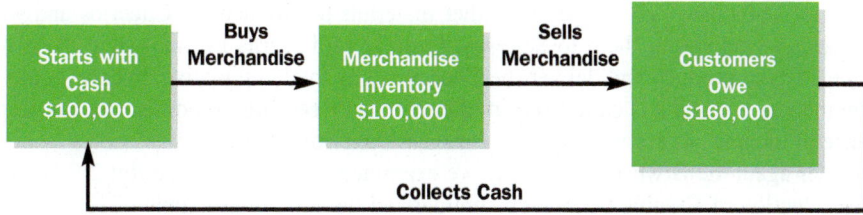

The box for the amounts owed to the entity by customers is larger than the other two boxes because the company's objective is to sell its goods at a price higher than it paid for them. The amount by which the selling price exceeds expenses is profit or income.

The Accounting Time Period

Because it is difficult to accurately measure the success of an ongoing operation, the only way to be certain of a business's success is to close its doors, sell all its assets, pay all liabilities, and return any leftover cash to the owner. Actually, in the 1400s, Venetian merchant traders did exactly that for each and every voyage. Investors provided cash to buy merchandise and pay the crew, and after the voyage the traders paid the investors whatever profits were generated on the voyage. Because that system would not be feasible for companies today, we need to measure performance over time periods shorter than the life of the company.

In the United States, the calendar year is the most popular time period for measuring income. However, about 35% of publicly traded U.S. companies use a **fiscal year** that differs from the calendar year. Established purely for accounting purposes, the fiscal year does not necessarily end on December 31. Many companies choose the end of calendar-year quarters (March 31, June 30, and September 30) as their fiscal year end. For example, Microsoft ends its fiscal year on June 30, and The Walt Disney Company uses September 30. Some companies select the low point in annual business activity as their fiscal year-end date. For example, Wal-Mart and Macy's use a fiscal year ending on January 31 after completing holiday and post-holiday sales. General Mills ends its fiscal year on the last Sunday in May, a low point in the company's operating cycle. In Japan, many companies, including such well-known companies as Sony, Toyota, Honda, and Toshiba, use a March 31 year end to coincide with that of the Japanese government.

fiscal year
The year established for accounting purposes, which may differ from the calendar year.

Users of financial statements would like information more than once a year. They want to know how well the business is doing at least each quarter. Therefore, companies also prepare financial statements for these **interim periods**—periods of less than a year. The SEC requires companies with publicly traded securities to officially file financial statements every quarter. However, in some countries such as those in the European Union, authorities require only semi-annual statements.

interim periods
The time spans established for accounting purposes that are less than a year.

Revenues and Expenses

revenue (sales, sales revenue)
The increase in net assets resulting from selling products or services. Revenues increase owners' equity.

expenses
Decreases in net assets as a result of consuming or giving up resources in the process of providing products or services to a customer. Expenses decrease owners' equity.

income (profits, earnings)
The excess of revenues over expenses.

retained earnings (retained income)
Total cumulative owners' equity generated by income or profits.

Now let's see how accountants measure income. Revenues and expenses are the key components. These terms apply to the inflows and outflows of assets that occur during a business's operating cycle. Companies obtain assets by selling products or services and use assets in producing and delivering those products or services. When they sell products or services, they record **revenue** (sometimes called **sales** or **sales revenue**), which is the increase in net assets resulting from selling products or services. Revenues increase owners' equity. In contrast, **expenses** are decreases in net assets as a result of consuming or giving up resources in the process of providing products or services to a customer. Expenses decrease owners' equity. **Income** (also known as **profits** or **earnings**) is the excess of revenues over expenses. If expenses exceed revenues, we call it a loss.

Revenues arise when General Mills ships a carton of Cheerios to Safeway. Expenses arise when General Mills uses oats, sugar, and other materials to produce the Cheerios and when it pays the costs of delivering them to Safeway. General Mills earns income when the revenues exceed the costs to produce and deliver the Cheerios. The total cumulative owners' equity generated by income or profits is called **retained earnings** or **retained income**. You can learn the importance of income or earnings from the Business First box on page 50.

Consider again the Biwheels Company we examined in Chapter 1. Exhibit 2-2 is almost a direct reproduction of Exhibit 1-2, which summarized the nine transactions of Hector Lopez's business. However, the company has now been incorporated with multiple stockholders, and the owners' equity account is no longer Hector Lopez, Capital. In Exhibit 2-2, it is Stockholders' Equity, which contains both Paid-in Capital and Retained Earnings.

EXHIBIT 2-2

Biwheels Company

Analysis of Transactions for January 2, 20X2, to January 12, 20X2 (in $)

		Assets		=	Liabilities		+	Stockholders' Equity	
Description of Transactions	Cash +	Merchandise Inventory +	Store Equipment =		Note Payable +	Accounts Payable +		Paid-in Capital +	Retained Earnings
(1) Initial investment	+400,000			=				+400,000	
(2) Loan from bank	+100,000			=	+100,000				
(3) Acquire store equipment for cash	−15,000		+15,000	=					
(4) Acquire inventory for cash	−120,000	+120,000		=					
(5) Acquire inventory on credit		+10,000		=		+10,000			
(6) Acquire inventory for cash plus credit	−10,000	+30,000		=		+20,000			
(7) Sale of equipment	+1,000		−1,000	=					
(8) Return of inventory acquired on January 6		−800		=		−800			
(9) Payment to creditor	−4,000			=		−4,000			
Balance January 12, 20X2	352,000 +	159,200 +	14,000 =		100,000 +	25,200 +		400,000	
		525,200				525,200			

EXHIBIT 2-3

Biwheels Company

Analysis of Transactions for January 20X2 (in $)

Description of Transactions	Cash	+	Accounts Receivable	+	Merchandise Inventory	+	Prepaid Rent	+	Store Equipment	=	Note Payable	+	Accounts Payable	+	Paid-in Capital	+	Retained Earnings
(1)–(9) See Exhibit 2-2 Balance, January 12, 20X2	352,000	+		+	159,200	+		+	14,000	=	100,000	+	25,200	+	400,000	+	
(10a) Sales on open account (inflow of assets)			+160,000							=							+160,000 (Sales Revenue)
(10b) Cost of merchandise inventory sold (outflow of assets)					–100,000					=							–100,000 (Cost of Goods Sold Expense)
(11) Collect accounts receivable	+5,000		–5,000							=							
(12) Pay rent in advance	–6,000						+6,000			=							
(13) Recognize expiration of rental services							–2,000			=							–2,000 (Rent Expense)
(14) Recognize expiration of equipment services									–100	=							–100 (Depreciation Expense)
Balance January 31, 20X2	351,000	+	155,000	+	59,200	+	4,000	+	13,900	=	100,000	+	25,200	+	400,000	+	57,900

583,100   583,100

BUSINESS FIRST

EARNINGS AND EARNINGS EXPECTATIONS

Earnings are a critical measure of company performance, and investors watch earnings carefully. Almost every day the financial press reports on current and prospective earnings. A focus for both investors and the press is "consensus earnings forecasts." A major source of consensus forecasts is Zacks Investment Research (another source is Thomson Reuters I/B/E/S). A large number of Wall Street analysts follow the stocks of any major corporation, and Zacks gathers the analysts' forecasts and publishes a continually updated average of the forecasts. These are important inputs to investors, even to sophisticated investors such as mutual fund managers. When a company announces its actual earnings, the press inevitably compares it with the consensus analysts' forecast. Any difference between the forecast and actual earnings is called an "earnings surprise." Most companies try to keep their earnings surprises to a minimum by providing guidance to analysts about what to expect.

Consider Apple's earnings announcements during 2010. The following table shows the Zacks consensus earnings forecast each quarter compared with the actual earnings:

Quarter	Reporting Date	Actual Earnings	Consensus Earnings	Earnings Surprise	Earnings Surprise %
Q1/2011	1/18/11	$6.43	$5.38	$1.05	19.52
Q2/2011	4/20/11	$6.40	$5.34	$1.06	19.85
Q3/2011	7/19/11	$7.79	$5.81	$1.98	34.08
Q4/2011	10/18/11	$7.05	$7.30	−$0.25	−3.42

Meeting earnings expectations is important. Investors derive information from earnings reports, and when the results surprise them, stock prices generally react. You might expect that a positive earnings surprise would lead to an increase in stock price and that a negative earnings surprise would lead to a stock price decrease. Apple met expectations in three of the four quarters of fiscal 2011. The positive earnings surprises in the second and third quarters (April and July) contributed to a 3.1% and 2.8% increase in stock price, respectively, in the two days following the announcements. Apple's failure to meet the consensus estimate in the fourth quarter (a negative 3.42% surprise) was followed by a 6.38% decrease in the stock price over the two days following the announcement. This seemingly disproportionate stock price decline is partly attributable to the fact that this was the first time in more than 6 years that Apple missed the quarterly analysts' earnings estimate. The first quarter seems to defy the simple expectation that a positive earnings surprise will be followed by an increase in stock price. Despite the 19.52% positive earnings surprise in January, Apple's stock fell 2.34% in the two days following the earnings announcement. Why might this occur? Other company, industry, and general economic news occurring around the time of the earnings announcement can also influence the stock price.

Sources: http://www.zacks.com/stock/news/46168/Record+1Q+for+Apple; http://www.zacks.com/stock/news/51710/Apple+Fires+All+Cylinders+in+Q2; http://www.zacks.com/stock/news/57331/Apple+Crushes+Estimates; http://www.zacks.com/stock/news/62929/Apple+Struggles+in+4Q; http://investing.businessweek.com/research/stocks/earnings/earnings.asp?ticker=APPL:US.

accounts receivable (trade receivables, receivables) *Amounts owed to a company by customers as a result of the company's delivering goods or services and extending credit in the ordinary course of business.*

Now consider some additional transactions that are shown in Exhibit 2-3, a continuation of Exhibit 2-2. Suppose Biwheels' sales for the entire month of January total $160,000 on open account. The cost to Biwheels of the inventory sold is $100,000. Selling on open account creates an account receivable. **Accounts receivable** (sometimes called **trade receivables** or simply **receivables**) are amounts owed to a company by customers as a result of the company's delivering goods or services to the customers and extending credit in the ordinary course of business. Thus, the January sales increase Biwheels' Accounts Receivable account by $160,000. Delivering merchandise to customers reduces its Merchandise Inventory account by $100,000.

Note that we record the January sales and other transactions illustrated here as summarized transactions. The company's sales, purchases of inventory, collections from customers, or disbursements to suppliers do not take place all at once. Actual accounting systems record every sale at the time of sale using a cash register, a scanner, or some other data entry device, and then summarize the data over some period of time, such as the month of January for our example.

The accounting for the summarized sales transaction has two phases, a revenue phase (10a) and an expense phase (10b):

	Assets		=	Liabilities	+	Stockholders' Equity
	Accounts Receivable	+ Merchandise Inventory				Retained Earnings
(10a) Sales on open account	+160,000		=			+160,000 (Sales Revenue)
(10b) Cost of merchandise inventory sold		−100,000	=			−100,000 (Cost of Goods Sold Expense)

To understand this transaction, think of it as two steps occurring simultaneously in the balance sheet equation: an inflow of assets in the form of accounts receivable (10a) in exchange for an outflow of assets in the form of merchandise inventory (10b). This exchange of assets does not affect liabilities, so to keep the equation in balance, stockholders' equity must increase by $60,000 [that is, $160,000 (Sales Revenue) − $100,000 (Cost of Goods Sold expense)]. Note that **cost of goods sold** expense (also called **cost of sales** or **cost of revenue**) is the original acquisition cost of the inventory that a company sells to customers during the reporting period.

As entry 10a shows, we record revenue from sales as an increase in the asset Accounts Receivable and an increase in Retained Earnings. In contrast, in entry 10b we record the cost of goods sold expense as a decrease in the asset Merchandise Inventory and a decrease in Retained Earnings. You can see that revenues are positive entries to the Retained Earnings account in the stockholders' equity section of the balance sheet, and expenses are negative entries to Retained Earnings. We illustrate these relationships as follows, where the arrows show the components of the various accounts:

cost of goods sold (cost of sales, cost of revenue) The original acquisition cost of the inventory that a company sells to customers during the reporting period.

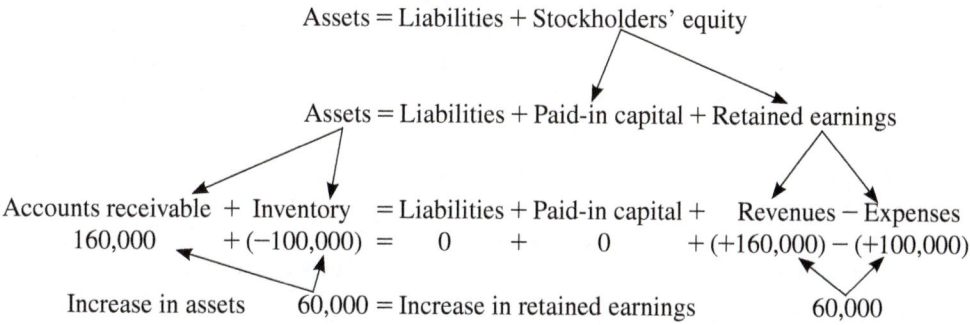

The ultimate purpose of sales is not to generate accounts receivable. Rather, Biwheels wants to collect these receivables in cash on a timely basis. The company may receive some cash shortly after a credit sale, and some customers may delay payments for long periods. Suppose Biwheels collects $5,000 of its $160,000 of accounts receivable during January. This summary transaction, call it transaction 11, increases Cash and decreases Accounts Receivable. It does not affect Retained Earnings.

	Assets				= Liabilities	+	Stockholders' Equity
	Cash	+ Accounts Receivable	+ Merchandise Inventory	=			Retained Earnings
(11) Collect accounts receivable	+5,000	−5,000			=		

We next consider how accountants decide when to record revenues in the books and how this affects measures of income.

Measuring Income

Accrual Basis and Cash Basis

accrual basis
Accounting method in which accountants record revenue as a company earns it and expenses as the company incurs them—regardless of when cash changes hands.

cash basis
Accounting method that recognizes revenue when a company receives cash and recognizes expenses when it pays cash.

There are two popular methods of measuring income, the accrual basis and the cash basis. Under the **accrual basis**, accountants record revenue as it is earned and record expenses as they are incurred, regardless of when cash changes hands. In contrast, the **cash basis** recognizes revenue when a company receives cash and recognizes expenses when it pays cash.

For many years, accountants debated the merits of accrual-basis versus cash-basis accounting. Supporters of the accrual basis maintained that the cash basis ignores activities that increase or decrease assets other than cash. Supporters of the cash basis pointed out that a company, no matter how well it seems to be doing, can go bankrupt if it does not manage its cash properly. Who is correct? In the end, the debate has been declared a draw. Companies prepare their income statements on an accrual basis, and they also prepare a separate statement of cash flows (described in Chapter 5). Although both cash and accrual bases have their merits, the accrual basis has the advantage of presenting a more complete summary of the entity's value-producing activities. It recognizes revenues as companies earn them and matches costs to revenues. We illustrated this accrual process in our analysis of the sale on open account in transaction 10. We recognized revenue although Biwheels received no cash, and we recorded an expense although, at the time of the sale, Biwheels paid no cash. Let's now take a look at some of the specifics of the accrual basis.

Recognition of Revenues

▶ **OBJECTIVE 2**

Determine when a company should record revenue from a sale.

revenue recognition
Criteria for determining whether to record revenue in the financial statements of a given accounting period. To be recognized, revenues must be earned and realized or realizable.

When accountants measure income on an accrual basis, they use a set of **revenue recognition** criteria, which determine whether to record revenue in the financial statements of a given accounting period. To be recognized under U.S. GAAP, revenues must ordinarily satisfy two criteria:

1. *They must be earned.* A company earns revenues when it has completed all (or substantially all) that it has promised to a customer. Typically, this involves the delivery of goods or services to a customer.
2. *They must be realized or realizable.* Revenues are realized when a company receives cash or claims to cash in exchange for goods or services. A "claim to cash" usually means a customer's promise to pay. Revenues are realizable when the company receives assets that are readily convertible into known amounts of cash or claims to cash. To recognize revenue on the basis of a promise to pay, the company must be relatively certain that it will receive the cash.

IFRS also contains criteria that companies must satisfy in order to recognize revenue. While the wording of the criteria differs, IFRS guidance typically results in revenue recognition occurring at the same time and in the same amount as does U.S. GAAP. The FASB and IASB are actively working on a revision of the rules for revenue recognition. The revision would clarify the principles for recognizing revenue and develop a common revenue standard for U.S. GAAP and IFRS. While final guidance is yet to be issued, changes are likely in the near future.

Revenue recognition for most retail companies, such as Wal-Mart, Safeway, and McDonald's, is straightforward. Such companies earn and realize revenue at the point of sale—when a customer makes a full payment by cash, check, or credit card and takes possession of the goods. Other companies may earn and realize revenue at times other than the point of sale. However, even in such cases, they do not recognize revenue until both earning and realization are complete.

Consider the following examples:

- The *Wall Street Journal* receives prepaid subscriptions. The *Wall Street Journal* realizes revenue when it receives the subscription, but it does not earn the revenue until delivery of each issue.
- A dealer in oriental rugs lets a potential customer take a rug home on a trial basis. The customer has possession of the goods, but the dealer records no revenue until the customer formally promises to accept and pay for the rug.

We elaborate further on revenue recognition in Chapter 6.

INTERPRETING FINANCIAL STATEMENTS

Suppose you are examining the 2013 financial statements of a new theater company. The theater sells a subscription series that allows patrons to attend all nine of its productions that occur monthly from September through May. During August and September, the company sold 1,000 subscriptions for the 2013–2014 season at $270 each and collected the cash. How much revenue from these subscriptions did the theater recognize in its financial statements for the year ended December 31, 2013?

Answer

At December 31, 2013, the theater has produced only four out of nine productions, so the company has earned only four-ninths of the total, or $120,000. Its total cash collections are $270,000. While the theater has realized all $270,000, it has earned only $120,000. Therefore, it recognizes and records only $120,000 of revenue in 2013.

Matching

We have seen how to recognize revenues on the accrual basis. What about expenses? There are two types of expenses in every accounting period: (1) those linked to the revenues earned that period, and (2) those linked to the time period itself. Expenses that are naturally linked to revenues are **product costs**. Examples include cost of goods sold and sales commissions. If there are no revenues, there is no cost of goods sold or sales commissions. When do we recognize product costs? Accountants match such expenses to the revenues they help generate. We recognize and record expenses in the same period that we recognize the related revenues, a process called **matching**.

While the concept of matching is straightforward, it can be difficult to link some expenses directly to specific revenues. Rent and many administrative expenses are examples. These expenses support a company's operations for a given period, so we call them **period costs**. We record period costs as expenses in the period in which the company incurs them. For example, rent expense arises because of the passage of time, regardless of the level of sales. Therefore, rent is an example of a period cost. Consider a General Mills warehouse. The rent expense for the month of May gives General Mills the right to use the building for the month. General Mills records the entire rent expense in May, regardless of whether May's sales are high or low.

To help us match expenses with revenues, we record purchases of some goods or services as assets because we want to match their costs with the revenues in future periods. For example, we might buy inventory that we will not sell until a future period. By recording this inventory first as an asset and then expensing it when we sell the item, we match the cost of the inventory with the revenue from the sale of the inventory. Another example is rent paid in advance. Suppose a firm pays annual rent of $12,000 on January 1 for the use of a building. We increase an asset account, Prepaid Rent, by $12,000 because we have not yet used the rental services. Each month we reduce the Prepaid Rent account by $1,000 and increase Rent Expense by $1,000, acknowledging that we use up the prepaid rent asset as we occupy the building.

Applying Matching

To focus on matching, assume that Biwheels Company has only two expenses other than the cost of goods sold: rent expense and depreciation expense. Rent is $2,000 per month, payable quarterly in advance. Biwheels makes a payment of $6,000 for store rent, covering January, February, and March of 20X2. (Assume that Biwheels made this initial payment on January 16, although rent is commonly paid at the beginning of the rental period.) This is transaction 12 in Exhibit 2-3.

The rent payment gives the company the right to use the store facilities for the months of January, February, and March. The use of the facilities constitutes a future benefit, so Biwheels records the $6,000 in an asset account, Prepaid Rent. Transaction 12, the rent payment, has no effect on stockholders' equity in the balance sheet equation. Biwheels simply exchanges one asset, Cash, for another, Prepaid Rent:

▶▶ **OBJECTIVE 3**

Use the concept of matching to record the expenses for a period.

product costs
Costs that are linked with revenues and are charged as expenses when the related revenue is recognized.

matching
The recording of expenses in the same time period that we recognize the related revenues.

period costs
Expenses supporting a company's operations for a given period. We record these expenses in the time period in which the company incurs them.

	Assets			=	Liabilities	+ Stockholders' Equity
	Cash	+	Prepaid Rent	=		
(12) Pay rent in advance	−6,000		+6,000	=		

At the end of January, Biwheels records transaction 13. It recognizes that the company has used 1 month (one-third of the total) of the rental services. Therefore, Biwheels reduces Prepaid Rent by $2,000. It also reduces the Retained Earnings account in stockholders' equity by $2,000 as Rent Expense for January.

			Assets	=	Liabilities	+	Stockholders' Equity
	Cash	+	Prepaid Rent	=			Retained Earnings
(13) Recognize expiration of rental services			−2,000	=			−2,000 (Rent Expense)

This recognition of rent expense means that Biwheels has used $2,000 of the asset, Prepaid Rent, in the conduct of operations during January. That $2,000 in rent was a period cost for January, and Biwheels recognized it as an expense at the end of that period.

Prepaid rent of $4,000 remains an asset on January 31. Why? The $4,000 is a future benefit for Biwheels. Suppose Biwheels had not prepaid the rent. It would then have to pay $2,000 in both February and March for rent. Therefore, the prepayment means that future cash outflows will be $4,000 less than they would have been without the prepayment.

The same matching concept that underlies the accounting for prepaid rent applies to **depreciation**, which is the systematic allocation of the acquisition cost of long-lived assets to the expense accounts of the particular accounting periods that benefit from the use of the assets. Depreciation applies to physical assets that a company owns, such as buildings, equipment, furniture, and fixtures, that the company expects to use for multiple periods. (Land is not subject to depreciation because it does not deteriorate over time.)

In both of these examples, prepaid rent and depreciation, the business purchases an asset that gradually wears out or is used. As a company uses an asset, it transfers more and more of the asset's original cost from the asset account to an expense account. The main difference between depreciation and prepaid rent is the length of time before the asset loses its usefulness. Buildings, equipment, and furniture remain useful for many years; prepaid rent and other prepaid expenses usually expire within a year.

Transaction 14 in Exhibit 2-3 records the depreciation expense for the Biwheels equipment. A portion of the original cost of $14,000 becomes depreciation expense in each month of the equipment's useful life. Assume that Biwheels will use the equipment for 140 months. Under the matching concept, the depreciation expense for January is ($14,000 ÷ 140 months), or $100 per month:

depreciation
The systematic allocation of the acquisition cost of long-lived assets to the expense accounts of the particular accounting periods that benefit from the use of the assets.

	Assets	=	Liabilities	+	Stockholders' Equity
	Store Equipment	=			Retained Earnings
(14) Recognize expiration of equipment services	−100	=			−100 (Depreciation Expense)

In this transaction, Biwheels decreases the asset account, Store Equipment, and also decreases the stockholders' equity account, Retained Earnings. Transactions 13 and 14 highlight the general concept of expense under the accrual basis. We can account for the purchase and use of goods and services—for example, inventories, rent, and equipment—in two basic steps: (1) the acquisition of the assets (transactions 3, 4, 5, and 6 in Exhibit 2-2 and transaction 12 in Exhibit 2-3), and (2) the expiration of the assets as expenses (transactions 10b, 13, and 14 in Exhibit 2-3). As these examples show, when a company uses the services represented by prepaid expenses and long-lived assets, it decreases both total assets and stockholders' equity. Remember that expense accounts are deductions from stockholders' equity.

Recognition of Expired Assets

You can think of assets such as inventory, prepaid rent, and equipment as costs that a company stores and carries forward to future accounting periods and then records as expenses when it uses them. For inventory, we record the expense when the company sells the item and recognizes revenue from the sale. For rent, we recognize the expense in the period to which the rent applies. For equipment, we split the total cost of the long-lived asset into smaller pieces and recognize one piece of that total cost as an expense in each of the accounting periods that benefits from the use of the equipment. In summary, inventory costs are *product costs* that accountants match to the revenues they help generate. Rent is a *period cost* that accountants record in the period it benefits. Because equipment benefits many periods, accountants spread its cost over those periods as depreciation expense:

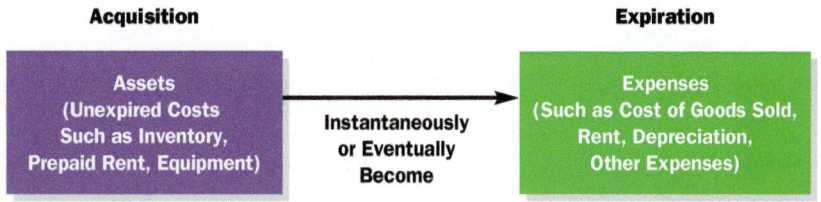

The analysis of the inventory, rent, and depreciation transactions in Exhibits 2-2 and 2-3 distinguishes between acquisition and expiration. Biwheels recorded inventory, rent, and equipment as assets when it acquired them. The unexpired costs of inventory, prepaid rent, and equipment then remain assets until used. When Biwheels uses them, they become expenses. What happens if Biwheels acquires assets and uses them right away? For example, companies often acquire services such as advertising and use them almost immediately. Conceptually, these costs are assets until the company uses them, at which time it recognizes them as expenses. For example, suppose General Mills purchased newspaper advertising for Wheaties for $1,000 cash. To abide by the acquisition–expiration sequence, we could analyze the transaction in two phases as in alternative 1 that follows:

		Assets		=	Liabilities +	Stockholders' Equity	
Transaction	**Cash**	**Other + Assets +**	**Prepaid Advertising =**			**Paid-in Capital +**	**Retained Earnings**
Alternative 1: Two Phases							
Phase (a) Prepay for advertising	−1,000		+1,000	=			
Phase (b) Use advertising			−1,000	=			−1,000 (Advertising Expense)
Alternative 2: One Phase							
Phases (a) and (b) together	−1,000			=			−1,000 (Advertising Expense)

In practice, however, if a company uses prepaid advertising and other similar services in the same accounting period that it acquires them, accountants may not bother recording them as assets. Instead, accountants frequently use the recording shortcut shown in alternative 2.

Although alternative 1 is technically correct, alternative 2 does not misstate the company's financial position as long as the advertising prepayment and the use of the advertising occur in the same accounting period.

Although this chapter focuses on the income statement, it is important to realize that the income statement is really just a way of explaining changes between one accounting period's balance sheet and the next period's balance sheet. It shows how the performance of management moved the company from its beginning financial position to its end-of-the-period position. The balance sheet equation shows revenue and expense items as components of stockholders' equity. The income statement simply collects all these changes in stockholders' equity for the accounting period and combines them in one place.

(1) Assets (A) = Liabilities (L) + Stockholders' equity (SE)

(2) Assets = Liabilities + Paid-in capital + Retained Earnings

(3) Assets = Liabilities + Paid-in capital + $\dfrac{\text{Cumulative}}{\text{Revenues}} - \dfrac{\text{Cumulative}}{\text{Expenses}}$

Revenue and expense accounts are nothing more than subdivisions of stockholders' equity—temporary stockholders' equity accounts. Their purpose is to summarize the dollar volume of sales and the various expenses so we can measure income.

The analysis of each transaction in Exhibits 2-2 and 2-3 illustrates the dual nature of the balance sheet equation, which must always remain in balance. If the items affected are all on one side of the equation, the total amount added must equal the total amount subtracted on that side. If the items affected are on opposite sides of the equation, then equal amounts are simultaneously added or subtracted on each side.

The striking feature of the balance sheet equation is its universal applicability. No one has ever conceived a transaction, no matter how complex, that we cannot analyze via the equation. Business leaders and accountants employ the balance sheet equation constantly to be sure they understand the effects of business transactions they are planning.

INTERPRETING FINANCIAL STATEMENTS

You are examining the financial statements of a company that started in business on January 1, 2013, and rented an office for $4,000 per month. It paid 8 months of rent in advance for a total of $32,000. During January, the company earned no revenue. How much rent expense do you expect to see on the company's financial statements for January?

Answer

Rent expense is $4,000 for January. Companies charge rent expense in the period to which the rental applies. It is a period cost that becomes an expense when the company uses the space rented, regardless of the level of sales for that period.

The Income Statement

▶▶ OBJECTIVE 4

Prepare an income statement and show how it is related to a balance sheet.

You have now seen how companies record revenues and expenses and use them to measure income. We next consider how companies report revenues, expenses, and income in their financial statements. Chapter 1 introduced the balance sheet as a snapshot-in-time summary of a company's financial status. To report a company's performance as measured by income during the accounting period, we need another basic financial statement, the income statement. An **income statement** (also called **statement of earnings** or **statement of operations**) is a report of all revenues and expenses pertaining to a specific time period. **Net income** (or **net earnings**) is the famous "bottom line" on an income statement—the remainder after deducting all expenses from revenues.

Sales revenue		$160,000
Deduct expenses		
Cost of goods sold	$100,000	
Rent	2,000	
Depreciation	100	
Total expenses		102,100
Net income		$ 57,900

EXHIBIT 2-4

Biwheels Company

Income Statement, for the Month Ended January 31, 20X2

Look back at Exhibit 2-3 and notice that four of the accounting events (transactions 10a, 10b, 13, and 14) affect Biwheels Company's Retained Earnings account through recognition of sales revenue, cost of goods sold expense, rent expense, and depreciation expense. Exhibit 2-4 shows how an income statement arranges these transactions to arrive at a net income of $57,900.

Because the income statement measures performance over a period of time, whether it be a month, a quarter, or a year, it must always indicate the exact period covered. In Exhibit 2-4, the Biwheels income statement clearly shows it covers the month ended January 31, 20X2.

Public companies in much of the world publish income statements quarterly. In some countries, companies publish only semiannual or annual statements. Worldwide, most companies prepare such statements monthly or weekly for internal management purposes. Some CEOs even ask for a daily income statement that summarizes the income of the previous day.

Decision makers both inside and outside the company use income statements to assess the company's performance over a span of time. The income statement shows how the entity's operations for the period have increased net assets (that is, assets minus liabilities) through revenues and decreased net assets through expenses. Net income measures the amount by which the increase in net assets (revenues) exceeds the decrease in net assets (expenses). Of course, expenses could exceed revenues, in which case the company experiences a **net loss**. Net income or net loss is one measure of the wealth an entity creates or loses from its operations during the accounting period. Tracking net income or loss from period to period and examining changes in its components helps investors and other decision makers evaluate the success of the period's operations.

For example, General Mills reported 2011 net earnings of $1,798.3 million, 17.5% higher than in 2010. Management explained that this increase was due in part to an almost 2% increase in sales, half of which was attributable to physical sales volume and half to small price increases, and in part to a favorable change in product mix. The majority of the increase in net earnings resulted from cost-saving initiatives, marketing spending efficiencies, and accounting adjustments that decreased some expense categories and reduced taxes. The CEO and chairman of the board of directors indicated: "We are generally pleased with our 2011 sales and profit results, which met the key targets we set for the year and represent performance consistent with our long-term growth model."

income statement (statement of earnings, statement of operations)
A report of all revenues and expenses pertaining to a specific time period.

net income (net earnings)
The remainder after deducting all expenses from revenues.

net loss
The difference between revenues and expenses when expenses exceed revenues.

Relationship Between the Income Statement and Balance Sheet

The income statement is the major link between two balance sheets:

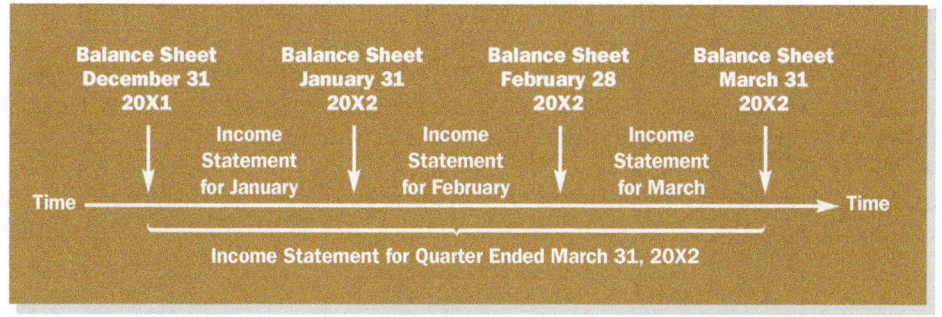

You can think of income statements as filling in the gaps between balance sheets. The balance sheets show the financial position of the company at discrete points in time, and the income statements explain the changes that have taken place between those points.

For example, the balance sheet for Biwheels Company on January 2, 20X2, showed assets of $500,000 and, to balance the equation, liabilities of $100,000 plus stockholders' equity of $400,000. There were no retained earnings. The January transactions analyzed in Exhibit 2-3 showed revenues of $160,000 and expenses of $102,100 recorded in the Retained Earnings account. The income statement in Exhibit 2-4 displays these revenues and expenses for the month of January and shows the resulting net income of $57,900. On the balance sheet on January 31, 20X2, the stockholders' equity account, Retained Earnings, will be $57,900 greater than on January 2.

Ethics, Depreciation, and Net Income

Sometimes measuring net income can cause ethical dilemmas for accountants. In Chapter 1, we learned about the ethical standards of accountants. It is usually easy to avoid conduct that is clearly unethical. However, ethical standards and accounting standards often leave room for individual interpretation and judgment. The most difficult ethical situations arise when there is strong pressure to take an action in the gray area between ethical and unethical or when two ethical standards conflict. Because net income is so important in measuring managerial performance, occasionally managers put pressure on accountants to report higher revenues or lower expenses than is appropriate. In the economic downturns of the last decade, authorities accused many companies of manipulating their income to make results look better than they actually were. For example, in 2002 authorities accused executives at **Enron** and **WorldCom** of manipulating net income, Enron by recognizing excess revenues and WorldCom by omitting required expenses. In 2004, the SEC accused insurance giant **AIG** of issuing "materially falsified financial statements … to paint a falsely rosy picture of [the company's] financial results to analysts and investors." The largest bankruptcy in U.S. history followed the collapse of **Lehman Brothers** in 2008. The company reported record profits in January 2008 and was bankrupt by the following September. Many believe that the collapse and bankruptcy of Lehman Brothers fueled the U.S. financial and economic crisis. Accounting scandals are not limited to U.S. companies. Early in 2009, the SEC charged an Indian company, **Satyam Computer Services**, with fraudulently overstating the company's revenue, income, and cash balances by more than $1 billion over a 5-year period.

One area that requires judgment, and therefore leaves room for ethical conflicts, is depreciation. Suppose you are an accountant for an airline with $15 billion of new airplanes. Management wants to depreciate the airplanes over 30 years—leading to depreciation of $500 million per year. You discover that most airlines depreciate similar airplanes over 15 years, which would mean $1 billion of annual depreciation. Management argues that airplanes such as these will physically last at least 30 years, and there is no reason not to use them for the entire 30-year period. You believe that technological change is likely to make them obsolete in 15 years, but such technological improvements are not assured and may not occur. With depreciation of $500 million, before-tax income for the company would be $400 million, so increasing depreciation to $1 billion will put the company in a loss position. If this happens, banks might ask for repayment of loans and force the company into bankruptcy. Should you prepare an income statement with $500 million of depreciation or insist on the larger $1 billion depreciation expense?

There is no obviously right answer to this question. The important point is that you recognize the ethical dimensions of this problem and weigh them when forming your opinion. The company might be in dire straits if you refuse to prepare an income statement with the $500 million of depreciation. However, if you truly believe that it is not proper to depreciate the airplanes over 30 years, you cannot ethically prepare an income statement with only $500 million of depreciation. Could management be right and you be wrong about the proper depreciation expense? Is management trying to influence its net income by manipulating its depreciation expense? Accountants must assert their judgments in cases such as this. Recognizing the ethical issues involved is an important part of making those judgments.

Summary Problem for Your Review

PROBLEM

Biwheels' transactions for January were analyzed in Exhibits 2-2 and 2-3. The balance sheet at January 31, 20X2, follows:

Biwheels Company

Balance Sheet, January 31, 20X2

Assets		Liabilities and Stockholders' Equity		
Cash	$351,000	Liabilities:		
Accounts receivable	155,000	Note payable		$100,000
Merchandise		Accounts payable		25,200
inventory	59,200	Total liabilities		125,200
Prepaid rent	4,000	Stockholders' equity:		
Store equipment	13,900	Paid-in capital	$400,000	
		Retained earnings	57,900	
		Total stockholders' equity		457,900
		Total liabilities and		
Total assets	$583,100	stockholders' equity		$583,100

The following transactions occurred during February:

15. Collections of accounts receivable, $130,000.
16. Payments of accounts payable, $15,000.
17. Acquisitions of inventory included $80,000 on open account and $10,000 acquired in exchange for cash.
18. Sales of merchandise for $176,000, of which $125,000 was on open account and $51,000 was for cash. The merchandise sold was carried in inventory at a cost of $110,000.
19. Recognition of rent expense for February.
20. Recognition of depreciation expense for February.
21. Borrowing of $10,000 from the bank, which Biwheels used to buy $10,000 of store equipment on February 28.

Required

1. Prepare an analysis of transactions, employing the balance sheet equation approach demonstrated in Exhibit 2-3.
2. Prepare a balance sheet as of February 28, 20X2, and an income statement for the month of February.

SOLUTION

1. The analysis of transactions is in Exhibit 2-5. All transactions are straightforward extensions or repetitions of the January transactions. Notice that some of these are summary transactions. For example, Biwheels made sales to many different customers; the $176,000 is the sum of all these sales. Likewise, Biwheels acquired the $90,000 of inventory from several suppliers at different times during February.
2. Exhibit 2-6 contains the balance sheet and Exhibit 2-7 the income statement, which were both described earlier. Notice that the balance sheet lists the ending balances in all the accounts in Exhibit 2-5. The income statement summarizes the revenue and expense entries in the Retained Earnings account.

EXHIBIT 2-5

Biwheels Company

Analysis of Transactions for February 20X2 (in $)

	Assets					=	Liabilities			Stockholders' Equity	
Description of Transactions	Cash	Accounts Receivable	Merchandise Inventory	Prepaid Rent	Store Equipment	=	Notes Payable	Accounts Payable	Paid-in Capital	Retained Earnings	
Balance, January 31, 20X2	351,000	155,000	59,200	4,000	13,900	=	100,000	25,200	400,000	57,900	
(15) Collect accounts receivable	+130,000	−130,000									
(16) Pay accounts payable	−15,000					=		−15,000			
(17) Acquire inventory on open account and for cash	−10,000		+90,000			=		+80,000			
(18a) Sales on open account and for cash	+51,000	+125,000				=				+176,000	(Sales Revenue)
(18b) Cost of inventory sold			−110,000			=				−110,000	(Cost of Goods Sold Expense)
(19) Recognize expiration of rental services				−2,000		=				−2,000	(Rent Expense)
(20) Recognize expiration of equipment services (depreciation)					−100	=				−100	(Depreciation Expense)
(21a) Borrow from bank	+10,000					=	+10,000				
(21b) Purchase store equipment	−10,000				+10,000	=					
Balance February 28, 20X2	507,000	150,000	39,200	2,000	23,800	=	110,000	90,200	400,000	121,800	
	722,000					=				722,000	

Assets		Liabilities and Stockholders' Equity		
Cash	$507,000	Liabilities:		
Accounts receivable	150,000	Notes payable	$110,000	
Merchandise inventory	39,200	Accounts payable	90,200	$200,200
Prepaid rent	2,000	Stockholders' equity:		
Store equipment	23,800	Paid-in capital	$400,000	
		Retained earnings	121,800	521,800
		Total liabilities and		
Total assets	$722,000	stockholders' equity		$722,000

Sales revenue		$176,000
Deduct expenses		
Cost of goods sold	$110,000	
Rent	2,000	
Depreciation	100	112,100
Net income		$ 63,900

Accounting for Dividends and Retained Earnings

Recall that companies record revenues and expenses for a particular time period in Retained Earnings, a stockholders' equity account. Because net income is the excess of revenues over expenses, the Retained Earnings account increases by the amount of net income reported during the period. If expenses exceed revenues, the Retained Earnings account decreases by the amount of the period's net loss.

▶▶OBJECTIVE 5

Account for cash dividends and prepare a statement of stockholders' equity.

Cash Dividends

Another decrease in the Retained Earnings account arises from **cash dividends**, distributions of cash to stockholders. Corporations pay out cash dividends to stockholders to provide a return on the stockholders' investment in the corporation. The ability to pay dividends is fundamentally a result of profitable operations. Retained earnings increase as profits accumulate, and they decrease as a company pays dividends.

cash dividends
Distributions of cash to stockholders that reduce retained earnings.

Although cash dividends decrease retained earnings, they are not expenses like rent and depreciation. Therefore, unlike rent and depreciation expense, we do not deduct dividends from revenues on the income statement. Why? Because dividends are not directly linked to the generation of revenue or the cost of operating activities. Rather, they are voluntary distributions of cash to stockholders, not a cost of doing business. Assume that on February 28, Biwheels declared and disbursed cash dividends of $50,000 to stockholders. We can analyze this transaction (22) as follows:

	Assets	=	Liabilities	+ Stockholders' Equity
	Cash	=		Retained Earnings
(22) Declaration and payment of cash dividends	−50,000	=		−50,000 (Dividends)

Cash dividends distribute some of the company's assets (cash) to shareholders, thus reducing the economic value of their remaining interest in Biwheels. Of course, companies must have sufficient cash on hand to pay cash dividends.

Transaction 22 presents the declaration and payment of a dividend as a single transaction. However, corporations usually approach dividend distributions in steps. The board of directors *declares*—announces its intention to pay—a dividend on one date (declaration date), payable to those *stockholders on record* as owning the stock on a second date (record date), and actually *pays* the dividend on a third date (payment date). The dividend amount reduces retained earnings and is recorded as a liability on the declaration date. On the payment date, both the dividend liability and cash decrease. We discuss dividends in more detail in Chapter 10.

Not all companies pay dividends. As of November 2012, eBay had never paid dividends. Microsoft and McDonald's paid no dividends during their early, high-growth years, but today they pay regular dividends. Starbucks paid its first dividend in 2010. As a successful company grows, the Retained Earnings account can increase rapidly if the company pays no dividends or dividends that are significantly less than its net income. Retained Earnings can easily be the largest stockholders' equity account. Its balance is the cumulative, lifetime earnings of the company less its cumulative, lifetime losses and dividends. For example, at the end of fiscal 2011, General Mills had retained earnings of $9,191.3 million, whereas paid-in capital was only $1,395.3 million.

Retained Earnings and Cash

The existence of retained earnings and cash enable a board of directors to declare a cash dividend. However, Cash and Retained Earnings are two entirely separate accounts, sharing no necessary relationship. Consider the following illustration:

Step 1. Assume an opening balance sheet of

Cash	$100	Paid-in capital	$100

Step 2. Purchase inventory for $50 cash. The balance sheet now reads

Cash	$ 50	Paid-in capital	$100
Inventory	50		
Total assets	$100		

Step 3. Now sell the inventory for $80 cash. This results in a Retained Earnings balance of $30, $80 in Revenues minus $50 in Cost of Goods Sold.

Cash	$130	Paid-in capital	$100
		Retained earnings	30
		Total owners' equity	$130

At this stage, the balance in Retained Earnings seems to be directly linked to the cash increase of $30. It is, but do not think that retained earnings is a claim against the cash specifically. Remember, it is a claim against total assets. We can clarify this relationship by examining the transaction that follows:

Step 4. Purchase inventory and equipment, in the amounts of $60 and $50, respectively. Now, the balance sheet reads

Cash	$ 20	Paid-in capital	$100
Inventory	60	Retained earnings	30
Equipment	50		
Total assets	$130	Total owners' equity	$130

What claim does the $30 in the Retained Earnings account represent? Is it a claim on cash? It cannot be because the company has $30 of retained earnings and only $20 in cash. The company reinvested part of the cash in inventory and equipment. This example helps to explain the nature of the Retained Earnings account. It is a residual claim, not a pot of gold. A residual claim means that if the company went out of business and sold its assets for cash, the owners would receive the amount left over after the company paid its liabilities. This amount might be either more or less than the current balance in the Cash account and more or less than the current balance in the Retained Earnings account.

Two examples highlight the lack of a direct relationship between cash and retained earnings. At the beginning of 2012 Royal Dutch Shell had retained earnings more than ten times larger than its cash balance: Cash, $11,292 million, and Retained Earnings, $162,987 million. On the same date, Amgen, one of the largest biotech companies in the world, had positive cash and negative retained earnings: Cash, $6,946 million, and Retained Earnings, $(8,919) million.

Statement of Stockholders' Equity

Because owners are interested in understanding the causes of changes in stockholders' equity of a company, accountants have created a financial statement to do just that. The **statement of stockholders' equity** (or **statement of shareholders' equity**) shows all changes during the year in each stockholders' equity account. It starts with the beginning balance in each account, followed by a list of all changes that occurred during the period, followed by the ending balance.

Changes in stockholders' equity arise from three main sources:

1. Net income or net loss. A period's net income (net loss) increases (decreases) the balance in the retained earnings portion of stockholders' equity.
2. Transactions with shareholders. For many companies, the most common transaction with shareholders is the declaration of dividends, which reduces retained earnings. Other transactions include issuing or repurchasing shares, which we discuss in Chapter 10.
3. **Other comprehensive income (OCI).** These are specific changes in stockholders' equity that do not result from net income or transactions with shareholders. Items classified as other comprehensive income increase or decrease stockholders' equity but are not recorded as part of paid-in capital or retained earnings. Rather, companies accumulate these items in a stockholders' equity account entitled **Accumulated Other Comprehensive Income (AOCI).** Most items of other comprehensive income, except for one item discussed in Chapter 11, are beyond the scope of this text.

Exhibit 2-8 shows Biwheels' statement of stockholders' equity for February. So far we have introduced only two stockholders' equity accounts for Biwheels, Paid-in Capital (with possible sub-accounts for par value and additional paid-in capital) and Retained Earnings. We will focus here on Retained Earnings because it is the only Biwheels stockholders' equity account that had changes in February.

Most companies, like Biwheels, will have only two items that affect retained earnings: net income (or loss) and dividends. Other transactions, most having to do with repurchases of a company's own common stock, can affect retained earnings. However, these transactions are less frequent, so we ignore them at this point.

If Biwheels had a net loss (negative net income) we would *subtract* the amount from the beginning balance of retained earnings. If accumulated net losses plus dividends exceed accumulated net income, retained earnings would be negative. Many companies with negative retained earnings use the more descriptive term **accumulated deficit**.

statement of stockholders' equity (statement of shareholders' equity)
A statement that shows all changes during the year in each stockholders' equity account.

other comprehensive income (OCI)
Changes in stockholders' equity that do not result from net income (net loss) or transactions with shareholders.

accumulated other comprehensive income (AOCI)
Stockholders' equity account that contains a cumulative total of all items classified as other comprehensive income.

accumulated deficit
A more descriptive term for retained earnings when the accumulated net losses plus dividends exceed accumulated net income.

	Paid-in Capital	Retained Earnings
Beginning balance, January 31, 20X2	$400,000	$57,900
Net income for February		63,900
Dividends declared		(50,000)
Ending balance, February 28, 20X2	$400,000	$71,800

EXHIBIT 2-8

Biwheels Company
Statement of Stockholders' Equity, for the Month Ended February 28, 20X2

Note how the income statement (Exhibit 2-7) and the changes in retained earnings (see Exhibit 2-8) are anchored to the balance sheet equation, where the bracketed items refer to retained earnings:

$$\text{Assets} = \text{Liabilities} + \text{Paid-in capital} + \text{Retained earnings}$$

$$[\text{Beginning balance} \quad + \text{Revenues} - \text{Expenses} - \text{Dividends}]$$
$$[\$57,900 \quad\quad + \$176,000 - \$112,100 - \$50,000]$$

$$\text{Ending retained earnings balance} = \$71,800$$

INTERPRETING FINANCIAL STATEMENTS

A company's income statement reveals revenues of $50,000 and expenses of $40,000. Its balance sheet shows that retained earnings grew from $15,000 at the beginning of the year to $17,000 at the end of the year. What can you conclude about dividends declared?

Answer

Because net income = (revenues − expenses), net income is ($50,000 − $40,000) = $10,000. Further, ending retained earnings = (beginning retained earnings + net income − dividends). This means that $17,000 = ($15,000 + $10,000 − dividends). Retained earnings would have been ($15,000 + $10,000) = $25,000 if the company had declared no dividends, but it was only $17,000. Therefore, the company must have declared ($25,000 − $17,000) = $8,000 in dividends.

Summary Problem for Your Review

PROBLEM

The following interpretations and remarks are common misinterpretations of financial statements. Explain fully the fallacy in each:

1. "Sales show the cash coming in from customers, and the various expenses show the cash going out for goods and services. The difference is net income."
2. Consider the following March 31, 2011, accounts of Sony Corporation, the large Japanese electronics company.

Sony Corporation
Stockholders' Equity (Yen in billions)

March 31	2010	2011
Stockholders' equity		
Common stock		
Authorized shares: 2010 and 2011, 3,600 million		
Issued and outstanding shares: 2010, 1,003.5 million; 2011, 1,003.6 million	¥ 626	¥ 626
Additional paid-in capital	1,158	1,160
Retained earnings	1,851	1,566
Other	(349)	(415)
Total stockholders' equity	¥3,286	¥2,937

A Sony employee commented, "Why can't Sony pay higher wages and dividends, too? It can use its more than ¥1.56 trillion (more than US$19.5 billion) of retained earnings to do so."

3. "The total Sony stockholders' equity measures the amount that the shareholders would get today if the corporation ceased business, sold its assets, and paid off its liabilities."

SOLUTION

1. Cash receipts and disbursements are not the basis for the accrual accounting recognition of revenues and expenses. Sales could easily be credit sales for which the company has not yet received cash, and expenses could be those that the company has incurred but not yet paid out (or paid out in a previous accounting period). Depreciation is an example where the expense recognition does not coincide with the payment of cash. Depreciation recorded in today's income statement may result from the use of equipment that the company acquired for cash years ago. Therefore, under accrual accounting, sales and expenses are not equivalent to cash inflows and outflows. To determine net income under accrual accounting, we subtract expenses from revenues (expenses are linked to revenues via matching). This can be quite different from cash inflows minus cash outflows.

2. As the chapter indicated, retained earnings is not cash. It is a stockholders' equity account that represents the accumulated increase in ownership claims due to profitable operations. This claim may be lowered by declaring cash dividends, but a growing company will need to reinvest cash in receivables, inventories, plant, equipment, and other assets necessary for expansion. Paying higher wages may make it impossible to compete effectively and stay in business. Paying higher dividends may make it impossible to grow. The level of retained earnings does not lead to a specific wage or dividend policy for the firm.

3. Stockholders' equity is the excess of assets over liabilities. If a company carried its assets in the accounting records at their current market values and listed the liabilities at their current market values, the remark would be true. However, many of the numbers on the balance sheet are historical numbers, not current numbers. Intervening changes in markets and general price levels in inflationary times may mean that some assets are woefully understated. Investors make a critical error if they think that balance sheets indicate current values for all assets.

Four Popular Financial Ratios

Now that you know the basics of balance sheets and income statements, you are ready to learn how investors use some of the information in these statements. Numbers are hard to understand out of context. Is $10 a lot to pay for a share of stock? Is $1 a good dividend? To show you how investors think about such questions, let's look at a few financial ratios that compare financial statement numbers in ways that help us to understand the economic meaning of the numbers.

> **▶▶ OBJECTIVE 6**
>
> Compute and explain earnings per share, price-earnings ratio, dividend-yield ratio, and dividend-payout ratio.

We compute a financial ratio by dividing one number by another. For a set of complex financial statements, we can compute literally hundreds of ratios. Every analyst has a set of favorite ratios, but **earnings per share (EPS)** of common stock is among the most frequently used. EPS is net income divided by the weighted-average number of common shares outstanding during the period over which the net income is measured. It is the only financial ratio required in the body of the financial statements. Publicly held companies must report it on the face of their income statements under both IFRS and U.S. GAAP. Let us now examine EPS and three other popular ratios.

> *earnings per share (EPS)*
> *Basic EPS is net income divided by the weighted-average number of common shares outstanding during the period over which the net income is measured.*

Earnings Per Share

EPS tells investors how much of a period's net income "belongs to" each share of common stock. When a company's owners' equity is relatively simple, computing EPS is straightforward, and the company reports only one number, basic EPS. General Mills reported basic EPS of $1.96, $2.32, and $2.80 in 2009, 2010, and 2011, respectively. The calculation for 2011 follows:

$$\text{EPS} = \frac{\text{Net income}}{\text{Average number of common shares outstanding}}$$

$$\text{2011 EPS} = \frac{\$1,798,300,000}{642,700,000} = \$2.80$$

Most income statements, including that of General Mills, show two EPS numbers, basic and diluted. At this point we focus only on basic EPS. Diluted EPS shows the potential decline in EPS if persons who have a right to acquire common shares at less than full market value, mainly due to stock option grants and debt that is convertible into common stock, exercise that right. We discuss diluted EPS in Chapter 10.

Investors interested in purchasing General Mills stock might be interested in the cause of the company's 20.7% increase in EPS from 2010 to 2011. From a review of the company's 10-K report, we can see that the increase in EPS was caused by an increase in net earnings, from $1,530.5 million in 2010 to $1,798.3 million in 2011, coupled with a decrease in the average number of common shares outstanding. The increase in net income, as noted previously, is the result of a modest increase in sales, cost-saving initiatives and efficiencies, and a reduction in taxes. The average number of common shares outstanding decreased because the company repurchased some of its own shares in the stock market. Investors can weigh the reported EPS numbers and management's explanation when forming their predictions of future EPS and deciding whether to invest in the stock.

Price-Earnings Ratio

price-earnings (P-E) ratio
Market price per share of common stock divided by earnings per share of common stock.

Another popular ratio is the **price-earnings (P-E) ratio**:

$$\text{P-E ratio} = \frac{\text{Market price per share of common stock}}{\text{Earnings per share of common stock}}$$

The numerator is typically the most recent market price for a share of the company's stock. The denominator is the EPS for the most recent 12 months. Thus, the P-E ratio varies throughout a given year, depending on the fluctuations in the company's stock price. For example, General Mills' P-E ratios at the end of fiscal 2011, 2010, and 2009 (on May 29, 2011, May 30, 2010, and May 31, 2009) were as follows:

$$2011 \text{ P-E} = \$39.29 \div \$2.80 = 14.0$$
$$2010 \text{ P-E} = \$36.65 \div \$2.32 = 15.8$$
$$2009 \text{ P-E} = \$25.59 \div \$1.96 = 13.1$$

earnings multiple
Another name for the P-E ratio.

Another name for the P-E ratio is the **earnings multiple**. It measures how much the investing public is willing to pay for a chance to share the company's potential earnings. Note especially that the marketplace determines the P-E ratio. Why? Because the market establishes the price of a company's shares. The P-E ratio may differ considerably for two companies within the same industry. It may also change for the same company through the years. General Mills' P-E increased 20.6% between 2009 and 2010. The low P-E ratio in 2009 may be partially a result of the company's low stock price during the overall market decline of 2008–2009. The 43.2% increase in the stock price from 2009 to 2010 may reflect both investors' belief that General Mills' EPS would continue to increase and the renewed market confidence that was present at that time. Notice that the stock price increase of 7.2% was modest from 2010 to 2011 when compared with the 20.7% increase in EPS. This resulted in an 11.4% decrease in the P-E ratio in 2011. In general, the P-E ratio indicates investors' predictions about the company's future net income. Investors apparently were less optimistic about the growth rate for General Mills' earnings at the end of 2011 than they were a year earlier. This may, in part, be due to the fact that cost-savings rather than sales growth caused most of the increased earnings in 2011, and there is a limit to the amount of costs that can be saved.

Consider Under Armour, a company that develops, markets and distributes performance apparel, footwear and accessories. You may be familiar with its products, which are sold worldwide to athletes of all levels. On December 31, 2011, Under Armour had a P-E of 38.19. Compare that with General Mills', which has consistently had a P-E ratio in the mid-teens. These ratios tell us that investors expect Under Armour's earnings to grow more rapidly than General Mills' earnings. The Business First box on page 67 illustrates the P-E ratios of some of the largest companies in the world.

BUSINESS FIRST

MARKET VALUE, EARNINGS, AND P-E RATIOS

Forbes ranks the largest global companies by a variety of criteria, including sales, profits, assets, and market value. The following table lists the 10 largest companies ranked on market value as measured by *Forbes* on March 11, 2011.

Company	Country	Market Value in Billions	EPS*	Stock Price*	P-E Ratio
ExxonMobil	U.S.	$407.2	$ 6.24	$ 82.12	13.2
Apple	U.S.	$324.3	$15.41	$351.99	22.8
PetroChina	China	$320.8	$12.70	$139.41	11.0
ICBC	China	$239.5	¥ 0.48**	¥ 4.30**	9.0
Petrobras-Petroleo	Brazil	$238.8	$ 3.88	$ 39.43	10.2
BHP Billiton***	Australia	$231.5	$ 4.29	$ 89.59	20.9
China Construction Bank	China	$224.8	¥ 0.56**	¥ 7.05**	12.6
General Electric	U.S.	$216.2	$ 1.06	$ 20.36	19.2
Microsoft	U.S.	$215.8	$ 2.73	$ 25.68	9.4
Royal Dutch Shell	Netherlands	$212.9	$ 3.28	$ 68.86	21.0

*Stock price is as of March 11, 2011, and EPS is for fiscal year-end closest to March 11, 2011. For most companies this was December 31, 2010.

**¥ = Chinese Yuan.

***Combined market value of BHP Billiton Ltd and BHP Billiton PLC (a dual-listed company with headquarters in Australia and the U.K.); Stock price shown is for the Australian registered BHP Billiton Ltd, which is the majority partner.

First, consider what companies are among the 10 largest market-cap companies. You might expect that there would be little movement in this list. However, just 2 years ago, 6 of the top 10 were U.S. companies (ExxonMobil, Wal-Mart, Microsoft, Procter & Gamble, AT&T, and Johnson & Johnson). In the last 2 years, 4 U.S. companies (Wal-Mart, Procter & Gamble, AT&T, and Johnson & Johnson) fell off the list and two other U.S. companies (Apple and General Electric) were added. Other new additions in 2011 were Petrobras-Petroleo, BHP Billiton, and China Construction Bank. Looking back just a little further, 6 years ago, 8 of the top 10 were U.S. companies and no company from China was in the top 25.

Note the concentration of firms on the list that are involved in energy production or mining. Five of the 10 companies are engaged in the energy business. ExxonMobil, Royal Dutch Shell, PetroChina, and Petrobras-Petroleo are all primarily involved in oil and gas exploration, production, development, and distribution. However, the companies also engage in development of renewable energies. BHP Billiton is a global mining company that mines numerous products including copper, silver, lead, zinc, iron ore, and coal. The company is also involved in oil and gas exploration, production, development, and marketing. While the companies operate in similar industries, their P-E ratios vary. Royal Dutch Shell and BHP Billiton have almost identical P-E ratios, at 21.0 and 20.9, respectively. On the other hand, PetroChina and Petrobras-Petroleo have P-E ratios that are approximately half of Royal Dutch Shell's, 11.0 and 10.2, respectively. This suggests that investors may expect variation in the rate of company growth, even within related industries.

Sources: Forbes.com, "The World's Biggest Public Companies," April 20, 2011; http://www.reuters.com/; Web sites for ExxonMobil, Apple, PetroChina, ICBC, Petrobras-Petroleo, BHP Billiton, China Construction Bank, General Electric, Microsoft, and Royal Dutch Shell.

INTERPRETING FINANCIAL STATEMENTS

From Microsoft's financial statements, you can determine that its basic EPS grew from $1.63 in 2009 to $2.73 in 2011, an increase of almost 67.5%. At the same time, its stock price increased from slightly less than $24 per share on June 30, 2009, to about $26 per share on June 30, 2011, an increase of only 8.3%. What happened to Microsoft's P-E ratio between 2009 and 2011? What would its price have been in 2011 if it had maintained its 2009 P-E ratio?

Answer

Microsoft's P-E in 2009 was ($24 ÷ $1.63) = 14.7, and by 2011 it had fallen to ($26 ÷ $2.73) = 9.5. If the company had a P-E ratio of 14.7 in 2011, its price would have been (14.7 × $2.73) = $40.13, or more than 1.5 times higher than it was.

Dividend-Yield Ratio

dividend-yield ratio
Common dividends per share divided by market price per share.

Individual investors are interested in the profitability of their personal investments in common stock. That profitability takes two forms: cash dividends and increases in the market price of the stock. Investors in common stock who seek regular cash returns on their investments pay particular attention to dividend ratios. One such ratio is the **dividend-yield ratio**, the common dividends per share divided by the current market price of the stock. General Mills' recent dividend-yield ratios were as follows:

$$2011 \text{ Dividend-yield} = \$1.12 \div \$39.29 = 2.85\%$$
$$2010 \text{ Dividend-yield} = \$\,.96 \div \$36.65 = 2.62\%$$
$$2009 \text{ Dividend-yield} = \$\,.86 \div \$25.59 = 3.36\%$$

Investors who favor high current cash returns do not generally buy stock in growth companies. Growth companies have conservative dividend policies because they use most of their profit-generated resources to help finance expansion of their operations. General Mills' dividend-yield is typical for a company with stable but not exceptional growth. According to General Mills' Web site, it targets a dividend yield in the 2% to 3% range. The actual dividend yields for 2009 through 2011 are consistent with this target. The ratio decreased in 2010 because the company experienced a significant increase in stock price as the market recovered from the lingering economic downturn. The ratio increased modestly in 2011 as both dividends and stock price rose.

Dividend-Payout Ratio

dividend-payout ratio
Common dividends per share divided by earnings per share.

Analysts are also interested in what proportion of net income a company elects to pay in cash dividends to its shareholders. The formula for computing the **dividend-payout ratio** is given here, followed by General Mills' recent ratios:

$$\text{Dividend-payout ratio} = \frac{\text{Common dividends per share}}{\text{Earnings per share}}$$
$$2011 \text{ Dividend-payout} = \$1.12 \div \$2.80 = 40.0\%$$
$$2010 \text{ Dividend-payout} = \$\,.96 \div \$2.32 = 41.4\%$$
$$2009 \text{ Dividend-payout} = \$\,.86 \div \$1.96 = 43.9\%$$

General Mills reports a relatively stable dividend-payout ratio. The company steadily increased both its dividends and EPS from 2009 to 2011. The General Mills' Web site notes that the company has paid regular dividends without interruption for 113 years and has experienced dividend growth at a 12 percent compound rate over the 2007 to 2011 time period. A stated goal of the company is to continue to increase dividends over time as earnings grow. Many companies elect to continue a stable or increasing pattern of dividends, even if this creates variations in its dividend-payout ratio.

Stock Price and Ratio Information in the Press

The business section of many daily newspapers in the United States reports market prices for stocks listed on major stock exchanges such as the NYSE, American Stock Exchange, or NASDAQ. The *Wall Street Journal* publishes end-of-day price quotes for the 1,000 largest stocks every day and shows more details on Saturdays. Consider the following stock quotations for General Mills in the Saturday, October 1, 2011, issue of the *Wall Street Journal*:

	52 Weeks							
YTD % CHG	High	Low	Stock	SYM	YLD %	P-E	LAST	NET CHG
8.15	40	34.54	GenMills	GIS	3.2	15	38.49	−0.42

These data represent trading on Friday, September 30. Notice that the fourth and fifth columns identify General Mills and show that its ticker symbol is GIS. All listed stocks have short ticker symbols that identify them. Stock exchanges created these symbols years ago to facilitate communication via ticker tape, but they remain effective for computer communication today.

The Portfolio

The Portfolio is your key to understanding a company's financial position and prospects using the three major financial statements—the balance sheet, the statement of earnings, and the statement of cash flows. It shows some of the most important financial ratios used in analyzing Starbucks' financial statements—and the statements of other companies. You can use this tool in financial statement analysis throughout the course.

As you review this portfolio, it is useful to be aware that, in addition to Starbucks' shareholders, there are other shareholders—referred to as a "noncontrolling interest"—who own a share of Starbucks' assets and income through their part-ownership of Starbucks' subsidiaries. Noncontrolling interests are discussed in Chapter 11. Ratios that relate to Starbucks' shareholders, such as Earnings per Common Share and Return on Common Stockholders' Equity, use only the amounts attributable to them. Ratios that relate to overall company performance use net income and total equity, which include both Starbucks' shareholders' interests and noncontrolling interests.

Current Ratio $= \dfrac{\$3,794.9}{\$2,075.8} = 1.83$

Starbucks has $1.83 in current assets for each $1 in current liabilities. *See Chapter 4.*

Starbucks Corporation
Consolidated Balance Sheets

In millions, except per share data

	Oct. 2, 2011	Oct. 3, 2010
ASSETS		
Current assets:		
Cash and cash equivalents	$ 1,148.1	$1,164.0
Short-term investments—available-for-sale securities	855.0	236.5
Short-term investments—trading securities	47.6	49.2
Accounts receivable, net	386.5	302.7
Inventories	965.8	543.3
Prepaid expenses and other current assets	161.5	156.5
Deferred income taxes, net	230.4	304.2
Total current assets	3,794.9	2,756.4
Long-term investments—available-for-sale securities	107.0	191.8
Equity and cost investments	372.3	341.5
Property, plant, and equipment, net	2,355.0	2,416.5
Other assets	297.7	346.5
Other intangible assets	111.9	70.8
Goodwill	321.6	262.4
TOTAL ASSETS	**$7,360.4**	**$6,385.9**

LIABILITIES AND EQUITY

Debt-to-Total-Assets Ratio $= \dfrac{\$2,973.1}{\$7,360.4} = .40$

Starbucks uses $.40 of debt financing for every $1 of total assets. *See Chapter 9.*

	Oct. 2, 2011	Oct. 3, 2010
Current liabilities:		
Accounts payable	$ 540.0	$ 282.6
Accrued compensation and related costs	364.4	400.0
Accrued occupancy costs	148.3	173.2
Accrued taxes	109.2	100.2
Insurance reserves	145.6	146.2
Other accrued expenses	319.0	262.8
Deferred revenue	449.3	414.1
Total current liabilities	2,075.8	1,779.1
Long-term debt	549.5	549.4
Other long-term liabilities	347.8	375.1
Total liabilities	2,973.1	2,703.6
Shareholders' equity:		
Common stock ($.001 par value)– authorized, 1,200.0 shares; issued and outstanding, 744.8 and 742.6 shares, respectively	0.7	0.7
Additional paid-in capital	1.1	106.2
Other additional paid-in capital	39.4	39.4
Retained earnings	4,297.4	3,471.2
Accumulated other comprehensive income	46.3	57.2
Total shareholders' equity	4,384.9	3,674.7
Noncontrolling interests	2.4	7.6
Total equity	4,387.3	3,682.3
TOTAL LIABILITIES and EQUITY	**$ 7,360.4**	**$6,385.9**

Book Value per Share of Common Stock $= \dfrac{(\$4,384.9 - 0)}{744.8} = \$5.89$

(The numerator is total shareholders' equity minus book value of preferred stock.) The shareholders' equity associated with each share of Starbucks' common stock is $5.89. *See Chapter 10.*

Market-to-Book $= \dfrac{\$37.29}{\$5.89} = 6.33$

The price of one share of Starbucks on Sunday, October 2, 2011, was $37.29, the closing price on Friday, September 30. The $5.89 amount is the book value per common share. Starbucks' market value is 6.33 times its book value. *See Chapter 10.*

$$\text{Gross Profit Percentage} = \frac{(\$11,700.4 - \$4,949.3)}{\$11,700.4} = 57.7\%$$

Starbucks' gross margin above the cost of items sold (including occupancy costs) is $.577 out of every $1 of sales. *See Chapter 4.*

Starbucks Corporation
Consolidated Statement of Earnings

In millions, except per share data

Fiscal year ended	Oct. 2, 2011
Total net revenues	$11,700.4
Cost of sales including occupancy costs	4,949.3
Store operating expenses	3,665.1
Other operating expenses	402.0
Depreciation and amortization expenses	523.3
General and administrative expenses	636.1
Total operating expenses	10,175.8
Gain on sale of properties	30.2
Income from equity investees	173.7
Operating income	1,728.5
Interest income and other, net	115.9
Interest expense	(33.3)
Earnings before income taxes	1,811.1
Income taxes	563.1
Net earnings including noncontrolling interests	1,248.0
Net earnings attributable to noncontrolling interests	2.3
Net earnings attributable to Starbucks	$ 1,245.7
Earnings per share—basic	$ 1.66
Earnings per share—diluted	$ 1.62
Weighted average shares outstanding:	
Basic	748.3
Diluted	769.7

Return on Sales $= \dfrac{\$1,248.0}{\$11,700.4} = 10.7\%$

For every $1 of sales Starbucks earns net income of $.107. *See Chapter 4.*

Earnings Per Common Share $= \dfrac{\$1,245.7}{748.3} = \$1.66$

This tells shareholders how much of Starbucks' net earnings applies to each share of common stock they own. *See Chapter 2.*

Price-Earnings Ratio $= \dfrac{\$37.29}{\$1.66} = 22.5$

The price of one share of Starbucks' stock on October 2, 2011, was $37.29. This ratio reveals how much value the market places on each dollar of Starbucks' current earnings. *See Chapter 2.*

$$\text{Inventory Turnover} = \frac{\$4,949.3}{[1/2 \times (\$965.8 + \$543.3)]} = 6.6$$

Starbucks has cost of sales that is 6.6 times its average inventory level. This means it holds its inventory an average of (365 ÷ 6.6) = 55.3 days. *See Chapter 7.*

$$\text{Accounts Receivable Turnover} = \frac{\$11,700.4}{[1/2 \times (\$386.5 + \$302.7)]} = 34.0$$

Assuming that all Starbucks' sales are on credit, it has credit sales that are 34.0 times its average receivables. This means that it collects its receivables in an average of (365 ÷ 34.0) = 10.7 days. *See Chapter 6.*

Starbucks Corporation
Consolidated Balance Sheets

In millions, except per share data

	Oct. 2, 2011	Oct. 3, 2010
ASSETS		
Current assets:		
Cash and cash equivalents	$ 1,148.1	$ 1,164.0
Short-term investments—available-for-sale securities	855.0	236.5
Short-term investments—trading securities	47.6	49.2
Accounts receivable, net	386.5	302.7
Inventories	965.8	543.3
Prepaid expenses and other current assets	161.5	156.5
Deferred income taxes, net	230.4	304.2
Total current assets	3,794.9	2,756.4
Long-term investments—available-for-sale securities	107.0	191.8
Equity and cost investments	372.3	341.5
Property, plant, and equipment, net	2,355.0	2,416.5
Other assets	297.7	346.5
Other intangible assets	111.9	70.8
Goodwill	321.6	262.4
TOTAL ASSETS	$ 7,360.4	$ 6,385.9

LIABILITIES AND EQUITY

$$\text{Return on Assets} = \frac{\$1,248.0}{[1/2 \times (\$7,360.4 + \$6,385.9)]} = 18.2\%$$

For each $1 of assets that Starbucks owns, it generates $.182 of net earnings. *See Chapter 4.*

	Oct. 2, 2011	Oct. 3, 2010
Current liabilities:		
Accounts payable	$ 540.0	$ 282.6
Accrued compensation and related costs	364.4	400.0
Accrued occupancy costs	148.3	173.2
Accrued taxes	109.2	100.2
Insurance reserves	145.6	146.2
Other accrued expenses	319.0	262.8
Deferred revenue	449.3	414.1
Total current liabilities	2,075.8	1,779.1
Long-term debt	549.5	549.4
Other long-term liabilities	347.8	375.1
Total liabilities	2,973.1	2,703.6
Shareholders' equity:		
Common stock ($.001 par value) — authorized, 1,200.0 shares; issued and outstanding, 744.8 and 742.6 shares, respectively	0.7	0.7
Additional paid-in capital	1.1	106.2
Other additional paid-in capital	39.4	39.4
Retained earnings	4,297.4	3,471.2
Accumulated other comprehensive income	46.3	57.2
Total shareholders' equity	4,384.9	3,674.7
Noncontrolling interests	2.4	7.6
Total equity	4,387.3	3,682.3
TOTAL LIABILITIES and EQUITY	$7,360.4	$ 6,385.9

$$\text{Return on Common Stockholders' Equity} = \frac{\$1,245.7}{[1/2 \times (\$4,384.9 + \$3,674.7)]} = 30.9\%$$

For each $1 invested or reinvested by common stockholders, Starbucks generates $.309 of net earnings. *See Chapter 4.*

Starbucks Corporation
Consolidated Statement of Earnings

In millions, except per share data

Fiscal year ended	Oct. 2, 2011
Net revenues	$ 11,700.4
Cost of sales including occupancy costs	4,949.3
Store operating expenses	3,665.1
Other operating expenses	402.0
Depreciation and amortization expenses	523.3
General and administrative expenses	636.1
Total operating expenses	10,175.8
Gain on sale of properties	30.2
Income from equity investees	173.7
Operating income	1,728.5
Interest income and other, net	115.9
Interest expense	(33.3)
Earnings before income taxes	1,811.1
Income taxes	563.1
Net earnings	$ 1,248.0
Net earnings attributable to noncontrolling interests	2.3
Net earnings attributable to Starbucks	$ 1,245.7
Earnings per share—basic	$ 1.66
Earnings per share—diluted	$ 1.62
Weighted average shares outstanding:	
Basic	748.3
Diluted	769.7

Starbucks Corporation
Consolidated Statement of Cash Flows

In millions

Fiscal year ended	Oct. 2, 2011
OPERATING ACTIVITIES:	
Net earnings	$1,248.0
Adjustments to reconcile net earnings to net cash provided by operating activities:	
Depreciation and amortization	550.0
Gain on sale of properties	(30.2)
Provision for impairments and asset disposals	36.2
Deferred income taxes, net	106.2
Equity in income of investees	(118.5)
Distributions of income from equity investees	85.6
Gain resulting from acquisition of joint ventures	(55.2)
Stock-based compensation	145.2
Excess tax benefit from exercise of stock options	(103.9)
Other	(2.9)
Cash provided/(used) by changes in operating assets and liabilities:	
Accounts receivable	(88.7)
Inventories	(422.3)
Accounts payable	227.5
Accrued taxes	104.0
Deferred revenue	35.8
Other operating assets	(22.5)
Other operating liabilities	(81.9)
Net cash provided by operating activities	1,612.4
INVESTING ACTIVITIES:	
Purchase of available-for-sale securities	(966.0)
Maturities and calls of available-for-sale securities	430.0
Acquisitions, net of cash acquired	(55.8)
Net (purchases)/sales of equity, other investments, and other assets	(13.2)
Additions to property, plant, and equipment	(531.9)
Proceeds from sale of property, plant, and equipment	117.4
Net cash used by investing activities	(1,019.5)
FINANCING ACTIVITIES:	
Proceeds from short-term borrowings	30.8
Purchase of noncontrolling interest	(27.5)
Proceeds from issuance of common stock	235.4
Excess tax benefit from exercise of stock options	103.9
Principal payments on long-term debt	(4.3)
Cash dividends paid	(389.5)
Repurchase of common stock	(555.9)
Other	(0.9)
Net cash used by financing activities	(608.0)
Effect of exchange rate changes on cash and cash equivalents	(0.8)
Net decrease in cash and cash equivalents	(15.9)
CASH AND CASH EQUIVALENTS:	
Beginning of period	1,164.0
End of period	$1,148.1

Free Cash Flow = ($1,612.4−$531.9) = $1,080.5

Starbucks generated $1,080.5 more cash from its operations than it needed to invest in maintaining and expanding its property, plant, and equipment. *See Chapter 5.*

Reading from left to right, General Mills' stock price increased by 8.15% between January 1 and September 30, 2011. The highest price at which General Mills' common stock sold in the preceding 52 weeks was $40.00 per share; the lowest price was $34.54. The current annual dividend yield is 3.2% based on the day's closing price of the stock. The P-E ratio is 15, also based on the closing price. The closing price—that is, the price of the last trade for the day—was $38.49, which was $.42 lower than the last trade on Thursday, September 29. That means that the closing price on September 29 was ($38.49 + $.42) = $38.91, and shareholders lost $.42 on each share they held on September 30.

Keep in mind that transactions in publicly traded shares are between individual investors in the stock, not between the corporation and the individuals. Thus, a "typical trade" results in the selling of, for example, 100 shares of General Mills stock held by Ms. Johnson in Minneapolis to Mr. Ruiz in Atlanta for $3,849 in cash. These parties would ordinarily transact the trade through their respective stockbrokers. The trade would not directly affect General Mills, except that it would change its records of shareholders to show that Ruiz, not Johnson, holds the 100 shares.

Summary Problem for Your Review

PROBLEM

On January 31, 2011, the first trading day after the Sunday, January 30 year end, The Home Depot stock sold at about $36.80 per share. The company had net income of $3,338 million for the fiscal year ending January 30, 2011, had an average of 1,648 million common shares outstanding during the year, and paid common dividends of $.945 per share. Calculate and interpret the following:

Earnings per share   Dividend-yield ratio
Price-earnings ratio   Dividend-payout ratio

SOLUTION (in millions of dollars)

$$\text{Earnings per share} = \$3,338 \div 1,648 = \$2.03$$
$$\text{Price-earnings ratio} = \$36.80 \div \$2.03 = 18.1$$
$$\text{Dividend-yield ratio} = \$.945 \div \$36.80 = 2.6\%$$
$$\text{Dividend-payout ratio} = \$.945 \div \$2.03 = 46.6\%$$

The Home Depot had net income of $2.03 for each share of its common stock. Its market price was 18.1 times its earnings. This is higher than the S&P 500 average P-E ratio as of January 1, 2011, and shows that investors expect continuing growth in The Home Depot's earnings. Home Depot paid out 46.6% of its income in dividends, which results in a 2.6% return for investors as of January 30, 2011. The dividend-yield ratio for the year ended January 30, 2011, is consistent with the historical average for Home Depot over the last 5 years. The dividend-payout ratio has been volatile over the last 5 years, ranging from a high of 56.9% in the fiscal year ended January 31, 2010, to a low of 24.1% for fiscal year ended January 28, 2007. Home Depot is apparently trying to maintain a record of steadily increasing dividend amounts despite fluctuating earnings.

Conceptual Framework

As we learned in Chapter 1, financial statements are based on a set of generally accepted accounting principles (GAAP) as determined by the Financial Accounting Standards Board (FASB) in the United States and the International Accounting Standards Board (IASB) in most of the rest of the world. How do these boards decide what is acceptable and what is unacceptable in financial reporting? Ideally, GAAP would be based on an agreed-upon objective of financial reporting, a set of overriding concepts, principles derived from the concepts, and rules for implementing the principles. Both the FASB and IASB have attempted to achieve this by developing conceptual frameworks. Although there are some differences in the FASB and IASB conceptual frameworks, the similarities are much greater than the differences. Further, the two standard setting bodies are working together on a common framework to serve as the basis for developing worldwide standards. We will focus primarily on the FASB framework, but the discussion would be similar for

▸▸ **OBJECTIVE 7**

Explain how the conceptual framework guides the standard setting process and how accounting regulators trade off relevance and faithful representation in setting accounting standards.

the IASB framework. Understanding the conceptual framework will help you understand why companies prepare financial statements the way they do.

Why is a conceptual framework necessary? When the FASB or IASB sets standards for financial reporting, they must make many judgments. Consider the accounting for the expiration of prepaid expenses. In the case of prepaid rent, it is easy to identify when the prepaid asset provides a benefit to the company. Rent becomes an expense in the period in which a company uses the rented facilities or equipment. However, some of the most difficult issues in accounting center on when a prepaid asset expires and becomes an expense. For example, some accountants believe that companies should first record research costs as an asset on the balance sheet and then gradually expense these costs in some systematic manner over a period of years. After all, companies engage in research activities because they expect them to create future benefits. However, both the IASB and the FASB have ruled that such costs have vague future benefits that are difficult to measure reliably. Therefore, companies must treat research costs as expenses when incurred. They do not appear on the balance sheet as assets. In contrast, under IFRS (but not U.S. GAAP) development costs that meet very specific criteria are considered assets and appear on the balance sheet.

Other difficult questions faced by the FASB and IASB include the following: Should companies record an expense when they issue stock options to executives? If so, how should the company measure the expense? How should companies measure and disclose the expense for retirement benefits? Should companies show assets and liabilities at historical cost or current market value? The list could go on and on. The existence of a conceptual framework helps standard setters when faced with such difficult questions.

What factors do the FASB and IASB consider when setting standards? They start with the **objective of financial reporting**—to provide information that is useful to present and potential investors and creditors and others in making investment, credit, and similar resource allocation decisions. Financial information is most useful to decision makers when it possesses certain qualitative characteristics, subject to practical constraints. As depicted in Exhibit 2-9, the conceptual framework identifies characteristics of information that lead to improved decision making. We next discuss these characteristics.

objective of financial reporting
To provide information that is useful to present and potential investors and creditors and others in making investment, credit, and similar resource allocation decisions.

EXHIBIT 2-9
Qualities That Increase the Value of Information

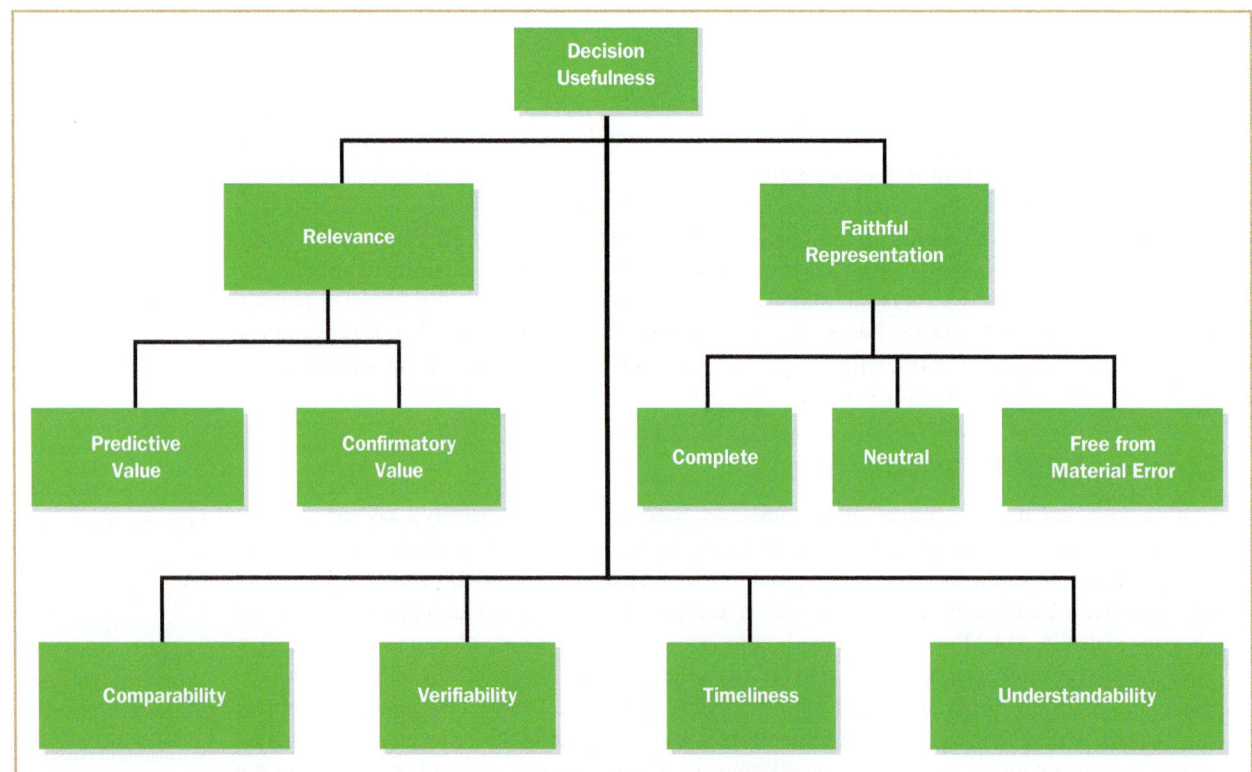

Characteristics of Decision-Useful Information

Relevance and faithful representation are the two main qualities that make accounting information useful for decision making. **Relevance** refers to whether the information makes a difference to the decision maker. If information has no impact on a decision, it is not relevant to that decision. The two attributes that can make information relevant are predictive value and confirmatory value. Information has **predictive value** if users of financial statements can use the information to help them form their expectations about the future. Information has **confirmatory value** if it can confirm or contradict existing expectations. Information that confirms expectations means that they become more likely to occur. Information that contradicts expectations will likely lead decision makers to change those expectations.

Users of financial statements want assurance that management has accurately and truthfully reported its financial results. Consequently, in addition to relevance, accountants want information to exhibit **faithful representation**—that is, information should truly capture the economic substance of the transactions, events, or circumstances it describes. Faithful representation requires information to be complete, neutral, and free from material errors. Information is complete if it contains all the information necessary to faithfully represent an economic phenomenon. It is neutral if it is free from bias—that is, the information is not slanted to influence behavior in a particular direction. Finally, information should be free from material errors. This does not mean the complete absence of errors. Much accounting information is based on estimates that are, by definition, imperfect. Being free from material errors simply means that estimates are based on appropriate inputs, which in turn are based on the best information available.

Accounting is filled with trade-offs between relevance and faithful representation. Consider the $4.0 billion balance sheet value of Weyerhaeuser Company's timberlands, which the company shows at historical cost. Some of the land was purchased more than 50 years ago. The balance sheet value faithfully represents the historical cost of the timberlands, but the cost of land 50 years ago is not very relevant to today's decisions. In contrast, the current value of the land is more relevant, but estimates of this current value are subjective and would be more difficult to represent faithfully. Which quality is more important? That answer depends on the specific decision being made. However, the most desirable information has both qualities: It is relevant and faithfully represents the phenomenon of interest. The prevailing view in the United States is that many current market value estimates, especially for property, plant, and equipment, are not sufficiently reliable to be included in the accounting records, even though they may be more relevant. However, under IFRS, companies can use current market values for such assets.

As you can see on the bottom of Exhibit 2-9, four characteristics can enhance both relevance and faithful representation. The first such characteristic is **comparability**—requiring all companies to use similar concepts and measurements and to use them consistently. It requires accounting systems to treat like phenomena the same and unlike phenomena differently. Comparability helps decision makers identify similarities in and differences between the phenomena being represented. Note that comparability requires **consistency**, using the same accounting policies and procedures from period to period. Information is more useful if decision makers can compare it with similar information about other companies or with similar information for other reporting periods. For example, financial results of two companies are hard to compare if the companies used different methods of accounting for the value of their inventory. Further, we cannot make useful comparisons over time if a company constantly changes its accounting methods.

The second enhancing characteristic is **verifiability**, which means that information can be checked to ensure it is correct. That is, knowledgeable and independent observers would agree that the information presented has been appropriately measured. For example, the historical cost of an item is verifiable because we can check the records to verify that the amounts are correct. In contrast, some estimates and appraisals are not easily verifiable.

Timeliness is obviously desirable. Information must reach decision makers while it can still influence their decisions. Information that is not available until after decision makers act is of little value.

Finally, information should be understandable. **Understandability** requires accountants to present information clearly and concisely. It does not require oversimplification of the data. That might fail to reveal important information. Complex phenomena sometimes require complex reporting. However, it is important to avoid unnecessary complexity.

---

relevance
The capability of information to make a difference to the decision maker.

predictive value
A quality of information that allows it to help users form their expectations about the future.

confirmatory value
A quality of information that allows it to confirm or contradict existing expectations.

faithful representation
A quality of information that ensures that it captures the economic substance of the transactions, events, or circumstances it describes. It requires information to be complete, neutral, and free from material errors.

comparability
A characteristic of information produced when all companies use similar concepts and measurements and use them consistently.

consistency
Using the same accounting policies and procedures from period to period.

verifiability
A characteristic of information that can be checked to ensure it is correct.

timeliness
A characteristic of information that requires information to reach decision makers while it can still influence their decisions.

understandability
A characteristic of information that requires information to be presented clearly and concisely.

Constraints

When setting standards that provide decision-useful information, there are practical constraints that must be considered. One is the cost-effectiveness constraint. Accounting should improve decision making. This is a benefit. However, accounting information is an economic good that is costly to produce and use. The **cost-effectiveness constraint** requires that standard setting bodies must choose rules whose decision-making benefits exceed the costs of providing the information. The FASB and IASB safeguard the cost effectiveness of their standards by (1) ensuring a standard does not "impose costs on the many for the benefit of a few," and (2) seeking alternative ways of handling an issue that are "less costly and only slightly less efficient."

cost-effectiveness constraint
Requirement that standard setting bodies choose rules whose decision-making benefits exceed the costs of providing the information.

The cost of providing information to the investing public includes expenses incurred by both companies and investors. Companies incur expenses for data collecting and processing, auditing, and educating employees. In addition, disclosure of sensitive information can lead to lost competitive advantages or increased labor union pressures. Investors' expenses include the costs of education, analysis, and interpretation.

The benefits of accounting information are often harder to pinpoint than the costs. For example, countries with emerging market economies often need to create an infrastructure of financial markets and relevant information to guide their economic development. However, the specific benefits of any particular proposal are harder to articulate than the general benefits of an intelligent system of accounting rules and procedures. While it can be difficult to explicitly identify and measure costs and benefits, standard setters attempt to weigh the cost effectiveness of a standard before its issuance.

Other Basic Concepts And Conventions

▶▶ **OBJECTIVE 8**

Explain how the following concepts affect financial statements: entity, going concern, materiality, stable monetary unit, periodicity, and reliability.

In addition to items in the conceptual framework, there are some basic concepts and conventions that are implicit in all financial statements. Now it is time to make some of these underlying assumptions explicit. In this section, we discuss the entity, going concern, materiality, stable monetary unit, periodicity, and reliability concepts and conventions.

The Entity Concept

The first basic concept or principle in accounting is the entity concept. As you learned in Chapter 1, an accounting entity is an organization or a section of an organization that stands apart from other organizations and individuals as a separate economic unit. Accounting draws sharp boundaries around each entity to avoid confusing its affairs with those of other entities.

An example of an entity is **Berkshire Hathaway Inc.**, an enormous entity that encompasses many smaller entities. Just a few of the companies that are part of the Berkshire Hathaway corporate entity are insurance companies such as GEICO, General Re, United States Liability Insurance Group, National Indemnity Company; food companies such as International Dairy Queen and See's Candies; jewelry companies such as Ben Bridge Jeweler, Helzberg Diamonds, and Borsheims Fine Jewelry; and numerous companies in the furniture, clothing, and other industries. Managers want accounting reports that are confined to their particular entities.

The entity concept helps the accountant relate events to a clearly defined area of accountability. For example, do not confuse business entities with personal entities. A purchase of groceries for merchandise inventory is an accounting transaction of a grocery store (the business entity), but the store owner's purchase of a DVD player with a personal check is a transaction of the owner (the personal entity).

Going Concern Convention

going concern (continuity)
A convention that assumes that an entity will persist indefinitely.

The **going concern (continuity)** convention is the assumption that an entity will persist indefinitely. This notion implies that a company will use its existing resources, such as plant assets, to fulfill its general business needs rather than sell them in tomorrow's real estate or equipment markets. For a going concern, it is reasonable to use historical cost to record long-lived assets.

The opposite view of this going concern convention is an immediate liquidation assumption, whereby a company values all items on its balance sheet at the amounts appropriate if the entity were to be liquidated in piecemeal fashion within a few days or months. Companies use this liquidation approach to valuation only when the probability is high that the company will be liquidated.

Materiality Convention

How does an accountant know what to include on the financial statements? There are a lot of rules and regulations about what must appear in those statements. However, some items are insignificant enough that they need not be reported. The **materiality** convention asserts that an item should be included in a financial statement if its omission or misstatement would tend to mislead the reader of the financial statements under consideration.

Most large items, such as buildings and machinery, are clearly material. Smaller items, though, may not be so clear-cut. Many acquisitions that a company theoretically should record as assets are immediately expensed because of their low dollar value. For example, coat hangers may last indefinitely but never appear in the balance sheet as assets. Many corporations require the immediate expensing of all outlays under a specified minimum, such as $1,000, regardless of the useful life of the asset acquired. The resulting $1,000 understatement of assets and stockholders' equity is considered too insignificant to be of concern. In fact, the FASB regularly includes the following statement in its standards: "The provisions of this statement need not be applied to immaterial items."

When is an item material? There will probably never be a universal, clear-cut answer. What is trivial to General Electric may be material to a local clothing boutique. A working rule is that an item is material if its proper accounting is likely to affect the decision of an informed user of financial statements. In sum, materiality is an important convention, but it is difficult to use anything other than prudent judgment to tell whether an item is material.

materiality
A convention that asserts that an item should be included in a financial statement if its omission or misstatement would tend to mislead the reader of the financial statements under consideration.

Stable Monetary Unit

The monetary unit (called the dollar in the United States, the yen in Japan, the euro in the European Union, and various names elsewhere) is the principal means for measuring financial statement elements. It is the common denominator for quantifying the effects of a wide variety of transactions. Accountants record, classify, summarize, and report in terms of the monetary unit. The ability to use historical-cost accounting depends on a stable monetary unit. A **stable monetary unit** is simply one that is not expected to change in value significantly over time—that is, a 2013 dollar has about the same value as a 2000 dollar. Although this is not precisely correct, with low levels of inflation, the changes in the value of the monetary unit do not cause great problems.

stable monetary unit
A monetary unit that is not expected to change in value significantly over time. For example, the dollar in the United States, the yen in Japan, and the euro in the European Union.

The Periodicity Convention

Earlier in the chapter we discussed the accounting time period. Recall that companies with publicly traded securities must file financial reports with the SEC on a quarterly and annual basis. However, companies frequently prepare monthly or even daily financial statements for internal use. For information to be useful, users must receive it on a timely basis. The **periodicity convention** requires that a company break up its economic activity into artificial time periods that will provide timely information to users.

periodicity convention
Related to the information characteristic of timeliness, this convention requires that a company break up its economic activity into artificial time periods that will provide timely information to users.

The Reliability Concept

Users of financial statements want assurance that management did not fabricate the numbers. Consequently, accountants regard reliability as an essential characteristic of measurement. **Reliability** is a quality of information that assures decision makers that the information captures the conditions or events it purports to represent. It is similar to representational faithfulness but also requires recording of data only when there is convincing evidence that can be verified by independent auditors.

reliability
A quality of information that assures decision makers that the information captures the conditions or events it purports to represent.

The accounting process focuses on reliable recording of events that affect an organization. Although many events may affect a company—including wars, elections, and general economic booms or depressions—accountants recognize only specified types of events as being reliably recorded as accounting transactions.

Suppose a top executive of ExxonMobil is killed in an airplane crash. The accountant would not record this event. Now suppose that ExxonMobil discovers that an employee has embezzled $1,000 in cash. The accountant would record this event. The death of the executive may have greater economic or financial significance for ExxonMobil than does the embezzlement, but the monetary effect is hard to measure in any reliable way.

The conceptual framework and these other concepts guide both standard setters and accountants. The standard setters use them to decide GAAP—principles that meet the concepts are preferred—and accountants use them to decide among alternative ways of recording and reporting transactions.

Highlights to Remember

1 **Explain how accountants measure income.** Accountants can measure income, the excess of revenues over expenses for a particular time period, on an accrual or cash basis. In accrual accounting, companies record revenue when they earn it and record expenses when they incur them. In cash accounting, companies record revenues and expenses only when cash changes hands. Accrual accounting is the standard basis for accounting today.

2 **Determine when a company should record revenue from a sale.** The concept of revenue recognition means that companies record revenues in the earliest period in which they are both earned and realized or realizable. Earning is typically tied to delivery of the product or service and realization requires a high probability that the company will receive the promised resources (usually cash). Recording revenues increases stockholders' equity.

3 **Use the concept of matching to record the expenses for a period.** Under matching, companies assign expenses to the period in which they use the pertinent goods and services to create revenues, or when assets have no future benefit. Recording expenses decreases stockholders' equity.

4 **Prepare an income statement and show how it is related to a balance sheet.** An income statement shows an entity's revenues and expenses for a particular period of time. The net income (loss) during the period increases (decreases) the amount of retained earnings on the balance sheet.

5 **Account for cash dividends and prepare a statement of stockholders' equity.** Cash dividends are not expenses. They are distributions of cash to stockholders that reduce retained earnings. Corporations are not obligated to pay dividends, but once the board of directors declares dividends they become a legal liability until paid in cash. The balance in retained earnings increases by the amount of net income and decreases by the amount of cash dividends. A statement of stockholders' equity shows how net income, transactions with shareholders, and other comprehensive income affect stockholders' equity accounts.

6 **Compute and explain EPS, P-E ratio, dividend-yield ratio, and dividend-payout ratio.** Ratios relate one element of a company's economic activity to another. EPS expresses overall earnings on a scale that individual investors can link to their own ownership level. The P-E ratio relates accounting earnings per share to market prices. The dividend-yield ratio relates dividends paid per share to market prices, and the dividend-payout ratio relates those same dividends to the earnings per share during the period.

7 **Explain how the conceptual framework guides the standard setting process and how accounting regulators trade off relevance and faithful representation in setting accounting standards.** The primary objective of financial reporting is to provide information that is useful to present and potential investors and creditors and others in making investment, credit, and similar resource allocation decisions. Relevance and faithful representation are the two main qualities that make information useful. Information is relevant if it has predictive and/or confirmatory value. Faithful representation is characterized by information that is (a) complete, (b) neutral, and (c) free from material error. Characteristics that enhance both relevance and faithful representation are (a) comparability, (b) verifiability, (c) timeliness, and (d) understandability.

8 **Explain how the following concepts affect financial statements: entity, going concern, materiality, stable monetary unit, periodicity, and reliability.** Authorities achieve comparability of financial statements by adopting concepts and conventions that all companies must use. Such concepts and conventions include the following: (a) accounting statements apply to a specific entity, (b) companies are assumed to be ongoing (not about to be liquidated), (c) items that are not large enough to be material need not follow normal rules, (d) accountants use the monetary unit for measurement despite its changing purchasing power over time, (e) accountants divide the economic activities into artificial time periods for reporting purposes, and (f) all transactions must have reliable measures.

Accounting Vocabulary

accounts receivable, p. 50
accrual basis, p. 52
accumulated deficit, p. 63
accumulated other compre-
    hensive income (AOCI),
    p. 63
cash basis, p. 52
cash cycle, p. 47
cash dividends, p. 61
comparability, p. 71
confirmatory value, p. 71
consistency, p. 71
continuity, p. 72
cost of goods sold, p. 51
cost of revenue, p. 51
cost of sales, p. 51
cost-effectiveness
    constraint, p. 72
depreciation, p. 54
dividend-payout
    ratio, p. 68
dividend-yield ratio, p. 68
earnings, p. 48
earnings multiple, p. 66

earnings per share (EPS),
    p. 65
expenses, p. 48
faithful representation, p. 71
fiscal year, p. 47
going concern, p. 72
income, p. 48
income statement, p. 57
interim periods, p. 47
matching, p. 53
materiality, p. 73
net earnings, p. 57
net income, p. 57
net loss, p. 57
objective of financial
    reporting, p. 70
operating cycle, p. 47
other comprehensive income
    (OCI), p. 63
period costs, p. 53
periodicity convention, p. 73
predictive value, p. 71
price-earnings (P-E)
    ratio, p. 66

product costs, p. 53
profits, p. 48
receivables, p. 50
relevance, p. 71
reliability, p. 73
retained earnings, p. 48
retained income, p. 48
revenue, p. 48
revenue recognition, p. 52
sales, p. 48
sales revenue, p. 48
stable monetary unit, p. 73
statement of earnings,
    p. 57
statement of operations,
    p. 57
statement of shareholders'
    equity, p. 63
statement of stockholders'
    equity, p. 63
timeliness, p. 71
trade receivables, p. 50
understandability, p. 71
verifiability, p. 71

Assignment Material

Questions

2-1 How long is a company's operating cycle?

2-2 What is the difference between a fiscal year and a calendar year? Why do companies use a fiscal year that differs from a calendar year?

2-3 "Expenses are negative stockholders' equity accounts." Explain.

2-4 What is the major defect of the cash basis of accounting?

2-5 What are the two criteria for the recognition of revenue?

2-6 Describe two scenarios where revenue is not recognized at the point of sale, one where recognition is delayed because the revenue is not yet earned, and one because it is not yet realized.

2-7 Distinguish product costs from period costs.

2-8 "Expenses are assets that have been used." Explain.

2-9 "Companies acquire goods and services, not expenses per se." Explain.

2-10 "The income statement is like a moving picture; in contrast, a balance sheet is like a snapshot." Explain.

2-11 Give two synonyms for income statement. Why is it important to learn synonyms that are used for various accounting terms?

2-12 Why might a manager put pressure on accountants to report higher revenues or lower expenses than accounting standards allow?

2-13 "Cash dividends are not expenses." Explain.

2-14 "Retained earnings is not a pot of gold." Explain.

2-15 What do users learn from the statement of stockholders' equity? What three types of changes are shown on the statement?

2-16 "An accounting entity is always a separate legal organization." Do you agree? Explain.

2-17 "Financial ratios are important tools for analyzing financial statements, but no ratios are shown on the statements." Do you agree? Explain.

2-18 "Fast-growing companies have high P-E ratios." Explain.

2-19 Give two ratios that provide information about a company's dividends, and explain what each means.

MyAccountingLab

2-20 "Companies with a high dividend-payout ratio are good investments because stockholders get more of their share of earnings in cash." Do you agree? Explain.

2-21 "Relevance and faithful representation are both desirable characteristics for accounting measurements, but often it is not possible to have both." Do you agree? Explain.

2-22 What two characteristics of accounting measurements make them relevant? Explain each.

2-23 Accounting numbers should be complete, neutral, and free from material errors. What characteristic of information do these criteria support?

2-24 How do accountants judge whether an item is reliable enough for reporting in the financial statements?

2-25 The concepts of materiality and cost-effectiveness can limit the amount of detailed information included in the financial statements. Explain how an accountant might use each to exclude an item from the statements.

Critical Thinking Questions

▶▶ **OBJECTIVES 1, 8**

2-26 Quarterly Versus Annual Financial Statements
In the United States, it is common to provide abbreviated financial data quarterly with full financial statements provided annually. In some countries companies provide only annual data. Discuss the trade-offs.

▶▶ **OBJECTIVE 1**

2-27 Accrual or Cash Basis
Which would you rather have, a cash-basis income statement or an accrual-basis income statement? Why?

▶▶ **OBJECTIVE 5**

2-28 Dividends and Stock Prices
Suppose a company was going to pay out one-half of its total assets as a cash dividend. What would you expect to happen to the value of the company's stock as a result of the dividend?

▶▶ **OBJECTIVE 6**

2-29 Interpretation of the P-E Ratio
Would you rather own a company with a high P-E ratio or a low P-E ratio? Why?

Exercises

▶▶ **OBJECTIVE 4**

2-30 Synonyms and Antonyms
Consider the following terms: (1) sales, (2) net earnings, (3) accumulated deficit, (4) unexpired costs, (5) prepaid expenses, (6) accounts receivable, (7) statement of earnings, (8) used-up costs, (9) net profits, (10) net income, (11) revenues, (12) retained earnings, (13) expenses, (14) statement of financial condition, (15) statement of income, (16) statement of financial position, (17) operating statement, and (18) cost of goods sold.

Group the items into two categories, those on the income statement and those on the balance sheet. Answer by indicating the numbered items that belong in each group. Specify items that are assets and items that are expenses.

▶▶ **OBJECTIVE 2**

2-31 Special Meanings of Terms
A news story described the disappointing sales of a new model car, the Jupiter. An auto dealer said, "Even if the Jupiter is a little slow to move out of dealerships, it is more of a plus than a minus. . . . We're now selling 14 more cars per month at $20,000 per car. That's $280,000 more income."

Is the dealer confused about accounting terms? Explain.

▶▶ **OBJECTIVE 1**

2-32 Cash Versus Accrual Accounting
Yankton Company had sales of $240,000 during 20X0, all on account. Accounts receivable for the year grew from $50,000 on January 1 to $110,000 on December 31. Expenses for the year were $170,000, all paid in cash.

1. Compute Yankton's net income on the cash basis of accounting.
2. Compute Yankton's net income on the accrual basis of accounting.
3. Which basis gives a better measure of Yankton's performance for 20X0? Why?

2-33 Nature of Retained Earnings

▶▶ **OBJECTIVE 5**

This is an exercise on the relationships between assets, liabilities, and ownership equities. The numbers are small, but the underlying concepts are large.

1. Assume an opening balance sheet of

Cash	$1,000	Paid-in capital	$1,000

2. Purchase inventory for $600 cash. Prepare a balance sheet. A heading is unnecessary in this and subsequent requirements.
3. Sell the entire inventory for $850 cash. Prepare a balance sheet. What does retained earnings represent and how is it related to other balance sheet accounts? Explain in your own words.
4. Buy inventory for $300 cash and equipment for $800 cash. Prepare a balance sheet. What does retained earnings represent and how is it related to other balance sheet accounts? Explain in your own words.
5. Buy inventory for $500 on open account. Prepare a balance sheet. What do retained earnings and account payable represent and how are they related to other balance sheet accounts? Explain in your own words.

2-34 Asset Acquisition and Expiration

▶▶ **OBJECTIVE 3**

The Greenley Company had the following transactions in July:

a. Paid $18,000 cash for rent for the next 6 months on July 1.
b. Paid $2,000 cash for supplies on July 3.
c. Paid $4,000 cash for an advertisement in the next day's *New York Times* on July 10.
d. Paid $8,000 cash for a training program for employees on July 17. The training was completed in July.

Show the effects on the balance sheet equation in two phases—at acquisition and on expiration at the end of the month of acquisition. Show all amounts in thousands.

2-35 Find Unknowns

▶▶ **OBJECTIVES 4, 5**

The following data pertain to Liverpool Auto, Ltd. Total assets at January 1, 20X1, were £110,000; at December 31, 20X1, they were £126,000. During 20X1, sales were £360,000, cash dividends declared were £5,000, and operating expenses (exclusive of cost of goods sold) were £210,000. Total liabilities at December 31, 20X1, were £55,000; at January 1, 20X1, they were £50,000. There was no additional investment by stockholders during 20X1.

Compute the following:

1. Stockholders' equity, January 1, 20X1, and December 31, 20X1
2. Net income for 20X1—ignore taxes
3. Cost of goods sold for 20X1

2-36 Recording Transactions

▶▶ **OBJECTIVES 1, 3, 4**

The Piedmont Company had the following transactions during June 20X1:

a. Collections of accounts receivable, $75,000.
b. Payment of accounts payable, $45,000.
c. Acquisition of inventory, $18,000, on open account.
d. Sale of merchandise, $30,000 on open account and $23,000 for cash. The sold merchandise cost Piedmont Company $28,000.
e. Depreciation on equipment of $1,000 in June.
f. Declared and paid cash dividends of $15,000.

Use the balance sheet equation format to enter these transactions into the books of Piedmont Company. Suppose that Piedmont has a cash balance of $15,000 at the beginning of June. What was the cash balance on June 30?

▶▶ OBJECTIVE 4

2-37 Income Statement

A statement of an automobile dealer follows:

Freeway Volvo, Inc.

Statement of Profit and Loss December 31, 20X0

Revenues		
Sales	$1,050,000	
Increase in market value of land and building	200,000	$1,250,000
Deduct expenses		
Advertising	100,000	
Sales commissions	50,000	
Utilities	20,000	
Wages	170,000	
Dividends	100,000	
Cost of cars purchased	700,000	1,140,000
Net profit		$ 110,000

List and describe any shortcomings of this statement.

▶▶ OBJECTIVES 4, 5

2-38 Income Statement and Retained Earnings

FedEx Corporation provides customers and businesses worldwide with a broad portfolio of transportation, e-commerce, and business services. In the year ended May 31, 2011, FedEx had revenues of $39,304 million and total expenses of $37,852 million. FedEx Corporation's retained earnings were $13,966 million at the beginning of the year and $15,266 million at the end of the year.

1. Compute FedEx Corporation's net income (loss) for the year ended May 31, 2011.
2. Compute the amount of cash dividends declared by FedEx during the year ended May 31, 2011.

▶▶ OBJECTIVES 4, 5

2-39 Balance Sheet Equation

(Alternates are 2-40 and 2-55.) Each of the following three columns is an independent case. For each case, compute the amounts ($ in thousands) for the items indicated by letters and show your supporting computations:

	Case		
	1	**2**	**3**
Revenues	$165	$ K	$290
Expenses	130	200	250
Dividends declared	—	7	Q
Additional investment by stockholders	—	40	35
Net income	E	30	P
Retained earnings			
Beginning of year	35	60	120
End of year	D	J	130
Paid-in capital			
Beginning of year	15	10	N
End of year	C	H	85
Total assets			
Beginning of year	80	F	L
End of year	95	280	M
Total liabilities			
Beginning of year	A	90	105
End of year	B	G	95

2-40 Balance Sheet Equation

(Alternates are 2-39 and 2-55.) Xcel Energy, provider of gas and electricity to customers in 12 Midwestern and Rocky Mountain states, has the following actual data ($ in millions) for the year 2011:

▶▶ OBJECTIVES 4, 5

Total expenses	$ B
Net income (loss)	841
Dividends	510
Assets, beginning of period	27,388
Assets, end of period	D
Liabilities, beginning of period	A
Liabilities, end of period	21,015
Shareholders' equity, beginning of period	8,189
Shareholders' equity, end of period	8,482
Retained earnings, beginning of period	1,702
Retained earnings, end of period	C
Total revenues	10,655

Find the unknowns ($ in millions), showing computations to support your answers.

2-41 Nonprofit Operating Statement

Examine the accompanying statement of the Berlin University Faculty Club. Identify the Berlin University classifications and terms that would not be used by a profit-seeking hotel and restaurant in the United States. Suggest alternate terms. (€ is the European euro.)

▶▶ OBJECTIVE 4

Berlin U Faculty Club

Statement of Income and Expenses for Fiscal Year

Food Service			
Sales		€548,130	
Expenses			
Food	€287,088		
Labor	272,849		
Operating costs	30,537	590,474	
Deficit			€ (42,344)
Bar			
Sales		90,549	
Expenses			
Cost of liquor	29,302		
Labor	5,591		
Operating costs	6,125	41,018	
Surplus			49,531
Hotel			
Sales		33,771	
Expenses		23,803	
Surplus			9,968
Total surplus from operations			17,155
General income (members' dues, room fees, etc.)			95,546
General administration and operating expenses			(134,347)
Deficit before university subsidy			(21,646)
University subsidy			23,000
Net surplus after university subsidy			€ 1,354

▶▶ OBJECTIVE 6

2-42 Earnings and Dividend Ratios

GlaxoSmithKline plc, the British pharmaceutical company, reported 2011 earnings of £5,458 million under IFRS. Cash dividends were £3,406 million. The company had an average of 5,099 million common shares outstanding. No other type of stock was outstanding. The market price of the stock at the end of the year was approximately £14.72 per share.

Compute (1) EPS, (2) P-E ratio, (3) dividend-yield, and (4) dividend-payout ratio.

▶▶ OBJECTIVE 6

2-43 Earnings and Dividend Ratios

Chevron Corporation is one of the largest oil companies in the world. The company's revenue in 2011 was $573.706 billion. Net income was $26.895 billion. EPS was $13.54. The company's common stock is the only type of shares outstanding.

1. Compute the average number of common shares outstanding during the year.
2. The dividend-payout ratio was 22.8%. What was the amount of dividends per share?
3. The market price of the stock at the end of the year was $106.40 per share. Compute (a) dividend-yield and (b) P-E ratio.

▶▶ OBJECTIVE 8

2-44 Assessing Materiality

On December 31, 2011, ExxonMobil, the large petroleum company, reported total assets of $331,052 million and annual net income of $41,060 million.

On the same date, Dayton Service Stations, Inc., operator of six gas stations in Dallas, reported total assets of $926,000 and annual net income of $224,000.

1. Suppose both companies made an investment of $250,000 in new equipment in January 2012. Would you expect the amount of detail about the investment that each company disclosed in its financial statements to differ? Why?
2. How would each company decide on its level of disclosure about the investment?

MyAccountingLab

Problems

▶▶ OBJECTIVES 1, 2, 3, 4

2-45 Fundamental Revenue and Expense

R. J. Sen Corporation was formed on June 1, 20X0, when some stockholders invested $100,000 in cash in the company. During the first week of June, the company spent $85,000 cash for merchandise inventory (sportswear). During the remainder of the month, total sales reached $115,000, of which $70,000 was on open account. The cost of the inventory sold was $60,000. For simplicity, assume that no other transactions occurred except that on June 28, R. J. Sen Corporation acquired $34,000 additional inventory on open account.

1. By using the balance sheet equation approach demonstrated in Exhibit 2-3 (p. 49), analyze all transactions for June. Show all amounts in thousands.
2. Prepare a balance sheet for June 30, 20X0.
3. Prepare two statements for June, side by side. The first should use the accrual basis of accounting to compute net income, and the second, the cash basis to compute the difference between cash inflows and cash outflows. Which basis provides a more informative measure of economic performance? Why?

▶▶ OBJECTIVE 2

2-46 Revenue Recognition

Footnote 1 to Microsoft's 2011 annual report contained the following:

Revenue Recognition

Revenue is recognized when persuasive evidence of an arrangement exists, delivery has occurred, the fee is fixed or determinable, and collectibility is probable . . . . Revenue for retail packaged products, products licensed to original equipment manufacturers (OEMs) . . . generally is recognized as products are shipped or made available. . . . Certain multi-year licensing arrangements include a perpetual license for current products combined with rights to receive future versions of software products on a when-and-if-available basis and are accounted for as subscriptions, with billings recorded as unearned revenue and recognized as revenue ratably over the billing coverage period... . Revenue related to our Xbox 360 gaming and entertainment console, Kinect for Xbox 360, games published by us, and other hardware components is generally recognized when ownership is transferred to the resellers. Revenue related to games published by third parties for use on the Xbox 360 platform is recognized when games are manufactured by the game publishers. Display advertising revenue is recognized as advertisements are displayed. Search advertising revenue is recognized when the ad appears in the search results or when the action necessary to earn the revenue has been completed. Consulting services revenue is recognized as services are rendered, generally based on the negotiated hourly rate in the consulting arrangement and the number of hours worked during the period.

1. Explain how Microsoft's revenue recognition policy meets the criteria of being earned and realized.
2. Discuss the accounting for multiyear licensing arrangements.
3. Discuss the accounting for revenue related to games published by third parties.

2-47 Analysis of Transactions, Preparation of Statements

▶▶ **OBJECTIVES 3, 4**

(Alternates are 2-48, 2-50, 2-52, and 2-54.) The Montero Company, a wholesale distributor of furnace and air conditioning equipment, began business on July 1, 20X2. The following summarized transactions occurred during July:

a. Montero's stockholders contributed $300,000 in cash in exchange for their common stock.
b. On July 1, Montero signed a 1-year lease on a warehouse, paying $48,000 cash in advance for occupancy of 12 months.
c. On July 1, Montero acquired warehouse equipment for $100,000. A cash down payment of $40,000 was made, and a note payable was signed for the balance.
d. On July 1, Montero paid $24,000 cash for a 2-year insurance policy covering fire, casualty, and related risks.
e. Montero acquired assorted merchandise for $35,000 cash.
f. Montero acquired assorted merchandise for $190,000 on open account.
g. Total sales were $205,000, of which $30,000 were for cash.
h. Cost of inventory sold was $155,000.
i. Rent expense was recognized for the month of July.
j. Depreciation expense of $2,000 was recognized for the month.
k. Insurance expense was recognized for the month.
l. Collected $45,000 from credit customers.
m. Disbursed $80,000 to trade creditors.
For simplicity, ignore all other possible expenses.

Required
1. By using the balance sheet equation format demonstrated in Exhibit 2-3 (p. 49), prepare an analysis of each transaction. Show all amounts in thousands. What do transactions (h)–(m) illustrate about the theory of assets and expenses? (Use a Prepaid Insurance account, which is not illustrated in Exhibit 2-3.)
2. Prepare an income statement for July on the accrual basis. Ignore income taxes.
3. Prepare a balance sheet for July 31, 20X2.

2-48 Analysis of Transactions, Preparation of Statements

▶▶ **OBJECTIVES 3, 4**

(Alternates are 2-47, 2-50, 2-52, and 2-54.) The Bekele Company was incorporated on April 1, 20X0. Bekele had 10 holders of common stock. Rosa Bekele, the president and chief executive officer, held 51% of the shares. The company rented space in chain discount stores and specialized in selling ladies' accessories. Bekele's first location was in a store that was part of The Old Market in Omaha.

The following events occurred during April:

a. The company was incorporated. Common stockholders invested $200,000 cash.
b. Purchased merchandise inventory for cash, $45,000.
c. Purchased merchandise inventory on open account, $35,000.
d. Merchandise carried in inventory at a cost of $37,000 was sold for cash for $25,000 and on open account for $75,000, for a grand total of $100,000. Bekele (not The Old Market) carries and collects these accounts receivable.

e. Collection of accounts receivable, $18,000. See transaction (d).

f. Payments of accounts payable, $30,000. See transaction (c).

g. Special display equipment and fixtures were acquired on April 1 for $36,000. Their expected useful life was 36 months. This equipment was removable. Bekele paid $12,000 as a down payment and signed a promissory note for $24,000. Also see transaction (k).

h. On April 1, Bekele signed a rental agreement with The Old Market. The agreement called for a flat $2,000 per month, payable quarterly in advance. Therefore, Bekele paid $6,000 cash on April 1.

i. The rental agreement also called for a payment of 10% of all sales. This payment was in addition to the flat $2,000 per month. In this way, The Old Market would share in any success of the venture and be compensated for general services such as cleaning and utilities. This payment was to be made in cash on the last day of each month as soon as the sales for the month had been tabulated. Therefore, Bekele made the payment on April 30.

j. Employee wages and sales commissions were all paid for in cash. The amount was $34,000.

k. Depreciation expense of $1,000 was recognized ($36,000 ÷ 36 months). See transaction (g).

l. The expiration of an appropriate amount of prepaid rental services was recognized. See transaction (h).

Required

1. Prepare an analysis of Bekele Company's transactions, employing the balance sheet equation approach demonstrated in Exhibit 2-3 (p. 49). Show all amounts in thousands.

2. Prepare a balance sheet as of April 30, 20X0, and an income statement for the month of April. Ignore income taxes.

3. Given these sparse facts, analyze Bekele's performance for April and its financial position as of April 30, 20X0.

▶▶ OBJECTIVES **1, 2**

2-49 Accrual Versus Cash-Based Revenues

(Alternate is 2-51.) Refer to the preceding problem. Suppose Bekele measured performance on the cash basis instead of on the accrual basis. Compute the cash receipts, cash disbursements, and net cash inflows (outflows) for April. Which measure, accrual-based net income or net cash inflows (outflows), provides a better measure of accomplishment? Why?

▶▶ OBJECTIVES **3, 4**

2-50 Analysis of Transactions, Preparation of Statements

(Alternates are 2-47, 2-48, 2-52, and 2-54.) H.J. Heinz Company's actual condensed balance sheet data for April 27, 2011, follow ($ in millions):

Cash	$ 724	Accounts payable	$ 1,500
Receivables	1,265	Other liabilities	7,549
Inventories	1,452		
Other assets	6,285	Shareholders' equity	3,182
Property, plant, and equipment	2,505		
Total	$12,231	Total	$12,231

The following summarizes a few transactions during May 2011 ($ in millions):

a. Ketchup carried in inventory at a cost of $4 was sold for cash of $3 and on open account of $8, for a grand total of $11.

b. Acquired inventory on account, $6.

c. Collected receivables, $5.

d. On May 2, used $12 cash to prepay some rent and insurance for 12 months. Heinz classifies prepaid expenses as Other Assets.

e. Payments on accounts payable (for inventories), $4.

f. Paid selling and administrative expenses in cash, $1.

g. Prepaid expenses of $1 for rent and insurance expired in May.

h. Depreciation expense of $2 was recognized for May.

Required
1. Prepare an analysis of Heinz's transactions, employing the balance sheet equation approach demonstrated in Exhibit 2-3 (p. 49). Show all amounts in millions.
2. Prepare a statement of earnings for the month ended May 31 and a balance sheet as of May 31. Ignore income taxes.

2-51 Accrual Versus Cash-Based Revenue

▶▶ OBJECTIVES 1, 2

(Alternate is 2-49.) Refer to the preceding problem. Suppose Heinz measured performance on the cash basis instead of the accrual basis. Compute the cash receipts, cash disbursements, and net cash inflows (outflows) during May. Which measure, net income or net cash inflows (outflows), provides a better measure of overall performance? Why?

2-52 Analysis of Transactions, Preparation of Statements

▶▶ OBJECTIVES 3, 4

(Alternates are 2-47, 2-48, 2-50, and 2-54.) Nestlé S.A. is a Swiss company that calls itself the world's leading nutrition, health, and wellness company. It produces many food products including Nestlé Milk Chocolate and Nescafé. Nestlé's condensed balance sheet data for July 1, 2011, reported under IFRS, follow (in millions of Swiss francs, CHF):

Cash	CHF 2,833	Accounts payable	CHF 11,137
Receivables	11,946	Other liabilities	37,081
Inventories	8,885	Owners' equity	52,472
Property, plant, and equipment	20,114		
Other assets	56,912		
Total	CHF100,690	Total	CHF100,690

The following summarizes a few transactions during July 2011 (CHF in millions):

a. Products carried in inventory at a cost of CHF500 were sold for cash of CHF350 and on open account of CHF400, for a grand total of CHF750.
b. Collection of receivables, CHF620.
c. Depreciation expense of CHF30 was recognized.
d. Selling and administrative expenses of CHF240 were paid in cash.
e. Prepaid expenses of CHF50 expired in July. These included fire insurance premiums paid in the previous year that applied to future months. The expiration increases selling and administrative expenses and reduces other assets.

Required
1. Prepare an analysis of Nestlé's transactions, employing the balance sheet equation approach demonstrated in Exhibit 2-3 (p. 49). Show all amounts in millions.
2. Prepare a statement of earnings before taxes. Also prepare a balance sheet as of July 31.

2-53 Prepare Financial Statements

▶▶ OBJECTIVES 3, 4

The Ludmilla Corporation does not use the services of a professional accountant. At the end of its second year of operations, 20X2, the company's office manager prepared its financial statements. Listed next in random order are the items appearing in these statements:

Accounts receivable	$ 32,400	Office supplies inventory	$ 2,000
Paid-in capital	100,000	Notes payable	8,000
Trucks	33,700	Merchandise inventory	61,000
Cost of goods sold	157,000	Accounts payable	14,000
Salaries expense	86,000	Notes receivable	2,500
Unexpired insurance	1,800	Utilities expense	5,000
Rent expense	19,500	Net income	8,200
Sales	285,000	Retained earnings	
Advertising expense	9,300	January 1, 20X2	18,000
Cash	14,800	December 31, 20X2	26,200

You are satisfied that the statements in which these items appear are correct, except for several matters that the office manager overlooked. The following information should have been entered on the books and reflected in the financial statements:

a. The amount shown for rent expense includes $2,000 that is actually prepaid for the first month in 20X3.
b. Of the amount shown for unexpired insurance, only $800 is prepaid for periods after 20X2.
c. Depreciation of trucks for 20X2 is $5,000.
d. $1,200 of the office supplies in the inventory shown earlier was actually issued and used during 20X2 operations.
e. Cash dividends of $4,000 were declared in December 20X2 by the board of directors. The company will distribute these dividends in February 20X3.

Prepare in good form the following corrected financial statements, ignoring income taxes:

1. Income statement for 20X2
2. Statement of changes in retained earnings for 20X2
3. Balance sheet at December 31, 20X2

It is not necessary to prepare a columnar analysis to show the transaction effects on each element of the accounting equation.

2-54 Transaction Analysis and Financial Statements, Including Dividends
(Alternates are 2-47, 2-48, 2-50, and 2-52.) Consider the following balance sheet of a wholesaler of children's toys:

Gecko Toy Company

Balance Sheet, December 31, 20X0

Assets		Liabilities and Stockholders' Equity		
		Liabilities		
Cash	$ 400,000	Accounts payable		$ 800,000
Accounts receivable	400,000	Stockholders' equity		
Merchandise inventory	860,000	Paid-in capital	$360,000	
Prepaid rent	45,000	Retained earnings	645,000	
Equipment	100,000	Total stockholders' equity		1,005,000
Total	$1,805,000	Total		$1,805,000

The following is a summary of transactions that occurred during 20X1:

a. Acquisitions of inventory on open account, $1 million.
b. Sales on open account, $1.5 million; and for cash, $200,000. Therefore, total sales were $1.7 million.
c. Merchandise carried in inventory at a cost of $1.3 million was sold as described in b.
d. The warehouse 12-month lease expired on October 1, 20X1. However, the company immediately renewed the lease at a rate of $84,000 for the next 12-month period. The entire rent was paid in cash in advance.
e. Depreciation expense for 20X1 for the warehouse equipment was $20,000.
f. Collections on accounts receivable, $1.25 million.
g. Wages for 20X1 were paid in full in cash, $200,000.
h. Miscellaneous expenses for 20X1 were paid in full in cash, $70,000.
i. Payments on accounts payable, $900,000.
j. Cash dividends for 20X1 were declared and paid in full in December, $100,000.

Required
1. Prepare an analysis of transactions, employing the balance sheet equation approach demonstrated in Exhibit 2-3 (p. 49). Show the amounts in thousands of dollars.
2. Prepare an ending balance sheet, a statement of income, and the retained earnings column of the statement of stockholders' equity for 20X1.

3. Reconsider transaction j. Suppose the dividends were declared on December 15, 20X1, payable on January 31, 20X2, to shareholders of record on January 20. Indicate which accounts and financial statements in requirement 2 would be changed and by how much. Be complete and specific.

2-55 Balance Sheet Equation

▶▶ **OBJECTIVES 4,5**

(Alternates are 2-39 and 2-40.) Merck & Co., Inc., the giant pharmaceutical company, had the following actual data for fiscal year ended December 31, 2011 ($ in millions):

Assets, beginning of period	$105,781
Assets, end of period	105,128
Liabilities, beginning of period	A
Liabilities, end of period	D
Other shareholders' equity, beginning of period	19,269
Other shareholders' equity, end of period	17,953
Retained earnings, beginning of period	37,536
Retained earnings, end of period	C
Total revenues	48,047
Cost of sales and all other expenses	41,775
Net earnings	B
Dividends and other decreases in retained earnings	4,818

Find the unknowns ($ in millions), showing computations to support your answers.

2-56 Two Sides of a Transaction

▶▶ **OBJECTIVES 3,4**

For each of the following transactions, show the effects on the entities involved. As was illustrated in the chapter, use the Assets = Liabilities + Owners' equity (A = L + OE) equation to demonstrate the effects. Using the accounts in the illustration below, show the dollar amounts and indicate whether the effects are increases or decreases.

ILLUSTRATION

The Nebraska State Hospital collects $1,000 from the Blue Cross Health Care Plan.

			A			=	**L**	**+ OE**
Entity	**Cash**	**+**	**Other Assets**	**+ Trucks**	**=**	**Liabilities**	
Hospital	+1,000		−1,000		=		
Blue Cross	−1,000				=	−1,000	

1. Borrowing of $150,000 on a home mortgage from Fidelity Savings by David Stratton.
2. Payment of $10,000 principal on the preceding mortgage. Ignore interest.
3. Purchase of a 2-year subscription to *Businessweek* magazine for $90 cash by Cindy Silverton.
4. Purchase of used trucks by the U.S. Postal Service for $10 million cash from FedEx. The trucks were carried in the accounts at $10 million (original cost minus accumulated depreciation) by FedEx.
5. Purchase of U.S. government bonds for $100,000 cash by Lockheed Corporation.
6. Cash deposits of $18 on the returnable bottles sold by Safeway Stores to a retail customer, Philomena Simon.
7. Collections on open account of $100 by an Office Depot store from a retail customer, Gerald Arrow.
8. Purchase of traveler's checks of $1,000 from American Express Company by William Spence.
9. Cash deposit of $600 in a checking account in Bank of America by Jeffrey Hoskins.
10. Purchase of a United Airlines "supersaver" airline ticket for $400 cash by Peter Tanlu on June 15. The trip will be taken on September 10.

▶▶ **OBJECTIVES 4, 5**

2-57 Net Income and Retained Earnings

McDonald's Corporation is a well-known fast-food restaurant company. The following data are from its 2011 annual report ($ in millions):

McDonald's Corporation

Retained earnings, December 31, 2010	$33,811.7	Dividends declared	$ 2,607.3
Revenues	27,006.0	Selling, general, and administrative expenses	2,393.7
Interest and other nonoperating expenses	517.5	Franchise restaurants—occupancy expenses	1,481.5
Provision for income taxes	2,509.1	Retained earnings, end of year	36,707.5
Food and paper expense	6,167.2		
Payroll and employee benefits	4,606.3	Occupancy and other operating expenses	3,827.6

1. Prepare the following for the year ended December 31, 2011:
   a. Income statement. Label the final three lines of the income statement as follows: income before provision for income taxes, provision for income taxes, and net income.
   b. The retained earnings column of the statement of stockholders' equity.
2. Comment briefly on the relative size of the cash dividend.

▶▶ **OBJECTIVES 4, 5**

2-58 Earnings Statement, Retained Earnings

General Mills, Inc. is a leading global manufacturer and marketer of branded consumer foods sold through retail stores and a supplier of branded and unbranded food products to the foodservice and commercial baking industries. The following amounts were in the financial statements contained in its annual report for the year ended May 29, 2011 ($ in millions):

Total sales	$14,880.2	Retained earnings at beginning of year (June 1, 2010)	$8,122.4
Cash	619.6		
Income taxes	721.1	Cost of sales	8,926.7
Accounts payable	995.1	Dividends declared	729.4
Total assets	18,674.5	Other expenses	3,434.1

Choose the relevant data and prepare (1) the income statement for the year and (2) the retained earnings column of the statement of stockholders' equity for the year. Label the final three lines of the income statement as follows: income before income taxes, provision for income taxes, and net income.

▶▶ **OBJECTIVE 6**

2-59 Financial Ratios

(Alternate is 2-60.) Following is a list of three well-known package delivery companies (**UPS** and **FedEx** from the United States and **Deutsche Post World Net**, owner of DHL, in Germany) and selected financial data of the sort typically included in letters sent by stock brokerage firms to clients. Note that € is the symbol for the euro, the European currency.

	Per Share Data			Ratios and Percentages		
Company	**Price**	**Earnings**	**Dividends**	**P-E**	**Dividend-Yield**	**Dividend-Payout**
FedEx	—	$4.61	—	20.3	—	10.4%
UPS	$72.56	—	—	18.7	2.9%	—
Deutsche Post	€11.88	€ .96	—	—	—	72.7%

The missing figures for this schedule can be computed from the data given.

1. Compute the missing figures and identify the company with the following:
   a. The highest dividend-yield
   b. The highest dividend-payout percentage
   c. The lowest market price relative to earnings
2. Assume you know nothing about any of these companies other than the data given and the computations you have made from the data. Which company would you choose as
   a. the most attractive investment? Why?
   b. the least attractive investment? Why?

2-60 Financial Ratios

▶▶ **OBJECTIVE 6**

(Alternate is 2-59.) Following is a list of three well-known petroleum companies and selected financial data of the sort typically included in letters sent by stock brokerage firms to clients.

Company	Per Share Data			Ratios and Percentages		
	Price	Earnings	Dividends	P-E	Dividend-Yield	Dividend-Payout
Royal Dutch Shell	$36.45	$ 4.98	$1.68	—	—	—
ExxonMobil	$84.76	—	—	10.05	2.2%	—
Chevron	—	$13.54	—	7.86	—	22.8%

The missing figures for this schedule can be computed from the data given.

1. Compute the missing figures and identify the company with the following:
   a. The highest dividend-yield
   b. The highest dividend-payout percentage
   c. The lowest market price relative to earnings
2. Assume that you know nothing about any of these companies other than the data given and the computations you have made from the data. Which company would you choose as
   a. the most attractive investment? Why?
   b. the least attractive investment? Why?

2-61 Revenue Recognition and Ethics

▶▶ **OBJECTIVE 2**

Diebold, Incorporated is an Ohio corporation that manufactures and sells automated teller machines (ATMs), bank security systems, and electronic voting machines. Its financial policies were called into question in May 2006 when the SEC opened an investigation into the company's revenue recognition policies.

From at least 2002 through 2007, Diebold recognized revenue on "F-term" orders, or Factory orders. In conjunction with many F-term orders, Diebold asked customers to sign a Memorandum of Agreement (MOA), which contained language stating that the customer had asked Diebold to hold the product for the customer's convenience. Diebold typically recognized revenue on the "ship to warehouse" date specified in the MOA, when it shipped the product from the factory to a Diebold warehouse. However, in some instances Diebold shipped product to the warehouse before the specified ship to warehouse date. While the MOAs specified the ship to warehouse dates, they did not always include fixed dates when product was to be shipped from the Diebold warehouse to the end customer. In addition, at the time of shipment to the warehouse, some of the ATMs were not complete as software had not been installed and/or quality testing had not been completed.

Comment on the ethical implications of Diebold's revenue recognition practices.

2-62 Relevance and Faithful Representation

▶▶ **OBJECTIVE 7**

Plum Creek Timber Company, Inc., is a Washington State forest products company. Its largest asset is Timber and Timberlands carried on its balance sheet at $3,377 million on December 31, 2011. This represents 79% of Plum Creek's total assets. A footnote indicates that "timber and timberlands ... are stated at cost." This means that the book value of the land and timber is the cost Plum Creek paid for it whenever it purchased the property. Also on Plum Creek's books are cash of $254 million; property, plant, and equipment of $138 million; and inventories of $53 million.

1. Does the timber and timberlands book value better meet the criterion of relevance or the criterion of faithful representation? Explain.
2. Plum Creek's total assets are the sum of the book value of timber and timberlands; cash; property, plant, and equipment; inventories; and several other relatively small assets. What problem do you see with adding these amounts together when measuring total assets?
3. Is there an alternative measure of the timber and timberlands that might be more relevant than the original cost? If so, what is it? Would your measure meet the criterion of faithful representation as well as the original cost does?

▶▶ **OBJECTIVE 8**

2-63 Continuity Convention and Liquidation
The following news report appeared in the financial press:

> *The Bulgarian national airline Balkan is to be placed in liquidation after its creditors today rejected a reorganization plan, legal administrators for the carrier said. With debts of €92 million to 2,200 creditors, Balkan began bankruptcy procedures in March. Creditors today rejected a restructuring for the airline and insisted on the sale of its assets to pay off its debts.*

Explain how the measurements used in the financial statements of Balkan would differ from those used in a similar airline that had not been placed in liquidation.

Collaborative Learning Exercise

▶▶ **OBJECTIVE 6**

2-64 Financial Ratios
Form groups of four to six persons each. Each member of the group should pick a different company and find the most recent annual report for that company.

1. Members should compute the following ratios for their company:
   a. EPS
   b. P-E ratio
   c. Dividend-yield ratio
   d. Dividend-payout ratio
2. As a group, list two possible reasons that each ratio differs across the selected companies. Focus on comparing the companies with the highest and lowest values for each ratio, and explain how the nature of the company might be the reason for the differences in ratios.

Analyzing and Interpreting Financial Statements

▶▶ **OBJECTIVES 4, 5**

2-65 Financial Statement Research
Select the financial statements of any company.

1. What was the amount of sales (or total revenues) and the net income for the most recent year?
2. What was the total amount of cash dividends for the most recent year?
3. What was the ending balance in retained earnings in the most recent year? What were the two most significant items during the year that affected the retained earnings balance?

▶▶ **OBJECTIVES 4, 5, 6**

2-66 Analyzing Starbucks' Financial Statements
Find the Starbucks financial statements for 2011 either on Starbucks' Web site or on the SEC's EDGAR Web site and answer the following questions:

1. What was the amount of net revenues (total sales) and net earnings for the year ended October 2, 2011?
2. How did Starbucks' net income and dividends affect its retained earnings?
3. What is Starbucks' EPS for the year ended October 2, 2011? Compute the P-E ratio, assuming the market price for Starbucks' stock was $35.93 at the time.
4. Suppose the average P-E ratio for companies at that time was 15. Do investors expect Starbucks' EPS to grow faster or slower than average? Explain.

2-67 Analyzing Financial Statements Using the Internet: Time Warner

Go to the Web site for **Time Warner** (www.timewarner.com). Click on Investor Relations. Find and open the most recent annual report.

Answer the following questions:

▸▸ **OBJECTIVES 1, 2, 3**

1. Refer to Time Warner's Statement of Income. What is the dollar amount of total revenues? What categories comprise its total revenues? Which category constitutes the largest percentage of total revenues?

2. Refer to Time Warner's Notes to Consolidated Financial Statements. Locate the footnote containing discussion of Time Warner's revenue recognition policies. Does Time Warner use a single revenue recognition policy to account for all of its different revenue generating activities? Find the portion of the footnote that discusses the revenue recognition policy for publishing activities. When does Time Warner recognize revenue from magazines? How does it account for subscriptions paid for in advance?

3. How much is Time Warner's "unearned revenue"? What does it represent and where is it found in the financial statements?

4. Does Time Warner prepare its income statement using the cash or accrual basis? What items on the balance sheet are clues to answering this question?

5. Do you think Time Warner is a profit-seeking organization? What clues on the financial statements help you answer this?

3

Recording Transactions

HAVE YOU EVER FLOWN ON Delta Air Lines? If so, your trip was just one of thousands of transactions that Delta had to record that day. With so many transactions happening, you might think that yours could get lost in the shuffle. Yet, you can read a report on your transaction combined with thousands of others in any major newspaper in articles based on press releases issued by the company. On April 26, 2011, Delta announced its earnings for the quarter ending March 2011. Here are some of the highlights of that announcement.

Total operating revenue was $7.7 billion in the March 2011 quarter, up 13% compared to operating revenue of $6.8 billion in the March 2010 quarter. Both higher passenger revenue and higher cargo revenue contributed to the increase. Passenger revenue rose 13%, or $769 million, and cargo revenue rose 42%, or $74 million. The increase in both revenue categories was attributable to higher volume and higher yields, despite the impact of severe winter weather and the catastrophic earthquake in Japan. Ed Bastian, Delta's president, said that the company expected double-digit unit revenue growth in the quarter ending June 2011.

Despite increased revenue, the company reported a net loss of $318 million for the quarter, $128 million worse than the net loss reported in the comparable quarter of 2010. The $610 million impact of 30% higher fuel prices was a major contributor to the weak income performance. Richard Andrew, Delta's CEO, commented that fuel costs are the biggest challenge facing the airline industry. Delta is engaged in numerous actions including fuel hedging, capacity reductions and changes in cost structure in an effort to offset the impact of fuel prices on net income.

Are you not seeing that trip to Disney World you took? The information contained in this news article comes directly from Delta's corporate headquarters and informs investors, stockholders, and other interested parties about the financial performance of the organization. Delta's corporate headquarters gets this information from the company's accounting records. Of course, these records contain every single Delta transaction, including your Disney World trip.

Delta's transactions can take many forms—for example, sale of tickets to passengers, sale of cargo transportation services, purchase of fuel for the planes, and payment of wages to employees. At the end of the month, quarter, or year, accountants compute the totals for each account and use them to prepare the reports that tell the financial story for that period. As you can see from Delta's press release, total operating revenue for the March 2011 quarter was $7.7 billion. After deducting expenses and other items, the net loss was $318 million. This indicates that, on average, Delta lost $.041 on each dollar of operating revenue [($318) million ÷ $7,700 million].

Information in press releases often leads to price changes in a company's stock. Delta's share price jumped by 7.3% on the day of the earnings announcement and increased by 12.35%

▶▶ **LEARNING OBJECTIVES** *After studying this chapter, you should be able to:*

1 Use double-entry accounting.

2 Describe the five steps in the recording process.

3 Analyze and journalize transactions and post journal entries to the ledgers.

4 Prepare and use a trial balance.

5 Close revenue and expense accounts and update retained earnings.

6 Correct erroneous journal entries and describe how errors affect accounts.

7 Explain how computers have transformed the processing of accounting data.

during the week following the announcement, to close at $10.46. The earnings release contained significant information and caused investors to change their valuation of Delta's shares. The investors viewed the press release as good news, despite the net loss and poor performance relative to the prior year. What could cause this positive response to seemingly negative news? While the company reported a net loss of $.38 per share, the analysts' estimate of EPS was a loss of $.50 per share. Delta outperformed the market's expectation. In addition, the company provided guidance that the coming quarter would bring higher revenues and controlled costs, leading to an expectation of better times ahead.

All companies, including Delta, have to develop systems for processing huge volumes of accounting data. Methods of processing the data have changed dramatically over time because computerized systems have replaced manual ones. However, the steps in recording, storing, and processing accounting data have not changed. Switching from pencil-and-paper accounting records to computerized ones is a little like switching from a car with a stick shift to one with an automatic transmission. You spend less time worrying about routine tasks, but you still need to understand how to use the vehicle. Whether a company enters data into the system by pencil, keyboard, or optical scanner, it must enter, summarize, and report the same basic data, and users must interpret the same basic financial statements.

To intelligently use the financial statements you learned about in the last two chapters, decision makers need to understand the methods accountants use to record and analyze the data in those statements. This chapter focuses on those methods. In particular, this chapter explains the double-entry accounting system that all companies use to record and process information about their transactions. As you will discover, a working knowledge of this system is essential for anyone engaged in business. Ultimately, accounting practices constitute a language that managers in all organizations use to understand the economic progress of their organizations. ●

What started as a crop dusting operation in 1924 has become one of the world's largest global airlines. Each year, more than 160 million travelers fly on Delta or one of its affiliated airlines. Delta must record millions of sales transactions each year. These transactions provide the basic information for the company's financial statements.

The Double-Entry Accounting System

▶▶ OBJECTIVE 1
Use double-entry accounting.

In large businesses such as Delta Air Lines, McDonald's, and Verizon, hundreds or thousands of transactions occur hourly. With so much activity, it might seem easy to lose track of one or two transactions. Even one lost transaction could create havoc on a company's accounting (just think of what happens when you miss one transaction in your checking account record). Such errors may lead to serious consequences. As a result, accountants must record these transactions in a systematic manner. Worldwide, the dominant recording process is a **double-entry system**, in which every transaction affects at least two accounts. Accountants analyze each transaction to determine which accounts it affects, whether to increase or decrease the account balances, and how much each balance will change. Accountants have used such a system for more than 500 years, as described in the Business First box on p. 93.

double-entry system

The method usually followed for recording transactions, whereby every transaction affects at least two accounts.

Recall the first three transactions of the Biwheels Company introduced in Chapter 1:

	A		**=**	**L**	**+**	**SE**
	Cash	**+ Store Equipment**	**=**	**Note Payable**	**+**	**Paid-in Capital**
(1) Initial investment by owner	+400,000		=			+400,000
(2) Loan from bank	+100,000		=	+100,000		
(3) Acquire store equipment for cash	−15,000	+15,000	=			

This balance sheet equation format illustrates the basic concepts of the double-entry system by showing two entries for each transaction. It also emphasizes that the equation Assets = Liabilities + Stockholders' Equity must always remain in balance. Unfortunately, this format is too cumbersome for recording each and every transaction that occurs. In practice, accountants record the individual transactions as they occur and then organize the elements of the transaction into accounts that group similar items together. For example, the Cash account collects all elements that affect cash.

general journal

A complete chronological record of an organization's transactions and how each transaction affects the balances in particular accounts.

The remainder of this chapter describes the elements of a double-entry system, focusing on how accountants use general journals and general ledgers to record, summarize, and report financial information. The **general journal** is a chronological record of an organization's transactions and how each transaction affects the balances in particular accounts. The **general ledger** is a collection of all ledger accounts that supports the organization's financial statements, where a **ledger account** is a listing of all the increases and decreases in a particular account. Let's begin with the general ledger.

general ledger

The collection of all ledger accounts that supports an organization's financial statements.

ledger account

A listing of all the increases and decreases in a particular account.

The General Ledger

T-account

Device used to portray the individual ledger accounts in the general ledger. Each T-account takes the form of the capital letter T and represents an individual ledger account. We accumulate the transactions that affect a particular ledger account within the related T-account.

The general ledger traditionally was a bound or loose-leaf book of ledger accounts, but today it is more likely to be a set of records in an electronic file. However, for simplicity's sake, you can think of the general ledger as a book with one page for each account. When you hear about "keeping the books" or "auditing the books," the word *books* refers to the general ledger, even if it is an electronic file. Accountants always keep the ledger accounts current in a systematic manner.

We use **T-accounts** to portray the individual ledger accounts in the general ledger. We call them T-accounts because they take the form of the capital letter T. Each T-account represents an individual account, such as Cash, Receivables, or Inventory. Within a T-account we accumulate the transactions that affect that particular ledger account. The vertical line in the T divides the account into left and right sides. Increases in the account go on one side of the vertical line and decreases on the other. The account title is shown on the horizontal line of the T.

Consider the format of the Cash T-account:

balance

A numerical total that is the net result of all activity recorded in an account as of a particular point in time. In a T-account the balance is the difference between the total left-side and right-side amounts in the T-account at any particular time. The balance in a general ledger account at the end of an accounting period is computed as the beginning balance in the account, plus the amount of the increases in the account during the period, minus the amount of the decreases.

	Cash	
Left side		Right side
Increases in cash		Decreases in cash

We record increases in asset accounts (such as Cash) on the left side of the T-account and decreases on the right side. We reverse this process for liabilities and owners' equity accounts—increases go on the right and decreases on the left. The **balance** in an account is the net result of all activity that has been recorded in the account as of a particular point in time. The balance in a T-account is

BUSINESS FIRST

DOUBLE-ENTRY ACCOUNTING: FIVE CENTURIES OF PROGRESS

Double-entry accounting is more than 500 years old. In the same decade that Columbus set sail for America, Luca Pacioli, an Italian friar and mathematician, published *Summa de Arithmetica, Geometria, Proportioni, et Proportionalita* ("Everything About Arithmetic, Geometry, and Proportions"), the first book that described a double-entry accounting system. Pacioli did not invent accounting. He simply described the system used by Venetian merchants. His system included journals and ledgers, with accounts for assets (including receivables and inventories), liabilities, equity, income, and expenses. His process included closing the books and preparing a trial balance. All these terms and concepts are still in use today, as described in this chapter. Pacioli also warned that "a person should not go to sleep at night until the debits equaled the credits," a good warning for accountants today.

The last five decades have seen more changes in accounting than did the preceding five centuries. First, automated data processing started replacing manual accounting systems. This, combined with the growth of complex business transactions, made accounting transactions more difficult and less transparent to financial statement users. Then a knowledge-based economy called into question an accounting system that focused mainly on physical assets.

The accounting scandals of the early twenty-first century put double-entry accounting at a crossroads. First, problems at Enron, WorldCom, Global Crossing, Tyco, Adelphia, and others caused critics to question the relevance of accounting in the modern business world. How could companies that had been reporting healthy financial results suddenly plunge into financial distress? Then some pundits blamed the financial crisis of 2008–2009 and the failure of companies such as AIG, Bear Stearns, and Merrill Lynch on financial reporting rules, especially the accounting for financial instruments. It is clear that reliable accounting systems are more important than ever. The discipline of a double-entry system cannot prevent managers and accountants from making bad decisions or entering fraudulent transactions in a company's books, but it does provide a framework for reporting economic results that is essential for disclosing information about a company to investors and potential investors.

In the 1920s, Werner Sombart, a German accountant, made the case that double-entry accounting played a major role in the development of capitalistic, market-based economies. This is reinforced in a recent book, *Double Entry: How the Merchants of Venice Created Modern Finance*. The events of the last decade prove its importance to the smooth functioning of worldwide capital markets. From Pacioli's time until today, double-entry accounting systems have kept confirming their value. To understand a market economy, one must understand the basics of double-entry accounting.

Sources: L. Pacioli, *Summa de Arithmetica, Geometria, Proportioni, et Proportionalita*, 1494; W. Sombart, *Der Moderne Kapitalismus*, 1924, and J. Gleeson-White, *Double Entry: How the Merchants of Venice Created Modern Finance*, W. W. Norton & Company, 2012.

the difference between the total left-side and right-side amounts in the T-account at any particular time. Asset accounts have left-side balances, that is, the total of the entries on the left side will be larger than the total of the entries on the right. In contrast, liability and owners' equity accounts have right-side balances. The balance in a general ledger account at the end of an accounting period is computed as the beginning balance in the account, plus the amount of the increases in the account during the period, minus the amount of the decreases.

The T-accounts for the first three Biwheels Company transactions are as follows:

Assets		=	Liabilities + Stockholders' Equity	

Cash			**Note Payable**	
Increases	Decreases		Decreases	Increases
(1) 400,000	(3) 15,000			(2) 100,000
(2) 100,000				

Store Equipment			**Paid-in Capital**	
Increases	Decreases		Decreases	Increases
(3) 15,000				(1) 400,000

Note that each of the three numbered transactions affects two accounts. Remember that, under the double-entry system, each transaction will affect at least two accounts so that the balance sheet is always in balance. In practice, we create accounts as we need them. We call the process of creating a new T-account in preparation for recording a transaction "opening the account." For transaction 1, we opened Cash and Paid-in Capital. For transaction 2, we opened Note Payable, and for transaction 3, we opened Store Equipment. We know that we need a new account when a transaction requires an entry to an account that we have not yet opened.

Each T-account summarizes the changes—increases and decreases—in a particular asset, liability, or owners' equity account. Because T-accounts show only amounts and not transaction descriptions, we identify each transaction in some way, such as by the numbering used in this illustration, by the date, or by both. This identification helps us to link the ledger entry to the transaction that caused it.

Take a look at the analysis of the entries for each Biwheels transaction. Notice that each transaction generates a left-side entry in one T-account and a right-side entry of the same amount in another T-account. When you analyze a transaction, it is helpful to initially pinpoint the effects (if any) on cash. Did cash increase or decrease? Then think of the effects on other accounts. It is frequently easier to identify the effects of a transaction on the Cash account than it is to identify the effects on other accounts.

1. Transaction: Initial investment by owners, $400,000 cash.

Analysis: The asset **Cash** increases.

The stockholders' equity **Paid-in Capital** increases.

Cash		Paid-in Capital	
(1) 400,000			(1) 400,000

2. Transaction: Loan from bank, $100,000.

Analysis: The asset **Cash** increases.

The liability **Note Payable** increases.

Cash		Note Payable	
(1) 400,000			(2) 100,000
(2) 100,000			

3. Transaction: Acquired store equipment for cash, $15,000.

Analysis: The asset **Cash** decreases.

The asset **Store Equipment** increases.

Cash		Store Equipment	
(1) 400,000	(3) 15,000	(3) 15,000	
(2) 100,000			

Ledger accounts contain a record of all the changes in specific assets, liabilities, and owners' equity. Accountants can prepare financial statements at any point in time if the account balances are up-to-date. The ledger accounts provide the information needed for the preparation of financial statements. For example, Biwheels' balance sheet after its first three transactions would contain the following account balances:

Assets		Liabilities and Stockholders' Equity	
Cash	$485,000	Liabilities	
Store equipment	15,000	Note payable	$100,000
		Stockholders' equity	
		Paid-in capital	400,000
Total	$500,000	Total	$500,000

Because Biwheels has just begun operations, there are no carry-over balances from the end of the previous accounting period. In the case of Store Equipment, Note Payable, and Paid-in Capital, there has been only one transaction up to this point, so the transaction amount becomes the account balance. For Cash, the balance of $485,000 is the difference between the total increase on the left side of ($400,000 + $100,000) = $500,000 and the total decrease of $15,000 on the right side.

Debits and Credits

You have just seen that the double-entry system features entries on left sides and right sides of various accounts. Accountants use the term **debit** (abbreviated dr.) to denote an entry or balance on the left side of any account and the term **credit** (abbreviated cr.) to denote an entry or balance on the right side. Popular usage ascribes other meanings to debit and credit, but in accounting they mean simply left-side entry and right-side entry. Some accountants use the word **charge** instead of debit, but there is no such synonym for credit. Just remember that debit refers to left and credit refers to right, and you will be fine.

Accountants use debit and credit as verbs, adjectives, and nouns. "Debit $1,000 to Cash" and "credit $1,000 to Accounts Receivable" are examples using debit and credit as verbs, meaning that you should place $1,000 on the left side of the Cash account and on the right side of the Accounts Receivable account. In "make a debit to Cash," debit is a noun, and in "Cash has a debit balance of $12,000," it is an adjective describing the balance. From this point on you will see the terms debit and credit again and again. Be sure you understand their uses completely before moving on.

debit
An entry or balance on the left side of any account.

credit
An entry or balance on the right side of any account.

charge
A word often used instead of debit.

Summary Problem for Your Review

PROBLEM

Suppose Biwheels' accountant asked you to do the following: "Debit Note Payable for $5,000 and credit Cash for $5,000."

1. Describe the transaction the accountant is asking you to record.
2. What are the balances in Cash and Note Payable after you record this transaction? Before the transaction the Cash balance was $486,000 and the Note Payable balance was $100,000.
3. After you correctly make the entries, the accountant tells you "I give you credit for correctly carrying out my instructions. If you had failed, it would be a debit on your record." What does she mean by "credit" and "debit" in this situation?

SOLUTION

1. Debiting the Note Payable account means to record an entry for $5,000 on the left side of the T-account. This decreases the Note Payable balance by $5,000 because Note Payable is a liability account. Crediting Cash for $5,000 means a right-hand entry to the Cash T-account, decreasing the balance in that asset account. Cash and Note Payable both decrease by $5,000, so the transaction represents a repayment of $5,000 of the note payable.
2. The Cash account will decrease by $5,000 to ($485,000 − $5,000) = $480,000. The Note Payable account will also decrease by $5,000 to ($100,000 − $5,000) = $95,000.
3. These are popular uses of the terms credit and debit—credit meaning praise or recognition and debit meaning blame. These definitions have nothing to do with the accounting uses of the terms. Remember, in accounting debit means left side and credit means right side, nothing more.

The Recording Process

In the preceding section, we entered Biwheels' transactions 1, 2, and 3 directly in the ledger accounts. In actual practice, accountants first record transactions in the general journal. The sequence of five steps in recording and reporting transactions is as follows:

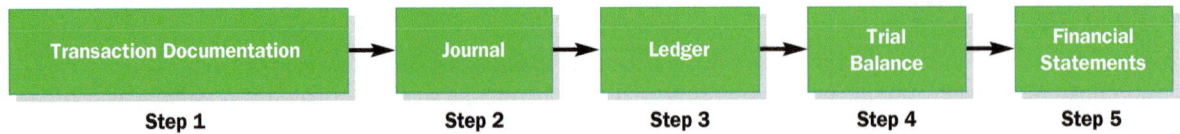

| Transaction Documentation | Journal | Ledger | Trial Balance | Financial Statements |
| Step 1 | Step 2 | Step 3 | Step 4 | Step 5 |

source documents

The original records supporting any transaction.

Step 1: The recording process begins with **source documents**. These are the original records supporting any transaction. Examples of source documents include sales slips or invoices, check stubs, purchase orders, receiving reports, cash receipt slips, and minutes of the board of directors. Most transactions generate a source document. For example, when a company sells a product to a customer, it creates a receipt for the sale. Companies keep source documents on file so they can use them to verify the details of a transaction and the accuracy of subsequent records, if necessary.

Step 2: In the second step of the recording process, we place an analysis of the transaction, based on the source documents, in the general journal, also called the **book of original entry**. Recall that the general journal is a chronological listing of transactions. It is basically a diary of all events (transactions) in an entity's life.

book of original entry

Another name for the general journal.

Step 3: The third step is to enter transactions into the ledger accounts. As we have seen, we enter each component into the left side or the right side of the appropriate accounts.

trial balance

A list of all the accounts in the general ledger together with their balances.

Step 4: The fourth step is the preparation of the **trial balance**, which is a list of all the accounts in the general ledger together with their balances. This list aids in verifying clerical accuracy and in preparing financial statements. Thus, we prepare it as needed, perhaps each month or each quarter as the firm prepares its financial statements. The timing of the first four steps varies. Transactions occur constantly so companies prepare source documents continuously. Depending on the size and nature of the organization, transaction summaries may occur continuously, weekly, or monthly. The timing of the steps in the recording process must conform to the needs of the users of the data.

Step 5: The final step, closing the books and preparing financial statements, occurs at least once a quarter, every 3 months, for publicly traded companies in the United States and at least annually for those reporting under IFRS. However, most companies prepare financial statements more frequently for management's benefit. For example, Springfield ReManufacturing Corporation, an employee-owned company in southern Missouri with more than 1,200 employees and sales of more than $400 million, prepares monthly financial statements. Springfield is a leader in "open book management," in which the company opens its accounting results to everyone in the firm. Management and all employees meet monthly to examine the results in detail. The company provides extensive training to employees on how the accounting process works and what the numbers mean. This management process has focused the attention of every employee and increased efficiency and profitability at Springfield.

Chart of Accounts

chart of accounts

A numbered or coded list of all account titles.

To ensure consistency in recording transactions, organizations specify a **chart of accounts**, which is a numbered or coded list of all account titles. This list specifies the accounts that the organization uses in recording its activities and is usually arranged in the order in which accounts appear in the financial statements. Accountants often use these account numbers as a shorthand way to identify the accounts. The following is the chart of accounts for Biwheels:

Account Number	Account Title	Account Number	Account Title
100	Cash	202	Note payable
120	Accounts receivable	203	Accounts payable
130	Merchandise inventory	300	Paid-in capital
140	Prepaid rent	400	Retained earnings
170	Store equipment	500	Sales revenue
170A	Accumulated	600	Cost of goods sold
	depreciation,	601	Rent expense
	store equipment	602	Depreciation expense
	(explained later)		

There is no universally agreed upon chart of accounts. The chart varies across companies as a function of the size, nature, and complexity of the organization. Large companies may have thousands of account numbers.

Journalizing Transactions

Let's examine step 2 in the recording process more closely. We call this step **journalizing**—the process of entering transactions into the general journal. A **journal entry** is an analysis of the effects of a single transaction on the various accounts, usually accompanied by an explanation. For each transaction, this analysis identifies the accounts to be debited and credited. The top of Exhibit 3-1 shows how to journalize the opening three transactions for Biwheels.

We will use the following conventions for recording journal entries in the general journal:

1. The date and identification number of the entry make up the first two columns.
2. The next column, Accounts and Explanation, shows the names of the accounts affected. At the left margin we place the title of the account or accounts to be debited. We indent the title of the account or accounts to be credited. Following the journal entry itself is the narrative explanation of the transaction. The length of the explanation depends on the complexity of the transaction and whether management wants the journal itself to contain all relevant information. Most often, explanations are brief because details are available in the supporting documents.
3. The Post Ref. (posting reference) column contains an identifying number from the chart of accounts that we use for cross-referencing to the ledger accounts.
4. The debit and credit columns show the amounts that we debit (left-entry) or credit (right-entry) to each account. It is customary not to use currency symbols (for example, dollar signs or yen or euro symbols) in either the journal or the ledger. Negative numbers never appear in the journal or the ledger. Instead, the side on which the number appears tells you whether to add or subtract the number in computing an account balance. Debits and credits tell the whole story in the recording process, so be sure you understand them fully.

Accountants often become so familiar with the various codes used in their company's chart of accounts that they think, talk, and write in terms of account numbers instead of account names. Thus, they might journalize Biwheels' entry 3, the acquisition of Store Equipment (Account 170) for Cash (Account 100), as follows:

20X2		dr.	cr.
Jan. 3	170	15,000	
	100		15,000

This journal entry employs the accountant's shorthand, which uses codes without account names. Its brevity and lack of explanation would hamper any outsider's understanding of the transaction, but the entry's meaning would be clear to any accountant within the organization.

▸▸OBJECTIVE 3

Analyze and journalize transactions and post journal entries to the ledgers.

journalizing
The process of entering transactions into the general journal.

journal entry
An analysis of the effects of a transaction on the various accounts, usually accompanied by an explanation.

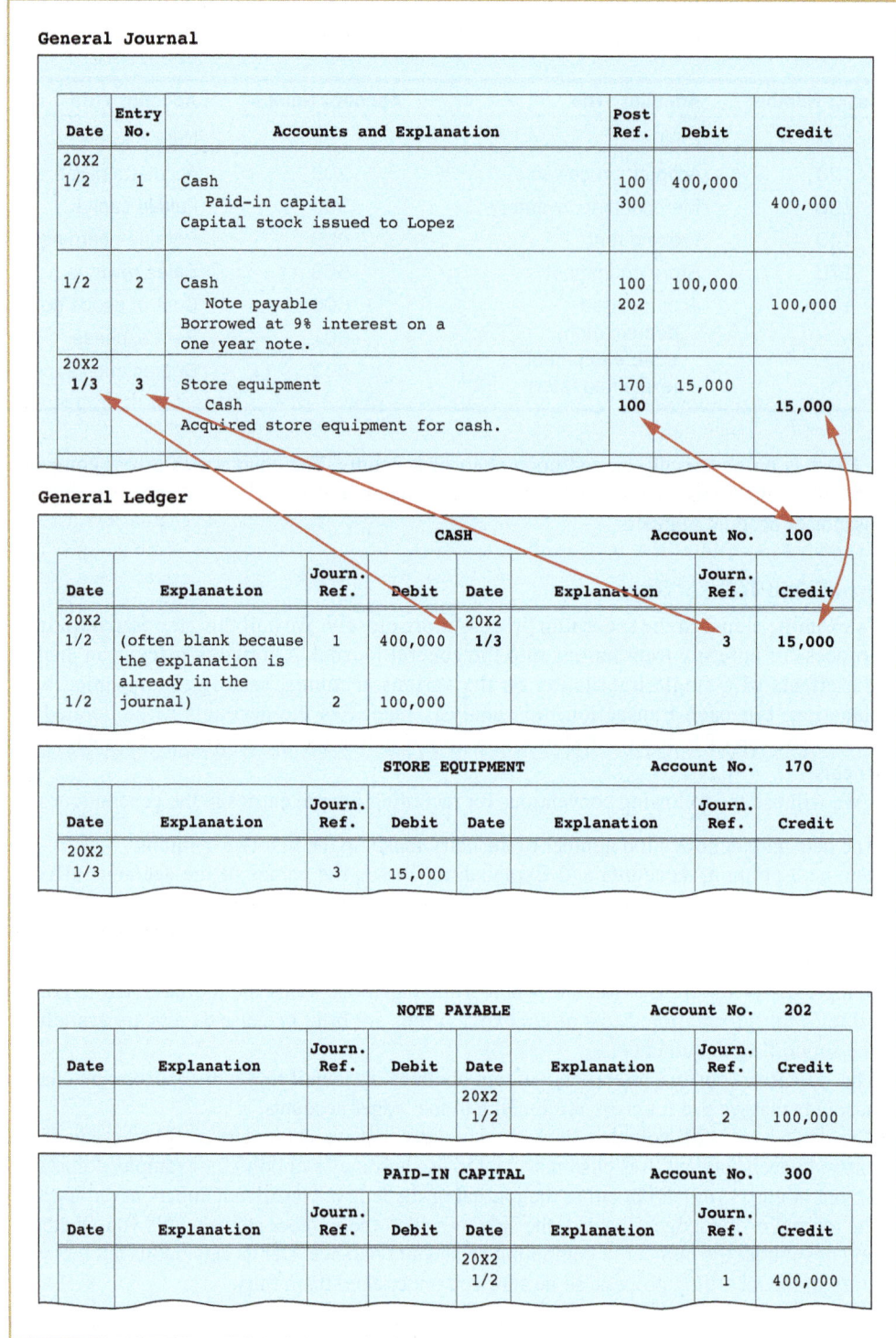

Posting Transactions to the General Ledger

We call step 3, the transferring of amounts from the general journal to the appropriate accounts in the general ledger, **posting**. To see how this works, consider transaction 3 for Biwheels as depicted in Exhibit 3-1. The red arrows in Exhibit 3-1 show how we post the $15,000 credit to the general ledger Cash account using the information and values from the journal entry recorded in the general journal. Note that the format of the sample general ledger in Exhibit 3-1 provides space for transferring all the information in the journal entry, not just the summary information allowed in the simplified T-account format. There are columns for dates, explanations, journal

posting

*The transferring of amounts from
the general journal to the appropriate accounts in the general ledger.*

	Cash			Account No.	100	
Date	**Explanation**	**Journ. Ref.**	**Debit**	**Credit**	**Balance**
20X2					
1/2	(often blank because the explanation is	1	400,000		400,000
1/2	already in the journal)	2	100,000		500,000
1/3		3		15,000	485,000

references, and amounts. The structure is repeated for debits on the left side of the page and for credits on the right side.

Because posting is strictly a mechanical process of moving numbers from the general journal to the general ledger, it is most efficiently done by a computer. The accountant journalizes a transaction in an electronic general journal, and the computer automatically transfers the information to an electronic version of the general ledger. There is also cross-referencing between the general journal and the general ledger. **Cross-referencing** is the process of using numbering, dating, and/or some other form of identification to relate each general ledger posting to the appropriate journal entry. A single transaction from the general journal might be posted to several different ledger accounts. Cross-referencing allows users to find all the components of the transaction in the general ledger no matter where they start. It also helps auditors to find and correct errors and reduces the frequency of errors.

General ledger entries do not always take the form of Exhibit 3-1. Exhibit 3-2 shows another popular general ledger format, one that has only one date column and one explanation column and adds an additional column to the presentation to provide a running balance of the account holdings. This format is very similar to the format found in a checkbook. The running balance feature is a useful addition because it provides a status report for an account at a glance. Although most accounting systems are now fully computerized, the reports generated by computers often look much like the paper-based general ledgers and general journals they replaced. After hundreds of years of use, these formats have become traditional and familiar.

cross-referencing
The process of using numbering, dating, and/or some other form of identification to relate each general ledger posting to the appropriate journal entry.

Analyzing, Journalizing, and Posting the Biwheels Transactions

We have seen that accountants review source documents about a transaction, mentally analyze the transaction, record that analysis in a journal entry in the general journal, and then post the results to the general ledger. We can now apply this process to additional transactions from the Biwheels Company. We will omit explanations for the journal entries because we already presented them in the original statement of the transaction. We indicate the posting of the elements of the transaction to the T-accounts by encircling the new number.

4. Transaction: Acquired merchandise inventory for cash, $120,000.

    Analysis: The asset **Merchandise Inventory** increases.

               The asset **Cash** decreases.

Journal Entry: Merchandise inventory.   120,000

               Cash   120,000

    Posting:

	Cash				Merchandise Inventory
(1)	400,000	(3)	15,000	(4)	(120,000)
(2)	100,000	(4)	(120,000)		

5. Transaction: Acquired merchandise inventory on credit, $10,000.

Analysis: The asset **Merchandise Inventory** increases.

The liability **Accounts Payable** increases.

Journal Entry: Merchandise inventory   10,000

Accounts payable   10,000

Posting:

Merchandise Inventory			Accounts Payable	
(4)	120,000		(5)	(10,000)
(5)	(10,000)			

simple entry

A journal entry for a transaction that affects only two accounts.

Transaction 5, like transactions 1, 2, 3, and 4, is a **simple entry** because the transaction affects only two accounts. Note that the balance sheet equation remains in balance with each new transaction.

6. Transaction: Acquired merchandise inventory for $10,000 cash plus $20,000 trade credit.

Analysis: The asset **Cash** decreases.

The asset **Merchandise Inventory** increases.

The liability **Accounts Payable** increases.

Journal Entry: Merchandise inventory   30,000

Cash   10,000

Accounts payable   20,000

Posting:

Cash					Accounts Payable	
(1)	400,000	(3)	15,000		(5)	10,000
(2)	100,000	(4)	120,000		(6)	(20,000)
		(6)	(10,000)			

Merchandise Inventory		
(4)	120,000	
(5)	10,000	
(6)	(30,000)	

compound entry

A journal entry for a transaction that affects more than two accounts.

Transaction 6 is a **compound entry**, which means that a single transaction affects more than two accounts. Whether transactions are simple (like transactions 1 through 5) or compound, the total of all left-side entries always equals the total of all right-side entries. The net effect is to keep the accounting equation in balance at all times:

$$\text{Assets} = \text{Liabilities} + \text{Stockholders' equity}$$
$$+30,000 - 10,000 = +20,000$$

7. Transaction: Sold unneeded showcase to neighbor for $1,000 cash. The cost of the showcase was $1,000.

Analysis: The asset **Cash** increases.

The asset **Store Equipment** decreases.

Journal Entry: Cash   1,000

Store equipment   1,000

Posting:

Cash				Store Equipment			
(1)	400,000	(3)	15,000	(3)	15,000	(7)	(1,000)
(2)	100,000	(4)	120,000				
(7)	(1,000)	(6)	10,000				

In transaction 7, one asset increases, and another asset decreases. The transaction affects only one side of the accounting equation because there is no entry to a liability or stockholders' equity account.

8. Transaction: Returned merchandise inventory to supplier for full credit, $800.

Analysis: The asset **Merchandise Inventory** decreases.

The liability **Accounts Payable** decreases.

Journal Entry: Accounts payable 800

Merchandise inventory 800

Posting:

Merchandise Inventory				Accounts Payable			
(4)	120,000	(8)	800	(8)	800	(5)	10,000
(5)	10,000					(6)	20,000
(6)	30,000						

9. Transaction: Paid cash to creditor, $4,000.

Analysis: The asset **Cash** decreases.

The liability **Accounts Payable** decreases.

Journal Entry: Accounts payable 4,000

Cash 4,000

Posting:

Cash				Accounts Payable			
(1)	400,000	(3)	15,000	(8)	800	(5)	10,000
(2)	100,000	(4)	120,000	(9)	4,000	(6)	20,000
(7)	1,000	(6)	10,000				
		(9)	4,000				

Transactions 7, 8, and 9 are all simple entries. In transactions 8 and 9, an asset and a liability both decrease an equal amount, retaining the equality of the balance sheet equation.

Revenue and Expense Transactions

Revenue and expense transactions deserve special attention because their relationship with the balance sheet equation is less obvious. Recall that the stockholders' equity section of the balance sheet equation includes both Paid-in Capital and Retained Earnings:

$$\text{Assets} = \text{Liabilities} + \text{Stockholders' equity}$$

$$\text{Assets} = \text{Liabilities} + (\text{Paid-in capital} + \text{Retained earnings})$$

Also, recall from Chapter 2 that, if we ignore dividends, retained earnings is merely accumulated revenue less accumulated expenses. Therefore, we can group the T-accounts as follows:

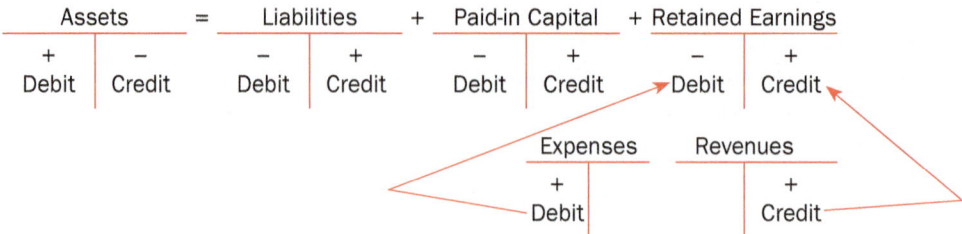

Revenues and expenses are part of retained earnings. You can think of them as separate compartments within the larger Retained Earnings account. Why don't we simply increase or decrease the Retained Earnings account directly, eliminating the need for separate Revenue and Expense accounts? To do so would make it more difficult to prepare an income statement because revenue and expense items would be mixed together in the Retained Earnings account. By accumulating information separately for categories of revenue and expense, we simplify the preparation of an income statement.

A revenue account accumulates items that increase retained earnings. Any credit to revenue is effectively a credit to retained earnings. Therefore, when we record Sales Revenue, we increase both revenues and retained earnings. Similarly, an expense account accumulates items that decrease retained earnings. A debit to expense is effectively a debit to retained earnings. Although a debit entry increases expenses, it results in a decrease in retained earnings. Thus, when we record Wage Expense, we increase expenses but decrease retained earnings. Revenue and expense accounts are fundamentally a part of stockholders' equity.

We can now examine a few transactions involving revenues and expenses. Consider Biwheels' transactions 10a and 10b:

10a. Transaction:	Sales on credit, $160,000.		
Analysis:	The asset **Accounts Receivable** increases.		
	Stockholders' equity, specifically **Retained Earnings**, increases because a revenue account, **Sales Revenue**, increases.		
Journal Entry:	Accounts receivable.	160,000	
	Sales revenue		160,000
Posting:			

Accounts Receivable		Sales Revenue	
(10a) (160,000)		(10a)	(160,000)

A credit, or right-side, entry in transaction 10a increases the Sales Revenue account, increasing the stockholders' equity account, Retained Earnings. In transaction 10b, a debit, or left-side, entry increases the expense account, Cost of Goods Sold. The effect is to decrease the stockholders' equity account, Retained Earnings.

10b. Transaction:	Cost of merchandise inventory sold, $100,000.		
Analysis:	The asset **Merchandise Inventory** decreases.		
	Stockholders' equity, specifically **Retained Earnings**, decreases because an expense account, **Cost of Goods Sold**, increases.		
Journal Entry:	Cost of goods sold	100,000	
	Merchandise inventory		100,000
Posting:			

Merchandise Inventory			Cost of Goods Sold	
(4)	120,000	(8) 800	(10b) (100,000)	
(5)	10,000	(10b) (100,000)		
(6)	30,000			

Before we continue, let's look for a minute at the logic illustrated by transactions 10a and 10b. These transactions illustrate the relationship of revenue and expense to retained earnings. Revenues increase Retained Earnings, a stockholders' equity account, because the revenue accounts and the stockholders' equity accounts are right-side balance accounts. Expenses decrease Retained Earnings because expenses are left-side balance accounts. They reduce the normal right-side balance of Retained Earnings. Therefore, increases in expenses are decreases in Retained Earnings and thereby in stockholders' equity. The following analysis shows that we could record the $160,000 in Sales Revenue and $100,000 in Cost of Goods Sold expense directly to the Retained Earnings account or first in separate revenue and expense accounts that are part of Retained Earnings. The latter alternative captures the most information and is the preferred approach.

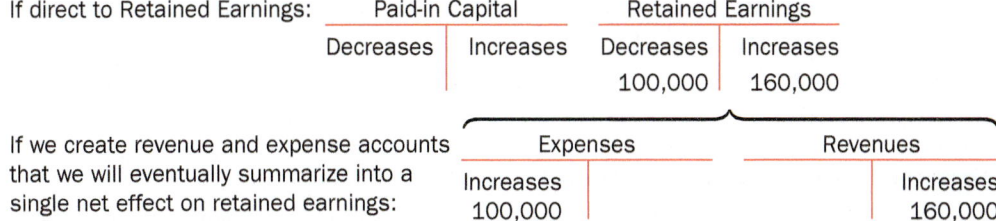

Exhibit 3-3 presents the rules of debit and credit and the normal balances of the accounts discussed in this section. It demonstrates the basic principles of the balance sheet equation and the double-entry accounting system:

$$\text{Left side} = \text{Right side}$$
$$\text{Debit} = \text{Credit}$$

The exhibit also emphasizes that revenues increase stockholders' equity. Therefore, we record them as credits. In contrast, expenses decrease stockholders' equity, and we record them as debits. Keeping separate accounts for revenues and expenses makes it easier to prepare an income statement. Revenues and expenses comprise the data used to calculate net income (or net loss) on the income statement, thereby providing a detailed explanation of how the period's transactions caused the balance sheet account, Retained Earnings, to change during the period.

EXHIBIT 3-3
Rules of Debit and Credit and Normal Balances of Accounts

Rules of Debit and Credit

Assets	=	Liabilities	+	Stockholders' Equity			
Assets	=	Liabilities	+	Paid-in Capital	+	Retained Earnings	

+	−	−	+	−	+	−	+
Increase	Decrease	Decrease	Increase	Decrease	Increase	Decrease	Increase
Debit	Credit	Debit	Credit	Debit	Credit	Debit	Credit
Left	Right	Left	Right	Left	Right	Left	Right
Normal Bal.			Normal Bal.		Normal Bal.		Normal Bal.

Expenses		Revenues	
+*	−	−	+
Increase	Decrease	Decrease	Increase
Debit	Credit	Debit	Credit
Left	Right	Left	Right
Normal Bal.			Normal Bal.

*Remember that increases in expenses decrease retained earnings.

Normal Balances

Assets	Debit
Liabilities	Credit
Stockholders' equity (overall)	Credit
Paid-in capital	Credit
Revenues	Credit
Expenses	Debit

Transaction 11 is the collection of some of the accounts receivable created by transaction 10a:

11. Transaction: Cash collected from debtors, $5,000.

Analysis: The asset **Cash** increases.

The asset **Accounts Receivable** decreases.

Journal Entry: Cash 5,000

Accounts receivable 5,000

Posting:

Cash				Accounts Receivable			
(1)	400,000	(3)	15,000	(10a)	160,000	(11)	(5,000)
(2)	100,000	(4)	120,000				
(7)	1,000	(6)	10,000				
(11)	(5,000)	(9)	4,000				

Prepaid Expenses and Depreciation Transactions

Recall from Chapter 2 that prepaid expenses, such as prepaid rent and depreciation expense, relate to assets having a useful life that will expire in the future. Biwheels' transactions 12, 13, and 14 demonstrate the journalizing and posting of prepaid rent expenses and depreciation of store equipment.

12. Transaction: Paid rent for 3 months in advance, $6,000.

Analysis: The asset **Cash** decreases.

The asset **Prepaid Rent** increases.

Journal Entry: Prepaid rent 6,000

Cash 6,000

Posting:

Cash				Prepaid Rent			
(1)	400,000	(3)	15,000	(12)	(6,000)		
(2)	100,000	(4)	120,000				
(7)	1,000	(6)	10,000				
(11)	5,000	(9)	4,000				
		(12)	(6,000)				

Transaction 12 represents the prepayment of rent as the acquisition of an asset. It affects only asset accounts—Cash decreases (a credit) and Prepaid Rent increases (a debit). Transaction 13 represents the subsequent expiration of one-third of the asset as an expense.

13. Transaction: Recognized expiration of rental services, $2,000.

Analysis: The asset **Prepaid Rent** decreases.

Stockholders' Equity, specifically **Retained Earnings** decreases because an expense account, **Rent Expense**, increases.

Journal Entry: Rent expense 2,000

Prepaid rent 2,000

Posting:

Prepaid Rent				Rent Expense			
(12)	6,000	(13)	(2,000)	(13)	(2,000)		

Be sure you understand that, in transaction 13, the effect of the $2,000 increase in Rent Expense is a decrease in retained earnings on the balance sheet.

14. Transaction: Recognized depreciation, $100.

Analysis: The asset-reduction account **Accumulated Depreciation, Store Equipment** increases.

Stockholders' equity, specifically **Retained Earnings**, decreases because the expense account, **Depreciation Expense**, increases.

Journal Entry: Depreciation expense 100

Accumulated depreciation,   100
store equipment....................................

Posting:

Accumulated Depreciation, Store Equipment		Depreciation Expense	
(14)	(100)	(14)	(100)

In transaction 14, we open a new account, Accumulated Depreciation, Store Equipment. As the name implies, **accumulated depreciation** (sometimes called **allowance for depreciation**) is the cumulative sum of all depreciation recognized since the date of acquisition of an asset. It is a **contra account**—a separate but related account that offsets or is a deduction from a companion account. A contra account has two distinguishing features: (1) It always has a companion account, and (2) it has a balance on the opposite side from the companion account. In our illustration, accumulated depreciation is a **contra asset** account because its companion account is an asset. We deduct the balance in the contra asset from the related asset account. Although the normal balance of the asset account is a debit, the normal balance of accumulated depreciation is a credit. The asset and contra asset accounts on January 31, 20X2, are as follows:

Asset:	Store equipment	$14,000
Contra asset:	Accumulated depreciation, store equipment	(100)
Net asset:	Book value	$13,900

The **book value**, also called **net book value**, **carrying amount**, or **carrying value**, is the balance of an account minus the balance of any associated contra accounts. In our example, the book value of Store Equipment is $13,900, the original acquisition cost ($14,000) less the contra account for accumulated depreciation ($100).

A Note on Accumulated Depreciation

Why do published annual reports routinely provide information on both the original cost of assets and the accumulated depreciation? For Biwheels, why don't we reduce Store Equipment directly by $100? Conceptually, we could. However, accountants have traditionally preserved the asset's original cost in the asset account throughout its useful life. They can then readily refer to that account to learn the asset's initial cost. Reports to management, government regulators, and tax authorities sometimes require such information. Moreover, the original $14,000 cost is the height of accuracy—it is a reliable, objective number. In contrast, the balance in Accumulated Depreciation is an estimate, the result of a calculation, the accuracy of which depends heavily on the accountant's less reliable prediction of an asset's useful life. Recall that we calculated the monthly depreciation of $100 by dividing the $14,000 cost by an assumed useful life of 140 months. We do not *know* how long an asset will be useful. In calculating depreciation, we make estimates that are imperfect, but there is no better way to allocate the cost of the equipment over the periods that it benefits.

Investors also find it useful to know the assets' original costs. They can estimate the age of the assets by dividing the balance in Accumulated Depreciation by the original cost of the assets. For example, recently **Delta Air Lines** had accumulated depreciation of $4,820 million on property and equipment of $25,135 million, making its property and equipment about 19% depreciated. Five years ago Delta's assets were 41% depreciated, so Delta has been replacing assets faster than it has been depreciating them. We can compare this with **American Airlines**, which has accumulated depreciation of $10,400 million on an original cost of $22,628 million. Therefore, its assets are ($10,400 ÷ $22,628) = 46% depreciated.

---

accumulated depreciation (allowance for depreciation)
The cumulative sum of all depreciation recognized since the date of acquisition of an asset.

contra account
A separate but related account that offsets or is a deduction from a companion account. An example is accumulated depreciation.

contra asset
A contra account whose companion account is an asset. A contra asset account has a credit balance. We deduct the balance in the contra asset from an asset account.

book value (net book value, carrying amount, carrying value)
The balance of an account shown on the books minus the value of any associated contra accounts. For example, the book value of equipment is its acquisition cost minus accumulated depreciation.

Summary Problem for Your Review

PROBLEM

An annual report of Kobe Steel, Ltd., one of the world's largest producers of iron and steel, showed the following (Japanese yen in billions):

Plant and equipment, at cost	¥2,987
Accumulated depreciation	2,019

1. Open T-accounts for (a) Plant and Equipment, at cost, (b) Accumulated Depreciation, and (c) Depreciation Expense. Enter the balances in the Plant and Equipment and Accumulated Depreciation T-accounts.
2. Assume that during the ensuing year Kobe Steel purchased additional plant and equipment for cash of ¥97 billion and incurred depreciation expense of ¥115 billion. Prepare the journal entries, and post to the T-accounts opened in question 1.
3. Show how Kobe Steel would present its plant and equipment accounts in its balance sheet after the journal entries in requirement 2.

SOLUTION

1 & 2. Amounts are in billions of Japanese yen.

Plant and Equipment, at Cost

Bal.	2,987	
(a)	97	
Bal.	3,084	

Accumulated Depreciation

	Bal.	2,019
	(b)	115
	Bal.	2,134

Depreciation Expense

(b)	115	

a. Plant and equipment, at cost		97	
Cash			97
b. Depreciation expense		115	
Accumulated depreciation			115

3. The plant and equipment section would appear as follows:

Plant and equipment, at cost	¥3,084
Less: Accumulated depreciation	2,134
Plant and equipment, net	¥ 950

Biwheels' Transactions in the Journal and Ledger

Exhibit 3-4 shows the journal entries for Biwheels' transactions 4 through 14 as analyzed in the previous section and as listed in the general journal. The posting reference (Post Ref.) column uses the account numbers from the Biwheels chart of accounts on page 97. These account numbers also appear on each account in the Biwheels general ledger. Exhibit 3-5 shows the Biwheels general ledger in T-account form.

EXHIBIT 3-4

Biwheels Company

General Journal

Date	Entry No.	Accounts and Explanation	Post Ref.	Debit	Credit
20X2	4	Merchandise inventory Cash Acquired inventory for cash	130 100	120,000	 120,000
	5	Merchandise inventory Accounts payable Acquired inventory on credit	130 203	10,000	 10,000
	6	Merchandise inventory Cash Accounts payable Acquired merchandise inventory for cash plus credit (This is an example of a *compound journal entry* whereby more than two accounts are affected by the same transaction)	130 100 203	30,000	 10,000 20,000
	7	Cash Store equipment Sold store equipment to business neighbor	100 170	1,000	 1,000
	8	Accounts payable Merchandise inventory Returned some inventory to supplier	203 130	800	 800
	9	Accounts payable Cash Payments to creditors	203 100	4,000	 4,000
	10a	Accounts receivable Sales revenue Sales to customers on credit	120 500	160,000	 160,000
	10b	Cost of goods sold Merchandise inventory To record the cost of inventory sold	600 130	100,000	 100,000
	11	Cash Accounts receivable Collections from debtors	100 120	5,000	 5,000
	12	Prepaid rent Cash Payment of rent in advance	140 100	6,000	 6,000
	13	Rent expense Prepaid rent Recognize expiration of rental service	601 140	2,000	 2,000
	14	Depreciation expense Accumulated depreciation, store equipment Recognize depreciation for January	602 170A	100	 100

Pause and trace each of the following journal entries to its posting in the ledger in Exhibit 3-5. Recall that the first three journal entries are in Exhibit 3-1 on page 98; the rest of them are in Exhibit 3-4.

1. Initial investment
2. Loan from bank
3. Acquired store equipment for cash
4. Acquired merchandise inventory for cash
5. Acquired merchandise inventory for credit
6. Acquired merchandise inventory for cash plus credit

EXHIBIT 3-5

Biwheels Company
General Ledger

Assets	=	Liabilities + Stockholders' Equity
(Increases on left, decreases on right)		(Decreases on left, increases on right)

Cash — Account No. 100

(1)	400,000	(3)	15,000
(2)	100,000	(4)	120,000
(7)	1,000	(6)	10,000
(11)	5,000	(9)	4,000
		(12)	6,000
1/31 Bal.	351,000		

Accounts Receivable — 120

(10a)	160,000	(11)	5,000
1/31 Bal.	155,000		

Merchandise Inventory — 130

(4)	120,000	(8)	800
(5)	10,000	(10b)	100,000
(6)	30,000		
1/31 Bal.	59,200		

Prepaid Rent — 140

(12)	6,000	(13)	2,000
1/31 Bal.	4,000		

Store Equipment — 170

(3)	15,000	(7)	1,000
1/31 Bal.	14,000		

Accumulated Depreciation, Store Equipment — 170A

		(14)	100

Note Payable — 202

		(2)	100,000

Accounts Payable — 203

(8)	800	(5)	10,000
(9)	4,000	(6)	20,000
		1/31 Bal.	25,200

Paid-in Capital — 300

		(1)	400,000

Retained Earnings — 400

		1/31 Bal.	57,900*

Expense and Revenue Accounts

Sales Revenues — 500

		(10a)	160,000

Cost of Goods Sold — 600

(10b)	100,000		

Rent Expense — 601

(13)	2,000		

Depreciation Expense — 602

(14)	100		

Note: An ending balance is shown on the side of the account with the larger total.

*The details of the revenue and expense accounts appear in the income statement. Their net effect is then transferred to a single account, Retained Earnings, in the balance sheet. In this case, ($160,000 − $100,000 − $2,000 − $100) = $57,900.

 7. Sold store equipment for cash
 8. Returned merchandise inventory for credit
 9. Paid cash to creditor
10a. Sales on credit
10b. Cost of merchandise inventory sold
 11. Collected cash from debtors
 12. Paid rent in advance
 13. Recognized expiration of rental services
 14. Recognized depreciation

As you trace these items, ask yourself why they appear on the left or right side of each account. You might find it useful to state the relationships explicitly as follows: "The initial investment was a debit to Cash and a credit to Paid-in Capital. The posting shows an entry on the left-hand side of the Cash account, which increases the balance in this asset account. It also shows a right-hand side entry to the Paid-in Capital account, which increases the balance in this stockholders' equity account."

Accountants may update the ledger account balances from time to time as desired. We will use double horizontal lines, as in Exhibit 3-5, to signify that we have updated these accounts. A single number labeled "balance" (or Bal.) immediately below the double lines summarizes all postings above the double lines. We use this balance as a starting point for computing the next updated balance.

The accounts in Exhibit 3-5 that contain only one number do not have a double line. Why? If there is only one number in a given account, this number automatically serves as the ending balance. For example, the Note Payable entry of $100,000 also serves as the ending balance for the account.

Preparing the Trial Balance

After posting journal entries to the ledger, accountants prepare a trial balance (see step 4 on p. 96). Recall that a trial balance is a list of all accounts with their respective balances. Accountants prepare it as a test or check—a trial, as the name says—before proceeding further. Thus, the purpose of the trial balance is twofold: (1) to help check on the accuracy of postings by proving whether the total debits equal the total credits, and (2) to establish a convenient summary of the balances in all accounts for the preparation of financial statements.

We can prepare a trial balance at any time the account balances are up-to-date. For example, we might prepare a trial balance for Biwheels on January 3, 20X2, after the company's first three transactions:

> ▶▶ **OBJECTIVE 4**
> Prepare and use a trial balance.

Biwheels Company

Trial Balance, January 3, 20X2, for the Period January 2–3, 20X2

Account Number	Account Title	Debit	Credit
		Balance	
100	Cash	$485,000	
170	Store equipment	15,000	
202	Note payable		$100,000
300	Paid-in capital		400,000
	Total	$500,000	$500,000

The more accounts a company has, the more detailed the trial balance becomes and the more essential it is for checking the clerical accuracy of the ledger postings. Although the trial balance assures the accountant that the debits and credits are equal, errors can still exist. For example, an accountant may misread a $10,000 cash receipt on account as a $1,000 receipt and record the erroneous amount in both the Cash and Accounts Receivable accounts. Both Cash and Accounts Receivable would be in error by offsetting amounts. The balance in Cash would be understated by $9,000 and the balance in Accounts Receivable would be overstated by $9,000. Or the accountant might record a $10,000 cash receipt on account as a credit to Sales Revenue instead of a credit reducing Accounts Receivable. Sales Revenue and Accounts Receivable would both be overstated by $10,000. Nevertheless, the trial balance would still show total debits equal to total credits.

EXHIBIT 3-6

Biwheels Company

*Trial Balance, January 31,
20X2, for the Period January 1
to January 31, 20X2*

	Debits	Credits
Cash	$ 351,000	
Accounts receivable	155,000	
Merchandise inventory	59,200	
Prepaid rent	4,000	
Store equipment	14,000	
Accumulated depreciation, store equipment		$ 100
Note payable		100,000
Accounts payable		25,200
Paid-in capital		400,000
Retained earnings		0*
Sales revenue		160,000
Cost of goods sold	100,000	
Rent expense	2,000	
Depreciation expense	100	
Total	$685,300	$685,300

*If a Retained Earnings balance existed at the start of the accounting period, it would appear here.
However, in our example, Retained Earnings was zero at the start of the period.

Exhibit 3-6 presents the trial balance based on the general ledger shown in Exhibit 3-5. Accountants normally prepare the trial balance with the balance sheet accounts listed first, assets, then liabilities, and then stockholders' equity, followed by the income statement accounts, revenues and expenses. Note that the Retained Earnings account listed in Exhibit 3-6, has no balance because it was zero at the beginning of the period in our example. All balance sheet accounts except Retained Earnings show their balances as of the date the trial balance is prepared. Retained Earnings shows the balance at the *beginning* of the period. Why? Because we have recorded the changes in Retained Earnings for the current period in separate revenue and expense accounts rather than directly into Retained Earnings, so Retained Earnings remains at its beginning balance. When accountants prepare formal balance sheets, they reduce the revenue and expense accounts to zero and add their net effect to the beginning balance in the Retained Earnings account to arrive at the correct ending balance in Retained Earnings.

Closing the Books and Deriving Financial Statements from the Trial Balance

OBJECTIVE 5

Close revenue and expense accounts and update retained earnings.

The trial balance is the springboard for the last step of the process, closing the books and preparing the balance sheet and the income statement, as shown in Exhibit 3-7. To **close the books** we transfer the balances in all revenue and expense accounts to Retained Earnings, which resets the revenue and expense accounts to zero so that they are ready to record the next period's transactions. Note that the balance in the Retained Earnings account in the balance sheet in Exhibit 3-7 is $57,900, although the amount of retained earnings in the trial balance is $0. Why? Because, after closing the books, the January 31 balance sheet shows the ending balance in Retained Earnings—the beginning balance of zero plus net income during the period. In future periods when we prepare a trial balance, the beginning balance will be the ending balance of the previous period. The beginning balance as of February 1 will be $57,900.

Let's examine the process of closing the books. Accountants make **closing entries** to transfer balances in the "temporary" stockholders' equity accounts (revenue and expense accounts) to the "permanent" stockholders' equity account, Retained Earnings. They may do this in two steps. First they transfer the amounts in each revenue and expense account to an Income Summary account, which becomes the basis for preparing the income statement. In the second step they transfer the amount in the Income Summary account to the permanent Retained Earnings account. Alternatively, accountants may transfer the revenue and expense accounts directly into the Retained Earnings account, bypassing the need for an Income Summary account. As a

close the books

To transfer the balances in all revenue and expense accounts to retained earnings, which resets the revenue and expense accounts to zero so that they are ready to record the next period's transactions.

closing entries

Journal entries that transfer balances in the "temporary" stockholders' equity accounts (revenue and expense accounts) to the "permanent" stockholders' equity account, Retained Earnings.

EXHIBIT 3-7

Biwheels Company

Trial Balance, Balance Sheet, and Income Statement

Biwheels Company
Trial Balance,
January 31, 20X2

	Debits	Credits
Cash	$351,000	
Accounts receivable	155,000	
Merchandise inventory	59,200	
Prepaid rent	4,000	
Store equipment	14,000	
Accumulated depreciation, store equipment		$ 100
Note payable		100,000
Accounts payable		25,200
Paid-in capital		400,000
Retained earnings		0*
Sales revenue		160,000
Cost of goods sold	100,000	
Rent expense	2,000	
Depreciation expense	100	
Total	$685,300	$685,300

*If there were a beginning balance in Retained Earnings, this balance would be added to the $57,900 from the income statement to compute Retained Earnings on the balance sheet.

Biwheels Company
Balance Sheet,
January 31, 20X2

Assets		
Cash		$351,000
Accounts receivable		155,000
Merchandise inventory		59,200
Prepaid rent		4,000
Store equipment	14,000	
Less: Accumulated depreciation	100	13,900
Total assets		$583,100

Liabilities and Stockholders' Equity		
Liabilities		
Note payable	$100,000	
Accounts payable	25,200	
Total liabilities		$125,200
Stockholders' equity		
Paid-in capital	$400,000	
Retained earnings	57,900	
Total stockholders' equity		457,900
Total liabilities and stockholders' equity		$583,100

Biwheels Company
Income Statement, for the Month Ended January 31, 20X2

Sales revenue		$160,000
Deduct expenses		
Cost of goods sold	$100,000	
Rent	2,000	
Depreciation	100	
Total expenses		102,100
Net income		$ 57,900

EXHIBIT 3-8

Biwheels Company

Closing the Accounts—Data are from Exhibit 3-7

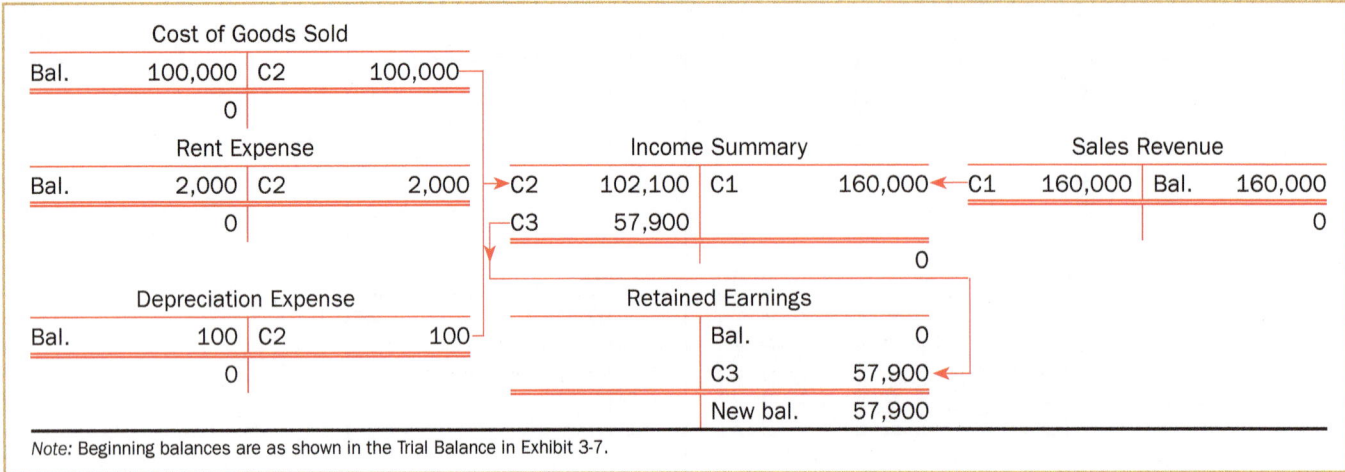

Note: Beginning balances are as shown in the Trial Balance in Exhibit 3-7.

student new to accounting, we recommend the use of the two-step approach to the closing process, which we demonstrate in Exhibit 3-8.

The process closes the revenue accounts in entry C1 and closes the expense accounts in entry C2, transferring the amounts in revenue and expense accounts to the Income Summary account. Then, as a final step, entry C3 transfers the total net income for the period from the Income Summary to Retained Earnings. Notice that we opened a new temporary account called Income Summary. We use it only momentarily to keep track of the process. You will never see an Income Summary account listed on a financial statement. We transfer the revenue and expense amounts into Income Summary and then immediately transfer the balance to Retained Earnings. Slight variations on this process occur in different companies, but the end result is always the same—revenue and expense account balances are reset to zero and the net income generated during the period increases retained earnings.

The following analysis gives the journal entries for the closing entries shown in Exhibit 3-8:

C1. Transaction:	Clerical procedure of transferring the ending balances of revenue accounts to the Income Summary account.	
Analysis:	The stockholders' equity account **Sales Revenue** decreases to zero.	
	The stockholders' equity account **Income Summary** increases.	
Journal Entry:	Sales revenue..................... 160,000	
	Income summary...............	160,000
C2. Transaction:	Clerical procedure of transferring the ending balances of expense accounts to the Income Summary account.	
Analysis:	The negative stockholders' equity (expense) accounts **Cost of Goods Sold**, **Rent Expense**, and **Depreciation Expense** decrease to zero.	
	The stockholders' equity account **Income Summary** decreases.	
Journal Entry:	Income summary.................... 102,100	
	Cost of goods sold..............	100,000
	Rent expense	2,000
	Depreciation expense	100
C3. Transaction:	Clerical procedure of transferring the ending balance of Income Summary account to the Retained Earnings account.	
Analysis:	The stockholders' equity account **Income Summary** decreases to zero.	
	The stockholders' equity account **Retained Earnings** increases.	
Journal Entry:	Income summary.................. 57,900	
	Retained earnings	57,900

Summary Problem for Your Review

PROBLEM

The balance sheet of Hassan Used Auto Company, on March 31, 20X1, follows:

Assets		Liabilities and Owner's Equity	
Cash	$ 10,000	Accounts payable	$ 3,000
Accounts receivable	20,000	Notes payable	70,000
Automobile inventory	100,000	Hassan, capital	57,000
Total assets	$130,000	Total liabilities and owner's equity	$130,000

The Hassan business is a proprietorship, thus the owner's equity account used here is Hassan, Capital.

Hassan rented operating space and equipment on a month-to-month basis. During April, the business had the following summarized transactions:

a. Invested an additional $20,000 cash in the business
b. Collected $10,000 on accounts receivable
c. Paid $2,000 on accounts payable
d. Sold autos for $120,000 cash
e. Cost of autos sold was $70,000
f. Replenished inventory for $60,000 cash
g. Paid rent expense in cash, $14,000
h. Paid utilities in cash, $1,000
i. Paid selling expense in cash, $30,000
j. Paid interest expense in cash, $1,000

Required

1. Open the following T-accounts in the general ledger: Cash; Accounts Receivable; Automobile Inventory; Accounts Payable; Notes Payable; Hassan, Capital; Sales; Cost of Goods Sold; Rent Expense; Utilities Expense; Selling Expense; and Interest Expense. Enter the March 31 balances in the appropriate accounts.
2. Journalize transactions a through j and post the entries to the ledger. Identify entries by transaction letter.
3. Prepare the trial balance at April 30, 20X1.
4. Prepare an income statement for April. Ignore income taxes.
5. Give the closing entries.

SOLUTION

The solutions to requirements 1 through 5 are in Exhibits 3-9 through 3-12. Exhibit 3-9 shows the journal entries. Exhibit 3-10 includes the appropriate opening balances and shows the posting of all transactions to the general ledger. Exhibit 3-11 presents the trial balance and the income statement. The closing entries appear in Exhibit 3-12.

EXHIBIT 3-9

Hassan Used Auto Company

General Journal

ENTRY	ACCOUNTS AND EXPLANATION	POST REF.*	DEBIT	CREDIT
a.	Cash	✓	20,000	
	Hassan, capital	✓		20,000
	Investment in business by Hassan			
b.	Cash	✓	10,000	
	Accounts receivable................	✓		10,000
	Collected cash on accounts			
c.	Accounts payable	✓	2,000	
	Cash.............................	✓		2,000
	Disbursed cash on accounts owed to others			
d.	Cash	✓	120,000	
	Sales Revenue	✓		120,000
	Sales for cash			
e.	Cost of goods sold	✓	70,000	
	Automobile inventory	✓		70,000
	Cost of inventory that was sold to customers			
f.	Automobile inventory..................	✓	60,000	
	Cash.............................	✓		60,000
	Replenished inventory			
g.	Rent expense	✓	14,000	
	Cash.............................	✓		14,000
	Paid April rent			
h.	Utilities expense	✓	1,000	
	Cash.............................	✓		1,000
	Paid April utilities			
i.	Selling expense.......................	✓	30,000	
	Cash.............................	✓		30,000
	Paid April selling expenses			
j.	Interest expense......................	✓	1,000	
	Cash.............................	✓		1,000
	Paid April interest expense			

*Ordinarily, account numbers are used to denote specific posting references. Otherwise, check marks are used to indicate that the entry has been posted to the general ledger.

EXHIBIT 3-10

Hassan Used Auto Company

General Ledger

	Cash					Accounts Payable		
Bal.*	10,000	(c)	2,000		(c)	2,000	Bal.*	3,000
(a)	20,000	(f)	60,000				Bal.	1,000
(b)	10,000	(g)	14,000					
(d)	120,000	(h)	1,000			Notes Payable		
		(i)	30,000				Bal.*	70,000
		(j)	1,000					
			108,000†			Cost of Goods Sold		
Bal.	52,000				(e)	70,000		

	Accounts Receivable					Selling Expense		
Bal.*	20,000	(b)	10,000		(i)	30,000		
Bal.	10,000							

	Automobile Inventory					Utilities Expense		
Bal.*	100,000	(e)	70,000		(h)	1,000		
(f)	60,000							
Bal.	90,000							

	Hassan, Capital		
		Bal.*	57,000
		(a)	20,000
		Bal.	77,000

	Sales Revenue		
		(d)	120,000

	Rent Expense	
(g)	14,000	

	Interest Expense	
(j)	1,000	

*Balances denoted with an asterisk are as of March 31; balances without asterisks are as of April 30. A lone number in any account also serves as an ending balance.

†Subtotals are included in the Cash account. They are not an essential part of T-accounts. However, when an account contains many postings, subtotals ease the checking of arithmetic.

EXHIBIT 3-11

Hassan Used Auto Company

Trial Balance and Income Statement, for the Month Ended April 30, 20X1

Account Title	Balance		Hassan Used Auto Company		
	Debit	Credit	*Income Statement, for the Month Ended April 30, 20X1*		
Cash	$ 52,000		Sales		$120,000
Accounts receivable	10,000		Deduct expenses		
Automobile inventory	90,000		Cost of goods sold	$70,000	
Accounts payable		$ 1,000	Rent expense	14,000	
Notes payable		70,000	Utilities expense	1,000	
Hassan, capital		77,000*	Selling expense	30,000	
Sales revenue		120,000	Interest expense	1,000	116,000
Cost of goods sold	70,000		Net income		$ 4,000
Rent expense	14,000				
Utilities expense	1,000				
Selling expense	30,000				
Interest expense	1,000				
Total	$268,000	$268,000			

*Beginning balance of $57,000 plus additional investment of $20,000.

EXHIBIT 3-12

Hassan Used Auto Company

Closing Entries

C1.	Sales Revenue..	120,000	
	Income summary...............................		120,000
C2.	Income summary.......................................	116,000	
	Cost of goods sold............................		70,000
	Selling expense		30,000
	Utilities expense...............................		1,000
	Rent expense		14,000
	Interest expense...............................		1,000
C3.	Income summary.......................................	4,000	
	Retained earnings............................		4,000

▶▶ **OBJECTIVE 6**

Correct erroneous journal entries and describe how errors affect accounts.

correcting entry

A journal entry that cancels a previous erroneous entry and adds the correct amounts to the correct accounts.

Effects of Errors

Now that we have completed all steps of the recording process, let's consider what happens when journal entries have errors. Suppose a journal entry contains an error. How do we correct it? If we discover the error immediately, we can rewrite the entry or reenter the correct data. However, if we detect the error after posting to ledger accounts, we must make a **correcting entry**. Correcting entries cancel a previous erroneous entry and add the correct amounts to the correct accounts. We record the correcting entry in the general journal and post it to the general ledger exactly as we would a regular entry. However, the end result is that we have corrected the balances in the accounts to what they should have been originally. Because we use the balances to prepare the financial statements, they must be correct.

Consider the following examples:

1. A company erroneously debited a $500 repair expense to the Equipment account on December 27. We discover the error on December 31:

CORRECT ENTRY	12/27	Repair expense	500	
		Cash.................................		500
ERRONEOUS ENTRY	12/27	Equipment	500	
		Cash.................................		500
CORRECTING ENTRY	12/31	Repair expense	500	
		Equipment..........................		500

The correcting entry shows a credit to Equipment to cancel or offset the erroneous debit to Equipment. It also debits Repair Expense, recognizing the amount that should have been recorded on December 27. Notice that the credit to Cash was correct, and therefore we did not change it.

2. A $3,000 collection on account was erroneously credited to Sales Revenue on November 2. We discover the error on November 28:

CORRECT ENTRY	11/2	Cash	3,000	
		Accounts receivable		3,000
ERRONEOUS ENTRY	11/2	Cash	3,000	
		Sales revenue		3,000
CORRECTING ENTRY	11/28	Sales revenue	3,000	
		Accounts receivable		3,000

The debit to Sales Revenue in the correcting entry offsets the incorrect credit to Sales Revenue. The credit to Accounts Receivable in the correcting entry recognizes the collected amount where it belongs, as a decrease in Accounts Receivable. Essentially, the correcting entry moves the $3,000 credit from the Sales Revenue account to the Accounts Receivable account. The debit to Cash in the original entry is correct, and thus we do not change it.

INTERPRETING FINANCIAL STATEMENTS

Suppose that on May 27, 20X0, a manager reported to the accounting department a purchase of equipment for $10,000 cash. The accountant recorded this transaction in the company's books. Subsequent review of the transaction revealed that the manager had been in error and that the $10,000 was for supplies that his department used up during May. Prepare a correcting entry. Would this situation raise any potential ethical issues? Explain.

Answer

| CORRECTING ENTRY | Supplies expense | 10,000 | |
| | Equipment | | 10,000 |

If it had gone undetected, the "error" would have kept the $10,000 expense from reducing income. This overstatement of income might have had a benefit for the manager, perhaps helping him meet a profit target needed for a bonus. The accountant would have an ethical obligation to investigate this transaction to make sure it was truly an error and not an attempt to manipulate income.

Temporary Errors

Undetected errors can affect a variety of accounts, including revenues and expenses for a given accounting period. Some errors are automatically corrected in the ordinary bookkeeping process in the next period. Such errors misstate net income in both periods, which could mislead users of the financial statements. However, by the end of the second period the errors cancel each other out, and they affect the balance sheet of only the first period, not the second.

Consider a payment of $1,000 made in December 20X1 to cover rent for the month of January 20X2. Instead of recording it as Prepaid Rent, the accountant listed the payment as Rent Expense in December:

INCORRECT ENTRY	12/X1	Rent expense...............................	1,000	
		Cash.......................................		1,000
		One month's rent		
CORRECT ENTRIES	12/X1	Prepaid rent................................	1,000	
		Cash.......................................		1,000
		Payment for January 20X2's rent		
	1/X2	Rent expense..............................	1,000	
		Prepaid rent		1,000
		Expiration of January 20X2's rent		

The effects of this recording error are (1) to overstate 20X1's rent expense (which understates pretax income and retained earnings) by $1,000 and understate 20X1's year-end assets by $1,000 (because the prepayment would not be listed as an asset), and (2) to understate 20X2's rent expense (which overstates pretax income) by $1,000. These errors have no effect on 20X2's ending assets or retained earnings balances. Why? Because, regardless of whether the accountant made the incorrect entry shown above or the correct entries shown above, by the end of January 20X2 the only asset effect is a $1,000 decrease in Cash. With regard to the balance in retained earnings, the total of the pretax incomes for the 2 years is the same with or without the error. The first year's understatement of pretax income by $1,000 offsets the second year's overstatement of $1,000. The retained earnings balance at the end of the second year is thus correct on a pretax basis.

Errors that Persist

Errors that do not automatically correct themselves will keep subsequent balance sheets in error until an accountant makes specific correcting entries. For example, overlooking a depreciation expense of $2,000 in 20X0 would (1) overstate pretax income, assets, and retained earnings by $2,000 in 20X0, and (2) continue to overstate assets and retained earnings on successive balance sheets for the life of the fixed asset. However, observe that the error would not affect pretax income for years after 20X0 unless accountants commit the same error again.

Incomplete Records

A company's accounting records are not always perfect. Someone may steal, lose, or destroy records, forcing accountants to make journal and ledger entries and create financial statements with incomplete information. Luckily, T-accounts can help accountants discover unknown amounts. For example, suppose the proprietor of a local sports shop asks your help in calculating her sales for 20X1. She provides the following accurate but incomplete information:

List of customers who owe money	
December 31, 20X0	$ 4,000
December 31, 20X1	6,000
Cash receipts from customers during 20X1 appropriately credited to customer's accounts	280,000

She further tells you that all sales were on credit, not cash. How can you use T-accounts to solve for the missing credit sales figure? There are two basic steps to follow:

Step 1: Enter all known items into the relevant T-account. In this case, we are looking for credit sales, which accountants debit to Accounts Receivable. By substituting S for the unknown credit sales, we can construct the following T-account:

Accounts Receivable			
Bal. 12/31/X0	4,000	Collections	280,000
Credit sales	S		
Total debits	(4,000 + S)	Total credits	280,000
Bal. 12/31/X1	6,000		

Step 2: Solve for the unknown. Finding this solution is a simple algebraic exercise. We can use the debit and credit relationships we have just learned to solve our problem:

$$\text{Total debits} - \text{Total credits} = \text{Balance}$$
$$(4,000 + S) - 280,000 = 6,000$$
$$S = 6,000 + 280,000 - 4,000$$
$$S = 282,000$$

The analyses of missing data become more complicated if there are more entries in a particular account or if there is more than one unknown value. Nevertheless, the idea is to fill in the account with all known debits, credits, and balances, and then solve for the unknown.

Data Processing and Accounting Systems

Data processing is a general term referring to the procedures used to record, analyze, store, and report on chosen activities. An accounting system is a data processing system. Today most accounting systems are computerized. Software packages are available in many sizes and types. Small companies might use QuickBooks, Sage 50 Accounting, NetSuite, or Microsoft Small Business Manager. Many large companies build their accounting systems around larger enterprise resource planning (ERP) systems. Two of the largest ERP companies are the German company SAP and its American rival Oracle. These systems are based on the structure of journal entries and ledger accounts used in this book. They take the drudgery out of bookkeeping, but they have not fundamentally changed the way companies keep their accounting records. Whether you enter transactions data into a book or into a computer, the transactions data in general ledgers and general journals remain the same. The main advantage of a computerized accounting program is that the computer can automatically carry out steps such as general-ledger postings and financial statement preparation.

Computers affect more than the processing of data and preparation of reports. When you check out at a Walgreens drugstore or H&M clothing store, the cash register often does more than just record a sale. It may be linked to a computer that also records a decrease in inventory. It may activate an order to a supplier if the inventory level is low. If a sale is on credit, the computer may check your credit limit, update the company's accounts receivable, and eventually prepare your monthly billing statement. Most importantly, the computer can automatically enter every transaction into the journal as it occurs, thereby reducing the amount of source-document paperwork and potential data entry errors.

Automation has consistently decreased the cost of data processing. Consider American Express, a financial services company that has almost 88 million credit card holders and is the world's largest credit issuer as measured by purchase volume. American Express recently reported annual purchase volume of $620 billion! Given the magnitude of sales, American Express would receive millions of separate sales slips daily if its system were manual. However, computers record most credit sales by reading the magnetic strips on credit cards. Grocery stores and other retail establishments get most payments by swiping a customer's credit card through a scanner. Most gas stations have the card-reading equipment built into the gasoline pumps, even eliminating the need for sales clerks. Information about each credit sale is electronically submitted to a central computer, which prepares all billing documents and financial statements. Companies automatically record millions of transactions into their general journals without any paperwork or keyboard entry, producing huge savings in time and money while increasing accuracy.

Computers also reduce the time it takes to close the books and prepare financial statements. IBM announced its financial results for the year ended December 31, 2011, in a Webcast at 4:30 PM ET on January 19, 2012. It took less than 3 weeks for a company with nearly $100 billion in sales to finalize its results. Computer-based systems have also allowed the SEC to require large companies to file 10-K reports within 60 days after year-end rather than the 90 days required until this decade. The most recent advance in data processing for financial reporting is the use of **XBRL** (eXtensible Business Reporting Language), an XML-based computer language that allows easy comparisons across companies. We describe this in the Business First box on page 120.

> **▸▸OBJECTIVE 7**
> Explain how computers have transformed the processing of accounting data.

data processing
The procedures used to record, analyze, store, and report on chosen activities.

XBRL
eXtensible Business Reporting Language, an XML-based computer language that allows easy comparisons across companies.

BUSINESS FIRST

DATA PROCESSING USING XBRL

The Internet has created new opportunities for companies to report and exchange financial information. The first step was putting financial statements on the Web in PDF format. This conveyed the information quickly and easily, but it did not allow analysis of the data. Some companies then made the statements available in Excel format. This allowed analysis between years and between different statements for the same company, but it did not allow intercompany analyses. To address this issue, an original group of 12 organizations (including the AICPA, Deloitte & Touche LLP, Ernst & Young LLP, Great Plains Software, KPMG LLP, Microsoft Corporation, and PricewaterhouseCoopers LLP) formed XBRL International in August 1999 to create a common XML-based language for the reporting of business information. In just over 10 years XBRL has become widely used throughout the world. You can view the current status of XBRL on the Web at www.xbrl.org.

One reason for the growth in usage of XBRL (eXtensible Business Reporting Language) is the growing number of regulators, lenders, and other consumers of financial information demanding information in this format. Since 2011 the SEC has required all companies to submit their financial statements in XBRL format.

When creating an XBRL submission for the SEC, companies choose electronic data tags from the U.S. GAAP taxonomy, which is an electronic description and classification system for financial statements, disclosures, and other reports. This data tagging system provides a unique electronically readable tag for each individual disclosure item in financial statements, footnotes, and financial statement schedules. These electronic tags enable computers to read the financial information. The SEC makes the following comparison on their Web site: "XBRL allows computers to read financial information and use it in analytical tools, much like bar codes applied to merchandise are used for computerized inventory controls." Once data are coded in XBRL, different types of reports using various subsets of the data can be produced with minimal effort. To facilitate international application of XBRL, the IASB and XBRL International have also developed an XBRL taxonomy that models the primary financial statements that a commercial and industrial entity may use to report under IFRS.

What are the benefits of XBRL? Users can download an XBRL document using one of many available XBRL reader software products. These software products can generate reports suitable for the individual user's needs. A recent report issued by EDGAR Online discloses how accountants, institutional investors, and attorneys are using the data to analyze company financial statements. Of the survey respondents, 74% indicated that they are using the data to perform industry or market financial analysis, 51% for benchmarking competitors or comparable companies, 40% for analyzing equity investment decisions, and 30% for identifying or evaluating mergers, acquisitions, and partnerships.

Another argument for the push to XBRL was that it would not only help investors compare and contrast companies, but that it would improve internal company reporting. For example, a company using XBRL should be able to quickly, efficiently, and cheaply assemble and integrate data from divisions that use different accounting systems, create a variety of reports with minimal effort, and expedite tax and other regulatory filings. While all of this and more is possible with XBRL, some company CFOs question the benefit to the company. Mathew Watson, senior director, external reporting and corporate accountant at Best Buy noted: "The argument that reporting language can be leveraged internally? We don't think that's the case. We think our internal mechanisms work well. XBRL is just a compliance need. The internal use of XBRL is not even on our horizon."

Proponents of XBRL also claim that it can improve the quality of financial reporting by making monitoring of reporting easier. Prior to the XBRL requirement, the SEC was able to review only a small percentage of the filings made by publicly traded companies. If companies submit financial statements in XBRL format, the SEC can use analytic software to electronically screen nearly all filings. Intra-industry and cross-industry analyses may reveal anomalies that lead to further investigation of the financial reports. Can this eliminate fraudulent reporting? No, but it might more quickly and easily identify problems, making accountants and executives think twice before deciding to manipulate their financial numbers.

Sources: XBRL International Web site (www.xbrl.org); E. Z. Taylor, and A. C. Dzuranin, "Interactive Financial Reporting: An Introduction to eXtensible Business Reporting Language (XBRL)," *Issues in Accounting Education*, Vol. 25, No. 1, 2010, pp. 71–83; M. Cohn, "Acc'ts Mining XBRL Data," *Webcpa*, August 1, 2011; D. Rosenbaum, "XBRL: What's It Good For?" *CFO.com*, July 28, 2011; Securities and Exchange Commission, *Summary of XBRL Information for Phase 3 Filers* (modified May 10, 2011) on SEC Web site (www.sec.gov/spotlight/xbrl/xbrlsummaryinfophase3-051011.shtml); "IASC Foundation and XBRL PFS Taxonomy Release," International Accounting Standards Board Press Release, 27 November 2002; N. Hannon, "Accounting Scandals: Can XBRL Help?" *Strategic Finance*, August 2002, pp. 61–62.

Highlights to Remember

1 Use double-entry accounting. Double-entry accounting refers to the fact that every transaction affects at least two accounts. For example, we not only keep track of an increase in cash, but we also keep track of whether that increase arose from making a sale or borrowing money. To help us understand the double-entry accounting system, we use a simplified version of general ledger accounts called T-accounts. Accountants at all levels use T-accounts to help think through complex transactions. Accountants use the terms debit and credit repeatedly. Remember that debit means "left side" and credit means "right side."

2 Describe the five steps in the recording process. There are 5 steps in the process that leads to the preparation of financial statements: (1) create source documents, (2) record transactions in a general journal, (3) post journal entries to the general ledger, (4) prepare a trial balance, and (5) close the books and prepare financial statements.

3 Analyze and journalize transactions and post journal entries to the ledgers. The general journal provides a chronological record of transactions. For each transaction it includes the date and an identification number for the transaction, the accounts affected, the amounts of the debits and credits, the identifying number used to post each account to the general ledger, and an explanation of the transaction. After we initially record transactions as journal entries in the general journal, we post the elements of each transaction to the proper accounts in the general ledger. The general ledger accounts accumulate all the transactions affecting the account over time. We determine the balance in a specific general ledger account by adding all debits and all credits and subtracting the totals.

4 Prepare and use a trial balance. Trial balances are internal reports that list each account in the general ledger together with the balance in that account as of the trial balance date. Accountants use trial balances for detecting errors in the accounts and in preparing financial statements. Trial balances that fail to balance are the result of errors in journalizing or posting. The good news is that the out-of-balance condition lets you know that an error has been made.

5 Close revenue and expense accounts and update retained earnings. At the end of each accounting period, accountants "close" the temporary revenue and expense accounts. This involves resetting them to zero by transferring their balances for the period into an Income Summary account, which we in turn transfer to the Retained Earnings account.

6 Correct erroneous journal entries and describe how errors affect accounts. Despite precautions, errors sometimes occur in accounting entries. Accountants correct such errors when discovered by making correcting entries that reverse the errors and adjust account balances so they equal the amounts that would have existed if the correct entries had been made.

7 Explain how computers have transformed the processing of accounting data. Computers are fast and efficient and enable the performance of repetitive tasks with complete accuracy, reducing human effort and errors. Many software packages are available to aid in the processing of accounting transactions. Computers perform tasks from initial recording of a sale, to journalizing and posting, to creation of trial balances and financial statements, and finally to sending financial information to interested parties over the Web.

Accounting Vocabulary

accumulated depreciation, p. 105

allowance for depreciation, p. 105

balance, p. 92

book of original entry, p. 96

book value, p. 105

carrying amount, p. 105

carrying value, p. 105

charge, p. 95

chart of accounts, p. 96

close the books, p. 110

closing entries, p. 110

compound entry, p. 100

contra account, p. 105

contra asset, p. 105

correcting entry, p. 116

credit, p. 95

cross-referencing, p. 99

data processing, p. 119

debit, p. 95

double-entry system, p. 92

general journal, p. 92

general ledger, p. 92

Assignment Material

MyAccountingLab

Questions

3-1 "Double entry means that amounts are shown in both the general journal and general ledger." Do you agree? Explain.

3-2 "Increases in cash and accounts payable are shown on the right side of their respective accounts." Do you agree? Explain.

3-3 "Debit and credit are used as verbs, adjectives, or nouns." Give examples of how credit may be used in these three meanings.

3-4 Name three source documents for transactions.

3-5 "The general ledger is the major book of original entry because it is more essential than the general journal." Do you agree? Explain.

3-6 "Revenue and expense accounts are really little stockholders' equity accounts." Explain.

3-7 Give two synonyms for book value.

3-8 "Accumulated depreciation is the total depreciation expense for the year." Do you agree? Explain.

3-9 What is a trial balance and what purpose does it serve?

3-10 "If debits equal credits in a trial balance, you can be assured that no errors were made." Do you agree? Explain.

3-11 What is the role of the Income Summary account when closing the books?

3-12 "In double-entry accounting, errors are not a problem because they are self-correcting." Do you agree? Explain.

3-13 Are all data processing systems for accounting computerized? Explain.

Critical Thinking Questions

▶▶ OBJECTIVE 2

3-14 The Chart of Accounts
You have just joined the accounting staff of a fast-food company. You are surprised that this company has a chart of accounts with twice as many accounts as the fast-food company you previously worked for, even though the current client's sales are one-half as large. You are tempted to write a very critical memo to your manager about this issue. You have asked a more experienced friend for advice. What might this friend ask about these clients?

▶▶ OBJECTIVE 3

3-15 The Relation of Expense and Retained Earnings Accounts
A fellow student asked you the following: "I understand that a debit increases an expense account. I also understand that a debit decreases retained earnings. But if an expense account is a part of retained earnings (a 'little' stockholders' equity account), how can a debit entry have a different effect on retained earnings than it does on an expense account?" Provide an explanation to the student.

▶▶ OBJECTIVE 3

3-16 Reconstructing Transactions
Your supervisor in the accounting department has asked you to trace transactions from the general journal to the general ledger. You are partway into the task when you find at the top of one page in the general journal that a coffee spill has obliterated part of a transaction. You can see that the debit portion of the transaction was for $1,000 to rent expense, but the credit portion is illegible. How might you go about recreating what happened?

▶▶ OBJECTIVE 7

3-17 Manual Versus Computerized Accounting Systems
As a new auditor, you have just been assigned to the audit of a company with a highly computerized accounting system. How would you expect an audit of such a system to differ from the audit of a small company whose records are maintained manually?

Exercises

3-18 Debits and Credits

▶▶ **OBJECTIVE 1**

For each of the following accounts, indicate whether it normally possesses a debit or a credit balance (use dr. or cr.):

1. Sales
2. Supplies Expense
3. Accounts Receivable
4. Accounts Payable
5. Supplies Inventory
6. Retained Earnings
7. Dividends Payable
8. Depreciation Expense
9. Paid-in Capital
10. Subscription Revenue
11. Equipment
12. Accumulated Depreciation
13. Cost of Goods Sold
14. Prepaid Rent

3-19 Debits and Credits

▶▶ **OBJECTIVE 1**

Indicate for each of the following transactions whether an accountant will debit or credit the account named in parentheses (use dr. or cr.):

1. Sold merchandise (Merchandise Inventory), $1,500
2. Bought merchandise on account (Merchandise Inventory), $4,000
3. Paid Napoli Associates $3,000 owed them (Accounts Payable)
4. Received cash from customers on accounts due (Accounts Receivable), $2,000
5. Bought merchandise on open account (Accounts Payable), $5,000
6. Borrowed money from a bank (Notes Payable), $10,000
7. Sold merchandise (Cost of Goods Sold) $1,500

3-20 Debits and Credits

▶▶ **OBJECTIVE 1**

For the following transactions, indicate whether the accountant for Jacksonville Company should debit or credit the account in parentheses (use dr. or cr.):

1. Jacksonville sold merchandise on credit (Accounts Receivable).
2. Jacksonville received interest on an investment (Interest Revenue).
3. Jacksonville declared dividends and paid them in cash (Retained Earnings).
4. Jacksonville paid wages to employees (Wages Expense).
5. Jacksonville sold merchandise for cash (Sales Revenue).
6. Jacksonville acquired a 4-year fire insurance policy (Prepaid Expenses).

3-21 True or False

▶▶ **OBJECTIVE 1**

Use T or F to indicate whether each of the following statements is true or false:

1. Repayments of bank loans should be charged to Notes Payable and credited to Cash.
2. Cash payments of accounts payable should be recorded by a debit to Cash and a credit to Accounts Payable.
3. Inventory purchases on account should be credited to Accounts Payable and debited to an expense account.
4. All credit entries are recorded on the right side of accounts and represent decreases in the account balances.
5. Cash collections of accounts receivable should be debited to Cash and credited to Accounts Receivable.
6. Credit purchases of equipment should be debited to Equipment and charged to Accounts Payable.

7. In general, entries on the right side of asset accounts represent decreases in the account balances.
8. Increases in asset and expense accounts should be recorded on the left side of the accounts.
9. Increases in retained earnings are recorded as credits.
10. Both decreases in assets and decreases in liabilities are recorded on the debit sides of accounts.
11. Asset debits should be on the right and liability debits should be on the left.
12. In some cases, increases in account balances are recorded on the right sides of accounts.

▶▶ OBJECTIVE 2

3-22 5-Step Recording Process

Suppose you buy a $125 pair of shoes for cash from **Nike** on November 12, 20X0. The shoes cost Nike $80. Follow the accounting for your purchase through the five steps that lead from recording your purchase to its inclusion in Nike's financial statements. List each step and what happens to the record of your purchase in the step.

▶▶ OBJECTIVE 3

3-23 Matching Transaction Accounts

Listed here are a series of accounts that are numbered for identification. Accompanying this problem are columns in which you are to write the identification numbers of the accounts affected by the transactions described. You may use the same account in several answers. For each transaction, indicate which account or accounts are to be debited and which are to be credited. The first transaction is completed for you.

1. Cash
2. Accounts Receivable
3. Inventory
4. Equipment
5. Accumulated Depreciation, Equipment
6. Prepaid Insurance
7. Accounts Payable
8. Notes Payable
9. Paid-in Capital
10. Retained Earnings
11. Sales Revenue
12. Cost of Goods Sold
13. Operating Expense

		Debit	Credit
(a)	Purchased new equipment for cash plus a short-term note	4	1, 8
(b)	Paid some old trade bills with cash	_____	_____
(c)	Made sales on credit: Inventory is accounted for as each sale is made	_____	_____
(d)	Paid cash for salaries and wages for work done during the current fiscal period	_____	_____
(e)	Collected cash from customers on account	_____	_____
(f)	Bought regular merchandise on credit	_____	_____
(g)	Purchased 3-year insurance policy on credit	_____	_____
(h)	Paid cash for inventory that arrived today	_____	_____
(i)	Paid off note owed to bank	_____	_____
(j)	To secure additional funds, 400 new shares of common stock were sold for cash	_____	_____
(k)	Recorded the entry for depreciation on equipment for the current fiscal period	_____	_____
(l)	Paid cash for ad in today's *Wall Street Journal*	_____	_____
(m)	Some insurance premiums have expired	_____	_____

3-24 Prepaid Expenses

▶▶ OBJECTIVE 3

Continental AG is a large German supplier of auto parts. Assume that Continental had €62.4 million of prepaid expenses on January 1, 2012. (€ stands for euro, the European currency.) This item mainly consists of prepayments of rent, leasing fees, interest, and insurance premiums. Assume all these prepayments were for services that Continental used during 2012 and that Continental spent €164 million in cash during 2012 for rent, leasing fees, and interest, of which €38 million was a prepayment of expenses for 2013.

1. Prepare a journal entry recognizing the use of the €62.4 million of prepaid expenses during 2012.
2. Prepare a compound journal entry for the cash payment of €164 million for rent, leasing fees, interest, and insurance premiums during 2012, with the proper amounts going to expense and prepaid expenses.

3-25 Journalizing and Posting

▶▶ OBJECTIVE 3

(Alternate is 3-26.) Prepare journal entries and post to T-accounts the following transactions of Toronto Building Supplies:

a. Cash sales, $10,000; items sold cost $4,500
b. Collections on accounts, $8,500
c. Paid cash for wages, $3,500
d. Acquired inventory on open account, $5,000
e. Paid cash for janitorial services, $550

3-26 Journalizing and Posting

▶▶ OBJECTIVE 3

(Alternate is 3-25.) Prepare journal entries and post to T-accounts the following transactions of Washington Real Estate Company:

a. Acquired office supplies of $900 on open account. Use a Supplies Inventory account.
b. Sold a house and collected an $9,000 commission on the sale. Use a Commissions Revenue account.
c. Paid cash of $750 to a local newspaper for current advertisements.
d. Paid $500 for a previous credit purchase of office supplies.
e. Recorded office supplies used of $300.

3-27 Reconstruct Journal Entries

(Alternate is 3-28.) Reconstruct the journal entries (with explanations) that resulted in the postings to the following T-accounts of Four Seasons Heating Contractors:

Cash				Equipment		Revenue from Fees	
(a) 70,000	(b) 1,500		(c) 15,000				(d) 87,000
	(c) 5,000						

Accounts Receivable		Note Payable	
(d) 87,000			(c) 10,000

Supplies Inventory		Paid-in Capital		Supplies Expense	
(b) 1,500	(e) 400		(a) 70,000	(e) 400	

3-28 Reconstruct Journal Entries

▶▶ OBJECTIVE 3

(Alternate is 3-27.) Reconstruct the journal entries (omit explanations) that resulted in the postings to the following T-accounts of a small fruit wholesaler:

Cash		Accounts Payable		Paid-in Capital	
(a) 50,000	(e) 18,000	(e) 18,000	(b) 80,000		(a) 50,000

Accounts Receivable	
(c) 110,000	

Inventory		Cost of Goods Sold		Sales Revenue	
(b) 80,000	(d) 68,000	(d) 68,000			(c) 110,000

▶▶ OBJECTIVES 3, 4

3-29 Trial Balance

Gamma Company had total assets (cash and inventories) of $50,000, total liabilities of $30,000, and stockholders' equity of $20,000 at the beginning of 20X0. During the year Gamma purchased inventory for $65,000 cash and sold all of that inventory for $100,000 cash. Total expenses other than cost of goods sold were $20,000, all paid in cash.

1. Enter the beginning balances into three T-accounts: Total Assets, Total Liabilities, and Stockholders' Equity.
2. Prepare journal entries for the transactions in 20X0. Post the inventory purchases, sales revenue, and expenses to the three T-accounts, opening new accounts for revenues and expenses as needed.
3. Prepare a trial balance at the end of 20X0.

▶▶ OBJECTIVE 5

3-30 Closing Accounts

Use the information for Gamma Company in Exercise 3-29. Prepare closing entries to transfer all temporary accounts to an Income Summary account, and then close the Income Summary account to Stockholders' Equity. Note that Stockholders' Equity includes both paid-in capital and retained earnings; there is no way to separate the two with the information given.

▶▶ OBJECTIVE 5

3-31 Closing Accounts and Preparing Financial Statements

Bonfiglio Company imports art and artifacts from Italy and Spain and sells them in its Bonfiglio Gallery in London. At the end of 20X2 Bonfiglio had the following trial balance:

Cash	£ 44,000	
Accounts receivable	23,000	
Inventories	75,000	
Fixed assets, net	121,000	
Accounts payable		£ 36,000
Paid-in capital		90,000
Retained earnings, Jan. 1, 20X2		92,000
Revenue		345,000
Cost of sales	165,000	
Operating expenses	135,000	
Totals	£563,000	£563,000

1. Prepare closing journal entries for Bonfiglio Company.
2. Prepare an income statement for 20X2 and a balance sheet for December 31, 20X2.

▶▶ OBJECTIVE 6

3-32 Effects of Errors

The bookkeeper of Rollins Legal Services included the cost of a new computer, purchased on December 30 for $5,000 and to be paid for in cash in January, as an operating expense instead of an addition to the proper asset account. What was the effect of this error ("no effect," "over-stated," or "understated" —use symbols N, O, or U, respectively) on the following?

1. Total assets as of December 31
2. Total liabilities as of December 31
3. Operating expenses for the year ended December 31
4. Profit from operations for the year
5. Retained earnings as of December 31 after the books are closed

▶▶ OBJECTIVE 6

3-33 Effects of Errors

Analyze the effect of the following errors on the net profit figures of Yokahama Trading Company (YTC) for 20X0 and 20X1. Choose one of three answers: understated (U), overstated (O), or no effect (N). Problem 1 has been answered as an illustration.

1. Example: Failure to adjust at end of 20X0 for prepaid rent that had expired during December 20X0. YTC charged the remaining prepaid rent in 20X1. Answer: 20X0: O; 20X1: U. (Explanation: In 20X0, expenses would be understated and profits overstated. This error would carry forward so expenses in 20X1 would be overstated and profits understated.)
2. YTC omitted recording depreciation on Office Machines in 20X0 only. Correct depreciation was taken in 20X1.

3. During 20X1, YTC purchased ¥40,000 of office supplies and debited Office Supplies, an asset account. At the end of 20X1, ¥10,000 worth of office supplies were left. No entry had recognized the use of ¥30,000 of office supplies during 20X1.

4. Machinery, with a cost of ¥500,000, bought in 20X0, was not entered in the books until paid for in 20X1. Ignore depreciation; answer in terms of the specific error described.

5. YTC debited 3 months' rent, paid in advance in December 20X0, for the first quarter of 20X1, directly to Rent Expense in 20X0. No prepaid rent was on the books at the end of 20X1.

Problems

MyAccountingLab

3-34 Account Numbers, Journal, Ledger, and Trial Balance

▶▶ OBJECTIVES 3, 4

Journalize and post the entries required by the following transactions for Francisco Furniture Repair Company. Prepare a trial balance as of April 30, 20X0, for the period April 1 to April 30, 20X0. Ignore interest. Use dates, posting references, and the following chart of accounts. As you identify the need for specific expense accounts, assign each expense account its own account number.

Cash	100	Note payable	130
Accounts receivable	101	Paid-in capital	140
Equipment	111	Retained earnings	150
Accumulated depreciation,		Sales revenue	200
equipment	111A	Expenses	300, 301, etc.
Accounts payable	120		

- April 1, 20X0. The Francisco Furniture Repair Company was formed with $100,000 cash on the issuance of common stock.
- April 2. Francisco acquired equipment for $70,000. Francisco made a cash down payment of $20,000. In addition, Francisco signed a note for $50,000.
- April 3. Sales on credit to repair furniture at a local hotel, $3,500.
- April 3. Supplies acquired (and used) on open account, $200.
- April 3. Wages paid in cash, $700.
- April 30. Depreciation expense for April, $2,000.

3-35 Account Numbers, T-Accounts, and Transaction Analysis

▶▶ OBJECTIVES 3, 4

Consider the following:

Vancouver Computing
Trial Balance, December 31, 20X0 ($ in thousands)

		Balance	
Account Number	Account Titles	Debit	Credit
10	Cash	$ 60	
20	Accounts receivable	115	
21	Note receivable	100	
30	Inventory	130	
40	Prepaid insurance	12	
70	Equipment	120	
70A	Accumulated depreciation, equipment		$ 30
80	Accounts payable		140
100	Paid-in capital		65
110	Retained earnings		182
130	Sales revenue		950
150	Cost of goods sold	550	
160	Wages expense	200	
170	Miscellaneous expense	80	
		$1,367	$1,367

The following information had not been considered before preparing the trial balance:

a. The $100,000 note receivable was signed by a major customer. It is a 3-month note dated November 1, 20X0. Interest earned during November and December was collected in cash at 4 PM on December 31. The interest rate is 6% per year.

b. The Prepaid Insurance account reflects a 1-year fire insurance policy acquired for $12,000 cash on September 1, 20X0.

c. Depreciation for 20X0 was $18,000.

d. Vancouver Computing paid wages of $12,000 in cash at 5 PM on December 31.

Required

1. Enter the December 31 balances in T-accounts in a general ledger. Number the accounts. Allow room for additional T-accounts.

2. Prepare the journal entries prompted by the additional information. Show amounts in thousands.

3. Post the journal entries to the ledger. Key your postings. Create logical new account numbers as necessary.

4. Prepare a new trial balance, December 31, 20X0.

▶▶ OBJECTIVE 4

3-36 Trial Balance Errors

Consider the following trial balance ($ in thousands):

Powell Paint Store
Trial Balance, Year Ended December 31, 20X0

Cash	$ 22	
Equipment	33	
Accumulated depreciation, equipment	15	
Accounts payable	42	
Accounts receivable	14	
Prepaid insurance	1	
Prepaid rent		$ 3
Inventory	129	
Paid-in capital		17
Retained earnings		10
Cost of goods sold	500	
Wages expense	100	
Miscellaneous expenses	80	
Advertising expense		30
Sales		788
Note payable	40	
	$976	$848

List and describe all the errors in the preceding trial balance. Be specific. On the basis of the available data, prepare a corrected trial balance.

▶▶ OBJECTIVES 3, 4

3-37 Journal, Ledger, and Trial Balance

(Alternates are 3-39 through 3-44.) The balance sheet accounts of Detroit Machinery, Inc., had the following balances on October 31, 20X0:

Cash	$ 41,000	
Accounts receivable	90,000	
Inventory	70,000	
Prepaid rent	2,000	
Accounts payable		$ 27,000
Paid-in capital		160,000
Retained earnings		16,000
	$203,000	$203,000

Following is a summary of the transactions that occurred during November:

a. Collections of accounts receivable, $75,000.
b. Payments of accounts payable, $14,000.
c. Acquisitions of inventory on open account, $80,000.
d. Merchandise carried in inventory at a cost of $70,000 was sold on open account for $96,000.
e. Recognition of rent expense for November, $1,000.
f. Wages paid in cash for November, $8,000.
g. Cash dividends declared and disbursed to stockholders on November 29, $10,000.

Required
1. Prepare journal entries.
2. Enter beginning balances in T-accounts. Post the journal entries to T-accounts. Use the transaction letters to key your postings.
3. Prepare a trial balance for the month ending November 30, 20X0.
4. Explain why accounts payable increased by so much during November.

3-38 Financial Statements

▶▶ **OBJECTIVES 4, 5**

Refer to problem 3-37. Prepare a balance sheet as of November 30, 20X0, and an income statement for the month of November. Prepare the retained earnings column of a statement of stockholders' equity. Prepare the income statement first.

3-39 Journal, Ledger, and Trial Balance

▶▶ **OBJECTIVES 3, 4**

(Alternates are 3-37 and 3-40 through 3-44.) The balance sheet accounts of Red Lake Appliance Company had the following balances on December 31, 20X1:

	Balance	
Account Title	**Debit**	**Credit**
Cash	$ 43,000	
Accounts receivable	29,000	
Merchandise inventory	120,000	
Accounts payable		$ 35,000
Notes payable		83,000
Paid-in capital		43,000
Retained earnings		31,000
Total	$192,000	$192,000

Operating space and equipment are rented on a month-to-month basis. A summary of January 20X2 transactions follows:

a. Collected $24,000 on accounts receivable.
b. Sold appliances for $60,000 cash and $45,000 on open account.
c. Cost of appliances sold was $56,000.
d. Paid $25,000 on accounts payable.
e. Replenished inventory for $64,000 on open account.
f. Paid selling expense in cash, $33,000.
g. Paid rent expense in cash, $7,000.
h. Paid interest expense in cash, $2,000.

Required
1. Open the appropriate T-accounts in the general ledger. In addition to the seven accounts listed in the trial balance of December 31, open accounts for Sales, Cost of Goods Sold, Selling Expense, Rent Expense, and Interest Expense. Enter the December 31 balances in the accounts.
2. Journalize transactions a through h. Post the entries to the ledger, keying by transaction letter.
3. Prepare a trial balance for the month ended January 31, 20X2.

▶▶ **OBJECTIVES 3, 4, 5**

3-40 Journal, Ledger, and Trial Balance
(Alternates are 3-37, 3-39, and 3-41 through 3-44.) Robert Kapela owned and managed a franchise of Ithaca Espresso, Incorporated. The company's balance sheet accounts had the following balances on September 1, 20X0, the beginning of a fiscal year:

Ithaca Espresso
Balance Sheet Accounts, September 1, 20X0

Cash	$ 13,000	
Accounts receivable	5,200	
Merchandise inventory	77,800	
Prepaid rent	4,000	
Store equipment	21,000	
Accumulated depreciation, store equipment		$ 6,150
Accounts payable		40,000
Paid-in capital		30,000
Retained earnings		44,850
	$121,000	$121,000

Summarized transactions for September were as follows:

a. Acquisitions of merchandise inventory on account, $41,000.
b. Sales for cash, $74,250.
c. Payments to creditors, $29,000.
d. Sales on account, $3,000.
e. Advertising in newspapers, paid in cash, $3,000.
f. Cost of goods sold, $45,000.
g. Collections on account, $6,000.
h. Miscellaneous expenses paid in cash, $8,000.
i. Wages paid in cash, $9,000.
j. Entry for rent expense. (Rent was paid quarterly in advance, $6,000 per quarter. Payments were due on February 1, May 1, August 1, and November 1.)
k. Depreciation of store equipment, $250.

Required

1. Enter the September 1 balances in T-accounts in a general ledger.
2. Prepare journal entries for each transaction.
3. Post the journal entries to the ledger. Key your postings by transaction letter.
4. Prepare an income statement for September and a balance sheet as of September 30, 20X0.

3-41 Journalizing, Posting, and Trial Balance

(Alternates are 3-37, 3-39, 3-40, and 3-42 through 3-44.) Tsugawa Nursery, a retailer of garden plants and supplies, had the accompanying balance sheet accounts on December 31, 20X0:

▶▶ OBJECTIVES 3, 4

Assets			Liabilities and Stockholders' Equity	
Cash		$ 24,000	Accounts payable*	$116,000
Accounts receivable		40,000	Paid-in capital	40,000
Merchandise inventory		131,000	Retained earnings	79,000
Prepaid rent		4,000		
Store equipment	$60,000			
Less: Accumulated depreciation	24,000	36,000		
Total		$235,000	Total	$235,000

*For merchandise only.

Following is a summary of aggregate transactions that occurred during 20X1:

a. Purchases of merchandise inventory on open account, $550,000.
b. Sales, all on credit, $810,000.
c. Cost of merchandise sold to customers, $536,000.
d. Disbursed $25,000 for the rent of the store. Add to Prepaid Rent.
e. Disbursed $165,000 for wages through November.
f. Disbursed $75,000 for miscellaneous expenses such as utilities, advertising, and legal help. (Debit Miscellaneous Expenses.)
g. On July 1, 20X1, loaned $40,000 to the office manager. He signed a note that will mature on July 1, 20X2, together with interest at 5% per annum. Interest for 20X1 is due on December 31, 20X1.
h. On August 1, 20X1, borrowed $80,000 from a supplier. The note is payable in 4 years. Interest is payable yearly on December 31 at a rate of 6% per annum.
i. Collections on accounts receivable, $692,000.
j. Payments on accounts payable, $472,000.

The following entries were made on December 31, 20X1:

k. Recognized rent expense for 20X1: $3,000 of prepaid rent is applicable to 20X2; the remainder expired in 20X1.
l. Depreciation for 20X1 was $6,000.
m. Wages earned by employees during December were paid on December 31, $6,000.
n. Interest on the loan made to the office manager was received. See transaction g.
o. Interest on the loan from the supplier was disbursed. See transaction h.

Required

1. Prepare journal entries in thousands of dollars.
2. Post the entries to T-accounts in the ledger, keying your postings by transaction letter.
3. Prepare a trial balance for the year ending December 31, 20X1.

▶▶ OBJECTIVES 3, 4, 5

3-42 Transaction Analysis, Trial Balance, and Closing Entries

(Alternates are 3-37, 3-39 through 3-41, 3-43, and 3-44.) Husker Auto Glass, Inc., had the accompanying balance sheet values on January 1, 20X0:

Husker Auto Glass, Inc.
Balance Sheet Accounts, January 1, 20X0

Cash	$ 8,000	
Accounts receivable	3,000	
Parts inventory	2,000	
Prepaid rent	2,000	
Trucks	36,000	
Equipment	8,000	
Accumulated depreciation, trucks		$15,000
Accumulated depreciation, equipment		5,000
Accounts payable		1,900
Paid-in capital		20,000
Retained earnings		17,100
Total	$59,000	$59,000

During January, the following summarized transactions occurred:

January	2	Collected accounts receivable, $2,500.
	3	Rendered services to customers for cash, $4,200 ($700 collected for parts, $3,500 for labor). Use two accounts, Parts Revenue and Labor Revenue.
	3	Cost of parts used for services rendered, $300.
	7	Paid legal expenses, $500 cash.
	9	Acquired parts on open account, $900.
	11	Paid cash for wages, $1,000.
	13	Paid cash for truck repairs, $500.
	19	Billed customer for services, $3,600 ($800 for parts and $2,800 for labor).
	19	Cost of parts used for services rendered, $500.
	24	Paid cash for wages, $1,400.
	27	Paid cash on accounts payable, $1,500.
	31	Rent expense for January, $1,000 (reduce Prepaid Rent).
	31	Depreciation for January: trucks, $600; equipment, $200.
	31	Paid cash to local gas station for gasoline for trucks for January, $300.
	31	Paid cash for wages, $800.

Required

1. Enter the January 1 balances in T-accounts. Leave room for additional accounts.
2. Record the transactions in the journal.
3. Post the journal entries to the T-accounts. Key your entries by date. (Note how keying by date is not as precise as by transaction number or letter. Why? There is usually more than one transaction on any given date.)
4. Prepare a trial balance for the month ended January 31, 20X0.
5. Prepare closing entries.

▶▶ OBJECTIVES 3, 4

3-43 Transaction Analysis, Trial Balance

(Alternates are 3-37, 3-39 through 3-42, and 3-44.) **McDonald's Corporation** is a well-known fast-food restaurant company. Examine the accompanying balance sheet values, which are based on McDonald's condensed quarterly report and actual terminology:

McDonald's Corporation
Balance Sheet Values, September 30, 2011 ($ in millions)

Cash	$ 2,389	
Accounts and notes receivable	1,204	
Inventories	115	
Prepaid expenses	714	
Property and equipment, at cost	35,220	
Other assets	5,518	
Accumulated depreciation		$12,882
Notes and accounts payable		750
Other liabilities		18,189
Paid-in capital		5,447
Retained earnings		35,330
Other stockholders' equity*	27,438	
Total	$72,598	$72,598

*These negative stockholders' equity items will be explained in later chapters.

Consider the following assumed partial summary of transactions for October 2011 ($ in millions):

a. Revenues in cash, company-owned restaurants, $1,550.
b. Revenues, on open account from franchised restaurants, $550. Open a separate revenue account for these sales.
c. Inventories acquired on open account, $827.
d. Cost of the inventories sold, $820.
e. Depreciation, $250. (Debit Depreciation Expense.)
f. Paid rent and insurance premiums in cash in advance, $142. (Debit Prepaid Expenses.)
g. Prepaid expenses expired, $137. (Debit Operating Expenses.)
h. Paid other liabilities in cash, $163.
i. Cash collections on receivables, $590.
j. Cash disbursements on notes and accounts payable, $747.
k. Paid interest expense in cash, $110.
l. Paid other expenses in cash, mostly payroll and advertising, $1,010. (Debit Operating Expenses.)

Required

1. Record the transactions in the journal.
2. Enter beginning balances in T-accounts. Post the journal entries to the T-accounts. Key your entries with the transaction letters used here.
3. Prepare a trial balance for the month ended October 31, 2011.

3-44 Transaction Analysis, Trial Balance

▶▶ **OBJECTIVES 3, 4**

(Alternates are 3-37 and 3-39 through 3-43.) Columbia Sportswear is one of the largest outdoor apparel, footwear, accessories, and equipment companies in the world. Examine the following balance sheet values, which are slightly revised from Columbia's annual report:

Columbia Sportswear Balance Sheet Values
December 31, 2011 ($ in millions)

Cash	$ 241.0	
Accounts receivable	351.5	
Prepaid expenses	36.4	
Inventories	365.2	
Property and equipment, net	250.9	
Other assets	137.5	
Accounts payable		$ 149.0
Other liabilities		159.0
Paid-in capital		49.9
Retained earnings		1,024.6
Total	$1,382.5	$1,382.5

Consider the following assumed partial summary of transactions for the first three months of 2012 ($ in millions):

a. Acquired inventories for $286.9 on open account.
b. Sold inventories that cost $239.7 for $423.5 on open account.
c. Collected $410.6 on open account.
d. Disbursed $231.3 on open accounts payable.
e. Paid cash of $15 for advertising expenses. (Use an Operating Expenses account.)
f. Paid rent and insurance premiums in cash in advance, $11. (Use a Prepaid Expenses account.)
g. Prepaid expenses expired, $18. (Use an Operating Expenses account.)
h. Other liabilities paid in cash, $22.3.
i. Interest expense of $4 was paid in cash. (Use an Interest Expense account.)
j. Depreciation of $16 was recognized. [Use an Operating Expenses account; instead of creating an Accumulated Depreciation account, reduce the Property and Equipment (net) account directly.]
k. Additional shares were sold for $6 in cash. (Record as an increase to Paid-in Capital.)

Required
1. Record the transactions in the journal.
2. Enter beginning balances in T-accounts. Post the journal entries to the T-accounts. Key your entries with the transaction letters used here.
3. Prepare a trial balance for the three months ended March 31, 2012.
4. Explain why cash increased during the first three months of 2012.

▶▶ **OBJECTIVE 5**

3-45 Preparation of Financial Statements from Trial Balance
PepsiCo produces snack foods such as Fritos and Lay's potato chips, as well as beverages such as Pepsi and Mug Root Beer. The company had the following condensed trial balance as of September 3, 2011, for the nine months ended September 3, 2011 ($ in millions):

PepsiCo Trial Balance

	Debits	Credits
Current assets	$ 17,834	
Property and equipment, net	20,737	
Intangible assets, net	34,131	
Other assets	2,676	
Current liabilities		$ 17,565
Long-term debt and other liabilities		33,810
Stockholders' equity*		21,379
Net revenue		46,346
Cost of sales	21,862	
Selling, general, and administrative expenses	16,995	
Other expenses	2,461	
Cash dividends declared	2,404	
Total	$119,100	$119,100

*Includes beginning retained earnings.

1. Prepare PepsiCo's income statement for the nine months ended September 3, 2011.
2. Prepare PepsiCo's balance sheet as of September 3, 2011.

3-46 Accumulated Depreciation

▶▶ OBJECTIVE 3

Johnson Matthey, the British specialty chemical company, had the following balances on its March 31, 2011, balance sheet [£ (British pound) in millions]:

Tangible fixed assets, at cost	£1,755.0
Less: Accumulated depreciation	847.3
Net tangible fixed assets	£ 907.7

Suppose that Johnson Matthey depreciates most of its tangible fixed assets over 15 years.

1. What is the approximate average age of Johnson Matthey's tangible fixed assets?
2. Johnson Matthey invested £115.1 million in tangible fixed assets during the prior year. Using this information and your answer to part 1, explain whether Johnson Matthey is growing or depleting its supply of fixed assets.

3-47 Effects of Errors

▶▶ OBJECTIVE 6

Toyota Motor Corporation is one of the world's largest automakers. The company reported pretax profit of ¥291,468 million in fiscal 2010 and pretax profit of ¥563,290 million in fiscal 2011. Assume that there are no income taxes so that these amounts are also after-tax amounts. Consider the following two independent scenarios.

1. Suppose Toyota built a new factory that began production at the beginning of fiscal 2010. Cost of the factory was ¥600,000 million, and its life was estimated to be 20 years. If Toyota neglected to take depreciation on the factory in fiscal 2010 but correctly charged one year's depreciation in fiscal 2011, what misstatements would exist on Toyota's 2010 financial statements? On its 2011 financial statements?
2. Suppose in fiscal 2010 Toyota incorrectly recorded ¥100,000 million of sales for orders of automobiles that were not delivered, and thus the revenue was not earned, until fiscal 2011. What errors would there be in the fiscal 2010 financial statements? In the fiscal 2011 financial statements? Assume that cost of goods sold averages 75% of sales.

3-48 Journal Entries, Posting

▶▶ OBJECTIVE 3

Sony Corporation is a leading international supplier of audio and video equipment. The Sony annual report at the end of the 2011 fiscal year included the following balance sheet items (Japanese yen in billions):

Cash	¥1,014
Receivables	744
Prepaid expenses	603
Land	146
Accounts payable, trade	793

Consider the following assumed transactions that occurred immediately subsequent to the balance sheet date (Japanese yen in billions):

a. Collections from customers	¥567
b. Purchase of land for cash	20
c. Purchase of 2-year insurance policy for cash	12
d. Disbursements to trade creditors	499

1. Enter the five account balances in T-accounts.
2. Journalize each transaction.
3. Post the journal entries to T-accounts. Key each posting by transaction letter.

▶▶ OBJECTIVE 3

3-49 Reconstructing Journal Entries, Posting
(Alternate is 3-50.) Procter & Gamble has brands such as Tide, Pampers, and Gillette. A partial income statement from its annual report for the fiscal year ending in June 30, 2011, showed the following actual numbers and nomenclature ($ in millions):

Net sales	$82,559
Costs and expenses	
Cost of products sold	40,768
Selling, general, and administrative expense	25,973
Interest expense	831
Other income, net	(202)
Income taxes	3,392
Total expenses	70,762
Net earnings	$11,797

1. Prepare six summary journal entries for the given data. Label your entries a through f. Omit explanations. For simplicity, assume that all transactions (except for cost of products sold) were for cash.
2. Post to T-accounts in a ledger for all affected accounts. Key your postings by transaction letter.

▶▶ OBJECTIVE 3

3-50 Reconstructing Journal Entries, Posting
(Alternate is 3-49.) Lowe's Companies, Inc., operates more than 1,700 home improvement retail stores in 50 states and Canada. A condensed income statement from its annual report for the nine months ending October 28, 2011, showed the following actual numbers and nomenclature ($ in millions):

Net sales		$38,579
Expenses		
Cost of sales	$25,208	
Selling, general, and administrative expenses	9,583	
Other expenses	2,271	
Total costs and expenses		37,062
Pretax earnings		$ 1,517

1. Prepare four summary journal entries for the given data. Label your entries a through d. Omit explanations. For simplicity, assume that all transactions except for cost of sales were for cash.
2. Post to T-accounts in a ledger for all affected accounts. Key your postings by transaction letter.

▶▶ OBJECTIVE 3

3-51 Plant Assets and Accumulated Depreciation
Norsk Hydro, the Norwegian-based global supplier of aluminum and aluminum products, had the following in its January 1, 2011, balance sheet (in millions of Norwegian Kroner, NOK):

Total property, plant, and equipment, at cost	NOK60,754
Less: Accumulated depreciation	35,905
Property, plant, and equipment, net	NOK24,849

1. Open T-accounts for (a) Property, Plant, and Equipment; (b) Accumulated Depreciation, Property, Plant, and Equipment; and (c) Depreciation Expense. Enter the balance sheet amounts into the T-accounts.
2. Assume that in 2011 Norsk Hydro purchased or sold no assets and that depreciation expense for 2011 was NOK2,952 million. Depreciation was the only item affecting the Property, Plant, and Equipment account in 2011. Prepare the journal entry, and post to the T-accounts.
3. Prepare the property, plant, and equipment section of Norsk Hydro's balance sheet at the end of 2011.
4. Land comprises $1,170 million of Norsk Hydro's property, plant, and equipment, and land is not depreciated. Comment on the age of the company's depreciable assets—that is, all property, plant, and equipment except land—at the December 31, 2011, balance sheet date.

3-52 Management Incentives, Financial Statements, and Ethics

Alicia Perez was controller of the vascular products division of a major medical instruments company. On December 30, 2012, Perez prepared a preliminary income statement and compared it with the 2012 budget:

▶▶ **OBJECTIVE 5**

Vascular Products Division
Income Statement, for the Year Ended December 31, 2012 ($ in thousands)

	Budget	Preliminary Actual
Sales revenue	$1,200	$1,600
Cost of goods sold	600	800
Gross margin	600	800
Other operating expenses	450	500
Operating income	$ 150	$ 300

The top managers of each division had a bonus plan that paid each a 10% bonus if operating income exceeded budgeted income by more than 20%. It was obvious to Perez that the vascular products division had easily exceeded the $180,000 of operating income needed for a bonus. In fact, she wondered if it would not be desirable to reduce operating income this year—after all, the higher the income this year, the higher top management is likely to set the budget next year. Besides, if some of December's sales could just be held back and recorded in January, the division would have a running start on next year.

Perez had always been a team player, and she saw holding back sales as the best strategy for her team of managers. Therefore, she recorded only $1,500,000 of sales in 2012—the other $100,000 was recorded as January 2013 sales. Operating income for 2012 then became $250,000 and there was a head start of $50,000 on 2013's operating income.

Comment on the ethical implications of Perez's decision.

Collaborative Learning Exercise

3-53 Income Statement and Balance Sheet Accounts

Form teams of two persons each. Each person should make a list of 10 account names, with approximately one-half being income statement accounts and one-half being balance sheet accounts. Give the list to the other member of the team, who is to write beside each account name the financial statement (I for income statement or B for balance sheet) on which it belongs. If there are errors or disagreements in classification, discuss the account and come to an agreement about which financial statement it belongs to.

▶▶ **OBJECTIVE 1**

Analyzing and Interpreting Financial Statements

3-54 Financial Statement Research

Select the financial statements of any company.

▶▶ **OBJECTIVE 3**

1. Prepare an income statement in the following format:
   Total sales (or revenue)
   Cost of goods sold
   Gross margin
   Other expenses
   Income before income taxes
   Be sure to include all revenue in the first line and all expenses (except income taxes) in either cost of goods sold or other expenses.
2. Prepare three summary journal entries for the income statement data you prepared. Use the given account titles and label your entries a, b, and c. Omit explanations. For simplicity, assume that all "other expenses" were paid in cash and all sales are on credit.
3. Post to T-accounts in a ledger for all affected accounts. Key your postings by transaction letter.

▸▸ OBJECTIVE 3

3-55 Analyzing Starbucks' Financial Statements

Using either the SEC EDGAR Web site or Starbucks' Web site, find Starbucks' 2011 financial statements. Note the following summarized items (dollars in millions) from the income statement for the year ended October 2, 2011:

Net revenues		$11,700.4
Cost of sales including occupancy costs	$4,949.3	
Store and other operating expenses	5,226.5	
Other income	(319.8)	
Interest expense	33.3	9,889.3
Pretax income		1,811.1
Income taxes		565.4
Net earnings		$ 1,245.7

1. Prepare six summary journal entries for the given data. Use Starbucks' account titles and label your entries a through f. Omit explanations. For simplicity, assume all transactions (except for cost of sales) were for cash. Assume cost of sales is 70% of the "cost of sales including occupancy costs," whereas occupancy costs are 30% and are paid in cash.
2. Starbucks' balance sheet shows $2,355.0 million of Property, Plant, and Equipment, net. Explain what the term "net" means and find both gross and net amounts for Property, Plant, and Equipment.

▸▸ OBJECTIVE 3

3-56 Analyzing Financial Statements Using the Internet: Delta

Go to www.delta.com. In the menu at the bottom of the home page, click on About Delta. Then locate Delta's Annual Reports under Investor Relations. Select the most recent annual report. Answer the following questions about Delta Air Lines, Inc.:

1. Locate Delta's accumulated depreciation balance on the balance sheet or in its property and equipment footnote. What is the dollar magnitude of accumulated depreciation at year end? Does this represent an expense for Delta? Why does Delta keep track of accumulated depreciation?
2. Does Delta include a line for depreciation on its Consolidated Statements of Operations? If so, what is the dollar amount reported? Locate the Property and Equipment (Long-Lived Assets) footnote. Does the footnote include a dollar amount for depreciation expense? If so, what is the dollar amount reported? If both numbers are reported, do they agree?

3. Locate Cash and Cash Equivalents at the end of the year on the Consolidated Balance Sheet. How much did cash and cash equivalents increase or decrease during the past year? Where would you look for a detailed explanation of the change in Cash?

4. Locate Shareholders' Equity on the Consolidated Balance Sheets. Does Delta's common stock have a par value per share? What is it? Consider two amounts: Common Stock and Additional Paid-in Capital. What is the dollar amount reported in each of these line items. How did these amounts arise?

5. Again, locate Shareholders' Equity on the Consolidated Balance Sheets. What does Delta report for Retained Earnings? Did Retained Earnings increase or decrease during the year? What could cause this change in Retained Earnings?

4 Accrual Accounting and Financial Statements

CHANCES ARE YOU or someone you know is one of the millions of customers who have purchased outdoor wear or accessories made by **Columbia Sportswear**, the Oregon-based designer and manufacturer of active outdoor apparel. Columbia is one of the largest outdoor apparel, footwear, accessories, and equipment companies in the world. The company has an international reputation based on innovation, quality, performance, functionality, and value—factors that have won over discerning shoppers. Columbia Sportswear's management team is concerned about these factors, and takes pride in its high customer satisfaction ratings. However, customer satisfaction alone does not pay their salaries, so managers also need to know whether the company is making a profit. Do managers have to turn to complicated equations and formulas to determine the company's profit? No, they can turn to Columbia Sportswear's financial statements—just as we can.

LEARNING OBJECTIVES *After studying this chapter, you should be able to:*

1 Understand the role of adjustments in accrual accounting.

2 Make adjustments for the expiration or consumption of unexpired costs.

3 Make adjustments for the earning of revenues received in advance.

4 Make adjustments for the accrual of unrecorded expenses.

5 Make adjustments for the accrual of unrecorded revenues.

6 Describe the sequence of steps in the recording process and relate cash flows to adjusting entries.

7 Prepare a classified balance sheet and use it to assess short-term liquidity.

8 Prepare single- and multiple-step income statements.

9 Use ratios to assess profitability.

Information in Columbia Sportswear's financial statements comes directly from the company's financial accounting system, which generates information useful in assessing the company's financial success. If you want to buy Columbia Sportswear's stock instead of its clothes, you need information about the company's financial position and prospects in order to judge whether it is a wise investment. To read and understand Columbia's financial statements and compare them to the statements of other companies, you must first understand the fundamentals of financial accounting. This includes the use of accrual accounting and the adjusting entries required before financial statements are prepared.

Financial managers in entities as large as **IBM** and as small as **Chez José Mexican Restaurant**, in nonprofit as well as for-profit organizations, and located in Spain, China, the United States, or elsewhere in the world, must understand the consequences of these adjustments when interpreting financial statements. ●

Columbia Sportswear distributes and sells products in more than 100 countries through a mix of wholesale distribution channels, direct-to-consumer channels, independent distributors, and licensees. The flagship store is located in downtown Portland, Oregon. Columbia's financial statements reflect the results of all this business activity, using the principles of accrual accounting discussed in this chapter.

Adjustments to the Accounts

explicit transactions

Observable events such as cash receipts and disbursements, credit purchases, and credit sales that trigger the majority of day-to-day routine journal entries.

implicit transactions

Events, such as the passage of time, that do not generate source documents or any visible evidence that the event actually occurred. We do not recognize such events in the accounting records until the end of an accounting period.

adjustments (adjusting entries)

End-of-period entries that assign the financial effects of implicit transactions to the appropriate time periods.

accrue

To accumulate a receivable (asset) or payable (liability) during a given period, even though no explicit transaction occurs, and to record a corresponding revenue or expense.

Accountants record the majority of a company's transactions in journals and ledgers as the events occur. However, no observable event triggers transactions such as those discussed in Chapter 3 for depreciation and the expiration of prepaid rent. The difference between these transactions and the majority of the transactions we have recorded to date stems from how obvious or explicit they are.

Explicit transactions are observable events, such as cash receipts and disbursements, credit purchases, and credit sales that trigger the majority of day-to-day routine journal entries. Every explicit transaction is prompted by an economic event that has occurred, and we know that the accountant must make an entry to record the event. Entries for these transactions are supported by source documents, for example, sales slips, purchase invoices, employee payroll checks, or other tangible evidence. Note that not all explicit transactions require an actual exchange of goods and services between the company and another party. For example, the loss of assets due to fire or theft is an explicit transaction, even though no market exchange occurs. In all cases, though, a specific observable event triggers the need to record a journal entry.

Implicit transactions are events, such as the passage of time, that do not generate source documents or any visible evidence that the event actually occurred. Because there is no specific notification to record such events, accountants do not formally recognize them in the accounting records until the end of an accounting period. For example, accountants prepare entries for depreciation expense or the expiration of prepaid rent from special schedules or memorandums at the end of an accounting period. An explicit event did not trigger such entries. Accountants recorded the related explicit transaction at the time the company purchased the depreciable asset or made the initial rent payment. We call the end-of-period entries that record these implicit events adjustments. **Adjustments** (also called **adjusting entries**) assign the financial effects of implicit transactions to the appropriate time periods. Thus, adjustments occur at periodic intervals, usually at the end of the accounting cycle when accountants are about to prepare the financial statements. They make adjustments by recording journal entries in the general journal and then posting them to the general ledger. After recognizing these adjustments for implicit transactions, they update the balances in the general ledger accounts through the end of the period and use these updated balances for preparing financial statements.

Adjusting entries are at the heart of accrual accounting. **Accrue** means to accumulate a receivable (asset) or payable (liability) during a given period, even though no explicit transaction occurs. The receivables or payables increase as time passes, even though no physical assets change hands. In order to maintain the equality of the balance sheet equation, as we accumulate the receivable or payable on the balance sheet, we must also recognize a revenue or expense on the income statement.

What routine business transactions require accruals? Examples are the wages earned by employees but not yet paid and the interest owed on borrowed money before the scheduled interest payment date. First, consider wages. Usually we recognize wage expense when a company pays its employees. However, suppose a company pays wages on Friday, and its accounting period ends on the following Wednesday. By the close of business on Wednesday, employees have earned 3 days' wages, but no explicit event has prompted the company to record an entry. The company must make an adjustment to recognize the wages for Monday, Tuesday, and Wednesday as an increase in both Wages Payable and Wage Expense. Because accruals are not based on explicit transactions, we do not record them on a day-to-day basis. Rather, we make adjusting entries at the end of each accounting period to recognize unrecorded but relevant accruals.

You will see that each adjustment affects both an income statement account and a balance sheet account. Adjusting entries never affect cash, as any entry with a cash impact is the result of an explicit transaction. The goal of adjusting entries is to ensure that all the company's assets, liabilities, and stockholders' equity accounts are properly reflected in the financial statements. In the adjusting process, we consider whether the passage of time or other events has led to the creation of assets, the consumption of assets, or the creation or discharge of liabilities.

Adjustments help match revenues and expenses to the appropriate accounting period and ensure the balance sheet correctly states assets and liabilities. For example, consider a $29 million annual contract for a baseball star, such as Alex Rodriguez, for the 2012 season. If the team pays all $29 million in cash in 2012, there is an explicit transaction. The team records a reduction in cash of $29 million and an expense of $29 million. In contrast, suppose the team pays only $20 million in cash and defers $9 million until 2013 or later. The $20 million cash payment is an explicit transaction that the team records as an expense in 2012. Because no explicit transaction for the additional $9 million occurs during 2012, the team does not routinely enter it into the accounting record. However, Rodriguez has earned the full $29 million as a result of playing the whole season and the team must eventually pay the remaining $9 million, so a liability exists. Further, the team incurred the entire $29 million for the benefit of the 2012 season, so the $9 million deferred payment is an expense for 2012. Thus, at the end of the period, when the team prepares the 2012 financial statements, an adjustment is necessary to record the deferred $9 million payment as an expense and to record a $9 million liability for its payment.

The principal adjustments arise from four basic types of implicit transactions:

   I. Expiration or consumption of unexpired costs
  II. Earning of revenues received in advance
 III. Accrual of unrecorded expenses
  IV. Accrual of unrecorded revenues

Let us now examine each of these four categories in detail.

I. Expiration or Consumption of Unexpired Costs

▶▶ OBJECTIVE 2

Make adjustments for the expiration or consumption of unexpired costs.

Some costs expire due to the passage of time. For example, initially a company engages in an explicit transaction that creates an asset. As the company consumes the asset, it must make an adjustment to reduce the asset and to recognize an expense. The key characteristic of unexpired costs is that an explicit transaction in the past created an asset, and subsequent implicit transactions recognize the consumption of this asset.

For example, refer back to page 104 of Chapter 3. Biwheels paid $6,000 in January to cover rent for the months of January, February, and March. The company initially recorded $6,000 of Prepaid Rent as an asset. As each day passed, Biwheels incurred rent expense and the asset declined in value. However, there is no benefit to recording daily adjusting entries. Rather, Biwheels made a $2,000 adjustment at the end of each month to reflect the gradual expiration of the rent costs. The adjusting entry reduced the asset, Prepaid Rent, and increased Rent Expense. Another example of adjusting for asset expiration is the expensing of Office Supplies Inventory. Suppose a company just initiating operations purchases $10,000 of Office Supplies Inventory on March 1, 2013. The company had no supplies inventory on hand prior to this purchase. At the time of the purchase an explicit transaction has occurred and the company records an increase (debit) to Office Supplies Inventory and a decrease (credit) to Cash. The journal entry to record this purchase is as follows:

Office supplies inventory	10,000	
Cash		10,000

At the end of March, the company determines that it has used $1,500 of the Office Supplies Inventory acquired on March 1. This requires the following adjusting entry to increase Office Supplies Expense (debit) and reduce Office Supplies Inventory (credit):

Office supplies expense	1,500	
Office supplies inventory		1,500

After recording this adjusting entry, the balance sheet will show only $8,500 ($10,000 – $1,500) in Office Supplies Inventory, and the income statement will show an expense of $1,500. Will failure to record an adjusting entry cause the balance sheet and income statement to be incorrect? Yes. Even though the balance sheet will balance, both the income statement and the balance sheet will be in error. If the company fails to make the preceding adjusting entry, Office Supplies Inventory is overstated by $1,500 and Office Supplies Expense is understated by $1,500. Understated expenses result in overstated net income and overstated Retained Earnings, a stockholders' equity account.

Another example of the expiration of unexpired costs is the recording of Depreciation Expense and Accumulated Depreciation. You can review the accounting for depreciation on page 105 of Chapter 3.

II. Earning of Revenues Received in Advance

unearned revenue (revenue received in advance, deferred revenue)
Represents cash received from customers who pay in advance for goods or services to be delivered at a future date.

Just as a company acquires assets and recognizes the related expense over time as it uses the assets, it may receive revenue in advance and then earn the revenue over time. **Unearned revenue** (also called **revenue received in advance** or **deferred revenue**) represents cash received from customers who pay in advance for goods or services that the company promises to deliver at a future date. The company receives cash before it earns the related revenue. This commitment to provide goods or services in the future is a liability, and the company must record both the receipt of cash and the liability. For instance, airlines often require advance payment for tickets. American Airlines recently showed a balance of almost $4.4 billion in an unearned revenue account labeled Air Traffic Liability. Over time, as customers take the flights they have paid for, American reduces the liability and increases revenue.

The analysis of adjusting entries for unearned revenue is easier to understand if we visualize the financial positions of both parties to a contract. For example, recall the Biwheels Company's January advance payment of $6,000 for 3 months' rent. Compare the financial impact on Biwheels Company with the impact on the company that owns the property (the landlord), who received the rental payment:

	Owner of Property (Landlord, Lessor)					Biwheels Company (Tenant, Lessee)				
	A	=	L	+	SE	A	=	L	+	SE
	Cash	=	Unearned Rent Revenue	+	Rent Revenue	Cash +	Prepaid Rent	=		Rent Expense
(a) Explicit transaction (advance payment of 3 months' rent)	+6,000	=	+6,000			−6,000	+6,000	=		
(b) January adjustment (for 1 month rent)		=	−2,000		+2,000		−2,000	=		−2,000
(c) February adjustment (for 1 month rent)		=	−2,000		+2,000		−2,000	=		−2,000
(d) March adjustment (for 1 month rent)		=	−2,000		+2,000		−2,000	=		−2,000

The journal entries for (a) and (b) follow:

OWNER (LANDLORD)

(a) Cash	6,000	
Unearned rent revenue		6,000
(b) Unearned rent revenue	2,000	
Rent revenue		2,000

[Entries for (c) and (d) are the same as for (b).]

BIWHEELS COMPANY (TENANT)

(a) Prepaid rent	6,000	
Cash		6,000
(b) Rent expense	2,000	
Prepaid rent		2,000

[Entries for (c) and (d) are the same as for (b).]

We are already familiar with the analysis from Biwheels' point of view. The $2,000 monthly entries for Biwheels are examples of the first type of adjustment, the expiration of a prepaid asset. From the viewpoint of the landlord, transaction (a) is an explicit transaction that recognizes the receipt of cash and an increase in Unearned Rent Revenue, a liability. Why record a liability? Because the landlord is now obligated to either deliver the rental services or refund the money if the services are not delivered. This account could be called Rent Collected in Advance or Deferred Rent Revenue instead of Unearned Rent Revenue. Regardless of the title, it is a liability account representing revenue collected in advance that the landlord has not earned, and it obligates the landlord to provide services in the future.

BUSINESS FIRST

FRANCHISES AND REVENUE RECOGNITION

In a franchise arrangement, a central organization, such as McDonald's or the National Basketball Association, sells the right to use the company name and company products to a franchisee. The franchisee also receives the benefit of advertising through the larger company, along with management assistance and product development. The Web site www.azfranchises.com reports that 300 different business categories use franchising to distribute goods and services to U.S. consumers. In *Entrepreneur Magazine*'s 2012 Franchise 500 rankings, the top 50 companies include 16 fast-food or family service restaurants, 9 companies that provide residential or commercial cleaning services, 5 personal services companies such as fitness centers and beauty salons, and 3 hotels.

One source estimates that there are 3,000 different franchise business companies operating more than 825,000 franchise outlets and employing more than 18 million people in the United States. The global franchising industry generates revenues of more than $2.1 trillion. Two of the largest global franchises are Subway with almost 35,000 outlets (30% outside the United States) and McDonald's with more than 26,000 franchise outlets (57% outside the United States). One important difference between Subway and McDonald's is that all of Subway's locations are franchises, while McDonald's operates 6,400 company-owned locations in addition to its franchise outlets.

Franchising raises an interesting accounting problem. How does the central organization account for the franchise fees? At first glance, it might seem clear that companies should record such fees as revenue when they receive the cash. However, under accrual accounting, companies should record revenue only after two conditions have been satisfied: (1) the company has completed the "work," that is, it has earned the revenue, and (2) there is reasonable assurance the company will actually collect the fee (it is realized in cash or will be collectible).

The Rocky Mountain Chocolate Factory is a franchisor of premium chocolate shops with more than 315 stores in the United States, Canada, and the United Arab Emirates. It provides an example of a company that collects franchise fees before it performs the related work. Rocky Mountain Chocolate sells its franchisees area development rights that grant the franchisee the exclusive right to develop outlets in a specific geographic area. In return for these rights, Rocky Mountain Chocolate Factory receives an initial franchise fee. Should Rocky Mountain Chocolate record the fee as revenue when it receives the cash? It should not because Rocky Mountain Chocolate's work is not done until the franchisee actually opens and operates the franchise stores. In the interim, Rocky Mountain Chocolate must report the fees as deferred revenue.

McDonald's is perennially named one of *Entrepreneur Magazine*'s top franchising organizations. In 2011, McDonald's had $85.9 billion in system-wide sales, of which franchisees and affiliates generated $67.6 billion. However, when we look at the income statement, we see total revenue of only $27.0 billion—$18.3 billion from company-owned restaurants and $8.7 billion from franchisees and affiliates. Why? McDonald's recognizes as revenues only the franchise fees, not the total product sales of its franchisees.

Sources: www.entrepreneur.com/franchises; www.azfranchises.com/franchisefacts.htm; McDonalds 2010 Annual Report; Rocky Mountain Chocolate Factory 2010 Annual Report.

Notice that transaction (a) does not affect the landlord's stockholders' equity because it does not recognize any revenue. Recall from Chapter 2 that companies cannot recognize revenue on the income statement until it is both earned and realized. While the landlord realized the $6,000 when it received the cash, it had not earned any revenue as of that date. The landlord earns and recognizes the revenue over time as the adjusting entries in transactions (b), (c), and (d) are recorded. The landlord simultaneously decreases (debits) Unearned Rent Revenue and increases (credits) the stockholders' equity account Rent Revenue. The net effect is an increase in stockholders' equity at the time the owner recognizes the revenue. If the landlord fails to record the adjusting entry represented in (b), liabilities are overstated by $2,000 and revenues are understated by $2,000. Understated revenues result in an understatement of both net income and stockholders' equity. Similarly, if Biwheels fails to record the adjusting entry represented previously, its assets are overstated by $2,000 and its expenses are understated by $2,000. When expenses are understated, both net income and stockholders' equity are overstated.

By looking at both sides of the Biwheels rent contract, you can see that adjustment categories I and II are really mirror images of each other. Why? If a contract causes one party to record a Prepaid Expense, it will cause the other party to record Unearned Revenue. This basic relationship holds for any prepayment situation, from a 2-year fire insurance policy to a 5-year magazine subscription. In the case of the magazine subscription, the buyer initially recognizes a Prepaid Expense (asset) and uses adjustments to allocate the initial cost to an expense account over the term of the subscription. In turn, the seller, the magazine publisher, initially records a liability, Unearned Subscription Revenue, on receipt of payment for the 5-year subscription and uses adjustments to recognize the revenue over the subscription term.

Another example is Starbucks, who lists Deferred Revenue of $449.3 million among its liabilities on October 2, 2011. Starbucks sells prepaid coffee cards (stored value cards) as well as gift certificates, both of which holders can redeem for a beverage or food item. Starbucks receives cash when customers purchase the card but cannot recognize revenue until the card or certificate is redeemed. Suppose Starbucks sells stored value cards and gift certificates totaling $10,000 on September 8. The explicit transaction creates a liability, Deferred Revenue, on the balance sheet and increases Cash. By the October 2 year-end, customers have redeemed cards and certificates worth $3,000. The company will recognize $3,000 in revenue on the income statement and reduce the Deferred Revenue account by $3,000. Another example of companies that receive revenue in advance is franchisors as described in the Business First box on page 145.

III. Accrual of Unrecorded Expenses

> **OBJECTIVE 4**
>
> Make adjustments for the accrual of unrecorded expenses.

Wages are an example of a liability that grows moment to moment as employees perform their duties. The services provided by employees represent expenses. It is unnecessary to make hourly, daily, or even weekly formal entries in the accounts for many accrued expenses, as the cost of such frequent recording would exceed the benefits. This is true, even though computers can perform these tasks effortlessly. The costs of computing are small, but in this case the benefits are even smaller. Accountants aggregate these costs only when they prepare financial statements, and this rarely needs to be done hourly or daily. Consequently, they make adjustments to bring each accrued expense (and corresponding liability) account up-to-date at the end of the accounting period, just before they prepare the formal financial statements. These adjustments are necessary to accurately match the expenses to the period in which they help generate revenues.

Accounting for Payment of Wages

Most companies pay their employees on a predetermined schedule. Assume that Columbia Sportswear pays its employees each Friday for services rendered during that week. Consider the following sample calendar for January:

January						
S	M	T	W	T	F	S
	1	2	3	4	5	6
7	8	9	10	11	12	13
14	15	16	17	18	19	20
21	22	23	24	25	26	27
28	29	30	31			

Because wage expenses accrue for an entire week before Columbia pays employees, wages paid on January 26 are compensation for work done during the week ended January 26. Assume the total wages paid on the four Fridays during January total $500,000, which is $125,000 per 5-day workweek, or $25,000 per day. Columbia makes routine entries for wage payments at the end of each week in January. As it pays wages, the company increases Wages Expense and decreases Cash. During the January shown in the preceding calendar, Columbia would pay wages on the 5th, 12th, 19th, and 26th. These events represent explicit transactions, prompted by writing payroll checks. At the end of January, the balance sheet shows the summarized amounts of these explicit transactions and their effect on the accounting equation:

	A	=	L	+	SE
	Cash	=			Wages Expense
(a) Routine entries for explicit transactions	−500,000	=			−500,000

Accounting for Accrual of Wages

Assume that Columbia Sportswear prepares financial statements on a monthly basis. In addition to the $500,000 actually paid to employees during the month of January, Columbia owes $75,000 for employee services rendered during the last 3 days of the month. The company will not pay the employees for these services until Friday, February 2. To ensure an accurate accounting of Wages Expense for the month of January, Columbia must make an adjustment. Transaction (a) shows the total of the routine entries for the explicit payment of wages to employees during January, and transaction (b) shows the adjusting entry to accrue wages for Monday, January 29, through Wednesday, January 31. Transaction (b) recognizes both the expense and the liability.

(a) Wages expense	500,000	
Cash		500,000
(b) Wages expense	75,000	
Accrued wages payable		75,000

If Columbia does not record transaction (b), both expenses and liabilities are understated by $75,000. Understated expenses result in the overstatement of both net income and stockholders' equity.

The total effect of wages on the balance sheet equation for the month of January, including transactions (a) and (b), is as follows:

	A	=	L	+	SE
	Cash	=	Accrued Wages Payable	+	Wages Expense
(a) Routine entries for explicit transactions	−500,000	=			−500,000
(b) Adjustment for implicit transaction, the accrual of unrecorded wages		=	+75,000		−75,000
Total effects	−500,000	=	+75,000		−575,000

The adjustment in entry (b) is the first adjusting entry we have examined that shows an expense offset by an increase in a liability instead of a decrease in an asset. The accountant's problem is different for this type of accrual than it was for prepaid rent. With prepaid rent, there is a record in the accounts of an asset, and the accountant might recognize the necessity for an adjustment by asking the following question: Is the asset balance shown on the books correct or is an adjustment required to reduce it? With accrued wages there is no asset account to prompt such a question. However, because most end-of-period adjustments are routine, accountants know to check for adjustments such as expired rent and accrued wages because they experience these items every period.

On February 2, Columbia will pay off the liability for the work performed during the last 3 days of January, together with the wages expense for February 1 and 2:

Wages expense (February 1 and 2)	50,000	
Accrued wages payable	75,000	
Cash		125,000
To record wages expense for February 1 and 2 and to pay wages for the week ended February 2		

These entries clearly demonstrate the matching principle. The routine entries and the adjusting entries match the wages expense to the periods in which they help generate revenues.

Accrual of Interest

Other examples of accrued expenses include sales commissions, property taxes, income taxes, and interest on borrowed money. Interest is the "rent" paid for the use of money, just as rent is paid for the use of buildings. The interest accumulates (accrues) as time passes, regardless of when a company actually pays cash for interest.

Assume that Columbia Sportswear borrowed $100,000 from **Wells Fargo Bank** on December 31, 2012. The terms of the loan require that Columbia repay the loan amount of $100,000 plus 6% interest on December 31, 2013. By convention, we express interest rates on an annual basis. We can calculate interest for any part of a year as follows:

$$\text{Principal} \times \text{Interest rate} \times \text{Fraction of a year} = \text{Interest}$$

Principal is the amount borrowed ($100,000). The interest rate is expressed as an annual percentage (6% or .06). For the full year, the interest expense is

$$\$100,000 \times .06 \times 1 = \$6,000$$

As of January 31, 2013, Columbia has had use of the $100,000 bank loan for 1 month or one-twelfth of a year. Columbia owes the bank for the use of this money, and the amount owed has accrued for the entire month of January. The amount of interest owed is ($100,000 $\times$ .06 $\times$ 1/12) = $500. The monthly cost of the loan is $500. The interest is not due to be paid until December 31, 2013. However, at the end of January, Columbia is liable for 1 month of accrued interest. We analyze and record the adjustment in the same way as the adjustment for accrued wages:

	A	=	L	+	SE
			Accrued Interest Payable		**Interest Expense**
Adjustment to accrue January interest not yet recorded		=	+500		−500

The adjusting journal entry is as follows:

Interest expense	500	
Accrued interest payable		500

At the end of January, Columbia owes Wells Fargo $100,500, not $100,000. The adjusting entry matches the $500 interest expense with the period in which Columbia had the benefit of the bank loan. If Columbia omits the adjusting entry, liabilities and expenses will both be understated at the end of January. Would the understatement of interest expense have other financial statement implications? Yes. If interest expense is understated, both net income and stockholders' equity are overstated.

Accrual of Income Taxes

As a company generates income, it accrues income tax expense. Income taxes exist worldwide, although rates and details differ from country to country. Corporations in the United States are subject to federal income taxes and, in most states, state income taxes. For many corporations, the federal plus state income tax rates are around 40%. Assuming a combined 40% tax rate, for every dollar of income a company makes, it accrues $.40 of income tax expense. Of course, the company does not pay $.40 in tax as it earns each dollar. Instead, taxes accrue over the accounting period, and the company makes an adjustment at the end of the period when it prepares financial statements.

Companies use various account titles to denote income taxes on their income statements: Income tax expense, provision for income taxes, and income taxes are most common. For multinational firms, income tax expense may include tax obligations in every country in which the firm operates. In preparing income statements, most companies calculate a subtotal called **income before income tax**, **earnings before income tax**, or **pretax income** and then show income taxes as a separate income statement item just before net income. This arrangement is logical because income tax expense is based on pretax income. The 2010 Columbia Sportswear annual report contains the format adopted by the vast majority of companies.

income before income tax (earnings before income tax, pretax income)
Income before the deduction of income tax expense.

Income before income tax	$104,891,000
Income tax expense	27,854,000
Net income	$ 77,037,000

Adidas, which reports under IFRS, uses a similar format for its 2010 income:

Profit before tax	€806,000,000
Income tax expense	238,000,000
Profit after tax	€568,000,000

IV. Accrual of Unrecorded Revenues

Just as the realization of unearned revenues is the mirror image of the expiration of prepaid expenses, the accrual of unrecorded revenues is the mirror image of the accrual of unrecorded expenses. Because the company has not received cash, there is no explicit transaction to trigger a journal entry. However, according to the revenue recognition principle, revenues affect stockholders' equity in the period a company earns them, not the period in which it receives cash. Thus, an adjustment is required to recognize revenues earned but not yet received.

▶▶ **OBJECTIVE 5**
Make adjustments for the accrual of unrecorded revenues.

Consider the $100,000 loan **Wells Fargo Bank** made to **Columbia Sportswear**. As of January 31, 2013, Wells Fargo Bank has earned $500 in interest on the loan. The following tabulation shows the mirror-image effect:

	Wells Fargo Bank as a Lender				Columbia Sportswear as a Borrower			
	A	= L +	SE		A =	L	+	SE
	Accrued Interest Receivable		Interest Revenue			Accrued Interest Payable		Interest Expense
January interest	+500	=	+500		=	+500		−500

Another example of accrued revenues and receivables is "unbilled" fees. Attorneys, public accountants, physicians, and advertising agencies may earn hourly fees during a particular month but not issue bills to their clients until the completion of an entire contract or engagement. Under the accrual basis of accounting, a company should record such revenues in the month in which it earns the revenues, not at a later time. For example, assume that a law firm renders $10,000 of services during January but does not bill for these services until March 31. Before the firm prepares financial statements for January, it makes the following adjustment for unrecorded revenues for the month:

	A	= L +	SE
	Accrued (Unbilled) Fees Receivable		Fee Revenue
Adjustment for fees earned	+10,000	=	+10,000

The journal entry to record these unrecorded revenues is shown here:

Accrued (unbilled) fees receivable	10,000	
Fee revenue		10,000

What happens if the law firm does not make this adjusting entry? Assets and revenues are both understated by $10,000. Understated revenues result in understated net income and understated stockholders' equity.

Utility companies often recognize unbilled revenues for utility services provided but not yet billed to customers. In fact, as of January 1, 2012, Northwest Natural, a utility that provides natural gas to more than 674,000 residential and business customers throughout Oregon and southwestern Washington, included almost as much Accrued Unbilled Revenue as Accounts Receivable among its current assets:

Accounts receivable	$77,449,000
Accrued unbilled revenue	$61,925,000

Ethics, Unearned Revenue, and Revenue Recognition

Deciding when unearned revenue becomes earned can pose ethical dilemmas for accountants. Suppose you are the accountant for a small company that receives a $100,000 cash payment on December 15, in exchange for a commitment to provide various consulting services at a later date. At the time the company receives the cash, you appropriately record an increase in Cash and an increase in the liability account, Unearned Revenue. As we saw earlier in this chapter, as the company provides the services, the appropriate accounting treatment is to decrease the Unearned Revenue account and recognize revenue on the income statement.

When you review the contract on December 31, you conclude that the company has performed $65,000 worth of the $100,000 in consulting services. You propose an adjusting entry to recognize $65,000 in revenue (credit) and to reduce the Unearned Revenue account (debit) by $65,000. Your boss, the CFO of the company, insists that the company has completed only $10,000 in services. He argues that recognition of only $10,000 in revenue is a more conservative estimate of the percentage of services performed. In addition, he reminds you that accountants should be conservative. In this context, **conservatism** means selecting methods of measurement that anticipate expenses and liabilities and defer recognition of revenues and assets, yielding lower immediate net income, lower assets, and lower stockholders' equity. Your boss argues that financial statements are less likely to mislead users if balance sheets report assets at lower rather than higher amounts, report liabilities at higher rather than lower amounts, and if income statements report lower rather than higher net income. He claims that it is unethical to overstate revenue and net income and understate liabilities, and that his lower estimate of $10,000 conservatively states revenue and net income.

You have overheard a conversation at the water cooler suggesting that the company expects sales to slow in the coming year, and you wonder whether that forecast has anything to do with the CFO's estimate. Could the CFO be attempting to "save" revenue to record in the coming year? Should you prepare an income statement that recognizes $10,000 of revenue associated with the service contract or insist on recording $65,000?

The issues in this scenario are complex. It is often difficult to determine exactly when consulting services have been performed. Two people, both acting in good faith, may give different estimates of the completion of these services. The $10,000 is a more conservative estimate of revenue earned. However, by reporting lower net income in the current period, the company will report higher net income in the following period. If the CFO's $10,000

conservatism

Selecting methods of measurement that anticipate expenses and liabilities and defer recognition of revenues and assets, yielding lower net income, lower assets, and lower stockholders' equity.

estimate is intended solely to manipulate the company's revenue and earnings trend, use of that estimate is unethical.

▶▶ OBJECTIVE 6

Describe the sequence of steps in the recording process and relate cash flows to adjusting entries.

The Adjusting Process in Perspective

Chapter 3 presented the various steps in the recording process as follows:

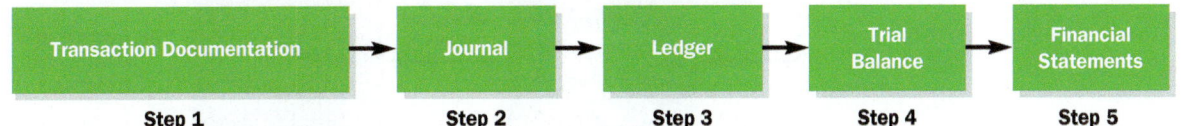

The final aim of the recording process is the preparation of accurate financial statements prepared on the accrual basis. To accomplish this goal, the process must incorporate adjusting entries to record implicit transactions. When we consider the adjustments, we can further divide the final three steps in the recording process as follows:

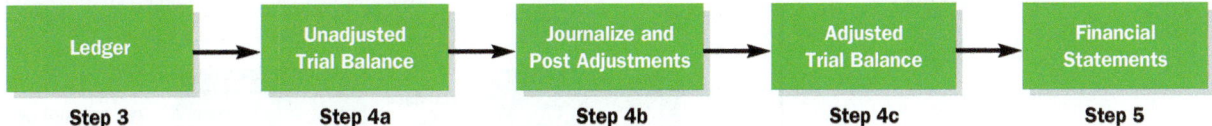

As you review these steps, remember that each adjusting entry affects at least one income statement account, a revenue or an expense, and one balance sheet account, an asset or a liability. Adjusting entries never debit or credit cash. Why? If transactions affect cash, they are explicit transactions that companies must record as they occur. The end-of-period adjustment process is reserved for implicit transactions that are a necessary component of the accrual basis of accounting.

Cash flows—that is, explicit transactions involving cash receipts or cash disbursements—may precede or follow the adjusting entry that recognizes the related revenue or expense. The diagrams that follow underscore the basic differences between the cash flows and the accrual accounting entries.

Entries for adjustments I and II, expiration or consumption of unexpired costs and earning of revenues received in advance, generally occur subsequent to the related cash flows. For example, at the time a company receives or disburses cash for rent, only the balance sheet is affected. The subsequent adjusting entry records the later impact on the income statement.

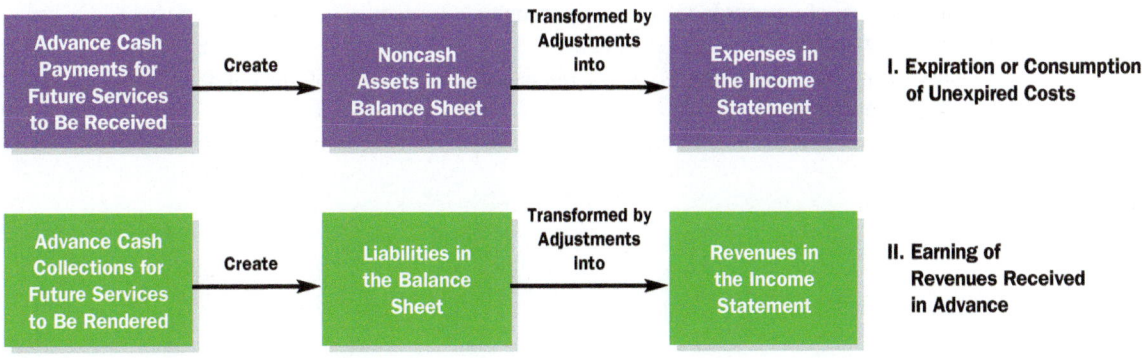

We make the entries for adjustments III and IV, accrual of unrecorded expenses and accrual of unrecorded revenues, before the related cash flows. The income statement is affected before the cash receipts and disbursements occur. The accounting entity computes the amount of goods or services provided or received prior to any cash receipt or payment. Exhibit 4-1 summarizes the major adjusting entries.

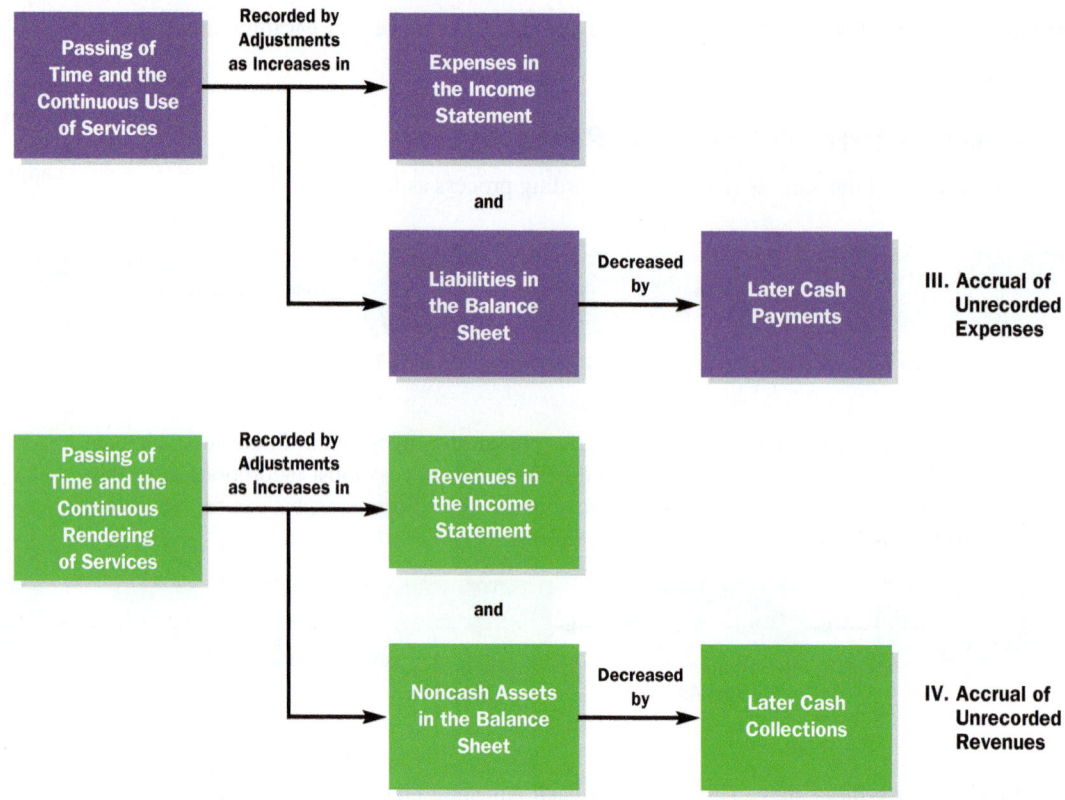

EXHIBIT 4-1

Summary of Adjusting Entries

	Adjusting Entry	Type of Account Debited	Type of Account Credited
I.	Expiration or consumption of unexpired costs	Expense	Prepaid expense, accumulated depreciation
II.	Earning of revenues received in advance	Unearned revenue	Revenue
III.	Accrual of unrecorded expenses	Expense	Payable
IV.	Accrual of unrecorded revenues	Receivable	Revenue

Summary Problem for Your Review

PROBLEM

1. Chan Audio Company is a retailer of stereo equipment that began operations on January 1, 20X0. One month later, on January 31, 20X0, the company's unadjusted trial balance consists of the following accounts and account balances:

Cash	$ 71,700	
Accounts receivable	160,300	
Note receivable	40,000	
Merchandise inventory	250,200	
Prepaid rent	15,000	
Store equipment	114,900	
Note payable		$100,000
Accounts payable		117,100
Unearned rent revenue		3,000
Paid-in capital		400,000
Sales		160,000
Cost of goods sold	100,000	
Wages expense	28,000	
Total	$780,100	$780,100

Consider the following adjustments on January 31:

a. January depreciation expense, $1,000.

b. On January 2, Chan paid $15,000 for rent in advance to cover the first quarter of 20X0, as shown by the $15,000 debit balance in the Prepaid Rent account. Adjust for the consumption of January rent.

c. Wages earned by employees during January but not paid as of January 31 totaled $3,750.

d. Chan borrowed $100,000 from the bank on January 1. The company recorded this explicit transaction when it borrowed the money, as shown by the $100,000 credit balance in the Note Payable account. Chan is to pay the principal and 6% interest 1 year later (January 1, 20X1). Chan has not yet made an adjustment for the recognition of January interest expense.

e. On January 1, Chan made a cash loan of $40,000 to a local supplier, as shown by the $40,000 debit balance in the Note Receivable account. The promissory note stated that the loan is to be repaid 1 year later (January 1, 20X1), together with interest at 4.5% per annum. On January 31, Chan needs to make an adjustment to recognize the interest earned on the note receivable.

f. On January 15, a nearby corporation paid Chan $3,000 cash as an advance rental for temporary use of Chan's excess storage space and equipment. The rental agreement covers the 3 months from January 15 to April 15. This $3,000 is the credit balance in the Unearned Rent Revenue account. On January 31, Chan needs to make an adjustment to recognize the rent revenue earned for one-half a month.

g. Chan must accrue income tax expense on January income at a rate of 40% of income before taxes.

Required

1. Enter the trial balance amounts in the general ledger. Set up the new asset account, Accrued Interest Receivable, and the new contra asset account, Accumulated Depreciation, Store Equipment. Set up the following new liability accounts: Accrued Wages Payable, Accrued Interest Payable, and Accrued Income Taxes Payable. Set up the following new expense and revenue accounts: Depreciation Expense, Rent Expense, Interest Expense, Interest Revenue, Rent Revenue, and Income Tax Expense.
2. Journalize adjustments (a) to (g) and post the entries to the ledger. Identify entries by transaction letter.
3. Prepare an adjusted trial balance as of January 31, 20X0.

Solution

The solutions to requirements 1 through 3 are in Exhibits 4-2, 4-3, and 4-4. Accountants often refer to the final trial balance, Exhibit 4-4, as the adjusted trial balance. Why? All the necessary adjustments have been made; thus, the trial balance provides the data necessary for creating the formal financial statements.

EXHIBIT 4-2

Chan Audio Company
Journal Entries

		Debit	Credit
(a)	Depreciation expense..	1,000	
	Accumulated depreciation, store equipment		1,000
	Depreciation for January		
(b)	Rent expense	5,000	
	Prepaid rent..		5,000
	Rent expense for January		
	$15,000 \div 3 = \$5,000$		
(c)	Wages expense..	3,750	
	Accrued wages payable..		3,750
	Wages earned in January but not paid		
(d)	Interest expense..	500	
	Accrued interest payable...		500
	Interest for January		
	$100,000 \times .06 \times 1/12 = \$500$		
(e)	Accrued interest receivable..	150	
	Interest revenue..		150
	Interest earned for January		
	$40,000 \times .045 \times 1/12 = \$150$		
(f)	Unearned rent revenue...	500	
	Rent revenue...		500
	Rent earned for January, rent per month,		
	$3,000 \div 3 = \$1,000$; for half a month, $500		
(g)	Income tax expense..	8,960	
	Accrued income taxes payable..		8,960
	Income tax on January income		
	$.40 \times (160,000 + 150 + 500 - 100,000 - 28,000 - 3,750 - 1,000 - 5,000 - 500)$ $= 8,960$		

EXHIBIT 4-3

Chan Audio Company

General Ledger

Assets	=	Liabilities + Stockholders' Equity	
(Increases Left, Decreases Right)		**(Decreases Left, Increases Right)**	

Cash		Note Payable		Paid-in Capital	
Bal. 71,700			Bal. 100,000		Bal. 400,000

Accounts Receivable		Accounts Payable		Sales	
Bal. 160,300			Bal. 117,100		Bal. 160,000

Note Receivable		Unearned Rent Revenue		Cost of Goods Sold	
Bal. 40,000		(f) 500	Bal. 3,000	Bal. 100,000	
			Bal. 2,500		

Merchandise Inventory				Wages Expense	
Bal. 250,200		Accrued Wages Payable		Bal. 28,000	
			(c) 3,750	(c) 3,750	
Prepaid Rent				Bal. 31,750	
Bal. 15,000	(b) 5,000	Accrued Interest Payable			
Bal. 10,000			(d) 500	Depreciation Expense	
				(a) 1,000	

Store Equipment		Accrued Income Taxes Payable			
Bal. 114,900			(g) 8,960	Rent Expense	
				(b) 5,000	

Accumulated Depreciation, Store Equipment				Interest Expense	
	(a) 1,000			(d) 500	

Accrued Interest Receivable				Interest Revenue	
(e) 150					(e) 150

				Rent Revenue	
					(f) 500

				Income Tax Expense	
				(g) 8,960	

EXHIBIT 4-4

Chan Audio Company

Adjusted Trial Balance, January 31, 20X0

Account Title	Balance		
	Debit	Credit	
Cash	$ 71,700		⎫
Accounts receivable	160,300		
Note receivable	40,000		
Accrued interest receivable	150		
Merchandise inventory	250,200		
Prepaid rent	10,000		
Store equipment	114,900		Balance
Accumulated depreciation, store equipment		$ 1,000	Sheet
Note payable		100,000	Exhibit 4-5
Accounts payable		117,100	
Unearned rent revenue		2,500	
Accrued wages payable		3,750	
Accrued interest payable		500	
Accrued income taxes payable		8,960	
Paid-in capital		400,000	⎭
Sales		160,000	⎫
Interest revenue		150	
Rent revenue		500	
Cost of goods sold	100,000		Income
Wages expense	31,750		Statement
Depreciation expense	1,000		Exhibits 4-9
Rent expense	5,000		and 4-10
Interest expense	500		
Income tax expense	8,960		⎭
Total	$794,460	$794,460	

Classified Balance Sheet

▶▶ OBJECTIVE 7

Prepare a classified balance sheet and use it to assess short-term liquidity.

classified balance sheet

A balance sheet that groups the accounts into subcategories to help readers quickly gain a perspective on the company's financial position and to draw attention to certain accounts or groups of accounts.

Once the company has recorded all necessary adjusting entries, it is ready to prepare the financial statements. As we saw in Chapter 1, balance sheet accounts are separated into the major categories of assets, liabilities, and owners' equity. A **classified balance sheet** further groups the accounts into subcategories to help readers quickly gain a perspective on the company's financial position and to draw attention to certain accounts or groups of accounts. Assets are frequently classified into two groups: current assets and noncurrent or long-term assets. Liabilities are similarly classified into current liabilities and noncurrent or long-term liabilities.

Current Assets and Liabilities

Current assets are cash and other assets that a company expects to convert to cash, sell, or consume during the next 12 months (or within the normal operating cycle if longer than 1 year). Similarly, **current liabilities** are those liabilities that come due within the next year (or within the normal operating cycle if longer than a year). Typically, we expect companies to pay current

EXHIBIT 4-5

Chan Audio Company

Balance Sheet, January 31, 20X0

Assets			Liabilities and Stockholders' Equity		
Current assets			Current liabilities		
Cash		$ 71,700	Accounts payable		$117,100
Accounts receivable		160,300	Unearned rent revenue		2,500
Note receivable		40,000	Accrued wages payable		3,750
Accrued interest receivable		150	Accrued interest payable		500
Merchandise inventory		250,200	Accrued income taxes payable		8,960
Prepaid rent		10,000	Note payable		100,000
Total current assets		532,350	Total current liabilities		232,810
Long-term assets			Stockholders' equity		
Store equipment	$114,900		Paid-in capital	$400,000	
Accumulated depreciation	(1,000)	113,900	Retained earnings	13,440	413,440
Total		$646,250	Total		$646,250

liabilities using assets classified as current. Identifying current assets and liabilities is useful in assessing the company's ability to meet obligations as they become due. For the most part, current assets give rise to the cash needed to pay current liabilities, so the relationship between these categories is important.

Exhibit 4-5 shows the classified balance sheet for Chan Audio Company, which we prepared from the adjusted trial balance for the company (shown in Exhibit 4-4). In the United States a classified balance sheet generally lists the current asset accounts in the order in which the assets are likely to be converted to cash during the coming year. Therefore, Cash appears first. In the case of Chan Audio, Accounts Receivable appears next because the firm should receive cash payments for these accounts within weeks or months. The Note Receivable and related Accrued Interest Receivable, the third and fourth accounts listed, are due January 1, 20X1, within the 1 year (or normal operating cycle) time frame for classification as current assets. Nonmonetary assets, such as inventories and prepaid expenses (in this case, Merchandise Inventory and Prepaid Rent), appear last in the current assets section of the balance sheet. Chan does not convert Prepaid Rent to cash, but it is a current asset in the sense that its existence reduces the obligation to pay cash within the next year.

As shown in Exhibit 4-5, we also list current liability accounts in the approximate order in which they will require the use of cash during the coming year. Wages tend to be paid weekly or monthly, whereas interest and taxes tend to be paid monthly, quarterly, or annually.

The difference between current assets and current liabilities is **working capital** (**net working capital** or **net current assets**). In the case of Chan Audio Company, the working capital on January 31, 20X0, is ($532,350 – $232,810) = $299,540. Working capital is important because it relates current assets and current liabilities. It normally increases in dollar amount as the company grows, so it is proportional to the size of the firm.

Formats of Balance Sheets

While all balance sheets contain the same basic information, the details and formats of balance sheets and other financial statements vary across companies and accounting jurisdictions. For example, consider the balance sheets of Columbia Sportswear for December 31, 2010, and December 31, 2009, as shown in Exhibit 4-6. The format and classifications are those actually used by Columbia. Note the absence of a separate subtotal for noncurrent assets and noncurrent liabilities. Some companies prefer to omit these subtotals when there are only a few items within a specific class. Exhibit 4-6 presents a classified balance sheet in the **report format** (assets at the top), which is different from the **account format** (assets on the left) illustrated in Exhibit 4-5. Either format is acceptable.

current assets
Cash and other assets that a company expects to convert to cash, sell, or consume during the next 12 months or within the normal operating cycle if longer than 1 year.

current liabilities
Liabilities that come due within the next year or within the normal operating cycle if longer than 1 year. Typically, we expect current liabilities to be paid using assets classified as current.

working capital (net working capital, net current assets)
The excess of current assets over current liabilities.

report format
A classified balance sheet with the assets at the top.

account format
A classified balance sheet with the assets on the left.

EXHIBIT 4-6

Columbia Sportswear Company

Consolidated Balance Sheets (in thousands)

	December 31	
	2010	**2009**
Assets		
Current assets		
Cash and cash equivalents	$ 234,257	$ 386,664
Short-term investments	68,812	22,759
Accounts receivable, net	300,181	226,548
Inventories, net	314,298	222,161
Deferred income taxes	45,091	31,550
Prepaid expenses and other current assets	28,241	32,030
Total current assets	990,880	921,712
Property, plant, and equipment, net	221,813	235,440
Intangible assets, net	40,423	27,127
Goodwill	14,470	12,659
Other noncurrent assets	27,168	15,945
Total assets	$1,294,754	$1,212,883
Liabilities and Shareholders' Equity		
Current liabilities		
Accounts payable	$ 130,626	$ 102,494
Accrued liabilities	102,810	67,312
Income taxes payable	16,037	6,884
Deferred income taxes	2,153	2,597
Total current liabilities	251,626	179,287
Income taxes payable	19,698	19,830
Deferred income taxes	—	1,494
Other long-term liabilities	21,456	15,044
Total liabilities	292,780	215,655
Shareholders' equity:		
Preferred stock; 10,000 shares authorized; none issued and outstanding	—	—
Common stock; (no par value) 125,000 shares authorized; 33,683 and 33,736 issued and outstanding	5,052	836
Retained earnings	950,207	952,948
Accumulated other comprehensive income	46,715	43,444
Total shareholders' equity	1,001,974	997,228
Total liabilities and shareholders' equity	$1,294,754	$1,212,883

Foreign companies and U.S. companies in certain industries may use formats that differ from those presented in Exhibits 4-5 and 4-6. Exhibit 4-7 shows a condensed balance sheet for Nokia Corporation, a Finnish company that is one of the world's largest makers of cell phones. Nokia prepares a classified balance sheet in a format that is common for companies reporting under IFRS. Note that Nokia lists noncurrent assets totaling €11,978 million before current assets totaling €27,145 million. The sequencing of the liabilities and equity side of the balance sheet is reversed relative to the ordering typical in a balance sheet prepared under U.S. GAAP. Nokia first lists shareholders' equity totaling €16,231 million, followed by noncurrent liabilities of €5,352 million and finally current liabilities of €17,540 million. Unilever Group is a dual-listed company consisting of Unilever NV headquartered in Rotterdam, Netherlands,

EXHIBIT 4-7

Nokia Corporation

Condensed Consolidated Balance Sheets (in millions of euros)

	December 31	
	2010	**2009**
Assets		
Noncurrent assets	€11,978	€12,125
Current assets	27,145	23,613
Total assets	€39,123	€35,738
Shareholders' Equity and Liabilities		
Total equity	€16,231	€14,749
Noncurrent liabilities	5,352	5,801
Current liabilities	17,540	15,188
Total shareholders' equity and liabilities	€39,123	€35,738

and Unilever PLC headquartered in London, England. The company operates as a single business and is the top maker of packaged consumer goods in the world. Unilever also uses IFRS to prepare its financial statements. Exhibit 4-8 shows balance sheets for Unilever for December 31, 2010, and December 31, 2009. Unilever lists noncurrent assets before current assets and then deducts current liabilities from current assets to give a direct measure of working capital (called net current assets or net current liabilities). Unilever reports negative working capital of €1,122 million as of December 31, 2010. After the calculation of a subtotal representing total assets less current liabilities, Unilever reports noncurrent liabilities and shareholders' equity. Recognize that, regardless of the format and modest differences in account naming conventions, balance sheets contain the same basic information.

Current Ratio

Current assets are an indicator, albeit an imperfect indicator, of how much cash a company will have on hand in the near future; current liabilities tell you how much debt the company will have to pay off with that cash in the near future. Comparing the two amounts helps financial statements users assess a business entity's **liquidity**, which is its ability to meet its near-term financial obligations with cash and near-cash assets as those obligations become due.

Investors use the **current ratio** (also called the **working capital ratio**), which we calculate by dividing current assets by current liabilities, to evaluate a company's liquidity. Chan Audio's current ratio is

$$\text{Current ratio} = \frac{\$532,350}{\$232,810} = 2.29$$

liquidity
An entity's ability to meet its near-term financial obligations with cash and near-cash assets as those obligations become due.

current ratio (working capital ratio)
Current assets divided by current liabilities.

A current ratio that is too low may indicate the company will have difficulty meeting its short-term obligations. Conversely, a current ratio that is too high may indicate excessive holdings of current assets such as cash, accounts receivable, or inventories. Excessive holdings of this nature are bad for a company because they tie up money that could be more effectively used elsewhere.

How do we assess this ratio? Is a higher current ratio always better? Other things being equal, the higher a company's current ratio, the more assurance creditors have that the company will be able to pay them in full and on time. However, as with all ratios, it can be misleading to draw conclusions from the numeric value of the ratio alone. In the case of the current ratio, it is important to consider the composition of current assets and current liabilities before drawing inferences. Suppose that just prior to the end of January, Chan Audio used $70,000 of its cash to pay off part of the outstanding balance in Accounts Payable. The restated current ratio is

$$\text{Current ratio} = \frac{\$532,350 - \$70,000}{\$232,810 - \$70,000} = 2.84$$

EXHIBIT 4-8

Unilever Group

Condensed Consolidated Balance Sheets (in millions of euros)

	December 31	
	2010	**2009**
Goodwill	€13,178	€12,464
Intangible assets	5,100	4,583
Property, plant, and equipment	7,854	6,644
Pension asset for funded schemes in surplus	910	759
Deferred tax assets	607	738
Other noncurrent assets	1,034	1,017
Total noncurrent assets	28,683	26,205
Inventories	4,309	3,578
Trade and other current receivables	4,135	3,429
Current tax assets	298	173
Cash and cash equivalents	2,316	2,642
Other financial assets	550	972
Noncurrent assets held for sale	876	17
Total current assets	12,484	10,811
Financial liabilities	(2,276)	(2,279)
Trade payables and other current liabilities	(10,226)	(8,413)
Current tax liabilities	(639)	(487)
Provisions	(408)	(420)
Liabilities directly associated with noncurrent assets held for sale	(57)	—
Total current liabilities	(13,606)	(11,599)
Net current assets/(liabilities)	(1,122)	(788)
Total assets less current liabilities	**€27,561**	**€25,417**
Financial liabilities due after one year	€7,258	€7,692
Noncurrent tax liabilities	184	107
Pensions/post-retirement health-care liabilities		
Funded schemes in deficit	1,081	1,519
Unfunded schemes	1,899	1,822
Provisions	886	729
Deferred tax liabilities	880	764
Other noncurrent liabilities	295	248
Total noncurrent liabilities	12,483	12,881
Share capital	484	484
Share premium	134	131
Other reserves	(5,406)	(5,900)
Retained profit	19,273	17,350
Shareholders' equity	14,485	12,065
Non-controlling interests	593	471
Total equity	15,078	12,536
Total capital employed	**€27,561**	**€25,417**

Even though the restated current ratio is higher than the previous value of 2.29, it is difficult to argue that Chan is more liquid as it has only $1,700 in cash. The relative liquidity of Chan under these two different scenarios depends on the company's ability to convert its noncash current assets such as Merchandise Inventory and Accounts Receivable to cash. This illustrates one of the difficulties in interpreting the current ratio; some current assets are less liquid than others and may take longer to convert to cash.

Variations of the current ratio attempt to distinguish among assets based on their relative level of liquidity. One common variation of the current ratio is the **quick ratio** (also known as the **acid test ratio**), which removes inventory (and potentially other less liquid assets such as prepaid expenses) from the numerator of the calculation. This ratio provides a more restrictive view of the company's liquidity. For example, in the initial scenario depicted for Chan Audio, the quick ratio is $[(\$532{,}350 - \$250{,}200) \div \$232{,}810] = 1.21$. In the second scenario, the quick ratio is $[(\$532{,}350 - \$250{,}200 - \$70{,}000) \div (\$232{,}810 - \$70{,}000)] = 1.30$.

An old rule of thumb was that the current ratio should be greater than 2.0. However, in strong economic times, when companies have good investment opportunities, current ratios are more commonly close to 1.0. And in 2011, following the very weak economies of the preceding few years, current ratios for many companies were well over 2.0. Why? Because companies were holding large amounts of cash. In making judgments about a company's liquidity, analysts do not focus on the ratio value in isolation; rather they compare a company's current ratio with those of past years, with those of similar companies, or with an industry norm. For example, on January 1, 2012, IBM's ratio was 1.21, compared with an industry median of about 2.5. Although only slightly greater than 1.0 and below the industry median, IBM's ratio is probably not a cause for concern. Over fiscal years 2006 through 2011, IBM's current ratio ranged from a low of 1.11 at December 31, 2009, to a high of only 1.36 at December 31, 2006. This consistently low current ratio suggests that IBM is comfortable operating with current assets only slightly larger than current liabilities. It is also common for firms in the utility industry to have low current ratios because of low levels of inventory and stable cash flows. For example, Pacific Gas & Electric, a regional gas and electric power company, had a current ratio of only 0.84 on January 1, 2012. On the other hand, Google's current ratio of 5.9 on the same day was almost five times as large as IBM's and seven times as large as that of Pacific Gas & Electric. You will find more information on working capital and the current ratio in the Business First box on page 162.

Although some people use the current or quick ratio to measure short-term debt-paying ability, a prediction of cash receipts and disbursements is more useful. Whether a company's level of cash is too low or too high really depends on the forecasts of operating requirements over the coming months. For example, a company such as a small comic book and baseball card retailer might need very little cash on hand because upcoming debts and operating needs will be small in the next few months. Conversely, Marvel Comics, the corporation that produces the comic books sold by the small retailer, will need millions of dollars in cash to meet upcoming debt and short-term operating needs. As a rule, companies should try to keep on hand only the cash necessary to meet disbursement needs and invest any temporary excess cash to generate additional income.

quick ratio (acid test ratio)
Variation of the current ratio that removes less liquid assets from the numerator. Perhaps the most common version of this ratio is (current assets – inventory) ÷ current liabilities.

INTERPRETING FINANCIAL STATEMENTS

Published annual reports typically contain condensed balance sheet information. This level of detail is appropriate for external analysts and investors. Is this same level of detail sufficient for internal use?

Answer

No. Firms prepare detailed balance sheets for their internal use. Suppose that you are the person responsible for managing inventory at Columbia Sportswear's flagship store in Portland, Oregon.

Rather than just knowing the total amount of inventory on hand, you would need to know what the inventory levels are for spring merchandise and for summer merchandise, for men's wear and women's wear, and for clothing and accessories. This detail and more is necessary for you to manage your operation and evaluate your performance. Outside investors are more concerned with the overall performance of Columbia Sportswear relative to competing retailers, so summarized company-wide information is sufficient.

Income Statement

We have seen that balance sheets provide decision makers with information about a company's ability to meet its short-term operating and debt needs. However, investors are also concerned about a company's ability to generate earnings and pay dividends. The income statement provides some of the information necessary to address these concerns. Income statements, like balance sheets, may include subcategories that help focus attention on certain accounts or groups of accounts. There are two commonly used income statement formats, the single-step income statement and the multiple-step income statement.

▶▶ **OBJECTIVE 8**
Prepare single- and multiple-step income statements.

BUSINESS FIRST

MANAGING WORKING CAPITAL

The main components of working capital for a typical company are accounts receivable plus inventories less accounts payable. Analysts must interpret fluctuations in working capital levels with care. All else equal, lower levels of receivables and inventories and higher levels of accounts payable will decrease working capital levels. Receivables may decrease because of declining sales, but they can also decrease when collection of receivables speeds up. Decreasing inventories may mean decreased ability to deliver orders on time. However, they may also mean the company is doing a better job anticipating customer demand. Accounts payable may increase for a variety of reasons: increasing inventory purchases in response to higher demand, the company's inability to meet its short-term obligations, or a conscious decision on the part of the company to effectively use supplier financing.

The traditional view is that large amounts of working capital and high current ratios are good—they show that a company is likely to remain solvent. However, large amounts of working capital may needlessly tie up funds that can be used profitably elsewhere in the company. Each dollar not invested in working capital is a dollar of cash available for investing in value-adding activities—activities that actually create and deliver products or services to customers. When companies have good investment opportunities, working capital levels tend to be lower. In the 1990s, the booming economy offered such opportunities and holding large amounts of inventories and accounts receivable fell out of fashion. The stated target of some firms was zero working capital and a current ratio of 1.0, and many companies made a concerted effort to reduce working capital and, hence, lower their current ratios.

The financial crisis of 2008 brought an economic slowdown and nearly frozen credit markets. Faced with declining revenues and an inability to borrow, the working capital of many U.S. companies began to creep back up. As sales levels declined, inventory levels rose and some companies faced an increase in receivables levels because customers took longer to pay. When faced with this situation, companies had to reexamine their working capital management. In an article published in *CFO World*, Brian Shanahan of REL Consultancy stated, "If you are looking for some kind of funding, with the exception of stealing money from someone, improving your working capital position is the cheapest way you can do it."

Consider Cytec Industries, a global supplier of specialty chemicals and materials. Despite a current ratio of 2.45 at the end of 2008, Cytec was faced with a liquidity challenge. While the current ratio was high, the company held only $55.3 million, less than 5% of current assets, in cash. Trade receivables of $448.8 million and inventories of $569.4 million comprised 37% and 47% of current assets, respectively. To ensure an adequate cash balance, the company began a concerted effort to improve its

working capital performance in 2009, including linking employee pay to the company's working capital goals.

Cytec's current ratio decreased 19% to 1.98 at the end of 2009. This lower current ratio does not necessarily indicate a reduction in liquidity or decreased efficiency in management of working capital. In fact, the opposite is true. Cytec dramatically improved the rate at which it collected accounts receivable in 2009, reducing the balance in Trade Accounts Receivable at year-end to $374.2 million (33% of current assets). As a result of improved inventory management, Cytec also reduced its inventory levels by 38% to $351.9 million by year-end 2009, down to 31% of current assets. Less money tied up in inventory leaves more available for other uses. These actions, along with others, resulted in $261.7 million in available cash at the end of 2009, a 373% increase!

Cytec's current ratio increased to 2.26 by the end of 2010. Remember that a higher current ratio does not always indicate improved liquidity. However, in this case, Cytec continued to improve its working capital management. The cash balance increased to $383.3 million or 29% of current assets, while accounts receivable and inventories fell to 28% and 27% of current assets, respectively. The company attributed these changes to continued increases in the rate of receivables collections, increased inventory sales, and successful inventory management.

Cytec is not alone in holding a large cash balance. According to a survey of U.S. finance executives done by *CFO*, U.S. nonfinancial companies held more than $2 trillion in cash and other liquid assets as of the end of June 2011. Due to the slow economic recovery, uncertain demand for products, and volatile world financial markets, companies continue to maintain large cash balances.

Thomson Reuters, the global provider of financial, legal, tax and accounting, health-care, and scientific information, data, and news, improved its working capital management in 2010. How did Thomson Reuters accomplish this? While Cytec achieved greater liquidity by effective management of receivables and inventories, Thomson Reuters has virtually no inventory, so inventory management improvements were not possible. Also, the company does much of its business outside the United States, where longer-term receivables collection times are the norm. As a result the company focused its efforts on its payable cycle, taking better advantage of supplier credit.

You can see that analysts must look beyond the current ratio value itself to gain an understanding of the actual performance of the company.

Sources: K. O'Sullivan, "Sitting Comfortably on a Cash Cushion," *CFO*, November 1, 2011, pp. 45–47; C. Doherty, "Working Capital Improvements," *CFO World*, September 2, 2011, http://www.cfoworld.co.uk/in-depth/financial-planning/3300926/working-capital-improvements; D. Katz, "Easing the Squeeze: The 2011 Working Capital Scorecard," *CFO*, July 15, 2011, pp. 44–51; Cytec Industries 2010 and 2009 Annual Reports; Thomson Reuters 2010 Annual Report.

Single- and Multiple-Step Income Statements

The adjusted trial balance for Chan Audio Company (Exhibit 4-4) provides the data for the two formats of income statements shown in Exhibits 4-9 and 4-10. Exhibit 4-9 presents a **single-step income statement**. Notice that it groups all types of revenue together (e.g., Sales Revenue, Rent Revenue, and Interest Revenue) and then deducts all expenses without reporting any intermediate subtotals. Exhibit 4-10 provides an example of a **multiple-step income statement**. Rather than grouping all revenues together and then subtracting all expenses, the multiple-step income statement combines revenues and expenses to highlight significant relationships. Regardless of the presentation format, the net income number is the same. There is no theoretical or practical reason to prefer one of these formats. Experienced readers of financial statements can easily adjust from one to another. As you begin to read and evaluate actual statements, do not let the superficial differences in presentation confuse you.

single-step income statement
An income statement that groups all revenues together and then lists and deducts all expenses without reporting any intermediate subtotals.

multiple-step income statement
An income statement that contains one or more subtotals that highlight significant relationships.

EXHIBIT 4-9

Chan Audio Company

Single-Step Income Statement for the Month Ended January 31, 20X0

Sales		$160,000
Rent revenue		500
Interest revenue		150
Total sales and other revenues		160,650
Expenses		
Cost of goods sold	$100,000	
Wages	31,750	
Depreciation	1,000	
Rent	5,000	
Interest	500	
Income taxes	8,960	
Total expenses		147,210
Net income		$ 13,440

EXHIBIT 4-10

Chan Audio Company

Multiple-Step Income Statement for the Month Ended January 31, 20X0

Sales		$160,000
Cost of goods sold		100,000
Gross profit		60,000
Operating expenses		
Wages	$31,750	
Depreciation	1,000	
Rent	5,000	37,750
Operating income		22,250
Other revenues and expenses		
Rent revenue	500	
Interest revenue	150	
Total other revenue	650	
Deduct: interest expense	500	150
Income before income taxes		22,400
Income taxes		8,960
Net income		$ 13,440

EXHIBIT 4-11

Columbia Sportswear Company

Consolidated Statements of Operations (in thousands)

| | Year Ended December 31 | |
	2010	2009
Net sales	$1,483,524	$1,244,023
Cost of sales	854,120	719,945
Gross profit	629,404	524,078
Selling, general, and administrative expenses	534,068	444,715
Net licensing income	(7,991)	(8,399)
Income from operations	103,327	87,762
Interest income, net	1,564	2,088
Income before income tax	104,891	89,850
Income tax expense	27,854	22,829
Net income	$ 77,037	$ 67,021

The majority of U.S. companies employ the multiple-step income statement format in their external financial statements. The Columbia Sportswear income statement (which the company calls a statement of operations) in Exhibit 4-11 is a multiple-step income statement. Let's take a closer look at the subtotals that commonly appear in a multiple-step statement. Most multiple-step income statements start with the separate computation and disclosure of **gross profit** (also called **gross margin**), which is the excess of sales revenue over the cost of the inventory that was sold. Chan reports a gross profit of $60,000 in Exhibit 4-10, and Columbia Sportswear's 2010 income statement shows a gross profit of $629,404,000.

The next section of a multiple-step income statement usually contains the **operating expenses**, which is a group of recurring expenses that pertain to the firm's routine, ongoing operations. Examples of such expenses are wages, rent, depreciation, and various other operation-oriented expenses, such as telephone, heat, and advertising. We deduct these operating expenses from the gross profit to obtain **operating income** (also called **operating profit** or **income from operations**). Chan reports operating income of $22,250 in Exhibit 4-10. In Exhibit 4-11, Columbia Sportswear groups all recurring operating expenses together into a category called Selling, General, and Administrative Expenses and subtracts them from gross profit. Finally, prior to computing income from operations, Columbia Sportswear also deducts from operating expenses a small amount of income from licensing activities. Be sure to note that, while Columbia subtracts Selling, General, and Administrative Expenses from gross profit when computing Income from Operations, it adds the line item called Net Licensing Income to gross profit because it is a revenue item, not an expense item. Columbia reports income from operations of $103,327,000 in 2010.

The next grouping in the multiple-step income statement contains **nonoperating revenues and expenses**, which are revenues and expenses that are not directly related to the mainstream of a firm's operations. Nonoperating revenues are usually minor in relation to the sales revenue shown in the first section of the multiple-step statement. Nonoperating expenses are also minor, with the possible exception of interest expense. Some companies have significant levels of debt (which causes high interest expense), whereas other companies incur little debt and have low interest expense. Chan Audio Company separately itemizes Interest Expense and Interest Revenue in Exhibit 4-10. In contrast, Columbia Sportswear nets Interest Expense and Interest Revenue on the income statement. In all financial statements, accountants use the label "net" to denote that some amounts have been offset in computing the final result. Thus, if a company reports net interest, it means that interest revenue and interest expense have been combined into one number, which may result in either an expense or a revenue. In the case of Columbia Sportswear, interest revenue exceeds interest expense in both years shown in Exhibit 4-11. Note that Interest Income, Net has been added to Income from Operations to arrive at Income before Income Tax. Users of financial statements usually regard interest revenue and interest expense as "other" or "nonoperating" items because they arise from lending and borrowing

---

gross profit (gross margin)

The excess of sales revenue over the cost of the inventory that was sold.

operating expenses

A group of recurring expenses that pertain to the firm's routine, ongoing operations.

operating income (operating profit, income from operations)

Gross profit less all operating expenses.

nonoperating revenues and expenses

Revenues and expenses that are not directly related to the mainstream of a firm's operations.

EXHIBIT 4-12

Unilever Group

Condensed Consolidated Income Statement for the Year Ended December 31, 2011 (in millions of euros)

Turnover	€46,467
Operating profit	6,433
Net finance costs	(448)
Other nonoperating income (loss)	260
Profit before taxation	6,245
Taxation	(1,622)
Net profit	€ 4,623

money—activities that are distinct from most companies' ordinary operations of selling goods or services. Exceptions occur in companies in the business of lending and borrowing money: banks, credit unions, insurance companies, and other financial intermediaries.

If income statements keep nonoperating revenues and expenses separate from operating revenues and expenses, we can easily compare operating income over time or between companies. Comparisons of operating income focus attention on selling the product and controlling the costs of doing so. Success in this arena is an important test of a company's health.

Note where income taxes appear in both the single-step and multiple-step income statements of Chan Audio in Exhibits 4-9 and 4-10, as well as in Columbia Sportswear's income statement in Exhibit 4-11. Most companies follow the practice of showing income taxes as a separate item immediately above net income, regardless of the grouping of other items on the income statement.

IFRS and U.S. GAAP are broadly similar with respect to the presentation of the income statement. The suggested income statement format for companies reporting under IFRS includes subtotals for gross profit and pretax income. This is similar, but not identical, to the U.S. multiple-step format. However, while IFRS allows companies to display expenses either by nature or by function, U.S. GAAP requires them to show expenses by function. The income statement of Nokia Corporation, the Finnish cell phone company referenced earlier in the chapter, is indistinguishable in format from the multiple-step income statement of Columbia Sportswear. However, you can see a few major format differences in a condensed version of the income statement of Unilever Group, the Anglo-Dutch consumer products giant, shown in Exhibit 4-12. The company reports Turnover of €46,467 million for the year ended December 31, 2011. The term **turnover**, used by some IFRS companies, is synonymous with sales or sales revenue. Unilever then reports operating profit of €6,433 million without itemizing the operating expenses. While you can deduce that operating expenses were (€46,467 million – €6,433 million) = €40,034 million, the income statement does not show them directly. The remainder of the statement is similar to those shown earlier.

Analysts and investors follow trends in corporate earnings. When observing earnings trends, it is important to distinguish between trends in operating versus nonoperating activities. There is a distinction between those circumstances where earnings growth is due to declining interest expense or increasing interest revenue and those circumstances where earnings growth is due to a dramatic increase in sales. The first two sources of earnings growth are not directly linked to the company's routine, ongoing activities. However, when demand for the product increases, the long-term potential for continued growth is improved. The need to use caution in interpreting changes in earnings is not limited to the distinction between operating and nonoperating earnings. For example, everything else equal, a reduction in research and development expense—an operating expense—will result in an improvement in current period earnings. However, the long-term implications for the company may be negative if research and development is crucial to the development of new products.

turnover
Sales or sales revenue.

Profitability Evaluation Ratios

For experienced managers, the income statement and balance sheet are key components of the "language of business." These managers can compare current period income with that of the previous quarter or prior year. They have a solid understanding of their competitors' financial

▶▶ **OBJECTIVE 9**
Use ratios to assess profitability.

statements and can evaluate how their company compares with the competition. How can individuals who do not have this deep company and industry knowledge use the financial statements to gain insights into the company's performance?

Earlier in this chapter, we saw that ratios such as the current ratio help give meaning to the numbers in the balance sheet. Similarly, ratios using income statement numbers are useful in evaluating a company's **profitability**, which is the ability of a company to provide its investors with a particular rate of return on their investment. If Mary invests $100 in Columbia Sportswear and receives $10 every year as a result, $10 is her return on investment. However, absolute amounts are hard to evaluate. What if Mary had given Columbia Sportswear $200? In that case, a return of $10 would not be as attractive. Thus, it is common to express the return as a **rate of return**, a return per dollar invested. In the case of a $100 investment, a $10 return is a 10% rate of return ($10 ÷ $100). For a $200 investment, a $10 return is a 5% rate of return ($10 ÷ $200).

Profitability measures are useful decision-making tools. Investors use them to distinguish among different investment opportunities. Managers know that their company's profitability measures will affect the investment decisions of investors and that high profitability makes it easier to raise capital by selling stock or issuing debt securities. From time to time, managers may have to decide whether to buy another company, a division of a company, or a machine that will be used in manufacturing a new product. In each case, the manager will evaluate the profitability of the project as part of making the decision.

Investors use trends in profitability measures over time, and within and across industries, as a basis for predictions and decisions. We provide a very brief introduction to four profitability ratios: gross profit percentage, return on sales, return on common stockholders' equity, and return on assets. Chapter 12 expands on the interpretation of these ratios and introduces additional measures of financial performance.

Gross Profit Percentage

A ratio based on gross profit (sales revenue minus cost of goods sold) is particularly useful to a retailer or manufacturer in choosing a pricing strategy and in judging its results. This measure, the **gross profit percentage**, or **gross margin percentage**, is defined as gross profit divided by sales revenue. Chan Audio Company's gross profit percentage for January is (numbers from Exhibit 4-10)

$$\text{Gross profit percentage} = \text{Gross profit} \div \text{Sales}$$
$$= \$60,000 \div \$160,000$$
$$= 37.5\%$$

We can also present this relationship as follows:

	Amount	Percentage
Sales	$160,000	100.0%
Cost of goods sold	100,000	62.5
Gross profit	$ 60,000	37.5%

Gross profit percentages vary greatly by industry. For example, software companies have high gross profit percentages (Microsoft's was almost 78% for the year ending June 30, 2011). Why? Because most costs in the software industry are in research and development and sales and marketing, not in cost of goods sold. In contrast, retail companies have lower gross margin percentages because product costs are their main expense. For example, for the year ended August 28, 2011, the gross profit percentage for Costco was 12.6%. Other gross margin percentages fall between the extremes, such as Intel's at 65.3% and Columbia Sportswear's at 42.4%.

Return on Sales or Net Profit Margin

Managers carefully follow the **return on sales ratio** (also known as the **profit margin ratio**), which shows the relationship of net income to sales revenue. This ratio gauges a company's ability to control the level of all its expenses relative to the level of its sales.

profitability
The ability of a company to provide investors with a particular rate of return on their investment.

rate of return
The return per dollar invested.

gross profit percentage (gross margin percentage)
Gross profit (sales revenue – cost of goods sold) divided by sales revenue.

return on sales ratio (profit margin ratio)
Net income divided by sales.

As with the gross profit percentage, the return on sales tends to vary by industry, but the range is not as great. We can compute Chan Audio's return on sales ratio as follows using numbers from Exhibit 4-9 or 4-10:

$$\text{Return on sales} = \text{Net income} \div \text{Sales}$$
$$= \$13,440 \div \$160,000$$
$$= 8.4\%$$

Columbia Sportswear reports a return on sales ratio of 5.2% ($77,037 ÷ $1,483,524) for the year ended December 31, 2010.

Return on Common Stockholders' Equity

The **return on common stockholders' equity ratio (ROE or ROCE)** also uses net income, but compares it with invested capital (as measured by average common stockholders' equity) instead of sales. Many analysts regard this ratio as the ultimate measure of overall accomplishment from the perspective of the shareholder. Chan Audio's common stockholders' equity on January 1 was paid-in capital of $400,000 and on January 30 was this $400,000 plus $13,350 of retained earnings, making January's average common stockholders' equity $406,720. Therefore, the company's return on common stockholders' equity for the month of January is

return on common stockholders' equity ratio (ROE or ROCE)
Net income divided by invested capital (measured by average common stockholders' equity).

$$\text{Return on common stockholders' equity} = \text{Net income} \div \text{Average common stockholders' equity}$$
$$= \$13,440 \div \$406,720$$
$$= 3.3\% \text{ (for 1 month)}$$

Return on Assets

The **return on assets ratio (ROA)** compares net income with invested capital as measured by average total assets. The company invests its resources in assets, which it uses to generate revenues and ultimately, net income. The return on assets ratio measures how effectively those assets generate profits. Assuming a balance in total assets of $620,000 as of January 1, we can calculate the return on assets ratio for Chan Audio for the month of January as follows:

return on assets ratio (ROA)
Net income divided by average total assets.

$$\text{Return on assets} = \text{Net income} \div \text{Average total assets}$$
$$= \$13,440 \div 1/2 \text{ (January 1 balance, } \$620,000$$
$$+ \text{ January 31 balance, } \$646,250)$$
$$= \$13,440 \div \$633,125$$
$$= 2.1\% \text{ (for 1 month)}$$

Other variations of the return on assets ratio are discussed in Chapter 12.

Chan Audio's 37.5% gross profit percentage is high compared with the average of 31.1% for the retail stereo industry. Chan Audio has also maintained excellent expense control as evidenced by its 8.4% return on sales, 39.6% return on common stockholders' equity (a monthly rate of 3.3% × 12 = 39.6% as an annual rate), and 25.2% return on assets (2.1% × 12 = 25.2%), which are higher than the annual returns earned by the industry over the same period.

Recent examples of annual return on sales, return on common stockholders' equity, and return on assets ratios for firms in different industries are shown here:

	Return on Sales (%)	Return on Common Stockholders' Equity (%)	Return on Assets (%)
Microsoft	33.1	54.0	28.2
Costco	1.6	12.4	5.8
McDonald's	20.6	34.5	15.9
CVS Caremark	3.6	9.3	5.5
Honda (Japan)	6.3	12.5	4.9
Google	29.0	20.7	17.3
Delta Air Lines	1.9	103.9	1.6
Starbucks	8.8	28.1	15.8

The return on stockholder's equity for **Delta Air Lines** may seem out of line, especially with its small returns on sales and assets. It is a result of very small stockholders' equity. This is an illustration that ratios can be distorted by extremely small denominators.

INTERPRETING FINANCIAL STATEMENTS

Which industry would you expect to have a higher gross margin percentage, the grocery industry or the pharmaceutical industry? Why?

Answer

There are many "right ways" to think about this issue. Whole Foods, a premium grocery store chain, has a gross margin of 35%, while Safeway's is 27%. The grocery industry is a retail activity where stores buy and resell items very quickly. As a result they can accept fairly low margins because they hold the inventory briefly and face little risk of failure. In contrast, the pharmaceutical industry has to develop drugs, seek government approval to market them, and then aggressively sell them. Thus, the pharmaceutical industry has high gross margin percentages. In 2010, Pfizer had a gross margin percentage of 76%. It is important to remember that Cost of Goods Sold excludes Selling, General, and Administrative Costs, which are larger relative to sales in the pharmaceutical industry than in the grocery industry. In addition, the pharmaceutical industry faces huge R&D costs, which accountants treat as a period cost instead of a product cost. So R&D, which may be 15% or more of sales in the pharmaceutical industry, is not part of Cost of Goods Sold and does not affect the gross margin percentage.

Summary Problem for Your Review

PROBLEM

Johnson & Johnson (maker of Tylenol, Band-Aid products, and other health-care and personal use products) reports a statement of earnings as follows:

Johnson & Johnson
Statement of Earnings for the Year Ended December 31, 2010
($ in millions except per share figures)

Sales to customers	$ 61,587
Cost of products sold	18,792
Gross profit	42,795
Selling, marketing, and administrative expenses	19,424
Research and development expense	6,844
Interest income	(107)
Interest expense	455
Other (income) expense, net	(768)
	25,848
Earnings before provision for taxes on income	16,947
Provision for taxes on income	3,613
Net earnings	$ 13,334
Basic net earnings per share	$ 4.85

1. Is this a single- or multiple-step income statement? Explain your answer.
2. What term would **Columbia Sportswear** use as a label for the line in Johnson & Johnson's statements having the $16,947 figure? (Refer to the Columbia Sportswear income statement in Exhibit 4-11 on page 164.)
3. Suggest an alternative term for Interest Income.
4. What is the amount of the famous "bottom line" that is so often referred to by managers?
5. Net earnings per share are defined as net earnings divided by the average number of common shares outstanding. Compute the average number of common shares outstanding during the year.

SOLUTION

1. As is often the case, Johnson & Johnson uses a hybrid of single- and multiple-step income statements. However, this one is closer to a multiple-step statement. A pure single-step statement would place Interest Income and Other Income with Sales to Customers to obtain total revenues and would not calculate a gross profit subtotal. A pure multiple-step statement would separate operating and nonoperating activities and provide a subtotal for income from operations.

2. Columbia Sportswear would use "income before income tax" to describe the $16,947 figure.

3. Interest Revenue.

4. The "bottom line" is net earnings of $13,334 million. The bottom line per average common share outstanding is $4.85.

5. Companies must show net earnings per share on the face of the income statement.

$$\text{Earnings per share (EPS)} = \text{Net earnings} \div \text{Average number of common shares outstanding}$$
$$\$4.85 = \$13,334,000,000 \div \text{Average common shares outstanding}$$
$$\text{Average shares} = \$13,334,000,000 \div \$4.85$$
$$\text{Average shares} = 2,749,278,351$$

Highlights to Remember

1 **Understand the role of adjustments in accrual accounting.** At the end of each accounting period, accountants must make adjustments so financial statements recognize revenues and expenses that do not result from explicit transactions.

2 **Make adjustments for the expiration or consumption of unexpired costs.** We record many costs initially as assets and recognize them as expenses as time passes. Examples are depreciation and the consumption of prepaid rent.

3 **Make adjustments for the earning of revenues received in advance.** Some companies receive payments for revenue before they earn the revenue. They initially recognize unearned revenue as a liability. As the revenue is earned, the company must reduce the liability and recognize the revenue. Examples are rental payments received in advance or payment for magazine subscriptions received in advance. To clarify these first two types of adjustments, you might view them as mirror images by looking at both sides of the adjustment simultaneously. For example, (a) the expiration of unexpired costs (the tenant's rent expense) is accompanied by (b) the earning of unearned revenues (the landlord's rent revenue).

4 **Make adjustments for the accrual of unrecorded expenses.** Companies may incur expenses before cash disbursements are made. Such expenses should be included in the income statement of the period when they are incurred, not in the period when they are paid. Examples are the accrual of wages or interest expense.

5 **Make adjustments for the accrual of unrecorded revenues.** Some revenues accrue before there is an explicit transaction. Interest revenue may be recorded before there is a legal obligation for receipt of payment. Similarly, utilities often provide services before a bill is issued. This results in the recognition of revenue and a receivable before the billing cycle sends out a request for payment. You can also view these final two types of adjustments as mirror images. For example, (a) the accrual of unrecorded expenses (a borrower's interest expense) is accompanied by (b) the accrual of unrecorded revenues (a lender's interest revenue).

6 **Describe the sequence of steps in the recording process and relate cash flows to adjusting entries.** The adjusting entries capture expense and revenue elements that either precede or follow the related cash flows. Entries for the expiration or consumption of unexpired costs and the earning of unearned revenues follow the cash flows, whereas entries for the accrual of unrecorded expenses and the accrual of unrecorded revenues precede the cash flows. The adjusting entries provide a mechanism for capturing implicit transactions that do not necessarily generate documents that lead to them being recorded.

7 **Prepare a classified balance sheet and use it to assess short-term liquidity.** Classified balance sheets divide accounts into subcategories. Assets and liabilities are separated into

current and long-term subcategories that are useful in analysis. For example, the difference between current assets and current liabilities is called working capital. The current ratio, defined as current assets divided by current liabilities, is used to help assess liquidity. The quick or acid test ratio, frequently computed as current assets minus inventory divided by current liabilities, is also useful.

8 **Prepare single- and multiple-step income statements.** Income statements may appear in single- or multiple-step format. Single-step statements group all revenue items together and all expense items together, whereas multiple-step statements calculate various subtotals such as gross profit and operating income. Regardless of the format, published income statements are highly condensed and summarized compared with reports used within an organization.

9 **Use ratios to assess profitability.** Analysts use ratios based at least partly on the income statement to assess profitability. Among the most useful are gross margin percentage (or gross profit percentage), return on sales, return on common stockholders' equity, and return on assets.

Accounting Vocabulary

account format, p. 157
accrue, p. 142
acid test ratio, p. 161
adjusting entries, p. 142
adjustments, p. 142
classified balance sheet,
   p. 156
conservatism, p. 150
current assets, p. 156
current liabilities, p. 156
current ratio, p. 159
deferred revenue, p. 144
earnings before income tax,
   p. 149
explicit transactions, p. 142
gross margin, p. 164
gross margin percentage,
   p. 166
gross profit, p. 164

gross profit percentage,
   p. 166
implicit transactions, p. 142
income before income tax,
   p. 149
income from operations,
   p. 164
liquidity, p. 159
multiple-step income
   statement, p. 163
net current assets, p. 157
net working capital, p. 157
nonoperating revenues and
   expenses, p. 164
operating expenses, p. 164
operating income, p. 164
operating profit, p. 164
pretax income, p. 149
profit margin ratio, p. 166

profitability, p. 166
quick ratio, p. 161
rate of return, p. 166
report format, p. 157
return on assets ratio (ROA),
   p. 167
return on common stock-
   holders' equity ratio
   (ROE, ROCE), p. 167
return on sales ratio, p. 166
revenue received in advance,
   p. 144
single-step income statement,
   p. 163
turnover, p. 165
unearned revenue, p. 144
working capital, p. 157
working capital ratio,
   p. 159

Assignment Material

MyAccountingLab

Questions

4-1 Give two examples of explicit transactions.

4-2 Give two examples of implicit transactions.

4-3 Give two synonyms for unearned revenue.

4-4 Distinguish between the accrual of wages and the payment of wages.

4-5 Give a synonym for income tax expense.

4-6 Explain why income tax expense is usually the final deduction on both single-step and multiple-step income statements.

4-7 "The accrual of previously unrecorded revenues is the mirror image of the accrual of previously unrecorded expenses." Explain by using an illustration.

4-8 What types of adjusting entries are made prior to the related cash flows? After the related cash flows?

4-9 Why are current assets and current liabilities grouped separately from long-term assets and long-term liabilities?

4-10 "Google is much more profitable than Amazon.com because its current ratio is nine times larger than Amazon's." Do you agree? Explain.

4-11 "Companies should always strive to avoid negative working capital." Do you agree? Explain.

4-12 Explain the difference between a single-step and a multiple-step income statement.

4-13 Why does interest expense typically appear below operating income on a multiple-step income statement?

4-14 The term "costs and expenses" is sometimes found instead of just "expenses" on the income statement. Would expenses be an adequate description? Why?

4-15 Name four popular ratios for measuring profitability, and indicate how to compute each of the four.

4-16 "Computer software companies are generally more profitable than grocery stores because their gross profit percentages are usually at least twice as large." Do you agree? Explain.

Critical Thinking Questions

4-17 Accounting Errors

You have discovered an error in which the tenant has "incorrectly" recorded as rent expense a $5,000 payment made on December 1 for rent for the months of December and January. As a young auditor you are not sure whether this must be corrected. You think it is a self-correcting error. What are the issues you should consider?

▸▸ **OBJECTIVE 2**

4-18 What Constitutes Revenue?

You have just started a program of selling gift certificates at your store. In the first month, you sold $7,000 worth and customers redeemed $2,300 of these certificates for merchandise. Your average gross profit percentage is 38%. What should you report as gift certificate revenue, and how much gross margin related to the gift certificates will appear in the income statement?

▸▸ **OBJECTIVE 3**

4-19 Operating Versus Nonoperating Expenses

You have recently begun a new job as an internal auditor for a large retail clothing chain. The company prepares a multiple-step income statement. You discover that a material amount of salaries expense was erroneously classified as a nonoperating expense. One of your co-workers argues that the error need not be corrected because the net income number is not affected by the misclassification. You disagree. Defend your position.

▸▸ **OBJECTIVE 8**

4-20 Accounting for Supplies

A company began business on July 1 and purchased $2,000 in supplies including paper, pens, paper clips, and so on. On December 31, as financial statements were being prepared, the accounting clerk asked how to treat the $2,000 that appeared in the Supplies Inventory account. What should the clerk do?

▸▸ **OBJECTIVE 2**

Exercises

4-21 True or False

Use T or F to indicate whether each of the following statements is true or false:

▸▸ **OBJECTIVES 2, 3**

1. Retained Earnings should be accounted for as a noncurrent liability.
2. Deferred Revenue will appear on the income statement.
3. Machinery used in the business should be recorded as a noncurrent asset.
4. A company that employs cash-basis accounting cannot have a Prepaid Expense account on the balance sheet.
5. From a single balance sheet, you can find stockholders' equity for a period of time but not for a specific day.
6. It is not possible to determine changes in the financial condition of a business from a single balance sheet.

4-22 Tenant and Landlord

The Klassen Company, a retail hardware store, pays quarterly rent on its store at the beginning of each quarter. The rent per quarter is $24,000. The owner of the building in which the store is located is the Resing Corporation.

▸▸ **OBJECTIVES 2, 3**

Using the balance sheet equation format (refer to page 144 for an example), analyze the effects of the following on the tenant's and the landlord's financial position:

1. Klassen pays $24,000 rent on July 1.
2. Adjustment for July.
3. Adjustment for August.
4. Adjustment for September. Also prepare the journal entries for Klassen and Resing for September.

> **OBJECTIVES 2, 3**

4-23 Customer and Airline
Kimberly Clark (KC), maker of Scott paper products, decided to hold a managers' meeting in Hawaii in February. To take advantage of special fares, KC purchased airline tickets in advance from Alaska Airlines at a total cost of $65,000. These were acquired on December 1 for cash.

Using the balance sheet equation format (refer to page 144 for an example), analyze the impact of the December payment and the February travel on the financial position of both KC and Alaska. Also prepare journal entries for February for both companies.

> **OBJECTIVE 4**

4-24 Accrual of Wages
Consider the following calendar:

September						
S	M	T	W	T	F	S
		1	2	3	4	5
6	7	8	9	10	11	12
13	14	15	16	17	18	19
20	21	22	23	24	25	26
27	28	29	30			

Miller's Department Store commenced business on September 1. It is open every day except Sunday. Its total payroll for all employees is $6,000 per day. Payments are made each Tuesday for the preceding week's work through Saturday.

Using the balance sheet equation format (refer to page 147 for an example), analyze the financial impact on Miller's of the following:

1. Disbursements for wages on September 8, 15, 22, and 29.
2. Adjustment for wages on September 30. Also prepare the journal entry required on September 30.

> **OBJECTIVE 4**

4-25 Accrued Vacation Pay
As of December 31, 2008, Delta Air Lines had the following account listed as a current liability on its balance sheet:

Accrued salaries and related benefits	$1,367,000,000

The "related benefits" include the liability for vacation pay. Under the accrual basis of accounting, vacation pay is ordinarily accrued throughout the year as workers perform service and earn vacation. For example, suppose a Delta baggage handler earns $1,350 per week for 50 weeks and also gets paid $2,700 for 2 weeks' vacation each year. Accrual accounting requires that the obligation for the $2,700 be recognized as it is earned instead of when the payment is disbursed. Thus, in each of the 50 work weeks, Delta would recognize a wage expense (or vacation pay expense) of ($2,700 ÷ 50) = $54.

1. Prepare Delta's weekly adjusting journal entry called for by the $54 example.
2. Prepare the entry for the $2,700 payment of vacation pay.

4-26 Placement of Interest in Income Statement

▶▶ OBJECTIVE 8

Two companies have the following balance sheets as of December 31, 20X8:

Sunriver Company

Cash	$ 75,000	Note payable*	$125,000
Other assets	150,000	Stockholders' equity	100,000
Total	$225,000	Total	$225,000

*6% annual interest.

Black Butte Company

Cash	$ 75,000	Stockholders' equity	$225,000
Other assets	150,000		
Total	$225,000		

In 20X9, each company had sales of $700,000 and operating expenses of $600,000. Sunriver had not repaid the $125,000 Note Payable as of December 31, 20X9. Neither company incurred any new interest-bearing debt in 20X9. Ignore income taxes. Did the two companies earn the same net income and the same operating income? Explain, showing computations of operating income and net income.

4-27 Effects of Interest on Lenders and Borrowers

▶▶ OBJECTIVES 4, 5

Bank of America loaned Miller Paint Company $1,500,000 on May 1, 20X0. The loan plus interest of 4% is payable on May 1, 20X1.

1. Using the balance sheet equation format (refer to page 149 for an example), prepare an analysis of the impact of the transaction on both Bank of America's and Miller's financial position on May 1, 20X0. Show the summary adjustments on December 31, 20X0, for the period May 1 to December 31. Prepare an analysis of the transaction that takes place on May 1, 20X1, when Miller repays its obligation.
2. Prepare adjusting journal entries for Bank of America and Miller on December 31, 20X0.
3. Prepare the entries that Bank of America and Miller would make on May 1, 20X1 when the loan and interest is repaid. These entries should include interest that accumulates between January 1, 20X1, and May 1, 20X1.

4-28 Identification of Transactions

▶▶ OBJECTIVE 1

Valenzuela Corporation's financial position is represented by the nine balances shown on the first line of the following schedule ($ in thousands). Assume that a single transaction took place for each of the following lines, and describe what you think happened, using one short sentence for each line.

	Cash	Accounts Receivable	Inventory	Equipment	Accounts Payable	Accrued Wages Payable	Unearned Rent Revenue	Paid-in Capital	Retained Earnings
Bal.	$19	$32	$54	$ 0	$29	$0	$0	$55	$21
(1)	29	32	54	0	29	0	0	65	21
(2)	29	32	54	20	29	0	0	85	21
(3)	29	32	66	20	41	0	0	85	21
(4A)	29	47	66	20	41	0	0	85	36
(4B)	29	47	58	20	41	0	0	85	28
(5)	34	42	58	20	41	0	0	85	28
(6)	14	42	58	20	21	0	0	85	28
(7)	19	42	58	20	21	0	5	85	28
(8)	19	42	58	20	21	2	5	85	26
(9)	19	42	58	19	21	2	5	85	25
(10)	19	42	58	19	21	2	3	85	27

▶▶ OBJECTIVES 2,3,4,5

4-29 Effects on Balance Sheet Equation

Following is a list of effects of accounting transactions on the balance sheet equation: Assets = Liabilities + Stockholders' equity.

a. Increase in assets, decrease in liabilities
b. Increase in assets, increase in liabilities
c. Decrease in assets, decrease in stockholders' equity
d. Decrease in assets, decrease in liabilities
e. Increase in assets, decrease in assets
f. Increase in liabilities, decrease in stockholders' equity
g. Decrease in assets, increase in liabilities
h. Decrease in liabilities, increase in stockholders' equity
i. Increase in assets, increase in stockholders' equity
j. None of these

Required

Which of the relationships previously identified by letter defines the accounting effect of each of the following transactions?

1. The adjusting entry to recognize periodic depreciation.
2. The adjusting entry to record Accrued Salaries.
3. The adjusting entry to record Accrued Interest Receivable.
4. The collection of interest previously accrued.
5. The settlement of an Account Payable by the issuance of a Note Payable.
6. The recognition of an expense that had been paid for previously. A "prepaid" account was increased on payment.
7. The earning of revenue previously collected. Unearned Revenue was increased when collection was made in advance.

▶▶ OBJECTIVES 2,3,4,5

4-30 Effects of Errors in Adjustments

What will be the effect—understated (U), overstated (O), or no effect (N)—on the income of the present and future periods if the following errors were made? In all cases, assume that amounts carried over into 20X1 would affect 20X1 operations via the routine accounting entries of 20X1.

	Period	
	20X0	**20X1**
1. Revenue has been collected in advance, but earned amounts have not been recognized at the end of 20X0. Instead, all revenue was recognized as earned in 20X1.	_____	_____
2. Revenue for services rendered has been earned, but the unbilled amounts have not been recognized at the end of 20X0.	_____	_____
3. Accrued wages payable have not been recognized at the end of 20X0.	_____	_____
4. Prepaid rent has been paid (in late 20X0), but no adjustment for rent used in 20X0 was made. The payments have been debited to prepaid rent. They were transferred to expense in mid-20X1.	_____	_____

▶▶ OBJECTIVES 2,3,4,5

4-31 Effects of Adjustments and Corrections

Listed here are a series of accounts that are numbered for identification.

1. Cash
2. Accounts Receivable
3. Notes Receivable
4. Inventory
5. Accrued Interest Receivable
6. Accrued Rent Receivable
7. Fuel on Hand

8. Prepaid Rent
9. Prepaid Insurance
10. Prepaid Repairs and Maintenance
11. Land
12. Buildings
13. Machinery and Equipment

14. Long-Term Debt	22. Salaries and Wages
15. Notes Payable	23. Insurance Expense
16. Accrued Wages and Salaries Payable	24. Repairs and Maintenance Expense
17. Accrued Interest Payable	25. Rent Expense
18. Unearned Subscription Revenue	26. Rent Revenue
19. Capital Stock	27. Subscription Revenue
20. Sales	28. Interest Revenue
21. Fuel Expense	29. Interest Expense

Required

All accounts needed to answer this question are listed previously. The same account may be used in several answers. Prepare any necessary adjusting or correcting entries called for by the following situations, which were discovered at the end of the calendar year. With respect to each situation, assume that no entries have been made concerning the situation other than those specifically described (i.e., no monthly adjustments have been made during the year). Consider each situation separately. These transactions were not necessarily conducted by one firm. Amounts are in thousands of dollars.

a. A $10,000 purchase of equipment on December 30 was erroneously debited to Long-Term Debt. The credit was correctly made to Cash.

b. A business made several purchases of fuel oil. Some purchases ($900) were debited to Fuel Expense, whereas others ($1,100) were charged to an asset account. An oil gauge revealed $400 of fuel on hand at the end of the year. There was no fuel on hand at the beginning of the year. What adjustment was necessary on December 31?

c. On April 1, a business took out a fire insurance policy. The policy was for 2 years, and the full premium of $3,600 was paid on April 1. The payment was debited to Insurance Expense on April 1. What adjustment was necessary on December 31?

d. On December 1, $6,000 was paid in advance to the landlord for 5 months' rent. The tenant debited Prepaid Rent for $6,000 on December 1. What adjustment is necessary on December 31 on the tenant's books?

e. Machinery is repaired and maintained by an outside maintenance company on an annual fee basis, payable in advance. The $1,800 fee for the year beginning September 1 was paid on September 1 and charged to Repairs and Maintenance Expense. What adjustment is necessary on December 31?

f. On November 16, $800 of machinery was purchased, $200 cash was paid down, and a 90-day, 5% note payable was signed for the balance. The November 16 transaction was properly recorded. Prepare the adjustment for the interest on December 31.

g. A publisher sells subscriptions to magazines. Customers pay in advance. Receipts are originally credited to Unearned Subscription Revenue. On June 1, $24,000 in 1-year subscriptions (all beginning on June 1) were collected and recorded. What adjustment was necessary on December 31?

h. On December 30, certain merchandise inventory was purchased for $1,300 on open account. The bookkeeper debited Machinery and Equipment and credited Accounts Payable for $1,300. Prepare a correcting entry.

i. A 120-day, 8%, $15,000 cash loan was made to a customer on November 1. The November 1 transaction was recorded correctly. What adjustment is necessary on December 31?

4-32 Working Capital and Current Ratio

Using the Columbia Sportswear balance sheet in Exhibit 4-6 on page 158, compute Columbia's working capital, current ratio, and quick ratio for 2010. Compute the quick ratio as (current assets − inventories) ÷ current liabilities.

▶▶ OBJECTIVE 7

4-33 Profitability Ratios

The Nestlé Group, the Swiss chocolate company, sells many other food items in addition to various types of chocolates. Sales in 2011 were CHF83,642 million (where CHF means Swiss francs), cost of goods sold was CHF44,127 million, net income was CHF9,487 million, average common stockholders' equity was CHF60,436 million, and average total assets were CHF112,866 million.

▶▶ OBJECTIVE 9

Compute Nestlé's gross profit percentage, return on sales, return on average common stockholders' equity, and return on average total assets.

▶ **OBJECTIVES 1, 7, 9**

4-34 Impact of Adjusting Entries on Ratios

Exercise 4-31 asked you to write adjusting/correcting entries for transactions (a) through (i). In this problem, consider the effect on the current ratio and return on sales if the adjusting/correcting entries were not made. Indicate whether the failure to record the adjusting/correcting entry will result in these ratios being understated (U), overstated (O), or no effect (N). If additional information is necessary before you can provide the correct response, indicate with (I). Prior to the adjusting entry, the current ratio exceeds 1.0 and the company operated at a profit.

	Current Ratio	Return on Sales
(a)	_____	_____
(b)	_____	_____
(c)	_____	_____
(d)	_____	_____
(e)	_____	_____
(f)	_____	_____
(g)	_____	_____
(h)	_____	_____
(i)	_____	_____

MyAccountingLab

Problems

▶ **OBJECTIVES 2,3,4,5**

4-35 Adjusting Entries

(Alternates are 4-37 through 4-39.) Susan Hatfield, certified public accountant, had the following transactions (among others) during 20X0:

1. For accurate measurement of performance and position, Hatfield uses the accrual basis of accounting. On August 1, she acquired office supplies for $3,000. Office Supplies Inventory was increased, and Cash was decreased by $3,000 on Hatfield's books. On December 31, her inventory of office supplies was $1,300.
2. On August 1, a client gave Hatfield a retainer fee of $48,000 cash for monthly services to be rendered over the following 12 months. Hatfield increased Cash and Unearned Fee Revenue.
3. Hatfield accepted an $8,000 note receivable from a client on October 1 for tax services. The note plus interest of 6% per year was due in 6 months. Hatfield increased Note Receivable and Fee Revenue by $8,000 on October 1.
4. As of December 31, Hatfield had not recorded $800 of unpaid wages earned by her secretary during late December.

For the year ended December 31, 20X0, prepare all adjustments called for by the preceding transactions. Assume that appropriate entries were routinely made for the explicit transactions described earlier. However, no adjustments have been made before December 31. For each adjustment, prepare an analysis in the same format used when the adjustment process was explained in the chapter (i.e., the balance sheet equation format). Also prepare the adjusting journal entry.

▶ **OBJECTIVE 8**

4-36 Multiple-Step Income Statement

(Alternates are 4-40 and 4-51.) From the following data, prepare a multiple-step income statement for the Huffman Company for the fiscal year ended May 31, 20X0 ($ in thousands except for percentage).

Sales	$2,800	Cost of goods sold	$1,800
Interest expense	138	Depreciation expense	160
Utilities expense	110	Rent revenue	80
Interest revenue	28	Wage expense	400
Income tax rate	40%		

4-37 Four Major Adjustments

(Alternates are 4-35, 4-38, and 4-39.) Leslie Baker, an attorney, had the following transactions (among others) during 20X0, her initial year in law practice:

▶▶ OBJECTIVES 2,3,4,5

a. On July 1, Baker leased office space for 1 year. The landlord (lessor) insisted on full payment in advance. Prepaid Rent was increased and Cash was decreased by $24,000 on Baker's books. Similarly, the landlord increased Cash and increased Unearned Rent Revenue.

b. On September 1, Baker received a retainer of $12,000 cash for services to be rendered to her client, a local trucking company, over the succeeding 12 months. Baker increased Cash and Unearned Fee Revenue. The trucking company increased Prepaid Expenses and decreased Cash.

c. As of December 31, Baker had not recorded $500 of unpaid wages earned by her secretary during late December.

d. During November and December, Baker rendered services to another client, a utility company. She had intended to bill the company for $5,400 services through December 31, but failed to do so.

Required

1. For the year ended December 31, 20X0, prepare all adjustments called for by the preceding transactions. Assume that appropriate entries were routinely made for the explicit transactions. However, no adjustments have been made before December 31. For each adjustment, prepare an analysis in the same format used when the adjustment process was explained in the chapter (i.e., the balance sheet equation format). Prepare two adjustments for each transaction, one for Baker and one for the other party to the transaction. In part (c), assume that the secretary uses the accrual basis for her entity.

2. For each transaction, prepare the journal entries for Leslie Baker and the other entities involved.

4-38 Four Major Adjustments

(Alternates are 4-35, 4-37, and 4-39.) Columbia Sportswear included the following items in its December 31, 2011, balance sheet ($ in thousands):

▶▶ OBJECTIVES 2,3,4,5

Prepaid expenses and other current assets	$36,392
Income taxes payable (a current liability)	12,579

1. Analyze the impact of the following assumed transactions on the financial position of Columbia as of January 31, 2012. Prepare your analysis in the same format used when the adjustment process was explained in the chapter. Also show adjusting journal entries.

a. On January 31, an adjustment of $728 thousand was made for the rental of various retail outlets that had originally increased Prepaid Expenses but had expired.

b. During December 2011, Columbia sold product for $1,019 thousand cash to Dick's Sporting Goods, but delivery was not made until January 28, 2012. Unearned Revenue had been increased in December. No other adjustments had been made since then. Prepare the adjustment on January 31.

c. Columbia had loaned cash to several of its independent retail distributors. As of January 31, 2012, the distributors owed $112 thousand of interest that had been unrecorded.

d. On January 31, Columbia increased its accrual of federal income taxes by $938 thousand.

2. Compute the ending balances on January 31, 2012, in Prepaid Expenses and in Income Taxes Payable.

4-39 Four Major Adjustments

(Alternates are 4-35, 4-37, and 4-38.) Alaska Airlines showed the following items in its balance sheet as of December 31, 2011, the end of the fiscal year ($ in millions):

▶▶ OBJECTIVES 2,3,4,5

Inventories and supplies	$ 44.3
Prepaid expenses and other current assets	93.0
Air traffic liability	489.4
Accrued wages, vacation, and payroll taxes	163.8

A footnote stated, "Passenger revenue is recognized when the passenger travels. Tickets sold but not yet used are reported as air traffic liability."

The 2011 income statement included the following ($ in millions):

Passenger revenues	$3,950.7
Wages and benefits expense	990.5

1. Analyze the impact of the following assumed 2012 transactions on the financial position of Alaska. Prepare your analysis in the same format used when the adjustment process was explained in the chapter. Also show adjusting journal entries.
   a. Rented sales offices for 1 year, beginning September 1, 2012, for $9 million cash.
   b. On December 31, 2012, an adjustment was made for the rent in requirement (a).
   c. Sold 20 charter flights to Apple Computer for $250,000 each. Cash of $5 million was received in advance on November 20, 2012. The flights were for transporting marketing personnel to business conventions.
   d. As the financial statements were being prepared on December 31, 2012, accountants for both Alaska and Apple Computer independently noted that the first 6 charter flights had occurred in December. The rest will occur in early 2013. An adjustment was made on December 31.
   e. Alaska loaned $30 million to Boeing. Interest of $1.8 million was accrued on December 31.
   f. Additional wages of $35 million were accrued on December 31.
2. At year-end, before the adjustments for the transactions described in parts (c) and (d) of number 1, the company had $378 million in the Air Traffic Liability account related to collections in advance for flights scheduled in 2013. Compute the proper year-end balance in the Air Traffic Liability account as of December 31, 2012.

▶▶ OBJECTIVES 8, 9

4-40 Gap Inc. Financial Statements

(Alternates are 4-36 and 4-51.) Gap Inc. is a specialty retailer of clothing, accessories, and personal care products for men, women, children, and babies. Products are sold under Gap, Old Navy, Banana Republic, Piperlime, and Athleta brands. Actual financial data and nomenclature from its January 29, 2011, annual report are given next ($ in millions):

Net sales	$14,664	Earnings before income taxes	$?
Gross profit	5,889	Income taxes	778
Operating income	1,968	Retained earnings	
Operating expenses	?	Beginning of year	10,815
Cost of goods sold	?	End of year	?
Interest income	14	Dividends declared	252
		Net earnings	?

1. Compute the missing values. Prepare a multiple-step statement of income for the year ended January 29, 2011.
2. Compute the ending balance in Retained Earnings as of January 29, 2011.
3. Compute the percentage of gross profit on sales and the percentage of net earnings on sales.
4. The average common stockholders' equity for the year was $4,485.5 million. What was the return on average common stockholders' equity?

▶▶ OBJECTIVES 3, 5

4-41 Accounting for Dues

(Alternate is 4-42.) The Sunset Beach Golf Club provided the following data from its comparative balance sheets:

	December 31	
	20X1	**20X0**
Dues receivable	$95,000	$75,000
Unearned dues revenue	—	$20,000

The income statement for 20X1, which was prepared on the accrual basis, showed Dues Revenue Earned of $590,000. No dues were collected in advance during 20X1.

Prepare the 20X1 journal entries and post to T-accounts for the following:

1. Earning of dues collected in advance.
2. Billing of dues revenue during 20X1.
3. Collection of dues receivable in 20X1.

4-42 Accounting for Subscriptions

▶▶ OBJECTIVES 3, 5

(Alternate is 4-41.) A French magazine company collects subscriptions in advance of delivery of its magazines. However, many magazines are delivered to magazine distributors (for newsstand sales), and these distributors are billed and pay later. The subscription revenue earned for the month of March on the accrual basis was €200,000 (€ refers to the euro). Other pertinent data were as follows:

	March	
	31	1
Unearned subscription revenue	€190,000	€140,000
Accounts receivable	7,000	9,000

Prepare journal entries and post to T-accounts for the following:

1. Collections of Unearned Subscription Revenue of €140,000 prior to March 1.
2. Billing of Accounts Receivable (a) of €9,000 prior to March 1, and (b) of €80,000 during March (credit Revenue Earned).
3. Collections of cash during March and any other entries that are indicated by the given data.

4-43 Financial Statements and Adjustments

▶▶ OBJECTIVES 7, 8

Rockwell Wholesalers, Inc. has just completed its fourth year of business in 20X1. A set of financial statements was prepared by the principal stockholder's eldest child, a college student who is beginning the third week of an accounting course. Following is a list (in no systematic order) of the items appearing in the student's balance sheet, income statement, and the retained earnings column of the statement of stockholders' equity:

Accounts receivable	$183,100	Advertising expense	$ 97,300
Note receivable	36,000	Cost of goods sold	590,000
Merchandise inventory	201,900	Unearned rent revenue	4,800
Cash	99,300	Insurance expense	3,500
Paid-in capital	620,000	Unexpired insurance	2,300
Building	300,000	Accounts payable	52,500
Accumulated depreciation, building	20,000	Interest expense	500
		Telephone expense	20,000
Land	169,200	Notes payable	2,500
Sales	936,800	Net income	58,626
Salary expense	124,300	Miscellaneous expense	3,400
Retained earnings, December 31, 20X0	164,000	Maintenance expense	4,800

Assume that the statements in which these items appear are current and complete, except for the following matters not taken into consideration by the student:

a. Salaries of $8,500 have been earned by employees for the last half of December 20X1. Payment by the company will be made on the next payday, January 2, 20X2.
b. Interest at 6% per annum on the Note Receivable has accrued for 2 months and is expected to be collected by the company when the Note is due on January 31, 20X2.

c. Part of the building owned by the company was rented to a tenant on November 1, 20X1, for 6 months, payable in advance. This rent was collected in cash and is represented by the item labeled Unearned Rent Revenue.

d. Depreciation on the building for 20X1 is $6,250.

e. Cash dividends of $60,000 were declared in December 20X1, payable in January 20X2.

f. Income tax at 40% applies to 20X1, all of which is to be paid in the early part of 20X2.

Required

Prepare the following corrected financial statements, showing appropriate support for the dollar amounts you compute:

1. Multiple-step income statement for the year ended December 31, 20X1
2. The retained earnings column of the statement of stockholders' equity for the year ended December 31, 20X1
3. Classified balance sheet at December 31, 20X1

▶▶ **OBJECTIVES 2, 4, 5**

4-44 Mirror Side of Adjustments

Problem 4-35 described some adjustments made by Susan Hatfield, CPA. Prepare the necessary adjustment as it would be made by the client in transactions (2) and (3), and by the secretary in transaction (4). For our purposes, assume that the secretary keeps personal books on the accrual basis.

▶▶ **OBJECTIVES 2,3,4,5**

4-45 Mirror Side of Adjustments

Problem 4-38 described some adjustments made by Columbia Sportswear. The adjustments are lettered (a) through (d). Prepare the necessary adjustment as it would be made by (a) landlords, (b) Dick's Sporting Goods, (c) retail distributors, and (d) the government taxing authorities. Assume that all use accrual accounting.

▶▶ **OBJECTIVES 2,3,4,5**

4-46 Mirror Side of Adjustments

Problem 4-39 described some adjustments made by Alaska Airlines. The adjustments are lettered (a) through (f). Repeat the requirements for each adjustment as it would be made by the other party in the transaction: specifically, (a) and (b) landlord, (c) and (d) Apple Computer, (e) Boeing, and (f) employees. Assume that all use accrual accounting.

▶▶ **OBJECTIVES 2, 4**

4-47 Journal Entries and Posting

Nike is a worldwide leader in the design, marketing, and distribution of athletic and sports-inspired footwear, apparel, equipment, and accessories. The company's May 31, 2011, balance sheet included the following ($ in millions):

	May 31	
	2011	**2010**
Prepaid expenses	594	873
Income taxes payable	117	59

Suppose that during the fiscal year ended May 31, 2011, $366 million in cash was disbursed and charged to Prepaid Expenses. Similarly, $145 million was disbursed for income taxes and charged to Income Taxes Payable.

1. Assume that the Prepaid Expenses account relates to outlays for miscellaneous operating expenses, for example, supplies, insurance, and short-term rentals. Prepare summary journal entries for (a) the disbursements, and (b) the expenses for fiscal 2011.

2. Assume that there were no other accounts related to income taxes. Prepare summary journal entries for (a) the disbursements, and (b) the expenses for fiscal 2011.

4-48 Advance Service Contracts

▶▶ OBJECTIVES **3, 5**

Diebold, Incorporated, a manufacturer of automated teller machines, showed the following current liability on the balance sheet on December 31, 2011 ($ amounts in thousands):

	December 31	
	2011	**2010**
Deferred revenue	$241,992	$205,173

The footnotes to the financial statements stated the following: "Deferred revenue is recorded for any services billed to customers in advance of the contract period commencing." Assume that service contracts typically cover a 12-month period and can begin at any given month during the year. Revenue is recognized ratably over the life of the contract period. ("Recognized ratably" means an equal amount per month.)

1. Prepare summary journal entries for the creation in 2010, and subsequent earning in 2011, of the deferred revenue of $205,173. Use the following accounts: Accounts Receivable, Deferred Revenue, and Income from Advance Billings.
2. A 1-year job contract was billed to Keystone Bank on January 1, 2011, for $36,000. Work began on January 2. The full amount was collected on February 15. Prepare all pertinent journal entries through February 28, 2011. Use the following accounts: Accounts Receivable, Deferred Revenue, and Income from Service Contracts.

4-49 Journal Entries and Adjustments

▶▶ OBJECTIVE **5**

Northwest Natural is a public utility in Oregon. The 2011 annual report included the following footnote:

Utility revenues, derived primarily from the sale and transportation of gas, are recognized upon delivery of gas commodity or service to customers. Revenues include accruals for gas delivered but not yet billed to customers based on estimates of deliveries from meter reading dates to month end (accrued unbilled revenue). Accrued unbilled revenues are dependent upon a number of factors that require management's judgment, including total gas receipts and deliveries, customer use by billing cycle and weather factors. Accrued unbilled revenues are reversed the following month when actual billings occur.

The income statements showed the following ($ in thousands):

For Year Ended December 31		
	2011	**2010**
Gross operating revenues	$848,796	$812,106
Income from operations	144,845	157,605

The balance sheets included the following as part of current assets ($ in thousands):

	December 31	
	2011	**2010**
Accounts receivable	$77,449	$67,969
Accrued unbilled revenue	61,925	64,803

Prepare the adjusting journal entry for (a) the unbilled revenues at the end of 2011, and (b) the eventual billing and collection of the unbilled revenues in 2012. Ignore income taxes.

▶▶ OBJECTIVE 7

4-50 Classified Balance Sheet, Current Ratio, and Quick Ratio

Amazon.com, Inc.'s balance sheet (slightly modified) for December 31, 2011, contained the following items ($ in millions):

Property and equipment, net	$ 4,417
Accrued expenses and other	3,751
Cash and cash equivalents	5,269
Other noncurrent assets	1,416
Inventories	4,992
Other current assets	351
Accounts payable	11,145
Marketable securities, short-term	4,307
Accounts receivable, net	?
Goodwill	1,955
Long-term liabilities	2,625
Stockholders' equity	7,757

1. Prepare a December 31, 2011, classified balance sheet for Amazon.com. Include the correct amount for Accounts Receivable.
2. Compute the company's working capital, current ratio, and quick ratio. Compute the quick ratio as (current assets – inventory) ÷ current liabilities.
3. Comment on the company's current and quick ratios. In 2010, the current ratio was 1.33 and the quick ratio was 1.02.
4. During 2011, Amazon decreased its Marketable Securities by $678. Suppose the company had not decreased its Marketable Securities but had instead decreased long-term investments (classified as Other Noncurrent Assets) by $678. How would this have affected Amazon's current ratio? How would it have affected the company's liquidity?

▶▶ OBJECTIVE 8

4-51 Multiple-Step Income Statement

(Alternates are 4-36 and 4-40.) Intel Corporation is one of the largest companies in the United States. Its annual report for the year ended December 31, 2011, contained the following data and actual terms ($ in millions):

Cost of sales	$20,242	Gross margin	$33,757
Research and development	8,350	Interest and other income, net	192
Marketing, general, and administrative	7,670	Provision for taxes	4,839
Amortization of acquisition-related intangibles	260	Gains (losses) on equity investments, net	112
Net revenue	?		

Prepare a multiple-step statement of income. Include the correct amount for Net Revenue.

▶▶ OBJECTIVES 8, 9

4-52 Single-Step Income Statement

Harley-Davidson is the parent company of Harley-Davidson Motor, Buell Motorcycle, and Harley-Davidson Financial Services. It is most well-known for producing heavyweight, custom, and touring motorcycles as well as parts, accessories, and apparel. Harley-Davidson Financial Services provides wholesale and retail financing and insurance programs to dealers and customers. A recent Harley-Davidson annual report contained the following slightly modified items ($ in thousands) for the year ending December 31, 2011:

Investment income	$ 7,963	Selling, administrative, and engineering expense	$1,060,943
Cost of goods sold	3,106,288	Interest expense	45,266
Financial services income	649,449	Provision for income taxes	244,586
Retained earnings at end of year	6,824,180	Cash dividends declared	111,011
Financial services expense	246,523	Net sales revenue	4,662,264
Other income	51,036		
Restructuring expense and asset impairment	67,992		

1. Prepare a combined single-step statement of income and retained earnings for the year.
2. Compute the percentage of gross profit on sales and the percentage of net income to sales.
3. The average stockholders' equity for the year was $2,313,561. What was the percentage of net income to average stockholders' equity?

4-53 Pharmaceutical Company Financial Statements

» **OBJECTIVES 7, 8, 9**

Merck & Co., Incorporated, is a global health-care company that offers prescription medicines, vaccines, biologic therapies, animal health, and consumer care products. The annual report for the year ended December 31, 2011, included the data (slightly modified) shown next ($ in millions). Unless otherwise specified, the balance sheet amounts are the balances as of December 31, 2011.

Sales	$48,047	Long-term debt	$15,525
Cash dividends declared	4,818	Cash and cash equivalents	13,531
Inventories	6,254	Accrued liabilities	9,731
Paid-in capital	17,953	Short-term investments	1,441
Other current assets	3,694	Taxes on income	942
Retained earnings		Property and equipment, net	16,297
December 31, 2010	37,536	Other noncurrent assets	52,192
December 31, 2011	?	Marketing and administrative expense	13,733
Trade accounts payable	2,462		
Other expenses, net	816	Research and development expense	8,467
Cost of sales	16,871		
Other current liabilities	3,271	Other noncurrent liabilities	16,415
Long-term investments	3,458	Income taxes payable	781
Interest expense, net	946	Accounts receivable	8,261

1. Prepare a combined multiple-step statement of income.
2. Prepare a classified balance sheet. Include the correct number for retained earnings.
3. The average common stockholders' equity for the year was $56,874 million. What was the percentage of net income to average common stockholders' equity?
4. The average total assets for the year were $105,454.5 million. What was the percentage of net income to average total assets?
5. Compute (a) gross profit percentage, and (b) percentage of net income to sales.

▶▶ **OBJECTIVES 7, 8**

4-54 Preparation of Financial Statements from Trial Balance

The Procter & Gamble Company is one of the largest consumer products companies in America. The (slightly modified) trial balance as of June 30, 2011, appears here:

The Procter & Gamble Company
Trial balance as of June 30, 2011 ($ in millions)

	Debits	Credits
Cash and cash equivalents	$ 2,768	
Accounts receivable	6,275	
Inventories	7,379	
Deferred income taxes	1,140	
Prepaid expenses and other current assets	4,408	
Property, plant, and equipment, at cost	41,507	
Accumulated depreciation		$ 20,214
Trademarks and other intangibles, net	32,620	
Goodwill	57,562	
Other noncurrent assets	4,909	
Debt due within one year		9,981
Accounts payable		8,022
Accrued and other liabilities		9,290
Long-term debt		22,033
Deferred income tax		11,070
Other noncurrent liabilities		9,957
Preferred stock		1,234
Common stock, stated value $1 per share		4,008
Additional paid-in capital		62,405
Retained earnings (June 30, 2010)		64,614
Accumulated other comprehensive loss*	2,054	
Reserve for ESOP debt retirement*	1,357	
Treasury stock*	67,278	
Noncontrolling interest*		361
Net sales		82,559
Cost of products sold	40,768	
Selling, administrative, and general expense	25,973	
Interest expense	831	
Other nonoperating income, net		202
Income taxes	3,392	
Cash dividends declared	5,729	
	$305,950	$305,950

*Part of stockholders' equity.

1. Prepare Procter & Gamble's income statement for the year ended June 30, 2011, using a multiple-step format.
2. Prepare Procter & Gamble's income statement for the year ended June 30, 2011, using a single-step format. Which format for the income statement is more informative? Why?
3. Prepare Procter & Gamble's classified balance sheet as of June 30, 2011.

4-55 Adjusting Entries and Ethics

By definition, adjusting entries are not triggered by an explicit event. Therefore, accountants must initiate adjusting entries. For each of the following adjusting entries, discuss a potential unethical behavior that an accountant or manager might undertake:

▶▶ **OBJECTIVES 2,3,4,5**

1. Recognition of expenses from the prepaid supplies account
2. Recognition of revenue from the unearned revenue account
3. Accrual of interest payable
4. Accrual of fees receivable

Collaborative Learning Exercise

4-56 Implicit Transactions

Form groups of from three to six "players." Each group should have a die and a paper (or board) with four columns labeled as follows:

▶▶ **OBJECTIVES 2,3,4,5**

1. Expiration or consumption of unexpired costs
2. Earning of unearned revenues
3. Accrual of unrecorded expenses
4. Accrual of unrecorded revenues

The players should select an order in which they want to play. Then, the first player rolls the die. If this player rolls a 5 or 6, the die passes to the next player. If the second player rolls a 1, 2, 3, or 4, this person must, within 20 seconds, name an example of a transaction that fits in the corresponding category; for example, if a 2 is rolled, the player must give an example of earning of unearned revenues. Each time a correct example is given, the player receives one point. If someone doubts the correctness of a given example, the player can challenge it. If the remaining players unanimously agree that the example is incorrect, the challenger gets a point and the player giving the example does not get a point for a correct example and is out of the game. If the remaining players do not unanimously agree that the answer is incorrect, the challenger loses a point and the player giving the example gets a point for a correct example. If a player fails to give an example within the time limit or gives an incorrect example, this person is out of the game (except for voting when an example is challenged), and the remaining players continue until everyone has failed to give a correct example within the time limit. Each correct answer should be listed under the appropriate column. The player with the most points is the group winner.

When all groups have finished a round of play, a second level of play can begin. The groups can get together and list all examples for each of the four categories by group. Discussion can establish the correctness of each entry; the faculty member or an appointed discussion leader will be the final arbitrator of the correctness of each entry. Each group gets one point for each correct example and loses one point for each incorrect entry. The group with the most points is the overall winner.

Analyzing and Interpreting Financial Statements

▶▶ OBJECTIVES 7, 9

4-57 Financial Statement Research
Select any two companies.

1. For each company, determine the amount of working capital and the current ratio.
2. Compare the current ratios. Which company has the larger ratio, and what do the ratios tell you about the liquidity of the companies?
3. Compute the gross margin percentage, the return on sales, and the return on common stockholders' equity.
4. Compare the profitability of the two companies.

▶▶ OBJECTIVES 2, 4

4-58 Analyzing Starbucks' Financial Statements
This problem develops skills in preparing adjusting journal entries. The balance sheet of Starbucks for the year ended October 2, 2011, included the following information (all $ amounts in millions).

	October 2, 2011	October 3, 2010
Prepaid expenses and other current assets	$161.5	$156.5
Other accrued expenses	319.0	262.8

Suppose that during the year ended October 2, 2011, $207.5 million cash was disbursed and debited to Prepaid Expenses and $279.3 million of liabilities classified as Other Accrued Expenses were paid in cash.

1. Assume that the Prepaid Expenses account relates to outlays for miscellaneous operating expenses, for example, supplies, insurance, and short-term rentals. Prepare summary journal entries for (a) the disbursements, and (b) the expenses (for our purposes, debit Operating Expenses) for the year ended October 2, 2011. Post the entries to T-accounts.
2. Prepare summary journal entries for (a) the disbursements, and (b) the expenses related to the Other Accrued Expenses account for the year ended October 2, 2011. (For our purposes, debit Operating Expenses.) Post the entries to T-accounts.

▶▶ OBJECTIVES 7, 9

4-59 Analyzing Financial Statements Using the Internet
Go to www.columbia.com to find Columbia Sportswear's home page. Under the About Us menu near the bottom of the page, select Investor Relations. Then select Financial Information and click on the most recent annual report. You may also select the most recent Form 10-K. Answer the following questions:

1. Name one item on Columbia Sportswear's balance sheet that most likely represents unexpired (prepaid) costs. Name one item that most likely represents the accrual of unrecorded expenses.
2. Does Columbia Sportswear prepare a single- or multiple-step income statement? How can you tell?

3. Determine Columbia Sportswear's gross profit percentage for the past 2 years. Is the change favorable? What does Columbia Sportswear's management say about the change? (Hint: Look in Management's Discussion and Analysis.) If nothing was said, why do you think management chose not to comment? How do you think management determines the reason that gross profit changed, given the condensed nature of the income statement?

4. Calculate Columbia Sportswear's current ratio for the past 2 years. Did this ratio improve or decline? Does management offer any comment about any particular problems that could have affected this ratio? Should management be concerned about changes in the current ratio?

5. Where can you find evidence in Columbia Sportswear's annual report that the financial statements were prepared using U.S. GAAP?

5

Statement of Cash Flows

COSTCO OPERATES NEARLY 600 MEMBERSHIP warehouses in the United States and seven other countries. You may be one of the more than 64 million members who shop in Costco stores. The company offers its members "low prices on a limited selection of nationally branded and private-label products in a wide range of merchandise categories." Costco began operations in 1983 with a single warehouse in Seattle, Washington. In just three decades it has grown into the third largest retailer based in the U.S. and the seventh largest retailer in the world.

Costco stocks a small number of items, about 3,600 compared with more than 100,000 at many department and grocery stores, and sells most items in large quantities. Its annual sales in fiscal 2011 were nearly $90 billion. Each year Costco needs cash to build new warehouses and stock them with merchandise. A quick look at the company's balance sheet tells you Costco has plenty of cash—more than $4 billion on August 28, 2011. However, if you truly want to see where Costco spends its cash, you should pay attention to one specific financial report—the statement of cash flows.

Costco reports the cash provided or used by the company for operating, investing, and financing activities, giving you a complete picture of how the company generated the money and how it was spent. For example, in recent years, operating activities such as selling merchandise and memberships have provided billions in cash for Costco ($3.2 billion in 2011). In contrast, investing and financing activities have used cash, primarily because Costco invested heavily in property and equipment and spent millions of dollars buying back shares of its own stock as well as paying dividends. The net result of these activities in 2011 was an increase in cash of $795 million over the previous year's balance. You can learn all of this from the company's statement of cash flows. ●

LEARNING OBJECTIVES *After studying this chapter, you should be able to:*

1 Identify the purposes of the statement of cash flows.

2 Classify activities affecting cash as operating, investing, or financing activities.

3 Compute and interpret cash flows from financing activities.

4 Compute and interpret cash flows from investing activities.

5 Use the direct method to calculate cash flows from operations.

6 Use the indirect method to explain the difference between net income and net cash provided by (used for) operating activities.

7 Understand why we add depreciation to net income when using the indirect method for computing cash flows from operating activities.

8 Show how the balance sheet equation provides a conceptual framework for the statement of cash flows.

9 Identify free cash flow, and interpret information in the statement of cash flows.

The critical importance of cash makes the statement of cash flows one of the key financial statements. The statement explains the changes that occur in the firm's cash balance during the year. The statement of cash flows allows both investors and managers to keep their fingers on the pulse of any company's lifeblood—cash. Attitudes toward holding cash vary. Some managers and investors like the safety of large amounts of cash. For example, after the great recession of 2008–2011 many companies held onto large amounts of cash to provide flexibility to meet unforeseen needs. **Microsoft**, for instance, held $57 billion in cash, cash equivalents, and short-term investments in early 2012. In contrast, other companies minimized cash holdings, even during the recession, because cash provides only small returns to the company.

Companies that lose too much cash may find it necessary to declare bankruptcy. **Bankruptcy** means that a company seeks court protection from its creditors under federal law. Court protection allows a firm to delay paying certain obligations while it negotiates with its creditors to reorganize its business and settle its debts. **Enron** and **General Motors** are recent examples of large and historically successful companies that entered bankruptcy and either liquidated entirely (Enron) or reorganized large portions of their business (GM). We observed bankruptcies of many large companies in the economic downturns of 2001–2002 and 2008–2011.

Although managers and investors benefit from watching cash flows, until recently many countries did not require a statement of cash flows. For example, India began to require such a statement about 10 years ago. Today, both the IASB and FASB require a statement of cash flows and have similar requirements for the statement. In this chapter, we examine cash flow statements and explain how managers and investors use the information in such statements.

Overview of Statement of Cash Flows

A balance sheet shows the amount of cash a company holds at the close of business on the balance sheet date. But it does not show how the company generated this cash balance. For that, you need a statement of cash flows. The **statement of cash flows** (or **cash flow statement**) reports

Costco attracts a wide variety of shoppers—old and young, urban and rural, and of all ethnic backgrounds—who buy memberships that allow them to purchase items in large quantities at low prices. Cash flows are critical to Costco.

bankruptcy
When a company seeks court protection from its creditors under federal law.

statement of cash flows (cash flow statement)
One of the basic financial statements that reports the cash receipts and cash payments of an entity during a particular period and classifies them as financing, investing, and operating cash flows.

the cash receipts and cash payments of an entity during a particular period and classifies them as financing, investing, or operating cash flows. Statements of cash flows, like income statements, show the performance of a company over a period of time. Both help explain why the balance sheet items have changed—the income statement shows details about how operating activities produce changes in retained earnings, while the statement of cash flows provides a detailed explanation of the changes in the cash account. As the following diagram shows, these statements link the balance sheets in consecutive periods:

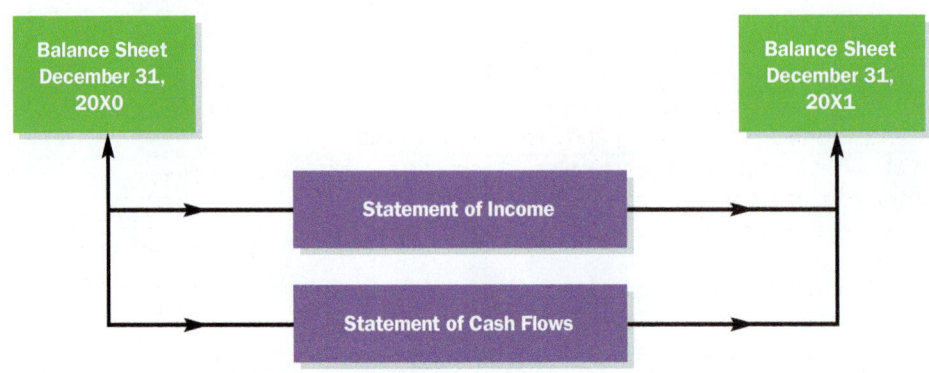

cash equivalents

Highly liquid short-term investments that a company can easily and quickly convert into cash, such as money market funds and Treasury bills.

> ▶▶ **OBJECTIVE 1**
>
> Identify the purposes of the statement of cash flows.

cash flows from operating activities

The first major section of the cash flow statement. It helps users evaluate the cash impact of management's operating decisions.

operating activities

Transactions that affect the purchase, processing, and selling of a company's products and services.

> ▶▶ **OBJECTIVE 2**
>
> Classify activities affecting cash as operating, investing, or financing activities.

cash flows from financing activities

The section of the statement of cash flows that helps users understand management's financing decisions.

Purposes of Cash Flow Statement

Why do managers and investors use a statement of cash flows?

1. It helps them understand the relationship of net income to changes in cash balances. Cash balances can decline despite positive net income and vice versa.
2. It reports past cash flows as an aid to
   a. predicting future cash flows,
   b. evaluating how management generates and uses cash, and
   c. determining a company's ability to pay interest, dividends, and debts when they are due.
3. It identifies specific increases and decreases in a firm's productive assets.

The statement of cash flows explains how a company generates cash during a period and how it uses cash. It helps investors assess how well management has managed cash. The importance of cash management is discussed in the Business First box on p. 191.

Before continuing with our discussion of cash flows, let's first be clear about what we mean by cash. Our use of the term refers not only to the currency and bank accounts that we all call cash but also to cash equivalents. **Cash equivalents** are highly liquid short-term investments that a company can easily and quickly convert into cash, such as money market funds and Treasury bills. Hereafter, when we refer to cash, we mean both cash and cash equivalents.

Typical Activities Affecting Cash

Managers affect cash as the result of three types of decisions: operating, financing, and investing decisions. Operating decisions affect the major day-to-day activities that generate revenues and expenses. The first major section of the statement of cash flows, **cash flows from operating activities**, summarizes the cash impact of such decisions. **Operating activities** are transactions that affect the purchase, processing, and selling of a company's products and services. For example, making sales, collecting accounts receivable, recording an expense for cost of goods sold, purchasing inventory, and paying accounts payable or employee wages are all operating activities. The thing these transactions have in common is that they are an integral part of the major income-generating activities of the company.

Managers make financing decisions when they decide whether and how to raise or repay cash. For example, when a company needs cash, financial managers may decide whether to

BUSINESS FIRST

CASH MANAGEMENT

The recession in 2008–2011 tested the cash management of many companies. During the later stages of this recession, companies were holding more cash than at any time in the last 40 years. For example, Google nearly quadrupled its holdings of cash and marketable securities in the 5 years leading up to 2012, Microsoft increased its cash and marketable securities from less than $24 billion at the end of 2008 to more than $57 billion in early 2012, and PepsiCo increased its cash from under $1 billion in 2007 to almost $6 billion in 2011. This was partly a reaction to the financial crisis in the early years of the recession when it was nearly impossible to raise cash. But the retention of cash also allowed these companies to be poised to invest when the economy turned around.

While some companies hoarded cash, others did not have enough cash to meet their obligations and had to file for bankruptcy. Probably the most famous bankruptcy was that of Lehman Brothers, a global financial services firm, in September 2008. Not only was Lehman's bankruptcy a major blow to the U.S. economy, dropping the Dow Jones Average by more than 500 points in one day, it inspired several books and even a popular movie, *Margin Call*. But many other familiar companies declared bankruptcy around that time, including Hollywood Video, Levitz, Sharper Image, Linens 'n Things, and Circuit City. More recently, as the recession continued, large companies such as General Motors, American Airlines, and MF Global followed suit. Let's look at one company's descent into bankruptcy, that of Blockbuster. The following table shows selected financial data for Blockbuster (in millions):

Year ended:	Jan. 2, 2011	Jan. 3, 2010	Jan. 4, 2009	Jan. 6, 2008
Total assets	$1,184	$1,538	$2,155	$2,734
Total liabilities	1,736	1,853	1,940	2,078
Net cash flow from operations	11	29	51	(56)
Capital expenditures	24	32	118	74

Until the year that ended on January 3, 2010, Blockbuster had total assets greater than total liabilities, leaving positive stockholders' equity. But total liabilities exceeded total assets for the last two years. Examination of the cash flow statement provides insight into Blockbuster's financial difficulties. In all 4 years Blockbuster spent more to purchase capital assets than it generated in operating cash flow. It is hard for a company to stay in business if its operations do not generate enough cash to cover its capital expenditures. So, as successful companies piled up cash, many less successful ones such as Blockbuster declared bankruptcy. Some, such as General Motors, used bankruptcy as a means of reorganizing and staying in business. Others, such as Linens 'n Things, reorganized under new ownership. But many bankrupt companies simply liquidated by selling their assets and using the proceeds to pay off some portion of their debts.

Sources: T. McGinty, and C. Tuna, "Jittery Companies Stash Cash," *Wall Street Journal* (November 3, 2009, p. A1); Blockbuster 10-K filings for years ending Jan. 2, 2011, Jan. 3, 2010, Jan. 4, 2009, and Jan. 6, 2008.

borrow money from a bank or other lender or issue additional capital stock. When there is excess cash, financial managers may decide to repay previous borrowings or to buy back previously issued stock. To understand financing decisions, we use the section of the statement of cash flows labeled **cash flows from financing activities**. **Financing activities** are a company's transactions that obtain resources by borrowing from creditors or selling shares of stock and use resources to repay creditors or provide a return to shareholders.

After raising capital, managers must decide how to invest the capital. These investing decisions include the choices to (1) acquire or dispose of plant, property, equipment, and other long-term productive assets, and (2) provide or collect cash as a lender or as an owner of securities. The statement of cash flows covers the results of investing decisions in a section labeled **cash flows from investing activities**. **Investing activities** are transactions that acquire or dispose of long-lived assets or acquire or dispose of securities held for investment purposes that are not cash equivalents. Thus, purchasing property or equipment is an investing activity, but purchasing inventory or prepaying rent are operating activities. Why? Because a company will generally use property and equipment for multiple years, whereas it will use inventory and prepaid rent within one year.

financing activities
A company's transactions that obtain resources by borrowing from creditors or selling shares of stock and use resources to repay creditors or provide a return to shareholders.

cash flows from investing activities
The section of the statement of cash flows that helps users understand management's investing decisions.

investing activities
Transactions that acquire or dispose of long-lived assets or acquire or dispose of securities held for investment purposes that are not cash equivalents.

EXHIBIT 5-1

**Typical Operating,
Investing, and Financing
Activities**

Cash Inflows	Cash Outflows
Operating activities	
Collections from customers	Cash payments to suppliers
Interest and dividends collected	Cash payments to employees
Other operating receipts	Interest and taxes paid
	Other operating cash payments
Investing activities	
Sale of property, plant, and equipment	Purchase of property, plant, and equipment
Sale of securities that are not cash equivalents	Purchase of securities that are not cash equivalents
Receipt of loan repayments	Making loans
Financing activities	
Borrowing cash from creditors	Repayment of amounts borrowed
Issuing equity securities	Repurchase of equity shares
Issuing debt securities	Payment of dividends

There is one more item you will see on the cash flow statements of companies with international operations—the effect of exchange rates on cash. Companies show this effect after the operating, investing, and financing activities. The effect of exchange rates is not a cash flow, but it appears on the cash flow statement because it is necessary for the reconciliation of cash balances at the beginning and end of the period. Consider a U.S. company with a bank account in London. The account balance is £100,000 at the beginning of the year when the exchange rate is 2 U.S. dollars for every British pound. The company would include this bank account as part of its total cash balance on a U.S. balance sheet at a value of (£100,000 × $2/£) = $200,000. Suppose there were no cash flows into or out of the bank account during the year, but the exchange rate changed to $1.7 per pound. At the end of the year, a U.S. balance sheet would include this bank account at a value of (£100,000 × $1.7/£) = $170,000. Cash measured in dollars fell by $30,000 in the absence of any cash flow. This change in cash is reported on the cash flow statement as the effect of exchange rates on cash.

Exhibit 5-1 shows typical operating, investing, and financing activities reported in a statement of cash flows. The fact that these activities affect cash should be fairly obvious and straightforward. What is not always obvious is the classification of these activities as operating, investing, or financing. Consider interest payments and dividend payments, for example. These both represent cash flows to those who supply capital to the firm. You might think they should be classified the same. However, U.S. GAAP classifies interest payments as cash flows associated with operations and dividend payments as financing cash flows. This classification maintains the long-standing distinction that transactions with owners (dividends) are not part of a company's routine operating activities and cannot be treated as expenses, whereas interest payments to creditors are expenses. In addition, both dividends and interest received are operating activities under U.S. GAAP. Most companies reporting under IFRS use the same method as those reporting under U.S. GAAP. However, companies using IFRS have other options. They may classify dividend or interest payments as either operating or financing activities. Further, IFRS allows companies to classify interest or dividend receipts as either operating or investing activities, as long as the classification is consistent across periods.

Preparing a Statement of Cash Flows

To see how various activities affect the statement of cash flows, consider the activities of Biwheels Company for January 20X2. We reproduce the company's transactions in balance sheet equation format in Exhibit 5-2 and display the resulting balance sheet and income statement in Exhibit 5-3. We use these exhibits to prepare a statement of cash flows for Biwheels for January 20X2. Notice that the cash balance for Biwheels increased from $0 at the beginning of

EXHIBIT 5-2

Biwheels Company

Analysis of Transactions for January 20X2 (in $)

Description of Transactions	Cash	+ Accounts Receivable	+ Merchandise Inventory	+ Prepaid Rent	+ Store Equipment	=	Note Payable	+ Accounts Payable	+ Paid-in Capital	+ Retained Earnings
(1) Initial investment	+400,000					=			+400,000	
(2) Loan from bank	+100,000					=	+100,000			
(3) Acquire store equipment for cash	−15,000				+15,000	=				
(4) Acquire inventory for cash	−120,000		+120,000			=				
(5) Acquire inventory on credit			+10,000			=		+10,000		
(6) Acquire inventory for cash plus credit	−10,000		+30,000			=		+20,000		
(7) Sale of equipment	+1,000				−1,000	=				
(8) Return of inventory acquired on January 6			−800			=		−800		
(9) Payment to creditor	−4,000					=		−4,000		
(10a) Sales on open account		+160,000				=				+160,000
(10b) Cost of merchandise inventory sold			−100,000			=				−100,000
(11) Collect accounts receivable	+5,000	−5,000				=				
(12) Pay rent in advance	−6,000			+6,000		=				
(13) Recognize expiration of rental services				−2,000		=				−2,000
(14) Depreciation					−100	=				−100
Balance, January 31, 20X2	351,000	+155,000	+59,200	+4,000	+13,900	=	100,000	+25,200	+400,000	+57,900

	Assets					=	Liabilities		+	Stockholders' Equity

583,100 = 583,100

EXHIBIT 5-3

Biwheels Company's Income Statement and Balance Sheet

Income Statement, for the Month Ended January 31, 20X2

Sales revenue		$160,000
Deduct expenses		
Cost of goods sold	$100,000	
Rent	2,000	
Depreciation	100	
Total expenses		102,100
Net income		$ 57,900

Balance Sheet, January 31, 20X2

Assets		Liabilities and Stockholders' Equity		
Cash	$351,000	Liabilities:		
Accounts receivable	155,000	Note payable		$100,000
Merchandise inventory	59,200	Accounts payable		25,200
Prepaid rent	4,000	Total liabilities		125,200
Store equipment, net	13,900	Stockholders' equity:		
		Paid-in capital	$400,000	
		Retained earnings	57,900	
		Total stockholders' equity		457,900
		Total liabilities and		
Total assets	$583,100	stockholders' equity		$583,100

the month to $351,000 at the end of the month. Because the statement of cash flows explains the changes in cash, the first step in developing the statement is always to compute the amount of the change, in this case an increase of $351,000. Next we examine the three sections of the statement of cash flows that combine to explain this $351,000 increase.

Cash Flows from Financing Activities

> **▶ OBJECTIVE 3**
>
> Compute and interpret cash flows from financing activities.

Although most companies list operating activities as the first section of the cash flow statement, we will begin our discussion with the more easily described and understood section, cash flows from financing activities. Further, financing activities were the first transactions in the launching of Biwheels Company. The financing activities section shows cash flows to and from providers of capital. The easiest way to determine cash flows from financing activities is to examine changes in the cash account in the balance sheet equation (or T-account) and identify those changes associated with financing activities. Exhibit 5-2 shows that Biwheels had two such transactions in January:

Transaction 1, Initial investment, $400,000

Transaction 2, Loan from bank, $100,000

Both of these transactions are cash inflows, that is, increases in cash. Therefore, Biwheels' cash flows from financing activities total $500,000:

Biwheels Company
Cash Flows from Financing Activities for the Month of January 20X2

Proceeds from initial investment	$400,000
Proceeds from bank loan	100,000
Net cash provided by financing activities	$500,000

If you did not have access to the balance sheet equation entries, you could also look at the changes in Biwheels' balance sheet during January. Note that all balance sheet accounts were zero at the beginning of the month. You can compute the increases in Note Payable and Paid-in Capital as follows:

	Balance, January 1, 20X2	Balance, January 31, 20X2	Increase (Decrease)
Note payable	$0	$100,000	$100,000
Paid-in capital	0	400,000	400,000

If stockholders' had invested $100,000 on December 31, 20X1 and the remaining $300,000 on January 2, 20X2, the cash inflow for January 20X2 from the investment would have been only $300,000:

	Balance, January 1, 20X2	Balance, January 31, 20X2	Increase (Decrease)
Paid-in capital	$100,000	$400,000	$300,000

Two general rules for financing activities are as follows:

- Increases in cash (cash inflows) stem from increases in liabilities or paid-in capital
- Decreases in cash (cash outflows) stem from decreases in liabilities or paid-in capital

You can see a list of some financing activities and their effect on cash in the first part of Exhibit 5-4. For example, selling common shares increases cash (+), paying dividends decreases cash (–), and converting debt into common stock has no effect on cash. In addition, note that the transactions classified as financing activities do not affect net income. The relevance of this distinction will become more evident when we discuss cash flows from operations.

Cash Flows from Investing Activities

The section of the cash flow statement called cash flows from investing activities lists cash flows from the purchase or sale of plant, property, equipment, and other long-lived assets. It is usually the second section in the cash flow statement. To determine the cash flows from investing activities, look at transactions that increase or decrease long-lived assets, loans, or securities that are

▶▶ **OBJECTIVE 4**
Compute and interpret cash flows from investing activities.

EXHIBIT 5-4

Analysis of Effects of Financing and Investing Transactions on Cash

Type of Transaction	Increase (+) or Decrease (–) in Cash
Financing Activities	
Increase long- or short-term debt	+
Reduce long- or short-term debt	–
Sell common shares	+
Repurchase common shares	–
Pay dividends	–
Convert debt to common stock	No effect
Investing Activities	
Purchase fixed assets for cash	–
Purchase fixed assets by issuing debt	No effect
Sell fixed assets for cash	+
Purchase for cash investment securities of other firms that are not cash equivalents	–
Sell for cash investment securities in other firms that are not cash equivalents	+
Make a loan to another company or person	–
Collect a loan	+

not considered cash equivalents. Biwheels has only one such asset, Store Equipment. There were two cash transactions relating to store equipment during January:

Transaction 3, Acquire store equipment for cash, $15,000

Transaction 7, Sale of asset [store equipment] for cash, $1,000

The first of these transactions is a use of cash, or a cash outflow. The second is a source of cash, or a cash inflow. The investing activities section of Biwheels' cash flow statement is as follows:

Biwheels Company
Cash Flows from Investing Activities
for the Month of January 20X2

Purchase of store equipment	$(15,000)
Proceeds from sale of store equipment	1,000
Net cash used by investing activities	$(14,000)

Notice that we place the cash outflows in parentheses. Because there is a net cash outflow, investing activities used cash during January. This contrasts with financing activities, which provided cash.

The second part of Exhibit 5-4 shows types of investing activities and their effects on cash. For example, selling investment securities (except for securities that are cash equivalents) increases cash (+) and making a loan decreases cash (–). Notice that buying or selling securities that are cash equivalents does not change cash. It simply turns one type of cash into another type of cash.

If you did not have access to the transactions listed in the balance sheet equation, you would need to look at changes in the long-lived assets, loans, and other investments on the balance sheet. Two general rules for investing activities are as follows:

- Increases in cash (cash inflows) stem from sale of long-lived assets, collection of loans made to others, and sale of investments
- Decreases in cash (cash outflows) stem from purchases of long-lived assets, granting of loans to others, and purchases of investments

Consider Biwheels' only long-lived asset, Store Equipment. Changes in the net amount of such assets generally result from three possible sources—(1) asset acquisitions, (2) asset disposals, and (3) depreciation expense for the period:

$$\text{Change in assets} = \text{Acquisitions} - \text{Disposals} - \text{Depreciation expense}$$

Asset acquisitions and disposals may involve cash, but depreciation has no impact on cash. It is not a cash outflow. Thus, it is important to identify how much of the change in the asset values resulted from the recognition of depreciation. From the balance sheet, we learn that the net amount of Biwheels' Store Equipment increased from $0 to $13,900 in January. From the income statement, we know that Depreciation Expense was $100. Thus, we know that the net acquisitions (that is, acquisitions less disposals) were $14,000:

$$\$13,900 = \text{Acquisitions} - \text{Disposals} - \$100$$
$$\text{Acquisitions} - \text{Disposals} = \$13,900 + \$100 = \$14,000$$

Only by knowing more about either the actual acquisitions or disposals can we break down net acquisitions into acquisitions and disposals. In this case we know that Biwheels' acquisitions were $15,000, so disposals must have been ($15,000 – $14,000) = $1,000. If we had not known the amount of acquisitions but knew that disposals were $1,000, we could compute acquisitions as ($14,000 + $1,000) = $15,000. Management has no problem examining financial records directly to determine the details about acquisitions and disposals, but investors have a more difficult time obtaining such details.

INTERPRETING FINANCIAL STATEMENTS

A company raised $1 million by selling common stock. The company put $400,000 into securities that are cash equivalents and used the other $600,000 to buy equipment. What are the effects of these transactions on the cash flow statement?

Answer

The $1 million appears as cash provided by financing activities. The $600,000 appears as a use of cash in the investing section.

Because the securities are cash equivalents, the $400,000 does not appear in the investing section; instead, it is simply a rearrangement of the form in which the company holds cash. The net increase in cash from these transactions is $400,000, or $1 million from financing less $600,000 used for investing.

Noncash Investing and Financing Activities

Some financing or investing activities do not affect cash. Companies list such activities in a separate schedule accompanying the statement of cash flows. In our example, Biwheels Company did not engage in any noncash investing or financing activities. However, suppose Biwheels' purchase of the store equipment was not for cash, but was financed as follows:

A. Biwheels acquired $8,000 of the store equipment by issuing common stock.
B. Biwheels acquired the other $7,000 of store equipment by signing a note payable for $7,000.

Also consider one other possible transaction:

C. Biwheels converted $50,000 of its original note payable to common stock. That is, Biwheels issued $50,000 of common stock in exchange for a reduction of $50,000 in the note payable.

These items would affect the balance sheet equation as follows:

	Cash	+	Store Equipment	=	Note Payable	+	Paid-in Capital
A.	0		+$8,000	=			+$ 8,000
B.	0		+$7,000	=	+$ 7,000		
C.	0			=	−$50,000		+$50,000

None of these transactions affect cash; therefore, they do not belong in a statement of cash flows. However, each transaction could just as easily involve cash. For example, in the first transaction, the company might issue common stock for $8,000 cash and immediately use the cash to purchase the fixed asset. The financing cash inflow and investing cash outflow would then both appear on the statement of cash flows. Because of the importance of these noncash investing and financing decisions, readers of financial statements want to be informed of such noncash activities. Companies must report such items in a schedule of noncash investing and financing activities. Biwheels Company's schedule for hypothetical transactions A, B, and C would be as follows:

Schedule of noncash investing and financing activities	
Common stock issued to acquire store equipment	$ 8,000
Note payable for acquisition of store equipment	$ 7,000
Common stock issued on conversion of note payable	$50,000

Summary Problem for Your Review

PROBLEM

Examine the entries to Biwheels' balance sheet equation for February 20X2 in Exhibit 2-5 (p. 60) and the final February transaction, transaction 22, declaration and payment of dividends of $50,000 (p. 61).

1. Identify the transactions that belong in the financing and investing sections of the statement of cash flows for February.
2. Assume that Biwheels has two additional transactions during February:
   a. Bought shares of common stock of Pacific Cycle for $12,000 cash.
   b. Bought a $30,000 storage shed for $8,000 cash and signed a note payable for the remaining $22,000. The company financed the $8,000 for the cash down payment by borrowing $8,000 cash from the bank and then using it for the down payment.

   How would these transactions affect the financing and investing sections of Biwheels' February statement of cash flows?
3. Prepare the financing and investing sections of Biwheels' statement of cash flows including all transactions in parts 1 and 2 of this problem. Include a schedule of noncash investing and financing activities if appropriate. Interpret the information you learn from these two sections.

SOLUTION

1. Only transaction 21, borrowing of $10,000 from the bank and using that $10,000 to buy store equipment, and transaction 22, payment of cash dividends of $50,000, involve financing or investing activities. The $10,000 loan is a financing activity, the $10,000 paid to buy the store equipment is an investing activity, and the $50,000 of dividends paid is a financing activity.
2. The $12,000 paid for Pacific Cycle shares is an investing activity. The purchase of the storage shed has three effects: (1) The $8,000 paid in cash is an investing activity, (2) the $8,000 borrowed from the bank is a financing activity, and (3) the $22,000 acquisition for a note payable is a noncash investing and financing activity.
3. The statement of cash flows would include the following. Note that we combined the two borrowings from the bank into one line: ($10,000 + $8,000) = $18,000.

Biwheels Company Cash Flows from Financing and Investing Activities for the Month of February 20X2	
Cash Flows from Investing Activities	
Acquisition of store equipment	$(10,000)
Purchase of Pacific Cycle common shares	(12,000)
Acquisition of storage shed	(8,000)
Net cash used for investing activities	$(30,000)
Cash Flows from Financing Activities	
Borrowing from banks	$ 18,000
Payment of dividends	(50,000)
Net cash used by financing activities	$(32,000)
Noncash Investing and Financing Activities	
Note payable financing for purchase of storage shed	$ 22,000

From these sections of the cash flow statement, we learn that in February Biwheels used a total of $62,000 in cash for investing and financing activities. Either the company used cash generated by operations or it depleted its cash balance to support these activities. Of the $30,000 spent for investing activities, $18,000 increased long-lived assets and $12,000 increased Biwheels' investment in the securities of another company, Pacific Cycle. We also learn that the $18,000 in cash inflows from financing was entirely debt financing, borrowing from banks. The company did not sell or buy back any shares of its common stock. The $50,000 cash outflow for dividends was larger than the additional borrowing, resulting in a net cash outflow of $32,000 from financing activities. Finally, Biwheels also invested another $22,000 in the storage shed and financed it with debt in the form of a note payable. This transaction involved both a financing activity and an investing activity, but it had no effect on cash.

Cash Flows from Operating Activities

Users of financial statements appreciate information about management's ability to make financial and investment decisions. However, they often are more concerned with assessing management's operating decisions. They focus on the first section of cash flow statements, cash flows from operating activities (or cash flows from operations), which shows the cash effects of transactions that involve the major income-generating activities of the company. As noted earlier, these are activities that affect the purchase, processing, and selling of a company's products and services—in other words, the transactions that affect the income statement.

Approaches to Calculating the Cash Flows from Operating Activities

Under current U.S. GAAP, companies can use either of two approaches to compute cash flows from operating activities (or cash flows from operations). The **direct method** subtracts operating cash disbursements from operating cash collections to arrive at net cash flow from operations. The **indirect method** starts with the accrual net income from the income statement and adjusts it to reflect only those income statement activities that involve actual cash receipts and cash disbursements. Both methods produce the same amount of net cash provided by (or used for) operating activities. The only difference is the format of the operating section of the cash flow statement.

Both the IASB and FASB prefer the direct method because it is a straightforward listing of cash inflows and cash outflows and is easier for investors to understand. As indicated in the Business First box on p. 200, the two Boards are likely to go a step further in the near future and issue a standard that requires companies to use the direct method. Although we will discuss the direct method first, you also need to understand the indirect method because many companies will continue to use it until the standards force them to change.

Before addressing the details of the direct and indirect methods, consider the types of cash flows that accountants classify as operating activities. Exhibit 5-5 lists many such activities.

direct method
A method for computing cash flows from operating activities that subtracts operating cash disbursements from operating cash collections to arrive at cash flows from operations.

indirect method
A method for computing cash flows from operating activities that adjusts the previously calculated accrual net income from the income statement to reflect only those income statement activities that involve actual cash receipts and cash disbursements.

EXHIBIT 5-5

Analysis of Effects of Operating Transactions on Cash

Type of Transaction	Increase (+) or Decrease (−) in Cash
Operating Activities	
Sell goods and services for cash	+
Sell goods and services on credit	No effect
Collect accounts receivable	+
Receive dividends or interest	+
Recognize cost of goods sold	No effect
Purchase inventory for cash	−
Purchase inventory on credit	No effect
Pay accounts payable	−
Accrue operating expenses	No effect
Pay operating expenses	−
Accrue taxes	No effect
Pay taxes	−
Accrue interest	No effect
Pay interest	−
Prepay expenses for cash	−
Record the use of prepaid expenses	No effect
Charge depreciation	No effect

BUSINESS FIRST

ACCOUNTING CHANGES ON THE HORIZON: FINANCIAL STATEMENT PRESENTATION

Generally accepted accounting principles (GAAP) are continually changing. Both the FASB and IASB issue new standards that either improve previous standards or address new issues that arise as the nature of business and the economy changes.

Most new accounting standards today involve a joint effort of the FASB and IASB. One such effort is the Financial Statement Presentation Project. As part of their effort to converge U.S. GAAP and IFRS, in April 2004 the FASB and IASB set out to work together on major revisions to the required format for companies' financial statements. We will discuss two changes that, if adopted, would directly alter the statement of cash flows. We will also discuss one change that would affect all three of the basic financial statements: the balance sheet, the income statement, and the statement of cash flows.

With respect to the statement of cash flows, the proposed standard would require the use of the direct method. Almost all companies today use the indirect method, so those companies would have to change the format of their statement. The proposed standard would also prohibit the combining of cash and cash equivalents. Companies would have to include all items currently called cash equivalents in their short-term investments section, not as part of cash.

Probably the most sweeping and controversial proposed change is to organize the basic financial statements into a set of categories that are more cohesive across the statements than are current statement formats. For the balance sheet and income statement, these categories would be similar, but not identical, to the statement of cash flows format that divides activities into operating, investing, and financing activities. For example, the balance sheet and income statement would have a Business section, which would be divided into operating and investing categories, and a Financing section, which would be separated into debt and equity categories. In addition, there would be a separate section for taxes payable, both current and deferred. A balance sheet would be organized something like this:

BUSINESS
  Operating assets and liabilities
  .
  .
  Investing assets and liabilities
  .
  .
FINANCING
  Debt category
  .
  .
  Equity category
  .
  .
INCOME TAXES

The Boards are still working on this project. Progress has been slow, and there is no projected date for releasing a proposed draft of the new standards. Nevertheless, many accountants believe that at some future date both Boards will require new presentation formats.

Sources: G. McClain, and A. J. McLelland, "Shaking Up Financial Statement Presentation," *Journal of Accountancy*, November 2008, pp. 56–64; Financial Accounting Standards Board, *Project Updates* (last update May 3, 2011), http://www.fasb.org/financial_statement_presentation.shtml.

These cash flows are associated with revenues and expenses on the income statement. Notice that recording revenue from the sales of goods or services does not necessarily increase cash. Only sales for cash immediately increase cash. There is no cash effect of credit sales until the customer actually pays. Biwheels must collect its accounts receivable to generate any cash. Similarly, cash received for services to be performed in the future is an operating cash inflow recognized in the statement of cash flows even though a company may not earn and record the revenue until a later period.

The cash effects of expenses are similar. Sometimes the cash outflow precedes the recording of the expense on the income statement. For example, Biwheels incurred a $6,000 cash outflow for prepaid rent in January and recorded the $6,000 as an asset. The entire $6,000 would appear on January's statement of cash flows. The company does not record rent expense on the income statement until later, when it uses the rented facilities. The entries that recognize rent expense and reduce the Prepaid Rent account do not affect cash.

In other cases, the cash outflow follows the recording of the expense, as may occur with payment of wages. The statement of cash flows reports wages when the company actually disburses cash to employees, not when it records the wages expense.

Let's examine the cost of goods sold expense. Accounting for the acquisition and sale of inventory usually requires recording three transactions: (1) purchase of inventory on credit, (2) payment of accounts payable, and (3) delivery of goods to the customer and thus the recording of an expense, where steps (2) and (3) may occur in either order. If the purchase of inventory is for cash, steps 1 and 2 combine to form a single transaction.

Consider the following Biwheels transactions. Biwheels bought a bicycle seat on credit for $30 on June 7. Biwheels sold the seat on June 29 and paid the supplier in full on July 7. Two transactions occurred during June:

1. June 7. The balance sheet accounts Merchandise Inventory and Accounts Payable increased by $30.
2. June 29. The balance sheet account Merchandise Inventory decreased by $30, and Biwheels recorded a $30 cost of goods sold expense on the income statement. (Note that Biwheels would also record the sales revenue and increase either cash or accounts receivable on June 29, but we are focusing here on the expense part of the transaction.)

At the end of June, no cash transaction had occurred. Neither purchasing inventory on credit nor charging cost of goods sold expense affects cash. The cash transaction occurs on July 7, when Biwheels pays $30 in cash to the supplier, thereby reducing its accounts payable by $30. The end result of the three transactions is a $30 expense and a $30 cash payment. However, Biwheels recorded the expense in June and the cash outflow in July. June's income statement would have a $30 expense, but June's cash flow statement would have no related cash outflow. In July, the situation would be reversed—the cash flow statement would have a $30 outflow, but there would be no expense on the income statement. Notice in Exhibit 5-5 that there is no effect on cash when we recognize cost of goods sold or purchase inventory on credit, but there is a decrease in cash when we pay accounts payable or purchase inventory for cash.

Now that you know some of the operating transactions that affect cash and how the cash inflow or outflow can occur at a different time than the recording of the related revenue or expense, let's examine the two formats used for showing the cash flow effects of operations.

Cash Flows from Operations—The Direct Method

The direct method consists of a listing of cash receipts (inflows) and cash disbursements (outflows). The easiest way to identify cash flows from operations using the direct method is to examine the Cash column of the balance sheet equation. The following entries from Exhibit 5-2 (p. 193) affect cash:

▶▶ **OBJECTIVE 5**

Use the direct method to calculate cash flows from operations.

Entry	Cash Effect
(1) Initial investment	+400,000
(2) Loan from bank	+100,000
(3) Acquire store equipment for cash	–15,000
(4) Acquire inventory for cash	*–120,000*
(6) Acquire inventory for cash plus credit	*–10,000*
(7) Sale of equipment	+1,000
(9) Payment to creditor	*–4,000*
(11) Collect accounts receivable	*+5,000*
(12) Pay rent in advance	*–6,000*

We know from the previous sections that transactions 1 and 2 are financing activities and transactions 3 and 7 are investing activities. Thus, the remaining transactions affecting cash must be operating activities. Therefore, the cash flows from operating activities must include transactions 4, 6, 9, 11, and 12, which are in bold italics. The statement follows:

Biwheels Company

Cash Flows from Operating Activities
For the Month of January 20X2

Cash payments for inventory (transactions 4 and 6)	$(130,000)
Cash payments to creditors for accounts payable (transaction 9)	(4,000)
Cash collections on accounts receivable (transaction 11)	5,000
Cash payments for rent (transaction 12)	(6,000)
Net cash used by operating activities	$(135,000)

A more common format for this statement lists the cash collections first. It also combines the cash payments for inventory and cash payments to creditors for accounts payable on one line, cash payments to suppliers:

Biwheels Company

Cash Flows from Operating Activities
For the Month of January 20X2

Cash collections	$ 5,000
Cash payments to suppliers	(134,000)
Cash payments for rent	(6,000)
Net cash used by operating activities	$(135,000)

Notice the small cash inflow generated by operations during January. All sales in January were credit sales, and Biwheels collected only $5,000 during the month. Operating cash outflows that exceed cash inflows are common in young, growing companies. Companies pay for items such as rent and inventories in advance of receiving cash for the sales that result from the use of these resources.

Cash Flows from Operations—The Indirect Method

> ▶▶ **OBJECTIVE 6**
>
> Use the indirect method to explain the difference between net income and net cash provided by (used for) operating activities.

The direct method gives a straightforward picture of where a company gets cash and how it spends cash. However, some users of financial statements may want to understand how the net cash flow from operating activities differ from net income. To show this, a company uses the indirect method. Let's examine the January indirect-method cash flow statement for Biwheels shown in Exhibit 5-6. The statement starts with net income, adds or subtracts a series of adjustments, and ends with net cash provided by (used for) operating activities. To construct this statement, we use January's income statement, the January 31 balance sheet from Exhibit 5-3 on p. 194, and the January 1 balance sheet where all accounts have a zero balance. Each income statement item has a related item or items in the statement of cash flows, although a transaction may appear on the two statements at different points in time. That is, each sale eventually results in cash inflows; each expense entails cash outflows at some time. However, a company often records a revenue in one accounting period and receives the related cash inflow in another. Similarly, it may record an expense in a period that differs from that in which it records the related cash outflow. The indirect method highlights the differences between (1) revenues and cash inflows, and (2) expenses and cash outflows in a given time period.

Look again at Exhibit 5-6. If all sales were for cash and all expenses were paid in cash as incurred, cash flows from operating activities would be identical to net income. Thus, you can think of the first line of Exhibit 5-6, net income, as what the cash flow from operating activities would be if all revenues were cash inflows and all expenses were cash outflows. The subsequent adjustments recognize the differences in timing between revenues and cash inflows and between expenses and cash outflows. Understanding these adjustments is key to understanding the indirect method. An alternative format that can help you become familiar with these adjustments is in Exhibit 5-7, where the middle column contains the adjustments shown in Exhibit 5-6. We will describe Exhibit 5-7 as we discuss each adjustment.

Net income		$ 57,900
Adjustments to reconcile net income to net cash provided (used) by operating activities:		
Depreciation		100
Increase in accounts receivable		(155,000)
Increase in inventory		(59,200)
Increase in accounts payable		25,200
Increase in prepaid rent		(4,000)
Net cash provided by (used for) operating activities		$(135,000)

EXHIBIT 5-6

Biwheels Company

Cash Flows from Operating Activities—Indirect Method, for the Month of January 20X2

ADJUSTMENT FOR DEPRECIATION The first adjustment is to add depreciation expense back to net income. We do this because we deducted depreciation of $100 when computing the net income of $57,900, but there is no related operating cash outflow in January. In fact, depreciation never entails an operating cash flow because the cash flow occurred as an investing activity when Biwheels paid for the equipment. Because we deducted $100 of depreciation in computing January's net income, adding it back simply cancels the deduction. There is no cash flow effect of depreciation. A word of caution—do not interpret the $100 depreciation add-back as a cash inflow. While line items in the financing and investing sections of a statement of cash flows represent cash inflows and cash outflows, the line items in the operating section of an indirect method statement are not cash flows. Rather, they are adjustments of net income. An adjustment similar to the one made for depreciation will apply to any expense for which there is never an operating cash outflow.

▸▸ **OBJECTIVE 7**

Understand why we add depreciation to net income when using the indirect method for computing cash flows from operating activities.

To highlight the effect of depreciation, let's for a moment assume that Biwheels received all $160,000 of revenue in cash and paid all $102,000 of nondepreciation expenses in cash. The income statement and statement of cash flows from operating activities would be as follows:

Income Statement		Cash Flows from Operating Activities	
Sales	$ 160,000	Cash inflows from sales	$160,000
Nondepreciation expenses	(102,000)	Cash outflows for expenses	(102,000)
Depreciation	(100)	Net cash provided by operating activities	$ 58,000
Net income	$ 57,900		

The only difference between net income and net cash provided by operating activities in this example is the $100 of depreciation. To compute the net cash provided by operating activities, we simply add the $100 to the net income: ($57,900 + $100) = $58,000. The center column of line D

EXHIBIT 5-7

Biwheels Company

Comparison of Net Income and Net Cash Provided by Operating Activities

Net Income		Adjustments		Cash Flows from Operating Activities	
A. Sales revenues	$160,000	Increase in accounts receivable	$(155,000)	Cash collections from customers	$ 5,000
		Increase in inventories	(59,200)		
B. Cost of goods sold	(100,000)	Increase in accounts payable	25,200	Cash payments to suppliers	(134,000)
C. Rent expense	(2,000)	Increase in prepaid rent	(4,000)	Cash payments for rent	(6,000)
D. Depreciation	(100)	Depreciation	100		0*
Net income	$ 57,900	Total adjustments	$(192,900)	Net cash provided by (used for) operating activities	$(135,000)

*Depreciation is not a cash flow.

of Exhibit 5-7 shows depreciation as one of the adjustments to net income when computing cash provided by operating activities.

Now suppose depreciation expense was $500 rather than $100. Net income would be ($160,000 − $102,000 − $500) = $57,500, and net cash provided by operating activities would still be $58,000, the sum of net income ($57,500) and depreciation ($500). Net cash provided by operating activities did not change with the increase in depreciation. That is, the amount of depreciation has no effect on the cash provided by operating activities. To calculate cash flows, we add back to net income exactly the same amount we subtracted for depreciation, essentially canceling the earlier deduction.

Depreciation is Biwheels' only expense for which there is never an operating cash flow. The related cash flow was an investing outflow at the time the company paid for the underlying asset. The remaining adjustments for Biwheels represent situations where timing creates differences between net income and cash flows from operations. That is, over time the total revenue or expense will equal the total operating cash inflow or outflow, but the company may report some revenues or expenses on the income statement in one period and the related cash inflows or outflows on the statement of cash flows in another period.

ADJUSTMENT FOR REVENUES Consider Biwheels' revenues. If all of Biwheels' sales were for cash, there would be no accounts receivable, the associated cash flows would occur at the time of sale, and the cash inflow would equal the sales revenue. However, Biwheels' January sales are all on open account. Thus, each sale initially increases accounts receivable, and the cash inflow occurs when Biwheels collects the receivable from the customer. You can compute the amount of cash collections from income statement and balance sheet data in two steps: (1) compute the total amount Biwheels could possibly collect in the month, which is the sales for the month plus the accounts receivable balance at the beginning of the month, and (2) from this you subtract the amount that Biwheels has not yet collected, the accounts receivable at the end of the month. This gives collections in January of $5,000:

Sales	$160,000
+ Beginning accounts receivable	0
Potential collections	160,000
− Ending accounts receivable	155,000
Cash collections from customers	$ 5,000

We can simplify this by subtracting the ending accounts receivable balance from the beginning accounts receivables balance to give us a single number representing the change in accounts receivable.

Beginning accounts receivable	$ 0
Less: Ending accounts receivable	155,000
Decrease (increase) in accounts receivable	$(155,000)

Don't be fooled by the signs. When the number is negative, accounts receivable has increased. When the number is positive, accounts receivable has decreased.

Combining the change in accounts receivable with sales gives us the amount of cash collected from customers during the period:

Sales	$160,000
Decrease (increase) in accounts receivable*	(155,000)
Cash collections from customers	$ 5,000

*The format "decrease (increase)" means that decreases are positive amounts and increases are negative amounts.

In the Biwheels example, accounts receivable increased by $155,000, meaning that collections from customers fell short of sales. So net income was overstated relative to the amount of operating cash flows received. Because Biwheels' accounts receivable increased in January, we deduct the $155,000 from net income to get cash provided by operating activities. Line A in Exhibit 5-7 shows this adjustment.

If accounts receivable had remained unchanged (that is, accounts receivable at the end of the month equaled the accounts receivable at the beginning of the month), cash collections would equal sales and no adjustment of net income would be necessary. If accounts receivable had decreased, meaning that collections exceeded sales, net income would be lower than cash flows from operations. We would then add the decrease in accounts receivable to sales to determine the cash collections.

INTERPRETING FINANCIAL STATEMENTS

Suppose all $160,000 of Biwheels' sales were for cash. Compute the cash collections from customers using the formula sales plus or minus the change in accounts receivable. Explain.

Answer

If all sales were for cash, accounts receivable would have remained at $0. Because there was no increase or decrease in accounts

receivable, there would be no adjustment of sales needed to compute cash collections from customers:

Sales	$160,000
Decrease (increase) in accounts receivable	0
Cash collections from customers	$160,000

ADJUSTMENT FOR COST OF GOODS SOLD Just as we adjusted sales to compute cash collections from customers, we can adjust cost of goods sold to compute cash outflow for payments to suppliers. To do this, we use one income statement account, Cost of Goods Sold, and two balance sheet accounts, Inventory and Accounts Payable. We adjust cost of goods sold to get cash payments to suppliers in two steps:

These two steps yield the following:

Step 1	
Cost of goods sold in January	$100,000
+ Ending inventory, January 31	59,200
Inventory available in January	159,200
– Beginning inventory, January 1	0
Inventory purchased in January	$159,200
Step 2	
Inventory purchased in January	$159,200
+ Beginning accounts payable, January 1	0
Total amount to be paid	159,200
– Ending accounts payable, January 31	(25,200)
Amount paid in cash during January	$134,000

In step 1, we compute the amount of inventory purchased in January, independent of whether we purchase the inventory for cash or credit. This requires two calculations: (1) adding the amount of inventory used in January (that is, the cost of goods sold) to the amount of inventory left at the end of January to get the total inventory available in January, and (2) deducting from that total the amount that was in inventory at the beginning of the month. This yields the total inventory purchased in January. It is important to understand that, in the Biwheels example, the beginning inventory balance was zero, so purchases and inventory available in January both equal $159,200. When a company has been in operation for multiple periods, this equality is unlikely.

If Biwheels had bought all of its inventory for cash, we could stop at this point. Its cash outflow to suppliers would equal the amount purchased, $159,200. However, because Biwheels purchased some inventory on credit, we must take step 2. This requires examining the activity in Biwheels' accounts payable as well as activity in inventory. If Biwheels had paid off all its accounts payable by the end of January, it would have paid an amount equal to the beginning accounts payable plus the purchases in January, a total of $159,200. Yet, $25,200 remained payable at the end of January, meaning that of the $159,200 of potential payments, Biwheels paid only ($159,200 – $25,200) = $134,000 in January.

As with the adjustment for revenues, we can simplify these two steps into one line each:

Cost of goods sold in January	$100,000
Step 1: Increase (decrease) in inventory during January	59,200
Step 2: Decrease (increase) in accounts payable during January	(25,200)
Payments to suppliers during January	$134,000

The first two lines show that Biwheels purchased $159,200 of inventory—$100,000 to meet sales demand and $59,200 to build up inventory. If all purchases were for cash, the payments to suppliers would have been $159,200. (If inventory had decreased during the month, the amount of purchases would be cost of goods sold minus the decrease in inventory.) However, because accounts payable increased by $25,200, Biwheels did not pay the entire $159,200 in January. Of the $159,200 potential cash outflow, Biwheels will pay $25,200 sometime after January, so the company paid only ($159,200 – $25,200) = $134,000 in January.

These adjustments that convert cost of goods sold into payments to suppliers are shown in line B of Exhibit 5-7. Because an increase in inventories requires extra cash, the cash flow from operations will be less than net income—that is, we subtract the $59,200 increase in inventories from net income when computing cash flows from operations. In contrast, when accounts payable increases we retain cash that accounting period, so we add the $25,200 increase in accounts payable to net income when computing cash flows from operations.

ADJUSTMENTS FOR OTHER EXPENSES Before considering line C in Exhibit 5-7, let's create a general approach to adjustments. Then we can apply the approach to line C.

- Adjust for revenues and expenses that do not require cash:
  Add back depreciation.
  Add back other expenses that do not require cash.
  Deduct revenues that do not generate cash.

- Adjust for changes in noncash assets and liabilities relating to operating activities:
  Add decreases in operating assets.
  Deduct increases in operating assets.
  Add increases in operating liabilities.
  Deduct decreases in operating liabilities.

Adjustments so far have included adding back the $100 of depreciation expense, deducting the $155,000 increase in accounts receivable (an operating asset), deducting the $59,200 increase in inventory (an operating asset), and adding the $25,200 increase in accounts payable (an operating liability). Take time to verify that each of these adjustments is consistent with the preceding general rules. We will see other adjustments similar to depreciation in later chapters.

Now let's consider Biwheels' adjustments for its other operating assets and liabilities. The only such asset or liability is Prepaid Rent, an asset account. It increased from $0 at the beginning of the month to $4,000 at the end of the month. Thus, we need to deduct $4,000 from net income to compute cash flow from operations, as shown in line C of Exhibit 5-7. This $4,000 adjustment is the result of paying $6,000 in cash for rent, but charging only $2,000 as an expense. This means that Biwheels' cash outflow for rent exceeded the rent expense by $4,000 in the month of January.

To summarize, look again at Exhibit 5-7. An indirect-method cash flow statement begins with the net income of $57,900 from the bottom of the first column of Exhibit 5-7, adds (deducts) the adjustments totaling $(192,900) in the middle column, and ends with the $(135,000) net cash used for operating activities in the right-hand column. The left-hand column calculates net income, the right-hand column calculates cash flows from operations, and the middle column shows line-by-line adjustments that represent all the differences between net income and cash flow from operations. Although Biwheels had a healthy net income of $57,900, it used $135,000 of cash to support its operations. Such a depletion of cash cannot continue indefinitely, regardless of how much income Biwheels generates. However, Biwheels is like other young, growing companies: It is using cash to build up its business in anticipation of positive cash flows being provided by operating activities in the future.

Reconciliation Statement

When a company uses the direct method for reporting cash flows from operating activities, users of the financial statements might miss information that relates net income to operating cash flows. Thus, those using direct-method statements must include a supplementary schedule reconciling net income to net cash provided by operations. Such a supplementary statement is effectively the operating section of an indirect method cash flow statement. In essence, companies that choose to use the direct method must also report using the indirect method. In contrast, those using the indirect method never explicitly report the information on a direct-method statement. The supplementary statement included with direct-method cash flow statements would be identical to the body of Exhibit 5-6, but it would be labeled "Reconciliation of Net Income to Net Cash Provided by Operating Activities."

The Statement of Cash Flows and the Balance Sheet Equation

To better understand how the cash flow statement relates to the other financial statements, let's examine the balance sheet equation. The balance sheet equation provides the conceptual basis for all financial statements, including the statement of cash flows. The equation can be rearranged as follows:

> ▶▶ **OBJECTIVE 8**
> Show how the balance sheet equation provides a conceptual framework for the statement of cash flows.

$$\text{Assets} = \text{Liabilities} + \text{Stockholders' equity}$$
$$\text{Cash} + \text{Noncash assets (NCA)} = \text{L} + \text{SE}$$
$$\text{Cash} = \text{L} + \text{SE} - \text{NCA}$$

Any change (Δ) in cash must be accompanied by a change in one or more items on the right side to keep the equation in balance:

$$\Delta \text{Cash} = \Delta \text{L} + \Delta \text{SE} - \Delta \text{NCA}$$

Therefore:

$$\text{Change in cash} = \text{Change in all noncash accounts}$$

or

$$\text{What happened to cash} = \text{Why it happened}$$

The statement of cash flows focuses on the changes in the noncash accounts as a way of explaining how and why the amount of cash has increased or decreased during a given period. Thus, changes in the accounts on the right side of the equation appear in the statement of cash flows when they involve the use or receipt of cash. The left side of the equation measures the net effect of the change in cash. Of course, transactions can occur that affect only the right side of the

EXHIBIT 5-8

Biwheels Company

Analysis of Operating Transactions for January 20X2 (in $)

	Cash	=	Liabilities	+	Stockholders' Equity	−	Noncash Assets				
Description of Transactions	**Cash**	**=**	**Accounts Payable**	**+**	**Retained Earnings**	**−**	**Accounts Receivable**	**Merchandise Inventory**	**Prepaid Rent**	**Store Equipment**
(4) Acquire inventory for cash	−120,000	=						+120,000		
(5) Acquire inventory on credit		=	+10,000					+10,000		
(6) Acquire inventory for cash plus credit	−10,000	=	+20,000					+30,000		
(8) Return of inventory acquired on January 6		=	−800					−800		
(9) Payment to creditor	−4,000	=	−4,000							
(10a) Sales on open account		=			+160,000		+160,000			
(10b) Cost of merchandise inventory sold		=			−100,000			−100,000		
(11) Collect accounts receivable	+5,000	=					−5,000			
(12) Pay rent in advance	−6,000	=							+6,000	
(13) Recognize expiration of rental services		=			−2,000				−2,000	
(14) Depreciation		=			−100					−100
Total Changes	**−135,000**	**=**	**+25,200**	**+**	**+57,900**	**−**	**+155,000**	**+59,200**	**+4,000**	**−100**

equation. For example, the purchase of equipment in exchange for common stock is a noncash investing and financing activity. Remember that such activities do not affect cash and do not appear in the statement of cash flows.

This same analysis can help explain the direct and indirect methods of reporting cash from operating activities. Exhibit 5-8 lists all of Biwheels' January transactions that we classify as operating activities. However, we have rearranged the columns in the format of the revised balance sheet equation presented above: $\Delta Cash = \Delta L + \Delta SE - \Delta NCA$. We list only the transactions that appear in the operating cash flows section of the statement of cash flows. Recall that operating activities are transactions that affect the purchase, processing, and selling of products or services.

Notice that the entries on the left side of the equal signs (those in the boxes) appear on the direct-method statement of cash flows from operations. They are the direct cash flows and total an outflow of $135,000. The changes in each account (that is, the bottom line for each column) on the right side of the equation (those circled) appear on the indirect-method statement. They also must total $135,000. Therefore, you can see that the direct- and indirect-method statements must always produce the same amount of net cash flow from operations. They differ only in format. The direct-method statement is a listing of all changes in cash, whereas the indirect-method statement shows the reasons for those changes. The following summarizes this analysis:

$$\Delta Cash = \Delta L + \Delta SE - \Delta NCA$$

$$\text{Direct method} = \text{Indirect method}$$

Examples of Statements of Cash Flows

Exhibit 5-9 shows the complete January indirect-method statement of cash flows for Biwheels. It shows that the total cash balance increased by $351,000, mainly due to $500,000 generated by financing activities. Of the $500,000 raised, operations used $135,000 and investing activities used $14,000, leaving the $351,000 balance.

EXHIBIT 5-9

Biwheels Company

Statement of Cash Flows
For January 20X2

Cash Flows from Operating Activities		
Net income	$ 57,900	
Adjustments to reconcile net income to net cash provided by (used for) operating activities		
Depreciation	100	
Increase in accounts receivable	(155,000)	
Increase in inventory	(59,200)	
Increase in accounts payable	25,200	
Increase in prepaid rent	(4,000)	
Net cash provided by (used for) operating activities		$(135,000)
Cash Flows from Investing Activities		
Purchase of store equipment	$ (15,000)	
Proceeds from sale of store equipment	1,000	
Net cash provided by (used for) investing activities		(14,000)
Cash Flows from Financing Activities		
Proceeds from initial investment	$400,000	
Proceeds from bank loan	100,000	
Net cash provided by (used for) financing activities		500,000
Net increase in cash		351,000
Cash, January 2, 20X2		0
Cash, January 31, 20X2		$ 351,000

EXHIBIT 5-10

Costco, Inc.

Statement of Cash Flows (in millions), for the Year Ended August 28, 2011

CASH PROVIDED (USED) BY OPERATIONS		
Net income		$ 1,542
Adjustments to reconcile net income to net cash provided by operating activities:		
Income charges not affecting cash		
Depreciation	855	
Other noncash charges	269	
Changes in operating assets and liabilities:		
Increase in merchandise inventories	(642)	
Increase in accounts payable	804	
Other operating assets and liabilities, net	370	
Net cash provided by operating activities		$ 3,198
CASH PROVIDED (USED) BY INVESTING ACTIVITIES		
Purchases of short-term investments	(3,276)	
Maturities of short-term investments	2,614	
Sales of investments	602	
Additions to property and equipment	(1,290)	
Proceeds from the sale of property and equipment	16	
Other investing activities, net	154	
Cash used by investing activities		(1,180)
CASH PROVIDED (USED) BY FINANCING ACTIVITIES		
Repayments of short-term borrowings	(105)	
Proceeds from short-term borrowings	79	
Cash dividend payments	(389)	
Repurchases of common stock	(624)	
Other financing activities, net	(238)	
Cash used by financing activities		(1,277)
Effect of exchange rate changes		54
Net increase in cash and equivalents		795
Cash and equivalents, beginning of year		3,214
Cash and equivalents, end of year		$ 4,009

You are now prepared to read most of the significant items on a real corporation's statement of cash flows. Consider Exhibit 5-10, Costco's statement of cash flows. We have simplified some items that were not covered in this chapter, but most of the items included should be familiar. Some terminology is slightly different from what we have used, but the meanings should be clear. Notice that Costco did almost the opposite of Biwheels. It generated substantial cash from operations and used that cash for both investing and financing activities.

Summary Problem for Your Review

PROBLEM

Examine the entries to Biwheels' balance sheet equation for February 20X2 in Exhibit 2-5 (p. 60) and the balance sheet and income statement in Exhibits 2-6 and 2-7 (p. 61).

1. Prepare a statement of cash flows from operating activities for February using the direct method.
2. Prepare a statement of cash flows from operating activities for February using the indirect method.
3. Give a one-line explanation of the insight most readily learned from each of the two statements.

SOLUTION

1. See Exhibit 5-11. The numbers come directly from the first column of Exhibit 2-5. The cash collections are $130,000 collected on accounts receivable and the $51,000 cash sales. The payments to suppliers include $15,000 paid on accounts payable and $10,000 for cash purchases.

2. See Exhibit 5-12. The net income and add-back of depreciation come from the income statement. The other adjustments are differences between January 31 and February 28 balances on the balance sheets.

3. The direct-method statement shows the large excess of cash collections over cash payments. The indirect-method statement shows that the net cash flow from operations exceeded net income by ($156,000 – $63,900) = $92,100 due primarily to the large increase in accounts payable and the depletion of inventory.

Cash collections from customers	$181,000
Cash payments to suppliers	(25,000)
Net cash provided by operating activities	$156,000

EXHIBIT 5-11

Biwheels Company

Statement of Cash Flows from Operating Activities— Direct Method, February 20X2

Net income	$ 63,900
Adjustments to reconcile net income to net cash provided by (used for) operating activities	
Depreciation	100
Decrease in accounts receivable	5,000
Decrease in inventory	20,000
Increase in accounts payable	65,000
Decrease in prepaid rent	2,000
Net cash provided by (used for) operating activities	$156,000

EXHIBIT 5-12

Biwheels Company

Statement of Cash Flows from Operating Activities— Indirect Method, February 20X2

The Importance of Cash Flow

Both the income statement and the statement of cash flows report on changes the company experiences during the period. Both are measures of performance over the period. You might wonder why accounting authorities require both. Because each one provides important, but different, information. The income statement shows how stockholders' equity increases (or decreases) as a result of operations. It matches revenues and expenses using the accrual concepts and provides a valuable measure of economic performance. In contrast, the statement of cash flows explains changes in the cash account rather than changes in owners' equity. The focal point of the statement of cash flows is the net cash flow from operating activities, often called simply cash flow. It measures a firm's performance in maintaining a strong cash position. In addition, users of financial statements often compare the cash flows from operating, investing, and financing activities. The Business First box on p. 212 describes some of these comparisons.

Many analysts focus on **free cash flow**—generally defined as net cash flow from operations less capital expenditures. This is the cash flow remaining after undertaking the firm's operations and making the investments necessary to ensure its continued operation. Some also subtract dividends, assuming they are necessary to keep the shareholders happy. Companies that cannot generate enough cash from operations to cover their investments need to raise more capital, either by selling assets or by issuing debt or equity. If investment is for growth, this situation may be acceptable. Wal-Mart had negative free cash flow for years as it built up its business. However, if the investment is merely to maintain the status quo, the company is probably in trouble. In the

▶▶ **OBJECTIVE 9**

Identify free cash flow, and interpret information in the statement of cash flows.

free cash flow
Generally defined as net cash flow from operations less capital expenditures.

BUSINESS FIRST

INTERPRETING OPERATING, INVESTING, AND FINANCING CASH FLOWS

Comparing net cash flow from operations with the net cash flow from investing and financing activities can tell a lot about a company. First, let's consider companies with positive net cash flow from operations. Those who have negative net cash flow from investing activities in the same period, that is, those who used funds to expand their investments in fixed assets, tend to be healthy, growing firms. In the early years these firms often have positive net cash flow from financing activities as the result of raising capital in the debt or equity markets. As they mature, the most successful of these companies begin to pay back debt and return capital to shareholders, making net cash flow from financing activities negative. For example, in the last two decades Starbucks has had consistently positive net cash flow from operations and negative net cash flow from investing activities as it expanded its operations globally. Until 2003 Starbucks generally raised capital, creating positive net cash flow from financing activities. Since 2003 Starbucks has used cash for financing activities, paying back debt holders and shareholders.

If companies with positive net cash flow from operations also have positive net cash flow from investing activities, analysts often question the company's future prospects. Such companies are depleting their asset bases, so they are not preparing for future growth. For example, Aquila Corporation, in the 2 years before its 2008 purchase by Great Plains Energy, reported $212 million net cash provided by operations and $786 million net cash provided by investing activities. Although operations were generating cash, Aquila needed to sell assets to generate additional cash to pay debts as they came due. The cash flow problems that necessitated Aquila's selling of assets were a main reason the shareholders approved the company's sale to Great Plains.

Companies with negative net cash flow from operations are generally in one of two categories: (1) young companies that have not yet reached the point of generating positive operating net cash flows, and (2) companies that are in trouble. In the first category are many biotechnology companies that must undertake years of R&D before having salable products. Pressure Biosciences, Inc., a Boston life-sciences company, is an example of a company that has not had positive operating net cash flow but continues to raise capital and invest in additional fixed assets. If such companies do not have positive net cash from financing activities, analysts examine whether their existing cash is likely to be enough to cover negative operating and investing cash flows long enough to reach profitability. Medivir AB, a Swedish biotech company, was in the same situation as Pressure Biosciences until 2011 when it achieved its first positive net cash flow from operations.

Companies with negative net cash flow from operations and positive net cash flow from investing activities are, either intentionally or unwittingly, liquidating the company. They are selling off their assets to support money-losing operating activities. Midway Games, the Chicago-based entertainment software company that published video games such as the *Mortal Kombat* series and *NBA Jam*, had such a situation in 2008, just prior to its 2009 bankruptcy filing.

Sources: Medivir AB 2011 Annual Report; Pressure Biosciences, Inc. 2010 Annual Report; Starbucks 2011 Annual Report; Midway Games 2008 Annual Report; W. Wong, "Midway Games, Known for Mortal Kombat, Files for Chapter 11," *Chicago Tribune* (February 12, 2009).

recession of 2008–2011, numerous companies experienced negative free cash flow, and many resorted to selling off assets to meet their cash needs. Examples of companies with negative free cash flow are **AMR Corp.**, parent of American Airlines, which experienced negative free cash flow for 3 years before its bankruptcy declaration in November 2011, and **Dynegy, Inc.**, the $2.3 billion electric energy company, which experienced negative free cash flow in 4 of the 5 years before its bankruptcy, also in November 2011. Biwheels Company has a large negative free cash flow for January, [$(135,000) − $15,000] = $(150,000), meaning that it must improve its net cash flow from operations or it will need to raise additional capital. In February its free cash flow improved to a positive ($156,000 − $10,000) = $146,000.

The Crisis of Negative Cash Flow

Although investors make important economic decisions on the basis of net income, the so-called bottom line, sometimes earnings numbers do not tell the full story of what is really happening inside a company. Take the classic case of **Prime Motor Inns**, once one of the world's largest hotel operators. At its peak, Prime reported earnings of $77 million on revenues of $410 million. Moreover, revenues had increased by nearly 11% from the preceding year. Despite its impressive earnings performance, Prime lacked the cash to meet its obligations and filed for Chapter 11 bankruptcy. Under bankruptcy protection, a firm's obligations to its creditors are frozen as management figures out how to pay those creditors. How can a firm with $77 million in earnings file for bankruptcy about a year later?

Although the company's business was owning and operating hotels, much of Prime's reported $77 million of earnings arose from selling hotels. When buyers found it difficult to obtain outside financing for these hotel sales, Prime financed the sales itself by accepting notes and mortgages receivable from buyers rather than receiving cash. Of course, Prime soon ran out of hotels to sell. In the year that Prime reported $77 million of net income, an astute analyst would have noted that Prime had a net cash *outflow* from operations of $15 million. The cash flow statement can provide insights that are not evident from the income statement alone.

INTERPRETING FINANCIAL STATEMENTS

What pattern in the cash flow statement would have helped to alert the careful analyst to a potential problem at Prime Motor Inns?

Answer

Prime was reporting large profits under accrual accounting, but operating cash flow was negative. Prime was financing sales by accepting notes and mortgages from buyers. This predicament would have been evident from the significant increases in these notes and mortgages receivable as compared with prior years.

Summary Problems for Your Review

PROBLEM

The Buretta Company uses U.S. GAAP and has prepared the data in Exhibit 5-13.

In December 20X2, Buretta paid $54 million cash for a new building acquired to accommodate an expansion of operations. The company financed this purchase partly by a new issue of long-term debt for $40 million cash. During 20X2, the company also sold fixed assets for $5 million cash. The assets were listed on Buretta's books at $5 million. All sales and purchases of merchandise were on credit.

Because the 20X2 net income of $4 million was the highest in the company's history, Alice Buretta, the company's president, was perplexed by the company's extremely low cash balance.

1. Prepare a statement of cash flows from the Buretta data in Exhibit 5-13. Ignore income taxes. Use the direct method for reporting cash flows from operating activities.
2. Prepare a supporting schedule that reconciles net income to net cash provided by operating activities.
3. What does the statement of cash flows tell you about Buretta Company? Does it help you reduce Alice Buretta's puzzlement? Why?

EXHIBIT 5-13

Buretta Company Financial Statements (in millions)

Income Statement (Including Changes in Retained Earnings)
For the Year Ended December 31, 20X2

Sales		$100
Less: Cost of goods sold		
Inventory, December 31, 20X1	$ 15	
Purchases	105	
Cost of goods available for sale	120	
Inventory, December 31, 20X2	(47)	73
Gross profit		27
Less: Other expenses		
General expenses	8	
Depreciation	8	
Property taxes	4	
Interest expense	3	23
Net income		4
Retained earnings, December 31, 20X1		7
Subtotal		11
Dividends declared and paid		1
Retained earnings, December 31, 20X2		$ 10

Balance Sheets for December 31

Assets			Liabilities and Stockholders' Equity		
	20X2	**20X1**		**20X2**	**20X1**
			Accounts payable	$ 39	$14
Cash	$ 1	$20	Accrued property		
Accounts receivable	20	5	tax payable	3	1
Inventory	47	15	Long-term debt	40	0
Prepaid general			Common stock	70	70
expenses	3	2			
Fixed assets, net	91	50	Retained earnings	10	7
			Total liabilities and		
Total assets	$162	$92	stockholders' equity	$162	$92

SOLUTION

1. See Exhibit 5-14. We can compute cash flows from operating activities as follows ($ in millions):

Sales	$100
Less increase in accounts receivable	(15)
(a) Cash collections from customers	$ 85
Cost of goods sold	$ 73
Plus increase in inventory	32
Purchases	105
Less: Increase in accounts payable	(25)
(b) Cash paid to suppliers	$ 80
General expenses	$ 8
Plus increase in prepaid general expenses	1
(c) Cash payment for general expenses	$ 9
(d) Cash paid for interest	$ 3
Property taxes	$ 4
Less: Increase in accrued property tax payable	(2)
(e) Cash paid for property taxes	$ 2

2. Exhibit 5-15 reconciles net income to net cash used by operating activities.
3. The statement of cash flows shows where cash has come from and where it has gone. Operations used $9 million of cash. Why? The statement in Exhibit 5-14, which uses the direct method, shows the result clearly: $94 million in cash paid for operating activities exceeded $85 million in cash received from customers. The reconciliation using the indirect method, in Exhibit 5-15, shows why, in a profitable year, operating cash flow could be negative. The three largest items that explain the difference in net income and net cash flow from operations are changes in inventory, accounts receivable, and accounts payable. Sales during the period were not collected in full because accounts receivable rose sharply, by $15 million—a 300% increase. Similarly, Buretta spent cash on inventory growth, although it financed much of that growth by increased accounts payable. In summary, the items

Cash flows from operating activities		
Cash collections from customers (a)		$ 85
Cash payments		
Cash paid to suppliers (b)	$(80)	
General expenses (c)	(9)	
Interest paid (d)	(3)	
Property taxes (e)	(2)	(94)
Net cash used by operating activities		(9)
Cash flows from investing activities		
Purchase of fixed assets (building)	(54)	
Proceeds from sale of fixed assets	5	
Net cash used by investing activities		(49)
Cash flows from financing activities		
Long-term debt issued	40	
Dividends paid	(1)	
Net cash provided by financing activities		39
Net decrease in cash		(19)
Cash balance, December 31, 20X1		20
Cash balance, December 31, 20X2		$ 1

EXHIBIT 5-14

Buretta Company

Statement of Cash Flows, for the Year Ended December 31, 20X2 (in millions)

EXHIBIT 5-15

EXHIBIT 5-15

Supporting Schedule to Statement of Cash Flows

Reconciliation of Net Income to Net Cash Used by Operating Activities, for the Year Ended December 31, 20X2 (in millions)

Net income (from income statement)	$ 4
Adjustments to reconcile net income to net cash used by operating activities:	
Add: Depreciation, which was deducted in the computation of net income but does not decrease cash	8
Deduct: Increase in accounts receivable	(15)
Deduct: Increase in inventory	(32)
Deduct: Increase in prepaid general expenses	(1)
Add: Increase in accounts payable	25
Add: Increase in accrued property tax payable	2
Net cash used by operating activities	$ (9)

in parentheses in Exhibit 5-15, large increases in accounts receivable ($15 million) and inventory ($32 million), plus an increase in prepaid expenses ($1 million), show that Buretta used $48 million of cash in operations. In contrast, the sum of the items not in parentheses shows that Buretta generated only $39 million in cash from operations, that is, ($4 million + $8 million + $25 million + $2 million). Thus, the company used a net amount of $9 million in operations ($39 million – $48 million).

Investing activities also consumed cash because Buretta invested $54 million in a building, and it received only $5 million from sales of fixed assets, leaving a net use of $49 million. Financing activities did generate $39 million cash, but that was $19 million less than the $58 million used by operating and investing activities ($9 million used in operations + $49 million used in investing).

Alice Buretta should no longer be puzzled by the reduction in cash. The statement of cash flows shows clearly that cash payments exceeded receipts by $19 million. However, she may still be concerned about the depletion of cash. Either the company must change operations so it does not require so much cash, it must curtail investment, or it must raise more long-term debt or ownership equity. Otherwise, Buretta Company will soon run out of cash.

PROBLEM

To understand how cash flow and net income vary during the life cycle of a business, consider the following example that portrays the 4-year life of a short-lived merchandising company, CB International. The first year the entrepreneurs bought twice as much as they sold because they were building their base inventory levels. CB International's suppliers offered payment terms that resulted in CB paying 80% of each year's purchases during that year and 20% in the next year. Sales were for cash with a sales price equal to twice the cost of the item. Selling expenses were constant over the life of the business, and CB International paid them in cash as incurred. At the end of the fourth year, CB International paid the suppliers in full and sold all the inventory. Use the following summary results to prepare four income statements and statements of cash flows from operations using both direct and indirect methods for CB International, one for each year of its life.

	Year 1	Year 2	Year 3	Year 4
Purchases	2,000 units	1,500 units	1,500 units	1,000 units
$1 each	$2,000	$1,500	$1,500	$1,000
Sales	1,000 units	1,500 units	2,000 units	1,500 units
$2 each	$2,000	$3,000	$4,000	$3,000
Cost of sales	$1,000	$1,500	$2,000	$1,500
Selling expense	$1,000	$1,000	$1,000	$1,000
Payments to suppliers*	$1,600	$1,600	$1,500	$1,300

*$(.8 \times \$2,000) = \$1,600; (.2 \times \$2,000) + (.8 \times \$1,500) = \$1,600; (.2 \times \$1,500) + (.8 \times \$1,500) = \$1,500;$
$(.2 \times \$1,500) + (1.0 \times \$1,000) = \$1,300.$

SOLUTION

	Year 1	Year 2	Year 3	Year 4	Total
Income statement					
Sales	$2,000	$3,000	$4,000	$3,000	$12,000
Cost of sales	1,000	1,500	2,000	1,500	6,000
Selling expenses	1,000	1,000	1,000	1,000	4,000
Net income	$ 0	$ 500	$1,000	$ 500	$ 2,000
Cash flows from operations: direct method					
Collections from customers	$2,000	$3,000	$4,000	$3,000	$12,000
Payments to suppliers	(1,600)	(1,600)	(1,500)	(1,300)	(6,000)
Payments for selling efforts	(1,000)	(1,000)	(1,000)	(1,000)	(4,000)
Net cash flow from operations	$ (600)	$ 400	$1,500	$ 700	$ 2,000
Cash flows from operations: indirect method					
Net income	$ 0	$ 500	$1,000	$ 500	$ 2,000
– Increase in inventory	(1,000)				(1,000)
+ Decrease in inventory			500	500	1,000
+ Increase in accounts payable	400				400
– Decrease in accounts payable		(100)		(300)	(400)
Cash flow from operations	$ (600)	$ 400	$1,500	$ 700	$ 2,000

Balance Sheet Accounts at the end of	Year 1	Year 2	Year 3	Year 4
Merchandise inventory	$1,000	$1,000	$500	$0
Accounts payable	$ 400	$ 300	$300	0

This problem illustrates the difference between accrual-based earnings and cash flows. Significant cash outflows occur for operations during the first year because payments to acquire inventory and for selling expenses exceed collections from customers. In fact, it is not until the third year that net cash flow from operations exceeds net earnings for the year.

Highlights to Remember

1 **Identify the purposes of the statement of cash flows.** The statement of cash flows focuses on the changes in cash and the activities that cause those changes. Accrual-based net income is a useful number, but we also ask the following questions: How did our cash position change? How much of the change in cash was caused by operations, how much by investing activities, and how much by financing activities?

2 **Classify activities affecting cash as operating, investing, or financing activities.** Operating activities are the typical day-to-day activities of the firm in acquiring or manufacturing products, selling them to customers, and collecting the cash. Investing activities involve buying and selling plant, property, and equipment or other long-lived productive assets, as well as buying and selling securities that are not classified as cash equivalents. It might include buying a whole company as well as specific assets. Financing activities involve raising or repaying capital such as borrowing from a bank, issuing bonds, repaying debt, or paying dividends to shareholders.

3 **Compute and interpret cash flows from financing activities.** Financing activities are transactions that obtain or repay capital. Cash flows from financing activities show whether a company borrows or repays money, issues additional securities, pays dividends, or buys back shares from stockholders.

4 **Compute and interpret cash flows from investing activities.** Investing activities are transactions that acquire or sell long-lived productive assets such as property or equipment and securities held for investment purposes that are not considered cash equivalents. Cash flows from investing activities show where management has elected to invest any funds raised or generated.

5 **Use the direct method to calculate cash flows from operations.** The direct method, preferred by the FASB and IASB, explicitly lists all cash inflows and cash outflows from operating activities. We can find the relevant cash flows in the cash column in the balance sheet equation. The advantage of the direct method is that it is straightforward and easy to understand.

6 **Use the indirect method to explain the difference between net income and net cash provided by (used for) operating activities.** The more commonly used method for calculating the net cash flow from operations is the indirect method, which starts with net income and adjusts it for the differences, typically account by account, between accrual net income and operating cash flow. Both the direct and indirect method yield the same net cash flow from operations; the only difference is the format of the presentation. The advantage of the indirect method is that it explicitly addresses the differences between net income and net cash from operations.

7 **Understand why we add depreciation to net income when using the indirect method for computing cash flows from operating activities.** Under the indirect method, we add depreciation expense back to net income because it is an expense that does not require the use of cash. Because we deduct depreciation when computing net income, adding it back simply eliminates the effect of deducting this noncash item. This adding back of depreciation expense sometimes causes some people to think of depreciation as a source of cash. This is not the case. Increasing depreciation does not affect cash flow.

8 **Show how the balance sheet equation provides a conceptual framework for the statement of cash flows.** The balance sheet equation is the conceptual base of all financial statements. By reconstructing the equation with cash isolated on the left side of the equal sign, we can see how the right-hand entries provide an explanation for the changes in cash. Increases in liabilities or stockholders' equity or decreases in noncash assets increase cash, whereas decreases in liabilities or stockholders' equity or increases in noncash assets decrease cash.

9 **Identify free cash flow, and interpret information in the statement of cash flows.** To understand how a company manages its cash, analysts often compare cash flows across operating, investing, and financing activities. Free cash flow, net cash flow from operations less capital expenditures and possibly dividends, is a metric that helps such comparisons.

Accounting Vocabulary

bankruptcy, p. 189
cash equivalents, p. 190
cash flow statement,
    p. 189
cash flows from financing
    activities, p. 190

cash flows from investing
    activities, p. 191
cash flows from operating
    activities, p. 190
direct method, p. 199
financing activities, p. 191

free cash flow, p. 211
indirect method, p. 199
investing activities, p. 191
operating activities, p. 190
statement of cash flows,
    p. 189

Assignment Material

MyAccountingLab

Note: Many of the questions, exercises, and problems do not require the use of the indirect method of reporting cash flow from operations. The following can be answered by reading only pages 188–202: Questions 5-1 through 5-17, Exercises 5-33 through 5-40, and problems 5-48 through 5-56.

Questions

5-1 "The statement of cash flows is an optional statement included by most companies in their annual reports." Do you agree? Explain.

5-2 What are the purposes of a statement of cash flows?

5-3 Define cash equivalents.

5-4 The statement of cash flows summarizes what three types of activities?

5-5 Name four major operating activities included in a statement of cash flows.

5-6 Name three major investing activities included in a statement of cash flows.

5-7 Name three major financing activities included in a statement of cash flows.

5-8 There is one item on a cash flow statement that is not a cash flow but affects cash. What is it and why do companies include it on their statements of cash flow?

5-9 Where does interest received or paid appear on the statement of cash flows under U.S. GAAP? Under IFRS?

5-10 Which of the following financing activities increase cash: increase long-term debt, repurchase common shares, or pay dividends? Which decrease cash?

5-11 Which of the following investing activities increase cash: purchase fixed assets by issuing debt, sell fixed assets for cash, collect a loan, or purchase equipment for cash? Which decrease cash?

5-12 Explain why increases in liabilities increase cash and increases in noncash assets decrease cash.

5-13 Why are noncash investing and financing activities listed on a separate schedule accompanying the statement of cash flows?

5-14 A company acquired a fixed asset in exchange for common stock. Explain how this transaction should be shown, if at all, in the statement of cash flows. Why is your suggested treatment appropriate?

5-15 Suppose a company paid off a $1 million short-term loan to one bank with the proceeds from an identical loan from another bank. The change in the short-term debt account would be zero. Should anything appear in the statement of cash flows? Explain.

5-16 What are the two major ways of computing net cash provided by operating activities?

5-17 Where does a company get the information included in the direct-method cash flow statement?

5-18 Why is there usually a difference between the cash collections from customers and sales revenue in a period's financial statements?

5-19 What two balance sheet accounts explain the difference between the cost of goods sold and the cash payments to suppliers?

5-20 What types of adjustments reconcile net income with net cash provided by operations?

5-21 "Net losses mean drains on cash." Do you agree? Explain.

5-22 The indirect method for reporting cash flows from operating activities can create an erroneous impression about noncash expenses (such as depreciation). What is the impression, and why is it erroneous?

5-23 An investor's newsletter had the following item: "The company expects increased cash flow in 2013 because depreciation charges will be substantially greater than they were in 2012." Comment.

5-24 "Depreciation is an integral part of a statement of cash flows." Do you agree? Explain.

5-25 "The balance sheet equation helps explain the income statement and balance sheet, but it is not useful in interpreting the statement of cash flows." Do you agree? Explain.

5-26 Demonstrate how the fundamental balance sheet equation can be recast to focus on cash.

5-27 A company operated at a profit for the year, but cash flow from operations was negative. Why might this occur? What industry or industries might find this a common occurrence?

5-28 A company operated at a loss for the year, but cash flow from operations was positive. Why might this occur? What industry or industries might find this a common occurrence?

Critical Thinking Questions

▶▶ **OBJECTIVE 9**

5-29 Cash Flow Patterns and Growth

You are considering an investment in a company that has negative cash flow from operations, negative cash flow from investing, and positive cash flow from financing. All the financing in the current year is from short-term debt. What does this pattern of cash flow tell you about the client's circumstance. How does this affect your investment decision?

▶▶ **OBJECTIVE 9**

5-30 Google and Cash Generation

On September 30, 2011, Google was generating increasing amounts of cash from operating activities each year and was unable to fully use it to grow the business. Hence, the levels of liquid investments were increasing so that cash, cash equivalents, and marketable securities comprised 62% of the company's assets. What would you imagine Google's management might have been considering as a means of using the cash and liquid investment assets?

▶▶ **OBJECTIVE 9**

5-31 Amazon and Negative Cash Flow from Operations

Between 2004 and 2010, Amazon.com, the industry leader in online sales of books and other consumer products, increased its free cash flow from $477 million to $2,516 million. Prior to 2002, Amazon had never generated positive net cash flow from operations. What does this tell you about the stage of growth that Amazon is in?

▶▶ **OBJECTIVE 9**

5-32 Failures to Generate Positive Net Cash Flow from Operations

You are discussing your investment strategies with a colleague who says, "I would never invest in a company that is not generating both positive earnings and positive net cash flow from operations." How do you respond?

Exercises

▶▶ **OBJECTIVE 3**

5-33 Simple Statement of Cash Flows from Financing Activities

Gumbo, Inc., is a seafood restaurant in New Orleans. Gumbo began business in January 20X1 when investors bought common stock for $100,000 cash. Gumbo also borrowed $55,000 from Stateside Bank on January 15, on which it paid interest of $3,000 on July 15. In January the company invested $80,000 in machinery and equipment and signed a monthly rental agreement on a building with rental payments of $4,000 a month. During 20X1 Gumbo had net income of $14,000 on sales of $249,000. On December 15 the company declared and paid cash dividends of $2,000 to its common stockholders. On December 31 the company paid $10,000 to buy common shares back from the stockholders.

Prepare a statement of cash flows from financing activities for the year 20X1.

▶▶ **OBJECTIVE 3**

5-34 Financing Activities, IFRS and U.S. GAAP

During 20X0, the Southampton Shipping Company, a company reporting under IFRS, refinanced its long-term debt. It spent £165,000 to retire long-term debt due in 2 years and issued £180,000 of 15-year bonds (£ signifies pound, the UK monetary unit). It then bought and retired common shares for cash of £35,000. Interest expense for 20X0 was £23,000, of which it paid £22,000 in cash; the other £1,000 was still payable at the end of the year. Dividends declared and paid during the year were £11,000.

Prepare a statement of cash flows from financing activities. Discuss the treatment of interest expense under IFRS compared with U.S. GAAP.

5-35 Investing Activities

▶▶ OBJECTIVE 4

Tasman Trading Company issued common stock for $320,000 on the first day of 20X0. The company bought fixed assets for $175,000 cash and inventory for $75,000 cash. Late in the year, it sold fixed assets for cash equal to their book value of $20,000. It sold one-half the inventory for $55,000 cash during the year. On December 15, the company used excess cash of $65,000 to purchase common stock of Fellski Company, which Tasman regarded as a long-term investment.

Prepare a statement of cash flows from investing activities for Tasman Trading Company.

5-36 Noncash Investing and Financing Activities

▶▶ OBJECTIVES 3, 4

Wellstone Company had the following items in its statement of cash flows or its schedule of non-cash investing and financing activities.

Note payable issued for acquisition of fixed assets	$144,000
Retirement of long-term debt	565,000
Common stock issued on conversion of preferred shares	340,000
Purchases of marketable securities	225,000
Mortgage assumed on acquisition of warehouse	530,000
Increase in accounts payable	47,000

Prepare a schedule of noncash investing and financing activities, selecting appropriate items from the preceding list.

5-37 Cash Received from Customers

▶▶ OBJECTIVE 5

Northgate Publishers, Inc., had sales of $900,000 during 20X1, 80% of them on credit and 20% for cash. During the year, accounts receivable increased from $60,000 to $90,000, an increase of $30,000. What amount of cash was received from customers during 20X1?

5-38 Cash Paid to Suppliers

▶▶ OBJECTIVE 5

Cost of Goods Sold for Northgate Publishers, Inc., during 20X1 was $600,000. Beginning inventory was $100,000, and ending inventory was $150,000. Beginning trade accounts payable were $24,000, and ending trade accounts payable were $42,000. What amount of cash did Northgate pay to suppliers?

5-39 Cash Paid to Employees

▶▶ OBJECTIVE 5

Northgate Publishers, Inc., reported Wage and Salary Expense of $220,000 on its 20X1 income statement. It reported cash paid to employees of $185,000 on its statement of cash flows. The beginning balance of Accrued Wages and Salaries Payable was $18,000. What was the ending balance in Accrued Wages and Salaries Payable? Ignore payroll taxes.

5-40 Simple Cash Flows from Operating Activities

▶▶ OBJECTIVE 5

Neptune Strategy, Inc., provides consulting services. In 20X1, net income was $185,000 on revenues of $460,000 and expenses of $275,000. The only noncash expense was depreciation of $35,000. The company has no inventory. Accounts receivable increased by $5,000 during 20X1, and accounts payable and salaries payable were unchanged.

Prepare a statement of cash flows from operating activities. Use the direct method. Omit supporting schedules.

5-41 Net Income and Cash Flow

▶▶ OBJECTIVE 6

Refer to Problem 5-40. Prepare a schedule that reconciles net income to net cash flow from operating activities.

5-42 Identify Operating, Investing, and Financing Activities

▶▶ OBJECTIVE 2

The following listed items were found on a recent statement of cash flows for Verizon Communications, Inc. For each item, indicate which section of the statement should contain the item—the operating, investing, or financing section. Also, indicate whether Verizon uses the direct or indirect method for reporting cash flows from operating activities.

a. Net income
b. Dividends paid
c. Proceeds from long-term borrowings

d. Capital expenditures
e. Proceeds from sale of common stock
f. Retirements of long-term borrowings
g. Change in inventories
h. Depreciation and amortization expense
i. Proceeds from dispositions [of assets]

▶▶ OBJECTIVES 5, 6

5-43 Simple Direct- and Indirect-Method Statements

Wayzata Company saw its cash plummet by $110,000 in 20X0. The company's president wants an explanation of what caused the decrease in cash despite income of $60,000. He has asked you to prepare both direct and indirect method statements of cash flows from operations for 20X0. You have discovered the following information:

- Sales, all on credit, were $560,000.
- Accounts receivable increased by $130,000.
- Cost of goods sold was $390,000.
- Payments to suppliers were $455,000.
- Accounts payable decreased by $40,000.
- Inventory increased by $25,000.
- Operating expenses were $95,000, all paid in cash except for depreciation of $30,000.
- Income tax expense was $15,000; taxes payable decreased by $5,000.

1. Prepare a statement of cash flows from operating activities using the direct method.
2. Prepare a statement of cash flows from operating activities using the indirect method.
3. Explain why cash decreased by $110,000 when net income was a positive $60,000.

▶▶ OBJECTIVE 7

5-44 Nature of Depreciation

This continues the previous Problem, 5-43. The president looked at the indirect-method cash flow statement and suggested a way to help the cash flow problem. He suggested tripling the depreciation from $30,000 to $90,000 a year. That way, the cash flow will improve by $60,000 annually. Explain why this reasoning is faulty.

▶▶ OBJECTIVE 7

5-45 Depreciation and Cash Flows

(Alternate is 5-67.) Sawadi Thai Restaurant had sales of $880,000, all received in cash. Total operating expenses were $580,000. All except depreciation were paid in cash. Depreciation of $90,000 was included in the $580,000 of operating expenses. Ignore income taxes.

1. Compute net income and net cash provided by operating activities.
2. Assume that nondepreciation expenses are the same as in part 1 but that depreciation is tripled. Compute net income and net cash provided by operating activities.

▶▶ OBJECTIVE 8

5-46 Balance Sheet Equation of Statement of Cash Flows

When you hear the name Rolls-Royce Holdings plc you probably think of luxury automobiles. However, today the company is mainly in aerospace, marine, and energy fields. The company's condensed December 31, 2011, balance sheet follows (in millions of British pounds):

Assets		Liabilities and Stockholders' Equity	
Cash and cash equivalents	£ 1,310	Trade and other payables	£ 6,236
Trade and other receivables	4,009	Other liabilities	5,668
Other assets	11,104	Stockholders' equity	4,519
Total assets	£ 16,423	Total liabilities and stockholders' equity	£ 16,423

1. Prepare a balance sheet equation for Rolls-Royce Holdings in a format that supports the statement of cash flows.
2. Suppose that during the next month trade and other receivables increased by £500, other assets increased by £300, trade and other payables decreased by £150, other liabilities decreased by £50, and stockholders' equity was unchanged. What would be the balance in cash and cash equivalents at the end of the month?

5-47 Free Cash Flow

▶▶ OBJECTIVE 9

GlaxoSmithKline, the global maker of medicines, vaccines, and consumer health-care products and headquartered in the United Kingdom, reported net cash inflow from operating activities of £6,250 million in 2011. The company included the following among its items in the investing and financing sections of its cash flow statement (in millions of British pounds):

Purchase of property, plant, and equipment	£ (923)
Purchase of intangible assets	(405)
Purchase of equity investments	(76)
Purchase of businesses, net of cash acquired	(264)
Dividends paid to shareholders	(3,406)

Compute GlaxoSmithKline's free cash flow in at least two ways. Discuss the adequacy of the company's free cash flow.

Problems

MyAccountingLab

5-48 Statement of Cash Flows, Effect of Exchange Rates, Japan

▶▶ OBJECTIVE 2

Kansai Electric supplies power to an area of Japan that includes Osaka and Kyoto. Its operating revenues are nearly ¥2.8 trillion (about $33 billion in U.S. dollars), and its assets are more than ¥7.3 trillion. The bottom of Kansai Electric's 2011 cash flow statement contained the following (in millions of Japanese yen, ¥):

Net cash provided by operating, investing, and financing activities	¥ 18,228
Effect of exchange rate changes on cash and cash equivalents	(303)
Net increase in cash and cash equivalents	17,925
Cash and cash equivalents, beginning of year	77,525
Cash and cash equivalents, end of year	¥ 95,450

Is the effect of exchange rate changes on cash and cash equivalents a cash flow? Explain why Kansai Electric included it on the company's cash flow statement.

5-49 Cash Flows from Financing Activities

▶▶ OBJECTIVE 3

ConAgra Foods, Inc. is one of North America's leading food companies with brands such as Banquet and Healthy Choice. Its 2011 sales exceeded $12 billion. ConAgra's 2011 statement of cash flows included the following items, among others ($ in millions):

Cash dividends paid	$ (374.5)
Repurchase of ConAgra Foods common shares	(825.0)
Additions to property, plant, and equipment	(466.2)
Depreciation and amortization	360.9
Exercise of stock options and issuance of other stock awards	59.7
Sale of property, plant, and equipment	18.9
Increase in inventories	(190.7)
Net income	818.8
Repayments of long-term debt	(294.3)
Other financing items	2.1

1. Prepare the section "Cash flows from financing activities" from ConAgra's 2011 annual report. All items necessary for that section appear in the preceding list. The list also includes some items from other sections that should not be included among the financing activities.
2. Did ConAgra's financing activities increase or decrease cash during 2011? By how much? What were the main causes of this increase or decrease?

5-50 Cash Flows from Investing Activities

Johnson & Johnson is a health-care company with headquarters in New Brunswick, New Jersey. Its revenues in the fiscal year ended January 1, 2012, were more than $65 billion. Following are items from the company's statement of cash flows for that year. The list includes all items in the investing activities section of the statement plus some items from the operating and financing sections.

Additions to property, plant, and equipment	$ (2,893)
Proceeds from long-term debt	4,470
Increase in accounts receivable	(915)
Proceeds from the disposal of assets	1,342
Dividends to shareholders	(6,156)
Acquisitions, net of cash acquired	(2,797)
Depreciation and amortization of property and intangibles	3,158
Purchases of investments	(29,882)
Sales of investments	30,396
Other (primarily purchases of intangibles)	(778)

Prepare the section "Cash flows from investing activities" for Johnson & Johnson for the fiscal year ending January 1, 2012.

5-51 Cash Flows from Investing Activities—IFRS

Vodafone Group Plc is a large UK-based telecommunications company that reports using IFRS. Its revenues in fiscal 2011 were more than £45 billion (where £ is the British pound). The company's statement of cash flows for fiscal 2011 contained the following items (British pounds in millions):

Purchase of interests in subsidiaries and joint ventures, net of cash acquired	£ (402)
Proceeds from issue of long-term borrowings	4,861
Purchase of intangible assets	(4,290)
Purchase of property, plant, and equipment	(4,350)
Increase in trade and other receivables	(387)
Purchase of investments	(318)
Disposal of property, plant, and equipment	51
Depreciation and amortisation	7,876
Disposal of investments	4,467
Repayment of borrowings	(4,064)
Dividends received from associates	1,424
Dividends received from investments	85
Interest received	1,659
Taxation on investing activities	(208)
Profit for the financial year	7,870

1. Prepare the section "Cash flows from investing activities" for Vodaphone for the 2011 fiscal year. Vodaphone includes interest and dividends received and the related taxes as investing activities. All items from the investing activities section are included in the preceding list, along with some items from other sections of the statement of cash flows.
2. Prepare the section "Cash flows from investing activities" for Vodaphone for the 2011 fiscal year using U.S. GAAP.

5-52 Noncash Investing and Financing Activities

▶▶ **OBJECTIVES 3, 4**

The Arcadia Company operates a chain of video game arcades. Among Arcadia's activities in 20X0 were the following:

1. The firm traded four old video games to another amusement company for one new Primeval Hunt game. The old games could have been sold for a total of $3,000 cash.
2. The company paid off $50,000 of long-term debt by paying $20,000 cash and signing a $30,000 6-month note payable.
3. The firm issued debt for $60,000 cash, all of which was used to purchase new games for its Northwest Arcade.
4. The company purchased the building in which one of its arcades was located by assuming the $100,000 mortgage on the structure and paying $20,000 cash.
5. Debt holders converted $65,000 of debt to common stock.
6. The firm refinanced debt by paying cash to buy back an old issue at its call price of $21,000 and issued new debt at a lower interest rate for $21,000.

Prepare a schedule of noncash investing and financing activities to accompany a statement of cash flows.

5-53 Statement of Cash Flows, Direct Method

▶▶ **OBJECTIVE 5**

(Alternates are 5-54 and 5-55.) Charleston Aerospace Company had cash and cash equivalents of $200 million on December 31, 2011. The following items are on the company's statement of cash flows ($ in millions) for the first 6 months of 2012:

Capital expenditures for property and equipment	$ (1,710)
Receipts from customers	9,455
Interest paid, net	(190)
Repurchase of common stock	(193)
Sales of marketable securities	191
Retirement of long-term debt	(160)
Payments to suppliers and employees	(7,499)
Issuance of common stock for employee stock plans	251
Dividend payments	(17)
Issuance of long-term debt	135
Other investing activity	(134)
Taxes paid	(167)

Prepare a statement of cash flows for the first 6 months of 2012 using the direct method. Include the balance of cash and cash equivalents at year-end 2011 and calculate the cash balance at June 30, 2012. Omit the schedule reconciling net income to net cash provided by operating activities and the schedule of noncash investing and financing activities.

5-54 Prepare a Statement of Cash Flows, Direct Method

▶▶ **OBJECTIVE 5**

(Alternates are 5-53 and 5-55.) Cascade Tile is a wholesale distributor of ceramic tiles. Its cash balance on December 31, 20X0, was $226,000, and net income for 20X1 was $312,000. Its 20X1 transactions affecting income or cash follow ($ in thousands):

1. Sales of $1,500 were all on credit. Cash collections from customers were $1,390.
2. The cost of items sold was $800. Purchases of inventory on account totaled $850; inventory and accounts payable were affected accordingly.
3. Cash payments on trade accounts payable totaled $815.
4. Accrued salaries and wages: total expense, $190; cash payments, $200.
5. Depreciation was $45.
6. Interest expense, all paid in cash, was $13.

7. Other expenses, all paid in cash, totaled $100.
8. Income taxes accrued were $40; income taxes paid in cash were $35.
9. A warehouse was purchased for $435 cash.
10. Long-term debt was issued for $125 cash.
11. Cash dividends of $41 were paid.

Prepare a statement of cash flows for 20X1 using the direct method for reporting cash flows from operating activities. Omit supporting schedules.

▶▶ OBJECTIVE 5

5-55 Prepare a Statement of Cash Flows, Direct Method
(Alternates are 5-53 and 5-54.) Hiramatsu Exports, Inc., is a wholesaler of Japanese goods. By the end of 20X0, the company's cash balance had dropped to ¥9 million, despite net income of ¥254 million in 20X0. Its transactions affecting income or cash in 20X0 were as follows (¥ in millions):

1. Sales were ¥2,610, all on credit. Cash collections from customers were ¥2,515.
2. The cost of items sold was ¥1,699.
3. Inventory increased by ¥56.
4. Cash payments on trade accounts payable were ¥1,758.
5. Payments to employees were ¥305; accrued wages payable decreased by ¥24.
6. Other operating expenses, all paid in cash, were ¥94.
7. Interest expense, all paid in cash, was ¥26.
8. Income tax expense was ¥105; cash payments for income taxes were ¥108.
9. Depreciation was ¥151.
10. A warehouse was acquired for ¥540 cash.
11. Equipment was sold for ¥47; original cost was ¥206, accumulated depreciation was ¥159.
12. The firm received ¥28 for issue of common stock.
13. Long-term debt was retired for ¥21 cash.
14. The company paid cash dividends of ¥98.

Prepare a statement of cash flows for 20X0 using the direct method for reporting cash flows from operating activities. Calculate the cash balance as of January 1, 20X0. Omit supporting schedules.

▶▶ OBJECTIVE 5

5-56 Prepare Statement of Cash Flows from Income Statement and Balance Sheet
(Alternate is 5-58.) During 20X1, Jacinta Manufacturing Company (JMC) declared and paid cash dividends of $10,000. Late in the year, JMC bought new welding machinery for a cash cost of $125,000, financed partly by its first issue of long-term debt. Interest on the debt is payable annually. JMC sold several old machines for cash equal to their aggregate book value of $5,000. The company pays taxes in cash as incurred. The following data are in thousands:

Jacinta Manufacturing Company
Income Statement for the Year Ended December 31, 20X1

Sales		$490
Cost of sales		300
Gross margin		190
Salaries	$82	
Depreciation	40	
Cash operating expenses	15	
Interest	2	139
Income before taxes		51
Income taxes		8
Net income		$ 43

Jacinta Manufacturing Company
Balance Sheets

	December 31		Increase
	20X1	**20X0**	**(Decrease)**
Assets			
Cash and cash equivalents	$125	$ 45	$ 80
Accounts receivable	45	60	(15)
Inventories	57	62	(5)
Total current assets	227	167	60
Fixed assets, net	190	110	80
Total assets	$417	$277	$140
Liabilities and Stockholders' Equity			
Accounts payable	$ 26	$ 21	$ 5
Interest payable	2	—	2
Long-term debt	100	—	100
Paid-in capital	220	220	—
Retained earnings	69	36	33
Total liabilities and stockholders' equity	$417	$277	$140

Prepare a statement of cash flows for 20X1. Use the direct method for reporting cash flows from operating activities. Omit supporting schedules. Assume that Jacinta paid expense items in cash unless balance sheet changes indicate otherwise.

5-57 Statement of Cash Flows, Direct Method

The J.M. Smucker Company had net sales of $4,826 million from selling products such as jam (Smucker's), peanut butter (Jif), and vegetable oils (Crisco) for the year ending April 30, 2011. The income statement showed operating expenses of $4,042 million, other expenses of $67 million, and income taxes of $238 million. The company's statement of cash flows, prepared under the indirect method, contained the items presented in the following table where negative numbers represent reductions in cash. Of the items listed, assume that Depreciation and amortization and Other net noncash expenses (benefits) affect operating expenses and that Other changes in current assets and liabilities, net affect other expenses.

▶▶ **OBJECTIVE 5**

	(in millions)
Proceeds from long-term debt	$ 400
Dividends paid	(194)
Additions to property, plant, and equipment	(180)
Purchases of marketable securities	(76)
Sales and maturities of marketable securities	57
Disposal of property, plant, and equipment	6
Repurchase of common stock	(389)
Other financing activities, net	13
Net income	479
Depreciation and amortization	240
Other net noncash expenses (benefits)	(7)
Changes in operating assets and liabilities	
Increase in trade receivables	(103)
Increase in inventories	(204)
Increase in accounts payable and accrued liabilities	85
Decrease in income taxes payable	(66)
Other changes in current assets and liabilities, net	(32)

1. Assume that these are all the items in Smucker's cash flow statement. Prepare the statement of cash flows for J.M. Smucker using the direct method for reporting cash flows from operating activities. Omit the schedule reconciling net income to net cash provided by operating activities.
2. Discuss the relation between operating cash flow and investing and financing needs.

▶▶ **OBJECTIVE 5**

5-58 Prepare Statement of Cash Flows from Income Statement and Balance Sheet
(Alternate is 5-56.) Cape Town Manufacturing had the following income statement and balance sheet items (in millions of rands, the South African currency):

Income Statement
For the Year Ended December 31, 20X1

Sales	R925
Cost of goods sold	(545)
Gross margin	380
Operating expenses	(220)
Depreciation	(60)
Interest	(15)
Income before taxes	85
Income taxes	(25)
Net income	60
Cash dividends declared and paid	(33)
Total increase in retained earnings	R 27

Balance Sheets

	December 31 20X1	December 31 20X0	Increase (Decrease)
Assets			
Cash	R 37	R 60	R (23)
Accounts receivable	230	150	80
Inventories	450	350	100
Total current assets	717	560	157
Fixed assets, gross	890	715	175
Accumulated depreciation	(570)	(550)	(20)
Fixed assets, net	320	165	155
Total assets	R1,037	R725	R312
Liabilities and stockholders' equity			
Trade accounts payable	R 515	R300	R215
Long-term debt	250	180	70
Stockholders' equity	272	245	27
Total liabilities and stockholders' equity	R1,037	R725	R312

During 20X1, Cape Town purchased fixed assets for R315 million cash and sold fixed assets for their book value of R100 million. Operating expenses, interest, and taxes were paid in cash. No long-term debt was retired.

Prepare a statement of cash flows for 20X1. Use the direct method for reporting cash flows from operating activities. Omit supporting schedules.

5-59 Statement of Cash Flows, Direct Method, Interest Expense, Australia
CSR Limited is a leading supplier of building and construction materials headquartered in Sydney, Australia. The company's 2011 total assets were more than A$2.2 billion, where A$ is the Australian dollar. The following items appeared in CSR's 2011 statement of cash flows (in millions), which it reports using the direct method:

▶▶ OBJECTIVE 5

Receipts from customers	A$ 3,400
Payments to suppliers and employees	(3,142)
Dividends and distributions received	7
Interest received	13
Other cash paid for operating activities	(28)
Net cash from operating activities	185
Purchase of property, plant, and equipment	(143)
Proceeds from sale of property, plant, and equipment	49
Net repayments of borrowings	(795)
Net cash from disposal of discontinued operations	1,873
Dividends paid	(307)
Capital return to CSR Limited shareholders	(661)
Other investing activities	(60)
Income taxes paid	(65)
Net cash from investing activities	1,719
Proceeds from issue of shares	3
Interest and other finance cost paid	(41)
Net cash from financing activities	(1,801)
Net increase in cash	?

1. Prepare a statement of cash flows for CSR Limited using the direct method. Include the proper amount for the net increase in cash. One item, interest paid, is included in a different section of the statement than it would be on a U.S. statement of cash flows. Place it in the section that makes the cash flows in each section total to the amounts given.
2. What does the placement of interest paid tell you about the GAAP used by CSR Limited? That is, does it report under IFRS or U.S. GAAP? Where would the interest paid be shown in a statement of cash flows using the other GAAP (IFRS or U.S. GAAP)?
3. Explain why CSR places interest paid where it does. Also explain why interest paid might be placed in the alternative section you indicated in requirement 2.

5-60 Reconcile Net Income and Net Cash Provided by Operating Activities
(Alternate is 5-63.) Refer to Problem 5-54 regarding Cascade Tile. Prepare a supporting schedule that reconciles net income to net cash provided by operating activities.

▶▶ OBJECTIVE 6

5-61 Cash Provided by Operations
Clorox Company is a leading producer of laundry additives, including Clorox liquid bleach. In the 6 months ended December 31, 2011, net sales of $2,526 million produced net earnings of $235 million. To calculate net earnings, Clorox recorded $89 million in depreciation and amortization. Other items of revenue and expense not requiring cash decreased net earnings by $21 million. Dividends of $159 million were paid during the period. Among the changes in balance sheet accounts during the period were the following ($ in millions):

▶▶ OBJECTIVE 6

Accounts receivable	$ 35	Decrease
Inventories	65	Increase
Accounts payable and accrued liabilities	136	Decrease
Income taxes payable	11	Decrease

Compute the net cash provided by operating activities using the indirect method.

▸▸ **OBJECTIVE 6**

5-62 Cash Flows from Operating Activities, Indirect Method

Sumitomo Metal Industries, Ltd., is a leading diversified manufacturer of steel products. During the year ended March 31, 2011, Sumitomo had a net loss of ¥36 billion on revenues of approximately ¥1,402 billion (or more than $17 billion in U.S. dollars). The following summarized information relates to Sumitomo's statement of cash flows:

	(billions of yen)
Depreciation and amortization	¥127
Repayments of long-term debt	130
Proceeds from long-term debt	74
Other noncash revenues and expenses, net	53
Decrease in receivables	37
Increase in inventories	14
Other, net	17
Acquisition of property, plant, equipment, and other assets	116
Increase in payables	18

Compute the net cash provided by operating activities using the indirect method. All the information necessary for that task is provided, together with some information related to other elements of the cash flow statement. Note that the format does not include parentheses to differentiate elements that increase cash from those that decrease cash, but the distinction should be clear from the captions (except for "Other noncash revenues and expenses, net" and "Other, net," which are both increases in cash).

▸▸ **OBJECTIVE 6**

5-63 Reconcile Net Income and Net Cash Provided by Operating Activities

(Alternate is 5-60.) Refer to Problem 5-55. Prepare a supporting schedule to the statement of cash flows that reconciles net income to net cash provided by operating activities.

▸▸ **OBJECTIVE 6**

5-64 Indirect Method: Reconciliation Schedule in Body of Statement

Refer to Problem 5-56. Prepare a statement of cash flows that includes a reconciliation of net income to net cash provided by operating activities in the body of the statement.

▸▸ **OBJECTIVE 6**

5-65 Cash Flows, Indirect Method

The Jawarski Company has the following balance sheet data ($ in millions):

	December 31				December 31		
	20X1	20X0	Change		20X1	20X0	Change
Current assets				Current liabilities			
Cash	$ 5	$ 21	$ (16)	(summarized)	$101	$ 26	$ 75
Receivables, net	53	15	38	Long-term debt	150	—	150
Inventories	94	50	44	Stockholders' equity	201	160	41
Total current assets	152	86	66				
Plant assets (net of accumulated depreciation)	300	100	200	Total liabilities and			
Total assets	$452	$186	$266	stockholders' equity	$452	$186	$266

Net income for 20X1 was $55 million. Net cash inflow from operating activities was $88 million. Cash dividends paid were $14 million. Depreciation was $40 million. Fixed assets were purchased for $240 million, $150 million of which was financed via the issuance of long-term debt outright for cash.

Georg Jawarski, the president and majority stockholder of the Jawarski Company, was a superb operating executive. He was imaginative and aggressive in marketing, and ingenious and creative in production. However, he had little patience with financial matters. After examining the most recent balance sheet and income statement, he muttered, "We've enjoyed 10 years of steady growth; 20X1 was our most profitable ever. Despite such profitability, we're in the worst cash position in our history. Just look at those current liabilities in relation to our available cash! This whole picture of the more you make, the poorer you get, just does not make sense. These statements must be wrong."

1. Prepare a statement of cash flows for 20X1 using the indirect method.
2. By using the statement of cash flows and other information, write a short memorandum to Jawarski, explaining why there is such a squeeze on cash.

5-66 Prepare Statement of Cash Flows

▶▶ **OBJECTIVES 5, 6**

The Feinstein Company has assembled the accompanying balance sheets and statement of income and retained earnings for 20X4.

Feinstein Company

Balance Sheets as of December 31 (in millions)

	20X4	20X3	Change
Assets			
Cash	$ 4	$ 22	$(18)
Accounts receivable	52	31	21
Inventory	70	50	20
Prepaid general expenses	4	3	1
Plant assets, net	207	150	57
	$337	$256	$ 81
Liabilities and shareholders' equity			
Accounts payable for merchandise	$ 74	$ 60	$ 14
Accrued tax payable	3	2	1
Long-term debt	54	—	54
Capital stock	100	100	—
Retained earnings	106	94	12
	$337	$256	$ 81

Feinstein Company

Statement of Income and Retained Earnings for the Year Ended December 31, 20X4 (in millions)

Sales		$282
Less: Cost of goods sold		
Inventory, December 31, 20X3	$ 50	
Purchases	185	
Cost of goods available for sale	235	
Inventory, December 31, 20X4	70	165
Gross profit		117
Less: Other expenses		
General expense	51	
Depreciation	40	
Taxes	10	101
Net income		16
Dividends declared and paid		4
Net income of the period retained		12
Retained earnings, December 31, 20X3		94
Retained earnings, December 31, 20X4		$106

On December 30, 20X4, Feinstein paid $103 million in cash to acquire a new plant to expand operations. This was partly financed by an issue of long-term debt for $54 million in cash. Plant assets were sold for their book value of $6 million during 20X4. Because net income was $16 million, the highest in the company's history, Isaac Feinstein, the chief executive officer, was distressed by the company's extremely low cash balance.

1. Prepare a statement of cash flows for 20X4 using the direct method for reporting cash flows from operating activities.

2. Prepare a schedule that reconciles net income to net cash provided by operating activities.
3. What is revealed by the statement of cash flows? Does it help you reduce Mr. Feinstein's distress? Why? Briefly explain to Mr. Feinstein why cash has decreased even though net income was $16 million.

▶▶ OBJECTIVE 7

5-67 Depreciation and Cash Flows

(Alternate is 5-45.) The following condensed income statement and reconciliation schedule are from the annual report of Tran Company ($ in millions):

Sales	$425
Expenses	350
Net income	$ 75

Reconciliation Schedule of Net Income to Net Cash Provided by Operating Activities	
Net income	$ 75
Add noncash expenses: Depreciation	25
Deduct net increase in noncash operating working capital	(17)
Net cash provided by operating activities	$ 83

A shareholder has suggested that the company switch from straight-line to accelerated depreciation on its annual report to shareholders, maintaining that this will increase the cash flow provided by operating activities. According to the stockholder's calculations, using accelerated methods would increase depreciation to $48 million, an increase of $23 million; net cash flow from operating activities would then be $106 million.

1. Suppose Tran Company adopts the accelerated depreciation method proposed. Compute net income and net cash flow from operating activities. Ignore income taxes.
2. Use your answer to requirement 1 to prepare a response to the shareholder.

▶▶ OBJECTIVES 6, 8

5-68 Balance Sheet Equation

(Alternate is 5-69.) Refer to Problem 5-66, Feinstein Company, requirement 1. Support the operating section of your cash flow statement by using a form of the balance sheet equation. (See Exhibit 5-8 on p. 208.) Use the equation Cash = Liabilities + Retained Earnings − Noncash Assets, and show how the direct-method and indirect-method statements arrive at the same total cash provided by operating activities.

▶▶ OBJECTIVE 8

5-69 Balance Sheet Equation

(Alternate is 5-68.) Examine the data for Cascade Tiles, Inc., in Problem 5-54. Support the operating section of your cash flow statement by using a form of the balance sheet equation. (See Exhibit 5-8 on p. 208.) Use the equation Cash = Liabilities + Retained Earnings − Noncash Assets, and show how the direct-method and indirect-method statements arrive at the same total cash provided by operating activities.

▶▶ OBJECTIVES 3, 4, 5, 6

5-70 Comprehensive Statement of Cash Flows

During the past 30 years, Only Toys, Inc., has grown from a single-location specialty toy store into a chain of stores selling a wide range of children's products. Its activities in 20X1 included the following:

1. The organization issued $1,906,000 in long-term debt; $850,000 of the proceeds was used to retire debt that became due in 20X1 and was listed on the books at $850,000.
2. The company purchased 40% of the stock of Bozeman Toy Company for $3,900,000 cash.
3. The firm purchased property, plant, and equipment for $1,986,000 cash, and sold property with a book value of $600,000 for $600,000 cash.
4. The company signed a note payable for the purchase of new equipment; the obligation was listed at $516,000.
5. Executives exercised stock options for 8,000 shares of common stock, paying cash of $170,000.
6. On December 30, 20X1, the firm bought Salzburg Musical Instruments Company by issuing common stock with a market value of $305,000.

7. The company issued common stock for $3,300,000 cash.

8. The firm withdrew $800,000 cash from a money market fund that was considered a cash equivalent.

9. The company bought $249,000 of treasury stock to hold for future exercise of stock options.

10. Long-term debt of $960,000 was converted to common stock.

11. Selected results for the year follow:

Net income	$ 809,000
Depreciation and amortization	615,000
Increase in inventory	72,000
Increase in accounts receivable	31,000
Increase in accounts and wages payable	7,000
Increase in taxes payable	35,000
Interest expense	144,000
Increase in accrued interest payable	15,000
Sales	9,850,000
Cash dividends received from investments	152,000
Cash paid to suppliers and employees	8,074,000
Cash dividends paid	240,000
Cash paid for taxes	390,000

Prepare a statement of cash flows for 20X1 using the direct method. Include a schedule that reconciles net income to net cash provided by operating activities. Also include a schedule of noncash investing and financing activities.

5-71 **Statement of Cash Flows, Direct and Indirect Methods**

Nordstrom, Inc., the Seattle-based fashion retailer, had the following income statement for the year ended January 28, 2012 ($ in millions):

▶▶ **OBJECTIVES 5, 6**

Total revenues		$10,877
Costs and expenses		
Cost of sales and related buying and occupancy costs	$6,592	
Selling, general, and administrative	3,036	
Interest expense	130	
Total costs and expenses		9,758
Earnings before income taxes		1,119
Income taxes		436
Net earnings		$ 683

The company's net cash provided by operating activities, prepared using the indirect method, was as follows ($ in millions):

Net earnings	$ 683
Adjustments to reconcile net earnings to net cash provided by operating activities	
Depreciation, amortization, and other noncash expenses	488
Changes in	
Accounts receivable	(98)
Merchandise inventories	(137)
Accounts payable	54
Accrued salaries, wages, and related benefits	6
Other liabilities	181
Net cash provided by operating activities	$1,177

Prepare a statement showing the net cash provided by operating activities using the direct method. Assume that accrued salaries, wages, and related benefits and other liabilities relate to selling, general, and administrative expenses, as do all components of depreciation, amortization, and other noncash expenses.

▶▶ OBJECTIVE 9

5-72 Free Cash Flow

A condensed version of the Kellogg Company statement of cash flows appears in Exhibit 5-16.

EXHIBIT 5-16

Kellogg Company and Subsidiaries

Consolidated Statement of Cash Flows, Year Ended December 31

(millions)	2011	2010	2009
Operating Activities			
Net earnings	$1,229	$ 1,240	$1,208
Items in net earnings not requiring (providing) cash			
Depreciation and amortization	369	392	384
Other noncash expenses (revenues)	(130)	(280)	(127)
Changes in operating assets and liabilities	127	(344)	178
Net cash provided by operating activities	1,595	1,008	1,643
Investing Activities			
Additions to properties	(594)	(474)	(377)
Other	7	9	7
Net cash used in investing activities	(587)	(465)	(370)
Financing Activities			
Reductions of notes payable	0	(1)	(1,354)
Issuances of notes payable	189	0	10
Issuances of long-term debt	895	987	1,241
Reductions of long-term debt	(945)	(1)	(482)
Net issuances of common stock	291	204	131
Common stock repurchases	(798)	(1,052)	(187)
Cash dividends	(604)	(584)	(546)
Other	15	8	5
Net cash used in financing activities	(957)	(439)	(1,182)
Increase (decrease) in cash and cash equivalents	$ 51	$ 104	$ 91

Use that statement to answer the following two questions.

1. What was Kellogg's free cash flow for each of the 3 years shown?
2. What does the free cash flow tell us about Kellogg's ability to generate sufficient cash flow from operations to cover ongoing investing activities and pay dividends to its shareholders?

▶▶ OBJECTIVES 3, 4

5-73 Miscellaneous Cash Flow Questions

McDonald's Corporation is a well-known provider of food services around the world. McDonald's statements of cash flows for 2011 and 2010 are reproduced with a few slight modifications as Exhibit 5-17. Use that statement to answer the following questions:

EXHIBIT 5-17

McDonald's Corporation

Consolidated Statement of Cash Flows, Years Ended December 31

(in millions)	2011	2010
Operating Activities		
Net income	$5,503	$ 4,946
Adjustments to reconcile to cash provided by operations		
Depreciation and amortization	1,415	1,276
Other noncash expenses	192	248
Changes in operating working capital items		
Accounts receivable	(161)	(50)
Inventories, prepaid expenses, and other current assets	(52)	(50)
Accounts payable	36	(40)
Income taxes	198	55
Other accrued liabilities	19	(43)
Cash provided by operations	7,150	6,342
Investing Activities		
Capital expenditures	2,730	(2,136)
Purchases of restaurant businesses	186	(183)
Sales of restaurant businesses and property	511	378
Other	166	(115)
Cash used for investing activities	2,571	(2,056)
Financing Activities		
Net short-term borrowings (repayments)	261	3
Long-term financing issuances	1,367	1,932
Long-term financing repayments	624	(1,147)
Treasury stock purchases	3,363	(2,699)
Common stock dividends	2,610	(2,408)
Other	436	590
Cash used for financing activities	4,533	(3,729)
Effect of exchange rates on cash and cash equivalents	(97)	34
Cash and equivalents increase (decrease)	A	591
Cash and equivalents beginning of year	B	1,796
Cash and equivalents at end of year	$ C	$ 2,387

1. In the financing activities section, all parentheses for 2011 have been removed. Which numbers should be put in parentheses?
2. In the investing activities section, all parentheses for 2011 have been removed. Which numbers should be put in parentheses?
3. The 2011 values for the change in cash and cash equivalents and for beginning and end-of-year balances have been omitted and replaced with the letters A, B, and C. Provide the proper values for these three missing numbers.
4. Suppose the balance in Retained Earnings at December 31, 2010, was $33,812 million. Compute the Retained Earnings balance at December 31, 2011. Assume that all dividends declared were paid in cash in 2011.
5. Comment on the relation between cash flow from operations and cash used for investing activities.

5-74 Interpretation of the Statement of Cash Flows and Ethics

Victoria, Inc., produces athletic wear. The company's peak year was 2008. Since then, both sales and profits have fallen. The following information is from the company's 2011 annual report ($ in thousands):

▶▶ **OBJECTIVE 9**

	2011	2010	2009
Net income	$1,500	$4,500	$7,500
Accounts receivable (end of year)	900	1,800	6,000
Inventory (end of year)	1,050	2,100	2,850
Net cash provided by operations	675	1,050	2,250
Capital expenditures	900	1,050	1,350
Proceeds from sales of fixed assets	2,700	1,500	2,250

During 2012, short-term loans of $9 million became due. Victoria paid off only $2.25 million and was able to extend the terms on the other $6.75 million. Accounts payable continued at a very low level in 2012, and the company maintained a large investment in corporate equity securities, enough to generate a $3,000,000 addition to net income and $900,000 of cash dividends in 2012. Victoria neither paid dividends nor issued stock or bonds in 2012. Its 2012 statement of cash flows was as follows:

Victoria, Inc.
Statement of Cash Flows for the Year Ended December 31, 2012 (in thousands)

Cash flows from operating activities		
Net income	$ 1,650	
Adjustments to reconcile net income to net cash provided by operating activities		
Add back noncash expenses:		
Depreciation and amortization	600	
Deduct noncash revenues:		
Investment revenue from equity investments, less $900 of dividends received*	(2,100)	
Net decrease in accounts receivable	150	
Net decrease in inventory	225	
Net cash provided by operating activities		$ 525
Cash flows from investing activities		
Purchase of fixed assets	(600)	
Insurance proceeds on building fire	3,000	
Sale of plant assets	3,750	
Purchase of corporate equity securities	(2,250)	
Net cash provided by investing activities		3,900
Cash flows from financing activities		
Principal payments on short-term debt to banks	(2,250)	
Purchase of treasury stock	(900)	
Net cash used for financing activities		(3,150)
Net increase in cash		1,275
Cash, December 31, 2011		1,800
Cash, December 31, 2012		$ 3,075

*$3,000 of revenue from equity investments was included in income. $900 of this was received in the form of dividends, so $2,100 of the income was not received in cash.

1. Interpret Victoria's statement of cash flows.
2. Describe any ethical issues relating to the strategy and financial disclosures of Victoria.

Collaborative Learning Exercise

5-75 Items in the Statement of Cash Flows
Form groups of four to six students each. Each member of the group should select a different company, find its statement of cash flows for a recent year, and make a list of the items included in each section of the statement: operating, investing, and financing activities. Be ready to explain the nature of each item.

1. As a group, make a comprehensive list of all items the companies listed under cash flows from operating activities. Identify those that are essentially the same but simply differ in terminology, and call them a single item. For each item, explain why and how it affects cash flows from operating activities. Note whether any of the companies selected use the direct method for reporting cash flows from operating activities. (Most companies use the indirect method, despite the fact that the FASB and IASB prefer the direct method.) If any use the direct method, separate the items listed under the direct method from those listed under the indirect method.

2. Make another comprehensive list of all items listed under cash flows from investing activities. Again, combine those that are essentially identical and differ only in terminology. For each item, explain why and how it affects cash flows from investing activities.

3. Make a third comprehensive list, this time including all items listed under cash flows from financing activities. Again, combine those that are essentially identical and differ only in terminology. For each item, explain why and how it affects cash flows from financing activities.

4. Reconvene as a class. For each of the three sections on the statement of cash flows, have groups sequentially add one item to the list of items included in the statement, simultaneously explaining why it is included in that section. Then identify the items that appear on nearly all cash flow statements and those that are relatively rare.

Analyzing and Interpreting Financial Statements

5-76 Financial Statement Research

Identify an industry and select two companies within that industry.

▶▶ **OBJECTIVE 9**

1. Determine whether net cash flow from operations is stable through time.
2. Relate net cash flow from operations to investing and dividend payment needs.
3. Compare net cash flow from operations to net income. Explain why they differ.

5-77 Analyzing Starbucks' Financial Statements

Find Starbucks' 2011 statement of cash flows either on Starbucks' Web site or using the SEC's EDGAR database.

▶▶ **OBJECTIVE 9**

1. Did Starbucks' net cash provided by operating activities increase or decrease between the year ended October 3, 2010, and the year ended October 2, 2011? By how much? What item contributed most to the change?
2. Did Starbucks' net cash used by investing activities increase or decrease between the year ended October 3, 2010, and the year ended October 2, 2011? By how much? What was the major cause of the change?
3. Explain to someone who's not an accountant what Starbucks did with the $1,612.4 million of cash generated by operating activities during the year ended October 2, 2011.
4. Suppose a friend of yours commented, "Starbucks must have poor financial management. It made a profit of $1,248.0 million in the year ended October 2, 2011, and it generated $1,612.4 million in cash from operations, yet it paid only $389.5 million in dividends. Its shareholders should expect more." Respond to your friend's comment.

5-78 Analyzing Financial Statements Using the Internet: Nike

Go to www.nikebiz.com and select Investors to locate Nike's most current financial information.

▶▶ **OBJECTIVE 9**

1. Take a look at Nike's Condensed Consolidated Statement of Cash Flows. Does Nike use the direct or indirect method? How can you tell?
2. Locate Management's Discussion and Analysis. Look under the section titled Liquidity and Capital Resources. What does management have to say about cash provided by operations?
3. Which is larger—cash provided (or used) by operations or net income for the period? Why is the cash provided by operations different from the amount of net income for the year?
4. Why does Nike add depreciation to net income in the operating activities section?
5. What were the primary uses of cash by investing activities in the most recent fiscal period?
6. What were the primary providers of cash or uses of cash by financing activities in the most recent fiscal period?

6 Accounting for Sales

NOT MANY COMPANIES SEEK THE permission of the Central Intelligence Agency (CIA) when naming products. Yet that is precisely what **System Development Laboratories** did in 1977 when it created a new type of database while working on a confidential project for the U.S. government. Called the "Oracle," this new relational database structure became the world's most popular database management system, and for the company, now called **Oracle Corporation**, it was an explosive sales success story. Revenues for 2011 exceeded $35 billion for sales of software and hardware systems and related services worldwide.

Recording and managing this sales revenue is important to Oracle's success. For every sale generated, the company must either collect cash or record an account receivable from the customer. The company must then collect the accounts receivable so it has adequate cash to continue its operations.

Managing accounts receivable and collecting cash are key activities for Oracle. The faster the company collects the cash, the less it will need to borrow (and the less interest it will pay). However, many customers need to obtain credit from their suppliers. Companies that push to collect cash too quickly may drive potential customers elsewhere. It took Oracle an average of 63 days to convert sales to cash in 2011. Oracle, like many other companies such as the major automobile firms, has a finance subsidiary that extends credit to its customers so that they can stretch payments over multiple years. **Ford Credit** and **GM Financial** often provide low interest car loans to help spur sales.

In a recent analysis of Oracle, a security analyst presented a prominent graph displaying the revenue growth in each part of Oracle's business. Such trends in revenue help analysts to understand what happened in the last year or the last quarter and to predict what may occur in the future. Recording revenue in the right time period is essential to measuring the rate of increase or decrease in sales. For Oracle, whose company name means "source of wisdom," efficient and accurate measurement of revenues and tracking of accounts receivables is smart business. ●

Recognition of Sales Revenue

Why is the timing of revenue recognition so important? It is critical to the measurement of net income in two ways. First, it directly increases net income by the amount of the revenue. Second, it reduces net income by triggering the recognition of certain expenses—for example, companies report the cost of the items sold in the same period in which they recognize the related revenue.

Changes in revenues and net income are especially important because of the profound effects they have on stock prices. For example, the Business First box on p. 240 shows how rapid earnings growth drove extraordinary increases in Intel's stock price in the 1990s and stagnant earnings growth arrested the increase in stock price from 2001 through the latter part of 2009. Both earnings and stock price began a slow and less predictable increase in 2010 and 2011. Sales and earnings growth are also important to managers because they often receive higher salaries or larger bonuses for increasing sales and net income. Therefore, they may prefer to recognize sales revenue as soon as possible. Owners and potential investors, however, want to be sure the economic benefits of the sale are certain before recognizing revenue.

To ensure that companies record revenues in the appropriate accounting period, both IFRS and U.S. GAAP require companies to meet certain criteria before recognizing revenue. Currently, companies adhering to U.S. GAAP must meet a two-pronged test for revenue recognition as described in Chapter 2: (1) A company must have delivered the goods or services to its customer, that is, it has *earned* the revenue; and (2) it must have received cash or an asset virtually assured of being converted into cash, that is, the revenue must be *realized* or *realizable*. While IFRS uses different terminology in its revenue recognition criteria, the underlying principles are similar. However, particularly in the United States, these seemingly simple criteria have led to an explosion of industry- or transaction-specific guidance that has increased the complexity of revenue recognition and can result in different accounting for transactions that are economically

In just over 30 years Oracle grew from a small company to one with the huge campus pictured here. Oracle is the world's largest enterprise software company. Its revenues exceeded $35 billion in 2011.

▶▶ **OBJECTIVE 1**

Recognize revenue items at the proper time on the income statement.

BUSINESS FIRST

THE INTEL DECADE OF THE 1990S ... AND THE RECKONING IN THE 2000S

Would you like to invest in a stock whose price increases 50-fold in just 10 years? Anyone who bought Intel's stock in 1990 already has. Intel stock purchased for $100 mid-1990 sold for about $5,000 in mid-2000.

If you had been able to read and understand Intel's financial statements in 1990, could you have predicted this large increase in stock price? Unfortunately, you probably could not. You also could not have predicted in 2000 that by mid-2010 your $5,000 investment would fall to under $1,800 and then climb again to more than $2,500 by early 2012. If understanding financial statements was sufficient for making good investment decisions, there would be a lot of rich accountants in this world. However, looking at Intel's financial statements from 1990 through 2000 helps explain why the company did so well over that period. The company's financial statements from 2000 through 2011 help explain its struggles over that decade, with a slight recovery in 2010 and 2011.

Intel's revenues increased from less than $4 billion in 1990 to nearly $34 billion in 2000, a rate of growth of more than 24% per year. Meanwhile, over the same period earnings per share grew from $.10 to $1.51, more than 31% per year. If investors in 2000 expected this growth to continue, it is no wonder they were willing to pay top dollar for shares of Intel.

Do Intel's financial statements since 2000 explain the cause of the decline in its stock price and its recent recovery? Partly. They certainly show that the anticipated growth did not occur. Revenues in 2009 were $35 billion, only $1 billion higher than in 2000. But revenues increased significantly to $43.6 billion and almost $54 billion in 2010 and 2011, respectively. Between 2000 and 2009, net income fell from $11 billion to $4 billion, and EPS fell from $1.51 to $.79, before recovering to nearly $13 billion and $2.46 in 2011. If investors had predicted these financial results, they would not have elected to hold Intel shares between 2000 and 2009. But remember, accountants simply report history—they do not predict future results.

Intel is still a much larger and stronger company than it was in 1990, and shareholders who bought shares in 1990 still have more than $2,500 for every $100 invested. However, those who invested in 2000 have seen half of their money melt away. What will the future hold? It depends in part on what revenues and income Intel will generate in the future. Its financial statements will gradually reveal whether purchasing Intel stock today will turn out to be a good investment.

Sources: Intel Annual Reports for 2000 and 2011; Yahoo Finance Historical Prices for Intel (http://finance.yahoo.com/q/hp?s=INTC&a=06&b=9&c=1986&d=02&e=28&f=2012&g=m&z=66&y=0).

---

similar. Therefore, the FASB and IASB entered into joint discussions in an attempt to improve accounting for revenues. This effort is about to conclude, and by the time you read this text the new standard may be in effect.

The new standard is expected to have a five-step process for revenue recognition:

Step 1: Identify the contract with a customer.

Step 2: Identify the separate performance obligations in the contract.

Step 3: Determine the transaction price.

Step 4: Allocate the transaction price to the separate performance obligations in the contract.

Step 5: Recognize revenue when (or as) the entity satisfies a performance obligation.

In plain English, this means that the company and customer must approve an agreement that specifies the sales price and the list of all the products and services that transfer to the customer as a result of the sale. The company then assigns a portion of the sales price to each product or service and records revenue when the customer receives each product or service. There are two major effects of this new revenue recognition process: (1) if the entire product and/or service is not provided to the customer at the point of sale, revenue is spread over the time periods in which the products and services are delivered, and (2) there is no realization criterion, that is, collectability of the sales price does not directly affect the recording of revenues.

Most companies recognize revenue at the point of sale and will continue to do so under the proposed guidance. Suppose you buy a compact disc at a local music store. The sale meets both the current and new revenue recognition tests at the time of purchase. It meets the new standard simply because the customer receives the product at the time of the sale. Under the old standard, the store earns the revenue because it delivers the merchandise at the point of sale, and the store realizes the revenue because it receives cash, a check, or a credit card slip, all of which it can readily convert to cash.

When the customer receives the entire product or service at the point of sale, the only thing that causes a difference between the old and new standards is the collectability of the sales price. Suppose a real estate company sells an acre of land in the desert to a customer for $10,000 and records an account receivable of $10,000. If there is a significant chance that the customer will not eventually pay the $10,000, current U.S. GAAP does not allow the recording of revenue. In contrast, the new standard would require recording the revenue but also require recognition that the account receivable may be uncollectible (the process for which we discuss later in the chapter).

When delivery of a product or service is spread over time, both the old and new standards require delaying revenue recognition at least until the company delivers the product or service to the customer. Consider the sale of magazine subscriptions where the subscriber makes payment upfront. Under current U.S. GAAP, the realization test for revenue recognition is met at the time the publisher receives payment. However, the publisher does not record revenue until it delivers the magazines and thereby earns the revenue. Under the new standards, revenue recognition would be determined by the delivery of the product, independent of the timing of cash collection. So both the old and new standards lead to recording revenue at the same time—at delivery of the product.

INTERPRETING FINANCIAL STATEMENTS

Consider two types of sales by **Starbucks**, over-the-counter sales and sales of "stored value" cards, such as gift cards. When would Starbucks recognize the revenue from each?

Answer

Starbucks recognizes revenues from over-the-counter sales at the point of sale—as it collects cash or records a credit card payment for the merchandise. In contrast, when it sells a stored value card, Starbucks initially records a liability, "deferred revenue." It then recognizes revenue when customers use their cards at retail stores. Only then has Starbucks earned the revenue by delivering the product to the customer.

A more complex example of services spread over time is long-term contracts. Suppose **Oracle** signs a $40 million contract with the U.S. government for designing and implementing an Enterprise Resource Planning system for a branch of Homeland Security. Oracle signs the contract and immediately begins work on January 2, 20X0. The expected completion date is December 31, 20X1. The government will pay Oracle upon completion of the project. Oracle expects to complete one-half of the project each year. When should Oracle record the $40 million of revenue on its income statement?

Because Oracle provides one-half of the services each year, it may seem logical that it should record half of the revenue each year—$20 million annually, even though delivery of the completed project will not occur until the end of 20X1. Under certain specified conditions, current U.S. GAAP does allow recognition of revenue during production. If Oracle's contract meets these conditions, Oracle will apply the **percentage of completion method**. This method recognizes revenue on long-term contracts as production occurs and, following the matching principle, also recognizes the associated expenses. Under this method, when Oracle recognizes one-half of the revenue in 20X0, it also recognizes the expenses incurred in fulfilling that half of the contract.

Under current U.S. GAAP, before applying the percentage of completion method, Oracle must determine the likelihood of receiving payment. If payment is questionable, the percentage of completion method is not appropriate. Generally, companies can count on the government and major corporations to make payments on their contracts. Because payment is virtually certain, the company realizes revenues as it earns them. In addition to the expectation of payment, the percentage of completion method is appropriate only if progress measures are dependable, contract obligations are explicit, and both the seller and buyer are expected

percentage of completion method
Method of recognizing revenue on long-term contracts as production occurs, rather than waiting until the final product is delivered. The company must also recognize the associated expenses.

to meet their obligations. If the project does not meet these criteria, especially if there is great uncertainty about whether the customer will pay at the end of the contract, companies reporting under current U.S. GAAP would delay recognition of both revenue and related expenses until completion of the contract, a method known as the **completed contract method**. In contrast, under current IFRS, companies use the percentage of completion method whenever the outcome of a contract can be estimated reliably.

The proposed new U.S. standard eliminates many of the hurdles to the application of the percentage of completion method. Not only does it converge the rules for percentage of completion as employed under U.S. GAAP and IFRS, but it also simplifies the accounting for long-term contracts relative to existing practice.

completed contract method

Method of recognizing revenue on long-term contracts that delays recognition of both revenue and related expenses until completion of the contract.

Measurement of Sales Revenue

▶ **OBJECTIVE 2**

Account for sales, including sales returns and allowances, sales discounts, and bank credit card sales.

After deciding *when to recognize* revenue, accountants must determine *how to measure* it. To measure revenue, accountants approximate the fair value of the asset inflow from the customer. That is, they measure revenue in terms of the cash-equivalent value of the asset received. A cash sale is simplest—it increases Sales Revenue, an income statement account, and increases Cash, a balance sheet account, by the amount of the cash received. Consider a $100 sale:

Cash	100	
Sales revenue		100

Accountants record a credit sale on open account much like a cash sale, except that it increases the balance sheet account Accounts Receivable instead of Cash:

Accounts receivable	100	
Sales revenue		100

Measuring revenue is more complex when the cash-equivalent value of the asset received is not obvious. When might this happen? One case is when a company receives goods or services instead of cash for a sale. In such a situation, the company must estimate the cash-equivalent value of the goods or services received. Even when a sale is for cash, the cash received may be less than the listed price of the item sold. For example, merchants may give discounts for prompt payment or for high-volume purchases. Or sometimes the customer is unable or unwilling to pay the full amount owed.

Some companies distinguish between gross sales and net sales when reporting revenues. **Gross sales** is the total amount of sales before deducting returns, allowances, and discounts. **Net sales** is the result after deducting such items. When a company makes such a distinction, it is the net sales, the amount actually received, that constitutes revenue to the company. We will next identify and examine returns, allowances, and discounts.

gross sales

The total amount of sales before deducting returns, allowances, and discounts.

net sales

The total amount of sales after deducting returns, allowances, and discounts.

Merchandise Returns and Allowances

Suppose a store recognizes revenue for a given sale at the point of that sale, but later the customer returns the merchandise. The purchaser may be unhappy with the product's color, size, style, or quality, or he or she simply may have a change of heart. The store calls these **sales returns**; the customer calls them **purchase returns**. Such merchandise returns are minor for manufacturers and wholesalers, but they are major for retail department stores. For instance, returns of 12% of gross sales are not abnormal for stores such as Nordstrom or Macy's.

Sometimes, instead of returning merchandise, the customer demands a reduction of the original selling price. For example, a customer may complain about scratches on a household appliance or about buying a pair of shoes for $40 on Wednesday and seeing the same shoes on sale for $29 on Thursday. Sellers often settle such complaints by granting a **sales allowance**, which we treat as a reduction of the original selling price (the purchaser calls this a **purchase allowance**).

Companies deduct both sales returns and sales allowances from gross sales to determine net sales. Instead of reducing the revenue (or sales) account directly, managers of retail stores typically

sales returns (purchase returns)

Merchandise returned by the customer.

sales allowance (purchase allowance)

Reduction of the original selling price.

use a contra revenue account, Sales Returns and Allowances, which combines both returns and allowances in a single account. Managers use a contra account to enable them to monitor changes in the level of returns and allowances, which may provide insights that are helpful in forecasting demand and managing inventory. For instance, a change in the percentage of returns in fashion merchandise may signal changes in customer tastes. Similarly, sellers of fashion or fad merchandise may find tracking of sales returns to be especially useful in assessing the quality of products and services from various suppliers. Also, if a company uses sales figures to determine commissions or bonuses, managers must know which sales personnel have especially high rates of sales returns or allowances. Because returns happen after the sales, accountants separately record returns and allowances to avoid going back and changing the original entries for the sale—a messy and unreliable process.

How does a retailer adjust gross sales for sales returns and allowances? Suppose your local outlet of **Talbots** has $900,000 gross sales on credit and $80,000 sales returns and allowances. The analysis of transactions would show the following:

	A	=	L	+	SE
Credit sales on open account	+900,000 Increase Accounts Receivable	=			+900,000 Increase Sales
Returns and allowances	−80,000 Decrease Accounts Receivable	=			−80,000 Increase Sales Returns and Allowances

The journal entries (without explanations) are as follows:

Accounts receivable.	900,000	
Sales.		900,000
Sales returns and allowances	80,000	
Accounts receivable		80,000

The income statement would begin as follows:

Gross sales	$900,000
Deduct: Sales returns and allowances	80,000
Net sales	$820,000
or	
Sales, net of $80,000 returns and allowances	$820,000

Managers react differently to this information than they would to knowing only that net sales were $820,000. They easily see that about 9% of the company's sales are either being returned or lost through price reductions. Then they can ask the following questions: How has this pattern changed through time? What can we do to reduce the extra service costs we incur to handle these special transactions? Should we modify our inventory selections or our inventory levels?

Trade and Cash Discounts

In addition to returns and allowances, trade and cash discounts also reduce reported sales amounts. **Trade discounts** are reductions to the gross selling price for a particular class of customers. An example is a discount for large-volume purchases. Suppose Tartan Wholesale Co. offers no discount on the first $10,000 of merchandise purchased per order, but a 2% discount on the next $10,000 of purchases and a discount of 3% on all sales in excess of $20,000. The gross sales revenue recognized from a sale with a trade discount is the price received after deducting the discount. Thus, a trade discount is simply a reduction in the gross sales price. Tartan Wholesale

trade discounts
Reductions to the gross selling price for a particular class of customers.

would record sale of merchandise listed at $25,000 less a trade discount as follows, where the sales amount is [$10,000 + (98% × $10,000) + (97% × $5,000)] = $24,650:

	A	=	L	+	SE
Sale with trade discount	+24,650	=			+24,650
	Increase Accounts Receivable or Cash				Increase Sales

Companies set trade discount terms to be competitive in industries where such discounts are common or to encourage certain customer behavior. For example, manufacturers with seasonal products (gardening supplies, snow shovels, fans, Christmas ornaments, and so on) might offer price discounts on early orders and deliveries to smooth out production throughout the year and to minimize the manufacturer's cost of storing the inventory. In deciding to accept early delivery, the buyer must weigh the storage costs it will incur against the reduced price the discount provides.

cash discounts

Reductions in the amount owed by customers due to prompt payment.

Another type of discount, **cash discounts**, rewards customers for prompt payment. Sellers quote the terms of the credit sale in various ways on the invoice:

Credit Terms	Meaning
n/30	The full billed price (gross price) is due on the thirtieth day after the invoice date.
1/5, n/30	A 1% discount can be taken for payment within 5 days of the invoice date; otherwise, the full billed price is due in 30 days.
15 E.O.M.	The full price is due within 15 days after the end of the month of sale; an invoice dated December 20 is due January 15.

For example, suppose a manufacturer sells $30,000 of computer equipment to Oracle on terms 2/10, n/60. Therefore, Oracle may remit $30,000 less a cash discount of (.02 × $30,000), or ($30,000 − $600) = $29,400, if it makes payment within 10 days after the invoice date. Otherwise, it must pay the full $30,000 within 60 days. We illustrate two approaches to accounting for this transaction, the gross method and the net method. If the manufacturer uses the gross method of accounting for cash discounts it would record the sale at the gross sales price of $30,000 as shown in entry 1 below. It would record entry 2 if Oracle pays within 10 days and entry 3 if Oracle pays the full amount in 60 days:

	A	=	L	+	SE
1. Sell at terms of 2/10, n/60	+30,000 Increase Accounts Receivable	=			+30,000 Increase Sales
Followed by either 2 or 3					
2. Either collect $29,400 ($30,000 less 2%)	+29,400 Increase Cash	=			−600 Increase Cash Discounts on Sales
	−30,000 Decrease Accounts Receivable				
or					
3. Collect $30,000	+30,000 Increase Cash	=			(No Effect)
	−30,000 Decrease Accounts Receivable				

The journal entries follow:

```
1. Accounts receivable  . . . . . . . . . . . . . . . .     30,000
        Sales. . . . . . . . . . . . . . . . . . . . . . . .              30,000
2. Cash  . . . . . . . . . . . . . . . . . . . . . . . . . .     29,400
   Cash discounts on sales  . . . . . . . . . . . . .        600
        Accounts receivable  . . . . . . . . . . . . .               30,000
   or
3. Cash  . . . . . . . . . . . . . . . . . . . . . . . . . .     30,000
        Accounts receivable  . . . . . . . . . . . . .               30,000
```

If the manufacturer uses the net method of accounting for the cash discounts, it would initially record the sale at the net price, as shown in entry 1 that follows. It would record entry 2 if Oracle pays within 10 days and entry 3 if Oracle pays the full amount in 60 days:

	A	=	L	+	SE
1. Sell at terms of 2/10, n/60	+29,400	=			+29,400
	[Increase Accounts Receivable]				[Increase Sales]
Followed by either 2 or 3					
2. Either collect $29,400 ($30,000 less 2%)	+29,400	=			(No Effect)
	[Increase Cash]				
	−29,400				
	[Decrease Accounts Receivable]				
or					
3. Collect $30,000	+30,000	=			+600
	[Increase Cash]				[Increase Interest Revenue]
	−29,400				
	[Decrease Accounts Receivable]				

The journal entries for the net method follow:

```
1. Accounts receivable. . . . . . . . . . . . . . . .     29,400
        Sales. . . . . . . . . . . . . . . . . . . . . . . .              29,400
2. Cash  . . . . . . . . . . . . . . . . . . . . . . . . . .     29,400
        Accounts receivable  . . . . . . . . . . . . .               29,400
   or
3. Cash  . . . . . . . . . . . . . . . . . . . . . . . . . .     30,000
        Accounts receivable  . . . . . . . . . . . . .               29,400
        Interest Revenue  . . . . . . . . . . . . . . .                  600
```

The net method assumes that the delayed receipt of cash is essentially a loan to the customer. Cash discounts encourage prompt payment and thus reduce the seller's need for cash. Early collection also reduces the risk of bad debts. Moreover, favorable credit terms with attractive cash discounts are a way to compete with other sellers.

Should purchasers take cash discounts? The answer is usually yes, but the decision depends on interest rates. Suppose Oracle decides to pay $30,000 in 60 days, not $29,400 in 10 days. It has the use of $29,400 for an extra 50 days (60 days – 10 days) for an "interest" payment of $600. If Oracle could borrow the $29,400 from the bank at a 10% annual interest rate, the interest cost for 50 days on $29,400 is [($29,400 × 10%) × (50 ÷ 365)] = $403. It is ($600 – $403) = $197 cheaper to borrow the money from the bank. If the company does not have the cash to pay now, it should borrow the money in order to take the cash discount. Only if Oracle cannot borrow the $29,400 for less than $600 of interest should it pass up the cash discount and pay $30,000 on the sixtieth day.

You could also calculate the annual interest rate implicit in the cash discount. The rate is ($600 ÷ $29,400) = 2.04% for the 50 days. During a year, there are (365 days ÷ 50 days) = 7.3 periods of 50 days. Thus, the annual rate is (2.04% per period × 7.3 periods per year) = 14.9%. Most well-managed companies, such as Oracle, can borrow for less than 14.9% interest per year, so they design their accounting systems to always take advantage of cash discounts. Usage of cash discounts varies through time and from one industry to another. You may be familiar with some gas stations that offer a lower price for cash payment, whereas other stations do not.

Recording Charge Card Transactions

In a sense, companies offer cash discounts when they accept charge cards such as **VISA**, **MasterCard**, and **American Express**. Why? These credit card companies charge retailers a fee, and the retailers receive an amount less than the listed sales price. Why do retailers accept these cards? There are three major reasons: (1) to attract credit customers who would otherwise shop elsewhere, (2) to get cash immediately instead of waiting for credit customers to pay their accounts, and (3) to avoid the cost of tracking, billing, and collecting customers' accounts.

Most large retailers deposit credit card charges in their bank accounts immediately via electronic transmissions, and those who still use paper charge slips generally deposit them daily (just like cash). The services of a credit card company cost money (in the form of service charges on every credit sale), and companies deduct this cost from gross sales in calculating net sales revenue. Card companies' service charges are typically from 1% to 4% of gross sales, with the large-volume retailers bearing the lowest cost as a percentage of sales. The arrangement for one large-volume retailer was 4.3 cents per transaction plus 1.08% of the gross sales using charge cards.

Suppose VISA charges a company a straight 3% of sales for its credit card services. Credit sales of $10,000 will result in cash of only [$10,000 – (.03 × $10,000)] = $9,700. Managers usually report the $300 amount separately for control purposes:

	A	=	L	+	SE
					+10,000 $\begin{bmatrix} \text{Increase} \\ \text{Sales} \end{bmatrix}$
Sales using VISA	+9,700 $\begin{bmatrix} \text{Increase} \\ \text{Cash} \end{bmatrix}$	=			−300 $\begin{bmatrix} \text{Increase} \\ \text{Cash Discounts} \\ \text{for Bank Cards} \end{bmatrix}$

Cash	9,700	
Cash discounts for bank cards	300	
Sales		10,000

By accounting for these cash discounts separately, managers can continuously evaluate whether the costs they incur are justified.

Accounting for Net Sales Revenue

Because we record cash discounts (when accounted for under the gross method) and sales returns and allowances as deductions from Gross Sales, a detailed income statement might contain multiple elements as follows (numbers assumed):

Gross sales		$1,000
Deduct:		
Sales returns and allowances	270	
Cash discounts on sales	20	290
Net sales		$ 710

Reports to shareholders typically omit details and show only net revenues. For example, Starbucks reports "total net revenues" of $11,700.4 million on its 2011 income statement. Some companies separate revenue into categories. For example, Oracle shows software revenues separately from service revenues, and Starbucks shows revenue from company-owned retail stores separately from revenue from licensing and foodservice activities.

Summary Problem for Your Review

PROBLEM

Carlos Lopez, marketing manager for Fireplace Distributors, sold 12 wood stoves to Woodside Condominiums, Inc. The sales contract was signed on April 27, 20X1. The list price of each wood stove was $1,200, but Lopez allowed a 5% quantity discount. He also offered a cash discount of 2% of the amount owed if Woodside paid by June 10. Fireplace Distributors delivered the wood stoves on May 10 and received the proper payment on June 9. The company uses the gross method of accounting for cash discounts.

1. How much revenue should Fireplace Distributors recognize in April, in May, and in June? Explain.
2. Suppose Fireplace Distributors has a separate account titled "Cash Discounts on Sales." What journal entry would it make on June 9 when it receives the cash payment?
3. Suppose Fireplace Distributors has another account titled "Sales Returns and Allowances." Suppose further that one of the wood stoves had a scratch and Fireplace Distributors allowed Woodside to deduct $100 from the total amount due. What journal entry would Fireplace Distributors make on June 9 when it receives the cash payment?

SOLUTION

1. Under current U.S. GAAP Fireplace Distributors would recognize revenue of $13,680 [(12 × $1,200) less a 5% quantity discount of $720] in May and none in April or June. The key to recognizing revenue is whether the revenue is earned and the asset received from the buyer is realized. Fireplace Distributors does not earn the revenue until it delivers the merchandise. Therefore, it cannot recognize revenue in April. Provided that Woodside Condominiums has a good credit rating, the receipt of cash is reasonably ensured before Fireplace Distributors actually receives the cash. Therefore, recognition of revenue need not be delayed until June. On May 10, both revenue recognition tests are met, and Fireplace Distributors would record the revenue on May's income statement. However, if Woodside had a poor credit rating, Fireplace Distributors would not recognize and record the revenue until it received the cash in June.

   Under the proposed new revenue recognition rules, Fireplace Distributors would recognize all of the revenue in May as it has fulfilled its obligation by delivering the product to Woodside.

2. The original revenue recorded was $13,680. The 2% cash discount is (2% × $13,680) = $273.60. Therefore, the cash received is ($13,680 − $273.60) = $13,406.40:

Cash	13,406.40	
Cash discounts on sales	273.60	
Accounts receivable		13,680.00

3. The only difference from requirement 2 is a $100 smaller cash receipt and a $100 debit to Sales Returns and Allowances:

Cash	13,306.40	
Cash discounts on sales	273.60	
Sales returns and allowances	100.00	
Accounts receivable		13,680.00

Credit Sales and Accounts Receivable

Cash sales are important for some companies, but most sales in today's world are on credit. Credit sales create challenges for measuring revenue and managing the company's assets because the company agrees to accept payment in the future for goods or services delivered today. Companies must manage these expected future payments, accounts receivable, to ensure their collection in a timely manner.

Uncollectible Accounts

▶▶ OBJECTIVE 3

Estimate and interpret uncollectible accounts receivable balances.

uncollectible accounts (bad debts)
Receivables determined to be uncollectible because customers are unable or unwilling to pay their debts.

bad debt expense
The loss that arises from uncollectible accounts.

Granting credit entails both costs and benefits. The main benefit is the boost in sales and profit that a company generates when it extends credit. Many potential customers would not buy if credit were unavailable, or they would buy from a competitor that offered credit. Among the costs of providing credit is the cost of administering and collecting the credit amount. Before a company grants credit, it reviews the customer's credit and payment history to decide whether to accept the customer. It must then track what a customer owes, send periodic bills, deposit payments, record the payment in the customer's account, and so forth. These steps require clerical time and effort. Another cost is the delay in receiving payment. The seller must finance its activities in other ways while awaiting payment. Perhaps the most significant cost is **uncollectible accounts** or **bad debts**—receivables that some credit customers are either unable or unwilling to pay. Accountants often call the loss that arises from uncollectible accounts **bad debt expense**.

The extent of nonpayment of debts varies. It often depends on the credit risks that managers are willing to accept. For instance, many smaller local establishments will accept a higher level of risk than will larger national stores such as Nordstrom. Why? Possibly because the local stores know their customers personally. The extent of nonpayments can also depend on the industry. For example, the problem of uncollectible accounts is especially difficult in the healthcare field. The Bayfront Medical Center of St. Petersburg, Florida, once reported bad debts equal to 21% of gross revenue.

Deciding When and How to Grant Credit

Competition and industry practice affect whether and how companies offer credit. They offer credit only when the additional earnings on credit sales exceed the costs of offering credit. Suppose 5% of credit sales are bad debts, administrative costs of a credit department are $5,000 per year, and $20,000 of credit sales (with earnings of $8,000 before credit costs) are achieved. Assume that the company would not receive any of the credit sales without granting credit. Offering credit is worthwhile because the additional earnings of $8,000 exceeds the credit costs of [(5% × $20,000) + $5,000] = $6,000.

Measurement of Uncollectible Accounts

Uncollectible accounts require special accounting procedures and thus deserve special attention. Consider an example. Suppose Compuport began business on January 2, 20X1 and had credit sales of $100,000 (200 customers averaging $500 each) during 20X1. Collections during 20X1 were $60,000. The December 31, 20X1, gross accounts receivable balance of $40,000 includes the accounts of 80 different customers who have not yet paid for their 20X1 purchases. Some of those still-uncollected sales may never be received from the customers. The outstanding balances are as follows:

Customer	Amount Owed
1. Jones	$1,400
2. Slade	125
⋮	⋮
42. Monterro	500
⋮	⋮
79. Weinberg	700
80. Porras	11
Total receivables	$40,000

How should Compuport account for these receivables? As Compuport's accountants, should we assume they will all be collected and report $40,000 of accounts receivable on the balance sheet? Or should we report only the amount Compuport expects to receive? If we assume some receivables will not be collected, how do we decide which are collectible and which are not? Of course, we would never have initially made a credit sale to someone we really believed would not pay us, and at the end of the year we are unlikely to know exactly which customers may not pay.

There are two basic ways to record uncollectibles, the specific write-off method and the allowance method. Under the specific write-off method, the company waits to see which specific customers do not pay and only then reduces the amount receivable. Under the allowance method, at the end of the accounting period the company estimates the portion of outstanding receivables that will not be collected and reports a net accounts receivable, the gross amount less the expected uncollectibles.

Specific Write-Off Method

A company that rarely experiences a bad debt might use the **specific write-off method** (or **direct write-off method**), which assumes that all sales are fully collectible until proven otherwise. If uncollectibles are small and infrequent, this practice will not misstate the economic situation in a material way. If Compuport adopts this method, it will reduce the Account Receivable when it identifies a specific customer account as uncollectible. Because Compuport deems no specific customer's account to be uncollectible at the end of 20X1, its December 31, 20X1, balance sheet would simply show Accounts Receivable of $40,000.

specific write-off method (direct write-off method)
A method of accounting for bad debt losses that assumes all sales are fully collectible until proven otherwise.

Now assume that during 20X2 Compuport identifies Jones and Monterro as customers who are not expected to pay. When the probability of collection from specific customers becomes small, Compuport recognizes the amounts in the particular customer's accounts as bad debt expense:

Specific Write-Off Method	A	= L +	SE
20X1 Sales	+100,000	=	+100,000
	[Increase Accounts Receivable]		[Increase Sales]
20X2 Write-off	–1,900	=	–1,900
	[Decrease Accounts Receivable]		[Increase Bad Debt Expense]

The journal entry for the $1,900 write-off is as follows:

Bad Debt Expense	1,900	
Accounts Receivable		1,900

The problem with the specific write-off method is that it fails to apply the matching principle of accrual accounting. The $1,900 bad debt expense recorded using the specific write-off method in 20X2 is related to (or caused by) the $100,000 of 20X1 sales. Matching requires recognition of the bad debt expense at the same time as the related revenue, that is, in 20X1, not 20X2. As a result of not matching expenses to revenues, the specific write-off method produces two errors in reported earnings. First, Compuport overstates its 20X1 income by $1,900 because the company reports no bad debt expense that year. Second, it understates its 20X2 income by $1,900. Why? Because Compuport charges 20X1's bad debt expense of $1,900 in 20X2. Equally important, the accounts receivable balance in 20X1 overstates the asset by $1,900. Compare the specific write-off method with a correct matching of revenue and expense:

	Specific Write-Off Method: Matching Violated		Matching Applied Correctly	
	20X1	**20X2**	**20X1**	**20X2**
Sales revenue	$100,000	$0	$100,000	$0
Bad debt expense	0	1,900	1,900	0
20X1 ending accounts receivable	40,000		38,100	

Another error in matching can arise if a customer pays an account that a company has previously written off as uncollectible. When such **bad debt recoveries** occur, we must capture the customer's true payment history. We accomplish this in two steps. First, we reverse the write-off, and then we handle the collection as a normal receipt on account. Suppose that in 20X3 Monterro unexpectedly pays the $500 that was written off in 20X2. The write-off must be reversed and the payment recorded:

Accounts receivable.	500	
Bad debt expense.		500
To reverse February 20X2 write-off of account of Monterro		
Cash	500	
Accounts receivable		500
To record the collection on account		

The reduction in 20X3's bad debt expense offsets the overstatement of 20X2's bad debt expense, so 20X2's income was understated and 20X3's income will be overstated.

The principal arguments in favor of the specific write-off method are based on cost-benefit and materiality. The method is simple, extremely inexpensive to use, and does not require estimation. Moreover, no great error in measurement of income or accounts receivable occurs if the amounts of bad debts are small and similar from one year to the next.

Allowance Method

Few companies use the specific write-off method because it violates the matching principle and most companies' bad debts are neither small nor similar from year to year. Instead, most companies estimate the amount of uncollectible accounts to be matched to each year's revenue. This method, known as the **allowance method**, has two basic elements: (1) an estimate of the amount of sales or receivables that will ultimately be uncollectible, and (2) a contra account that contains the estimated uncollectible amount to be deducted from the total accounts receivable. We usually call the contra account **allowance for uncollectible accounts** (or **allowance for doubtful accounts**, or **allowance for bad debts**). It contains the amount of receivables the company estimates to be uncollectible from as-yet unidentified customers. In other words, using this contra account allows accountants to recognize bad debts in general during the proper period, before they identify uncollectible accounts from specific individuals in the following periods.

Returning to our example, suppose that Compuport knows from experience that it will not collect about 2% of sales. Therefore, the company estimates that it will not collect (2% × $100,000) = $2,000 of the 20X1 sales. However, on December 31, 20X1, it does not know which customers will fail to

bad debt recoveries

Accounts receivable that were previously written off as uncollectible but then collected at a later date.

allowance method

A method of accounting for bad debt losses that uses (1) estimates of the amount of sales or receivables that will ultimately be uncollectible, and (2) a contra account that contains the estimated uncollectible amount to be deducted from the total accounts receivable.

allowance for uncollectible accounts (allowance for doubtful accounts, allowance for bad debts)

A contra asset account that measures the amount of receivables estimated to be uncollectible.

pay their accounts. Compuport can still acknowledge the $2,000 of expected bad debts in 20X1, before it identifies the specific accounts of Jones and Monterro in 20X2. The effects of the allowance method on the balance sheet equation in the Compuport example follow:

	A	=	L	+	SE
Allowance method					
20X1 Sales	+100,000	=			+100,000
	⎡ Increase Accounts Receivable ⎤				⎡ Increase Sales ⎤
20X1 Allowance	−2,000	=			−2,000
	⎡ Increase Allowance for Uncollectible Accounts ⎤				⎡ Increase Bad Debt Expense ⎤
20X2 Write-off	+1,900	=			(No Effect)
	⎡ Decrease Allowance for Uncollectible Accounts ⎤				
	−1,900				
	⎡ Decrease Accounts Receivable ⎤				

The associated journal entries are as follows:

20X1 Sales	Accounts receivable.	100,000	
	Sales.		100,000
20X1 Allowances	Bad debt expense	2,000	
	Allowance for uncollectible accounts . .		2,000
20X2 Write-offs	Allowance for uncollectible accounts.	1,900	
	Accounts receivable, Jones		1,400
	Accounts receivable, Monterro.		500

The first journal entry represents many (200 in this example) individual sales to specific customers in 20X1 and the related increases in accounts receivable. The second entry records the estimate of bad debt expenses for 20X1, which results in an increase to the Allowance for Uncollectible Accounts. In 20X2, after exhausting all practical means of collection, Compuport decides the Jones and Monterro accounts are uncollectible, and the third entry writes off these accounts. Recording the $1,900 write-off for Jones and Monterro in 20X2 reduces their individual subsidiary accounts, reduces the general ledger Accounts Receivable account, and reduces the Allowance for Uncollectible Accounts balance to $100.

The separate entries to the Jones and Monterro subsidiary ledger accounts emphasize that companies keep separate accounts receivable records for each individual customer, showing all sales and payments in the customer's subsidiary ledger account. The total of all a particular customer's net sales less payments and any amounts written off is the amount receivable from that customer. At any point in time, the sum of the balances of all customer accounts in the subsidiary ledger must equal the accounts receivable balance in the general ledger. We illustrate this process in Exhibit 6-1, where panel A shows the accounts at the end of 20X1 (before the write-off) and panel B shows the accounts after the write-off.

The allowance method is superior in measuring annual accrual accounting income and in measuring the year-end accounts receivable asset accurately. Under this method Compuport deducts from 20X1 sales the $2,000 of those sales that it believes it will never collect. This matches the bad debt expense to the sales that generated the bad debts. In addition, the balance sheet shows a more conservative receivable balance of $38,000 at December 31, 20X1.

EXHIBIT 6-1

Compuport General Ledger, December 31, 20X1

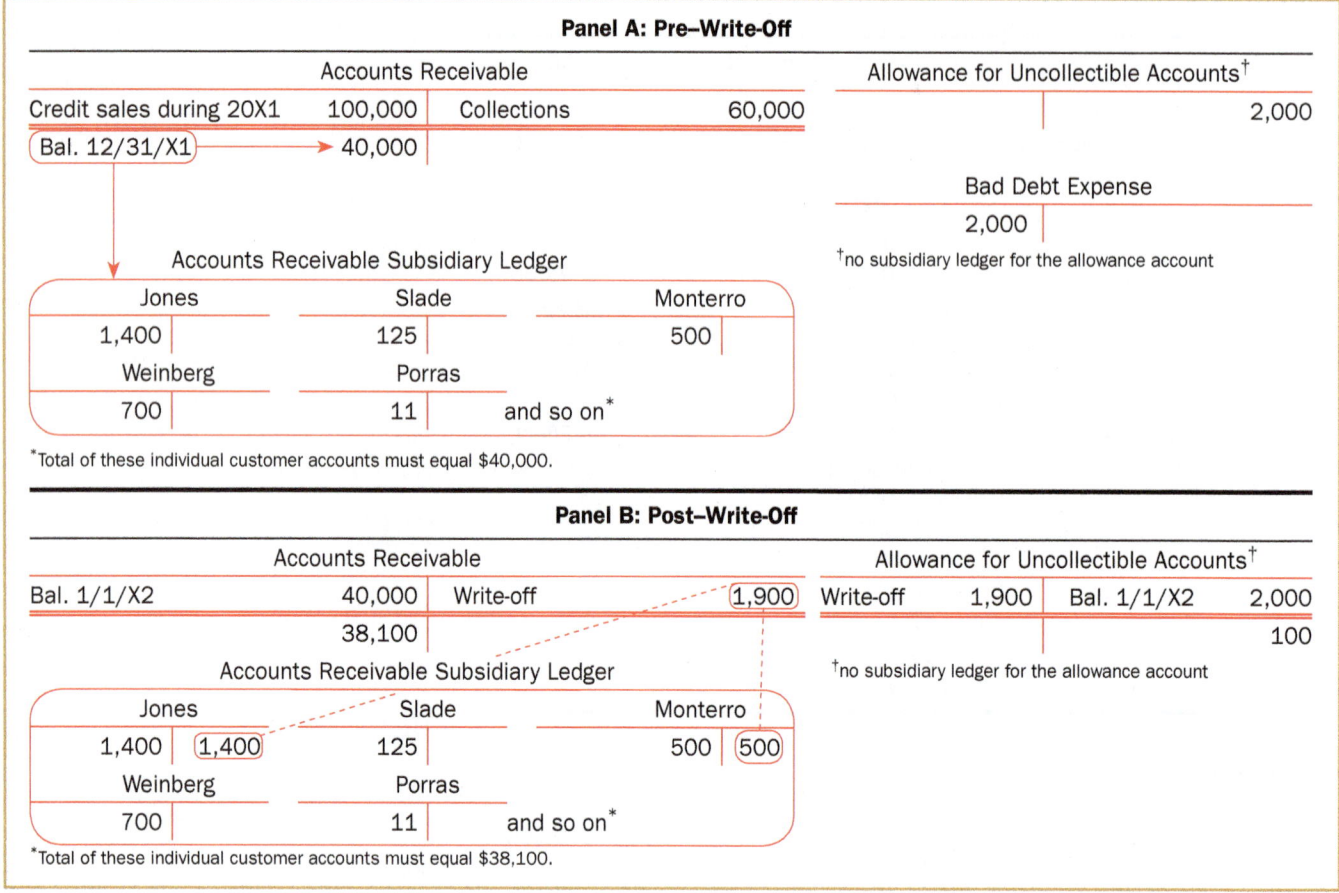

The allowance method results in the following presentation in the Compuport balance sheet at December 31, 20X1:

Accounts receivable	$40,000
Less: Allowance for uncollectible accounts	2,000
Net accounts receivable	$38,000

Oracle discloses its allowance for uncollectible accounts in the caption for Trade Receivables:

($ in millions)	2011	2010
Trade receivables, net of allowances for doubtful accounts of $372 and $305 as of May 31, 2011 and 2010, respectively	$6,628	$5,585

The allowance method relies on historical experience and information about economic circumstances (growth versus recession, interest rate levels, and so on) and customer composition. Of course, companies revise estimates when conditions change. For example, if a local employer closed or drastically reduced employment and many local customers were suddenly unemployed, Compuport might increase expected bad debts. Oracle discloses the following in its 2011 annual report:

We record allowances for doubtful accounts based upon a specific review of all significant outstanding invoices. For those invoices not specifically reviewed, provisions are provided at differing rates, based upon the age of the receivable, the collection history associated with the geographic region that the receivable was recorded in and current economic trends. We write-off a receivable and charge it against its recorded allowance when we have exhausted our collection efforts without success.

We next examine three methods of estimating bad debts when applying the allowance method.

Applying the Allowance Method Using a Percentage of Sales

How do managers and accountants estimate the amount of bad debts in the allowance method? Companies that express the amount as a percentage of total credit sales use the **percentage of sales method**, which relies on historical relationships between credit sales and uncollectible accounts adjusted for current economic conditions. This method is often referred to as an income statement approach because the computation of bad debt expense is a function of an income statement value, credit sales, not a function of the balance in Accounts Receivable. It was the method used in the previous section that introduced the allowance method. In our example, Compuport managers determined a rate of 2% of credit sales, for a total of (2% × $100,000) = $2,000, based on experience. To arrive at the 2% rate they might look at the last 4 years and divide the total of all bad debts by the total of all credit sales to calculate that over time they failed to collect 2% of credit sales.

percentage of sales method
An approach to estimating bad debt expense and uncollectible accounts based on the historical relationship between credit sales and uncollectible accounts adjusted for current economic conditions.

INTERPRETING FINANCIAL STATEMENTS

How does the ultimate write-off of the Monterro and Jones accounts affect total assets reported on the balance sheet?

Answer
The ultimate write-off has no effect on total assets:

	Before Write-Off	After Write-Off
Accounts receivable	$40,000	$38,100
Allowance for uncollectible accounts	2,000	100
Book value (net realizable value)	$38,000	$38,000

Applying the Allowance Method Using a Percentage of Accounts Receivable

A second method of estimating the amount of bad debts is the **percentage of accounts receivable method**, which bases estimates of uncollectible accounts on the historical percentage of ending accounts receivable that subsequently prove to be uncollectible, not on the percentage of credit sales that become uncollectible. This method focuses on the ending Accounts Receivable balance and estimates the percentage of those receivables that is unlikely to be collected. As a result of this focus on the ending accounts receivable balance, we refer to this method as a balance sheet approach. The Allowance for Uncollectible Accounts contra account should show the estimated amount of bad debts contained in the end-of-period accounts receivable, that is, the bad debt percentage multiplied by the ending accounts receivable. We then calculate the needed adjustment to the Allowance for Uncollectible Accounts to achieve the desired ending balance in the Allowance account. Consider the historical experience in the following table:

percentage of accounts receivable method
An approach to estimating bad debt expense and uncollectible accounts that bases estimates of uncollectible accounts on the historical percentage of ending accounts receivable that subsequently prove to be uncollectible.

	Accounts Receivable at End of Year	Bad Debts Deemed Uncollectible and Written Off in Subsequent Year
20X1	$100,000	$ 3,500
20X2	80,000	2,450
20X3	90,000	2,550
20X4	110,000	4,080
20X5	120,000	5,600
20X6	112,000	2,200
Six-year total	$612,000	$20,380

Average percentage not collected = ($20,380 ÷ $612,000) = 3.33%

At the end of 20X7 the accounts receivable balance is $115,000. We compute the 20X7 addition to the Allowance for Uncollectible Accounts as follows:

1. Divide total bad debt losses of $20,380 by total ending accounts receivable of $612,000 to calculate the historical average uncollectible percentage of 3.33%.
2. Apply the percentage from step 1 to the ending Accounts Receivable balance for 20X7 to determine the ending balance that should be in the Allowance account at the end of the year: (3.33% × $115,000) = $3,830.
3. Prepare an adjusting entry to bring the Allowance to the appropriate amount determined in step 2. Suppose that, prior to the adjusting entry, the books show a $700 credit balance in the Allowance account at the end of 20X7. Then the adjusting entry needed for 20X7 is ($3,830 – $700), or $3,130, to record the Bad Debt Expense. The journal entry is as follows:

Bad debt expense	3,130	
Allowance for uncollectible accounts		3,130
To bring the Allowance to $3,830, the level justified		
by bad debt experience during past 6 years		

The percentage of accounts receivable method differs from the percentage of sales method in two ways: (1) The percentage is based on the ending accounts receivable balance instead of credit sales, and (2) the dollar amount calculated using the percentage is the appropriate ending balance in the allowance account, not the amount added to the account for the year.

Applying the Allowance Method Using the Aging of Accounts Receivable

We can refine the percentage of accounts receivable approach by considering the composition of the end-of-year accounts receivable based on the age of the debt. This **aging of accounts receivable method** directly incorporates the customers' payment histories. As more time elapses after the sale, collection becomes less likely. The seller may send the buyer a late notice 30 days after the sale and a second reminder after 60 days, make a phone call after 90 days, and place the account with a collection agency after 120 days. Companies that analyze the age of their accounts receivable for credit management purposes naturally incorporate this information into accounting estimates of the allowance for uncollectibles. For example, the $115,000 balance in Accounts Receivable on December 31, 20X7, for Compuport might be aged as shown in Exhibit 6-2. Experience has shown that only 0.1% of receivables less than 30 days old become uncollectible, while 1% of those between 31 and 60 days, 5% of those between 61 and 90 days, and 90% of those over 90 days old are ultimately not collected. We can apply these percentages to the outstanding balance in receivables in each age category to estimate that Compuport will not collect $3,772 of the $115,000 accounts receivable.

This aging schedule in Exhibit 6-2 produces a different target balance for the Allowance account than the balance that resulted from the percentage of accounts receivable method: $3,772 versus $3,830. Therefore, the journal entry is slightly different. Given the same

aging of accounts receivable method

An approach to estimating bad debt expense and uncollectible accounts that considers the composition of year-end accounts receivable based on the age of the debt.

EXHIBIT 6-2

Compuport

Aging of Accounts Receivable, 20X7

Name	Total	1–30 Days	31–60 Days	61–90 Days	More Than 90 Days
Oxwall Tools	$ 20,000	$20,000			
Chicago Castings	10,000	10,000			
Estee	20,000	15,000	$ 5,000		
Sarasota Pipe	22,000		12,000	$10,000	
Ceilcote	4,000			3,000	$1,000
Other accounts (each detailed)	39,000	27,000	8,000	2,000	2,000
Total	$115,000	$72,000	$25,000	$15,000	$3,000
Historical bad debt percentages		0.1%	1%	5%	90%
Bad debt allowance to be provided	$ 3,772 =	$ 72 +	$ 250 +	$ 750 +	$2,700

$700 credit balance in the Allowance account, the journal entry to record the Bad Debt Expense is ($3,772 − $700) = $3,072:

Bad debt expense	3,072	
Allowance for uncollectible accounts.		3,072
To bring the Allowance to $3,772, the level justified by prior experience using the aging method		

Whether a company uses the percentage of sales, percentage of accounts receivable, or aging of accounts receivable method to estimate bad debt expense and the Allowance for Uncollectible Accounts, the subsequent accounting for write-offs is the same—a decrease in Accounts Receivable and a decrease in the Allowance for Uncollectible Accounts.

Bad Debt Recoveries and the Allowance Method

Now let's consider bad debt recoveries under the allowance method. As described on p. 250, we reverse the write-off and then handle the collection as a normal receipt on account. Return to the earlier Compuport example and assume that we wrote off Monterro's account for $500 in February 20X2 and then unexpectedly collected it in January 20X3. The following journal entries produce a complete record of the transactions in Monterro's individual accounts receivable account:

20X1	Accounts receivable, Monterro	500	
	Sales.		500
	To record sales of $500 to Monterro, a specific customer		
Feb. 20X2	Allowance for uncollectible accounts.	500	
	Accounts receivable, Monterro.		500
	To write off uncollectible account of Monterro		
Jan. 20X3	Accounts receivable, Monterro	500	
	Allowance for uncollectible accounts		500
	To reverse February 20X2 write-off of account of Monterro		
	Cash	500	
	Accounts receivable, Monterro.		500
	To record the collection on account		

Note that these 20X2 and 20X3 entries have no effect on the level of bad debt expense estimated for 20X1. At the end of 20X1, using one of the three estimation methods we just examined, Compuport estimated bad debt expense and end-of-period uncollectibles. We do not change these estimates, even if future uncollectibles are greater or less than expected. The errors in estimate affect future periods but do not produce adjustments of prior periods.

INTERPRETING FINANCIAL STATEMENTS

Examine the trade receivables balances of Oracle as of May 31, 2011 and 2010, shown on page 252. Compute the gross accounts receivable on May 31, 2011 and 2010. Did the percentage of accounts receivable deemed uncollectible increase or decrease in 2011?

Answer

Oracle's gross accounts receivable balances were as follows:

2011:	$6,628 million + $372 million = $7,000 million;
2010:	$5,585 million + $305 million = $5,890 million.

In 2010, Oracle deemed ($305 ÷ $5,890) = 5.18% of the accounts receivable to be uncollectible; in 2011 it was ($372 ÷ $7,000) = 5.31%. Therefore, the company expected a slightly higher default percentage in 2011 than in 2010. The change may have resulted from a change in actual experience or may have resulted from the company's belief that the continuing recession would cause default rates to increase.

BUSINESS FIRST

MANAGING ACCOUNTS RECEIVABLE

Years ago, a current ratio (current assets ÷ current liabilities) of 2 to 1 was normal, but increasingly aggressive companies have driven their current ratios below 1. This is not accidental. It happens because these companies view most current assets as money that is not available to help expand the company. To reduce the current ratio, companies are concentrating on reducing current assets, including accounts receivable. However, reductions in accounts receivable must not undermine the company's relationships with its customers.

Cash and receivables management involves careful planning of receipts and disbursements. When you can accurately predict future cash flows, you avoid the need to keep idle cash "just in case." Many companies find their major problem in collecting receivables is disputes over amounts billed. If companies discover disputes when a bill is overdue and lose more time in solving the problem, significant payment delays result. One solution is to provide records on a Web site so customers can see exactly what the selling company has recorded. Early contact between the seller's accounts receivable staff and the buyer's accounts payable staff may promptly resolve disputes. Well-managed companies are glad to work closely with customers and suppliers to complete their business in a timely and accurate manner.

Burlington Northern Santa Fe, the railroad company with nearly $20 billion of revenue and $70 billion of assets, speeded collection by breaking its receivable management into two steps. What it calls "days-to-bill" measures the time between providing service and billing the customer, whereas "days-to-pay" measures the time between billing and collection. To reduce days-to-bill, the company executed technology initiatives to eliminate errors and get the billing process out of human hands. It reduced bills in process on any given day to 15,000 from about 50,000 a decade earlier. By working closely with customers to resolve disputes, the company also cut its collection period significantly; in 2011 the company collected receivables in an average of 19 days compared with more than 30 days a decade earlier.

Sources: R. Myers, "Cash Crop: The 2000 Working Capital Survey," *CFO Magazine*, August 2000; Burlington Northern Santa Fe Corporation 2011 Annual Report.

Assessing the Level of Accounts Receivable

▶▶ **OBJECTIVE 4**

Assess the level of accounts receivable.

In addition to accounting properly for bad debts, managers seek to manage bad debt levels appropriately. The more credit a company provides, the greater the sales but also the greater the chances of bad debts occurring. Management and financial analysts ask questions such as the following: Can the firm increase sales without excessive growth in receivables? Do bad debt expenses rise sharply when sales grow, indicating a reduction in the credit quality of the company's customers? The secret to managing accounts receivable is to allow enough credit to facilitate sales but not allow collections to lag and receivables to build up, as illustrated in the Business First box above.

accounts receivable turnover
Credit sales divided by average accounts receivable for the period during which the sales are made.

One measure of the ability to control receivables is the **accounts receivable turnover**—credit sales divided by the average accounts receivable for the period during which the sales were made:

$$\text{Accounts receivable turnover} = \text{Credit sales} \div \text{Average accounts receivable}$$

This ratio indicates how rapidly collections occur. Suppose you made $100 in credit sales each day, 365 days per year, and you collected cash for every sale 10 days after the sale. In this instance, annual credit sales would be (365 × $100) = $36,500, and average accounts receivable would be (10 days × $100 per day) = $1,000, giving an accounts receivable turnover of ($36,500 ÷ $1,000) = 36.5. If the turnover were 12, it would indicate that, on average, the company collects receivables after 1 month. Higher turnovers indicate that a company collects its receivables quickly—lower turnovers indicate slower collection cycles. Competitive conditions in the industry often drive the ratio. Changes in the ratio provide important guidance concerning changes in the company's policies, changes in the industry's competitive environment, and changes in general economic conditions. For example, a decline in the general level of economic activity will slow collections across the board, and this turnover measure will tend to decline for all firms.

Suppose credit sales for Compuport in 20X8 were $1 million and beginning and ending accounts receivable were $115,000 and $112,000, respectively. The accounts receivable turnover ratio would be computed as:

$$\text{Accounts receivable turnover} = \$1{,}0000{,}000 \div \left[1/2 \times (\$115{,}000 + \$112{,}000)\right] = 8.81$$

We can also assess receivables levels in terms of how many days it takes to collect them. This alternative to the turnover ratio has an appealing direct interpretation. How long does it take on average to get my money after I make a sale? The **days to collect accounts receivable**, or **average collection period**, is 365 divided by the accounts receivable turnover. For our example,

$$\begin{aligned}\text{Days to collect accounts receivable} &= 365 \text{ days} \div \text{Accounts receivable turnover}\\ &= 365 \text{ days} \div 8.81\\ &= 41.4 \text{ days}\end{aligned}$$

days to collect accounts receivable (average collection period)
365 divided by accounts receivable turnover.

When we try to compare accounts receivable turnover or average collection period across companies, we encounter a major problem. Companies do not disclose their credit sales, only total sales. Thus, computations available to the public are generally based on total sales. This means that two factors affect accounts receivable turnover and average collection period, the percentage of sales that are on credit and the credit collection experience. For example, jewelry retailers take twice as long to collect receivables as do bookstores. But this may be due more to the fact that jewelers have a larger percentage of sales on credit rather than a difference in experience in collecting accounts receivable. Nevertheless, managers, who have access to credit sales data, can use these measures to monitor the success of their collection efforts.

Summary Problem for Your Review

PROBLEM

The balance sheet of **VF Corporation**, the large apparel company with brands such as JanSport, Nautica, Wrangler, Lee, and The North Face, showed accounts receivable at December 31, 2011, of $1,120,246,000, net of allowances of $54,010,000. Suppose a large discount chain that owed VF $8 million announced bankruptcy on January 2, 2012. VF managers decided that chances for collection were virtually zero and immediately wrote off the account. Show the accounts receivable and allowance account balances after the write-off, and explain the effect of the write-off on income for the year beginning January 1, 2012.

SOLUTION

The write-off does not affect the net accounts receivable. Nevertheless, both gross accounts receivable and the allowance for doubtful accounts change. Gross accounts receivable were $1,174,256,000 at January 2 and the allowance was $54,010,000, giving a net accounts receivable of $1,120,246,000. When VF takes the write-off, gross accounts receivable decrease by $8 million, but the allowance does also, with the following result:

Gross receivables ($1,174,256,000 − $8,000,000)	$1,166,256,000
Less: Allowance for doubtful accounts	
($54,010,000 − $8,000,000)	46,010,000
Net receivables	$1,120,246,000

There would be no effect on VF Corporation's 2012 net income.

Accounting for and Managing Cash

▸▸OBJECTIVE 5

Manage cash and explain its importance to the company.

All revenues are expected to generate cash at some point. We next discuss the reporting and managing of cash. Many companies combine cash and cash equivalents on their balance sheets. Recall that cash equivalents are highly liquid short-term investments that can easily and quickly be converted into cash. For example, the 2011 balance sheet of Oracle begins with "Cash and cash equivalents … $16,163 million." Oracle describes its cash equivalents as "deposits held at major banks, money market funds, Tier 1 commercial paper, corporate notes, U.S. Treasury obligations, U.S. government agency and government sponsored enterprise obligations, and other securities with original maturities of 90 days or less." Although this is a long complex list of items, they all share one characteristic: Oracle will have cash in hand when the securities mature (within no more than 90 days), or Oracle can easily sell these marketable items to other people and receive cash immediately.

Cash means the same thing to organizations that it does to individuals. It is not just paper money and coins, but it also includes other items that a bank will accept for deposit, including money orders and checks. However, banks do not treat all items accepted for deposit the same. For example, although a bank may add all deposits to the accounts of bank customers on the date received, the bank may not provide the depositor with access to the funds until the check "clears" through the banking system (until the bank receives payment from the check writer's bank). If the check fails to clear because its writer has insufficient funds, the bank deducts the amount of the check from the depositor's account.

A bank employee may talk about a deposit being "credited" to the account of a customer of the bank. A manager of the company making the deposit may be confused by the term "credited." He regarded the deposit as a debit to cash. Why would a banker say the customer's account is "credited"? Deposits in the bank are assets to the depositor but they are a liability to the bank. Suppose a company receives a check from a customer and deposits the check in its bank account. The company debits its Cash account (an asset account) to show the increase in the asset Cash. The offsetting credit might be to Sales if the check came from a sales transaction or to Accounts Receivable if it arose from collection of an account. In contrast, when the bank receives the check, it credits its liability account Deposits to acknowledge the increase in the amount it owes the company depositing the check.

Compensating Balances

compensating balances

The required minimum balances a company must keep on deposit designed to partially compensate the bank for providing a loan to the company.

Frequently, the entire cash balance in a bank account is not available for unrestricted use. Why? Because banks often require companies to maintain **compensating balances**, which are required minimum balances on deposit designed to partially compensate the bank for providing a loan to the company.

Compensating balances increase the effective interest rate that the borrower pays. For a loan of $100,000 at 8% per year, the annual interest will be $8,000. With a 10% compensating balance, the borrower can use only $90,000 of the loan, raising the effective interest rate on the usable funds to ($8,000 ÷ $90,000) = 8.9%.

To ensure that financial statements provide a true picture concerning cash, annual reports must disclose significant compensating balances. For example, a footnote in the annual report of Chiquita Brands International, the distributor of Chiquita and Fresh Express brand produce, disclosed the following: "The company had €5 million ($6 million) … of cash equivalents in a compensating balance arrangement… ." Without such disclosures, analysts and investors might think that a company has more cash available than it really does.

Management of Cash

Cash is usually a small portion of the total assets of a company. Yet, companies manage cash especially carefully. Why? First, although the cash balance may be small at any one time, the flow of cash can be enormous. Weekly receipts and disbursements of cash may be many times as large as the cash balance. Second, because cash is the most liquid asset, it is enticing to thieves and embezzlers. If someone steals a $200 jacket, he or she may be able to get only $40 from selling stolen goods, but if the same person steals $200 cash, he or she will have $200. Third, adequate cash is essential to the smooth functioning of operations. Companies need it for everything from routine purchases to major investments, from purchasing lunch for a visiting business partner to purchasing another company. Finally, because cash itself does not earn income, it is important not to hold excess cash. The treasury department is responsible for managing the levels of cash efficiently and for ensuring that the company deposits unneeded cash in income-generating accounts.

Most organizations have detailed, well-specified procedures for receiving, recording, and disbursing cash. These are part of an organization's **internal control system** (or **internal controls**), which provides checks and balances that ensure all company actions are proper and are consistent with management's goals and objectives. Internal control of cash is especially important because of its vulnerability to theft or embezzlement. Companies should have a policy to immediately deposit cash in a bank account, and they should periodically reconcile the company's books with the bank's records. To **reconcile a bank statement** means to verify that the bank balance and the accounting records are in agreement. The two balances are rarely identical. A company records a deposit when it sends money to the bank and records a payment when it writes a check. The bank, however, records the deposit when it is received, probably a day or two after the company recorded it. The bank typically receives and processes a check written by a company when the payee deposits it and it clears through the banking system, possibly days or weeks after the company issues it. For more on bank reconciliations see Appendix 6.

Additional internal control procedures set up to safeguard cash include the following:

1. Have different individuals receive cash than those who disburse cash.
2. Have different individuals handle cash than those who access accounting records.
3. Immediately record and deposit cash receipts.
4. Make disbursements using serially numbered checks and require proper authorization by someone other than the person writing the check.
5. Reconcile bank accounts monthly.

Why are such internal controls necessary? Consider a person who handles cash and makes entries into the accounting records. That person could take $200 in cash and cover it up by making the following entry in the books:

Operating expenses	200	
Cash		200

Besides guarding against dishonest actions, internal control procedures help ensure that accounting records are accurate. For example, suppose a company writes a check but does not record it in the books. The bank reconciliation will not balance. With serially numbered checks, it is possible to trace items from the checkbook to a bank statement and identify the unrecorded check.

Overview of Internal Control

Companies design internal control systems to protect all their assets, not just cash, and to help managers maintain accurate financial records. For example, we do not want a manager to expose the company to huge speculative losses from unauthorized trading of exotic derivative securities. Here internal controls ensure that managers make decisions consistent with corporate strategy. Nor should a salesperson at a clothing store be able to walk out of the store with holiday gifts for the family without paying for them. Here internal control refers to the protection of firm assets from theft and loss. An electronic tag on a leather coat is an internal control device and so is the requirement that two people have to approve checks over $5,000.

In its broadest sense, internal controls refer to both administrative controls and accounting controls:

▶▶OBJECTIVE 6
Develop and explain internal control procedures.

1. **Administrative controls** are methods and procedures that facilitate management planning and control of operations. They include the formal organizational chart that spells out responsibilities and reporting relationships, as well as departmental budgeting procedures, reports on performance, and procedures for granting credit to customers.

accounting controls

The methods and procedures for authorizing transactions, safeguarding assets, and ensuring the accuracy of the financial records.

2. **Accounting controls** include the methods and procedures for authorizing transactions, safeguarding assets, and ensuring the accuracy of the financial records. Good accounting controls help to maximize efficiency and to minimize waste, errors, and fraud.

We focus on internal accounting controls, which have the following objectives:

1. Authorization. Ensure that managers execute transactions in accordance with management's general or specific intentions.
2. Recording. Ensure that accountants accurately record authorized transactions.
3. Safeguarding. Provide appropriate restrictions on access to assets.
4. Reconciliation. Ensure that accountants regularly verify records against other independently kept records and/or confirm them by physical counts or examinations.
5. Valuation. Ensure that accountants periodically review recorded amounts for impairment of values and necessary write-downs.
6. Operational Efficiency. In addition to preventing errors and fraud, good internal control systems promote efficient actions.

The first three general objectives—authorization, recording, and safeguarding—relate to a system of accountability to prevent errors and irregularities. The fourth and fifth objectives—reconciliation and valuation—aid in detecting errors and irregularities. The last objective recognizes that an internal control system's purpose is as much a positive one (promoting efficiency) as a negative one (preventing errors and fraud).

The Accounting System

An entity's accounting system is a set of records, procedures, internal controls, and equipment that collect, organize, and report the continuous flow of information about the events affecting the entity's financial performance and position. Chapters 3 and 4 provided an overview of the heart of the accounting system—including source documents, journal entries, postings to ledgers, trial balances, adjustments, and financial reports. The system handles repetitive, voluminous transactions, which fall primarily into four categories:

1. Cash disbursements
2. Cash receipts
3. Purchase of goods and services, including employee payroll
4. Sales and delivery of goods and services

The volume of the physical records is often staggering. For example, telephone and credit card companies process millions of transactions daily. Computers and data processing systems make it possible. Well-designed and well-run accounting systems are positive contributions to organizations and the economy. Credit card companies, for example, use sophisticated systems to evaluate transactions on your credit card and may refuse a credit transaction that seems likely to be a fraudulent use of your card by an unauthorized party. Although such refusals sometimes inconvenience a legitimate card holder, they more frequently foil criminal use. Another example is **FedEx Corporation**, which created a dominant position in the overnight delivery market by developing an efficient system for continuously tracking items from pickup to delivery. Finally, **Wal-Mart**'s extraordinary success as a low-price retailer is due in part to its integrated inventory control and ordering system that allows its computers to interact automatically with suppliers, whether they are companies such as **Procter & Gamble** in the United States or **Shenzhen Zuonmens Industrial** in China, to generate orders and reduce delivery times.

Checklist of Internal Control

Good systems of internal control have certain features in common. We have summarized these features in a checklist of internal control—the best practices that managers use to create or evaluate specific procedures for cash, purchases, sales, payroll, and the like.

1. **Reliable Personnel with Clear Responsibilities.** The most important control element is personnel. Incompetent or dishonest individuals undermine any system. Thus, good procedures to hire, train, motivate, and supervise employees are essential. Companies should give individuals authority, responsibility, and duties commensurate with their abilities, interests, experience, and reliability. Employees should be evaluated periodically against their responsibilities.

The wrong, lowest-cost talent is expensive in the long run, not only because of fraud but also because of poor productivity.

Clear responsibilities means having policies and procedures that specify such details as having sales clerks sign sales slips, inspectors sign initial packing slips, and workers sign time cards and requisitions. For example, grocery stores often assign each cashier a separate money tray so management can reward efficiency and easily trace shortages. It has been estimated that retailers lose more than 2% of sales to theft and mistakes—and employee theft causes much larger losses than shoplifting.

2. **Separation of Duties.** Separation of duties makes it hard for one person, acting alone, to defraud the company. This is why large movie theaters have a cashier selling tickets and an usher taking them. The cashier takes in cash, the usher keeps the ticket stubs, and a third person compares the cash with the number of stubs.

However, separation of duties is not foolproof. Suppose the ticket seller pockets the cash and issues a fake ticket. If the ticket seller and usher collude, the usher might accept the fake ticket, destroy it, and allow entry. Separation of duties alone does not prevent such collusive theft. Better supervision of the ticket seller and the usher is the primary method of preventing such collusion. Or, even in the absence of collusion, if the fake ticket is a good forgery, the usher may not be able to detect the ticket seller's theft.

Here are two examples where separation of duties would lead to better internal control:

- In a computer system, a person with custody of assets should not have access to programming or any input of records. In a classic example, a programmer in a bank rounded transactions to the next lower cent instead of the nearest cent and had the computer put the fraction of a cent into his account. A customer amount of $10.057 became $10.05, and the programmer's account received $.007. With millions of transactions, the programmer's account grew very large.

- The same individual should not authorize payments and also sign the check in payment of the bill. Similarly, an individual who handles cash receipts should not have the authority to indicate which accounts receivable should be written off as uncollectible. The latter separation of powers prevents the following embezzlement: A bookkeeper opens the mail, removes a $1,000 check from a customer, and somehow cashes it. To hide the theft, the bookkeeper prepares the following journal entry to write off an amount owed by a customer:

Allowance for bad debts	1,000	
Accounts receivable		1,000

3. **Proper Authorization.** General authorizations are usually written policies, such as definite limits on what price to pay (whether to fly economy or first class), on what price to receive (whether to offer a sales discount), on what credit limits to grant to customers, and so forth. Specific authorizations require that a designated manager explicitly approve deviations from the limits set by general authorization. For example, a senior manager may need to approve overtime or the board of directors may need to approve large expenditures for capital assets.

4. **Adequate Documents.** Companies have a variety of documents and records, from source documents (such as sales invoices and purchase orders) to journals and ledgers. Immediate, complete, and tamper-proof recording of data is the goal. Companies minimize recording errors by optically scanning bar-coded data, by prenumbering and accounting for all source documents, by using devices such as cash registers, and by designing forms for ease of recording. When a merchant offers a customer a free item if a red star comes up on the cash register receipt, it is partly a way to ensure that sales clerks actually ring up the sale and charge the proper amount.

5. **Proper Procedures.** Most organizations use procedure manuals to specify the flow of documents and provide information and instructions to facilitate record keeping. Well-designed routines permit specialization of effort, division of duties, and automatic checks on each step in the routine.

6. **Physical Safeguards.** Companies minimize losses of cash, inventories, and records by using safes, locks, guards, guard dogs, and special lighting and limiting access to sensitive areas. For example, many companies require all visitors to sign a register and wear a name tag, and they may restrict access to certain places by having card scanners that grant admission only to authorized personnel.

BUSINESS FIRST

LACK OF INTERNAL CONTROLS AND THE $346,770 OVERDRAFT

Banks need tight internal controls on their ATMs because they dispense cash. This is important not only to protect cash but also to maintain customer confidence. Think about how bank internal control procedures should stop potential thieves. Automated teller machines (ATMs) require the use of a customer's personal identification number (the "pin" number). As a secondary precaution, ATMs normally restrict withdrawals to a maximum amount, perhaps $300 per day, per account. To keep thieves from randomly guessing pin numbers, computers track "unauthorized" accesses. After several incorrect pin numbers, the ATM keeps the card and notifies the user to reclaim it at the bank.

Given such controls, how could someone take $346,770 from Karen Smith's bank account via ATMs? It all started when she left her bank card in her wallet, which was locked inside her van during a high school football game. Two thieves broke into the van, stole the bank card, and started visiting local ATMs.

Karen's big mistake was storing her pin number on her social security card, which she kept in the stolen wallet. But that alone was not enough. Oregon TelCo Credit Union happened to be updating some computer programs, and its $200 limit per account per day was inoperative—a severe lapse in controls. To access all the funds in Karen's account, the thieves put the card in and withdrew $200, time after time. When one ATM ran out of bills, the thieves visited another on a circuitous, five-county, 500-mile route.

Another internal control should have limited the thieves to the balance in Karen's account, which was much less than $346,770. Something else went wrong. Banks generally do not allow access to deposits made in an ATM until at least the next banking day so the bank can verify the deposit. Unfortunately, the TelCo system was giving immediate credit for deposits made into automated tellers. The thieves "deposited" $820,500 by inserting empty deposit envelopes and recording large deposits on the ATM keypad. They exhausted the cash in the ATMs in their five-county area by 2:30 AM and headed to Reno to buy a new truck and enjoy their wealth.

One piece of TelCo's internal control worked. Hidden cameras photographed the thieves. From the videos, the police were able to identify and arrest the perpetrators, a husband and wife team with more than 20 felony convictions between them.

Sources: "Survey: Level Four Finds ATM Security Is Top Concern for U.S. Consumers," ATMmarketplace.com, February 17, 2009; *New York Times*, February 12, 1995, p. 36.

7. **Vacations and Rotation of Duties.** Rotating employees and requiring them to take vacations ensures at least two employees know how to do each job so an absence due to illness or a sudden resignation does not create major problems. Further, employees are less likely to engage in fraudulent activities if they know that another employee periodically performs their duties and might discover the fraud. A company might accomplish rotation of duties by the common practice of having employees such as receivables and payables clerks occasionally exchange duties. In addition, a receivables clerk may handle accounts from A to C for 3 months, and then be rotated to accounts M to P for 3 months, and so forth.

8. **Independent Check.** All phases of the system should undergo periodic review by outsiders such as independent public accountants or internal auditors. By first evaluating the system of internal control and testing the extent to which employees follow the appropriate procedures, the auditor decides on the likelihood of undetected errors. When internal controls are weak, auditors will examine many transactions to provide reasonable assurance that they discover errors if any exist. If internal controls are strong, the auditor can use a smaller sample to develop confidence in the accuracy of the accounting records.

9. **Cost-Benefit Analysis.** Highly complex systems can strangle people in red tape, impeding instead of promoting efficiency. The right investments in the accounting system can produce huge benefits. No internal control is perfect, but adequate internal control is essential, as illustrated in the Business First box above. The goal is not total prevention of fraud or implementation of operating perfection; instead, the goal is the design of a cost-effective tool that helps achieve efficient operations and minimizes temptation.

Reports on Internal Controls

The Sarbanes-Oxley Act requires U.S. companies to publicly report on the adequacy of their internal controls. In addition, the company's auditor must also issue a report attesting to management's assessment. Oracle reported the following about its internal controls in its 2011 10-K report to the SEC:

> Our management is responsible for establishing and maintaining adequate internal control over financial reporting . . . [W]e conducted an evaluation of the effectiveness of our internal control over financial reporting as of May 31, 2011 . . . . Our internal control over financial reporting includes policies and procedures that provide reasonable assurance regarding the reliability of financial reporting and the preparation of financial statements for external reporting purposes in accordance with U.S. generally accepted accounting principles . . . . The effectiveness of our internal control over financial reporting as of May 31, 2011, has been audited by Ernst & Young LLP, an independent registered public accounting firm.

THE AUDIT COMMITTEE Management's responsibility for the entity's financial statements and internal controls extends upward to the board of directors. In the United States the SEC requires publicly traded companies to have an **audit committee**, which oversees the internal accounting controls, financial statements, and financial affairs of the corporation. While audit committees are not required everywhere, their use is increasing throughout the world. Audit committees provide contact and communication among the board, the external auditors, the internal auditors, the financial executives, and the operating executives.

Audit committee members in the United States must be "outside" board members, that is, board members who are not managers of the company. They are considered to be more independent than the "inside" directors—employees who serve as part of the corporation's management. Oracle has a typical board composition. Of its twelve directors in 2012, four are also members of management (including founder and CEO Lawrence Ellison) and eight are "outside" directors—four executives or retired executives from other companies, two academics, a consultant, and a venture capitalist. Oracle has a combined Finance and Audit Committee that includes only outside directors. It met 17 times in 2011, more than any other board committee.

audit committee
A committee of the board of directors that oversees the internal accounting controls, financial statements, and financial affairs of the corporation.

Highlights to Remember

1 Recognize revenue items at the proper time on the income statement. Companies currently recognize revenue when a sale meets two criteria: (1) the revenue is earned, and (2) the asset received in return is realized or realizable. A proposed new standard may change this to eliminate the formal realization criterion. The new standard would also spread the recognition of revenue over time when products or services are not all transferred to the customer at the point of sale. Nevertheless, the most common situation is one where delivery of the product and recognition of revenue both occur at the point of sale.

2 Account for sales, including sales returns and allowances, sales discounts, and bank credit card sales. At the moment a sale occurs and meets the revenue recognition requirements, a company records the full amount of the sale. This allows the sales revenue for the year to show the full level of economic activity, regardless of whether the sale is on account or for cash. The sale increases an asset account and increases the sales revenue account. For credit sales we also need to maintain a subsidiary ledger that contains detailed records about the individual customers and the amounts owed by each customer. In addition, a company may not collect the total sales it initially recorded. It may offer various discounts or allowances, which it deducts from gross sales to arrive at net sales on the income statement. Sales returns and allowances arise when customers return merchandise or receive discounts due to damaged goods or errors in filling the order. Customers sometimes receive a cash discount as a result of prompt payment. Similarly, bank cards charge a known discount or service fee to compensate the bank for its collection services. One type of discount, a trade discount, is not deducted from gross sales to get net sales but is a reduction in gross sales itself.

3 **Estimate and interpret uncollectible accounts receivable balances.** Potential uncollectible accounts reduce the amount of accounts receivable reported on the balance sheet. Reporting the uncollectible portion of credit sales requires estimates that may be based on a percentage of credit sales, a percentage of accounts receivable, or an aging of accounts receivable. These estimates permit the financial statements to (1) properly reflect asset levels on the balance sheet, and (2) properly match bad debt expense with revenue on the income statement.

4 **Assess the level of accounts receivable.** Companies and analysts use ratios to assess the level of accounts receivable. The accounts receivable turnover ratio and the days to collect accounts receivable both relate the balance in accounts receivable to the level of credit sales during the year. Comparisons with other companies is problematic because companies do not disclose credit sales. However, examination of a particular company over time draws attention to unusual circumstances and possible problems.

5 **Manage cash and explain its importance to the company.** Cash is the fuel that runs a company and must be available to meet obligations as they come due. Managing cash requires vigilance. Protecting cash from theft or loss, adequately planning for the availability of cash as needed, and reconciling the firm's accounting records with the bank's records are just some of the issues management must address.

6 **Develop and explain internal control procedures.** It is tempting to delegate internal control decisions to accountants. However, managers at all levels have a major responsibility for the success of internal controls. To help monitor internal control, boards of directors appoint audit committees, which oversee accounting controls, the financial statements, and general financial affairs of the company. Managers and accountants should recognize that the role of an internal control system is as much a positive one (enhancing efficiency) as a negative one (reducing errors and fraud). A checklist for effective internal control includes the following: (1) reliable personnel with clear responsibilities, (2) separation of duties, (3) proper authorization, (4) adequate documents, (5) proper procedures, (6) physical safeguards, (7) vacations and rotation of duties, (8) independent check, and (9) cost-benefit analysis.

Appendix 6: Bank Reconciliations

> ▶▶ **OBJECTIVE 7**
>
> Prepare a bank reconciliation.

An important part of internal control of cash is to reconcile bank statements. The top part of Exhibit 6-3 shows the cash transactions during January 20X2 for Ruiz Company and its bank, **Bank of America**, in a T-account format. The bottom part of the exhibit lists Ruiz Company's journal entries for its cash transactions. The cash balance on January 31 is an asset (Cash in Bank, a receivable from the bank) of $8,000 on the depositor's books and a liability (Deposits, a payable to the depositor) of $10,980 on the bank's books. The purpose of a bank reconciliation is to explain the differences between the bank's balance and the depositor's balance.

First, let's review how banks use the terms debit and credit. Banks credit the depositor's account for additional deposits because the bank has a liability to the depositor and the bank's credit entry increases its liability. Banks debit the account for checks written by the depositor and paid by the bank because they reduce the bank's liability to the depositor. For example, on January 8, when the bank pays the $2,000 check drawn by the depositor on January 5, the bank's journal entry would be as follows:

Jan. 8	Deposits....................................	2,000	
	Cash....................................		2,000
	To decrease the depositor's account		

Ruiz Company performs a monthly bank reconciliation to make sure the company and the bank have recorded the same deposits and withdrawals. Reconciliations also ensure that the depositor has recorded all fees and charges and any direct deposits recorded by the bank. Bank reconciliations take many forms, but the objective is to explain all differences in the cash balances shown on the bank statement and in the depositor's general ledger at a given date. Exhibit 6-4 is Ruiz's bank reconciliation for January using the data in Exhibit 6-3.

EXHIBIT 6-3

Cash Transactions January 20X2

Ruiz Company Records

Cash in Bank

1/1/X2 Bal.	11,000	1/5	2,000
1/10	4,000	1/15	3,000
1/24	6,000	1/19	5,000
1/31	7,000	1/29	10,000
	28,000		20,000
1/31/X2 Bal.	8,000		

Bank of America Records

Deposits

1/8	2,000	1/1/X2 Bal.	11,000
1/20	3,000	1/11	4,000
1/28	5,000	1/26	6,000
1/31	20[*]		
	10,020		21,000
		1/31/X2 Bal.	10,980

[*]Service charge for printing checks.

Ruiz Company General Journal

Date		Debit	Credit
1/5	Accounts payable	2,000	
	Cash		2,000
	Check No. 1		
1/10	Cash	4,000	
	Accounts receivable		4,000
	Deposit slip No. 1		
1/15	Income taxes payable	3,000	
	Cash		3,000
	Check No. 2		
1/19	Accounts payable	5,000	
	Cash		5,000
	Check No. 3		
1/24	Cash	6,000	
	Accounts receivable		6,000
	Deposit No. 2		
1/29	Accounts payable	10,000	
	Cash		10,000
	Check No. 4		
1/31	Cash	7,000	
	Accounts receivable		7,000
	Deposit No. 3		

EXHIBIT 6-4

Ruiz Company Bank Reconciliation, January 31, 20X2

Balance per books (also called *balance per check register, register balance*)	$ 8,000
Deduct: Bank service charges for January not recorded on the books (also include any other charges by the bank not yet deducted)*	20
Adjusted (corrected) balance per books	$ 7,980
Balance per bank (also called *bank statement balance, statement balance*)	$10,980
Add: Deposits not recorded by bank (also called *unrecorded deposits, deposits in transit*), deposit of 1/31	7,000
Subtotal	$17,980
Deduct: Outstanding checks, check of 1/29	10,000
Adjusted (corrected) balance per bank	$ 7,980

*Note that new entries on the depositor's books are required for all previously unrecorded additions and deductions made to achieve the adjusted balance per books.

This popular reconciliation format has two major sections. The first section begins with the balance in the company's books, that is, the balance in the Cash T-account. The accountant then makes adjustments for items not entered on the books but already entered by the bank. An example is the $20 service charge. The accountant records these adjustments in the records of the company, in this case deducting the $20 service charge. The second section begins with the balance reported by the bank. Adjustments are made for items entered in the company's books but not yet entered by the bank. These items normally adjust automatically as deposits and checks reach the bank for processing. After adjustments, each section should end with identical adjusted cash balances. This is the amount that should appear as Cash in Bank on the depositor's balance sheet.

Ruiz Company must also use a journal entry to record any entries made in the bank's books that also belong in the books of Ruiz. The bank reconciliation indicates that Ruiz must enter the bank service charge in its books:

Jan. 31	Bank service charge expense	20	
	Cash		20
	To record bank charges for printing checks		

Accounting Vocabulary

Assignment Material

Questions

6-1 What is the two-pronged test for revenue recognition under current U.S. GAAP?

6-2 Describe the timing of revenue recognition under current U.S. GAAP for a defense contractor in the United States on a $50 million long-term government contract with work spread evenly over 5 years.

6-3 The proposed joint FASB/IASB standard on revenue recognition has a five-step process for revenue recognition. What are the five steps?

6-4 What will be the major effects on revenue recognition if the proposed joint FASB/IASB standard is adopted?

6-5 Why is measuring revenue for a noncash sale more complex than it is for a cash sale?

6-6 Why is the realizable value of a credit sale often less than that of a cash sale?

6-7 Distinguish between a sales return and a sales allowance.

6-8 Distinguish between a trade discount and a cash discount.

6-9 "Trade discounts should not be recorded by the accountant." Do you agree? Explain.

6-10 "Retailers who accept VISA or MasterCard are foolish because they do not receive the full price for merchandise they sell." Comment.

6-11 Describe the difference between the gross and net methods of accounting for cash discounts.

6-12 What is the cost-benefit relationship in deciding whether to offer credit to customers, and whether to accept bank credit cards?

6-13 Distinguish between the allowance method and the specific write-off method for bad debts.

6-14 "The Allowance for Uncollectible Accounts account has no subsidiary ledger, but the Accounts Receivable account does." Explain.

6-15 "Under the allowance method, there are three popular ways to estimate the bad debt expense for a particular year." Name the three.

6-16 What is meant by "aging of accounts"?

6-17 Distinguish between the percentage of sales approach to applying the allowance method and the aging of accounts receivable approach.

6-18 Explain why a write-off of a bad debt should be reversed if collection occurs at a later date.

6-19 Granting credit has two major impacts on a company, one good and one bad. Describe both.

6-20 What is the relationship between the average collection period and the accounts receivable turnover?

6-21 Describe and give two examples of cash equivalents.

6-22 "A compensating balance essentially increases the interest rate on money borrowed." Explain.

6-23 "Cash is only 3% of our total assets. Therefore, we should not waste time designing systems to manage cash. We should use our time on matters that have a better chance of affecting our profits." Do you agree? Explain.

6-24 It is common in sub shops and pizza parlors around the Baruch College campus to find signs that say "Your purchase is free if the clerk does not give you a receipt" or "Two free lunches if your receipt has a red star." What is management trying to accomplish with these free offers?

6-25 "The cash balance on a company's books should always equal the cash balance shown by its bank." Do you agree? Explain.

6-26 List five internal control procedures used to safeguard cash.

6-27 "If everyone were honest, there would be no need for internal controls to safeguard cash." Do you agree? Explain.

6-28 Distinguish between internal accounting control and internal administrative control.

6-29 "The primary responsibility for internal controls rests with the outside auditors." Do you agree? Explain.

6-30 What is the primary responsibility of the audit committee?

6-31 Prepare a checklist of important factors to consider in judging an internal control system.

6-32 "The most important element of successful control is personnel." Explain.

6-33 What is the essential idea of separation of duties?

6-34 Study Appendix 6. When a company makes a bank deposit, it debits its cash account. Why might a bank say the company's account was "credited"?

MyAccountingLab

Critical Thinking Questions

▶▶ OBJECTIVE 1

6-35 Revenue Recognition

A newly created weekly free newspaper has approached your bank seeking a loan. Although the newspaper is free, it gets significant revenue from advertising. In the first 2 months of operations, it reported profits of $10,000. It has receivables of $70,000 on $200,000 of advertising revenue. Some of the revenue reported for these 2 months included special promotional pricing that gave advertisers 4 months of ads for the price of 2 months. All this promotional revenue was included in the income statement for 2 months. Comment on the reported profit.

▶▶ OBJECTIVE 2

6-36 Bank Credit Cards

If a company accepts bank credit cards, why might it accept specific cards instead of all of them? For example, some retailers accept VISA and MasterCard, but not American Express or Diner's Club, while the exact opposite is true for some restaurants.

▶▶ OBJECTIVE 1

6-37 Criteria for Revenue Recognition

We generally treat revenue as earned when the company delivers merchandise to the customer. At that moment, what additional uncertainty remains about the proper amount of revenue that will ultimately be realized? Would this change under the new revenue recognition criteria under consideration?

▶▶ OBJECTIVE 1

6-38 Revenue Recognition and Evaluation of Sales Staff

Revenue on an accrual-accounting basis is usually recognized as it is earned. Revenue in cash-basis accounting must be received in cash. Is accrual-basis or cash-basis recognition of revenue more relevant for evaluating the performance of a company's sales staff? Why?

Exercises

▶▶ OBJECTIVE 1

6-39 Revenue Recognition

Sierra Logging Company hired Reid Construction Company to build a new bridge across the Brown Trout River. The bridge would extend a logging road into a new stand of timber. The contract called for a payment of $12 million on completion of the bridge. Work was begun in 20X0 and completed in 20X2. Total costs were as follows:

20X0	$ 2 million
20X1	3 million
20X2	5 million
Total	$10 million

1. Suppose the accountant for Reid Construction Company judged that Sierra Logging might not be able to pay the $12 million.
   a. How much revenue would you recognize each year under current revenue-recognition standards?
   b. How much revenue would you recognize each year under the proposed revenue-recognition standards?
2. Suppose Sierra Logging is a subsidiary of a major wood products company. Therefore, receipt of payment on the contract is reasonably certain. How much revenue would you recognize each year under current revenue-recognition standards?

▶▶ OBJECTIVE 2

6-40 Noncash Sales

Suppose Accenture sold software with a retail value of $240,000 to Atlanta Pictures, Inc. Instead of receiving cash, Accenture received 22,000 shares of Atlanta Pictures stock, which at the time was selling for $10 per share. What revenue should Accenture recognize on the sale? Prepare the journal entry for this sale.

▶▶ OBJECTIVE 2

6-41 Net Revenue and Noncash Sales—Auto Dealership

Northend Motors sold a new BMW to Salvador Frezatti. The list price of the new car was $40,000. Mr. Frezatti traded in a 5-year old Audi that has a Blue Book value of $15,000. Northend also offered a 10% trade discount off the list price. So Mr. Frezatti paid cash of $21,000. After getting home, Mr. Frezatti discovered that the BMW had a scratch in the passenger-side door, and Northend offered an allowance of $1,000 to cover the repair.

Prepare a schedule showing both the gross revenue and the net revenue for Northend Motors from this transaction.

6-42 Revenue Recognition, Cash Discounts, and Returns

▶▶ OBJECTIVES 1, 2

Royalton Bookstore ordered 1,000 copies of an introductory physics textbook from **Prentice Hall** on July 17, 20X0. The books were delivered on August 12, at which time a bill was sent requesting payment of $90 per book. However, a 2% discount was allowed if Prentice Hall received payment by September 12. Royalton Bookstore sent the proper payment, which was received by Prentice Hall on September 10. On December 18, Royalton Bookstore returned 60 books to Prentice Hall for a full cash refund.

1. Prepare the journal entries (if any) for Prentice Hall on (a) July 17, (b) August 12, (c) September 10, and (d) December 18. Include appropriate explanations. Assume that Prentice Hall uses the gross method for cash discounts.
2. Suppose this was the only sales transaction in 20X0. Prepare the revenue section of Prentice Hall's income statement.

6-43 Sales Returns and Discounts

▶▶ OBJECTIVE 2

Fresno Fruit Wholesalers had gross sales of $850,000 on credit during the month of March. Sales returns and allowances were $50,000. Cash discounts granted were $35,000 and were accounted for using the gross method.

Prepare an analysis of the impact of these transactions on the balance sheet equation. Also show the journal entries. Prepare a detailed presentation of the revenue section of the income statement. Assume the appropriate amount of receivables was collected.

6-44 Gross and Net Methods for Cash Discounts

▶▶OBJECTIVE 2

Midvale Manufacturing, Incorporated, reported the following in 20X0 ($ in thousands):

Sales	$680
Cash discounts on sales	20

1. Assume that Midvale uses the gross method of accounting for cash discounts.
   a. Prepare the revenue section of the 20X0 income statement.
   b. Prepare journal entries for the initial revenue recognition for 20X0 sales and the collection of accounts receivable. Assume that all sales were on credit and all accounts receivable for 20X0 sales were collected in 20X0. Omit explanations.
2. Assume that Midvale uses the net method of accounting for cash discounts.
   a. Prepare the revenue section of the 20X0 income statement.
   b. Prepare journal entries for the initial revenue recognition for 20X0 sales and the collection of accounts receivable. Assume that all sales were on credit and all accounts receivable for 20X0 sales were collected in 20X0. Omit explanations.
   c. Suppose the customers passed up the $20,000 cash discounts and paid the full $680,000. Prepare the journal entry for the collection of the accounts receivable.

6-45 Cash Discounts Transactions

▶▶ OBJECTIVE 2

Grodahl Electronics is a wholesaler that sells on terms of 2/10, n/30. Suppose it sold video equipment to **Costco** for $600,000 on open account on January 10. Payment (net of cash discount) was received on January 19. By using the balance sheet equation framework, analyze the two transactions for Grodahl Electronics using the gross method for cash discounts. Also prepare journal entries.

6-46 Entries for Cash Discounts and Returns on Sales

▶▶ OBJECTIVE 2

The Walla Walla Wine Company, a wholesaler of Washington state wines, sells on credit terms of 2/10, n/30. It uses the gross method for cash discounts. Consider the following transactions:

June 9	Sales on credit to Westlake Wine Mercantile, $40,000.
June 11	Sales on credit to Marty's Liquors, $15,000.
June 18	Collected from Westlake Wine Mercantile.
June 26	Accepted the return of six cases from Marty's Liquors, $1,000.
July 10	Collected from Marty's Liquors.
July 12	Westlake Wine Mercantile returned some defective wine that it had acquired on June 9 for $100. Walla Walla issued a cash refund immediately.

Prepare journal entries for these transactions. Omit explanations. Assume the full appropriate amounts were exchanged.

OBJECTIVE 2

6-47 Credit Terms, Discounts, and Annual Interest Rates

As the struggling owner of a new restaurant, you suffer from a habitual shortage of cash. Yesterday the following invoices arrived:

Vender	Face Amount	Terms
Hong Fruit & Vegetables	$ 700	n/30
Rose Exterminators	90	EOM
Iowa Meat Supply	850	15, EOM
John's Fisheries	1,000	1/10, n/30
Garcia Equipment	2,000	2/10, n/30

1. Write out the exact meaning of each of the terms.
2. You can borrow cash from the local bank on a 10-, 20-, or 30-day note bearing an annual interest rate of 14%. Should you borrow to take advantage of the cash discounts offered by the last two vendors? Why? Show computations. For interest rate computations, assume a 360-day year.

OBJECTIVE 2

6-48 Accounting for Credit Cards

Michelle's Classic Clothing Store has extended credit to customers on open account. Its average experience for each of the past 3 years has been as follows:

	Cash	Credit	Total
Sales	$500,000	$300,000	$800,000
Bad debt expense	—	5,000	5,000
Administrative expense	—	8,000	8,000

Michelle Lebeck is considering whether to accept bank cards (for example, VISA or MasterCard). She has resisted because she does not want to bear the cost of the service, which would be 4% of gross sales.

The representative of VISA claims that the availability of bank cards would have increased overall sales by at least 10%. Regardless of the level of sales, the new mix of the sales would be 50% bank card and 50% cash.

1. How would a bank card sale of $300 affect the accounting equation? Where would the discount appear on the income statement?
2. Should Lebeck adopt the bank card if sales do not increase? Base your answer solely on the sparse facts given here.
3. Repeat requirement 2, but assume that total sales would increase 10%.

OBJECTIVE 2

6-49 Trade-ins Versus Discounts

Many states base their sales tax on gross sales less any discount. Trade-in allowances are not discounts, so companies cannot deduct them from the sales price for sales tax purposes. Suppose Jit Eap had decided to trade in his old car for a new one with a list price of $32,000. He will pay cash of $20,000 plus sales tax. If he had not traded in a car, the dealer would have offered a discount of 15% of the list price. The sales tax is 7%.

How much of the $12,000 price reduction should be called a discount? How much a trade-in? Mr. Eap wants to pay as little sales tax as legally possible.

OBJECTIVE 3

6-50 Uncollectible Accounts

During 20X1, the Downtown Department Store had credit sales of $900,000. The store manager expects that 2% of the credit sales will never be collected, although no accounts are written off until 10 assorted steps have been taken to attain collection. The 10 steps require a minimum of 14 months.

Assume that during 20X2, specific customers are identified who are never expected to pay $16,000 that they owe from the sales of 20X1. All 10 collection steps have been completed.

1. Show the impact on the balance sheet equation of the preceding transactions in 20X1 and 20X2 under (a) the specific write-off method, and (b) the allowance method. Which method do you prefer? Why?
2. Prepare journal entries for both methods. Omit explanations.

6-51 Specific Write-off Versus Allowance Methods

▶▶ OBJECTIVE 3

The Empire District Electric Company serves customers in the region where the states of Kansas, Missouri, Arkansas, and Oklahoma come together. Empire District uses the allowance method for recognizing uncollectible accounts. The company's January 1, 2012, balance sheet showed accounts receivable of $42,296,000, which was shown net of uncollectible accounts of $1,138,000.

1. Suppose Empire District wrote off a specific uncollectible account for $30,000 on January 2, 2012. Assume this was the only transaction affecting the accounts receivable or allowance accounts on that day. Give the journal entry to record this write-off. What would the balance sheet show for accounts receivable at the end of the day on January 2.
2. Suppose Empire District used the specific write-off method instead of the allowance method for recognizing uncollectible accounts. Give the journal entry to record this write-off. Compute the accounts receivable balance that would be shown on the January 2, 2012, balance sheet.

6-52 Allowance Method and Correcting Entries

▶▶ OBJECTIVE 3

The Good Samaritan Hospital uses the allowance method in accounting for bad debts. A journal entry was made for writing off the accounts of Jane Peterson, Eunice Belmont, and Samuel Goldman. Do you agree with this entry? If not, show the correct entry and the correcting entry.

Bad debt expense	16,205	
Accounts receivable		16,205

6-53 Bad Debts

▶▶ OBJECTIVE 3

Prepare all journal entries for 20X2 concerning the following data for a medical clinic that performs elective laser surgery that corrects vision. Such procedures are not covered by third-party payers such as Blue Cross or Medicare. Consider the following balances of the medical clinic on December 31, 20X1: Gross Receivables from Individual Patients, $250,000 and Allowance for Doubtful Receivables, $50,000, which makes Net Receivables $200,000. During 20X2, total billings to individual patients were $2.5 million. Past experience indicated that 10% of such individual billings would ultimately be uncollectible. Write-offs of receivables during 20X2 were $240,000.

6-54 Bad Debt Allowance

▶▶ OBJECTIVE 3

Kansas Furniture Mart had sales of $1,150,000 during 20X1, including $600,000 of sales on credit. Balances on December 31, 20X0, were Accounts Receivable, $120,000, and Allowance for Bad Debts, $10,000. For 20X1 collections of accounts receivable were $560,000. Bad debt expense was estimated at 2% of credit sales, as in previous years. Write-offs of bad debts during 20X1 were $9,000.

1. Prepare journal entries concerning the preceding information for 20X1.
2. Show the ending balances of the balance sheet accounts on December 31, 20X1.
3. Based on the given data, would you advise Eleanor Sarkowski, the president of the store, that the 2% estimated bad debt rate appears adequate?

6-55 Bad Debt Recoveries

▶▶ OBJECTIVE 3

Southcenter Variety Store has many accounts receivable. The Southcenter balance sheet, December 31, 20X1, showed Accounts Receivable, $950,000, and Allowance for Uncollectible Accounts, $40,000. In early 20X2, write-offs of customer accounts of $31,000 were made. In late 20X2, a customer, whose $10,000 debt had been written off earlier, won a $1 million sweepstakes cash prize. The buyer immediately remitted $10,000 to Southcenter. The store welcomed the purchaser's money and return to high credit standing.

Prepare the journal entries for the $31,000 write-off in early 20X2 and the $10,000 receipt in late 20X2.

▸▸ OBJECTIVE 3

6-56 Subsidiary Ledger

A custom furniture company made credit sales of $840,000 in 20X1 to 100 customers: Ferrara, $5,000; Cerruti, $7,000; others, $828,000. Total collections during 20X1 were $760,000 including $5,000 from Cerruti, but nothing was collected from Ferrara. At the end of 20X1, an allowance for uncollectible accounts was provided of 2.5% of credit sales. 20X1 is the company's first year of operations.

1. Set up general ledger accounts for Accounts Receivable, Allowance for Uncollectible Accounts, and Bad Debt Expense plus a subsidiary ledger for Accounts Receivable. The subsidiary ledger should consist of two individual accounts plus a third account called Others. Post the entries for 20X1. Prepare a statement of the ending balances of the individual accounts receivable to show that they reconcile with the general ledger account.
2. On March 24, 20X2, the Ferrara account was written off. Give the journal entry.

▸▸ OBJECTIVE 4

6-57 Accounts Receivable Turnover and Average Collection Period

Vulcan Materials Company, the nation's largest producer of construction aggregates, is headquartered in Birmingham, Alabama. The company had 2011 sales of $2,565 million. Beginning and ending net accounts receivable as of December 31, 2010 and 2011 were $261 million and $299 million, respectively.

Compute Vulcan's accounts receivable turnover and average collection period for the fiscal year. Assume all sales are on open account.

▸▸ OBJECTIVE 4

6-58 Accounts Receivable Ratios

Bayer Group, the German chemical and pharmaceutical company, is the third largest pharmaceutical company in the world. It had the following results in 2009–2011 (in millions of euros):

	2009	2010	2011
Sales	€31,168	€35,088	€36,528
Ending accounts receivable	€ 6,106	€ 6,668	€ 7,061

Compute the accounts receivable turnover and the average collection period for 2010 and 2011. Did Bayer's ratios improve or decline in 2011 compared with 2010? Assume all sales are on credit.

▸▸ OBJECTIVE 5

6-59 Compensating Balances

Morneau Company borrowed $200,000 from **Citibank** at 8% interest. The loan agreement stated that a compensating balance of $25,000 must be kept in the Morneau checking account at Citibank. The total Morneau cash balance at the end of the year was $45,000.

1. How much usable cash did Morneau Company receive for its $200,000 loan?
2. What was the real interest rate paid by Morneau?
3. Prepare a footnote for the annual report of Morneau Company explaining the compensating balance.

▸▸ OBJECTIVE 6

6-60 Internal Control Weaknesses

Identify the internal control weaknesses in each of the following situations, and indicate what change or changes you would recommend to eliminate the weaknesses:

1. The internal audit staff of Wichita Aerospace, Inc., reports to the controller. The company conducts internal audits only when a department manager requests one, and audit reports are confidential documents prepared exclusively for the manager. The company does not allow internal auditors to talk to the external auditors.
2. Liz Paltrow, president of Southwestern State Bank, a small-town Wyoming bank, wants to expand the size of her bank. She hired Fred Gladstone to begin a foreign loan department. Gladstone had previously worked in the international department of a London bank. Paltrow told him to consult with her on any large loans, but she never specified exactly what was meant by "large." At the end of Gladstone's first year, Paltrow was surprised and pleased by Gladstone's results. Although he had made several loans larger than any made by other

sections of the bank and had not consulted with her on any of them, Paltrow hesitated to say anything because the financial results were so good. She certainly did not want to upset the person most responsible for the bank's excellent growth in earnings.

3. Isabelle Reed is in charge of purchasing and receiving watches for Import Jewelry, Inc., a chain of jewelry stores. Reed places orders, fills out receiving documents when the watches are delivered, and authorizes payment to suppliers. According to Import Jewelry's procedures manual, Reed's activities should be reviewed by a purchasing supervisor. However, to save money, the supervisor was not replaced when she resigned 3 years ago. No one seems to miss the supervisor.

6-61 Assignment of Duties

▶▶ OBJECTIVE 6

Fleetfoot Wholesalers is a distributor of several popular lines of sports and leisure shoes. It purchases merchandise from several suppliers and sells to hundreds of retail stores. Here is a partial list of the company's necessary office routines:

1. Verifying and comparing related purchase documents: purchase orders, purchase invoices, receiving reports, etc.
2. Preparing vouchers for cash disbursements and attaching supporting purchase documents
3. Signing vouchers to authorize payment (after examining vouchers with attached documents)
4. Preparing checks to pay for the purchases
5. Signing checks (after examining voucher authorization and supporting documents)
6. Mailing checks
7. Daily sorting of incoming mail into items that contain money and items that do not
8. Distributing the mail: money to cashier, reports of money received to accounting department, and remainder to various appropriate offices
9. Making daily bank deposits
10. Reconciling monthly bank statements

The company's chief financial officer has decided that no more than five people will handle all these routines, including himself as necessary.

Prepare a chart to show how these operations could be assigned to the five employees, including the chief financial officer. Use a row for each of the numbered routines and a column for each employee: Financial Officer, A, B, C, D. Place a check mark for each row in one or more of the columns. Observe the rules of the textbook checklist for internal control, especially separation of duties.

6-62 Simple Bank Reconciliation

▶▶ OBJECTIVE 7

Study Appendix 6. East End Hospital has a bank account. Consider the following information:

a. Balances as of July 31: per books, $50,000; per bank statement, $35,860.
b. Cash receipts of July 31 amounting to $9,000 were recorded and then deposited in the bank's night depository. The bank did not include this deposit on its July statement.
c. The bank statement included service charges of $140.
d. Patients had given the hospital some bad checks amounting to $11,000. The bank marked them NSF and returned them with the bank statement after charging the hospital for the $11,000. The hospital had made no entry for the return of these checks.
e. The hospital's outstanding checks amounted to $6,000.

Required

1. Prepare a bank reconciliation as of July 31.
2. Prepare the hospital journal entries required by the given information.

Problems

MyAccountingLab

6-63 Revenue Recognition on Long-term Contracts

▶▶ OBJECTIVE 1

On January 2, 20X0, Kowalski Construction Company signed a contract to provide paved roads to a new housing development. The project will last 2 years, and the total payment will be $4 million, to be paid at completion of the project. Kowalski's budgeted cost for the project is $3 million. Work will progress evenly over the 2 years. On December 31, 20X0, Kowalski's accountant asks you what revenue should be recorded for 20X0. Costs of $1.5 million were incurred during 20X0.

1. Suppose Kowalski uses the percentage of completion method. What revenue should be recorded for 20X0? What profit is recognized in 20X0?
2. Suppose Kowalski uses the completed contract method. What revenue should be recorded for 20X0? What profit is recognized in 20X0?
3. Assume that the contract was with a large corporation that is very stable. Under current U.S. GAAP, which method should Kowalski use?
4. Assume that the contract is with a small developer and the economy has taken a downturn during 20X0, making payment of the final contract price highly uncertain. However, Kowalski Company still believes it will receive payment and continues working on the project. Under current U.S. GAAP, which method should Kowalski use?
5. How would your answers to requirement 4 change if Kowalski were reporting under IFRS rather than U.S. GAAP?

▶▶ OBJECTIVE 2

6-64 Bank Cards

VISA and MasterCard are used to pay for a large percentage of retail purchases. The financial arrangements are similar for both bank cards. A news story provided the following example.

Assume that a cardholder charges $500 for a dress to her VISA card. The merchant would then deposit the sales draft with its bank, which immediately credits $500 less a small transaction fee (say 4% of the sale) to the merchant's account. The bank that issued the customer her card then pays the merchant's bank $500 less a 3% transaction fee, allowing the merchant's bank a 1% profit on the transaction.

1. Prepare the journal entry for the sale by the merchant.
2. Prepare the journal entries for the merchant's bank concerning (a) the merchant's deposit, and (b) the collection from the customer's bank that issued the card.
3. Prepare the journal entry for the customer's bank that issued the card.
4. The national losses from bad debts for bank cards have recently been about 5% of the total billings to cardholders. If so, how can the banks justify providing this service if their revenue from processing is typically 3%–4%?

▶▶ OBJECTIVE 2

6-65 Sales Returns and Allowances

Crown Crafts, Inc., produces children's products such as infant and toddler bedding, bibs, soft goods, and accessories. Major customers include Wal-Mart and Target. A footnote to the company's 2011 financial statements states that it records sales when goods are shipped to customers, and these sales are reported net of allowances for estimated returns and allowances. The first line of Crown Crafts' income statement was (in thousands) "Net sales … $89,971."

1. Suppose customer returns in 2011 were 2.5% of gross sales and sales allowances were 1.5% of gross sales. Assume that the company also gave customers cash discounts of $1,240,000. Compute the amount of gross sales. Assume the gross method for accounting for cash discounts. Round to the nearest thousand.
2. Crown Crafts had only one line for net sales on its income statement. Prepare a more detailed presentation of sales, beginning with gross sales and ending with net sales.

▶▶ OBJECTIVE 2

6-66 Gross and Net Methods for Cash Discounts

Belkin Company offers a cash discount of 2% if payment is received within 15 days, with full payment due in 30 days. Belkin sold some merchandise to Alvarez Company for $10,000 on June 1.

1. Suppose that on June 14, Alvarez Company paid the appropriate amount to Belkin.
   a. Prepare Belkin Company's journal entries on June 1 and June 14 assuming that Belkin used the gross method to account for cash discounts.
   b. Prepare Belkin Company's journal entries on June 1 and June 14 assuming that Belkin used the net method to account for cash discounts.
2. Suppose instead, that on June 30 Alvarez Company paid the appropriate amount to Belkin.
   a. Prepare Belkin Company's journal entries on June 1 and June 30 assuming that Belkin used the gross method to account for cash discounts.
   b. Prepare Belkin Company's journal entries on June 1 and June 30 assuming that Belkin used the net method to account for cash discounts.

6-67 Allowance for Credit Losses

▶▶ OBJECTIVE 3

Tompkins Financial Corporation, a multibank holding company headquartered in Ithaca, New York, reported the following changes in the company's Allowance for Loan and Lease Losses account as of December 31, 2011 ($ in thousands):

	2011
Reserve at beginning of year	$27,832
Provisions charged to operations	8,945
Recoveries on loans and leases	1,048
Loans and leases charged off	(10,232)
Reserve at end of year	$27,593

1. Terminology in bank financial statements sometimes differs slightly from that in statements of industrial companies. Explain what is meant by "allowance for loan and lease losses," "provisions charged to operations," and "loans and leases charged off."
2. Prepare the 2011 journal entries to record the writing off of specific credit losses, the recovery of previously written-off credit losses, and the charge for credit losses against 2011 income. Omit explanations.
3. Suppose the bank analyzed its loans at the end of 2011 and decided that an allowance for loan and lease losses equal to $30 million was required. Compute the provision that would be charged in 2011.
4. The bank had income before income taxes of $51,923,000 in 2011. Compute the income before income taxes if the reserve for loan and lease losses at the end of 2011 had been $30 million.

6-68 Aging of Accounts

▶▶ OBJECTIVE 3

Consider the following analysis of Accounts Receivable, February 28, 20X0:

Name of Customer	Total	Remarks
Akita Nurseries	$ 25,000	20% over 90 days,
		80% 61–90 days
Michael's Landscaping	8,000	75% 31–60 days,
		25% under 30 days
Rose's Garden Supply	12,000	60% 61–90 days,
		40% 31–60 days
Loring Farm	20,000	All under 30 days
Hjortshoj Florists	4,000	25% 61–90 days,
		75% under 30 days
Other accounts (each detailed)	80,000	50% under 30 days,
		30% 31–60 days,
		15% 61–90 days,
		5% over 90 days
Total	$149,000	

Prepare an aging schedule, classifying ages into four categories: 1–30 days, 31–60 days, 61–90 days, and over 90 days. Assume that the prospective bad debt percentages for each category are .2%, .8%, 10%, and 85%, respectively. What is the ending balance in Allowance for Uncollectible Accounts?

▶▶ OBJECTIVE 3

6-69 Percentage of Ending Accounts Receivable

Consider the following data:

	Accounts Receivable at End of Year	Accounts Receivable Deemed Uncollectible and Written Off During Subsequent Years
20X1	$216,000	$ 8,000
20X2	170,000	7,572
20X3	195,000	7,000
20X4	230,000	10,300
20X5	275,000	13,000
20X6	240,000	9,820

The unadjusted credit balance in Allowance for Uncollectible Accounts at December 31, 20X7, is $600. By using the percentage of ending accounts receivable method, prepare an adjusting entry to bring Allowance for Uncollectible Accounts to the appropriate amount at December 31, 20X7, when the Accounts Receivable balance is $250,000. Base your estimate of the percentage on the actual loss experience in the prior 6 years. Assume that all write-offs occur before the end of the year following the sale.

▶▶ OBJECTIVE 3

6-70 Estimates of Uncollectible Accounts

Ramsey Company has made an analysis of its sales and accounts receivable for the past 5 years. Assume that all accounts written off in a year related to sales of the preceding year and were part of the accounts receivable at the end of that year. That is, no account is written off before the end of the year of the sale, and all accounts remaining unpaid are written off before the end of the year following the sale. The analysis showed the following:

	Sales	Ending Accounts Receivable	Bad Debts Written Off During the Year
20X1	$680,000	$ 90,000	$12,000
20X2	750,000	97,000	15,500
20X3	750,000	103,000	14,000
20X4	850,000	114,000	16,500
20X5	840,000	110,000	17,630

The balance in Allowance for Uncollectible Accounts on December 31, 20X4, was $16,100. Use all the relevant data above in answering the following questions.

1. Determine the bad debt expense for 20X5 and the balance of the Allowance for Uncollectible Accounts for December 31, 20X5, using the percentage of sales method.
2. Repeat requirement 1 using the percentage of ending accounts receivable method.

▶▶ OBJECTIVE 3

6-71 Percentage of Sales and Percentage of Ending Accounts Receivable

Cottonwood Equipment Company had credit sales of $7 million during 20X0. Most customers paid promptly (within 30 days), but a few took longer; an average of 1.1% of credit sales were never paid. On December 31, 20X0, accounts receivable were $480,000. The Allowance for Bad Debts account, before any recognition of 20X0 bad debts, had a $1,200 debit balance.

Cottonwood produces and sells mountaineering equipment and other outdoor gear. Most of the sales (about 80%) come in the period of March through August; the other 20% is spread almost evenly over the other 6 months. Over the last 6 years, an average of 17% of the December 31 balance in accounts receivable has not been collected.

1. Suppose Cottonwood Equipment uses the percentage of sales method to calculate an allowance for bad debts. Present the accounts receivable and allowance accounts as they should appear on the December 31, 20X0, balance sheet. Give the journal entry required to recognize the bad debt expense for 20X0.

2. Repeat requirement 1, except assume that Cottonwood Equipment uses the percentage of ending accounts receivable method.
3. Which method do you prefer? Why?

6-72 Student Loans

▶▶ OBJECTIVE 3

The 2011 annual report of the University of Washington includes information about its receivables from student loans in a footnote to the financial statements ($ in thousands):

	2011	2010
Student loans	$78,876	$79,643
Less: Allowances	(9,207)	(9,136)
Total, net	$69,669	$70,507

1. Compare the quality of the loans outstanding at the end of 2011 with the quality of those outstanding at the end of 2010.
2. Suppose the university had granted $500,000 of additional loans before the end of 2011. Using the allowance method, which accounts would be affected by the additional loans and by how much? Use the bad debt percentage for loans outstanding at the end of 2011.

6-73 Discounts and Doubtful Items

▶▶ OBJECTIVE 3

Eli Lilly, a major pharmaceutical company, includes the following in its December 31, 2011, balance sheet ($ amounts in millions):

Accounts receivable, net of allowances of $110.1	$3,597.7

1. Compute the ratio of the allowance for doubtful items to gross accounts receivable for December 31, 2011. In 2009, this ratio was 3.4%. What are some possible reasons for the changes in this ratio?
2. Independent of the actual balances, prepare a journal entry to write off an uncollectible account of $210,000 on January 2, 2011.

6-74 Uncollectible Accounts

▶▶ OBJECTIVE 3

Google Inc., is a global technology company that has been an innovative leader in Web search. Its balance sheet on December 31, 2011, included the following data ($ in millions):

Accounts receivable, net of allowance of $133	$5,427

1. The company uses the allowance method for accounting for bad debts. The company added $214 million to the allowance during the year ending December 31, 2011. Write-offs of uncollectible accounts were $182 million. Show (a) the impact on the balance sheet equation of these transactions, and (b) the journal entries.
2. Calculate the allowance balance on December 31, 2010.
3. Suppose Google had used the specific write-off method for accounting for bad debts. By using the same information as in requirement 1, show (a) the impact on the balance sheet equation, and (b) the journal entry.
4. How would these Google balance sheet amounts on December 31, 2011, have been affected if the specific write-off method had been used up to that date? Be specific.

6-75 Uncollectible Accounts

▶▶ OBJECTIVE 3

Oracle is the world's largest supplier of database software. Its balance sheet included the following presentation:

	May 31	
	2011	**2010**
	($ in millions)	
Trade receivables, net of allowance for doubtful accounts of $372 and $305 as of May 31, 2011 and 2010, respectively	$6,628	$5,585

During 2011, Oracle added $180 million to its allowance for doubtful accounts.

1. Calculate the write-offs of uncollectible accounts.
2. Show the impact on the balance sheet equation of these transactions.
3. Give the journal entries needed to record these transactions.

▶▶ **OBJECTIVE 3**

6-76 Negative Balance in Allowance for Bad Debts Account
This problem is an extension of Exercise 6-54. Only the amount of write-off of bad debts is different.

Kansas Furniture Mart had sales of $1,150,000 during 20X1, including $600,000 of sales on credit. Balances on December 31, 20X0, were Accounts Receivable, $120,000, and Allowance for Bad Debts, $10,000. For 20X1 collections of accounts receivable were $560,000. Bad debt expense was estimated at 2% of credit sales, as in previous years. Suppose a recession hit during 20X1 and the write-off of bad debts was $25,000, which is much higher than expected.

1. What is the balance in the Allowance for Bad Debts account at the end of 20X1? If left unadjusted, how would this affect the Net Accounts Receivable? Does this seem reasonable?
2. What should Kansas Furniture Mart do to rectify this situation?

▶▶ **OBJECTIVE 4**

6-77 Average Collection Period
Consider the following:

	20X3	20X2	20X1
Sales	$2,000,000	$2,500,000	$2,400,000
	December 31		
	20X3	20X2	20X1
Accounts receivable	$ 170,000	$ 190,000	$ 180,000

Of the total sales, 70% are on account.

Compute the days to collect accounts receivable for the years 20X2 and 20X3. Comment on the results.

▶▶ **OBJECTIVE 4**

6-78 Classic Case of Sales, Accounts Receivable, and Ethics
Writing in *Corporate Cashflow*, Howard Schillit described how the market value of Comptronix fell from $238 million to $67 million in a few hours when it was revealed that management had "cooked the books." Comptronix provided contract manufacturing services to makers of electronic equipment. Its 1991 financial results looked strong.

However, the relationship between sales and accounts receivable sent signals to knowledgeable analysts.

	1991	1990	Change
Sales	$102.0 million	$70.2 million	+45%
Accounts receivable	12.6 million	12.0 million	+ 5%
Accounts receivable turnover	8.1	5.9	

1. Discuss the relationship that you would expect between sales and accounts receivable in a normal situation.
2. What unethical actions might cause sales to grow so much faster than accounts receivable? What unethical actions might cause the opposite, that is, for accounts receivable to grow faster than sales?
3. What is the most likely type of "cooking the books" that occurred at Comptronix?

▶▶ **OBJECTIVE 5**

6-79 Managing Cash
Volvo Group, the Swedish auto company, had 2011 sales of SEK310 billion, where SEK stands for Swedish kroner. Among the SEK353 billion in total assets on its balance sheet were cash and cash equivalents of SEK30 billion. The company has many internal controls related to cash.

A new employee in the internal audit department asked why so much effort was put into monitoring cash when it was less than 9% of total assets. Prepare an answer for the new employee.

6-80 Audit Committee Role

▶▶ OBJECTIVE 6

In a recent court decision, a U.S. corporation was required to delegate certain responsibilities to its audit committee. The audit committee was required to do the following:

a. Consult with its independent auditors before deciding any significant or material accounting question or policy.
b. Retain independent auditors to perform quarterly reviews of all financial statements prior to public issuance.
c. Conduct internal audits, with personnel reporting directly to the audit committee (internal auditors must report quarterly to the audit committee).
d. Retain or dismiss independent and internal auditors.
e. Consult with the independent auditors on their quarterly reviews of financial statements.
f. Review all monthly corporate and division financial statements and the auditor's management letter.
g. Receive quarterly reports from independent auditors on internal control deficiencies.
h. Review and approve all reports to shareholders and the SEC before dissemination.

The court also ruled that the audit committee must be composed of at least three outside directors who have no business dealings with the firm other than directors' fees and expense reimbursements.

1. Prepare a partial corporation organization chart to depict these requirements. Use boxes only for Audit Committee, Independent Auditors, Internal Auditing, Finance Vice President, and Board of Directors. Connect the appropriate boxes with lines: solid lines for direct responsibility and dashed lines for information and communications. Place letters on these lines to correspond to the requirements specified by the court decision.
2. Identify the main elements of the chapter checklist of internal control that seem most relevant to this system design.

6-81 Embezzlement of Cash Receipts

▶▶ OBJECTIVE 6

Rapid Repair Company is a small auto body shop. It has only a few employees.

The owner of Rapid Repair, who is also its president and general manager, makes daily deposits of customer checks in the company bank account and writes all checks issued by the company. The president also reconciles the monthly bank statement with the books when the bank statement is received in the mail.

The assistant to Rapid Repair's president renders secretarial services, which include taking dictation, typing letters, and processing all mail, both incoming and outgoing. Each day the assistant opens the incoming mail and gives the president the checks received from customers. The vouchers attached to the checks are separated by the assistant and sent to the bookkeeper, along with any other remittance advices that have been enclosed with the checks.

The bookkeeper makes prompt entries to credit customers' accounts for their remittances. From these accounts, the bookkeeper prepares monthly statements for mailing to customers.

Other employees include mechanics and other auto repair personnel.

For the thefts described next, explain briefly how each could have been concealed and what precautions you would recommend for forestalling the theft and its concealment:

1. The president's assistant takes some customers' checks, forges the company's endorsements, deposits the checks in a personal bank account, and destroys the check vouchers and any other remittance advices that have accompanied these checks.
2. The same action is taken as in requirement 1, except that the vouchers and other remittance advices are sent intact to the bookkeeper.

6-82 Film Processing

▶▶ OBJECTIVE 6

Write no more than one page about the possible areas where internal controls should be instituted in the following business described briefly. Keep in mind the size of the business, and do not suggest controls of a type impossible to set up in a firm of this sort. Make any reasonable assumptions about management duties and policies not expressly described.

You have a film-developing service in Houston, with 12 employees driving their own cars 6 days a week to contact about 40 stores each, where film is left to be picked up and developed. Drivers bring film in one day and return the processed film the second or third day. Store managers pay the driver in cash the amount customers pay for the developing, less a percentage for the stores' work as agents. The driver then turns this cash in to the Houston office, where all film is developed and books are kept. Between 6 and 10 employees work at the Houston office, depending on the volume of work. You run the office and have one full-time accounting-clerical employee. Route drivers are paid monthly by miles of route covered.

▶▶ OBJECTIVE 6

6-83 Casino Skimming

An article in the *Wall Street Journal* reported that about $7 million in quarters disappeared from the slot machines of four casinos of **Argent Corporation** in an 18-month period. The coins weighed nearly 150 tons, and the odds against such a payout to players of the slot machines is 1 in 3,875,000,000,000,000,000,000,000,000,000,000,000,000,000,000,000,000—an extremely unlikely event, to say the least. The disappearance was part of the biggest known skim operation ever. Skimming is taking a portion of gambling revenues before they can be counted for tax purposes.

Internal control is especially important in casinos. Meters in the slot machines record the winnings paid to customers. Coins are taken immediately to the slot counting room when machines are emptied. In the counting rooms, coins are weighed, and a portion is returned to the change booths.

What items in the chapter checklist of internal control seem especially important concerning slot machine operations? How could the money from slot machine operations have been stolen in such large amounts?

▶▶ OBJECTIVE 6

6-84 Employee Dishonesty

Consider the following true newspaper reports of dishonesty:

1. At a small manufacturer, supervisors had access to time cards and handed out W-2 forms each year. The supervisors pocketed $80,000 a year in the paychecks for phantom workers.
2. A manager at a busy branch office of a copying service had a receipt book of his own. Jobs of $200 and $300 were common. The manager stole cash by simply giving customers a receipt from his book instead of one of the company's numbered forms.
3. A purchasing agent received tiny kickbacks on buttons, zippers, and other trims used at a successful dress company. The agent got rich, and the company was overcharged $10 million.

Specify what control or controls would have helped avoid each of the listed situations.

▶▶ OBJECTIVE 6

6-85 Internal Control Weaknesses

Identify the internal control weaknesses in each of the following situations.

1. Richard Tuiamu, a football star at the local university, was hired by football supporter R.U. Shore to work in the accounting department of Shore Machining during summer vacation. Providing summer jobs is one way Shore supports the team. After a week of training, Tuiamu opened the mail containing checks from customers, recorded the payment in the books, and prepared the bank deposit slip.
2. Juan Vargas manages a local franchise of a major 24-hour convenience store. Vargas brags that he keeps labor costs well below the average for such stores by operating with only one clerk. He has not granted a pay increase in 4 years. He loses a lot of clerks, but he can find replacements.
3. Clarence Opheim operates an **Exxon** service station. Because it takes much extra time for attendants to walk from the gas pumps to the inside cash register, Opheim placed a locked cash box next to the pumps and gave each attendant a key. Cash and credit card slips are placed in the cash box. Each day the amounts are counted and entered in total into the cash register.
4. Lazlo Galetta trusts his employees. The former manager purchased fidelity bonds on employees who handle cash. Galetta decided that such bonds showed a lack of trust, so he ceased purchasing them. Besides, the money saved helped Galetta meet his budget for the year.

6-86 Cooking the Books

▶▶ OBJECTIVE 6

In *The Accounting Wars*, author Mark Stevens presents a chapter on "Book Cooking, Number Juggling, and Other Tricks of the Trade." He quotes Glen Perry, a former chief accountant of the SEC's Enforcement Division: "Companies play games with their financial reports for any number of reasons, the most common being the intense pressure on corporate management to produce an unbroken stream of increasing earnings reports." Stevens then lists Perry's "terrible 10 of accounting frauds—ploys used to misrepresent corporate financial statements." Among the ten are the following:

1. Recognition of revenues before they are realized
2. Recognition of rentals to customers as sales
3. Improper cutoffs at year-end
4. Creation of fraudulent year-end transactions to boost earnings
5. Failure to recognize losses through write-offs and allowances
6. Inconsistent accounting practices without disclosures
7. Capitalization or improper deferral of expenses

Suppose you were a division manager in a major corporation. Give a brief, specific example of each of the 7 methods.

6-87 Bank Reconciliation

▶▶ OBJECTIVE 7

Study Appendix 6. The City of Rockport has a checking account with First Bank. The city's cash balance on February 28, 20X1, was $30,000. The deposit balance on the bank's books on February 28, 20X1, was also $30,000. The following transactions occurred during March.

Date	Check Number	Amount	Explanation
3/1	261	$11,500	Payment of previously billed consulting fee
3/6	262	9,500	Payment of accounts payable
3/10		12,000	Collection of taxes receivable
3/14	263	15,000	Acquisition of equipment for cash
3/17		16,000	Collection of license fees receivable
3/28	264	8,000	Payment of accounts payable
3/30	265	21,000	Payment of interest on municipal bonds
3/31		25,000	Collection of taxes receivable

All cash receipts are deposited via a night depository system after the close of the municipal business day. Therefore, the receipts are not recorded by the bank until the succeeding day.

On March 31, the bank charged the City of Rockport $100 for miscellaneous bank services.

1. Prepare the journal entries on the bank's books for check 262 and the deposit of March 10.
2. Prepare the journal entries for all March transactions on the books of the City of Rockport.
3. Post all transactions for March to T-accounts for the City's Cash in Bank account and the bank's Deposit account. Assume only checks 261 to 263 have been presented to the bank in March, each taking 4 days to clear the bank's records.
4. Prepare a bank reconciliation for the City of Rockport, March 31, 20X1. The final three City of Rockport transactions of March had not affected the bank's records as of March 31. What adjusting entry in the books of the City of Rockport is required on March 31?
5. What would be the cash balance shown on the balance sheet of the City of Rockport on March 31, 20X1?

6-88 Ethics and Bank Reconciliations

▶▶ OBJECTIVE 7

Study Appendix 6. The Farmington Chamber of Commerce recently hired you as an accounting assistant. On assuming your position on September 15, one of your first tasks was to reconcile the August bank statement. Your immediate supervisor, Ms. Robitelli, had been in charge of nearly all accounting tasks, including paying bills, preparing the payroll, and recording all transactions in the books. She has been very helpful to you, providing assistance on all the tasks she has asked you to do. The reconciliation was no different. Without assistance, you were able to locate the following information from the bank statement and the Chamber's books:

Balance per books	$16,610
Balance per bank statement	16,600
Bank service charges	30
NSF check returned	3,000
Deposits in transit	4,600
Outstanding checks	9,850

You also found a deposit on the bank statement of $3,300 that was incorrectly recorded as $3,030 on the Chamber's books.

When you could not reconcile the book and bank balances, you asked Ms. Robitelli for help. She responded that an additional $2,500 deposit was in transit.

1. Assume the information you obtained without Ms. Robitelli's help is accurate and complete. Prepare the August bank reconciliation with the original information, showing that the book and the bank balances do not reconcile.
2. Prepare a reconciliation using the new number, $7,100, for deposits in transit.
3. Why might Ms. Robitelli have instructed you to add $2,500 to the deposits in transit? What might she be trying to hide? If there were deceit, when might it be discovered?
4. What actions would you take if you were the accounting assistant?
5. By coincidence, you noticed a $2,500 cancelled check, signed by Ms. Robitelli, to an individual whose name you did not recognize. How would this change your answer to number 4?

Collaborative Learning Exercise

▶▶ OBJECTIVE 1

6-89 Revenue Recognition

Form groups of three to six students. Each student should pick one of the six industries listed below. The Standard Industrial Classification (SIC) number is provided for each industry. This number may be helpful in locating companies in that industry, especially if using search routines in electronic media.

- 2721—Periodicals Publishing and Printing

  Marvel Entertainment Group or **Readers Digest Association**

- 4512—Air Transportation, Scheduled

  Alaska Air Group or **Southwest Airlines Company**

- 4911—Electric Services

  Duke Power or **Puget Sound Energy**

- 6311—Life Insurance

  Allstate Corporation or **USLIFE, Incorporated**

- 7811—Motion Picture, Videotape Production

  Dick Clark Productions or **Walt Disney Company**

- 8062—General Medical and Surgical Hospitals

  Columbia/HCA Healthcare or **Regency Health Services**

Members of each group should learn as much as possible about the revenue recognition issues in their industry. Select at least two companies in the industry, and examine the description of each company's revenue recognition policies in the footnotes (usually in footnote 1 or 2) to the financial statements. Two possible companies are listed for each industry, but do not feel restricted to using the companies listed.

After the individual research on a particular industry, get together as a team and report on what each member has learned. Compare and contrast the issues relating to when revenue is earned and realized in each industry. Discuss why issues that are important in one industry are unimportant in another.

Analyzing and Interpreting Financial Statements

6-90 Financial Statement Research

Select an industry and choose two companies within that industry.

Calculate the accounts receivable turnover and days to collect accounts receivable for the two companies for 2 years and comment on the results.

▶▶ **OBJECTIVE 4**

6-91 Analyzing Starbucks' Financial Statements

Find Starbucks' 2011 financial statements either through the SEC EDGAR database or on Starbucks' Web site.

▶▶ **OBJECTIVES 2, 4**

1. Starbucks combines cash and cash equivalents on the balance sheet. Examine the first footnote to the financial statement and determine how Starbucks defines cash equivalents.
2. The first line of Starbucks' income statement is "Net revenues." From the Revenue Recognition section of footnote 1 to the financial statements, determine what items are deducted from gross revenue to yield net revenue.
3. Calculate the days to collect accounts receivable for the year ended October 2, 2011, assuming all sales were on account.

6-92 Analyzing Financial Statements Using the Internet: Oracle

Go to www.sec.gov to search for Oracle Corporation in the EDGAR database or go to the Oracle Web site. Find Oracle Corporation's latest 10-K filing under Investor Relations and SEC Filings.

Answer the following questions about the company:

▶▶ **OBJECTIVES 1, 3**

1. Under Part I, Item 1, how does Oracle categorize its products and services? What are its operating segments?
2. Examine the Revenue Recognition accounting policy in the Notes to Consolidated Financial Statements. When does Oracle recognize revenue from new software licenses? For software license updates and product support contracts?
3. Examine Oracle's balance sheet. Which method of accounting for uncollectible accounts does the company use? How can you tell?
4. Compute Oracle's allowance for uncollectible accounts as a percentage of trade accounts receivable in the most recent 2 years. What does this tell you about the company's expectation about possible nonpayment of accounts?

7

Inventories and Cost of Goods Sold

HAVE YOU EVER GONE to your local hardware store and been frustrated because it did not have what you wanted? A goal of **The Home Depot** is to help you avoid this frustration. The company meets this goal by keeping a large inventory—up to 40,000 different items, more than three times the number at a typical hardware store. As former CEO and Chairman Bernie Marcus said, one of the three main values at The Home Depot is assortment: "everything a do-it-yourselfer needs to complete a project."

Inventory requires a large investment by retail companies—$10.3 billion at The Home Depot, as of January 29, 2012, about 26% of the company's total assets—and accounting for this inventory is important. By carefully monitoring inventory levels, The Home Depot makes sure it does not lose sales by having too little inventory and does not lose money by investing in too much inventory. ●

In Chapter 6, we learned how to account for sales revenues. Of course, when a company sells a product, it also incurs costs. For example, The Home Depot must buy the tools it sells. Similarly, a **Toyota** dealership has to pay for every car it sells. Both companies must recognize the cost of the products sold along with the related revenues.

Determining the cost of the Toyota sold is easy enough—the dealer simply looks up the cost on the invoice for the specific car sold. Unfortunately, the calculations are not always that simple. Because The Home Depot purchases products such as tools in quantity and holds them in inventory, it is often difficult to trace the precise cost of a single product. As a result, companies must develop procedures to determine the value of their inventories and the cost of goods sold. The Home Depot had sales of $70.4 billion in the year ended January 29, 2012, with cost of goods sold of $46.1 billion. This provides a gross margin of $24.3 billion or 34.5% of sales, up from 30% in 1999.

This chapter examines various methods of valuing and accounting for inventories that companies such as Toyota and The Home Depot use to calculate cost of sales, inventory, and gross margin measures. You will find different inventory accounting practices around the globe.

LEARNING OBJECTIVES *After studying this chapter, you should be able to:*

1 Link inventory valuation to gross profit.

2 Use both perpetual and periodic inventory systems.

3 Calculate the cost of merchandise acquired.

4 Compute income and inventory values using the three principal inventory valuation methods allowed under both U.S. GAAP and IFRS and the one method allowed only by U.S. GAAP.

5 Use the lower-of-cost-or-market method to value inventories under both U.S. GAAP and IFRS.

6 Show the effects of inventory errors on financial statements.

7 Evaluate the gross profit percentage and inventory turnover.

8 Describe characteristics of LIFO and how they affect the measurement of income (Appendix 7A).

9 Determine inventory costs for a manufacturing company (Appendix 7B).

Companies in the same industry often use different methods and even a single company may use different methods for different products. By understanding these diverse practices, you should be able to distinguish differences between companies that are simply the result of different accounting practices from those reflecting real economic differences.

Gross Profit and Cost of Goods Sold

For merchandising firms, an initial step in assessing profitability is determining gross profit (also called profit margin or gross margin), which you learned in Chapter 4 is the difference between sales revenues and the cost of goods sold. Sales revenues must cover the cost of goods sold and provide a gross profit sufficient to cover all other costs including R&D, selling and marketing, administration, and so on. As illustrated in Exhibit 7-1, companies report products being held prior to sale as inventory, a current asset on the balance sheet. When they sell the goods, the cost of the inventory becomes an expense, cost of goods sold or cost of sales, on the income statement. We deduct this expense from net sales to determine gross profit, and we deduct additional expenses from gross profit to determine operating income. The Business First box on page 287 provides additional information about **The Home Depot** and other retailers.

The Basic Concept of Inventory Accounting

In theory, accounting for inventory and cost of goods sold is very simple. Suppose Christina sells T-shirts. Periodically, she orders many shirts of various sizes and colors. They sell, she orders more, and her business operating cycle continues on in this way. After a year, Christina prepares financial statements to evaluate her success. To calculate the value of inventory on hand, she counts all the inventory items remaining at year-end. She then develops a

The aisles of The Home Depot are stacked high with products so customers can find what they need. These products are the company's inventories, and managing its inventories is essential to The Home Depot. Recording this inventory on its balance sheet and recognizing cost of goods sold when a customer buys an item are important steps in measuring the company's assets and income. We learn about inventory accounting in this chapter.

> ▶▶ **OBJECTIVE 1**
> Link inventory valuation to gross profit.

285

EXHIBIT 7-1

**Merchandising Company
(Retailer or Wholesaler)**

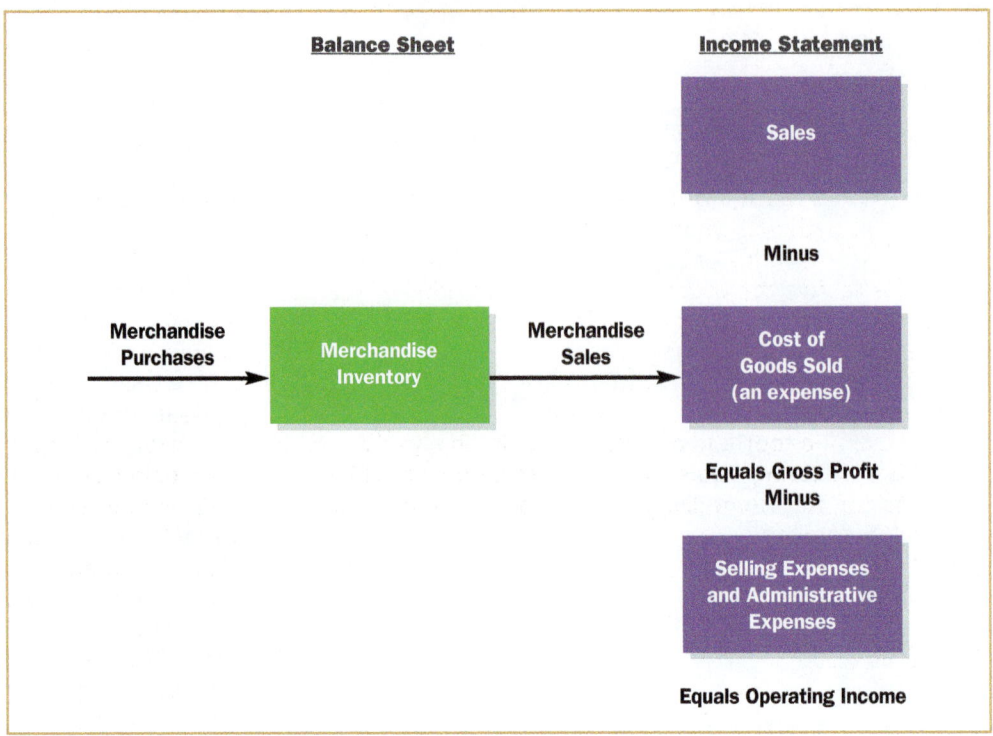

---

cost valuation

Process of assigning a specific value from the historical-cost records to each item in ending inventory.

cost valuation by assigning a specific value from the historical-cost records to each item in ending inventory. If the shirts cost $5 each and there are 100 shirts remaining in inventory, Christina's total ending inventory is valued at $500. Suppose she had no shirts at the beginning of the year, and total purchases for the year were $26,000. Cost of goods sold for the year would be $25,500 ($26,000 of available shirts minus $500 of unsold shirts). Notice that the key to calculating Christina's cost of goods sold is knowing the value of the remaining unsold inventory and subtracting that amount from the total value of the inventory items available for sale during the year.

In this example the sequence of events was simple. There was no beginning inventory and Christina acquired all items at the same price, $5 per shirt. Rarely is the economic process this simple. In the following sections, we show you the major techniques companies use for measuring inventories and examine problems that arise in using these techniques. As a manager or investor, you want to know how inventory accounting methods can affect reported earnings and how events such as inflation or changing inventory levels affect inventory values and thereby affect earnings. Let's begin by examining two major types of systems for keeping inventory records.

perpetual inventory system

An inventory system that keeps a continuous record of both inventories on hand and cost of goods sold that helps managers control inventory levels and prepare interim financial statements.

physical count

The process of identifying, counting, and assigning a specific cost to all items in inventory.

inventory shrinkage

Losses of inventory from theft, breakage, or loss.

Perpetual and Periodic Inventory Systems

There are two main systems for keeping merchandise inventory records: perpetual and periodic. A **perpetual inventory system** keeps a continuous record of both inventories on hand and cost of goods sold that helps managers control inventory levels and prepare interim financial statements. To verify this continuous record-keeping process, companies periodically physically count and value the inventory. A **physical count** is the process of identifying, counting, and assigning a specific cost to all items in inventory. Companies should perform physical counts at least annually to verify the accuracy of the perpetual records. The Home Depot discusses these issues in the notes to its financial statements: "Independent physical inventory counts or cycle counts are taken on a regular basis in each store and distribution center to ensure that amounts reflected in the accompanying Consolidated Financial Statements for Merchandise Inventories are properly stated."

The physical count helps management remove damaged or obsolete goods from inventory. It also helps reveal **inventory shrinkage**, which refers to losses of inventory from theft, breakage, or loss. Inventory shrinkage can be quite large in some businesses. The perpetual system also

BUSINESS FIRST

INVENTORY MANAGEMENT AND MERCHANDISING

Following its founding in Atlanta in 1978, The Home Depot's growth was phenomenal, and it was added to the Dow Jones Industrial Average in 1999. Despite sales declines during the economic recession of 2008–2011, The Home Depot currently ranks as one of the nation's largest retailers. The company's more than 2,200 stores are concentrated in the United States, its territories, Canada, and Mexico. An acquisition in 2006 also gave Home Depot a foothold of seven stores in China.

The following table compares revenue and EPS growth for The Home Depot with that of three other large U.S. retailers.

4-year Average Annual Growth Rates		
	Revenue	**EPS**
The Home Depot	−2%	2%
Wal-Mart	4	10
JCPenney	−3	NM[*]
Lowe's	1	−6

[*]Not meaningful.

Note that during the years ending from January 2008 through January 2012 these four companies had very different economic experiences. This period included a major recession. Thus, while Wal-Mart enjoyed a 10% increase in EPS on a 4% annual growth in sales, JCPenney experienced a 3% decline in sales and EPS went from a positive $4.90 to a negative $.70. In the table this change is shown as NM for "not meaningful."

The Home Depot attends to details, monitoring its inventory and its vendors. When General Electric (GE) experienced shortages in light bulb inventories, Bernie Marcus, The Home Depot founder and CEO, immediately cut a deal with Phillips, the Dutch electronics company, to replace GE as the light bulb supplier. The Home Depot also seeks new opportunities. In surveys of customers, they found GE was named the third best brand for water heaters, despite the fact that GE did not make water heaters. What's the solution? Pay GE a royalty for use of the name, pay Rheem to manufacture water heaters with the GE name, and become the exclusive distributor for a great product. The company also recently rolled out new product lines including new Dewalt hand tools and new paints by Glidden and Martha Stewart.

The Home Depot uses advanced technology. Inventory tracking and order placement occurs through wireless pen-based PCs that staff wheel up and down aisles to transmit current inventory counts and to execute orders based on a database of sales history and forecasts. The Home Depot's credit approvals take less than a second, an industry standard. The company pioneered self-checkout in its industry and now offers digitized catalogs and the "Buy Online Pickup In-Store" option to encourage Web sales.

Of course, today no one is safe from competition or from macro factors such as the global recession of 2008–2009 and the European debt crisis of 2011–2012. Lowe's is running hard as the second player in this market. Although it is only 72% the size of The Home Depot, Lowe's managed to generate revenue growth in the last 4 years. Nevertheless, EPS declined. Stay tuned.

Sources: The Home Depot 2011 Annual Report; Wal-Mart 2012 Annual Report; JCPenney 2012 Annual Report; Lowe's Companies, Inc., 2012 Annual Report; "Profit in a Big Orange Box," *Forbes*, January 24, 2000, pp. 122–128; "Home Depot Headed to $39 Even with Housing in the Dumps," *Forbes.com*, August 26, 2011. Note that each of these annual reports is for the year ending in January or February of 2012, however, they label the reports differently. The Home Depot calls it the 2011 annual report and Wal-Mart calls it the 2012 annual report.

provides managers with information to aid in pricing and ordering because inventory records are always up-to-date. Once cumbersome and expensive, perpetual inventory systems are inexpensive today due to technology such as computerized inventory systems and optical scanning equipment at checkout counters.

Previous chapters have used the perpetual system to record inventory transactions without referring to it by name. It works as follows:

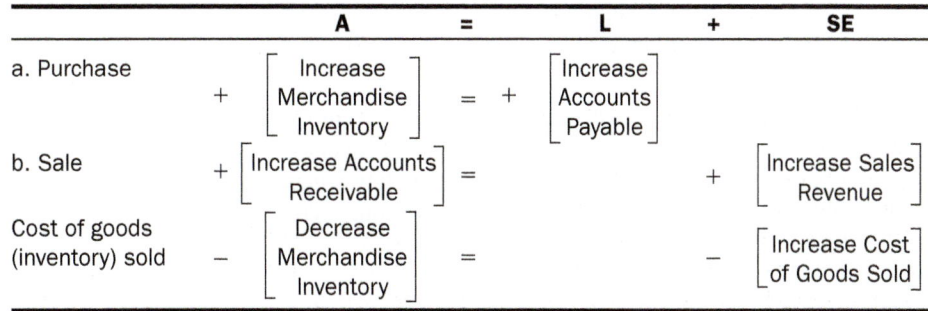

	A	=	L	+	SE
a. Purchase	+ [Increase Merchandise Inventory]	=	+ [Increase Accounts Payable]		
b. Sale	+ [Increase Accounts Receivable]	=		+	[Increase Sales Revenue]
Cost of goods (inventory) sold	− [Decrease Merchandise Inventory]	=		−	[Increase Cost of Goods Sold]

In the perpetual inventory system, the journal entries are as follows:

a. When inventory is purchased:
   Merchandise inventory. xxx
     Accounts payable (or cash)   xxx
b. When inventory is sold:
   Accounts receivable (or cash). xxx
     Sales revenue.   xxx

   Cost of goods sold xxx
     Merchandise inventory.   xxx

Thus, in the perpetual inventory system, we record the sale of an item and the accompanying inventory reduction simultaneously.

In contrast, a **periodic inventory system** does not maintain a day-to-day record of inventories or of the cost of goods sold. Instead, we compute the cost of goods sold and an updated inventory balance only at the end of an accounting period, when we take a physical count of inventory. We used this periodic inventory system in the example of Christina's T-shirt business.

Under the periodic system, calculations for the cost of goods sold start by computing the **cost of goods available for sale**—the opening inventory for the period plus purchases during the period. From this amount, we subtract the ending inventory value, determined by the physical count, to compute the cost of goods sold. Therefore, in the periodic system the cost of goods sold is a residual amount. The logic is that if we had inventory available and it is no longer on hand, then we sold it. Of course, practically speaking, if someone stole the item, its cost will also be included in cost of goods sold.

$$\underbrace{\text{Beginning inventory} + \text{Purchases}}_{\text{Goods available for sale}} - \underbrace{\text{Ending inventory}}_{-\text{ Inventory leftover}} = \underbrace{\text{Cost of goods sold}}_{=\text{ Cost of goods sold}}$$

Journal entries for a periodic system appear below. A detailed explanation of these entries accompanies the discussion of Exhibit 7-4 later in the chapter:

a. When inventory is purchased:
   Purchases xxx
     Accounts payable (or cash)   xxx
b. When inventory is sold:
   Accounts receivable (or cash). xxx
     Sales revenue   xxx
c. At the end of an accounting period:
   Cost of goods sold xxx
     Purchases   xxx
     Inventory (beginning).   xxx

   Inventory (ending) xxx
     Cost of goods sold   xxx

Exhibit 7-2 compares the perpetual and periodic inventory systems. Note that only the perpetual system provides a continuous assessment of inventory levels and helps managers restock with the right merchandise in a timely and effective manner. As implementation costs have fallen with the use of computerized systems, more companies find that these benefits justify the slightly higher cost of the perpetual system.

periodic inventory system
An inventory system that computes the cost of goods sold and an updated inventory balance only at the end of an accounting period when the company takes a physical count of inventory.

cost of goods available for sale
Sum of opening inventory for the period plus purchases during the period.

EXHIBIT 7-2

Inventory Systems

Periodic System		Perpetual System
Beginning inventories (by physical count)	$xxx	Cost of goods sold (kept on a day-to-day basis instead of determined periodically)*
Add: Purchases	xxx	
Cost of goods available for sale	xxx	
Less: Ending inventories (by physical count)	xxx	
Cost of goods sold	$xxx	

*Such a condensed figure does not preclude the presentation of a supplementary schedule similar to that on the left.

Physical Inventory

Good inventory control procedures require a physical count of items held in inventory at least annually in both periodic and perpetual inventory systems. In a periodic system, the count must occur at the end of the accounting period because it is used to determine the amount of inventory on hand for computing cost of goods sold. In a perpetual system, the count can occur during the year because its goal is simply to check the accuracy of the accounting system's record of inventory on hand. The physical count is an imposing, time-consuming, and expensive process. You may have seen "Closed for Inventory" signs posted on the doors of businesses that you frequent. To simplify counting and valuation, firms often choose fiscal year ends that fall when inventory levels are low and physical counts are easier. For example, The Home Depot, Sears, JCPenney, and Lowe's all have late January or early February year-ends, which follow the holiday season.

The physical inventory is so important to income determination that external auditors usually observe the client's physical count and confirm the accuracy of the subsequent valuation. Often audit firms hire outside experts to assist them. For example, assessing a jeweler's inventory might require an expert to test the color, size, clarity, and imperfections in the diamonds on hand. Similarly, the client and auditor might rely on an engineer to measure the physical dimensions of an electric utility's coal pile so they can accurately estimate the volume and weight without actually weighing the coal itself.

A classic case of inventory fraud is the Salad Oil Swindle of 1963. Late that year an obscure company named Allied Crude Vegetable Oil and Refining was unable to repay its loans. Collateral for the loans had been $175 million worth of vegetable oil inventory supposedly stored in 40 converted gasoline storage tanks in Bayonne, New Jersey. Investigation revealed that, instead of vegetable oil, the tanks contained seawater, soap stock, and sludge.

Allied used ingenious techniques to hide its shortfall from the watchful auditors. Because the 40 storage tanks were connected by pipes, Allied pumped a small quantity of vegetable oil from tank to tank during the week required to complete the inventory count. The auditors counted the same vegetable oil over and over. Moreover, the company never completely filled any tank with oil. Each tank had one opening, and Allied welded a closed pipe beneath each opening. Each pipe held a few hundred pounds of real oil. When the auditors took samples, they were actually testing what was in this pipe, not what was in the tank. After authorities discovered the fraud, they opened a faucet on one tank, and water poured out for 12 days.

Cost of Merchandise Acquired

Regardless of whether a company uses the periodic or perpetual system, the basis of inventory accounting is the cost of the merchandise a company purchases or produces for resale. What makes up that cost? To be more specific, does that cost include all or part of the following: invoice price, transportation charges, trade and cash discounts, cost of handling and placing the item in stock, storage, purchasing department, receiving department, and other indirect charges?

▶▶ OBJECTIVE 3
Calculate the cost of merchandise acquired.

Companies generally include the invoice price plus the directly identifiable inbound transportation charges less any offsetting discounts in the cost of merchandise. Many companies treat the costs of the purchasing and receiving departments as period costs and charge them on the income statement as they occur. However, some companies, including **The Home Depot**, include these costs in the cost of merchandise. The Home Depot's notes to its financial statements describe this as follows: "Cost of Sales includes the actual cost of merchandise sold and services performed, the cost of transportation of merchandise from vendors to the Company's stores, locations or customers, [and] the operating cost of the Company's sourcing and distribution network.... The cost of handling and shipping merchandise from the Company's stores, locations, or distribution centers to the customer is classified as SG&A [Selling, General and Administrative expense]."

Transportation Charges

F.O.B. destination

Seller pays freight costs from the shipping point of the seller to the receiving point of the buyer.

F.O.B. shipping point

Buyer pays freight costs from the shipping point of the seller to the receiving point of the buyer.

The major cost of transporting merchandise is typically the freight charges from the shipping point of the seller to the receiving point of the buyer. When the seller bears this cost, the sales invoice reads free onboard or **F.O.B. destination**. When the buyer bears this cost, it reads **F.O.B. shipping point**.

In theory, we should add any transportation costs borne by the buyer to the cost of the inventory acquired. In practice, though, it is not always easy to identify the transportation costs associated with specific inventory items. Companies tend to order several different items and have them shipped at the same time.

freight in (inward transportation)

An additional cost of the goods acquired during the period, which is often shown in the purchases section of an income statement.

Sometimes managers want to keep freight costs separate from other inventory costs. For example, management may want to see how freight costs change over time and to compare costs using rail service with costs using trucks. Consequently, accountants frequently use a separate transportation cost account, calling it Freight In, Transportation In, Inbound Transportation, or Inward Transportation. **Freight in** (or **inward transportation**) appears in the purchases section of an income statement as an additional cost of the goods acquired during the period. It becomes part of the cost of goods available for sale, and because it increases cost of goods sold, Freight In affects the gross profit section of the buyer's income statement.

INTERPRETING FINANCIAL STATEMENTS

Suppose that Huang Company bought several items of inventory that were shipped in a single load. If Huang Company paid the shipping costs, should it assign total freight costs to each of the components of the shipment based on weight, value, number of items, volume of the item, or some other process?

Answer

Each of these bases of assignment might be correct in certain cases. For example, if the product is coal, weight would be a very good basis for assigning delivery costs. If the product is jewelry, the company might consider assigning costs based on the number of items and their value because the shipping costs would depend on packing and handling of the item and insurance for its value in case it were lost or damaged. Thus, assigning shipping costs for purchased inventory would require extensive analysis to pick the best approach, followed by a lot of clerical work to apply the technique. Because of these difficulties and the modest benefit to the company from all this work, many companies do not assign freight costs to inventories. Instead, they charge them to expense when incurred.

Returns, Allowances, and Discounts

In Chapter 6, you learned about sales returns, allowances, and discounts. The accounting for purchase returns, purchase allowances, and cash discounts on purchases is just the opposite of their sales counterparts. Using the periodic inventory system, suppose a company's gross purchases are $960,000 and purchase returns and allowances are $75,000. The summary journal entries are as follows:

Purchases	960,000	
Accounts payable		960,000
Accounts payable	75,000	
Purchase returns and allowances		75,000

EXHIBIT 7-3

Detailed Gross Profit Calculation
($ in thousands)

Gross sales				$1,740
Deduct: Sales returns and allowances		$ 70		
Cash discounts on sales		100	170	
Net sales			1,570	
Deduct: Cost of goods sold				
Merchandise inventory, December 31, 20X1		100		
Purchases (gross)		$960		
Deduct: Purchase returns and allowances	$75			
Cash discounts on purchases	5	80		
Net purchases		880		
Add: Freight in		30		
Total cost of merchandise acquired		910		
Cost of goods available for sale		1,010		
Deduct: Merchandise inventory, December 31, 20X2		140		
Cost of goods sold			870	
Gross profit			$ 700	

Suppose also that the company takes cash discounts of $5,000 on payment of the remaining $885,000 = ($960,000 – $75,000) of payables. The summary journal entry is as follows:

Accounts payable	885,000	
Cash discounts on purchases		5,000
Cash		880,000

To calculate cost of goods available for sale, we deduct Cash Discounts on Purchases and Purchase Returns and Allowances from Gross Purchases.

Car dealers sometimes sell cars "below cost" or "$100 below invoice." Do dealers lose money on such sales? Probably not, because gross invoice cost to the dealer and final cost of goods sold may differ. Dealers receive incentives from the manufacturers such as volume discounts or special discounts to push particular models. The dealer's invoice shows the list price before discounts and allowances, not the final net dealer cost.

A detailed gross profit section in the income statement is often arranged as in Exhibit 7-3. Although management may find such detail valuable, the summary presentation shown below is much more common in the annual report to shareholders:

Net sales	$1,570
Cost of goods sold	870
Gross profit	$ 700

Comparing Accounting Procedures for Periodic and Perpetual Inventory Systems

Suppose GoodEarth Products, Incorporated, has a balance of $100,000 in merchandise inventory at the beginning of 20X2 (December 31, 20X1). A summary of transactions for 20X2 follows:

a. Purchases	$990,000
b. Purchase returns and allowances	80,000

Net purchases were therefore $990,000 less $80,000, or $910,000. The physical count of the ending inventory for 20X2 led to a cost valuation of $140,000. Note how we use these figures to compute the $870,000 cost of goods sold:

Beginning + Net purchases inventory	−	Ending inventory	=	Cost of goods sold
$100,000 + $910,000	−	$140,000	=	$870,000
Cost of goods available for sale	−	Cost of goods leftover	=	Cost of goods sold
$1,010,000	−	$140,000	=	$870,000

The periodic and perpetual procedures would record these transactions differently. As the left side of Exhibit 7-4 shows, in the perpetual system we directly increase the Inventory account by the $990,000 in purchases (entry a) and decrease it by the $80,000 in returns and allowances (entry b) and the $870,000 cost of goods sold (entry c). These summary numbers reflect the total impact on each account during the period, but in fact the Inventory account and the Cost of Goods Sold account would each change continuously as items were received, returned, or sold. The following T-accounts summarize how these items would appear in the general ledger (dollar amounts in thousands):

Inventory				**Cost of Goods Sold**	
Balance 12/31/X1	100	(b)	80	(c)	870
(a)	990	(c)	870		
Balance 12/31/X2	140			Balance 12/31/X2	870

Although the method seems to create the correct $140,000 final inventory balance, recall that the company will also conduct a physical count at least once a year to verify the number. Often there are minor differences between the valuation determined by the physical count and the value shown in the perpetual record. Such differences, often due to clerical error or shrinkage, result in appropriate adjustments to increase or decrease inventory and cost of sales. Suppose a physical count had been taken at the end of the year and had yielded a value of $135,000. We would then make the following journal entry (in thousands):

Inventory shrinkage expense	5	
Inventory		5

Under the perpetual system it is necessary to take a periodic physical inventory to assess the accuracy of the inventory balance, but it need not be taken at year-end. If this physical count occurred two months before year-end and showed a $5,000 difference between the physical inventory and the perpetual inventory amounts, the adjusting journal entry to conform the accounting records to the physical count would be the same.

Under the periodic system on the right side of Exhibit 7-4, we record purchases and purchase returns and allowances in separate accounts, as entries (a) and (b) indicate. We call the system "periodic" because we do not compute the cost of goods sold or the inventory amount on a daily basis. Entries (d1) and (2) at the bottom of Exhibit 7-4 show how we update these accounts during the eventual periodic calculation of cost of goods sold.

Entry (d1) transfers the beginning inventory balance, purchases, and purchase returns and allowances, totaling $1,010,000, to cost of goods sold. This is the cost of goods available for sale. Next, we physically count the ending inventory and compute its cost. Entry (d2) recognizes the $140,000 ending inventory and reduces the $1,010,000 cost of goods available for sale by $140,000 to obtain a final cost of goods sold of $870,000. The

EXHIBIT 7-4

GoodEarth Products, Incorporated

Comparison of Journal Entries for Perpetual and Periodic Inventory Systems ($ amounts in thousands)

	Perpetual Records			Periodic Records		
a. Gross purchases:	Inventory	990		Purchases	990	
	Accounts payable. .		990	Accounts payable.		990
b. Returns and allowances:	Accounts payable . . .	80		Accounts payable	80	
	Inventory.		80	Purchase returns and allowances		80
c. As goods are sold:	Cost of goods sold . .	870		No entry		
	Inventory.		870			
d. At the end of the accounting period:	d1. ⎱ No entry d2. ⎰			d1. Cost of goods sold	1,010	
				Purchase returns and allowances . . .	80	
				Purchases		990
				Inventory		100
				d2. Inventory.	140	
				Cost of goods sold		140

following T-accounts show how these journal entries affect the general ledger accounts under the periodic system (dollar amounts in thousands):

Inventory				Cost of Goods Sold			
Balance 12/31/X1	100	(d1)	100	(d1)	1,010	(d2)	140
(d2)	140						
Balance 12/31/X2	140			Balance 12/31/X2	870		

Purchases				Purchase Returns and Allowances			
(a)	990	(d1)	990	(d1)	80	(b)	80

Notice that both systems reach the same result, Inventory of $140,000 and Cost of Goods Sold of $870,000. In the periodic system the Purchases and Purchase Returns and Allowances accounts are used during the year, but are closed at year-end in the adjusting journal entry that calculates Cost of Goods Sold.

Principal Inventory Valuation Methods

Each period, accountants must divide the cost of goods available for sale between cost of goods sold and cost of items remaining in ending inventory. Under a perpetual system, we must determine a cost for each item sold. Under a periodic system, we instead must determine the specific costs of the items remaining in ending inventory. In both systems, we must determine the costs of individual items using an inventory valuation method. Four principal inventory valuation methods are commonly used in the United States: specific identification; first-in, first-out (FIFO); last-in, first-out (LIFO); and average cost. Companies reporting under IFRS cannot use LIFO. The most popular method worldwide is the average cost method, and the next most common choice is FIFO. In this section, we explain and compare these methods.

If unit prices and costs did not fluctuate, all four inventory methods would show identical results. However, prices change, and these changes raise central issues concerning cost of goods sold (income measurement) and inventories (asset measurement). As a simple example of the valuation method choices facing management, consider Emilio, a new vendor of a cola drink at the fairgrounds, who begins the week with no inventory. He buys one can of cola on Monday for 30¢, a second can on Tuesday for 40¢, and a third can on Wednesday for 56¢. He then sells one can on Thursday for 90¢.

▶▶**OBJECTIVE 4**

Compute net income and inventory values using the three principal inventory valuation methods allowed under both U.S. GAAP and IFRS and the one method allowed only by U.S. GAAP.

As Exhibit 7-5 shows, Emilio's choice of inventory method can significantly affect the amounts reported as cost of goods sold and ending inventory. The gross profit for Monday through Thursday ranges from 34¢ to 60¢, depending on the method chosen and how that method splits the acquisition costs between ending inventory and cost of goods sold. By using Exhibit 7-5 as a guide, we now examine each of the four methods in detail.

Specific Identification

specific identification method

This inventory method concentrates on physically linking the particular items sold with the cost of goods sold that a company reports.

The **specific identification method** concentrates on physically linking the particular items sold with the cost of goods sold that a company reports. Emilio could mark each can with its cost and record that cost as cost of goods sold when he hands the can to a customer. If he reached for the Monday can instead of the Wednesday can, the specific identification method would show different results. Thus, Exhibit 7-5 indicates that gross profit for operations of Monday through Thursday could be 60¢, 50¢, or 34¢, depending on the particular can Emilio hands to the customer. He could choose which can to sell and affect reported results by doing so. Because the specific item handed to the customer determines the cost of goods sold, the specific identification method may permit managers to manipulate income and inventory values by filling a sales order from a number of physically equivalent items with different historical costs. This would be true for Emilio. Each can is identical. It would not be true for a car dealer for whom each car has a unique identification number indicating its features such as color, style, engine, sound system, and so forth.

Specific identification is relatively easy to use for expensive low-volume merchandise, such as custom artwork, diamond jewelry, and automobiles. However, many organizations have inventory items that are insufficiently valuable to warrant such individualized attention. Nevertheless, the use of bar codes and scanning equipment is making specific identification economically feasible in more and more circumstances.

FIFO

first-in, first-out (FIFO)

This method of accounting for inventory assigns the cost of the earliest acquired units to cost of goods sold.

EXHIBIT 7-5

Emilio's Cola Sales

Comparison of Inventory Methods (all monetary amounts are in cents)

FIFO refers to **first-in, first-out**. The FIFO method is a cost assignment method and does not track the actual physical flow of individual items, except by coincidence. For identical units, it assigns the cost of the earliest acquired units (those that were "first-in") to cost of goods sold. Thus, under FIFO, we assume that Emilio sells the Monday can of cola first—regardless of

	(1) Specific Identification			(2) FIFO	(3) LIFO	(4) Average Cost
	(1A)	(1B)	(1C)			
Income Statement for the Period Monday Through Thursday						
Sales	90	90	90	90	90	90
Deduct cost of goods sold						
1 30¢ (Monday) unit	30			30		
1 40¢ (Tuesday) unit		40				
1 56¢ (Wednesday) unit			56		56	
1 average cost unit						
[(30¢ + 40¢ + 56¢) ÷ 3 = 42¢]						42
Gross profit for Monday through Thursday	60	50	34	60	34	48
Thursday's Ending Inventory, Two Units						
Monday unit @ 30¢		30	30		30	
Tuesday unit @ 40¢	40		40	40	40	
Wednesday unit @ 56¢	56	56		56		
Average cost units @ 42¢						84
Total ending inventory on Thursday	96	86	70	96	70	84

the actual can he delivers to the customer. As a result, we assign the costs of the more recently acquired cans to the units in ending inventory.

By using the more recent costs to measure the ending inventory, FIFO provides inventory valuations that closely approximate the actual market value of the inventory at the balance sheet date. In addition, in periods of rising prices, FIFO leads to higher net income. Note that gross profit is 60¢ in Exhibit 7-5 under FIFO because we charge the oldest, lowest-cost unit to cost of goods sold. Higher reported incomes may favorably affect investor attitudes toward the company. Similarly, higher reported incomes may lead to higher salaries, higher bonuses, or higher status for the management of the company. Unlike specific identification, FIFO specifies the order in which acquisition costs become cost of goods sold, so management cannot affect income by choosing to sell one identical item instead of another.

LIFO

LIFO refers to **last-in, first-out**. Whereas FIFO associates the most recent costs with ending inventories, LIFO assigns the costs of the most recently acquired units to cost of goods sold. The LIFO method assumes that a company sells the stock acquired most recently before it sells older stock. Thus, under LIFO, we assume that Emilio sells the Wednesday can of cola—regardless of the actual can he delivers from the cooler.

last-in, first-out (LIFO)
This inventory method assigns the cost of the most recently acquired units to cost of goods sold.

LIFO provides an income statement perspective in the sense that net income measured using LIFO combines current sales prices and the most recent acquisition costs. In contrast, the balance sheet includes older costs which, in a period of rising prices, may be far below current prices. In a period of rising prices and constant or growing inventories, LIFO yields lower net income as shown by the 34¢ gross margin in Exhibit 7-5. Why is lower net income such an important feature of LIFO? In the United States, LIFO is an acceptable inventory accounting method for income tax purposes. When a company reports lower income to the tax authorities, it pays lower taxes. It is not surprising that over 5,000 U.S. corporations use LIFO for at least some of their inventories to take advantage of this tax benefit. However, the U.S. Internal Revenue Code includes the LIFO Conformity rule, which requires companies that use LIFO for tax purposes to also use it for financial reporting purposes.

You might think of LIFO as the good news/bad news method. Lower income taxes provide the good news, but the accompanying bad news is lower reported profits. During a period of higher inflation some years ago, the *Wall Street Journal* reported that many small firms changed from FIFO to LIFO. As an example, when Becton, Dickinson and Company changed to LIFO its annual report stated that its "change to the LIFO method ... for both financial reporting and income tax purposes resulted in improved cash flow due to lower income taxes paid." Indeed, some observers maintain that executives of U.S. companies are guilty of serious mismanagement by not adopting LIFO when its adoption would result in significantly lower taxable income.

Debates about the permissibility of LIFO in the United States for tax purposes and financial reporting purposes have been frequent for decades, rising and falling as inflation rates have made the tax effects increase and decrease in importance. The economic effects can be very significant. For example, in 2010, ExxonMobil had $21.3 billion of cumulative reductions in taxable income as a result of using LIFO. If forced to switch to FIFO and pay taxes on that difference, it would represent $7.5 billion in taxes at a 35% tax rate. In a 2007 reform proposal, the House Ways and Means Committee estimated that repealing LIFO would raise approximately $106 billion in additional tax revenues for the federal government. That bill did not pass, but tax reform and LIFO repeal continue to be considered. The current move toward adoption of IFRS in the United States increases the focus on this issue since LIFO is not acceptable under IFRS.

One reason that IFRS prohibits LIFO is that it permits management to influence reported income by the timing of purchases of inventory items. Consider Emilio's case as described in Exhibit 7-5. Suppose that acquisition prices increase from 56¢ on Wednesday to 68¢ on Thursday, the day of the sale of the one unit. How does the acquisition of one more unit on Thursday affect net income? Under LIFO, if Emilio acquired an additional unit on Thursday for 68¢, the cost of goods sold would change to 68¢, and profit would fall by 12¢. In contrast, under FIFO, cost of goods sold and gross profit would be unchanged by the acquisition of the additional unit.

	LIFO		FIFO	
	As in Exhibit 7-5	**If One More Unit Acquired**	**As in Exhibit 7-5**	**If One More Unit Acquired**
Sales	90¢	90¢	90¢	90¢
Cost of goods sold	56	68	30	30
Gross profit	34¢	22¢	60¢	60¢
Ending inventory				
First purchase, Monday	30¢	30¢		
Second purchase, Tuesday	40	40	40¢	40¢
Third purchase, Wednesday		56	56	56
Fourth purchase, Thursday				68
	70¢	126¢	96¢	164¢

To learn more about LIFO and its effects on companies' financial statements, see Appendix 7A.

Average Cost

average cost method

This inventory method computes an average unit cost by dividing the total acquisition cost of all items available for sale by the number of units available for sale.

The **average cost method** computes an average unit cost by dividing the total acquisition cost of all items available for sale by the number of units available for sale. Picture Emilio dropping his cooler and not knowing which can was in front. Exhibit 7-5 shows the calculations Emilio would make to average the costs of these units. The average cost is $[(30¢ + 40¢ + 56¢) \div 3] = 42¢$

To better understand the average cost method, assume that Emilio bought two cans instead of one on Monday at 30¢ per can. To get the weighted average, we must consider not only the price paid, but also the number of units purchased as follows:

$$\text{Average cost} = \text{Cost of goods available for sale} \div \text{Units available for sale}$$
$$\text{Average cost} = [(2 \times 30¢) + (1 \times 40¢) + (1 \times 56¢)] \div 4$$
$$= 156¢ \div 4$$
$$= 39¢$$

weighted-average cost method

Average cost method used in conjunction with the periodic inventory system.

moving-average cost method

Average cost method used in conjunction with the perpetual inventory system.

The average cost method produces a gross profit somewhere between that obtained under FIFO and that under LIFO (48¢ as compared with 60¢ and 34¢ in Exhibit 7-5). When The Home Depot recently adopted the average cost method for its Canadian operations, it described this change in accounting principle in note 3 to its annual financial statements. The note discussed the new accounting system that was required to support the change: "[T]he Company implemented a new enterprise resource planning ('ERP') system, including a new inventory system, for its retail operations in Canada.... The new ERP system allows the Company to utilize the weighted-average cost method, which the Company believes will result in greater precision in the costing of inventories and a better matching of cost of sales with revenue generated." Proper design and implementation of the information management systems is crucial to enable companies to capture the right information at the right time to produce the financial statements they need to run their businesses effectively. Note that The Home Depot footnote refers to the weighted-average cost method. When average cost is adopted along with a periodic inventory system we refer to it as the **weighted-average cost method**. If average cost is used in conjunction with a perpetual inventory system we call it the **moving-average cost method**.

Cost Flow Assumptions

Because the actual physical flow of identical products is less important to the financial success of most businesses than is the flow of the units' costs through the financial statements, the accounting profession has concluded that companies may choose any of the allowable methods to record cost of goods sold. Basically, the units are all the same, but their costs differ, so managing the assignment of these differing costs is more important than is tracing where each specific unit goes. Because only the specific identification method is linked to the physical flow of merchandise, accountants often refer to the other inventory methods as cost flow assumptions. For example, when we decide to match the cost of the first inventory item purchased with the sales revenue from the first item sold to calculate the gross profit from the sale, we are adopting the FIFO cost flow assumption.

	(1) Specific Identification			(2) FIFO	(3) LIFO	(4) Average Cost
	(1A)	**(1B)**	**(1C)**			
Sales, 2 units @ 90 on Friday	180	180	180	180	180	180
Cost of goods sold						
(Thursday ending inventory from Exhibit 7-5)	96	86	70	96	70	84
Gross profit, Friday only	84	94	110	84	110	96
Gross profit, Monday through						
Thursday (from Exhibit 7-5)	60	50	34	60	34	48
Gross profit, Monday through						
Friday (3 cans sold)	144	144	144	144	144	144

Notice that the cost flow assumptions do not affect the cumulative gross profit over the life of a company. Suppose Emilio sells his remaining two cans of inventory for 90¢ per can on Friday and enters a more attractive business. Exhibit 7-6 shows Friday's gross profit and the cumulative gross profit for the entire week. As you can see, the gross profit for Friday varies with the cost flow assumption used. However, the last line of the exhibit shows that the cumulative gross profit over the life of Emilio's business would total $1.44 under any of the inventory methods. What makes the choice of method important is the need to match particular costs to particular periods during the life of the business in order to prepare periodic financial statements and evaluate performance.

Inventory Cost Relationships

Note that all inventory methods work with the same basic numbers. Nothing in our choice of methods affects accounts payable. We record inventory purchases at actual cost and recognize a liability in the same amount under all these methods. All that changes is how we allocate those actual costs between ending inventory and cost of sales when we prepare financial statements.

Recall that during a period of rising prices, FIFO yields higher inventory and higher gross profit than does LIFO or average cost. This result is consistent with the balance sheet equation that requires that $A = L + SE$. If inventory is higher under FIFO (higher assets) and the equation is to balance, either liabilities or stockholders' equity must also be higher. Higher gross profit under FIFO implies higher net income and higher stockholders' equity (SE in the equation).

There are, of course, relationships other than those of the accounting equation that come into play in the various inventory methods. Consider also the link between cost of goods sold and the valuation of ending inventory. Emilio's three cola cans had a total cost of goods available for sale of $1.26. At the end of the period, Emilio must allocate this $1.26 either to cans sold or to cans in ending inventory. The higher the cost of goods sold, the lower the ending inventory. Exhibit 7-7 illustrates that interdependence. At one extreme, FIFO treats the 30¢ cost of the first can acquired as cost of goods sold and 96¢ as ending inventory. At the other extreme, LIFO treats the 56¢ cost of the last can acquired as cost of goods sold and 70¢ as ending inventory.

Application of the Consistency Convention

Although companies can choose any allowable inventory cost flow assumption, the consistency convention discussed in Chapter 2 requires that the chosen method be consistently applied over time. Interpreting financial performance over time involves comparing the results of different periods. If accounting methods for inventory were changed often, meaningful comparisons over time would be impossible.

Occasionally, a change in market conditions or other circumstances may justify a change in inventory method. A significant increase in inflation motivated more than 40 companies to switch to LIFO in the 1970s to capture tax benefits. With its auditor's approval, a firm may change its inventory method to one that it and its auditor think better represents the firm's economic situation. However, the firm has to note the change in its financial statements as The Home Depot did when adopting the weighted-average method in Canada. The auditor must also refer to the change in its audit opinion. This alerts financial statement readers to the possible effects of the change on their analysis.

EXHIBIT 7-7

Emilio's Cola Sales, Monday Through Thursday

Diagram of Inventory Methods (all monetary amounts are in cents)

	Beginning Inventory	+	Purchases	−	Cost of Goods Sold	=	Ending Inventory	
FIFO	0	+ 126	{ 1 @ 30 1 @ 40 1 @ 56	−	1 @ 30	=	{ 1 @ 40 1 @ 56 }	96
LIFO	0	+ 126	{ 1 @ 30 1 @ 40 1 @ 56	− 1 @ 56	=	{ 1 @ 30 1 @ 40 }	70
Specific identification	0	+ 126	{ 1 @ 30 1 @ 40 1 @ 56	− 1 @ 30 or − 1 @ 40 or − 1 @ 56	= = =	{ 1 @ 40 1 @ 56 } 96 or { 1 @ 30 1 @ 56 } 86 or { 1 @ 30 1 @ 40 } 70	
Average cost	0	+ 126	{ 1 @ 30 1 @ 40 1 @ 56	− 1 @ 42	=	2 @ 42	84

Summary Problem for Your Review

PROBLEM

Examine Exhibit 7-8. The company uses the periodic inventory system. By using these facts, prepare a columnar comparison of income statements for the year ended December 31, 20X2. Compare the FIFO, LIFO, and weighted-average inventory methods. Remember that when average cost is used with a periodic inventory system, it is called the weighted-average cost method. Assume that other expenses are $1,000. The income tax rate is 40%.

EXHIBIT 7-8

Facts for Summary Problem

	Purchases	Sales (units)	Inventory
December 31, 20X1			200 @ $5 = $1,000
January 25	170 @ $6 = $1,020		
January 29		150*	
May 28	190 @ $7 = $1,330		
June 7		230*	
November 20	150 @ $8 = $1,200		
December 15	___ ___	100*	
Total	510 $3,550	480*	
December 31, 20X2			230 @ ?

*Selling prices were $9, $11, and $13, respectively, providing total sales of:

150 @ $ 9 = $1,350		Beginning inventory	$1,000
230 @ $11 = $2,530		Purchases	$3,550
100 @ $13 = $1,300		Cost of goods available	
Total sales 480 $5,180		for sale	$4,550

EXHIBIT 7-9

Comparison of Inventory Methods for the Year Ended December 31, 20X2

SOLUTION

See Exhibit 7-9.

	FIFO		LIFO		Weighted Average
Sales, 480 units		$5,180		$5,180	$5,180
Deduct cost of goods sold					
Beginning inventory, 200 @ $5	$1,000		$1,000		$1,000
Purchases, 510 units (from Exhibit 7-8)*	3,550		3,550		3,550
Available for sale, 710 units†	$4,550		$4,550		$4,550
Ending inventory, 230 units†					
150 @ $8	$1,200				
80 @ $7	560	1,760			
Or					
200 @ $5			$1,000		
30 @ $6			180	1,180	
Or					
230 @ $6.408					1,474
Cost of goods sold, 480 units		2,790		3,370	3,076
Gross profit		2,390		1,810	2,104
Other expenses		1,000		1,000	1,000
Income before income taxes		1,390		810	1,104
Income taxes at 40%		556		324	442
Net income		$ 834		$ 486	$ 662

*Always equal across all three methods.
†These amounts will generally not be equal across the three methods because beginning inventories will typically be different. They are equal here only because beginning inventories were assumed to be equal.
‡Under FIFO, the ending inventory is composed of the last purchases plus the second-last purchases, and so forth, until the costs of 230 units are compiled. Under LIFO, the ending inventory is composed of the beginning inventory plus the earliest purchases of the current year until the costs of 230 units are compiled. Under weighted average, the ending inventory and cost of goods sold are accumulations based on an average unit cost. The latter is the cost of goods available for sale divided by the number of units available for sale: ($4,550 ÷ 710) = $6.408.

Lower-of-Cost-or-Market Method

Sometimes companies cannot easily sell obsolete or damaged inventory items at amounts equal to or above their historical cost. In such a case, the historical cost overstates the value of the inventory. To avoid overstating the inventory, we use the **lower-of-cost-or-market method (LCM)**. LCM requires companies to compare the current market price of inventory with its historical cost derived under whichever inventory method the company has adopted and then report the lower of the two as the inventory value.

How companies measure current market price depends on whether they use IFRS or U.S. GAAP. Under IFRS the market price is **net realizable value**—the net amount the company expects to receive when it sells the inventory. Under U.S. GAAP it is usually **current replacement cost**—what it would cost to buy the inventory item today.

Consider the following example of a U.S. company. The Ripley Company has 100 units in its ending FIFO inventory on December 31, 20X1. Ripley tentatively computed its gross profit for 20X1 as follows:

Sales		$2,180
Cost of goods available for sale	$1,980	
Ending inventory of 100 units, at cost	790	
Cost of goods sold		1,190
Gross profit		$ 990

▶▶ **OBJECTIVE 5**
Use the lower-of-cost-or-market method to value inventories under both U.S. GAAP and IFRS.

lower-of-cost-or-market method (LCM)
A comparison of the current market price of inventory with its historical cost derived under whichever inventory method the company has adopted. LCM requires reporting the lower of the two as the inventory value.

net realizable value
The net amount the company expects to receive when it sells the inventory.

current replacement cost

What it would cost a company to buy an inventory item today.

write-down

A reduction in the recorded historical cost of an item in response to a decline in value.

Assume a sudden decline in replacement costs of this inventory during the final week of December from $7.90 per unit to $4 per unit and a corresponding decline in net realizable value to $5 per unit. Ripley Company expects these declines to be permanent. Under U.S. GAAP, an inventory write-down of ($7.90 – $4.00) × 100 units, or $390, is in order. A **write-down** reduces the recorded historical cost of an item in response to a decline in value. When a write-down occurs, the new $4 per unit replacement cost becomes, for accounting purposes, the unexpired cost of the inventory. Thus, if replacement prices subsequently rise to $8 per unit in January 20X2, the assigned cost of each unit will remain $4. In short, the lower-of-cost-or-market method as applied under U.S. GAAP would regard the $4 replacement cost of December 31 as the "new historical cost" of the inventory. The journal entry required to record the write-down is as follows:

Loss on write-down of inventory (or cost of goods sold).........	390	
Inventory		390
To write down inventory from $790 cost to $400 market value		

The write-down of inventories increases cost of goods sold in 20X1 by $390. Therefore, reported income for 20X1 would be lowered by $390:

	Before $390 Write-Down	After $390 Write-Down	Difference
Sales	$2,180	$2,180	
Cost of goods available	$1,980	$1,980	
Ending inventory	790	400	–$390
Cost of goods sold	$1,190	$1,580	+$390
Gross profit	$ 990	$ 600	–$390

Why is the decline in net realizable value an important criterion for the write-down? Because, if the market replacement cost falls but selling prices and net realizable value remain the same, the items still have their original earning power. No loss has occurred, and no reduction in the book value of the inventory is necessary. The $390 write-down is needed only when both the replacement cost and net realizable value fall. Why? Because then the original $790 historical cost cannot be recovered in the future. The $390 is considered to have expired during 20X1, and the write-down causes it to be included in cost of sales in the year the decline occurred.

How would LCM differ if Ripley Company used IFRS? Because the net realizable value is $5 per unit, the write-down would be only ($7.90 – $5.00) × 100 units, or $290. Except for the amount, the accounting for the decline in inventory value would be the same as under U.S. GAAP. However, if the net realizable value subsequently increases, IFRS allows companies to reverse the write-down. They can increase the inventory value up to the amount of the original cost. This decreases cost of sales and increases profit in the year the recovery occurs.

Conservatism in Action

LCM is an example of conservatism. As discussed in Chapter 4, conservatism means selecting methods of measurement that anticipate expenses and liabilities and defer recognition of revenues and assets, yielding lower net income, lower assets, and lower stockholders' equity. We illustrated conservatism in accounts receivable with the use of an allowance for bad debts. We estimated and recorded losses on uncollectible accounts before they were certain. With inventories, conservatism dictates that we use the LCM method.

Accountants believe that erring in the direction of conservatism is better than erring in the direction of overstating assets and net income. The accountant's conservatism balances management's optimism. Management prepares the financial statements, but the conservatism principle moderates management's human tendency to hope for, and expect, the best.

Compared with a pure cost method, the lower-of-cost-or-market method reports less net income in the period of decline in the market value of the inventory and more net income in the period of sale. The lower-of-cost-or-market method affects how much income the Ripley Company reports in each year, but not the total income over the company's life. Exhibit 7-10 underscores this point, using the U.S. GAAP rule for LCM. Suppose Ripley goes out of business

EXHIBIT 7-10

The Ripley Company
Effects of Lower-of-Cost-or-Market

	Cost Method		Lower-of-Cost-or-Market Method	
	20X1	**20X2**	**20X1**	**20X2**
Sales	$2,180	$ 800	$2,180	$ 800
Cost of goods available	1,980	790	1,980	400
Ending inventory	790	—	400*	—
Cost of goods sold	1,190	790	1,580	400
Gross profit	$ 990	$ 10	$ 600	$ 400
Combined gross profit for 2 years				
Cost method: $990 + $10 =		$1,000		
LCM method: $600 + $400 =				$1,000

*The inventory is shown here after being written down by $390, from $790 to $400. For internal purposes, many accountants prefer to show the write-down separately, presenting a gross profit before write-down of inventory, the write-down, and a gross profit after write-down.

in early 20X2. That is, it acquires no more units. There are no sales in 20X2 except for the disposal of the inventory for $800 (100 units × $8 per unit = $800). The LCM method will affect neither combined gross profit nor combined net income for the two periods, as the bottom of Exhibit 7-10 reveals. The LCM method simply transfers $390 of profit from 20X1 to 20X2. The only difference under IFRS is that $290 of profit would move from 20X1 to 20X2.

A full-blown lower-of-cost-or-market method is rarely encountered in practice. Why? Because it is expensive to get the correct replacement costs of hundreds or thousands of different products in inventory. Further, the benefit from doing so does not justify the cost. Auditors do watch for price trends in the industry that might indicate a serious concern. In particular, they watch for subclasses of inventory that are obsolete, shopworn, or otherwise of only nominal value and apply LCM selectively to such inventory.

Effects of Inventory Errors

Inventory errors can arise from many sources. For example, incorrect physical counts can occur when accountants miss goods that were in receiving or shipping areas instead of in the inventory stockroom. Or a clerk might hit a 5 on the keyboard instead of a 6.

An undiscovered inventory error usually affects two reporting periods. The error will cause misstated amounts in the period in which the error occurred, but the effects will then be counterbalanced by identical offsetting amounts in the following period. Why? Because the ending inventory of one period becomes the beginning inventory of the next period. Consider the income statements shown in Panel A of Exhibit 7-11. Ending inventory for 20X7 is actually $70,000. However, the physical count of ending inventory for 20X7 is erroneous, reporting ending inventory of only $60,000. What is the impact of this error? The ending inventory valuation is $10,000 too low and cost of goods sold is $10,000 too high. This overstatement of cost of goods sold results in 20X7 pretax income being $10,000 too low. With a tax rate of 40%, net income will be $6,000 too low.

Panel B of Exhibit 7-11 shows the effects of the uncorrected error on the following year, 20X8. We assume that the operations during 20X8 duplicate those of 20X7, except that the ending inventory is correctly counted as $40,000. The 20X8 beginning inventory of $60,000 is $10,000 too low and produces cost of goods sold that is too low leading to a gross profit and pretax income that are too high by $10,000. After taking taxes into consideration, 20X8 net income is high by $6,000. The counterbalancing errors in 20X8 exactly offset the errors in 20X7. Note that the retained earnings at the end of 20X8 is as it should be. Why? Because the net income in 20X7 is understated by $6,000, but the net income in 20X8 is overstated by $6,000.

From the balance sheet equation and this example we can develop a handy rule of thumb. If ending inventory is understated, retained earnings is understated. If ending inventory is overstated, retained earnings is overstated. However, from our example we note that the inventory error is $10,000 while the net income error is $6,000. How can they be different? The inventory error is before tax and the net income error is after tax. The difference of $4,000 is in taxes payable. In the first year when margins are too low, taxes are too low as well. So net income is understated by $6,000 and taxes payable are understated by $4,000.

▶▶ **OBJECTIVE 6**
Show the effects of inventory errors on financial statements.

EXHIBIT 7-11

Effects of Inventory Errors (in thousands)

PANEL A				
20X7	Correct Reporting		Incorrect Reporting*	Effects of Errors
Sales		$980		$980
Deduct: Cost of goods sold				
Beginning inventory	$100		$100	
Purchases	500		500	
Cost of goods available for sale	600		600	
Deduct: Ending inventory	70		60	Understated by $10
Cost of goods sold		530		540	Overstated by $10
Gross profit		450		440	Understated by $10
Other expenses		250		250	
Income before income taxes		200		190	Understated by $10
Income tax expense at 40%		80		76	Understated by $4
Net income		$120		$114	**Understated by $6** ┐
Ending balance sheet items				
Inventory		$ 70		$ 60	Understated by $10
Retained earnings includes current net income		120		114	Understated by $6
Income tax liability†		80		76	Understated by $4

*Because of error in ending inventory.
†For simplicity, assume that the entire income tax expense for the year will not be paid until the succeeding year. Therefore, the ending liability will equal the income tax expense.

PANEL B				
20X8	Correct Reporting		Incorrect Reporting*	Effects of Errors
Sales		$980		$980
Deduct: Cost of goods sold				
Beginning inventory	$ 70		$ 60	Understated by $10
Purchases	500		500	
Cost of goods available for sale	570		560	Understated by $10
Deduct: Ending inventory	40		40	
Cost of goods sold		530		520	Understated by $10
Gross profit		450		460	Overstated by $10
Other expenses		250		250	
Income before income taxes		200		210	Overstated by $10
Income tax expense at 40%		80		84	Overstated by $4
Net income		$120		$126	**Overstated by $6** ┘
Ending balance sheet items				
Inventory		$ 40		$ 40	**Correct**
Retained earnings includes				
Net income of previous year		120		114	Counterbalanced and
Net income of current year		120		126	thus now correct in total
Two-year total		$240		$240	
Income tax liability				
End of previous year		80		76	Counterbalanced and thus
End of current year		80		84	now correct in total†
Two-year total		$160		$160	

*Because of error in beginning inventory.
†The $84 really consists of the $4 that pertains to income of the previous year plus $80 that pertains to income of the current year.

Summary Problem for Your Review

PROBLEM

At the end of 20X1, an error was made in the count of physical inventory that overstated the ending inventory value by $2,000. The error went undetected. The subsequent inventory at the end of 20X2 was done correctly. Assess the effect of this error on income before tax, tax expense, net income, and retained earnings for 20X1 and 20X2, assuming a 40% tax rate.

SOLUTION

	20X1	20X2
Beginning inventory	OK	$2,000 too high
Purchases	OK	OK
Goods available for sale	OK	$2,000 too high
Ending inventory	$2,000 too high	OK
Cost of goods sold	$2,000 too low	$2,000 too high

Note that 20X1 ending inventory becomes 20X2 beginning inventory, reversing the effects on Cost of Goods Sold. The 20X1 Cost of Goods Sold being too low causes 20X1 pretax income to be too high by $2,000. Therefore, taxes will be too high by (.40 × $2,000) = $800, and net income will be too high by $1,200, causing retained earnings to be too high by $1,200 also. In 20X2, the effects reverse and by year-end retained earnings is correctly stated.

Cutoff Errors and Inventory Valuation

The accrual basis of accounting should include the physical counting and careful valuation of inventory at least once yearly. Auditors routinely search for **cutoff errors**, which are failures to record transactions in the correct time period. For example, suppose a company with a periodic inventory system and a calendar year-end conducts a physical inventory on December 31. Inventory purchases of $100,000 arrive in the receiving room during the afternoon of December 31. Accountants include the $100,000 acquisition in Purchases and Accounts Payable, but the people counting the inventory fail to include it in the ending inventory count. Such an error would understate ending inventory, thereby overstating cost of goods sold and understating gross profit. This error would be self-correcting in the subsequent year.

Suppose that, in addition to the inventory count error, accountants did not record the acquisition in Purchases and Accounts Payable until January 2. The errors in the inventory count and in accounting for purchases would understate purchases, the ending inventory, and accounts payable as of December 31. However, cost of goods sold and gross profit would be correct because the $100,000 error in purchases and the $100,000 error in ending inventory offset each other. On the balance sheet there is an error in total assets, due to understated Inventory and an equal error in total liabilities, due to understated Accounts Payable.

The correct time to record purchases and sales is keyed to the legal transfer of ownership. Consider an order for goods that a supplier ships FOB shipping point. Technically, the receiving company should record the value of the goods on its financial statements when the supplier ships the goods. However, in practice, the receiving company may not actually record the goods until they are received. As long as both the shipment and delivery of the goods occur in the same accounting period, this discrepancy in the recording of inventory has no financial statement impact. However, at year-end management must determine whether there are goods in transit that should be recorded, even though not yet received. The records would need to be adjusted accordingly to reflect the in transit items.

Auditors are especially careful about cutoff tests because errors are easy to make. Moreover, the pressure for profits sometimes causes managers to manipulate the accounting for sales

cutoff error
Failure to record transactions in the correct time period.

and purchases at year-end. Selectively omitting items from the physical inventory count while accurately recording the purchase can increase cost of goods sold while selectively omitting a purchase while counting the inventory physically can decrease cost of goods sold. The first case understates earnings and the second case overstates them. It is easy to imagine circumstances under which management might choose to overstate earnings, but why would management choose to understate earnings? Suppose that managers earn a bonus for increasing earnings by at least 10% over the prior year, but there is no extra bonus if the increase exceeds 10%. As year-end approaches, the company is on target to increase earnings by 15%. If management could manipulate inventories and reduce the earnings increase from 15% to 10% they would still receive their current-year bonus. This manipulation would create a self-correcting error that would overstate earnings in the next year and make it easier to earn next year's bonus.

Similar incentives sometimes tempt managers to deliberately include sales orders placed near year-end (instead of bona fide completed sales) in revenues. For example, a news story about **McCormick & Company**, a firm known for its spices, reported, "The investigation also found that improprieties included the company's accounting for sales. In a longstanding practice, the company recorded as sales, goods that had been selected and prepared for shipment rather than waiting until after they had been shipped as is the customary accounting practice." Sometimes managers will accelerate the recognition of revenues in order to meet a sales- or profit-based target and therefore earn a bonus. This is an obvious ethical lapse.

The Importance of Gross Profits

▶▶ **OBJECTIVE 7**

Evaluate the gross profit percentage and inventory turnover.

We began this chapter by discussing gross profits, which are equal to sales revenue less the cost of goods sold. Management and investors closely watch gross profit and how it changes over time. We now return to the gross profit concept and examine how it can help us understand an industry or a company and how changes in gross profit over time for either an industry or a company are helpful to management and investors.

Gross Profit Percentage

As first introduced in Chapter 4, analysts often express gross profit as a percentage of sales. Consider the following information for a hypothetical **Safeway** grocery store:

	Amount	Percentage
Sales	$10,000,000	100%
Net cost of goods sold	7,500,000	75%
Gross profit	$ 2,500,000	25%

The gross profit percentage—gross profit divided by sales—is 25% for this store. The following table illustrates the extent to which gross profit percentages vary across industries.

Company	Gross Profit Percentage
Ford Motor Company; Automobiles	22%
The Home Depot; Building supplies	34
Merck; Pharmaceuticals	81
Whole Foods; Specialty grocery retailer	38
Safeway; Grocery retailer	31
Sysco; Grocery wholesaler	20

Sources: Fidelity.com company analysis features, 2012.

wholesaler

A company that sells in large quantities to retail companies instead of individuals.

retailer

A company that sells items directly to the public—to individual buyers.

What accounts for this wide variation in gross profit percentage? The nature of the business plays a major role. **Wholesalers**, such as **Sysco**, sell in larger quantities and incur fewer selling costs because they sell to retail companies instead of individuals. As a result of competition and high volumes, they have smaller gross profit percentages than do retailers. **Retailers**, such as Safeway and **Whole Foods**, sell directly to the public—to individual buyers—and typically have higher gross profit margins than wholesalers in the same industry. Also note that the specialty retailer, Whole Foods, commands a higher markup on its products than Safeway, the regular grocery retailer. Drug manufacturers, such as Merck, earn high gross profits because of high drug prices, caused by the need for substantial R&D outlays (sometimes more than 15% of sales) and allowed by patent protection on specific drugs. In contrast, auto manufacturers face more direct competition and earn lower gross profit percentages.

Consider a pharmaceutical company that must incur large R&D costs to generate any sales from a drug. Accounting practice treats the R&D costs as a period cost when incurred instead of a product cost to be matched to future sales of the drug. Why? Because it is impossible to know, as a company incurs R&D costs, whether it will ultimately produce a viable drug whose therapeutic value will allow recovery of the costs of development. But the pharmaceutical company still must generate enough revenue and cash flow to cover the costs of R&D, so it needs high gross margin percentages. The Business First box on p. 306 elaborates on some of the reasons a pharmaceutical company such as Merck or Eli Lilly has high gross margin percentages.

Gross margin percentages tend to be fairly stable over time. Even during the recession of 2008–2011, most of these companies had gross margin percentages very similar to the ones shown above, except that Ford reported a gross profit percentage of only 2% in 2008. The Home Depot has not recovered to 2006 sales levels. Sales have fallen by 25% since then, but the gross profit percentage has actually ticked up very slightly.

Estimating Intraperiod Gross Profit and Inventory

To avoid costly physical counts of inventory, some companies use the gross profit percentage to estimate ending inventory balances for monthly or quarterly reports. For example, suppose sales of a particular Home Depot store have historically resulted in a gross profit percentage of 30%. The accountant assumes that gross profit continues to be 30% of sales and estimates the cost of goods sold for quarterly sales of $10 million as follows (in millions):

$$\text{Sales} - \text{Cost of goods sold} = \text{Gross profit}$$
$$S - COGS = .30 \times S$$
$$\$10.0 - COGS = .30 \times \$10.0$$
$$COGS = \$7.0$$

If we know the store's beginning inventory is $5 million and purchases are $7.1 million, we can then estimate ending inventory to be $5.1 million as follows (in millions):

$$\text{Beginning inventory} + \text{Purchases} - \text{Ending inventory} = COGS$$
$$BI + P - EI = COGS$$
$$\$5.0 + \$7.1 - EI = \$7.0$$
$$EI = \$5.1$$

This estimation method is not acceptable for audited year-end financial statements.

Gross Profit Percentage and Turnover

Retailers often attempt to increase total profits by increasing sales levels. They may lower prices and hope to increase their total gross profits by selling their inventories more quickly, replenishing, selling again, and so forth. In essence, they are accepting a lower gross profit per unit but are expecting to increase total sales more than enough to compensate. With a higher volume of sales activity, a smaller gross margin per unit sold can provide higher total profits. This is one of the reasons that stores such as Costco, Wal-Mart, and The Home Depot do well.

To relate sales levels to inventory levels we measure **inventory turnover**—cost of goods sold divided by the average inventory held during a given period. Average inventory is usually computed simply as the sum of beginning inventory and ending inventory divided by 2. For The Home Depot store in the previous example, the average inventory is [($5.0 million + $5.1 million) ÷ 2] = $5.05 million. The quarterly inventory turnover is computed as follows:

$$\text{Inventory turnover} = \text{Cost of goods sold} \div \text{Average inventory}$$
$$= \$7.0 \text{ million} \div \$5.05 \text{ million} = 1.4$$

Suppose sales double if The Home Depot lowers its prices by 5%. Sales revenue on the current level of business drops from $10 million to (0.95 × $10 million), or $9.5 million. But the

inventory turnover
The cost of goods sold divided by the average inventory held during a given period.

BUSINESS FIRST

PHARMACEUTICALS—PRICING AND AVAILABILITY

Nothing is more important than your health, and nothing is more contentious than how much drugs cost, who should pay for them, and where in the world they will be available. Eli Lilly is a major pharmaceutical company with worldwide sales of $23.1 billion and a gross profit percentage of 85%. Part of the reason for this high gross margin is that Lilly spends 21% of sales on research and development, producing the next generation of life-saving, life-extending, and life-improving drugs. Lilly deducts these R&D expenses after the computation of gross profit.

Lilly has addressed the question, "Are Drug Prices Fair?" in several of its annual reports and other publications. For example, in 2009 the company's Web site presented a 48-page document entitled, "Medicines and Miracles, Improving Health … Improving Life." In that document Lilly argues that many widely held beliefs about the high cost of drugs are based on incomplete or misunderstood data. In 2012 the Web site included a speech by John Lechleiter, chairman and CEO, discussing "Return on Innovation." A few of the ideas are summarized below.

Lilly stresses that today's medicines are more expensive than in the past, but they do more than ever before. Modern medicines are more cost-effective than other treatments. A year's treatment with new antipsychotic drugs costs about the same as 1 week of hospitalization for a patient with schizophrenia and improves the patient's quality of life. Much of the public outcry over pharmaceutical costs is not about the cost of a specific drug, but about the total cost of all drugs. Lilly indicates that medicines account for about 10% of health-care spending in the United States and this has been remarkably stable since 1960. Indeed, Lilly indicates that the average American spends more on tobacco and alcohol than he or she spends on over-the-counter and prescription medicines combined.

Lilly's answer to the debate about drug prices is that pharmaceuticals are a good value in the fight against disease and preserving the quality of life. Today we are learning a great deal about genetics, gene mapping, and how genetic makeup causes treatments to succeed for one patient and fail for another. All of these developments have the potential to alter the costs of finding successful treatments and using them effectively for the right patients. Lechleiter illustrates efforts to tailor drugs to individuals, citing the use of personal characteristics such as age or weight; established biomarkers such as blood sugar levels for people with diabetes; and new innovations in bio-imaging and the use of genetic screens.

Pharmaceutical companies in the developed world are for-profit companies and have been criticized for ignoring solutions to important diseases in lesser-developed countries because the affected populations could not pay. Merck's expensive decision some years ago to successfully pursue a cure for a major disease prevalent almost exclusively in Africa is one of several exceptions. Both humanitarian groups and political pressure have helped encourage compromises that extend the availability of drugs to poor populations. For example, the Gates Foundation has invested more than $1.6 billion to speed vaccine development and provide immunization to the world's poor.

Lechleiter also provides several compelling reminders of the role of medicines in our health. For centuries, life expectancy was 20–25 years, growing to 35 years by 1800 and 47 years in 1900. But the explosive growth was to 78 years in 2000, a 66% increase in 100 years. In the first half of the twentieth century the gains were from fewer people dying of infectious diseases, partly due to cleaner water, better sanitation, and better diet. But the discovery of insulin early in the century and of penicillin in the 1940s followed by a stream of new classes of antibiotics played a huge role in increasing life span. And in more recent years numerous new therapies have led to a nearly 60% decline in death from coronary heart disease. Similarly, the 5-year survival rate for all cancers together has increased from 50% in 1975 to nearly 70% today. The drugs may be expensive, but they do extend our lives and improve the quality of life during those extended years.

Sources: Eli Lilly 1999, 2003, 2008, and 2012 Annual Reports; *BusinessWeek*, April 26, 2004, p. 65; Eli Lilly Web site, http://www.lilly.com/news/speeches/Pages/101029.aspx.

store sells twice as many units, so total revenue becomes (2 × $9.5 million), or $19 million. How profitable is this store? Cost of goods sold doubles from $7 million to $14 million. Total gross profit is ($19 million − $14 million) = $5 million. So gross profit during the quarter is $2 million higher as a result of the lower price. The inventory turnover doubles: $14 million divided by $5.05 million (the unchanged average inventory) is 2.8. However, the gross profit percentage falls from 30% to 26% ($5 million divided by $19 million).

EXHIBIT 7-12

The Home Depot Store

*Effects of Increased
Inventory Turnover
($ in millions)*

		Unit Sales Increase		
	Original	**20%**	**50%**	**100%**
PANEL A				
No change in sales price				
Sales	$10.00	$12.00	$15.00	$20.00
Cost of goods sold (70%)	7.00	8.40	10.50	14.00
Gross profit (30%)	$ 3.00	$ 3.60	$ 4.50	$ 6.00
Inventory turnover	1.4	1.7	2.1	2.8
PANEL B				
5% reduction in sales price				
Sales (95% of above)	$ 9.50	$11.40	$14.25	$19.00
Cost of goods sold (as above)	7.00	8.40	10.50	14.00
Gross profit (26% of sales)	$ 2.50	$ 3.00	$ 3.75	$ 5.00
Inventory turnover (as above)	1.4	1.7	2.1	2.8

Is the company better off? Maybe. Certainly, the current month's gross profit is larger. However, long-term strategic concerns raise the question, "Is this new sales level sustainable?" For some products, when prices fall, consumers sharply increase purchases and stockpile the extras for later consumption. There is little increase in underlying demand, just a shift of future purchases to the present. Therefore, the current increase in sales could result in decreased future sales.

Another strategic question is "What will the competition do?" If The Home Depot's increased sales came at a competitor's expense, the competitor's response may be a similar decrease in prices. The competition might recover most of its old customers, with each buying a little more at the new price than they did at the old. Assuming all competitors decrease prices similarly, the whole market would see perhaps a 20% sales growth, not a doubling of sales. In that case, The Home Depot store would be no better off overall because the 20% sales growth would just cover the 5% price reduction.

Exhibit 7-12 illustrates two principles. Panel A shows that if a firm can increase inventory turnover while maintaining a constant gross profit percentage, it should do so. To increase inventory turnover means that a firm supports sales levels with less inventory. It can do this by more frequently restocking, for example. However, as Panel B shows, if the increased inventory turnover results from sales growth driven by a decrease in sales price, the gross profit percentage may fall. The desirability of the change depends on whether the sales gain could offset the decreased margin.

In The Home Depot store example, when a 5% price reduction produces only a 20% increase in units sold, the new gross profit of $3 million is just equal to the initial gross profit. Any sales increase less than 20% would result in a decreased gross profit. However, at any sales increase greater than 20%, the new gross profit would exceed the original $3 million. For example, at a 50% increase in sales volume, the new gross profit of $3.75 million exceeds the original by ($3.75 million – $3 million) = $.75 million. The lesson of Exhibit 7-12 is that you cannot focus on only one number or measure of company performance. Paying too much attention to one measure could cause you to miss the fact that another measure is falling fast.

Earlier you saw the industry variability in gross profit percentages. The same variability applies to inventory turnover percentages, as the following table illustrates:

Company	Gross Profit Percentage	Inventory Turnover
Ford Motor Company	22%	16
The Home Depot	34	4
Merck	81	2
Whole Foods	38	18
Safeway	31	11
Sysco	20	16

Source: Fidelity.com company analysis features, 2012.

As you can see, the companies with the higher gross profit percentages tend to have lower inventory turnover. Compare Ford and Sysco with Home Depot and Merck. But there is substantial variation around this pattern. As noted earlier for gross profit percentage, turnover is fairly stable by company over time. Only two of the six companies experienced changes in their turnover ratios during the last 3 years and then only slightly. However, within industries there is substantial variation. For example, Fidelity.com provides an industry average value for inventory turnover as well as turnover ratios by company. For Ford the turnover ratio is 16, which is substantially higher than the reported automobile industry average of 9. Similarly, Whole Foods' inventory turnover of 18 far exceeds the Food and Staples Retail average of 10, while Safeway's 11 is about average.

The inventory turnover measure is especially effective for assessing companies in the same industry. If one industry member has a higher turnover than another, it is probably more efficient. That is, the higher turnover indicates an ability to use smaller inventory levels to attain high sales levels. This is good because it reduces the investment in inventory. Such a company has fewer products sitting on display shelves or in warehouses and uses less capital in maintaining, moving, and displaying inventory items. Thus, Whole Foods is outperforming Safeway on two measures—displaying both a higher gross profit percentage and a higher turnover.

In evaluating accounting measures of performance, we must always consider the effects of different accounting choices. Within industries, companies typically choose similar inventory cost methods (LIFO or FIFO), but this is not always true. So one explanation for differences in gross profit percentages or inventory turnovers in a comparison between companies is a difference in inventory cost flow assumption. However, such an issue could not explain this comparison of Whole Foods and Safeway.

Do the mental experiment. Assume a period of rising prices and that one firm uses LIFO and one uses FIFO. Assume their sales levels and other economic outcomes are identical. The one using LIFO shows a lower gross profit because cost of goods sold is higher. That same firm has higher inventory turnover because its inventory levels are lower. Thus, in our example, differences in inventory accounting could not explain the advantage that Whole Foods has on both measures.

Gross Profit Percentages And Accuracy of Records

Auditors, including those from the IRS, use the gross profit percentage to help satisfy themselves about the accuracy of records. For example, the IRS compiles gross profit percentages by types of retail establishment. If a company shows an unusually low percentage compared with similar companies, IRS auditors may suspect that the company has tried to avoid taxes by failing to record all cash sales. Similarly, managers watch changes in gross profit percentages to judge operating profitability and to monitor how well a company is controlling employee theft and shoplifting.

Internal Control of Inventories

In many organizations, inventories are more easily accessible than cash. Therefore, they can become an easy target for thieves. Retail merchants must contend with inventory shrinkage, a polite term for shoplifting by customers and embezzling by employees. The importance of shrinkage is clear from a recent annual report of The Home Depot that says, "Our second priority is to increase gross profit through shrink reduction, distribution efficiencies, an improved pricing model, the expansion of private brand offerings and increased foreign sourcing. In 2008, inventory shrink decreased as a result of several focused initiatives." The report for the year ending in January 2012 refers to unchanged shrinkage over the prior year. Improvement does not always happen, but shrinkage is always important to monitor and minimize.

A University of Florida study sponsored by the National Retail Federation estimated that U.S. retailers lose $37 billion annually to inventory shrinkage, the largest percentage of it due to employee theft. Average inventory shrinkage for retailers is 1%–3% of sales depending on the retail category. The study is discussed at Multichannelmerchant.com, which presents a number of possible interventions that retailers can use to reduce theft. These interventions include cameras to monitor customer and employee behavior, analysis of data to identify fraudulent returned merchandise and who is making the returns, merchandise sensors to identify merchandise that has not been paid for, and perhaps most importantly, improved hiring and training practices for employees. Experts on controlling inventory shrinkage generally agree that the best deterrent is an alert employee at the point of sale.

At the National Retail Federation's Loss Prevention Conference in June 2012, shrinkage control was one of four key focus points, along with emerging technologies, safety, and crisis management. The conference Web site noted that "One of the core principles of a loss prevention program is reducing shrink."

Shrinkage in Perpetual and Periodic Inventory Systems

Measuring inventory shrinkage is straightforward for companies that use a perpetual inventory system. Shrinkage is simply the difference between the cost of inventory identified by a physical count and the inventory balance in the company's general ledger. A periodic inventory system has no continuing balance of the inventory account. Cost of goods sold automatically includes inventory shrinkage. Why? Beginning inventory plus purchases less ending inventory measures all inventory that has flowed out, whether it went to customers, shoplifters, or embezzlers, or was simply lost or broken. In a periodic inventory system, a major decrease in gross profit percentage could point to increased shrinkage as the problem.

Summary Problem for Your Review

PROBLEM

Hewlett-Packard (HP) designs, manufactures, and services a broad array of products including perhaps your calculator or printer. Some results of product sales for the year ended October 31, 2011, were as follows ($ in millions):

Sales of products	$127,245
Cost of merchandise sold	93,397
Beginning merchandise inventory	6,466
Ending merchandise inventory	7,490

1. Calculate the 2011 gross profit and gross profit percentage for HP.
2. Calculate the inventory turnover ratio.
3. What gross profit would have been reported if inventory turnover in 2011 had been 9, the gross profit percentage remained the same as that calculated in requirement 1, and the level of inventory was unchanged?

SOLUTION

(Monetary amounts are in millions.)

1. Gross profit = Sales − Cost of merchandise sold
     = $127,245 − $93,397
     = $33,848

   Gross profit percentage = Gross profit ÷ Sales
     = $33,848 ÷ $127,245
     = 26.6%

2. Inventory turnover = Cost of merchandise sold ÷ Average merchandise inventory
     = $93,397 ÷ [($6,466 + $7,490) ÷ 2]
     = $93,397 ÷ $6,978
     = 13.4

3. To respond to this question you must first see that a lower inventory turnover given a constant average inventory implies a decrease in sales. Decreased sales with a constant gross profit percentage implies decreased total gross profit. With these relationships in mind, answering the question is a process of working backward based on the ratios and relationships.

$$\text{Cost of merchandise sold} = \text{Inventory turnover} \times \text{Average merchandise inventory}$$
$$= 9 \times \$6,978$$
$$= \$62,802$$
$$\text{Gross profit percentage} = (\text{Sales} - \text{Cost of merchandise sold}) \div \text{Sales}$$
$$26.6\% = (S - \$62,802) \div S$$
$$.266 \times S = S - \$62,802$$
$$S - (.266 \times S) = \$62,802$$
$$S \times (1 - .266) = \$62,802$$
$$S = \$62,802 \div (1 - .266)$$
$$S = \$85,561$$
$$\text{Gross profit} = \text{Sales} - \text{Cost of merchandise sold}$$
$$= \$85,561 - \$62,802$$
$$= \$22,759$$

At a turnover of 9 and a constant gross profit percentage, the gross profit would have been $22,759. As you would expect given our calculations, the gross profit percentage remains at ($22,759 ÷ $85,561) = 26.6%.

Highlights to Remember

1 Link inventory valuation to gross profit. We link inventory valuation to gross profit because the inventory valuation involves allocating the cost of goods available for sale between cost of goods sold (used in computing gross profit—sales less cost of goods sold—on the income statement) and ending inventory (a current asset on the balance sheet).

2 Use both perpetual and periodic inventory systems. Under the perpetual inventory system, we continuously track inventories and cost of goods sold by recording cost of goods sold at the time of each sale. Under the periodic inventory system, we compute cost of goods sold using an adjusting entry at year-end. Under both systems, accountants conduct physical counts of inventory. They count the goods on hand and calculate a cost for each item from purchase records. Under the periodic system, the physical inventory count must be performed at year-end as it is the basis for the year-end adjusting entry to recognize cost of goods sold. Under the perpetual system, the physical inventory is used to confirm the accounting records. Differences, if any, lead to adjustments to cost of goods sold and ending inventory.

3 Calculate the cost of merchandise acquired. The cost of merchandise acquired is the invoice price of the goods plus directly identifiable inbound transportation costs less any cash or quantity discounts and less any returns or allowances.

4 Compute income and inventory values using the three principal inventory valuation methods allowed under both U.S. GAAP and IFRS and the one method allowed only by U.S. GAAP. Valuation of inventories involves the assignment of specific historical costs of acquisition either to units sold or to units remaining in ending inventory. Four major inventory valuation methods are in use in the United States: specific identification, average cost, FIFO, and LIFO. IFRS does now allow LIFO. Specific identification is most common for low-volume, high-value products such as automobiles, boats, or jewelry. FIFO attributes the most recent, current prices to inventory items. LIFO attributes the most recent, current prices to cost of sales. When prices are rising and inventories are constant or growing, LIFO net income is less than FIFO net income. LIFO is popular in the United States among companies who face rising prices, for whom lower profits under LIFO mean lower taxes. The U.S. tax law allows companies to use LIFO for tax purposes only if they also use it for financial reporting purposes. LIFO also allows management to affect its income by the timing of purchases of inventory. Average cost provides results between LIFO and FIFO for both the income statement cost of sales and the balance sheet inventory number.

5 Use the lower-of-cost-or-market method to value inventories under both U.S. GAAP and IFRS. Conservatism leads to the lower-of-cost-or-market (LCM) method, which treats cost as the maximum value of inventory. U.S. companies must reduce inventory carrying amounts to replacement cost (with a corresponding increase in cost of goods sold) when inventory replacement prices fall below historical cost levels and net realizable values also decline. IFRS uses net realizable value instead of replacement cost in applying LCM.

6 **Show the effects of inventory errors on financial statements.** The nature of accrual accounting for inventories creates a self-correcting quality about errors in counting or valuing the ending inventory. This occurs because the ending inventory in one period becomes the beginning inventory of the subsequent period.

7 **Evaluate the gross profit percentage and inventory turnover.** Financial analysts and managers use gross profit percentages as a measure of profitability and inventory turnover as a measure of efficient asset use. They compare these measures with prior levels to examine trends and with current levels of other industry members to assess relative performance.

Appendix 7A: Characteristics and Consequences of LIFO

Although LIFO is prohibited under IFRS, it is widely used in the United States, has strong tax benefits for certain companies, and has some unusual features in application. Because of its dominant role in inventory accounting in the United States, we give LIFO a little extra attention in this appendix.

▶▶ **OBJECTIVE 8**

Describe characteristics of LIFO and how they affect the measurement of income.

LIFO and Inflation

Inflation is a key factor driving companies to use LIFO. When inflation is low, as it has been for most of the last three decades, the tax and income differences are small. The inventory method chosen matters little. Low inflation has been the norm in the United States during most of the last hundred years, but in the 1970s, the inflation rate in the United States reached double digits for the first time. In response, more than 40 U.S. corporations switched from FIFO to LIFO, deciding the benefit of lower income taxes exceeded the cost of reporting lower profits. These tax savings were not trivial. For example, by switching from FIFO to LIFO, **DuPont** saved more than $200 million in taxes in the first year, and it anticipated greater savings in the future.

Why did some firms remain on FIFO? Some firms should choose FIFO because for them it lowers taxes. Even when prices were rising in general, some industries, such as computer manufacturing, faced declining costs and prices, so FIFO minimized their reported income and taxes. For those who could have lowered taxes by using LIFO, possible reasons to remain on FIFO include the high bookkeeping costs of implementing the switch, reluctance by management to make an accounting switch that reduces reported income and possibly reduces management bonuses, fear that banks would view the reduction in income unfavorably in loan negotiations, and belief that lower reported income would result in a lower stock price.

Holding Gains and Inventory Profits

LIFO's income statement orientation provides a particular economic interpretation of operating performance in inflationary periods, based on replacement of inventory. A merchant such as Emilio in the example beginning on page 293 is in the business of buying and selling on a daily basis. To continue in business, he must be able to maintain his stock of cola and must make sufficient profit on each transaction to make it worth his while to run the soda stand. So, before Emilio can feel he has really made a profit, he will need to restock inventory and be ready for the next day. If he must spend 56¢ to replace the can he sold, this 56¢ cost of acquiring the item today is the current replacement cost of the inventory. Under LIFO, we calculate his profit to be 34¢ because we use that recent inventory acquisition cost of 56¢ to measure cost of goods sold. So LIFO approximates a replacement cost view of the transaction.

In contrast, FIFO measures profit using the 30¢ can acquired on Monday as cost of goods sold and reports a profit of 60¢. The difference between the 60¢ FIFO profit and the 34¢ LIFO profit is 26¢, which is also the difference between the historical cost of 30¢ under FIFO and the recent replacement cost of 56¢ under LIFO. This 26¢ difference occurs because prices are rising. We call it a **holding gain** or an **inventory profit**—the increase in the replacement cost of the inventory held during the current period. The idea is that between Monday and Thursday, Emilio's first can of cola acquired for 30¢ became more valuable as prices rose, and because he held it as inventory during those days he experienced a 26¢ gain.

holding gain (inventory profit)

Increase in the replacement cost of the inventory held during the current period.

Because LIFO matches the most recent acquisition costs with sales revenue, LIFO cost of goods sold typically offers a close approximation to replacement cost, and reported net income rarely contains significant holding gains. In contrast, FIFO reports a profit of 60¢ including the economic profit of 34¢ calculated as sales price less replacement costs, plus the inventory profit or holding gain of 26¢ that arose because the value of the inventory item rose with the passage of time.

LIFO Layers

The ending inventory under LIFO will have one total value, but it may contain prices from many different periods. For example, Emilio's ending inventory contained two cans, one acquired on Monday at 30¢ and one acquired on Tuesday at 40¢. We call each distinct cost element of inventory a **LIFO layer** or a **LIFO increment**—a separately identifiable addition to inventory at an identifiable cost level. As a company grows, the LIFO layers accumulate one after another over the years. Suppose Emilio's business grew for years, ending each year with two more cans in inventory than were there the year before. Each year would contribute an identifiable LIFO layer, much like the annual rings on a tree. After 4 years of inventory growth and rising prices, his ending inventory might be structured as follows:

LIFO layer (LIFO increment)
A separately identifiable addition to LIFO inventory at an identifiable cost level.

Year 1	Layer 1—1 can @ .30	
	Layer 2—1 can @ .40	$ .70
Year 2	Layer 3—2 cans @ .45	.90
Year 3	Layer 4—2 cans @ .50	1.00
Year 4	Layer 5—2 cans @ .55	1.10
Total inventory—8 cans		$3.70

Some LIFO companies have inventories that include layers that date back as far as 1940, when companies first used LIFO. Reported LIFO inventory values may therefore be far below the market value or current replacement value of the inventory. This means that the book values reported on the balance sheet will have little relevance to investors interested in assessing the current value of the assets of the company. Although LIFO better presents the economic reality on the income statement, FIFO provides more up-to-date valuations of inventory on the balance sheet.

LIFO Inventory Liquidations

The existence of old LIFO layers can cause problems in income measurement when inventories decrease after a period of rising prices. Examine Exhibit 7-13. Suppose Harbor Electronics bought 100 units of inventory at $10 per unit on December 31, 20X0, to begin its business operations. The company bought and sold 100 units each year, 20X1–20X4, at the purchase and selling prices shown. The example assumes replacement costs and sales prices rise by the same amount, with a difference between the two of $3 per unit. In 20X5, Harbor sold its remaining 100 units, but purchased none.

Compare the gross profit each year under LIFO with that under FIFO in Exhibit 7-13. LIFO gross profit was consistently less than FIFO gross profit because prices were rising, and the LIFO cost of goods sold reflected the latest prices, whereas the FIFO cost of goods sold did not. What happened in 20X5? The old 20X0 inventory became the cost of goods sold under LIFO because Harbor depleted its inventory. As a result, gross profit under LIFO soared to $1,300, well above the FIFO gross profit, which was stable at $500. In general, when the physical amount of inventory decreases in a period of rising prices, under LIFO the cost of goods sold consists of low-acquisition-cost inventory associated with old LIFO layers. This is called a **LIFO liquidation**. This treatment can create a very low cost of goods sold and high gross profit.

LIFO liquidation
A decrease in the physical amount in inventory causing old, low LIFO inventory acquisition costs to become the cost of goods sold, resulting in a high gross profit.

We saw above that FIFO leads to recognition of a small holding gain being recognized each year due to the increase in value of items held in inventory. In this example, you could think of the annual $200 difference in gross profit as reported under LIFO and FIFO in years 20X1 through 20X4 as being due to recognition of an annual $200 holding gain under FIFO. In contrast, a LIFO company would recognize all of the holding gain in the final year, creating a difference of $800 ($1,300 – $500) in gross profit in the year of the LIFO liquidation.

				FIFO			LIFO		
Year	Purchase Price Per Unit	Selling Price Per Unit	Revenue	Cost of Goods Sold	Gross Profit	Ending Inventory	Cost of Goods Sold	Gross Profit	Ending Inventory
20X0	$10	—	—	—	—	$1,000	—	—	$1,000
20X1	12	$15	$1,500	$1,000	$ 500	1,200	$1,200	$ 300	1,000
20X2	14	17	1,700	1,200	500	1,400	1,400	300	1,000
20X3	16	19	1,900	1,400	500	1,600	1,600	300	1,000
20X4	18	21	2,100	1,600	500	1,800	1,800	300	1,000
20X5		23	2,300	1,800	500	0	1,000	1,300	0
Total			$9,500	$7,000	$2,500		$7,000	$2,500	

EXHIBIT 7-13

Harbor Electronics

Effect of Inventory Liquidations Under LIFO (Purchases and Sales of 100 Units 20X1–20X4, Purchases but No Sales in 20X0; Sales but No Purchases in 20X5)

For example, LIFO inventory liquidations by Ford Motor Company decreased its 2010 cost of sales by $4 million. In a sense, a LIFO liquidation means that the current year's income includes the cumulative inventory profit from years of increasing prices. An analyst tracking Ford's profitability would notice that its profits in 2010 were not due solely to producing and selling automobiles that year. It was partly due to the company's inventory accounting process. Ford is a large and complex company, and it uses LIFO for only part of its inventory, 31% in 2010. Moreover, the prices of various parts of its inventories move in different directions. So, while Ford had LIFO liquidations for part of its inventory in 2010, overall its LIFO inventory grew, as we will discuss more fully below.

The effect of LIFO liquidations is potentially large, and security analysts incorporate the effect of the choice between LIFO and FIFO on net income in their overall evaluation of a company's performance. The difference between a company's inventory valued using LIFO and what it would be under FIFO, its **LIFO reserve**, is helpful in making these estimates. Companies that use LIFO must explicitly measure and report their LIFO reserve on the balance sheet itself or in the footnotes.

Refer to Exhibit 7-13. What is the Harbor Electronics' LIFO reserve at the end of 20X1? It is ($1,200 – $1,000) = $200, the difference in the LIFO and FIFO ending inventories. Note that it is the same as the difference in gross profit of $200 in 20X1. What about year 20X2? The LIFO reserve is $400 (FIFO ending inventory of $1,400 less LIFO ending inventory of $1,000). This difference represents the cumulative effect on earnings (or gross profit) during the first 2 years the company was in business. The specific effect on earnings during 20X2 is the change in the LIFO reserve, or $200. Exhibit 7-14 summarizes these effects.

From Exhibit 7-14, note that the *annual* difference between gross profit using FIFO and gross profit using LIFO is the yearly change in the LIFO reserve. Finally, when Harbor sells all of the inventory in 20X5, the liquidation of the LIFO inventory leads to recognition of higher

LIFO reserve

The difference between a company's inventory valued at LIFO and what it would be under FIFO.

EXHIBIT 7-14

Harbor Electronics

Annual and Cumulative Effects of LIFO Reserve

	Ending Inventory				Gross Profit Effect	
Year	FIFO	LIFO	LIFO Reserve	Change in Reserve	Current	Cumulative
20X0	$1,000	$1,000	$ 0	$ 0	$ 0	$ 0
20X1	1,200	1,000	200	200	200	200
20X2	1,400	1,000	400	200	200	400
20X3	1,600	1,000	600	200	200	600
20X4	1,800	1,000	800	200	200	800
20X5	0	0	0	(800)	(800)	0

earnings under LIFO than under FIFO by the entire amount of the LIFO reserve. LIFO recognizes inventory profits when a company reduces its inventory levels. The balance of the LIFO reserve at any point in time indicates the *cumulative* difference between FIFO and LIFO gross profit over all prior years.

How significant are the effects of LIFO? Ford Motor Company reported 2010 inventory of $5.9 billion. Ford used LIFO for some of its inventories. If it had used FIFO for all inventories, the total inventory would have been $865 million higher (a 15% difference). This means that over time, Ford has reported lower income on its tax returns by $865 million and paid lower taxes of approximately $346 million ($865 million times the approximate tax rate of 40%) as a result of its decision to use LIFO instead of FIFO.

This savings amounts to an interest-free loan from the government. If Ford were to switch to FIFO or go out of business, the recognition of cost of goods sold based on old inventory costs would create a large LIFO liquidation, and all these delayed taxes would become due. In the meantime, Ford has the use of some $346 million it has not yet had to pay in taxes.

Adjusting from LIFO to FIFO

Typically, disclosures in the annual report are sufficient to permit detailed analysis of LIFO effects. Ford Motor Company's 2010 report allows us to compare results under LIFO with what Ford would have reported under FIFO:

Ford Motor Company ($ in millions)

| | 2010 Inventory | | Cost of Goods Sold |
	Beginning	Ending	
LIFO	$5,041	$5,917	$104,451
LIFO reserve	798	865	67[*]
FIFO	$5,839	$6,782	$104,384

[*]Change in LIFO reserve is an increase of $67 = ($798 − $865). Therefore, cost of goods sold is $67 less under FIFO then under LIFO.

Note that Ford's LIFO reserve increased from $798 million to $865 million during 2010. This increase of $67 million in the LIFO reserve is exactly the amount by which the cost of goods sold for the year as computed under LIFO exceeds the cost of goods sold as it would be computed under FIFO.

INTERPRETING FINANCIAL STATEMENTS

In contrast to the effect on cost of goods sold in a specific year, we can examine the cumulative effect of the inventory accounting choice over time. The end-of-year level of the LIFO reserve allows us to answer the question, "During the years that **Ford** has used LIFO, what has been the total, cumulative effect on cost of goods sold?" To see this, do the mental experiment of having Ford sell all of its 2010 year-end inventory for $9,000 million in early 2011. How would profit from this liquidation differ between LIFO and FIFO given inventory levels that would exist at year-end 2010 under each method?

Answer

This complete liquidation would produce gross profit under LIFO that is $865 million higher than gross profit as it would be reported under FIFO. This $865 million difference in gross profit in the final liquidation year is equal to the cumulative amount by which gross profits were lower under LIFO in past years. The hypothetical liquidation of Ford inventories would show the following (in millions):

	LIFO	FIFO	Difference
Sales	$9,000	$9,000	—
Cost of goods sold	5,917	6,782	865
Gross profit	$3,083	$2,218	($865)

Summary Problem for Your Review

PROBLEM

"When prices are rising, FIFO produces profits that confuse economic profit and holding gains because more resources are needed to maintain operations than were previously required to purchase the same inventory that was just sold." Do you agree? Explain.

SOLUTION

Yes, FIFO profits combine economic profits and holding gains, but well-trained analysts and managers know that. LIFO often gives a better measure of "distributable" income than FIFO. Recall Emilio's Cola Sales example in Exhibit 7-5 on page 294. The gross profit under FIFO was 60¢, and under LIFO it was 34¢. The (60¢ – 34¢) = 26¢ difference is a fool's profit because it must be reinvested to maintain the same inventory level as prior to the sale. It arises from a profit on holding inventory as prices change instead of the profit from buying at wholesale and selling at retail.

Appendix 7B: Inventory in a Manufacturing Environment

Yes, In this we examined inventory accounting from the viewpoint of a merchandiser. When a company manufactures products, the accounting issues change. The cost of inventory is a combination of the acquisition cost of raw material; the wages paid to workers who combine the raw materials into finished products; and an allocation of the costs of space, energy, and equipment used by the workers as they transform the various elements into a finished product.

> ▶▶ **OBJECTIVE 9**
> Determine inventory costs for a manufacturing company.

Consider how we accumulate costs in a manufacturing environment for Packit, a company that makes backpacks. The raw materials are heavy fabric, glue, and thread. The transformation occurs when workers use cutters to make the panels that other workers sew and glue together. The costs of manufacture certainly include the wages paid to workers and raw materials, but they also include depreciation on the manufacturing building, depreciation on the sewing machines and cutters, and utilities to support the effort in the form of heat, power, and light. The finished goods are backpacks.

The accounting process is easiest to understand when calculating the cost of a complete year of production using the periodic approach. In the following example, Packit produced 40,000 children's backpacks during its first year in business at a total cost of $800,000, providing a cost per backpack of $20.00 ($800,000 ÷ 40,000 units). At year-end, if Packit has sold all 40,000 backpacks, the financial statements would include $800,000 in cost of goods sold.

Packit Company—Year 1

Beginning inventory	—
Fabric purchased and used	$200,000
Wages paid to workers	300,000
Thread and glue used	50,000
Depreciation on building and equipment	220,000
Utilities	30,000
Total costs to manufacture	$800,000
Cost per backpack ($800,000 ÷ 40,000)	$ 20.00

In the preceding example, Packit transformed all materials acquired during the year into finished products and sold all those products before year-end. In reality, if we take a snapshot of the typical backpack manufacturer at year-end, we would observe bolts of fabric, spools of thread, and gallons of glue waiting to be put into production. We call these items that are held for use in the manufacturing of a product **raw material inventory**. In addition, we would also observe fabric already cut but not assembled and some partially completed backpacks. We refer to the material, labor, and other costs accumulated for partially completed items as **work in process inventory**. When manufacture

raw material inventory
The cost of materials held for use in the manufacturing of a product.

work in process inventory
The cost incurred for partially completed items, including raw materials, labor, and other costs.

finished goods inventory
The accumulated costs of manufacture for goods that are complete and ready for sale.

is complete and the goods are ready to deliver to customers, we call the inventory **finished goods inventory**. Exhibit 7-15 shows the accounting system for managing these costs for Packit's second year of production. During this second year, Packit completed 48,000 backpacks and sold 44,000. Some remain in the assembly process at year-end, and Packit holds unused fabric, thread, and glue in preparation for future production.

The schematic in Exhibit 7-15 captures the production process. You might think of each of the accounts as corresponding to a physical reality. The raw material is stored in a locked room, ready for use. The work in process is located in the production room, and as it is finished it is physically transferred to a storage site. When Packit sells goods, it removes the items sold from that storage site and gives them to the customer in exchange for cash or an account receivable. Raw materials, work in process, and finished goods are all forms of inventory and appear on the balance sheet as current assets. They are simply in different stages of completion. The

EXHIBIT 7-15

Packit Company Accounting for Manufacturing Costs—Year 2

Raw Material Inventory

Fabric purchased	$270,000	→ 270,000 310,000
Thread and glue purchased	65,000	→ 65,000
	$335,000	Balance 25,000

Work in Process Inventory

Raw material is transferred into production		→ 310,000 948,000
Wages earned	$380,000	→ 380,000
Depreciation	240,000	→ 240,000
Utilities	40,000	→ 40,000
	$660,000	Balance 22,000

48,000 Backpacks with a cost of $948,000 are finished and transferred to finished goods

(average cost = $19.75 = $948,000 ÷ 48,000 units)

Finished Goods Inventory

948,000   869,000

Balance   79,000

44,000 Backpacks with a cost of $869,000 are sold and shipped to customers

(44,000 units × $19.75 = $869,000)

Cost of Goods Sold

→ 869,000

The summary journal entries to record these events for year 2 would be as follows:

PURCHASE OF RAW MATERIAL:

Raw material inventory.	335,000	
Accounts payable.		335,000

PRODUCTION ACTIVITY:

Work in process inventory	310,000	
Raw material inventory		310,000

Work in process inventory	660,000	
Wages payable.		380,000
Accumulated depreciation.		240,000
Utilities payable		40,000

COMPLETION OF PRODUCTION:

Finished goods inventory	948,000	
Work in process inventory.		948,000

act of sale converts the asset into an expense, cost of goods sold, that Packit will report on its income statement. At the end of year 2, Packit will show total inventory on its balance sheet of $126,000, as follows:

Raw materials inventory	$ 25,000
Work in process inventory	22,000
Finished goods inventory	79,000
Total inventory	$126,000

Accounting Vocabulary

average cost method, p. 296
cost of goods available for
　sale, p. 288
cost valuation, p. 286
current replacement cost,
　p. 300
cutoff error, p. 303
finished goods inventory,
　p. 316
first-in, first-out (FIFO), p. 294
F.O.B. destination, p. 290
F.O.B. shipping point, p. 290
freight in, p. 290
holding gain, p. 311

inventory profit, p. 311
inventory shrinkage, p. 286
inventory turnover, p. 305
inward transportation, p. 290
last-in, first-out (LIFO),
　p. 295
LIFO increment, p. 312
LIFO layer, p. 312
LIFO liquidation, p. 312
LIFO reserve, p. 313
lower-of-cost-or-market
　method (LCM), p. 299
moving-average cost method,
　p. 296
net realizable value, p. 299

periodic inventory system,
　p. 288
perpetual inventory system,
　p. 286
physical count, p. 286
raw material inventory, p. 315
retailer, p. 304
specific identification
　method, p. 294
weighted-average cost
　method, p. 296
wholesaler, p. 304
work in process inventory,
　p. 315
write-down, p. 300

Assignment Material

Questions

7-1 Express the cost of goods sold section of the income statement as an equation.

7-2 When a company records a sales transaction, it also records another related transaction. Explain the related transaction.

7-3 "There are two steps in conducting a physical count of inventories." What are they?

7-4 Distinguish between the perpetual and periodic inventory systems.

7-5 "An advantage of the perpetual inventory system is that a physical count of inventory is unnecessary. The periodic method requires a physical count to compute cost of goods sold." Do you agree? Explain.

7-6 Distinguish between F.O.B. destination and F.O.B. shipping point.

7-7 "Freight out should be classified as a direct offset to sales, not as an expense." Do you agree? Explain.

7-8 Name the four inventory cost flow assumptions or valuation methods that are commonly used in the United States. Give a brief phrase describing each.

7-9 For which of the following items would a company be likely to use the specific identification inventory method?

a. Corporate jet aircraft
b. Large sailboats
c. Pencils
d. Diamond rings
e. Timex watches
f. Automobiles
g. Books
h. Compact discs

7-10 If a company uses a FIFO cost flow assumption, will it report the same cost of goods sold using the periodic inventory method that it reports using the perpetual method? Why or why not?

MyAccountingLab

7-11 Why is LIFO a good news/bad news inventory method?

7-12 "Purchases of inventory at the end of a fiscal period can have a direct effect on income under LIFO." Do you agree? Explain.

7-13 "Gamma Company has six units of inventory, two purchased for $4 each and four purchased for $5 each. Thus, the weighted-average cost of the inventory is ($4 + $5) ÷ 2 = $4.50 per unit." Do you agree? Explain.

7-14 Assume that the physical level of inventory is the same at the beginning and end of the year and that the cost of inventory items is rising. Which will produce a higher ending inventory value, LIFO or FIFO?

7-15 Will LIFO or FIFO produce higher cost of goods sold during a period of falling prices? Explain.

7-16 "There is a single dominant reason why more and more U.S. companies have adopted LIFO." What is the reason?

7-17 What does *market* mean in the application of the lower-of-cost-or-market method of inventory accounting?

7-18 "The lower-of-cost-or-market method is inherently inconsistent." Do you agree? Explain.

7-19 "Inventory errors are counterbalancing." Explain.

7-20 "Gross profit percentages help in the preparation of interim financial statements." Explain.

7-21 The branch manager of a national retail grocery chain has stated, "My managers are judged more heavily on the basis of their merchandise-shrinkage control than on their overall sales volume." Why? Explain.

7-22 Study Appendix 7A. "An inventory profit is a fictitious profit." Do you agree? Explain.

7-23 Study Appendix 7A. LIFO can produce absurd inventory valuations. Why?

7-24 Study Appendix 7A. What is an inventory holding gain (or inventory profit)?

7-25 Study Appendix 7A. What generally happens to income when a company liquidates old LIFO inventory layers?

7-26 Study Appendix 7B. What are the three types of inventory in a manufacturing company? Which of the three is usually the largest?

Critical Thinking Questions

▸▸ OBJECTIVE 2

7-27 Periodic Versus Perpetual Inventory Systems

The Zen Bootist manufactures sheepskin slippers, mittens, gloves, jackets, and leather sandals to sell at craft fairs and similar events. The majority of the company's transactions occur over the winter gift-giving season. As the business has grown, the owner has become concerned about how to account for certain items and has asked your advice about whether to use the periodic or perpetual inventory system. What do you say?

▸▸ OBJECTIVE 4

7-28 Purchasing Operations and LIFO Versus FIFO

Suppose a company bases its evaluation of the purchasing officer for a refinery on the gross margin on the oil products produced and sold during the year. During the year, the price of a barrel of oil increased from $80 to $90. The value of the inventory of oil at the beginning of the year is $80 or less per barrel. On the last day of the year, the purchasing agent is contemplating the purchase of additional oil at $90 per barrel. Is the agent more likely to purchase additional oil if the company uses the FIFO or LIFO method for its inventories? Explain.

▸▸ OBJECTIVE 6

7-29 Effect of Overstating Inventories

Phar Mor was a large, rapidly growing pharmacy chain that proved to have overstated assets by more than $400 million. Top executives accomplished the overstatement by inflating the company's inventories at numerous store locations. How would this affect the income statements of Phar Mor?

▸▸ OBJECTIVE 7

7-30 Deciding on a Discount Policy

You are debating with your boss about whether to give customers a 2% discount for quantity purchases. You favor the idea, but your boss says, "Why give money away? If the customer buys more, we are out 2%." How do you reply?

Exercises

7-31 Gross Profit Section

▶▶ OBJECTIVES **1, 3**

Given the following, prepare a detailed gross profit section for Kuperstein's Jewelry Wholesalers for the year ended December 31, 20X8 ($ in thousands), computing the amount for Gross Sales.

Cash discounts on purchases	$ 6	Cash discounts on sales	$ 4
Sales returns and allowances	50	Purchase returns and allowances	27
Gross purchases	650	Freight in	50
Merchandise inventory, December 31, 20X7	103	Merchandise inventory, December 31, 20X8	185
Gross profit	356		

7-32 Gross Margin Computations and Inventory Costs

▶▶ OBJECTIVES **1, 3**

On January 15, 20X4, Violet Muir valued her inventory at cost, $41,000. Her statements are based on the calendar year, so you find it necessary to establish an inventory figure as of January 1, 20X4. You find that from January 2 to January 15, sales were $71,200; sales returns, $2,300; goods purchased and placed in stock, $54,000; goods removed from stock and returned to suppliers, $1,000; and freight in, $400. Calculate the inventory cost as of January 1, assuming that goods are priced to provide a 24% gross profit.

7-33 Journal Entries

▶▶ OBJECTIVE **2**

Coppola Company had sales of $19 million during the year. The goods cost Coppola $17 million. Give the journal entry or entries at the time of sale under the perpetual and periodic inventory systems.

7-34 Valuing Inventory and Cost of Goods Sold

▶▶ OBJECTIVE **4**

Crowe Metals, Ltd., had the following inventory transactions during the month of March (in British pounds, £):

3/1 beginning inventory	3,000 units @ £2.00	£6,000
Week 1, purchases	2,000 units @ £2.10	4,200
Week 2, purchases	2,000 units @ £2.20	4,400
Week 3, purchases	1,000 units @ £2.30	2,300
Week 4, purchases	1,000 units @ £2.50	2,500

On March 31, a count of the ending inventory was completed, and 4,000 units were on hand. By using the periodic inventory system, calculate the cost of goods sold and ending inventory using LIFO, FIFO, and weighted-average inventory methods.

7-35 Entries for Purchase Transactions

▶▶ OBJECTIVES **2, 3**

The Schubert Company is a Swiss wholesaler of office supplies. Its unit of currency is the Swiss franc (CHF). Schubert uses a periodic inventory system. Prepare journal entries for the following summarized transactions (omit explanations):

Aug. 2	Purchased merchandise on account, CHF350,000, terms 2/10, n/45.
Aug. 3	Paid cash for freight in, CHF15,000.
Aug. 7	Schubert complained about some defects in the merchandise acquired on August 2. The supplier hand-delivered a credit memo granting an allowance of CHF32,000.
Aug. 11	Cash disbursement to settle purchase of August 2.

7-36 Cost of Inventory Acquired

▶▶ OBJECTIVE **3**

On July 5, Horwath Company purchased on account a shipment of sheet steel from Northwest Steel, Co. The invoice price was $195,000, F.O.B. shipping point. Shipping cost from the steel mill to Horwath's plant was $10,000, which was paid directly to the shipping company. When inspecting the shipment, the Horwath receiving clerk found several flaws in the steel. The clerk informed Northwest's sales representative of the flaws, and after some negotiation, Northwest granted an allowance of $9,000.

To encourage prompt payment, Northwest grants a 2% cash discount to customers who pay their accounts within 30 days of billing. Horwath paid the proper amount on August 1.

1. Compute the total cost of the sheet steel acquired.
2. Prepare the journal entries for the transaction assuming a periodic inventory system. Omit explanations.

▶▶ OBJECTIVE 2

7-37 Entries for Periodic and Perpetual Systems

Rajiv, Co., had inventory and accounts payable of $110,000 on December 31, 20X7. Data for 20X8 follow:

Gross purchases on account	$980,000
Cost of goods sold	920,000
Inventory, December 31, 20X8	100,000
Purchase returns and allowances	70,000

By using the data, prepare comparative journal entries, including closing entries, for both a perpetual and a periodic inventory system.

▶▶ OBJECTIVES 2, 3

7-38 Entries for Purchase Transactions

Swahili Imports uses a periodic inventory system. Prepare journal entries for the following summarized transactions for 20X1 (omit explanations). For simplicity, assume the beginning and ending balances in accounts payable were zero.

1. Purchases (all using trade credit), $900,000
2. Purchase returns and allowances, $40,000
3. Freight in, $74,000 paid in cash
4. Payment for all credit purchases, less returns and allowances and cash discounts on purchases of $18,000

▶▶ OBJECTIVES 2, 3

7-39 Journal Entries, Periodic Inventory System

Refer to the data in the preceding problem. Inventories were $71,000 on December 31, 20X0, and $120,000 on December 31, 20X1. Sales were $1,200,000. Prepare summary journal entries for 20X1 for sales and cost of goods sold (omit explanations).

▶▶ OBJECTIVES 2, 3

7-40 Journal Entries, Periodic Inventory System

Consider the following data taken from the adjusted trial balance of the Newport Boat Company, December 31, 20X3 ($ in millions):

Purchases (on account)	$140	Sales (on account)	$239
Sales returns and allowances	5	Purchase returns and allowances	6
Freight in (paid in cash)	14	Cash discounts on sales	8
Cash discounts on purchases	1	Other expenses	80
Inventory (beginning of year)	25		

Prepare summary journal entries. The ending inventory was $35 million.

▶▶ OBJECTIVE 3

7-41 Reconstruction of Transaction

Apple Computer, Inc., produces the well-known iMacs, iPhones, and iPads. Consider the following account balances ($ in millions):

	September 24, 2011	September 25, 2010
Inventories	$776	$1,051

The cost of the inventories purchased (or produced) during the 12 months between September 25, 2010, and September 24, 2011, was $64,156,000,000. The income statement for the 2011 fiscal year had an item "cost of sales." Compute its amount.

7-42 Reconstruction of Records

▶▶ **OBJECTIVES 3, 7**

An earthquake caused heavy damage to the Sellwood Antique Store on May 3, 20X8. All merchandise was destroyed. Some accounting data are missing. In conjunction with an insurance investigation, you have been asked to estimate the cost of the inventory destroyed. The following data for 20X8 (recorded before the earthquake) are available:

Cash discounts on purchases	$ 2,000	Inventory, December 31, 20X7	$38,000
Gross sales	280,000	Purchase returns and allowances	7,000
Sales returns and allowances	24,000	Inward transportation	4,000
Gross purchases	159,000	Gross profit percentage on net sales	45%

7-43 Cost of Inventory Destroyed by Fire

▶▶ **OBJECTIVES 1, 3, 7**

Nguyen Company's insurance agent requires an estimate of the cost of merchandise lost by fire on March 9. Merchandise inventory on January 1 was $70,000. Purchases since January 1 were $170,000; freight in, $15,000; and purchase returns and allowances, $10,000. Sales are made at a gross margin of 20% of sales and totaled $200,000 up to March 9. What was the cost of the merchandise destroyed?

7-44 Inventory Shortage

▶▶ **OBJECTIVES 1, 7**

An accounting clerk of the Blakely Company absconded with cash and a truck full of electronic merchandise on May 14, 20X4. The following data have been compiled for 20X4:

Beginning inventory, January 1	$ 55,000
Sales to May 14, 20X4	300,000
Average gross profit rate	25%
Purchases to May 14, 20X4	210,000

Compute the estimated cost of the ending inventory and indicate how you could use that value to estimate the cost of the missing merchandise.

7-45 Inventory Errors

▶▶ **OBJECTIVE 6**

At the end of his first business year, Clifford Hudsick counted and priced the inventory. A few very high-value items were hidden in a dark corner of the storage shelves and Clifford understated his 20X5 ending inventory by $20,000. His business financial statements and his tax return were affected. Assume a 40% tax rate.

1. Calculate the effect on taxable income, taxes, net income, and retained earnings for 20X5.
2. Repeat requirement 1 for 20X6, assuming the 20X6 ending inventory is correctly calculated.

7-46 Decision About Pricing

▶▶ **OBJECTIVE 7**

Burlingame Gems, Inc., a retail jewelry store, had gross profits of $1,320,000 on sales of $2,500,000 in 20X3. Average inventory was $1,000,000.

1. Compute inventory turnover.
2. Anne Scott, owner of Burlingame Gems, is considering whether to become a "discount" jeweler. For example, Anne believes that a reduction of 10% in average selling prices would increase inventory turnover in 20X4 to 1.5 times per year. Beginning and ending inventory would be unchanged. Suppose Anne's beliefs are valid. What would her new gross profit percentage be? Would the total gross profit in 20X4 have improved? Show computations.

▶▶ **OBJECTIVE 4**

7-47 LIFO and FIFO

The inventory of the Roseburg Sand and Gravel Company on June 30 shows 1,000 tons at $9 per ton. A physical inventory on July 31 shows a total of 1,200 tons on hand. Revenue from sales of gravel for July totals $102,000. The following purchases were made during July:

July 8	5,000 tons @ $10 per ton
July 13	1,000 tons @ $11 per ton
July 22	800 tons @ $12 per ton

1. Compute the inventory cost as of July 31 using (a) LIFO, and (b) FIFO.
2. Compute the gross profit using each method.

▶▶ **OBJECTIVE 5**

7-48 Lower-of-Cost-or-Market

(Alternate is 7-74.) Crowell Company uses the inventory method "cost or market, whichever is lower." There were no sales or purchases during the periods indicated, although selling prices generally fluctuated in the same directions as replacement costs. Crowell makes adjustments for LCM each quarter. At what amount would you value merchandise on the dates that follow using U.S. GAAP? Using IFRS?

	Invoice Cost	**Replacement Cost**	**Realizable Value**
December 31, 20X1	$200,000	$185,000	$195,000
April 30, 20X2	200,000	190,000	210,000
August 31, 20X2	200,000	220,000	225,000
December 31, 20X2	200,000	180,000	190,000

▶▶ **OBJECTIVES 3, 7**

7-49 Reconstructing Transactions and Explaining Margins

Consider the following account balances of Costco Wholesale Corporation, the Seattle-based warehouse store operator ($ in millions):

	August 28 2011	**August 29 2010**
Merchandise inventories	$6,638	$5,638

On Costco's income statement for the fiscal year 2011, the cost of the merchandise sold was $77,739 million. Compute the net cost of the acquisition of inventory for the fiscal year ending August 28, 2011. The annual report discussed the gross profit percentage (Costco calls it gross margin) and why it fell from 10.83% in 2010 to 10.69% in 2011. Provide two possible reasons for a decline in the gross profit percentage.

▶▶ **OBJECTIVE 7**

7-50 Gross Profit Percentage

Toys "R" Us operates more than 1,500 stores in the United States and abroad. Like most retailers, the managers of Toys "R" Us monitor the company's gross margin percentage. The following information is from the company's income statement (in millions):

	For the Year Ended		
	January 28, 2012	**January 29, 2011**	**January 30, 2010**
Sales	$13,909	$13,864	$13,568
Cost of sales	8,939	8,939	8,790

Compute the gross profit percentage for each of the 3 years. Comment on the changes in gross profit percentage.

7-51 Profitability and Turnover

▶ **OBJECTIVE 7**

Parr Building Supply began 20X9 with inventory of $240,000. Parr's 20X9 sales were $1,200,000, purchases of inventory totaled $1,035,000, and ending inventory was $275,000.

1. Prepare a statement of gross profit for 20X9.
2. What was Parr Building Supply's inventory turnover?

Problems

7-52 Detailed Income Statement

▶ **OBJECTIVE 3**

(Alternate is 7-55.) Following are accounts taken from the adjusted trial balance of the Morlan Bathroom Supply Company, December 31, 20X5. The company uses the periodic inventory system. All amounts are in thousands.

Sales salaries and commissions	$160	Freight in	$ 55
Inventory, December 31, 20X4	200	Miscellaneous expenses	13
Allowance for bad debts	14	Sales	1,066
Rent expense, office space	10	Bad debt expense	8
Gross purchases	700	Cash discounts on purchases	15
Depreciation expense, office equipment	3	Inventory, December 31, 20X5	300
		Office salaries	46
Cash discounts on sales	16	Rent expense, selling space	50
Advertising expense	45	Income tax expense	4
Purchase returns and allowances	40	Sales returns and allowances	50
Delivery expense	20	Office supplies used	6
		Depreciation expenses, trucks, and store fixtures	29

Prepare a detailed multiple-step income statement for 20X5.

7-53 Perpetual Inventory Calculations

▶ **OBJECTIVES 2, 4**

Platt Electric is a wholesaler for commercial builders. The company uses a perpetual inventory system and a FIFO cost-flow assumption. The data concerning a particular product for the year 20X8 follows:

	Units Purchased	Units Sold	Balance
December 31, 20X7			100 @ $5 = $500
February 10, 20X8	80 @ $6 = $ 480		
April 14		60	
May 9	110 @ $7 = $ 770		
July 14		120	
October 21	100 @ $8 = $ 800		
November 12		75	
Total	290 $2,050	255	

Calculate the ending inventory balance in units and dollars.

▶▶ OBJECTIVE 7

7-54 Gross Profit and Turnover

Retailers closely watch a number of financial ratios, including the gross profit (gross margin) percentage and inventory turnover. Suppose the results for the furniture department in a large store in a given year were as follows:

Sales	$6,000,000
Cost of goods sold	3,600,000
Gross profit	$2,400,000
Beginning inventory	$1,300,000
Ending inventory	$1,100,000

1. Compute the gross profit percentage and the inventory turnover.
2. Suppose the retailer is able to maintain a reduced average inventory of $1,000,000 during the succeeding year. What inventory turnover would have to be obtained to achieve the same $2,400,000 gross profit? Assume that the gross profit percentage is unchanged.
3. Suppose the retailer maintains inventory at the $1,000,000 level throughout the succeeding year but cannot increase the inventory turnover from the level in requirement 1. What gross profit percentage would have to be obtained to achieve the same total gross profit?
4. Suppose the average inventory of $1,200,000 is maintained. Compute the total gross profit in the succeeding year if there is
   a. a 10% increase of the gross profit percentage (that is, 10% of the percentage, not an additional 10 percentage points) and a 10% decrease of the inventory turnover.
   b. a 10% decrease of the gross profit percentage and a 10% increase of the inventory turnover.
5. Why do retailers find the preceding types of ratios helpful?

▶▶ OBJECTIVE 3

7-55 Detailed Income Statement

(Alternate is 7-52.) Sears Holdings Corporation is a major retailer. The company's annual report contained the following actual data, which has been somewhat summarized, for the year ended January 28, 2012 ($ in millions):

Net revenues	$41,567
Purchases of inventory	30,422
Selling and administrative expenses	10,664
Depreciation and amortization	853
Other operating expenses	585
Interest expense (net)	289
Other income	39
Income taxes	1,369

The balance sheets included the following actual data ($ in millions of dollars):

	January 28 2012	January 29 2011
Inventories	8,407	8,951

Prepare a detailed multiple-step income statement that includes the calculation of Cost of Goods Sold and ends with Net Earnings.

7-56 Comparison of Inventory Methods

▸▸ OBJECTIVE 4

(Alternates are 7-67 and 7-69.) Contractor Supply Company is a wholesaler for commercial builders. The company uses a periodic inventory system. The data concerning Kemtone cooktops for the year 20X8 follow:

	Units Purchases	Units Sold	Balance
December 31, 20X7			110 @ $50 = $5,500
February 10, 20X8	80 @ $60 = $ 4,800		
April 14		60	
May 9	120 @ $70 = $ 8,400		
July 14		120	
October 21	100 @ $80 = $ 8,000		
November 12		80	
Total	300 $21,200	260	
December 31, 20X8			150 @ ?

The sales during 20X8 were made at the following selling prices:

60 units	@ $ 90 =	$ 5,400
120 units	@ 100 =	12,000
80 units	@ 110 =	8,800
260		$26,200

1. Prepare a comparative statement of gross profit for the year ended December 31, 20X8, using FIFO, LIFO, and average cost inventory methods. Remember that when average cost is used with the periodic inventory system we refer to it as the weighted-average method.
2. By how much would income taxes differ if Contractor Supply Company had used LIFO instead of FIFO for Kemtone cooktops? Assume a 40% income tax rate.

7-57 Effects of Late Purchases

▸▸ OBJECTIVE 4

(Alternates are 7-68 and 7-70.) Refer to the preceding problem. Suppose 100 extra units had been acquired on December 30, 20X8, for $80 each, a total of $8,000. How would net income and income taxes have been affected under FIFO and under LIFO? Show a tabulated comparison.

7-58 LIFO, FIFO, and Lower-of-Cost-or-Market

▸▸ OBJECTIVES 4, 5

Altobelli Company began business in Chicago on March 15, 20X0. The following are Altobelli's purchases of inventory:

March 17	100 units @ $10 =	$1,000
April 19	50 units @ $12 =	600
May 14	100 units @ $13 =	1,300
Total		$2,900

On May 25, the company sold 130 units, leaving inventory of 120 units. Altobelli Company's accountant was preparing a balance sheet for June 1, at which time the replacement cost of the inventory was $12 per unit.

1. Suppose Altobelli Company uses LIFO without applying lower-of-cost-or-market. Compute the June 1 inventory amount.
2. Suppose Altobelli Company uses lower-of-LIFO-cost-or-market. Compute the June 1 inventory amount.

3. Suppose Altobelli Company uses FIFO without applying lower-of-cost-or-market. Compute the June 1 inventory amount.
4. Suppose Altobelli Company uses lower-of-FIFO-cost-or-market. Compute the June 1 inventory amount.

▶▶ OBJECTIVE 6

7-59 Inventory Errors
(Alternate is 7-66.) The following data are from the 20X1 income statement of the Atiyeh Rug Emporium ($ in thousands):

Sales		$1,650
Deduct cost of goods sold		
Beginning inventory	$ 390	
Purchases	820	
Cost of goods available for sale	1,210	
Deduct: Ending inventory	370	
Cost of goods sold		840
Gross profit		810
Other expenses		610
Income before income taxes		200
Income tax expense at 40%		80
Net income		$ 120

The ending inventory was overstated by $20,000 because of errors in the physical count. The income tax rate was 40% in 20X1 and 20X2.

1. Which items in the income statement are incorrect and by how much? Use O for overstated, U for understated, and N for not affected. Complete the following tabulation (amounts in thousands):

	20X1	20X2
Beginning inventory	N	O $20
Ending inventory	?	?
Cost of goods sold	?	?
Gross margin	?	?
Income before income taxes	?	?
Income tax expense	?	?
Net income	?	?

2. What is the dollar effect of the inventory error on retained earnings at the end of 20X1 and at the end of 20X2?

▶▶ OBJECTIVE 4

7-60 LIFO, FIFO, and Prices Rising and Falling
The Stern Company uses a periodic inventory system. Inventory on December 31, 20X1, consisted of 10,000 units @ $10 = $100,000. Purchases during 20X2 were 13,000 units. Sales were 12,000 units for sales revenue of $19 per unit.

1. Prepare a four-column comparative statement of gross margin for 20X2:
   a. Assume purchases were at $12 per unit. Assume FIFO and then LIFO.
   b. Assume purchases were at $8 per unit. Assume FIFO and then LIFO.
2. Explain the differences between LIFO and FIFO gross margin in both (a) and (b) in requirement 1.
3. Assume an income tax rate of 40%. Suppose all transactions were for cash. Which inventory method in requirement (1a) would result in more cash for Stern Company and by how much?
4. Assume an income tax rate of 40%. Suppose all transactions were for cash. Which inventory method in requirement (1b) would result in more cash for Stern Company and by how much?

7-61 LIFO, FIFO, and Cash Effects

▶▶ OBJECTIVE 4

In 20X8, Mehrabi Company had sales revenue of £444,000 for a line of woolen scarves. The company uses a periodic inventory system. Pertinent data for 20X8 included the following:

Inventory, December 31, 20X7	14,000 units @ £6 =	£ 84,000
January purchases	22,000 units @ £7 =	154,000
July purchases	30,000 units @ £8 =	240,000
Sales for the year	40,000 units	

1. Prepare a statement of gross margin for 20X8. Use two columns, one assuming LIFO and one assuming FIFO.
2. Assume a 40% income tax rate. Suppose all transactions were for cash. Which inventory method would result in more cash for Mehrabi Company, and by how much?

7-62 FIFO and LIFO

▶▶ OBJECTIVE 4

Two companies, the Lastin Company and the Firstin Company, are in the scrap metal warehousing business as arch competitors. They are about the same size, and in 20X1 coincidentally encountered seemingly identical operating situations. Only their inventory accounting systems differed. Lastin uses LIFO, and Firstin uses FIFO.

Their beginning inventory was 11,000 tons; it cost $50 per ton. During the year, each company purchased 50,000 tons at the following prices:

- 30,000 @ $60 on March 17
- 20,000 @ $70 on October 5

Each company sold 46,000 tons at average prices of $100 per ton. Other expenses in addition to cost of goods sold, but excluding income taxes, were $600,000. The income tax rate is 40%.

1. Compute net income for the year for both companies. Show your calculations.
2. As a manager, which method would you prefer? Why? Explain fully. Include your estimate of the overall effect of these events on the cash balances of each company, assuming all transactions during 20X1 were direct receipts or disbursements of cash.

7-63 Effects of LIFO and FIFO

▶▶ OBJECTIVE 4

The Brachman Company is starting in business on December 31, 20X0. In each half year, from 20X1 through 20X3, it expects to purchase 1,000 units and sell 500 units for the amounts listed below. In 20X4 it expects to purchase and sell 500 units in each half year. In 20X5, it expects to purchase no units and sell all remaining units for the amount indicated in the following table:

	20X1	20X2	20X3	20X4	20X5
Purchases					
First 6 months	$1,000	$2,000	$3,000	$1,500	0
Second 6 months	2,000	2,500	3,000	2,000	0
Total	$3,000	$4,500	$6,000	$3,500	0
Sales (at selling price)	$5,000	$5,000	$5,000	$5,000	$15,000

Assume that there are no costs or expenses other than those shown above. The tax rate is 40%, and taxes for each year are payable on December 31 of each year. Brachman Company is trying to decide whether to use periodic FIFO or LIFO throughout the 5-year period.

1. What was net income under FIFO for each of the 5 years? Under LIFO? Show calculations.
2. Explain briefly which method, LIFO or FIFO, seems more advantageous, and why.

▶▶ OBJECTIVE 4

7-64 Effects of LIFO on Purchase Decisions

The M. J. Chan Corporation is nearing the end of its first year in business. The following purchases of its single product have been made:

	Units	Unit Price	Total Cost
January	1,000	$ 9	$ 9,000
March	1,000	10	10,000
May	1,000	11	11,000
July	1,000	13	13,000
September	1,000	14	14,000
December	4,000	15	60,000
	9,000		$117,000

Sales for the year will be 5,000 units for $120,000. Expenses other than cost of goods sold will be $31,000.

The president is undecided about whether to adopt FIFO or LIFO for income tax purposes. The company has ample storage space for up to 7,000 units of inventory. Inventory prices are expected to stay at $15 per unit for the next few months.

1. What would be the net income before taxes, the income taxes, and the net income after taxes for the year under (a) FIFO, or (b) LIFO? Income tax rates are 40%.
2. If the company sells its year-1 year-end inventory in year 2 @ $25 per unit and goes out of business, what would be the net income before taxes, the income taxes, and the net income after taxes under (a) FIFO, and (b) LIFO? Assume that other expenses in year 2 are $30,000.
3. Repeat requirements 1 and 2, assuming that the 4,000 units @ $15 purchased in December were not purchased until January of the second year and were then sold in year 2. Generalize on the effect on net income of the timing of purchases under FIFO and LIFO.

▶▶ OBJECTIVE 8

7-65 Changing Quantities and LIFO Reserve

Study Appendix 7A. Consider the following data for the year 20X8:

	Units	Unit Cost
Beginning inventory	2	*
Purchases	3	24
	3	28
Ending inventory	2	†

*FIFO, $20; LIFO, $12.
†To be computed.

1. Prepare a comparative table computing the cost of goods sold using columns for FIFO and LIFO. In a final column, show (a) the difference between FIFO and LIFO inventories (the LIFO reserve) at the beginning of the year and at the end of the year, and (b) how the change in this amount explains the difference in cost of goods sold.
2. Repeat requirement 1, except assume that the ending inventory consisted of zero units.
3. In your own words, explain why, for a given year, the increase in the LIFO reserve measures the amount by which cost of goods sold is higher under LIFO than FIFO.

▶▶ OBJECTIVE 6

7-66 Inventory Errors, 3 Years

(Alternate is 7-59.) In early 20X4 at the Westfall Company, a team of internal auditors discovered that the ending inventory for 20X1 had been overstated by $10 million. Furthermore, the ending inventory for 20X3 had been understated by $5 million. The ending inventory for December 31, 20X2, was correct. The income tax rate is 40%.

1. Prepare a tabulation covering each of the 3 years that indicates which of the following items in the income statement are incorrect and by how much.
   Beginning inventory
   Cost of goods available

Ending inventory
Cost of goods sold
Gross margin
Income before income taxes
Income tax expense
Net income

2. Is the amount of retained earnings correct at the end of 20X1, 20X2, and 20X3? If it is erroneous, indicate the amount and whether it is overstated (O) or understated (U).

7-67 Comparison of Inventory Methods

▶▶ **OBJECTIVE 4**

(Alternates are 7-56 and 7-69.) **Dell Computer Company** produces computers. The following
data and descriptions are from the company's annual report ($ in millions):

	February 3	January 28
	2012	2011
Inventories	$1,404	$1,301

Assume that Dell uses the periodic inventory system. Suppose a division of Dell had the
accompanying data concerning the purchase and resale of computers ($ are not in millions):

	Units	Total
Inventory (January 28, 2011)	100	$ 40,000
Purchase (February 20, 2011)	200	100,000
Sales, March 17, 2011 (at $900 per unit)	150	
Purchase (June 25, 2011)	160	96,000
Sales, November 7, 2011 (at $1,000 per unit)	160	

1. For these computers only, prepare a tabulation of the cost of goods sold section of the income
statement for the year ended February 3, 2012. Support your computations. Show your tabulation for four different inventory methods: (a) FIFO, (b) LIFO, (c) average cost known as
weighted-average for periodic inventory systems, and (d) specific identification. For requirement (d), assume that the purchase of February 20 was identified with the sale of March 17.
Also assume that the sale of November 7 included the sale of half of the units in beginning
inventory and the remainder from the purchase of June 25.
2. By how much would income taxes differ if Dell used (a) LIFO instead of FIFO for this
inventory item, and (b) LIFO instead of weighted average? Assume a 40% tax rate.

7-68 Effects of Late Purchases

▶▶ **OBJECTIVE 4**

(Alternates are 7-57 and 7-70.) Refer to the preceding problem. Suppose the **Dell** division acquired
50 extra computers at $700 each on February 2, 2012, at a total additional cost of $35,000. How
would gross profit and income taxes be affected under FIFO (that is, compare FIFO results before
and after the purchase of 50 extra computers) and under LIFO (that is, compare LIFO results
before and after the purchase of 50 extra computers)? Show computations and explain.

7-69 Comparison of Inventory Methods

▶▶ **OBJECTIVE 4**

(Alternates are 7-56 and 7-67.) **Texas Instruments** is a major producer of semiconductors and
other electrical and electronic products. Semiconductors are especially vulnerable to price fluctuations. The following are from the company's annual report ($ in millions):

	December 31	
	2011	2010
Inventories	$1,788	$1,520

Texas Instruments uses a variety of inventory methods, but for this problem assume it uses
only FIFO.

Assume Texas Instruments had the accompanying data concerning one of its semiconductors. Assume a periodic inventory system.

	Purchases		Sales (units)	Balance
December 31, 2010				80 @ $5 = 400
February 25, 2011	50 @ $6 =	$ 300		
March 29			60*	
May 28	80 @ $7 =	$ 560		
June 7			90*	
November 20	90 @ $8 =	$ 720		
December 15			40*	
Total	220	$1,580	190	
December 31, 2011				110 @ ?

*Selling prices were $11, $12, and $13, respectively.

	60	@ $11 =	$ 660
	90	@ 12 =	1,080
	40	@ 13 =	520
Total sales	190		$2,260

Summary of costs to account for is as follows:

Beginning inventory	$ 400
Purchases	1,580
Cost of goods available for sale	$1,980
Other expenses for this product	$ 600
Income tax rate, 40%	

1. Prepare a comparative income statement for the 2011 fiscal year for the product in question. Use the FIFO, LIFO, and average cost inventory methods. Remember that when a periodic inventory system is used the average cost method is known as weighted-average cost.
2. By how much would income taxes have differed if Texas Instruments had used LIFO instead of FIFO for this product?
3. Suppose Texas Instruments had used the specific identification method. Compute the gross margin (or gross profit) under two different scenarios; if the ending inventory had consisted of (a) 90 units @ $8 and 20 units @ $7, or (b) 60 units @ $5 and 50 units @ $8.

▶▶ OBJECTIVE 4

7-70 Effects of Late Purchases
(Alternates are 7-57 and 7-68.) Refer to the preceding problem. Suppose Texas Instruments had acquired 50 extra units @ $8 each on December 30, 2011, at a total additional cost of $400. How would income before income taxes have been affected under FIFO? That is, compare FIFO results before and after the purchase of 50 extra units. Under LIFO? That is, compare LIFO results before and after the purchase of 50 extra units. Show computations and explain.

▶▶ OBJECTIVE 4

7-71 Classic Switch from LIFO to FIFO
Effective January 1, 1970, Chrysler Corporation adopted the FIFO method for inventories previously valued by the LIFO method. The 1970 annual report stated, "This … makes the financial statements with respect to inventory valuation comparable with those of the other United States automobile manufacturers."

The *Wall Street Journal* reported the following:

The change improved Chrysler's 1970 financial results several ways. Besides narrowing the 1970 loss by $20 million it improved Chrysler's working capital.

The change also made the comparison with 1969 earnings look somewhat more favorable because, upon restatement, Chrysler's 1969 profit was raised by only $10.2 million from the original figures.

Finally, the change helped Chrysler's balance sheet by boosting inventories, and thus current assets, by $150 million at the end of 1970 over what they would have been under LIFO. As Chrysler's profit has collapsed over the last two years and its financial position tightened, auto analysts have eyed warily Chrysler's shrinking ratio of current assets to current liabilities.

To get the improvements in its balance sheet and results, however, Chrysler paid a price. Roger Helder, vice president and comptroller, said Chrysler owed the government $53 million in tax savings it accumulated by using the LIFO method since it switched from FIFO in 1957. The major advantage of LIFO is that it holds down profit and thus tax liabilities. The other three major auto makers stayed on the FIFO method. Mr. Helder said Chrysler now has to pay back that $53 million to the government over 20 years, which will boost Chrysler's tax bills about $3 million a year.

Given the content of this chapter, do you think the Chrysler decision to switch from LIFO to FIFO was beneficial to its stockholders? Explain, being as specific as you can.

7-72 LIFO, FIFO, Purchase Decisions, and Earnings per Share

▶▶ **OBJECTIVES 4, 8**

Kansas Seed Corn Supplies, a company with 100,000 shares of common stock outstanding, had the following transactions during 20X1, its first year in business:

Sales	1,000,000 pounds @ $5
Purchases	900,000 pounds @ $2
	300,000 pounds @ $3

The current income tax rate is a flat 40%; the rate next year is expected to be 35%.

It is December 20 and Brian Fleming, the president, is trying to decide whether to buy the 400,000 pounds he needs for inventory now or early next year. The current price is $4 per unit. Prices on inventory are expected to remain stable; in any event, no decline in prices is anticipated.

Fleming has not chosen an inventory method as of yet, but will pick either LIFO or FIFO. Other expenses for the year will be $1.4 million.

1. Using LIFO, prepare a comparative income statement assuming the 400,000 pounds (a) are not purchased, and (b) are purchased. The statement should end with reported earnings per share.
2. Repeat requirement 1, using FIFO.
3. Comment on the preceding results. Which method should Fleming choose? Why? Be specific.
4. Suppose that in year 2 the tax rate drops to 35%, prices remain stable, 1.1 million pounds are sold @ $5, enough pounds are purchased at $4 so the ending inventory will be 800,000 pounds, and other expenses are reduced to $800,000.
   a. Prepare a comparative income statement for the second year showing the impact of each of the four alternatives in year one (LIFO and FIFO with and without the late purchase) on net income and earnings per share for the second year.
   b. Explain any differences in net income that you encounter among the four alternatives.
   c. Why is there a difference in ending inventory values under LIFO, even though the same amount of physical inventory is in stock?
   d. What is the total cash outflow for income taxes for the 2 years together under the four alternatives?
   e. Would you change your answer in requirement 3 now that you have completed requirement 4? Why?

7-73 Eroding the LIFO Base

▶▶ **OBJECTIVES 4, 8**

Study Appendix 7A. Many companies on LIFO are occasionally faced with strikes or material shortages that necessitate a reduction in their normal inventory levels to satisfy current sales demands. A few years ago, several large steel companies requested special legislative relief from the additional taxes that ensued from such events.

A news story stated the following:

> As steelworkers slowly streamed back to the mills this week, most steel companies began adding up the tremendous losses imposed by the longest strike in history. At a significant number of plants across the country, however, the worry wasn't losses but profits—"windfall" bookkeeping profits that for some companies may mean painful increases in corporate income taxes.
>
> These outfits have been caught in the backfire of a special mechanism for figuring up inventory costs on tax returns. It's known to accountants as LIFO, or last in, first out. Ironically, it's designed to slice the corporate tax bill in a time of rising prices.
>
> Biggest Bite—Most of the big steel companies—16 out of the top 20—as well as 40 percent of all steel warehousers, use LIFO accounting in figuring their taxes. But the tax squeeze from paper LIFO profits won't affect them all equally. It will put the biggest bite on warehousers that kept going during the strike—and as a result, the American Steel Warehouse Assn. may ask Congress for a special tax exemption on these paper profits... .
>
> Companies such as Ryerson and Castle have been caught because they have had to strip their shelves bare in order to satisfy customer demands during the strike. And they probably won't be able to rebuild their stocks by the time they close their books for tax purposes.

To see how this situation can happen, consider the following example. Suppose a company adopted LIFO in 1976. At December 31, 20X8, its LIFO inventory consisted of three "layers":

From 1976	110,000	units @	$1.00	$110,000
From 1977	50,000	units @	1.10	55,000
From 1978	30,000	units @	1.20	36,000
				$201,000

In 20X9, prices rose enormously. Data follow:

Sales	500,000	units @ $3.00 =	$1,500,000
Purchases	340,000	units @ $2.00 =	$ 680,000
Operating expenses			$ 500,000

A prolonged strike near the end of the year resulted in a severe depletion of the normal inventory stock of 190,000 units. The strike was settled on December 28, 20X9. The company intended to replenish the inventory as soon as possible. The applicable income tax rate is 40%.

1. Compute the income taxes for 20X9.
2. Suppose the company had been able to meet the 500,000-unit demand out of current purchases. Compute the income taxes for 20X9 under those circumstances.

▶▶ **OBJECTIVE 5**

7-74 Lower-of-Cost-or-Market

(Alternate is 7-48.) A U.S. camera company's annual report stated, "Inventories are stated at the lower of cost or market. The cost of most inventories in the U.S. is determined by the last-in, first-out (LIFO) method." Assume severe price competition in 20X8 necessitated a write-down on December 31 for a class of camera inventories with a LIFO cost of $13 million. The appropriate valuation at market was deemed to be $9 million.

1. Assume sales of this line of camera for 20X8 were $20 million, and cost of goods sold was $14 million, and that the product line was terminated in 20X9 and the remaining inventory was sold for $8 million. Prepare a statement of gross margin for 20X8 and 20X9. Show the results under a strict LIFO cost method in the first two columns and under a lower-of-LIFO-cost-or-market method in the next two columns.

2. Assume the company did not discontinue the product line. Instead, a new marketing campaign spurred market demand. Replacement cost of the cameras in the December 31 inventory was $10 million on January 31, 20X9. What inventory valuation would be appropriate on January 31, 20X9, if the company still holds the inventory?

7-75 LIFO Reserve

Study Appendix 7A. **Whirlpool Corporation** reported 2011 pretax operating profit of $792 million. Footnotes to Whirlpool's financial statements read, "Inventories are stated at first-in, first-out ('FIFO') cost, except U.S. production inventories, which are stated at last-in, first-out ('LIFO') cost." The footnote showed that if the FIFO method of inventory accounting had been used for all inventories, they would have been $203 and $149 million higher than reported at December 31, 2011 and 2010, respectively.

▶▶ OBJECTIVE 8

1. Calculate the 2011 pretax income that Whirlpool would have reported if the FIFO inventory method had always been used for all inventories.
2. Suppose Whirlpool's income tax rate is 34%. What were Whirlpool's 2011 income taxes using LIFO? What would they have been if Whirlpool had used FIFO?
3. Was Whirlpool's use of LIFO a good choice from a tax perspective? What is the cumulative financial effect of the choice?

7-76 LIFO Reserve

Study Appendix 7A. **Brunswick Corporation** reported total inventories of $532.6 million on January 1, 2012. Some inventories were valued using FIFO and some using LIFO. A footnote to the financial statements indicated the following: "Inventories valued at the last-in, first-out method (LIFO) … were $119.8 million and $118.2 million lower than the FIFO cost of inventories at December 31, 2011 and 2010, respectively."

▶▶ OBJECTIVE 8

1. Has the cost of Brunswick's LIFO inventories generally been increasing or decreasing? Explain.
2. Suppose Brunswick sold its entire inventory for $1,000 million the subsequent year and did not replace it. Compute the gross profit from the sale of this inventory (a) as Brunswick would report it using its current inventory methods, and (b) as it would have been reported if Brunswick had always used FIFO instead of LIFO. Which inventory method creates higher gross profit? Explain.

7-77 Inventory Errors

IBM had inventories of $2.6 billion at December 31, 2011, and $2.5 billion a year earlier.

▶▶ OBJECTIVE 6

1. Suppose the beginning inventory for fiscal 2011 had been overstated by $20 million because of errors in physical counts. There were no other inventory errors. Which items in the financial statements would be incorrect and by how much? Use O for overstated, U for understated, and N for not affected. Assume a 40% tax rate and state dollar amounts in millions.

	Effect on Fiscal Year	
	2011	**2010**
Beginning inventory	O by $20	N
Ending inventory	?	?
Cost of sales	?	?
Gross profit	?	?
Income before taxes on income	?	?
Taxes on income	?	?
Net income	?	?

2. What is the dollar effect of the inventory error on retained earnings at the end of fiscal 2011 and 2010?

▶▶ OBJECTIVE 8

7-78 LIFO Liquidation and Ethics

Study Appendix 7A. A LIFO liquidation increases earnings, and management can choose to create a LIFO liquidation by deciding when inventory is replaced. Delaying replacement by a few days at year-end can create a LIFO liquidation and improve earnings. Scholars are often interested in learning whether management actually makes choices such as a LIFO liquidation in order to increase earnings.

Discuss the implications of a managerial decision from an ethical position. Also state whether you believe it is likely that scholars would observe a pattern in LIFO liquidation decisions when they study a large number of companies. Such a study might ask the question: What did analysts expect earnings to be and what were they actually? Furthermore, they might focus on companies that would have reported earnings below analysts' expectations had they not recognized LIFO liquidations. Specifically, were LIFO liquidations more likely for companies that would otherwise report earnings below what the analysts were forecasting?

▶▶ OBJECTIVE 8

7-79 Year-End Purchases and LIFO Layers

Study Appendix 7A. A company engaged in the manufacture and sale of dental supplies maintained an inventory of gold for use in its business. The company used LIFO for the gold content of its products.

On the final day of its fiscal year, the company bought 10,000 ounces of gold at $1,600 per ounce. Had the purchase not been made, the company would have penetrated its LIFO layers for 8,000 ounces of gold acquired at $750 per ounce.

The applicable income tax rate is 40%.

1. Compute the effect of the year-end purchase on the income taxes of the fiscal year.
2. On the second day of the next fiscal year, the company resold the 10,000 ounces of gold to its suppliers. What do you think the IRS should do if it discovers this resale? Explain.

▶▶ OBJECTIVE 7

7-80 Comparison of Gross Profit Percentages and Inventory Turnover

JCPenney and Kmart (since a 2005 merger it is Sears/Kmart) are long-time competitors in the retail business, although they target slightly different markets. The gross margin for each company and average inventory follow for the indicated years (both have January year-ends; 2011 refers to the year ending in January of 2012):

JCPenney

	2011	2003	1995
Retail sales	$17,260	$32,347	$20,380
Cost of goods sold	11,042	22,573	13,970
Gross profit	6,218	9,774	6,410
Average inventory	3,065	4,938	3,711

Sears/Kmart

	2011	2003	1995
Retail sales	$41,567	$30,762	$34,025
Cost of goods sold	30,966	26,258	25,992
Gross profit	10,601	4,504	8,033
Average inventory	8,679	5,311	7,317

Calculate gross profit percentages and inventory turnovers for 2011, 2003, and 1995 for each company and compare them. What trends do you observe? Which company appears to perform better? To what extent do their different performances seem to relate to their relative positions in the retail market?

▶▶ OBJECTIVE 8

7-81 LIFO and Ethical Issues

Study Appendix 7A. Yokohama Company is a wholesaler of musical instruments. Yokohama has used the LIFO inventory method for more than 40 years. Near the end of 20X8, before computing cost of goods sold, the company's inventory of a particular instrument listed three LIFO layers, two of which were from earlier years and one from 20X8 purchases:

	No. of Units	Unit Cost
Layer one	4,500	$40
Layer two	2,500	50
20X8 Purchases	29,500	60
Total available	36,500	

In 20X8, Yokohama sold 32,000 units, leaving 4,500 units in inventory.

On December 27, 20X8, Yokohama had a chance to buy a minimum of 15,000 units of the instrument at a unit cost of $70. The offer was good for 10 days, and delivery would be immediate on placing the order.

Helen Tagnetta, chief purchasing manager of Yokohama, was trying to decide whether to make the purchase and, if it is made, whether to make it in 20X8 or 20X9. The controller had told her that she should buy immediately because the company would save almost $80,000 in taxes. The combined federal and state income tax rate is 45%.

1. Explain why nearly $80,000 of taxes would be saved.
2. Are there any ethical considerations that would influence this decision? Explain.

7-82 Inventory Shrinkage

▶▶ **OBJECTIVE 2**

Lola, owner of Aboy Hardware Company, was concerned about her control of inventory. In December 20X7, she installed a computerized perpetual inventory system. In April, her accountant brought her the following information for the first 3 months of 20X8:

Sales	$700,000
Cost of goods sold	610,000
Beginning inventory (per physical count)	135,000
Merchandise purchases	630,000

Lola had asked her public accounting firm to conduct a physical count of inventory on April 1. The CPAs reported inventory of $140,000.

1. Compute the ending inventory shown in the books by the new perpetual inventory system.
2. Provide the journal entry to reconcile the book inventory with the physical count. What is the corrected cost of goods sold for the first 3 months of 20X8?
3. Do your calculations point out areas about which Lola should be concerned? Why?

7-83 Cheating on Inventories

▶▶ **OBJECTIVE 6**

The *Wall Street Journal* reported, "Cheating on inventories is a common way for small businesses to chisel on their income taxes.... A New York garment maker, for example, evades a sizable amount of income tax by undervaluing his firm's inventory by 20% on his tax return. He hides about $500,000 out of a $2.5 million inventory."

The news story concluded, "When it's time to borrow, business owners generally want profits and assets to look fat." The garment maker uses a different fiscal period for financial statements to his bank: "After writing down the inventory as of Dec. 31, he writes it up six months later when the fiscal year ends. In this way, he underpays the IRS and impresses his banker. Some describe that kind of inventory accounting as WIFL—Whatever I Feel Like."

1. At a 40% income tax rate, what amount of federal income taxes would the owner evade according to the news story?
2. Consider the next year. By how much would the ending inventory have to be understated to evade the same amount of income taxes?

Use the following table and fill in the blanks:

	Honest Reporting		Dishonest Reporting	
	First Year	Second Year	First Year	Second Year
Beginning inventory	$ 3,000,000	$?	$ 3,000,000	$?
Purchases	10,000,000	$10,000,000	10,000,000	10,000,000
Available for sale	13,000,000	?	13,000,000	?
Ending inventory	2,500,000	2,500,000	2,000,000	?
Cost of goods sold	$10,500,000	$?	$11,000,000	$?
Income tax savings @ 40%*	$ 4,200,000	$?	$?	$?
Income tax savings for 2 years together	$?		$?	

*This is the income tax effect of only the cost of goods sold. To shorten and simplify the analysis, sales and operating expenses are assumed to be the same each year.

▶▶ OBJECTIVE 9

7-84 Manufacturing Costs

Study Appendix 7B. Stephen Bedford made custom T-shirts for himself and his friends for years before trying to treat it seriously as a business. On January 1, 20X1, he decided to become more serious. He bought some screening equipment for $5,000. Depreciation of the screening equipment for the month of January is $750. He acquired 2,000 shirts for $6,000 and rented a studio for $500 per month. During the month, he paid an assistant $1,600 and together they created three designs, screened 1,500 shirts, and sold 1,200 at $10 each. At month-end, there were 500 shirts unused, 300 finished shirts ready for sale, and Sam was trying to figure out how he was doing.

1. Calculate the cost of goods sold and the value of ending inventory (including raw material and finished goods).
2. Prepare an income statement for Stephen's first month of operations. Assume a 40% tax rate.

Collaborative Learning Exercise

▶▶ OBJECTIVE 4

7-85 Understanding Inventory Cost Assumptions

Form groups of three students each. (If there are more than three students in a group, extras can be paired up.) Each student should select or be assigned one of these three inventory methods:

1. Specific identification
2. FIFO
3. LIFO

Consider the following information from the annual report of Simpson Corporation. Simpson uses the LIFO method to account for its inventories ($ amounts are in millions).

For the year ended March 31, 20X1 (fiscal year 20X1)	
Sales	$967
Cost of goods sold (using LIFO)	534
Other operating expenses	417
Operating income	$ 16
Purchases of inventory in fiscal 20X9	$562
At March 31, 20X1	
Inventories @ LIFO	$169
Inventories @ FIFO	181
At March 31, 20X0	
Inventories @ LIFO	$141
Inventories @ FIFO	152

Assume that Simpson had exactly the same physical sales in the next fiscal year (20X2) as in fiscal 20X1, but sales prices rose slightly so that total fiscal 20X2 sales were $1,000. Assume that other operating expenses in fiscal 20X2 were exactly the same as in fiscal 20X1. Further assume Simpson bought just enough inventory in fiscal 20X2 to replace what the company sold, but because of a 5% price increase on April 1, purchases of inventories in fiscal 20X2 were $561. (Note that if there had been no price increase, the purchases of inventories would have equaled last year's LIFO cost of goods sold, $534.) FIFO inventory on March 31, 20X2, was $190.

1. Compute operating income for Simpson for the year ended March 31, 20X2, using the inventory method to which you were assigned. Those using the LIFO and FIFO methods have all the information needed for the calculations. Those using specific identification must make some assumptions, and their operating income numbers will depend on the assumptions made.
2. Explain to the other members of the group how you computed the operating income, including an explanation of how you chose the assumptions you made.

Analyzing and Interpreting Financial Statements

7-86 Financial Reporting Research

Select an industry and identify two firms within that industry.

▸▸ **OBJECTIVES 4, 7**

1. Identify the inventory accounting method used by each.
2. Calculate gross profit percentages and inventory turnovers for 2 years for each firm. Comment on the comparison and any trends.

7-87 Analyzing Starbucks' Financial Statements

Refer to the fiscal 2011 financial statements for Starbucks either at http://investor.starbucks.com or on the SEC's EDGAR Web site. Assume that Starbucks uses the periodic inventory method.

▸▸ **OBJECTIVES 3, 7**

1. Compute the amount of merchandise inventory purchased during the year ended October 2, 2011. (*Hint:* Use the inventory T-account.) Assume that 80% of the costs listed under "Cost of sales including occupancy costs" are cost of sales. The other 20% are occupancy costs.
2. Compute the inventory turnover for Starbucks for the year ended October 2, 2011.
3. Calculate the gross margin percentage for each of the last 3 years. Use total net revenues and cost of sales including occupancy costs to compute the gross margin. Comment on any changes.

7-88 Analyzing Financial Statements Using the Internet: Deckers Outdoor Corporation

Go to Deckers Outdoor Corporation's latest annual report information on its Web site. Deckers Outdoor Corporation is the exclusive licensee for the manufacture of Teva footwear. Use the latest 10-K filing to find financial report data.

▸▸ **OBJECTIVES 4, 7**

Answer the following questions about Deckers:

1. What percentage of revenues does Teva represent? Have revenues related to Teva products increased or decreased over the past few years?
2. Read the Summary of Significant Accounting Policies section of the Notes to Consolidated Financial Statements. How are inventories valued and accounted for? Why do you think the company uses this particular costing method?
3. Locate the income statement. How much gross profit is reported for the most recent year? What is the gross profit percentage? Have these amounts increased or decreased compared with the previous year? What explanation does management give for the changes? (*Hint:* Look in the Management's Discussion and Analysis section.)

8 Long-Lived Assets

THE NAME NM Electronics is probably not familiar to you. **NM Electronics** is the name that Gordon E. Moore and Robert Noyce gave their fledgling company at the time of its founding in 1968. In 1969, Moore and Noyce changed the name of their company to Integrated Electronics, or Intel for short. On November 15, 1971, **Intel Corporation** introduced the first microprocessor. Since that time, microprocessors have become the brain of millions of devices that have changed the way we live. For example, microprocessors can be found in computers, washing machines, smart phones, gaming consoles, and cars to name only a few products that we use every day. Since their introduction more than 40 years ago, microprocessors have become faster and more powerful, while decreasing in size and cost. Intel is the largest semiconductor manufacturer in the world, operating plants 24/7 in many countries around the globe.

In the early years, Intel's manufacturing processes were relatively primitive. Former Intel Chairman Andy Grove, quoted on Intel's Web site, said, "The fab area looked like Willy Wonka's factory, with hoses and wires and contraptions chugging along—the semiconductor equivalent of the Wright Brothers' jury-rigged airplane. It was state-of-the-art manufacturing at the time, but by today's standards, it was unbelievably crude." Most of the assembly work was done by hand in non-sterile manufacturing facilities. Today, Intel has a huge investment in its manufacturing facilities. Currently, the building of one plant costs in excess of $5 billion. As noted on the Intel Web site, microprocessor-controlled robots transport the silicon wafers through the manufacturing process, and work is performed in cleanrooms that are atmospherically isolated from the external environment and 10,000 times cleaner than a hospital operating room. This type of manufacturing requires an incredible investment in appropriate ventilation and air filter equipment to maintain the required temperature, humidity, pressurization, and cleanliness. Huge air filtration systems completely change the air in cleanrooms about 10 times per minute. Intel's 2011 financial statements show gross investment in Machinery and Equipment of approximately $34.4 billion and in Land and Buildings of over $17.9 billion. In 2011 alone, Intel spent slightly over $10.7 billion to purchase new property, plant, and equipment. ●

▶▶ LEARNING OBJECTIVES *After studying this chapter, you should be able to:*

1 Distinguish a company's expenses from expenditures that it should capitalize.

2 Measure the acquisition cost of tangible assets such as land, buildings, and equipment.

3 Compute depreciation for buildings and equipment using various depreciation methods.

4 Recalculate depreciation in response to a change in estimated useful life or residual value.

5 Differentiate financial statement depreciation from income tax depreciation.

6 Explain the effect of depreciation on cash flow.

7 Account for expenditures after acquisition.

8 Compute gains and losses on the disposal of fixed assets and consider the impact of these gains and losses on the statement of cash flows.

9 Determine the balance sheet valuation of tangible assets for companies who use the revaluation method allowed under IFRS.

10 Account for the impairment of tangible assets.

11 Account for intangible assets, including impairment.

12 Explain the reporting for goodwill.

13 Interpret the depletion of natural resources.

By now, you should understand how to account for short-lived assets, such as inventory. We match their costs to the single period in which we recognize the associated revenues. What about assets that a company does not use quickly? Many long-lived assets, such as buildings and heavy machinery, help generate revenues in multiple periods, and companies must spread the costs of such assets across those periods. To qualify for the treatment discussed in this chapter companies must actually use the assets in their day-to-day operations and not hold them for purposes of resale or investment. A company should classify an unused building or land that it holds for speculative purposes as an investment rather than as property, plant, and equipment.

How important are long-lived assets? Depending on the industry, they can be the most important assets a company owns. For example, consider the net property, plant, and equipment accounts as presented on the balance sheets of the following companies ($ in millions) for fiscal year 2011:

Intel is the world's largest semiconductor chip maker, based on revenue. With greater than 80% market share in the global microprocessor market, the Intel logo is familiar to consumers worldwide. Semiconductor manufacturing requires huge investments in facilities and equipment. We learn about the accounting for physical assets used in manufacturing and intangible assets, such as the Intel logo, in this chapter.

Company	Total Assets	Property, Plant, and Equipment	
		Property, Plant, and Equipment, net	Percentage of Total Assets
Bank of America	$2,129,046	$13,637	0.6
Time Warner	67,801	3,963	5.8
Microsoft	108,704	8,162	7.5
Deckers	1,146	90	7.9
Google	72,574	9,603	13.2
Coca-Cola	79,974	14,939	18.7
Starbucks	7,360	2,355	32.0
Intel	71,119	23,627	33.2
Chevron	209,474	122,608	58.5
Duke Energy	62,526	42,661	68.2

Why do these numbers vary so greatly? Because different types of businesses require different types of assets. **Bank of America** (B of A) is one of the largest banks in the world, providing a range of banking and nonbanking financial services. At the end of 2011, it had more than $2.1 trillion in assets, less than 1% in the form of property, plant, and equipment. Almost 42% of B of A's assets were in the form of loans. Fifty-nine percent of **Time Warner**'s assets are in the form of nonphysical assets such as copyrights and tradenames, whereas only 5.8% is in the form of property, plant, and equipment. **Deckers** "designs, manufactures, and markets innovative function-oriented footwear and apparel" under such brand names as Teva, Simple, Ugg, and Tsubo. The company outsources most of the manufacturing to Asian and Costa Rican subcontractors and has little need for fixed assets. **Microsoft** and **Google** are high-tech companies that rely on intellectual property, not physical assets. These companies generate large amounts of cash that they then invest. Microsoft's balance sheet shows significant current and long-term investments, but little property, plant, and equipment (frequently referred to as PP&E). More than 60% of Google's assets are in the form of cash and marketable securities, and only 13.2% are in the form of property, plant, and equipment. **Coca-Cola**'s balance sheet has net property, plant, and equipment totaling 18.7% of total assets with various long-term nonphysical assets and investments comprising 49.4% of total assets. **Starbucks** leases most of its locations, but it has made substantial investments in both store equipment and leasehold improvements, which are long-term investments to improve leased facilities. As noted previously, Intel's manufacturing process requires a significant investment in buildings and equipment, which comprise 33.2% of its assets. More than 58% of **Chevron**'s total assets are in the form of property, plant, and equipment, including oil wells, drilling rigs, buildings, and gas pumps. **Duke Energy** is a utility company with a significant percentage of its assets in the form of electric generation plants, electric and natural gas distribution and transmission facilities, and equipment.

Accounting for long-lived assets presents some interesting and unique concerns. One important consideration is when to charge the cost of a long-lived asset as an expense on the income statement. For example, if an asset helps generate revenue for 10 years, how much of its cost should we assign to each of the 10 years the company uses the asset? The answer to this question depends on the method chosen for recording depreciation. Remember, depreciation is a systematic and rational system for allocating the cost of the asset over its useful life. This chapter explores depreciation—both understanding the nature of depreciation and learning about various depreciation methods. However, we begin with a look at long-lived assets in general.

Overview of Long-Lived Assets

Most business entities hold major assets such as land, buildings, equipment, and patents that they use in operations. These long-lived assets help produce revenues over multiple periods by facilitating the production of goods or services and the sale of these items to customers. Because these assets are necessary in day-to-day operations, companies do not sell them in the ordinary course of business. However, replacement of these assets is an essential part of the successful operation of a business. Keep in mind that one company's long-lived asset might be another company's short-lived asset. For example, a delivery truck is a long-lived asset for most companies, but a truck dealer would regard a delivery truck as short-lived merchandise inventory.

tangible assets (fixed assets, plant assets)
Physical items that can be seen and touched, such as land, buildings, and equipment.

Long-lived assets can be either tangible or intangible. **Tangible assets** (also called **fixed assets** or **plant assets**) are physical items that you can see and touch. Examples are land, buildings, and equipment. In contrast, **intangible assets** lack physical substance. They generally consist of contractual rights, legal rights, or economic benefits. Examples are patents, trademarks, and copyrights. Financial instruments such as accounts receivable, notes receivable, and investments in bonds and stocks also lack physical substance, but these assets are not classified as intangibles for accounting purposes. Accounts and notes receivable represent claims to cash and are accounted for as discussed in Chapter 6. Investments in bonds and stocks aren't classified as intangible assets because they are not part of the operating activities of the company. We discuss such investments in Chapter 11. Intangible assets are becoming increasingly important in today's economy, as described in the Business First box on p. 341.

intangible assets
Assets that lack physical substance. They consist of contractual rights, legal rights, or economic benefits. Examples are patents, trademarks, and copyrights.

BUSINESS FIRST

VALUING RECORDED AND UNRECORDED ASSETS

The historical-cost model of accounting for long-lived assets has both strengths and weaknesses. Historical costs are observable, verifiable, and reliable, resulting in long-lived assets being fairly valued at acquisition. Companies can then select a depreciation method to allocate the acquisition cost over the useful life of the asset, matching costs with revenues generated. However, from the moment of acquisition throughout the life of the assets, book value may be out of touch with market value, and the depreciation expense may be unrelated to the change in market value for the period. These characteristics of historical accounting are very serviceable as long as we remember the strengths and weaknesses of the model.

The bigger problem is that the current accounting model does not treat certain things as assets, even though they provide undeniable future benefits to the company and represent significant expenditures by corporations. Companies worldwide invest heavily in intangibles such as research and development (R&D), business processes and software, brand enhancement, and employee training. For many companies the spending on such activities surpasses what is spent on tangible assets, yet the benefits provided by these activities are not reflected in the balance sheet.

Much of the money spent on intangible capital goes for the development of human capital, expenditures for advertising, and R&D. Ed Michaels of McKinsey & Company says, "For many companies today, talented people are the prime source of competitive advantage." Investors and analysts realize this, and the high stock prices attached to Apple, Google, and Facebook are in part recognition of what the very able employees of those firms can do. However, the financial statements do not (and cannot independently and reliably) report a value for this human capital. A key reason is that the firm does not own these talented employees; it only "rents" them. Talent is always susceptible to being lured away. How do the financial statements help us to assess these elements? Companies with great human capital grow faster and earn more than the others. We can measure their growth and earnings and compare them using financial accounting outcomes.

While companies do not record these expenditures as assets on their balance sheets, people are interested in the value of these unrecorded assets. Consider Coca-Cola. Coca-Cola sells for more per ounce than does RC Cola, Jones Soda, or a number of other very tasty competitors. Part of the reason is the century of advertising and impression making that is Coke's history. The brand name is an asset, and yet the financial statements do not reflect it. Each year, Interbrand, one of the world's leading brand consultancies, prepares a ranking of the 100 Best Global Brands. In 2011, Interbrand ranked Coca-Cola #1 and assigned the Coca-Cola brand a value of $71,861 million, up 2% from its estimate in 2010! Note that Coca-Cola's total recorded assets at the end of 2011 were $79,974 million, a number only slightly higher than the unrecorded estimated brand value. In the United States, companies expense advertising costs as incurred and do not recognize the internal generation of a brand asset. The accounting process provides information on the amount companies currently spend on these efforts, and we can assess its effectiveness by looking at the outcomes. When Coke grows rapidly and earns high profits, we can see the evidence of a devoted workforce and a great brand.

The difficulty and uncertainty inherent in the assignment of value to unrecorded intangible assets is evident by a comparison of brand value estimates and rankings. Millward Brown is a global marketing research company. One of its divisions, Millward Brown Optimor, developed the BrandZ Top 100 Most Valuable Global Brand rankings, which valued the Coca-Cola brand at $73,752 million in 2011 and ranked it #6 behind Apple, Google, IBM, McDonald's, and Microsoft.

Sources: J. Byrne, "The Search for the Young and Gifted: Why Talent Counts," *BusinessWeek*, October 4, 1999, pp. 108–109; http://www.interbrand.com/en/best-global-brands/Best-Global-Brands-2011.aspx; http://www.millwardbrown.com/libraries/optimor_brandz_files/2011_brandz_top100_chart.sflb.ashx.

We do not account for all long-lived physical assets in the same way. Among tangible assets, land is unique—it does not wear out or become obsolete. Therefore, we report land in the financial records at historical cost and do not depreciate it. Most other long-lived tangible assets wear out, become inadequate for a given company's use, or become obsolete. As a company uses these assets over time, accountants convert their historical cost to expense. There are similar differences in the way we account for various types of intangible assets, depending on their characteristics.

amortization

When referring to long-lived assets, it usually means the allocation of the costs of intangible assets to the periods that benefit from these assets.

depletion

The process of allocating the cost of natural resources to the periods that benefit from their use.

▶▶ OBJECTIVE 1

Distinguish a company's expenses from expenditures that it should capitalize.

---

expenditures

Purchases of goods or services, whether for cash or credit.

capitalize

To record the purchase price of an asset in a long-term asset account, recognizing that it will have benefits lasting more than a year.

In practice, accountants use more than one term to describe the allocation of costs over time. For tangible assets such as buildings, machinery, and equipment, they call it depreciation. They use **amortization** to refer to the allocation of the costs of intangible assets to the periods that benefit from these assets. Finally, for natural resources, they call it **depletion**.

Contrasting Long-Lived Asset Expenditures with Expenses

When a company purchases an asset, management must decide whether the asset will be used only within the current accounting year or whether it will be used over multiple years. We call all purchases of goods or services, whether for cash or on credit, **expenditures**. As explained in Chapter 2, companies make expenditures to purchase assets. For those assets to remain on the balance sheet they must continue to provide future economic benefits to the company and be reliably measured. Companies use the benefits provided by some assets, such as advertising services, almost immediately, so they record such expenditures directly as expenses. Companies use the benefits of other assets, such as prepaid rent, within a year, so the expenditures are classified as current assets for a short period before companies recognize them as expenses. Finally, companies **capitalize** assets that have benefits lasting more than a year; that is, they record the purchase price in a long-term asset account and recognize part of the purchase price as an expense each period as they use the asset. Capital expenditures result in new long-lived assets, or they increase the capacity, efficiency, or useful life of existing long-lived assets.

The Decision to Capitalize

Sometimes it is difficult to decide whether to capitalize or expense a particular expenditure. Consider the expenditure for work performed on an engine. The company should capitalize this expenditure only if it increases the capacity, efficiency, or useful life of the engine beyond initial expectations. If it merely keeps the engine running as expected, it is an expense. In the absence of contradictory evidence, most accountants would call it an expense. Why? Because accountants and auditors watch for tendencies to understate current expenses, thereby overstating income, through the unjustified capitalization of expenditures that should be expensed.

Wherever doubt exists, accountants tend to charge an expense instead of an asset account for repairs, parts, and similar items. Conservatism leads us to guard against earnings patterns that are unusually high and increasing, which can mislead investors. Furthermore, often such expenditures are minor in magnitude, so the cost-benefit test of record keeping and the concept of materiality justify this choice. For instance, many companies charge to expense all expenditures that are less than a specified minimum dollar amount such as $100, $1,000, or $5,000. The minimum dollar amount is primarily a function of the size of the company

Ethics: Capitalization versus Expense

Because decisions about whether to expense or capitalize expenditures require judgment, this is an area that management may inappropriately try to influence in order to increase reported net income. Suppose that you run the internal audit department of a large U.S. corporation. As part of the routine internal audit work, one of your staff members uncovers $2 billion in expenditures that the company has capitalized, although no one in the department is able to find authorization for capital spending in that amount. You begin to suspect that the $2 billion really represents operating costs that accountants have shifted to capital expenditure accounts, making the company appear more profitable. The choice of whether to capitalize or expense the $2 billion has a material effect on the company's financial performance. When you question the person in charge of capital spending about the transaction, he states that the expenditure represents "prepaid capacity," a term that is not familiar to you in spite of your extensive background in accounting. Accountants at various levels within the organization repeatedly stonewall your efforts to obtain clarification of these expenditures. Ultimately, you decide to undertake a detailed investigation. When you reveal your intentions to your company's CFO, he asks you to delay the investigation until after the current quarter, indicating that he intends to take care of the problem in the subsequent quarter.

Now you are faced with a difficult decision. Should you pursue the investigation despite the CFO's request to delay? After all, the CFO is your boss, and he and others higher up in the organization have suggested that you postpone or abandon your investigation. You have no hard evidence of wrongdoing, and if the CFO does in fact correct the problem prior to year-end, the annual financial results will be correctly stated. However, the evasiveness of company executives when questioned about these capital expenditures and the lack of documentation for them suggests that the $2 billion disbursement is just the tip of the iceberg. If you and your staff pursue this investigation and find inappropriate accounting for capital expenditures, the findings could be very detrimental to the company and your fellow employees.

This is a situation similar to the one that confronted Cynthia Cooper and her audit staff at WorldCom. We know what decision Ms. Cooper made. She and her audit team contacted the head of WorldCom's audit committee and KPMG, WorldCom's new outside auditor. Further investigation revealed one of the biggest accounting scandals in U.S. history. On June 25, 2002, WorldCom disclosed that it had wrongly treated $3.8 billion in operating costs, primarily access fees that WorldCom paid to other phone companies for the use of their lines, as capital expenditures. Rather than immediately expensing these costs, WorldCom capitalized the $3.8 billion as an asset. This allowed WorldCom to expense the $3.8 billion as depreciation (or amortization) on the income statement over time rather than expensing it immediately. The decision to capitalize rather than expense these costs enhanced the company's net income in the period in which it capitalized the costs, but it would decrease future periods' income as WorldCom depreciated the capitalized costs. As a result of this and other accounting manipulations, several WorldCom executives, including the CEO and CFO, were convicted of conspiracy, securities fraud, and making false financial filings and were sentenced to time in prison.

Acquisition Cost of Tangible Assets

Accounting for a long-lived asset begins with its purchase. The acquisition cost of a long-lived asset is the cash-equivalent purchase price, including incidental costs to complete the purchase, to transport the asset, and to prepare it for its intended use. Consider the following categories of tangible assets.

▶▶ **OBJECTIVE 2**

Measure the acquisition cost of tangible assets such as land, buildings, and equipment.

Land

The acquisition cost of land includes charges to the purchaser for the cost of land surveys, legal fees, title fees, transfer taxes, and even the demolition costs of old structures that must be torn down to get the land ready for its intended use. If the purchaser assumes the seller's obligation for unpaid taxes, mortgages, or encumbrances on the property, it also capitalizes these costs. Consider the following example for the acquisition of a piece of land to be used as the site of a new building to house company headquarters. There is an existing building on the land that must be torn down. All of the following items become part of the capitalized value of the land:

Purchase price	$500,000
Closing costs, including attorney's fees	9,500
Title search and transfer taxes	1,000
Costs of demolition of old building	6,000
Costs of clearing, grading, and filling in preparation for new building	19,000
Assumption of unpaid property taxes	10,000
Proceeds from the sale of materials salvaged from the old building	(2,500)
Total acquisition cost	$543,000

Under historical-cost accounting, companies report land on the balance sheet at its original cost. After years of rising real estate values and inflation, the carrying amount of land is often far below its current market value. Consider that in 1970, Intel purchased its first piece of property, a 26-acre pear orchard in Santa Clara, California. Should land acquired and held since 1970 still appear at its 1970 cost on balance sheets prepared more than 40 years later? Yes. U.S. GAAP requires companies to carry land at its original historical cost, unless the fair value of the land has fallen below that original cost.

Buildings and Equipment

The cost of buildings, plant, and equipment should include all costs of acquisition and preparation for use. Consider the following example for used packaging equipment:

Invoice price, gross	$100,000
Deduct 2% cash discount for payment within 30 days	(2,000)
Invoice price, net	98,000
State sales tax at 8% of $98,000	7,840
Transportation costs	3,000
Installation costs	8,000
Repair costs prior to use	7,000
Total acquisition cost	$123,840

As you can see, several individual costs make up the total acquisition cost. We capitalize the total of $123,840 and add it to the Equipment account. Why do we include repair costs in the amount that we capitalize as the acquisition cost of the asset? Normally, we would expense repair costs on the income statement as the costs are incurred. The difference is that repair costs incurred prior to the first use of an asset are part of getting the asset ready to use and, therefore, we include them in the acquisition cost on the balance sheet. In contrast, after the equipment is in use, we should charge ordinary repair costs as expenses on the income statement.

Companies usually pay for capital expenditures with cash or other **monetary assets**—assets that are fixed in terms of the units of currency and easily convertible into cash. Accounts receivable represent an example of a monetary asset. However, a company may elect to pay for fixed assets with **nonmonetary assets**—items that are less liquid than monetary assets and whose price in terms of units of currency is more susceptible to change over time. The practice of exchanging nonmonetary assets is particularly common for start-up companies. If they do not have sufficient cash but have stock that is highly valued, companies may pay for assets using their own stock. For example, the owner of a piece of land might sell it to a company in exchange for stock because the owner could either sell the stock immediately or hold the stock in hopes that it would increase in value. We generally record a nonmonetary exchange at the fair value of the asset surrendered, land in this example, or the fair value of the consideration received, stock in this example, whichever is the more clearly evident.

The **fair value** of an asset is the price for which a company could sell the asset to an independent third party. When a stock trades actively, we typically assume that the fair value of the stock is the best indicator of the value of the transaction. After all, if we asked four different appraisers to appraise the land, they would probably arrive at four different values, while the stock exchange determines a value for shares of stock at any given point in time. Suppose that Woodside Corporation sold land to Tryon Company in exchange for shares of Tryon stock. Tryon is a publicly traded stock whose share price is observable each day. An appraiser valued the land at $100,000, whereas the stock had a market value at the time of the sale of $108,000. Tryon would record the following entry, ignoring the $100,000 appraised value in favor of the market value of the stock:

Land	108,000	
Paid-in capital		108,000
Purchase of land in exchange for $108,000 of common stock		

If Tryon's stock is not publicly traded and no market price for the stock is determinable, Tryon would record the transaction at the appraised value of $100,000.

There is detailed accounting guidance that addresses the situation where two companies exchange physical assets. While these rules are beyond the scope of this text, the underlying goal remains to record the acquired asset at fair value.

Basket Purchases

Frequently, companies acquire more than one long-lived asset for a single overall purchase price. The acquisition of two or more assets for a lump-sum cost is sometimes called a **basket purchase** or **lump-sum purchase**. The acquisition cost of a basket purchase is divided among the assets

---

monetary assets
Assets that are fixed in terms of units of currency and easily convertible into cash.

nonmonetary assets
Assets that are less liquid than monetary assets and whose price in terms of units of currency is more susceptible to change over time.

fair value
The value of an asset based on the price for which a company could sell the asset to an independent third party.

basket purchase (lump-sum purchase)
The acquisition of two or more assets for a lump-sum cost.

purchased according to some estimate of the relative fair values of the assets. For instance, suppose Intel acquires land and a building for $1 million. How much of the $1 million should Intel allocate to land and how much to the building? If an independent appraiser indicates that the fair values of the land and the building are $480,000 and $720,000, respectively, the $1 million cost would be allocated as follows:

	(1)	(2)	(3)	(2) × (3)
	Appraised Value	**Weighting**	**Total Cost to Allocate**	**Allocated Costs**
Land	$ 480,000	480 ÷ 1,200 (or 40%)	$1,000,000	$ 400,000
Building	720,000	720 ÷ 1,200 (or 60%)	1,000,000	600,000
Total	$1,200,000			$1,000,000

Allocating a basket purchase cost to the individual assets can significantly affect future reported income if the useful lives of the assets differ. In our example, if Intel allocates less cost to the land, it allocates more cost to the building, which is depreciable. In turn, future depreciation expenses are higher, and operating incomes are lower.

Accounting Alternatives Subsequent to Acquisition

All companies throughout the world initially record long-lived assets at their acquisition cost. However, subsequent to acquisition there are two possible accounting methods. The most popular is the cost method. U.S. GAAP requires the cost method, IFRS allows it, and most companies worldwide use it. Under the cost method, companies carry assets at their cost less depreciation. Under certain circumstances a company may write down the asset value, but it can never increase the value. Most of this chapter focuses on the cost method. The alternative method, allowed only by IFRS, is the revaluation method. It is used mostly in Europe, especially in the Netherlands, Denmark, and the United Kingdom. Under this method, companies carry long-lived assets at their fair value. We discuss the revaluation method briefly starting on page 358. Here we discuss depreciation as employed in the cost method and demonstrate several depreciation methods.

Depreciation of Buildings and Equipment

After purchasing tangible long-lived assets other than land, a company must depreciate the assets. Those new to accounting frequently misunderstand depreciation. It is not a process of valuation. In everyday use, we might say that an auto depreciates in value, meaning that its current market value declines. However, to an accountant, depreciation is not a technique for approximating current values such as replacement costs or resale values. It is simply a system for cost allocation. For purposes of financial reporting, both U.S. GAAP and IFRS allow companies to freely select the depreciation method they believe best portrays their economic circumstance as long as the selected method is systematic and rational.

Depreciation is one of the key factors distinguishing accrual accounting from cash-basis accounting. If a company purchases a long-lived asset for cash, strict cash-basis accounting would treat the entire cost of the asset as an expense in the period of acquisition. In contrast, accrual accounting initially capitalizes the cost and then allocates it in the form of depreciation over the periods the company uses the asset. This more effectively matches expenses with the revenues produced.

The cost a company allocates as depreciation over the total useful life of the asset is the **depreciable value** (also **depreciable base** or **allocation base**). It is the difference between the total acquisition cost and the estimated residual value. The **residual value**, also known as **terminal value, disposal value, salvage value,** and **scrap value,** is the amount a company expects to receive from sale or disposal of a long-lived asset at the end of its useful life. The **useful life** or **service life** of an asset is the shorter of the physical life of the asset or the economic life of the asset. The economic life of an asset and its physical life need not be the same. The physical life of an asset depends on the wear and tear it takes while in use. At some point,

> **OBJECTIVE 3**
>
> Compute depreciation for buildings and equipment using various depreciation methods.

depreciable value (depreciable base, allocation base)
The cost a company allocates as depreciation over the total useful life of an asset. It is the difference between the total acquisition cost and the estimated residual value.

residual value (terminal value, disposal value, salvage value, scrap value)
The amount a company expects to receive from sale or disposal of a long-lived asset at the end of its useful life.

useful life (service life)
The shorter of the physical life or the economic life of an asset.

a company can no longer use a piece of equipment in the production process due to deterioration. However, a company may decide to replace equipment prior to the end of its physical life. Such replacement depends on economic factors rather than physical ones. For example, given the rapidly increasing speed and decreasing cost of computers, most companies replace them long before they physically wear out. That is, their economic life is shorter than their physical life. Both the residual value and useful life are estimates company management must make at the time it acquires the asset, and these estimates can greatly affect a company's net income.

Depreciation methods differ primarily in the amount of cost allocated to each accounting period. A list of depreciation amounts for each period of an asset's useful life is a **depreciation schedule**. We use the following symbols and amounts to compare various annual depreciation schedules for a $41,000 delivery truck purchased by Chang Company on January 1, 20X1:

depreciation schedule
The list of depreciation amounts for each period of an asset's useful life.

Symbols	Amounts for Illustration
Let	
C = total acquisition cost on January 1, 20X1	$41,000
R = estimated residual value	$ 1,000
n = estimated useful life (in years or miles)	4 years
	200,000 miles
D = amount of annual depreciation expense	Various

Straight-Line Depreciation

straight-line depreciation
A method that spreads the depreciable value evenly over the useful life of an asset.

Straight-line depreciation spreads the depreciable value evenly over the useful life of an asset. It is by far the most popular method for financial reporting purposes. In fact, a recent survey showed that more than 98% of major companies use straight-line depreciation for at least some of their fixed assets. While straight-line depreciation may not be the best representation of the actual use rate of an asset, its popularity stems from its simplicity in both theory and application.

Exhibit 8-1 shows the balance sheet values for Chang Company's truck using straight-line depreciation. At the end of the fourth year, the truck has a remaining net book value of $1,000, which is the estimated residual value. The annual depreciation expense charged to Chang's income statement is as follows:

$$\text{Depreciation expense} = \frac{(\text{Acquisition cost} - \text{Estimated residual value})}{\text{Years of estimated useful life}}$$

$$D = \frac{(C - R)}{n}$$

$$D = \frac{(\$41,000 - \$1,000)}{4}$$

$$D = \$10,000 \text{ per year}$$

EXHIBIT 8-1

Chang Company

Straight-Line Depreciation Schedule

	Balances at End of Year			
	1	2	3	4
Equipment (at original acquisition cost)	$41,000	$41,000	$41,000	$41,000
Less: Accumulated depreciation (the portion of original cost that has already been charged to operations as an expense)	10,000	20,000	30,000	40,000
Net book value (the portion of original cost that has not yet been charged to operations)	$31,000	$21,000	$11,000	$ 1,000

Depreciation Based on Units

In some cases, time is not the determining factor of the useful life of an asset. When physical wear and tear determines the useful life of the asset, accountants may base depreciation on units of service or units of production instead of units of time (years). Depreciation based on units of service is known as **units-of-production depreciation** or the **activity method** and, in some circumstances, results in a better matching of costs and revenues. In our example, Chang's truck has a useful life of 200,000 miles, so depreciation computed on a per mile basis is as follows:

$$\text{Depreciation expense per unit of service} = \frac{(\text{Acquisition cost} - \text{Estimated residual value})}{\text{Estimated units of service}}$$

$$D = \frac{(C - R)}{n}$$

$$D = \frac{(\$41,000 - \$1,000)}{200,000 \text{ miles}}$$

$$D = \$.20 \text{ per mile}$$

units-of-production depreciation (activity method)
A depreciation method based on units of service or units of production when physical wear and tear is the dominating influence on the useful life of the asset.

If employees drive the truck 65,000 miles in the first year of use, depreciation expense for that year will be $(65,000 \times \$.20) = \$13,000$.

For some assets, such as transportation equipment, units-of-production depreciation may be more logical than the straight-line method. However, the units-of-production depreciation method is not widely used, probably for several reasons:

1. When the usage of an asset is fairly constant across time, unit-based depreciation produces approximately the same yearly depreciation expense as does straight-line depreciation.

2. Straight-line depreciation is easier. Under straight-line, we can determine the entire depreciation schedule at the time of acquisition; however, under units-of-production depreciation, we must keep detailed records of units of service to determine the amount depreciated each year.

Declining-Balance Depreciation

Any pattern of depreciation that writes off depreciable value more quickly than does the straight-line method is considered **accelerated depreciation**. Companies use a number of accelerated depreciation methods, but we will illustrate only the **double-declining-balance (DDB) method**, also known as 200% declining-balance method. We compute DDB depreciation as follows:

1. Compute the straight-line rate by dividing 100% by the useful life stated in years. Then double the straight-line rate. In our example, the straight-line rate is $(100\% \div 4) = 25\%$. The DDB rate is $(2 \times 25\%)$, or 50%.

2. To compute the depreciation on an asset for any year, ignore the estimated residual value and multiply the asset's net book value at the beginning of the year by the DDB rate.

accelerated depreciation
Any depreciation method that writes off depreciable value more quickly than does the straight-line method.

double-declining-balance (DDB) method
A common form of accelerated depreciation. It is computed by doubling the straight-line rate and multiplying the resulting DDB rate by the asset's beginning net book value.

We can apply the DDB method to Chang Company's truck as follows:

$$\text{DDB rate} = 2 \times (100\% \div n)$$

$$\text{DDB rate, 4-year life} = 2 \times (100\% \div 4) = 50\%$$

$$\text{DDB depreciation} = \text{DDB rate} \times \text{Beginning net book value}$$

For year 1: $D = .50 \times (\$41,000)$
$= \$20,500$

For year 2: $D = .50 \times (\$41,000 - \$20,500)$
$= \$10,250$

For year 3: $D = .50 \times (\$41,000 - \$20,500 - \$10,250)$
$= \$5,125$

For year 4: $D = .50 \times (\$41,000 - \$20,500 - \$10,250 - \$5,125)$
$= \$2,563$

In this example, the depreciation amount for each year is one-half the preceding year's depreciation. However, this halving is a special case that happens only with a 4-year life asset. Remember, the basic approach of DDB is to apply the depreciation rate to the beginning net book value. Applying the constant DDB rate to the declining net book value results in lower depreciation in each successive year. Although we illustrated the declining-balance method with DDB, other versions use different multiples. For example, the 150% declining-balance method multiples the straight-line rate by 1.5 instead of doubling it. In the case of the asset with a 4-year life, the 150% declining-balance rate is (1.5 × 25%) = 37.5%.

Comparing and Choosing Depreciation Methods

Exhibit 8-2 compares the results of straight-line and DDB depreciation for Chang Company's truck. Note that the DDB method, when strictly applied, provides $38,438 of total depreciation and does not allocate the full $40,000 depreciable value to expense. Some companies compensate for this by adjusting the depreciation schedule part way through the asset's depreciable life. One such adjustment is illustrated in the last two columns of Exhibit 8-2, where additional depreciation is added in the last year to reach the residual value. In addition, if the residual value is large enough, application of DDB may result in fully depreciating an asset prior to the end of its useful life. Because you cannot depreciate an asset below its estimated residual value, a company may simply stop taking depreciation once the residual value has been reached. Alternatively, a company may compensate for this by modifying the depreciation schedule toward the end of the asset life so that the depreciation in the final years brings the net book value at the end of use to exactly the residual value.

Companies do not necessarily use the same depreciation method for all types of depreciable assets. Although **Intel** uses straight-line depreciation for all assets, a recent **Boeing** annual report states, "The principal methods of depreciation are as follows: buildings and land improvements, 150% declining balance; and machinery and equipment, sum-of-the-years' digits." We do not cover the computations for sum-of-the-years' digits depreciation in this text; however, it is an alternative accelerated depreciation method.

How does a company choose among the alternatives? In some cases, tradition leads a company to select the method used by other companies in its industry to enhance comparability. Sometimes one method provides superior matching of expense and revenue, as units-of-production depreciation does for certain types of equipment and manufacturing processes. Sometimes companies choose the method most consistent with the life cycle cost of the asset. Suppose a type of equipment requires little maintenance in the first years of its life, but increasing maintenance in later

EXHIBIT 8-2

Chang Company

Depreciation: Two Popular Methods
(assume equipment costs $41,000, 4-year life, and estimated residual value of $1,000)

	Straight-Line*		Declining-Balance at Twice the Straight-Line Rate (DDB)[†]		Modified DDB—Depreciation Schedule Adjustment in Year 4[‡]	
	Annual Depreciation	**Book Value**	**Annual Depreciation**	**Book Value**	**Annual Depreciation**	**Book Value**
At acquisition		$41,000		$41,000		$41,000
Year 1	$10,000	31,000	$20,500	20,500	$20,500	20,500
Year 2	10,000	21,000	10,250	10,250	10,250	10,250
Year 3	10,000	11,000	5,125	5,125	5,125	5,125
Year 4	10,000	1,000	2,563	2,562	4,125	1,000
Total	$40,000		$38,438		$40,000	

*Depreciation is the same each year, 25% of ($41,000 – $1,000).

[†](100% ÷ 4) = 25%. The DDB rate is 50%. Then 50% of $41,000; 50% of ($41,000 – $20,500); 50% of [$41,000 – ($20,500 + $10,250)]; etc. Unmodified, this method will not fully depreciate the existing book value.

[‡]The depreciation schedule adjustment occurs in year 4, and the depreciation amount is the amount needed to reduce the book value to the estimated salvage value.

Summary Problem for Your Review

PROBLEM

"The net book value of plant assets that appears on the balance sheet is the amount that would be spent today for their replacement." Do you agree? Explain.

SOLUTION

No. Net book value of plant assets on the balance sheet is the result of deducting accumulated depreciation from original historical cost. It is a result of cost allocation, not valuation. The depreciation process does not attempt to reflect all the technological and economic events that may affect replacement value. Consequently, there is no assurance that net book value will approximate replacement cost.

years. Accelerated depreciation with decreasing depreciation charges each year, plus rising maintenance costs each year, may provide a more constant cost per year. Thus, the choice depends on the nature of the industry, as well as the equipment and the goals of management.

As noted earlier, both IFRS and U.S. GAAP allow companies to select the depreciation method as long as it is systematic and rational. Also, both sets of standards determine the depreciable value by subtracting the residual value from the original cost. However, IFRS requires companies to separately depreciate each component of a property, plant, and equipment asset if the component cost comprises a significant portion of the total cost—a method known as **component depreciation**. For example, significant components of a building include the electrical system, the heating and cooling system, the plumbing system, and the roof, to name a few. A company using IFRS must assign each component its own useful life for depreciation purposes. The heating and cooling system may depreciate over 20 years, while the roof depreciates over 30 years.

component depreciation
A depreciation approach required by IFRS where each component of a property, plant, and equipment asset must be depreciated separately if the component cost comprises a significant portion of the total cost.

Changes in Estimated Useful Life or Residual Value

A company estimates the useful life and residual value of an asset at the time of its acquisition. The information on which the company bases these estimates may change with time. If new information becomes available and the use of the revised estimate would result in a material change in depreciation expense, the company must adopt the new estimate and revise the depreciation schedule. Accounting for changes in estimated useful life or residual value is prospective in nature. In other words, the company does not go back and revise the depreciation expense taken in prior periods. Rather, it recomputes depreciation expense for the period in which it revises the estimate and for all future periods.

Refer to the straight-line depreciation schedule for Chang Company's truck as shown in Exhibit 8-2. Chang originally estimated a residual value of $1,000 and a useful life of 4 years for the truck. Suppose that at the beginning of year 4, Chang determines that it will continue to use the truck for 2 more years rather than 1 more year. As of the beginning of year 4, Chang has recorded a total of $30,000 in depreciation expense, $10,000 in year 1, $10,000 in year 2, and $10,000 in year 3. The net book value of the truck at the beginning of year 4 is $11,000 as shown in Exhibit 8-2. Chang still expects the residual value to be $1,000. Chang must allocate the remaining $10,000 in allowable depreciation expense over a total of 2 years: ($10,000 ÷ 2) = $5,000. The revised depreciation schedule for Chang is as follows:

▶▶ **OBJECTIVE 4**
Recalculate depreciation in response to a change in estimated useful life or residual value.

	Annual Depreciation	**Book Value**
At acquisition		$41,000
Year 1	$10,000	31,000
Year 2	10,000	21,000
Year 3	10,000	11,000
Year 4	5,000	6,000
Year 5	5,000	1,000
Total	$40,000	

Contrasting Income Tax and Shareholder Reporting

▶▶ **OBJECTIVE 5**
Differentiate financial statement depreciation from income tax depreciation.

In accounting for long-lived assets, reporting to stockholders and reporting to the income tax authorities often differ. Reports to stockholders and filings with the SEC must abide by GAAP. In contrast, reports to income tax authorities must abide by the income tax rules and regulations. Frequently GAAP rules and tax rules differ. Therefore, keeping two sets of records is necessary.

Depreciation for Tax Reporting Purposes

Modified Accelerated Cost Recovery System (MACRS)
The underlying basis for computing depreciation for tax purposes.

While Congress makes some changes to the U.S. tax code almost every year, since 1986 the underlying basis for computing depreciation for tax purposes has been the **Modified Accelerated Cost Recovery System (MACRS)**. The MACRS depreciation schedule is based on the declining-balance depreciation method discussed previously and differs from financial reporting depreciation in most cases. One important difference is that MACRS classifies depreciable assets into property classes and specifies the useful lives to be used for tax depreciation purposes for each property class. Frequently, useful lives for tax purposes are shorter than the useful lives used for financial reporting purposes. Remember that the shorter the life, the earlier a company recognizes depreciation expense. Higher expenses reported for tax purposes mean lower taxable net income, which means lower income taxes payable. MACRS allows for higher depreciation and lower taxes in the early years of an asset's service life than does the straight-line method commonly used for financial reporting. This is reversed in the later years of an asset's life. However, because of the time value of money, the company benefits from the delay in paying taxes.

Another important difference relates to residual values. Remember that the residual value reduces the depreciable value of an asset. For financial reporting purposes companies cannot depreciate an asset below its estimated residual value. However, MACRS assumes that all assets have a zero residual value. This allows a company to depreciate the entire historical cost for tax purposes, potentially increasing the total amount of depreciation expense.

Shareholder Reporting

Companies typically use MACRS for tax purposes because it provides larger tax deductions earlier in the life of the assets. Why does the tax code provide this benefit? Before MACRS was adopted, taxpayers and the government often spent significant time and money arguing about the specific choices that the company made with regard to the depreciable life of the asset, its salvage value, or other features of the depreciation method. By specifying one attractive accelerated method, tax authorities were able to eliminate most such disputes. In addition, the adoption of MACRS made the tax law favorable toward the economy by supporting companies in their desire to acquire and use long-lived productive assets.

There are several practical reasons for adopting straight-line depreciation for financial reporting, namely, simplicity, convenience, and reporting of higher earnings in early years than would be reported under accelerated depreciation. Managers tend not to choose accounting methods that reduce reported earnings substantially in the early years of long-lived assets.

Depreciation and Cash Flow

▶▶ **OBJECTIVE 6**
Explain the effect of depreciation on cash flow.

Too often, nonaccountants confuse the relationships among depreciation expense, income tax expense, cash, and accumulated depreciation. For example, the business press contains misleading quotations such as "… we're looking for financing of $3.75 billion. Of that, about 60% will be recovered in depreciation and amortization." As another example, consider a *BusinessWeek* news report concerning an airline company: "And with a hefty boost from depreciation and the sale of $6 million worth of property, its cash balance rose by $10 million in the year's first quarter."

These statements imply that depreciation somehow generates cash. It does not. Depreciation simply allocates the original cost of an asset to the periods in which the company uses the asset—nothing more and nothing less. Furthermore, accumulated depreciation is merely the portion of an asset's original cost that has been recorded as depreciation expense in prior periods—not a pile of cash waiting to be used.

Effects of Depreciation on Cash

To illustrate depreciation's relationship to cash, consider Acme Service Company, which began business with cash and common stockholders' equity of $100,000. Acme immediately acquired equipment for $40,000 cash. The equipment had an expected 4-year life and an estimated residual value of zero. The first year's operations generated cash sales of $103,000 and cash operating expenses of $53,000.

Straight-line depreciation on the equipment would be ($40,000 ÷ 4) = $10,000 in each year. Assume that depreciation would be $20,000 in the first year if Acme selected an accelerated depreciation method. Note from the first two columns of Exhibit 8-3 that the reported pretax income differs as a result of the depreciation method chosen, but cash flow from operations is the same. Comparing the pretax amounts stresses the role of depreciation expense most vividly. Why? Because before taxes, the only balance sheet accounts affected by changes in the depreciation method are Accumulated Depreciation and Retained Earnings. Depreciation does not affect the before-tax ending cash balances.

Now suppose that for financial reporting purposes, U.S. GAAP allowed Acme to write off the entire $40,000 in the first year but still treat it as an investing activity. What would Acme report as pretax income and cash provided by operations? Pretax income would be only ($103,000 – $53,000 – $40,000) = $10,000. However, the increase in cash would remain at $50,000. Why? Because cash received from sales of $103,000 and cash expenses of $53,000 would not change, leaving the $50,000 cash provided by operations unchanged.

Effects of Depreciation on Income Taxes

Now consider the after-tax portions of Exhibit 8-3 in the two rightmost columns. Depreciation is a deductible noncash expense for income tax purposes. Thus, the higher the depreciation a company deducts on its tax return in any given year, the lower the taxable income, and the lower the cash paid for income taxes. In short, if tax depreciation expense is higher, taxes are lower and the company keeps more cash for use in the business.

To emphasize the relationship between depreciation and cash and to simplify the comparison, we assume the depreciation method used for financial reporting is the same as for tax purposes. From the last two columns of Exhibit 8-3, you can see that Acme would pay $16,000 of income taxes in the first year using straight-line depreciation, but only $12,000 using accelerated depreciation. Therefore, compared with the straight-line depreciation method, the accelerated method conserves $4,000 in cash. Depreciation does not generate cash, but it does have a cash benefit if it results in lower taxes.

EXHIBIT 8-3

Acme Service Company

Income Statement and Statement of Cash Flows ($ in thousands)

	Before Taxes		After Taxes	
	Straight-Line Depreciation	**Accelerated Depreciation**	**Straight-Line Depreciation**	**Accelerated Depreciation**
Income Statement				
Sales	$103	$103	$103	$103
Operating expenses	53	53	53	53
Depreciation expense	10	20	10	20
Pretax income	40	30	40	30
Income tax expense (40%)	—	—	16	12
Net income	$ 40	$ 30	$ 24	$ 18
Statement of Cash Flows				
Cash collections	$103	$103	$103	$103
Cash operating expenses	53	53	53	53
Cash tax payments	—	—	16	12
Cash provided by operations*	$ 50	$ 50	$ 34	$ 38

*Sometimes called *cash flow from operations, net cash provided by operations,* or just *cash flow.* It is simply cash collected on sales less all operating expenses requiring cash and less cash paid for income taxes.

Summary Problems for Your Review

PROBLEM

"Accumulated depreciation provides cash for the replacement of fixed assets." Do you agree with this quotation from a business magazine? Explain.

SOLUTION

Accumulated depreciation does not generate cash. It is the sum of all the noncash depreciation expense recognized since the date a company acquired an asset. It in no way represents a stockpile of cash for replacement.

PROBLEM

Review the important chapter illustration in the section "Depreciation and Cash Flow" on page 351. Suppose Acme Service had acquired the equipment for $80,000 instead of $40,000. The estimated residual value remains zero, the useful life remains 4 years, and sales and operating expenses are unchanged.

1. Prepare a revised Exhibit 8-3. As in Exhibit 8-3, assume the same depreciation method is used for financial reporting and tax reporting. Assume an income tax rate of 40% and round all income tax computations to the nearest thousand.
2. Indicate the major items affected by the change. Also tabulate all differences between the final two columns in your revised exhibit as compared with the final two columns in Exhibit 8-3.

SOLUTION

1. The revised income statements and statement of cash flows information are in Exhibit 8-4. Examine Exhibit 8-4 before attempting requirement 2.

EXHIBIT 8-4

Acme Service Company

Income Statement and Statement of Cash Flows ($ in thousands)

	Before Taxes		After Taxes	
	Straight-Line Depreciation	Accelerated Depreciation	Straight-Line Depreciation	Accelerated Depreciation
Income Statement				
Sales	$103	$103	$103	$103
Operating expenses	53	53	53	53
Depreciation expense	20	40	20	40
Pretax income	30	10	30	10
Income tax expense (40%)	—	—	12	4
Net income	$ 30	$ 10	$ 18	$ 6
Statement of Cash Flows				
Cash collections	$103	$103	$103	$103
Cash operating expenses	53	53	53	53
Cash tax payments	—	—	12	4
Cash provided by operations	$ 50	$ 50	$ 38	$ 46

2. The following comparisons of Exhibits 8-4 and 8-3 are noteworthy. The change in depreciation does not affect sales, cash operating expenses, or cash provided by operations before

income taxes. Because of higher depreciation, net income is lower in all four columns of Exhibit 8-4 than it was in Exhibit 8-3. Comparison of the final two columns of the exhibits follows:

	As Shown in		
	Exhibit 8-4	Exhibit 8-3	Difference
Straight-line depreciation	20	10	10 Higher
Accelerated depreciation	40	20	20 Higher
Pretax income based on			
Straight-line depreciation	30	40	10 Lower
Accelerated depreciation	10	30	20 Lower
Income tax expense based on			
Straight-line depreciation	12	16	4 Lower
Accelerated depreciation	4	12	8 Lower
Net income based on			
Straight-line depreciation	18	24	6 Lower
Accelerated depreciation	6	18	12 Lower
Cash provided by operations based on			
Straight-line depreciation	38	34	4 Higher
Accelerated depreciation	46	38	8 Higher

Especially noteworthy is the phenomenon that higher tax depreciation not only decreases net income but also decreases cash outflows for income taxes. As a result, cash provided by operations increases.

Expenditures after Acquisition

In addition to the initial investment at acquisition, companies incur ongoing expenditures associated with the operation of long-lived assets. For example, repairs and maintenance costs are necessary to maintain a fixed asset in operating condition. **Repairs** include the occasional costs of restoring a fixed asset to its ordinary operating condition after breakdowns, accidents, or damage. **Maintenance** includes the routine recurring costs of activities such as oiling, polishing, painting, and adjusting that are necessary to keep a fixed asset in operating condition. Accountants generally combine repair and maintenance costs in a single account and regard them as expenses of the current period.

In contrast, an **improvement** (sometimes called a **betterment** or a **capital improvement**) is an expenditure that increases the future benefits provided by an existing fixed asset by decreasing its operating cost, increasing its rate of output, improving its safety, reducing its rate of pollution, or prolonging its useful life. Repairs and maintenance maintain the level of an asset's future benefits, whereas improvements increase those benefits. We generally capitalize improvements. Examples of capital improvements or betterments include the rehabilitation of an apartment house that will allow increased rents and the rebuilding of a machine that increases its speed or extends its useful life.

Suppose Chang Company's $41,000 delivery truck with a 4-year life and $1,000 residual value, presented earlier in the chapter, experiences a major overhaul costing $7,000 at the start of year 3. Chang depreciated the truck using straight-line depreciation during the first 2 years of use. If this overhaul extends the useful life of the truck from 4 to 5 years, the accounting is as follows:

1. Increase the book value of the truck ($41,000 − $20,000 = $21,000 at the end of year 2) by $7,000. Thus, we add $7,000 to the existing Equipment account.

▶▶ **OBJECTIVE 7**
Account for expenditures after acquisition.

repairs
The occasional costs of restoring a fixed asset to its ordinary operating condition after breakdowns, accidents, or damage.

maintenance
The routine recurring costs of activities such as oiling, polishing, painting, and adjusting that are necessary to keep a fixed asset in operating condition.

improvement (betterment, capital improvement)
An expenditure that increases the future benefits provided by an existing fixed asset by decreasing its operating cost, increasing its rate of output, improving its safety, reducing its rate of pollution, or prolonging its useful life.

2. Revise the depreciation schedule to spread the revised book value of the truck over the remaining 3 years, as follows (assume Chang continues to use straight-line depreciation):

	Original Depreciation Schedule		Revised Depreciation Schedule	
	Year	Amount	Year	Amount
	1	$10,000	1	$10,000
	2	10,000	2	10,000
	3	10,000	3	9,000*
	4	10,000	4	9,000
			5	9,000
Accumulated depreciation		$40,000		$47,000†

*New depreciable amount is [($41,000 − $20,000 + $7,000) − $1,000 residual value] = $27,000. New depreciation expense is $27,000 divided by the remaining useful life of 3 years, or $9,000 per year.

†Recapitulation: Original cost	$41,000
Major overhaul	7,000
	48,000
Less: Residual	1,000
Depreciable amount	$47,000

Gains and Losses on Sales of Tangible Assets

Earlier in this chapter you learned how to account for property, plant, and equipment assets at the date of acquisition, how to account for expenditures related to the assets during their useful lives, and how to compute depreciation. However, companies sometimes sell an asset before the end of its useful life. When they sell assets, gains or losses are inevitable. We measure these gains or losses by the difference between the proceeds received and the net book value (net carrying amount) of the asset being sold.

Recording Gains and Losses

Consider Chang Company's delivery truck from our earlier example. Suppose Chang sells the truck for $21,000 in cash at the very beginning of year 3. Chang depreciated the asset using straight-line depreciation during the first 2 years of its life, giving the asset a $21,000 net book value at the beginning of year 3. Because the asset sells for exactly its net book value, there is no gain or loss on the transaction. Chang simply exchanges one asset, equipment, carried on the books at $21,000, for another asset, cash, of $21,000. Chang would eliminate the equipment asset and its accumulated depreciation from the records and record the cash received. The sale would have the following effects:

A				=	L	+	SE
+$21,000	−	$41,000	+ $20,000	=	$0	+	$0
Increase Cash		Decrease Equipment	Decrease Accumulated Depreciation				

Note that the disposal of the truck requires the removal of its book value, which appears in two accounts, Equipment and Accumulated Depreciation. We remove the original acquisition cost of $41,000 from the Equipment account and the $20,000 in accumulated depreciation on the truck from the Accumulated Depreciation account. Remember that a reduction in the balance in Accumulated Depreciation increases assets, hence the + sign associated with Accumulated Depreciation in the illustration.

Suppose the selling price was $27,000 instead of $21,000. The sale would result in a gain of $6,000, the difference between the sale proceeds and the net book value of the asset being sold:

Sale proceeds		$27,000
Less: Book value		
Cost	$ 41,000	
Accumulated depreciation	(20,000)	21,000
Gain		$ 6,000

This sale would have the following effects on the accounting equation:

A			=	L	+	SE
+$27,000 −	$41,000 +	$20,000	=	$0 +		$6,000
[Increase Cash]	[Decrease Equipment]	[Decrease Accumulated Depreciation]				[Increase SE Gain on Sale of Equipment]

Now suppose the selling price was $17,000 instead of $21,000. The sale would result in a $4,000 loss with the following effects:

A			=	L	+	SE
+$17,000 −	$41,000 +	$20,000	=	$0 −		$4,000
[Increase Cash]	[Decrease Equipment]	[Decrease Accumulated Depreciation]				[Decrease SE Loss on Sale of Equipment]

Exhibit 8-5 shows the T-account presentations and journal entries for these transactions. Note again that we must eliminate both the original cost of the equipment and the accompanying accumulated depreciation when we sell the asset. The net effect is to eliminate the $21,000 carrying amount of the equipment (cost of $41,000 less accumulated depreciation of $20,000).

Income Statement Presentation

In most instances, gains or losses on the disposition of plant assets are not significant enough to appear as separate line items on the income statement. In such cases, companies include these gains and losses as part of "Other Income" or "Other Expense" on the income statement and do

EXHIBIT 8-5

Journal and Ledger Entries

Gain or Loss on Sale of Equipment ($ in thousands)

Sale at $27,000:

		Cash	Equipment	Gain on Sale of Equipment
		27 |	* 41 | 41	| 6
Cash	27			
Accumulated depreciation	20		Accumulated Depreciation	
Equipment.		41	20 |* 20	
Gain on sale of equipment . .		6		

Sale at $17,000:

		Cash	Equipment	Loss on Sale of Equipment
		17 |	* 41 | 41	4 |
Cash	17			
Accumulated depreciation . .	20		Accumulated Depreciation	
Loss on sale of equipment . .	4		20 |* 20	
Equipment.		41		

*Beginning balance.

not separately identify them. The following three lines from the 2011 DuPont income statement illustrate this treatment ($ amounts in millions):

Sales	$37,961
Other income, net	758
Total	$38,719

Footnote 3 to DuPont's financial statements reveals that the item Other Income, net includes a net gain of $90 million arising from the sale of assets. The use of the term "net" gain suggests that DuPont sold some assets at a gain and other assets at a loss, with the gains exceeding the losses by $90 million. The $90 million net gain is not material to analysts in evaluating the company, so DuPont does not include a separate income statement line for it. To put things in perspective, the $90 million is small relative to the almost $38 billion in sales and the $758 million in Other Income, net reported on the 2011 income statement. It is also small relative to the more than $48.5 billion in assets on DuPont's December 31, 2011, balance sheet.

Some companies follow DuPont's example and list other income, including gains from the sale of assets, with sales revenue at the very top of the income statement. Others exclude such gains (or losses) from the computation of major profit categories such as gross profit or operating profit. The Coca-Cola Company took the latter approach in its 2011 financial statements. On its income statement Coca-Cola added $529 million of Other Income, net after calculating gross profit and operating income. The Management Discussion and Analysis reveals that Other Income, net includes "dividend income, rental income, gains and losses related to the disposal of property, plant and equipment …" as well as other income and expense items. When interpreting a company's income statement, it is important to know which approach a company has taken with regard to other income and other expense categories.

Asset Sales and the Statement of Cash Flows

The sale of fixed assets has implications for the statement of cash flows. Sales of fixed assets are investing activities. The previous examples demonstrate three different scenarios. In the first case (case A), Chang's truck sells for exactly its net book value of $21,000. In the second case (case B), it sells for $27,000 in cash resulting in a gain of $6,000. In the final case (case C), it sells for $17,000 in cash creating a loss of $4,000. In each case, the investing section of the statement of cash flows shows the actual cash received, labeled as "Proceeds from the sale of fixed assets." This is the only impact on the body of the cash flow statement if Chang Company uses the direct method for presenting cash flows from operating activities. If it uses the indirect method, the cash flows from operating activities section starts with net income. Because gains or losses from the sale of fixed assets affect net income but do not represent cash transactions above and beyond the cash proceeds shown in the investing section, Chang must remove these gains or losses from net income to calculate operating cash flows.

Suppose Chang Company uses the indirect method and has net income of $50,000 before accounting for the sale of the truck. To simplify the illustration, we assume no tax effects. The following table depicts the effects of the sale of the truck on net income:

	Income Before Sale	Gain (Loss)	Income After Sale
Case A: Sale at $21,000	$50,000	0	$50,000
Case B: Sale at $27,000	$50,000	$6,000	$56,000
Case C: Sale at $17,000	$50,000	($4,000)	$46,000

Net income includes the gain or loss on the sale of the truck. Therefore, the reconciliation of net income and cash flows from operating activities must remove the noncash gain or loss from net income. In case A, the $50,000 in reported net income does not include any gain or loss on the sale of the truck. Therefore, in arriving at cash flows from operating activities, we do not adjust net income. In case B, net income of $56,000 includes a $6,000 noncash gain, which we must deduct from net income to arrive at net cash provided by operating activities. Subtracting the

$6,000 gain does not imply a use of cash. It simply offsets the effect of the $6,000 gain included in net income. In case C, net income of $46,000 includes the $4,000 loss. Like depreciation expense, this loss does not represent a cash disbursement. The company did not pay someone $4,000 in cash to take possession of the truck! Therefore, we must add back to net income the loss on the sale of the truck to offset its earlier deduction. The net cash provided by operating activities is the same in each case. The sale of the truck did not affect operating cash flows. Recall that in every case, the investing section of the cash flow statement includes all of the cash received upon sale of the asset.

INTERPRETING FINANCIAL STATEMENTS

In January 20X2, Olsson Company sells a building that had an original historical cost of $850,000 and accumulated depreciation of $575,000 at the time of sale. It sells the building for cash and records a pretax gain of $75,000.

1. Indicate how these facts affect the statement of cash flows, prepared on a direct method basis, for the year ended December 31, 20X2. Ignore any tax consequences.
2. Indicate how these facts affect the statement of cash flows, prepared on an indirect method basis, for the year ended December 31, 20X2. Ignore any tax consequences.

Answer

1. The net book value of the building at the date of sale is ($850,000 − $575,000) = $275,000 and the gain on the sale is $75,000. The sale is an investing activity, so Olsson Company

shows cash proceeds of $350,000 from the sale of the building in the investing section of the cash flow statement. The $350,000 is derived as follows:

$$\text{Gain on sale} = \text{Selling price} - \text{net book value}$$
$$\$75,000 = \text{Selling price} - \$275,000$$
$$\$350,000 = \text{Selling price}$$

Under the direct method there is no other impact on the statement of cash flows.

2. Under the indirect method, Olsson Company still shows the total cash proceeds of $350,000 from the sale of the building in the investing section. In addition, Olsson must deduct the gain of $75,000 from net income in the operating section of the statement of cash flows. This is necessary because the gain is included in net income, but it does not represent additional cash received from the sale. All of the cash received is classified as an investing activity.

Summary Problem for Your Review

PROBLEM

Refer to Exhibit 8-2 on page 348. Suppose the estimated residual value had been $5,000 instead of $1,000.

1. Compute depreciation for each of the first 2 years using straight-line and double-declining-balance (DDB) methods.
2. Assume that the company uses DDB depreciation and sells the equipment for $20,000 cash at the end of the second year. Compute the gain or loss on the sale. Show the effects of the sale in the Equipment and Accumulated Depreciation T-accounts. Where and how would the sale appear in the income statement? Where and how would the sale appear in the statement of cash flows?
3. Assume that the company uses straight-line depreciation and sells the equipment for $20,000 cash at the end of the second year. Compute the gain or loss on the sale. Compare this amount to the gain or loss computed in the previous question.

SOLUTION

1.

	Straight-Line Depreciation = (C − R) ÷ n	DDB Depreciation = Rate* × (Beg. Book Value)
Year 1	($41,000 − $5,000) ÷ 4 = $9,000	.50 × $41,000 = $20,500
Year 2	($41,000 − $5,000) ÷ 4 = $9,000	.50 × ($41,000 − $20,500) = $10,250

*Rate = 2 × (100% ÷ n) = 2 × (100% ÷ 4) = 50%.

2.

Selling price	$20,000
Net book value of equipment sold is [$41,000 – ($20,500 + $10,250)] or ($41,000 – $30,750) =	10,250
Gain on sale of equipment	$ 9,750

The effect of removing the book value is a $10,250 decrease in assets. Note that the effect of a decrease in Accumulated Depreciation (by itself) is an increase in assets.

Equipment

Acquisition cost	41,000	Cost of equipment sold	41,000

Accumulated Depreciation

Accumulated depreciation on equipment sold	30,750	Depreciation for Year 1	20,500
		Year 2	10,250
			30,750

The company may show the $9,750 gain as a separate item on the income statement labeled Gain on Sale of Equipment or Gain on Disposal of Equipment. Alternatively, it may combine the gain with similar transactions in the account Other Gains and Losses or Other Income, net. On the statement of cash flows, the company will show the $20,000 cash received as an inflow from investing activities. If it uses the direct method for reporting cash flows from operating activities, there is no further entry. If it uses the indirect method, it must deduct the $9,750 gain from net income in computing cash flows from operating activities.

3.

Selling price	$20,000
Net book value of equipment sold is [$41,000 – ($9,000 + $9,000)] or ($41,000 – $18,000) =	23,000
Loss on sale of equipment	$ 3,000

Even though the sales price is the same as in requirement 2, there is a loss of $3,000 instead of a gain of $9,750 because the book value is $12,750 higher. The amount of the gain or loss on equipment being disposed of depends on the depreciation method used.

Revaluation of Tangible Assets

The market value of tangible assets can either increase or decrease over time. Do the accounting rules allow companies to revalue the assets upward if the value increases or downward if the value decreases? Upward revaluations are infrequent and exist only for companies reporting under IFRS when they elect the revaluation method for long-lived assets. Downward revaluations are mandated under both IFRS and U.S. GAAP and occur when events or circumstances result in the impairment of property, plant, and equipment. An asset is considered to be **impaired** when it ceases to have economic value to the company at least as large as the carrying value (book value) of the asset.

impaired

When an asset ceases to have economic value to the company at least as large as the book value of the asset.

▶▶ **OBJECTIVE 9**

Determine the balance sheet valuation of tangible assets for companies who use the revaluation method allowed under IFRS.

Revaluation Method Under IFRS

Companies reporting under IFRS and electing the revaluation method carry their fixed assets at fair value regardless of whether the adjustment to fair value results in an increase or decrease in carrying value. Fair value, which is the amount for which the asset could be exchanged between knowledgeable, willing parties in an arm's length transaction, is usually determined by hiring an appraiser who uses market-based evidence. Under the revaluation method, companies can revalue plant assets up to fair value, resulting in a revaluation gain, or down to fair value, resulting in a revaluation loss. Companies typically do not include revaluation gains in net income; rather they recognize revaluation gains as part of other comprehensive income and accumulate such gains in stockholders' equity. However, a company would credit the revaluation gain to income if it reverses a revaluation loss that was previously recognized as a reduction of income. Revaluation losses first appear in other comprehensive income, offsetting previous revaluation gains accumulated in stockholders' equity on the same asset. The remainder is a loss on the income statement.

Once a company begins to make revaluation adjustments, it must continue to make them regularly so that the carrying amounts of the assets remain current. Also, if a company revalues any assets, it must revalue all other assets in the same asset category. While IFRS allows the revaluation method, it is more costly to implement due to the need for recurring appraisals and is used infrequently in practice.

Impairment of Assets

Downward revaluations due to impairment occur under both U.S. GAAP and IFRS. Both U.S. GAAP and IFRS require that, at each reporting date, companies assess whether impairment indicators exist for long-lived assets. Companies must review assets for impairment whenever indicators suggest that impairment is possible. Indicators that may lead to a review for impairment include, but are not limited to, a significant decline in the market price of an asset, a significant change in the manner in which an asset is being used, an adverse change in legal or business environment, evidence of obsolescence or physical damage, or a forecast indicating that the company will experience continuing losses associated with the use of the asset.

▶▶ **OBJECTIVE 10**
Account for the impairment of tangible assets.

Suppose that Intel, a company reporting under U.S. GAAP, owns equipment with a net book value of $150,000. Due to a change in technology and product demand, Intel determines that it must review the asset for impairment. U.S. GAAP requires a two-step process. The first step in the impairment review is a **recoverability test** that compares the sum of the expected future net cash flows from the use of the asset plus its expected future disposal value with the current carrying value of the asset. If the sum of the estimated cash flows plus disposal value is greater than the carrying value, the asset is not impaired. If the sum of the estimated cash flows plus disposal value is less than the carrying value, Intel must consider the asset to be impaired. Suppose Intel estimates the total expected future net cash flows to be $127,000. Because this is less than the carrying value of $150,000, there is evidence of impairment. Thus Intel proceeds to the second step, computation of the dollar amount of the impairment loss.

recoverability test
The first step in the asset impairment review process under U.S. GAAP. The test compares the sum of the expected future net cash flows from the use of the asset plus its expected future disposal value with the current carrying value of the asset.

The impairment loss is the amount by which the carrying value of the asset exceeds its fair value. If there is an active market for the asset being evaluated, the fair value is the current market price. In the absence of an active market, Intel must estimate the fair value using appropriate valuation techniques. One such valuation technique estimates the fair value of an asset as the *present value* of the expected future net cash flows generated by the asset. (Present value, the value today of future cash flows, is described in Appendix 9 to Chapter 9.) Notice that Intel used the sum of all expected future net cash flows to determine whether impairment occurred. Under this valuation technique it would use the present value of those expected future net cash flows to calculate the magnitude of the loss. Assume that the market price (fair value) of the equipment in our example is known and is $105,000. Therefore, Intel must record an impairment loss of $45,000:

Net book value of the equipment	$150,000
Minus: Fair value of the equipment	105,000
Impairment loss	$ 45,000

The entry to record the impairment loss is as follows:

Loss on impairment	45,000	
Accumulated depreciation		45,000

Intel reports this loss as part of continuing operations. If the dollar amount is large enough, the loss may appear as a separate line item on the income statement. Otherwise, Intel is likely to combine it with other expenses. In this example, the new carrying value of the asset is $105,000. Even if the fair value of the equipment increases above $105,000 in the future, Intel cannot write the asset back up above $105,000. Under U.S. GAAP, once an impairment loss is recorded, it cannot be restored.

The Management Discussion and Analysis (MD&A) in Intel's 2011 annual report explains its impairment review process: "We assess property, plant and equipment for impairment when events or changes in circumstances indicate that the carrying value of the assets or the asset grouping may not be recoverable.... We measure the recoverability of assets that will continue to be used in our operations by comparing the carrying value of the asset grouping to our estimate of the related total future undiscounted net cash flows. If an asset grouping's carrying value is not recoverable through the related undiscounted cash flows, the asset grouping is considered to be impaired. The impairment is measured by comparing the difference between the asset group-ing's carrying value and its fair value." The MD&A goes on to indicate that impairments (and additional depreciation on assets whose useful lives were shortened) ranged from $10 million to $75 million per quarter during the 2009 through 2011 time period.

How would Intel's impairment accounting change if it reported under IFRS? The company would use a single-step process that compares the carrying value (that is, net book value) of the asset with its **recoverable amount**, defined as the higher of (1) fair value minus the cost to sell, and (2) the value in use, calculated as the present value of expected future net cash flows. If the carrying value is greater than the recoverable amount, Intel would recognize an impairment loss for the difference. Suppose that the value in use is $100,000 and that Intel would incur a cost of $7,500 to sell the asset. Its recoverable amount would be $100,000, the higher of the following:

1. Fair value less cost to sell: ($105,000 – $7,500) = $97,500
2. Value in use: $100,000

Therefore, the impairment loss would be ($150,000 – $100,000) = $50,000. Unless Intel used the revaluation method and had recognized previous revaluation gains on this asset, it would recognize the $50,000 as a loss on its income statement.

Under U.S. GAAP, the impairment test for long-lived assets that a company is *holding for resale* differs slightly from that described earlier for assets in use. The impairment loss, if any, is the excess of the carrying value of the asset over the fair value less the cost to sell, or $97,500 given the preceding information. If Intel were intending to sell the previously described asset, under U.S. GAAP the impairment loss would be ($150,000 – $97,500) = $52,500. Further, if the asset's fair value less cost to sell subsequently increased from $97,500 to $110,000, Intel would write the asset back up to $110,000. Following an impairment loss, companies can write up assets held for resale as long as the write-up never results in a value in excess of the net book value of the asset at the time of the original impairment.

Intangible Assets

We now turn our attention to another group of long-lived assets—intangibles. These assets are not physical items, but instead are rights or claims to expected benefits that are often contractual in nature.

Under U.S. GAAP, the accounting for intangible assets depends on two factors: (1) whether a company acquires the intangible from an external party or develops it internally, and (2) whether the intangible asset has a finite or indefinite life. Consider the first of these factors. A company's balance sheet lists an intangible asset only if the company purchased the rights to the asset from an external party. It does not list equally valuable assets created by internal expenditures. For example, footnote 14 of Intel's 2011 annual report indicates that in 2011, as part of acquisitions, Intel paid $4,961 million to other companies for identifiable intangible assets and intellectual property developed by those companies. Intel recorded the $4,961 mil-lion as intangible assets in 2011. In contrast, suppose Intel spent $4,961 million to internally develop similar intangible assets. Intel would charge this $4,961 million to expense, and it would not recognize assets.

Why is there a discrepancy between the accounting treatment for externally acquired and internally developed items? One of the criteria for recognition of an asset is that the future benefits provided by that asset can be quantified with a reasonable degree of precision. The FASB believes that it is difficult for management to value the results of its internal research and development efforts honestly and objectively. As a result, U.S. GAAP requires companies

recoverable amount

Under IFRS, the higher of (1) fair value minus the cost to sell, and (2) the value in use, calculated as the present value of expected future net cash flows.

▸▸ **OBJECTIVE 11**

Account for intangible assets, including impairment.

BUSINESS FIRST

RESTATING FINANCIAL STATEMENTS TO SHOW RESEARCH AND DEVELOPMENT

Under U.S. GAAP, most companies must immediately expense internal R&D expenditures. Why? The FASB decided that it is hard to determine whether R&D will be valuable, and, if it is valuable, it is hard to estimate the value and predict the period of time over which a company will realize this value. However, some analysts believe it is important to treat R&D as an asset in order to fully understand the total commitment of resources a company has made. They assume a useful life and develop a hypothetical value for internal R&D expenditures.

To illustrate, consider the following data for Eli Lilly. R&D spending in the 5-year period 2006–2010 rose 56.1% from $3,129.3 million in 2006 to $4,884.2 million in 2010 and totaled $19,667.6 million. Suppose Lilly capitalized these amounts each year as they were incurred and then amortized them over the subsequent 4 years on a straight-line basis (25% per year). Under this procedure, the $3,129.3 million spent in 2006 would appear as an asset of $3,129.3 million at year-end 2006 and would give rise to amortization of $782.3 million in each of the next 4 years. By the end of 2010, it would be fully amortized and would not appear as an asset.

Consider Lilly's financial statements for 2010. If Lilly was allowed to capitalize R&D, we can calculate the 2010 R&D expense of $3,695.8 million and the R&D asset of $10,921.3 million as shown in the table below.

Assuming capitalization of R&D, how would the financial statements differ from what Eli Lilly reported under U.S. GAAP? Net earnings for 2010 would be higher

because R&D expense on the income statement would be $3,695.8 million, instead of the $4,884.2 million actually recorded in 2010. This lowers the R&D expense by $1,188.4 million. On the balance sheet, assets would be higher by $10,921.3 million or about 35% greater than the actual reported total assets of $31,001.4 million. Of course, if assets are higher, there needs to be an offsetting effect on the other side of the balance sheet equation, and retained earnings and some liabilities for taxes would also be higher.

Lilly and other pharmaceutical companies are extreme cases because R&D expenses are typically more than 15% of sales (about 21.2% for Lilly in 2010). Some young, biotech start-ups have even more substantial R&D spending on a proportional basis. Indeed, some of these start-ups have no sales, and if they expense R&D immediately for accounting purposes, they sometimes have essentially no assets. Yet these companies may have very high market values because the ideas they have generated have great potential. Research-intensive firms and young start-up firms are two examples where adjustments to the data from the historical-cost accounting model are often useful for analyzing the firm. The 4-year amortization period in this example is arbitrary and was chosen in part to simplify the example. In various industries, different assumptions might be appropriate depending on the rate of technological change.

(all dollar amounts in millions)

Year of R&D Expenditure	R&D Expenditure	2010 Income Statement R&D Expense*	% of Annual R&D Spending Unamortized at End of 2010	Balance Sheet Asset—12/31/10
2006	$3,129.3	$ 782.3	0	$ 0.00
2007	3,486.7	871.7	25	871.7
2008	3,840.9	960.2	50	1,920.5
2009	4,326.5	1,081.6	75	3,244.9
2010	4,884.2	—	100	4,884.2
Total 2010 Value		$3,695.8		$10,921.3

Source: http://investor.lilly.com/secfiling.cfm?filingID=1193125-11-41620.
*Each expense amount is 25% of the original R&D expenditure in column 2.

to immediately expense the costs of internal research and development, despite the fact that the company surely expects future benefits. However, when one company purchases the results of another company's efforts, the negotiated purchase price represents a verifiable historical cost from the perspective of the purchaser. These negotiated acquisition costs are capitalized.

This discrepancy has generated significant debate. In recent years we have seen an increase in the number of firms in the economy that are "knowledge-based" businesses. The value of these firms lies in intangibles such as internal research and development activities and intellectual capital. However, under existing U.S. GAAP, if a company does not acquire these resources externally, it cannot record them as assets. Some analysts believe that R&D and perhaps other expenditures for intellectual capital should be capitalized, and they adjust the financial statements accordingly, as shown in the Business First box on page 361.

U.S. GAAP allows an exception to the automatic expensing of internal research and development costs for computer software companies. These companies can capitalize some of the costs of developing and producing software. Companies in this industry expense R&D costs up to the time when the company considers the software product to be technologically feasible. After that point, and until the product goes into production, they capitalize R&D costs. They then amortize these capitalized amounts over the estimated product life. This exception can have a significant impact on the financial statements of companies in the software development industry. Consider **BMC Software**, one of the world's largest software companies. For the year ended March 31, 2011, BMC recognized $176.5 million in R&D expense on the income statement. Review of BMC's balance sheet shows a noncurrent asset, Software Development Costs, net, with a balance of $193.8 million. Note 1 reveals that the company capitalized $124.0 million in R&D costs and recorded amortization of $75.7 million during the year.

IFRS takes a different approach to accounting for R&D, separating research costs from development costs. The IFRS standards define research costs as costs incurred for current or planned investigations undertaken with the prospect of gaining new scientific or technical knowledge and understanding. Companies cannot capitalize research costs. The standards define development costs as costs incurred for the application of research findings or specialist knowledge to production, production methods, services, or goods prior to the commencement of commercial product or use. Companies must capitalize development costs when it is sufficiently certain that the future economic benefits to the company will cover the related development costs. **Bayer AG**, a large German pharmaceutical company that prepares its financial statements under IFRS, has over 300 operating companies worldwide and engages in significant research and development activity. Bayer's income statement for the 2011 fiscal year includes €2,932 million in research and development expenses. Does Bayer capitalize any development expenditures? No. It discusses its development expenditures in the footnotes in its 2011 annual report: "Since our own development projects are often subject to regulatory approval procedures and other uncertainties, the conditions for the capitalization of costs incurred before receipt of approvals are not normally satisfied."

Once a company has capitalized a purchased intangible asset, the remaining question is how to account for that asset going forward. Under U.S. GAAP the accounting treatment depends on whether the asset has a finite life or an indefinite life. Companies do not routinely amortize intangible assets deemed to have indefinite lives. Instead, they evaluate these assets periodically for impairment. In contrast, companies amortize finite-lived intangible assets over their estimated useful lives. The useful life of an intangible asset is the shorter of its economic useful life or its legal life, if any. Because of obsolescence, the economic lives of intangible assets are often shorter than their legal lives. To gain a better understanding of this process, we now examine some specific intangible assets that have finite lives and hence are subject to amortization.

Examples of Intangible Assets

patents

Grants made by the federal government to an inventor, bestowing (in the United States) the exclusive right to produce and sell a given product, or to use a process, for up to 20 years.

Patents are grants made by the federal government to the inventor of a product or process, bestowing (in the United States) the exclusive right to produce and sell a given product, or use a process, for up to 20 years. After that time, others can manufacture the product or use the process. Suppose a company acquires a newly patented product from an inventor for $170,000. Although the remaining legal life of this patent is 20 years, because of fast-changing technology, the economic life of the patent is only 5 years. The company would amortize the asset over 5 years, the shorter of the economic or legal life, making the annual amortization expense ($170,000 ÷ 5) = $34,000.

copyrights

Exclusive rights to reproduce and sell a book, musical composition, film, or similar creative item.

Copyrights are exclusive rights to reproduce and sell a book, musical composition, film, or similar creative item. In the United States, the federal government issues these rights and provides protection to a company or individual for the life of the creator plus 70 years. The

INTERPRETING FINANCIAL STATEMENTS

Suppose a major pharmaceutical company acquires a biotechnology company that is heavily involved in research and development activities. The research and development of the biotech firm has resulted in only one patented process. However, it has an extensive research pipeline. It is this pipeline that is of most interest to the pharmaceutical company. The total purchase price is $100 million. An independent valuation of the fair value of the one patent acquired in the transaction set the value at $15 million. The remainder of the purchase price is attributable to the pipeline, which is commonly called "Purchased In-Process Research and Development (IPRD)." How should the pharmaceutical company account for this acquisition?

Answer

The company would record the patent as an intangible asset valued at $15 million. It is evident that the pharmaceutical company believes the research pipeline has future benefit or it would not have been willing to pay $100 million for the biotech company. The accounting treatment of in-process R&D acquired in an acquisition has been a matter of considerable disagreement in recent years. Some argue that these costs, or a portion of these costs, should be treated as an asset. After all, one of the criteria for recognition of an asset is the provision of future benefits. Others argue that the benefits to be derived from the purchased IPRD are too uncertain to meet asset-recognition criteria. Before 2009, U.S. GAAP required companies to expense IPRD in the period of acquisition. However, under current U.S. GAAP, the pharmaceutical company would capitalize the $85 million of purchased in-process R&D. The IPRD asset would be considered an indefinite-life intangible asset subject to impairment but not amortization.

initial costs of obtaining copyrights from the government are nominal; however, a company may pay a large sum to purchase an existing copyright from the owner. For example, a publisher of paperback books will sometimes pay the author of a popular novel in excess of $1 million for the writer's copyright. Although copyrights have a long legal life, their economic lives are frequently significantly shorter.

Trademarks are distinctive identifications of a manufactured product or of a service, taking the form of a name, a sign, a slogan, a logo, or an emblem. Well-known examples include the distinctive cursive script logo for Coca-Cola, the McDonald's Golden Arches and the Nike Swoosh logo. Trademarks, trade names, trade brands, secret formulas, and similar items are property rights with economic lives that depend on their estimated length of use. If you look at Coca-Cola's balance sheet, you see no accounting recognition of its secret formula. The company did not purchase the formula, rather it was developed internally. As a result, Coca-Cola did not record an asset. In fact, the story is that Coca-Cola chose to keep the formula a secret instead of patenting it because it did not want the patent protection to expire, leaving others free to produce the product. The Coca-Cola balance sheet also does not report an intangible asset for the Coca-Cola trademark, although Coke has spent millions of advertising dollars creating public awareness of the brand and millions more dollars protecting it from infringement. Coca-Cola's balance sheet does show an account entitled Trademarks. What does this account represent? Coca-Cola acquired the trademarks of such companies as *Fanta* and *Minute-Maid*, so it lists them as intangible assets. Similarly, PepsiCo includes a trademark value for *Gatorade* among its intangible assets because it purchased the trademark rights when it bought Quaker Oats Company.

Franchises and **licenses** are legal contracts that grant the buyer the right to sell a product or service in accordance with specified conditions. An example is a local Starbucks franchise. The buyer obtains the right to use the Starbucks name, to acquire branded products such as cups, and to share in advertising and special promotions. In exchange, the franchisee promises to follow Starbucks procedures and maintain standards of quality, cleanliness, and pricing. Other private sector companies may award franchises for car dealerships, fast-food restaurants, hotel operations, or gasoline stations. These types of franchise agreements typically have a finite life. While the terms of franchise agreements can differ significantly, most often franchisees capitalize the up-front franchise fee and amortize that fee over the life of the franchise agreement.

Government agencies may grant franchises or operating licenses to a company, awarding it the right to use publicly held property in the operation of its business. Examples include the use of public property for the placement of telephone or electric utility lines, or the use of the airwaves for broadcasting purposes. The lengths of the franchises vary from 1 year to perpetuity. As mentioned previously, one of the factors that determines the accounting for externally acquired intangible assets is whether the asset has a finite or an indefinite life.

trademarks
Distinctive identifications of a manufactured product or of a service, taking the form of a name, a sign, a slogan, a logo, or an emblem.

franchises (licenses)
Legal contracts that allow the buyer the right to sell a product or service in accordance with specified conditions.

A **leasehold** is the right to use a fixed asset (such as a building or some portion thereof) for a specified period of time beyond 1 year. Companies often classify leaseholds with plant assets on the balance sheet, although they are technically intangible assets. A company that owns its own plant clearly counts that plant as a tangible asset. However, if a company leases the plant, then it owns only the right to use the leased plant, not the plant itself. Because the leasehold provides future benefits (in this case, the use of the plant) but does not give the company ownership of the plant, it is an intangible asset. We discuss leases of this type in Chapter 9.

Related to a leasehold is a **leasehold improvement**, which occurs when a tenant spends money to add new materials or improvements to a leased property. These improvements become part of the leased property and revert to the landlord at the end of the lease. A leasehold improvement can take various forms. Examples are the installation of new fixtures, panels, walls, and air-conditioning equipment that the lessee must leave on the premises when a lease expires. Companies generally amortize the costs of leasehold improvements over the life of the lease, even if the physical life of the leasehold improvement is longer. For example, Costco amortizes its leasehold improvements over "the shorter of the useful life or lease term."

Impairment of Intangible Assets

The U.S. GAAP and IFRS rules governing impairment of finite-life intangible assets are the same as those for long-lived tangible assets discussed on pages 359–360. However, the rules for impairment of indefinite-life intangibles differ slightly from those for tangible assets. U.S. GAAP does not require a recoverability test for indefinite-life intangibles. Rather, a company compares the carrying value of the intangible asset with its fair value. If the carrying value is less than the fair value, no impairment has occurred. If the carrying value is greater than the fair value, the company must recognize an impairment loss equal to the carrying amount less the fair value.

The comparison of carrying value to fair value may not need to be performed every year. GAAP guidance issued in July 2012 allows a company to perform an optional qualitative assessment to determine whether the company believes it is "more likely than not" that an indefinite-lived intangible is impaired. If this assessment suggests that the likelihood of impairment is less than 50%, the company is not required to perform any additional testing. In other words, the company is not required to perform the comparison of the carrying value of the asset to its fair value. If the assessment suggests that the likelihood of impairment is greater than 50%, additional testing is required. This optional qualitative assessment is consistent with a previously adopted proposal related to the testing for goodwill impairment. The IFRS requirements for indefinite-life intangibles are more complex and beyond the scope of this text.

Goodwill

All of the intangible assets discussed so far are separately identifiable. In other words, they are assets that one company could sell to another. Goodwill is an intangible asset that cannot be separated from the company that owns it and therefore it cannot be sold or transferred. A company can recognize **goodwill** only when it buys another company. Goodwill is the excess of the amount paid for the acquired company over the fair value of its identifiable net assets. We discuss goodwill in more detail in Chapter 11.

Assume that Millard Corporation purchases Tigner Company for a total of $10 million in cash. At the time of the acquisition, Tigner has total assets with a fair value of $19 million and total liabilities with a fair value of $13 million. Therefore, the fair value of the assets less the liabilities of Tigner is $6 million. Nevertheless, Millard has agreed to pay $10 million for Tigner. Chapter 11 discusses the reasons why one company might pay a premium for another company and how the purchase price would be allocated to various assets and liabilities. In our example, Millard accounts for the business combination with a summary journal entry that looks like this (in millions of dollars):

Goodwill	4	
Total assets of Tigner	19	
Total liabilities of Tigner.		13
Cash		10

Millard records goodwill as a noncurrent asset on its books.

BUSINESS FIRST

IMPACT OF GOODWILL IMPAIRMENTS

The recession and credit crisis that began in 2008 resulted in extremely high levels of goodwill impairment on the books of companies worldwide. A study performed by KPMG LLP indicates that goodwill impairments peaked at $340 billion in 2008 and declined to $92 billion in 2009 and $39 billion in 2010. In addition, only 7% of companies studied recorded a goodwill impairment loss in 2010 compared with approximately 12% in 2009 and 17% in 2008.

While goodwill impairment losses overall were on the decline, some industries continued to be hard-hit. The KMPG study shows that the hardest hit industry in terms of actual dollar impairment losses in 2010 was the diversified financial services industry, which accounted for almost 36% of the total impairment losses. Bank of America (B of A) is one of the largest firms in this industry. Through its numerous subsidiaries in the United States and in international markets, the bank offers a full range of banking and nonbanking financial services in all 50 states and the District of Columbia, as well as in 40 foreign countries. B of A's retail banking footprint covers approximately 80% of the U.S. population, and in the United States alone it serves approximately 57 million consumer and small business customers. B of A has achieved this prominent position partly through a long history of mergers and acquisitions, frequently involving the acquisition of battered companies. A table showing recent material acquisitions appears below.

Acquired Company	Year Purchase Closed	Purchase Price
FleetBoston Financial	2004	$47 billion
MBNA	2006	$35 billion
The United States Trust Company	2007	$3.3 billion
LaSalle Bank Corporation	2007	$21 billion
Countrywide Financial	2008	$4.4 billion
Merrill Lynch	2009	$50 billion

These acquisitions increased B of A's market position in a number of different areas of financial services. MBNA was heavily into credit card services. US Trust was primarily a wealth management firm. The acquisition of Countrywide Financial gave B of A a substantial market share of the mortgage business. And the acquisition of Merrill Lynch, which was poised on the edge of bankruptcy, gave B of A increased presence in the investment banking arena. These acquisitions resulted in the presence of goodwill on Bank of America's balance sheet. At the beginning of 2010, the company's balance sheet listed goodwill of $86,314 million, or about 4% of total assets.

As required under U.S. GAAP, B of A performs goodwill impairment reviews whenever circumstances indicate that impairment may have occurred. Such circumstances occurred in both the third and fourth quarters of 2010. During the third quarter of 2010, the Dodd-Frank Wall Street Reform and Consumer Protection Act was signed into law. Among other things, the law placed a limit on fees charged to merchants when customers use debit cards, an action that B of A expected would reduce the future revenues generated by its debit card business. As a result of its review and testing procedures, the company recorded a $10.4 billion write-off of goodwill during the quarter ended September 30, 2010. During the fourth quarter of 2010, the company performed an additional review related to the goodwill associated with the acquisition of Countrywide. The review indicated that it was likely that there had been a decline in the fair value of goodwill as a result of "increased uncertainties, including existing and potential litigation exposure and other related risks, higher servicing costs including loss mitigation efforts, foreclosure related issues and the redeployment of centralized sales resources to address servicing needs." As a result of its testing procedures and analysis, B of A recorded a $2.0 billion goodwill impairment during the fourth quarter. These two impairment charges reduced goodwill by 14.4%. As of December 31, 2010, goodwill comprised 3.3% of total assets, down slightly from a year earlier.

While the balance sheet impact was not large, the effect of the combined $12.4 billion in goodwill impairment charges on B of A's 2010 income was substantial. For the full year ending December 31, 2010, B of A reported a net loss of $2,238 million and a net loss per common share of $.37. Excluding the goodwill impairment charges, the company would have reported net income of $10,162 million and EPS of $.86.

Sources: "Evaluating Impairment Risk: Goodwill Impairment Continues Its Downward Trend in 2010," http://www.kpmginstitutes.com/taxwatch/insights/2011/evaluating-impairment-risk-in-2010.aspx; "KPMG Study Reveals Dramatic Decrease in Goodwill Impairment for U.S.–Based Companies," http://www.pro2net.com/x69718.xml; Bank of America 2010 10-K.

Companies do not amortize goodwill. However, they must review goodwill for impairment whenever events or circumstances suggest the possibility of impairment. As an example, the credit crisis of 2008–2009 certainly qualifies as an event suggesting the need for impairment review by many companies. The details of the goodwill impairment test are beyond the scope of this text book. However, if a company determines that the goodwill is not worth its carrying value, the company must write down the goodwill to its current fair value, which in some cases might be zero. The Business First box on page 365 gives an example of goodwill impairments.

Depletion of Natural Resources

▶▶ **OBJECTIVE 13**

Interpret the depletion of natural resources.

Our final group of long-lived assets is natural resources (sometimes called wasting assets), such as minerals, oil, and timber. Depletion is the accounting mechanism used to allocate the acquisition cost of natural resources over time. Depletion differs from depreciation because depletion focuses specifically on the physical use and exhaustion of the natural resources, whereas depreciation focuses more broadly on any reduction of the economic value of a fixed asset, including physical deterioration and obsolescence.

Accountants usually classify the costs of natural resources as noncurrent assets. However, buying natural resources is actually like buying massive quantities of inventories under the ground (iron ore) or above the ground (timber). Depletion expense is the measure of the portion of this "long-term inventory" that a company uses up in a particular period. For example, a coal mine may have a total cost of $20 million and originally contain an estimated 1 million tons of usable coal. The depletion rate would be ($20 million ÷ 1 million tons) = $20 per ton. If the company mined 100,000 tons during the first year, the depletion expense would be (100,000 tons × $20), or $2 million for that year. Each year the company would measure the amount of coal extracted and record the amount of depletion based on that usage.

As our coal mine example shows, companies measure depletion on a units-of-production basis. They may directly reduce the asset account, or they may accumulate depletion in a separate contra account similar to accumulated depreciation. Environmental laws and ethical responsibility often lead a firm to expend substantial amounts to return the site to a safe and attractive condition after exhausting the natural resources. When calculating the depletion per unit, companies add these expected future costs when computing the total costs subject to depletion. Therefore, the depletion per unit includes not only the original cost of the resources but also future restoration costs. The companies add the portion of depletion that represents future costs for site restoration to an Asset Retirement Liability account that grows as extraction continues.

Highlights to Remember

1 Distinguish a company's expenses from expenditures that it should capitalize. Accountants must choose between capitalizing or expensing each expenditure. They should capitalize expenditures that meet the criteria for asset recognition and should expense the others. Capitalized items that provide benefits for multiple periods are considered long-lived assets.

2 Measure the acquisition cost of tangible assets such as land, buildings, and equipment. The acquisition cost includes an asset's purchase price and all incidental costs necessary to get it ready for its intended use.

3 Compute depreciation for buildings and equipment using various depreciation methods. Depreciation is a systematic allocation of historical cost over the useful life of the asset. Three common depreciation methods discussed in the text are straight-line, double-declining-balance (DDB), and units-of-production depreciation. The straight-line method results in a constant amount of depreciation expense per year of use. We calculate it by dividing depreciable value (original historical cost less estimated residual value) by the shorter of the physical life or the economic life. DDB is a declining-balance method that records the largest annual depreciation expense in the first full year of use and declining amounts thereafter. The annual depreciation charge is a percentage of the book value at the beginning of the year. For DDB the percentage is twice the percentage used for straight-line, that is, $2 \times (100\% \div \text{years of life})$. Units-of-production depreciation is based on the physical use of the asset, for example miles driven for a vehicle. The cost per unit is the depreciable value divided by the estimated units of use from the asset. We multiply this cost per unit by the actual units of use to determine the annual depreciation.

4 **Recalculate depreciation in response to a change in estimated useful life or residual value.** New information may cause the initial estimate of useful life or residual value to be revised. If the use of the new estimate would result in a significant change in depreciation expense, the new estimate must be adopted and the depreciation schedule revised. A change in estimate is treated as a prospective adjustment. The company does not go back and revise the depreciation expense taken in prior periods. Rather, the company recomputes depreciation expense for the period in which it revises the estimate and all future periods.

5 **Differentiate financial statement depreciation from income tax depreciation.** Financial reports to shareholders and filings with the SEC often differ from the reports filed with the tax authorities. Rules governing financial statement presentation produce information useful to investors and managers. Tax rules governing determination of tax obligations achieve political and economic goals and give taxpayers the right to make certain choices with an eye for maximizing expenses and therefore minimizing the tax obligation. Therefore, companies keep two sets of records to satisfy these two purposes.

6 **Explain the effect of depreciation on cash flow.** By itself, depreciation does not provide cash. However, companies deduct depreciation for income tax purposes. Therefore, the larger the depreciation reported on the tax return in any given year, the lower the annual pretax income and the lower the amount of taxes a company pays the taxing authorities. By paying less in taxes a company retains a greater amount of cash.

7 **Account for expenditures after acquisition.** Companies should immediately expense any expenditures that represent routine repairs or maintenance of fixed assets. In contrast, they should capitalize improvements that increase the future benefits provided by a fixed asset.

8 **Compute gains and losses on the disposal of fixed assets and consider the impact of these gains and losses on the statement of cash flows.** Gains and losses on the disposal of fixed assets arise because the proceeds of the sale are not identical to the book value (original historical cost less accumulated depreciation) of the asset sold. If the proceeds exceed the book value, the company realizes a gain on its income statement. If the proceeds are less, it records a loss. On the statement of cash flows, the cash proceeds from the sale of fixed assets constitute cash provided by investing activities. The sale of fixed assets has no effect on the calculation of cash flows from operations under the direct method. However, when calculating cash flow from operations using the indirect method, the starting point is net income, which includes any gains or losses from fixed asset sales. To adjust net income in calculating net cash provided by operating activities, we subtract gains from, or add losses to, net income.

9 **Determine the balance sheet valuation of tangible assets for companies who use the revaluation method allowed under IFRS.** IFRS permits the revaluation of fixed assets to fair value. Under IFRS, companies can revalue fixed assets to fair value regardless of whether fair value is higher or lower than the carrying value of the assets.

10 **Account for the impairment of tangible assets.** Events or circumstances may arise that cause an asset to have an economic value to the company that is smaller than the carrying value of that asset. The FASB has implemented a two-step process to test for the impairment of tangible assets. The first step is a recoverability test, which compares the total expected future net cash flows from the asset and its eventual disposition with the carrying value of the asset. If the carrying value is greater than the future cash flows, the asset is considered to be impaired. If the assets are held for use, the impairment loss is the amount by which the carrying value of the asset exceeds its fair value. If the assets are held for resale purposes, the impairment loss is the amount by which the carrying value of the asset exceeds its fair value less the cost to sell. IFRS employs an impairment test that requires an asset to be recognized at the lower of its net book value or its recoverable amount.

11 **Account for intangible assets, including impairment.** Intangible assets are not physical in nature. Instead, they are legal or contractual rights. Examples include patents, trademarks, and copyrights. Companies capitalize such assets when purchased from external parties. Some purchased intangibles have finite lives. Companies amortize these intangibles over their useful lives. The remaining net book value appears on the balance sheet as an asset.

Other purchased intangible assets have indefinite lives. Companies do not amortize indefinite-life intangibles. However, all recorded intangibles are subject to impairment and companies must write them down if their fair value is less than their book value. Companies do not capitalize internally created intangible assets. Instead, they expense such outlays as incurred.

12 **Explain the reporting for goodwill.** Goodwill is an intangible asset measured as the excess of the purchase price of an acquired company over the fair value of its identifiable assets less its identifiable liabilities. Companies do not amortize goodwill but must write it down when they deem its value to be impaired.

13 **Interpret the depletion of natural resources.** Depletion refers to the accounting process for allocating the cost of natural resources over the periods of extraction. Companies typically use the units-of-production method to allocate the cost of acquiring natural resources. In some cases, companies expect to incur future costs to mitigate environmental damage and return the site to an acceptable condition. Accountants estimate these future costs and include them in the annual depletion charges to appropriately match the full cost to the revenues generated over time.

Accounting Vocabulary

accelerated depreciation, p. 347
activity method, p. 347
allocation base, p. 345
amortization, p. 342
basket purchase, p. 344
betterment, p. 353
capital improvement, p. 353
capitalize, p. 342
component depreciation, p. 349
copyrights, p. 362
depletion, p. 342
depreciable base, p. 345
depreciable value, p. 345
depreciation schedule, p. 346
disposal value, p. 345
double-declining-balance (DDB) method, p. 347

expenditures, p. 342
fair value, p. 344
fixed assets, p. 340
franchises, p. 363
goodwill, p. 364
impaired, p. 358
improvement, p. 353
intangible assets, p. 340
leasehold, p. 364
leasehold improvement, p. 364
licenses, p. 363
lump-sum purchase, p. 344
maintenance, p. 353
Modified Accelerated Cost Recovery System (MACRS), p. 350
monetary assets, p. 344
nonmonetary assets, p. 344

patents, p. 362
plant assets, p. 340
recoverability test, p. 359
recoverable amount, p. 360
repairs, p. 353
residual value, p. 345
salvage value, p. 345
scrap value, p. 345
service life, p. 345
straight-line depreciation, p. 346
tangible assets, p. 340
terminal value, p. 345
trademarks, p. 363
units-of-production depreciation, p. 347
useful life, p. 345

Assignment Material

Questions

8-1 Distinguish between *tangible* and *intangible assets*.

8-2 Distinguish among *amortization*, *depreciation*, and *depletion*.

8-3 "The cash discount on the purchase of equipment is income to the buyer during the year of acquisition." Do you agree? Explain.

8-4 Many companies expense all expenditures that are less than a predetermined dollar amount. What is the justification for this policy?

8-5 "When an expenditure is capitalized, we credit the stockholders' equity account." Do you agree? Explain.

8-6 "Accumulated depreciation is a sum of cash being accumulated for the replacement of fixed assets." Do you agree? Explain.

8-7 "The accounting process of depreciation is allocation, not valuation." Explain.

8-8 Criticize the following statement: "Depreciation is the loss in value of a fixed asset over a given span of time."

8-9 "Keeping two sets of books is immoral and unnecessary." Do you agree? Explain.

8-10 "Accelerated depreciation saves cash but shows lower net income." Explain.

8-11 "A change in the estimated useful life of a fixed asset requires restatement of depreciation expense in prior periods." Do you agree? Explain.

8-12 Contrast repairs and maintenance expenditures with expenditures for capital improvements or betterments.

8-13 The manager of a division reported to the president of the company, "Now that our major capital improvements are finished, the division's expenses will be much lower." Is this really what this manager means to say? Explain.

8-14 What determines the gain or loss on the sale of fixed assets?

8-15 Name and describe four kinds of intangible assets.

8-16 "We account for internally acquired patents differently than we account for externally acquired patents." Explain the difference.

8-17 "Accountants cannot capitalize improvements made to leased property by a tenant because the improvements become part of the leased property and therefore belong to the lessor." Do you agree? Explain.

8-18 XYZ Company's only transaction in 20X1 was the sale of a fixed asset for $20,000 cash. The only line item on the income statement was "Gain on sale of fixed assets,

$5,000." Correct the following statement of cash flows, assuming the company uses the indirect method for reporting cash flows from operating activities. How would your answer change if the company uses the direct method?

Cash flows from operating activities	
Gain on sale of fixed assets	$ 5,000
Cash flows from investing activities	
Proceeds from sale of fixed assets	20,000
Total increase in cash	$25,000

8-19 The Lawrence Company sold fixed assets with a book value of $8,000 and recorded a gain of $6,000. How should the company report this on the statement of cash flows prepared using the indirect method?

8-20 "In a basket purchase, all assets that are part of the purchase must be depreciated over the same useful lives." Do you agree? Explain.

8-21 "The recoverability test determines the magnitude of the impairment loss on a piece of equipment used in the manufacturing process." Do you agree? Explain.

8-22 Under IFRS, how would a company record the revaluation of fixed assets to reflect an increase in fair value?

8-23 How do U.S. GAAP and IFRS differ with regard to accounting for the impairment of fixed assets held for use?

Critical Thinking Questions

8-24 Production Facilities and Depreciation

A manager in a company reporting under U.S. GAAP complained about the amount of depreciation charged on the plant for which she was responsible: "The market value of my plant just continues to increase, yet I am hit with large depreciation charges on my income statement and the value of my plant and equipment on the balance sheet goes down each year. This doesn't seem fair." Comment on this statement, focusing on the relation of asset values on the balance sheet to market values of the assets.

▶▶ **OBJECTIVES 2, 3**

8-25 Research and Development and the Recognition of Intangible Assets

In the United States, most R&D expenditures are charged directly to expense. Under IFRS, companies recognize development costs as assets when it is likely that the resultant future economic benefits will cover the development costs. Suppose you are manager of an R&D department. Which method of accounting for R&D would be most consistent with the information you use for decision making? Explain.

▶▶ **OBJECTIVE 11**

8-26 Capital Investment and the Statement of Cash Flows

Growing companies often need capital to purchase or build additional facilities. There are many potential sources of such capital. Describe how an investor might use the statement of cash flows to learn how a company financed its capital expansion.

▶▶ **OBJECTIVE 2**

▸▸ **OBJECTIVES 2, 9**

8-27 Accounting Valuation of Fixed Assets

Consider two types of assets held by IBM: land purchased in 1912 when the company was known as the Computing-Tabulating-Recording Company, and machinery purchased and installed at its manufacturing plant in 2012. How close do you suppose the December 31, 2013, balance sheet value of each asset is to the fair value of the asset at that date, assuming the company uses U.S. GAAP? What if IBM uses IFRS?

Exercises

▸▸ **OBJECTIVES 1, 2**

8-28 Computing Acquisition Costs

Suppose Emory University acquired a 20-acre parcel of land immediately adjacent to its existing facilities on January 2, 2012. The land included a warehouse, parking lots, and driveways. The university paid $800,000 cash and also gave a note for $3 million, payable at $300,000 per year plus interest of 5% on the outstanding balance.

The university demolished the warehouse at a cash cost of $150,000 so it could be replaced with a new classroom building. For construction of the building, the university made a cash down payment of $3 million and gave a mortgage note of $7 million. The mortgage was payable at $250,000 per year plus interest of 5% on the outstanding balance.

1. Calculate the cost that Emory University should add to its Land account and its Building account.
2. Prepare journal entries (without explanations) to record the preceding transactions.

▸▸ **OBJECTIVES 1, 2, 7**

8-29 Government Equipment: Computing Acquisition Costs

An office of the IRS acquired some used computer equipment. Installation costs were $10,000. Repair costs prior to use were $15,000. The purchasing manager, with a salary of $56,000 per annum, spent 1 month evaluating equipment and completing the transaction. The invoice price was $450,000. The seller paid its salesman a commission of 5% and offered the buyer a cash discount of 2% if the invoice was paid within 60 days. Freight costs were $7,400, paid by the purchaser. Repairs during the first year of use were $18,000.

Compute the total capitalized cost to be added to the Equipment account. The seller was paid within 60 days.

▸▸ **OBJECTIVE 2**

8-30 Basket Purchase

On February 21, 20X2, Speed-Tune, an auto service chain, acquired an existing building and land for $920,000 from a local gas station that had failed. The tax assessor had placed an assessed valuation of $300,000 on the land and $500,000 on the building as of January 1, 20X2.

Land	$300,000
Building	500,000
Total	$800,000

How much of the $920,000 purchase price should be attributed to the building? Why?

▸▸ **OBJECTIVES 3, 8**

8-31 Journal Entries for Depreciation

(Alternates are 8-32 and 8-33.) On January 1, 20X1, the Dallas Auto Parts Company acquired nine identical assembly robots for a total of $594,000 cash. The robots had an expected useful life of 10 years and an expected residual value of $54,000 in total. Dallas uses straight-line depreciation.

1. Set up T-accounts and prepare the journal entries for the acquisition and for the first annual depreciation charge. Post to T-accounts.
2. On December 31, 20X3, Dallas sold one of the robots for $40,000 in cash. The robot had an original cost of $66,000 and an expected residual value of $6,000. Prepare the journal entry for the sale.
3. Refer to requirement 2. Suppose Dallas had sold the robot for $62,000 cash instead of $40,000. Prepare the journal entry for the sale.

▸▸ **OBJECTIVES 3, 8**

8-32 Journal Entries for Depreciation

(Alternates are 8-31 and 8-33.) The Alaska Airlines balance sheet dated December 31, 2011, included the following ($ in millions):

Property and equipment	
Aircraft and other flight equipment	$4,041.8
Other property and equipment	762.3
Deposits for future flight equipment	262.5
	5,066.6
Less: Accumulated depreciation and amortization	1,665.1
Net property and equipment	$3,401.5

Assume that on January 1, 2012, Alaska acquired new maintenance equipment for $990,000 cash. The equipment had an expected useful life of 5 years and an expected residual value of $90,000. Alaska uses straight-line depreciation.

1. Prepare the journal entry that would be made annually for depreciation on the new equipment.
2. Suppose Alaska sold some of the equipment it originally purchased on January 1, 2012. The equipment being sold had an original cost of $330,000 and an expected residual value of $30,000. Alaska sold the equipment for $220,000 cash 2 years after the purchase date. Prepare the journal entry for the sale.
3. Refer to requirement 2. Suppose Alaska had sold the equipment for $180,000 cash, instead of $220,000. Prepare the journal entry for the sale.

8-33 Journal Entries for Depreciation

▶▶ OBJECTIVES 3, 8

(Alternates are 8-31 and 8-32.) The Coca-Cola Company's annual report for the year ended December 31, 2011, included the following ($ in millions):

Property, plant, and equipment	$ 23,151
Less: Accumulated depreciation	8,212
	$ 14,939

Assume that on January 1, 2012, Coca-Cola acquired some new bottling equipment for $1.6 million cash. The equipment had an expected useful life of 4 years and an expected residual value of $400,000. Coca-Cola uses straight-line depreciation.

1. Prepare the journal entry that Coca-Cola would make annually for depreciation on the new equipment.
2. Suppose Coca-Cola sold some of the equipment it had purchased on January 1, 2012. The equipment being sold had an original cost of $80,000 and an expected residual value of $15,000. Coca-Cola sold the equipment for $42,000 cash 2 years after the purchase date. Prepare the journal entry for the sale.
3. Refer to requirement 2. Suppose Coca-Cola had sold the equipment for $51,000 cash, instead of $42,000. Prepare the journal entry for the sale.

8-34 Simple Depreciation Computations

▶▶ OBJECTIVE 3

A company acquired the following assets:

a. Conveyor, 5-year useful life, $48,000 cost, straight-line method, $5,000 expected residual value
b. Truck, 3-year useful life, $18,000 cost, DDB method, $1,500 expected residual value

Compute the first 3 years of depreciation for each asset.

8-35 Units-of-Production Depreciation Method

▶▶ OBJECTIVES 3, 8

The Rockland Transport Company has many trucks that have an estimated useful life of 200,000 miles. The company computes depreciation on a mileage basis. Suppose Rockland purchases a new truck for $100,000 cash. Its expected residual value is $10,000. Its mileage during year 1 is 60,000 and during year 2 is 90,000.

1. What is the depreciation expense for each of the 2 years?
2. Compute the gain or loss if Rockland sells the truck for $40,000 at the end of year 2.

▶▶ OBJECTIVE 3

8-36 Fundamental Depreciation Approaches
(Alternates are 8-37 through 8-39.) U-Haul acquired new trucks for $1.4 million. Their estimated useful life is 4 years, and estimated residual value is $200,000.

Prepare a depreciation schedule similar to Exhibit 8-2, p. 348, comparing straight-line and DDB depreciation.

▶▶ OBJECTIVE 3

8-37 Units-of-Production, Straight-Line, and DDB
(Alternatives are 8-36, 8-38, and 8-39.) Roche Bay Mining Company buys special drills for $640,000 each. Each drill can extract about 150,000 tons of ore, after which it has a $40,000 residual value. Roche Bay bought one such drill in early January 20X1. Projected tonnage figures for the drill are 70,000 tons in 20X1, 45,000 tons in 20X2, and 35,000 tons in 20X3. The drill is scheduled for sale at the end of the third year at the $40,000 residual value. Roche Bay is considering units-of-production, straight-line, or DDB depreciation for the drill.

Compute depreciation for each year under each of the three methods.

▶▶ OBJECTIVE 3

8-38 Comparison of Popular Depreciation Methods
(Alternates are 8-36, 8-37, and 8-39.) Port Townsend Cedar Company acquired a saw for $34,000 with an expected useful life of 5 years and a $2,000 expected residual value. Prepare a tabular comparison (similar to Exhibit 8-2, p. 348) of the annual depreciation and book value for each year under straight-line and DDB depreciation. If these two methods were available for tax reporting purposes, which would a company prefer to use?

▶▶ OBJECTIVE 3

8-39 Fundamental Depreciation Policies
(Alternates are 8-36 through 8-38.) Suppose the printing department of Geico Insurance acquired a new press for $360,000. The equipment's estimated useful life is 8 years and estimated residual value is $40,000.

Prepare a depreciation schedule similar to Exhibit 8-2, p. 348, comparing straight-line and DDB depreciation. Show all amounts in thousands of dollars (rounded to the nearest tenth). Limit the schedule to the first 3 years of useful life. Show the depreciation for each year and the book value at the end of each year.

▶▶ OBJECTIVE 3

8-40 Accumulated Depreciation
Ceradyne, Inc., reported the following items on its December 31, 2011, balance sheet ($ in thousands):

Property, plant, and equipment, net	$428,562
Accumulated depreciation	185,186

1. Compute Ceradyne's historical cost of property, plant, and equipment on December 31, 2011.
2. If Ceradyne uses a 12-year economic life for computing straight-line depreciation on most of its assets, are most of its assets more than or less than 5 years old? Explain how you can determine this.

▶▶ OBJECTIVE 4

8-41 Revision of Useful Life and Residual Value Estimates
Nowling Company buys a machine for $85,000 on January 1, 2012. A residual value of $5,000 and a useful life of 10 years are estimated at the acquisition date. Nowling uses straight-line depreciation. Early in 2016, Nowling discovers that a competitor has come out with a new product that will reduce demand for Nowling's product. As a result, it estimates that the machine will no longer be of use after 2018. Nowling believes it will be able to sell the machine to a scrap dealer for $8,000 at that time.

Prepare a depreciation schedule comparing the original depreciation schedule (for 2012–2021) with the depreciation schedule based on the revised estimates of useful life and residual value (for 2012–2018). Show all amounts in thousands of dollars (rounded to the nearest tenth).

▶▶ OBJECTIVE 6

8-42 Depreciation, Income Taxes, and Cash Flow
Fleck Company began business with cash and common stockholders' equity of $150,000. The same day, December 31, 20X1, the company acquired equipment for $60,000 cash. The equipment had an expected useful life of 5 years and an expected residual value of $5,000. The first year's operations generated cash sales of $190,000 and cash operating expenses of $100,000.

1. Prepare an analysis of income and cash flow for the year 20X2, using the format illustrated in Exhibit 8-3 (p. 351). Assume (a) straight-line depreciation, and (b) DDB depreciation. Assume an income tax rate of 40%. Fleck pays income taxes in cash. The company uses the same depreciation method for reporting to shareholders and to income tax authorities.
2. Examine your answer to requirement 1. Does depreciation provide cash? Explain as precisely as possible.
3. Suppose Fleck doubled its 20X2 depreciation under straight-line and DDB methods. How would this affect the before-tax cash flow? Be specific.

8-43 MACRS versus Straight-Line Depreciation

> ▶▶ **OBJECTIVE 5**

Durham Machinery bought special tooling equipment for $2.6 million. For financial reporting purposes, the estimated useful life is 5 years, with no residual value. For tax purposes, assume MACRS specifies a 3-year, DDB depreciation schedule. Durham Machinery uses the straight-line depreciation method for reporting to shareholders.

1. Explain the two factors that account for the acceleration of depreciation for tax purposes.
2. Compute the first year's depreciation (a) for shareholder reporting, and (b) for tax purposes. (Ignore complications in the tax law that are not introduced in this text.)

8-44 Leasehold Improvements

> ▶▶ **OBJECTIVES 7, 11**

Suppose Domino's Pizza has a 10-year lease on space in a suburban shopping center. Near the end of the sixth year of the lease, Domino's exercised its rights under the lease, removing walls and replacing floor coverings and lighting fixtures. Domino's will not be able to remove these improvements at the end of the lease term. The cost of these improvements was $180,000. The useful life of the redesigned facilities of these improvements was predicted to be 12 years.

What accounts would be affected by the $180,000 expenditure? What would be the annual amortization?

8-45 Capital Expenditures

> ▶▶ **OBJECTIVES 1, 7**

Consider the following transactions:

a. Acquired building for a down payment plus a mortgage payable
b. Paid delinquent real estate taxes on a building at the time of its acquisition
c. Acquired new air-conditioning system for the building
d. Paid interest on building mortgage
e. Paid principal on building mortgage
f. Paid cash dividends
g. Paid travel expenses of sales personnel
h. Paid janitorial wages
i. Paid security guard's wages

Required

Answer the following by letter:

1. Indicate which transactions are capital expenditures.
2. Indicate which transactions are expenses in the current year.

8-46 Capital Expenditures

> ▶▶ **OBJECTIVES 1, 7, 11**

Consider each of the following transactions. For each one, indicate whether it is a capital expenditure (C) or an expense in the current year (E).

1. Paid a consultant to advise on marketing strategy
2. Installed new lighting fixtures in a leased building
3. Paid for routine maintenance on equipment
4. Developed a patent that cost $50,000 in R&D
5. Paid for overhaul of machinery that extends its useful life
6. Acquired a patent from General Electric for $40,000
7. Paid for a tune-up on one of the autos in the company's fleet

▶▶ OBJECTIVES 4, 7

8-47 Repairs and Improvements

Yakima Wheat Company acquired harvesting equipment for $90,000 with an expected useful life of 5 years and a $10,000 expected residual value. Yakima Wheat used straight-line depreciation. During its fourth year of service, cash expenditures related to the equipment were as follows:

1. Oiling and greasing, $200.
2. Replacing belts and hoses, $450.
3. Major overhaul during the final week of the year, including the replacement of an engine. The useful life of the equipment was extended from 5 to 7 years. The cost was $27,000. The residual value is now expected to be $11,000, instead of $10,000.

Indicate in words how each of the three items would affect the income statement and the balance sheet in the fourth year. Prepare a tabulation that compares the original depreciation schedule with the revised depreciation schedule.

▶▶ OBJECTIVE 8

8-48 Disposal of Equipment

The Outpatient Clinic of Eastside Hospital acquired X-ray equipment for $29,000 with an expected useful life of 5 years and a $4,000 expected residual value. The hospital uses straight-line depreciation. The clinic sold the equipment at the end of the fourth year for $14,000 cash.

1. Compute the gain or loss on the sale. Show the effects of the sale on the balance sheet equation, identifying all specific accounts by name. Where and how would the sale appear on the income statement?
2. (a) Show the journal entry for the transaction in requirement 1.
   (b) Repeat 2a, assuming that the cash sales price was $8,500 instead of $14,000.

▶▶ OBJECTIVE 8

8-49 Gain or Loss on Sale of Fixed Assets

Bella's Pizza Company purchased a delivery van in early 20X1 for $55,000 and depreciated it on a straight-line basis over its useful life of 5 years. Estimated residual value was $5,000. The company sold the van in early 20X4 after recognizing 3 years of depreciation.

1. Suppose Bella's Pizza received $27,000 cash for the van. Compute the gain or loss on the sale. Prepare the journal entry for the sale of the van.
2. Suppose Bella's Pizza received $14,000 cash for the van. Compute the gain or loss on the sale. Prepare the journal entry for the sale of the van.

▶▶ OBJECTIVE 8

8-50 Gain or Loss on Disposal of Equipment—Cash Flow Implications

Icarus Software Company sold five computers. It had purchased the computers 5 years ago for $120,000, and accumulated depreciation at the time of sale was $80,000.

1. Suppose Icarus received $40,000 cash for the computers. How would the company show the sale on its statement of cash flows?
2. Suppose Icarus received $50,000 cash for the computers. How would the company show the sale on its statement of cash flows (including the schedule reconciling net income and net cash provided by operating activities).
3. Redo requirement 2 assuming cash received was $30,000.

▶▶ OBJECTIVES 11, 12

8-51 Various Intangible Assets and Impairment

(Alternative is 8-52.) Consider the following:

1. On December 29, 20X1, a publisher acquires the paperback copyright for a book by Steven King for $3 million. Most sales of this book are expected to take place uniformly during 20X2 and 20X3. What is the amortization for 20X2?
2. In 20X1, Company C spent $6 million in its research department, which resulted in new valuable patents. In late December 20X1, Company D paid $6 million to an outside inventor for some valuable new patents. Under U.S. GAAP, how would the income statements for the year ended December 31, 20X1, for each company be affected? How would the balance sheets as of December 31, 20X1, be affected?
3. On December 28, 20X8, Black Electronics Company purchased a patent for a piece of equipment for $500,000. The patent has 10 years of its legal life remaining. Technology

changes fast, so Black Electronics expects the patent to be worthless in 5 years. What is the amortization for 20X9?

4. (a) During the fiscal year ending December 31, 20X3, Samela Corporation paid $12 million in cash for Haddock Company. At the time of the acquisition, the total assets of Haddock had a fair value of $22 million and the total liabilities had a fair value of $15 million. What journal entry would Samela Corporation make to record the acquisition of Haddock? (b) On December 31, 20X4, Samela Corporation performed a recovery test, which determined that the goodwill recorded in the initial transaction had become impaired. A further review indicated that the fair value of the goodwill was $3 million. Does Samela need to make a journal entry to recognize the impairment of goodwill? If so, prepare the entry.

8-52 Various Intangible Assets

▸▸ OBJECTIVE 11

(Alternative is 8-51.) Consider the following:

1. On December 31, 2012, Sony Corporation purchased a patent on some broadcasting equipment for $900,000. The patent has 16 years of its legal life remaining. Because technology moves rapidly, Sony expects the patent to be worthless at the end of 6 years. What is the amortization for 2013?

2. Consider alternative scenarios (a) and (b).
   a. Suppose that Amgen, a biotech firm with over $15 billion in revenues, spent $3,167 million in its research departments in 2011. These expenditures resulted in valuable new patents.
   b. Suppose that in late December 2011, Amgen had paid $3,167 million to various outside companies for the same new patents.
   How would alternatives (a) and (b) affect Amgen's income statement for the year ended December 31, 2011? How would they affect Amgen's balance sheet on December 31, 2011?

3. Analogic Corporation included $1.594 million of software as an asset on its 2011 balance sheet. The notes indicated that "Software development costs incurred subsequent to establishing technological feasibility through general release of the software products are capitalized. Technological feasibility is demonstrated by the completion of a detailed program design. Capitalized costs are amortized on a straight-line basis over the economic lives of the related products, generally three years." Suppose that Analogic spent the same amount on this activity every year but had always used an estimated economic life of 4 years rather than 3 years. How would the income statement and balance sheet differ if the life had always been 4 years rather than 3?

8-53 IFRS Revaluation of Fixed Assets

▸▸ OBJECTIVE 9

Bauer Corporation prepares financial statements using IFRS and has elected the revaluation method of accounting for its fixed assets. Bauer has a December 31 fiscal year-end and revalues its fixed assets at the end of each fiscal year. On January 1, 2012, the company purchased land at a cost of €200,000. Consider the two alternative scenarios that follow:

1. The fair value of the land at December 31, 2012, was €190,000. By December 31, 2013, the fair value of the land had increased to €230,000. What is the financial statement impact of revaluation for the year ended December 31, 2012? December 31, 2013?

2. The fair value of the land at December 31, 2012, was €250,000. By December 31, 2013, the fair value of the land had decreased to €185,000. What is the financial statement impact of revaluation for the year ended December 31, 2012? December 31, 2013?

8-54 Computation of Impairment on Long-Lived Assets

▸▸ OBJECTIVE 10

Vincent Corporation acquired an office building that it rents to a variety of small businesses. The building had an original cost of $15 million, and at the end of 20X5 it had a net book value of $11 million. Due to a change in zoning regulations effective January 20X6, Vincent believes the building has become less desirable and expects rental rates to decline. The company estimates that the fair market value of the building has decreased from $19 million to $7.5 million as a result of the zoning change. Vincent deems it necessary to review the building for possible impairment.

1. Suppose that the sum of the expected future net cash flows from the use of the building plus its eventual disposal value is estimated to be $9 million. Compute the amount of the impairment loss, if any, that Vincent should recognize on the building, assuming that Vincent prepares its financial statements using U.S. GAAP.

2. Now assume that Vincent uses IFRS. Vincent has elected historical cost as the basis of valuing its fixed assets and carries the building at a net book value of $11 million. The sum of the expected future net cash flows is estimated to be $9 million and the present value of these cash flows is $7.4 million. Vincent estimates that if it were to sell the building, it would incur a selling cost of $.1 million. Compute the impairment loss, if any, that Vincent should recognize on the building.

8-55 Depletion

▶▶ **OBJECTIVE 13**

A zinc mine contains an estimated 1,250,000 tons of zinc ore. The mine cost $14.4 million. The tonnage mined during 20X1, the first year of operations, was 150,000 tons.

1. What was the depletion for 20X1?
2. Suppose that in 20X2 a total of 120,000 tons were mined. What depletion expense would be charged for 20X2?

Problems

8-56 Popular Depreciation Methods

▶▶ **OBJECTIVE 3**

The 2011 annual report of **Alaska Airlines** contained the following footnote:

> PROPERTY, EQUIPMENT, AND DEPRECIATION—*Property and equipment are recorded at cost and depreciated using the straight-line method over their estimated useful lives, which are as follows:*

Aircraft and related flight equipment	15–20 years
Buildings	25–30 years
Capitalized leases & leasehold improvements	Shorter of lease term or estimated useful life
Minor building and land improvements	10 years
Computer hardware and software	3–5 years
Other furniture and equipment	5–10 years

Consider a **Boeing** 737-100 airplane that Alaska acquired for $50 million. Its useful life is 20 years, and its expected residual value is $6 million. Prepare a tabular comparison of the annual depreciation and book value for each of the first 3 years of service life under straight-line and DDB depreciation. Show all amounts in thousands of dollars (rounded to the nearest thousand). (Note that this is a comparison of methods used for reporting to shareholders. Such methods may differ from those used for reporting to the income tax authorities.) *Hint*: See Exhibit 8-2 on page 348.

8-57 Reconstruction of Plant Asset Transactions

▶▶ **OBJECTIVE 8**

The annual report of **General Mills**, maker of *Wheaties*, *Cheerios*, and *Betty Crocker* baking products, for the year ended May 29, 2011, contained the following ($ in millions):

	May 29, 2011	May 30, 2010
Total land, buildings, and equipment	$7,492.1	$6,949.7
Less: Accumulated depreciation	4,146.2	3,822.0
Net land, buildings, and equipment	$3,345.9	$3,127.7

During fiscal 2011, depreciation expense was $472.6 million, and General Mills acquired land, buildings, and equipment worth $848.8 million. Assume that no gain or loss arose from the disposition of land, buildings, and equipment and that General Mills received cash of $158.0 million from such disposals.

Compute (1) the original historical cost of assets sold or retired during fiscal 2011, (2) the amount of accumulated depreciation associated with the assets sold or retired, and (3) the book value of the assets sold or retired. *Hint*: The use of T-accounts may help your analysis.

8-58 Depreciation

Asahi Kasei Corporation has sales nearly the equivalent of US$10 billion. The company included the following in its balance sheet for the year ended March 31, 2011 (¥ in millions):

Property, plant, and equipment, net of accumulated depreciation	
Buildings and structures	¥177,789
Machinery, equipment, and vehicles	144,220
Land	55,243
Lease assets	5,463
Construction in progress	22,173
Other	13,466
Total property, plant, and equipment, net	¥418,354

Footnote 8 contains the following:

Accumulated depreciation comprises the following (¥ in millions):	
Buildings and structures	¥ 231,474
Machinery, equipment, and vehicles	1,047,912
Lease assets	3,118
Other	105,252
Total accumulated depreciation	¥1,387,756

Footnote 2 says, "Depreciation is provided for under the declining-balance method for property, plant, and equipment, except for buildings which are depreciated using the straight-line method, at rates based on estimated useful lives of the assets, principally, ranging from 5 years to 60 years for buildings and from 4 years to 22 years for machinery, equipment and vehicles."

1. Compute the original acquisition cost of each of the categories of assets listed under Property, Plant, and Equipment.
2. Explain why Asahi Kasei shows no accumulated depreciation for land or construction in progress.
3. Suppose Asahi Kasei had used straight-line instead of declining-balance depreciation for all asset categories. How would this affect the preceding values shown for Property, Plant, and Equipment?

8-59 Reconstruction of Plant Asset Transactions

The Ford Motor Company's footnotes included the following ($ in millions):

Ford Motor Company

	December 31	
	2011	2010
Property		
Land, plant, equipment, and other	$48,104	$49,454
Less: Accumulated depreciation	32,874	33,900
Net land, plant, equipment, and other	15,230	15,554
Special tools, net	6,999	7,473
Net automotive sector property	$22,229	$23,027

The notes to the income statement for 2011 revealed depreciation and amortization expense of $3,533 million. The account Special Tools, net is increased by new investments in tools, dies, jigs, and fixtures necessary for new models and production processes. Ford then amortizes these investments over various periods and reduces the account directly. When special tools are disposed of, the account is reduced by the net book value. (Note that Ford uses the term amortization rather than depreciation for the decline in the carrying amount of these special tools.)

Hint: Analyze with the help of T-accounts.

1. Assume that Ford spent $2,000 million on special tools in 2011. The company disposed of special tools with a net book value of $700 million. How much amortization did Ford record on special tools in 2011?
2. Given your answer to requirement 1, estimate the cost of the new acquisitions of land, plant, and equipment. Assume all disposals of plant and equipment involved fully depreciated assets with zero book value.

▶▶ OBJECTIVE 3

8-60 Average Age of Assets

Walgreens is a drugstore chain operating more than 8,200 stores in 50 states, the District of Columbia, Guam, and Puerto Rico. Walgreens typically builds rather than buys stores, so it can pick prime locations. Net property, plant, and equipment comprised almost 42% of Walgreens assets as of August 31, 2011. The company had the following on its August 31, 2011, balance sheet ($ in millions):

Total property, plant, and equipment	$ 15,834
Less: Accumulated depreciation	4,308
	$ 11,526

A footnote states that "depreciation is provided on a straight-line basis over the estimated useful lives of owned assets." Annual depreciation expense is approximately $804 million. Assume a zero salvage value for all of the assets.

1. Estimate the average useful life of Walgreens depreciable assets.
2. Estimate the average age of Walgreens depreciable assets on August 31, 2011.

▶▶ OBJECTIVE 6

8-61 Depreciation, Income Tax, and Cash Flow

(Alternates are 8-62 and 8-63.) Sanchez Metal Products Company had the following balances, among others, at the end of December 20X1: Cash, $300,000; Equipment, at cost $400,000; Accumulated Depreciation, $100,000. Total revenues (all in cash) were $950,000. All operating expenses except depreciation were for cash and totaled $600,000. Straight-line depreciation expense was $60,000. Depreciation expense would have been $100,000 if Sanchez had used accelerated depreciation.

1. Assume zero income taxes. Fill in the first two columns of blanks in the accompanying table. Show the amounts in thousands.

Table for Problem 8-61
($ amounts in thousands)

	1. Zero Income Taxes		2. 40% Income Taxes	
	Straight-Line Depreciation	Accelerated Depreciation	Straight-Line Depreciation	Accelerated Depreciation
Revenues (all cash)	$	$	$	$
Cash operating expenses	_____	_____	_____	_____
Cash provided by operations before income taxes				
Depreciation expense	_____	_____	_____	_____
Pretax income				
Income tax expense	_____	_____	_____	_____
Net income	$_____	$_____	$_____	$_____
Supplementary analysis				
Cash provided by operations before income taxes	$	$	$	$
Income tax payments	_____	_____	_____	_____
Net cash provided by operations	$_____	$_____	$_____	$_____

2. Fill in the last two columns of blanks in the table above. Assume an income tax rate of 40%. Assume also that Sanchez uses the same depreciation method for reporting to shareholders and to income tax authorities.

3. Compare your answers to requirements 1 and 2. Does depreciation provide cash? Explain as precisely as possible.
4. Refer to requirement 2. Assume that Sanchez had used straight-line depreciation for reporting to shareholders and to income tax authorities. Indicate the change (increase or decrease and amount) in the following balances if Sanchez had used accelerated depreciation for shareholder and tax reporting instead of straight-line: Cash, Accumulated Depreciation, Pretax Income, Income Tax Expense, and Retained Earnings.
5. Refer to requirement 1 where there are zero taxes. Suppose depreciation was doubled under both straight-line and accelerated methods. How would this affect cash? Be specific.

8-62 Depreciation, Income Taxes, and Cash Flow

▶▶ **OBJECTIVE 6**

(Alternates are 8-61 and 8-63.) The 2011 annual report of Wal-Mart, a major retailing company, listed the following property and equipment ($ in millions):

Property and equipment, at cost	$148,584
Less: Accumulated depreciation	43,486
Property and equipment, net	$105,098

The cash balance was $7,395 million. Depreciation expense during the year was $7,641 million. The condensed income statement follows ($ in millions):

Revenues	$421,849
Expenses	(396,307)
Operating income	$ 25,542

For purposes of this problem, assume that all revenues and expenses, excluding depreciation, are for cash. Thus, cash operating expenses in millions of dollars were ($396,307 – $7,641) = $388,666.

Table for Problem 8-62
($ amounts in millions)

	1. Zero Income Taxes		2. 40% Income Taxes	
	Straight-Line Depreciation	Accelerated Depreciation	Straight-Line Depreciation	Accelerated Depreciation
Revenues (all cash)	$	$	$	$
Cash operating expenses	_____	_____	_____	_____
Cash provided by operations before income taxes				
Depreciation expense	_____	_____	_____	_____
Pretax income				
Income tax expense	_____	_____	_____	_____
Net income	$_____	$_____	$_____	$_____
Supplementary analysis				
Cash provided by operations before income taxes	$	$	$	$
Income tax payments	_____	_____	_____	_____
Net cash provided by operations	$_____	$_____	$_____	$_____

1. Wal-Mart uses straight-line depreciation. If accelerated depreciation had been used, assume that depreciation would have been $9,641 million. Assume zero income taxes. Fill in the first two columns of blanks in the accompanying table ($ in millions).
2. Fill in the last two columns of blanks in the table above. Assume an income tax rate of 40%. Assume also that Wal-Mart uses the same depreciation method for reporting to shareholders and to income tax authorities.
3. Compare your answers to requirements 1 and 2. Does depreciation provide cash? Explain as precisely as possible.

4. Refer to requirement 2. Assume that Wal-Mart had used straight-line depreciation for reporting to shareholders and to income tax authorities. Indicate the change (increase or decrease and amount) in the following balances if Wal-Mart had used accelerated depreciation for shareholder and tax reporting instead of straight-line during that year: Cash, Accumulated Depreciation, Pretax Income, Income Tax Expense, and Retained Earnings. What would be the new balances in Cash and Accumulated Depreciation?

5. Refer to requirement 1 where there are zero taxes. Suppose Wal-Mart increased depreciation by an extra $2,750 million under both straight-line and accelerated methods. How would cash be affected? Be specific.

▶▶ OBJECTIVE 6

8-63 Depreciation, Income Taxes, and Cash Flow

(Alternates are 8-61 and 8-62.) Carrefour is the world's second-largest retailer, just behind Wal-Mart. Carrefour operates more than 9,500 stores in four different grocery store formats: hypermarkets, supermarkets, cash & carry, and convenience. While headquartered in France, over 57% of the company's sales are made in other countries. The company's 2010 annual report showed the following balances (€ in millions):

Revenues	€ 89,325
Operating expenses	(87,489)
Operating income	€ 1,836

Carrefour had depreciation expense of €1,633 million (included in operating expenses). The company's ending cash balance was €3,271 million.

Carrefour reported its property and equipment (called tangible fixed assets by Carrefour) in the following way (€ in millions):

Gross tangible fixed assets	€33,726
Less: Accumulated depreciation	18,429
Net tangible fixed assets	€15,297

For purposes of this problem, assume all revenues and expenses, excluding depreciation, are for cash. Also, you may round all values computed in the table to the nearest million euros.

Table for Problem 8-63
(amounts in millions of euros)

	1. Zero Income Taxes		2. 60% Income Taxes	
	Straight-Line Depreciation	**Accelerated Depreciation**	**Straight-Line Depreciation**	**Accelerated Depreciation**
Revenues (all cash)	€	€	€	€
Cash operating expenses	_____	_____	_____	_____
Cash provided by operations before income taxes				
Depreciation expense	_____	_____	_____	_____
Pretax income				
Income tax expense	_____	_____	_____	_____
Net income	€	€	€	€
Supplementary analysis				
Cash provided by operations before income taxes	€	€	€	€
Income tax payments	_____	_____	_____	_____
Net cash provided by operations	€	€	€	€

1. Carrefour used straight-line depreciation. If accelerated depreciation had been used, assume that depreciation would have been €2,363 million. Assume zero income taxes. Fill in the first two columns of blanks in the accompanying table (in millions of euros).

2. Fill in the last two columns of blanks in the table above. Assume an income tax rate of 60%. Assume also that Carrefour uses the same depreciation method for reporting to shareholders and to income tax authorities.

3. Compare your answers to requirements 1 and 2. Does depreciation provide cash? Explain as precisely as possible.

4. Refer to requirement 2. Carrefour used straight-line depreciation for reporting to shareholders and to income tax authorities. Indicate the change (increase or decrease and amount) in the following balances if Carrefour had used accelerated depreciation for shareholder and tax reporting instead of straight-line: Cash, Accumulated Depreciation, Pretax Income, Income Tax Expense, and Retained Earnings. What would be the new balances in Cash and Accumulated Depreciation?

5. Refer to requirement 1 where there are zero taxes. Suppose the company had doubled its depreciation under both straight-line and accelerated methods. How would this affect cash? Be specific.

8-64 Rental Vehicles

AMERCO is the holding company for U-Haul International and its subsidiaries. Footnote 3 from the annual report for fiscal year 2011 indicated:

▶▶ **OBJECTIVES 3, 8**

> *Property, plant and equipment are stated at cost. Depreciation is computed for financial reporting purposes using the straight-line or an accelerated method based on a declining balance formula over the estimated useful lives.... Routine maintenance costs are charged to operating expense as they are incurred. Gains and losses on dispositions of property, plant and equipment are netted against depreciation expense when realized.*

1. Assume that U-Haul acquires some new trucks on January 1, 2011, for $100 million. The useful life is 1 year. Expected residual values are $82 million. Prepare a summary journal entry for depreciation on these trucks for 2011. The 2011 fiscal year ends on March 31, 2011.

2. Prepare a summary journal entry for depreciation for the first 9 months of fiscal 2012 (April 1, 2011 through December 31, 2011).

3. Assume that U-Haul sells the trucks for $88 million cash on December 31, 2011. Prepare the journal entry for the sale. U-Haul considers the trucks to be "revenue-earning equipment."

4. What is the total depreciation expense on these trucks for fiscal 2012? If U-Haul could have exactly predicted the $88 million proceeds when it originally acquired the trucks, what would depreciation expense have been in fiscal 2011? In fiscal 2012? Explain.

8-65 Nature of Research Costs

Julene Pief, a distinguished scientist of international repute, had developed many successful drugs for a well-established pharmaceutical company. Having an entrepreneurial spirit, Julene persuaded the board of directors that she should resign her position as vice president of research and launch a subsidiary company to produce and market some powerful new drugs for treating arthritis. However, she did not predict overnight success. Instead, she expected to gather a first-rate research team that might take 3–5 years to generate any marketable products. Furthermore, she admitted that the risks were so high that conceivably no commercial success might result. Nevertheless, she had little trouble obtaining an initial investment of $8 million. The Pief Pharmaceuticals Company was 70% owned by the parent and 30% by Julene.

▶▶ **OBJECTIVE 11**

Julene assembled a team of researchers and began operations. By the end of the first year of the life of the new subsidiary, it had expended $3 million on research activities, mostly for researchers' salaries but also for related research costs.

The subsidiary had developed no marketable products, but Julene and other top executives were extremely pleased with the overall progress and were very optimistic about developing such products within the next 3 or 4 years.

How would you account for the $3 million? Would you write it off as an expense in year 1? Could it be capitalized as an intangible asset? If so, would you carry it indefinitely? Or would you write it off systematically over 3 years or some longer span? Why?

▶▶ **OBJECTIVES 2, 7**

8-66 Meaning of Book Value

Wagner Company purchased an office building 20 years ago for $1.3 million, $500,000 of which was attributable to land. The mortgage has been fully paid. The current balance sheet follows:

Cash		$ 300,000	Stockholders' equity	$1,000,000
Land		500,000		
Building at cost	$ 800,000			
Accumulated depreciation	(600,000)			
Net book value		200,000		
Total assets		$1,000,000		

The company is about to borrow $1.8 million on a first mortgage to modernize and expand the building. This amounts to 60% of the combined appraised fair value of the land and building before the modernization and expansion.

Prepare a balance sheet after the loan is made and the building is expanded and modernized. Comment on its significance.

▶▶ **OBJECTIVE 4**

8-67 Change in Service Life

Suppose that a major airline extended the useful lives of its Boeing 727-100 aircraft from 16 years to 20 years. As a result, depreciation and amortization expense was decreased by $9,000,000. The company's financial statements also contained the following data: depreciation expense, $235,518,000 and net income, $42,233,000.

The cost of the Boeing 727-100 aircraft subject to depreciation was $800 million. Residual values were predicted to be 10% of acquisition cost.

Assume a combined federal and state income tax rate of 46% throughout all parts of these requirements.

1. Was the effect of the change in estimated useful life a material difference? Explain, including computations.
2. Examination of the annual report of a competitor airline indicated that the competitor used a 10-year life. Suppose the company making the change in estimate had changed to a 10-year life instead of a 20-year life on its 727-100 equipment. Estimated residual value is 10%. Compute the new depreciation and net income. For purposes of this requirement, assume that the equipment cost $800 million and has been in service 1 year and that reported net income based on a 20-year life was $42,233,000.

▶▶ **OBJECTIVE 8**

8-68 Disposal of Equipment

(Alternate is 8-69.) Suppose American Airlines acquired a new Boeing 747 airplane for $250 million. Its expected residual value was $70 million. The company's annual report indicated that straight-line depreciation was used based on an estimated service life of 25 years. Assume the company records gains or losses, if any, in Other Income (Expense).

Show all amounts in millions of dollars.

1. Assume that American sold the equipment at the end of the sixth year for $220 million cash. Compute the gain or loss on the sale. Show the effects of the sale on the balance sheet equation, identifying all specific accounts by name. Where and how would the sale appear on the income statement?
2. (a) Show the journal entries for the transaction in requirement 1. (b) Repeat 2a, assuming that the cash sales price was $195 million instead of $220 million.

▶▶ **OBJECTIVE 8**

8-69 Disposal of Property and Equipment

(Alternate is 8-68.) Rockwell Automation is a leading provider of industrial automation power and controls. The annual report indicates that the company uses straight-line depreciation for its property and equipment. In addition, the annual report said, "Gains or losses on property transactions are recorded in income in the period of sale or retirement."

Suppose Rockwell received $5 million for property and equipment that it sold.

1. Assume that Rockwell originally acquired the total property and equipment in question for $60 million and received the $5 million in cash. There was a loss of $8.5 million on the sale.

Compute the accumulated depreciation on the property and equipment sold. Show the effects of the sale on the balance sheet equation, identifying all specific accounts by name.
2. (a) Show the journal entry and postings to T-accounts for the transaction in requirement 1.
   (b) Repeat 2a, assuming that the cash sales price was $18 million cash instead of $5 million.

8-70 Gain on Airplane Crash

▶▶ **OBJECTIVE 8**

A few years ago, a Delta Air Lines 727 crashed in Dallas. The crash resulted in a gain of $.11 per share for Delta. How could this happen? Consider the accounting for airplanes. Airlines insure their craft at market value, $6.5 million for Delta's 727. However, the planes' book values are often much less because of large accumulated depreciation amounts. The book value of Delta's 727 was only $962,000.

1. Suppose Delta received the insurance payment and immediately purchased another 727 for $6.5 million. Compute the effect of the insurance payment on pretax income. Also compute the effect on Delta's total assets.
2. Do you think a casualty should generate a reported gain? Why?

8-71 Disposal of Equipment

▶▶ **OBJECTIVE 8**

Lufthansa's policy of rolling over entire fleets of aircraft in roughly 10 years—before the aircrafts have outlived their usefulness—began when seven first-generation 747s were sold. The 747s were bought 6 to 9 years earlier for $22–$28 million each and sold for about the same price.

1. Assume an average original cost of $25 million per aircraft, an average original expected useful life of 10 years, and a $3.5 million expected residual value for each aircraft. Also assume the planes were on average 8 years old at the time of disposal. Use straight-line depreciation. Compute the total gain or loss on the sale of the seven planes. Assume each plane sold for $25 million.
2. Prepare a summary journal entry for the sale.

8-72 Software Development Costs

▶▶ **OBJECTIVE 11**

Microsoft, Incorporated, is one of the largest producers of software for personal computers. Special rules apply to accounting for the costs of developing software for sale or lease. Companies expense such costs until the technological feasibility of the product is established. Thereafter, they should capitalize these costs and amortize them over the life of the product.

One of Microsoft's divisions began working on some special business applications software. Suppose the division had spent $900,000 on the project by the end of 20X7, but it was not yet clear whether the software was technologically feasible.

On July 1, 20X8, after spending another $400,000, management decided that the software was technologically feasible. During the second half of 20X8, the division spent another $2 million on this project. In December 20X8, the company announced the product, with deliveries to begin in March 20X9. The division incurred no R&D costs for the software after December 20X8.

1. Prepare journal entries to account for the R&D expenses for the software for 20X7 and 20X8. Assume that the division paid all expenditures in cash.
2. Would any R&D expenses affect income in 20X9?

8-73 Basket Purchase and Intangibles

▶▶ **OBJECTIVES 2, 11**

A tax newsletter stated, "When a business is sold, part of the sales price may be allocated to tangible assets and part to a 'covenant not to compete.' How this allocation is made can have important tax consequences to both the buyer and seller."

A large law firm, organized as a professional services corporation, purchased a successful local firm for $100,000. The purchase included both tangible assets, which have an average remaining useful life of 10 years, and a 3-year covenant not to compete. Suppose the buyer has legally supportable latitude concerning how to allocate this amount, as follows:

	Allocation One	Allocation Two
Covenant	$ 72,000	$ 48,000
Tangible assets	28,000	52,000
Total for two assets	$100,000	$100,000

1. For income tax purposes, which allocation would the buyer favor? Why?
2. For shareholder reporting purposes, which allocation would the buyer favor? Why?

▸▸ OBJECTIVE 3

8-74 Depreciation Policies and Ethics

Some companies have depreciation policies that differ substantially from the norm of their industry. For example, **Cineplex Odeon** (now operating as **AMC Theaters** in the United States and **Cineplex Entertainment** in Canada) depreciated its theater seats, carpets, and related equipment over 27 years, much longer than most of its competitors. Another example is **Waste Management**. Compared with industry norms, Waste Management used longer useful lives and larger salvage values for garbage trucks and container assets.

Growing companies can increase their current income by depreciating fixed assets over a longer period of time or by utilizing a higher estimated salvage value. Sometimes companies lengthen the depreciable lives or increase the salvage value estimates of their fixed assets when a boost in income is desired. Comment on the ethical implications of the choice of useful life or salvage value for depreciation purposes, with special reference to the policies of Cineplex Odeon and Waste Management.

Collaborative Learning Exercise

▸▸ OBJECTIVE 3

8-75 Accumulated Depreciation

Form groups of at least four students (this exercise can be done as an entire class, if desired). Individual students, on their own, should select a company and find the fixed asset section of its most recent balance sheet. From the balance sheet (and possibly the footnotes) find the original acquisition cost of property, plant, and equipment (the account title varies slightly by company) and the accumulated depreciation on property, plant, and equipment. Compute the ratio of accumulated depreciation to original acquisition cost. Also note the depreciation method used and the average economic life of the assets, if given. (For an extra bonus, find a company that uses accelerated depreciation for reporting to shareholders; such companies are harder to find.)

When everyone gets together, make four columns on the board or on a piece of paper. Find the 25% of the companies with the highest ratios of accumulated depreciation to original acquisition cost and list them in the first column. Then list the 25% with the next highest ratios in the second column, and so on. As a group, make a list of explanations for the rankings of the companies. What characteristics of the company, its industry, or its depreciation methods distinguish the companies with high ratios from those with low ratios?

Analyzing and Interpreting Financial Statements

▸▸ OBJECTIVES 2, 3

8-76 Financial Statement Research

Select two distinct industries and identify two companies in each industry.

1. Identify the depreciation methods used by each company.
2. Calculate gross and net plant, property, and equipment as a percentage of total assets for each company. What differences do you observe between industries? Within industries?
3. Do the notes disclose any unusual practices with regard to long-lived assets?

▸▸ OBJECTIVES 3, 4

8-77 Analyzing Starbucks' Financial Statements

Find the financial statements of **Starbucks** for the year ended October 2, 2011, and look at footnote 1. Depreciation and amortization expense was $523.3 million for the year ended October 2, 2011, according to the Consolidated Statement of Earnings.

1. What lives does Starbucks use for depreciating and amortizing its property, plant, and equipment and its intangible assets?
2. Suppose Starbucks extended the lives of all its depreciable assets by 50% so depreciation was smaller each year. Estimate the effect of this on net earnings reported in the year 2011. Assume that the average tax rate in the current income statement applied to this change in depreciation and that depreciation for financial reporting purposes was the same as that for tax purposes.

8-78 Analyzing Financial Statements Using the Internet

▶▶ OBJECTIVES 3, 6, 11

Go to www.intel.com to find Intel's home page. Select Investor Relations from the bottom navigation menu. Then select Financials and Filings from the left navigation menu. You can access the 10-K filings by clicking on Annual Reports, 10-Ks, and Proxy Statements or SEC Filings. From there you can open the most recent 10-K.

Answer the following questions about Intel:

1. What is the nature of Intel's operations? What type of property, plant, and equipment would you expect Intel to include in the account Property, Plant, and Equipment on its balance sheet?
2. In which section of its financial statements does Intel provide information on the method of depreciation used for property, plant, and equipment? What other disclosures concerning depreciable assets are available in this same location?
3. Does Intel have any intangible assets? Where in the footnotes does Intel provide information about the nature of any intangible assets? What type of intangibles does Intel hold? Does Intel amortize the intangibles? If so, what amortization method is used? How are intangible assets categorized on the balance sheet?
4. What does the amount listed on the balance sheet for Property, Plant, and Equipment represent—cost, market, or some other amount? If Intel purchases no additional property and equipment assets, what will happen to the net book value over time?
5. How much depreciation and amortization expense did Intel report, as shown in its most recent annual report? Why is this amount not obvious from looking at the income statement? Which financial statement provides the depreciation and amortization amount?

9 Liabilities and Interest

WHEN YOU HAVE a taste for a hamburger, you might stop by Jack in the Box. Originally just a drive-through hamburger restaurant, Jack in the Box has expanded to more than 2,221 hamburger outlets in 29 states. The company owns and operates about 30% of these units with the rest franchise-operated. The 2011 consolidated statement of earnings included $1.4 billion in company restaurant sales and $282 million in franchise revenue. In addition to its hamburger restaurants, the San Diego-based company acquired Qdoba Mexican Grill in 2003 and now operates 583 Qdoba locations in 42 states selling south-of-the-border fare.

As it expanded, Jack in the Box borrowed money to finance the opening of new locations. In the first quarter of 2012 the company opened 16 new Jack in the Box restaurants and 15 new Qdoba locations. And the financing is not just for opening new restaurants. In the same quarter the company also purchased 11 restaurants from franchisees to convert them to company-owned locations. In a press release the company indicated that it expected to open 30–35 new Jack in the Box restaurants and 70–90 Qdoba restaurants in 2012. It estimated that these investments will involve $90 to $100 million in capital expenditures.

Where will this $100 million come from? In 2011 the company generated $124 million in cash flow from operations, and it does not pay dividends. So the growth could be financed from operating cash flow. But the company has many choices to make. In 2011 it repurchased common stock for $193 million, which was more than twice the level of stock repurchases made during the prior year. The company did not issue any new long-term debt in 2011, although it issued $200 million in 2010.

As of January 22, 2012, the company's total liabilities exceeded $1 billion, of which $472.8 million was long-term debt. The long-term debt included a revolving credit arrangement, a term loan, and some capital lease obligations, all of which we will discuss in this chapter. The footnotes to the 2011 10-K show that the company has a significant repayment obligation in 2015 when it must repay $395 million of long-term debt.

Why would Jack in the Box want to take on so much debt? Why does any company borrow money? Companies borrow because management believes that remaining competitive requires continual growth. If the company can use the borrowed funds to continue increasing sales and earnings per share, both management and shareholders will benefit. The key to a company's successful borrowing is that it must earn more using the borrowed funds than it pays for them. Also, the company must expect to be able to repay the loan when it becomes

---

▶▶ LEARNING OBJECTIVES *After studying this chapter, you should be able to:*

1 Account for current liabilities.

2 Measure and account for long-term liabilities.

3 Account for bond issues over their entire life.

4 Value and account for long-term lease obligations.

5 Evaluate pensions and other postretirement benefits.

6 Interpret deferred tax assets and liabilities; and restructuring and contingent liabilities.

7 Use ratio analysis to assess a company's debt levels.

8 Compute and interpret present and future values (Appendix 9).

due. The organizations that make the loans are also concerned that the money be used for productive purposes and that the borrower is able to meet the interest and principal obligations when they come due.

Companies are not the only ones that borrow money. For example, when individuals seek to buy a car or a house, lenders assess the buyer's financial position carefully and pay special attention to the size of the down payment the buyer will make. Why? Because the larger the down payment, the more "equity" the borrower has in the purchase and therefore, the more reason the borrower has to continue to make payments. The higher the likelihood of repayment, the more comfortable the lender is making the loan. This translates into lower interest rates for the borrower. The financial crisis in 2008–2009 showed what can happen if lenders are not vigilant in requiring significant equity investments from home purchasers. Many banks are still holding loans that borrowers are not able to repay.

Similarly, potential investors in the common stock or bonds of a company carefully evaluate the amount of debt the company has relative to the amount of stockholders' equity to assess the potential risk of their investment. Thus, GAAP provides a definition of what constitutes a liability and describes how best to disclose liabilities to readers of financial statements. ●

Liabilities in Perspective

As we learned earlier, liabilities are a company's obligations to pay cash or to provide goods and services to other companies or individuals. Liabilities include wages due to employees, payables to suppliers, taxes owed the government, interest and principal due to lenders, obligations from losing a lawsuit, and so on. A liability arises whenever an organization recognizes an obligation before paying it.

This is a typical Jack in the Box restaurant. Jack in the Box must buy, build, or lease a building and acquire equipment and inventories before it can generate any sales. To expand the number of locations, Jack in the Box borrows money, creating a liability. In this chapter we see how to account for such liabilities.

Investors, financial analysts, management, and creditors consider existing liabilities of the firm when valuing the firm's common stock, when considering a new loan to the company, and when making many other decisions. Problems arise when companies appear to have excessive debt or seem unable to meet existing obligations. For example, if suppliers who normally sell on credit conclude that a customer's debt is excessive, they might refuse to ship new items or may ship only collect on delivery (COD). Also, lenders may refuse to provide new loans when debt is excessive. Customers, worried that the company will not be in business long enough to honor warranties, may prefer to buy elsewhere. Of course, once creditors and customers lose confidence, debt problems can escalate quickly. Because excessive debt levels can cause major problems, analysts and investors pay close attention to debt levels.

Let's look at how Jack in the Box reports its liabilities. Exhibit 9-1 shows its balance sheet presentation of liabilities. As is common practice, Jack in the Box classifies its liabilities as either current or long-term (noncurrent), which helps readers of financial statements interpret the immediacy of the company's obligations. In Chapter 4, we learned that current liabilities are obligations that come due within the next year or within the company's normal operating cycle, whichever is longer. Jack in the Box Company includes the portion of long-term obligations due within the next year ($16 million on September 30, 2012) as a part of the company's current liabilities.

long-term liabilities

Obligations that come due more than 1 year after the balance sheet date.

In contrast, **long-term liabilities** are those that fall due more than 1 year after the balance sheet date. Companies pay some long-term obligations gradually, in yearly or monthly installments. Some obligations are paid in one large sum at maturity. In either case, companies must provide a summary of the repayment schedule over the next 5 years in the footnotes to their financial statements. Jack in the Box shows that repayments are $16 million and $31 million for the next 2 years, but it must repay $371 million in 2015. Knowing that such a large repayment is due will focus the attention of management on strategies for financing the repayment and will focus the attention of analysts on what sources of cash might support the repayment.

In the general ledger, companies keep separate accounts for different liabilities, such as wages, salaries, commissions, interest, and similar items. In the annual report, however, companies often combine these liabilities and show them as a single current liability labeled "accrued liabilities" or "accrued expenses payable." Sometimes they omit the adjective "accrued" and call these liabilities simply "taxes payable," "wages payable," and so on. Some omit the term "payable" and simply use "accrued wages" or "accrued taxes." Jack in the Box combines all accrued liabilities except accounts payable on its balance sheet.

Accountants generally measure liabilities in terms of the amount of cash needed to pay off an obligation or the cash value of products or services to be delivered. For current liabilities, which we examine next, measurement is relatively easy, and the accounting process is straightforward.

EXHIBIT 9-1

Jack in the Box Inc.

Liabilities Section, Consolidated Balance Sheets as of September 30, 2012, and October 2, 2011 (dollars in millions)

	2012	2011
Current liabilities		
Current maturities of long-term debt	$ 16	$ 21
Accounts payable	95	94
Accrued expenses	164	168
Total current liabilities	275	283
Long-term debt, net of current maturities	405	447
Other long-term liabilities	371	291
Deferred income taxes	0	5
Total liabilities	$1,051	$1,026

Accounting for Current Liabilities

We record some current liabilities as a result of a transaction with an outside entity, such as a lender or supplier. We record other liabilities with an adjusting journal entry to acknowledge an obligation arising over time, such as interest or wages. Let's take a look at the accounting procedures for several different types of current liabilities.

▶▶OBJECTIVE 1
Account for current liabilities.

Accounts Payable

Accounts payable are amounts owed to suppliers. Jack in the Box lists them as a separate item under current liabilities, as do more than 90% of major U.S. companies. However, a few companies combine accounts payable with accrued liabilities. Large sums of money flow through the accounts payable system. Therefore, accountants carefully design data processing and internal control systems for these transactions. The objective is to ensure that the company writes checks only for legitimate obligations of the company.

Internal control systems generally require managers to make all payments by check. Why? Prenumbered checks make record keeping easy, and companies can thus trace exactly where their money is going.

Good systems also require source documents, sometimes paper documents but increasingly electronic records, to support all checks. First, there must be a **purchase order**, which specifies the quantities and prices of items ordered. Second is the **receiving report**, which indicates the items received by the company and their condition. Then accountants match the purchase order and receiving report to the **invoice**, a bill from the seller that indicates the number of items shipped, their price, and any additional costs (such as shipping), along with the terms of payment. This process permits periodic, systematic reviews to ensure that the system is working, and it leaves a trail that is easy to follow in case an error arises. Because multiple people are involved, the system is designed to avoid errors or to detect them early before their consequences are serious. Many systems allow checks only to approved vendors and require a high-level employee to approve all additions to the approved-vendor list. Some corporations even generate automatic payments when an approved supplier's computer has provided the proper source information.

purchase order
A source document that specifies the items ordered and the price to be paid by the ordering company.

receiving report
A source document that specifies the items received by the company and the condition of the items.

invoice
A bill from the seller to a buyer indicating the number of items shipped, their price, and any additional costs (such as shipping), along with payment terms, if any.

Notes Payable

When companies take out loans, they generally sign promissory notes. A **promissory note**, often called a note payable, is a written promise to repay the loan principal plus interest at specific future dates. Most promissory notes are payable to banks. Notes that are payable within a year are included with current liabilities; others are classified as long-term liabilities. Many companies also have **commercial paper**, a debt contract issued by prominent companies that borrow directly from investors. The liability created by commercial paper always falls due in 9 months or less, usually in 60 days after issuance, so it is a current liability.

Companies also establish lines of credit. A **line of credit** establishes a predetermined maximum amount that a company can borrow from a given lender without significant additional credit checking or other time-consuming procedures. Lines of credit have no fixed repayment schedules. They can benefit both lenders and borrowers. The lender gets the advantage of not having to run credit checks and prepare extensive paperwork every time the borrower wants a loan. The borrower gets the advantage of having a preset amount of borrowing available. Jack in the Box calls its $400 million line of credit maturing on June 29, 2015, a "revolving credit facility." As of September 30, 2012, Jack in the Box showed $250 million as debt under the line of credit. Part of the $250 million is classified as current and part is classified as a long-term liability based on the repayment schedule.

As another example, Coca-Cola explained the $12,135 million of loans and notes payable on its 2011 balance sheet in footnote 10 in the 10-K as follows:

promissory note
A written promise to repay principal plus interest at specific future dates.

commercial paper
A short-term debt contract issued by prominent companies that borrow directly from investors.

line of credit
An agreement with a bank to provide short-term loans up to some predetermined maximum, without significant additional credit checking or other time-consuming procedures.

Loans and notes payable consist primarily of commercial paper issued in the United States. As of December 31, 2011, and 2010 we had $12,135 million and $7,535 million, respectively, in outstanding commercial paper borrowings.... In addition, we had approximately $5,685 million in lines of credit and other short-term credit facilities as of December 31, 2011, of which $736 million was outstanding.

Coca-Cola borrows more in the commercial paper market than it does from banks because the interest rates are lower in the commercial paper market. However, only companies with the visibility and creditworthiness of Coca-Cola can issue commercial paper.

Accrued Employee Compensation

Accrued liabilities are expenses that a company has recognized on the income statement but not yet paid. Our first example of an accrued liability is obligations to employees for payment of wages. Many companies have a separate current liability account for such items, with a title such as salaries, wages, and commissions payable, but Jack in the Box combines this liability with the other accrued expenses.

In earlier chapters, we assumed that an employee who earned $100 per week received $100 in cash on payday each week. In reality, however, payroll accounting is never that easy. For example, employers must withhold some employee earnings and pay them instead to the government, insurance companies, labor unions, charitable organizations, and so forth. Some of this withholding is legally mandated and some is provided as a service to the employee.

Consider the withholding of income taxes and the employees' portion of Social Security taxes (also called Federal Insurance Contributions Act or FICA taxes). For simplicity, assume that a particular Jack in the Box restaurant has a $100,000 monthly payroll and that the only amounts it withholds are $15,000 for income taxes and $7,000 for Social Security taxes. The withholdings are not additional employer costs. They are part of the employee wages and salaries that the company pays to third parties on behalf of the employees. The journal entry for this $100,000 payroll is as follows:

Compensation expense....................	100,000	
Salaries and wages payable		78,000
Income tax withholding payable		15,000
Social Security withholding payable		7,000

Companies must also deal with payroll taxes and fringe benefits. These are employee-related costs in addition to salaries and wages. Payroll taxes are amounts paid to the government for items such as the employer's portion of Social Security, federal and state unemployment taxes, and workers' compensation taxes. Fringe benefits include employee pensions, life and health insurance, and vacation pay. At many organizations, the fringe benefits exceed 30% of salary. Thus, a person who earns $30,000 per year in salary effectively costs the company $30,000 plus 30% of $30,000, or $39,000. A company must accrue liabilities for each of these costs. If the company has not yet paid them at the balance sheet date, it must include them among its current liabilities.

Note that there are two parts to Social Security taxes. Employers withhold one part from the employees' wages and pay a similar amount themselves. Suppose the Jack in the Box restaurant pays its portion of the FICA tax in an amount equal to the $7,000 withheld from the employee and also pays 10% of gross wages into a retirement account. The following journal entry summarizes the effect on the Jack in the Box financial statements:

Employee benefit expense..................	17,000	
Employer Social Security payable...........		7,000
Pension liability payable		10,000

Income Taxes Payable

In nearly every country in the world, corporations must pay income taxes as a percentage of their earnings. Instead of paying one lump sum at tax time, corporations make periodic installment payments based on their estimated tax for the year. Therefore, the accrued but unpaid liability for income taxes at year-end is generally much smaller than the annual income tax expense.

To illustrate, suppose a corporation has an estimated taxable income of $100 million for the calendar year 20X0. At a 40% tax rate, the company's estimated taxes for the year are $40 million. It would make payments as follows:

	April 15	June 15	September 15	December 15
Estimated taxes (in millions)	$10	$10	$10	$10

The company must file a final income tax return and make a final payment by March 15, 20X1. Suppose the actual taxable income for the year was $110 million instead of the estimated $100 million. Total tax would then be $44 million. On March 15, the corporation must pay the $4 million additional tax on the extra $10 million of taxable income. The accrued liability on December 31, 20X0, would appear in the current liability section of the balance sheet as follows:

Income taxes payable	$4,000,000

For simplicity, the illustration assumed equal quarterly payments. However, the estimated taxable income for a calendar year may change as the year unfolds, and quarterly payments would change to reflect the revised estimate of income. Regardless of how a company changes its estimates, there will almost always be a tax payment or refund due on March 15, and there will be an appropriate accrual adjustment at year-end.

Current Portion of Long-Term Debt

Companies report the portion of their long-term debt that represents payments due within a year as a current liability. As the year progresses and payments are made, this balance changes. Payments reduce the current obligation, but payments that were previously between 12 and 24 months away become current. As new financial statements are prepared, they must include the correct balance in the current portion of long-term debt account. This requires a journal entry to reclassify a noncurrent liability as a current liability. Suppose a company started 2012 with $750,000 in the current portion of long-term debt account. During the year, payments reduce the account to zero. But the passage of time now requires moving to current liability status $1 million in payments due in 2013 that were previously classified as noncurrent. To accomplish this, the company would make the following reclassification journal entry:

Long-term debt	1,000,000	
Current portion of long-term debt		1,000,000

Sales Tax

When retailers collect sales taxes, they do so on behalf of the state or local government. For example, if a customer pays a 7% sales tax on sales of $10,000, the total collected by the company will be ($10,000 + $700), or $10,700. The transaction would affect the balance sheet as follows:

A	=	L	+	SE
+10,700	=	+700		+10,000
[Increase Cash or Accounts Receivable]		[Increase Sales Tax Payable]		[Increase Sales]

The sales shown on the income statement would be $10,000, not $10,700. The sales tax never affects the income statement, as it is neither revenue nor expense to the company. The company is simply serving as a collection agency for the taxing authority. The $700 received for taxes increases the current liability account, Sales Tax Payable, which appears on the balance sheet until the company pays it to the government. The journal entries for the sale and the subsequent payment to the government (without explanations) are as follows:

Cash or accounts receivable	10,700	
Sales		10,000
Sales tax payable		700
Sales tax payable	700	
Cash		700

Returnable Deposits

Occasionally, customers deposit money with suppliers that will be returned in full. Well-known examples of such deposits are those for returnable containers such as soft drink bottles, oil drums, or beer kegs. Also, many landlords require security deposits that are to be returned in full at the end of a lease, as long as the tenants do not damage the property.

Companies that receive deposits record them as a form of payable, although the word "payable" may not be a part of their specific account name. The accounting entries by the recipients of deposits have the following basic pattern:

1. Deposit received	Cash	100,000	
	Deposits Payable		100,000
2. Deposit returned	Deposits Payable	100,000	
	Cash		100,000

The account Deposits Payable is a current liability of the company receiving the deposit.

Unearned Revenue

In Chapter 4, you learned that unearned revenue arises when a company collects cash before it earns the related revenue. These unearned revenues are usually current liabilities because they typically require a company either to deliver the product or service or to make a full refund within a year. Examples of unearned revenues include lease rentals, magazine subscriptions, insurance premiums, airline or theater ticket sales sold in advance, and repair service contracts signed in advance. The journal entries to record $100,000 of prepayments for services and the subsequent performance of those services and appropriate revenue recognition are as follows:

Cash	100,000	
Unearned sales revenue		100,000
To record advance collections from customers		
Unearned sales revenue	100,000	
Sales.		100,000
To record sales revenue when services are performed for customers who paid in advance		

Any portion of collections received in advance that the company will not earn within the year or operating cycle is classified as a noncurrent liability.

Companies use a variety of account titles for revenues collected in advance of being earned. For example, **Time Warner Cable** lists them as "Deferred Revenue and Subscriber-related Liabilities," **The New York Times Company** calls them "Unexpired Subscriptions," and **Monster Worldwide, Inc.**, operator of one of the largest job-search Web sites, simply lists them as "Deferred Revenues."

INTERPRETING FINANCIAL STATEMENTS

Consider a basketball team that sells season tickets for $100 each, collected at the beginning of the season. The accounting period is a calendar year, but typically 40% of the games occur in November and December, whereas the other 60% occur in January and February. The team sells all of its 15,000 seats to season ticket holders for the 20X0–20X1 season. Indicate how these facts would affect the income statement and the balance sheet for 20X0 and the income statement for 20X1.

Answer

In 20X0, the team would collect ($100 × 15,000) = $1,500,000. However, it would earn only 40% of those collections, or $600,000, in 20X0, so the 20X0 income statement would show only $600,000 of revenue. The 20X0 balance sheet would show a current liability of (60% × $1,500,000) = $900,000, labeled Revenue Received in Advance, Unearned Revenue, or Deferred Revenue. This $900,000 is deferred, and the team will recognize it as income on the 20X1 income statement when it earns the revenue by playing the remaining games.

Product Warranties

warranty
A promise to repair or replace a defective product, usually for problems that arise within a specified period of time or usage.

Some current liabilities are difficult to measure precisely. For example, when a company sells a product, it often provides a product **warranty**, which is a promise to repair or replace a defective product, usually for problems that arise within a specific period of time or usage. For example, an auto company might provide a warranty on the drive train of a car for 5 years or 50,000 miles.

This product warranty creates a liability, but the exact amount of the liability will not be known until the end of the warranty period.

If warranty obligations are material, a company must accrue them when it sells the products because the obligation arises at the time of sale, not when the customer receives actual repair services. For example, **Ford Motor Co.** described its warranty accounting in the notes in the 2011 10-K as follows: "Estimates are used to account for certain items such as marketing accruals, warranty costs, employee benefit programs, etc. Estimates are based on historical experience.... Estimated warranty costs are accrued for at the time the vehicle is sold to a dealer."

Like Ford, other companies estimate their warranty expense at the time of sale based on past experience with replacing or remedying defective products. Although estimates should be close, they are rarely precisely correct. Assume that a company has $20 million in sales and has found that warranty expense averages about 3% of sales. The accounting entry related to the warranty obligation resulting from the $20 million in sales is as follows:

Warranty expense	600,000	
Liability for warranties (or some similar title).		600,000
To record the estimated liability for warranties arising from current sales; the provision is 3% of current sales of $20 million, or $600,000		

When a customer makes a valid $1,000 warranty claim and receives services, the company records an entry such as the following:

Liability for warranties	1,000	
Cash, accounts payable, accrued wages payable, and similar accounts		1,000
To record the acquisition of supplies, outside services, and employee services to satisfy claims for repairs		

If the estimate for warranty expense is accurate, the entries for all claims will total about $600,000. If additional information makes it clear that the claims will differ from $600,000, we adjust the liability accordingly. For example, suppose we get information that quality problems are causing excessive warranty claims so we expect total claims to be $700,000 rather than the original estimate of $600,000. We then need to add $100,000 to the Liability for Warranties account and charge an additional $100,000 to Warranty Expense.

Companies reporting under IFRS include warranty liabilities in a category called provisions. **Provisions** are liabilities of uncertain timing or amount. They are obligations arising from a past event that are likely to be honored and for which the company can make a reliable estimate of the amount. For example, the Italian auto manufacturer **Fiat** included the following in its "Other Provisions" footnote 27 to its 2011 financial statements (in millions of euros):

provisions
Liabilities of uncertain timing or amount.

	At 31 December 2010	Charge	Utilization	Release to Income	Other Changes	At 31 December 2011
Warranty Provisions	€970	€1,421	€(1,135)	€(202)	€2,476	€3,530

The *charge* is the 2011 warranty expense, *utilization* is the amount paid for warranty claims in 2011, and *release to income* is amounts arising from changes in warranty estimates during 2011. If there had been no "*other changes*," warranty obligations would have increased by (€1,421 million – €1,135 million – €202 million) = €84 million. However, because Fiat gained a controlling interest in Chrysler during 2011, under IFRS accounting standards it had to include Chrysler's warranty obligations on its consolidated financial statement. Including Chrysler accounts for most of the increase in Fiat's warranty provisions. Issues involving the consolidation of multiple companies are addressed in detail in Chapter 11.

This concludes our discussion of current liabilities. Now let's proceed to long-term liabilities.

Long-Term Liabilities

▶▶ **OBJECTIVE 2**

Measure and account for long-term liabilities.

Long-term liabilities are obligations that are not due for at least a year. How do lenders and borrowers measure the value of such obligations? They usually use the time value of money, which refers to the fact that a dollar you expect to pay or receive in the future is not worth as much as a dollar you have today. If you are not comfortable with the concept and computations involving the time value of money, especially present values, it is important to study Appendix 9 carefully. As you will see, accounting has embraced present value approaches in valuing bonds, leases, pensions, and other long-term liabilities. We start with an analysis of bonds and notes.

Corporate Bonds

bonds

Formal certificates of debt that include (1) a promise to pay interest in cash at a specified annual rate, plus (2) a promise to pay the principal of the bond at a specific maturity date.

Many corporations have heavy demands for borrowed capital, so they often borrow from the general public by issuing corporate bonds in the financial markets. **Bonds** are formal certificates of debt that include (1) a promise to pay interest in cash at a specified annual rate (often called the **nominal interest rate**, **contractual rate**, **coupon rate**, or **stated rate**), plus (2) a promise to pay the principal (often called the **face amount, face value**, or par value) of the bond at a specific maturity date. Bonds generally pay interest every 6 months. Fundamentally, bonds are individual promissory notes issued to many lenders.

nominal interest rate (contractual rate, coupon rate, stated rate)

A contractual rate of interest paid on bonds.

We often call bonds **negotiable** financial instruments or securities because one lender can transfer them to another. Sometimes companies use bonds to borrow directly from a financial institution such as a pension plan or insurance company. We call such bonds **private placements** because the general public does not hold or trade them. Private placements provide more than half the capital borrowed by corporations in the United States. They are popular because they are generally easy to arrange and they allow the lender to evaluate the creditworthiness of the borrower very carefully and directly. Borrowers and lenders can tailor specific features of the bond to meet their special needs.

face amount (face value)

The loan principal or the amount that a borrower promises to repay at a specific maturity date.

Specific Bond Characteristics

negotiable

Legal financial contracts that can be transferred from one lender to another.

There are many ways that issuers can tailor bonds to their needs. In this section, we discuss just some of the provisions companies can put into bonds.

private placements

Bonds issued by corporations when money is borrowed directly from a financial institution. The general public does not hold or trade such bonds.

PREFERENCE IN LIQUIDATION—MORTGAGE BONDS AND SUBORDINATED DEBENTURES Bond provisions help determine bondholders' priority for claims when a company is in **liquidation**, which means converting assets to cash and paying off outside claims. For example, **mortgage bonds** are secured by the pledge of specific property. In case of default, mortgage bondholders have the first right to proceeds from the sale of the pledged property.

liquidation

Converting assets to cash and paying off outside claims.

In contrast, debenture holders have a lower priority claim to recover their loan amount. A **debenture** is a debt security with a general claim against the company's total assets, instead of a specific claim against a particular asset. At liquidation, a debenture bondholder shares the available assets with other general creditors, such as trade creditors who seek to recover their accounts payable claims, with one exception. If debenture bonds are **subordinated**, the bondholders have claims against only the assets that remain after satisfying the claims of other, more senior general creditors.

mortgage bond

A form of long-term debt that is secured by the pledge of specific property.

To clarify these ideas, suppose a liquidating company has a single asset, a building, and sells it for $115,000 cash. The company's liabilities total $160,000 as follows:

debenture

A debt security with a general claim against all assets, instead of a specific claim against particular assets.

Liabilities	
Accounts payable	$ 50,000
First mortgage bonds	80,000
Subordinated bonds	30,000
Total liabilities	$160,000

subordinated debentures

Debt securities whose holders have claims against only the assets that remain after satisfying the claims of other, more senior general creditors.

The mortgage bondholders, having a direct claim on the building, will receive their full $80,000. The trade creditors (the company's suppliers, to whom the company owes money) will receive the remaining $35,000 for their $50,000 claim ($.70 on the dollar). The subordinated debenture claimants will get what is left over—nothing.

Instead, suppose the $30,000 of bonds were not subordinated. The bondholders would have a general claim on assets equivalent to that of the account payable claims held by the company's suppliers. The company would then use the $35,000 of cash remaining after paying $80,000 to the mortgage holders to settle the claims of the suppliers and bondholders proportionally as follows:

Liabilities		Payments	
Accounts payable	$ 50,000	(5/8 × 35,000) =	21,875
First mortgage bonds	80,000		80,000
Unsubordinated bonds	30,000	(3/8 × 35,000) =	13,125
	$160,000		$115,000

In order of priority, we have the mortgage bond, then unsubordinated debentures and accounts payable, and finally any subordinated debenture. Because interest rates are higher for riskier bonds, mortgage bonds would have the lowest interest rate and unsubordinated debentures would have the next lowest. Subordinated debentures would carry the highest interest rate.

PROTECTION OF BONDHOLDERS—BOND COVENANTS Many bonds contain **protective covenants** or simply **covenants**. Covenants generally restrict the ability of the borrower to take certain actions or give the lender the ability to force early payment under certain conditions. For example, a covenant might require immediate repayment of the loan if the borrower misses an interest payment, it may restrict sale of particular properties, or it may restrict the payment of dividends unless the borrower has generated additional earnings since issuing the debt. In general, covenants protect the bondholders' interests. Based on the concept that less risky bonds pay lower interest, covenants can make the bond safer and therefore lower the interest rate.

Covenants that give bondholders the right to demand repayment of the loan principal may require the borrower to maintain a sufficient level of retained earnings (which can serve to limit dividend payments), a sufficient ratio of stockholders' equity to debt (which can limit new debt issuance), or sufficient levels of cash and accounts receivable. Covenants might also prohibit the issuance of additional debt without first repaying the existing debt.

For example, in footnote 7 of the 2011 10-K, Jack in the Box indicated that its borrowings are subject to "a number of customary covenants under our credit facility, including limitations on additional borrowings, acquisitions, loans to franchisees, capital expenditures, lease commitments, stock repurchases, dividend payments, and requirements to maintain certain financial ratios." Lenders generally tailor bond covenants to specific borrowers and situations. In general, the more covenants there are, the more restricted the borrower is, and the more attractive the arrangement is to the lender. You can find more information on bond covenants in the Business First box on page 396.

CALLABLE, SINKING FUND, AND CONVERTIBLE BONDS Additional bond provisions can make bonds more or less attractive. Some bonds are **callable**, which means that the issuer has the option to redeem them before maturity. Typically, the redemption price exceeds the face value of the bond by an amount referred to as a **call premium**. To illustrate, consider a $1,000 bond issued in 2014 with a 2034 maturity date that is callable any time after 2024 for a price of $1,050. The call premium is $50 per $1,000 bond. Callable bonds are good for the borrower because the borrower has a choice to redeem the bond early or wait to maturity. However, it creates uncertainty for the lender, who might therefore require a higher interest rate on callable bonds. The call premium compensates the lender for the risk of unexpected early redemption.

Sinking fund bonds require the issuer to make annual payments into a sinking fund. A **sinking fund** is a pool of cash or securities set aside solely for meeting certain obligations. It is an asset generally listed under "other assets." The sinking fund helps assure the bondholders that the company will have cash to repay the bond's principal at maturity.

Convertible bonds are bonds that may, at the holder's option, be exchanged for other securities, usually for a preset number of shares of the issuing company's common stock. Under U.S. GAAP, companies list convertible bonds with debt. In contrast, under IFRS convertible bonds have both debt and equity components: (1) The value of the debt component is the present value of interest and principal payments at the market rate of interest at issue for bonds of a similar risk level but without the conversion feature, and (2) the equity component is the excess that investors

protective covenant (covenant)
A provision in a bond that restricts the ability of the borrower to take certain actions or gives the lender the ability to force early payment under certain conditions.

callable bonds
Bonds subject to redemption before maturity at the option of the issuer.

call premium
The amount by which the redemption price of a callable bond exceeds face value.

sinking fund bonds
Bonds that require the issuer to make annual payments to a sinking fund.

sinking fund
A pool of cash or securities set aside for meeting certain obligations.

convertible bonds
Bonds that may, at the holder's option, be exchanged for other securities, usually for a preset number of shares of the issuing company's common stock.

BUSINESS FIRST

BOND COVENANTS

A bond is a promise to pay interest and to repay principal at specific times. However, investors have learned that to control the risk that a borrower will be unable to pay in the future, it is useful to limit the borrower's freedom in a number of ways by writing restrictions into the bond contract. These covenants take many forms and may limit the ability to pay dividends or to borrow additional amounts, or they may require maintenance of certain ratios, such as debt-to-equity, current ratio, and so on.

For such covenants to be powerful, they typically require the borrower to provide the lender with audited financial statements and require the auditor to provide assurance that no violations of the covenants have occurred. If a company violates a covenant, the debt typically comes due immediately. Although the lender may not require repayment in full when this happens, the default provides the opportunity for the lender to renegotiate the terms of the loan. That may involve earlier repayment, a higher interest rate, issuance of common stock, or some other remedy.

Covenants tend to evolve in response to observed risks. It is currently common for bonds to have a "change of control" feature, which means that when the ownership of the equity (common stock) of a company changes hands such that a new entity controls 50% or more of the stock, the bonds become immediately due and payable. This feature might be called the RJR provision because it became common after Kohlberg, Kravis, Roberts & Co. (KKR), a leveraged buyout firm, acquired R.J. Reynolds Tobacco Company

(RJR) for $31.4 billion in a hostile takeover in 1989. RJR had various bonds outstanding when KKR acquired it. In the acquisition, KKR issued many additional bonds that were equal to RJR's existing bonds in seniority. In the process, the new company became very debt heavy, and investors worried that the merged company would not be able to repay the existing bondholders. Existing bonds fell approximately 14% in value on the day KKR and RJR announced the takeover. Thereafter, many lenders inserted a change-of-control feature into their bonds to ensure they had the right to get their full face (maturity) value back whenever a takeover occurred.

The availability of credit and the terms required vary greatly over time and between grade A borrowers and very risky borrowers. In 2006 interest rates were low and some lenders, seeking higher returns, were willing to offer "covenant-lite" loans, knowing that by requiring fewer protective covenants they could earn higher interest rates. In the credit crisis of 2008–2009 these conditions changed sharply, and credit markets were much less receptive to risky debt and weak covenants. The price of risky debt fell sharply and market rates rose to 20%. By 2012 the environment changed again, interest rates on risky corporate debt dropped to the vicinity of 7% and lenders again offered some covenant-lite loans in search of higher interest rates.

Sources: Slate.com, "Covenant-lite," Tuesday, February 22, 2011; Kohlberg, Kravis, Roberts & Co. Web site (www.kkr.com).

pay above the initial value of the debt. By increasing the attractiveness of the bond to lenders, sinking fund covenants and conversion features lower the interest rate the issuer must pay. An equivalent statement is that these features increase the amount that the investor would pay for the bond at any specific coupon rate of interest.

Bond Interest Rates, Bond Discount, and Bond Premium

market rate
The rate available on investments in similar bonds at a moment in time.

bond discount (discount on bonds)
The excess of face amount over the proceeds on issuance of a bond.

bond premium (premium on bonds)
The excess of the proceeds from issuance over the face amount of a bond.

The interest rate is a key factor for all bonds, but there are multiple interest rates that define the cash flows the bond provides and also how much the bond is worth. Recall that the nominal interest rate or coupon rate determines the amount of each semiannual interest payment. In contrast, the **market rate** is the rate available on investments in similar bonds at a moment in time. It is the amount of interest that investors require to purchase the bond. If the market rate differs from the coupon rate, the issuing company will not receive the face amount when it issues the bond. When the market rate exceeds the coupon rate, the bond sells at a discount—the **bond discount** (or **discount on bonds**) is the amount by which the face amount exceeds the proceeds from the bond. When the coupon rate exceeds the market rate, the bond sells at a premium—the **bond premium** (or **premium on bonds**) is the excess of the proceeds over the face amount.

Note that premiums and discounts do not reflect the creditworthiness of the issuer. Instead, they simply reflect differences between the coupon rate and the market rate. These differences often result from changes in market interest rates between the time a company sets the terms of the bond and when it actually issues the bond. Note further that the coupon rate is generally fixed for the entire life of the bond. In contrast, market rates of interest associated with a company's bonds change regularly as general credit conditions change and as the specific riskiness of the issuer changes.

Consider a $1,000 2-year bond with a coupon rate of 10% that pays interest every 6 months until maturity and pays the face amount at maturity. Exhibit 9-2 shows the bond's market values at three different market interest rates. It calculates the present value of the annuity of interest payments and adds that to the present value of the repayment of face value at maturity. Note the following:

1. Although we express the quoted bond interest rates as annual rates, companies generally pay bond interest semiannually. Thus, a 10% bond really pays 5% interest each semiannual period. A 2-year bond has 4 periods, a 10-year bond has 20 periods, and so on.
2. The higher the market rate of interest, the lower the present value of the bond payments.
3. When the market interest rate equals the coupon rate of 10%, the bond is worth the face value of $1,000. We say such a bond is issued at par.
4. When the market interest rate is 12%, which exceeds the 10% coupon rate, the bond sells at a *discount*. The company receives $965.35, $34.65 less than the par value of $1,000.
5. When the market interest rate is 8%, which is less than the 10% coupon rate, the bond sells at a *premium*. The company receives $1,036.30, $36.30 more than the par value of $1,000.

The initial bond discount or bond premium depends on the market interest rate at the time the company issues the bond. After issuance, market interest rates may vary and the market value of the bond will move up or down as interest rates change. Bondholders can sell their bonds in the marketplace, and the price they will receive depends on the current market rate for similar

EXHIBIT 9-2

Computation of Market Value of $1,000 Face Value, 10% Coupon, 2-Year Bond *(in dollars)*

	Present Value Factor	Total Present Value	Sketch of Cash Flows by Period				
			0	1	2	3	4
Valuation at market rate of 10% per year, or 5% per half-year							
Principal, 4-Period line, Table 9A-2 (.8227 × $1,000) = $822.70	.8227	822.70					1,000
Interest, 4-Period line, Table 9A-3 (3.5460 × $50) = $177.30	3.5460	177.30		50	50	50	50
Total: Bond sells at Par		1,000.00					
Valuation at market rate of 12% per year, or 6% per half-year							
Principal	.7921	792.10					1,000
Interest	3.4651	173.25		50	50	50	50
Total: Bond sells at a Discount		965.35					
Valuation at market rate of 8% per year, or 4% per half-year							
Principal	.8548	854.80					1,000
Interest	3.6299	181.50		50	50	50	50
Total: Bond sells at a Premium		1,036.30					

yield to maturity

The interest rate at which all contractual cash flows for interest and principal have a present value equal to the current price of the bond.

bonds, not the market rate in effect at the time of issue. We call the current market rate for a bond the **yield to maturity**. It is the interest rate at which all contractual cash flows for interest and principal have a present value equal to the current price of the bond. The price of the bond at any point in time is what investors are willing to pay for this specific promise of interest and principal payments from this specific issuer after considering other bond offerings from other issuers.

What determines the market interest rate or the yield to maturity? There are many factors, including general economic conditions, industry conditions, risks of the use of the proceeds, and specific features of the bonds. However, we can summarize these in three basic components: the real interest rate, the inflation premium, and the firm-specific risk component.

real interest rate

The return that investors demand because they are delaying their consumption.

inflation premium

The extra interest that investors require because the general price level may increase between now and the time they receive their money.

firm-specific risk

The risk that the firm will not repay the loan or will not pay the interest on time.

1. The **real interest rate** is the return that investors demand because they are delaying their consumption. If you could have a dollar now or later, now is generally better. The real rate of interest historically has been in the 3% range.
2. The **inflation premium** is the extra interest that investors require because the general price level may increase between now and the time they receive their money. This is an expectation, and peoples' expectations vary widely. In some countries inflation rates have exceeded 100% per year. In the United States and most developed countries recent inflation rates have been closer to 3% per year or less.
3. Finally, there is the **firm-specific risk**, referring to the risk that the firm will not repay the loan or will not pay the interest on time. In either event, the investor could lose everything and at a minimum will have to pursue legal avenues to collect the money due. The amount associated with firm-specific risk ranges widely from 1% or 2% for firms with very good credit ratings to 10% or more for firms facing financial distress.

The first two components reflect general economic conditions. The third is company-specific and creates different rates for different companies. Creditors look carefully at the riskiness of the companies in which they invest. For example, compare a $1,000 bond issued by the U.S. government with $1,000 bonds issued by **Verizon** and **Rite Aid**. In 2012, the U.S. government bond had a yield to maturity of just below 2% per year for a 10-year bond and just over 3% for a 30-year bond. As the time to maturity becomes longer, investors generally require a higher interest rate. At the same time, similar Verizon bonds with about 10 years to maturity paid 3%, and the Rite Aid bonds paid 9%. From this we can conclude that Verizon bonds are riskier than U.S. government bonds, and Rite Aid bonds are even more risky. These rates are low by historical standards. *Kiplinger Personal Finance* in September 2011 reminded us that sometimes (but rarely) you get a higher dividend return on common stock than the yield on the corporation's debt. They cited Verizon as an example because the common stock yielded 5.5% while one of its bonds yielded about 3%.

Assessing the Riskiness of Bonds

Although assessing the riskiness of bonds is essential, many creditors cannot spend the time to do an in-depth analysis of each bond offering. Thus, commercial services have developed evaluation systems to rate bonds according to their creditworthiness. **Mergent, Inc.** (formerly **Moody's**) and **Standard & Poor's** (S&P), a division of **McGraw-Hill**, are perhaps the best known.

Higher rated bonds are safer, and companies with better ratings generally pay lower interest rates. For example, examine the following average interest rates for bonds in each rating category. The rates, for June of each year, are from the Mergent Bond Record. Aaa is the highest rating and Baa is the lowest rating shown.

Rating	Aaa	Aa	A	Baa
2011[*]	5.02	5.26	5.52	6.10
2008	5.68	6.11	6.43	7.07
2003	4.97	5.72	5.92	6.19
1998	6.53	6.78	6.88	7.13
1993	7.33	7.51	7.74	8.07
1988	9.86	10.13	10.42	11.00

*The 2011 data are from December 2011.

Note that rates increase from left to right as ratings decrease. Investors will accept a lower yield for debt issued by the least risky companies. In addition, rates in every category fell steadily between 1988 and 2003. However, all climbed in 2008, reflecting a market-wide increase in risk. Rates fell again in the next few years, reflecting actions by the government to support the economic recovery by creating a low interest rate environment.

To assign the ratings, Mergent often interviews company management in addition to analyzing financial data such as sales levels, profitability, and the debt level. In the United States, debt obligations are legally enforceable, and many examples exist where creditors have forced a company to liquidate to pay interest or to repay principal. This is what caused the collapse of Enron, Borders, Lehman Brothers, and many other companies in recent years.

Financial analysts must adapt to the realities facing specific companies. In Japan, for example, debt ratios tend to be much higher than they are in the United States. This difference partly reflects banking practices. Japanese banks lend very large sums to the biggest and most creditworthy corporations. Although the transaction has the form of debt, it tends to be part of a long-term relationship between bank and customer. The banks end up with long-term rights that look somewhat like the rights of a U.S. shareholder.

Issuing and Trading Bonds

A syndicate of investment bankers called **underwriters** generally manages the issuance of a corporation's bonds. The syndicate typically buys the entire issue of bonds from the corporation, thus guaranteeing that the company will obtain the funds it needs. The syndicate then sells the bonds to the general investing public. The investment banker who manages the underwriting syndicate often helps the company set the terms of the bond contract—terms such as the time to maturity, interest payment dates, coupon interest rates, and size of the bond issue. After a company initially issues bonds, the bondholders can often trade the bonds in markets or on exchanges such as the NYSE. You can find corporate bond prices in newspaper business sections and financial Web sites. For example, on April 20, 2012, *Barron's* included the following information on General Electric Capital (GE) and Goldman Sachs Group bonds:

underwriters
A group of investment bankers that buys an entire bond or stock issue from a corporation and then sells the securities to the general investing public.

	Coupon	Maturity	Last Price	Yield
General Electric	2.300	April 27, 2017	100.304	2.235
Goldman Sachs	5.750	Jan. 24, 2022	114.826	5.113

Bonds typically have a face value of $1,000, but we usually express their values in terms of percentages of face value. GE's 2.3% coupon bonds maturing in 2017 sell for $1,003.04 (100.304% of $1,000) and have a yield to maturity of 2.235%. The Goldman bonds have a higher yield, 5.113%, indicating greater risk. Both bonds have coupon rates greater than the yield rate, so the price of each is greater than $1,000.

Bond Accounting

Let's look next at how we account for bonds. The body of a company's balance sheet usually summarizes the various types of bonds and other long-term debt on one line. However, most companies show details about bonds in the footnotes. In Exhibit 9-1, Jack in the Box showed $405 million of long-term debt, net of current maturities, on its balance sheet as of September 30, 2012. Footnote 7 provided more details, showing two different borrowings, each carrying an interest rate of 2.5% over LIBOR. **LIBOR** is the London Interbank Offering Rate, a fluctuating interest rate for loans between banks in London. LIBOR provides an observable basis for use in loan contracts that specify changing interest rates over time. Jack in the Box's long-term debt also included a capital lease obligation that we will discuss shortly.

Some other companies show more details. For example, in 2011 Coca-Cola had an extensive footnote describing borrowing activity. Coca-Cola issued $2.9 billion of new long-term debt in 2011 and used over half of the $2.9 billion to reduce the level of commercial paper outstanding. Even so, the year ended with $12.2 billion of current liabilities related to commercial paper. Royal Dutch Shell reported $30 billion of long-term debt in 2011 out of a total of $37 billion of total debt. Debt was 13% of total capital as noted in the four pages of footnotes providing details

▶▶**OBJECTIVE 3**
Account for bond issues over their entire life.

LIBOR
London Interbank Offering Rate, a fluctuating interest rate for loans between banks in London.

and discussing strategies. As the company indicated in its 2011 10-K, "A key measure of Shell's capital structure management is the proportion of debt to equity."

To understand what these accounts mean, we look at how a company records the issuance of bonds, the periodic interest payments, and the retirement of bonds.

Bonds Issued at Par

Suppose that on December 31, 20X0, Delta Company issued 10,000 2-year, 10% debentures, at par. That means the company received exactly the amount of the bond principal or face value, and the market rate is equal to the coupon rate of 10%. Because bonds typically have a principal or face value of $1,000 each, the total issue is for (10,000 × $1,000) = $10 million. (Notice that this bond is identical to those valued in Exhibit 9-2 on page 397.) The interest expense equals the amount of the interest payments, (5% × $10 million) = $500,000 each 6 months for a total of $2,000,000 over the four semiannual periods. Exhibit 9-3 shows how the bonds affect Delta's balance sheet equation throughout their life, assuming the company does not retire them before maturity.

The journal entries for the issue, interest, and maturity of the bonds are as follows:

1.	Cash		10,000,000	
		Bonds payable		10,000,000
	To record proceeds upon issuance of 10% bonds maturing on December 31, 20X2			
2–5.	Interest expense		500,000	
		Cash		500,000
	To record four payments of interest, one each 6-month period			
6.	Bonds payable		10,000,000	
		Cash		10,000,000
	To record payment of maturity value of bonds and their retirement			

Entry 1 records the issuance of the bonds, entries 2–5 are the four identical interest payments, and entry 6 is the repayment of principal at maturity.

The issuer's balance sheets at June 30, 20X1, December 31, 20X1, and June 30, 20X2 (after the respective semiannual interest payments) all show the following:

Bonds payable, 10% due December 31, 20X2	$10,000,000

Bonds Issued at a Discount

Now suppose Delta issues its 10,000 bonds when annual market interest rates are 12%, which is a 6% rate for each 6-month period. From Exhibit 9-2 we can see that Delta receives $965.35 for each bond, for total proceeds of (10,000 × $965.35) = $9,653,500. Therefore, the company recognizes a discount of ($10,000,000 − $9,653,500) = $346,500 at issuance. The discount results

EXHIBIT 9-3

Bond Transactions: Issued at Par

($ in thousands)

	A	=	L	+	SE	
	Cash	=	**Bonds Payable**	+	**Retained Earnings**	
Issuer's records						
1. Issuance	+10,000	=	+10,000			
2–5. Semiannual interest (repeated twice a year for 2 years)	−500	=			−500	⎡Increase Interest Expense⎤
6. Maturity value (final payment)	−10,000	=	−10,000			

from the fact that the market rate exceeds the coupon rate and the company has use of only $9,653,500, not $10,000,000. The journal entry at issue is as follows:

Cash	9,653,500	
Discount on bonds payable	346,500	
Bonds payable		10,000,000

The discount on bonds payable is a contra liability account. The bonds payable account usually shows the face amount, and we deduct the discount amount from the face value to get the amount shown on the balance sheet, often referred to as the net carrying amount, the net liability, or simply the book value:

Issuer's Balance Sheet	December 31, 20X0
Bonds payable, 10%, due December 31, 20X2	$10,000,000
Deduct: Discount on bonds payable	346,500
Net liability (book value)	$ 9,653,500

For bonds issued at a discount, interest takes two forms—semiannual cash outlays of (5% × $10 million) = $500,000 plus an "extra" lump-sum cash payment of $346,500 at maturity (total payment of $10,000,000 at maturity when Delta actually borrowed only $9,653,500). For the issuer, the $346,500 is another cost of using the borrowed funds over the four semiannual periods. For the investor, the $346,500 represents extra interest revenue in addition to the coupon payments. The issuer should spread the extra $346,500 over all four periods, not simply charge it to expense at maturity. We call the spreading of the discount over the life of the bonds **discount amortization**.

How much of the $346,500 should Delta amortize each semiannual period? To determine this, companies use **effective interest amortization**, also called the **compound interest method**. Under this method, each period bears a total interest expense equal to the net liability (the face amount less unamortized discount) at the beginning of the period multiplied by the market interest rate in effect when the debt was issued. The difference between the total interest expense and the interest payment is the amortization of the discount.

Exhibit 9-4 shows the effective interest amortization schedule for our example. The interest expense each period is the market rate of interest at issue times the net liability at the

discount amortization
The spreading of bond discount over the life of the bonds as interest expense.

effective interest amortization (compound interest method)
A method of amortization of bond discounts and premiums whereby each period bears a total interest expense equal to the net liability at the beginning of the period multiplied by the market interest rate in effect when the debt was issued.

EXHIBIT 9-4
Effective Interest Amortization of Bond Discount

	(1) Beginning Net Liability	(2) Interest Expense* @ 6%**	(3) Nominal Interest† @ 5%	(4) Discount Amortized (2) – (3)	(5) Ending Unamortized Discount	(6) Ending Net Liability $10,000,000 – (5)
For 6 Months Ended						
12/31/X0	—	—	—	—	$346,500	$ 9,653,500
6/30/X1	$9,653,500	$ 579,207	$ 500,000	$ 79,207	267,293†	9,732,707
12/31/X1	9,732,707	583,959	500,000	83,959	183,334	9,816,666
6/30/X2	9,816,666	588,997	500,000	88,997	94,337	9,905,663
12/31/X2	9,905,663	594,337	500,000	94,337	0	$10,000,000§
		$2,346,500	$2,000,000	$346,500		

*Market interest rate when issued times beginning net liability, column (1).

**To avoid rounding errors, an unrounded actual effective rate slightly under 6% was used. The table used to calculate the proceeds of the issue has too few significant digits to calculate the exact present value of a number as large as $10 million. The more exact issue price would be $9,653,489.

†Nominal (coupon interest) rate times par value (face value) for 6 months.

†($346,500 – $79,207) = $267,293; ($267,293 – $83,959) = $183,334; etc.

§This is the face amount that Delta will repay on December 31, 20X2, when the bond matures.

beginning of the period (see column 2). Notice that interest expense increases each semi-annual period as the net liability increases until the net liability equals the maturity value of $10,000,000. The cash payment, column 3, is a constant $500,000 based on the nominal (coupon) interest rate, and the difference between the interest expense and the cash payment is the amount of discount amortized, shown in column 4. The amortization decreases the unamortized discount, column 5, which then increases the net liability, causing the interest expense to increase each period.

The balance sheet disclosure of the bond payable is the ending net liability, calculated as the difference between the face value and the unamortized discount. The balance sheet values for each six months, after payment of the interest due on that date, are as follows:

Delta's Balance Sheets	December 31, 20X0	June 30, 20X1	December 31, 20X1	June 30, 20X2	December 31, 20X2*
Bonds payable, 10%, due 12/31/X2	$10,000,000	$10,000,000	$10,000,000	$10,000,000	$10,000,000
Deduct: Unamortized discount	346,500	267,293	183,334	94,337	—
Net liability	$ 9,653,500	$ 9,732,707	$ 9,816,666	$ 9,905,663	$10,000,000

*Before payment at maturity.

Exhibit 9-5 shows the balance sheet equation for the effective interest method of amortizing the bond discount. The journal entries follow:

12/31/X0	1.	Cash	9,653,500	
		Discount on bonds payable	346,500	
		Bonds payable		10,000,000
6/30/X1	2.	Interest expense	579,207	
		Discount on bonds payable		79,207
		Cash		500,000
12/31/X1	3.	Interest expense	583,959	
		Discount on bonds payable		83,959
		Cash		500,000
6/30/X2	4.	Interest expense	588,997	
		Discount on bonds payable		88,997
		Cash		500,000
12/31/X2	5.	Interest expense	594,337	
		Discount on bonds payable		94,337
		Cash		500,000
12/31/X2	6.	Bonds payable	10,000,000	
		Cash		10,000,000

Bonds Issued at a Premium

Accounting for bonds issued at a premium is not difficult after you have mastered bond discounts. The key idea remains that the interest expense is the market rate of interest at issue times the net liability (book value of the bond). Bond premiums differ from bond discounts in the following ways:

1. The cash proceeds *exceed* the face amount.
2. We *add* the amount of the account Premium on Bonds Payable to the face amount of the bond to determine the net liability reported in the balance sheet.
3. Amortization of the bond premium causes interest expense to be *less than* the cash payment for interest.

To illustrate, suppose Delta issued the 10,000 bonds when annual market interest rates were 8% and semiannual rates were 4%. From Exhibit 9-2 on page 397, we can see that Delta receives

EXHIBIT 9-5

Delta Company

Balance Sheet Equation Effects of Effective Interest Amortization of Bond Discount (rounded to thousands of dollars)

	A	=	L			+	SE
	Cash	=	**Bonds Payable**	+	**Discount on Bonds Payable**	+	**Retained Earnings**
1. Issuance	+ 9,654	=	+10,000		−346 ⎡Increase⎢Discount⎦		
Semiannual interest for 6 months ended:							
2. 6/30/X1	−500	=			+79		−579
3. 12/31/X1	−500	=			+84 ⎡Decrease		−584 ⎡Increase
4. 6/30/X2	−500	=			+89 ⎢Discount		−589 ⎢Interest
5. 12/31/X2	−500	=			+94		−594 ⎦Expense
6. Maturity value, 12/31/X2 (final payment)	−10,000	=	−10,000		0		
Bond-related totals	− 2,346	=	+ 0		+ 0	+	−2,346

$1,036.30 for each bond, for total proceeds of $(10,000 \times \$1,036.30) = \$10,363,000$. Exhibit 9-6 shows how to apply the effective interest method to the bond premium. The key concept remains the same as that for amortization of a bond discount: The interest expense (column 2) equals the net liability each period (column 1) multiplied by the market interest rate in effect when the bond was issued. Balance sheets show the net liability calculated as the face amount plus unamortized premium.

EXHIBIT 9-6

Effective Interest Amortization of Bond Premium

For 6 Months Ended	(1) Beginning Net Liability	(2) Interest Expense* @ 4%**	(3) Nominal Interest† @ 5%	(4) Premium Amortized (3) – (2)	(5) Ending Unamortized Premium	(6) Ending Net Liability $10,000,000 + (5)
12/31/X0	—	—	—	—	$363,000	$10,363,000
6/30/X1	$10,363,000	$ 414,517	$ 500,000	$ 85,483	277,517‡	10,277,517
12/31/X1	10,277,517	411,098	500,000	88,902	188,615	10,188,615
6/30/X2	10,188,615	407,542	500,000	92,458	96,157	10,096,157
12/31/X2	10,096,157	403,843	500,000	96,157	0	10,000,000
		$1,637,000	$2,000,000	$363,000		

*Market interest rate when issued times beginning net liability, column (1).
**To avoid rounding errors, an unrounded actual effective rate slightly under 4% was used.
†Nominal (coupon interest) rate times par value (face value) for 6 months.
‡($363,000 – $85,483) = $277,517; ($277,517 – $88,902) = $188,615; etc.

Delta's Balance Sheets	December 31, 20X0	June 30, 20X1	December 31, 20X1	June 30, 20X2	December 31, 20X2*
Bonds payable, 10% due 12/31/X2	$10,000,000	$10,000,000	$10,000,000	$10,000,000	$10,000,000
Add: Premium on bonds payable	363,000	277,517	188,615	96,157	0
Net liability	$10,363,000	$10,277,517	$10,188,615	$10,096,157	$10,000,000

*Before payment at maturity.

Exhibit 9-7 shows the effects on the balance sheet equation, and the journal entries are as follows:

12/31/X0	1.	Cash	10,363,000	
		Premium on bonds payable		363,000
		Bonds payable		10,000,000
6/30/X1	2.	Interest expense.....................	414,517	
		Premium on bonds payable	85,483	
		Cash		500,000
12/31/X1	3.	Interest expense.....................	411,098	
		Premium on bonds payable	88,902	
		Cash		500,000
6/30/X2	4.	Interest expense.....................	407,542	
		Premium on bonds payable	92,458	
		Cash		500,000
12/31/X2	5.	Interest expense.....................	403,843	
		Premium on bonds payable	96,157	
		Cash		500,000
12/31/X2	6.	Bonds payable	10,000,000	
		Cash		10,000,000

Companies frequently issue bonds between interest payment dates. When this occurs, the company adjusts the bond price for the interest that is already accrued as of the issue date. For example, if a $1,000 bond that will pay interest of $20 on June 30 is issued on March 31, the issuer would collect $10 of interest from the buyer on March 31 and then pay $20 3 months later.

Cash Flow Statement Effects

The issuance of bonds is a financing activity, so companies show the cash received as a cash inflow from financing activities on the statement of cash flows. Payments at maturity are also financing cash outflows. Semiannual interest payments are operating cash outflows

EXHIBIT 9-7

Delta Company

Balance Sheet Equation Effects of Effective Interest Amortization of Bond Premium
(rounded to thousands of dollars)

	A	=	L		+	SE
	Cash	**=**	**Bonds Payable**	**+ Premium on Bonds Payable**	**+**	**Retained Earnings**
Issuer's records						
1. Issuance	+10,363	=	+10,000	+363 ⎡Increase⎤		
				⎣Premium⎦		
Semiannual interest 6 months ended						
2. 6/30/X1	−500	=		−85		−415
3. 12/31/X1	−500	=		−89 ⎡Decrease⎤		−411 ⎡Increase⎤
4. 6/30/X2	−500	=		−93 ⎣Premium⎦		−407 ⎢Interest⎥
5. 12/31/X2	−500	=		−96		−404 ⎣Expense⎦
6. Maturity value, 12/31/X2 (final payment)	−10,000	=	−10,000	0		
Bond-related totals	− 1,637	=	+ 0	+ 0	+	−1,637

under U.S. GAAP, as are all interest payments. Most companies using IFRS also classify the interest payments as operating activities, although they are allowed to list them with financing activities.

The amortization of bond discounts and premiums does not affect cash. Thus, it does not appear in the operating section of a direct method statement of cash flows. However, suppose a company uses the indirect method. The amortization of bond discount would be like depreciation, a noncash expense. You would add the amortization of bond discount to (or deduct the amortization of bond premium from) net income to get cash flow from operating activities. Such an adjustment in the indirect method of reporting cash flows from operations is necessary to adjust interest expense as reported on the income statement to the actual cash payment for interest.

Summary Problem for Your Review

PROBLEM

Suppose that on December 31, 2013, **Procter & Gamble** issued $12 million of 10-year, 10% debentures. Assume that the annual market interest rate at issuance was 14%.

1. Compute the proceeds from issuing the debentures.
2. Prepare an analysis of the following items: (a) issuance of the debentures, (b) first two semiannual interest payments, and (c) payment of the maturity value. Use the balance sheet equation (similar to the presentation in Exhibit 9-5, page 403). Round to the nearest thousand dollars. Use a bond discount account.
3. Prepare journal entries for the items in requirement 2. Use a bond discount account.

SOLUTION

1. Because the market interest rate exceeds the nominal rate, the proceeds will be less than the face amount. Proceeds are the present value (PV) of the 20 interest payments of $600,000 and the $12 million maturity value at 7% per semiannual period:

PV of interest payments: (10.5940 × $600,000)	$6,356,400
PV of maturity value: (.2584 × $12,000,000)	3,100,800
Total proceeds	$9,457,200

2. See Exhibit 9-8.

EXHIBIT 9-8

Analysis of Procter & Gamble's Bond Transactions

(in thousands of dollars)

	A	=	L			+	SE	
	Cash	=	Bonds Payable	+	Discount on Bonds Payable	+	Retained Earnings	
Procter & Gamble's records								
(a) Issuance	+9,457		+12,000		−2,543 [Increase			
(b) Semiannual interest					Discount]			
6 Months ended								
6/30/14	−600				+62 [Decrease		−662* [Increase	
12/31/14	−600				+66 [Discount]		−666*	Interest
(c) Maturity value								[Expense]
(final payment)	−12,000		−12,000					
Bond-related totals†	−14,543		0		0		−14,543	

*(7% × $9,457) = $662; [7% × ($9,457 + $62)] = $666.

†Totals after payment at maturity and all 20 entries for discount amortization and interest payments are made.

3. 12/31/13:	Cash	9,457,200	
	Discount on bonds payable	2,542,800	
	Bonds payable		12,000,000
6/30/14:	Interest expense	662,004*	
	Discount on bonds payable		62,004
	Cash		600,000
	*($9,457,200 × .07) = $622,004		
12/31/14:	Interest expense	666,344*	
	Discount on bonds payable		66,344
	Cash		600,000
	*[($9,457,200 + $62,004) × .07] = $666,344		
Maturity:	Bonds payable	12,000,000	
	Cash		12,000,000

Early Extinguishment

early extinguishment

When a company chooses to redeem its own bonds before maturity.

You have seen how companies account for bonds they hold until maturity. However, some companies redeem or pay off their bonds earlier, either by purchases on the open market or by exercising their rights to redeem callable bonds. We call it an **early extinguishment** when a company chooses to redeem its own bonds before maturity. When a company extinguishes debt early, it recognizes the difference between the cash paid and the net liability (face value less unamortized discount or plus unamortized premium) as a gain or loss.

Consider the bonds Delta issued at a discount (see Exhibit 9-4, page 401). Suppose Delta purchases all its bonds on the open market for $960 per $1,000 of face value on December 31, 20X1 (after paying all interest payments and recording amortization for 20X1):

Net liability:		
Face or par value	$10,000,000	
Deduct: Unamortized discount on bonds*	183,334	$ 9,816,666
Cash required, 96% of $10,000,000		9,600,000
Difference, gain on early extinguishment of debt		$ 216,666

*See Exhibit 9-4. Of the original $346,500 discount, Delta has amortized ($79,207 + $83,959) = $163,166, leaving $183,334 of the discount unamortized.

Exhibit 9-9 presents an analysis of the transaction. Delta would show the $216,666 gain on extinguishment of debt on its income statement. The journal entry on December 31, 20X1, is as follows:

Bond payable	10,000,000	
Discount on bonds payable		183,334
Gain on early extinguishment of debt		216,666
Cash		9,600,000
To record open market acquisition of entire issue of 10% bonds at 96% of par		

Noninterest-Bearing Notes and Bonds

zero coupon bond

A bond or note that pays no cash interest payments during its life.

Some notes and bonds do not provide semiannual interest payments. Instead, they simply pay a lump sum at a specified date. For example, consider **zero coupon bonds**. These bonds provide no cash interest payments during their life. The name, zero coupon, is completely descriptive. To

EXHIBIT 9-9

Delta Company

Analysis of Early Extinguishment of Debt on Issuer's Records (rounded to thousands of dollars)

	A	=	L		+	SE
	Cash	=	**Bonds Payable** +	**Discount on Bonds Payable**	+	**Retained Earnings**
Redemption, December 31, 20X1	–9,600	=	–10,000	+183 ⌈Decrease⌊Discount⌋	+217	⌈Gain on Early⌊Extinguishment⌋

call such bonds noninterest-bearing, however, is misleading. Investors demand interest revenue. Otherwise, why would they invest? Therefore, companies sell zero coupon bonds and notes for less than the face or maturity value. The investor determines a bond's market value at the issuance date by calculating the present value of its maturity value, using the market rate of interest for bonds having similar terms and risks. For accounting purposes, the issuer amortizes the discount as interest expense over the life of the bond and the investor recognizes interest revenue in a similar manner.

Instead of collecting semiannual or other periodic payments, banks often discount both long- and short-term notes when making loans. Consider a 2-year, "noninterest-bearing," $10,000 face value note issued by Gamma Company on December 31, 20X0, when annual market interest rates were 10% (5% semiannually). In exchange for a promise to pay $10,000 on December 31, 20X2, the bank provides Gamma with cash equal to the present value of the $10,000 payment:

$$\text{PV of \$1.00 from Table 9A-2, 5\% column, 4-period row} = 0.8227$$
$$\text{PV of \$10,000 note} = (\$10,000 \times .8227) = \$8,227$$

The note requires no specific interest payments. However, there is **implicit interest** (or **imputed interest**), which is a form of interest expense that is not explicitly stated in a loan agreement. The imputed interest amount is based on an **imputed interest rate**, which is the market rate that equates the proceeds of the loan with the present value of the loan payments.

In this example, the $10,000 payment on December 31, 20X2, will consist of $8,227 repayment of principal and ($10,000 – $8,227) = $1,773 of imputed interest. At issue, Gamma shows the note on its balance sheet as follows:

implicit interest (imputed interest)
An interest expense that is not explicitly stated in a loan agreement.

imputed interest rate
The market interest rate that equates the proceeds from a loan with the present value of the loan payments.

Note payable, due December 31, 20X2	$10,000
Deduct: Discount on note payable	1,773
Net liability	$ 8,227

Exhibit 9-10 shows how Gamma recognizes interest expense for each semiannual period.

Each amortization of the discount decreases the discount account and increases the net liability. The appropriate journal entries follow:

12/31/X0	Cash	8,227	
	Discount on note payable	1,773	
	Note payable		10,000
6/30/X1	Interest expense.	411	
	Discount on note payable		411
12/31/X1	Interest expense.	432	
	Discount on note payable		432
6/30/X2	Interest expense.	454	
	Discount on note payable		454
12/31/X2	Interest expense.	476	
	Discount on note payable		476
	Note payable	10,000	
	Cash.		10,000

EXHIBIT 9-10

Analysis of Transactions of Borrower, Discounted Notes

	A	=	L	+		+	SE
	Cash	=	Notes Payable	+	Discount on Notes Payable	+	Retained Earnings
Proceeds of loan	+8,227	=	+10,000	–1,773	⎡Increase⎤		
Semiannual amortization					⎣Discount⎦		
6 Months ended:							
6/30/X1		=		+411			–411
12/31/X1		=		+432	⎡Decrease⎤		–432	⎡Increase⎤
6/30/X2		=		+454	⎣Discount⎦		–454	Interest
12/31/X2		=		+476			–476	⎣Expense⎦
Payment of note	–10,000	=	–10,000				
Note-related totals	– 1,773	=	+ 0	+ 0		+	–1,773

Accounting for Leases

▶▶OBJECTIVE 4

Value and account for long-term lease obligations.

Included among its long-term liabilities, Jack in the Box has a long-term liability called Capital Lease Obligations. Why do we treat some leases as liabilities, but not others? Because sometimes a company signs a lease that gives it most of the privileges and obligations of ownership. It uses the lease as the method of financing the asset, so its payment obligations are similar to those of a company that issues debt and buys the asset. Other times a company signs a lease that simply gives it permission to use the asset for a specific period of time but does not convey most of the privileges and obligations of ownership. This type of lease qualifies as a simple rental expense.

Leasing is a big business. Companies can acquire almost any asset imaginable via a lease contract. A **lease** is a contract whereby a **lessor** (owner) grants the use of property to a **lessee** in exchange for regular payments. Legal title to the property remains with the lessor, but the lessee uses the property as it would use property it owns. Our discussion focuses on leasing from the lessee's point of view. From an accounting perspective, whether we record a lease as a liability depends on whether it is a capital (finance) lease or an operating lease.

Operating and Capital (Finance) Leases

Accountants categorize leases into two categories, capital and operating. **Capital leases** (called **finance leases** under IFRS) transfer most of the risks and benefits of ownership to the lessee. Many such leases are similar to installment sales in which the purchaser pays the price of an item over time along with interest payments. Accountants require companies to record such leased items as if the lessee had borrowed the money and purchased the leased asset. In other words, the economic substance of the transaction prevails over the legal form. The property is accounted for as an asset, and the obligation to pay for it is treated as a liability.

The lease structure determines whether a lessee treats a lease as an operating or capital lease for accounting purposes. Under U.S. GAAP, a lease is a capital lease if it meets one or more of the following conditions:

1. The lessor transfers ownership of the asset to the lessee by the end of the lease term.
2. The lease contains a **bargain purchase option**—that is, a provision that states that the lessee can purchase the asset from the lessor at the end of the lease for substantially less than the asset's expected fair value.
3. The lease term equals or exceeds 75% of the estimated economic life of the property.
4. At the start of the lease term, the present value of minimum lease payments is at least 90% of the property's fair value.

lease

A contract whereby an owner (lessor) grants the use of property to a second party (lessee) in exchange for regular payments.

lessor

The owner of property who grants usage rights to the lessee.

lessee

The party who has the right to use leased property and makes lease payments to the lessor.

capital lease (finance lease)

A lease that transfers most risks and benefits of ownership to the lessee.

bargain purchase option

A provision that states that the lessee can purchase the asset from the lessor at the end of the lease for substantially less than the asset's expected fair value.

BUSINESS FIRST

ON THE HORIZON

On July 21, 2012, the IASB and the FASB continued their discussion of new lease accounting standards. Over the last 2 years the primary focus has been to extend accounting treatment similar to the treatment of financing leases to all leases that extend beyond 1 year. This would lead to additional recognition of Capital Lease Assets and Capital Lease Obligations on corporate balance sheets. An exposure draft was issued in August 2010 and extensive public debate followed. In response the boards have agreed to re-expose a revised standard.

The new proposal clarifies a number of implementation issues regarding what leases are and are not covered and how both lessees and lessors are treated. Leases of less than 1 year are not covered by the proposed standard nor are leases providing the right to explore for or use natural resources or leases of biological assets. U.S. GAAP would exclude timber leases and IFRS would exclude service concession arrangements.

Another change is to create an alternative approach to the reporting, measurement, and timing of expense recognition for certain leases, notably leases of property including land or buildings or both. Specifically, the expense recognition would occur on a straight-line basis over the life of the asset regardless of the timing of lease payments. Lease expense would be disclosed as one amount in the income statement rather than separating the amortization of the asset and using the effective interest rate method for the liability.

The boards are working through some final technical items before issuing the revised exposure draft (ED). Given that 2 years have passed since the issuance of the prior ED, a final standard is likely to still be years away from implementation.

Leases reported under IFRS have similar but less detailed requirements to qualify as a finance (capital) lease. Essentially, the lease must cover substantially all of the asset's life and the present value of the lease payments must be approximately equal to the asset's fair value. The FASB and IASB are reconsidering how to classify leases, and the current discussion suggests that in the future companies may be required to account for all leases extending beyond 1 year as capital leases (see the Business First box above).

All other leases are **operating leases**. Examples are an office rented by the month and a car rented by the day. Companies account for operating leases as ordinary rent expenses. Operating leases are not recognized as liabilities on the balance sheet.

Managers cannot classify a lease however they wish—the lease either meets the requirements of a capital (finance) lease or it does not. When there are bright-line rules that determine the accounting treatment of a transaction, managers may choose to structure the transaction to achieve the accounting result they prefer. For leases this could mean writing the lease so it does not meet any of the criteria of a capital lease and therefore does not appear as a liability on the balance sheet.

Consider a simple example to see how the accounting differs for operating and capital leases. Suppose the Bestick Company can acquire a truck with a useful life of 4 years and no residual value under either of the following options:

operating lease
Leases that should not be recognized as liabilities on the balance sheet, but should be accounted for by the lessee as ordinary rent expenses.

Buy Outright	or	Capital (Finance) Lease
Borrow $50,000 cash and agree to repay it in four equal installments at 12% interest compounded annually. Use the $50,000 to purchase the truck.		Rental cost of $16,462 per year, payable at the end of each of 4 years; ownership of the truck transfers to Bestick at the end of the lease.

There is no basic difference between the outright purchase option, financed with debt, and an irrevocable (noncancelable) 4-year lease. The Bestick Company uses the asset for its entire useful life and must pay for repairs, property taxes, and other operating costs under either plan. Thus, the lease is a capital (finance) lease.

Companies make most lease payments at the start of each period, but to ease our computations we assume that each payment of $16,462 will occur at the end of the year. To make the comparison between capital leasing and purchasing, we need to calculate payments on the $50,000 loan under the purchase option:

$$
\begin{aligned}
\text{Let } X &= \text{loan payment} \\
\$50,000 &= \text{PV of annuity of } \$X \text{ per year for 4 years at } 12\% \\
\$50,000 &= 3.0373 \times X \\
X &= \$50,000 \div 3.0373 \\
X &= \$16,462 \text{ per year}
\end{aligned}
$$

Note that this loan payment is exactly equal to the lease payment. Thus, from Bestick's perspective, both the outright purchase and the capital lease create an obligation for four $16,462 payments that have a present value of $50,000.

Suppose GAAP allowed Bestick to treat this lease contract as an operating lease. At the end of each year the journal entry would be as follows:

Rent expense	16,462	
Cash		16,462
To record lease payment		

No leasehold asset or lease liability would appear on the balance sheet.

Now suppose Bestick accounts for the lease as a capital lease as both U.S. GAAP and IFRS require for the example described. Then it must recognize both a leasehold asset and a lease liability on its balance sheet valued at the present value of future lease payments, initially $50,000 in this illustration. The signing of the capital lease requires the following journal entry:

Truck leasehold	50,000	
Capital lease liability, current		10,462
Capital lease liability, long-term		39,538
To record lease creation		

Note that the $50,000 liability has two components. The current liability is the portion of the first-year payment that reduces the liability, calculated as the difference between the payment due in the first year and the first year's interest: [$16,462 − (12% × 50,000)] = $10,462. The remainder of the liability ($50,000 − $10,462 = $39,538), is a long-term liability.

Bestick then amortizes the asset over 4 years. Straight-line amortization, the most common method, is ($50,000 ÷ 4) = $12,500 annually.

The yearly journal entries for the leasehold amortization expense are as follows:

Leasehold amortization expense	12,500	
Truck leasehold		12,500

In addition, Bestick must record the annual lease payment. Each lease payment consists of interest expense plus an amount that reduces the outstanding liability. We use the effective interest method, as Exhibit 9-11 demonstrates. The yearly journal entries for lease payments are as follows:

	Year 1		Year 2		Year 3		Year 4	
Interest expense	6,000		4,745		3,339		1,764	
Lease liability	10,462		11,717		13,123		14,698	
Cash		16,462		16,462		16,462		16,462

EXHIBIT 9-11

Bestick Company
Schedule of Capital Lease Payments

End of Year	(1) Capital Lease Liability at Beginning of Year	(2) Interest Expense at 12% per Year	(3) Cash for Capital Lease Payment	(4) Reduction in Lease Liability (3) – (2)	(5) Capital Lease Liability at End of Year (1) – (4)
1	$50,000	$6,000	$16,462	$10,462	$39,538
2	39,538	4,745	16,462	11,717	27,821
3	27,821	3,339	16,462	13,123	14,698
4	14,698	1,764	16,462	14,698	0

The January 1, 2012, balance sheet of Continental Airlines illustrates presentation of leased assets and the associated liabilities:

(in millions)	January 1, 2012
Assets	
Capital leases—Other property and equipment	$170
Less: Accumulated amortization	17
	$153
Liabilities	
Current maturities of capital leases	$ 3
Long-term obligations under capital leases	193
Total obligations under capital leases	$196

INTERPRETING FINANCIAL STATEMENTS

Explain why the $153 million net asset value of capital leases for Continental Airlines on January 1, 2012, is not the same as the $196 million of obligations under capital leases.

Answer

When a company initiates a lease, the amounts of the capital-lease asset and the capital-lease obligation are identical. Their values first diverge and then converge over time because of the accounting process. Companies typically amortize assets using the straight-line basis. In contrast, they reduce the liability each period using the effective interest method. Under this method, each lease payment includes the payment of interest and the reduction of principal. Because interest is largest in the early years of the lease, reductions in the principal of the lease obligation start off small. Hence, we expect the amount of liability to exceed that of the asset in most cases. The difference will grow in the early years of the lease and decrease during the later years as illustrated in the next section.

Note 15 of the 10-K provides additional detail about Continental's leasing. It provides a table that shows total payments of $6.5 billion over the lives of the leases for aircraft acquired under operating leases and $5.5 billion for facilities and other assets acquired under operating leases. In contrast, the payments under capital leases are $.6 billion. Operating leases are some twenty times larger. The changes to U.S. GAAP and IFRS currently under consideration would require all longer term leases to be capitalized. If these changes are implemented, Continental would reflect much higher liabilities on its balance sheet.

Differences in Income Statements

The Bestick Company example allows us to compare the accounting treatment of operating and capital (finance) leases. But remember that the specifics of the contract will actually dictate which treatment is appropriate under U.S. GAAP. Exhibit 9-12 summarizes the major differences. The cumulative expenses are the same, $65,848, but the timing differs. Capital leases recognize larger expenses than operating leases in the early years and smaller expenses in later years. Therefore, immediate reported income is lower for capital leases. The longer the lease, the more pronounced the differences.

EXHIBIT 9-12

Bestick Company

Comparison of Annual Expenses: Operating Versus Capital Leases

	Operating Lease Method	Capital Lease Method			Differences	
Year	(a) Lease Payment*	(b) Amortization of Asset†	(c) Interest Expense‡	(d) Total Expense (b) + (c)	(e) Difference in Pretax Income (a) – (d)	(f) Cumulative Difference in Pretax Income
1	$16,462	$12,500	$ 6,000	$18,500	$(2,038)	$(2,038)
2	16,462	12,500	4,745	17,245	(783)	(2,821)
3	16,462	12,500	3,339	15,839	623	(2,198)
4	16,462	12,500	1,764	14,264	2,198	0
Cumulative expenses	$65,848	$50,000	$15,848	$65,848	$ 0	

*Rent expense for the year under the operating-lease method.
†($50,000 ÷ 4) = $12,500.
‡From Exhibit 9-11.

An operating lease affects the income statement as rent expense, which is the amount of the lease payment. A capital lease affects the income statement as amortization (of the asset) plus interest expense (on the liability).

Differences in Balance Sheets and Cash Flow Statements

The difference between operating and capital (finance) leases on the balance sheet is straightforward. At the inception of the lease, operating leases do not affect the balance sheet, whereas capital leases create both an asset and a liability. Note that this difference is critical to the calculation of the return on assets (ROA) and also to ratios such as the debt-to-equity ratio introduced later in this chapter.

The effects on the statement of cash flows are less obvious. Operating leases affect only cash flows from operations. All cash payments for operating leases are operating cash outflows. In contrast, capital (finance) leases affect both operating and financing cash flows. The cash lease payment has two components: interest expense and reduction of the lease liability. For Bestick Company, the first year's lease payment of $16,462 includes an interest expense of $6,000 and a reduction in the lease liability of $10,462, as you can see in Exhibit 9-11. The $6,000 interest expense is an operating cash outflow under U.S. GAAP. The lease reduction of $10,462 is a financing cash outflow. In the second year, the operating cash outflow is $4,745, and the financing cash outflow is $11,717. Notice that the operating cash outflow systematically declines throughout the life of the lease, whereas the financing cash outflow grows. The only difference under IFRS is that the cash flow for interest payments can be classified as a financing item.

Summary Problem for Your Review

PROBLEM

Suppose that on December 31, 20X0, the Sanchez Company enters into a lease to use a machine for 3 years with payments at the end of each year. Lease payments for the 3-year term of the lease are as follows:

Year 1	$ 40,000
Year 2	40,000
Year 3	40,000
Total lease payments	$120,000

Sanchez treats the lease as a capital (finance) lease and uses an interest rate of 10%.

1. Calculate the amount Sanchez should record as the carrying value of the capital-lease asset and the capital-lease liability as of the beginning of the lease on 12/31/X0.
2. How will Sanchez record the first year's payment?
3. How will the lease affect the first year's income statement?
4. How will the lease affect the first year's statement of cash flows?
5. How does the capital lease result differ from the result if the lease was classified as an operating lease?

SOLUTION

1. The present value of a 3-year annuity of $40,000 per year discounted at 10% will be the initial value of the asset and the liability. From Table 9A-3, the present value factor is 2.4869.

$$(2.4869 \times \$40,000) = \$99,476$$

2. The first year's payment is $40,000, part of which is interest and part of which is principal repayment. The interest portion is $(.10 \times \$99,476) = \$9,948$. The journal entry is as follows:

Interest expense	9,948	
Capital lease liability	30,052	
Cash		40,000

3. The first year's income statement will show an expense of $9,948 for interest. It will also show amortization expense on the capital-lease asset, assuming straight-line amortization, of $(\$99,476 \div 3) = \$33,159$.
4. The total cash outflow for the first year is $40,000. The interest portion, $9,948, is an operating cash outflow. The reduction of the lease obligation of $30,052 is a financing cash outflow.
5. If this was an operating lease, no asset or liability would be recorded. In each year of the lease, the full $40,000 payment would be rent expense. On the statement of cash flow, the entire $40,000 rent payment would be classified as an operating cash flow. For a capital lease, an asset and a liability would appear on the balance sheet, and in each year the expense would be the sum of the interest expense and the amortization expense. For the first year, this would be $(\$9,948 + \$33,159) = \$43,107$. The statement of cash flows would show the interest payment as operating and the repayment of principal as financing.

Other Long-Term Liabilities, Including Pensions and Deferred Taxes

We next explore some other long-term liabilities that commonly appear on balance sheets—pensions, other postretirement benefits, deferred taxes, restructuring liabilities, and contingent liabilities.

Pensions and Other Postretirement Benefits

Many U.S. companies provide benefits for retired employees. Accountants classify these benefits in two categories: **pensions**, which are payments to former employees after they retire, and **other postretirement benefits**, which primarily consist of health insurance but also include any other benefits. Let's first consider pensions.

PENSIONS Pensions are divided into defined contribution plans and defined benefit plans. In a **defined contribution pension plan** the employer makes annual contributions directly into a fund belonging to the employee according to a plan document. The contributions are invested by a plan trustee. Accounting for a defined contribution pension plan, such as a 401k plan, is straightforward. Suppose that a company records salaries and wages for employees of $100,000

> **▶▶ OBJECTIVE 5**
> Evaluate pensions and other postretirement benefits.

pensions
Payments to former employees after they retire.

other postretirement benefits
Non-pension benefits provided to retired workers, such as life and health insurance.

defined contribution pension plan

A pension plan where the employer makes annual contributions directly into a fund belonging to the employee, according to a plan document. The employee's retirement benefit depends on the amount in the fund at retirement.

in a given month, and that employees pay 8% of their salaries and wages into a pension fund, and the company matches that amount. The journal entry for the company would be:

Wages and salaries expense	100,000	
Pension expense.	8,000	
Cash—payments to employees		92,000
Cash—payments to pension fund.		16,000

The employee's retirement pay will depend on the amount in the fund at the time he or she retires. If the fund has performed well, the employee's payments are higher than if the fund has performed poorly. The company has no obligation beyond its initial contribution. In essence, all the risks and rewards associated with fund performance rest with the employee. The expense to the company is the annual payment it makes into the plan, typically a percentage of the employee's income.

defined benefit pension plan

A pension plan where the employer guarantees the employee a specific amount of retirement pay based on factors such as pay earned during final years and total years of service.

In contrast, in a **defined benefit pension plan** the employer guarantees the employee a specific amount of retirement pay, normally a certain percentage of their last few years of pay, with the percentage depending on the employee's total years of service. These plans create a liability for the company. Why? Because such a plan guarantees employees a specific amount of retirement pay. The company is obligated to make these pension payments after the employee retires. The obligation is the present value of the expected future pension payments to existing retired employees and to future retirees. This present value depends on many assumptions: when current employees will retire, what their salaries will be in their final years of employment, how long they will live and collect benefits, and the interest rate used to calculate present values.

Under current U.S. GAAP, companies report the total value of this pension obligation in footnotes to their financial statements. Previously, companies could simply promise benefits to employees and accrue pension liabilities, without setting assets aside. However, if a company then went bankrupt, workers and retirees were left without pension benefits.

To protect workers, U.S. tax laws now provide incentives for companies to make payments into a pension fund that is separate from the company's assets and controlled by a trustee. The money in this fund is available only to pay future pensions. Footnotes to the financial statements reveal the fair value of the assets in the pension fund. If the fair value of the assets is less than the present value of a company's pension obligations, a company lists a net liability on its balance sheet for the excess obligation. If the fair value of the assets is greater than the present value of a company's pension obligations, a company lists a net asset on the balance sheet.

Jack in the Box's footnotes disclose that it has both defined contribution and defined benefit plans. However, note 11 of the 2012 10-K revealed that "In fiscal 2010, the Board of Directors approved changes to our qualified plan whereby participants no longer accrue benefits effective December 31, 2015, and the plan was closed to new and rehired employees effective January 1, 2011." Pension fund assets on September 30, 2012, were $312 million but the present value of pension fund liabilities was $466 million. Because pension obligations were greater than the invested assets, Jack in the Box included a ($466 million – $312 million) = $154 million liability among its other long-term liabilities on the balance sheet.

How do companies account for pension expenses year by year? To apply the matching principle, they must charge the pension expense to the years an employee works. Each year that an employee works generates an additional claim to retirement pay. The additional claim is an expense of the year the employee works, not the year the company distributes the retirement pay.

The defined benefit pension obligation in a given year increases by the amount of the service cost, the present value of the expected future pension benefits earned by current employees that year, plus the interest cost, the increased present value of payments owed to current and former employees because the payments are now 1 year closer. It decreases by the amount of payments to retirees because the company owed these amounts at the beginning of the year but no longer owes them at the end of the year. Finally, the obligation can change by an amount that depends primarily on actuarial assumptions and plan changes that are beyond the scope of this text.

At the same time, pension assets increase (decrease) by the amount of gains (losses) on the assets during the year, decrease by cash payments to retirees, and increase by any contributions from the company or participants.

Consider Jack in the Box's experience in the year ended September 30, 2012. Its net pension liability started at $93 million and ended at $154 million. Why did it increase by $61 million?

First, the company's net pension obligation increased by $112 million because of a $134 million increase in future obligations less $22 million in benefits paid in fiscal 2011. The pension assets increased by almost $51 million because of a $53 million increase in market value, a contribution by the company to the pension fund of $19 million, and cash payments to retirees of $22 million. Because the obligation increased by $112 million and the assets increased by $51 million, the net liability increased by $61 million.

OTHER POSTRETIREMENT BENEFITS Companies may give their retirees health-care benefits that can be expensive. Accounting for the expense of health insurance and similar postretirement benefits is similar to accounting for pensions. The key difference is that most companies do not set aside specific assets on behalf of employees. This is due to the fact that, unlike pensions, U.S. federal tax law does not give any incentive for setting assets aside to fund health-care benefits for retirees. As a result, companies record the full present value of expected payments for other postretirement benefits as a liability. Companies recognize any increase in the liability as a current expense.

Jack in the Box's liability for other postretirement benefits is included in other liabilities on the balance sheet and explained in the footnotes. It was $29.6 million on October 2, 2011, the end of the prior year. During fiscal 2012, the company paid $1.5 million for health insurance and other benefits to retirees, incurred other postretirement benefit expenses of $2.6 million, and had an actuarial loss (which caused an increase in expected future payments and therefore an increase in the liability) of $6.6 million, causing the postretirement benefits liability to increase by ($2.6 million + $6.6 million − $1.5 million) = $7.7 million. Thus, the liability on September 30, 2012, was $37.3 million. The summary journal entries to record the $2.6 million expense, the $1.5 million payment, and the $6.6 million actuarial loss are as follows:

Other postretirement benefits expense	2,600,000	
Postretirement benefits liability		2,600,000
Postretirement benefits liability	1,500,000	
Cash		1,500,000
Actuarial loss on postretirement benefits (expense).	6,600,000	
Postretirement benefits liability		6,600,000

Liabilities for pensions and other postretirement benefits can be very large. For example, in early 2009 **Ford Motor Company** had an excess of pension liabilities over funded assets of nearly $12 billion and other postretirement benefits liabilities of more than $16 billion. These combined liabilities represented about 13% of Ford's total assets. In December 2009 Ford fully funded a Trust to pay many of these obligations as a result of an agreement with the United Auto Workers, a major labor union representing Ford employees. Nonetheless, as of December 31, 2011, Ford still had an excess of pension liabilities over funded assets of $9 billion, and the shortfall had increased by $2.7 billion during the year.

It is important to recognize that the funding status of a pension plan can change very quickly. Because most companies invest their pension assets in the stock and bond markets, the value of the pension assets fluctuates with the market. **Medtronic**, the Minneapolis-based medical technology company, had net assets of $133 million because pension assets exceeded pension obligations in 2008. However, because of the drop in stock prices in 2008–2009, its 2010 balance sheet included a $299 million liability for underfunded benefit plans. By April 29, 2011, due to good returns and large funding contribution, the liability had been reduced to $156 million. However, it soared again to a $486 million liability at April 27, 2012.

Internationally, practice concerning pensions and other postretirement benefits varies widely. For example, many countries provide the majority of retirement income through individual savings. Others do so through tax-supported government programs similar to the U.S. Social Security Administration. In these cases actual company pensions are rare, so there is nothing to report.

Deferred Taxes

We have previously seen that delaying the payment of taxes from the time a company earns income to when it pays cash to the U.S. government leads to short-term taxes payable. Another source of difference between income tax expense and income tax payments arises because a nation's tax rules differ from the GAAP requirements for financial reporting. Some differences between GAAP reporting and tax laws cause companies to record income tax expenses

▶▶ **OBJECTIVE 6**

Interpret deferred tax assets and liabilities; and restructuring and contingent liabilities

deferred income tax liability

An obligation arising because the difference between GAAP reporting and tax laws requires companies to record income tax expense on the income statement before they are obligated to make payment to the tax authorities.

deferred income tax asset

An asset arising because the difference between GAAP reporting and tax laws requires companies to pay taxes to the tax authorities before they record income tax expense on the income statement.

permanent differences

Differences between net income and taxable income that arise because some revenue or expense items are recognized for either tax or financial reporting purposes, but not for both.

temporary differences

Differences between net income and taxable income that arise because some revenue and expense items are recognized at different times for tax purposes than for financial reporting purposes.

tax rate

The percentage of taxable income paid to the government.

before they pay the taxes. This creates a **deferred income tax liability**. Other differences cause companies to pay taxes before they record the related income for financial reporting, which creates **deferred income tax assets**. For example, Jack in the Box reported income tax expense of $30.6 million in 2012. However, Jack in the Box was currently obligated to pay $37.2 million in income taxes, including $6.6 million of taxes that had previously been deferred.

The differences between income tax expense and income taxes actually paid arise because accountants designed GAAP to provide useful information to investors, whereas governments write the tax code to generate tax revenue and to provide specific incentives to companies. Revenue recognition and expense recognition rules for tax purposes can differ from GAAP rules on two dimensions: (1) whether to recognize an item (permanent differences), and (2) when to recognize it (temporary differences). **Permanent differences** arise when a company recognizes a revenue or expense item for either tax or financial reporting purposes but not for both. **Temporary differences** arise when a company recognizes some revenue or expense item at a different time for tax purposes than for financial reporting purposes.

To save their companies money, good managers work to pay the least amount of income tax at the latest possible moment permitted within the law. As a result, they delay the reporting of taxable revenue as long as possible, while deducting tax-deductible expense items as quickly as possible. Corporations pay taxes to the government as follows:

$$\text{Taxes paid or payable} = \text{Income tax rate} \times (\text{Taxable revenue} - \text{Tax-deductible expenses})$$

The **tax rate** is the percentage of taxable income paid to the government. U.S. corporate tax rates in 2012 ranged from 15% on incomes of less than $50,000 to 35% on incomes of more than $335,000. Many states also levy an income tax, with tax rates varying from state to state. To simplify our illustrations, we generally assume a flat total tax rate of 40%. This is a reasonable approximation of the combination of the federal 35% rate plus a state tax rate. We next provide illustrations of a permanent difference (municipal bond interest) and a temporary difference (depreciation).

PERMANENT DIFFERENCES To consider permanent differences, suppose a company in New York state owns a bond issued by the city of New York and periodically receives interest on it. For financial reporting, the company reports this interest revenue on the income statement. Under U.S. federal law, bondholders do not pay taxes on interest received from municipal bonds issued by cities, states, and towns. Similarly, a New York State corporation pays no state income tax on interest received from New York State bond issuers. Therefore, the interest revenue will never appear on the company's federal or state tax return.

Dealing with this permanent difference is straightforward. We include the interest revenue for financial reporting, but we never recognize an income tax expense related to this revenue on our financial statements, and we never have to pay income tax on the revenue received. Therefore, permanent differences do not create deferred taxes.

Suppose the New York state company has a 40% combined federal and state tax rate and reports $100 of pretax income, of which $20 is revenue from nontaxable municipal bonds. It will pay taxes on only ($100 − $20) = $80 of income, resulting in taxes of ($80 × 40%) = $32. As a percentage of pretax income, the tax rate appears to be ($32 ÷ $100) = 32%, rather than the 40% nominal tax rate.

TEMPORARY DIFFERENCES Let's consider a common source of temporary differences, depreciation. Many companies use accelerated depreciation for tax purposes (MACRS) and straight-line depreciation for financial reporting. Suppose Webster Company earns $40,000 per year before deducting depreciation and taxes, and pays taxes at a rate of 40% of taxable income. Webster acquires a $10,000 asset with a 2-year useful life. It can deduct the $10,000 immediately for tax purposes and will depreciate it at $5,000 per year for financial reporting.

Exhibit 9-13 shows that Webster will pay taxes of $12,000 the first year and $16,000 the second, a total of $28,000 or 40% of the $70,000 total income. What should Webster report as income tax expense each year for financial reporting purposes? One approach is to report the amount Webster actually pays to the government each year, but neither U.S. GAAP nor IFRS permits this alternative. Instead, both require Webster to report the amount that it would have paid if the pretax income used for financial reporting had also been reported to the tax authorities. If taxable income had been $35,000 each year, the tax would have been

	Financial Reporting		Income Tax Returns	
	Year 1	Year 2	Year 1	Year 2
Income before depreciation and taxes	$40,000	$40,000	$40,000	$40,000
Depreciation	5,000	5,000	10,000	0
Pretax income	$35,000	$35,000	$30,000	$40,000
Taxes payable at 40%			$12,000	$16,000

EXHIBIT 9-13

Webster Company
Income for Financial Reporting and Income Tax Return

(40% × $35,000) = $14,000 annually. Therefore, the income statement for financial reporting would show the following:

	Year 1	Year 2	2-Year Totals
Pretax income	$35,000	$35,000	$70,000
Tax expense (40% of $35,000)	14,000	14,000	28,000
Net income	$21,000	$21,000	$42,000

This method matches the income tax expense with the financial reporting revenues and expenses to which it relates.

How do we account for this income tax expense? The tax payable to the government in year 1 is $12,000, but we record a tax expense of $14,000. Think of it as a current payable for the $12,000 currently owed to the government and a $2,000 liability that arises because of predictable future taxes. This $2,000 liability is a deferred tax liability because it will be paid only when a future tax return is filed. The journal entry is as follows:

Income tax expense	14,000	
Deferred tax liability		2,000
Cash (or taxes payable)		12,000

We show the deferred tax liability of $2,000 on the balance sheet. It equals the tax rate of 40% times the $5,000 temporary difference in depreciation expense ($5,000 on the books versus $10,000 on the tax return).

Remember that differences between reported income and taxable income result in deferral of taxes, not cancellation of taxes. Thus, we recognize a liability for future taxes equal to today's tax savings. In year 2, the tax payable to the government is $16,000, but the company again records a tax expense of $14,000. Therefore, the company pays the $2,000 that it treated as a deferred tax liability in year 1. The journal entry in the second year is as follows:

Income tax expense	14,000	
Deferred tax liability	2,000	
Cash (or taxes payable)		16,000

In this example, we create the deferred tax liability in year 1 and reverse it in year 2. Because Webster will pay the $2,000 in the next year, it is a current liability. However, if we depreciate an asset over 10 years, the deferred tax liability would take 10 years to reverse. Deferred taxes that become due in more than 1 year are long-term liabilities.

The balance sheet of nearly every company contains deferred tax liabilities. For example, footnote 10 disclosed that Jack in the Box had deferred tax assets of $194 million and deferred tax liabilities of $51 million on its balance sheet as of September 30, 2012. The deferred tax liability is due primarily to the timing of depreciation on property and equipment. If Jack in the Box had used straight-line depreciation for both financial and tax reporting, it would have already paid $27 million more to the government in taxes. As it stands, it will still pay the $27 million, but it has delayed the payment and thereby can earn interest on the money in the meantime. The remaining $24 million arises from the timing of amortization for intangible assets.

The major source of Jack in the Box's deferred tax assets is pensions and other postretirement benefits. The company recognizes the expense for book purposes when the obligation is created, but the tax authorities do not allow the deduction until the payments are actually made. The accounting is exactly opposite from the depreciation case, and a deferred tax asset is created in the initial year and then reverses in subsequent years.

Summary Problem for Your Review

PROBLEM

The Solar Kitchen Corporation began business on January 1, 20X0, to manufacture and sell energy-efficient additions to provide solar-heated eating areas next to existing kitchens. Because of good styling and marketing to an energy-conscious public, sales soared. During 20X0, the following transactions occurred:

a. On January 1, Solar Kitchen sold 1,000 new shares of common stock at $100 per share.
b. The company immediately invested one-half of the proceeds from the stock sale in tax-free municipal bonds yielding 6% per annum. It held the bonds throughout the year, resulting in interest revenue of ($50,000 × .06) = $3,000.
c. Sales for the year were $450,000, with operating expenses of $380,000 reported under GAAP (exclusive of income tax expense).
d. Tax depreciation exceeded depreciation for financial reporting by $30,000.

Required

1. Calculate earnings before tax for financial reporting.
2. Calculate income tax payable to the tax authorities and income tax expense for financial reporting using a 40% tax rate.
3. Make the appropriate journal entry. Assume the 40% tax rate is expected to be maintained.

SOLUTION

1. Earnings before taxes for financial reporting are as follows:

Sales revenue	$450,000
Interest revenue	3,000
Less: Operating expenses	(380,000)
Pretax income	$ 73,000

2. Tax calculations follow:

	Reporting to Tax Authorities	Financial Reporting
Earnings before tax	$73,000	$73,000
Permanent differences		
Nontaxable interest revenue	(3,000)	(3,000)
Subtotal	70,000	70,000
Temporary differences		
Depreciation	(30,000)	—
Earnings on which tax is based	40,000	70,000
Tax rate	.40	.40
Income tax payable	$16,000	
Income tax expense for financial reporting		$28,000

3.

Income tax expense	28,000	
Income tax payable.		16,000
Deferred tax liability		12,000

Restructuring Liabilities

Many companies record restructuring charges, which often involve significant liabilities for future costs. A **restructuring** is a significant makeover of part of the company. It typically involves closing one or more plants, reducing the size of the workforce, and terminating or relocating various activities. For example, Medtronic recorded $261 million in restructuring charges in 2011, $50 million in 2010, and $120 million in 2009. At year-end 2011, Medtronic disclosed a remaining liability of $204 million for restructuring costs. Note that the charge against the income statement is in anticipation of costs the company expects to incur as it executes the plan. The liability at year-end is for the remaining unexecuted costs.

Companies reporting under IFRS include restructuring liabilities under provisions. For example, Nestlé, the Swiss-based packaged food company, reported the following restructuring transactions in the "Provisions" footnote to its 2011 financial statements (in millions of Swiss francs, CHF):

	Restructuring
At 31 December 2010	CHF798
Provisions made in the period	115
Amount used	(187)
Unused amounts reversed	(61)
Currency retranslations	(33)
At 31 December 2011	CHF632

Nestlé describes the restructuring charges as follows: "Restructuring provisions are expected to result in future cash outflows when implementing the plans (usually over the following two to three years)." The provisions footnote also describes environmental and litigation costs.

Contingent Liabilities

The liabilities you have learned about so far are all concrete. We are confident about the existence of the liability, even if we have to estimate its amount. In contrast, a **contingent liability** is a potential (possible) liability that depends on a future event arising out of a past transaction. If the probability that the event will occur is high and the company can reasonably estimate the amount of the obligation, the company should include the liability and its amount on the balance sheet. More often, a contingent liability has an indefinite amount. A common example is a lawsuit. These are possible obligations of indefinite amounts. Why? If a judge rules against the company, it will be obligated to pay an amount that is currently unknown. However, the judge may rule in the company's favor, in which case there is no obligation.

If the probability that the future event will occur is not sufficiently high, or if a company cannot reasonably estimate the dollar amount of the potential liability, it does not report a dollar amount on its balance sheet. In this situation, some companies list contingent liabilities without a dollar amount on the balance sheet after long-term liabilities but before stockholders' equity. For example, in 2011 Medtronic had a caption "Commitments and Contingencies" on its balance sheet with no amount specified. The line item referred to three different footnotes describing various contingencies. Footnote 16 was the longest, running three pages and describing in detail numerous lawsuits and investigations by various government agencies. Even in the absence of a balance sheet line item such as Medtronic's "Commitments and Contingencies," companies will provide footnote discussion of contingent liabilities. Companies discuss environmental issues, product safety, potential strikes, and any other contingent event that might affect the company. The Business First box on page 420 describes an example of the evolution of a contingent liability to a definite liability—one where the final amount of the liability evolved over more than 20 years after Dow Corning first reported it as a contingent liability.

restructuring
A significant makeover of part of the company typically involving the closing of plants, firing of employees, and relocation of activities.

contingent liability
A potential liability that depends on a future event arising out of a past transaction.

BUSINESS FIRST

CONTINGENT LIABILITIES AT DOW CORNING, INC.

A well-known product liability issue involved Dow Corning, Inc. At December 31, 2011, the balance sheet showed $1.6 billion as an "Implant Reserve" among long-term liabilities. The origins of this reserve date back to the 1980s, when the company began facing accusations from patients who were unhappy with silicone breast implants made by the company that were surgically implanted for reconstructive or cosmetic purposes. The accusations became lawsuits over time. Gradually the number of lawsuits increased and some were resolved. Throughout the 1980s, the notes disclosed the litigation in detail, but the balance sheet and income statement did not show specific numbers.

In 1991, the company recorded $25 million of pretax costs for the pending litigation; in 1992, it recorded another $69 million. Each of these amounts was a best estimate of future costs to be incurred. The products from which the claims stemmed were produced and delivered years before. In fact, production of all silicone implants ceased in 1992.

The liability estimates provided through 1992 were woefully inadequate. In 1993, Dow Corning recorded another pretax charge of $640 million. Combined with expected insurance coverage exceeding $600 million, the expected total cost of litigation exceeded $1.2 billion. Even that was still well short of the $1.6 billion still shown in 2011.

Dow Corning joined other manufacturers in 1994 to structure a settlement that would properly compensate plaintiffs, minimize legal costs, and allow the companies to survive. The deal required an agreement between the plaintiffs, the companies, and the insurance carriers. In late 1994 agreement seemed close. Dow Corning provided another pretax charge of $241 million. At that time, there were more than 19,000 pending lawsuits on this product.

In May 1995, Dow Corning declared bankruptcy. Too many plaintiffs were unwilling to agree to the settlement. Bankruptcy changed the company's whole litigation situation and left the final outcome very much in doubt. In 1998, Dow Corning recorded another pretax charge of $1.1 billion as its estimate of total additional costs to be incurred on all claims in bankruptcy, including the breast implant controversy. That is the last significant charge made for implant costs. Since then the liability labeled "Implant Reserve," representing the present value of expected future settlements, has generally decreased. However, at the end of 2011 it was still $1.6 billion. In 2011, Dow Corning earned $1 billion on sales of $6.4 billion. Its total stockholders' equity was $3.6 billion. You can see that this liability remains a significant drag on Dow Corning, although the notes indicate it expects to be able to fund its remaining obligations from operating cash flow.

This saga underscores the difficulty of predicting the cost of litigation. Any time your initial estimate of $25 million is off by a factor of 100 and it takes 20 years to uncover the truth, you know that there was great uncertainty in the original predictions.

Sources: Dow Corning annual reports for 1991–2011 (included since 2003 with the 10-K filings of Corning Corporation).

Debt Ratios and Interest-Coverage Ratios

▶▶ OBJECTIVE 7

Use ratio analysis to assess a company's debt levels.

debt-to-equity ratio
Total liabilities divided by total shareholders' equity.

long-term-debt-to-total-capital ratio
Total long-term debt divided by total shareholders' equity plus total long-term debt.

debt-to-total-assets ratio
Total liabilities divided by total assets.

We have emphasized the link between the interest rate required by lenders and the risk associated with the loan. When people take out loans to buy a car or a house, the interest rate on the loan is smaller if the down payment is larger. Lenders believe that the higher the down payment, the less risk they bear. How does this concept work for corporations? Potential creditors often use debt ratios to measure the extent to which a company has used borrowing to finance its activity. The more the borrowing and the less the stockholders' equity, the riskier it is to lend money to the firm. Investors and analysts use a variety of ratios to help assess the risk imposed by a company's borrowing:

$$\text{Debt-to-equity ratio} = \frac{\text{Total liabilities}}{\text{Total shareholders' equity}}$$

$$\text{Long-term-debt-to-total-capital ratio} = \frac{\text{Total long-term debt}}{\text{Total shareholders' equity} + \text{Total long-term debt}}$$

$$\text{Debt-to-total-assets ratio} = \frac{\text{Total liabilities}}{\text{Total assets}}$$

$$\text{Interest-coverage ratio} = \frac{\text{Pretax income} + \text{Interest expense}}{\text{Interest expense}}$$

Note that the first three ratios are alternate ways of expressing the proportion of the firm's resources obtained from creditors. The higher the proportion, the riskier the firm and the higher the interest rate it must pay. The fourth ratio, the interest-coverage ratio (also known as the **times-interest-earned ratio**), more directly measures the firm's ability to meet its interest obligations. It measures the amount of pretax income available in relation to the company's interest expense. The lower the ratio, the more likely the company will have difficulty meeting its interest obligations. A minimum level of this ratio is common in debt covenants.

interest-coverage ratio (times-interest-earned ratio)
Pretax income plus interest expense divided by interest expense.

Debt burdens vary greatly from firm to firm and industry to industry. For example, retailing companies, utilities, and transportation companies tend to have debt of more than 60% of their assets, which gives a debt-to-equity ratio of 1.5. Jack in the Box has a debt-to-equity ratio of 2.5, which is up from 1.8 three years ago. Computer companies and drug companies generally have lower debt levels. Microsoft's debt-to-equity ratio is .72 and Pfizer's is 1.28. Debt-to-equity ratios that were believed to be too high a few years ago are becoming commonplace today. The average debt-to-equity ratio for major U.S. industrial companies grew from about 1.5 in 1960 to more than 2.0 today.

INTERPRETING FINANCIAL STATEMENTS

In comparing two companies, you observe that one company has little debt with a debt-to-total-assets ratio of 20%. The second company has a much higher ratio of 80%. How would you expect their interest-coverage ratios to compare?

Answer

A low debt-to-total-assets ratio is generally associated with a high interest-coverage ratio. Why? Because low relative debt means low interest costs. Interest costs are low for two reasons: (1) a small amount of debt on which to pay interest, and (2) low interest rates because a small amount of borrowing creates less risk and lower interest rates than large borrowings. All else equal, when debt levels and interest costs are low, we expect interest coverage to be high.

Highlights to Remember

1 Account for current liabilities. Liabilities are obligations to pay money or to provide goods or services. An entity's liability level is important to analysts because unpaid liabilities may produce difficulties ranging from an inability to raise additional capital to forced liquidation. To help assess debt levels, financial statements typically separate liabilities requiring payment within 1 year as current liabilities. Accounting for current liabilities is a straightforward extension of procedures covered in earlier chapters. Companies record transactions as they occur, and accruals at the end of a period capture incomplete transactions such as accruing interest, wages, utilities, or taxes.

2 Measure and account for long-term liabilities. Long-term liabilities involve more complex contracts that convey many rights and responsibilities over long periods of time. Companies initially record bonds, a common long-term liability, at the amount received from investors at issue. During the life of the bond, a company recognizes interest expense each period.

3 Account for bond issues over their entire life. The value of bonds at the date of issue is the present value of the future interest payments plus the present value of the principal payment, both calculated using the initial market rate of interest appropriate to the company's risk level and the current level of expected inflation. During the life of a bond, companies recognize interest expense using the effective interest method each period. They determine the interest paid or payable by multiplying the coupon rate of interest specified in the bond contract by the face value. They determine the interest expense by multiplying the market interest rate when the bond was issued times the book value of the bond (the net liability). The difference between the interest paid and the interest expense is the amount of the bond discount or premium that the company amortizes during the period. Amortizing a bond discount increases interest expense and amortizing a bond premium decreases it.

4 **Value and account for long-term lease obligations.** Leases are contracts that grant the lessee the right to use property owned by the lessor. Because many leases involve long time periods and place many of the risks of ownership on the lessee, GAAP contains rules to classify some leases as capital (or finance) leases. Companies account for a capital lease as if they had purchased the asset. They create both an asset and a liability when they sign a capital lease. The initial asset and liability values are both equal to the present value of payments required under the lease. The companies amortize the asset over its economic life. They divide the lease payments into interest expense and loan repayment portions using the effective interest amortization method. During the life of the lease, the book value of the liability is typically larger than the book value of the asset because of the different amortization methods used. On the statement of cash flows, the portion of the lease payment representing interest is an operating cash outflow under U.S. GAAP, and the portion representing a reduction in the lease liability is a financing cash outflow. Leases that do not meet the criteria for classification as capital leases are treated as operating leases. Companies record no asset or liability and treat payments made under the operating lease as rent expense.

5 **Evaluate pensions and other postretirement benefits.** Under defined benefit pension plans and other postretirement benefit plans, companies must recognize measurable obligations for future pension payments and other benefits. Historical precedent leads to footnote disclosure for much of the pension information. On the income statement, the matching principle leads companies to record annually the change in their liability for future obligations for pensions and other postretirement benefits. In essence, companies record the change in the liability as an expense during the current period. Pension disclosures involve footnote presentations of the present value of the obligation, as well as the value of pension assets set aside with a trustee on behalf of the employees. For life and health insurance obligations to future retirees, companies often do not set aside assets. Thus, financial statements of such companies present a significant liability equal to the present value of anticipated future payments for life and health insurance. Both pensions and insurance obligations depend on complex forecasts of future costs, retiree life expectancies, and so forth.

6 **Interpret deferred tax assets and liabilities; and restructuring and contingent liabilities.** Deferred tax liabilities arise because tax deductions such as depreciation expense on the company's tax return often precede the charging of the related expense on the company's books. When this happens, the immediate tax payable is less than it would appear to be if one examined the financial reports. Deferred tax assets arise when items such as pension costs are expensed for financial reporting purposes well before they are paid and become deductible for tax purposes. When this happens, the immediate tax payable is higher than it would appear to be if one examined the financial reports. To help investors understand the long-run tax obligations of the company, companies report tax expense as if they were paying taxes on the net income reported to shareholders. The company recognizes a deferred tax liability to reflect predictable higher taxes in the future, when these temporary differences in the recording of depreciation expense will reverse. Conversely it recognizes a deferred tax asset to reflect predictably lower taxes in the future. Restructuring liabilities are obligations associated with formal plans for future costs of closing plants, separating workers, and disposing of assets. Contingent liabilities are potential liabilities arising from past events with uncertain future outcomes.

7 **Use ratio analysis to assess a company's debt levels.** Debt ratios and interest coverage ratios are two measures used to evaluate the level of a company's indebtedness. The more debt a company has, the more problems it will face if cash flow is inadequate to meet liabilities as they come due.

Appendix 9: Compound Interest, Future Value, and Present Value

▶▶ OBJECTIVE 8
Compute and interpret present and future values.

principal
The amount borrowed or the amount to be repaid.

interest
The cost the borrower pays the lender to use the principal.

Interest is the cost of using money. This appendix teaches you what you need to know about interest to understand the accounting for long-term liabilities. Our discussion of interest uses amounts from interest tables to solve problems; however, many of you will be using Excel, another spreadsheet, or financial calculators to make these calculations. The mechanism is not important, but the principles are paramount to understanding these liabilities.

When you borrow money, the amount borrowed is the loan **principal**. **Interest** is the cost the borrower pays the lender (investor) to use the principal. It is the rental charge for cash, just as you pay rental charges to use an automobile or an apartment. For the investor, interest is the return on investment or the fee received for lending money. Contracts that bear interest have many forms, from simple short-term promissory notes to multimillion-dollar issues of bonds.

Calculating the amount of interest depends on the **interest rate** (a specified percentage of the principal) and the interest period (the time period over which the borrower uses the principal).

We calculate **simple interest** by multiplying an interest rate by an unchanging principal amount. If the borrower pays interest in cash at the end of each period, the principal amount does not change, and simple interest is appropriate. However, more common is **compound interest**, which we calculate by multiplying an interest rate by a principal amount that increases each time interest is accrued but not paid. We add the accumulated interest to the principal, and the total becomes the new principal for the next period.

Future Value

Consider an example. Suppose Christina's T-shirt business has $10,000 in cash that it does not need at this moment. Instead of holding the $10,000 in her business checking account, which does not pay interest, Christina deposits $10,000 in an account that pays 10% yearly interest, compounded annually. She plans to let the $10,000 remain in the account and earn interest for 3 years. After 3 years, she will withdraw all the money. The amount Christina will have in the account after 3 years, including principal and interest, is the **future value** of the $10,000 investment.

Let's compute the future value of Christina's investment after 3 years. Compound interest provides interest on both the principal and the previously accrued but unpaid interest. Christina earns interest in year 1 on $10,000: (10% × $10,000) = $1,000. If she does not withdraw the interest, the principal for year 2 includes the initial $10,000 deposit plus the $1,000 of interest earned in the first year, $11,000. She earns interest in year 2 on the $11,000: (10% × $11,000) = $1,100. In the third year she will earn interest on $12,100: (10% × $12,100) = $1,210. The future value (FV) of the $10,000 deposit at the end of 3 years with annual compound interest at 10% is $13,310:

	Principal	Compound Interest	Balance End of Year
Year 1	$10,000	$10,000 × .10 = $1,000	$11,000
Year 2	11,000	11,000 × .10 = 1,100	12,100
Year 3	12,100	12,100 × .10 = 1,210	13,310

More generally, suppose you invest S dollars for two periods and earn interest at an interest rate i. After one period, the investment would be increased by the interest earned, Si. You would have $S + Si = S(1 + i)$. In the second period, you would again earn interest ($i[S(1 + i)]$). After two periods, you would have the following:

$$[S(1 + i)] + (i[S(1 + i)]) = S(1 + i)(1 + i) = S(1 + i)^2$$

The general formula for computing the FV of S dollars in n years at interest rate i is

$$FV = S(1 + i)^n$$

In general, n refers to the number of periods the funds are invested. Periods can be years, months, days, or any other time period. However, the interest rate must be consistent with the time period. That is, if n refers to months, i must be expressed as $i\%$ per month.

The "force" of compound interest can be staggering. For example,

Compound Interest at 10%	Future Values of $10,000 at End of		
	10 Years	20 Years	40 Years
$10,000 × (1.10)^{10}$ = $10,000 × 2.5937 =	$25,937		
$10,000 × (1.10)^{20}$ = $10,000 × 6.7275 =		$67,275	
$10,000 × (1.10)^{40}$ = $10,000 × 45.2593 =			$452,593

Calculating future values and compound interest by hand is tedious and time consuming. Fortunately, there are tables, calculators, or software to do the work. We use tables in this appendix. For example, Table 9A-1 on page 425 shows the future values of $1 for various periods and interest rates. Each number in the table is the solution to the expression $(1 + i)^n$. Each column represents a specific interest rate, i, and each row represents a number of periods, n. Notice that the 3-year, 10% future value factor is 1.3310 (the third row, seventh column). We calculated this number as $(1 + .10)^3$. This is consistent with our preceding example where we show that $10,000 grows to $13,310 over 3 years [($10,000 × 1.3310) = $13,310].

Suppose you want to know how much $800 will grow to if left in the bank for 9 years at 8% interest. Multiply $800 by $(1 + .08)^9$. You can find the value for $(1 + .08)^9$ in the 9-period row and 8% column of Table 9A-1.

$$\$800 \times 1.9990 = \$1,599.20$$

The examples in this text use the factors from Table 9A-1 and similar tables in this appendix, which we have rounded to four decimal places. If you use tables with different rounding, or if you use a hand calculator or personal computer, your answers may differ slightly from those given because of a small rounding error.

Present Value

present value (PV)
The value today of a future cash inflow or outflow.

Accountants generally use present values to record long-term liabilities. The **present value (PV)** is the value today of a future cash inflow or outflow.

Suppose you invest $1.00 today. As you learned in the discussion of future values, the $1.00 will grow to $1.06 in 1 year at 6% interest—that is, ($1 × 1.06) = $1.06. At the end of the second year, its value is [($1 × 1.06) × 1.06] = [$1 × (1.06)^2] = $1.124.

Once you know how to calculate the future value of S dollars invested at a known interest rate i for n periods, you can reverse the process to calculate the present value of a future amount. Let PV be the present value, or value today, and FV be the future value, the value at some future date. Using the equation for future value

$$FV = PV(1 + i)^n$$

we can rearrange terms to compute the present value, PV:

$$PV = \frac{FV}{(1 + i)^n}$$

If you expect to receive $1.00 in 1 year, it is worth ($1 ÷ 1.06) = $.9434 today. Suppose you invest $.9434 today. In 1 year, you will have ($.9434 × 1.06) = $1.00. Thus, $0.9434 is the present value of $1.00 a year later, at 6%. If you will receive the dollar in 2 years, its present value is [$1.00 ÷ (1.06)^2] = $.8900. If you invest $.89 today at 6% interest, it will grow to $1.00 at the end of 2 years. The general formula for the PV of an FV that you will receive or pay in n periods at an interest rate of i% per period is as follows:

$$PV = \frac{FV}{(1 + i)^n} = FV \times \frac{1}{(1 + i)^n}$$

discounted values
Another name for present values.

discount rates
Interest rates used to compute present values.

discounting
The process of finding the present value.

Table 9A-2 on page 426 gives factors for $1/(1 + i)^n$ (which is the present value of $1.00) at various interest rates over several different periods. You may hear present values called **discounted values**, interest rates called **discount rates**, and the process of finding the present value called **discounting**. You can think of present values as discounting (decreasing) the value of a future cash inflow or outflow. Why do we discount the value? Because you will receive or pay the cash in the future, not today, so it is worth less in today's dollars.

Assume a prominent city issues a 3-year noninterest-bearing note payable that promises to pay a lump sum of $1,000 exactly 3 years from now. You desire a rate of return of exactly 6%, compounded annually. Recall from Chapter 4 that we defined the rate of return to be the return per dollar invested or the amount an investor earns expressed as a percentage of the amount invested. How much should you be willing to pay now for the 3-year note? The situation is sketched as follows:

End of Year	0	1	2	3
	Present Value			Future Value
	? ←			$1,000

Future Value of $1

$$FV = (1 + i)^n$$

Periods	3%	4%	5%	6%	7%	8%	10%	12%	14%	16%	18%	20%	22%	24%	25%
1	1.0300	1.0400	1.0500	1.0600	1.0700	1.0800	1.1000	1.1200	1.1400	1.1600	1.1800	1.2000	1.2200	1.2400	1.2500
2	1.0609	1.0816	1.1025	1.1236	1.1449	1.1664	1.2100	1.2544	1.2996	1.3456	1.3924	1.4400	1.4884	1.5376	1.5625
3	1.0927	1.1249	1.1576	1.1910	1.2250	1.2597	1.3310	1.4049	1.4815	1.5609	1.6430	1.7280	1.8158	1.9066	1.9531
4	1.1255	1.1699	1.2155	1.2625	1.3108	1.3605	1.4641	1.5735	1.6890	1.8106	1.9388	2.0736	2.2153	2.3642	2.4414
5	1.1593	1.2167	1.2763	1.3382	1.4026	1.4693	1.6105	1.7623	1.9254	2.1003	2.2878	2.4883	2.7027	2.9316	3.0518
6	1.1941	1.2653	1.3401	1.4185	1.5007	1.5869	1.7716	1.9738	2.1950	2.4364	2.6996	2.9860	3.2973	3.6352	3.8147
7	1.2299	1.3159	1.4071	1.5036	1.6058	1.7138	1.9487	2.2107	2.5023	2.8262	3.1855	3.5832	4.0227	4.5077	4.7684
8	1.2668	1.3686	1.4775	1.5938	1.7182	1.8509	2.1436	2.4760	2.8526	3.2784	3.7589	4.2998	4.9077	5.5895	5.9605
9	1.3048	1.4233	1.5513	1.6895	1.8385	1.9990	2.3579	2.7731	3.2519	3.8030	4.4355	5.1598	5.9874	6.9310	7.4506
10	1.3439	1.4802	1.6289	1.7908	1.9672	2.1589	2.5937	3.1058	3.7072	4.4114	5.2338	6.1917	7.3046	8.5944	9.3132
11	1.3842	1.5395	1.7103	1.8983	2.1049	2.3316	2.8531	3.4785	4.2262	5.1173	6.1759	7.4301	8.9117	10.6571	11.6415
12	1.4258	1.6010	1.7959	2.0122	2.2522	2.5182	3.1384	3.8960	4.8179	5.9360	7.2876	8.9161	10.8722	13.2148	14.5519
13	1.4685	1.6651	1.8856	2.1329	2.4098	2.7196	3.4523	4.3635	5.4924	6.8858	8.5994	10.6993	13.2641	16.3863	18.1899
14	1.5126	1.7317	1.9799	2.2609	2.5785	2.9372	3.7975	4.8871	6.2613	7.9875	10.1472	12.8392	16.1822	20.3191	22.7374
15	1.5580	1.8009	2.0789	2.3966	2.7590	3.1722	4.1772	5.4736	7.1379	9.2655	11.9737	15.4070	19.7423	25.1956	28.4217
16	1.6047	1.8730	2.1829	2.5404	2.9522	3.4259	4.5950	6.1304	8.1372	10.7480	14.1290	18.4884	24.0856	31.2426	35.5271
17	1.6528	1.9479	2.2920	2.6928	3.1588	3.7000	5.0545	6.8660	9.2765	12.4677	16.6722	22.1861	29.3844	38.7408	44.4089
18	1.7024	2.0258	2.4066	2.8543	3.3799	3.9960	5.5599	7.6900	10.5752	14.4625	19.6733	26.6233	35.8490	48.0386	55.5112
19	1.7535	2.1068	2.5270	3.0256	3.6165	4.3157	6.1159	8.6128	12.0557	16.7765	23.2144	31.9480	43.7358	59.5679	69.3889
20	1.8061	2.1911	2.6533	3.2071	3.8697	4.6610	6.7275	9.6463	13.7435	19.4608	27.3930	38.3376	53.3576	73.8641	86.7362
21	1.8603	2.2788	2.7860	3.3996	4.1406	5.0338	7.4002	10.8038	15.6676	22.5745	32.3238	46.0051	65.0963	91.5915	108.4202
22	1.9161	2.3699	2.9253	3.6035	4.4304	5.4365	8.1403	12.1003	17.8610	26.1864	38.1421	55.2061	79.4175	113.5735	135.5253
23	1.9736	2.4647	3.0715	3.8197	4.7405	5.8715	8.9543	13.5523	20.3616	30.3762	45.0076	66.2474	96.8894	140.8312	169.4066
24	2.0328	2.5633	3.2251	4.0489	5.0724	6.3412	9.8497	15.1786	23.2122	35.2364	53.1090	79.4968	118.2050	174.6306	211.7582
25	2.0938	2.6658	3.3864	4.2919	5.4274	6.8485	10.8347	17.0001	26.4619	40.8742	62.6686	95.3962	144.2101	216.5420	264.6978
26	2.1566	2.7725	3.5557	4.5494	5.8074	7.3964	11.9182	19.0401	30.1666	47.4141	73.9490	114.4755	175.9364	268.5121	330.8722
27	2.2213	2.8834	3.7335	4.8223	6.2139	7.9881	13.1100	21.3249	34.3899	55.0004	87.2598	137.3706	214.6424	332.9550	413.5903
28	2.2879	2.9987	3.9201	5.1117	6.6488	8.6271	14.4210	23.8839	39.2045	63.8004	102.9666	164.8447	261.8637	412.8642	516.9879
29	2.3566	3.1187	4.1161	5.4184	7.1143	9.3173	15.8631	26.7499	44.6931	74.0085	121.5005	197.8136	319.4737	511.9516	646.2349
30	2.4273	3.2434	4.3219	5.7435	7.6123	10.0627	17.4494	29.9599	50.9502	85.8499	143.3706	237.3763	389.7579	634.8199	807.7936

$$PV = \frac{1}{(1 + i)^n}$$

Periods	3%	4%	5%	6%	7%	8%	10%	12%	14%	16%	18%	20%	22%	24%	25%
1	.9709	.9615	.9524	.9434	.9346	.9259	.9091	.8929	.8772	.8621	.8475	.8333	.8197	.8065	.8000
2	.9426	.9246	.9070	.8900	.8734	.8573	.8264	.7972	.7695	.7432	.7182	.6944	.6719	.6504	.6400
3	.9151	.8890	.8638	.8396	.8163	.7938	.7513	.7118	.6750	.6407	.6086	.5787	.5507	.5245	.5120
4	.8885	.8548	.8227	.7921	.7629	.7350	.6830	.6355	.5921	.5523	.5158	.4823	.4514	.4230	.4096
5	.8626	.8219	.7835	.7473	.7130	.6806	.6209	.5674	.5194	.4761	.4371	.4019	.3700	.3411	.3277
6	.8375	.7903	.7462	.7050	.6663	.6302	.5645	.5066	.4556	.4104	.3704	.3349	.3033	.2751	.2621
7	.8131	.7599	.7107	.6651	.6227	.5835	.5132	.4523	.3996	.3538	.3139	.2791	.2486	.2218	.2097
8	.7894	.7307	.6768	.6274	.5820	.5403	.4665	.4039	.3506	.3050	.2660	.2326	.2038	.1789	.1678
9	.7664	.7026	.6446	.5919	.5439	.5002	.4241	.3606	.3075	.2630	.2255	.1938	.1670	.1443	.1342
10	.7441	.6756	.6139	.5584	.5083	.4632	.3855	.3220	.2697	.2267	.1911	.1615	.1369	.1164	.1074
11	.7224	.6496	.5847	.5268	.4751	.4289	.3505	.2875	.2366	.1954	.1619	.1346	.1122	.0938	.0859
12	.7014	.6246	.5568	.4970	.4440	.3971	.3186	.2567	.2076	.1685	.1372	.1122	.0920	.0757	.0687
13	.6810	.6006	.5303	.4688	.4150	.3677	.2897	.2292	.1821	.1452	.1163	.0935	.0754	.0610	.0550
14	.6611	.5775	.5051	.4423	.3878	.3405	.2633	.2046	.1597	.1252	.0985	.0779	.0618	.0492	.0440
15	.6419	.5553	.4810	.4173	.3624	.3152	.2394	.1827	.1401	.1079	.0835	.0649	.0507	.0397	.0352
16	.6232	.5339	.4581	.3936	.3387	.2919	.2176	.1631	.1229	.0930	.0708	.0541	.0415	.0320	.0281
17	.6050	.5134	.4363	.3714	.3166	.2703	.1978	.1456	.1078	.0802	.0600	.0451	.0340	.0258	.0225
18	.5874	.4936	.4155	.3503	.2959	.2502	.1799	.1300	.0946	.0691	.0508	.0376	.0279	.0208	.0180
19	.5703	.4746	.3957	.3305	.2765	.2317	.1635	.1161	.0829	.0596	.0431	.0313	.0229	.0168	.0144
20	.5537	.4564	.3769	.3118	.2584	.2145	.1486	.1037	.0728	.0514	.0365	.0261	.0187	.0135	.0115
21	.5375	.4388	.3589	.2942	.2415	.1987	.1351	.0926	.0638	.0443	.0309	.0217	.0154	.0109	.0092
22	.5219	.4220	.3418	.2775	.2257	.1839	.1228	.0826	.0560	.0382	.0262	.0181	.0126	.0088	.0074
23	.5067	.4057	.3256	.2618	.2109	.1703	.1117	.0738	.0491	.0329	.0222	.0151	.0103	.0071	.0059
24	.4919	.3901	.3101	.2470	.1971	.1577	.1015	.0659	.0431	.0284	.0188	.0126	.0085	.0057	.0047
25	.4776	.3751	.2953	.2330	.1842	.1460	.0923	.0588	.0378	.0245	.0160	.0105	.0069	.0046	.0038
26	.4637	.3607	.2812	.2198	.1722	.1352	.0839	.0525	.0331	.0211	.0135	.0087	.0057	.0037	.0030
27	.4502	.3468	.2678	.2074	.1609	.1252	.0763	.0469	.0291	.0182	.0115	.0073	.0047	.0030	.0024
28	.4371	.3335	.2551	.1956	.1504	.1159	.0693	.0419	.0255	.0157	.0097	.0061	.0038	.0024	.0019
29	.4243	.3207	.2429	.1846	.1406	.1073	.0630	.0374	.0224	.0135	.0082	.0051	.0031	.0020	.0015
30	.4120	.3083	.2314	.1741	.1314	.0994	.0573	.0334	.0196	.0116	.0070	.0042	.0026	.0016	.0012
40	.3066	.2083	.1420	.0972	.0668	.0460	.0221	.0107	.0053	.0026	.0013	.0007	.0004	.0002	.0001

The factor in the period 3 row and 6% column of Table 9A-2 is .8396. The present value of the $1,000 payment is ($1,000 × .8396) = $839.60. You should be willing to pay $839.60 for the $1,000 that you will receive in 3 years.

Suppose we compound interest semiannually instead of annually. How much should you be willing to pay now? Remember to pay attention to the number of periods involved, not just the number of years. The 3 years become six interest payment periods. The rate per period is one-half the annual rate, or (6% ÷ 2) = 3%. The factor in the period 6 row and 3% column of Table 9A-2 is .8375. You should now be willing to pay ($1,000 × 0.8375), or only $837.50 instead of $839.60. Why do you pay less? Because, with more frequent compounding the original investment will grow faster.

To see how present values work, let's return to our example. Suppose Christina's financial institution promised to pay her a lump sum of $13,310 at the end of 3 years for her investment. How much does she need to deposit to earn a 10% rate of return, compounded annually? Using Table 9A-2, the period 3 row and the 10% column show a factor of .7513. Multiply this factor by the future amount and round to the nearest dollar:

$$PV = .7513 \times \$13,310 = \$10,000$$

Present Value of an Ordinary Annuity

An **ordinary annuity** is a series of equal cash flows that take place at the end of successive periods of equal length. In other words, an annuity pays you the same amount at the end of each period for a set number of periods. We denote its present value as PV_A. Assume that you buy a note from an insurance company that promises to pay $1,000 at the end of each of 3 years. How much should you be willing to pay for this note if you desire a rate of return of 6%, compounded annually?

ordinary annuity
A series of equal cash flows that take place at the end of successive periods of equal length.

You could solve this problem using Table 9A-2. First, find the present value of each payment you will receive, and then add the present values as in Exhibit 9-14. You should be willing to pay $943.40 for the first payment, $890.00 for the second, and $839.60 for the third, a total of $2,673.00.

Table 9A-3 on page 428 provides a shortcut method for calculating the present value of an annuity. We can calculate the present value in Exhibit 9-14 as follows:

$$
\begin{aligned}
PV_A &= (\$1,000 \times .9434) + (\$1,000 \times .8900) + (\$1,000 \times .8396) \\
&= \$1,000 \times (.9434 + .8900 + .8396) \\
&= \$1,000 \times 2.6730 \\
&= \$2,673.00
\end{aligned}
$$

The three terms in parentheses are the first three numbers from the 6% column of Table 9A-2, and their sum is in the third row of the 6% column of Table 9A-3: (.9434 + .8900 + .8396) = 2.6730. This shortcut is especially valuable if the cash payments or receipts extend over many periods. Consider an annual cash payment of $1,000 for 20 years at 6%. The present value, calculated from Table 9A-3, is ($1,000 × 11.4699) = $11,469.90. To use Table 9A-2 for this calculation, you would have to perform 20 calculations and then add up the 20 products.

You can calculate the factors in Table 9A-3 using the following general formula:

$$PV_A = \frac{1}{i}\left[1 - \frac{1}{(1 + i)^n}\right]$$

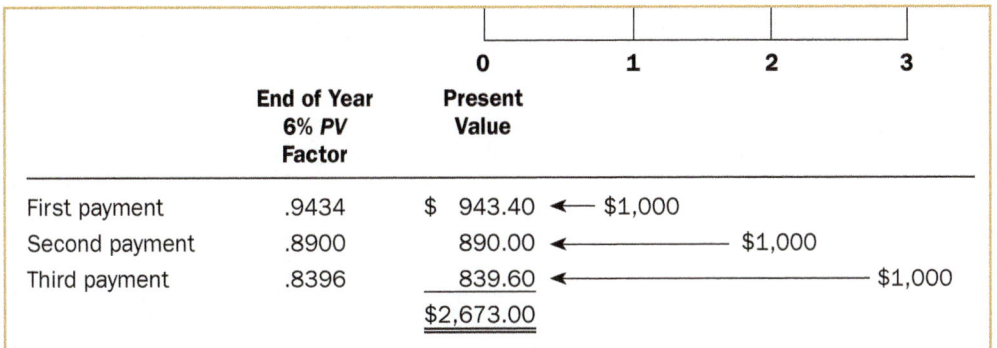

EXHIBIT 9-14

PV **of Three Annual $1,000 Payments**

	End of Year 6% PV Factor	Present Value			
			0	1	2	3
First payment	.9434	$ 943.40 ← $1,000			
Second payment	.8900	890.00 ←	$1,000		
Third payment	.8396	839.60 ←			$1,000
		$2,673.00			

Present Value of Ordinary Annuity of $1

$$PV_A = \frac{1}{i}\left[1 - \frac{1}{(1+i)^n}\right]$$

Periods	3%	4%	5%	6%	7%	8%	10%	12%	14%	16%	18%	20%	22%	24%	25%
1	.9709	.9615	.9524	.9434	.9346	.9259	.9091	.8929	.8772	.8621	.8475	.8333	.8197	.8065	.8000
2	1.9135	1.8861	1.8594	1.8334	1.8080	1.7833	1.7355	1.6901	1.6467	1.6052	1.5656	1.5278	1.4915	1.4568	1.4400
3	2.8286	2.7751	2.7232	2.6730	2.6243	2.5771	2.4869	2.4018	2.3216	2.2459	2.1743	2.1065	2.0422	1.9813	1.9520
4	3.7171	3.6299	3.5460	3.4651	3.3872	3.3121	3.1699	3.0373	2.9137	2.7982	2.6901	2.5887	2.4936	2.4043	2.3616
5	4.5797	4.4518	4.3295	4.2124	4.1002	3.9927	3.7908	3.6048	3.4331	3.2743	3.1272	2.9906	2.8636	2.7454	2.6893
6	5.4172	5.2421	5.0757	4.9173	4.7665	4.6229	4.3553	4.1114	3.8887	3.6847	3.4976	3.3255	3.1669	3.0205	2.9514
7	6.2303	6.0021	5.7864	5.5824	5.3893	5.2064	4.8684	4.5638	4.2883	4.0386	3.8115	3.6046	3.4155	3.2423	3.1611
8	7.0197	6.7327	6.4632	6.2098	5.9713	5.7466	5.3349	4.9676	4.6389	4.3436	4.0776	3.8372	3.6193	3.4212	3.3289
9	7.7861	7.4353	7.1078	6.8017	6.5152	6.2469	5.7590	5.3282	4.9464	4.6065	4.3030	4.0310	3.7863	3.5655	3.4631
10	8.5302	8.1109	7.7217	7.3601	7.0236	6.7101	6.1446	5.6502	5.2161	4.8332	4.4941	4.1925	3.9232	3.6819	3.5705
11	9.2526	8.7605	8.3064	7.8869	7.4987	7.1390	6.4951	5.9377	5.4527	5.0286	4.6560	4.3271	4.0354	3.7757	3.6564
12	9.9540	9.3851	8.8633	8.3838	7.9427	7.5361	6.8137	6.1944	5.6603	5.1971	4.7932	4.4392	4.1274	3.8514	3.7251
13	10.6350	9.9856	9.3936	8.8527	8.3577	7.9038	7.1034	6.4235	5.8424	5.3423	4.9095	4.5327	4.2028	3.9124	3.7801
14	11.2961	10.5631	9.8986	9.2950	8.7455	8.2442	7.3677	6.6282	6.0021	5.4675	5.0081	4.6106	4.2646	3.9616	3.8241
15	11.9379	11.1184	10.3797	9.7122	9.1079	8.5595	7.6061	6.8109	6.1422	5.5755	5.0916	4.6755	4.3152	4.0013	3.8593
16	12.5611	11.6523	10.8378	10.1059	9.4466	8.8514	7.8237	6.9740	6.2651	5.6685	5.1624	4.7296	4.3567	4.0333	3.8874
17	13.1661	12.1657	11.2741	10.4773	9.7632	9.1216	8.0216	7.1196	6.3729	5.7487	5.2223	4.7746	4.3908	4.0591	3.9099
18	13.7535	12.6593	11.6896	10.8276	10.0591	9.3719	8.2014	7.2497	6.4674	5.8178	5.2732	4.8122	4.4187	4.0799	3.9279
19	14.3238	13.1339	12.0853	11.1581	10.3356	9.6036	8.3649	7.3658	6.5504	5.8775	5.3162	4.8435	4.4415	4.0967	3.9424
20	14.8775	13.5903	12.4622	11.4699	10.5940	9.8181	8.5136	7.4694	6.6231	5.9288	5.3527	4.8696	4.4603	4.1103	3.9539
21	15.4150	14.0292	12.8212	11.7641	10.8355	10.0168	8.6487	7.5620	6.6870	5.9731	5.3837	4.8913	4.4756	4.1212	3.9631
22	15.9369	14.4511	13.1630	12.0416	11.0612	10.2007	8.7715	7.6446	6.7429	6.0113	5.4099	4.9094	4.4882	4.1300	3.9705
23	16.4436	14.8568	13.4886	12.3034	11.2722	10.3711	8.8832	7.7184	6.7921	6.0442	5.4321	4.9245	4.4985	4.1371	3.9764
24	16.9355	15.2470	13.7986	12.5504	11.4693	10.5288	8.9847	7.7843	6.8351	6.0726	5.4509	4.9371	4.5070	4.1428	3.9811
25	17.4131	15.6221	14.0939	12.7834	11.6526	10.6748	9.0770	7.8431	6.8729	6.0971	5.4669	4.9476	4.5139	4.1474	3.9849
26	17.8768	15.9828	14.3752	13.0032	11.8258	10.8100	9.1609	7.8957	6.9061	6.1182	5.4804	4.9563	4.5196	4.1511	3.9879
27	18.3270	16.3296	14.6430	13.2105	11.9867	10.9352	9.2372	7.9426	6.9352	6.1364	5.4919	4.9636	4.5243	4.1542	3.9903
28	18.7641	16.6631	14.8981	13.4062	12.1371	11.0511	9.3066	7.9844	6.9607	6.1520	5.5016	4.9697	4.5281	4.1566	3.9923
29	19.1885	16.9837	15.1411	13.5907	12.2777	11.1584	9.3696	8.0218	6.9830	6.1656	5.5098	4.9747	4.5312	4.1585	3.9938
30	19.6004	17.2920	15.3725	13.7648	12.4090	11.2578	9.4269	8.0552	7.0027	6.1772	5.5168	4.9789	4.5338	4.1601	3.9950
40	23.1148	19.7928	17.1591	15.0463	13.3317	11.9246	9.7791	8.2438	7.1050	6.2335	5.5482	4.9966	4.5439	4.1659	3.9995

Applied to our illustration we have the following:

$$PV_A = \frac{1}{.06}(1 - .83962) = \frac{.16038}{.06} = 2.6730$$

In particular, note that the higher the interest rate, the lower the present value factor in Table 9A-3. Why? Because, at a higher interest rate, you would need to invest less now to obtain the same stream of future annuity payments. For example, for a 10-year annuity the factor declines from 7.7217 for 5% to 6.1446 for 10%.

Summary Problems for Your Review

PROBLEM

To make sure you understand present values, use Table 9A-2 to obtain the present values of the following:

1. $1,600, at 20%, to be received at the end of 20 years
2. $8,300, at 10%, to be received at the end of 12 years
3. $8,000, at 4%, to be received at the end of 4 years

SOLUTION

1. $1,600 × (.0261) = $41.76
2. $8,300 × (.3186) = $2,644.38
3. $8,000 × (.8548) = $6,838.40

PROBLEM

To make sure you understand present values of annuities, use Table 9A-3 to obtain the present values of the following ordinary annuities:

1. $1,600 to be received at the end of each year for 20 years, assuming interest at 20%
2. $8,300 to be received at the end of each year for 12 years, assuming interest at 10%
3. $8,000 to be received at the end of each year for 4 years, assuming interest at 4%

SOLUTION

1. $1,600 × (4.8696) = $7,791.36
2. $8,300 × (6.8137) = $56,553.71
3. $8,000 × (3.6299) = $29,039.20

Accounting Vocabulary

bargain purchase option, p. 408
bond discount, p. 396
bond premium, p. 396
bonds, p. 394
call premium, p. 395
callable bonds, p. 395
capital lease, p. 408
commercial paper, p. 389
compound interest, p. 423
compound interest method, p. 401
contingent liability, p. 419

contractual rate, p. 394
convertible bonds, p. 395
coupon rate, p. 394
covenant, p. 395
debenture, p. 394
debt-to-equity ratio, p. 420
debt-to-total-assets ratio, p. 420
deferred income tax asset, p. 416
deferred income tax liability, p. 416

defined benefit pension plan, p. 414
defined contribution pension plan, p. 414
discount amortization, p. 401
discount on bonds, p. 396
discount rates, p. 424
discounted values, p. 424
discounting, p. 424
early extinguishment, p. 406
effective interest amortization, p. 401
face amount, p. 394

Assignment Material

MyAccountingLab

Questions

9-1 Distinguish between current liabilities and long-term liabilities.

9-2 Name and briefly describe five items that are often classified as current liabilities.

9-3 "Withholding taxes really add to employer payroll costs." Do you agree? Explain.

9-4 "Product warranties expense should not be recognized until actual repair services are performed. Until then you don't know which products might require warranty repairs." Do you agree? Explain.

9-5 Distinguish between a mortgage bond and a debenture. Which is safer?

9-6 Distinguish between subordinated and unsubordinated debentures.

9-7 Bond covenants usually restrict the borrower's rights in various ways. An example might be a restriction that no additional long-term debt could be issued unless the debt-to-total assets ratio was below .50. Who benefits from such a covenant? How?

9-8 Many callable bonds have a call premium for "early" calls. Who does the call premium benefit—the issuer or the purchaser of the bond? How?

9-9 How does reporting for convertible bonds differ under IFRS compared with U.S. GAAP?

9-10 "When a company buys back bonds that it has issued, it always pays the book value to the bondholders. Therefore, there is never a gain or loss on extinguishing bonds." Do you agree? Explain.

9-11 "The face amount of a bond is what you can sell it for." Do you agree? Explain.

9-12 "The quoted bond interest rates imply a rate per annum, but the bond markets do not mean that rate literally." Explain.

9-13 A company plans to issue bonds with a coupon rate of 10%. At what market rates will the bonds be issued at a discount? At what market rates will they be issued at a premium?

9-14 "When a bond is issued at a discount, there are two components of interest expense." Explain.

9-15 What are the three main differences between accounting for a bond discount and accounting for a bond premium?

9-16 A company reported interest payments in the financing activities section of the statement of cash flows. Does the company report under IFRS or U.S. GAAP? Explain.

9-17 "A company that issues zero coupon bonds recognizes no interest expense until the bond matures." Do you agree? Explain.

9-18 "When accounting for a lease, it is necessary to determine whether the lease is a capital lease or a finance lease." Do you agree? Explain.

9-19 Certain leases are essentially equivalent to purchases financed with debt. A company must account for such leases as if the asset had been purchased. Explain.

9-20 "A capital (or finance) lease results in both an asset and a liability on a company's balance sheet." Explain.

9-21 "A capital (or finance) lease and operating lease are recorded differently on the balance sheet, but their effect on the income statement is the same." Do you agree? Explain.

9-22 Discuss which characteristics of a lease are evaluated in deciding whether it is a capital (or finance) lease.

9-23 "Because a company never knows how much it will have to pay for pensions, no pension liability is recognized. Pension obligations are simply explained in a footnote to the financial statements." Do you agree? Explain.

9-24 Compare and contrast permanent differences and temporary differences between GAAP and tax reporting.

9-25 "Differences in tax and GAAP rules lead to more depreciation being charged on tax statements than on financial reports to the public." Do you agree? Explain.

9-26 "It is unethical for big companies to recognize a large income tax expense on their income statements reported to the public but to pay a small amount to the government." Do you agree? Explain.

9-27 "A contingent liability is a liability having an estimated amount." Do you agree? Explain.

9-28 Name four ratios that help analysts assess a company's risk. Give a brief explanation of each.

9-29 Refer to Appendix 9. How are Table 9A-2 (p. 426) and Table 9A-3 (p. 428) related to each other?

Critical Thinking Questions

9-30 Lenders and Covenants
Why would a lender want to add a covenant specifying a maximum debt-to-total-assets ratio to a loan contract?

▶▶ **OBJECTIVE 7**

9-31 Refinancing Bonds
Your treasurer is new to the job and has just noticed that your bonds are trading below par (i.e., at a discount). This officer recommends that you retire the bonds by issuing new bonds because you will have a gain in the process and will reduce your interest payments. Do you believe you should accept the treasurer's recommendation?

▶▶ **OBJECTIVE 3**

9-32 Cash Interest Versus Interest Expense
As a lender, you are contemplating a covenant that is based on the interest-coverage ratio. A young member of your organization with a new MBA degree has suggested that you calculate the ratio using actual cash interest payments each period instead of interest expense each period. You have been asked to discuss this proposal. What do you say?

▶▶ **OBJECTIVE 7**

9-33 Lottery Winnings
The New York Lottery provides prizes that start at $3 million and rise each time someone fails to win the lottery. Participants in the lottery are permitted to choose to receive a lump-sum payment or 26 annual payments as an annuity. A recent winner of $20 million was surprised to receive a check for less than $10 million. How could you explain this to the winner?

▶▶ **OBJECTIVE 8**

Exercises

9-34 Accrued Employee Compensation
Choi Company had total compensation expense for March of $40,000. The company paid $30,000 to employees during March, and it will pay the remainder in April.

▶▶ **OBJECTIVE 1**

1. Prepare the journal entry for recording the compensation expense for March.
2. Suppose salaries and wages payable were $8,000 at the beginning of March. Compute salaries and wages payable at the end of March.

9-35 Sales Taxes
Most of the food sold in retail stores in California is not subject to sales taxes (e.g., candy), but some items are (e.g., soft drinks). Apparently, the candy lobbyists were more effective than soft drinks lobbyists when dealing with the state legislature. Most cash registers are designed to record taxable sales and nontaxable sales and automatically add the appropriate sales tax.

▶▶ **OBJECTIVE 1**

The sales for the past week in the local **Whole Foods** grocery store were $180,000 cash, of which $60,000 was taxable at a rate of 9%. By using the $A = L + SE$ equation, show the impact on the entity, both now and when the sales taxes are paid at a later date. Also prepare corresponding journal entries.

▶▶ OBJECTIVE 1

9-36 Product Warranties

During 20X0, the Ashley Appliance Company had cash sales of $800,000. The company estimates that the cost of servicing products under warranty will average 3% of sales.

1. Prepare journal entries for sales revenue and the related warranty expense for 20X0. Assume all sales are for cash.
2. The liability for warranties was $12,000 at the beginning of 20X0. Expenditures (all in cash) to satisfy warranty claims during 20X0 were $21,400, of which $4,000 was for products sold in 20X0. Prepare the journal entry for the warranty expenditures.
3. Compute the balance in the Liability for Warranties account at the end of 20X0.

▶▶ OBJECTIVE 1

9-37 Unearned Revenues

The **Reader's Digest Association, Inc.,** one of the largest publishers of magazines in the world, had unearned revenues of $340.4 million on its March 31, 2012, balance sheet. The company showed $244.6 million as a current liability and $95.8 million was reported as long term. Suppose that during April, Reader's Digest delivered magazines with a sales value of $30 million to prepaid subscribers and sold subscriptions for $35 million cash.

1. Prepare journal entries for the new subscriptions and the deliveries to prepaid subscribers.
2. Compute the amount in the unearned revenue account at the end of April 2012.

▶▶ OBJECTIVES 1, 2

9-38 Liabilities on the Balance Sheet

Krispy Kreme Company, the doughnut company, had the following items on its January 29, 2012, balance sheet (in thousands):

Cash and cash equivalents	$ 44,319
Accounts payable	10,494
Total stockholders' equity	249,126
Accrued liabilities	28,800
Inventories	16,497
Current maturities of long-term debt	2,224
Long-term debt, less current maturities	25,369
Other long-term obligations	18,935

Prepare the liabilities section of Krispy Kreme's balance sheet. Include only the items that are properly included in liabilities. Separate current and long-term liabilities.

▶▶ OBJECTIVES 1, 6

9-39 Various Liabilities

1. **Whirlpool Corporation** sells electric appliances, including automatic washing machines. Suppose that experience in recent years has indicated that warranty costs average 3.0% of sales. Sales of washing machines for April were $5.0 million. Cash disbursements and obligations for warranty service on washing machines during April totaled $144,000. Prepare the journal entries prompted by these facts. Omit explanations.
2. **Pepsi-Cola Bottling Company of New York** gets cash deposits for its returnable bottles. In November, it received $72,000 cash and disbursed $68,000 for bottles returned. Prepare the journal entries concerning the receipts and returns of deposits. Omit explanations.
3. **Citibank** received a $14,000 savings deposit on April 1. On June 30, it recognized interest thereon at an annual rate of 2%. On July 1, the depositor closed her account with the bank. Prepare the bank's necessary journal entries. Omit explanations.
4. The Village Theater sold, for a total of $180,000 cash, 600 season tickets in advance of December 31 for six plays, each to be held in successive months, beginning in January.
   a. What is the effect on the balance sheet of December 31? What is the appropriate journal entry for the sale of the tickets? Omit explanations.
   b. What is the effect on the balance sheet of January 31? What is the related journal entry for January? Omit explanations.

5. Suppose a tabloid newspaper has lost a lawsuit. Damages were set at $500,000. The newspaper plans to appeal the decision to a higher court. The newspaper's attorneys are 90% confident of a reversal of the lower court's decision. What liability, if any, should be shown on the newspaper's balance sheet?

9-40 Priorities of Claims

▸▸ OBJECTIVES 1, 2

Bram Real Estate Corporation is being liquidated. It has one major asset, an office building, which was converted into $16.4 million cash. The stockholders' equity has been wiped out by past losses. The following claims exist: Accounts Payable, $4 million; Debentures Payable, $5 million; and First Mortgage Payable, $11 million.

1. Assume that the debentures are not subordinated. How much will each class of claimants receive?
2. Suppose the debentures are subordinated.
   a. How much will each class of claimants receive?
   b. How much will each class receive if the cash proceeds from the sale of the building amount to only $12.5 million?

9-41 Discounted Present Value and Bonds

▸▸ OBJECTIVE 3

On December 31, 20X1, Hartley Company issued a 3-year $10,000 bond that promises an interest rate of 12%, payable 6% semiannually. Compute the discounted present value of the principal and the interest as of December 31, 20X1, if the market rate of interest for such securities is 12%, 14%, and 10%, respectively. Show your computations, including a sketch of cash flows. Round to the nearest dollar.

9-42 Criteria for Capital Leases

▸▸ OBJECTIVE 4

Indicate which of the following leases would be a capital (financing) lease and which would be an operating lease:

1. Rental of a warehouse for $10,000 per month, renewable annually.
2. Rental of a crane for $9,000 per month on a 6-year lease, with an option to buy for $10,000 at the end of the 6 years when its fair value is $150,000.
3. Rental of an automobile on a 6-month lease for $500 per month. The auto will be returned to the dealer after the 6 months.
4. Rental of a computer for $500 per month on a 5-year lease. At the end of 5 years, the computer is expected to have a fair market value of zero.
5. Rental of 10 forklifts for $1,400 per month on an 8-year lease. The value of the forklifts at the end of 8 years is uncertain, but the total economic life is not expected to be more than 10 years.

9-43 Accounting for Pensions

▸▸ OBJECTIVE 5

Merinoff Company's 20X0 pension expense was $800,000, of which it paid $500,000 in cash to a trustee. By using the balance sheet equation format, show which accounts were affected by these data. Prepare the corresponding journal entry.

9-44 Deferred Taxes

▸▸ OBJECTIVE 6

Procter & Gamble Company's (P&G) net sales in 2011 exceeded $82 billion. On its income statement, P&G reported the following earnings from continuing operations ($ in millions):

Earnings before income taxes	$15,189
Income taxes	3,392
Net earnings	$11,797

Taxes due on 2011 taxable income and payments to the government for income taxes related to operations in 2011 were $3,263 million. Assume that the income tax expense and these income tax payments were the only tax-related transactions during 2011.

Prepare the journal entry that recognizes the income tax expense and the income tax payment.

▶▶ OBJECTIVE 7

9-45 Debt and Interest-Coverage Ratios

The Empire District Electric Company, headquartered in Joplin, Missouri, provides electric services and also distributes natural gas to customers primarily in the states of Missouri, Kansas, Oklahoma, and Arkansas. A devastating tornado with winds exceeding 200 miles per hour hit Joplin on May 22, 2011, killing over 160 people. Property damage was extensive with a path of destruction over 13 miles long and up to three-fourths of a mile wide. For Empire District, 4,000 power poles and 100 miles of electric lines were down; six substations were damaged leaving approximately 20,000 customers without power. The company suspended its dividend in the face of storm costs that might reach $30 million.

The following summary financial items are taken from the financial statements for the year ending December 31, 2011 (dollars in thousands):

Total assets	$2,021,835
Current liabilities	97,029
Shareholders' equity	693,989
Interest expense	41,302
Pretax income	96,273

Assume that all long-term liabilities are in the form of long-term debt. Compute the following four ratios. In one sentence per ratio, explain what it tells you about Empire District.

1. Debt-to-equity
2. Long-term-debt-to-total-capital
3. Debt-to-total-assets
4. Interest-coverage ratio

▶▶ OBJECTIVE 8

9-46 Exercises in Compound Interest

Study Appendix 9. Then answer the following questions:

1. You deposit $10,000. How much will you have in 4 years at (a) 8% compounded annually, and (b) at 12% compounded annually?
2. A savings and loan association offers depositors a $10,000 lump-sum payment 4 years hence. (a) How much will you be willing to deposit if you desire an interest rate of 8% compounded annually? (b) How much at an interest rate of 12%?
3. Repeat requirement 2, assuming an interest rates of 6% and do the calculation twice, assuming (a) annual and then (b) semiannual compounding.

▶▶ OBJECTIVE 8

9-47 Exercises in Compound Interest

Study Appendix 9. A reliable friend has asked you for a loan. You are pondering various proposals for repayment.

1. Repayment of a $30,000 lump sum 4 years hence. How much will you lend if your desired rate of return is (a) 10% compounded annually, and (b) 20% compounded annually?
2. Repeat requirement 1, but assume the interest rates are compounded semiannually.
3. Suppose the loan is to be paid in full by equal payments of $8,000 at the end of each of the next 4 years. How much will you lend if your desired rate of return is (a) 10% compounded annually, and (b) 20% compounded annually?

▶▶ OBJECTIVE 8

9-48 Compound Interest and Journal Entries

Study Appendix 9. Benenson Company bought some equipment on a contract entailing a €200,000 cash down payment and an €800,000 lump sum to be paid at the end of 4 years. The same equipment can be purchased for €788,000 cash.

1. Prepare the journal entry for the acquisition of the equipment.
2. Prepare journal entries at the end of each of the first 2 years. Ignore entries for depreciation.

9-49 Exercises in Compound Interest

▶▶ **OBJECTIVE 8**

Study Appendix 9. Then answer the following questions:

1. It is your sixtieth birthday. You plan to work 5 more years before retiring. Then you want to spend $20,000 for a Mediterranean cruise. What lump sum do you have to invest now to accumulate the $20,000? Assume your minimum desired rate of return is as follows:
   a. 5%, compounded annually
   b. 10%, compounded annually
   c. 20%, compounded annually
2. You want to spend $5,000 on a vacation at the end of each of the next 5 years. What lump sum do you have to invest now to take the five vacations? Assume that your minimum desired rate of return is as follows:
   a. 5%, compounded annually
   b. 10%, compounded annually
   c. 20%, compounded annually

9-50 Exercises in Compound Interest

▶▶ **OBJECTIVE 8**

Study Appendix 9. Then answer the following questions:

1. At age 60, you find that your employer is moving to another location. You receive termination pay of $600,000. You have some savings and wonder whether to retire now.
   a. If you invest the $600,000 now at 8%, compounded annually, how much money can you withdraw from your account each year so at the end of 5 years there will be a zero balance?
   b. If you invest the $600,000 now at 10%, compounded annually, how much money can you withdraw from your account each year so at the end of 5 years there will be a zero balance?
2. At 16%, compounded annually, which of the following plans is more desirable in terms of present value? Show computations to support your answer.

	Annual Cash Inflows	
Year	Mining	Farming
1	$100,000	$ 20,000
2	80,000	40,000
3	60,000	60,000
4	40,000	80,000
5	20,000	100,000
	$300,000	$300,000

9-51 Basic Relationships in Interest Tables

▶▶ **OBJECTIVE 8**

Study Appendix 9. Then answer the following questions:

1. Suppose you borrow $50,000 now at 16% interest compounded annually. The borrowed amount plus interest will be repaid in a lump sum at the end of 6 years. How much must be repaid? Use Table 9A-1 and the basic equation FV = Present amount × Future value factor.
2. Repeat requirement 1 using Table 9A-2 and the basic equation PV = Future amount × Present value factor.
3. Assume the same facts as in requirement 1, except that the loan will be repaid in equal installments at the end of each of 5 years. How much must be repaid each year? Use Table 9A-3 and the basic equation PV_A = Future annual amounts × Conversion factor.

9-52 Discounted Present Value and Leases

▶▶ **OBJECTIVES 4, 8**

Study Appendix 9. Suppose Wal-Mart signed a 10-year lease for a new store location. The lease calls for an immediate payment of $50,000 and annual payments of $40,000 at the end of each of the next 9 years. Wal-Mart expects to earn 16% interest, compounded annually, on its investments. What is the present value of the lease payments?

MyAccountingLab **Problems**

9-53 Accounting for Payroll

▶▶ OBJECTIVE 1

For the week ended January 27, the Massengill Company had a total payroll of $100,000. The company withheld three items from employees' paychecks: (1) Social Security (FICA) tax of 7.1% of the payroll; (2) income taxes, which average 22% of the payroll; and (3) employees' savings that are deposited in their Credit Union, which are $6,000. Massengill paid all three items together with the wages on January 30.

1. Use the balance sheet equation to analyze the transactions on January 27 and January 30.
2. Prepare journal entries for the recording of the items in requirement 1.
3. In addition to the payroll, Massengill pays (1) payroll taxes of 9% of the payroll, (2) health insurance premiums of $7,000, and (3) contributions to the employees' pension fund of $8,000. Prepare journal entries for the recognition and payment of these additional expenses.

9-54 Liabilities on the Balance Sheet—IFRS

▶▶ OBJECTIVES 1, 2

ArcelorMittal, headquartered in Luxembourg, is the largest steel producer in the world. It reports using IFRS. Following are items from the company's December 31, 2010, balance sheet (in millions of U.S. dollars):

Liabilities held for sale and distribution	$ 2,037
Long-term debt, net of current portion	19,292
Short-term debt and current portion of long-term debt	6,716
Long-term provisions	1,738
Property, plant, and equipment	54,344
Trade accounts payable and other	13,256
Deferred employee benefits	7,180
Total noncurrent liabilities	?
Trade accounts receivable	5,725
Short-term provisions	1,343
Other long-term obligations	1,865
Total current liabilities	30,723
Inventories	19,583
Deferred tax liabilities	4,006
Accrued expenses and other liabilities	6,900
Income tax liabilities	471
Total liabilities	64,804

Prepare the liabilities section of ArcelorMittal's balance sheet. Classify liabilities into current and noncurrent portions. Omit items that are not liabilities. Include the appropriate number for total noncurrent liabilities.

9-55 Convertible Bonds—IFRS and U.S. GAAP

▶▶ OBJECTIVE 2

Brock Company issued $100,000 convertible 5-year bonds with a face value of $100,000 on January 1, 20X0. The coupon rate on the bonds was 6%, and Brock received $100,000 cash for the bonds. Interest is paid semiannually. The market rate for similar bonds without a conversion factor was 10%. Each $1,000 bond is convertible into 20 shares of Brock Company common stock. At the time of issue of the bonds, Brock common stock sold for $42 per share.

1. How would Brock Company report the issuance of the bonds using U.S. GAAP?
2. How would Brock Company report the issuance of the bonds using IFRS?

9-56 Convertible Bonds

▶▶ OBJECTIVE 2

Sometimes companies find it desirable to include a convertibility option to sell bonds at a reasonable interest rate. Siemens AG, the huge German electronics company, issued €2.5 billion of convertible bonds some years ago with a coupon rate of 1.375%, which is less interest than Siemens would have paid if the bonds were not convertible. Each €1,000 bond is convertible into 17.8 common shares of Siemens stock.

In 2011, Siemens had revenues of more than €74 billion and a net income of over €6.3 billion. The company pays dividends of €3.00 per share.

1. Compute the annual interest received by the holders of the convertible bonds.
2. The current price of one share of Siemens common stock in June 2012 was €65.70. If you held some of the Siemens convertible bonds, would you immediately convert your bonds to common stock? Why or why not?
3. Suppose the maturity date of the convertible bonds was rapidly approaching. Would you convert your holdings of the convertible bonds if the price of Siemens stock were only €62 per share? If the price were €50 per share? Explain.

9-57 Bonds Issued at Par

▸▸ **OBJECTIVE 3**

(Alternative is 9-58.) On December 31, 20X1, Northeast Financial, Corp., issued $20 million of 8-year, 10% debentures at par. Interest is paid semiannually.

1. Compute the proceeds from issuing the debentures.
2. Using the balance sheet equation format, prepare an analysis of this bond transaction. Show entries for the issuer concerning (a) issuance, (b) first semiannual interest payment, and (c) payment of maturity value.
3. Show all the corresponding journal entries keyed as in requirement 2.
4. Show how the bond-related accounts would appear on the balance sheet as of December 31, 20X1, and June 30, 20X2. Assume that the semiannual interest payment due on June 30, 20X2, has been made.

9-58 Bonds Issued at Par

▸▸ **OBJECTIVE 3**

(Alternative is 9-57.) On December 31, 2009, Idaho Mining, Inc., issued $50 million of 10-year, 6% debentures at par.

1. Compute the proceeds from issuing the debentures.
2. By using the balance sheet equation format, prepare an analysis of this bond transaction. Show entries for the issuer concerning (a) issuance, (b) first semiannual interest payment, and (c) payment of maturity value.
3. Show the corresponding journal entries for (a), (b), and (c) in requirement 2.
4. Show how the bond-related accounts would appear on the balance sheet as of December 31, 2009, and June 30, 2010. Assume that the semiannual interest payment due on June 30, 2010, the balance sheet date, has been made.

9-59 Bond Discount Transactions

▸▸ **OBJECTIVE 3**

(Alternates are 9-60 and 9-62.) On March 1, 2009, Oregon Gas & Electric issued $100 million of 20-year, 9% debentures. Proceeds were $91,420,000, implying a market interest rate of 10%. Show all amounts in thousands of dollars.

1. By using the balance sheet equation format, prepare an analysis of bond transactions. Assume effective interest amortization. Show entries for the issuer concerning (a) issuance, (b) first semiannual interest payment, and (c) payment of maturity value.
2. Show all the corresponding journal entries for (a), (b), and (c) in requirement 1.
3. Show how the bond-related accounts would appear on the balance sheets as of March 1, 2009, and March 1, 2010. Assume the March 1 interest payment and amortization of bond discount have been made.

9-60 Bonds Issued at a Discount

▸▸ **OBJECTIVE 3**

(Alternates are 9-59 and 9-62.) On January 1, 20X0, Washington Park District issued $20 million of 5-year, 6% debentures. Interest is paid semiannually. The market interest rate at issuance was 10%.

1. Compute the proceeds from issuing the debentures.
2. By using the balance sheet equation format, prepare an analysis of this bond transaction. Show entries for the issuer concerning (a) issuance, (b) first semiannual interest payment, and (c) payment of maturity value.
3. Show the corresponding journal entries for (a), (b), and (c) in requirement 2.
4. Show how the bond-related accounts would appear on the balance sheets as of January 1, 20X0, and July 1, 20X0. Assume Washington Park District has already recorded the semiannual interest payment and amortization due on the balance sheet dates.

▶▶ OBJECTIVE 3

9-61 Bond Amortization Schedule

Consider a $10 million issue of 5-year, 6% debentures when the market interest rate was 10%. It was issued on January 1, 20X0.

1. Prepare a table showing the interest expense and the unamortized discount and ending liability balance for each semiannual period. Use Exhibit 9-4 on page 401 as an example. (*Hint*: Use a spreadsheet.)
2. Prepare the journal entry for recording interest for the 6-month period ended when the bond matures on December 31, 20X4.

▶▶ OBJECTIVE 3

9-62 Bond Discount Transactions

(Alternates are 9-59 and 9-60.) Assume that on December 31, 2009, Oslo Dahler issued NKR20 million of 10-year, 10% debentures. Proceeds were NKR15,762,000; therefore, the market rate of interest was 14%. (NKR is the Norwegian kroner.)

1. By using the balance sheet equation format, prepare an analysis of transactions for Oslo Dahler. Key your transactions as follows: (a) issuance, (b) first semiannual interest using effective interest amortization of bond discount, and (c) payment of maturity value. Round all amounts to the nearest thousand.
2. Prepare corresponding journal entries for (a), (b), and (c) in requirement 1.
3. Show how the bond-related accounts would appear on Oslo Dahler's balance sheets as of December 31, 2009, and at the end of the following year, December 31, 2010. Assume that Oslo Dahler has already recorded the semiannual interest payments and amortization.

▶▶ OBJECTIVE 3

9-63 Bonds Issued at a Premium

(Alternate is 9-64.) On January 1, 20X0, Global Travel issued $6 million of 5-year, 10% debentures. The market interest rate at issuance was 8%. Interest is paid semiannually.

1. Compute the proceeds from issuing the debentures.
2. By using the balance sheet equation format, prepare an analysis of this bond transaction. Show entries for the issuer concerning (a) issuance, (b) first semiannual interest payment, and (c) payment of maturity value.
3. Show the corresponding journal entries for (a), (b), and (c) in requirement 2.
4. Show how the bond-related accounts would appear on the balance sheets as of January 1, 20X0, and July 1, 20X0. Assume the semiannual interest payments and amortization due on the balance sheet date have been recorded.
5. Calculate the interest expense for the 6-month period ending December 31, 20X0.

▶▶ OBJECTIVE 3

9-64 Bond Premium Transactions

(Alternate is 9-63.) Assume that on December 31, 20X0, Colorado Woolens issued $10 million of 10-year, 10% debentures. Proceeds were $11,359,000; therefore, the market rate of interest was 8%.

1. By using the balance sheet equation format, prepare an analysis of transactions for Colorado Woolens. Key your transactions as follows: (a) issuance, (b) first semiannual interest using effective interest amortization of bond premium, and (c) payment of maturity value. Round all amounts to the nearest thousand.
2. Prepare corresponding journal entries for (a), (b), and (c) in requirement 1.
3. Show how the bond-related accounts would appear on Colorado Woolens' balance sheets as of December 31, 20X0, and June 30, 20X1. Assume that the semiannual interest payment and amortization have been recorded.
4. Calculate the interest expense for the 6-month period ending December 31, 20X1.

▶▶ OBJECTIVE 3

9-65 Interest Expense on the Cash Flow Statement—IFRS and U.S. GAAP

Siemens AG is Europe's largest conglomerate. It is headquartered in Berlin and Munich. The amounts that follow are in millions of euros (€). The company's statement of cash flows for the year ending September 30, 2011, uses the indirect method of calculating cash flow from operations. It begins with €7,011 of income from continuing operations, adds back depreciation, and makes other adjustments to income that would be familiar. However, Siemens reports under IFRS and therefore its statements contain a few unusual items. In the operating section there is a deduction of €491, which removes the net interest income from operating income.

The Consolidated Statements of Income show interest income of €2,207 and interest expense of (€1,716), which nets to €491. In the operating section of the Statement of Cash Flows there is an addition for interest received (€787), and in the Financing section there is a deduction for interest paid (€475). What item(s) in this statement would be shown differently if Siemens reported using U.S. GAAP? Why is the interest expense amount different than the interest paid amount?

9-66 Early Extinguishment of Debt

▶▶ OBJECTIVE 3

(Alternative is 9-67.) On December 31, 20X0, Limestone Charters issued $20 million of 10-year, 12% debentures. Interest is paid semiannually. The market interest rate at issuance was 14%. One year later, on December 31, 20X1 (after all interest payments and amortization had been recorded for 20X1), the company purchased all the debentures for $19 million. Throughout their life, the debentures had been held by a large insurance company.
Show all amounts in thousands of dollars. Round to the nearest thousand.

1. Compute the gain or loss on early extinguishment.
2. By using the balance sheet equation, present an analysis of the December 31, 20X1, transaction on the issuer's books.
3. Show the appropriate journal entry.
4. At what price on December 31, 20X1, could Limestone Charters redeem the bonds and realize a $1,000,000 *gain*?

9-67 Early Extinguishment of Debt

▶▶ OBJECTIVE 3

(Alternative is 9-66.) On December 31, 20X0, a Zurich real estate holding company issued CHF10 million of 10-year, 8% debentures. The market interest rate at issuance was 8%. Suppose that on December 31, 20X1 (after all interest payments had been recorded for 20X1), the company purchased all the debentures for CHF9 million. The debentures had been held by a large insurance company throughout their life. (CHF represents Swiss francs.)
Show all amounts in thousands of Swiss francs.

1. Compute the gain or loss on early extinguishment.
2. By using the balance sheet equation, present an analysis of the December 31, 20X1, transaction on the holding company's books.
3. Show the appropriate journal entry.

9-68 Noninterest-Bearing Notes

▶▶ OBJECTIVE 3

On January 2, a local bookstore borrowed from a bank on a 1-year note. The face value of the note was $80,000. However, the bank deducted its interest "in advance" at 5% of the face value. Show the effects on the borrower's records at inception and at the end of the year:

1. Using the balance sheet equation, prepare an analysis of transactions.
2. Prepare journal entries. Omit explanations.
3. What was the real rate of interest?

9-69 Zero Coupon Bonds

▶▶ OBJECTIVE 3

Issuers of "deep-discount" or "zero coupon" debt securities must use an effective interest approach to amortization of discount for both tax reporting and reporting to the public. Similarly, buyers of such securities must record interest income under the effective interest rate method.

1. Assume that, in order to develop improvements for the Kindle, Amazon.com issues a 10-year zero coupon bond having a face amount of $50,000,000 to yield 10%. For simplicity, assume that the 10% yield is compounded annually. Prepare the journal entry for Amazon.com (the issuer).
2. Prepare the journal entry for interest expense for the first full year and the second full year using (a) straight-line, and (b) effective interest amortization.
3. Assume an income tax rate of 40%. How much more income tax for the first year would the issuer have to pay because of applying effective interest instead of straight-line amortization?
4. What kinds of borrowers might prefer these investments over bonds that pay interest immediately?

▶▶ OBJECTIVE 3

9-70 Zero Coupon Bonds

The state of Illinois issues zero coupon bonds as part of its Illinois College Savings Bonds series. This bond series had different maturity dates and the different maturities led to very different prices. Suppose that in late 2012, the state issued 9,000 such bonds with a total $90 million maturity value. Each bond had a maturity value of $10,000, and bonds ranged in price from $9,500 for a 3-year bond to $5,219 for an 11-year bond. Consider one of the 11-year zero coupon bonds issued on December 31, 2012, for $5,219. To maintain consistency with other bond yields that we work with, assume that the interest rate is compounded semiannually.

1. Compute the market interest rates for the 11-year zero coupon bond.
2. Is this higher or lower than the rate on the 3-year bonds? You can answer this question by asking what the price of the 3-year bond would be at exactly the 11-year rate and comparing that number with the actual sales price.
3. Prepare the state's journal entry for one 11-year bond at issuance. Do not use a discount account.
4. Prepare the state's journal entry for recording interest expense on the 11-year bonds for the first 6 months of 2013. Round to the nearest dollar.
5. Compute the liability that Illinois would show on its balance sheet for this bond on June 30, 2013.

▶▶ OBJECTIVE 4

9-71 Capital (Financing) Lease

On December 31, 20X0, the Jackson Building Maintenance Services acquired cleaning equipment on a capital lease for three annual lease payments of $30,000 each on December 31, 20X1, 20X2, and 20X3. The implicit interest rate was 10% compounded annually.

1. Compute the present value of the capital lease.
2. Prepare journal entries at the inception of the lease on December 31, 20X0, and for each of the 3 years. Distinguish between the short and long-term classifications of the lease liability.

▶▶ OBJECTIVE 4

9-72 Comparison of Operating and Capital (Financing) Lease

Refer to the preceding problem. Compare income statement and balance sheet effects of treating the lease as a capital lease rather than an operating lease. Ignore income taxes. You can do this by filling in the blanks in the following table.

	Operating Lease	Capital Lease	Difference
Total expenses			
20X1	?	?	?
20X2	?	?	?
Two years together	?	?	?
End of 20X1			
Total assets	?	?	?
Total liabilities	?	?	?
Retained earnings	?	?	?
End of 20X2			
Total assets	?	?	?
Total liabilities	?	?	?
Retained earnings	?	?	?

▶▶ OBJECTIVE 4

9-73 Capital or Operating Lease

On December 31, 20X0, the law firm of Preston, Gomez, and Bergman is offered 30 laptop computers for the firm's partners. It can either (a) buy them outright for $100,000 cash, or (b) lease them on a noncancelable lease whereby rental payments would be made at the end of each year for 3 years. The computers will become obsolete and worthless at the end of 3 years. The company can borrow $100,000 cash on a 3-year loan payable at maturity at 8% compounded annually.

1. Compute the annual rental payment, assuming that the lessor desires an 8% rate of return per year.
2. Suppose the lease could be accounted for as an operating lease. What annual journal entry would the company make?
3. The lease is a capital lease. Prepare an analytical schedule of each lease payment. Show the lease liability at the beginning of the year, and interest expense, lease payment, and lease

liability at the end of the year. You need not differentiate between current and noncurrent liabilities in this analysis.

4. Prepare an analysis of transactions for the capital lease, using the balance sheet equation format.

5. Prepare yearly journal entries for the capital lease. Omit explanations.

9-74 Leases

▶▶ OBJECTIVE 4

The following information appeared in a footnote to the 2011 annual report of Delta Air Lines, Incorporated:

The following table summarizes, as of December 31, 2011, our minimum rental commitments under capital leases ... with initial or remaining terms of more than 1 year:

Years Ending December 31 (in millions)	
2012	$ 221
2013	196
2014	168
2015	155
2016	163
Thereafter	323
Total minimum lease payments	$1,226
Less: Lease payments that represent interest	(489)
Present value of future minimum capital lease payments	$ 737

1. Suppose the minimum capital lease payments are made in equal amounts on March 31, June 30, September 30, and December 31 of each year. Compute the interest and principal to be paid on capital leases during the first half of fiscal 2012. Perform calculations in millions with two decimal places. Assume an interest rate of 8% per annum, compounded quarterly.

2. Prepare the journal entries for the lease payments in requirement 1 on March 31 and June 30, 2012. Omit explanations.

3. Delta has well over $1,000 million per year in operating leases. Suppose an analyst thought it appropriate to treat some of Delta's operating leases as if they were capital leases. Assume that the payments on these operating leases were $1,000 million per year for 15 years made annually at year-end. If these operating leases were treated as capital leases and capitalized at 8% compounded annually, how much would long-term debt increase? Do calculations to the closest million. Delta's long-term debt and capital leases total $11,847 million. What percentage increase in long-term debt would result from capitalizing these operating leases?

9-75 Leases

▶▶ OBJECTIVES 4, 7

Consider footnote 7 from the 2011 annual report of FedEx:

We utilize certain aircraft, land, facilities, retail locations, and equipment under capital and operating leases that expire at various dates through 2046. ... A summary of future minimum lease payments under capital leases and noncancelable operating leases with an initial or remaining term in excess of one year at May 31, 2011, is as follows (in millions):

	Capital Leases	Operating Leases
2012	$ 25	$ 1,794
2013	119	1,654
2014	2	1,465
2015	2	1,354
2016	2	1,192
Thereafter	13	6,533
Total	$163	$13,992

1. Compute the net present value of the operating lease payments as of May 31, 2011. Use a 10% implicit interest rate. For ease of computation, assume each payment is made on May 31 of the designated year (i.e., the first $1,794 million payment is made on May 31, 2012) and that the final payment, labeled "Thereafter," is made on May 31, 2017.

2. Suppose FedEx were to capitalize the operating leases examined in requirement 1. Show the journal entries necessary to do the following (omit explanations):

   a. Capitalize the leases on June 1, 2011. Ignore any prior period adjustments, and do not break the lease obligation into current and long-term portions.

   b. Record the first payment on May 31, 2012.

3. FedEx's total assets on May 31, 2011, were $27,385 million, and its total stockholders' equity was $15,220 million. Compute its total debt-to-equity ratio. Then, suppose FedEx capitalized its operating leases using the present value calculated in requirement 1. Recompute the debt-to-equity ratio. What difference does capitalizing the operating leases make to the debt-to-equity ratio? Explain.

▶▶ OBJECTIVE 4

9-76 Capital Leases

The Home Depot is the leading retailer in the home improvement industry and one of the 10 largest retailers in the United States. The company included the following on its January 29, 2012, balance sheet and footnotes ($ in millions):

Capital lease assets	$588
Capital lease obligations (long term)	$420
Capital lease obligations (current)	29
Total capital lease obligations	$449

Total capital lease payments, scheduled for the fiscal year ending in 2013, are $106,000,000.

1. Prepare the journal entry for the $106,000,000 lease payments. Remember that the lease payments will include the principal payments due for the year plus interest expense accrued for the year.

2. Suppose that the capital lease assets have an average remaining life of 20 years and that no new leases are signed in the fiscal year ending in 2013. Compute the balance in the capital lease asset account and the total in the capital lease obligations account (long-term and current combined) as of the year ending in 2013.

3. Explain why the amount in the capital lease assets account is not equal to the amount in the lease obligations accounts.

▶▶ OBJECTIVE 5

9-77 Pension Liabilities

According to note 15 in its 10-K, **Boeing Company**, the aircraft and aerospace manufacturer, had pension obligations of $67,651 million and obligations for postretirement benefits other than pensions of $7,997 million at the end of 2011. The fair value of plan assets in the pension plan was $51,051 million, and the fair value of plan assets for postretirement benefits other than pensions was $102 million. Total retained earnings was $27,524 million. The total market value of Boeing common stock was approximately $53.33 billion in June 2012.

1. Comment on the confidence that employees might have about receiving the benefits due to them.

2. Recognizing pensions and other postretirement benefits as liabilities on the balance sheet has been a controversial topic. Do you think this is important information to disclose to shareholders? Why or why not?

▶▶ OBJECTIVE 5

9-78 Pensions

Alcoa, Inc., is the world's leader in the production and fabrication of aluminum and aluminum products. The company has had a defined benefit pension plan for many years. Footnote W of the 10-K for December 31, 2011, reports pension obligations of $13,526 million. On the same date its pension assets totaled $10,311 million.

1. What is the impact of this defined benefit pension plan on Alcoa's balance sheet on December 31, 2011? Comment on how comfortable employees should be that they will receive their full pension benefits.

2. Optional question: What factors affect the balances in the Pension Assets and Pension Obligations accounts other than pension expense and pension funding?

▶▶ OBJECTIVE 6

9-79 Deferred Taxes

The Home Depot reported earnings from continuing operations before the provision for income taxes of $6,068 million for the year ending January 29, 2012, in its 10-K. Footnote 6 revealed that the provision for income taxes was $2,185 million and that the current amount paid to the federal, state, and foreign governments was $1,950 million.

1. Compute the earnings from continuing operations after taxes.
2. Prepare the journal entry to record taxes on ordinary activities. Omit explanation.
3. Explain why the amount of income taxes paid to the government was not the same as the amount of income taxes recorded on the income statement.

9-80 Deferral of Taxes and Reversal of Temporary Differences

> ▸▸ **OBJECTIVE 6**

Assad Company bought an asset for $400,000 on January 1, 20X0. The asset has a 10-year life and zero salvage value for both financial reporting and tax purposes. Assad uses straight-line depreciation for financial reporting purposes and DDB depreciation for tax purposes. The DDB schedule switches to straight-line depreciation for the remaining book value when the resulting straight-line depreciation exceeds the amount of depreciation on the original DDB schedule. This results in the following depreciation charges:

Year	Straight-line Depreciation	DDB Depreciation
20X0	$40,000	$80,000
20X1	40,000	64,000
20X2	40,000	51,200
20X3	40,000	40,960
20X4	40,000	32,768
20X5	40,000	26,214
20X6	40,000	26,214
20X7	40,000	26,214
20X8	40,000	26,214
20X9	40,000	26,214

The company's tax rate is 40%.

1. Compute the amount in the deferred tax account at the end of each year.
2. Is the deferred tax account an asset or a liability? Explain.
3. What is the amount in the deferred tax account at the end of the life of the asset? Explain what caused the deferred tax account to reach this value at the end of the asset's life.
4. Suppose that in 20X1, the company earns $80,000 before considering depreciation charges and depreciation is the only source of either permanent or timing differences for tax purposes. Compute the tax provision and the amount of current tax due to the government.

9-81 The Income Tax Footnote

> ▸▸ **OBJECTIVE 6**

Alcoa had sales of $24,951 million in 2011 and generated income from continuing operations before income taxes of $1,063 million. In its 10-K for 2011, Alcoa provided information about taxes in footnote T:

The provision (benefit) for income taxes on income (loss) from continuing operations consisted of the following:

	2011	2010
	($ in millions)	
Current		
Federal	$ 10	$ 33
Foreign	427	409
State and local	(1)	(7)
	436	435
Deferred		
Federal	28	37
Foreign	(211)	(320)
State and local	2	(4)
	(181)	(287)
Net tax expense	$255	$148

1. Provide the journal entries to record income tax expense for 2011.
2. Compute income (loss) from continuing operations for 2011.

▶ OBJECTIVE 7

9-82 Debt-to-Equity Ratios

The total debt and stockholders' equity for three companies follows. The companies are described as follows:

- **General Electric** is a multinational technology and services company and is a large, well-established company.
- **Google** is a fast-growing company focusing on Internet search.
- **Amgen** is a biotechnology company pioneering the development of products based on advances in recombinant DNA.

	Total Debt		Stockholders' Equity	
(in millions)	2011	2004	2011	2004
General Electric	$599,108	$623,303	$118,134	$110,821
Google	11,610	285	46,241	589
Amgen	29,842	9,516	19,029	19,705

1. Compute debt-to-equity ratios for each company for 2004 and 2011.
2. Discuss the differences in the ratios across firms.
3. Discuss the changes in individual company ratios from 2004 to 2011.

▶ OBJECTIVE 2

9-83 Review of Chapters 8 and 9

The Kroger Company, a Cincinnati-based supermarket chain, operates nearly 2,500 stores throughout the United States. The company's annual report for the fiscal year ended January 28, 2012, contained the following ($ in millions):

The Kroger Company

	January 28	January 29
	2012	2011
Property, plant, and equipment, at cost	$28,071	$26,716
Less: Accumulated depreciation and amortization	13,607	12,569
Net property, plant, and equipment	$14,464	$14,147
Current portion of long-term debt	$ 1,315	$ 588
Long-term debt less current portion	6,850	7,303

Kroger's statement of cash flows listed capital investments of $1,898 million and depreciation and amortization of $1,638 million for the fiscal year ended January 28, 2012. Assume that all capital investments and all depreciation and amortizations were for property, plant, and equipment. (The use of T-accounts should help your analysis.)

1. Compute the dollar amounts of the following:
   a. Accumulated depreciation relating to properties and plants disposed of during the fiscal year ended January 28, 2012.
   b. Original acquisition cost of properties and plants disposed of during the fiscal year ended January 28, 2012.
2. Compute the dollar amount of the net increase or decrease in total long-term debt during the fiscal year ended January 28, 2012.

▶ OBJECTIVES 1, 2

9-84 Liabilities for Frequent Flier Miles and Ethics

Most airlines in the United States have frequent flier programs that grant free flights if a customer accumulates enough flight miles on the airline. For example, **United Airlines** offers a free domestic flight for every 25,000 miles flown on United. United describes its program as follows in a footnote to the 2011 financial statements:

In the case of the sale of air services, the Company recognizes a portion of the ticket sales as revenue when the air transportation occurs and defers a portion of the ticket sale representing the value of the related miles. The adoption of Accounting Standards Update 2009-13, Multiple-Deliverable Revenue Arrangements—a consensus of the FASB Emerging Issues Task Force ("ASU 2009-13") resulted in the revision of this accounting, effective January 1, 2011.

Under the Company's prior accounting policy, the Company estimated the weighted average equivalent ticket value by assigning a fair value to the miles that were issued in connection with the sale of air transportation. The equivalent ticket value is a weighted average ticket value of each outstanding mile, based upon projected redemption patterns for available award choices when such miles are consumed. The fair value of the miles was deferred and the residual amount of ticket proceeds was recognized as passenger revenue at the time the air transportation was provided.

The Company began applying the new guidance in 2011 and determines the estimated selling price of the air transportation and miles as if each element is sold on a separate basis. The total consideration from each ticket sale is then allocated to each of these elements individually on a pro rata basis. The estimated selling price of miles is computed using an estimated weighted average equivalent ticket value that is adjusted by a sales discount that considers a number of factors, including ultimate fulfillment expectations associated with miles sold in flight transactions to various customer groups.

In its 2011 annual report, United Continental Holdings, the parent company for the newly merged United and Continental, reported a current liability of $2.4 billion and a long-term liability of $3.3 billion for frequent flyer deferred revenue. These are very large numbers equal to approximately 15% of passenger revenue.

The notes indicated that the new accounting policy decreases the value of miles that the Company records as deferred revenue and increases the passenger revenue recorded at the time air transportation is provided. Not only does the required financial accounting under GAAP sometimes change, but also firms think about the "real cost" of frequent flyer miles differently. Some airlines believe the cost is about $70 per flight while others think it is more like $10 per flight. It depends on what the airline considers to be the marginal cost of an extra passenger. If the flights are usually full, the marginal cost is high because a frequent flyer ticket might push out a full-fare ticket worth several hundred dollars. If flights usually have open seats, putting a frequent flyer in the seat costs only insurance and very modest jet fuel.

Suppose airlines use one estimate of the cost of these "free" flights for their internal decision making and another for computing the liability for their publicly reported balance sheet. Comment on the ethical issues.

9-85 Present Value and Sports Salaries

▶▶ **OBJECTIVE 8**

Study Appendix 9. On December 13, 2007, Alex Rodriguez signed a 10-year, $275 million contract with the New York Yankees. Five years into the contract, it remains the largest sports contract according to Wikipedia. In fact, the second highest contract is Alex Rodriguez's prior contract with the Texas Rangers. The contract has some built-in bonuses. Rodriguez receives an extra $6 million for each occurrence of passing the lifetime home run records of Willie Mays (660), Babe Ruth (714), Hank Aaron (755), and Barry Bonds (762). And if he passes Bonds for the all-time lead, there is another $6 million bonus. At the end of the 2012 baseball season, he had 647 home runs.

Assume that all payments in the contract are paid on January 2 of the respective years, beginning on January 2, 2008. The contract includes a $10 million signing bonus paid out as follows: $2 million on January 2, 2008; $1 million paid January 2 of each year 2009–2013; and $3 million on January 2, 2014. The salary is as follows (in millions):

2008	$27	2013	$28
2009	$32	2014	$25
2010	$32	2015	$21
2011	$31	2016	$20
2012	$29	2017	$20

Assume that the appropriate discount rate is 10%.

1. What was the present value of the contract on January 2, 2008?
2. How much present value (as of January 2, 2008) did Rodriguez lose by receiving the $10 million signing bonus over 5 years instead of immediately?
3. Do you agree that the contract was worth $275 million? Explain.
4. Give the journal entry to record his 2013 salary and bonus, assuming it is paid in cash along with any bonuses and that he does, in 2013, pass the home run record of Willie Mays.

Collaborative Learning Exercises

OBJECTIVE 3

9-86 Characteristics of Bonds

Form groups of three to six persons each. Each person should select a company that has long-term debt in the form of bonds (or debentures). Pick one of the company's bonds, and note the interest rate on the bond. If the company does not list bonds individually, you may need to select one of the groups of bonds that it presents.

Find out as much as you can about the factors that might explain the bond's interest rate. Among the items to look for are characteristics of the bond (such as the size of the issue, the length of the term, and any special features such as subordination, convertibility, and covenants) and characteristics of the company (such as its industry, its debt-to-equity ratio, and its interest-coverage ratio). Also, try to find out when the bond was issued and the level of prevailing interest rates at the time of issue. (Companies do not usually show the issue date in the footnotes to their financial statements. You might try looking at past annual reports to see when the bonds first appeared on the financial statement.) Prevailing interest rates may be represented by the rates on U.S. Treasury securities. Note the amount by which the interest rate of the bond exceeds the rate of a U.S. Treasury security of the same duration.

After students have performed their independent research, they should get together and compare results. Do the factors identified explain the differences in rates across the companies? How do the factors relate to the riskiness of the bonds? Is the amount by which the bond interest rate exceeds the U.S. Treasury rate related to the bond's riskiness?

OBJECTIVE 5

9-87 Accounting for Pensions

Form groups of two or more students. Divide each group into two debate teams. Each team should be assigned one of the two following positions:

1. Pensions and other postretirement benefits are legitimate liabilities of a company and should be recognized as such on their balance sheets. They are expenses of the periods in which the benefiting employees work, so the obligation to pay them should be accrued at that time.
2. Pensions and other postretirement benefits may be legal liabilities of a company but their measurement is very uncertain. Current accounting requirements provide a sense of certainty and precision that is inappropriate. One issue is that the present values rely on assumptions about time to retirement, time in retirement, and levels of earnings to be experienced by the pension fund investments, which are notoriously hard to estimate. Moreover, there are many examples of troubled firms winning concessions from unionized workers that actually change the future benefit streams. The profession should develop a new model for measuring and reporting pension liabilities.

Each team can be given 5–10 minutes to defend its position, followed by approximately 2 minutes each for rebuttals. Then a general class discussion of the issues can follow. The class might take a vote on which group made the most convincing argument.

Analyzing and Interpreting Financial Statements

9-88 Financial Statement Research

Select any two companies from the airline industry, and find each company's footnote describing its leases. (Possible companies include Alaska Airlines, American Airlines, Delta Air Lines, United, and US Airways, but do not feel restricted to these.) Compute each company's debt-to-equity ratio under each of three assumptions:

▸▸ **OBJECTIVE 7**

1. With leases as reported
2. With all leases treated as operating leases
3. With all leases treated as capital leases

For this calculation assume all operating lease payments due after the fifth year are spread evenly over years 6–15. That is, one-tenth of the remaining lease payments will be made each of the next 10 years. Use a 10% interest rate for computing the present value of the operating leases. Comment on the differences made by the three treatments of leases. Also, comment on the differences in ratios between the two companies.

9-89 Analyzing Starbucks' Financial Statements

Find Starbucks' financial statements for the fiscal year ended October 2, 2011, either via the Starbucks Web site or on the SEC's EDGAR database. Focus on the liabilities section of the balance sheet and footnote 10.

▸▸ **OBJECTIVE 7**

1. Compute the following ratios at October 2, 2011. Assess the changes in these ratios. The values at September 28, 2008, are provided for comparison:
   a. Debt-to-equity ratio: 9/28/2008 = 1.28
   b. Debt-to-total-assets ratio: 9/28/2008 = .56
2. Comment on Starbucks' amount of long-term liabilities compared with its amount of current liabilities.

9-90 Analyzing Financial Statements Using the Internet: Macy's, Inc.

Go to www.macysinc.com to find financial information for Macy's. Select For Investors, and click on the most recent annual report or 10-K.

Answer the following questions about Macy's and its long-term debt:

▸▸ **OBJECTIVES 2, 4, 5**

1. Locate the discussion of Lease Obligations in the Notes to Consolidated Financial Statements. Macy's has both capital leases and operating leases. What percentage of its future lease commitments are for capital leases?
2. How do the operating lease payments affect Macy's financial statements? Explain how these operating leases are considered "invisible debt."
3. What items comprise Macy's long-term debt? Was any long-term debt issued in the most recent year? Was any long-term debt retired in the most recent year?
4. Describe who is eligible for Macy's pension and other postretirement benefits. How are these items reported on the financial statements? What discount rate is used for determining the present value of these items? Does this rate differ from the rate used a year ago? If so, what difference does that make on the present value of the obligations?

10 Stockholders' Equity

United Parcel Service (UPS) has a distinctive brown fleet of trucks and a distinguished position as the world's largest package delivery company. Each business day, the company's 398,000 employees deliver packages for 1.1 million shippers to 7.7 million recipients in more than 220 countries. In 2011 UPS delivered 4.01 billion packages, an average of 15.4 million pieces per day. To do this requires a global fleet of about 101,000 delivery vehicles including more than 520 aircraft. Almost 2,000 of the delivery vehicles use alternative fuels, including hybrid electric, all electric, or compressed natural gas.

UPS has been one of the key beneficiaries of the shift to Web-based businesses. The firm continues to serve old-line, bricks-and-mortar companies, but the nature of the business is being transformed to a "time-definite" service. Companies once shipped items without knowing their precise arrival day or time. Today, UPS assures a package's time of arrival and provides the ability to monitor its progress constantly. Domestically, customers can select same-day, next-day, two-day, or three-day delivery options at differing price points. Many of these delivery options allow the customer to specify a time-of-day cut-off for their delivery. Internationally, UPS offers a selection of guaranteed day and time-definite shipping services. Customers have efficient electronic access to the information that allows them to request a pickup and track an order. They rely on UPS for full logistics support for ordering, scheduling, shipping, and receiving. UPS offers warehousing and order fulfillment services for small- to medium-size firms through its UPS Logistics segment. In addition to its package delivery service and logistical support, UPS has a company called **UPS Capital** that lends businesses money, finances inventory, and even buys accounts receivable.

▶▶ **LEARNING OBJECTIVES** *After studying this chapter, you should be able to:*

1. Describe the rights of common shareholders.

2. Account for common stock, including payment of cash dividends.

3. Contrast bonds, preferred stock, and common stock.

4. Explain the characteristics and use of stock option and restricted stock plans.

5. Identify the economic characteristics of and account for stock splits.

6. Account for both large- and small-percentage stock dividends.

7. Explain and report stock repurchases and other treasury stock transactions.

8. Record issuance of stock for noncash consideration and conversions of debt into equity or of preferred stock into common stock.

9. Understand restrictions on retained earnings and interpret other components of stockholders' equity.

10. Use the rate of return on common equity and book value per share.

Supporting the worldwide delivery service requires very modern, high-tech processing. UPS Worldport is the largest fully automated package handling facility in the world. Located near the company's air hub in Louisville, Kentucky, Worldport is a 5.2 million square foot facility equipped with overhead cameras that read smart labels and have the capacity to guide sorting of 416,000 packages per hour. Similar high-tech facilities were constructed in 2006 at the Cologne/Bonn airport in Germany and in 2008 in Tamworth, England. Also in 2008 the company opened a major air hub in Shanghai, China, serving all of China and providing direct service to the Americas, Europe, and the rest of Asia. In 2010, the company replaced a hub in the Philippines with a new hub in Shenzhen, China. This new hub has slashed a day off shipment time-in-transit for customers in the region. And, in 2011, the company announced plans to significantly expand the facility in Cologne, Germany, to meet increased demand.

UPS has been a public company since November 10, 1999. When UPS chose to "go public," it found a receptive audience, raising some $5.5 billion by selling more than 109 million shares at approximately $50 per share. UPS used the proceeds of the sale not only to fund its aggressive growth and development plans but also to purchase shares from employee shareholders. The company had been employee-owned for years, and the public offering allowed employees to realize the value of their long-term investment in the company. Even now, employees and retirees own most of the outstanding shares. In the United States, the SEC regulates public companies such as UPS, as described in the Business First box on p. 450. ●

UPS has become the world's largest package delivery company and a leading global provider of specialized transportation and logistics services. UPS employees control the company through their voting rights as shareholders. The public has relied on UPS for delivery services for more than a century but has only had access to UPS stock since it became a public company in 1999.

BUSINESS FIRST

PUBLIC COMPANIES

The U.S. Securities Acts of 1933 and 1934 created the Securities and Exchange Commission (SEC) in response to economic and political pressure associated with the stock market crash of 1929 and the Great Depression. The SEC regulates accounting practices and ensures that companies with publicly traded securities provide information to shareholders on a timely basis. The SEC Web site (www.sec.gov) indicates that "companies with more than $10 million in assets whose securities are held by more than 500 owners must file annual and other periodic reports." This requirement has been in place since 1964. In early 2012, the SEC's Advisory Committee on Small and Emerging Companies recommended that the SEC raise the 500 shareholder threshold to 1,000 and exclude certain employees from the shareholder count. This recommendation will require final approval from the SEC before it can be implemented. Companies that meet the filing requirements must submit quarterly and annual reports (forms 10-Q and 10-K, respectively). They also file special reports (form 8-K) whenever something material happens to the company. All corporate filings with the SEC are accessible on the SEC Web site, and Web sites of individual companies often link to SEC filings, usually in a section called "Investor Relations."

Security analysts closely monitor the quarterly results of public companies. We often observe large changes in market value and significant selling or buying of shares based on the results of one quarter of business. Some investors and managers believe this motivates an excessively short-term view in management decision making. They think a "closely held" private company has much more freedom to take the long view. Private companies can make investments that will take years to bear fruit and can accept short-term negative results in search of longer-term successes. When a company such as UPS chooses to have an initial public offering (IPO) and allow its shares to trade widely, it is agreeing to comply with costly and complicated SEC rules in exchange for access to a large pool of capital.

The majority of companies that most of us know are well-established companies that issued their common stock years ago. However, entrepreneurs are continually forming new corporations. Silicon Valley in California, Silicon Alley in New York City, and other high-tech locations originated thousands of new ventures in the last two decades. Most of these firms failed, but a few are thriving, including Amazon.com, eBay, Yahoo!, and Google.

A complicated marketplace exists for the funding of new ventures. New corporations often start with a few investors and then seek additional funding as their original ideas prove to be possible, exciting, and profitable. Groups of investors called venture capitalists support exciting ideas early in the process. If a company successfully implements these ideas, it may issue additional shares to the public through an IPO. An underwriting firm generally manages the IPO, and it sells shares to individual investors and to institutional investors such as pension funds, insurance companies, and mutual funds. Regardless of who owns the firm and whether it is public or private, the accounting procedures are very similar.

There is considerable variability in the number of IPOs from year to year. With the economic crisis, the number of U.S. and foreign issuer IPOs fell from 207 in 2007 to only 31 in 2008 and 54 in 2009. As the economic recovery began, the number increased to 142 and 116, in 2010 and 2011, respectively. One of the offerings in the fourth quarter of 2011 was Groupon, a company that sells internet coupons. Groupon raised $700 million in its IPO, making it the largest IPO by a U.S. internet company since Google raised $1.7 billion in 2004. Initially offered at $20 per share, Groupon ended its first day of trading at $26.11 per share, up 30.6%. While impressive, this 30.6% increase does not compare with the 109% first day increase in the stock price of LinkedIn Corporation, the professional networking company that went public on May 19, 2011. LinkedIn stock, which was initially offered at $45 per share, closed at $94.25 on the first day of trading. These dramatic stock price increases are seldom sustained. As of October 25, 2012, Groupon was trading at $4.46, but LinkedIn's price had increased to $105.72.

Facebook went public on May 18, 2012, and was one of the most anticipated IPOs in history. But it did not go well. The original offering price was $38 per share and investors clamored for more shares than originally offered. The volume was so large that it contributed to some technology problems at NASDAQ, the listing exchange. As of October 25, 2012, the stock price had fallen to $22.56, well below the offering price. Lawsuits by shareholders against Facebook, NASDAQ, and the underwriters citing multiple errors are moving through the courts.

Sources: www.sec.gov; D. A. Westenberg, *2010 IPO Report*, Wilmer Cutler Pickering Hale and Dorr LLP, http://www.ipoguidebook.com/files/upload/2010_IPO_report.pdf; http://www.hoovers.com/ipo-central/ipo-scorecard-biggest-first-days/100004166-1.html; http://www.hoovers.com/ipo-central/ipo-performance/100004163-1.html; A. Barr, and C. Baldwin, "Groupon's IPO Biggest by U.S. Web Company Since Google," ThomsonReuters, November 4, 2011, http://www.reuters.com/assets/print?aid=USTRE7A352020111104; S. Johnson, "SEC Advised to Dial Back 'Facebook Rule' for Small Companies," CFO.com, February 1, 2012; "Its IPO Botched, Facebook Looks Hard at Nasdaq," NYTimes.com, July 1, 2012.

Background on Stockholders' Equity

Thus far, we have focused primarily on transactions affecting assets and liabilities. Now we examine stockholders' equity in more detail. After all, stockholders such as those of UPS want to know details about their investments. Moreover, stockholders supply a significant portion of the capital that corporations employ, so knowing the rights and responsibilities of stockholders is important to understanding how companies raise capital.

The accounting equation must balance. If we know the amounts of assets and liabilities, stockholders' equity is the residual, the difference between the assets and liabilities. This is why we call the stockholders the residual claimants to the corporation. When a company goes out of business, sells its assets, and pays creditors out of the proceeds, the stockholders receive whatever, if anything, is left. It is now time to address issues relating to how we classify and report transactions between a company and its shareholders and how analysts use this information to evaluate the company.

We show the owners' equity section of the balance sheet from the UPS 2011 annual report in Exhibit 10-1. Some of what appears there is no surprise because common stock and retained earnings are old friends at this point. However, UPS has two classes of common stock and also lists additional paid-in-capital, accumulated other comprehensive loss, deferred compensation obligations, treasury stock, and noncontrolling interests. We will discuss most of these additional components of equity in this chapter. Noncontrolling interests are introduced in Chapter 11.

The retained earnings are a result of the historic profitability of UPS that has enabled it to finance much of its growth by retaining earnings in the business. Assets of the company reported in the balance sheet at December 31, 2011, total $34.7 billion, and total stockholders' equity of $7.1 billion represents 20.5% of total assets. Note that these accounting values do not correspond to the market value of UPS. The stock closed at approximately $73 per share at year-end 2011, which means the total market value of equity was $70.4 billion ($73 per share times 965 million class A and class B shares held by investors). This is almost 10 times greater than its book value of $7.1 billion.

A number of the accounting practices for shareholders' equity are based on legal characteristics of corporations, so we make frequent reference to the rights and privileges of shareholders and the consequences of various financing decisions on the firm and its owners. For example, UPS has two classes of common stock. This dual class system is common in companies that have a strong founder or family owned component. Martha Stewart Living, Google, Estée Lauder, Berkshire Hathaway, and Ford Motor Company all have dual class structures. In fact, a 2007 study reported that 11.5% of the firms that traded on the NYSE in that year were dual class firms. In the case of UPS, prior to going public in 1999 the company was employee-owned and UPS employees and retirees still hold the class A common stock, which is not publicly traded. The class A shares have 10 votes each, while class B shares have 1 vote each. Thus, the employees control votes for electing the board of directors, approving mergers, and other significant

EXHIBIT 10-1

UPS Shareowners' Equity
(in millions)

	December 31	
	2011	**2010**
Class A common stock (240 and 258 shares issued in 2011 and 2010)	$ 3	$ 3
Class B common stock (725 and 735 shares issued in 2011 and 2010)	7	7
Additional paid-in capital	—	—
Retained earnings	10,128	10,604
Accumulated other comprehensive loss	(3,103)	(2,635)
Deferred compensation obligations	88	103
Less: Treasury stock (2 shares in 2011 and 2010)	(88)	(103)
Total Equity for Controlling Interests	7,035	7,979
Noncontrolling Interests	73	68
Total Shareowners' Equity	$ 7,108	$ 8,047

corporate decisions. Class A shares are directly convertible into class B shares. During 2011, employees converted 21 million shares of class A stock to class B stock, probably so the employees could sell the shares and receive cash. At $73 per share, this represents a sale of $1.5 billion in ownership by long-term employees to new investors.

Internationally, there are substantial differences in the structure of corporate/business activity. For example, in some countries large corporations are primarily privately owned by a few individuals, instead of having broad public ownership and public financial reporting as in the United States. In other countries banks provide the majority of financing, so large public issuances of shares are rare. Many formerly planned economies have been transitioning from state-owned-and-operated business entities into private ones. In many countries the government remains the largest employer because it owns economic entities such as power producers, phone providers, and airlines, not to mention the mail system, which remains a government monopoly even in the United States. However, from an accounting perspective, worldwide movement toward IFRS and efforts to converge IFRS with U.S. GAAP have significantly reduced the international variation in accounting for stockholders' equity.

Accounting For Common Stock in Publicly Held Corporations

▶▶ OBJECTIVE 1

Describe the rights of common shareholders.

Although specific laws vary by jurisdiction, the process of incorporating is similar worldwide. In the United States, a company incorporates in accordance with state law, while in most of the world the national government determines corporate law. Each of the 50 U.S. states has its own system of corporate law. While state-to-state differences exist, state laws share many similarities. The Model Business Corporation Act prepared by the American Bar Association and adopted by almost half of the 50 states has reduced variation across states. Regardless of the state in which a company incorporates, it must file **articles of incorporation** with the secretary of state. These documents become the company's **corporate charter**.

articles of incorporation (corporate charter)

Documents a company must file with the secretary of state at the time at which it incorporates.

Corporate charters specify, among other things, the type and number of shares that a company can issue. While a company can issue different types of stock, it must have at least one class of stock that has all the rights, risks, and rewards of ownership. It is this class of stock that we typically refer to as common stock. The rights of common stockholders (or shareholders) generally include the right to (1) vote, (2) share in corporate profits through the declaration of dividends and/or appreciation of the share price, (3) share in any assets left at liquidation, and (4) possibly acquire shares of subsequent issues of stock. The extent of an individual stockholder's power is determined by the number and type of shares held.

Corporations hold annual meetings of shareholders, where they take votes on important matters. For example, the shareholders elect the board of directors. They also vote on such matters as changes to employee bonus plans, selection of outside auditors, and merger proposals. Large corporations make heavy use of the proxy system. A **corporate proxy** is a written authority granted by individual shareholders to others (usually members of corporate management) to cast the shareholders' votes. By using a proxy, shareholders may express (vote) their preference without traveling to the site of the annual meeting.

corporate proxy

A written authority granted by individual shareholders to others (usually members of corporate management) to cast the shareholders' votes.

The ultimate power to manage a corporation almost always resides with the common shareholders, but shareholders of publicly owned corporations usually delegate that power to the company's top managers. The modern large corporation frequently has a team of professional managers including a chief executive officer (CEO), a chief operating officer (COO), a chief financial officer (CFO), and perhaps a chief information or technology officer (CIO or CTO). Collectively these leaders are sometimes referred to as the "C-suite," named after the use of chief in their titles.

Increasingly, companies require top managers to own a significant number of shares in the firm because they believe that managers who own shares directly or hold stock options to acquire shares are more likely to share a common economic interest with shareholders. When the company's stock rises in value, the managers benefit personally. When the company's stock declines in value, the managers experience a loss in wealth. Of course, management ownership of stock has an associated risk as well. Top management may manipulate corporate financial performance in order to maximize their short-term personal wealth at the expense of long-term company performance.

preemptive rights

The right of stockholders to acquire a proportional amount of any new issues of capital stock.

Stockholders also may have **preemptive rights**, which are the rights to acquire a proportional amount of any new issues of capital stock. Whenever a company issues new shares of

BUSINESS FIRST

CORPORATE GOVERNANCE

Large-scale frauds in corporate America led to the passage of the Sarbanes-Oxley (SOX) legislation in 2002. The act created a new Public Company Accounting Oversight Board (PCAOB) with broad power to register, inspect, investigate, and discipline public accounting firms and set standards for public audits. The five members of the PCAOB are appointed by the SEC in consultation with the Chairman of the Federal Reserve Board and the Secretary of the Treasury. Two members must be CPAs, and the other three must not be. The act specifies rules of behavior for registered public accounting firms, including requiring rotation of the lead partner on an audit every 5 years. It prohibits public accounting firms from performing most "nonaudit" services for their audit clients. These services include financial information systems design and implementation, bookkeeping, and internal audit functions. Each annual report must include an "internal control report," including management's assertions and supporting attestation by the auditor. The SEC now requires every company to adopt a code of ethics for senior financial officers.

Sarbanes-Oxley, together with recent SEC regulations, significantly changed the corporate governance environment. The historical legal notion was that the shareholders elected a board of directors to represent them and to oversee the functioning of professional managers. However, various frauds revealed problems in the system. Some directors were neither as qualified nor as hard working as the shareholders expected. Managers, especially the CEO, often selected their friends for board membership, creating a board that was not a critical independent component of the corporate governance structure. Shareholders could vote for or against nominees, but they could not select candidate A over candidate Z. The post Sarbanes-Oxley environment requires increased independence between directors and management. For example, SOX increased the responsibilities of the board's audit committee and required that an independent director, who is professionally qualified for the role, must chair the audit committee. In the United States, we are seeing increasing pressure to separate the positions of CEO and chair of the board of directors. This concept of a nonexecutive chair has been common in other countries for some years. In fact, a group of European institutional investors is supporting efforts in U.S. companies to separate CEO and board chair positions. These changes are transforming the composition of boards of directors and the way shareholders influence the management of corporations.

Sources: Sarbanes-Oxley Act of 2002, *Pub.L. 107-204*, 116 *Stat.* 745, http://www.gpo.gov/fdsys/pkg/PLAW-107publ204/content-detail.html; Reuters, "International Investors Announce Support for Independent Chairman at ExxonMobil Corporation," May 19, 2008.

---

stock, more people can become owners, in which case each existing shareholder's percentage of ownership decreases. The preemptive privilege allows present shareholders to purchase additional shares directly from the corporation before it can sell new shares to the general public. In this way, the existing shareholders are able to maintain their percentage of ownership. Such rights are much more common in Europe than in the United States.

Perhaps the most important right of common shareholders is limited liability. Recall from Chapter 1 that limited liability means the creditors of the corporation have claims only on the assets owned by the corporation, not on the assets of the owners of the corporation. In contrast, the creditors of a partnership have potential rights against the savings, homes, and automobiles of the individual partners.

Despite state-level registration of corporations in the United States, since the 1930s there has been significant federal regulation of corporations. A major increase in such regulation occurred with the passage of the Sarbanes-Oxley Act in 2002, as described in the Business First box above.

Issuing Common Stock

The articles of incorporation referenced earlier establish the maximum number of shares of stock a company can legally issue. We call these **authorized shares**. When the company receives cash or other consideration in exchange for authorized stock certificates, the shares become **issued shares**. We call shares that are issued and held by the stockholders **outstanding shares**. Often the articles of incorporation specify the process whereby the shareholders can authorize additional shares in the future.

▶▶ **OBJECTIVE 2**

Account for common stock, including payment of cash dividends.

authorized shares
The maximum number of shares of stock that a company can legally issue under the articles of incorporation.

issued shares
The aggregate number of shares sold to the public.

outstanding shares
Issued shares held by the stockholders.

To account for the issuance of stock in exchange for cash, we record the receipt of cash and create a common stock account to represent the ownership interest. At the end of January 2012, UPS stock was selling for around $75 per share, so if UPS issued 1 million additional shares it would record the stock sale as follows:

Cash	75,000,000	
Common stock.		75,000,000

Many U.S. companies, however, record their common stock issuance in two accounts—par value and additional paid-in capital. Traditionally, par value was set as part of the articles of incorporation and was originally intended as a measure of protection for creditors because it established the minimum legal liability of a stockholder. In other words, if a company's assets were not sufficient to cover its liabilities, stockholders who had contributed less than the par value per share could be required to increase their investment. In addition, depending on state law, par value could limit the amount available to distribute to shareholders in the form of dividends. In this way, creditors would be assured the corporation would have at least a minimum amount of ownership capital—for example, $1 for each share issued. Currently, the concept of par value is not economically relevant and companies authorizing new share issuances frequently issue stock without a specified par value. However, corporations that have authorized shares with designated par values typically continue to distinguish par value from additional paid-in capital in the financial statements. Internationally, most companies using IFRS report a single capital account—for example, Volkswagen, the German automaker, refers to Subscribed Capital, and Carrefour, the French supermarket chain, calls it simply Capital.

While the UPS balance sheet as presented in Exhibit 10-1 shows no par value in its equity section, examination of the footnotes indicates that all UPS shares have a par value of $.01 each. The entry to record issuance of 1 million additional shares at $75 per share would separate out par value as follows:

Cash	75,000,000	
Common stock		10,000
Additional paid-in capital		74,990,000

Later in this chapter we discuss why the December 31, 2011, UPS balance sheet shows no dollar amount assigned to Additional Paid-in Capital.

Some companies use the term "stated value" rather than "par value." Similarly, the language used to describe additional paid-in capital varies widely. For economic purposes, most of these distinctions are of little importance. However, you encounter them in annual reports and should understand their meaning. The following illustrates the diversity of practice:

Company	Par Value per Share	Name for Additional Paid-in Capital
American Greetings	$1.00	Capital in excess of par value
McDonald's	.01	Additional paid-in capital
Home Depot	.05	Paid-in capital
ExxonMobil	No par value	No separate account
Royal Dutch Shell	Nominal value €.07	Balances combined in Ordinary share capital

treasury stock

A company's own stock that it has purchased and holds for later use.

Sometimes a company buys back shares of stock from its own shareholders. It might buy them to reduce shareholder claims permanently. Alternatively, companies may hold the shares for later use, usually to distribute as part of employee bonuses or stock purchase plans. We call such temporarily held shares **treasury stock**. Treasury shares are considered issued, but because the company holds them, they are no longer considered outstanding. For example, as of December 31, 2011, UPS had authorized a combined total of 10.2 billion shares of class A and class B stock. Issued shares totaled 965 million, of which UPS had reacquired 2 million shares that it lists as treasury stock. Therefore, 963 million shares were outstanding as shown in detail below.

Number of Shares (in millions)	
Authorized	10,200
Deduct: Unissued	9,235
Issued	965
Deduct: Shares held in treasury	2
Total shares outstanding	963

Cash Dividends

We first introduced cash dividends in Chapter 2. Remember that dividends are proportional distributions of income to shareholders, usually in the form of cash. In the United States companies typically pay dividends in equal amounts each quarter, although the board may declare, change, or eliminate a dividend at any time. Some firms tend to pay a special, larger dividend once per year.

Companies do not automatically pay dividends. A company's board of directors votes to approve each dividend. We call the date on which the board formally announces that it will pay a dividend the **declaration date**. On this date, the cash dividend becomes a liability. The board specifies a future date as the **date of record**. All stockholders owning stock on that date will receive the dividend. A person who holds the stock on the declaration date but sells before the date of record will not receive the dividend. The actual **payment date** is the day the company distributes the cash; it usually follows the date of record by a few days or weeks.

A company records entries for cash dividends at two times, when it creates the liability and when it pays the dividend. Suppose a company declares a $20,000 dividend on September 26 to stockholders of record on October 25. The payment date is November 15. The necessary entries are as follows:

declaration date
The date the board of directors formally announces that it will pay a cash dividend. On this date, the dividend becomes a liability.

date of record
The date that determines which shareholders will receive a cash dividend.

payment date
The date a company pays cash dividends.

Date of Declaration

Sept. 26	Retained earnings.	20,000	
	Dividends payable.		20,000

To record the declaration of dividends to be paid on November 15 to shareholders of record as of October 25

Date of Payment

Nov. 15	Dividends payable	20,000	
	Cash		20,000

To pay dividends declared on September 26 to shareholders of record as of October 25

If a company prepares a balance sheet between declaration and payment, it will include the Dividends Payable account as a current liability. The amount of cash dividends declared by a board of directors depends on many factors, primarily the market expectations, the current and predicted earnings, and the corporation's current cash position and financial plans concerning spending on plant assets and repayments of debts. Remember that payment of cash dividends requires cash. Thus, the single biggest factor affecting the size of dividends is the availability of cash that the company has not otherwise committed.

Investors expect companies that have historically paid regular dividends to continue to do so. General Electric is an example of a company that had paid dividends every quarter for more than 100 years. Its dividend increased each year, from quarterly payments of $.08 per share in 1995 to $.31 per share in 2008, until the financial crisis caused the board of directors to reduce the quarterly dividend to $.10 in June 2009. With the modest economic recovery, the board increased the quarterly dividend to $.17 in December 2011. Investors also expect that companies that have not paid dividends because cash was better used to finance expansion will continue to identify growth opportunities requiring additional investment. eBay is an example of a growing company that does not pay cash dividends.

What other factors might affect the company's decision to pay a dividend? In some states and some countries, the dividend decision depends on the amount of retained earnings because the law forbids dividend payments exceeding the company's retained earnings balance. A similar limitation may occur because of bond covenants that restrict dividend payments. Ultimately, investors carefully watch changes in dividend patterns. If a company has maintained a series of uninterrupted dividends over a span of years, it will make an effort to continue such payments, even in the face of net losses. In fact, companies occasionally borrow money for the sole purpose of maintaining dividend payments.

Elimination and initiation of dividend payments are big events that cause investors to pause and consider carefully what the company's decision means about the future. This careful consideration is necessary because the meaning of dividend changes can be confusing. Consider a company that initiates or increases a dividend. The good news is that the company has resources to distribute to shareholders while continuing to grow and do business. The bad news is that the company appears to no longer anticipate enough profitable future investments to use all the cash it generates.

Preferred Stock

> ▶▶ **OBJECTIVE 3**
> Contrast bonds, preferred stock, and common stock.

preferred stock
Stock that offers the stockholder different rights and preferential treatment relative to common stockholders.

The two most common types of stock are common stock and preferred stock. Common stock, as the name implies, is the most basic type. All corporations have it, and the shareholders who own it have the rights discussed earlier. **Preferred stock** offers the stockholder different rights and preferential treatment relative to common stockholders. The terms of preferred stock can include almost any arrangement the company and stockholders agree upon. For example, preferred stockholders often surrender the right to vote. In exchange, they usually have a right to dividends before common shareholders can receive a dividend. Often the amount of the preferred dividend is expressed as the product of a prespecified dividend rate times the stock's par value. For example, a $100 par, 5% preferred stock would pay a $5 dividend. In addition to preferential dividend treatment, preferred stockholders frequently have a preferred claim on assets in liquidation. Therefore, at liquidation, after distributing assets to satisfy the claims of all creditors, preferred stockholders receive any available company assets, up to the amount of a specified liquidation value, before common stockholders receive anything.

Preferred stock is like common stock in that dividends are not a legal obligation until the board of directors declares them. However, unlike common stock dividends, the amount of the preferred stock dividend is generally specified and does not change over time. While not evident on the December 31, 2011, balance sheet, a review of the footnotes indicates that UPS has 200 million authorized preferred shares. As of the balance sheet date, the company had issued no preferred shares.

Cumulative Dividends

cumulative
A characteristic of preferred stock that requires that undeclared dividends accumulate and the company must pay them before it can pay any dividends to common stockholders.

dividend arrearages (dividends in arrears)
Accumulated unpaid dividends on preferred stock.

What happens when the board votes to skip a preferred stock dividend? Just because a company can decide not to pay the dividend now may not mean that the company has completely avoided the obligation. Preferred stock dividends are often **cumulative**. Cumulative preferred stock requires that undeclared dividends accumulate and the company must pay them in the future before it can pay any dividends to common stockholders. From the standpoint of a common shareholder, accumulated unpaid dividends, called **dividend arrearages** or **dividends in arrears**, are somewhat like debt obligations. Why? Because a company must pay them before the common shareholders can receive dividends. Moreover, in the event of liquidation, a company must pay cumulative unpaid preferred dividends before common stockholders receive any cash.

To illustrate the operation of cumulative preferred stock, consider Exhibit 10-2. Panel A contains the stockholders' equity of Acumulado Corporation on December 31, 20X0, and panel B shows the consequences of subsequent years of net income and dividends.

Acumulado's board of directors elected not to declare and pay preferred dividends in 20X1 and 20X2. This decision makes economic sense, given that Acumulado Corporation posted losses both years. You may be thinking that the company had more than enough in retained earnings to be able to pay the dividends despite the losses, but retained earnings is not the same as cash. The large retained earnings balance resulted from many prior years of profitable operations, but in those prior years the company reinvested the cash generated by operations into productive business assets. When a firm encounters losses such as Acumulado experienced in 20X1 and 20X2, cash flow may be reduced, and there may be insufficient cash available to pay dividends.

EXHIBIT 10-2

Acumulado Corporation Preferred Dividends

PANEL A

Stockholders' Equity, December 31, 20X0:

Preferred stock, no par, cumulative, $5 annual dividend per share	
Issued and outstanding, 1,000,000 shares	$ 50,000,000
Common stock, no par, 5,000,000 shares	100,000,000
Retained earnings	400,000,000
Total stockholders' equity	$550,000,000

PANEL B

	Net Income	Preferred Dividends Declared	Preferred Dividends In Arrears	Common Dividends Declared	Ending Balance, Retained Earnings
20X0					$400,000,000
20X1	$ (4,000,000)	—	$ 5,000,000	—	396,000,000
20X2	(4,000,000)	—	10,000,000	—	392,000,000
20X3	21,000,000	$ 3,000,000	12,000,000	—	410,000,000
20X4	49,000,000	17,000,000	—	$ 2,000,000	440,000,000
20X5	32,000,000	5,000,000	—	17,000,000	450,000,000

Even though the company skipped making the $5 million annual preferred dividend payments, its obligation to make those payments remained and accumulated, becoming $10 million by the end of 20X2. When operating results improved in 20X3, the board declared and paid a partial dividend of $3 million, leaving $2 million additional arrearages, which raised the total arrearage to $12 million. In 20X4, Acumulado had a banner year and improved profitability and cash flow enough to pay a full dividend and more. Dividends to preferred shareholders of $17 million cover not only the 20X4 dividend of $5,000,000 but also all accumulated dividends in arrears. With accumulated preferred dividends now completely paid, the firm may pay a dividend to the common shareholders for the first time in 4 years. Note that the ending balance in retained earnings in each year is equal to the beginning balance, plus net income (or minus a net loss) minus dividends declared.

Would you rather own cumulative or noncumulative preferred stock? In the preceding example, a holder of noncumulative preferred stock would receive nothing in 20X1 or 20X2, $3 million in 20X3, and $5 million in 20X4. In contrast, the owner of cumulative shares received $3 million in 20X3 and $17 million in 20X4. The cumulative feature is certainly preferred, but as with most choices, it is not free. Because cumulative preferred shares are more secure, they typically pay dividends at a lower rate than noncumulative shares. The cumulative feature must be explicit in the contract. It is not automatic.

Preference in Liquidation

In addition to the cumulative dividend feature, preferred stock usually has a specific **liquidating value**—the amount a company needs to pay to all preferred stockholders, in addition to any dividends in arrears, before it distributes any assets to common stockholders if the company is liquidated. The stock certificate generally states the exact liquidating value, which is often the same as par value. Because par value often defines the liquidating value and may define the amount of the dividend, it is economically important for preferred stock.

Consider an illustration of the liquidation of assets when short- and long-term debt, preferred stock, and common stock are all present. Exhibit 10-3 shows how to distribute cash to different claimants. The priority of the claims generally decreases as you move down the chart. The first column presents the book values. The next seven columns show the distributions to each class of claimant under different circumstances.

When there is not enough cash to go around, common stockholders are always the last to get paid and often wind up getting nothing, as is the case in the last five columns of Exhibit 10-3. However, in those instances when there is excess cash available, common stockholders receive

liquidating value
The amount a company needs to pay to all preferred stockholders, in addition to any dividends in arrears, before it distributes any assets to common stockholders if the company is liquidated.

EXHIBIT 10-3

Liquidation of Claims Under Various Alternatives
(in thousands)

	Account Balances	Assumed Total Cash Proceeds to Be Distributed						
		$1,500	$1,000	$500	$450	$350	$200	$100
Accounts payable	$ 100	$ 100	$ 100	$100	$100	$100	$100	$ 50*
Unsubordinated debentures	100	100	100	100	100	100	100	50*
Subordinated debentures	200	200	200	200	200	150		
Preferred stock ($100 par value and $120 liquidating value per share)	100	120	120	100	50			
Common stock and retained earnings	500	980	480					
Total liabilities and shareholders' equity	$1,000							
Total cash proceeds distributed		$1,500	$1,000	$500	$450	$350	$200	$100

*Ratio of 50:50 because each has a $100,000 claim.

that excess, as is the case in Exhibit 10-3 when the total cash proceeds are $1,500. This illustrates the risks and rewards of common stock ownership. When things go well, common shareholders do very well. When things go badly, common shareholders are the first to suffer. Keep in mind, though, that both common and preferred stockholders are protected by limited liability. They do not have to add additional personal assets to the company when it cannot repay its debts.

Other Features of Preferred Stock

In addition to being cumulative and having liquidation value, preferred stock may have other features. As with our discussion of debt, each feature affects the attractiveness of the stock issue. If you add the cumulative feature to a 5% preferred, investors will pay more for a share of preferred stock. Another way to express the same idea is to say that if you add the cumulative feature to a preferred share, you reduce the size of the fixed dividend that investors require to be willing to invest in the preferred stock.

Each of the following features can also affect the attractiveness of preferred stock. For example, a holder of participating preferred stock ordinarily receives a fixed dividend but can receive higher dividends when the company has a very good year—one in which common stockholders receive especially large dividends. **Participating** means that holders of these preferred shares participate in the growth of the company because they share in growing dividends. If preferred stock does not have the participation feature, the dividend received by the preferred stockholder is capped at the prespecified rate. If preferred stock is **callable**, the issuing company has the right to purchase the stock back from the owner at specified dates upon payment of the **call price**, or **redemption price**. This call price is typically set above the par value or issuance price of the stock to compensate investors for the fact that the stock can be bought back at the issuer's choice. Recall from Chapter 9 that bonds may also be callable.

Convertible preferred stock gives the owner the option to exchange the preferred share for a prespecified number of shares of common stock. Because the ability to convert the stock can be quite valuable in future years if common stock prices grow significantly, convertible securities typically carry a lower dividend rate. For example, a regular preferred stock with an 8% dividend might sell for the same price as a 6% convertible preferred stock. As with the call feature, the conversion feature may be applied to bonds as well as to preferred stock.

It is not possible to describe every imaginable kind of preferred stock because individual investors and issuers have the opportunity to develop a unique security that exactly meets their needs, and they can adapt that security to the particular market conditions they face at the time. In fact, the investment banking community works hard to develop new types of preferred stock that exactly fit the particular needs of certain investors and therefore provide less expensive capital for the issuing company.

participating
A characteristic of preferred stock that allows holders of shares to participate in the growth of the company because they share in growing dividends.

callable
A characteristic of bonds or preferred stock that gives the issuer the right to purchase the bonds or stock back from the owner at a fixed price.

call price (redemption price)
The price at which an issuer can buy back a callable preferred stock or bond. The price is typically above the par value.

convertible
A characteristic of bonds or preferred stock that gives the owner the option to exchange the bonds or shares of preferred stock for a prespecified number of shares of common stock.

Comparing Bonds and Preferred Stock

Preferred stocks and bonds share certain characteristics. Both are contracts between an investor and an issuer that spell out each party's rights and responsibilities. Preferred stocks and bonds each pay a specific return to the investor. However, they differ as to the size and nature of those returns. We call the return to bondholders "interest," and it appears as an expense on the earnings statement of the company issuing the bond. In the United States, most interest income is taxable to the recipient and tax deductible to the issuing company. In contrast, the specific return to preferred shareholders is a "dividend" and represents a distribution of profits. Dividends do not reduce net earnings and are not tax deductible to the issuer. Dividends reduce the Retained Earnings account directly. For the recipient, dividends may be fully taxed, partly taxed, or untaxed, depending on whether the stockholder is an individual, a corporation, or a special entity such as a pension plan or an insurance company. The maximum tax rate on most dividends received by individuals was 15% from 2003 through 2012. However, the tax rate on dividends is the topic of frequent political debate and is subject to change over time. In fact, dividend tax rates for high income earners increased to 20% in 2013.

Preferred stocks and bonds also differ in that bonds have specific maturity dates, at which time the company must repay the principal amount, but most preferred stock has an unlimited life. From the investor's perspective, such preferred stock is riskier than bonds because it never matures and the company is not required to declare dividends. It is not always easy to determine whether a security is a debt or an equity instrument. Some preferred stock, for example, does have a mandatory redemption date. This makes it so similar to a bond that both U.S. GAAP and IFRS require companies to classify such a preferred stock as if it were debt.

Summary Problem for Your Review

PROBLEM

From the following data, prepare the stockholders' equity section of the balance sheet for Sample Corporation, December 31, 20X1:

Additional paid-in capital, preferred stock	$ 50,000
Additional paid-in capital, common stock	1,000,000
9% preferred stock, $50 par value, callable at $55, authorized 20,000 shares, issued and outstanding 12,000 shares	?
Common stock, stated value $2 per share, authorized 500,000 shares, issued 400,000 shares	?
Dividends payable	90,000
Retained earnings	2,000,000

SOLUTION

Dividends payable is a liability. Therefore, it does not appear in the stockholders' equity section of the balance sheet:

Sample Corporation, Balance Sheet (Partial), Stockholders' Equity, December 31, 20X1

9% preferred stock, $50 par value, callable at $55, authorized 20,000 shares, issued and outstanding 12,000 shares		$ 600,000
Common stock, stated value $2 per share, authorized 500,000 shares, issued 400,000 shares		800,000
Additional paid-in capital		
Preferred	$ 50,000	
Common	1,000,000	1,050,000*
Retained earnings		2,000,000
Total stockholders' equity		$4,450,000

*Many presentations would not show the detailed breakdown of additional paid-in capital into preferred and common portions.

Stock Options and Restricted Stock

▶▶ **OBJECTIVE 4**

Explain the characteristics and use of stock option and restricted stock plans.

Existing companies occasionally issue additional shares to investors, executives, or current shareholders. There are several motivations and several mechanisms for additional stock issues. When a firm simply wants to raise additional equity capital, the process is much like the original stock issue described earlier. Investors provide cash and receive additional new shares in exchange. If a firm wants to distribute shares to employees, there are numerous means to accomplish the distribution. We examine two methods—the use of stock options and restricted stock—to increase the number of shares held by employees.

Stock Options

stock options

Rights to purchase a specific number of shares of a corporation's capital stock at a predetermined price for a specific time period.

exercise price (strike price)

The predetermined price that an employee must pay to purchase a share of stock in a stock option plan.

vested options

Options that the holders have the power to exercise.

Stock options give the holder the right to purchase a specific number of shares of a corporation's capital stock at a predetermined price, known as the **exercise price** or **strike price**, for a specific time period. Companies often give options to employees as part of their compensation. The company typically gives (or grants) the options to an employee with the provision that the employee must remain with the company for a period of time before being allowed to exercise the options, at which point the options become **vested options**—options that the holders have the power to exercise. Once vested, the employee may exercise the options anytime before they expire, usually for another 5 years or so. Stock options are especially valuable to executives and other employees because they can gain the benefits of stock price increases without bearing the risks of price declines. Shareholders can also benefit from stock options because they motivate employees to work hard and to make decisions that increase the value of their shares.

Stock options awarded to employees are a form of compensation like salaries and wages. Although it is logical to treat them as an expense, neither U.S. GAAP nor IFRS required expensing of options until 2005. Now companies must recognize the fair value of options, measured at the date the options are granted, as an expense spread over the period between the grant date and the date the options vest. Because the market price of employee stock options is not observable, measurement of the fair value of employee stock options is based on an option-pricing model. In arriving at fair value, option-pricing models take into consideration multiple factors, including the exercise price, expected life of the option, share price, expected volatility of the share price, expected dividends, and the risk-free interest rate over the term of the option. Footnote disclosure of stock option plans is detailed and includes information about the number and characteristics of options outstanding and the assumptions used in the option-pricing model.

Accounting for options was one of the most contentious accounting issues ever addressed by standard setters. Both the FASB and IASB faced immense political pressure from large companies and some of their supporters in government to prevent the expensing of stock options. In the United States, Congress considered several bills that would prohibit the FASB from requiring companies to expense stock options. Nevertheless, in 2004 the IASB issued a standard that required expensing the fair value of options, and the FASB followed suit in 2005 with a nearly identical standard. The European Union endorsed the IASB standard, and the U.S. Congress never passed blocking legislation.

Suppose that Harris Corporation has an incentive compensation plan that includes the granting of stock options to key executives. On January 1, 2011, Harris granted these executives options on 10,000 shares. Each option gives the holder the right to buy a share at an exercise price of $50. The options vest at the end of 3 years. At the grant date, the fair value of the options, based on an options pricing model, is $6 per share or $60,000 (10,000 options × $6 fair value per option) in total. This $60,000 represents the total compensation expense that the company must allocate over the 3 years between the grant date, January 1, 2011, and the vesting date, December 31, 2013. The journal entry to recognize compensation expense of $20,000 (=$60,000 ÷ 3 years) in 2011 would be as follows:

Compensation expense, stock options	20,000	
Additional paid-in capital—stock options		20,000

Assuming no employees forfeit their options during the vesting period, the company would record similar entries in 2012 and 2013. If some employees do forfeit options by leaving the company prior to vesting, the total amount of compensation expense will be less than $60,000 and the dollar amount of the annual entries is adjusted accordingly.

Now, suppose executives exercise options for all 10,000 shares in 2014. If the par value per share is $1, the journal entry in 2014 would be as follows:

Cash	500,000	
Additional paid-in capital—stock options	60,000	
Common stock		10,000
Additional paid-in capital—common stock . .		550,000
To record issue of 10,000 shares, par value $1, upon exercise of options with an exercise price of $50 per share		

Note that the impact of the 2014 journal entry is a net increase in Additional Paid-in Capital of $490,000 ($550,000 − $60,000). The financial statement impact of the journal entry is indistinguishable from the issuance of new shares at the exercise price of $50, which may differ significantly from the market price at the time of issuance. Suppose the market price in 2014 was $44. An executive would simply buy shares in the open market for $44 instead of exercising the option and paying $50 per share. Harris Corporation would record no transaction. However, if the market price were $60, the executive would exercise the option to buy at $50 and have the opportunity to either sell immediately and capture the $10 per share gain or hold the shares in hopes of further appreciation.

If the options were not exercised by the expiration date, Harris would record the following journal entry:

Additional paid-in capital—stock options	60,000	
Additional paid-in capital—common stock. .		60,000
To record the expiration of 10,000 options		

Restricted Stock

Many companies use restricted stock plans instead of stock option plans to motivate their employees. Granting **restricted stock** is like paying employees with common stock instead of cash. Restricted stock typically has constraints that prohibit employees from selling the stock until it vests and require employees to forfeit the stock if they leave the company prior to the end of the vesting period. Some firms also require that the stock be sold back to the issuing company if the employee decides to sell. Similar to the accounting for a stock option plan, a restricted stock plan requires a company to record a salary and wage expense over the vesting period in an amount equal to the value of the stock awarded. Each period the expense is offset by an increase to paid-in capital. Employees receive an asset that will increase and decrease in value exactly in proportion to the increases and decreases in value experienced by shareholders. In addition, employees holding restricted stock receive the same dividends that common stockholders receive.

A major benefit of restricted stock over stock options is that it still retains some value, even when stock prices fall sharply. A major problem for many high-tech companies that lost 90% of their value in the early 2000s was that their stock options became worthless and often remained so. The cycle repeated itself in 2007–2009, although in that period it was the shares of financial services companies that dropped the most. When the stock market was rising annually, the recipient of stock options got something that turned out to be very valuable. As the stock market fell from 2000 to 2002 and from 2007 to 2009, it became evident that stock options did not always pay off. Proponents of restricted stock believe it is better than options because it truly aligns managerial benefits with shareholder benefits. In contrast, stock options benefit managers the most when the company earns very large returns. Therefore, managers receiving stock options may have incentives to undertake riskier projects than shareholders prefer.

In addition to granting stock options, UPS granted 3.9 million units of restricted stock to employees in 2011. During the year, 8.3 million restricted stock units vested. The company recognized compensation expense related to stock-based items such as options and restricted stock units of $524 million.

restricted stock

Stock awarded to employees with certain constraints. These constraints typically prohibit employees from selling the stock until it vests and require employees to forfeit the stock if they leave the company prior to the end of the vesting period.

INTERPRETING FINANCIAL STATEMENTS

UPS had 2011 operating income of $6,080 million. This included a deduction of $524 million for stock-based compensation. If UPS had not recognized any of this stock-based compensation as an expense, what operating income would the company have reported? Would you regard this as a material item in UPS's income statement? Why or why not?

Answer

Operating income would have been higher by $524 million: ($6,080 million + $524 million) = $6,604 million. This is 8.6% higher than the reported amount. This could definitely make a difference to users of the information, so it is a material item.

Stock Splits and Stock Dividends

Stock options and restricted stock put additional shares in the hands of employees. Companies can also issue additional shares to current shareholders in several other ways. We examine two of these ways: the stock split and the stock dividend.

Accounting for Stock Splits

▸▸ **OBJECTIVE 5**

Identify the economic characteristics of and account for stock splits.

stock split

Distribution of additional shares to existing stockholders without any additional consideration provided by the stockholders to the firm. The par value, if any, of the stock is adjusted.

A **stock split** refers to the distribution of additional shares to existing stockholders without any additional consideration provided by the stockholders to the firm. Issuance of one additional share for each share currently owned is a "two-for-one" split. For example, suppose the Allstar Equipment Company has 100,000 shares outstanding with a market value of $150 per share and par value of $10 per share. The total market value of the stock is thus $15 million. Suppose Allstar Equipment gives each shareholder an additional share for each share owned. The total number of shares would increase to 200,000. If nothing else about the company changes (assets, liabilities, and equity all stay the same), the total market value of the outstanding stock should still be $15 million. With 200,000 shares outstanding, though, the market value per share should drop to $75. Shareholders are as well-off as they were before because they have paid no additional money and they still have the same proportional ownership interest in the company.

So why bother? Good question—there is no perfect answer. Many companies do split their stock. A common result is that stock price falls 50% in a two-for-one split. Thus, one good explanation for issuing a split is that it causes the stock price to fall on a per share basis. If investors like to invest $1,000–$20,000 at a time, and stocks trade in units of 100 shares, you can see that investors would prefer stocks trading in a range between $10 and $200 per share. Most stocks do trade in that range and companies that split are often at the high end of that range. However, there is no rule about optimal share prices. Berkshire Hathaway is an example of a company whose Class A common stock trades at about $130,000 per share at this writing.

Some people argue that a stock split is a way to communicate with shareholders and remind them that their company is growing. It is true that after two two-for-one stock splits, investors realize that they have four times as many shares as they originally purchased. However, we would expect a similar pleased reaction from an investor who still had the same original number of shares that were now valued at four times their purchase price.

Would the accountant need to do anything to acknowledge Allstar's stock issuance of 100,000 additional shares? There are now twice as many shares outstanding but the company has received nothing in exchange for those shares. The same total par value of common stock account balance now represents twice as many shares. The company will adjust the original $10 par value of the stock by half. In other words, after the split, Allstar will have 200,000 shares outstanding, each with a par value of $5. Nothing changes in the stockholders' equity section, except the description of shares authorized, issued, and outstanding and the stated par value per share. The aggregate par value is unchanged, no cash has changed hands, each owner has the same proportionate interest as before, and each has the same relative voting power. Therefore, the accountant does not make a journal entry to record the stock split.

Stock splits increase the number of shares outstanding and decrease the per share price. Successful growing companies often split their stock. Companies having financial problems may want to do the opposite. A **reverse stock split** decreases rather than increases the number of shares outstanding without changing the total amount of owners' equity. This results in an increase in the price per share. Stock exchanges may eliminate trading in the stock of a company if its share price is too small—a procedure called delisting. A reverse stock split may bring the stock price back up to an acceptable level.

reverse stock split

A decrease rather than an increase in the number of shares outstanding without changing the total amount of owners' equity.

While stock splits do not require an accounting journal entry, they are not without financial implications. The change in par value requires that the company change all records and documents that refer to par value to reflect the new par value. In addition, the company may recall the existing stock certificates and issue new ones with the adjusted par value. As a result, large stock distributions are frequently accounted for as a stock dividend rather than as a stock split. We discuss this situation in the next section.

Accounting for Stock Dividends

Stock dividends are also distributions of additional shares to existing shareholders without additional consideration provided by the stockholder. However, the relative number of new shares issued is usually smaller than in a split, although this is not a requirement. More importantly, a stock dividend increases the number of shares but does not change the per share par value. Consequently, the total par value of common stock reported on the balance sheet increases.

LARGE-PERCENTAGE STOCK DIVIDENDS Large-percentage stock dividends, also known as *stock splits effected in the form of a stock dividend*, occur when the number of new shares issued exceeds 20% to 25% of the shares outstanding prior to the distribution. Companies account for large-percentage stock dividends at par or stated value. That means that an accounting entry simply transfers the par or stated value of the new shares from the retained earnings or additional paid-in capital account to the common stock account. While the debit side of this entry can, in practice, be to either retained earnings or additional paid-in capital, for our purposes we will assume the debit is to retained earnings.

As in the case of stock splits, the market value of the outstanding shares tends to adjust completely when a firm issues a stock dividend, provided that the firm lowers the per share cash dividend proportionately. Consider the Allstar Equipment Company and the effect of possible stock dividends on share price. The original $150 share price would fall to $120 with a 25% stock dividend [$15,000,000 ÷ (100,000 shares + 25,000 shares)] and to $75 with a 100% dividend. The total market value of the company stays at $15 million in all cases.

Suppose the Allstar Equipment Company chose to double the number of outstanding shares by issuing a 100% stock dividend. The total amount of stockholders' equity would be unaffected. However, its composition would change as shown in panel A of Exhibit 10-4. From a shareholder's

> ▶▶ **OBJECTIVE 6**
>
> Account for both large- and small-percentage stock dividends.

stock dividend
Distribution of additional shares to existing shareholders without additional consideration provided by the stockholders. The par value, if any, of the stock is not adjusted.

EXHIBIT 10-4

Stock Dividends

Allstar Example: Originally 100,000 Shares; $10 Par Value and $150 Market Value per Share

PANEL A: LARGE STOCK DIVIDEND (100%)				
Issue 100,000 new $10 Par Value Shares Accounted for at Par				
Retained earnings......................			1,000,000	
Common stock......................				1,000,000
	Common Stock	**Additional Paid-in Capital**	**Retained Earnings**	**Owners' Equity**
Original	$1,000,000	$4,000,000	$ 6,000,000	$11,000,000
100% Dividend	1,000,000		(1,000,000)	
Result	$2,000,000	$4,000,000	$ 5,000,000	$11,000,000
PANEL B: SMALL STOCK DIVIDEND (2%)				
Issue 2,000 new $10 Par Value Shares Accounted for at Market Price of $150				
Retained earnings......................			300,000	
Common stock......................				20,000
Additional paid-in capital..............				280,000
	Common Stock	**Additional Paid-in Capital**	**Retained Earnings**	**Owners' Equity**
Original	$1,000,000	$4,000,000	$6,000,000	$11,000,000
2% Dividend	20,000	280,000	(300,000)	
Result	$1,020,000	$4,280,000	$5,700,000	$11,000,000

perspective, this is essentially identical to a two-for-one stock split. The shareholder has twice as many shares, each with a market value that is reduced by half, and an ownership interest that is unchanged. Firms often prefer to account for a stock split as a stock dividend because it saves clerical costs. The company does not need to receive permission for a change in par value, and it does not have to exchange stock certificates.

However, the company does have an economic decision to make. What happens to the cash dividend? One possibility is to adjust the cash dividend proportionately. For a 100% stock dividend or a two-for-one stock split, this means that the cash dividend per share is cut in half and total cash dividends remain unchanged. It is at least as common for the company to increase the total cash dividend being paid, indicating that the cash dividend per share has been cut by less than half. Investors watch changes to cash dividends associated with stock splits and stock dividends carefully to assess the company's belief about future cash flow and future investment opportunity.

SMALL-PERCENTAGE STOCK DIVIDENDS Companies account for stock dividends of less than 20% to 25% at market value, not at par value. This rule is partly the result of tradition and partly due to the fact that small-percentage stock dividends are more likely to accompany increases in the total dividend payments or other changes in the company's financial policies. Security analysts argue that the decision to increase total cash dividends communicates management's conviction that future cash flows will rise to support these increased distributions. This is a positive statement about the firm's prospects.

Panel B of Exhibit 10-4 illustrates the effects of a 2% stock dividend. As before, the individual shareholder receives no assets from the corporation, and the corporation receives no consideration from the shareholder. One possible economic effect of a stock dividend is to signal increased cash dividends. Suppose the board of the company in our example consistently voted to pay annual cash dividends of $1 per share. Often companies maintain this cash dividend per share after a small stock dividend. After a 2% stock dividend, the owner of 1,000 shares can now expect a future annual cash dividend of ($1 × 1,020 shares) = $1,020 instead of ($1 × 1,000 shares) = $1,000. In this case, when a company maintains its dividend rate per share, announcing a stock dividend of 2% has the same economic effect as announcing an increase of 2% in the cash dividend.

The company records small-percentage stock dividends (under 20–25%) by transferring the market value of the additional shares from retained earnings to common stock and additional paid-in capital. We refer to this transfer as a "capitalization of retained earnings." U.S. practice concerning the use of market values in accounting for small-percentage stock dividends is arbitrary and is not consistently adopted worldwide.

Summary Problem for Your Review

PROBLEM

Charlie Company distributes a 2% stock dividend on its 1 million outstanding $5 par common shares. The stockholders' equity section before the dividend was as follows:

Common stock, 1,000,000 shares, $5 par value	$ 5,000,000
Additional paid-in capital in excess of par	20,000,000
Retained earnings	75,000,000
Total stockholders' equity	$100,000,000

The common stock was selling on the open market for $150 per share when Charlie Company distributed the dividend. How will the stock dividend affect the stockholders' equity section? If net income were $10.2 million next year, what would be the earnings per share before considering the effects of the stock dividend and after considering the effects of the stock dividend?

SOLUTION

	Before 2% Stock Dividend	Changes	After 2% Stock Dividend
Common stock, 1,000,000 shares, $5 par value	$ 5,000,000	+(20,000 @ $5)	$ 5,100,000
Additional paid-in capital	20,000,000	+[20,000 @ ($150 − $5)]	22,900,000
Retained earnings	75,000,000	−(20,000 @ $150)	72,000,000
Total	$100,000,000		$100,000,000

Earnings per share before considering the effects of the stock dividend would be ($10,200,000 ÷ 1,000,000), or $10.20. After the dividend earnings per share would be ($10,200,000 ÷ 1,020,000), or $10.

Note that the stock dividend has no effect on net income, the numerator of the earnings-per-share computation. However, it does affect the denominator and causes a small decrease in EPS.

Why Use Stock Splits and Dividends?

Experts debate the importance of stock splits and stock dividends even as companies continue to use them. We have reviewed the arguments surrounding the use of stock splits and stock dividends to control the price per share. Wal-Mart, for example, split two-for-one on 11 occasions since its public offering on October 1, 1970. In early February 2012 it was selling at almost $62 per share. An initial investment of $1,650 in 100 shares in 1970 would have grown to 204,800 shares worth $12,697,600. Without splits the price per share would have been $126,976.

Often a stock split or stock dividend accompanies other announcements, such as new corporate investment strategies or changes in cash dividend levels. Suppose the firm has traditionally paid a special cash dividend at year-end, but plans to expand production substantially, which absorbs available cash and makes the payment of this special dividend difficult. The firm might combine the announcement of the planned expansion with an announcement of a small stock dividend. The small-percentage stock dividend does not draw on cash immediately, but provides stockholders with a likely increase in future cash dividends in proportion to the percentage of new shares issued.

Fractional Shares

Corporations ordinarily issue shares in whole units. When shareholders are entitled to stock dividends in amounts equal to fractional units, corporations issue additional shares for whole units plus cash equal to the market value of the fractional amount.

For example, suppose a corporation issues a 3% stock dividend. A shareholder has 160 shares. The market value per share on the date of issuance is $40. Par value is $2. The shareholder would be entitled to (.03 × 160) = 4.8 shares. The company would issue four shares plus (.8 × $40) = $32 cash. The journal entry is as follows:

Retained earnings (4.8 × $40)	192	
Common stock, at par (4 × $2)		8
Additional paid-in capital (4 × $38)		152
Cash (.8 × $40)		32

To issue a stock dividend of 3% to a holder of 160 shares

The Investor's Accounting for Dividends and Splits

So far, we have focused on how the corporation deals with stock splits and dividends. What about the stockholder? Consider the investor's recording of the transactions described so far. Suppose Jesse bought 1,000 shares of the original issue of Allstar Equipment Company stock for $50 per share:

Investment in Allstar common stock	50,000	
Cash		50,000

To record investment in 1,000 shares of an original issue of Allstar Equipment Company common stock at $50 per share

If Jesse sold the shares to Katrina at a price other than $50, Jesse would record a gain or loss and Katrina would carry the shares at the amount she paid Jesse. Meanwhile, this sale would not affect the stockholders' equity of Allstar Equipment Company. The company would simply change its underlying shareholder records to delete Jesse and add Katrina as a shareholder.

Assuming Jesse did not sell any of his 1,000 shares, the following examples show how he would record the stock split, cash dividends, and stock dividends—treating each as an independent event, not as sequential events. Note that several events that produced journal entries for Allstar do not cause entries for Jesse:

a. Stock split at two-for-one:	No journal entry, but Jesse would make a memorandum in the investment account to show that he now owns 2,000 shares at a cost of $25 each, instead of 1,000 shares at a cost of $50 each.	

b. Cash dividends of $2 per share:	Cash	2,000	
	Dividend income.		2,000
	To record cash dividends on Allstar Equipment Company stock		

Or:	Alternatively, Jesse might use the following two entries:		
Date of declaration:	Dividends receivable	2,000	
	Dividend income.		2,000
	To record dividends declared by Allstar Equipment Company		
Date of receipt:	Cash	2,000	
	Dividends receivable.		2,000
	To record the receipt of cash dividends		

c. Stock dividends of 2% (small-percentage stock dividend):	No journal entry, but Jesse would make a memorandum in the investment account to show that [assuming the stock split in (a) had not occurred] he now owns 1,020 shares at an average cost of ($50,000 ÷ 1,020 shares), or $49.02 per share.	
d. Stock split in form of a 100% dividend (large-percentage stock dividend):	No journal entry, but Jesse would make a memorandum in the investment account to show that [assuming the stock splits and stock dividends in (a) and (c) had not occurred] he now owns 2,000 shares at an average cost of $25 instead of 1,000 shares at $50. Note that this memorandum has the same effect as the memorandum in (a) above.	

Summary Problem for Your Review

Baker Company has 2,000 shares of $10 par common stock outstanding and splits its stock five-for-one. How will the split affect its balance sheet and its earnings per share? How would your answer change if the company said that the split was effected in the form of a stock dividend?

SOLUTION

The total amount of stockholders' equity would not change, but there would be 10,000 outstanding shares at $2 par, instead of 2,000 shares at $10 par. Earnings per share would be one-fifth of that previously reported, assuming no change in total net income applicable to the common stock.

If the question were framed as "the company recently issued a five-for-one stock split effected in the form of a stock dividend," then Baker Company would maintain the original par value per share, and a journal entry would increase the par value account for common stock by $80,000 (8,000 additional shares times $10 par value per share) and reduce retained earnings by $80,000, leaving total stockholders' equity unchanged and EPS at one-fifth its original value.

Retained earnings.	80,000	
Common stock (at par)		80,000

Repurchase of Shares

So far, we have seen how companies sell shares and how they sometimes issue additional shares to current shareholders. You should not think, though, that stock always flows out of a company. Sometimes companies repurchase shares, usually for one of two purposes: (1) to reduce shareholder claims permanently, called retiring stock, and (2) to hold shares temporarily for later use, most often to be granted as part of employee option, bonus, or stock purchase plans. As we learned earlier in this chapter, we call temporarily held shares treasury stock or treasury shares.

Why do companies repurchase their own stock? There are numerous possible motivations. If management believes that the stock is undervalued by the market, they may attempt to increase the share price by reducing the number of available shares. Alternatively, a company may need shares to distribute to employees as part of a stock option or employee stock purchase plan. If the company issues previously unissued shares to employees, it increases the total number of shares outstanding and dilutes ownership rights. By repurchasing shares to offset those distributed to employees, the company can maintain a stable number of shares outstanding. Or the company may simply have more cash than it requires for ongoing investment in new projects, and the board of directors may decide to return some capital to its shareholders. It could pay higher cash dividends, but often the board prefers repurchasing shares. Why? For one thing, buybacks allow the company to return cash to shareholders without creating expectations of permanent increases in dividends. Further, buybacks put the cash in the hands of shareholders who want it, because shareholders decide whether to sell or hold their shares. Yet another reason is to defend against a hostile takeover of the company. By repurchasing its own stock, a company can keep it out of the hands of "outsiders." Whatever the motivation, stock buybacks are common.

By repurchasing shares, a company liquidates some shareholders' claims, and total stockholders' equity decreases by the amount of the repurchase. We discuss accounting for permanent and temporary repurchases using the illustration of the Allstar Equipment Company. Recall that Allstar shares have a market value of $150 per share. We also need to know Allstar's **book value per share of common stock**—total common shareholders' equity divided by the number of outstanding common shares. Allstar's total stockholders' equity of $11 million combines the original purchase price of shares in the past (par value plus additional paid-in capital) with the periodic earnings of the firm that have remained in the business (retained earnings). Allstar's book value per share is ($11,000,000 ÷ 100,000 shares) = $110 per share.

> ▶▶ **OBJECTIVE 7**
> Explain and report stock repurchases and other treasury stock transactions.

book value per share of common stock
Total common stockholders' equity divided by the number of common shares outstanding.

Retirement of Shares

In most U.S. states, once a company has repurchased shares it may retire them or hold them for reissue. Suppose the board of Allstar Company purchases and retires 5% of its outstanding shares at $150 per share for a total of (5,000 shares × $150), or $750,000 cash. Allstar originally issued these shares at $50 per share. The repurchase reduces total stockholders' equity by $750,000. How much of this do we charge against the common stock, additional paid-in capital, and retained earnings accounts? We reduce the common stock account by the par or stated value of the reacquired shares. For Allstar the repurchase price exceeds the par value. The most common approach to accounting for the excess is to first reduce the additional paid-in capital account by the amount of capital contributed by the original purchasers of the shares that Allstar retired and reduce retained earnings by any remaining repurchase amount. However, depending on circumstances, alternative allocations of the excess repurchase price over par value between additional-paid in capital and retained earnings are possible. We illustrate the most common approach in the following journal entry, which reverses the original paid-in capital (both par value and additional paid-in capital) and charges the excess cost of the reacquired shares to retained earnings. The impact of this journal entry on Allstar's equity accounts is illustrated in panel A of Exhibit 10-5.

EXHIBIT 10-5

Stock Repurchase

Allstar Example

PANEL A: REPURCHASED SHARES RETIRED

	Before Repurchase of 5% of Outstanding Shares	Changes Because of Retirement	After Repurchase of 5% of Outstanding Shares
Common stock, 100,000 shares @ $10 par	$ 1,000,000	−(5,000 shares @ $10 par) = −$50,000	$ 950,000
Additional paid-in capital	4,000,000	−(5,000 shares @ $40) = −$200,000	3,800,000
Total paid-in capital	5,000,000		4,750,000
Retained earnings	6,000,000	−(5,000 @ $100*) = −$500,000	5,500,000
Stockholders' equity	$11,000,000		$10,250,000
Book value per common share:			
$11,000,000 ÷ 100,000 shares	$ 110.00		
$10,250,000 ÷ 95,000 shares			$ 107.89

*$150 acquisition price less the $50 (or $10 + $40) originally paid in.

PANEL B: REPURCHASED SHARES HELD AS TREASURY STOCK

	Before Repurchase of 5% of Outstanding Shares	Changes Because of Treasury Stock	After Repurchase of 5% of Outstanding Shares
Common stock, 100,000 shares @ $10 par	$ 1,000,000		$ 1,000,000
Additional paid-in capital	4,000,000		4,000,000
Total paid-in capital	$ 5,000,000		$ 5,000,000
Retained earnings	6,000,000		6,000,000
Total equity before treasury stock	$11,000,000		$11,000,000
Deduct:			
Cost of treasury stock		$750,000	(750,000)
Total stockholders' equity			$10,250,000

Common stock	50,000	
Additional paid-in capital	200,000	
Retained earnings	500,000	
Cash		750,000

To record retirement of 5,000 shares of stock for $150 cash per share. The original paid-in capital is $50 per share ($10 par value + $40 additional paid-in capital). We reduce retained earnings by the additional $100 cost per share.

In addition, the company cancels the stock certificates and no longer considers the shares either outstanding or issued. The retired shares are like authorized but unissued shares.

Note how the book value per share of the outstanding shares has declined from $110.00 to $107.89 [($11,000,000 − $750,000) ÷ 95,000 shares]. We call this phenomenon **dilution**— a reduction in shareholders' equity per share or EPS that arises from changes among shareholders' proportionate interests. As a rule, boards of directors avoid dilution unless expected future profits will more than compensate for a temporary undesirable reduction in book value per share.

dilution
Reduction in stockholders' equity per share or EPS that arises from changes among shareholders' proportional interests.

Let's look again at the stockholders' equity of UPS in Exhibit 10-1. Subsequent to its IPO in 1999, UPS engaged in several share repurchases. As of fiscal year-end December 31, 2011, UPS had 240 million class A shares and 725 million class B shares issued, compared with 258 million class A and 735 million class B shares issued 1 year earlier. What caused the decrease in the number of issued shares during 2011? Footnote 10 reveals that, with regard to class A shares, in 2011 the company repurchased and retired 7 million shares, issued 10 million shares primarily as part of employee stock award plans, and that employees converted 21 million class A shares to class B, for a net decrease of 18 million shares. With regard to class B shares, the company repurchased and retired 31 million shares and issued 21 million shares in exchange for class A stock, for a net decrease of 10 million shares.

This type of share activity helps explain the absence of any dollar amount assigned to Additional Paid-in Capital on the UPS balance sheet. After UPS issued class B shares in the 1999 IPO, the balance in Additional Paid-in Capital was $5,096 million as of December 31, 1999. However, examination of Exhibit 10-1 shows a zero balance in Additional Paid-in Capital at the end of fiscal years 2010 and 2011. What happened to the $5,096 million in Additional Paid-in Capital? The most significant reduction occurred in fiscal year 2000 when UPS used the proceeds from the IPO to repurchase class A shares from shareholders. The company paid $4,070 million to repurchase shares via a tender offer and paid $1,395 million for other class A share repurchases. A **tender offer** is a public invitation to all stockholders of a particular class of stock to offer their shares for sale at a specified price, during a specified time, subject to certain conditions. Due to the circumstances and conditions of this repurchase, UPS accounted for the repurchase and retirement of the shares by reducing Common Stock and Additional Paid-in Capital as follows (dollars in millions):

tender offer
A public invitation to all stockholders of a particular class of stock to offer their shares for sale at a specified price, during a specified time, subject to certain conditions.

Common stock—Class A	1	
Additional paid-in capital	5,464	
Cash		5,465

This activity was partially offset by the issuance of shares under stock option plans that increased Additional Paid-in Capital by $635 million; resulting in a December 31, 2000, balance in Additional Paid-in Capital of only $267 million ($5,096 million + $635 million − $5,464 million). In subsequent years, the company continued to reduce Additional Paid-in Capital by repurchasing and retiring stock, with the result that by the end of 2010 the balance in Additional Paid-in Capital was zero.

Also note that Retained Earnings declined by $476 million, from $10,604 million at December 31, 2010, to $10,128 million at December 31, 2011, despite 2011 net income of $3,804 million. After dividends of $2,086 million, we would expect Retained Earnings to increase by ($3,804 million − $2,086 million) = $1,718 million. What caused Retained Earnings to fall $2,194 million = ($1,718 million + $476 million) below expectations? Common stock repurchases and retirements reduced Retained Earnings by $2,194 million. Why did they reduce Retained Earnings instead of Additional Paid-in Capital? Additional Paid-in Capital cannot fall below zero—that is, it can't have a debit balance. Once stock repurchases have reduced additional paid-in capital to zero, further repurchases must reduce retained earnings.

Treasury Stock

Now suppose Allstar's board of directors decides not to retire the 5,000 repurchased shares but to hold them temporarily as treasury stock. Perhaps the company needs the shares for an employee stock purchase plan or for executive stock options. The repurchase still decreases stockholders' equity. It is NOT an asset. Why? Because a company cannot own part of itself.

If treasury stock is not an asset, then what is it? The Treasury Stock account is a contra account to owners' equity, just as Accumulated Depreciation is a contra account to related fixed-asset accounts. Like retiring shares, Allstar's purchase of treasury stock decreases stockholders' equity by $750,000 (5,000 shares purchased at $150 per share). Unlike the accounting for retirements, common stock at par value, additional paid-in capital, and retained earnings do not change with treasury stock purchases. Instead, Allstar debits the Treasury Stock account for $750,000 as shown in the following journal entry:

Treasury stock.	750,000	
Cash		750,000

To record repurchase of 5,000 shares of stock for $150 cash per share. Shares to be held in treasury.

We deduct the amount in the treasury stock account from total stockholders' equity. Panel B of Exhibit 10-5 shows Allstar's stockholders' equity section before and after the purchase of the treasury shares. Treasury shares do not receive dividends, do not vote, and do not have liquidation rights because they are not considered outstanding shares.

Shares issued	100,000
Less: Treasury stock	5,000
Total shares outstanding	95,000

Companies usually resell treasury shares at a later date, perhaps through an employee stock purchase plan. Exhibit 10-6 shows the outcomes when Allstar reissues these treasury shares above or below the acquisition cost. Panel A shows the journal entry for reissue at $180 (above the $150 acquisition cost) and panel B shows the result for reissue at $120 (below the $150 acquisition cost). Panel C presents the different shareholder equity sections for each outcome.

As discussed previously, the specific accounting practices for purchases and sales of a company's own stock vary depending on whether the repurchase is considered permanent or temporary. However, one rule remains constant: transactions involving the sale or repurchase of a company's own stock never produce expenses, losses, revenues, or gains on the income statement. Why? A corporation's own capital stock is part of its capital structure. It is not an asset of the corporation. A company cannot make profits or losses by buying or selling its own stock.

There is no important difference between unissued shares and treasury shares. In our example, Allstar could accomplish the same objective by (1) acquiring 5,000 shares, retiring them, and issuing 5,000 "new" shares; or (2) acquiring 5,000 shares for the treasury and then reselling them. In fact, in some states treasury stock is not allowed. Companies in those states must retire repurchased shares. Although some account balances within stockholders' equity would differ under these alternatives, neither the number of shares outstanding nor the total stockholders' equity would change.

EXHIBIT 10-6

Reissuance of Treasury Shares

Allstar Repurchased 5,000 Shares for $150 per Share Creating a Treasury Stock Balance of $750,000

PANEL A: REISSUE AT $180 PER SHARE

Cash	900,000	
Treasury stock		750,000
Additional paid-in capital		150,000

PANEL B: REISSUE AT $120 PER SHARE

Cash	600,000	
Additional paid-in capital	150,000	
Treasury stock		750,000

PANEL C: COMPARATIVE BALANCES

	With 5,000 Shares in Treasury @ $150	Reissued @ $180	Reissued @ $120
Common stock	$ 1,000,000	$ 1,000,000	$ 1,000,000
Additional paid-in capital	4,000,000	4,150,000	3,850,000
Total paid-in capital	5,000,000	5,150,000	4,850,000
Retained earnings	6,000,000	6,000,000	6,000,000
Deduct treasury stock	(750,000)		
Total stockholders' equity	$10,250,000	$11,150,000	$10,850,000

Effects of Repurchases on Earnings Per Share (EPS)

Repurchasing shares, whether they are retired or held in treasury, reduces the number of shares outstanding. This tends to increase EPS. For example, suppose that Allstar generates net income of $950,000 each year and that using $750,000 to repurchase shares would not reduce future net income. Under these circumstances, repurchasing 5,000 shares increases EPS by $.50:

EPS = net income ÷ average number of shares outstanding

EPS before repurchase = $950,000   ÷   100,000 shares = $ 9.50

EPS after repurchase = $950,000   ÷   95,000 shares = $10.00

In contrast, using $750,000 to pay cash dividends leaves the number of shares unchanged at 100,000 and the EPS at $9.50. See the Business First box on page 472 for a comparison of how companies use dividends, splits, and repurchases.

INTERPRETING FINANCIAL STATEMENTS

As a manager, would you choose to distribute cash to your investors as a dividend or via share repurchase? How does this decision affect the financial statements?

Answer

The text raises several issues. One question pertains to the future. If you begin paying dividends, investors will expect you to continue to do so. Thus, you would want to assess future cash flow and your ability and desire to continue dividend payments before initiating dividends. A one-time distribution is probably better as a share repurchase, as are distributions that are likely to be highly variable over time. Shareholders often prefer repurchases because they can choose to participate or not, and if they do participate they pay taxes only on their gains. The tax benefit to repurchases is even greater in countries where the tax on capital gains is less than that on dividends.

As a manager, you would note that neither dividends nor repurchases affect the income statement, and they have the same effect on total financing cash flows. You might also note that dividends reduce only retained earnings, whereas the effect of share repurchases depends on the book value of the shares, the market value of the shares, and whether they are retired or held in treasury.

BUSINESS FIRST

STOCK SPLITS, DIVIDENDS, AND REPURCHASES

Companies differ widely in how they distribute resources to their shareholders. Consider four relatively young and very successful companies: Apple, Cisco Systems, Microsoft, and eBay. All four have had numerous stock splits. Apple had two-for-one stock splits in 1987, 2000, and 2005. Cisco Systems issued nine stock splits between 1990 and 2000. eBay split its stock three-for-one less than a year after it went public in 1998 and has had three additional two-for-one stock splits. Microsoft has split its stock nine times since its initial public offering in 1986.

These companies differ significantly in their use of cash dividends. Apple paid dividends from 1987 until 1995, when it stopped paying dividends. In August 2012 Apple initiated a quarterly dividend of $2.65 per share, its first dividend in 17 years. Microsoft did not pay a dividend until 2003, when it announced its first dividend. Since then, the dividend amount has been increased annually and was at $.20 per share per quarter in 2012. In addition, in 2004 Microsoft paid a special dividend of $3.00 per share. Cisco paid its first cash dividend on April 20, 2011, after years of taking the position that the share repurchase program, not the distribution of cash dividends, was in the best interests of the shareholders. eBay has never paid a cash dividend, and according to its Web site, it *"presently intends to continue this policy."*

All four companies have repurchased common stock, in most cases to offset the shares issued under employee stock plans. These companies are highly profitable and have substantial amounts of cash and marketable securities. As of the end of 2011, Apple had cash and short-term investments of $30.2 billion, representing 22% of total assets. Cisco had cash and short-term investments of $44.6 billion or 51% of total assets. Microsoft had cash and short-term investments of $51.7 billion or 46% of total assets. Ebay's balance sheet showed cash and short-term investments of $5.9 billion or 21.7% of total assets. When companies carry large amounts of cash and marketable securities on their balance sheets, investors frequently start calling for cash dividends or stock repurchases.

Sources: Cisco, Microsoft, Apple, and eBay Web sites and SEC filings.

Other Issuances of Common Stock

▶ OBJECTIVE 8

Record issuance of stock for noncash consideration and conversions of debt into equity or of preferred stock into common stock.

Companies do not always receive cash when they issue common stock. A company may issue shares for other assets or in exchange for its own corporate security—a bond or preferred stock.

Noncash Exchanges

A company may issue its stock to acquire land, a building, or common stock of another company, or to compensate a person or company for services received. The buyer and seller should both record the transaction at the "fair value" of either the securities or the exchanged assets or services, whichever is easier to determine objectively.

Conversion of Securities

Some companies issue bonds or preferred stock that allow the owner to convert them into common stock under prespecified conditions. The conversion feature makes the securities more attractive to investors and increases the price the issuer receives (or, equivalently, reduces the interest or dividend the company must pay). If the owner of convertible securities exercises the conversion privilege, the issuer simply adjusts the accounts as if it had issued the common stock initially. This may have significant effects on the company's proportion of debt and equity, and it may eliminate some substantial cash commitments previously associated with bond interest or preferred stock dividends.

For example, suppose Purchaser Company paid $160,000 for an investment in 5,000 shares of the $1 par value convertible preferred stock of Issuer Company in 20X1. In 20X8, Purchaser Company converted the preferred stock into 10,000 shares of Issuer Company common stock ($1 par value). Exhibit 10-7 shows the effect on the accounts of Issuer Company.

Purchaser Company also experiences a change in form of the investment, with no change in historical cost. The carrying value, or book value, of the investment remains $160,000. To show

EXHIBIT 10-7

Analysis of Convertible Preferred Stock

	Assets	=	Liabilities +		Stockholders' Equity		
					Additional Paid-in	**Common**	**Additional Paid-in**
	Cash	**=**		**Preferred Stock +**	**Capital, Preferred +**	**Stock +**	**Capital, Common**
20X1: Issuance of preferred	+160,000	=		+5,000	+155,000		
20X8: Conversion of preferred		=		–5,000	–155,000	+10,000	+150,000

The journal entries would be as follows:

On Issuer's Books

20X1: Cash	160,000	
Preferred stock, convertible.		5,000
Additional paid-in capital, preferred		155,000
To record issuance of 5,000 shares of $1 par preferred stock convertible into two common shares for one preferred share		
20X8: Preferred stock, convertible	5,000	
Additional paid-in capital, preferred	155,000	
Common stock.		10,000
Additional paid-in capital, common.		150,000
To record the conversion of 5,000 preferred shares to 10,000 common shares ($1 par)		

that the investment is now common stock instead of preferred stock, Purchaser Company might transfer the $160,000 from one investment account to another. Alternatively, it might change subsidiary records that document the composition of a single general ledger account called Investments.

Retained Earnings Restrictions

The most closely watched part of stockholders' equity, both by shareholders and creditors, is retained earnings. Boards of directors can make decisions that benefit shareholders but hurt creditors. For example, directors might pay excessive dividends that jeopardize payments of creditors' claims. To protect creditors, state laws or contractual obligations often restrict dividend-declaring power. For example, authorities in some jurisdictions do not permit boards to declare dividends if those dividends would cause stockholders' equity to be less than total paid-in capital. Therefore, retained earnings must exceed the cost of treasury stock. If there is no treasury stock, retained earnings must be positive. This restriction limits payments and thus protects the position of the creditors. Furthermore, many lenders require debt covenants that restrict certain uses of cash, such as dividend payments.

To reflect these limitations, management may designate a portion of retained earnings as being unavailable for dividends or otherwise restricted. Most companies with restrictions of retained earnings disclose them in the footnotes. Occasionally, restrictions appear as a line item on the balance sheet called **restricted retained earnings** or **appropriated retained earnings**—a part of retained earnings that companies cannot reduce by dividend declarations. In Europe, companies often use the term reserves to refer to restricted retained earnings. Accountants use the term **reserve** in many ways, but we will use it to mean only one thing: restrictions of dividend declarations. In the United States, reserves are not common. When they exist, they generally represent a statement by the board of directors of its intent to restrict dividend payments to retain cash for a particular purpose such as a plant expansion. In many countries, laws further restrict the payment of dividends, resulting in a shareholders' equity line called legal reserves.

▶▶ **OBJECTIVE 9**

Understand restrictions on retained earnings and interpret other components of stockholders' equity.

restricted retained earnings (appropriated retained earnings)
Any part of retained earnings that companies may not reduce by dividend declarations.

reserve
A restriction of dividend-declaring power as denoted by a specific subdivision of retained earnings.

Other Components of Stockholders' Equity

With regard to UPS, we have explained activity in the familiar equity accounts: common stock, additional paid-in capital and retained earnings, and also explained treasury stock. Three other elements commonly appear in stockholders' equity and deserve brief mention here. First, the UPS shareholders' equity in Exhibit 10-1 included a deduction of $3,103 million labeled Accumulated Other Comprehensive Loss. Recall from Chapter 2 that other comprehensive income is the change in stockholders' equity in the accounting period that does not result from net income or transactions with shareholders. Just as retained earnings is the accumulation of net income (less dividends), accumulated other comprehensive income (loss) is the accumulation of other comprehensive income over current and prior periods. In the case of UPS, the single largest factor in the Accumulated Other Comprehensive Loss account at December 31, 2011, was unrecognized pension and post-retirement benefit costs.

The second element of UPS' shareholders' equity that we have not discussed explicitly is Deferred Compensation Obligations. UPS is one of many companies that enhance the commitment of its employees to work hard and provide good service by rewarding them with shares of stock. Here, employees have delayed their right to receive shares for purposes of estate planning and tax management. As of December 31, 2011, UPS recognizes the obligation to deliver shares in the future in a Deferred Compensation Obligations account valued at $88 million. Note that UPS reflects an equal amount in treasury stock. The company holds in treasury the shares that it will be required to deliver to employees to cover these obligations.

The third unfamiliar element in Exhibit 10-1 is Noncontrolling Interests. We discuss noncontrolling interests in Chapter 11.

Financial Ratios Related to Stockholders' Equity

rate of return on common stockholders' equity (rate of return on equity, ROE, ROCE)
Net income less preferred dividends divided by average common equity.

Analysts answer many questions pertaining to stockholders' equity by using ratios. One important question is "How effectively does the company use resources provided by the shareholders?" To assess this, analysts relate the net income generated by the firm to the historic investment by its shareholders. We introduced the **rate of return on common stockholders' equity** or more simply, the **rate of return on equity** (**ROE** or **ROCE**) in Chapter 4. However, at that point we did not explicitly consider the impact of preferred stock on the calculation. If a company has preferred stock, we must deduct preferred stock dividends from net income in computing the numerator. The denominator is the average of the beginning and ending common equity balances. The common equity balance is the total stockholders' equity less the preferred stock at book value (or at liquidating value if it exceeds the book value). The formula for computing ROE follows:

$$\text{Rate of return on common equity} = \frac{(\text{Net income} - \text{Preferred dividends})}{\text{Average common equity}}$$

The calculations for Calvin Company are in Exhibit 10-8, with panel A presenting comparative stockholders' equity for 2 years together with earnings information and panel B using that information to calculate ROE.

ROE varies considerably among companies and industries and from year to year, as is evident in the following table:

	2011	2008	2005
UPS	50.2	31.7	23.3
McDonald's	37.9	30.1	17.7
ExxonMobil	26.2	38.5	33.9

ROE patterns often spark questions that increase your understanding of the company. Both UPS and McDonald's experienced increasing ROE over the 3 years shown. However, in the case of UPS, the increase is driven primarily by decreasing shareowners' equity resulting from share repurchases and retirements. Net income was $3,870 million in 2005 and $3,804 million in 2011, while average equity decreased from $16,631 million in 2005 to $7,577.5 million in 2011. McDonald's, on the other hand, saw net income increase from $2,602.2 million to $5,503.1 million

EXHIBIT 10-8

Calvin Company Owners' Equity

PANEL A

	December 31	
	20X2	**20X1**
Stockholders' equity:		
10% preferred stock, 100,000 shares, $100 par	$ 10,000,000	$ 10,000,000
Common stock, 5,000,000 shares, $1 par	5,000,000	5,000,000
Additional paid-in capital	35,000,000	35,000,000
Retained earnings	87,000,000	83,000,000
Total stockholders' equity	$137,000,000	$133,000,000
Net income for the year ended December 31, 20X2	$11,000,000	
Preferred dividends @ $10 per share	1,000,000	
Net income available for common stock	$10,000,000	

PANEL B: ROE

$$\text{Rate of return on common equity} = \frac{\text{Net income } - \text{ Preferred dividends}}{\text{Average common equity}}$$

$$= \frac{\$11,000,000 \ - \ \$1,000,000}{\frac{1}{2}[(\$133,000,000 \ - \ \$10,000,000) + (\$137,000,000 \ - \ \$10,000,000)]}$$

$$= \frac{\$10,000,000}{\frac{1}{2}(\$123,000,000 + \$127,000,000)}$$

$$= \frac{\$10,000,000}{\$125,000,000} = 8.0\%$$

from 2005 to 2011, respectively, while equity stayed relatively constant. The fluctuations in ExxonMobil's ROE over the years examined is due primarily to fluctuations in net income, which in turn was driven in part by fluctuations in oil prices.

A second ratio is book value per common share, introduced earlier in this chapter. When preferred stock is present, the calculation of the book value per share of common stock adjusts for the preferred. The calculation for Calvin Company using 20X2 data from panel A of Exhibit 10-8 follows:

$$\begin{array}{l}\text{Book value per share} \\ \text{of common stock}\end{array} = \frac{\begin{array}{l}\text{(Total stockholders' equity} \\ - \text{ Book value of preferred stock)}\end{array}}{\text{Number of common shares outstanding}}$$

$$= \frac{\$137,000,000 \ - \ \$10,000,000}{5,000,000} = \$25.40$$

The market value of a stock is usually more than its book value, but not always. This relationship is often captured by calculating a **market-to-book ratio**—market price per share divided by book value per share. Consider UPS. It had a market value of $80.52 and a book value of $7.70 in early 2012. This gives a market-to-book ratio of 10.5 to 1. Other comparisons are shown below (taken from Yahoo!'s financial site in March 2012) with each company's ratio compared with its value in 2009:

market-to-book ratio
Market value per share divided by book value per share.

	Market-to-Book Ratios	
	2011	**2009**
UPS	10.5	8.1
McDonald's	6.8	4.8
ExxonMobil	2.6	3.1

Shareholders value a stock based on what they believe the future earning power will be, not based on the historical cost of assets. Book values are balance sheet values that show a mix of the historical cost and the market values of assets. A higher market-to-book ratio reflects the expectation of higher earnings potential due to perceived growth opportunities, competitive advantage, or less risk.

What do these differences in values mean in the real world? A market value well above the book value may be appropriate if the company has many unrecorded assets (such as successful internal R&D activities or a superior distribution network) or appreciated assets (such as real estate).

Highlights to Remember

1 **Describe the rights of common shareholders.** On the balance sheet, stockholders' equity is the book value of the residual interests of a corporation's owners. By incorporating, the company provides limited liability for its owners and provides them with various rights, including the right to vote for the board of directors.

2 **Account for common stock, including payment of cash dividends.** When shares of common stock are issued, the company will typically record the receipt of an asset and show an increase in common stock at par or stated value with the remainder of the consideration received shown as additional paid-in capital. When a dividend is paid it represents a reduction of an asset and an offsetting reduction of retained earnings. Issuance of common stock increases shareholders' equity, and payment of dividends decreases shareholders' equity, but different accounts are affected by the two transactions.

3 **Contrast bonds, preferred stock, and common stock.** Bonds, preferred stock, and common stock are all claims on the assets of the corporation. Bonds are the senior claim and are specific legal obligations with required dates for payment of interest and repayment of principal. Preferred stock may have many specific rights attached to it, but unlike interest on bonds, dividends become obligations only when the board of directors declares them. In addition, preferred stock usually has no maturity date. Preferred shareholders typically receive dividends and repayment in the event of liquidation before common shareholders. We often call common stock the residual claim because common shareholders receive what is left after paying all other obligations. In liquidation of a failed company, common shareholders may receive little or nothing. However, when a company grows rapidly and prospers, the value of the common stock will increase much more than the value of either bonds or preferred stock.

4 **Explain the characteristics and use of stock option and restricted stock plans.** Companies use stock option and restricted stock plans to provide additional compensation to employees in the form of rights to acquire shares of company stock. Stock options allow the employee to acquire shares of stock at a prespecified price at the end of the vesting period. Accountants value the options using an option-pricing model and expense the value of the options as compensation over the vesting period of the plan. Restricted stock plans award stock to employees with certain constraints that typically prohibit employees from selling the stock until it vests. The value of the stock granted to the employees represents the compensation expense, which is allocated over the vesting period.

5 **Identify the economic characteristics of and account for stock splits.** Stock splits alter the number of shares held by the owners, without altering the economic claims of the shareholders. As a result, no change typically occurs in the total market value of the company, but the value of individual shares changes in proportion to the size of the split. A two-for-one split would typically cause the market price per share to decline by 50%.

6 **Account for both large- and small-percentage stock dividends.** Accounting for stock dividends involves rearranging the owners' equity account balances. We can rearrange par value accounts, paid-in capital accounts, and retained earnings without changing the total owners' equity. The exact procedure depends on the size of the stock dividend.

7 **Explain and report stock repurchases and other treasury stock transactions.** Companies sometimes repurchase shares of their own stock in the open market. These shares may later be retired, resold, or used to meet obligations under option agreements. If a company holds such shares temporarily rather than retiring them, they are treasury shares and are deducted from stockholders' equity. Transactions in the company's own stock never give rise to gains and losses and do not affect the income statement. Such transactions with the shareholders give rise to changes in the cash and equity accounts.

8 Record issuance of stock for noncash consideration and conversions of debt into equity or of preferred stock into common stock. Issuance of stock in exchange for noncash consideration should be recorded at the fair value of the stock or the fair value of the consideration, whichever is more evident. Generally, when investors convert debt into common stock, we transfer the book values of the debt into owners' equity. When investors convert preferred stock into common stock, the amount of owners' equity does not change. We transfer the book value of the converted preferred stock into common stock accounts. Part is shown as par or stated value and the remainder as additional paid-in capital.

9 Understand restrictions on retained earnings and interpret other components of stockholders' equity. Management may designate a portion of retained earnings as being unavailable for dividends or otherwise restricted. These restrictions protect creditors. Stockholders' equity may include additional accounts that involve other stock activities and the accumulation of other comprehensive income.

10 Use the rate of return on common equity and book value per share. Security analysts use the return on common stockholders' equity as a primary ratio to assess the effectiveness of management and the profitability of the firm. Analysts often compare the market value per share with the book value per share. A high ratio of market value to book value generally means good growth prospects and possibly unrecorded assets, such as internally developed patents.

Accounting Vocabulary

appropriated retained earnings, p. 473
articles of incorporation, p. 452
authorized shares, p. 453
book value per share of common stock, p. 467
call price, p. 458
callable, p. 458
convertible, p. 458
corporate charter, p. 452
corporate proxy, p. 452
cumulative, p. 456
date of record, p. 455
declaration date, p. 455
dilution, p. 469

dividend arrearages, p. 456
dividends in arrears, p. 456
exercise price, p. 460
issued shares, p. 453
liquidating value, p. 457
market-to-book ratio, p. 475
outstanding shares, p. 453
participating, p. 458
payment date, p. 455
preemptive rights, p. 452
preferred stock, p. 456
rate of return on common stockholders' equity (rate of return on equity, ROE, ROCE), p. 474
redemption price, p. 458

reserve, p. 473
restricted retained earnings, p. 473
restricted stock, p. 461
reverse stock split, p. 462
stock dividends, p. 463
stock options, p. 460
stock split, p. 462
strike price, p. 460
tender offer, p. 469
treasury stock, p. 454
vested options, p. 460

Assignment Material

Questions

10-1 What is the purpose of preemptive rights?

10-2 "Common shareholders have limited liability." Explain.

10-3 Can a share of common stock be outstanding but not authorized or issued? Why?

10-4 "Treasury stock is unissued stock." Do you agree? Explain.

10-5 "Cumulative dividends are liabilities that must be paid to preferred shareholders before any dividends are paid to common shareholders." Do you agree? Explain.

10-6 "The liquidating value of preferred stock is the amount of cash for which it can currently be exchanged." Do you agree? Explain.

10-7 What are convertible securities?

10-8 In what respects is preferred stock similar to debt and in what respects is it similar to common stock?

10-9 Which are riskier—bonds or preferred stock? Why? Whose perspective are you taking—the issuer's or the investor's?

10-10 Why do U.S. GAAP and IFRS require recognition of an expense when a company grants stock options to its employees?

MyAccountingLab

10-11 Why do you suppose companies offer their employees stock options instead of simply paying higher salaries?

10-12 Why might an employee prefer a restricted stock award rather than a stock option award?

10-13 "The only real dividends are cash dividends." Do you agree? Explain.

10-14 "A 2% stock dividend increases every shareholder's fractional portion of the company by 2%." Do you agree? Explain.

10-15 "A stock split can be achieved by means of a stock dividend." Do you agree? Explain.

10-16 "When companies repurchase their own shares, the accounting depends on the purpose for which the shares are purchased." Explain.

10-17 "When a company retires shares, it must pay the stockholders an amount equal to the original par value and additional capital contributed for those shares plus the stockholders' fractional portion of retained earnings." Do you agree? Explain.

10-18 Why might a company decide to buy back its own shares instead of paying additional cash dividends?

10-19 "Treasury stock is not an asset." Explain.

10-20 "Gains and losses are not possible from a corporation acquiring or selling its own stock." Do you agree? Explain.

10-21 What is the proper amount to record for an asset newly acquired through an exchange (e.g., an exchange of land for securities)? Explain.

10-22 Why does a conversion option make bonds or preferred stock more attractive to investors?

10-23 Restrictions on dividend-declaring power may be voluntary or involuntary. Give an example of each.

10-24 Why might a board of directors voluntarily restrict its dividend-declaring power?

10-25 "A company's ROE indicates how much return an investor makes on the investment in the company's shares." Do you agree? Explain.

10-26 "A common stock selling on the market far below its book value is an attractive buy." Do you agree? Explain.

Critical Thinking Questions

▶▶ **OBJECTIVE 7**

10-27 Company Share Prices and Intentions to Repurchase Shares
Your friend has thought about repurchases of common stock by the issuing company and has concluded that this is unethical. Specifically, this friend says that the company knows more than you do and if the company decides to repurchase shares, it is taking advantage of shareholders. How do you respond?

▶▶ **OBJECTIVE 7**

10-28 The Prohibition on Income Recognition from Trading in the Company's Shares
Your friend has considered stock repurchases. He thinks that it is proper for the company to buy its own shares and subsequently reissue them, recognizing a profit on the reissuance that would be reported on the income statement. How do you respond?

▶▶ **OBJECTIVE 2**

10-29 The Meaning of Par Value
Your friend has decided that par value of common stock is a meaningless notion and complicates accounting practice without adding value to the financial statements. How do you respond?

▶▶ **OBJECTIVES 5, 6**

10-30 Changes in Stock Prices When the Shares Are Split
Your friend has developed a stock investing strategy that suggests you should always buy the shares of companies when they split their stock or issue large stock dividends. How do you respond?

Exercises

▶▶ **OBJECTIVE 2**

10-31 Distinctions between Terms
Disposal Services, Inc., a waste management company, had 3.5 million shares of common stock authorized on August 31, 20X2. Shares issued were 2 million. There were 375,000 shares held in the treasury. How many shares were issued and outstanding? How many shares were unissued? Label your computations.

10-32 Distinctions between Terms

▶▶ **OBJECTIVE 2**

On December 31, 2011, IBM Corporation had 4,687.5 million shares of common stock authorized. There were 2,182.5 million shares issued, and 1,019.3 million shares held as treasury stock. How many shares were issued and outstanding? How many shares were unissued? Label your computations.

10-33 Preferences as to Assets

▶▶ **OBJECTIVE 3**

The following are account balances of Reliable Autos, Inc. ($ in thousands): Common Stock and Retained Earnings, $350; Accounts Payable, $350; Preferred Stock (5,000 shares; $20 par and $24 liquidating value per share), $100; Subordinated Debentures, $250; and Unsubordinated Debentures, $150. Prepare a table showing the distribution of the cash proceeds on liquidation and dissolution of the corporation under varying assumptions. Assume cash proceeds of the following ($ in thousands): $1,400, $1,100, $750, $550, $400, and $200, respectively.

10-34 Issuance of Common Shares

▶▶ **OBJECTIVE 2**

Kawasaki Heavy Industries is a large Japanese company that makes ships, aircraft engines, and many other products in addition to motorcycles. Its 2011 sales of ¥1,226,949 million were equivalent to $15,843 million. Kawasaki's financial statements indicate (yen in millions):

Common stock, 1,670,646,460 shares issued in 2011	
Total paid-in capital from the 2011 issue of stock	¥158,591

1. Assume all 1,670,646,460 shares had been issued at the same time at a ¥62 par value per share. Prepare the journal entry.
2. Is the relationship between the allocation of the total selling price between the Common Stock account and the Additional Paid-in Capital or Capital Surplus account different from what one might expect to find for a U.S. company? Explain.

10-35 Cumulative Dividends

▶▶ **OBJECTIVES 2, 3**

The Atkinson Data Services Corporation was founded on January 1, 20X1.

Preferred stock, no par, cumulative $4 annual dividend per share	
Issued and outstanding, 1,000,000 shares	$ 50,000,000
Capital stock, no par, 6,000,000 shares	90,000,000
Total stockholders' equity	$140,000,000

The corporation's subsequent net incomes (losses) were as follows:

20X1	$ (5,000,000)
20X2	(4,000,000)
20X3	16,000,000
20X4	20,000,000
20X5	14,000,000

Assume the board of directors declared dividends to the maximum extent permissible by law. The state prohibits dividend declarations that cause negative retained earnings.

1. Tabulate the annual dividend declarations on preferred and common shares. There is no treasury stock.
2. How would the total distribution to common shareholders change if the preferred stock were not cumulative?

▸▸ OBJECTIVES **2, 3**

10-36 Cumulative Dividends

In recent years, the McFarlane Company had severe cash flow problems. In 20X0, the company suspended payment of cash dividends on common stock. In 20X1, it ceased payment on its $3 million par value 6% cumulative preferred stock. No common or preferred dividends were paid in 20X1 or 20X2. In 20X3, McFarlane's board of directors decided that $1.0 million was available for cash dividends.

Compute the preferred stock dividend and the common stock dividend for 20X3.

▸▸ OBJECTIVE **2**

10-37 Cash Dividends

Honda, the Japanese automobile company, declared and paid cash dividends in fiscal 2011 of ¥51 per share on 1,807.3 million shares. The declaration preceded the payment by 1 month.

Prepare the journal entries relating to the declaration and payment of fiscal 2011 dividends by Honda.

▸▸ OBJECTIVE **4**

10-38 Exercise of Stock Options

On January 1, 2013, Lyndon Systems granted its top executives options to purchase 6,000 shares of common stock (par $2) at an exercise price of $20 per share, the market price on January 1. The options have an estimated fair value of $8 per option and may be exercised over a 4-year span, starting 3 years hence. Suppose all options are exercised 3 years hence, when the market value of the stock is $45 per share.

1. Prepare the journal entries Lyndon would record to account for compensation expense on December 31, 2013, December 31, 2014, and December 31, 2015.
2. Prepare the appropriate journal entry for the exercise of the options on the books of Lyndon Systems.
3. Discuss the economic benefits to managers and the benefits to the company from these options.

▸▸ OBJECTIVES **5, 6**

10-39 Stock Split versus Stock Dividend

An annual report of Pacific Foods Company included the following in the statement of consolidated retained earnings:

Charge for stock split	$4,401,000

The balance sheets before and after the split showed the following:

	After	Before
Common stock, $1 par value	$13,203,000	$8,802,000

Define stock split. What did Pacific Foods do to achieve its stock split? Does this conflict with your definition? Explain fully.

▸▸ OBJECTIVES **5, 6**

10-40 Stock Splits

On April 25, 2012, Coca-Cola announced its first stock split in 16 years and only its eleventh stock split since the stock began trading in 1919. In July the stockholders approved the two for one split, which gave each shareholder one additional share of stock for each share held on July 27, 2012. Assume the balance sheet just prior to the stock split is as follows:

Common stock, $0.25 par value; Authorized—5,600 million shares;	
Issued—3,520 million shares	$ 880
Capital surplus	11,212
Reinvested earnings	53,550
Accumulated other comprehensive income (loss)	(2,703)
Treasury stock at cost—1,257 million shares	(31,304)
	$31,635

1. Assume Coca-Cola accounts for this as a true stock split. Provide any journal entries necessary to record the split. Prepare Coca-Cola's stockholders' equity section immediately after the split.
2. Now assume that Coca-Cola accounts for this as a stock split effected in the form of a 100% stock dividend. Prepare any journal entries necessary to record the split. Prepare Coca-Cola's stockholders' equity section immediately after the split.

10-41 Reverse Stock Split

According to a news story, "The shareholders of QED approved a 1-for-10 reverse split of QED's common stock." Accounting for a reverse stock split applies the same principles as accounting for a regular stock split. QED Exploration, Incorporated, is an oil development company operating in Texas and Louisiana. QED's stockholders' equity section before the reverse split included the following:

Common stock, authorized 30,000,000 shares, issued 23,530,000 shares	$ 287,637
Additional paid-in capital	3,437,547
Retained income	2,220,895
Less: Treasury stock, at cost, 1,017,550 shares	(305,250)
Total stockholders' equity	$5,640,829

1. Prepare QED's stockholders' equity section after the reverse stock split.
2. Comment on possible reasons for a reverse split.

10-42 Cash and Stock Dividends

Tompkins Financial Corporation is a financial services holding company headquartered in Ithaca, New York, that offers banking, insurance, and wealth management services. It pays cash dividends quarterly and also issues stock dividends periodically.

1. At March 31, 2012, Tompkins had 11,233,280 issued shares with a par value of $.10 per share and 93,433 shares held in treasury. On April 25, 2012, the company announced that its Board of Directors approved payment of a regular quarterly cash dividend of $.36 per share, payable on May 15, 2012, to common shareholders of record on May 7, 2012. Assume no shares were acquired or sold by the company after March 31. Give the journal entry to record the declaration of the cash dividend.
2. At December 31, 2009, Tompkins had 9,785,265 issued shares with a par value of $.10 per share and 81,723 shares held in treasury. On January 27, 1010, the company announced that its board of directors approved payment of a regular quarterly cash dividend of $.3091 per share, payable on February 25, 2010, to common shareholders of record on February 5, 2010. The board also approved the payment of a 10% stock dividend distributable on February 25, 2010, to common shareholders of record on February 5, 2010. The share price was $36.93 when the stock dividend was issued. Assume no shares were acquired or sold by the company after December 31. Prepare the journal entry to record Tompkins' stock dividend.
3. Tompkins issued 10% stock dividends in 1995, 2003, 2005, 2006, and 2010. In 1998 Tompkins issued a three-for-two split. If an investor purchased 100 shares in 1994, how many shares would the investor have in 2012?

10-43 Treasury Stock

Assume that during 2011, Tompkins Financial Corporation repurchased 1,500 of its own shares at an average price of $38.67 per share. Par value was $.10 per share. Assume the shares were originally issued for $28.

1. Prepare the journal entry for the 2011 purchase of shares assuming that they were treated as treasury shares.
2. Assume instead, that Tompkins did not add the repurchased shares to treasury stock. Instead, it canceled the shares and returned them to unissued status. This is accounted for with a debit to Capital Stock at Par Value, a debit to Additional Paid-in Capital for the surplus created by the initial issuance, and a debit to Retained Earnings for the remainder. Give the actual entry Tompkins made.

▶▶ OBJECTIVE 10

10-44 Book Value and Return on Equity

Nelson Company had net income of $14 million in 20X8. The stockholders' equity section of its 20X8 annual report follows ($ in millions):

	20X8	20X7
Stockholders' equity		
8% Preferred stock, $50 par value, 400,000 shares authorized, 300,000 shares issued	$ 15.0	$ 15.0
Common stock, $1 par, 5 million authorized, 2 million and 1.8 million issued	2.0	1.8
Additional paid-in capital	32.0	30.0
Retained earnings	71.0	65.2
Total stockholders' equity	$120.0	$112.0

1. Compute the book value per share of common stock at the end of 20X8.
2. Compute the rate of return on common equity for 20X8.
3. Compute the amount of cash dividends on common stock declared during 20X8. (*Hint:* Examine the retained earnings T-account.)

▶▶ OBJECTIVE 10

10-45 Financial Ratios and Stockholders' Equity

Consider the following data for New York Bankcorp:

	December 31	
	20X2	20X1
Stockholders' equity		
Preferred stock, 200,000 shares, $20 par	$ 4,000,000	$ 4,000,000
Common stock, 4,000,000 shares, $2 par	8,000,000	8,000,000
Additional paid-in capital	5,000,000	5,000,000
Retained income	3,000,000	1,400,000
Total stockholders' equity	$20,000,000	$18,400,000

Net income was $2.8 million for 20X2. The preferred stock is 10%, cumulative. The par value of the preferred stock is also its liquidation value. The regular annual dividend on the preferred stock was declared and paid and the common shareholders received dividends of $.20 per share. The market price of the common stock on December 31, 20X2, was $13.20 per share.

Compute the following statistics for 20X2: rate of return on common equity, earnings per share of common stock, price-earnings ratio, dividend-payout ratio, dividend-yield ratio, and book value per share of common stock.

▶▶ OBJECTIVES 2, 3

10-46 Stockholders' Equity Section

The following are data for the Foin Corporation on December 31, 20X8:

6% cumulative preferred stock, $40 par value, callable at $42, authorized 100,000 shares, issued and outstanding 100,000 shares	$ 4,000,000
Treasury stock, common (at cost)	5,000,000
Additional paid-in capital, common stock	9,000,000
Dividends payable	200,000
Retained earnings	15,000,000
Additional paid-in capital, preferred stock	1,250,000
Common stock, $2.50 par value per share, authorized 1.8 million shares, issued 1.2 million shares of which 60,000 are held in the treasury	3,000,000

Prepare a detailed stockholders' equity section as it would appear in the balance sheet at December 31, 20X8.

10-47 Effects on Stockholders' Equity

▶▶ OBJECTIVES
2, 3, 6, 7

Indicate the effect (+, −, or 0) on total stockholders' equity of McKenzie Services Corporation for each of the following:

1. Declaration and issuance of a stock dividend on common stock
2. Sale of 100 shares of McKenzie Services by Jay Smith to Ray Fauley
3. Net earnings for the period of $600,000
4. Issuance of a stock dividend on common stock
5. Failing to declare a regular dividend on cumulative preferred stock
6. Declaration of a cash dividend of $50,000 in total
7. Payment of item 6
8. Purchase of 10 shares of treasury stock for $1,200 cash
9. Sale of treasury stock, purchased in item 8, for $1,400
10. Sale of treasury stock, purchased in item 8, for $1,000

Problems

MyAccountingLab

10-48 Dividends and Cumulative Preferred Stock

▶▶ OBJECTIVES 2, 3

Yanity Interiors, Inc., maker of seats and other interior equipment for Boeing aircraft, started 20X8 with the following balance sheet:

6% Cumulative convertible preferred stock, par value $10 a share, authorized 150,000 shares; issued 54,749 shares	$ 547,490
Common stock, par value $.20 a share, authorized 2,000,000 shares, issued 1,520,320 shares	304,064
Additional paid-in capital	2,063,351
Retained earnings	2,463,951
Less: Treasury stock, at cost	
Preferred stock, 6,008 shares	(75,100)
Common stock, 9,309 shares	(167,549)
Total stockholders' equity	$5,136,207

1. Suppose Yanity Interiors had paid no dividends, preferred or common, in the prior year, 20X7. All preferred dividends had been paid through 20X6. Management decided at the end of 20X8 to pay $.08 per share common dividends. Calculate the preferred dividends that would be paid during 20X8. Prepare journal entries for recording the declaration and payment of preferred and common dividends. Assume no preferred or common shares were issued or purchased during 20X7 or 20X8.
2. Suppose 20X8 net income was $500,000. Compute the 20X8 ending balance in the Retained Earnings account.

10-49 Dividend Reinvestment Plans

▶▶ OBJECTIVES 1, 2

Many corporations have automatic dividend reinvestment plans. Individual shareholders may elect not to receive their cash dividends. Instead, an equivalent amount of cash is invested in additional stock (at the current market value) that is issued to the shareholder.
Royal Dutch Shell had total assets of $345.3 billion at December 31, 2011, and declared a quarterly cash dividend of $.42 per share in the fourth quarter of 2011.

1. Suppose holders of 15% of the company's 6.2 billion outstanding shares decided to reinvest in the company under an automatic dividend reinvestment plan instead of accepting the cash. The market price of the shares on issuance was $50 per share. Prepare the journal entry or entries for these transactions. For purposes of this problem assume Shell shares have no par and no stated value.
2. One of the members of your investment club expressed the following opinion: Stockholders participating in dividend reinvestment programs pay taxes on dividends not really received. If a company would refrain from paying dividends only to take them back as reinvestments, it would save paperwork, and the stockholder would save income tax. Do you agree with these remarks? Explain in detail.

▶▶ OBJECTIVE 1

10-50 Multiple Classes of Common Stock

In 2011 *Fortune* magazine listed **Royal Dutch Shell** as the world's second largest corporation when ranked on sales and tenth largest when ranked on market value. Shell has multiple forms of common stock. It offers class A and class B shares. Class A shares pay cash dividends in euros, unless the shareholder elects otherwise. Class B shares pay dividends in pounds sterling (UK currency) unless the shareholder elects otherwise. In addition, for U.S. shareholders, Shell provides ADRs (American Depository Receipts), which pay dividends in U.S. dollars.

1. Consider why a company would choose to create multiple classes of common stock.
2. Why would a European-based integrated petroleum company present its IFRS financial statements in U.S. dollars as the reporting currency?

▶▶ OBJECTIVES 2, 6

10-51 Dividends

(Alternate is 10-52.)

1. Hubbard Company issued 500,000 shares of common stock, $4 par, for $25 cash per share on March 31, 20X1. Prepare the journal entry.
2. Hubbard Company declared and paid a cash dividend of $1 per share on March 31, 20X2. Prepare the journal entry. Assume only the 500,000 shares from requirement 1 are outstanding.
3. Hubbard Company had retained earnings of $10 million by March 31, 20X5. The market value of the common shares was $50 each. A common stock dividend of 5% was declared, and shares were issued on March 31, 20X5. Prior to the stock dividend 500,000 shares were outstanding. Prepare the journal entry. Also present a tabulation that compares the stockholders' equity section before and after the declaration and issuance of the stock dividend. Include at the bottom of the tabulation the effects on the overall market value of the stock, the total shares outstanding, and the number of shares and percentage of ownership of an individual owner who originally bought 5,000 shares.
4. What journal entries would be made by the investor who bought 5,000 shares of Hubbard common stock and held this investment throughout the time covered in requirements 1, 2, and 3?
5. Refer to requirement 4. Suppose the investor sold 200 shares for $58 each the day after receiving the stock dividend. Prepare the investor's journal entry for the sale of the shares.

▶▶ OBJECTIVES 2, 6

10-52 Dividends

(Alternate is 10-51.)

1. Sanchez Company issued 700,000 shares of common stock, $1 par, for $9 cash per share on December 31, 20X5. Prepare the journal entry.
2. Sanchez Company declared and paid a cash dividend of $.60 per share on December 31, 20X6. Prepare the journal entry. Assume only the 700,000 shares from requirement 1 are outstanding.
3. Sanchez Company had retained earnings of $7 million by December 31, 20X9. The market value of the common shares was $30 each. A common stock dividend of 2% was declared, and shares were issued on December 31, 20X9. Prior to the stock dividend 700,000 shares were outstanding. Prepare the journal entry. Also present a tabulation that compares the stockholders' equity section before and after the declaration and issuance of the stock dividend. Also include at the bottom of the tabulation the effects on the overall market value of the stock, the total shares outstanding, and the number of shares and percentage of ownership of an individual owner who originally bought 10,000 shares.
4. What journal entries would be made by the investor who bought 10,000 original-issue shares of Sanchez Company common stock and held this investment throughout the time covered in requirements 1, 2, and 3?
5. Refer to requirement 4. Suppose the investor sold 2,000 shares for $33 each the day after receiving the stock dividend. Prepare the investor's journal entry for the sale of the shares.

▶▶ OBJECTIVE 4

10-53 Stock Options

On January 1, 2013, Sikes Company granted stock options to 100 key employees. Each employee received 300 options. Each option entitles the employee to purchase one share of $1 par value common stock at a price of $25. The options vest 3 years from the date of the grant. Sikes employed an option pricing model to determine a fair value of $5 per option as of the grant date.

1. What journal entry would Sikes make during 2013?
2. What journal entry would Sikes make during 2014?

3. What journal entry would Sikes make during 2015?
4. What journal entry would Sikes record to recognize the exercise of 70% of the options in January 2016, when the market price per share was $40?
5. Assume that the remaining 30% of the options expired unexercised. What journal entry would Sikes make to record the expiration?

10-54 Meaning of Stock Splits and Dividends

▶▶ OBJECTIVES 2, 6

A January 31 announcement to shareholders of Premier Financial, a California savings and loan company, stated that the company had "good news" for stockholders. The announcement went on to explain that the board raised the quarterly cash dividend 12% and then declared a five-for-four stock split in the form of a 25% stock dividend. The additional shares were to be distributed on March 15 to shareholders of record on February 15.

On March 16, the board approved a merger between Premier Financial and a large U.S. steel company. The agreement called for a cash payment of $33.60 on each outstanding United Financial share. The original offer (in early February) was $42 per share for the 5.8 million shares outstanding.

1. As a recipient of the letter of January 31, you were annoyed by the five-for-four stock split. Prepare a letter to the chairman indicating the reasons for your displeasure.
2. Prepare a response to the unhappy shareholder in requirement 1.
3. A shareholder of Premier Financial wrote to the chairman in early March: "I'm confused about the change in the agreed upon price per share. I owned 100 shares and thought I'd receive $4,200. Now the price has dropped from $42.00 to $33.60." Prepare a response to the shareholder.

10-55 Stock Dividend and Fractional Shares

▶▶ OBJECTIVE 6

The Rupley Company declared and distributed a 5% stock dividend. The stockholders' equity before the dividend was as follows:

Common stock, 5,000,000 shares, $1 par	$ 5,000,000
Additional paid-in capital	20,000,000
Retained earnings	50,000,000
Total stockholders' equity	$75,000,000

The market price of Rupley's shares was $10 when the stock dividend was distributed. Rupley paid cash of $15,000 in lieu of issuing fractional shares.

1. Prepare the journal entry for the declaration and distribution of the stock dividend.
2. Show the stockholders' equity section after the stock dividend.
3. How did the stock dividend affect total stockholders' equity? How did it affect the proportion of the company owned by each shareholder?

10-56 Issuance and Retirement of Shares, Cash Dividends

▶▶ OBJECTIVES 2, 7

On January 2, 20X1, Willamette Investment Company began business by issuing 30,000 shares at $1 par value for $300,000 cash. The cash was invested, and on December 26, 20X1, all investments were sold for $315,000 cash. Operating expenses for 20X1 were $5,000, all paid in cash. Therefore, net income for 20X1 was $10,000. On December 27, the board of directors declared a $.10 per share cash dividend, payable on January 15, 20X2, to owners of record on December 31, 20X1. On January 30, 20X2, the company bought and retired 2,000 of its own shares on the open market for $8.00 each.

1. Prepare journal entries for issuance of shares, declaration and payment of cash dividends, and retirement of shares.
2. Prepare a balance sheet as of December 31, 20X1.

10-57 Issuance, Splits, and Dividends
(Alternate is 10-58.)

▶▶ OBJECTIVES 2, 5, 6

1. Almer Company issued 100,000 shares of common stock, $5 par, for $40 cash per share on December 31, 20X1. Prepare the journal entry.
2. Almer Company had retained earnings of $3.5 million by December 31, 20X5. The board of directors declared a two-for-one stock split and immediately exchanged two $2.50 par shares

for each share outstanding. Prepare the journal entry, if any. Present the stockholders' equity section of the balance sheet before and after the split.

3. Repeat requirement 2, but assume that instead of exchanging two $2.50 par shares for each share outstanding, one additional $5 par share was issued for each share outstanding. Almer said it issued a two-for-one stock split "effected in the form of a stock dividend."

4. What journal entries would be made by the investor who bought 2,000 shares of Almer Company common stock and held this investment throughout the time covered in requirements 1, 2, and 3?

▶▶ OBJECTIVES 2, 5, 6

10-58 Issuance, Splits, and Dividends
(Alternate is 10-57.)

1. Suppose **AT&T** had originally issued 200 million shares of common stock, $1 par, for $15 cash per share many years ago. Prepare the journal entry.

2. Suppose AT&T had retained earnings of $5 billion by December 31, 20X2. The board of directors declared a two-for-one stock split and immediately exchanged two $.50 par shares for each share outstanding. Prepare the journal entry, if any. Present the stockholders' equity section of the balance sheet before and after the split.

3. Repeat requirement 2, but assume that one additional $1 par share was issued by AT&T for each share outstanding (instead of exchanging shares) and accounted for as a two-for-one stock split "effected in the form of a stock dividend."

4. What journal entries would be made by the investor who bought 1,000 shares of AT&T common stock and held this investment throughout the time covered in requirements 1, 2, and 3?

▶▶ OBJECTIVES 5, 6

10-59 Stock Split and 100% Stock Dividend
The Moser Company wants to double its number of shares outstanding. The company president asks the controller how a two-for-one stock split differs from a 100% stock dividend. Moser has 300,000 shares ($1 par) outstanding at a market price of $20 per share.
The current stockholders' equity section is as follows:

Common shares, 300,000 issued and outstanding	$ 300,000
Additional paid-in capital	2,300,000
Retained earnings	4,500,000

1. Prepare the journal entry for a two-for-one stock split.
2. Prepare the journal entry for a 100% stock dividend.
3. Explain the difference between a two-for-one stock split and a 100% stock dividend.

▶▶ OBJECTIVE 7

10-60 Treasury Stock
(Alternate is 10-66.) **Minnesota Mining and Manufacturing Company (3M)** presented the following data in its 2011 annual report:

	December 31	
	2011	**2010**
	(in millions)	
Stockholders' equity:		
Common stock, $.01 par value	$ 9	$ 9
Additional paid-in capital	3,767	3,468
Retained earnings	28,348	25,995
Treasury stock	(11,679)	(10,266)
Other comprehensive income (loss)	(5,025)	(3,543)
Total stockholders' equity	$15,420	$15,663

1. During 2011, 3M reacquired 31.3 million treasury shares for $2,701 million. Give the journal entry to record this transaction. On average, what did 3M pay per share repurchased?

2. 3M also issued some treasury shares as part of its employee stock option and investment plans. What was the cost of treasury shares issued in 2011?
3. Suppose that on January 2, 2012, 3M used cash to reacquire 100,000 shares for $89 each and held them in the treasury. Prepare the journal entry. What is the new stockholders' equity total after the acquisition of treasury stock?
4. Suppose the 100,000 shares of treasury stock acquired in requirement 3 are sold for $96 per share. Prepare the journal entry.
5. Ignore requirement 4. Suppose the 100,000 shares of treasury stock are sold for $60 per share. Prepare the journal entry.

10-61 Treasury Shares

▶▶ **OBJECTIVE 7**

During 2011 outstanding common shares of General Electric (GE) decreased from 10,615,376,000 to 10,537,017,000. GE declared dividends of $6,458,000,000. The treasury stock account had a beginning balance of $31,938,000,000 and an ending balance of $31,769,000,000. The total cost of purchases of treasury shares in 2011 was $2,067,000,000. During 2011 GE stock fluctuated substantially from a high of $21.65 in the first quarter to a low of $14.02 during the fourth quarter. Over the last few years, GE stock prices have been lower than the historical average. As recently as late 2007, the stock was selling near $40 per share. Assume that the average price of treasury stock purchased in 2011 was $17.68 per share and the average carrying value of treasury stock disposals was $30 per share.

1. Compute the carrying value of the treasury shares sold during 2011.
2. What was the net increase (or decrease) in number of treasury shares in 2011?
3. Comment on the decision to buy/sell treasury stock during the year.

10-62 Repurchase of Shares and Book Value per Share

▶▶ **OBJECTIVE 7**

ExxonMobil repurchased common shares during 2011 and, as a result, the Treasury Stock account increased by $20,324 million. The market price of ExxonMobil shares averaged $81.50 per share during the year. There were 8,019 million shares issued and 3,285 million shares in the treasury at year-end. The condensed 2011 shareholders' equity section of the balance sheet showed the following (dollars in millions):

Common stock, no par	$ 9,512
Earnings reinvested	330,939
Treasury stock	(176,932)
Other	(2,774)
Total stockholders' equity	$160,745

1. Estimate the number of shares repurchased for the treasury.
2. Compute the book value per share at December 31, 2011.

10-63 Retirement of Shares

▶▶ **OBJECTIVE 7**

Sage Financial Systems, Inc., has the following:

Common stock, 6,000,000 shares, $2 par value	$ 12,000,000
Paid-in capital in excess of par	42,000,000
Total paid-in capital	54,000,000
Retained earnings	10,000,000
Stockholders' equity	$ 64,000,000
Overall market value of stock @ assumed market price of $28 per share	$168,000,000
Book value per share = $64,000,000 ÷ 6,000,000 = $10.67	

The company used cash to reacquire and retire 300,000 shares for $28 each. Prepare the stockholders' equity section before and after this retirement of shares. Also prepare the journal entry.

▶▶ OBJECTIVE 7

10-64 Disposition of Treasury Stock
Marshall Company bought 10,000 of its own shares for $12 per share. The shares were held as treasury stock. This was the only time Marshall had ever purchased treasury stock.

1. Marshall sold 5,000 of the shares for $13 per share. Prepare the journal entry.
2. Marshall sold the remaining 5,000 shares later for $11 per share. Prepare the journal entry.
3. Repeat requirement 2, assuming the shares were sold for $9 instead of $11 per share.
4. Did you record gains or losses in requirements 1, 2, and 3? Explain.

▶▶ OBJECTIVES 2, 9

10-65 Effects of Treasury Stock on Retained Earnings
Assume that Lawson Company has retained earnings of $16 million, paid-in capital of $48 million, and treasury stock at a cost of $12 million.

1. Tabulate the effects of cash dividend payments of (a) $8 million, and (b) $2 million on retained earnings and total stockholders' equity.
2. Why do many states forbid the payment of dividends if retained earnings do not exceed the cost of any treasury stock on hand? Explain, using the numbers from your answer to requirement 1.

▶▶ OBJECTIVE 7

10-66 Treasury Stock
(Alternate is 10-60.) Johannesburg Company has the following [in rands (R), the South African unit of currency]:

Common stock, 2,000,000 shares, R3 par value	R 6,000,000
Paid-in capital in excess of par	34,000,000
Total paid-in capital	40,000,000
Retained income	18,000,000
Stockholders' equity	R58,000,000
Overall market value of stock @ assumed market price of R40 per share	R80,000,000
Book value per share = R58,000,000 ÷ 2,000,000 = R29	

1. The company used cash to reacquire 150,000 shares for R40 each and held them in the treasury. Prepare the stockholders' equity section after the acquisition of treasury stock. Also prepare the journal entry.
2. Suppose all the treasury stock is sold for R50 per share. Prepare the journal entry.
3. Suppose all the treasury stock is sold for R30 per share. Prepare the journal entry.
4. Recalculate book value after each preceding transaction.

▶▶ OBJECTIVE 8

10-67 Convertible Securities
Suppose Walla Walla Company had paid $175,000 to Freewater Company for an investment in 10,000 shares of the $5 par value preferred stock of Freewater Company. The preferred stock was later converted into 10,000 shares of Freewater Company common stock ($1 par value).

1. Using the balance sheet equation, prepare an analysis of transactions of Walla Walla Company and Freewater Company.
2. Prepare the journal entries to accompany your analysis in requirement 1.

▶▶ OBJECTIVES 2, 4

10-68 Issue of Common Shares
Ahlbrandt Corporation had the following stockholders' equity on December 31, 2011:

Common stock: authorized 250,000,000 shares with $.01 par value, issued and outstanding 61,766,000 shares	$ 618,000
Additional paid-in capital	694,296,000
Accumulated deficit	(162,402,000)
Total stockholders' equity	$532,512,000

In 2011 the company approved an employee stock purchase plan that allows employees to purchase stock at 85% of the fair market value. When employees participate in this plan, Ahlbrandt recognizes compensation expense in the amount of the 15% discount. Compensation expense recognized in 2011 was $816,000. Assume an average market price of $20 per share. Net income for the year was $35,686,000. No dividends were paid.

1. Prepare the journal entry for the issuance of stock under the stock purchase plan in 2011.
2. At the end of 2011 Ahlbrandt had an accumulated deficit of ($162,402,000). At the current rate of earnings, how many years will it be before Ahlbrandt could pay a dividend of $1 per share without exhausting retained earnings?

10-69 Noncash Exchanges

▶▶ **OBJECTIVE 2**

Suppose Clair Company acquires some equipment from Marseilles Company in exchange for issuance of 10,000 shares of Clair's common stock. The equipment was carried on Marseilles's books at the €530,000 original cost less accumulated depreciation of €100,000. Clair's stock actively trades and has a current market value is €55 per share. Its par value is €1 per share.

1. By using the balance sheet equation, show the effects of the transaction on the accounts of Clair Company and Marseilles Company.
2. Show the journal entries on the books of Clair Company and Marseilles Company.

10-70 Covenants and Leases and Buying and Selling Stock

▶▶ **OBJECTIVE 2**

Mitchell Energy and Development Corporation was one of the country's largest oil and gas producers before it was purchased by **Devon Energy**. Some years ago, the notes to its financial statements revealed the existence of certain debt agreement restrictions on the level of consolidated stockholders' equity as well as on various asset-to-debt ratios. These bank credit agreements required that consolidated stockholders' equity be maintained at a level equal to at least $300,000,000 and also required the maintenance of specified financial and oil and gas reserve and/or asset value to debt ratios.

1. Given the existence of the asset-to-debt covenants, was Mitchell more likely to be able to enter into operating leases or capital leases without violating the covenants?
2. If Mitchell Energy and Development had refused to agree to these conditions at the time of the debt issues, how would it have affected the market price of the debt it issued?
3. Before being acquired, Mitchell issued 4.68 million additional shares at $53 per share. Give the journal entry to record the issue, assuming no par stock.
4. Devon Energy subsequently agreed to buy Mitchell Energy by giving each shareholder in Mitchell Energy $31 in cash and .585 shares of Devon Energy for each share of Mitchell Energy. Devon's shares were valued at $50.76. How much profit would an investor who bought 1,000 shares of Mitchell Energy at $53 per share just before the acquisition make when the merger was complete?

10-71 Financial Ratios

▶▶ **OBJECTIVE 10**

Consider the following data from two companies in very different industries. **Adobe Systems** is a software company. **Empire District** is an electric utility serving the Midwest. (Amounts except earnings per share and market price are in millions.)

	Total Assets	Total Liabilities	Net Income	Earnings per Share	Market Price per Share
Adobe Systems	$8,991	$3,208	$833	$1.67	$34.31
Empire District	2,022	1,328	55	1.31	21.09

1. Compute the market-to-book ratio, the price-earnings ratio (P-E), and the rate of return on common stockholders' equity for both Adobe Systems and Empire District. Use ending stockholders' equity rather than average stockholders' equity for computing return on equity.
2. Explain what might cause the differences in these ratios between the two companies.

▶▶ **OBJECTIVES 2, 7, 10**

10-72 Classic Case of Shareholders' Equity Section

Enron Corporation was a worldwide energy company with annual revenues in excess of $40 billion in 1999. Its main activities were in natural gas and electricity. Enron's collapse was one of the most spectacular events of the recent past. Enron filed for bankruptcy protection on December 2, 2001, and 2 years later its common stock shares were trading at $.04 per share. Events surrounding Enron led to the failure of its audit firm, **Arthur Andersen**. The data here are from the company's 1999 annual report ($ in millions).

For the Year Ended December 31	1999	1998
Other stockholders' equity	895	70
Common stock held in treasury, 1,337,714 shares and 9,333,322 shares, respectively	(49)	(195)
Common stock, no par value, 1,200,000,000 shares authorized, 716,865,081 shares and 671,094,552 shares issued, respectively	6,637	5,117
Retained earnings	2,698	2,226
Preferred stock, cumulative, no par value, 1,370,000 shares authorized, 1,296,184 shares and 1,319,848 shares issued, respectively	130	132
Accumulated other comprehensive income (loss)	(741)	(162)

1. Prepare the stockholders' equity section of Enron's 1999 balance sheet. Include the amount for total stockholders' equity.
2. Enron paid $355 million of cash dividends on common stock and $66 million of cash dividends on preferred stock in 1999. Compute Enron's net income for 1999.
3. Explain Enron's net acquisition or disposition of treasury shares during 1999. Include the increase or decrease in total number of shares and the average cost per share of those acquired or sold. What is the average purchase price (cost) of the shares remaining in the treasury at the end of 1999?
4. Calculate book value per share at December 31, 1999, and the market-to-book ratio on that date, given a market price per share of about $45.
5. The price per share peaked in 2000 at about $91. Estimate the loss in total market value for Enron from its peak until December 2003. Assume 716 million shares outstanding.

▶▶ **OBJECTIVE 4**

10-73 Stock Options and Ethics

Bristol-Myers Squibb is one of the largest pharmaceutical companies in the world. In 2002 the company granted executives options to purchase 40,112,732 shares of common stock. Suppose all shares were granted with an exercise price of $37.55 per share, which was the market price of the stock on the date the options were granted, and all options could be exercised anytime between 3 and 5 years from the grant date, provided that the executive still works for Bristol-Myers Squibb. Under the rules in place for accounting for stock options in 2002, Bristol-Meyers Squibb was not required to record an expense on its income statement for the compensation expense related to these options. However, the company was required to disclose information about the stock options, including the impact the options would have had on income if they had been expensed.

Assume that at the same time the stock options were issued, Bristol-Myers Squibb also issued warrants with the same $37.55 exercise price that are exercisable any time in the next 5 years. The company received $12 for each such warrant.

1. Under the rules in place in 2002, no expense was recorded. How would this answer differ in 2012?
2. How much value was there to the executive for each stock option issued in 2002? Given the vesting and exercise provisions, how much might executives have realized from these options by 2012? Use one of the Web-based financial sites to review the price performance of Bristol-Myers over these 10 years.
3. How much did it cost the firm for each stock option that was issued?
4. Might the fact that individual executives hold stock options affect their decisions about declaring dividends? Comment on the ethics of this influence.

Collaborative Learning Exercise

10-74 Market-to-Book and ROE
Form groups of three to six students each. Each student should pick two companies, preferably from different industries. Find the appropriate data and compute the market-to-book ratio and the ROE for each company.

▶▶ **OBJECTIVE 10**

Assemble the group and list the companies selected, together with their market-to-book ratio and ROE. Rank the companies from highest to lowest on market-to-book ratio. Then rank them on ROE.

Explain why companies rank as they do in each list. Are the rankings similar; that is, is the ranking based on market-to-book similar to the ranking based on ROE? Explain why you would or would not expect similarity in the rankings.

Analyzing and Interpreting Financial Statements

10-75 Financial Statement Research
Select a company and use its financial statements to answer the following questions:

▶▶ **OBJECTIVE 2**

1. Identify each transaction that affected stockholders' equity during the most recent 2 years.
2. Indicate which accounts were affected and by how much.
3. List any transactions that appear unusual. For example, many companies have a change in shareholders' equity that arises from tax benefits related to stock options. This and a few other common transactions are beyond our scope in this introductory course.

10-76 Starbucks' Annual Report
Find **Starbucks**' financial statements for the fiscal year ended October 2, 2011, either via the Starbucks Web site or on the SEC's EDGAR database.

▶▶ **OBJECTIVES 2, 10**

1. Prepare the journal entries to record any dividends declared and dividends paid in the year ended October 2, 2011.
2. How much cash did Starbucks generate from the issuance of common stock in the year ended October 2, 2011? How much cash did Starbucks use to repurchase common stock in the year ended October 2, 2011?
3. Compute Starbucks' return on common equity and book value per share in fiscal 2010 and 2011. Comment on the changes in the two ratios between 2010 and 2011.

10-77 Analyzing Financial Statements Using the Internet: United Parcel Service
Go to www.ups.com to find the home page of **United Parcel Service** (UPS). Click on the Investors link near the bottom of the page. Click on Financials to locate UPS's latest annual report.
Answer the following questions about UPS:

▶▶ **OBJECTIVES 1, 3, 4, 5, 6**

1. Identify the classes of stock that UPS has authorized as of the end of its most recent fiscal period, with their par values. Have all the shares in each category been issued? Can you tell if the shares were issued above par? How? What features distinguish the different classes of stock?
2. How many additional shares of common stock is UPS able to issue as of its most recent balance sheet date? If these shares were all issued and outstanding, how would the values reported on the balance sheet change? Does UPS have any treasury stock?
3. Has the number of issued shares in each category of common stock changed over the past year? If so, what caused the changes?
4. Did UPS declare any stock splits or stock dividends during its most recent 2-year comparative reporting period? If so, what effect did these have on the number of shares of stock outstanding? Why do you think UPS would want to declare a stock split or stock dividend?
5. Does UPS have a stock-based compensation plan?

11 Intercorporate Investments and Consolidations

HAVE YOU EVER wondered how the drink we know as Coca-Cola was created? John Pemberton, an Atlanta pharmacist, mixed up a sweet syrup one day in 1886. Curious about its taste, he took it next door to Jacob's Pharmacy, where it was mixed with carbonated water and made available for sale. Pemberton's bookkeeper named the creation Coca-Cola. On average, during the remainder of the year 1886, Jacob's sold nine drinks a day. The drink grew in popularity, and by 1895, Coca-Cola Company's annual report stated that Coca-Cola was sold in every state and territory in the United States. Currently, people around the globe consume Coca-Cola Company products 1.7 billion times every day—about 19,400 beverages every second.

How did the company experience such explosive growth? Acquisitions have contributed to this growth. One of Coca-Cola's first significant acquisitions was the purchase of Minute-Maid Corporation in 1960, which added fruit juice drinks to its product portfolio. The pattern of acquiring other companies has continued over the years, including recent acquisitions of Odwalla in 2001 and Energy Brands in 2007. These companies are all subsidiaries that Coca-Cola consolidates into one set of financial statements.

Another key to Coca-Cola's growth is its international distribution network. In 1899, the company sold the rights to bottle Coca-Cola in most of the United States for $1. By 1959, Coca-Cola was being distributed by 1,700 bottlers, operating in more than 100 countries. Bottling operations extended to China in 1981, to Russia in 1985, and to Vietnam in 1994. What is the relationship today between Coca-Cola and the bottling companies? Does Coca-Cola own the bottling companies? Or are the bottlers totally independent companies? Alternatively, does Coca-Cola have a partial ownership interest in the bottlers? In fact, all of these scenarios exist.

consolidated financial statements
The financial statements that result when the financial records of two or more separate legal entitles are combined into a single set of statements.

Pick up the annual report of most major or even middle-sized companies and you find **consolidated financial statements**. Consolidated financial statements result when the financial records of two or more separate legal entities are combined into a single set of statements. Coca-Cola describes its policies as follows: "Our Company consolidates all entities that we control by ownership of a majority voting interest.... We use the equity method to account

---

▶▶ **LEARNING OBJECTIVES** *After studying this chapter, you should be able to:*

1 Explain why corporations invest in one another.

2 Account for short-term investments in debt securities and equity securities.

3 Report long-term investments in bonds.

4 Contrast the equity and market methods of accounting for investments.

5 Understand the reasons for business combinations and prepare consolidated financial statements.

6 Incorporate noncontrolling interests into consolidated financial statements.

7 Explain the economic meaning and financial reporting of goodwill.

for investments in [nonconsolidated] companies, if our investment provides us with the ability to exercise significant influence over operating and financial policies of the investee." The company goes on to state that its investments in debt and equity securities, other than investments accounted for under the equity method, are classified as trading, available-for-sale, or held-to-maturity and accounted for at fair value or cost. In this chapter we will explain how and why the accounting methods used by Coca-Cola to account for its ownership interest in other companies depend on the percentage of the company that Coca-Cola owns. ●

An Overview of Corporate Investments

Companies invest in debt and equity securities for a variety of reasons. When a firm has excess cash, smart managers invest the cash rather than holding it in the company's checking account. While some bank accounts pay interest, companies seek enhanced returns from both short- and long-term debt securities issued by governments, banks, or other corporations.

Companies also invest in marketable equity securities of other companies. Sometimes this is simply a way to invest excess cash, and sometimes it is a strategic decision that gives the investor company some influence over the investee. After companies invest in equity securities of another company, their accountants must report on the financial results of these linked entities. Current accounting procedures for intercorporate linkages use one of three approaches based on how much influence the investor has over the investee, as measured by the percentage of ownership: (1) up to 20%, (2) between 20% and 50%, and (3) above 50%. After identifying the appropriate accounting procedure, there is a question about *where* to report the investment asset

Coca-Cola has a global presence. Its products are sold in more than 200 countries. In addition, Coca-Cola has an ownership interest in companies worldwide. Coca-Cola prepares consolidated financial statements that include the financial results for all of the brands it produces and for all of the companies that it controls.

▶▶ OBJECTIVE 1

Explain why corporations invest in one another.

493

on the balance sheet, among current or long-term assets. This classification is based on purpose or intent. An investment is a current asset if it is a short-term investment, one the owner expects to convert to cash within 1 year. All debt securities that mature within 1 year meet this standard. Debt or equity investments that a company plans to hold longer than a year are noncurrent assets and usually appear as either a separate investments category or as a part of "other" assets.

Coca-Cola's 2011 balance sheet includes investments in several line items. For example, the company lists $1,088 million in Short-term Investments and $144 million in Marketable Securities as current assets. Noncurrent investments include $7,233 million in Equity Method Investments, $1,141 million in Other Investments, Principally Bottling Companies, and $3,495 million in noncurrent Other Assets.

Short-Term Investments

<table>
<tr><td>

▶▶ OBJECTIVE 2

Account for short-term investments in debt securities and equity securities.

</td></tr>
</table>

As its name implies, a **short-term investment** is a temporary investment of otherwise idle cash in marketable securities. **Marketable securities** are notes, bonds, or stocks that can be readily sold on stock exchanges or over-the-counter markets. A company's short-term investment portfolio contains debt and equity securities that are highly liquid (easily convertible into cash), have readily determinable fair values, and relatively stable prices.

Ordinarily, companies expect to convert items classified as short-term investments into cash within a year after the date on the balance sheet. While a company may not convert some of these securities into cash within 12 months, we still classify them as current assets because management intends to convert them into cash as needed. The key point is that conversion to cash is easily available at the option of management.

Short-term debt securities are primarily government- and business-issued notes and bonds with maturities of 1 year or less. Debt securities also include short-term obligations of banks, called **certificates of deposit**, and **commercial paper**, consisting of short-term notes payable issued by large corporations with top credit ratings. **U.S. Treasury obligations**, which refer to interest-bearing notes, bonds, and bills issued by the federal government, are also classified as debt securities. All these debt securities may be held until maturity or may be resold in securities markets.

Short-term equity securities consist of securities representing ownership interests, such as common and preferred stock, in other corporations. Companies, as well as individuals, regularly buy and sell equity securities on the NYSE or other stock exchanges. If the investing firm intends to sell the equity securities it holds within a year or within its normal operating cycle, then we classify the securities as short-term investments.

At acquisition, companies record these securities at cost, including commissions, fees, and transfer taxes. How they are reported after acquisition depends on whether they are classified as trading securities, available-for-sale securities, or held-to-maturity securities. **Trading securities** are short-term investments, including both debt and equity securities, acquired by the company with the intent to resell them shortly for purposes of short-term profits. Companies list such securities among current assets on their balance sheets and measure them at fair value (basically market value). The primary holders of trading securities are financial institutions, although some large nonfinancial companies such as Intel also hold trading securities.

Held-to-maturity securities are debt securities that the company purchases with the intent to hold them until they mature. Equity securities do not have maturity dates and, therefore, cannot be classified as held-to-maturity. Held-to-maturity securities are shown on the balance sheet at amortized cost, not at fair value. Recall from Chapter 9 that the amortized cost of a debt security is the original cost adjusted for the amortization of any discount or premium. In Chapter 9 we examined the amortization of premiums and discounts on bonds payable by the issuer of the debt. Corporations that invest in bonds use the same approach, as illustrated later in this chapter. Unlike trading securities, which are always classified as short term because of the owner's intention, held-to-maturity securities are classified according to the time remaining until they mature. If the time to maturity is less than a year, they are short-term investments and thus current assets. Otherwise, they are long-term investments and classified as noncurrent assets.

Available-for-sale (AFS) securities include all debt and equity securities that are not classified as trading securities or held-to-maturity securities. They include equity securities that the company does not intend to sell in the immediate future and debt securities that the company neither plans to sell shortly nor to hold to maturity. Available-for-sale securities are listed on

short-term investment
A temporary investment of otherwise idle cash in marketable securities.

marketable securities
Notes, bonds, or stocks that can readily be sold on stock exchanges or over-the-counter markets.

short-term debt securities
Primarily government- and business-issued notes and bonds with maturities of 1 year or less. May also include certificates of deposit, commercial paper, and U.S. Treasury obligations.

certificates of deposit
Short-term obligations of banks.

commercial paper
Short-term notes payable issued by large corporations with top credit ratings.

U.S. Treasury obligations
Interest-bearing notes, bonds, and bills issued by the federal government.

short-term equity securities
Securities representing ownership interests in other corporations such as common or preferred stock that are held with the intention to liquidate within 1 year.

trading securities
Short-term investments in equity or debt securities that management intends to resell shortly for short-term profits.

held-to-maturity securities
Debt securities that the investor purchases with the intent to hold them until maturity.

the balance sheet at their fair values. Individual available-for-sale securities can be classified as either current or noncurrent depending on whether the company considers them to be part of working capital.

In the preceding discussion we indicate that trading and available-for-sale securities are shown on the balance sheet at their fair values. In the event that a company holds an investment in a security that does not have a readily available fair value, the security will be carried on the books at its original cost. While this circumstance can occur, it is not the norm. Throughout the remainder of this section, we assume the availability of a market price.

available-for-sale securities
Investments in equity or debt securities that are not classified as trading securities or held-to-maturity securities.

Changes in Market Prices of Securities

You now know how companies show trading, available-for-sale, and held-to-maturity securities on the balance sheet. How do we show the returns (interest, dividends, and market price changes) on these investments?

Held-to-maturity investments are straightforward because interest revenue is the only return reported on such securities. Changes in market value are ignored. Interest revenue appears directly on the income statement, increasing income and therefore increasing stockholders' equity. The effective interest rate method is used to measure the revenue over time as described in Chapter 9.

Reported returns on trading securities and available-for-sale securities come in two forms: (1) dividend or interest revenue, and (2) changes in market value. Companies always record the former on the income statement when earned. However, they report changes in market value differently for trading securities than for available-for-sale securities. For both trading and available-for-sale securities, fluctuations in market value result in an **unrealized gain** when the price of a security increases and an **unrealized loss** when the price of a security decreases. As the market value of *trading* securities changes, companies report these unrealized gains and losses on the income statement. In contrast, unrealized gains and losses that arise as market values of *available-for-sale* securities rise and fall do not affect the income statement. Instead, we include such unrealized gains and losses in other comprehensive income.

unrealized gain (loss)
The gain (loss) recognized when the market price of a trading or available-for-sale investment security increases (decreases).

In Chapter 2 we noted that other comprehensive income is a summary of all changes in equity except those arising from net income or from transactions with stockholders. Both U.S. GAAP and IFRS offer two presentation formats for other comprehensive income. Companies may present a single statement of total comprehensive income that includes the components of both net income and other comprehensive income. Alternatively, they can report two separate but adjoining statements—one containing the components of net income and one presenting the components of other comprehensive income. Notice that increases in prices of both trading securities and available-for-sale securities increase stockholders' equity, and decreases in prices decrease stockholders' equity. However, for trading securities, the increase or decrease is included in retained earnings because the unrealized gains and losses are included in net income. For available-for-sale securities, the increase or decrease is reflected in stockholders' equity as part of accumulated other comprehensive income.

We call this method of accounting for trading securities and available-for-sale securities at their fair values the market method. Under the **market method**, the asset values reported on the balance sheet are the market values of the publicly traded securities. Suppose two companies acquired identical assets at the same price on the same day, but one company classified them as trading securities and the other classified them as available-for-sale securities. The two companies would report identical asset values on their balance sheets, but they would differ in how they report changes in those market values. Assume the portfolio of assets purchased by the two companies cost $50 million and had market values at the end of four subsequent periods as shown in Exhibit 11-1.

market method
Method of accounting that reports short-term investments in publicly traded securities in the balance sheet at their fair values. For trading securities changes in market value are included in net income; for available-for-sale securities changes in fair value are included in other comprehensive income.

Exhibit 11-1 shows the financial statement presentation for the four periods, ignoring income tax effects. Most companies present the securities at market value, shown as a single line item on the balance sheet. In fact, the adjustment for the unrealized gain or loss due to changes in market value is likely made to a fair value adjustment account, which has a debit balance if the market value is higher than cost and a credit balance if the market value is below cost. The balance in the fair value adjustment account is added to (debit balance) or subtracted from (credit balance) the cost of the investment to determine the amount reflected on the balance sheet. The footnotes explain the change in the value of the investment from period to period attributable to acquisitions, sales, and unrealized gains or losses.

EXHIBIT 11-1

Financial Statement Presentation

Trading Securities and Available-for-Sale Securities ($ in millions)

	End of Period			
	1	**2**	**3**	**4**
Assumed market value at the end of each period	$50	$45	$47	$54
Balance Sheet Presentation				
Assets—both methods				
Short-term investment at cost	$50	$50	$50	$50
Fair value adjustment—unrealized gain (loss)	0	(5)	(3)	4
Carrying value/fair value	$50	$45	$47	$54
Stockholders' equity—Trading securities only				
Unrealized gain (loss) included in Retained earnings	$ 0	$ (5)	$ (3)	$ 4
Stockholders' equity—Available-for-sale securities only				
Unrealized gain (loss) included in Accumulated other comprehensive income	$ 0	$ (5)	$ (3)	$ 4
Income statement—Trading securities only				
Unrealized gain (loss) on changes in market value	$ 0	$ (5)	$ 2	$ 7
Other comprehensive income—Available-for-sale securities only				
Unrealized gain (loss) on changes in market value	$ 0	$ (5)	$ 2	$ 7

The unrealized gain (loss) for trading securities affects net income and therefore also increases (decreases) retained earnings. Over the four periods, the loss of $5 million and subsequent gains of $2 million and $7 million provide a cumulative net increase in retained earnings of $4 million by the end of period 4 ($9 million of gains less $5 million of losses).

For securities classified as available-for-sale, companies include the unrealized gains and losses as part of other comprehensive income for the period. The cumulative stockholders' equity effects appear in Accumulated Other Comprehensive Income, not in Retained Earnings. Notice that we use the term unrealized gain (loss) to describe two different items in Exhibit 11-1: (1) the effect on net income for trading securities, and (2) the effect on other comprehensive income for available-for-sale securities. This is common, and you will need to determine the precise meaning of the term from its context.

The journal entries ($ amounts in millions) for the two classes of securities for periods 2, 3, and 4 would appear as follows (shown without explanations):

Period	Trading securities		Available-for-sale (AFS) securities	
2	Unrealized loss[*] 5		Unrealized loss[†] 5	
	Trading securities, net[‡]	5	AFS securities, net[‡]	5
3	Trading securities, net[‡] 2		AFS securities, net[‡] 2	
	Unrealized gain[*]	2	Unrealized gain[†]	2
4	Trading securities, net[‡] 7		AFS securities, net[‡] 7	
	Unrealized gain[*]	7	Unrealized gain[†]	7

[*]Shown on the income statement.
[†]Shown as part of other comprehensive income in a combined statement of income and comprehensive income or in a separate statement of other comprehensive income.
[‡]Entry would likely be made to a Fair Value Adjustment account rather than directly to Trading or AFS Securities. If the Fair Value Adjustment account is used, the balance in Trading or AFS Securities would stay constant at $50. The Fair Value Adjustment account would have a credit balance of $5 at the end of period 2, a credit balance of $3 at the end of period 3, and a debit balance of $4 at the end of period 4. We allow for either accounting treatment by identifying this as Trading or AFS Securities, net.

The details in Exhibit 11-2 are taken from note 3 of Coca-Cola's 2011 annual report. Coca-Cola had investments classified as trading, available-for-sale, and held-to-maturity. Of the $211 million in trading securities, the company included $138 million in Marketable Securities and $73 million in Other Assets. While not detailed in the footnote excerpt in Exhibit 11-2, the complete footnote indicates that of the $1,401 million in available-for-sale securities at December 31, 2011, Coca-Cola included $5 million in Marketable Securities, $986 in Other Investments, Principally Bottling Companies, and $410 in Other Assets. The company classified a majority of held-to-maturity securities as cash equivalents because they are investments in very short-term U.S. Treasury obligations.

EXHIBIT 11-2

Coca-Cola Company

Note 3: Investments

Trading Securities

As of December 31, 2011 and 2010, our trading securities had a fair value of $211 million and $209 million, respectively. The Company had net unrealized losses on trading securities of $5 million, $3 million and $16 million as of December 31, 2011, 2010, and 2009. The Company's trading securities were included in the following captions in our consolidated balance sheet (in millions):

December 31,	2011	2010
Marketable Securities	$138	$132
Other Assets	73	77
Total trading securities	$211	$209

Available-for-Sale and Held-to-Maturity Securities

As of December 31, 2011 and 2010, available-for-sale and held-to-maturity securities consisted of the following (in millions):	Cost	Gross Unrealized Gains	Gross Unrealized Losses	Estimated Fair Value
2011				
Available-for-sale securities:				
Equity securities	$ 834	$237	$—	$1,071
Debt securities	332	1	(3)	330
	$1,166	$238	$(3)	$1,401
Held-to-maturity securities:				
Bank and corporate debt	$ 113	—	—	$ 113
2010				
Available-for-sale securities:				
Equity securities	$ 209	$267	$(5)	$ 471
Debt securities	14	—	—	14
	$ 223	$267	$(5)	$ 485
Held-to-maturity securities:				
Bank and corporate debt	$ 111	—	—	$ 111

During 2011, the company experienced net unrealized losses ($5 million) on its trading portfolio and net unrealized gains ($235 million) on its available-for-sale securities. Held-to-maturity securities are not adjusted to fair value, so no unrealized gain or loss is reported. It should be noted that, at each reporting date, companies must reassess the appropriateness of the classification of securities into the trading, available-for-sale, and held-to-maturity categories. They must reclassify securities if the company's intention with respect to those securities has changed and account for any transfers between categories at fair value on the date of the transfer.

Comprehensive Income

Net income and other comprehensive income combine to form **comprehensive income**—a summary of all changes in equity except those arising from transactions with stockholders. Two similar firms, one with trading securities and one with available-for-sale securities, would not report comparable net income but would have comparable comprehensive income. There are other items included in comprehensive income besides net income and changes in the value of available-for-sale securities, but they are beyond the scope of this text.

comprehensive income
Net income plus other comprehensive income that includes all changes in equity except those arising from transactions with stockholders.

In the stockholders' equity section of the balance sheet, Coca-Cola reports Accumulated Other Comprehensive Income (Loss) of $(2,703) million in 2011 and $(1,450) million in 2010. These are cumulative amounts. The Accumulated Other Comprehensive Loss account increased by $1,253 million during 2011. Contributing to the $1,253 increase in Accumulated Other Comprehensive Income (Loss) is the $235 million in net unrealized gains on Coca-Cola's available-for-sale securities.

INTERPRETING FINANCIAL STATEMENTS

Suppose Chavez Company had $100,000 of marketable securities on its balance sheet at the beginning of 20X0 and the market value of these securities increased to $108,000 during 20X0. Regardless of whether these are trading securities or available-for-sale securities, when the market value of the securities increases by $8,000, the marketable securities asset increases by $8,000. What other change in the balance sheet is necessary to keep the balance sheet equation in balance if these are trading securities? If they are available-for-sale securities? Ignore any tax consequences.

Answer

Unrealized gains and losses on trading securities, the annual change in market value each period, appear on the income statement.

Therefore, if Chavez Company's securities are trading securities, its net income will include the $8,000 gain, and the retained earnings component of stockholders' equity will increase by $8,000, balancing the $8,000 increase in assets.

Because gains and losses on available-for-sale securities are not part of net income, they do not affect retained earnings. Rather, if Chavez Company's securities are available-for-sale securities, the $8,000 gain will increase other comprehensive income, which increases a separate part of stockholders' equity, accumulated other comprehensive income. As explained in Chapter 2, other comprehensive income includes all changes in equity that are not part of net income and are not the result of transactions with stockholders.

Market Method and the Statement of Cash Flows

Consider the cash flow statement of a company with investments classified as trading, available-for-sale, or held-to-maturity. Companies typically classify cash expenditures for the purchase of, and cash receipts from the sale of, investment securities as investing activities in the statement of cash flows. However, cash payments and receipts for the purchase and sale of trading securities may be classified as operating cash flows if acquired for purposes of resale and carried at market value. The financial institutions that are the primary holders of trading securities consider the buying and selling of trading securities to be part of their normal operating activities. The classification of these activities as operating recognizes that for banks and brokers, trading securities are similar to the inventory of other types of business entities.

A company will classify any dividends or interest received on investments in debt or equity securities as operating cash flows, regardless of whether it classifies the investments as trading, available-for-sale, or held-to-maturity. Other than the cash receipts and disbursements from the sale or purchase of securities and dividends and interest received, what other items related to investments in marketable debt and equity securities will appear on the statement of cash flows? If the company prepares a direct method statement of cash flows, no other adjustments are necessary.

Now suppose the company uses the indirect method for its statement of cash flows. Net income will include realized gains and losses resulting from the sale of investments. These realized gains and losses are similar to the realized gains and losses on the sale of physical assets discussed in Chapter 8. An adjustment for the gain or loss is needed in the operating section of the statement of cash flows, with the result that the total cash receipts can be shown in the investing section of the statement. The company will add back any realized loss and subtract any realized gain in the reconciliation of net income to operating cash flows. Unrealized gains and losses on trading securities are included in net income but do not represent cash receipts or disbursements. Therefore, companies must subtract unrealized gains and add unrealized losses to net income to properly reflect operating cash flow. The unrealized gains and losses on available-for-sale securities accounted for using the market method are part of other comprehensive income, not net income, so no adjustments are needed in the statement of cash flows.

Fair Value Option

The fair value option under U.S. GAAP allows, but does not require, companies holding held-to-maturity and available-for-sale securities to account for these investments as if they were trading securities. In other words, it allows held-to-maturity and available-for-sale securities to be marked to fair value with unrealized gains or losses included in net income. The election of the fair value option is made for individual securities at the time of acquisition and is irrevocable. So far, relatively few companies have chosen this option. IFRS allows the fair value option, but the circumstances under which it is allowed are more restrictive than under U.S. GAAP.

Long-Term Investments in Bonds

Chapter 9 explained how firms account for bonds payable. The issuer amortizes bond discounts and premiums as periodic adjustments of interest expense using the effective-interest method. Investing firms use a similar method to account for investments in bonds held to maturity.

▸▸ **OBJECTIVE 3**

Report long-term investments in bonds.

Bonds Held to Maturity

Exhibit 11-3 should look familiar. It is like Exhibit 9-4 on page 401, but it takes the perspective of the investor rather than the issuer. Therefore, we use the phrase *book value* to refer to the first and last columns instead of the label *net liability* used in Exhibit 9-4. Recall that book value is a general term for the amounts reported in the financial statements.

Exhibit 11-3 shows the values for 10,000, 2-year bonds paying interest semiannually with a face value of $1,000 each and a 10% coupon rate (5% interest every 6 months). The bonds were issued on December 31, 20X0, to yield 12%. Because they pay only a 10% coupon interest rate, they are sold at a discount. Therefore, an investor acquiring the whole issue would pay only $9,653,500. Interest revenue takes two forms—four semiannual cash receipts of $500,000 (5% × $10 million), plus a lump-sum receipt of $346,500 ($10 million face value less amount paid at issue) at maturity.

The extra $346,500 to be paid at maturity (the discount) needs to be allocated to revenue over the 2-year term using the effective interest method. Therefore, like the issuer, the investor amortizes the discount:

	6/30/X1	12/31/X1	6/30/X2	12/31/X2
Semiannual interest revenue:				
Cash interest payments, .05 × $10 million	$500,000	$500,000	$500,000	$500,000
Amortization of $346,500 discount*	79,207	83,959	88,997	94,337
Semiannual interest revenue	$579,207	$583,959	$588,997	$594,337

*For the amortization schedule, see column 4 of Exhibit 11-3. Note that ($79,207 + $83,959 + $88,997 + $94,337) = $346,500.

As Exhibit 11-3 shows, the discount makes up the difference between the coupon interest rate of 10% and the market interest rate of 12%. Amortization of a discount increases the interest revenue. Investor accounting for bonds issued at a premium is similar, except that amortization of a premium decreases the interest revenue of investors.

Exhibit 11-4 shows how the investor and the issuer account for the bonds throughout the bonds' lives. Note that interest revenue for the investor and interest expense for the issuer are identical in each period.

EXHIBIT 11-3

Effective Interest Amortization of Bond Discount by the Investor

For 6 Months Ended	(1) Beginning Book Value	(2) Effective Interest @ 6%*	(3) Nominal Interest @ 5%	(4) Discount Amortized (2)–(3)	Period End Values		
					Face Amount	Unamortized Discount	Ending Book Value
12/31/X0	—	—	—	—	$10,000,000	$346,500	$ 9,653,500
6/30/X1	$9,653,500	$579,207	$500,000	$79,207	10,000,000	267,293[†]	9,732,707
12/31/X1	9,732,707	583,959	500,000	83,959	10,000,000	183,334[†]	9,816,666
6/30/X2	9,816,666	588,997	500,000	88,997	10,000,000	94,337	9,905,663
12/31/X2	9,905,663	594,337	500,000	94,337	10,000,000	0	10,000,000

* Effective market interest rate when issued times beginning book value, column (1). To avoid rounding errors, an unrounded actual effective rate slightly under 6% was used in the calculation of effective interest in column (2).

[†]$($346,500 − $79,207) = $267,293; ($267,293 − $83,959) = $183,334; etc.

EXHIBIT 11-4
Accounting for Bonds

	Investor's Records			Issuer's Records		
12/31/X0	1. Investment in bonds............	9,653,500		1. Cash	9,653,500	
	Cash		9,653,500	Discount on bonds payable	346,500	
				Bonds payable.............................		10,000,000
6/30/X1	2. Cash	500,000		2. Interest expense	579,207	
	Investment in bonds............	79,207		Discount on bonds payable		79,207
	Interest revenue		579,207	Cash		500,000
12/31/X1	Cash	500,000		Interest expense	583,959	
	Investment in bonds............	83,959		Discount on bonds payable		83,959
	Interest revenue		583,959	Cash		500,000
6/30/X2	Cash	500,000		Interest expense	588,997	
	Investment in bonds............	88,997		Discount on bonds payable		88,997
	Interest revenue		588,997	Cash		500,000
12/31/X2	Cash	500,000		Interest expense	594,337	
	Investment in bonds............	94,337		Discount on bonds payable		94,337
	Interest revenue		594,337	Cash		500,000
12/31/X2	3. Cash	10,000,000		3. Bonds payable	10,000,000	
	Investment in bonds		10,000,000	Cash		10,000,000

Early Extinguishment of Investment

Suppose in our example that the issuer buys back all its bonds on the open market for $9.6 million on December 31, 20X1 (after all interest payments and amortization were recorded for 20X1). The investor's loss is calculated in panel A of Exhibit 11-5. The journal entries for the investor and the issuer are shown in panel B.

EXHIBIT 11-5
Early Extinguishment

PANEL A: INVESTOR'S LOSS

Carrying amount		
Face or par value	$10,000,000	
Deduct: Unamortized discount on bonds[*]	183,334	$9,816,666
Cash received		9,600,000
Difference, loss on sale		$ 216,666

[*]The remaining discount is ($88,997 + $94,337) = $183,334, or ($346,500 − $79,207 − $83,959) = $183,334.

PANEL B: JOURNAL ENTRIES AT DECEMBER 31, 20X1

Investor's Records			Issuer's Records		
Cash...	9,600,000		Bonds payable..................................	10,000,000	
Loss on disposal of bonds.............	216,666		Discount on bonds payable............		183,334
Investment in bonds....................		9,816,666	Gain on early		
To record the sale of bonds			extinguishment of debt		216,666
on the open market			Cash		9,600,000
			To record the repurchase of		
			bonds on the open market		

Recall that this same extinguishment of debt was initially analyzed from the issuer's viewpoint in Chapter 9 on page 406. For the issuer to extinguish the bonds early, either the bond must grant the issuer the right to repay the debt early or the investor must choose to sell the bonds back to the issuer.

The Market and Equity Methods for Intercorporate Equity Investments

Many companies invest in the equity securities of another company. The accounting for equity securities from the issuer's point of view was discussed in Chapter 10. The investor's accounting depends on the relationship between the "investor" and the "investee." The question is: How much can the investor influence the operations of the investee? For example, the holder of a small number of shares in a company's stock cannot affect how the company invests its money, conducts its business, or declares and pays its dividends. We call this type of investor a passive investor. Such investors use the market method described earlier, report the investment at market value, and record dividends as income when received.

As investors acquire more substantial holdings of a company's stock, they have increased influence. A stockholder with 2% or 3% ownership of a company has little difficulty making appointments to speak with company management. At 5% ownership, U.S. law requires the investor to report the ownership publicly in a filing with the SEC. As ownership interest rises to 20% and beyond, the investor begins to affect decisions, to appoint directors, and so on.

Once the investor has significant influence, defined as 20%–50% ownership unless a company can clearly demonstrate otherwise, the market method no longer reflects the economic relationship between the influential investor and the investee (or **affiliated company**). Circumstances may exist that indicate that an investment of 20% or more does not result in significant influence: for example, if the investee opposes the investor's acquisition of its stock or if the investor tries and fails to obtain representation on the investee's board of directors. Alternatively, circumstances may indicate that an investment of slightly less than 20% still gives the investor significant influence. An investor that has significant influence, but not a sufficient ownership interest to have control (generally assumed to be 50% or more), must use the **equity method**, which records the investment at acquisition cost and makes adjustments for the investor's share of dividends and earnings or losses experienced by the investee after the date of investment. Under the equity method, the investor's share of the investee's earnings increases the book value at which the investment is carried and reported. Likewise, dividends received from the investee and the investor's share of the investee's losses reduce this carrying amount. The equity method is used under both U.S. GAAP and IFRS, with some minor differences.

How do companies apply the market and equity methods? Suppose Buyit Corporation invests $80 million in each of two companies, Passiveco and Influential. Influential has a total market value of $200 million, generates earnings of $30 million, and pays dividends of $10 million. Because of its $80 million investment, Buyit owns 40% ($80 million ÷ $200 million) of Influential and must account for that investment using the equity method. Passiveco, however, is four times larger. It has a total market value of $800 million, generates earnings of $120 million, and pays dividends of $40 million. Buyit thus owns only 10% ($80 million ÷ $800 million) of Passiveco and uses the market method to account for this investment.

We compare the methods in Exhibit 11-6. Panel A shows the effects on the balance sheet equation, and panel B shows the different journal entries for the two cases. The example assumes that the market values of Passiveco and Influential do not change during the period.

Under the market method, Buyit recognizes income from Passiveco when dividends are received. Although the income statement and retained earnings are affected, Buyit's investment account is unaffected by the receipt of dividends. It remains at $80 million. In contrast, under the equity method, Buyit recognizes income as Influential earns it instead of when Influential pays dividends. Cash dividends from Influential do not affect Buyit's net income; they increase cash and decrease the investment balance. Buyit's claim on Influential grows by its share of Influential's net income and the dividend is a partial liquidation of Buyit's "claim." It would be double-counting to include the $4 million of dividends as income after the $12 million of income is already recognized in Buyit's income statement as it is earned. Thus the investment account grows by $8 million during the year ($12 million of income less $4 million of dividends received).

▶▶ OBJECTIVE 4

Contrast the equity and market methods of accounting for investments.

affiliated company
A company that has 20%–50% of its voting shares owned by another company.

equity method
Accounting for an investment at acquisition cost adjusted for the investor's share of dividends and earnings or losses of the investee after the date of investment. Used by investors that have significant influence over, but do not control, the investee.

EXHIBIT 11-6

Comparing Market and Equity Methods

(in millions of dollars)

PANEL A: EFFECTS ON THE BALANCE SHEET EQUATION

	Market Method—Passiveco*				Equity Method—Influential**			
	A		=	L + SE	A		=	L + SE
	Cash + Investment		=	Liab. + SE	Cash + Investment		=	Liab. + SE
1. Acquisition	−80	+80	=		−80	+80	=	
2. a. Net income of Passiveco	No entry and no effect							
b. Net income of Influential						+12	=	+12
3. a. Dividends from Passiveco	+4		=	+4				
b. Dividends from Influential	___	___		___	+4	−4	=	___
Effect for year	−76	+80	=	+4	−76	+88	=	+12

*Passiveco: Under the market method, the investment account is unaffected. The dividend increases the cash amount by $4 million. Dividend revenue increases stockholders' equity by $4 million.

**Influential: Under the equity method, the investment account has a net increase of $8 million for the year. The dividend increases the cash account by $4 million and reduces investments. Investment revenue increases stockholders' equity by $12 million.

PANEL B: JOURNAL ENTRIES

Market Method—Passiveco				Equity Method—Influential		
1. Investment in Passiveco	80			1. Investment in Influential...............	80	
Cash...		80		Cash..		80
2. No entry				2. Investment in Influential...............	12	
				Investment revenue[†]		12
3. Cash	4			3. Cash	4	
Dividend revenue[†].......................		4		Investment in Influential		4

[†]Frequently called "equity in earnings of affiliated companies."

[‡]Frequently called "dividend income."

The major reason for using the equity method instead of the market method is that the equity method does a better job of recognizing increases or decreases in the economic resources that the investor can influence. The reported net income of an "equity" investor (an investor who owns more than 20% but less than 50% of a company and thus uses the equity method) is increased by its share of net income or decreased by its share of net loss recognized by the investee. The dividend payment, which the equity investor might influence, does not affect the investor's net income.

Coca-Cola accounts for a significant number of its investments in other companies using the equity method. Footnote 6 to the 2011 financial statements indicates that the company accounts for its ownership interests in Coca-Cola Hellenic, Coca-Cola FEMSA, and Coca-Cola Amatil using the equity method. At December 31, 2011, Coca-Cola owned approximately 23%, 29%, and 29%, respectively, of the common shares of these companies. The 2011 balance sheet reports Equity Method Investments of $7,233 million (9.0% of total assets), and the 2011 income statement includes Equity Income of $690 million.

Changes in Level of Ownership

As a company buys or sells shares of stock in another company, the appropriate accounting method for the investment may change. If the company uses the equity method and the level of investment decreases, it may be appropriate to change to the market method. Alternatively, if the level of investment increases, it may become appropriate to begin consolidating the affiliated company. The company simply discontinues the original method and applies the new method going forward. The existing balance in the equity method investment account becomes the new cost basis for the securities under either the market method or consolidation.

If, on the other hand, the company is using the market method and the level of investment increases, a switch to the equity method may be necessary. Such was the case for Coca-Cola in 2011, when it made an additional investment in **Coca-Cola Central Japan Company**. In this case, the company adjusts the market-method investment value to equal the balance that would have existed if the equity method had always been used, and it applies the equity method going forward. Finally, if a consolidated company ceases to meet the criteria for consolidation, the investor must switch to the equity method. This is not difficult because, as we will see later in the chapter, such a consolidating investor would already use the equity method to account for the investment on its non-consolidated books.

Equity Method and the Statement of Cash Flows

Consider the cash flow statement for a company with equity affiliates (firms for which the investor uses the equity method). If it uses the direct method to report cash flows from operating activities, no special problem arises because only the cash received from the affiliate as a dividend appears as an operating cash flow. However, suppose the company uses the indirect method. Because net earnings are increased (decreased) by the investor's share of its affiliates' earnings (losses), we must adjust reported income for the noncash portion of the income or loss from affiliates. Consider our earlier example of Buyit and Influential. Buyit included in its net income $12 million of investment revenue from Influential. However, its cash flow from Influential was only the $4 million of dividends. Because net income includes $12 million, the indirect method must decrease net earnings by ($12 million − $4 million) = $8 million, the amount of the equity in earnings that the investor did not receive in cash.

Fair Value Option

As with market-method investments, companies may elect to use the fair value option for investments that would otherwise be accounted for under the equity method. If an investor chooses the fair value option, it adjusts the investment to fair value with changes due to market price increases or decreases (unrealized gains or losses) recognized as part of net income. The investor would no longer record its share of the net income or loss of the investee in the investment account. Nor would it reduce the investment account for its share of the investor's dividends. Dividends would be recorded as revenue in the period received. IFRS does not allow the use of the fair value option for equity method investments.

Summary Problem for Your Review

PROBLEM

The following is a summary of material from a **Dow Chemical** December 31 annual report ($ in millions):

	$:
Marketable securities and interest-bearing deposits	706
	:
Total current assets	8,847
Investments:	
Investment in nonconsolidated affiliates	1,359
Other investments	2,872
Noncurrent receivables	390
Total investments	4,621
Properties	24,276
Less: Accumulated depreciation	15,786
Net property	8,490
Goodwill	1,834
Deferred charges and other assets	1,707
Total assets	$25,499

Note that the statements are somewhat compressed and no detail for current assets is shown.

1. Suppose that as of the balance sheet date Marketable Securities included a $24 million portfolio of equity securities. The market values of these securities on the following March 31, June 30, and September 30 were $20, $23, and $28 million, respectively. Compute the following:
   a. Carrying amount of the portfolio on each of the three dates
   b. Gain (loss) on the portfolio for each of the three quarters
2. Suppose the $2,872 million of Other Investments included a $9 million investment in the debentures of an affiliate that was being held to maturity. The debentures had a par value of $10 million and a 10% nominal rate of interest, payable June 30 and December 31. Their market rate of interest when the investment was made was 12%. Prepare the journal entry made by Dow to record the semiannual receipt of interest on June 30.
3. Suppose Dow's nonconsolidated affiliates (20%–50% owned companies) reported total net income of $200 million. Dow received cash dividends of $70 million from these companies. No other transactions occurred. Prepare the pertinent journal entries. Assume that on average Dow owns 40% of the companies.

SOLUTION

1. Amounts are in millions.
   a. Market: $20, $23, and $28.
   b. ($20 − $24) = $4 loss; ($23 − $20) = $3 gain; ($28 − $23) = $5 gain. Gain or loss would be reported in the income statement for trading securities or in other comprehensive income for securities available for sale.

2.

Cash	500,000[*]	
Other investments (in bonds)	40,000[***]	
Interest revenue.		540,000[**]

To record 6 months interest revenue, interest received in cash, and amortization.
$$^*(.5 \times .10 \times \$10,000,000) = \$500,000$$
$$^{**}(.5 \times .12 \times \$9,000,000) = \$540,000$$
$$^{***}(\$540,000 - \$500,000) = \$40,000$$

3.

Investments in nonconsolidated affiliates	80,000,000	
Investment revenue		80,000,000

To record 40% share of $200 million income

Cash	70,000,000	
Investments in nonconsolidated affiliates		70,000,000

To record dividends received from nonconsolidated affiliates

Consolidated Financial Statements

So far we have dealt with partial ownership of one company by another. Sometimes, though, one company owns enough of another to essentially have control over its decisions. This is the case where one company buys 100% of another company. In other cases, one company buys a majority (more than 50%) share of a second company and effectively takes control of that second company. In cases where one company has control over another, a parent–subsidiary relationship exists. The **parent company** is the owner, and the **subsidiary** is the "owned" company that is controlled by the parent.

Why have subsidiaries? Why not integrate the smaller companies into the larger parent to create a single legal entity? The reasons include limiting the liabilities in a risky venture, saving income taxes, conforming to government regulations with respect to a part of the business, doing business in a foreign country, and expanding in an orderly way while retaining the ability to subsequently sell or spin off the separate corporate subsidiary. For example, there are often tax advantages for the sellers when an acquisition involves selling the capital stock of a going concern instead of its individual assets. Sometimes foreign subsidiaries face more favorable treatment from their country of residence than a foreign parent corporation would experience.

parent company
A company owning more than 50% of the voting shares of another company, called the subsidiary company.

subsidiary
A corporation owned or controlled by a parent company through the ownership of more than 50% of the voting stock.

Or, as when Merck spun off Medco, the transaction was easier and less costly because Medco was an existing separate subsidiary corporation.

Parent and subsidiary companies must prepare *consolidated financial statements*. However, before we discuss such statements, let's examine corporate mergers, a common means by which consolidated entities arise.

Corporate Mergers

Corporate mergers can be a little like marriages. The challenge is to combine and retain the right combination of people and products to succeed over the long haul. Microsoft, Intel, Google, Facebook, and other technology companies often buy smaller, innovative young companies to capture their new ideas and, often, their talented employees. Consider Facebook. Founded in 2005, Facebook has made multiple acquisitions in its short history. When interviewed at Startup School 2010, Facebook CEO Mark Zuckerberg said, "We have not once bought a company for the company. We buy companies to get excellent people." The April 2012 acquisition of Instagram for $1 billion appears to be one of the first Facebook acquisitions that was product-driven. Since going public in 1986, Microsoft has purchased over 140 companies. Google has acquired over 70 companies, including well-known companies such as YouTube.

In other cases, firms combine large similar companies hoping to integrate the firms and create cost savings by eliminating duplications. For example, British Petroleum merged with AMOCO in 1998 becoming BP Amoco. In April 1999, BP Amoco announced its intention to acquire ARCO to form BP, one of the largest companies in the world. It took a year of negotiation and compromise in the structure of the deal to finally gain full approval of the acquisition in April 2000. Combining three companies with very similar operations created the opportunity for major savings when BP eliminated many redundant, repetitive activities and applied best practices throughout the combined entity. The opportunity for cost savings was a major factor in the consolidation of the oil industry during this time frame as Exxon Corp. and Mobil Corp. also completed their merger in 1999.

Companies with complementary products may also merge. In 2006, Walt Disney, Inc., well known for its theme parks and animated films, acquired Pixar, a company that made computer-generated children's films. Pixar brought new energy and technology to Disney's well-established film business and huge distribution network. See the Business First box on p. 506 for insights from a *Forbes* article on creating successful acquisitions.

Sometimes companies sell parts of themselves when they purchase another company. In some cases the sale is for strategic reasons, and in other cases regulators demand it. For example, the U.S. government challenged BP Amoco's acquisition of ARCO. BP agreed to sell ARCO's Alaskan assets and some of its own assets in the North Sea in order to obtain regulatory approval. Similarly, the Federal Trade Commission (FTC) required restructuring of many of Exxon and Mobil's gas stations to avoid monopolization.

Just as not all marriages work, not all business combinations work. This outcome is disturbingly common. A 2004 study by Bain and Company found that 70% of mergers failed to increase shareholder value, and a 2007 study found that over 90% of mergers in Europe failed to reach financial goals. When combinations fail, one solution is to sell the subsidiary to another company. For example, Coca-Cola acquired Columbia Pictures in 1982. Despite winning an Oscar for the movie *Gandhi*, Columbia failed to bring the desired returns, and Coca-Cola sold the company to Sony in 1989. Even business combinations within the same industry frequently fail. Consider Ford Motor Company, which acquired Jaguar in 1989, the car division of Volvo in 1999, and Land Rover in 2000. As the auto industry struggled, Ford sold Jaguar and Land Rover to the Indian automotive group Tata in June 2008. By June 2009, sales for Jaguar and Land Rover had fallen 32%, and Tata posted its first loss in 7 years. Volvo stopped posting profits in 2005 after quality issues contributed to a 22% decline in U.S. sales. Ford sold Volvo in 2010 to China's Zhejiang Geely Holding Group.

Not all disposals of parts of a company involve sales. Merck, a prominent pharmaceutical company, spun off its Medco unit when their merger failed to deliver the expected benefits. This means that Merck distributed its shares in Medco directly to Merck shareholders so they became the owners of Medco. Merck, a high-margin company that develops and then manufactures branded, patent-protected drugs, earned no benefits from owning Medco, a low-margin company that distributed drugs to patients.

BUSINESS FIRST

CREATING SUCCESSFUL ACQUISITIONS

How does a company increase the odds that its business combination will be one of the successful ones? A KPMG study cited shoddy due diligence, a lack of synergy between the two companies, too little planning, and poor execution as common reasons for failure. A successful acquisition avoids these pitfalls. More specifically, *Forbes* recommends the following:

1. Do not wait for a deal to come to you. Investment bankers and company brokers seek buyers for companies that want to be acquired. However, *Forbes* advises acquirers to take an active approach. Find the right partner and convince them to be acquired instead of choosing among companies that are for sale.
2. Stick to your knitting. Expansion should be aimed at increasing what you already do. Periodically, conglomerate mergers have been popular. These combinations of very diverse businesses on the grounds that good managers can manage anything and larger companies are better have failed at an even higher rate than usual.
3. Know what you are buying. "Due diligence" is the phrase for carefully investigating the target company. It is the corporate equivalent of kicking the tires or having a mechanic examine a potential

used-car purchase. Important questions to ask include: What is the order backlog? Will critical employees stay? Is debt subject to a change of ownership clause? Are there unrecorded liabilities resulting from environmental pollution or deferred maintenance that leaves plant, property, and equipment in need of repair? The list is long.

4. Learn their tribal customs. Companies have different work cultures. Consider a U.S. company headed by a rapid decision maker. The U.S. buyer might be willing to sign a merger agreement immediately, but a Swiss seller might want to think about it. Although a U.S. buyer might be able to act alone, a Chinese seller might seek a consensus among many managers. Processes for sealing the deal differ.
5. Start integration well before the deal is closed. The most difficult task is the merger of workforces and overcoming cultural differences. It must start early and receive total attention.

Notice that the accounting issues do not make the list of do's and don'ts. There are important steps in bringing the financial accounting for the combining companies together, but they are rarely critical to their success.

Sources: L. Kroll, "The Race to Embrace," *Forbes*, October 30, 2000, pp. 184–191.

Spin-offs often separate dissimilar business segments to create opportunities for more creative and innovative growth. Managers of the spin-off company can be compensated more directly based on the performance of the new, often smaller, company. A study of 146 spin-offs over 30 years concluded that investments in shares of spin-off firms outperformed the stock market by an average of 35% in their first 3 years as separate companies. As an example, Cadbury Schweppes plc (since acquired by Kraft) spun off Dr Pepper Snapple Group in 2008. Dr Pepper has since launched several new products and in May 2011 raised its annual dividend by 28%, the second annual dividend increase since being spun off.

Overview of Consolidated Statements

Now let's look specifically at consolidated statements. U.S. GAAP requires consolidated financial statements when one company directly or indirectly has a controlling financial interest in another company. The usual condition leading to the consolidation of financial statements under U.S. GAAP is ownership of a majority voting interest (more than 50% of the voting stock) of another company. There are limited circumstances—beyond the scope of this text—where consolidation may be appropriate when less than 50% of the stock is held by the parent company. In addition, there are infrequent circumstances when an investor owns a majority of the voting stock but does not consolidate. This is the case when control is considered temporary. Another example is Ford Motor Company's acquisition of S.C. Automobile Craiova S.A. from the Romanian government. The purchase agreement allows the Romanian government substantial control for a number of years following the acquisition. As a result, Ford does not consolidate S.C. Automobile Craiova S.A.

EXHIBIT 11-7

Before and After the Acquisition, Parent (P) Buys Subsidiary (S) for $213

($ in millions)

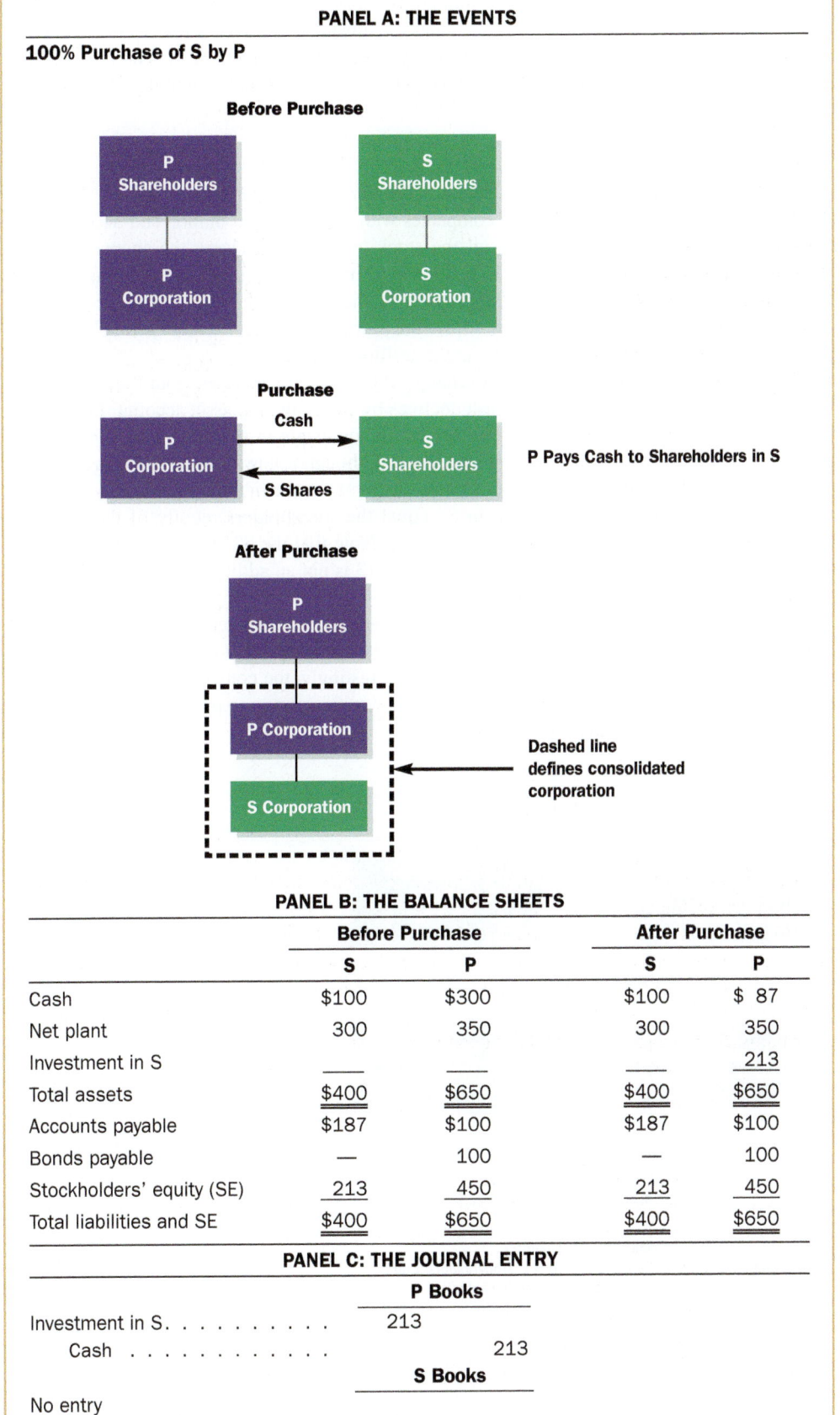

PANEL A: THE EVENTS

100% Purchase of S by P

Before Purchase

P Shareholders

S Shareholders

P Corporation

S Corporation

Purchase

Cash

P Corporation → S Shareholders

S Shares ←

P Pays Cash to Shareholders in S

After Purchase

P Shareholders

P Corporation

S Corporation

Dashed line defines consolidated corporation

PANEL B: THE BALANCE SHEETS

	Before Purchase		After Purchase	
	S	**P**	**S**	**P**
Cash	$100	$300	$100	$ 87
Net plant	300	350	300	350
Investment in S	——	——	——	213
Total assets	$400	$650	$400	$650
Accounts payable	$187	$100	$187	$100
Bonds payable	—	100	—	100
Stockholders' equity (SE)	213	450	213	450
Total liabilities and SE	$400	$650	$400	$650

PANEL C: THE JOURNAL ENTRY

P Books

Investment in S.	213	
Cash		213

S Books

No entry

IFRS also requires consolidated statements when one company has control over another, but it defines "control" slightly differently, relying more on subjective judgment rather than ownership percentages.

In accounting for parent/subsidiary relationships, subsidiaries remain separate legal entities from their parents. One parent can have numerous subsidiaries. For example, Coca-Cola has more than 40 subsidiaries. So how do we account for subsidiaries if they are separate legal entities? We start by keeping records for the subsidiary that are independent of the parent's records. Then we combine the financial statements of the parent company with those of its subsidiaries to create consolidated statements.

The Acquisition

To illustrate consolidated financial statements, consider two companies: the parent (P) and a subsidiary (S). Initially, they are separate companies with assets of $650 million and $400 million, respectively. On January 1, P acquires all the stock of S by purchasing the shares from the company's current stockholders for $213 million paid in cash. We illustrate this transaction in panel A of Exhibit 11-7 on page 507. Panel B shows the balance sheets of the two companies before and after this transaction. Panel C shows the journal entry for the acquisition. Figures in this and subsequent tables and discussion are in millions.

This purchase transaction is a simple exchange of one asset for another, from P's perspective. In terms of the balance sheet equation, cash declines by $213, and the asset account, Investment in S, increases by the same amount (remember that amounts are in millions). The subsidiary S is entirely unaffected from an accounting standpoint, although it now has one centralized owner with unquestionable control over economic decisions S may make in the future. In this example, the purchase price and the "Investment in S" equal the stockholders' equity of the acquired company, although this need not always be the case. Note that the $213 purchase price is paid to the former owners of S as private investors. The $213 is not an addition to the existing assets and stockholders' equity of S. That is, the books of S are unaffected by P's investment and by P's subsequent accounting for the investment. The transaction is between P and the individual stockholders of S. S still exists as a separate legal entity, but with a new owner, P.

Each legal entity keeps its own set of books. Interestingly, the consolidated entity does not keep a separate set of books. Instead, accountants use working papers to prepare the consolidated statements as shown schematically in Exhibit 11-8.

EXHIBIT 11-8

Preparing Consolidated Statements

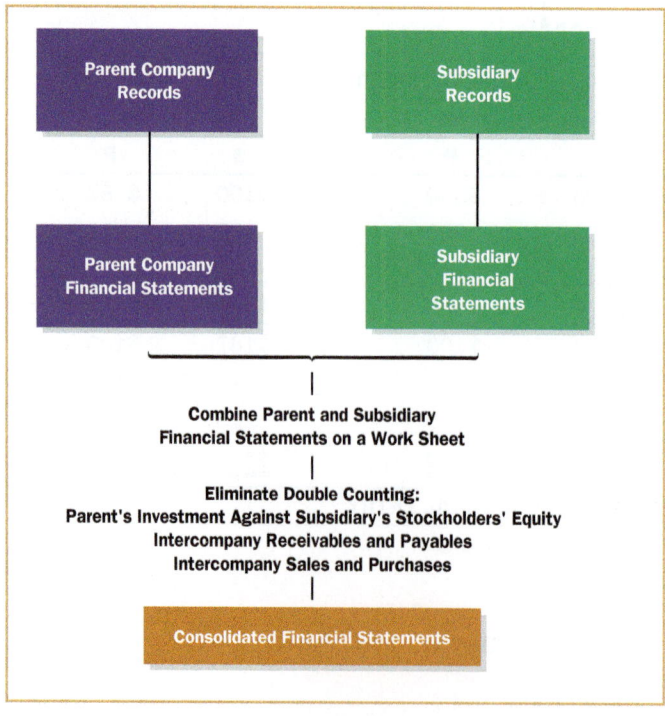

How do we consolidate the financial statements? Basically, we add up the individual financial statement values of the parent and the subsidiary. Consider a consolidated balance sheet prepared immediately after P's acquisition of S. The consolidated statement shows the details of all assets and liabilities of both the parent and the subsidiary. The Investment in S account on P's books represents P's investment in S, which is really composed of all the assets and liabilities of S. This same amount is represented in S's books by stockholders' equity. If the consolidated statements simply add the individual balance sheet values of S and P, the $213 amount is represented twice, once as P's Investment in S account, and again in S's stockholders' equity. The consolidated statements should not count this amount twice because the result would misstate the true assets and liabilities. We avoid this double-counting by eliminating the Investment in S account on P's books, and the stockholders' equity on S's books.

On the work sheet for consolidating the balance sheets, the journal entry to eliminate the double-counting of ownership interest is as follows:

Stockholders' equity (on S books)	213	
Investment in S (on P books)		213

Separately, after the purchase, P has assets of $650 and S has assets of $400, so you might think the consolidated company would have assets totaling $1,050. However, when we consolidate and eliminate the double-counting of the investment amount in S as shown in the preceding journal entry, the consolidated assets are ($1,050 – $213), or $837. The consolidated result, expressed in terms of the accounting equation, shows consolidated liabilities of $387 and stockholders' equity of $450 as follows:

100% Ownership							
	Assets			**=**	**Liabilities**	**+**	**Stockholders' Equity**
	Investment in S	**+**	**Cash and Other Assets**	**=**	**Accounts Payable, etc.**	**+**	**Stockholders' Equity**
P's accounts, Jan. 1							
Before acquisition			650	=	200	+	450
Acquisition of S	+213		−213	=			
S's accounts, Jan. 1			400	=	187	+	213
Intercompany eliminations	−213		___	=	___		−213
Consolidated, Jan. 1	0	+	837	=	387	+	450

After Acquisition

After the initial acquisition, P accounts for its long-term investment in S by the same equity method used to account for an unconsolidated ownership interest of 20%–50%. Suppose S has a net income of $50 million for the 12 months immediately after the acquisition (year 1). The parent company uses the equity method to account for the net income of its subsidiary by increasing its Investment in S account and its Stockholders' Equity account (in the form of retained earnings) by 100% of $50 million.

The income statements for the year are as follows (numbers in millions assumed):

	P (only)	S (only)	Consolidated
Sales	$900	$300	$1,200
Expenses	800	250	1,050
Operating income	100	50	150
Investment revenue*	50	—	—
Net income	$150	$ 50	$ 150

*Pro rata share (100%) of subsidiary net income, often called equity in earnings of affiliate or subsidiary.

P's parent-company-only income statement would show its own sales and expenses plus its proportional share of S's net income (as the equity method requires). This is the leftmost column of the preceding table. The income statement for P shows the same $150 million net income as the consolidated income statement. The difference is that P's "parent-only" income statement shows its 100% share of S as a single $50 million item, whereas the consolidated income statement combines the detailed revenue and expense items for P and S. The journal entry on P's parent-only books to record its 100% share of S's net income is as follows:

Investment in S.	50	
Investment revenue*		50

*Or "equity in net income of subsidiary."

To avoid counting the $50 million net income twice in the consolidated statements—once as S's net income and again as P's investment revenue—P must eliminate it in consolidation. Thus, after P records this year's net income, the amount that will eliminate the Investment in S account on the work sheet used for consolidating the balance sheets is ($213 + $50) = $263, which is the new balance in the Investment in S account on P's books and the new Stockholders' Equity balance on the books of S.

Exhibit 11-9 reflects the changes in P's accounts, S's accounts, and the consolidated accounts ($ in millions). Consolidated statements sum the individual accounts of two or more separate legal entities. We prepare them periodically via work sheets.

Intercompany Eliminations

When accountants consolidate the financial records of two companies, they must avoid double-counting any items. Exhibit 11-9 emphasizes elimination of the parent's investment account and the subsidiary's owners' equity. In many cases, the parent and subsidiary do business together, which leads to another type of double-counting. For example, suppose S charges P $12 for products that cost S $10, and the sale is made on credit. The two firms make the following journal entries on their separate books:

P's Records			**S's Records**		
Merchandise inventory.	12		Accounts receivable.	12	
Accounts payable.		12	Sales revenue		12
			Cost of goods sold	10	
			Merchandise Inventory		10

EXHIBIT 11-9

Consolidation Work Sheet

	Assets			=	Liabilities	+	Stockholders' Equity
	Investment in S	+	Cash and Other Assets	=	Accounts Payable, etc.	+	Stockholders' Equity
P's account							
Beginning of year	213	+	437	=	200	+	450
Operating income			+100	=			+100*
Share of S income	+50			=			+50*
End of year	263	+	537	=	200	+	600
S's accounts							
Beginning of year			400	=	187	+	213
Net income			+50	=			+50*
End of year			450	=	187	+	263
Intercompany eliminations	−263			=			−263
Consolidated, end of year	0	+	987	=	387	+	600

*Changes in the retained earnings portion of stockholders' equity.

However, has anything happened economically? No—as far as the consolidated entity is concerned, the product is just moved from one location to another. If P paid cash to S, the cash just shifts from "one pocket to another." So this transaction is not an important one from the perspective of the consolidated company, and it should be eliminated. It is important that each separate legal entity keeps track of its own transactions for its own records. When we consolidate, we eliminate the intercompany receivable and payable, eliminate the costs and revenues, and ensure that the consolidated entity carries the inventory at its original cost, $10. We eliminate these items with the following consolidation journal entries on the consolidation work sheet:

Accounts payable (P).	12	
Accounts receivable (S).		12
Sales revenue (S)	12	
Cost of goods sold (S)		10
Merchandise Inventory (P).		2

The parenthetical letters show whose records contain the underlying account balances. Remember, neither company records these entries on its individual records. They exist only in the consolidation work sheet.

Noncontrolling Interests

Our example of the consolidation of P and S assumes P purchased 100% of S. However, companies often purchase less than 100% of a subsidiary. One company can control another with just 51% of the shares. For example, Coca-Cola owns more than 50% but less than 100% of many companies. Coca-Cola consolidates each company into its consolidated financial statements but recognizes the claim on some of the consolidated assets held by other owners. These claims are called noncontrolling interests. **Noncontrolling interests** represent the claims of nonmajority shareholders in the assets and earnings of a company whose accounts are consolidated into the accounts of the majority shareholder. On its consolidated 2011 earnings statement, Coca-Cola shows a reduction of net income of $62 million due to noncontrolling interests. On the consolidated balance sheet, Coca-Cola shows $286 million of noncontrolling interests. Note that the labels are identical: noncontrolling interests. Thus, it is up to you, the reader, to know that the $62 million on the income statement is the current year increase, whereas the $286 million on the balance sheet is the cumulative effect.

To apply this concept to our example, assume that our parent company (P) bought only 90% of S. Exhibit 11-10 on page 512, using the basic figures of the previous example, shows the overall approach to a consolidated balance sheet immediately after the acquisition. In panel A, the graphic shows that some shareholders of S continue to have a noncontrolling interest in the consolidated entity. P pays $192 million for 90% of S (.90 × $213 million). The noncontrolling interest is 10%, or $21 million. (All dollar amounts are rounded to the nearest million.) Panel B illustrates that P's balance sheet shows the $192 million investment, and in consolidation we show the noncontrolling interest at $21 million, the amount by which the $213 million of net assets added in consolidation exceeds P's investment of $192 million. You can think of the noncontrolling interest as representing the interests of those shareholders who own the 10% of the subsidiary stockholders' equity that is not owned by the parent company.

Suppose the 90% acquisition occurred on January 1 and S has net income of $50 million for the year. P and S follow the same procedures in their individual income statements, regardless of whether P owns 100% or 90% of S. P reports either 100% or 90% of S's earnings as a line item on P's income statement labeled something like Equity in Earnings of Subsidiary. However, the presence of a noncontrolling interest changes the consolidated income statement. In consolidation, all the income is combined, and then the 10% share attributable to noncontrolling shareholders is subtracted. We illustrate this in panel A of Exhibit 11-11 on page 513. Note that the parent-only income statement shows net income of $145, as does the consolidated income statement in the far right column.

Panel B shows how the noncontrolling interest from the income statement during the year increases the level of the noncontrolling interest on the balance sheet at year-end. Note that the noncontrolling interest of $21 that existed on January 1 increased by $5 during the year to reflect the noncontrolling shareholders' 10% interest in the year's net income of $50. As indicated in

▶▶ **OBJECTIVE 6**

Incorporate noncontrolling interests into consolidated financial statements.

noncontrolling interests
The claims of nonmajority shareholders in the assets and earnings of a company whose accounts are consolidated into the accounts of the major shareholder.

the intercompany elimination near the bottom of panel B, the eliminating entry on the work sheet used for consolidating the balance sheets is as follows:

Stockholders' equity (on S books)	263	
Investment in S (on P books).		237
Noncontrolling interest (on consolidated statements) . . .		26

EXHIBIT 11-10
90% Purchase of S: P Pays Cash to Some S Shareholders; Some S Shareholders Retain Noncontrolling Interest *($ in millions)*

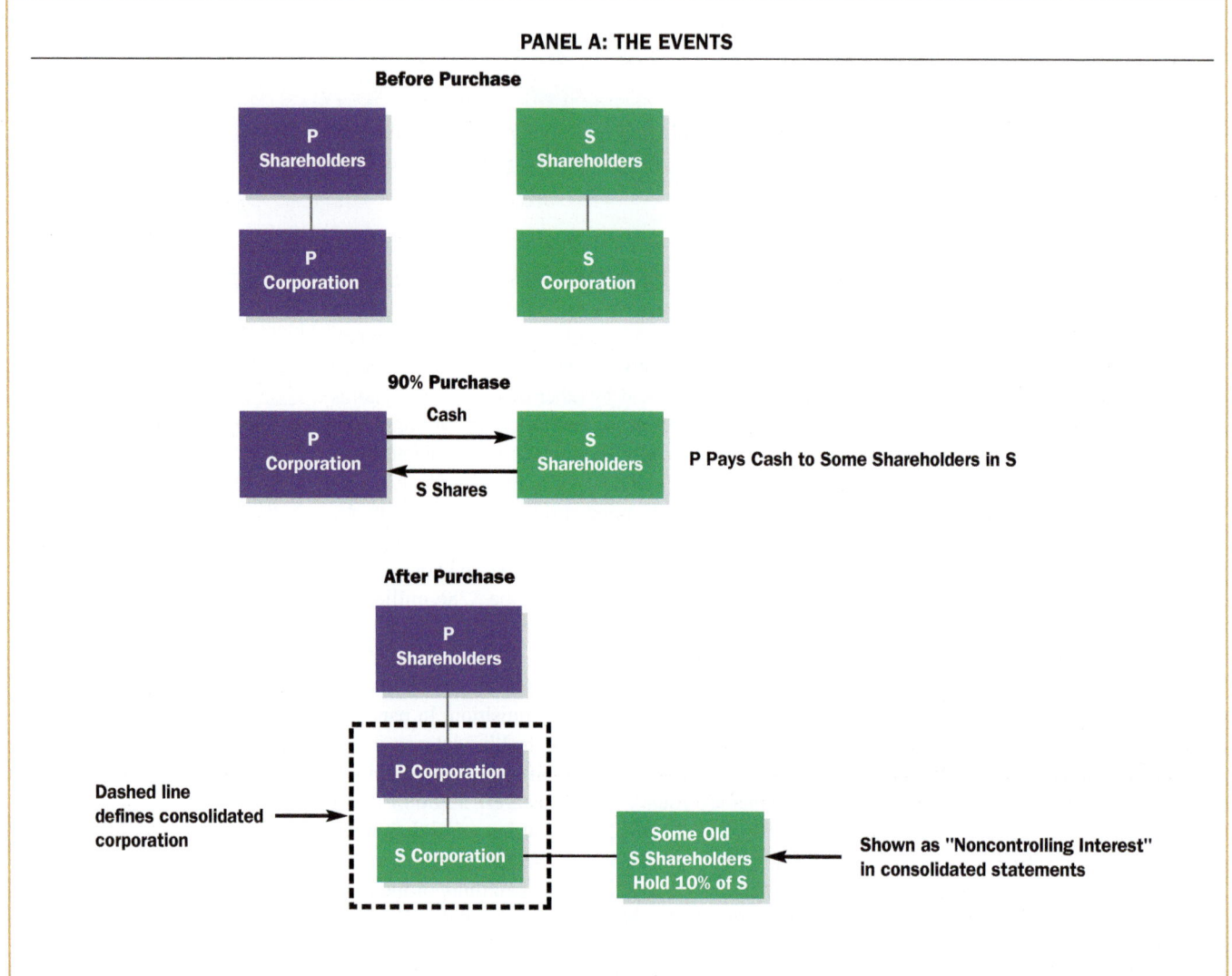

PANEL A: THE EVENTS

Before Purchase

90% Purchase
Cash
S Shares
P Pays Cash to Some Shareholders in S

After Purchase

Dashed line defines consolidated corporation

Some Old S Shareholders Hold 10% of S

Shown as "Noncontrolling Interest" in consolidated statements

PANEL B: 90% OWNERSHIP

	Assets		=	Liabilities	+	Stockholders' Equity		
	Investment in S	+ Cash and Other Assets	=	Accounts Payable, etc.	+	Noncontrolling Interest	+	Stockholders' Equity
P's accounts, Jan. 1								
Before acquisition		650	=	200			+	450
Acquisition of 90% of S	+192	−192	=					
S's accounts, Jan. 1		400	=	187			+	213
Intercompany eliminations	−192	___	=	___		+21		−213
Consolidated, Jan.1	0	+ 858	=	387	+	21	+	450

EXHIBIT 11-11
Effect of 90% Ownership During the Year

PANEL A: THE INCOME STATEMENT

	P	S	Consolidated
Sales	$900	$300	$1,200
Expenses	800	250	1,050
Operating income	100	50	150
Investment revenue*	45	—	
Net income	$145	$ 50	
Noncontrolling interest (10%) in subsidiary's net income			5
Net income to consolidated entity			$ 145

*Pro rata share (90%) of subsidiary net income, often called equity in earnings of affiliate or subsidiary.

PANEL B: THE BALANCE SHEET

	Assets		=	Liabilities	+	Stockholders' Equity		
	Investment in S	+	Cash and Other Assets =	Accounts Payable, etc.	+	Noncontrolling Interest	+	Stockholders' Equity
P's accounts								
Beginning of year, before acquisition			650 =	200			+	450
Acquisition	+192		−192 =					
Operating income			+100 =					+100
Share of S income	+45		=					+45
End of year	237	+	558 =	200			+	595
S's accounts								
Beginning of year			400 =	187			+	213
Net income			+50 =					+50
End of year		+	450 =	187			+	263
Intercompany eliminations	−237		=			+26†		−263
Consolidated, end of year	0	+	1,008 =	387	+	26†	+	595

†Beginning noncontrolling interest plus noncontrolling interest in net income: [$21 + (.10 × $50)] = ($21 + $5) = $26.

Summary Problem for Your Review

PROBLEM

1. Review the section on noncontrolling interests on pages 511–513. Suppose P buys 60% of the stock of S for a cost of (.60 × $213), or $128 million. The total assets of P consist of this $128 million plus $522 million of other assets, a total of $650 million. P's liabilities and stockholders' equity can be found in Exhibit 11-7. The assets, liabilities, and equity of S are unchanged from the amounts given in Exhibit 11-7 on page 507. Prepare an analysis showing what amounts would appear in a consolidated balance sheet immediately after the acquisition.
2. Suppose S has a net income of $50 million for the year, and P has an operating income of $100 million. Other details of their income statements are as described in the example on page 511 in this section. Prepare an analysis showing what amounts would appear in a consolidated income statement and year-end consolidated balance sheet.

SOLUTION

1.

	Assets		=	Liabilities	+	Stockholders' Equity		
	Investment in S	+ Cash and Other Assets	=	Accounts Payable, etc.	+	Noncontrolling Interest	+	Stockholders' Equity
P's accounts, January 1:								
Before acquisition		650	=	200			+	450
Acquisition of 60% of S	+128	–128	=					
S's accounts, January 1		400	=	187			+	213
Intercompany eliminations	–128		=			+85		–213
Consolidated, January 1	0	+ 922	=	387	+	85	+	450

2.

	P	S	Consolidated
Sales	$900	$300	$1,200
Expenses	800	250	1,050
Operating income	100	50	150
Pro rata share (60%) of subsidiary net income*	30	—	
Net income	$130	$ 50	
Noncontrolling interest (40%) in subsidiary's net income			20
Net income to consolidated entity			$ 130

*Also called investment revenue or equity in earnings of affiliate or subsidiary.

The balance sheet equation that shows the details of this analysis is in Exhibit 11-12.

EXHIBIT 11-12
Balance Sheet Equation for Summary Problem

	Assets		=	Liabilities	+	Stockholders' Equity		
	Investment in S	+ Cash and Other Assets	=	Accounts Payable, etc.	+	Noncontrolling Interest	+	Stockholders' Equity
P's accounts								
Beginning of year	128	+ 522*	=	200			+	450
Operating income		+100	=				+	+100
Share of S income	+30		=					+30
End of year	158	+ 622	=	200			+	580
S's accounts								
Beginning of year		400	=	187			+	213
Net income		+50	=					+50
End of year		450	=	187			+	263
Intercompany eliminations	–158		=			+105†		–263
Consolidated, end of year	0	+ 1,072	=	387	+	105†	+	580

*($650 beginning of year – $128 for acquisition) = $522.
†[$85 beginning of year + (.40 × $50)] = ($85 + $20) = $105.

Purchase Price not Equal to Book Value

When one company acquires another, the amount paid is usually higher and occasionally lower than either the book value or the fair value of the net assets owned by the acquired company. So far, we have assumed that the total amount paid, the book value, and the fair value of the subsidiary's net assets were all the same. When these amounts differ, the acquiring company uses the actual amount paid as the basis for accounting for the acquisition.

▶▶ OBJECTIVE 7

Explain the economic meaning and financial reporting of goodwill.

In a typical case, the acquiring company pays more than the fair value of the net assets acquired, which in turn is greater than the book value of the net assets. In such a case, consolidation requires a two-step adjustment. First, the initial consolidated statement must show all acquired assets and liabilities at their fair market values. Second, if the purchase price exceeds the fair market value of the acquired net assets, the consolidated statement must show an asset called goodwill. As discussed in Chapter 8, goodwill is the excess of the cost of an acquired company over the sum of the fair market value of its identifiable individual assets less its identifiable individual liabilities.

Why do companies pay more than the fair value of the net assets when acquiring a company? As you might suspect, the final price paid by the purchaser of an ongoing business is the culmination of a bargaining process. Therefore, the exact amount paid for goodwill is subject to the negotiations concerning the total purchase price. The accounting value assigned to goodwill initially is the residual amount arising from the difference between the total purchase price and the valuation that can be attached to specific assets and liabilities. Imagine a company that publishes a popular magazine with a large subscription and advertising base, in both hard copy and electronic formats. It has simple physical assets—a building, desks, and computers, a printing press, and some paper and ink—and possibly some recognized intangible assets such as purchased copyrights. Yet, a purchaser may be willing to pay more than the value of these recognized physical and intangible assets to acquire the company because it also has unrecognized intangible assets. Such assets include existing contracts, subscribers, advertising customers, and name recognition—so the going concern, the familiar magazine, is worth more than the collection of physical and recognized intangible assets. If the existing magazine continued and you bought similar assets and created a new competing magazine, profits would likely be a long-time coming.

Goodwill can be a significant portion of consolidated assets. Coca-Cola reported $12,219 million of goodwill at December 31, 2011. This is 15.3% of the total consolidated assets of Coca-Cola. Also, the balance in Goodwill increased from $11,665 million to $12,219 million from December 31, 2010, to December 31, 2011. The only way this can occur is if Coca-Cola purchased another company. In fact, in 2011 Coca-Cola acquired the Great Plains Coca-Cola Bottling Company for $360 million, a portion of which it attributed to goodwill. It also acquired the remaining ownership interest in Honest Tea, Inc. that it had not already owned. Prior to acquiring the remaining interest, Coca-Cola accounted for its investment in Honest Tea using the equity method. The acquisition of the remainder of Honest Tea required Coca-Cola to consolidate. As with the Great Plains acquisition, there was an increase in goodwill as a result of this purchase.

Accounting for Goodwill

To see the impact of goodwill on the consolidated statements, refer to our example in Exhibit 11-7 where P acquired a 100% interest in S. Suppose P paid $253 million rather than $213 million. Therefore, P recorded the investment at its $253 million cost. Upon examining S's assets, accountants found that a building with a book value of $20 million had a fair market value of $35 million. Fair market values of all other assets equaled their book values. This means that, of the $40 million excess of purchase price over book value of net assets, we can attribute $15 million to identifiable assets (the building), and the remaining $25 million is goodwill. The eliminating entry on the work sheet for consolidating the balance sheet, illustrated in Exhibit 11-13, is as follows (in millions of dollars):

Stockholders' equity (on S books)	213	
Goodwill (on consolidated balance sheet)	25	
Building (added to S's book value only on consolidated balance sheet)	15	
Investment in S (on P's books)		253

EXHIBIT 11-13

Creating Goodwill as of January 1

	Assets			=	Liabilities	+	Stockholders' Equity
	Investment in S	+ Cash and Other Assets +	Goodwill	=	Accounts Payable, etc.	+	Stockholders' Equity
P's accounts							
Before acquisition		650		=	200	+	450
Acquisition of S	+253	−253		=			
S's accounts		400		=	187	+	213
Intercompany eliminations	−253	+15†	+25*	=			−213
Consolidated	0	+ 812	+ 25*	=	387	+	450

*The 25 million "goodwill" would appear in the consolidated balance sheet as a separate intangible asset account. It is often shown as the final item in a listing of assets.

†The $15 million increase to cash and other assets shows the increase due to the market value of the building exceeding its book value.

impairment of goodwill

Reductions of the goodwill account because the value of the goodwill falls below its current carrying amount. The decrease in value is charged to expense.

Subsequent to the acquisition, under both IFRS and U.S. GAAP, the goodwill will decrease only if the acquiring company does not maintain the value of the goodwill. If the value of the goodwill decreases—called **impairment of goodwill**—the consolidated company must reduce the goodwill account by the amount of the decrease in value and charge that amount as an expense. In contrast, the consolidated company will depreciate any amount of purchase price assigned to an identifiable asset over the remaining life of that asset. Thus, a company that plans to maintain the value of the goodwill and wants to report high net income may prefer to assign the excess of the purchase price over the book value to goodwill rather than to identifiable assets.

Summary of Accounting for Equity Securities

Exhibit 11-14 summarizes the basic relationships in intercorporate investments. As we have seen, the accounting for investments in common stock depends on the nature of the investment:

1. Investments that represent more than a 50% ownership interest are usually consolidated. A subsidiary is a corporation controlled by another corporation. The usual condition for control is ownership of a majority (more than 50%) of the outstanding voting stock.
2. The equity method is generally used for a 20%–50% interest because such a level of ownership creates a presumption that the owner has the ability to exert significant influence. Under the equity method, the investor records its cost at the date of acquisition in an investment asset account. Each period, the investor adjusts the investment account and the income statement for its share of the earnings or losses of the investee for the current period. Dividends received from the investee reduce the carrying amount of the investment.
3. Marketable equity securities are generally carried at market value when ownership is below 20%. These investments are passive in the sense that the investor exerts no significant influence on the investee. Unrealized gains and losses appear in the income statement for trading securities and in a combined statement of income and comprehensive income or a separate statement of other comprehensive income for available-for-sale securities.

EXHIBIT 11-14
Summary of Accounting for Equity Securities

Percentage of Ownership	Type of Accounting	Balance Sheet Effects	Income Statement Effects	Major Journal Entries
100%	Consolidation	Individual assets, individual liabilities added together For subsidiaries purchased for more than the fair value of identifiable net assets, goodwill is shown	Individual revenues, individual expenses added together If goodwill exists, it must be checked for impairment	In work sheets for preparing consolidated statements, to eliminate reciprocal accounts, to avoid double-counting, and to recognize any goodwill
Greater than 50% and less than 100%	Consolidation	Same as 100% ownership, but recognition given to noncontrolling interest	Same as 100% ownership, but recognition given to noncontrolling interest near bottom of statement when consolidated net income is computed	Same as 100% ownership, but recognition of noncontrolling interests is included in work sheet entries

20% to and including 50%	Equity method	Investment carried at cost plus pro rata share of subsidiary earnings less dividends received	Equity in earnings (losses) of *affiliated* or *associated* companies shown on one line as addition to (deduction from) income	Investment xx
				  Equity in earnings xx
				To record earnings
				
				Cash xx
				  Investment xx
				To record dividends received

Less than 20%	Market method	Investment carried at market value	For trading securities, annual changes affect the income statement
			
			For available-for-sale securities there is no effect on the income statement, the changes appear in other comprehensive income.
				Marketable securities xx
				  Income statement
				    gain or loss xx
				To record appreciation
				
				Marketable securities xx
				  Other comprehensive
				    income xx
				To record appreciation

Highlights to Remember

1 Explain why corporations invest in one another. Corporate investments arise for many reasons. Some investments may create a relationship that leads to communication and sharing of information and talent. Other business combinations are driven by efforts to integrate firms and create cost reductions. As investments increase in size, the investor obtains more influence over the investee, leading to changes in the behavior of both parties. When investments exceed 50% ownership of the investee, the investor obtains control sufficient to dictate behavior. The owner controls decision making and dictates what is made, to whom it is sold, from whom parts are purchased, how activity is financed, whether dividends are paid, what new assets are purchased, and so on.

2 Account for short-term investments in debt securities and equity securities. The accounting for intercorporate investments depends on the purpose of the investment, on whether it is an equity or debt security, and on the level of control the investor has over the issuer of the security. For debt securities and equity securities that are classified as trading or available-for-sale, companies show the investment at market value on the balance sheet. Trading securities are held to be resold, and the unrealized gains and losses from changes in market value go directly to the income statement. The unrealized gains and losses on securities that are classified as available-for-sale are part of other comprehensive income.

3 Report long-term investments in bonds. When the investor's intention is to hold debt securities to maturity, the investor's accounting uses the effective interest rate method in the same manner that the issuer does. That is, the investor amortizes any discount or premium, which affects interest revenue.

4 Contrast the equity and market methods of accounting for investments. For equity securities held for the long term, the accounting is linked to the investor's level of control of the issuer of the equity security. For ownership interests of less than 20%, accounting for equity securities requires classification as either available-for-sale or trading, and under either classification, the investor carries the investments at fair value. As the ownership interest ranges from 20% to 50%, the increasing control the investor can exert over the issuer leads to earnings recognition in the income statement, proportional to the percentage of ownership. Under the equity method, the investor increases the investment account by the share of the issuer's earnings (or decreases the investment account by a proportionate share of losses). When the investor receives dividends, it decreases the investment account with no effect on earnings.

5 Understand the reasons for business combinations and prepare consolidated financial statements. As the ownership interest exceeds 50%, the investor controls the subsidiary. Consolidation, which involves combining all the assets and liabilities of the related corporate entities, is appropriate. For 100% owned subsidiaries, the consolidating process requires creation of a consolidation work sheet that includes entries to eliminate the double-counting of the parent's ownership in the subsidiary that would result from a straight combining of financial statements. Also, the work sheet must eliminate all intercompany transactions such as sales, receivables, and payables.

6 Incorporate noncontrolling interests into consolidated financial statements. Noncontrolling interests are the rights of nonmajority shareholders in consolidated subsidiaries that are more than 50% owned by the majority stockholder and therefore consolidated by the parent. Noncontrolling interests are treated much like the equity interests of an investor. On the income statement, net income available to common shareholders of the consolidated entity is reduced by the proportional interests of the noncontrolling shareholders. On the balance sheet, the noncontrolling interests are a measure of the equity claims of noncontrolling shareholders on the assets of consolidated subsidiaries.

7 Explain the economic meaning and financial reporting of goodwill. Goodwill refers to the excess of the purchase price of an acquired company over the fair value of its identifiable net assets. Economically, it arises because the acquired firm has created the ability to earn extraordinary returns by creating market power. The market power might take the form of brand recognition, a superior location, or a highly motivated sales staff. From an accounting perspective, companies record goodwill only when it is acquired by purchasing a controlling interest in another company. Companies do not amortize goodwill; they write it off (reduce it) only when management concludes that the value of the goodwill has declined (is impaired).

Accounting Vocabulary

affiliated company, p. 501
available-for-sale (AFS)
   securities, p. 495
certificates of deposit, p. 494
commercial paper, p. 494
comprehensive income, p. 497
consolidated financial
   statements, p. 492
equity method, p. 501

held-to-maturity
   securities, p. 494
impairment of goodwill, p. 516
market method, p. 495
marketable securities, p. 494
noncontrolling interests, p. 511
parent company, p. 504
short-term debt
   securities, p. 494

short-term equity
   securities, p. 494
short-term investment, p. 494
subsidiary, p. 504
trading securities, p. 494
unrealized gain (loss), p. 495
U.S. Treasury
   obligations, p. 494

Assignment Material

Questions

11-1 Why might a company invest in the securities of another company?

11-2 Distinguish among trading securities, available-for-sale securities, and held-to-maturity securities.

11-3 "The cost method is applied to investments in short-term securities." Do you agree? Explain.

11-4 "Increases in the market price of short-term investments become gains on the income statement; decreases become losses." Do you agree? Explain.

11-5 Does an unrealized gain or loss on trading securities require recognition in a statement of cash flows? Would your answer change if the securities are classified as available-for-sale?

11-6 Suppose an investor buys a $1,000 face value bond for $950, a discount of $50. Will amortization of the discount increase or decrease the investor's interest income? Explain.

11-7 What is the equity method?

11-8 "The equity method is usually used for long-term investments." Do you think this is appropriate? Explain.

11-9 Contrast the *market* method with the *equity* method.

11-10 What criterion is used to determine whether a parent–subsidiary relationship exists? Are U.S. GAAP and IFRS the same or different? Explain.

11-11 Why have subsidiaries? Why not have the corporation take the form of a single legal entity?

11-12 Suppose Company A buys 100% of the common shares of Company B for cash. How does Company B record the receipt of this cash on its books?

11-13 Why does consolidating a balance sheet require "eliminating entries"?

11-14 "A consolidated income statement will show more income than a parent-company-only statement when both the parent and subsidiary have positive net income." Do you agree? Explain.

11-15 What is a noncontrolling interest?

11-16 Distinguish between *control of* a company and *significant influence over* a company.

11-17 "Goodwill is the excess of purchase price over the book values of the individual assets acquired." Do you agree? Explain.

11-18 Does GAAP require amortization of goodwill against net income? If not, when does goodwill decrease?

11-19 Why might a company prefer to own a 19.9% interest in an affiliate instead of a 20.1% interest?

11-20 When is there justification for not consolidating majority-owned subsidiaries?

11-21 Suppose P company received $20,000 in cash dividends from Y company, a 40% owned affiliated company. Y company's net income was $80,000. How will P's statement of cash flows show these items using the direct method?

11-22 Why do noncontrolling interests arise in connection with consolidated statements but not with investments in affiliated companies accounted for under the equity method?

11-23 Would you expect the consolidated income statement to report higher net income than shown in the parent's separate financial statements? Explain.

MyAccountingLab

Critical Thinking Questions

11-24 Consequences of Marking to Market

As president of a young technology company, you and your chief financial officer are discussing your great success in investing in other high-growth companies in your industry. When you raised $20 million in capital, you actually needed $10 million immediately so you invested the other $10 million in a portfolio of dynamic companies that you accounted for as available-for-sale securities. Over the last year, the value of these companies doubled. How will next year's reported income compare with this year's if you liquidate that portfolio and invest it in the core business?

▶▶ OBJECTIVE 2

11-25 Scoping Out an Acquisition Strategy

You recently hired a young MBA who advises you to grow more aggressively and who suggests that you should do so by acquiring other small companies. Your cookware and tableware importing business has been quite successful, but you are not sure that this new employee's plan to acquire a series of retail cooking/kitchenware stores makes sense. What issues would you raise in discussing this proposal?

▶▶ OBJECTIVE 5

▶▶ **OBJECTIVE 4**

11-26 Accounting Consequences of Changing Ownership Interest

You own 19% of a company that you do business with and are considering buying another 5% of the company. The company provides a great product and great service. The company's share price has been rising because of its potential. However, it is currently not profitable from an accounting perspective because the company is doing a great deal of research and development. You have asked your CFO to advise you about the consequences of this increase in your owner-ship position. What would you expect the CFO to say?

▶▶ **OBJECTIVE 5**

11-27 Transactions Between Companies

Your company has sales of $100 million and profits of $10 million. A similar, smaller company with sales of $25 million and profits of $5 million appears to be an attractive merger candidate. You currently buy 50% of the smaller company's production. The CEO has indicated that this would be a great acquisition because it would increase sales by 25% and profits by 50%. As CFO, what issues do you raise concerning this proposed purchase and the CEO's analysis.

Exercises

▶▶ **OBJECTIVE 2**

11-28 Trading Securities

The Lapinski Company has a portfolio of trading securities consisting of common and pre-ferred stocks. The portfolio cost $160 million on January 1. The market values of the portfolio were as follows ($ in millions): March 31, $155; June 30, $135; September 30, $152; and December 31, $160.

1. Prepare a tabulation showing the balance sheet presentations and income statement presenta-tions for quarterly reporting purposes.
2. Show the journal entries for quarters 1, 2, 3, and 4.

▶▶ **OBJECTIVE 2**

11-29 Available-for-Sale Securities

The Brixey Company has a portfolio of securities identical to that of the Lapinski Company (see Exercise 11-28). However, Brixey classified the portfolio as available-for-sale securities. The portfolio cost $160 million on January 1. The market values of the portfolio were as follows ($ in millions): March 31, $155; June 30, $135; September 30, $152; and December 31, $160.

1. Prepare a tabulation showing the balance sheet presentations and income statement presenta-tions for quarterly reporting purposes.
2. Show the journal entries for quarters 1, 2, 3, and 4.

▶▶ **OBJECTIVE 3**

11-30 Bond Discount Transactions

On December 31, 20X1, a company purchased $1 million of 10-year, 10% debentures for $885,300. The market interest rate was 12%.

1. Using the balance sheet equation format, prepare an analysis of bond transactions for the investor. Assume effective interest amortization. Show entries for the investor concerning (a) purchase, (b) first semiannual interest payment, and (c) payment of maturity value.
2. Show the journal entries that correspond to (a), (b), and (c) of requirement 1.
3. Show how the bond investment would appear on the balance sheets as of December 31, 20X1, and June 30, 20X2.

▶▶ **OBJECTIVE 3**

11-31 Bond Premium Transactions

On December 31, 20X1, the Bavetta Company purchased $2 million of 5-year, 10% debentures for $2,162,220. The market interest rate was 8%.

1. Using the balance sheet equation format, prepare an analysis of transactions for the investor's records. Key your transactions as follows: (a) purchase, (b) first semiannual interest payment using effective interest amortization of bond premium, and (c) payment of maturity value.
2. Prepare the journal entries that correspond to (a), (b), and (c) of requirement 1.
3. Show how the bond-related accounts would appear on the balance sheets as of December 31, 20X1, and June 30, 20X2.

▶▶ **OBJECTIVES 2, 4**

11-32 Market Method or Equity Method

Fairbanks Outdoor Equipment acquired 25% of the voting stock of Bearpaw Snowshoes for $60 million cash. In year 1, Bearpaw had a net income of $32 million and paid a cash dividend of $12 million.

1. Using the equity and the market methods, show the effects of the three transactions on the accounts of Fairbanks Outdoor Equipment. Use the balance sheet equation format. Also show the corresponding journal entries. Assume constant market value for Bearpaw.
2. Which method, equity or market, would Fairbanks use to account for its investment in Bearpaw? Explain.

11-33 Equity Method

Hartman Company acquired 35% of the voting stock of Zhou Company for $90 million cash. In year 1, Zhou had a net income of $50 million and paid cash dividends of $30 million.

Prepare a tabulation that uses the equity method of accounting for Hartman's investment in Zhou. Show the effects on the balance sheet equation. What is the year-end balance in the Investment in Zhou account under the equity method?

11-34 Consolidated Statements

  ▶▶ OBJECTIVE 5

Tomasco and Wooten Companies had the following balance sheets at December 31, 20X8 ($ in thousands):

	Tomasco	Wooten
Assets		
Cash	$ 600	$100
Net plant	1,700	400
Total assets	$2,300	$500
Liabilities and stockholders' equity		
Accounts payable	275	$ 80
Long-term debt	425	195
Stockholders' equity	1,600	225
Total liabilities and stockholders' equity	$2,300	$500

On January 1, 20X9, Tomasco purchased 100% of the common stock of Wooten for $225,000.

1. Prepare a balance sheet for Tomasco Company immediately after its purchase of Wooten Company.
2. Prepare a balance sheet for the consolidated entity immediately after the purchase of Wooten Company.
3. Suppose Tomasco Company had net income of $250,000 in 20X9 (before recognizing its share of Wooten's income) and Wooten Company had net income of $45,000 in 20X9. Neither company sold items to the other. What was the 20X9 consolidated net income?

11-35 Noncontrolling Interest

  ▶▶ OBJECTIVE 6

Suppose P company owns 90% of S company and S company earns $300,000. What is the amount of the noncontrolling interest shown in P company's consolidated income statement? What is the amount of the noncontrolling interest shown in S company's individual income statement?

11-36 Goodwill

  ▶▶ OBJECTIVE 7

Giannacarro, Inc., purchased 100% of the common shares of Arietta for $290,000 on January 1, 20X7. Arietta's balance sheet just before the acquisition was as follows ($ in thousands):

Cash	$ 90
Net fixed assets	220
Total assets	$310
Liabilities	$240
Stockholders' equity	70
Total liabilities and stockholders' equity	$310

The fair market values of Arietta's assets and liabilities were equal to their book values.

1. Compute the amount of goodwill Giannacarro would recognize on this purchase. Where would this goodwill appear on Giannacarro's financial statements?

2. Giannacarro's 20X7 net income from all operations excluding those of Arietta was $100,000. Arietta had a net loss of $5,000. Assume there were no intercompany transactions. Compute consolidated net income for 20X7.

3. Repeat requirement 2 assuming Giannacarro concluded goodwill was impaired by $20,000.

4. How much goodwill appears on the consolidated balance sheet after requirement 3?

▶▶ **OBJECTIVE 4**

11-37 Affiliated Companies

Suppose Zerba Company owns 30% of Stallings Company. Stallings Company earns $180,000 and pays total dividends of $40,000 to its shareholders. What appears on the income statement of Zerba Company as a result of Stallings' activity? What would be the change in the account titled Investment in Equity Affiliates on Zerba's balance sheet?

▶▶ **OBJECTIVES 4, 5**

11-38 Consolidations versus the Equity Method

Some years ago, Japan's finance ministry issued a directive requiring the 600 largest Japanese companies to produce consolidated financial statements. The previous practice had been to use parent-company-only statements. The change was intended to put a stop to the practice of "window dressing" the parent company financial results by shoving losses onto the subsidiaries. When a parent company needed to show a bigger profit, it might sell its product to subsidiaries at an inflated price. Or the parent company might charge higher rent to a subsidiary company renting space from the parent.

Could a parent company follow these practices and achieve window dressing in its parent-only financial statements if it used the equity method of accounting for its intercorporate investments? Explain.

MyAccountingLab **Problems**

▶▶ **OBJECTIVE 2**

11-39 Trading Securities

Before its acquisition by Royal Dutch Shell, Pennzoil Company held a portfolio of trading equity securities that cost $660,100,000 and had a market value of $955,182,000 on January 1. Assume that the same portfolio was held until the end of the first quarter of the year. The market value of the portfolio was $980,160,000 at January 31, $940,000,000 at February 29, and $960,000,000 at March 31.

1. Prepare a tabulation showing the balance sheet presentation and income statement presentation for monthly reporting purposes.

2. Show the journal entries for January, February, and March.

3. How would your answer to requirement 1 change if the securities were classified as available-for-sale?

▶▶ **OBJECTIVE 2**

11-40 Short-Term Investments

The VanDuzer Company has the following footnote to its financial statements:

Note 4: Short-Term Investments
The company holds the following short-term investments at December 31 (in thousands):

	Cost	Market Value
Trading securities		
U.S. government bonds	$670,000	$680,000
Held-to-maturity securities		
Bonds issued by Beta Corp.	540,000	560,000
Available-for-sale securities		
Common shares of Gamma Corp.	600,000	770,000

1. Compute the amount that VanDuzer would show on its balance sheet for short-term investments.

2. Suppose the market values of the three securities at the beginning of the year had been as follows (in thousands):

U.S. government bonds	$700,000
Bonds issued by Beta Corp.	580,000
Common shares of Gamma Corp.	710,000

Prepare journal entries to recognize the changes in market values that would be recorded in VanDuzer's books at the end of the year.

11-41 Early Extinguishment of an Investment

On December 31, 20X2, an insurance company purchased $10 million of 10-year, 10% debentures for $8,852,950. On December 31, 20X3 (after all interest payments and amortization had been recorded for 20X3), the insurance company sold all the debentures for $9.2 million. The market interest rate at purchase when the bonds were issued was 12%. Interest payments are semiannual.

▶▶ **OBJECTIVE 3**

1. Compute the gain or loss on the sale for the insurance company (i.e., the investor).
2. Prepare the appropriate journal entries for the insurance company (i.e., the investor).

11-42 Consolidated Statements, Noncontrolling Interests

Consider the following for Ferchland Company (the parent) as of December 31, 20X8:

▶▶ **OBJECTIVES 5, 6**

	Ferchland	Subsidiary*
Assets	$800,000	$200,000
Liabilities to creditors	$300,000	$ 80,000
Stockholders' equity	500,000	120,000
Total	$800,000	$200,000

*70% owned by Ferchland.

The $800,000 in assets held by Ferchland includes an $84,000 investment in the 70% owned subsidiary. The $84,000 includes Ferchland's pro rata share of the subsidiary's net income for 20X8. Ferchland's sales were $890,000 and operating expenses were $802,000. These figures exclude any pro rata share of the subsidiary's net income. The subsidiary's sales were $550,000 and operating expenses were $500,000. Prepare a consolidated income statement and a consolidated balance sheet. Assume neither Ferchland nor its subsidiary sold items to the other.

11-43 Consolidated Financial Statements and Noncontrolling Interest

The parent company owns 70% of the common stock of Company S-1 and 60% of the common stock of Company S-2. The balances as of December 31, 20X4, in the condensed accounts follow:

▶▶ **OBJECTIVES 5, 6**

	($ in thousands)		
	Parent	**S-1**	**S-2**
Sales in 20X4	320,000	80,000	100,000
Investment in subsidiaries*	58,000	—	—
Other assets	152,000	90,000	20,000
Liabilities to creditors	110,000	20,000	5,000
Expenses in 20X4	300,000	90,000	90,000
Stockholders' equity, including current net income	100,000	70,000	15,000

*Accounted for using the equity method.

Prepare a consolidated balance sheet as of December 31, 20X4, and a consolidated income statement for 20X4 ($ in millions of dollars). Assume none of the companies sold items to each other.

11-44 Consolidated Financial Statements

Company P acquired a 100% voting interest in Company S for $120 million cash at the start of the year. Immediately before the business combination, each company had the following condensed balance sheet accounts ($ in millions):

▶▶ **OBJECTIVE 5**

	P	S
Cash and other assets	$600	$160
Accounts payable, etc.	$150	$ 40
Stockholders' equity	450	120
Total liab. and stk. eq.	$600	$160

1. Prepare a tabulation of the consolidated balance sheet accounts immediately after acquisition. Use the balance sheet equation format.
2. Suppose P and S have the following results for the year:

	P	S
Sales	$700	$180
Expenses	550	170

Prepare income statements for the year for P, S, and the consolidated entity. Assume neither P nor S sold items to the other.

3. Present the effects of the operations for the year on P's accounts and on S's accounts, using the balance sheet equation. Also tabulate the consolidated balance sheet accounts at the end of the year. Assume that liabilities are unchanged.
4. Suppose S paid a cash dividend of $6 million. What accounts in requirement 3 would be affected and by how much?

▶▶ OBJECTIVES 5, 6

11-45 Noncontrolling Interests

This alters problem 11-44. However, this problem is self-contained because all the facts are reproduced as follows: Company P acquired a 60% voting interest in Company S for $72 million cash at the start of the year. Immediately before the business combination, each company had the following condensed balance sheet accounts ($ in millions):

	P	S
Cash and other assets	$600	$160
Accounts payable, etc.	$150	$ 40
Stockholders' equity	450	120
Total liab. and stk. eq.	$600	$160

1. Prepare a tabulation of the consolidated balance sheet accounts immediately after acquisition. Use the balance sheet equation format.
2. Suppose P and S have the following results for the year:

	P	S
Sales	$700	$180
Expenses	550	170

Prepare income statements for the year for P, S, and the consolidated entity. Assume neither P nor S sold items to the other.

3. Using the balance sheet equation format, present the effects of the operations for the year on P's accounts and on S's accounts. Also tabulate consolidated balance sheet accounts at the end of the year. Assume that liabilities are unchanged.
4. Suppose S paid a cash dividend of $5 million. What accounts in requirement 3 would be affected and by how much?

▶▶ OBJECTIVES 5, 7

11-46 Goodwill and Consolidations

This alters problem 11-44. However, this problem is self-contained because all the facts are reproduced as follows: Company P acquired a 100% voting interest in Company S for $150 million cash at the start of the year. Immediately before the business combination, each company had the following condensed balance sheet accounts ($ in millions):

	P	S
Cash and other assets	$600	160
Accounts payable, etc.	$150	$ 40
Stockholders' equity	450	120
Total liab. and stk. equity	$600	$160

1. Assume the fair values of the individual assets and liabilities of S were equal to their book values. Prepare a tabulation of the consolidated balance sheet accounts immediately after the acquisition. Use the balance sheet equation format.
2. Suppose the book values of the S individual assets are equal to their fair market values except for equipment. The net book value of equipment is $40 million and its fair market value is $50 million. The equipment has a remaining useful life of 5 years. Straight-line depreciation is used.
   a. Describe how the consolidated balance sheet accounts immediately after the acquisition would differ from those in requirement 1. Be specific as to accounts and amounts.
   b. By how much will consolidated income differ in comparison with the consolidated income that would be reported if all equipment had fair value equal to its book value on S's books as in requirement 1?

11-47 Purchased Goodwill

▶▶ OBJECTIVES 5, 7

Consider the following balance sheets ($ in millions):

	Company A	Company B
Cash	$ 150	$ 15
Inventories	65	25
Plant assets, net	65	30
Total assets	$ 280	$ 70
Common stock and paid-in surplus	$ 80	$ 30
Retained earnings	200	40
Total liab. and stk. equity	$ 280	$ 70

Company A paid $90 million to Company B stockholders for all their stock. The "fair value" of the plant assets of Company B is $40 million. The fair value of cash and inventories is equal to their carrying amounts. Companies A and B continued to keep separate books.

1. Prepare a tabulation showing the balance sheets of companies A and B, intercompany eliminations, and the consolidated balance sheet immediately after the acquisition.
2. Suppose that $50 million instead of $40 million of the total purchase price of $90 million could logically be assigned to the plant assets. How would the consolidated accounts be affected?
3. Refer to the facts in requirement 2. Suppose Company A had paid $100 million instead of $90 million. State how your tabulation in requirement 2 would change.

11-48 Allocating Total Purchase Price to Assets

▶▶ OBJECTIVES 5, 7

Two Hollywood companies had the following balance sheet accounts as of December 31, 20X7 ($ in millions):

	Lexia	Hudson Productions		Lexia	Hudson Productions
Cash and receivables	$ 60	$ 44	Current liabilities	$ 100	$ 40
Inventories	240	6	Common stock	200	20
Plant assets, net	300	190	Retained earnings	300	180
Total assets	$600	$240	Total liab. and stk. eq.	$ 600	$240
Net income for 20X7	$ 38	$ 8			

On January 4, 20X8, these entities combined. Lexia issued $360 million of its shares (at market value) in exchange for all the shares of Hudson, a motion picture division of a large company. The inventory of films acquired through the combination had been fully amortized on Hudson's books.

During 20X8, Hudson received revenue of $42 million from the rental of films from its inventory. Lexia earned $40 million on its other operations (i.e., excluding Hudson) during 20X8. Hudson broke even on its other operations (i.e., excluding the film rental contracts) during 20X8.

1. Prepare a consolidated balance sheet for the combined company immediately after the combination. Assume $160 million of the purchase price was assigned to the inventory of films. The fair values of all other Hudson assets and liabilities were equal to their book values.

2. Prepare a comparison of Lexia's consolidated net income between 20X7 and 20X8, where the cost of the film inventories would be amortized on a straight-line basis over 4 years. What would be the net income for 20X8 if the $160 million were assigned to goodwill instead of the inventory of films and goodwill was not amortized?

▶▶ **OBJECTIVE 5**

11-49 Prepare Consolidated Financial Statements

From the following data, prepare a consolidated balance sheet and a multiple-step income statement for Amundsen Data Corporation. All data are in millions and pertain to operations for 20X2 or to balances on December 31, 20X2:

Short-term investments at current market value	$ 45
Income tax expense	90
Accounts receivable, net	110
Noncontrolling interest in subsidiaries	90
Inventories at average cost	390
Dividends declared and paid on preferred stock	10
Equity in earnings of affiliated companies	20
Paid-in capital in excess of par	82
Interest expense	30
Retained earnings	223
Investments in affiliated companies	110
Common stock, 10 million shares, $1 par	10
Depreciation and amortization	40
Accounts payable	205
Cash	60
First mortgage bonds, 10% interest, due December 31, 20X8	90
Property, plant, and equipment, net	120
Preferred stock, 2 million shares, $50 par, dividend rate is $5 per share, each share is convertible into one share of common stock	100
Accrued income taxes payable	35
Cost of goods sold and operating expenses, exclusive of depreciation and amortization	785
Subordinated debentures, 11% interest, due December 31, 20X9	100
Noncontrolling interest in subsidiaries' net income	20
Goodwill	100
Net sales and other operating revenue	1,060

▶▶ **OBJECTIVE 5**

11-50 IFRS Consolidations

In the 2011 annual report **Royal Dutch Shell** reports that it prepares its financial statements "under the provisions of the Companies Act 2006 and Article 4 of the International Accounting Standards (IAS) Regulation." The statements are prepared "in accordance with International Financial Reporting Standards (IFRS) as adopted by the European Union."

1. Footnote 1 goes on to state that there are no material differences from IFRS as issued by the IASB, and "therefore the Consolidated Financial Statements have been prepared in accordance with IFRS as issued by the IASB." Speculate as to why this extra language would be appropriate or necessary in Shell's financial statements.

2. Footnote 10 explains that although Shell has a 52% interest in **Aera**, an exploration and production company in the United States, it does not consolidate Aera. Speculate as to why accounting for Aera using the equity method might be appropriate under IFRS.

11-51 Equity Method and Cash Flows

▶▶ **OBJECTIVE 4**

Moscow Resources Company owns a 35% interest in Siberia Mining Company. Moscow uses the equity method to account for the investment. During 20X6, Siberia had net income of 180 million rubles and paid cash dividends of 40 million rubles. Moscow's net income, including the effect of its investment in Siberia, was 500 million rubles.

1. In reconciling Moscow's net income with its net cash provided by operating activities, the net income must be adjusted for Moscow's pro rata share of the net income of Siberia. Compute the amount of the adjustment. Will it be added to or deducted from net income?
2. Under the direct method, will the dividends paid by Siberia affect the amounts Moscow lists under operating, investing, or financing activities? By how much? Will the amount(s) be cash inflows or cash outflows?

11-52 Effect of Transactions Under the Equity Method

▶▶ **OBJECTIVE 4**

Ford Motor Company's 2011 financial statements revealed that it has extensive equity method investments. In total, the balance sheet showed equity investments of $2,569 million at December 31, 2010, and $2,936 million at December 31, 2011. During 2011 Ford included equity income of $500 million in its income statement, and footnote 11 indicates that approximately $316 million in dividends was received from equity investees.

1. Compute the approximate change in Ford's equity investment asset that cannot be explained by either increases (decreases) due to its share in earnings (losses) or decreases due to dividends received. You may find a T-account will help your analysis.
2. Ford uses the indirect method to construct its cash flow statement. Indicate how these transactions with equity investees would be shown in the statement of cash flows.

11-53 Equity Method, Consolidation, and Noncontrolling Interests

▶▶ **OBJECTIVES 4, 5, 6**

On January 2, 20X6, Gernon Shoe Company purchased 40% of Sports Clothing Company (SCC) for $2.0 million cash. Before the acquisition, Gernon had assets of $10 million and stockholders' equity of $8 million. SCC had stockholders' equity of $5 million and liabilities of $1 million, and the fair values of its assets and liabilities were equal to their book values.

SCC reported 20X6 net income of $600,000 and declared and paid dividends of $150,000. Assume that Gernon and SCC had no sales to one another. Separate income statements for Gernon and SCC were as follows:

	Gernon Shoe Company	Sports Clothing Company
Sales	$12,500,000	$4,600,000
Expenses	11,100,000	4,000,000
Operating income	$ 1,400,000	$ 600,000

1. Prepare the journal entries for Gernon Shoe (a) to record the acquisition of SCC, and (b) to record its share of SCC net income and dividends for 20X6.
2. Prepare Gernon Shoe's income statement for 20X6 and calculate the balance in its Investments in SCC account as of December 31, 20X6.
3. Suppose Gernon had purchased 80% of SCC for $4 million. Using the balance sheet equation format, prepare a tabulation of the consolidated balance sheet immediately after acquisition. Prepare the journal entries for both Gernon and SCC to record the acquisition. Omit explanations.
4. Prepare a consolidated income statement for 20X6, using the facts of requirement 3.

11-54 Equity Investments and Noncontrolling Interests

▶▶ **OBJECTIVES 4, 6**

Xerox has equity investments, and several of its consolidated subsidiaries have noncontrolling interests outstanding. Xerox's consolidated income statement for 2011 shows the following (dollars in millions):

Income before income taxes and equity income	$1,565
Income taxes	(386)
Equity in net income of unconsolidated affiliates	149
Net income	1,328
Less: Net income attributable to noncontrolling interests	33
Net income attributable to Xerox	$1,295

1. Assuming each of the equity companies is 40% owned by Xerox, estimate the 2011 earnings for these companies.
2. Independent of requirement 1, assume that each of the noncontrolling interests is a 20% interest, estimate the 2011 earnings of these companies.
3. Xerox prepares a cash flow statement using the indirect method. On it, net income is adjusted by $86 million for undistributed earnings of affiliated companies. Estimate dividends received from equity investees.

▶▶ OBJECTIVE 7

11-55 Goodwill

URS Corporation is an integrated engineering, construction, and technical services company that operates in nearly 50 countries. According to the company Web site, URS offers program management, planning, design and engineering; systems engineering and technical assistance; construction and construction management; operations and maintenance; and decommissioning services. In 2010, revenues totaled $9,177.1 million with net income of $287.0 million. In 2011, revenues increased slightly to $9,545.0 million, but URS had a net loss of $465.8 million, due primarily to an impairment of goodwill of $825.8 million.

1. URS's 2010 balance sheet showed goodwill of $3,393.2 million out of total assets of $7,351.4 million and its 2011 balance sheet showed goodwill of $2,773.0 million out of total assets of $6,862.6 million. Express goodwill as a percentage of total assets for each year, and indicate what that suggests about the company's growth.
2. From the information provided, can you determine whether URS engaged in any new acquisitions in 2011?
3. What happened to the excess earnings capacity of URS during 2011? How is this reflected in the company's income statement and balance sheet?

▶▶ OBJECTIVE 5

11-56 The Value of a Stock for Stock Exchange
On October 27, 2003, the following appeared in a news release:

> Bank of America Corporation and FleetBoston Financial Corporation today announced a definitive agreement to merge, creating the nation's premier financial services company. The company will bring unmatched convenience, innovation and resources to customers and clients throughout the nation and around the world.
>
> The merger, to be accomplished through a stock-for-stock transaction, establishes a new Bank of America that will serve approximately 33 million consumer relationships, with leading market shares throughout the Northeast, Southeast, Midwest, Southwest and West regions of the United States... .
>
> Under terms of the agreement, FleetBoston Financial stockholders will receive .5553 shares of Bank of America common stock for each of their shares. The exchange ratio was derived from the share price of Bank of America at the close of business on October 22, 2003, to establish the transaction's value at almost $47 billion, or $45 per FleetBoston Financial share.

Following this announcement, FleetBoston shares rose sharply and Bank of America shares dropped approximately 10%.

Discuss these events. How is this different than Bank of America agreeing to pay $45 per share in cash?

11-57 Intercorporate Investments and Statements of Cash Flow

▶▶ **OBJECTIVE 4**

The 20X6 balance sheet of Dietrich Resources, Corp., contained the following three assets:

	20X6	20X5
Long-term debt investments held to maturity	$ 166,000	$ 166,000
Investment in Modoc Mining Company, 43% owned	$ 941,000	$ 861,000
Investment in Sutter Gold Company, 25% owned	$1,144,000	$1,054,000

The long-term-debt investments were shown at cost, which equaled maturity value. Interest income was $16,000 for these debt investments, which had been owned for several years. The equity method was used to account for both Modoc Mining and Sutter Gold. Results for 20X6 included the following:

	Modoc Mining Company	Sutter Gold Company
Dietrich Resources, Corp., pro rata share of net income	$130,000	$90,000

Dietrich Resources received some dividends from affiliates. Estimate the dividend amounts using the pro rata share of net income and the changes in the investment accounts.

A schedule that reconciles net income to net cash provided by operating activities contained the following:

Net income	$796,000
Depreciation	130,000
Increase in noncash working capital	(15,000)

Note: The increase in noncash working capital is the net change in current assets and liabilities other than cash.

Given the available data, complete the reconciliation of net income to cash from operations.

11-58 Intercorporate Investments and Ethics

▶▶ **OBJECTIVE 4**

Lee Adsitt and Alex Wiren were best friends at a small undergraduate college and they fought side by side in the jungles of Vietnam. On returning to the United States, they went their separate ways to pursue MBA degrees, Lee to a prestigious East Coast business school and Alex to an equally prestigious West Coast school. However, 40 years later, their paths crossed again.

By 2003, Alex had become president and CEO of Hayden Electronics after 15 years with the firm. Lee had started working for American Airlines, but had left after 9 years to start his own firm, Adsitt Transport. In April 2008, Adsitt Transport was near bankruptcy when Lee approached his old friend for help. Alex Wiren answered his friend's call, and Hayden Electronics bought 19% of the stock of Adsitt Transport.

In 2013, Adsitt was financially stable and Hayden was struggling. In fact, Alex Wiren thought his job as CEO might be in jeopardy if Hayden did not report income up to expectations. Late in 2013, Alex approached Lee with a request—quadruple Adsitt's dividends so Hayden could recognize $760,000 of investment income. Hayden had listed its investment in Adsitt as an available-for-sale security. Although Adsitt had never paid dividends of more than 25% of net income, and it had plenty of use for excess cash, Lee felt a deep obligation to Alex. Thus, he agreed to a $4 million dividend on net income of $4.5 million.

1. Why does the dividend policy of Adsitt Transport affect the income of Hayden Electronics? Is this consistent with the intent of the accounting principles relating to the market and equity methods for intercorporate investments? Explain.
2. Comment on the ethical issues in the arrangements between Lee Adsitt and Alex Wiren.

Collaborative Learning Exercise

▶▶ OBJECTIVE 5

11-59 International Perspective on Consolidation

Form groups of four to six students. Each student should pick a country from the following list:

Australia	Japan
United Kingdom	Sweden
India	China

Find out the policy on consolidating financial statements in the country you select. If possible, find out when consolidated statements were first required and what criteria are used to determine what subsidiaries should be consolidated. If the country has adopted IFRS, see if you can determine how IFRS differs from prior, local GAAP.

Meet as a group and share your information. What generalizations can you draw from the policies you found? Propose explanations for the differences you find among countries. Discuss the effect of consolidation policies on comparisons of financial statements across countries.

Analyzing and Interpreting Financial Statements

▶▶ OBJECTIVE 5

11-60 Financial Statement Research

Select five companies in any industry. Review each company's financial statements to determine whether an acquisition occurred during the most recent year. For each acquisition, identify as much as possible concerning each of the following:

1. What was the purchase price? Did the acquiring company use cash or stock?
2. What percentage of the target was purchased?
3. Can you determine whether the acquired company was previously either a customer or a supplier of the acquiring company? If so, which one?

▶▶ OBJECTIVES 2, 7

11-61 Starbucks' Annual Report

Starbucks includes the following items on its balance sheet for the year ended October 2, 2011, and October 3, 2010 (amounts in millions):

	2011	2010
Short-term investments—Available-for-sale securities	$855.0	$236.5
Short-term investments—Trading securities	47.6	49.2
Long-term investments—Available-for-sale securities	107.0	191.8
Equity and cost investments	372.3	341.5

The investments are carried at fair value, except for the Equity and Cost Investments.

1. Estimate the effect on 2011 earnings before tax from changes in value of the investments that are accounted for as Available-for-Sale Securities.
2. Estimate the effect on 2011 earnings before tax from changes in value of the investments that are accounted for as Trading Securities. While this is an unrealistic assumption for trading securities, assume that no trading securities were sold or acquired in 2011.
3. Starbucks' goodwill increased from $262.4 million at the beginning of fiscal 2011 to $321.6 million at the end of the year. Starbucks did not recognize any goodwill impairment charges during fiscal 2011. What is the most likely cause of the $59.2 million increase in goodwill?

▶▶ OBJECTIVES 2, 4, 7

11-62 Analyzing Financial Statements Using the Internet

Go to www.ford.com to locate the Ford home page. Click on the More Ford link near the top of the page. Select Investors from the drop-down menu. Then select the most recent annual report under the category Financial Reports and SEC Filings.

Answer these questions about Ford.

1. Does Ford prepare consolidated statements and what is the basis for consolidation?
2. How does Ford determine the companies it reports on the equity method?
3. What information does Ford provide about the investments that it accounts for using the equity method? Consider the balance sheet, income statement, and footnotes in your answer.
4. What information does Ford provide about its marketable securities shown on the consolidated balance sheets? Can you tell which ones are classified as trading securities?
5. Did Ford include any goodwill on its balance sheet? Why would Ford want to pay more than the value of the net assets of a company it acquired?

12 Financial Statement Analysis

NO DOUBT YOU HAVE seen the Nike trademark Swoosh on a wide range of products, from running shoes to swimwear to golf accessories. Nike is the world's #1 shoemaker, designing and selling shoes for a variety of sports, including football, basketball, baseball, soccer, golf, tennis, and running. Footwear sales comprised almost 56% of Nike's 2012 revenue, up from 52% in 2008. The remaining 44% of Nike's 2012 revenue came from the sale of athletic apparel and equipment.

Nike operates on a May 31 fiscal year-end. During the 12 months ending May 31, 2012, Nike shares traded at a low of $78.58 on August 19, 2011, and at a high of $114.40 on May 3, 2012, representing a 46% increase from low to high. Google Finance reported a closing price for Nike of $108.18 on May 31, 2012, as compared with a price of $57.05 at the close of fiscal 2009. This represents an increase of almost 90%. During June 2012 the price fell to $87.78, a drop of 19%. What caused the fluctuation in Nike's stock price? Can the fluctuation be explained by changes in Nike's sales or earnings? Or are other factors at work? Did Nike's competitors experience similar fluctuations in stock price? Or is the variance unique to Nike?

In prior chapters, we concentrated on how to collect financial data and how to prepare and evaluate financial statements. In financial statement analysis, we interpret these financial data to more fully understand the story they tell about the company. However, understanding Nike requires more than just understanding its financial statements. You must be attuned to economy-wide forces such as the rate of inflation, demographic shifts, interest rate changes, and unemployment, as well as industry- and firm-specific factors. When we talk about the economy, it is the global economy. Nike manufactures its products primarily in China, Vietnam, and Indonesia. While almost 37% of Nike's sales occur in North America, China accounts for approximately 11%, and emerging markets account for 14%. Sales in both China and the emerging markets sector are growing much faster than in North America. North American sales increased by 17% from 2011 to 2012, compared with a 23% increase for China and a 25% increase in emerging markets. In understanding Nike's current and future performance,

---

▶▶ **LEARNING OBJECTIVES** *After studying this chapter, you should be able to:*

1 Locate and use sources of information about company performance.

2 Analyze the performance of a company using trend analysis, common-size financial statements, and segment disclosures.

3 Use basic financial ratios to guide your thinking.

4 Evaluate corporate performance using various metrics, including ROA, ROE, and EVA.

5 Calculate EPS when a company has preferred stock or dilutive securities.

6 Understand the nature of irregular items and how to adjust for them.

7 Use financial information to help assess a company's value.

separate analyses of domestic and international growth and profitability will improve the accuracy of forecasts for the whole company.

Let's look at the performance of the stock market during the 12 months from the end of May 2011 to May 31, 2012, to help evaluate the fluctuation in Nike's stock price. Looking at market-level data underscores the importance of market-wide factors on a company's stock price. The S&P 500 stood at 1,345 on May 31, 2011, and at 1,310 a year later. But that 2.6% decline hardly tells the story. During the 12 months ending May 31, 2012, the S&P hit a low of 1,099 on October 3, 2011, and a high of 1,419 on April 2, 2012, which represents a 29% increase from low to high. Recall that during that same 12 months Nike's stock went up by 46% from its low (on August 19, 2011) to its high (on May 3, 2012). This suggests that the fluctuation in Nike's stock price was partly the result of overall market effects and partly due to industry- and firm-specific factors.

At the firm-specific level, Nike's sales revenue was up almost 16% in fiscal year 2012 relative to 2011. In the best of circumstances revenue increases translate into similar or higher increases in earnings. However, Nike's earnings were up only 4% in that same time period. Why did Nike's earnings grow more slowly than sales? The financial statements and related disclosures reveal several factors that contributed to the slower growth in earnings. While Nike initiated price increases and enjoyed lower air freight costs, these benefits were more than offset by increased product costs, higher discounts on close-out sales, an unanticipated customs assessment, and a higher effective tax rate.

People perform financial analysis for different reasons. Suppliers want to see if a customer is likely to be able to pay for items purchased on credit or if it can afford a price increase. Customers want to know if a company will still be operating a year from now and therefore

Nike is the largest seller of athletic footwear and athletic apparel in the world. The company sells products to retail accounts, directly to consumers through Nike-owned retail stores and internet sales, and through a mix of independent distributors and licensees. The company operates more than 400 retail stores outside the United States. A Nike store in Beijing is pictured.

financial statement analysis
Using financial data to assess some aspect of a company's performance.

able to honor a warranty. Managers, creditors, investors, and the CEO's mother all have their reasons for reading the statements. Regardless of your interest in the company, **financial statement analysis** involves using financial data to assess some aspect of a company's performance. Our focus is on the investor. Investors read financial statements either to check on their current investments or to plan future investments. They analyze these statements and other material to determine whether their beliefs about the company have been borne out and to develop expectations about the future.

How do we use financial statements to forecast the future? We begin with a solid understanding of the company's past performance. Throughout the book we have shown you various ratios and other tools of analysis, so you should have some understanding of how to assess performance. This chapter integrates the tools you have already seen and teaches you several new ones as we focus on the techniques investors use to improve their investment decisions. ●

Sources of Information about Companies

▶▶ OBJECTIVE 1

Locate and use sources of information about company performance.

Publicly available information takes many forms. The now familiar annual report is one form, known for its completeness and its reliability, given the attestation of an independent registered public accounting firm or auditor. In addition to the financial statements (income statement, balance sheet, statement of cash flows, and statement of stockholders' equity), annual reports usually contain the following:

1. Footnotes to the financial statements
2. A summary of significant accounting policies used
3. Management's discussion and analysis (MD&A) of the financial results
4. The report of the Independent Registered Public Accounting Firm
5. Management's statement of its responsibility for the financial statements
6. Management's report on internal controls
7. Selected comparative financial data for a series of years
8. Narrative information about the company

These sections of the annual report are important to financial analysis. Footnotes are so important that at the bottom of most financial statements there is language that directs the reader to the footnotes. Some analysts and other financial statement users read the footnotes and the MD&A before examining the financial statements themselves. These two sections of the annual report provide a context for interpreting the numbers reported in the financial statements.

In addition to the annual reports distributed to shareholders, companies with stock traded in the United States must also submit reports to the SEC. Some of the most important are the annual 10-K, the quarterly 10-Q, and the periodic 8-K, which is issued whenever material events occur. Form 10-K contains information not included in the annual report to shareholders, although many companies now provide the full 10-K to shareholders. Form 10-Q includes unaudited quarterly financial statements, so it provides more timely, although less complete, information than does the annual report and 10-K. Form 8-K notifies investors of any unscheduled material event, such as a change in the board of directors or management, a change in auditors, significant asset sales, or bankruptcy.

In addition, companies issue proxy statements in connection with shareholder meetings. These statements contain useful information such as the qualifications of board members, executive compensation and stock option awards, and audit fee disclosures. The SEC requires other reports for specific events, such as the issuance of common shares or debt. All SEC filings are available to investors. See the SEC Web site (www.sec.gov) for easy access to EDGAR (**E**lectronic **D**ata **G**athering, **A**nalysis, and **R**etrieval), the SEC electronic information source. Many companies include links to their SEC filings from their corporate Web sites.

Companies issue annual reports and SEC Form 10-K and 10-Q filings well after the events being reported have occurred. For example, a company classified by the SEC as a large accelerated filer must file its 10-K within 60 days after the end of the fiscal year and its 10-Q within 40 days after the quarter end. In addition to 8-Ks, you can find more timely information in periodic company press releases, which highlight company developments. The Internet allows almost immediate access to company press releases, which are generally available on company Web sites. In addition, most companies hold public quarterly conference calls with security analysts to discuss new developments and make these calls accessible to investors via Webcasts.

Numerous online services compile and sell databases of press releases and other corporate information. Investors also rely on articles in the general financial press such as the *Wall Street Journal*, *BusinessWeek*, *Forbes*, *Fortune*, and *Barron's*. Trade and industry-specific publications and Web sites are useful information sources. For example, the *Industry Standard* (www.thestandard.com) and *Red Herring* (www.redherring.com) concentrate on news about high-tech companies. Services such as **Value Line**, **Moody's**, and **Standard and Poor's** (S&P) provide investors with useful information, as do credit agencies such as **Dun & Bradstreet**. In addition, stockbrokers prepare company analyses for their clients, and private investment services and newsletters supply analysts' reports and stock recommendations to their subscribers. **Google** is one of several sources of free information (www.GoogleFinance.com). On its Web site you can find current share prices and trading volumes, historical charts of that data, and summary financial information. You can also have Google push information to your e-mail on specific companies, industries, and so forth.

The Internet has transformed investing. Investors can purchase and sell securities electronically without ever talking to a broker. Internet sites provide continuous information about security prices and access to analysts' reports on various industries and securities. Rapid dissemination of information made possible by the Internet can help investors make investment decisions, but it can also quickly spread false rumors as illustrated in the Business First box on page 536.

Some investors request even more information than the public data described above. Banks or other creditors making multimillion-dollar loans may ask for a set of projected financial statements or other estimates of predicted results, known as **pro forma statements**. Although we can gain much information from other sources, our discussion focuses on analyzing the information contained in the financial statements themselves.

pro forma statements
A set of projected financial statements or other estimates of predicted results.

Objectives of Financial Statement Analysis

Different types of investors expect different types of returns. If you are a stockholder, you expect an increase in the value of the stock you hold. If you have invested in a company with a history of paying dividends, you also expect a dividend. If you have loaned the firm money, you expect to receive interest and the return of the amount loaned. Although the types of returns they expect are different, equity investors and creditors both risk not receiving the expected return. Therefore, both stockholders and creditors use financial statement analysis to help (1) predict expected returns, and (2) assess the risks associated with those returns.

The primary concerns of creditors are short-term liquidity and long-term solvency. **Short-term liquidity** refers to an organization's ability to meet current payments, such as interest, wages, and taxes, as they become due. **Long-term solvency** refers to a company's ability to generate enough cash to repay long-term debts as they mature.

short-term liquidity
An organization's ability to meet current payments, such as interest, wages, and taxes, as they become due.

In contrast, equity investors, while concerned about liquidity and solvency, are typically more interested in profitability and future security prices. Why? Because dividend payments depend, in part, on how profitable operations are, and stock prices depend on the market's assessment of the company's future prospects. Investors gain when they receive dividends and when the value of their securities rises. Rising profits spur both events, and declining profits have negative implications for both dividend policy and stock price. A struggling company may elect to reduce or even terminate its dividend. The 2008–2009 economic downturn, which led to falling profits and declining share prices, caused many companies, even some of the largest and best-known companies, to reduce or suspend dividends. For example, after 71 years of steady or increasing dividends, **General Electric** reduced its dividend by 68% in 2009 as its stock price fell from nearly $42 in late 2007 to a low of $7.06 the week of March 2, 2009. Since then, the annual dividend has been increased three times from $0.40 per share to $0.68 per share. At about the same time, **Dow Chemical**, a company that had never decreased its dividend in its 114-year history, reduced its dividend by 64%. This contributed to a 17% drop in Dow's share price in the week of the dividend announcement. Dividend cuts were also common in Europe during this time period. For example, in May 2009 **BT Group Plc**, the United Kingdom's largest phone company, cut its dividend by 89%.

long-term solvency
An organization's ability to generate enough cash to repay long-term debts as they mature.

Not all companies that experience a downturn in earnings cut dividends. While **Nike**'s stock price declined as income fell in fiscal year 2009, Nike actually increased the per share dividend to $0.98 in 2009 from $0.875 in 2008. Also, note that not all successful companies pay dividends.

BUSINESS FIRST

TRUTH, LIES, AND RUMORS IN THE DIGITAL AGE

"A lie can travel halfway around the world while the truth is still putting on its shoes." —attributed to *Mark Twain*

Web sites and focused business newscasts have increased the speed with which information reaches the markets. In addition, the widespread use of smart phones and similar devices allows access to such information anytime and anyplace, enabling prompt action. However, the availability and widespread dissemination of information does not make it trustworthy. For example, Apple shares opened at a price of $104.00 on October 3, 2008. That day the CNN citizen journalism Web site, iReport.com, reported that Apple CEO Steve Jobs was rushed to the hospital after a major heart attack. The rumor, which was false, caused Apple's shares to drop to an 18-month low of $94.65. While the market partially recovered, closing at $97.07, many investors took losses as they sold on the downslide.

As the world's largest company by market capitalization, Apple is often in the midst of information and misinformation. Speculation about an Apple TV has been rampant for some time, but on Sunday, May 13, 2012, the rumors took on substance as Apple became linked to the alleged purchase of a German company, Loewe, which makes sleek TV sets and speakers. The price action on Monday, May 14, was not in Apple, but in Loewe's, which opened at €6.0, up more than 40% from €4.28, the closing price the previous day. After numerous efforts to correct the record and deny the rumors, Loewe's price was still at €5.70 on May 18, although it was back to about €5.0 a month later.

Some erroneous information is released by people who hope to benefit. Mark Jakob fabricated a news release about Emulex, a designer, developer, and supplier of networking products. In the time period immediately after the news release, Mr. Jakob netted $241,000 in profit by trading on Emulex stock. However, he ultimately had to pay $455,642 to settle an SEC lawsuit against him and was sentenced to 44 months in prison.

Other situations result from a series of human and computer errors. One of the most bizarre tales of erroneous information involves United Airlines. An old *Chicago Tribune* article on the 2002 United Airlines bankruptcy filing resurfaced on the Internet on September 8, 2008. Traders reacted to this old bankruptcy announcement as though it were new information, triggering a sell-off of shares. United shares opened at $12.17 on September 8, 2008, and fell to a low of $3.00 within moments of the article being posted to the Bloomberg News service. NASDAQ officials briefly halted trading on the stock. Trading resumed after United issued a statement denying the rumor, and the shares closed at $10.92. See the stock price graph below.

How could this happen? An article in the *New York Times* reported that the problem began shortly after midnight on Sunday, September 7, 2008. A link to an article originally published in the *Chicago Tribune* in 2002 appeared in the "Most Viewed" section of the business page of a south Florida newspaper. A spokesperson

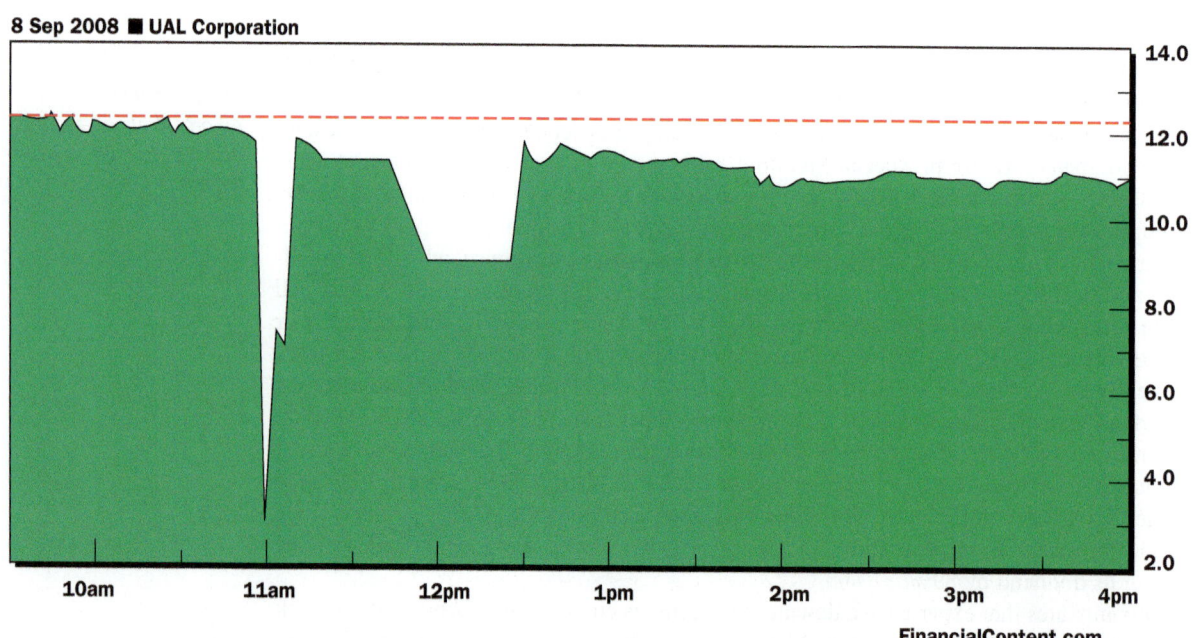

8 Sep 2008 ■ UAL Corporation

FinancialContent.com

for the *Chicago Tribune* claimed that a single click on the archived article in the middle of the night on a Sunday could have positioned it on the "Most Viewed" list. Within a minute, the automated scanning system of Google News located the link and followed it to the article, entitled "United Airlines Files for Bankruptcy," in the *South Florida Sun-Sentinel*'s archives. Google's system treated the article as though it was new.

On Monday morning, September 8, a researcher at an investment newsletter, *Income Securities Advisors, Inc. (ISA)*, did a Google search using the words "bankruptcy" and "2008." The search brought up the *South Florida Sun-Sentinel* Web site reference to the United Airlines bankruptcy filing. Neither the specific date of the article nor the actual date of the United bankruptcy filing appeared in the *Sun-Sentinel* article, and the

Web page, dated September 7, 2008, seemed current. The *ISA* researcher posted a summary of the article. Bloomberg has its own news group but also distributes stories from select third-party providers. Bloomberg distributed a news headline, citing the *South Florida Sun-Sentinel* article, and the share sell-off began.

These events demonstrates how quickly information, both factual and false, can be transmitted in the digital age.

Sources: R. Andrews, "Apple TV Rumor Mill Makes Millions as iTV 'Confirmed,'" May 14, 2012, PaidContent Web site; "United Incident Reinforces the Need for Web Strategy," September 15, 2008, *PR Week*, p. 8; N. Cohen, "Spinning a Web of Lies at Digital Speed," *New York Times*, October 13, 2008, Section B, p. 3; M. Helft, "How Series of Mistakes Hurt Shares of United," *New York Times*, September 15, 2008, Section C, p. 1; *WSJ* Staff Reporter, "Emulex Stock Saboteur Agrees to Pay $455,642 to Settle SEC Civil Suit," *Wall Street Journal*, July 25, 2001, p. B4; B. Snyder, "United Stock Tanks on False Bankruptcy Rumors" (http://industry.bnet.com/travel/1000193/united-stock-tanks-on-false-bankruptcy-rumors/).

For example, despite its enormous profitability, Microsoft did not pay a dividend until 2002, and Google has yet to pay a dividend.

Profitability is important not only to equity investors but also to creditors. Why? Because the profitable operations that allow for dividends and drive stock prices to higher levels also provide the cash to repay loans and finance growth. Investors and creditors are concerned with the future, while financial statements deal solely with past events. But trends in past sales, operating expenses, and net income often continue, so financial statement analysis of past performance is often a good indicator of future performance.

Evaluating Trends and Components of the Business

The next two sections discuss two of the most popular techniques for analyzing financial statements—trend analysis and common-size financial statements. We apply these two techniques to the same company, Nike, at both the total firm and the segment level. A third technique, ratio analysis, should already be familiar because you have encountered ratios in earlier chapters. Nevertheless, a later section of this chapter consolidates and adds to your knowledge of ratio analysis.

> ▶▶ OBJECTIVE 2
>
> Analyze the performance of a company using trend analysis, common-size financial statements, and segment disclosures.

Trend Analysis

Annual reports contain balance sheets for the current and prior year, and they contain the other financial statements for the current and previous 2 years. In addition, they include key financial data for at least the last 5 years and often for up to 10 years. In evaluating trends, we may or may not find these numbers to be adequate. Supplemental sources provide longer and richer access to information by archiving and adjusting older data. For example, Capital IQ Compustat provides 20 years of financial information extracted from financial statements. Mergent Online is a subscriber database that provides Internet access to complete company financial data, along with other information. Free online databases such as Reuters, Google, and Yahoo! offer historical records of select financial performance measures, and you can access SEC filings at www.sec.gov.

In **trend analysis** you compare financial trends and changes from one year to the next and identify patterns. You then ask why that trend exists and whether you expect it to continue. If sales have been growing steadily but inventories have not, can this continue? Will future

> *trend analysis*
>
> *An analysis technique that compares financial trends and changes from one year to the next and identifies patterns that have occurred in the past.*

inventory growth require substantial additional investment? If inventories have been growing steadily but sales have not, why is the company holding so much inventory?

Trend analysis prompts investors to ask what could cause the trends to end. The housing and credit crisis of the mid- to late 2000s saw an unprecedented decline in interest rates as the Federal Reserve Bank attempted to jump-start the slumping economy. The Fed intends to keep rates low until 2014, but if the economy recovers, will the Fed raise interest rates? And if so, by how much? Rising interest rates hurt many industries. Banks must pay more for the money that they lend. Automobile manufacturers are hurt because car buyers face higher car payments when interest rates rise and therefore buy fewer cars. The same analysis follows for builders of new houses. In contrast, rising interest rates can help companies such as The Home Depot, which serves the homeowners' needs for home improvement materials. Why? Because people who want a nicer home may conclude that interest rates are too high and decide to remodel their existing home. These examples illustrate how you might think about trends in sales and profits in particular industries.

To see how trend analysis works, let's examine the income statements and balance sheets of Nike as shown in Exhibits 12-1 and 12-2. The first two columns show Nike's information for 2012 and 2011. The third column shows the dollar amount of the change in each item from 2011 to 2012. Finally, the fourth column shows the percentage change, computed as follows:

$$\text{Percentage change 2011 to 2012} = \frac{2012 \text{ amount} - 2011 \text{ amount}}{2011 \text{ amount}} \times 100$$

For example, Nike's Revenues increased by $3,266 million or 15.7%:

$$\text{Percentage change} = \frac{\$24,128 - \$20,862}{\$20,862} \times 100 = 15.7\%$$

At the same time, Nike's Cost of Sales increased $2,303 million or 20.3%:

$$\text{Percentage change} = \frac{\$13,657 - \$11,354}{\$11,354} \times 100 = 20.3\%$$

You can add or subtract the dollar change amounts in the third column to obtain meaningful subtotals. However, you must use care when considering the effect of increases or decreases on

EXHIBIT 12-1

Nike, Inc.

Consolidated Statements of Income ($ in millions, except per share data and percentages)

	For the Year Ended May 31, 2012	For the Year Ended May 31, 2011	Increase (Decrease)	
			Amount	Percentage*
Revenues	$24,128	$20,862	$3,266	15.7%
Cost of sales	13,657	11,354	2,303	20.3%
Gross margin	10,471	9,508	963	10.1%
Selling and administrative expense	7,431	6,693	738	11.0%
Interest expense, net	3	4	(1)	(25.0%)
Other expense (income), net	54	(33)	87	NM
Income before income taxes	2,983	2,844	139	4.9%
Income taxes	760	711	49	6.9%
Net income	$ 2,223	$ 2,133	$ 90	4.2%
Basic earnings per share	$ 4.83	$ 4.48	$ .35	7.8%
Diluted earnings per share	$ 4.73	$ 4.39	$ .34	7.7%
Dividends declared per common share	$ 1.39	$ 1.20	$ .19	15.8%

*Percentage column numbers cannot be added. NM indicates not meaningful.

EXHIBIT 12-2

Nike, Inc.

Consolidated Balance Sheets ($ in millions, except percentages)

	May 31, 2012	May 31, 2011	Increase (Decrease)	
			Amount	Percentage*
Assets:				
Cash and equivalents	$ 2,317	$ 1,955	$ 362	18.5%
Short-term investments	1,440	2,583	(1,143)	(44.3%)
Accounts receivable, net	3,280	3,138	142	4.5%
Inventories	3,350	2,715	635	23.4%
Deferred income taxes	274	312	(38)	(12.2%)
Prepaid expenses and other current assets	870	594	276	46.5%
Total current assets	11,531	11,297	234	2.1%
Property, plant, and equipment, net	2,279	2,115	164	7.8%
Identifiable intangible assets, net	535	487	48	9.9%
Goodwill	201	205	(4)	(2.0%)
Deferred income taxes and other assets	919	894	25	2.8%
Total assets	$15,465	$14,998	$ 467	3.1%
Liabilities and Shareholders' Equity:				
Current portion of long-term debt	$ 49	$ 200	$ (151)	(75.5%)
Notes payable	108	187	(79)	(42.2%)
Accounts payable	1,588	1,469	119	8.1%
Accrued liabilities	2,053	1,985	68	3.4%
Income taxes payable	67	117	(50)	(42.7%)
Total current liabilities	3,865	3,958	(93)	(2.3%)
Long-term debt	228	276	(48)	(17.4%)
Deferred income taxes and other liabilities	991	921	70	7.6%
Shareholders' Equity:				
Common stock at stated value				
Class A convertible	—	—	—	—
Class B	3	3	0.0	0.0%
Capital in excess of stated value	4,641	3,944	697	17.7%
Accumulated other comprehensive income	149	95	54	56.8%
Retained earnings	5,588	5,801	(213)	(3.7%)
Total shareholders' equity	10,381	9,843	538	5.5%
Total liabilities and shareholders' equity	$15,465	$14,998	$ 467	3.1%

*Percentage column numbers cannot be added.

Source: Reuters (www.reuters.com).

revenue and expense accounts. Increases in revenues and increases in expenses have offsetting effects on net income. In Exhibit 12-1, the increase of $3,266 million in Revenues is offset by the increase in Cost of Sales of $2,303 million. While the sign of the change in Revenues and the sign of the change in Cost of Sales are both positive, they have opposite effects on gross margin and net income. The increase in Revenues increases the gross margin. The increase in Cost of Sales decreases the gross margin. In dollar terms, the increase in Revenues of $3,266 million exceeds the increase in Cost of Sales of $2,303 million, resulting in a $963 million increase in gross margin. However, the percentage increase in gross margin is only 10.1% compared with the revenue growth of 15.7%. This is troubling. Analysts would hope to see revenue growth that is more rapid than the growth in cost of sales. When cost of sales grows more rapidly than revenues, it means that the company is facing cost increases that it cannot fully pass on to its customers. It is not benefiting from economies of scale.

Similarly, Selling and Administrative Expense increased by $738 million or 11.0%. This increase in Selling and Administrative Expense was less than the 15.7% increase in Revenue and suggests that the company was able to contain these costs in the face of increasing sales. Note that although you can add the changes in dollars as you move down the column, you cannot add the changes stated in percentage terms.

Finally, nonoperating activities had a modest impact on the income statement in 2011 and 2012. Other Expense (income), net changed from income of $33 million in 2011 to expense of $54 million in 2012. This represents an increase in net expense of $87 million from 2011 to 2012. Interest Expense, net decreased from $4 million in 2011 to $3 million in 2012. This represents a small change in terms of dollars but a 25% decrease when viewed as a percentage.

In its income statement, Nike does not distinguish between operating and nonoperating revenues and expenses. Many companies make such a distinction. They label selling and administrative expense as operating and would likely classify other expense (income) and interest expense as nonoperating. However, there is not universal agreement on the distinction between operating and nonoperating activities. When you are comparing companies, it is important to recognize differences in classification. Often, operating activities are the more persistent and material aspects of corporate performance and receive more attention from analysts.

We need both dollar and percentage changes to identify trends and understand their true meaning. For example, the 15.7% Revenue increase of $3,266 million is associated with a smaller $2,303 million increase in Cost of Sales. As noted above, however, the fact that revenue grew by a larger dollar amount is not the most important fact. The disturbing fact is that the Cost of Sales grew at a higher rate (20.3%) than did revenue. In this case, the percentage information is most relevant to the analyst.

Although it is always possible to compute and interpret dollar changes, some percentage changes are not meaningful. Look at Exhibit 12-1. For example, Nike nets other income and expense into a single line item on the income statement. As noted previously, the net amount was income of $33 million in 2011 and an expense of $54 million in 2012. It is not meaningful to compute a percentage change in this case. This $87 million increase in net expenses is designated as not meaningful (NM) in the percentage change column because changes from income to expense are hard to measure and evaluate on a percentage basis. Another problem computing percentage change amounts arises when a company has a balance in a particular account that is not present in the preceding year. While not an issue for Nike in the 2 years under consideration, you don't have to look far to find an example in Nike's earlier financial statements. Nike included three expense items on the 2009 income statement that did not appear on the 2008 income statement: Restructuring Charges, Goodwill Impairment, and Intangible and Other Asset Impairment. If you try to compute the percentage increase between 2008 and 2009, the denominator of the percentage change calculation is zero and the percentage is undefined.

So far, our discussion of trends has focused on the income statement. However, balance sheet trends are also important. In Exhibit 12-2, the 2.3% decrease in total current liabilities and 17.4% decrease in long-term debt are favorable when compared with the 2.1% increase in total current assets and 3.1% increase in total assets. But it is not the percentage changes alone that are important. The changes suggest the important fact that assets grew without a corresponding increase in liabilities. It is evident that Nike relies primarily upon shareholders' equity to finance its activity. In fact, shareholders' equity grew 5.5% during the year, enough to finance all of the asset growth and to contribute to the reduction in current liabilities and long-term debt.

Changes on the income statement and the balance sheet should also be examined in conjunction with each other. From Exhibit 12-1, we observe that Nike experienced a 15.7% increase in revenue in 2012 relative to 2011. Increased sales activity frequently results in increased levels of accounts receivable if the company sells on account and increased levels of inventory if management wants to be sure it has sufficient product to deliver to the customer. This suggests that the observed increase in revenue on the income statement may be accompanied by increases in accounts receivable and inventory. Analysis of Nike's balance sheets in Exhibit 12-2 reveals that Accounts Receivable increased 4.5% and Inventories increased 23.4%. The relative size of the change in receivables is good news. The 4.5% increase in receivables is much smaller than the growth in revenue, suggesting that the company did not increase revenue by issuing excessive or questionable credit. However, the 23.4% increase in inventories is disturbing since they increased at a faster rate than revenue. Moreover, inventories grew more rapidly than did cost of sales. This suggests that not only did Nike fail to pass rising costs on to its customers by increasing product prices but also that it was investing in more units of inventory to support its sales levels.

Changes in dollar amounts and percentages such as those referenced in the previous paragraph help analysts see patterns. Although recognizing patterns is key, understanding what caused those patterns is even more important. What possible explanations exist for the changes in various financial statement accounts, such as sales revenue, inventory, and receivables? Where would we look for answers? One source used by analysts is the section of the company's annual report and 10-K called the **management discussion and analysis (MD&A)**. In the United States, the SEC dictates the content of the MD&A. It concentrates on explaining the major changes in the company's operating results, liquidity, and capital resources. The MD&A includes, but is not limited to, disclosures about a company's capital resources and liquidity, including off-balance sheet arrangements and capital expenditures; the results of operations, including discussion of trends in sales and expenses and an explanation of any unusual or infrequent events; disclosures about contractual obligations and commitments and trading activities; discussion of critical accounting policies and estimates; and the impact of adoption of new accounting policies.

management discussion and analysis (MD&A)
A section of the annual report and 10-K, the content of which is dictated by the SEC, that concentrates on explaining the major changes in operating results, liquidity, and capital resources.

Let's return to the relationship of revenues, cost of sales, inventory, and receivables and see if we can explain the trends in these financial statement items. Nike discusses several issues surrounding the 15.7% growth in revenue. One factor is how currencies change in value. Nike reports its results in U.S. Dollars. What happens when sales occur outside the United States? For example, when sales occur in China the currency is the Renminbi (RMB), and the RMB appreciated relative to the dollar during the year ended May 31, 2012. Each sale in China translates into more revenue in dollars in 2012 than it did in 2011. Overall, Nike revealed that on a currency neutral basis, revenue was up only 14%, so approximately 2% of the revenue growth came from currency changes.

Analyzing revenue growth requires that we understand the sources of revenue. For example, Nike reports revenue by product line. The primary product lines are footwear, apparel, and equipment. Revenue grew at different rates across these segments: equipment revenues increased by 18%, followed by footwear at 17%, and apparel at 15%. Nike also reports its results by geographic area. The largest geographic area was North America, which accounted for $8.8 billion in sales in 2012 or 36.6% of total revenue. The fastest growing region was Emerging Markets, which grew by 25% but only accounted for $3.4 billion or 14.1% of total revenue. Overall, Nike revealed that revenues increased due to price increases but noted that these increases were not enough to offset higher product costs from its suppliers, higher discounts on close-out sales, and increased spending on the digital business. As a result, gross margins only increased by 10.1%.

On the balance sheet, changes in accounts receivable and inventories link closely to revenue changes. In this instance Nike was able to control accounts receivable well. They increased by only 4.5% in 2012. Inventories, however, increased by 23.4%, notably more than the revenue increase. The MD&A reveals that the increase was attributable in part to higher costs per unit of product. There were also significant increases in the number of units in inventory, due partly to the increase in the number of Nike Brand stores from 487 in 2011 to 557 in 2012.

What additional questions arise from analyzing trends in Nike's financial statements? Let's start by considering the income statement in Exhibit 12-1. As you already know, Nike's Revenues and Cost of Sales both increased in 2012. The $3,266 million increase in Revenues outpaced the $2,303 million increase in Cost of Sales. So the company's gross margin, as measured in dollars, was $963 million greater in 2012 than in 2011. At this point, it appears that Nike is on track to report higher net income in 2012 because the gross margin is up 10.1%. However, closer scrutiny of the income statement reveals that net income in 2012 was up only 4.2%. How do we explain this? Selling and administrative expenses increased by 11.0%, a more rapid rate of increase than gross margin, putting downward pressure on the growth in net income. A major contributing factor was the change in Other Expense (Income), net, which went from income of $33 million in 2011 to expense of $54 million in 2012. The key elements contributing to the $54 million expense in 2012 were foreign currency losses and a charge for restructuring activity in Western Europe. The foreign currency issues are complex. Earlier we saw that foreign currency changes enhanced revenue growth by 2%, but the Other Expense item indicates that foreign currency exchange rates also produced some increased costs (foreign currency losses). The MD&A indicated that the two largely offset each other.

Net income increased only 4.2%. But earnings per share (EPS) increased by almost 8% on both a basic and fully diluted basis. The MD&A reveals that the larger percentage increase in EPS arose from the continuation of the share repurchase program authorized in 2008, which approved repurchase of $5 billion in Nike shares. During 2012, the number of outstanding shares in Nike decreased by 3% with a corresponding increase in EPS.

Examination of the balance sheet in Exhibit 12-2 also raises some interesting questions. Why did Short-Term Investments decrease by 44.3%? Does this represent a change in investment strategy? Why did the Current Portion of Long-Term Debt decrease by 75.5% and Notes Payable decrease 42.2%? Has there been a change in financing strategy? Why did total current assets increase by 2.1% while total current liabilities decreased by 2.3%? Has there been a change in working capital management? Why did Identifiable Intangible Assets increase by 9.9% and Goodwill decrease by 2.0%? The answers to these questions say a lot about how management runs a company, how it will perform in the future, and whether it would be a good investment.

As indicated earlier, an analyst might note that Nike's revenues increased by 15.7% while net income increased by only 4.2%. When relationships do not look as good as expected, the question is whether a crisis exists. When relationships look better than expected, the question is whether the company can sustain the improvement. To see how trends develop over time, analysts often look at more than 2 years of financial information. Exhibit 12-3 shows a 5-year summary of key items for Nike, which enables you to compute a longer trend. For example, percentage changes in revenue are as follows:

2012	**2011**
$\dfrac{\$24{,}128 - \$20{,}862}{\$20{,}862} \times 100 = 15.7\%$	$\dfrac{\$20{,}862 - \$19{,}014}{\$19{,}014} \times 100 = 9.7\%$
2010	**2009**
$\dfrac{\$19{,}014 - \$19{,}176}{\$19{,}176} \times 100 = (.8\%)$	$\dfrac{\$19{,}176 - \$18{,}627}{\$18{,}627} \times 100 = 2.9\%$

The 15.7% increase in sales in 2012 is significantly higher than the sales growth experienced in prior years. This contrasts with 2010, when sales revenue fell by .8% despite the start of the economic recovery.

compound annual growth rate (CAGR)
Year-over-year growth rate over a specified period of time.

By applying the present value techniques of Chapter 9, we can compute the **compound annual growth rate (CAGR)** in sales for the 4-year period. The CAGR is the year-over-year growth rate over a specified period of time and can be computed using the following formula:

$$\text{CAGR} = \left[\frac{\text{Ending sales value}}{\text{Beginning sales value}}\right]^{(1/\#\text{ of years})} - 1$$

In this case, a 4-year annual growth rate for sales of 6.68% will increase revenue from the initial 2008 level of $18,627 to that of 2012, $24,128. We obtained this precise growth rate with a calculator. However, you can use the tables in Chapter 9 to approximate this value. The future value multiple is 2012 sales divided by 2008 sales, or ($24,128 ÷ $18,627) = 1.295324. In Table 9A-1, p. 425, the future value factor for 4 years for 6% is 1.2625 and for 7% is 1.3108. The observed value of 1.295324 falls about two-thirds of the way between these two values, so the CAGR must be close to 6.7%. The 6.68% value we computed qualifies. The growth rate in revenue will reflect multiple factors. As prices rise, there would be some growth just because of higher per unit prices, even if units sold did not grow. But units sold could also grow both because of increased sales in existing markets and existing stores and also because of new stores and new markets. In this 4-year period, annual growth rates varied from slightly negative in 2010 to very positive in 2012 as the world moved through and began to recover from the recession.

While the 6.68% may seem like a reasonable growth rate for Nike, given the short time period analyzed here, the impact of a single observation can have significant impact on the CAGR. If you use the CAGR for purposes of forecasting a company's future performance, you must exercise caution and not simply extrapolate from the past.

Common-Size Statements

common-size statements
Financial statements in which components are expressed as relative percentages.

To make it easier to evaluate a company's performance over time or to compare companies that differ in size, we often analyze income statements and balance sheets using **common-size statements** in which we express the components as relative percentages. Nike's common-size

EXHIBIT 12-3

Nike, Inc.

Selected Financial Data from Item 6 of the 2012 10-K
(*$ in millions, except per share data and financial ratios*)

	2012	2011	2010	2009	2008
Year ended May 31					
Revenues	$24,128	$20,862	$19,014	$19,176	$18,627
Gross Profit	10,471	9,508	8,800	8,604	8,387
Gross margin %	43.4%	45.6%	46.3%	44.9%	45.0%
Restructuring and impairment	—	—	—	596	—
Net income	2,223	2,133	1,907	1,487	1,883
Basic EPS	4.83	4.48	3.93	3.07	3.80
Diluted EPS	4.73	4.39	3.86	3.03	3.74
Cash dividends declared per share	1.39	1.20	1.06	0.98	0.875
Price range of common stock					
High	$114.40	$ 92.30	$ 78.55	$ 70.28	$ 70.60
Low	$ 78.58	$ 67.21	$ 50.16	$ 38.24	$ 51.50
At May 31					
Cash and equivalents	$ 2,317	$ 1,955	$ 3,079	$ 2,291	$ 2,134
Short term investments	1,440	2,583	2,067	1,164	642
Inventories	3,350	2,715	2,041	2,357	2,438
Working capital	7,666	7,339	7,595	6,457	5,518
Total assets	15,465	14,998	14,419	13,250	12,443
Long-term debt	228	276	446	437	441
Redeemable preferred stock	0.3	0.3	0.3	0.3	0.3
Shareholders' equity	10,381	9,843	9,754	8,693	7,825
Year-end stock price	108.18	84.45	72.38	57.05	68.37
Market capitalization	49,546	39,523	35,032	27,698	33,577
Financial Ratios					
Return on equity	22.0%	21.8%	20.7%	18.0%	25.4%

statements appear in Exhibit 12-4, side by side with the income statements from Exhibit 12-1 and balance sheets from Exhibit 12-2.

The income statement percentages are based on sales revenue equal to 100%. We express each element of the income statement as a percentage of revenues. In 2011, Nike's gross margin was 45.6%, falling to 43.4% in 2012. To better understand this gross margin, we might compare it with a specific competitor's values or with industry averages. For example, Under Armour reported a gross margin of 48.4%, and VF (whose many brands include The North Face and Wrangler) reported a gross margin of 45.8% for the year ended December 31, 2011. Both Under Armour and VF outperformed Nike on gross margin. The year-over-year decline in Nike's gross margin may not be alarming, but it is still worth determining if the margins of other firms in the industry are following a similar trend or if Nike's decline is unusual. In fact, both Under Armour and VF experienced declines of a similar magnitude. Although the use of common-size financial statements facilitates the comparison of different sized firms, size can matter by creating economies of scale. Moreover, finding truly comparable companies can be difficult because of differences in business mix. Under Armour is less about footwear and more about apparel, and it is also much smaller with revenue of only $1.5 billion versus Nike's $24 billion. Similarly, VF is smaller than Nike with revenue of $9.4 billion. VF's 10-K identifies it as a "worldwide leader in branded lifestyle apparel, footwear and related products." In this sense it resembles Nike. In addition to The North Face and Wrangler, VF brands include JanSport, Eagle Creek, Lee, and Nautica. In 2011, VF purchased Timberland, a footwear company to be sure, but not exactly a sports and athletic shoe company. In addition, differences other than size may need to

EXHIBIT 12-4

Nike, Inc.

Common-Size Statements (in millions, except percentages)

	For the Year Ended May 31			
	2012		2011	
Statements of Income				
Revenues	$24,128	100.0%	$20,862	100.0%
Cost of sales	13,657	56.6%	11,354	54.4%
Gross margin	10,471	43.4%	9,508	45.6%
Selling and administrative expense	7,431	30.8%	6,693	32.1%
Interest expense, net	3	0.0%	4	0.0%
Other expense (income), net	54	0.2%	(33)	(0.2)%
Income before income taxes	2,983	12.4%	2,844	13.6%
Income taxes	760	3.1%	711	3.4%
Net income	$ 2,223	9.2%	$ 2,133	10.2%

	May 31			
	2012		2011	
Balance Sheets				
Assets:				
Cash and equivalents	$ 2,317	15.0%	$ 1,955	13.0%
Short-term investments	1,440	9.3%	2,583	17.2%
Accounts receivable, net	3,280	21.2%	3,138	20.9%
Inventories	3,350	21.7%	2,715	18.1%
Deferred income taxes	274	1.8%	312	2.1%
Prepaid expenses and other current assets	870	5.6%	594	4.0%
Total current assets	11,531	74.6%	11,297	75.3%
Property, plant, and equipment, net	2,279	14.7%	2,115	14.1%
Identifiable intangible assets	535	3.5%	487	3.2%
Goodwill	201	1.3%	205	1.4%
Deferred income taxes and other assets	919	5.9%	894	6.0%
Total assets	$15,465	100.0%	$14,998	100.0%
Liabilities and Shareholders' Equity:				
Current portion of long-term debt	$ 49	0.3%	$ 200	1.3%
Notes payable	108	0.7%	187	1.2%
Accounts payable	1,588	10.3%	1,469	9.8%
Accrued liabilities	2,053	13.3%	1,985	13.2%
Income taxes payable	67	0.4%	117	0.8%
Total current liabilities	3,865	25.0%	3,958	26.4%
Long-term debt	228	1.5%	276	1.8%
Deferred income taxes and other liabilities	991	6.4%	921	6.1%
Shareholders' Equity:				
Common stock at stated value				
Class A convertible	—	—	—	—
Class B	3	0.0%	3	0.0%
Capital in excess of stated value	4,641	30.1%	3,944	26.3%
Accumulated other comprehensive income	149	1.0%	95	0.6%
Retained earnings	5,588	36.1%	5,801	38.7%
Total shareholders' equity	10,381	67.1%	9,843	65.6%
Total liabilities and shareholders' equity	$15,465	100.0%	$14,998	100.0%

Note: Some percentages are off by .1% due to rounding.

be considered. For example, a manufacturing company's choice of depreciation method affects the reported gross margin, because it impacts cost of sales.

The behavior of each expense in relation to changes in total revenue is often revealing and common-size financial statements facilitate this analysis. That is, which expenses go up or down as sales fluctuate? Consider Nike's cost of sales divided by revenues. We previously mentioned that the primary reason for the increase in cost of sales in dollar terms was the increase in product input costs from suppliers. This increase in the numerator partially explains why cost of sales increased as a percentage of sales. However, management also offered higher discounts on close-out sales to help manage inventory levels, which also increased the cost of sales as a percentage of sales by decreasing the denominator. Another major cost, selling and administrative expense, also increased in dollar terms year-over-year but represented a lower percentage of sales in 2012.

The balance sheet percentages in Exhibit 12-4 are based on total assets equal to 100%. We refer to them as **component percentages** because they measure each component of the financial statements as a percentage of the total. As with the income statement, you must look for changes in balance sheet relationships. Nike's percentage of current assets is relatively stable—74.6% of assets in 2012 and 75.3% in 2011. But within the current asset category there is notable fluctuation. Short-Term Investments decreased from $2,583 million or 17.2% of total assets in 2011 to $1,440.0 million or 9.3% of total assets in 2012. Why? We previously noted a surprisingly large increase in inventories, and Nike must pay for those inventories. Accounts payable grew much more slowly than did inventories, so short-term investments were likely liquidated to help fund the increased inventories and to increase the level of cash and equivalents. Prepaid Expenses and Other Current Assets also grew from 4.0% to 5.6% of assets, representing another draw on short-term investments. The mix of long-term assets was reasonably stable between 2011 and 2012.

On the liability side of the balance sheet, total current liabilities decreased slightly as a percentage of total assets. What caused this decrease? It is due in part to the $151 million decrease in the Current Portion of Long-term Debt (down from 1.3% to .3% of total assets) and the $79 million decrease in Notes Payable (down from 1.2% to .7% of total assets). Changes in noncurrent liabilities were minimal and largely offsetting. The remaining significant observation is the increase in funding from shareholders' equity. Equity increased from 65.6% of total assets to 67.1% from 2011 to 2012. This year-over-year increase is part of a longer-term trend. In 2008, equity was only 62.9% of total assets. In 2012, despite significant stock repurchases and the declaration of $639 million in cash dividends, total shareholders' equity increased. This is attributable primarily to Nike's $2,223 million in net income and the proceeds from the issuance of shares to employees under stock option plans.

component percentages
Elements of financial statements that express each component as a percentage of the total.

INTERPRETING FINANCIAL STATEMENTS

Common-size financial statements are useful in comparing companies that are significantly different in size. However, when you engage in comparisons across companies, you must consider the accounting choices made by the companies in arriving at the numbers presented on the financial statements. Name two accounting choices that impact the comparability of financial statements. You may need to think back to previous chapters to respond to this question.

Answer

1. Depreciation method. The use of straight-line versus accelerated depreciation methods can have a significant effect on the income statement and on property, plant, and equipment values on the balance sheet.

2. Lease structure. A lease agreement structured as a capital lease will increase both assets and liabilities relative to a lease structured as an operating lease. Income statement values also vary because an operating lease results in rent expense, whereas a capital lease results in depreciation expense and interest expense.

Segment Reporting

Our analysis of trends and common-size statements has focused on the company as a whole. However, it is often useful to analyze individual segments of the business. A required footnote to financial statements provides information on the sales revenue, profits, and assets of each operating segment.

When employing financial analysis techniques, analysts often consider the different business and geographic segments of a company's activities. In its 2012 annual report Nike divides its business in two ways, by product line and by geographic segments. It identifies four major product lines: footwear, apparel, equipment, and other. The footwear, apparel, and equipment categories include all the Nike-brand sales activity except Nike Golf. Nike classifies Nike Golf with non-Nike brand products such as those manufactured under the Cole Haan, Converse, Hurley, and Umbro brands in the "other" category.

In May 2012, Nike announced its intention to divest both the Cole Haan and Umbro brands in order to focus its efforts toward driving the growth of the Nike, Jordan, Converse, and Hurley brands. The press release provided important information to analysts by reporting that the brands to be divested had provided $797 million in revenue and a combined loss before interest and taxes of $43 million in 2012. To predict outcomes in 2013, analysts need to know what is stable and what is changing, and these announcements provided that information.

For segment reporting purposes, Nike breaks its Nike-brand activity into seven operating segments that reflect its internal organization as of May 31, 2012. It separates Nike-brand footwear, apparel, and equipment sales activity into six geographic regions (North America, Western Europe, Central & Eastern Europe, Greater China, Japan, and Emerging Markets) and one segment (the Global Brand Division) representing licensing businesses that are not part of a geographic operating segment. Nike's nonbrand products (along with Nike Golf) comprise an additional segment called Other Businesses.

The SEC requires companies to report their segments based on the way they manage the company. Companies change these management practices over time. For example, in 2009 Nike-brand activity had only four geographic regions; the United States, EMEA (Europe, Middle East, and Africa), Asia Pacific, and the Americas.

Panel A of Exhibit 12-5 displays revenues, earnings before net interest and taxes (EBNIT), and net income after taxes for the company as a whole as reported in Nike's 2012 annual report. EBNIT is the primary financial measure used by Nike to evaluate the performance of the operating segments. The ratios of EBNIT to sales and after-tax return on sales in panel A are computed from these figures and both are down significantly in 2012 relative to the prior 2 years. Without further information about operating segment results, these aggregate figures cannot answer questions such as the following: What contribution did each geographic segment or product line make to Nike's total revenue? What contribution did each segment make to Nike's net income? Are sales of one segment driving the change in EBNIT to sales or is the company experiencing reduced profitability in all segments?

Panel B of Exhibit 12-5 helps answer these questions by showing Nike's operating segment disclosures taken from footnote 17 of its 2012 annual report. Nike reports revenues and EBNIT for its six geographic segments, North America, Western Europe, Central & Eastern Europe, Greater China, Japan, and Emerging Markets, and its two other segments, Global Brand and Other Businesses.

Nike does not calculate the EBNIT to sales ratios by region as we do in panel B, but doing so provides useful information. Specifically, note that the return is much higher in Greater China than in other regions and that Western Europe fell noticeably in 2011 and 2012 as economic conditions in that region worsened. Analysts use such information to predict future revenues and income. Worsening or improvement of the economic environment in a region informs estimates of the growth in revenues and EBNIT in that region, which leads to improved forecasts for the company. Similarly, management uses segment information to guide strategic decisions, such as where to advertise, where to increase inventories, and where to open and close stores.

One of the first things you may notice is that aggregated segment revenues and EBNIT figures from panel B do not agree with the total revenue and EBNIT figures in panel A. For example, panel A reports 2012 revenues of $24,128 million and EBNIT of $2,986 million, whereas panel B reports 2012 revenues of $24,167 million and EBNIT of $3,902 million. Why? For internal reporting, Nike does not allocate activity attributable to the corporate office to the segments. This makes the aggregate segment revenues and expenses differ from the overall corporate totals.

Nike's 2012 sales revenue as reported on the income statement was up 15.7% relative to 2011. However, EBNIT was up only 4.8% from $2,848 million to $2,986 million. As a result, the EBNIT to sales ratio for the combined segments fell from 13.7% to 12.4%. The segment revenue and profit information shown in panel B of Exhibit 12-5 reveals that not all segments are equally responsible for the decline in the EBNIT to sales ratio. The EBNIT to sales ratios

Panel A: Consolidated Income Statement Data and EBNIT to Sales Information

| | For the Year Ended May 31 | | |
	2012	2011	2010
Revenues	$24,128	$20,862	$19,014
Income before net interest and taxes	$ 2,986	$ 2,848	$ 2,523
Net income (after taxes)	$ 2,223	$ 2,133	$ 1,907
EBNIT to sales	12.4%	13.7%	13.3%
After-tax return on sales	9.2%	10.2%	10.0%

Panel B: Segment Disclosures (all income figures shown before net interest and taxes)

	Revenues	EBNIT	EBNIT to Sales Ratio
Year Ended May 31, 2012			
North America	$ 8,839	$2,007	22.7%
Western Europe	4,144	597	14.4%
Central & Eastern Europe	1,200	234	19.5%
Greater China	2,539	911	35.9%
Japan	829	136	16.4%
Emerging Markets	3,410	853	25.0%
Global Brand Divisions	111	(1,177)	NM
Other Businesses	3,095	341	11.0%
Total	$24,167	$3,902	16.1%
Year Ended May 31, 2011			
North America	$ 7,579	$1,736	22.9%
Western Europe	3,868	730	18.9%
Central & Eastern Europe	1,040	244	23.5%
Greater China	2,060	777	37.7%
Japan	766	114	14.9%
Emerging Markets	2,736	688	25.1%
Global Brand Divisions	96	(971)	NM
Other Businesses	2,786	335	12.0%
Total	$20,931	$3,653	17.5%
Year Ended May 31, 2010			
North America	$ 6,697	$1,538	23.0%
Western Europe	3,839	807	21.0%
Central & Eastern Europe	999	249	24.9%
Greater China	1,742	637	36.6%
Japan	882	180	20.4%
Emerging Markets	2,198	521	23.7%
Global Brand Divisions	86	(866)	NM
Other Businesses	2,564	298	11.6%
Total	$19,007	$3,364	17.7%

NM indicates not meaningful.

EXHIBIT 12-5

Nike, Inc.

Consolidated and Segment Data (in millions, except percentages)

for North America remained reasonably stable, but the ratios for Western Europe and Central & Eastern Europe both dropped significantly (at least 4 percentage points each) and even Greater China dropped 1.8 percentage points from 37.7% in 2011 to 35.9% in 2012. The footnotes also reveal that sales are growing at differing rates around the world. They are growing at single-digit rates in Western Europe and Japan from 2010 through 2012. They even fell in Japan from 2010 to 2011. In contrast, they are growing above 24% each year in the Emerging Markets from 2010 through 2012. Less than half of Nike's sales are now in North America. Nike-branded product sales in North America constituted 37% of total sales in 2012. Clearly, if you want to forecast Nike's future performance, you must understand not only economic and demographic trends in the United States but also trends around the globe.

INTERPRETING FINANCIAL STATEMENTS

In 2012, almost 37% of **Nike**'s $24,128 million in sales were domestic sales and 63% were foreign sales. Suppose you predicted North American sales to increase 2% and foreign sales to grow 5%. What would be your prediction of domestic, foreign, and total sales for the year 2013? What is the predicted company-wide sales growth rate?

Answer

1. Domestic sales (.37 × $24,128 × 1.02) = $9,105.9 million.
2. Foreign sales (.63 × $24,128 × 1.05) = $15,960.7 million.

3. Projected total sales would be $25,066.6 for a growth rate of about 3.9% The careful reader will note that $24,128 million in sales is the corporate level after recognizing certain overheads. The detail shows $24,167 as the gross number before corporate overhead allocation. Unless the corporate overheads differ remarkably by region, the sales number chosen will not make a significant difference in the analysis.

Financial Ratios

▶▶ **OBJECTIVE 3**

Use basic financial ratios to guide your thinking.

The cornerstone of financial statement analysis is the use of ratios. Exhibit 12-6 on pp. 549–550 groups some of the most popular ratios into four categories. You have encountered most of these ratios in earlier chapters, as indicated in the second column (a dash in the column means that this chapter introduces the ratio for the first time). We provide this summary to avoid the need to search for definitions in prior material.

We focus on the use of ratios by investors. However, managers also use ratios to guide, measure, and reward workers. If managers compensate workers for actions that make the company more profitable, workers are likely to do the right thing. Thus, some companies give workers a bonus if the company generates a return on equity (ROE) in excess of a predetermined benchmark or if earnings per share (EPS) exceeds a specific number.

Given recent corporate scandals where companies manipulated accounting records to inflate earnings, many companies are broadening their incentive programs to include nonaccounting measures as well as accounting numbers. For example, **Duke Energy** decided that profit may not be the right measure for rewarding employees. Suppose profit increases because you raise more capital and expand the company. Should the workers necessarily earn more? Duke Energy elected to reward workers based on two factors: success in meeting goals and ROE. For one worker, the goal might be reduced injuries, and for another, improved customer service. However, everyone earns more for meeting ROE targets. ROE is a good measure of efficiency because companies can improve ROE by increasing profitability and also by increasing the efficiency with which it employs assets.

Claw-back provisions are another corporate response to concerns about managers manipulating their earnings to generate positive performance and enhance compensation and bonuses. Claw-back provisions allow companies to reduce bonuses retroactively if they learn that the earnings and revenue levels that produced the bonuses were not legitimate. In addition, many companies are extending the period of time over which bonuses are earned to give managers a longer-term perspective.

Recall that debt contracts also employ financial ratios. For example, Duke Energy discloses that its credit agreements contain various financial and other covenants. Violation of the covenants could result in accelerated due dates and/or termination of the agreements. Examples would include maintaining a debt-to-equity ratio below a certain level or maintaining an interest-coverage ratio above a certain level.

Evaluating Financial Ratios

No single ratio by itself provides a sufficient basis for assessing a company's financial performance. Rather, we examine a set of ratios and perform other types of analyses, including review of nonfinancial information describing the firm's activities. However, financial ratios are a good place to start. The easy part of ratio analysis is the computation of the numerical values. Once

EXHIBIT 12-6

Some Typical Financial Ratios Applied to Nike, Inc. ($ in millions, except per share data*)

(see Exhibits 12-1 and 12-2 on pages 538 and 539 for data)

Typical Name of Ratio	Introduced in Chapter	Numerator	Denominator	Using Appropriate Nike Numbers Applied to May 31 of Year	
				2012	2011
Short-term liquidity ratios					
Current ratio	4	Current assets	Current liabilities	$11{,}531 \div 3{,}865 = 2.98$	$11{,}297 \div 3{,}958 = 2.85$
Quick ratio	4	Current assets minus inventories	Current liabilities	$(11{,}531 - 3{,}350) \div 3{,}865 = 2.12$	$(11{,}297 - 2{,}715) \div 3{,}958 = 2.17$
Accounts receivable turnover	6	Credit sales	Average accounts receivable	$24{,}128 \div [\tfrac{1}{2}(3{,}280 + 3{,}138)] = 7.52$	$20{,}862 \div [\tfrac{1}{2}(3{,}138 + 2{,}650)] = 7.21$
Average collection period (in days)	6	365	Accounts receivable turnover	$365.0 \div 7.52 = 48.5$	$365.0 \div 7.21 = 50.6$
Inventory turnover	7	Cost of sales	Average inventory at cost	$13{,}657 \div [\tfrac{1}{2}(3{,}350 + 2{,}715)] = 4.50$	$11{,}354 \div [\tfrac{1}{2}(2{,}715 + 2{,}041)] = 4.77$
Long-term solvency ratios					
Total-debt-to-total-assets	9	Total liabilities[1]	Total assets	$(15{,}465 - 10{,}381) \div 15{,}465 = 32.9\%$	$(14{,}998 - 9{,}843) \div 14{,}998 = 34.4\%$
Total-debt-to-total-equity	9	Total liabilities[1]	Stockholders' equity	$(15{,}465 - 10{,}381) \div 10{,}381 = 49.0\%$	$(14{,}998 - 9{,}843) \div 9{,}843 = 52.4\%$
Interest coverage[2]	9	Earnings before interest expense and taxes	Interest expense	$(2{,}983 + 33) \div 33 = 91.4$	$(2{,}844 + 34) \div 34 = 84.6$
Profitability ratios					
Return on common stockholders' equity (ROE)	4[3], 10	Net income minus preferred dividends	Average common stockholders' equity	$2{,}223 \div [\tfrac{1}{2}(10{,}381 + 9{,}843)] = 22.0\%$	$2{,}133 \div [\tfrac{1}{2}(9{,}843 + 9{,}754)] = 21.8\%$
Gross profit rate or percentage	4	Gross profit or gross margin	Sales	$10{,}471 \div 24{,}128 = 43.4\%$	$9{,}508 \div 20{,}862 = 45.6\%$
Return on sales or profit margin	4	Net income	Sales	$2{,}223 \div 24{,}128 = 9.2\%$	$2{,}133 \div 20{,}862 = 10.2\%$
Total asset turnover	—	Sales	Average total assets	$24{,}128 \div [\tfrac{1}{2}(15{,}465 + 14{,}998)] = 1.58$	$20{,}862 \div [\tfrac{1}{2}(14{,}998 + 14{,}419)] = 1.42$
EBIT to sales[2]	—	Earnings before interest expense and taxes	Sales	$(2{,}983 + 33) \div 24{,}128 = 12.5\%$	$(2{,}844 + 34) \div 20{,}862 = 13.8\%$
Return on assets (ROA)	4[4]	Earnings before interest expense and taxes	Average total assets	$(2{,}983 + 33) \div [\tfrac{1}{2}(15{,}465 + 14{,}998)] = 19.8\%$	$(2{,}844 + 34) \div [\tfrac{1}{2}(14{,}998 + 14{,}419)] = 19.6\%$
Earnings per share, basic (EPS)	2	Net income minus preferred dividends, if any	Average common shares outstanding	$2{,}223 \div 460.0 = \$4.83$	$2{,}133 \div 475.5 = \$4.49^{[5]}$

EXHIBIT 12-6 (Continued)

Some Typical Financial Ratios Applied to Nike, Inc. ($ in millions, except per share data)

(see Exhibits 12-1 and 12-2 on pages 538 and 539 for data)

Typical Name of Ratio	Introduced in Chapter	Numerator	Denominator	Using Appropriate Nike Numbers Applied to May 31 of Year	
				2012	2011
Market price and dividend ratios					
Price-earnings (P-E)	2	Market price of common share (assume $108.18 and $84.45)	Earnings per share	108.18 ÷ 4.83 = 22.4	84.45 ÷ 4.49 = 18.8
Book value per common share	10	Common stockholders' equity	Number of common shares outstanding	10,381 ÷ 458 = $22.67	9,843 ÷ 468 = $21.03
Market-to-book	10	Market price of common share	Book value per common share	108.18 ÷ 22.67 = 4.77	84.45 ÷ 21.03 = 4.02
Dividend-yield	2	Dividends per common share	Market price of common share	1.39 ÷ 108.18 = 1.3%	1.20 ÷ 84.45 = 1.4%
Dividend-payout	2	Dividends per common share	Earnings per share (EPS)	1.39 ÷ 4.83 = 28.8%	1.20 ÷ 4.48 = 26.8%

*most ratios are pure numbers since they are the result of dividing one dollar amount by another. EPS is an exception and is identified with a $ sign.
[1]Total liabilities computed as (Total assets – Total shareholders' equity).
[2]Interest expense is shown net of interest income in the income statement. Interest expense is shown separately in Exhibit 12.1 of the 10-K and that interest expense number is used here.
[3]The ROE introduced in Chapter 4 did not allow for subtraction of preferred stock dividends because preferred stock had yet to be introduced.
[4]The version of ROA computed in Chapter 4 uses after-tax net income in the numerator.
[5]$4.49 differs from the $4.48 reported because of rounding errors in $2,133 and $475.5.

Note: Year 2010 data required (in millions): Accounts receivable, $2,650; Inventory, $2,041; Stockholders' equity, $9,754; and Total assets, $14,419.
Number of common shares outstanding required (in millions) at May 31, 2012, and May 31, 2011, were 458 and 468, respectively.
Average common shares outstanding (in millions) in 2012 and 2011 were 460.0 and 475.5, respectively.

you have computed a set of ratios, you must decide what the ratios tell you about performance. There are three approaches to evaluating financial ratios: (1) **time-series comparisons** of a company's own historical ratios, (2) **benchmark comparisons** with general rules of thumb or "best practices," and (3) **cross-sectional comparisons** with ratios of other companies or with industry averages.

A few words of caution about these three types of comparisons are in order. When comparing a company's ratios in a time-series analysis, you must be aware of structural shifts in the company. For example, major acquisitions or divestitures complicate comparisons across time. Consider the merger of AOL and Time Warner in early 2000. Time Warner was a media conglomerate whose activities included a cable television system servicing a significant percentage of U.S. households, publishing, music and entertainment, and film libraries. At the time of the merger, AOL was the nation's largest Internet service provider. The financial statements of the combined enterprise bore little resemblance to those of either of the original companies. And the merger did not meet expectations. Time Warner spun off AOL in 2009, again disrupting time-series analysis of its financial ratios.

Comparisons to benchmarks are easy to implement. But you must identify the right benchmarks for the comparisons to be meaningful. Rules of thumb vary from industry to industry and are susceptible to change over time. For example, the traditional rule of thumb for the current ratio was 2 to 1 or higher. Improvements in working capital management enable many companies to operate with a much lower current ratio. A current ratio of 1 to 1 is generally considered sufficient for a company with strong and stable cash flows, whereas a company with weak cash flows should maintain a higher current ratio. Another example is the total liabilities to total shareholders' equity ratio. In its publication, *Key Business Ratios*, Dun & Bradstreet, a financial services firm, observes that the total liabilities to total shareholders' equity ratio should not exceed 100%. However, it is not uncommon for companies in some industries to have substantially higher ratios. For example, Duke Energy, Consolidated Edison, and Spectra Energy had ratios of 173%, 238%, and 216%, respectively, in early 2012.

Cross-sectional comparisons require the identification of comparable companies or a set of norms for a specific industry. On the surface, this may appear straightforward. However, identification of similar companies or the appropriate industry is often difficult. We have already noted the difficulty of finding a perfect match for Nike. But consider Berkshire Hathaway, Inc., which is a holding company comprised of many subsidiaries engaged in diverse business activities. One of Berkshire Hathaway's largest business segments is property and casualty insurance, including GEICO, one of the largest auto insurers in the United States, and General Re, one of the largest reinsurers in the world. Therefore, it might seem reasonable to compare Berkshire Hathaway to other insurance companies. However, Berkshire Hathaway's other business holdings include three jewelry companies, four furniture retailers, several finance and financial products companies, a newspaper publisher, multiple apparel and footwear companies, a candy manufacturer, and numerous other companies in diverse industries. In 2011 Berkshire Hathaway bought Lubrizol, and in 2009 it acquired the 77.4% of Burlington Northern Railway that it did not already own. Berkshire Hathaway made very focused and preferred investments in Goldman Sachs and Bank of America during the recession as these financial icons faced challenges. Although many companies operate in multiple industries, Berkshire Hathaway is an extreme example. Segment disclosures provide useful information about the performance of different segments and assist the analyst in finding appropriate comparable companies, but the information is limited in scope. For more on Berkshire Hathaway see the Business First box on page 552.

How can we find comparable companies? Historically, companies were classified according to the Standard Industry Classification (SIC) system. In 1997, the government introduced the North American Industry Classification System (NAICS). Both of these systems assign industry codes to companies based on their business activities. Several financial information services use these classification systems to provide average values for selected financial ratios and representative financial statements. Risk Management Association (formerly Robert Morris Associates), Dun & Bradstreet (D&B), and Standard and Poor's have provided these averages for many years. In addition, numerous online financial service providers compile industry information. Google Finance, Yahoo! Finance, Hoover's Online, and Reuters are examples. Regardless of the service you use to gather industry data, be alert to differences in computing ratios. Because there are no universally agreed upon formulas for most financial ratios except for EPS, you must know the computational formula employed before using such ratios.

time-series comparisons
Comparisons of a company's financial ratios with its own historical ratios.

benchmark comparisons
Comparisons of a company's financial ratios with general rules of thumb or "best practices."

cross-sectional comparisons
Comparisons of a company's financial ratios with the ratios of other companies or with industry averages.

BUSINESS FIRST

WARREN BUFFETT: NOTHING TO HIDE

Warren Buffett, Chairman of Berkshire Hathaway, is one of the most successful and well-known investors in the world. He is #3 on *Forbes Magazine*'s 2012 list of the richest people in the world and #2 in the United States behind Bill Gates. His wealth derives from his skill as a manager and investor. The company's 10-K describes Buffet's strategy as follows: "Our long-held acquisition strategy is to purchase businesses with consistent earning power, good returns on equity and able and honest management, at sensible prices." Note that consistent earning power and returns on equity can be assessed with ratios built from accounting information. The history of performance since 1965 shows the success of the strategy. During that 47-year period, the book value per share of the stock has increased at a compound annual rate of 19.8%. In contrast, the S&P has increased at a compound annual rate of 9.2%.

In some cases Berkshire Hathaway owns all of a subsidiary, but in many cases it holds a partial stake. For example, it owns 13% of American Express, 8.8% of Coca-Cola, 5.5% of IBM, and 7.6% of Wells Fargo. Buffett points out that accounting practice often misleads investors who do not fully understand it. Because Berkshire Hathaway owns less than 20% of each of these companies and does not hold them for short-term profit, it accounts for them using the market method and classifies them as available-for-sale securities. As such, Berkshire Hathaway included only the dividends received from them, $862,000, in net income in 2011. Buffett believes that recognizing a pro rata share of the net income of the four companies, $3.3 billion, as would be done using the equity method, is a more useful measure of performance. In terms of ratio analysis, net income is part of both return on sales and return on equity, and Buffett would argue that the market method of accounting systematically understates the operating performance of his conglomerate. In choosing to focus on book value per share, he has chosen a metric that does capture performance differently since it is based on changes in total owners' equity, which includes changes in market values of those security holdings.

Buffett's annual letter to his shareholders is a must-read for investors. The full text of his letters since 1977 is available on the Berkshire Hathaway Web site at www.berkshirehathaway.com/letters/letters.html. In his 2011 letter, Buffett says:

Our primary focus is on building operating earnings. Over time, the businesses we currently own should increase their aggregate earnings, and we hope also to *purchase some large operations that will give us a further boost. We now have eight subsidiaries that would each be included in the Fortune 500 were they standalone companies. That leaves only 492 to go. My task is clear, and I'm on the prowl.*

Generally, Buffett believes in reinvesting earnings and using cash generated to invest in other companies. Berkshire Hathaway does not pay dividends. But recently it has launched a share repurchase program, again with a clearly stated strategy; buy when the market price is lower than 110% of book value per share. Per the 2011 annual letter:

At our limit price of 110% of book value, repurchases clearly increase Berkshire's per-share intrinsic value. And the more and the cheaper we buy, the greater the gain for continuing shareholders. Therefore, if given the opportunity, we will likely repurchase stock aggressively at our price limit or lower.

Buffett is often a contrarian. In the early 1990s, he wrote one of only three letters supporting mandatory expensing of stock options received by the congressional committee investigating the accounting treatment. His view did not carry the day then, but in 2004 the FASB issued a standard requiring that stock options be expensed. Once again, Buffett was ahead of his time in understanding the need for financial transparency.

With regard to the tendency of some in the business world to blindly rely on historical models as guides to the future, Buffett offered the following advice in his 2008 letter:

Investors should be skeptical of history-based models. Constructed by a nerdy-sounding priesthood using esoteric terms such as beta, gamma, sigma and the like, these models tend to look impressive. Too often, though, investors forget to examine the assumptions behind the symbols. Our advice: Beware of geeks bearing formulas. If merely looking up past financial data would tell you what the future holds, the Forbes 400 (list of richest people) would consist of librarians.

Sources: Berkshire Hathaway Web site, www.berkshirehathaway.com; Berkshire Hathaway 2011 10-K.

Let's examine some specific ratios by comparing those for **Nike** from Exhibit 12-6 with both industry norms and the performance of specific competitors. The ratios shown in the following table have all been discussed in previous chapters. D&B provides the following industry ratios based on 60 companies in the sporting and recreational goods industry:

	Current Ratio (times)	Average Collection Period (days)	Total Liabilities to Stockholders' Equity** (%)	Return on Sales (%)	Return on Stockholders' Equity (%)
60 Companies					
Upper quartile	3.6	15.0	36.2	3.5	23.5
Median	2.4	26.3	63.0	2.0	8.9
Lower quartile	1.6	44.5	155.5	0.5	2.7
Nike*	3.0	48.5	49.0	9.2	22.0

*Ratios are from Exhibit 12-6. Consult Exhibit 12-6 for an explanation of the components of each ratio.

**In Exhibit 12-6, this ratio is identified as Total-debt-to-total-equity.

D&B calculates the ratios for each firm in the industry sample and ranks the individual ratios from best to worst. The median is the ratio ranked in the middle. The ratio ranked halfway between the median and the best value is the upper quartile. The lower quartile is the ratio ranked halfway between the median and the worst value. The concept of best and worst must be viewed with caution. Analysts may differ in their opinions about what is good and what is bad. For example, a short-term creditor might consider a very high current ratio to be good because it suggests the assets are available to repay the debt. From an investor's perspective, however, a very high current ratio may indicate that the company is maintaining higher levels of inventory and receivables than is desirable. Both the creditor and the investor should consider the composition and liquidity of current assets when assessing the current ratio. A high current ratio with current assets comprised primarily of slow-moving inventory may not indicate strong short-term liquidity.

When compared with the D&B ratios, Nike is between the median and the upper quartile of the current ratio, which measures short-term liquidity. Nike's 48.5-day collection period places it in the lower quartile. Suppose, like Nike, your company has an average receivables collection period that is much longer than the industry median of 26.3 days. One explanation might be that the company offers longer credit terms than those of its peers as a way to attract customers. An alternative explanation is that many firms in the industry give large discounts for cash purchases, whereas your company does not. A company with many cash sales may have a short average collection period for total sales, even though there are long delays in receiving payments for items sold on credit. Unfortunately, it is frequently difficult for an investor to obtain information on credit terms or the percentage of sales that were made on credit. An additional ratio that would be useful in assessing Nike's short-term liquidity is the inventory turnover ratio. D&B does not provide industry norms for this ratio.

Nike's total liabilities are 49.0% of stockholders' equity, placing it between the industry median and upper quartile. Typically, companies with lower levels of debt in relation to ownership capital are in a stronger position when business conditions deteriorate. Why? Because even when revenues decline, interest expenses and maturity dates do not change. Nike's ratio reflects a comparatively low level of risk or uncertainty with regard to its ability to meet outstanding debt obligations.

Investors are particularly interested in profitability ratios. Nike is in the upper quartile of the return on sales ratio, suggesting that it is able to generate greater income per dollar of sales than more than 75% of the comparative firms. Nike's common-size income statements can help you understand how it achieves a higher level of return on sales than the average firm in the industry. Nike's ROE of 22.0% is more than twice the industry median of 8.9% but slightly below the upper quartile of 23.5%. We explore Nike's ROE in more depth later in the chapter.

Overall, Nike does not perform like the median firm in the industry. What could cause Nike's ratios to differ from the norms reported by D&B? D&B includes 60 companies in this industry classification, including companies that manufacture all types of sporting equipment from marine pleasure craft to bowling balls. Although Nike manufactures sporting equipment, it focuses on footwear and apparel. Perhaps we should compare Nike with the apparel industry or the leather products industry or the rubber and plastics footwear industry. Many companies, including Nike, fall into more than one SIC or NAICS category, making it difficult to select the appropriate industry for comparison. Perhaps we should compare Nike to individual companies that are more similar.

Hoover's Online identifies Nike's top competitors as adidas, Fila Korea, and New Balance. Adidas prepares its financial statements in accordance with IFRS, making direct comparisons complex without a thorough understanding of the differences between U.S. GAAP and IFRS. Fila Korea and New Balance are private companies that do not disclose financial data to the public. Hoover's also lists Under Armour (UA), VF Corporation (VFC), and K-Swiss (KSWS) as competitors for Nike. While none of these three firms is a perfect match for Nike, each shares product lines with Nike, and all four companies compete for consumer dollars. Under Armour operates primarily in the athletic apparel market; VF Corporation is a holding company that owns numerous footwear and apparel companies; and K-Swiss competes with Nike on apparel, footwear, and accessories. All four companies sell primarily through third-party retailers, and all place heavy emphasis on brand management. From the chart below, you can see that the choice of comparable firms can alter your perception of a company's relative performance. The use of these specific competitors also allows us to compare inventory turnover ratios.

Specific Competitor Ratio Comparisons

	Current Ratio (times)	Average Collection Period (days)	Inventory Turnover (times)	Total Liabilities to Stockholders' Equity (%)	Return on Sales* (%)	Return on Stockholders' Equity* (%)
UA	3.8	29.3	2.8	44.4	6.6	17.1
VFC	1.9	36.9	4.1	51.4	9.3	21.2
KSWS	4.3	37.7	2.2	32.3	(24.0)	(32.2)
Nike	3.0	48.5	4.5	49.0	9.2	22.0

*Income is after-tax income before discontinued operations.

Does the comparison of ratios across companies provide easy answers for the investor? Generally not. While Nike's average collection period of 48.5 days is closer to VFC and KSWS than it is to the industry median of 26.3 days or to UA's collection period of 29.3 days, we still don't know why there is a difference across this peer group. Nike's total liabilities to stockholders' equity ratio is also more in line with UA and VFC than it is to the higher industry median of 63.0% or to KSWS's lower ratio of 32.3%. And Nike's inventory turnover ratio, while similar to VFC's, is twice that of KSWS. However, both the comparisons to D&B industry data and the comparisons to three specific competitors show Nike to have superior levels of return on sales and return on stockholders' equity.

In addition to comparing ratios at a single point in time, changes in a company's ratios over time alert investors and creditors to problems. For example, a decrease in inventory turnover may suggest that a company's sales staff is no longer doing a very good job or that the company's products have fallen out of favor with the buying public. An alternative to the "sales are falling" explanation is the "inventory is rising" explanation. Manufacturing may be producing inventory at a pace beyond what current buyers want. Alternatively, a company may stockpile inventory in anticipation of price increases or inventory shortages. In both cases, inventory builds faster than sales and turnover falls. However, one explanation for rising inventory (over-manufacturing) is cause for concern, whereas the other may represent good inventory planning.

The Risk Management Association provides a series of comparative financial ratios by NAICS classifications sorted by firm size. For example in NAICS 339920, Sporting and Athletic Goods Manufacturing, they provide benchmarking information for firms of very different sizes, ranging from firms with sales of up to $1 million to firms with sales over $25 million. The data show that size can matter. For example, the average inventory turnover for firms below $1 million in sales was 5.0 while it was 3.4 for firms with sales over $25 million. More significant was the range in values for the upper quartile where smaller firms had turnovers of 14.6 versus 4.5 for larger firms. Note that by these classifications, Nike is very large in comparison to the industry, with sales over $25 billion. This is another example of why comparative analysis must be done carefully.

In this section, we focused primarily on liquidity and solvency ratios. Now we turn our attention to ratios used to assess the role of operating performance and financing decisions in the overall success of the company.

Operating Performance and Financing Decisions

On pages 165–168 of Chapter 4, you learned about several ratios used to measure profitability: return on sales (also called the profit margin ratio), return on common stockholders' equity (ROE or ROCE), and return on assets (ROA). Both operating performance and financing decisions affect these measures of profitability. **Financial management** is concerned with where the company gets cash and how it uses that cash to its benefit. **Operating management** is concerned with the day-to-day activities that generate revenues and expenses. In many scenarios, it is useful to focus on operating efficiency and financing decisions separately. We begin with a discussion of a version of ROA that measures a company's operating performance independent of how the company finances those operations. We then consider the impact of debt versus equity financing on the return to investors, using ROE. We expand on the traditional ROE calculation with a discussion of Economic Value Added (EVA), introduced by **Stern Stewart & Company**. Finally, no discussion of financing alternatives is complete without consideration of income tax effects and alternative measures of financing risk.

▶▶ OBJECTIVE 4
Evaluate corporate performance using various metrics, including ROA, ROE, and EVA.

financial management
Decisions concerned with where the company gets cash and how it uses that cash to its benefit.

operating management
Decisions concerned with the day-to-day activities that generate revenues and expenses.

Operating Performance

In general, we evaluate the overall success of an investment by comparing investment returns with the amount of investment initially made:

$$\text{Rate of return on investment} = \frac{\text{Income}}{\text{Invested capital}}$$

However, there are several possible definitions of income and invested capital. The appropriate definition of these terms depends on how we intend to use the resulting rate of return measure. For example, depending on the setting, we may define income as net income, income from operations, earnings before interest and taxes (**EBIT**), or some other variation. We may also use different definitions of invested capital. Sometimes we define invested capital as common stockholders' equity and other times as total capital provided by both debt and equity sources. The purpose of the analysis drives these choices. For example, a stockholder might be more concerned about ROE (Net income ÷ Average common stockholders' equity), whereas a lender (who has first claim on the resources generated by the company) would be more concerned with how effectively the company uses its total assets to generate returns for all suppliers of capital (EBIT ÷ Average total assets).

EBIT
Earnings before interest and taxes.

Suppose we are interested in assessing a firm's use of assets independently of how it financed those assets. In this case, neither return calculation introduced in Chapter 4 is appropriate. If we are interested in assessing this on a pretax basis, we should use pretax ROA, calculated as follows:

$$\text{Pretax ROA} = \frac{\text{EBIT}}{\text{Average total assets}} \qquad (1)$$

Alternatively, an analyst might be interested in measuring ROA after taxes but independent of financing. In this case, the ROA calculation would be as follows:

$$\text{After-tax ROA} = \frac{\big\{\text{After-tax net income} + [\text{Interest expense} \times (1 - \text{tax rate})]\big\}}{\text{Average total assets}}$$

The denominator of both ROA calculations is average total assets, those claimed by all providers of capital (stockholders and debt holders). To be consistent, the numerators also include income available to all providers of capital. Because net income measures only income available to equity holders after paying interest to debt holders, we adjust net income by adding back interest expense, either before or after taxes.

As you can see, ROA has multiple definitions in practice, depending on the numerator and denominator used in its calculation. Our discussion focuses on the version of ROA defined in equation 1 above. We could use the more precise term **pretax and pre-interest return on total assets** to identify this version of ROA, but the terminology would be cumbersome. Thus, for the remainder of this chapter, we use ROA to mean only the formula in equation 1. This is the computation shown in Exhibit 12-6 on p. 549.

pretax and pre-interest return on total assets
A version of ROA defined as earnings before interest and taxes divided by average total assets.

To further explore ROA, we can decompose the right side of equation 1 into two important ratios:

$$\frac{\text{EBIT}}{\text{Average total assets}} = \frac{\text{EBIT}}{\text{Sales}} \times \frac{\text{Sales}}{\text{Average total assets}} \tag{2}$$

EBIT-to-sales

A variation of return on sales computed as earnings before interest and taxes divided by sales.

total asset turnover

A ratio that measures the sales a company is able to generate for each dollar invested in assets. Computed as: Sales divided by average total assets.

The first term on the right side of equation 2, computed as earnings before interest and taxes divided by sales, is a variation of return on sales, which we refer to as **EBIT-to-sales**. This ratio measures how much profit, before deducting taxes and the cost of debt financing, a company generates for each dollar of sales. The second term is the **total asset turnover** ratio, computed as sales divided by average total assets. This ratio measures the sales a company is able to generate for each dollar invested in assets. Thus, for Nike in 2012 we can express the equation as follows:

Return on total assets = EBIT-to-sales × Total asset turnover
19.8% = 12.5% × 1.58 times

Exhibit 12-7 displays these relationships for Nike for 2012.

This equation highlights that the EBIT-to-sales and total asset turnover ratios each contribute to the rate of return on total assets. Firms can achieve the same ROA with different combinations of EBIT-to-sales and total asset turnover. Understanding the industry provides insights. Companies in some industries have heavy fixed-capacity constraints, lengthy time to add new manufacturing capacity, and barriers that prevent new firms from entering the industry, allowing existing firms to charge high prices. Utilities and communications firms are traditional examples. These industries are likely to display high EBIT-to-sales and relatively low total asset turnover. Companies in other industries have few barriers to entry, intense competition, and commodity-like products. Firms in these industries generally have low EBIT-to-sales and high total asset turnover. Grocery stores are a good example.

Just as decomposing ROA helps us understand what drives the operating performance of a company, we can apply a similar decomposition to ROE. In this case, the numerator is after-tax net income and the invested capital is average common stockholders' equity. Why use income

EXHIBIT 12-7

Major Ingredients of Return on Total Assets for Nike, Inc.

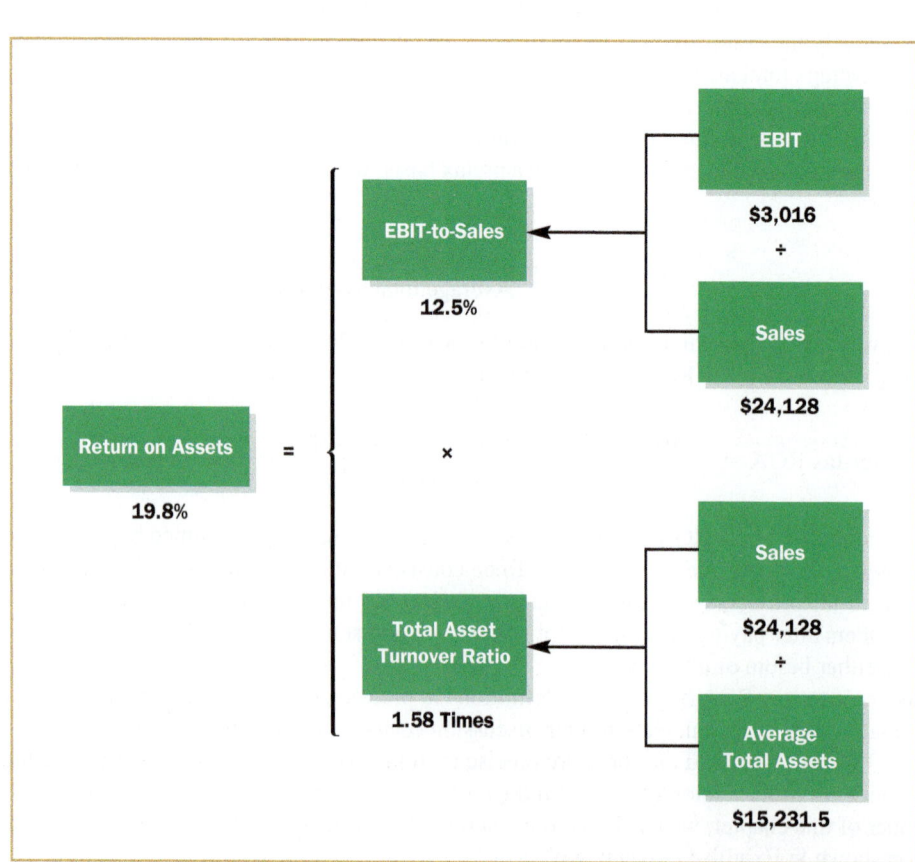

after deducting taxes and interest expense in this computation? Because the numerator should represent the income that is available to common stockholders. The company must pay both interest and taxes before there is any return remaining for stockholders. In addition to the return on sales (here with after-tax net income in the numerator) and total asset turnover, the decomposition has a third component called the **financial leverage ratio**. This ratio, computed as average total assets divided by average common stockholders' equity, indicates the proportion of total assets financed by common stockholders relative to those financed by creditors and preferred stockholders and emphasizes the impact of financing decisions on ROE. Some analysts call this decomposition the DuPont analysis because a talented group of financial analysts working at DuPont developed it many years ago. The decomposition is as follows:

financial leverage ratio
Ratio of average total assets divided by average total common stockholders' equity. Indicates the proportion of total assets financed by common stockholders relative to those financed by creditors and preferred stockholders.

$$\text{ROE} = \text{Return on sales} \times \text{Total asset turnover} \times \text{Financial leverage ratio}$$

$$= \frac{\text{Net income}}{\text{Sales}} \times \frac{\text{Sales}}{\text{Average total assets}} \times \frac{\text{Average total assets}}{\text{Average common stockholders' equity}}$$

For Nike, in 2012 the ROE decomposes as follows:

$$\text{ROE} = \text{Return on sales} \times \text{Total asset turnover} \times \text{Financial leverage ratio}$$

$$21.9\% = 9.2\% \times 1.58 \times 1.51$$

The first three items are calculated in Exhibit 12-6 and financial leverage is calculated as: $[1/2 \ (15,465 + 14,998)] \div [1/2 \ (10,381 + 9,843)] = (15,231.5 \div 10,112) = 1.51$. In Exhibit 12-6 ROE is reported as 22.0% when the ratio is calculated directly as Net income divided by average common stockholders' equity. When ROE is decomposed into the DuPont analysis, the value shown is 21.9%. The difference is simply due to rounding of the individual components of the DuPont decomposition. The introduction of the financial leverage ratio in the computation of ROE leads us to a discussion of financing decisions.

Financing Decisions

Good financial performance requires an appropriate balance of debt and equity financing. In addition to deciding how much debt is appropriate, a firm must decide how much to borrow short term and how much to borrow by issuing bonds or other long-term debt. Companies must repay or refinance short-term debt quickly. When a borrower encounters trouble and cannot repay, it becomes difficult to refinance. Lenders prefer healthy, profitable borrowers, not troubled ones. Such problems are especially severe during periods when interest rates are rising because each new refinancing occurs at a higher interest rate, and the cash flow needed to cover interest payments increases.

In most cases, companies should finance long-term investments with long-term capital: long-term debt or stock. Debt is often a more attractive vehicle to companies than is common stock because (1) a company can deduct interest payments but not dividends for income-tax purposes, and (2) the existing shareholders retain the same ownership rights to voting and profits. Most companies have a combination of long-term debt and stockholders' equity. We call the total long-term financing the **capitalization**, or simply the **capital structure**, of a corporation. Suppose a company's capital structure consists of long-term debt (bonds payable) and common stock. The common shareholders enjoy the benefits of all income in excess of interest expense and taxes.

capitalization (capital structure)
The total long-term financing of a company, consisting of long-term debt and stockholders' equity.

Trading on the equity (also referred to as using **financial leverage**, **leveraging**, or, in the United Kingdom, **gearing**) means using interest-bearing debt to try to enhance the rate of return on common stockholders' equity. There are costs and benefits to shareholders from trading on the equity. The costs are interest payments and increased risk, and the benefit is the larger potential return to the common shareholders—as long as overall income is large enough.

trading on the equity (financial leverage, leveraging, gearing)
Using interest-bearing debt to enhance the rate of return on common stockholders' equity.

To illustrate, imagine companies A, B, and C shown in Exhibit 12-8. The three companies are in the same industry, each has $80,000 in assets, and each has the same ROA in a given year. However, the annual ROA varies from 20% in year 1, to 10% in year 2, and 5% in year 3. The three companies have chosen very different capital structures. Company A has no debt, Company B has $30,000 in debt, and Company C has $60,000 in debt. Company B pays 10% interest, whereas the more heavily indebted Company C must pay 12%. How do the shareholders fare in these three companies in different years?

EXHIBIT 12-8

Trading on the Equity Effects of Debt on Rates of Return

	(1) Income Before Interest Expense (ROA × Assets)*	(2) Interest Expense (Debt × Interest Rate)†	(3) Net Income (Loss) (1) – (2)	(4) Stockholders' Equity	(5) Return on Equity (3) ÷ (4)
Year 1: 20% ROA					
Company A	$16,000	$ 0	$16,000	$80,000	20%
Company B	16,000	3,000	13,000	50,000	26%
Company C	16,000	7,200	8,800	20,000	44%
Year 2: 10% ROA					
Company A	$ 8,000	$ 0	$ 8,000	$80,000	10%
Company B	8,000	3,000	5,000	50,000	10%
Company C	8,000	7,200	800	20,000	4%
Year 3: 5% ROA					
Company A	$ 4,000	$ 0	$ 4,000	$80,000	5%
Company B	4,000	3,000	1,000	50,000	2%
Company C	4,000	7,200	(3,200)	20,000	(16%)

*All three companies have $80,000 in assets.

†Company A, no debt; Company B, $30,000 in debt at 10%; Company C, $60,000 in debt at 12%.

Exhibit 12-8 summarizes the results. The first column gives EBIT (income before interest expense and taxes). To examine financial leverage, this example focuses on interest and ignores taxes. Recall from equation 1 that we calculate the return on assets as follows:

$$\text{ROA} = \frac{\text{EBIT}}{\text{Average total assets}}$$

Therefore, EBIT equals ROA times average total assets. In this example, we assume the same ROA, and therefore the same EBIT, for each firm in a given year, but we vary the ROA from one year to the next. We can calculate EBIT each year by multiplying ROA for the year times the constant asset level of $80,000. The interest expense differs by company because each has a different level of debt, but for a given company it does not change from year to year. Our primary concern is the effect of financial leverage on the ROE.

What do we learn from Exhibit 12-8? First, a debt-free, or unlevered, company has identical ROA and ROE. Note that equity-financed, unlevered Company A's ROE and ROA are identical in years 1, 2, and 3: 20%, 10%, and 5%, respectively. Second, when a company with debt has an ROA greater than its interest rate, ROE exceeds ROA. This situation is called *favorable financial leverage* and describes both Company B and Company C in year 1. They earn 20% on their assets and pay either 10% or 12% on their debt. The earnings in excess of the interest cost increase earnings available to shareholders and increase ROE.

Year 2 is interesting because Company B has an ROA of 10%, which equals its interest rate. Thus, like Company A, Company B has ROE of 10%. In contrast, Company C experiences *unfavorable financial leverage*. Because its 10% ROA is less than its 12% interest cost, its ROE falls sharply to 4%. Year 3 further stresses the effects of financial leverage in years when the company performs poorly. When ROA falls noticeably below the firm's interest cost, ROE also falls sharply. Company B's ROE falls to 2%, whereas the more highly leveraged Company C faces a loss year and negative ROE.

When a company is unable to earn at least the interest rate on the money borrowed, the ROE is lower than it would be for a debt-free company. If earnings are low enough that the company cannot pay the interest and principal payments on debt, it may be forced into bankruptcy. The possibility of bankruptcy increases the risk to the common stockholders even more than it does to debt holders. Remember, debt holders collect their claims before stockholders do.

The more stable a company's income, the less dangerous it is to trade on the equity. Therefore, regulated industries, such as electric, gas, and telephone companies, have tended to have a heavier proportion of debt than do manufacturers of computers or high-tech companies. Historically, these regulated companies had a stable customer base and were somewhat protected from competition. Government regulations helped ensure that prices would be sufficiently high to ensure a profit. The breakup of **AT&T** as the dominant national phone company and recent efforts to deregulate electric utilities have produced changes in these historical patterns of financial leverage. Many utilities still have debt levels left over from their stable, regulated past. However, deregulation has made their returns much less stable and, therefore, their stock a more risky investment. The prudent use of debt is part of intelligent financial management.

Economic Value Added

We calculate ROA and ROE directly from financial statement information. Both ratios measure performance by relating an income statement number to investment levels reported on the balance sheet. **Economic Value Added (EVA)** is a related performance measure, developed and trademarked by Stern Stewart & Company. EVA measures the residual wealth of a company after deducting its cost of capital from operating profit. The idea is that a firm must earn more than it pays for capital if it is to increase in value. This is like saying that a firm must earn more than the interest expense on borrowing for borrowing to be favorable for the equity holders. When we refer to capital in EVA, we are referring to all capital, both debt and equity. The cost of that capital is a weighted average of interest cost and the returns required by equity investors.

Economic Value Added (EVA)
Measure of the residual wealth of a company after deducting its cost of capital from operating profit.

Assume that a company has a weighted-average after-tax cost of capital of 10% and $1 million in capital. The company is adding value if its net operating profit after tax exceeds 10% of $1 million, or $100,000. If the net operating profit after tax is $120,000, for example, we would calculate the EVA as ($120,000 – $100,000) = $20,000. If this firm generates only $70,000 of net operating profit after tax, we would say that EVA is ($70,000 – $100,000) = negative $30,000. In the latter case, the company is losing value. If such losses are expected to continue, it would be preferable to dissolve the company and return the capital to its creditors and owners.

In applying EVA, managers often adjust the accounting results reported under GAAP because they believe GAAP does not always reflect true economic value. Without exploring all such adjustments, we consider one: research and development (R&D) expenditures. Although U.S. GAAP requires most companies to expense R&D immediately, all agree that R&D has some economic value and that expensing all R&D may be an overly conservative approach. EVA proponents argue that it is better to arbitrarily assume a 5-year life for R&D than no life, and they restate the financial statements accordingly.

You saw an example of such a restatement on page 361 in Chapter 8 in the Business First Box. As a reminder, suppose a company capitalized the $50,000 it spent each year on R&D and assigned a 5-year life to the resulting asset. After the first 4 years, annual amortization of R&D on the income statement would equal the amount spent, $50,000. Whether the $50,000 is expensed each year as R&D expense or as amortization expense, net income is the same after the first 4 years. However, both assets and stockholders' equity will be higher during the initial years if the company capitalizes and amortizes the expenditure.

Many companies have adopted EVA as an internal management tool, including **Coca-Cola**, **Whole Foods**, **Herman Miller**, and **K-Swiss**. They believe that this procedure helps them allocate, manage, and redeploy scarce capital resources such as heavy equipment, working capital, and real estate.

Income Tax Effects of Financing Decisions

Because interest payments, but not dividends, are tax deductible by the company, if everything else is equal, the use of debt can be less costly to the corporation than is the use of equity. Consider raising additional capital of $10 million either through long-term debt or through preferred stock. Typically, preferred stock is part of shareholders' equity, and any dividends paid to preferred stockholders are not deductible for income tax purposes. Furthermore, the rate of preferred dividends is usually higher than the rate of interest on long-term debt because the preferred stockholders have greater risk due to their lower priority claim on the total assets of a company. Assume an interest rate of 6% for debt, a preferred dividend rate of 7%, and an income tax rate of 40%. Exhibit 12-9 shows the effects on net income of electing to raise capital through long-term debt versus preferred stock.

EXHIBIT 12-9

Income Tax Effects of Financing Decisions

	$10 Million Long-Term Debt	$10 Million Preferred Stock
Income before interest expense (assumed)	$5,000,000	$5,000,000
Interest expense at 6% of long-term debt	600,000	—
Income before income taxes	4,400,000	5,000,000
Income tax expense at 40%	1,760,000	2,000,000
Net income	$2,640,000	$3,000,000
Dividends to preferred shareholders at 7%	—	700,000
Net income available to common stockholders	$2,640,000	$2,300,000
Pretax cost of capital raised	6%	7%
After-tax cost of capital raised		
($360,000* ÷ $10,000,000)	3.6%	
($700,000 ÷ $10,000,000)		7%

*Interest expense		$600,000
Less income tax savings because of interest deduction:		
(.40 × $600,000)		240,000
Interest expense after tax savings		$360,000

When you examine Exhibit 12-9, you should note three points:

1. Interest is tax deductible, so its after-tax cost can be considerably less than that of dividends on preferred stock (3.6% versus 7%). In other words, using debt makes net income attributable to common shareholders substantially higher.
2. Interest is an expense, whereas preferred dividends are not. Therefore, using preferred shares makes net income higher ($3 million versus $2.64 million). Note that trading on the equity can benefit the common stockholders by the issuance of either long-term debt securities or preferred stock, provided that the additional assets generate sufficient earnings.
3. Failure to pay interest can lead to bankruptcy, which gives creditors rights to control or liquidate the company. The consequences of failure to pay dividends are less severe.

Measuring Safety

Investors in debt securities want to be sure that the company's future operations will provide enough cash to cover scheduled payments of interest and principal. Debt securities often have provisions aimed at reducing debt-holder risk, such as the right to repossess assets or the right to receive payment before common stockholders. However, because such provisions take effect only when the company is in danger of defaulting on the loans, they are nowhere near as valuable as a pattern of earnings growth. Debt holders prefer to avoid the trouble and costs of foreclosure or bankruptcy litigation. They would much rather have a steady stream of interest and repayments of principal provided by a company with good, steady earnings. They do not want to be in the position of **Lehman Brothers'** bondholders, waiting several years after the company declared bankruptcy and then receiving only a fraction of each dollar owed them.

Debt-to-equity ratios, discussed in Chapter 9, are popular measures of risk. However, they do not focus directly on the major concern of the holders of long-term debt: the ability of the company to make interest payments and repay debt on schedule. The interest-coverage ratio, calculated as EBIT divided by interest expense, focuses on interest-paying ability. In Exhibit 12-6, interest coverage for Nike is 91.4 times in 2012. This coverage ratio is up from 84.6 in 2011 and 49.7 in 2009. This partially reflects the profound downward trend in interest rates since the recession and partially the continued repayment of long-term debt totaling $243 million in the last 3 years.

A rule of thumb or benchmark for debt investors is that the interest coverage should be at least five times, even in the poorest year in a span of 7 to 10 years. The numerator in this ratio is computed on a before-tax basis because interest expense is deductible for income tax purposes. In effect, all EBIT is available to pay interest; companies pay taxes only on the amount remaining after paying interest. This tax-deductibility feature is a major reason companies use long-term debt much more widely than they use preferred stock.

Prominence of Earnings per Share

Throughout this text, we regard earnings as a basic reporting element in the financial statements. We often express earnings on a per share basis (EPS), and EPS is itself a component in other ratios. Up to this point, we have kept EPS simple by assuming the company has only common stock. In reality, EPS can be more complicated. We now turn to several issues that complicate the computation of EPS: changes in the number of common shares outstanding during the year, the presence of preferred stock, and the existence of convertible securities.

> ▶▶ **OBJECTIVE 5**
> Calculate EPS when a company has preferred stock or dilutive securities.

Weighted-Average Shares and Preferred Stock

When a company has only common stock outstanding, the primary complication is calculation of the weighted-average number of common shares outstanding in the following equation (numbers assumed):

$$\text{Earnings per share of common stock} = \frac{\text{Net income}}{\text{Weighted-average number of common shares outstanding during the period}}$$

$$= \frac{\$1,000,000}{800,000} = \$1.25$$

How would we calculate the 800,000 weighted-average shares in the denominator? Suppose 750,000 shares were outstanding at the beginning of a fiscal year, and the company issued 200,000 additional shares 3 months before the end of the fiscal year. The weighted average is based on the number of months that the shares were outstanding during the year. We can do the basic computation in two different ways:

750,000 × Weighting of 12/12	=	750,000	750,000 × 9/12	=	562,500
200,000 × Weighting of 3/12	=	50,000	or 950,000 × 3/12	=	237,500
Weighted-average shares		800,000			800,000

In this example, the number of shares outstanding rose because the company issued additional shares during the year. This might have occurred because executives exercised stock options and acquired more shares. Alternatively, the company might have issued a block of additional shares to outside investors at the current market price. Over the 2010–2012 time period, Nike received proceeds totaling almost $1.2 billion from the issuance of stock. The number of shares outstanding could also decline during the year if the company purchases shares for the treasury or retires shares. For example, from 2010 through 2012, Nike expended $4.4 billion to repurchase shares of stock.

A second complication arises if shares of nonconvertible preferred stock are outstanding. To compute the earnings applicable to common stock, we deduct the dividends on preferred stock for the current period, even if the company does not pay the dividends (numbers assumed):

$$\text{Earnings per share of common stock} = \frac{\text{Net income} - \text{Preferred dividends}}{\text{Weighted-average number of common shares outstanding during the period}}$$

$$= \frac{\$1,000,000 - \$200,000}{800,000} = \$1.00$$

We have treated Nike as if it had no preferred stock outstanding because the balance sheet does not show any. However, in reading the footnotes one learns that Sojitz America is the sole owner of some redeemable preferred stock with a par value of $.3 million. Why doesn't the preferred stock appear on Nike's balance sheet? Nike's balance sheet is reported in millions of dollars. Because of the small magnitude of the preferred stock, considerably less than a million dollars, it does not appear. There is a cumulative dividend of $.10 per share per year. These numbers are sufficiently immaterial that ignoring them in our analysis is reasonable, but it is a reminder that the footnotes are an integral part of the financial statements and a full reading is part of a complete analysis.

To ensure comparability of historical summaries of EPS, we must also adjust for changes in capitalization structure, for example, stock splits and stock dividends. As an example, Nike's

Web site indicates that Nike's common stock has split five times since 1983, with the most recent two-for-one stock split occurring in April 2007. In the 2007 annual report, Nike reports 2006 EPS of $2.69. If you look at the 2006 annual report, the EPS reported is $5.37. Why did Nike adjust the 2006 EPS when it published the 2007 annual report? Because the investor wants to be able to compare the year-to-year performance in terms of the current number of shares. Because each 2006 share outstanding counts as two 2007 shares, Nike adjusted the 2006 EPS to allow meaningful comparisons.

Basic and Diluted EPS

EPS calculations become a bit more complex when companies have convertible securities, stock options, or other financial instruments that holders can exchange for, or convert into, common shares. For example, suppose that a firm with net income of $10.5 million has outstanding preferred stock that is convertible into common stock.

Convertible preferred stock at 5%, $100 par, each share convertible into two common shares	100,000 shares
Average common shares outstanding	1,000,000 shares

The basic EPS computation follows:

Computation of earnings per share	
Net income	$10,500,000
Less: Preferred dividends (0.05 × $100 × 100,000 shares)	500,000
Net income available to common stockholders	$10,000,000
Earnings per share of common stock ($10,000,000 ÷ 1,000,000 shares)	$ 10.00

However, note the effect on EPS if the preferred shareholders converted, that is, exchanged their preferred shares for shares of common stock. EPS will be "diluted," or reduced. We can calculate EPS as if conversion had occurred at the beginning of the period. The company would pay no preferred dividends, but there would be 200,000 more common shares outstanding:

Net income	$10,500,000
Less: Preferred dividends	0
Net income available to common stockholders	$10,500,000
Earnings per share of common stock—assuming conversion ($10,500,000 ÷ 1,200,000 shares)	$ 8.75

The dilution of EPS caused by the conversion of the preferred stock is ($10.00 – $8.75) = $1.25 per share. Diluted EPS assumes the conversion of all potentially dilutive securities. In 2012, Nike reported basic EPS of $4.83 and diluted EPS of $4.73. The modest difference in the two EPS measures indicates that Nike had few potentially dilutive securities.

INTERPRETING FINANCIAL STATEMENTS

You are considering an investment in a company, and as part of your analysis you decide to compute P-E and dividend-yield ratios. When you examine the company's income statement, you find that it reports both basic and diluted earnings per share figures, and they are significantly different. Which earnings per share figure should you use in your ratio computations and why?

Answer

You should use basic earnings per share in the dividend-yield ratio. The market price represents the value of a share of stock currently outstanding and dividends are paid on outstanding shares. So the earnings per share used should reflect the shares actually outstanding, not the number of shares that would be outstanding if potentially dilutive securities were converted to common stock. The answer is not so obvious for the P-E ratio. If you think conversion is likely and will therefore reduce your claims to future net income, you might want to use diluted EPS.

Disclosure of Irregular Items

One of the goals of financial statement analysis is to evaluate or estimate a firm's future prospects. When forecasting the future, we need to distinguish the elements of the current financial statements that reflect ordinary recurring activity of the firm from those that represent one-time events or items that are not likely to be repeated. These irregular items fall into four major categories: unusual or nonrecurring items, extraordinary items, discontinued operations, and changes in accounting principle.

Unusual or Nonrecurring Items

A **nonrecurring (unusual) item** is an income statement item that is either unusual in nature or infrequent in occurrence, but not both. We expect nonrecurring items to be infrequent for a given firm. These items are generally classified as operating expenses, with any necessary discussion or explanation in the footnotes. Examples include the impairment of property, plant, and equipment; impairment of goodwill; and restructuring charges. Unusual items represent the most frequent of the four categories of irregular items.

The years 2012 and 2011 for Nike were not characterized by large, unusual items. We already noted one reasonably small exception, a restructuring charge in Western Europe that involved $24 million and was included in Other Expense, net. If we look back to 2009 we see $596 million in restructuring charges and impairments. You can see this in the 5-year summary in Exhibit 12-3 on p. 543. In 2009, Nike, like so many other companies, was dealing with the financial crisis, which greatly reduced the value of the company and thereby impaired goodwill. Moreover, the economic downturn necessitated major realignment of production and sales activity to deal with reduced demand. Restructuring charges capture those efforts from a financial standpoint.

Accounting guidance requires separate disclosure of material nonrecurring items. As a result, material nonrecurring items are typically shown as separate line items in the income statement as Nike did in 2009, or at least separately identified in the footnotes and MD&A as Nike did in 2012. Materiality will determine the appropriate disclosure. In fact, in 2009 Nike showed the $195 million of restructuring charges, $199 million of goodwill impairment, and $202 million in impairment of intangible and other assets as three separate line items. Our summary in Exhibit 12-3 aggregates the three items into a single line item of $596 million.

As we covered in Chapters 8 and 11, a company must evaluate fixed assets, intangible assets, and goodwill for impairment. If the impairment tests indicate that the assets have become impaired in value, an impairment loss is recorded on the income statement. That is exactly what happened to Nike in 2009. In 2008, Nike purchased Umbro, a leading United Kingdom-based global soccer company. However, in 2009 the decline in consumer demand and weakness in the worldwide economy suggested that goodwill and the Umbro trademark recorded in the acquisition should be tested for impairment. Impairment tests resulted in goodwill impairment of $199 million and other asset (trademark) impairment of $202 million. Three years later, in 2012, Nike announced its plans to sell Umbro and focus attention on better-performing subsidiaries.

As discussed in Chapter 9, restructuring costs result from a significant makeover of part of a company that typically involves closing one or more plants, reducing the size of the workforce, and terminating or relocating activities. As a result of restructuring in 2009, Nike reduced its workforce by 5% and incurred "pre-tax restructuring charges of $195 million, primarily consisting of severance costs related to the workforce reduction." Combined, the restructuring and impairments increased expenses by $596 million, accounting for over 75% of the increase in operating expenses in 2009. In 2012, such events were largely absent with no significant impairments and a modest restructuring charge disclosed only in footnotes. The flexibility in timing and presentation of impairment and restructuring expenses has raised questions of earnings management over the years.

How would an analyst use information about unusual items to project future income from continuing operations? An analyst who concludes that similar costs will continue in future years might base predictions on income as reported, without adjusting out the effect of unusual items. An analyst who believes the restructuring and impairment charges are truly unusual and unlikely to recur in future years might ignore the expense of $596 million in projecting the future. In that

---

▶▶ **OBJECTIVE 6**

Understand the nature of irregular items and how to adjust for them.

---

nonrecurring items (unusual items)

An income statement item that is either unusual in nature or infrequent in occurrence but not both. These items are not expected to happen often for a given firm.

case, the analyst would base projections on pretax income from continuing operations before deducting impairment and restructuring charges.

Because companies report unusual items with other expenses, they report such items on a before-tax basis. These items reduce pretax income and income tax expense. If we assume a 40% tax rate, the unusual items reported in 2009 reduced pretax income by $596 million and therefore reduced the tax provision by 40% of $596 million, or $238 million. The after-tax effect would be ($596 – $238) = $358 million. An analyst who elects to ignore the effect of the impairment and restructuring charges in estimating future after-tax net income would add back $358 million to reported after-tax net income for 2009.

Since Nike reported material restructuring and impairment charges only in 2009 and not in the other 4 years, they appear to be truly nonrecurring items. Life would not be quite as easy for the equity analyst trying to assess the future earnings of Timberland before its purchase by VF Corporation. Timberland reported restructuring costs every year from 2005 through 2008 in amounts ranging from $.925 million to $24.7 million and impairment costs every year from 2008 through 2010 ranging from $.925 million to $14.0 million. Although it is important to highlight these costs, it is not obvious that they are truly unusual or nonrecurring. In fact, the ongoing appearance of these costs on the income statement suggests the opposite. A footnote in Timberland's 2008 annual report describes the restructuring costs as related to severance, store closures, lease termination costs, and impairment of property, plant, and equipment. A footnote in the 2010 annual report describes the impairments as decreasing the goodwill by $5.395 million, trademarks by $7.014 million, and other intangible assets by $1.542 million. Even after VF Corporation purchased Timberland in June 2011, the problems were not all solved. In the fourth quarter of 2011, VF reported further transaction and restructuring costs related to the Timberland purchase totaling $6.7 million.

For decision-making and forecasting purposes, companies may also adjust their income for the effects of nonrecurring or unusual items. See the Business First Box on page 565 for discussion of additional means of measuring performance.

Extraordinary Items

extraordinary items
Items that are both unusual in nature and infrequent in occurrence that are shown separately, net of tax, on the income statement.

Extraordinary items result from events that are both unusual in nature and infrequent in occurrence. Write-downs of receivables, inventories, and intangibles are not extraordinary items. Neither are gains or losses on the sale or impairment of fixed assets. Why? Because they represent ordinary business risk. The effects of a strike and many foreign currency revaluations are also ordinary items. However, the financial effects of an earthquake or government expropriation are generally extraordinary items. Interestingly enough, we do not consider the effects of most floods as extraordinary. Why not? Because most floods occur in areas that are prone to certain amounts of flooding; thus, a flood in such locations is not an unusual occurrence. Accountants treat an event or transaction as ordinary unless the evidence clearly supports its classification as extraordinary.

Accountants exclude extraordinary items from regular operating income calculations and present each event or item that is considered extraordinary on a separate line on the income statement, generally below the presentation of after-tax operating income. Companies report these items net of tax, which means that the figure presented includes any tax effect attributable to the item. For example, Duke Energy reported an extraordinary item (gain) of $67 million after tax on its 2008 income statement. The $67 million was a one-time gain resulting from a ruling of the Public Utilities Commission of Ohio and was 5% of income before extraordinary items.

Surprisingly, U.S. authorities did not allow companies to account for the terrorist attacks of September 11, 2001, as an extraordinary item. The FASB's Emerging Issues Task Force (EITF) decided that, although the events of September 11 were definitely extraordinary, treating the financial effects of those events as extraordinary items would not be an effective means of communicating with stockholders. In a news release on October 1, 2001, the EITF observed "that the economic effects of the events were so extensive and pervasive that it would be impossible to capture them in any one financial statement line item."

Discontinued Operations

discontinued operations
A component of the business that is distinguishable from the rest of the entity, both operationally and for financial reporting purposes, that a company disposes of or makes plans to dispose of. The results are reported separately, net of tax, on the income statement.

Discontinued operations occur when a company disposes of (i.e., closes or sells), or makes plans to dispose of, a component of the business that is distinguishable from the rest of the entity, both operationally and for financial reporting. If a company discontinues such a component,

BUSINESS FIRST

BEYOND GAAP FINANCIAL METRICS

While metrics based on GAAP financial statement data provide valuable information to financial statement users, some companies attempt to extend the use of metrics to include aspects of performance that seem to defy traditional measurement techniques. For example, Wells Fargo computes a "happy-to-grumpy" ratio in an effort to assess whether its goal of developing a more engaged workforce is meeting with success. Other companies attempt to measure attributes such as customer satisfaction, innovation, brand loyalty, and service quality. Presumably, an increase in these attributes leads to increased sales. But the establishment of a link between these metrics and financial performance has proven to be a challenge.

You won't see Wells Fargo's "happy-to-grumpy" ratio in an SEC filing. However, some metrics based on nonfinancial information are reported because they complement traditional financial statement measures. Consider Southwest Airlines. In its 2011 10-K, Southwest reported a number of nonfinancial metrics that offer insight into Southwest's performance. Examples include the number of passengers, revenue passenger miles (RPMs) computed as the number of fare-paying passengers multiplied by the number of miles they travel, available seat miles (ASMs) computed as the number of available seats (whether occupied or not) multiplied by the number of miles traveled, and the load factor computed as RPM divided by ASM. The load factor shows how many available seats an airline actually sold relative to its total capacity. These metrics are considered valuable enough that Airlines for America (A4A), a trade association of the U.S. airlines (formerly the Air Transport Association), provides industry-wide figures to be used for comparison purposes, and analysts focused on the industry are attuned to the relative performance of different airlines. Other industries also report nonfinancial measures such as number of subscribers, number of advertisers, unit sales, or rate of occupancy.

Metrics that employ financial statement numbers in combination with nonfinancial data are frequently cited as indicators of performance. In the retail sector, companies use sales revenue to compute valuable metrics such as same store sales, sales per square foot, and sales per employee. For example, in its 2011 annual report, Target Corporation reported revenues per square foot of $294, which is up from $287 in 2009 but well below the $318 generated in 2007.

Companies may also report non-GAAP financial measures. The SEC defines a non-GAAP financial measure as a numerical measure of a company's historical or future financial performance, financial position, or cash flows that excludes amounts that are included in a GAAP measure or includes amounts that are excluded in GAAP measures. An example of a non-GAAP financial measure is a measure of operating income that excludes one or more expense or revenue items that are identified as "nonrecurring." An example of a non-GAAP financial ratio is a measure of operating margin that is calculated by dividing operating income by revenue, where either revenue or operating income, or both, are not calculated in accordance with GAAP.

Southwest reports a "non-GAAP" operating income that it calculates by adjusting GAAP operating income for the effect of fuel hedging activity. Southwest, like many energy users, often enters into contracts to acquire large quantities of fuel in future years at prices that are agreed to today. These contracts are hedges because they protect Southwest from large fluctuations in prices over time. Southwest argues that GAAP accounting misrepresents the cost of operating the airline in a specific year because GAAP recognizes gains and losses on hedging positions in years other than the year when the related fuel is consumed.

The release of non-GAAP financial measures, particularly variations of earnings, became so prevalent in the late 1990s and early 2000s that the SEC now requires specific disclosures. If a company publicly releases any material information in earnings announcements, press releases, or SEC filings that includes a non-GAAP financial measure, the SEC requires the company to also present the most directly comparable financial measure calculated in accordance with GAAP and a reconciliation of the differences between the non-GAAP measure and the comparable GAAP measure. Companies presenting non-GAAP financial measures must also provide a statement disclosing why management believes that presentation of the non-GAAP metric provides useful information to investors regarding the company's financial condition and results of operations.

The magnitude of the difference in GAAP and non-GAAP financial measures can be significant. In its third quarter 2012 earnings announcement, Hewlett-Packard (HP) reported non-GAAP net earnings of $1,973 million and non-GAAP diluted EPS of $1.00 for the 3 months ended July 31, 2012. The comparable GAAP figures were a net loss of $8,857 million and GAAP diluted EPS of $(4.49)! A summary of the adjustments appear below.

In millions, except per share data	Net Income	Impact per Diluted Share
GAAP results	$(8,857)	$(4.49)
Non-GAAP adjustments:		
Amortization of purchased intangible assets	476	0.25
Impairment of goodwill and purchased intangible assets	9,188	4.66
Restructuring charges	1,795	0.91
Acquisition-related charges	3	—
Wind down of nonstrategic businesses	108	0.05
Adjustments for taxes	(740)	(0.38)
Adjusted results	$ 1,973	$ 1.00

Hewlett-Packard believes that providing non-GAAP measures alongside the related GAAP measures in its announcements and SEC filings "provides investors with greater transparency to the information used by HP's management in its financial and operational decision-making and allows investors to see HP's results 'through the eyes' of management."

Sources: S. Leibs, "Measuring Up," *CFO*, June 1, 2007 (www.cfo.com/article.cfm/9214066); Southwest Airlines 2011 10-K (http://www.fuelteam.wallst.com/modules/secfilings/draw-Filing.asp?docKey=136-000119312512049647-78H1ENULTC34KBNHGKB6F132BC&formType=10-K&date=2/9/2012&docFormat=PDF); Conditions for Use of Non-GAAP Financial Measures, Securities and Exchange Commission (www.sec.gov/rules/final/33-8176.htm); "HP Reports Third Quarter 2012 Results," HP Web site, August 22, 2012 (http://www.hp.com/hpinfo/newsroom/press/2012/120822a.html?mtxs=rss-corp-news).

it should report the results of continuing operations separately from the operating results of the discontinued operations, although it must still report both on the income statement. This separation distinguishes the operations that are expected to continue from those that will not continue, enhancing the analyst's ability to forecast future performance. Companies must also separately report any gain or loss from the disposal of a discontinued operation. Like extraordinary items, discontinued operations are shown on the income statement net of tax.

In comparative income statements over multiple years, the statements must show the income or loss of the discontinued operations separately for all years in which that discontinued component operated. Otherwise, the company's current financial status, which no longer includes the discontinued component, would not be comparable to its past financial status. Because income statements reflect 3 years of comparative data, in the year a company makes the decision to discontinue an operation, it reports the effect separately for the current year and restates the prior 2 years to isolate the operations of the discontinued portion of the business. When evaluating a firm's income patterns through time, an analyst may need to estimate the amount of income attributable to discontinued operations in years prior to those restated by the company.

One of Nike's competitors, K-Swiss, reported a loss from discontinued operations in 2011. In July 2010, K-Swiss purchased Form Athletics as part of an overall strategy to enter the action sports market. However, during the third quarter of 2011, management decided not to continue operating in this line of business, so K-Swiss' income statement showed the 2011 after-tax results for Form Athletics, including an after-tax loss of $5,949,000 on the discontinued unit, as follows:

Loss from continuing operations	(64,522,000)
Loss from discontinued operations, less applicable income taxes	(5,949,000)
Net loss	$(70,471,000)

Changes in Accounting Principle

Changes in accounting principles occur under two circumstances: (1) when a company voluntarily changes from one acceptable accounting method to another, and (2) when a standard-setting authority issues a new accounting standard. In the year of the change in accounting principle, the company uses the newly adopted method to prepare the financial statements. Then, in most cases, the company makes a retrospective adjustment to the financial statements of all prior periods that are presented. This restates prior period financial statements to reflect the newly adopted accounting principle and makes prior periods consistent with the year of the change. The company also makes a cumulative adjustment to the beginning balance in Retained Earnings for the earliest year presented.

International Issues

Internationally, a variety of factors complicate financial statement analysis. Throughout the text, we consider differences in accounting methods used under U.S. GAAP and IFRS. When companies use different methods to generate the numbers in the financial statements, ratios based on those numbers may not be comparable. This is one of the reasons that we did not include a comparison of Nike to adidas in this chapter. In addition, we should stress the obvious but easily forgotten differences in the language of reporting and the currency of measurement. For example, most U.S. analysts cannot read financial statements in Japanese and do not readily "have a feel for" the value of yen versus dollars. Last, but not least, is the fact that different structures for security markets, different tax laws, and different preferences among citizens of different countries all affect the relative value of financial assets.

Valuation Issues

Accounting data are critically important to determining the value of a company. We have already examined a number of ratios that help in this effort. Exhibit 12-10 presents fundamental price and valuation information for Nike (NKE), Under Armour (UA), VF Corporation (VFC), and K-Swiss (KSWS) gathered from Reuters (www.reuters.com) as of August 13, 2012, as well as a few figures drawn from each company's most recent annual report. Information provided by Reuters is similar to that provided by many financial services. When using information gathered from outside sources, be sure you thoroughly understand the items reported. For example, the price to book, total-debt-to-equity, current, and quick ratios in Exhibit 12-10 are based on figures from the most recent quarterly financial statements. Many of the other reported values, such as the P-E ratio, ROA, ROE, and the 1-year growth rates are based on the most recent 12 months. This is often abbreviated as TTM for trailing twelve months. As a result, the values for Nike presented in Exhibit 12-10 do not necessarily correspond to the values reported in Exhibit 12-6, which used data from the fiscal year ended May 31, 2012.

> ▶▶ **OBJECTIVE 7**
> Use financial information to help assess a company's value.

Valuation techniques are beyond the scope of this textbook, and we do not attempt to reach conclusions regarding the appropriateness of the reported stock prices. Rather, our intent is to demonstrate that much of the information needed for valuation is readily available and related to the outputs of financial statement analysis. Reviewing this information gives us an opportunity to emphasize the importance of financial information in valuation and to explain a few common ratios and values to which we have not given significant attention. We next describe and compare key information shown in Exhibit 12-10 for four companies: Nike (NKE), Under Armour (UA), VF Corporation (VFC), and K-Swiss (KSWS). We then elaborate briefly on the P-E ratio.

Some Basic Comparisons

The four stocks traded at very different prices on August 10, 2012, and all have shown significant share price variation during the period from August 2011 to August 2012. UA and VFC are trading above the middle of their respective 52-week price ranges. NKE is trading just below its midpoint, and KSWS is trading near the low end of its range. Beta is a measure of how closely the price of the company's stock follows general market conditions. A value of 1.0 indicates the stock price moves proportionally to the market. NKE and VFC's have betas below 1.0 suggesting that their prices move slightly less than the market. For example, on a typical day, if the market moved up 10%, NKE's price would be expected to move up only 8.6%, whereas VFC's would move 9.1%. UA and KSWS, on the other hand, have betas in excess of 1.0. If the market moved up 10%, UA and KSWS would be expected to move 15.7% and 10.9%, respectively.

The latest annual EPS of each company is based on the most recent quarter. Reuters provides EPS information on a quarterly basis, and we have accumulated the most recent four quarters to provide an annual TTM number. They are widely divergent. VFC has earnings of $8.28 per share, and Nike has earnings of $4.73 per share. VFC has earnings per share that are 1.75 as large as Nike's, and we might expect that VFC's share price would be 1.75 times larger than Nike's $94.50. That implies that VFC would trade at $165.38, but it does not; it trades at $147.33. This difference is captured in the difference in P-E ratios. Nike's is 19.97 while VFC's is only 17.79.

EXHIBIT 12-10

Industry Fundamentals

Nike (NKE), Under Armour (UA), VF Corporation (VFC), and K-Swiss (KSWS)

PRICE AND VALUATION

Ticker Symbol	Current Price August 10, 2012	52-Week Range	Beta	Latest Annual EPS (TTM)	Price-Earnings
NKE	$ 94.50	78.50–114.81	0.86	$4.73	19.97
UA	$ 56.76	26.31–58.48	1.57	$0.94	60.12
VFC	$147.33	104.02–156.15	0.91	$8.28	17.79
KSWS	$ 3.04	2.47–6.60	1.09	–$1.60	n/a

Ticker Symbol	Price/Sales	Price/Book	Price/Cash Flow	Analyst Rating
NKE	1.78	4.17	16.38	2.30
UA	3.65	8.60	43.42	2.46
VFC	1.56	3.57	14.45	1.86
KSWS	0.44	0.73	n/a	2.75

GROWTH RATES AND DIVIDENDS

Ticker Symbol	Latest Annual Revenue (mil)	1-yr Revenue Growth	5-yr Revenue Growth	Latest Annual EPS (TTM)	1-yr EPS Growth	5-yr EPS Growth
NKE	$24,128.0	15.66%	8.13%	$4.73	7.75%	10.10%
UA	$ 1,622.5	38.42%	27.88%	$0.94	38.23%	18.62%
VFC	$10,358.6	22.81%	8.76%	$8.28	54.09%	11.04%
KSWS	$ 244.7	23.80%	–11.32%	–$1.60	n/a	n/a

Ticker Symbol	Latest Annual Dividend/Share	Dividend Yield	5-yr Dividend Growth Rate
NKE	$1.39	1.52	14.38%
UA	$0.00	0.00	0.00%
VFC	$2.70	1.92	6.11%
KSWS	$0.00	0.00	0.00%

FINANCIAL STRENGTH

Ticker Symbol	Total Debt/Equity	Long-term Debt/Equity	Current Ratio	Quick Ratio
NKE	3.71	2.20	2.98	2.12
UA	10.72	4.57	3.09	1.58
VFC	55.59	40.46	1.89	1.00
KSWS	3.75	0.06	4.63	2.34

EFFICIENCY

Ticker Symbol	Current Inventory Turnover	Current Receivable Turnover	Total Asset Turnover	Revenue/Employee (000s)	Income/Employee (000s)
NKE	4.50	7.52	1.58	$548.4	$50.5
UA	2.44	10.31	1.83	$300.4	$18.5
VFC	3.95	10.66	1.28	$178.6	$16.0
KSWS	1.86	6.83	1.04	$401.8	–$93.3

PROFITABILITY

Ticker Symbol	Gross Margin	Operating Margin	Pretax Margin	After-tax Profit Margin
NKE	43.40%	12.36%	12.36%	9.21%
UA	47.93%	10.26%	9.87%	6.16%
VFC	44.93%	12.16%	11.70%	8.98%
KSWS	33.29%	–21.70%	–21.57%	–23.23%

MANAGEMENT EFFECTIVENESS

Ticker Symbol	Return on Assets	5-yr Avg. Return on Assets	Return on Equity	5-yr Avg. Return on Equity
NKE	14.59%	14.13%	21.98%	21.49%
UA	11.28%	11.21%	16.20%	15.54%
VFC	11.46%	9.45%	21.12%	16.77%
KSWS	–24.16%	–5.18%	–31.85%	–6.16%

Data as of August 13, 2012.

Source: Reuters (www.reuters.com).

UA has a modest EPS of $.94 but a high P/E of 60.12. This suggests that investors expect UA to grow rapidly and generate rising EPS in years to come. KSWS had negative earnings and trades near the lower end of its 52-week range. It does not have a meaningful P-E because the denominator is negative, but it has a positive share price, since things could improve. Note that the P-E ratio shown by Reuters is not the result of dividing the current price by the prior year's EPS. Rather, the reported P-E ratio uses the most recent 12-months' earnings (TTM) in the denominator.

Exhibit 12-10 also includes items that relate stock price to sales, to book value, and to cash flow. Not only does UA have the largest P-E ratio but also the largest ratios of Price to Sales, to Book, and to Cash Flow. The final item in the Price and Valuation section is the Analyst Ratings. The number reported is the average of the analysts' rankings where a 1 is associated with a "buy" rating, a 2 represents an "outperform" rating, a 3 suggests a "hold," and a 5 represents a "sell" rating. Thus the lower the average of analysts' rankings, the more favorable is their view of the stock. By this measure, VFC receives the most enthusiastic support from analysts, possibly because its relatively low P-E ratio suggests that analysts believe it is underpriced.

The Growth Rates and Dividends portion of Exhibit 12-10 displays the most recent annual revenue (aggregated over the most recent 4 quarters), EPS, and dividends per share to provide a sense of size differences among the companies. Nike is the largest of the four with respect to revenues. This section of the exhibit gives growth rates for 1 and 5 years for revenue and EPS, and a 5-year growth rate for dividends. NKE, UA, and VFC have experienced positive growth in revenues over the last 5 years and even higher growth in the most recent 12 months. KSWS experienced a negative revenue growth over the 5-year interval but reported positive revenue growth in the most recent 12 months. KSWS reported negative EPS in the most recent year, so EPS growth rates are not reported. Neither UA nor KSWS declared dividends. VFC reported an annual per share dividend almost twice that of NKE. However, NKE reports a higher 5-year dividend growth rate.

The data in the Financial Strength section of the exhibit are outputs of ratio analysis. You should be familiar with the four ratios in this section. However, note that Reuters defines total debt as both short- and long-term debt but does not include operating liabilities such as accounts payable and accrued expenses. Note the differences in capital structure. NKE's total-debt-to-equity ratio of 3.71 is the lowest of the four firms, followed by KSWS with a ratio of 3.71. VFC's ratio of 55.59 is by far the largest, suggesting more reliance on borrowing. The current and quick ratios are more similar across the four firms than are the longer-term debt ratios. But note that VFC has the highest long-term ratios and the lowest current and quick ratios. High debt-to-equity ratios and low short-term liquidity ratios both suggest higher levels of borrowing, be it long-term financing or short-term operating liabilities.

The Efficiency section of Exhibit 12-10 displays both standard ratios such as inventory and accounts receivable turnovers and information about performance per employee. We can see that the companies vary with regard to inventory, receivable, and total asset turnovers. KSWS is the least efficient on every standard turnover measure. There is wider variation in the revenue-per-employee and income-per-employee metrics. While each NKE employee has generated an average of $548,400 in revenue in the last 12 months, each VFC employee has generated only $178,600.

The Profitability section of the exhibit displays four measures of profitability per dollar of sales: gross margin, operating margin, pretax margin, and after-tax profit margin. Note that NKE, UA, and VFC have fairly similar gross margins ranging from 47.93% for UA to 43.40% for NKE. However, after accounting for all operating expenses and nonoperating activity, the resultant after-tax profit margins are more divergent. NKE reports an after-tax profit margin of 9.21%, approximately 50% higher than that reported for UA. KSWS reports the lowest values for all four metrics. In fact, the operating, pretax, and after-tax margins for KSWS are all negative!

The Management Effectiveness portion of Exhibit 12-10 presents the return on assets and return on equity for the four firms and the 5-year average levels for these ratios. NKE has the highest levels on every measure. Reuters reports negative values for KSWS for all profitability measures other than gross margin. The situation appears to be worsening. The most recent year's measures for KSWS are worse than the 5-year averages. This highlights the importance of considering more than 1 year's performance.

So what might an analyst conclude? There are always more questions. What is the company planning? How many new products are in the pipeline? How are competitors changing the industry dynamics? Analysts would pursue answers to these and other questions before reaching a conclusion. And we saw their conclusions in the Analyst Rating column in the Price and Valuation section of Exhibit 12-10. From the analysts' perspectives, VFC is viewed most favorably with a rating of 1.86. The other three stocks have ratings above 2.

Price-Earnings Ratios and Growth

Some consider the P-E ratio a useful valuation tool. The ratio relates the price of a company's stock to the earnings it is generating. Some argue that low P-E stocks might be undervalued and high P-E stocks might be overvalued. This is the view of analysts called "value investors." These investors seek securities that the market is currently undervaluing. They would not blindly buy low P-E stocks, but they would use a low P-E ratio as a screen to identify securities that may be candidates for purchase. They would then consider many other factors in selecting the best investments.

The opposite view is that the best investments are growth stocks. "Growth investors" believe that high P-E stocks are likely to be high-growth stocks. The price is "high" because investors see strong growth prospects ahead. Again, the growth investor would use high P-Es to identify a group of stocks to evaluate more carefully.

Who is right? How do we relate P-E ratios to growth? When are we paying too much for future growth? As of August 10, 2012, the average P-E on stocks in the S&P 500 was 15.89. This is near the long-term norm of around 15. A few years ago, as the recession began, P-E levels peaked at more than 45. P-E ratios vary for different groups of stocks with the average for the smaller firms in the Russell 2000 index at 31.40 and the average for the technology-rich NASDAQ 100 at 11.72. We normally expect higher P-E ratios to be associated with faster growing firms, and the high average ratio for the Russell 2000 is consistent with that belief. However, the low ratio for the NASDAQ 100 might be surprising, since it suggests low growth expectations for tech firms. The P-E ratios for the four firms in our sample range from negative and not meaningful for KSWS, to 17.79 and 19.97 for VFC and NKE, respectively, to a high of slightly over 60 for UA. The question for investors is whether these P-E ratios properly capture their expectations of future growth rates.

price-earnings growth (PEG) ratio

Price-earnings ratio divided by the earnings growth rate.

One metric that relates P-E ratios directly to earnings growth rates is the **price-earnings growth (PEG) ratio**. To compute the PEG ratio, we divide the P-E ratio by the earnings growth rate. We can calculate the P-E ratio and the earnings growth rate based on historical earnings, current earnings, or forecasted earnings. Many analysts prefer a current P-E ratio and a forecasted 5-year earnings growth rate. Due to the variation in computational methods, information sources report widely different numbers.

How do we interpret the PEG ratio? A PEG ratio greater than 1.0 indicates that the stock may be overvalued or that the market expects future EPS growth to be greater than that currently reflected in the analysts' consensus forecast EPS. Growth stocks typically have a PEG ratio greater than 1.0 because investors are willing to pay more for a stock that they expect to grow rapidly. Stocks with a PEG ratio less than 1.0 may be undervalued, or the market may believe the earnings growth estimate reflected in the consensus forecast is too high.

Relating Cash Flow and Net Income

Although this chapter focuses on evaluating a company's performance based on various earnings metrics (e.g., EPS, P-E, PEG), we would be remiss if we did not mention the important role of cash flow. In fact, valuation models frequently use estimated cash flows, not forecasted earnings. It is important to realize that net income and cash flow do not always move together. Both net income and cash flow from operations are positive for the healthiest of firms. However, there are four possible combinations of positive and negative net income and cash flow from operations, and it is useful to think about what they might mean.

Relationship	1	2	3	4
Cash flow from operations	+	+	−	−
Net income	+	−	+	−

In relationship 1, the two positive values confirm the profitability of the company. In the fourth case, the uniform negative values are again in agreement. When either of these patterns appears and continues for multiple periods, the implications are straightforward.

What about relationship 2? This is common in some industries. Consider high capital investment industries with large depreciation charges or rapidly growing companies in capital-intensive industries. If a growing company uses a declining-balance depreciation method, large depreciation charges may create losses even though operating cash flow is positive. One should examine several years to assess the pattern. Another example is real estate, where the economic returns to the company include both current operating performance and appreciation of the underlying property. The accounting model does not record appreciation in real estate, so it does not appear in the income statement. Thus, you could have negative net income even though cash flow was sufficient to cover all expenses and the investment was appreciating consistently.

Relationship 3, negative cash flow and positive net earnings may be a red flag for trouble, but it may also represent the case of a rapidly growing firm. The difference between cash flow from operations and net income is depreciation and accruals of current operating assets and liabilities. A very rapidly growing firm may be investing heavily in inventory for new stores and granting credit to new customers with the result that inventories and accounts receivable are growing very quickly and using cash in the process. This may be a good situation as long as the company can meet the growing customer demand and pay its current obligations. We also observe this pattern in cases where sales revenue is not growing quickly, but inventory and accounts receivable are increasing. This situation tends to indicate bad management, slow-moving merchandise, and failure to manage credit. This pattern often precedes bankruptcy. In order to interpret relationship 3 for a given firm, you need to understand the firm and the industry in which it operates.

Analysts often use the relationship between cash flow from operations and net income as one of a set of indicators that address the issue of earnings quality. Earnings quality is not a well-defined or well-understood concept. However, analysts generally agree that companies should not recognize revenues prematurely and should not defer expenses inappropriately. Historically, some companies have intentionally or unintentionally engaged in accounting choices that lower the quality of earnings numbers. For example, by capitalizing costs that it should have expensed, WorldCom reported higher earnings than it should have. As a result, although earnings were higher in dollar magnitude, the quality of those earnings was lower. There is no single means to assess earnings quality. However, one ratio that some analysts use is a comparison of cash flow from operations to net income. We would expect this ratio to be consistently greater than 1. Why? Because net income includes an expense for depreciation, but cash flow from operations does not contain the related cash outflow. (The cash outflow is an investing activity at the time the company pays for the asset.) If the ratio is significantly less than 1, this may be an indication of low-quality earnings and a pending cash flow crisis.

Summary Problem for Your Review

PROBLEM

Exhibit 12-11 contains balance sheets and income statements for Kellogg Company. Kellogg is the world's leading producer of cereal, as well as convenience foods such as cookies, crackers, toaster pastries, cereal bars, and assorted other products.

1. Compute the following ratios for 2011: (a) current ratio, (b) quick ratio, (c) average collection period, (d) inventory turnover, (e) total asset turnover, (f) return on sales, (g) financial leverage ratio, and (h) ROE. Define the quick ratio as current assets minus inventories divided by current liabilities. Assume all sales are on credit.
2. Compare your computed values with the values for General Mills reported below.

General Mills	
Current ratio	1.03
Quick ratio	0.65
Average collection period (days)	27.20
Inventory turnover (times)	6.87
Total asset turnover (times)	0.84
Return on sales	9.54%
Financial leverage ratio	2.95
ROE	24.51%

EXHIBIT 12-11

**Kellogg Company
and Subsidiaries**

*Consolidated Balance Sheets
and Statements of Earnings
($ in millions, except
per share data)*

Consolidated Balance Sheets	December 31, 2011	December 31, 2010
Assets:		
Current assets		
Cash and cash equivalents	$ 460	$ 444
Accounts receivable, net	1,188	1,190
Inventories	1,132	1,056
Other current assets	247	225
Total current assets	3,027	2,915
Property, net	3,281	3,128
Goodwill	3,623	3,628
Other intangibles, net	1,454	1,456
Other assets	516	720
Total assets	$11,901	$11,847
Liabilities and Equity:		
Current liabilities		
Current maturities of long-term debt	$ 761	$ 952
Notes payable	234	44
Accounts payable	1,189	1,149
Other current liabilities	1,129	1,039
Total current liabilities	3,313	3,184
Long-term debt	5,037	4,908
Deferred income taxes	637	697
Pension liability	560	265
Other liabilities	592	639
Total liabilities	10,139	9,693
Equity		
Common stock, $.25 par value, 1,000,000,000 shares authorized; Issued: 419,484,087 shares in 2011 and 419,272,027 shares in 2010	105	105
Capital in excess of par value	522	495
Retained earnings	6,721	6,122
Treasury stock, at cost: 62,182,500 shares in 2011 and 53,667,635 shares in 2010	(3,130)	(2,650)
Accumulated other comprehensive income (loss)	(2,458)	(1,914)
Total Kellogg Company equity	1,760	2,158
Noncontrolling interests	2	(4)
Total equity	1,762	2,154
Total liabilities and equity	$11,901	$11,847

EXHIBIT 12-11
(Continued)

Kellogg Company and
Subsidiaries
Consolidated Balance Sheets
and Statements of Earnings
($ in millions, except
per share data)

Consolidated Statements of Earnings

	Year Ended December 31, 2011	Year Ended December 31, 2010	Year Ended December 31, 2009
Net sales	$ 13,198	$ 12,397	$ 12,575
Cost of goods sold	7,750	7,108	7,184
Selling, general, and administrative expense	3,472	3,299	3,390
Operating profit	1,976	1,990	2,001
Interest expense	233	248	295
Other income (expense), net	(11)	0	(22)
Income before income taxes	1,732	1,742	1,684
Income taxes	503	502	476
Net income	1,229	1,240	1,208
Net loss attributable to noncontrolling interests	(2)	(7)	(4)
Net income attributable to Kellogg Company	$ 1,231	$ 1,247	$ 1,212
Earnings per share—Basic	$ 3.40	$ 3.32	$ 3.17
Earnings per share—Diluted	$ 3.38	$ 3.30	$ 3.16

SOLUTION

1. Amounts are in millions of dollars.
   a. Current ratio = Current assets ÷ Current liabilities
      = $3,027 ÷ $3,313 = .91
   b. Quick ratio = (Current assets – Inventories) ÷ Current liabilities
      = ($3,027 – $1,132) ÷ $3,313 = 0.57
   c. Average collection period = (Average accounts receivable × 365) ÷ Sales
      = {[($1,188 + $1,190) ÷ 2] × 365} ÷ $13,198 = 32.9
   d. Inventory turnover = Cost of goods sold ÷ Average inventory
      = $7,750 ÷ [($1,132 + $1,056) ÷ 2] = 7.08
   e. Total asset turnover = Sales ÷ Average total assets
      = $13,198 ÷ [($11,901 + $11,847) ÷ 2] = 1.11
   f. Return on sales = Net income ÷ Sales
      = $1,229 ÷ $13,198 = 9.31%
   g. Financial leverage ratio = Average total assets ÷ Average equity
      = [($11,901 + $11,847) ÷ 2] ÷ [($1,762 + $2,154) ÷ 2] = 6.06
   h. ROE = Net income ÷ Average stockholders' equity
      = $1,231 ÷ [($1,760 + $2,158) ÷ 2] = 62.84%
2. Kellogg has a return on equity ratio (62.84%) that is more than double the value reported by General Mills (24.51%). The return on sales, total asset turnover, and financial leverage ratios give some insight into what is driving the difference in ROE. The companies have very similar return on sales ratios suggesting similar performance in controlling expenses relative to sales levels. Without the ability to compare common-size income statements, it is difficult to say why Kellogg has a slightly lower ratio (9.31% for Kellogg versus 9.54% for General Mills). Kellogg has a higher asset turnover ratio (1.11) indicating that it is able to generate more sales per dollar of assets than General Mills (.84). Again, without more information it is difficult to know why Kellogg's total asset turnover ratio is higher. The inventory turnover ratio does suggest that Kellogg turns its inventory at a faster rate (7.08 times per year compared with General Mills' 6.87), but it is slower to collect cash than General Mills as evidenced by the longer average collection period (Kellogg 32.9 days versus General Mills 27.2 days).

The big driver of Kellogg's higher ROE is the successful use of financial leverage. Kellogg reports a leverage ratio of 6.06 compared with General Mills' 2.95.

With regard to short-term liquidity ratios, General Mills reports higher current and quick ratios than Kellogg. Without access to the General Mills balance sheet, it is impossible to compare the composition of the current assets of the two companies. However, on the surface, General Mills' ratios suggest greater short-term liquidity.

Highlights to Remember

1 **Locate and use sources of information about company performance.** Financial and operating information is available from many sources, including company Web sites, the financial business press, analyst reports, and financial services companies. Various regulations in the United States require the issuance of annual and quarterly reports and govern their content. In addition, publicly traded companies must disclose particular information by filing a 10-K, an 8-K, and other forms with the SEC on a periodic basis.

2 **Analyze the performance of a company using trend analysis, common-size financial statements, and segment disclosures.** Companies provide financial information to aid investors in assessing the risk and return of a potential investment. Creditors are particularly concerned about the solvency and liquidity of the issuer, whereas equity investors are more interested in profitability. Numerous tools are available to assist both creditors and equity investors. Trend analysis is a form of financial statement analysis that concentrates on changes in the financial statements through time. It involves comparing relationships for a period of years or quarters. We construct common-size financial statements by expressing the elements of the balance sheet as a percentage of total assets and the elements of the income statement as a percentage of total revenue. Common-size statements enhance the ability to compare one company with another or to conduct a trend analysis over time. Segment disclosures allow analysis of separate business units.

3 **Use basic financial ratios to guide your thinking.** Basic financial ratios allow us to put numbers in perspective. By relating one part of the financial statements to another, ratios facilitate questions such as "Given the change in revenues, was the change in accounts receivable reasonable?" and "Is the company's inventory level, given its size, comparable to industry norms?" The chapter reviews the ratios presented throughout the text and adds some new ratios. Liquidity ratios deal with the immediate ability to make payments. Solvency ratios deal with the longer-term ability to meet obligations. Creditors often incorporate such ratios into debt covenants to protect lenders' rights. Investors use profitability ratios to assess operating efficiency and performance.

4 **Evaluate corporate performance using various metrics, including ROA, ROE, and EVA.** Return on assets (ROA) is a type of return on investment that relates earnings before interest and taxes (EBIT) to average total assets. We can subdivide ROA into EBIT-to-sales times total asset turnover. Return on equity (ROE) is the most fundamental profitability ratio for equity investors because it relates income to the shareholders' investment. We can subdivide ROE into the after-tax return on sales, total asset turnover, and financial leverage. EVA refers to Economic Value Added. It compares a company's adjusted earnings number with the minimum amount that it should have earned given the total capital in use. If the adjusted earnings exceed the required return, calculated as the weighted-average cost of capital times the capital in use, then the company has added economic value during the period.

5 **Calculate EPS when a company has preferred stock or dilutive securities.** Earnings per share (EPS) is a fundamental measure of performance. This chapter introduces some complexities in calculating EPS. Because preferred shares receive preference as to dividends, we deduct preferred dividends from earnings in the numerator. Because shares outstanding may change during the year, the denominator is the weighted-average number of shares outstanding over the year. The presence of options and convertible securities creates a potential to issue new shares that dilute current shareholders' interests. Therefore, companies report both basic and diluted EPS when significant potentially dilutive securities exist.

6 **Understand the nature of irregular items and how to adjust for them.** Unusual items, extraordinary items, discontinued operations, and changes in accounting principle are categories of irregular items. Separate disclosure of these items allows analysts to refine forecasts of future performance based on current operations. Income statements include unusual items with other expenses on a before-tax basis, but identify them separately. In contrast, income statements show extraordinary items and discontinued items separately, below earnings from operations and net of their individual tax effects. Changes in accounting principle are usually accounted for retrospectively.

7 **Use financial information to help assess a company's value.** To assess a company's valuation, you can use actual performance information reported by one of the readily available data providers. These sources report ratio values along with additional performance measures, including price-to-sales, price-to-book, and price-to-earnings. Analysts may see an investment opportunity when a company stands out on financial metrics including ROA and ROE and is growing quite rapidly but is not the highest priced based on P-E, price-to-sales, and price-to-book ratios.

Accounting Vocabulary

benchmark comparisons, p. 551
capital structure, p. 557
capitalization, p. 557
common-size
   statements, p. 542
component percentages, p. 545
compound annual growth
   rate (CAGR), p. 542
cross-sectional
   comparisons, p. 551
discontinued operations, p. 564
EBIT, p. 555
EBIT-to-sales ratio, p. 556

Economic Value Added
   (EVA), p. 559
extraordinary items, p. 564
financial leverage, p. 557
financial leverage ratio, p. 557
financial management, p. 555
financial statement
   analysis, p. 534
gearing, p. 557
leveraging, p. 557
long-term solvency, p. 535
management discussion and
   analysis (MD&A), p. 541

nonrecurring items, p. 563
operating management, p. 555
pretax and pre-interest return
   on total assets, p. 555
price-earnings growth
   (PEG) ratio, p. 570
pro forma statements, p. 535
short-term liquidity, p. 535
time-series comparisons, p. 551
total asset turnover, p. 556
trading on the equity, p. 557
trend analysis, p. 537
unusual items, p. 563

Assignment Material

Questions

12-1 In addition to the basic financial statements, what information is usually presented in a company's annual report?

12-2 Give at least three sources of information for investors besides a company's annual report.

12-3 "Financial statements report on history. Therefore, they are not useful to creditors and investors who want to predict future returns and risk." Do you agree? Explain.

12-4 How do information demands of creditors differ from those of equity investors?

12-5 "It's always a bad sign when revenues increase at a faster percentage rate than net income increases." Do you agree? Explain.

12-6 Suppose you want to evaluate the financial performance of a company over the last 5 years. What factors might affect the comparability of a firm's financial ratios over such a long period of time?

12-7 How do common-size statements aid comparisons across companies?

12-8 What information is presented in the MD&A section of annual reports?

12-9 Suppose you compared the financial statements of an airline and a grocery store. Which would you expect to have the higher values for the following ratios: debt-to-equity ratio, current ratio, inventory turnover ratio, average accounts receivable collection period, and ROE? Explain.

12-10 Whole Foods is a high-end grocery store specializing in natural and organic foods, as well as gourmet take-out foods. Whole Food stores are frequently located in up-scale neighborhoods. WinCo Foods is a warehouse-style food store chain with a large selection of

MyAccountingLab

nonbrand name food products, as well as fresh meat, produce, bakery items, and bulk foods. WinCo stores are typically located in outlying areas where real estate is less costly. Which of the two companies would you expect to have the higher gross profit margin? The higher total asset turnover? Explain.

12-11 Name three types of comparisons that are useful in evaluating financial ratios.

12-12 Suppose you work for a small manufacturing company and the president said that you must improve your current ratio. Would you interpret this to mean that you should increase it or decrease it?

12-13 Suppose the current ratio for your company changed from 2 to 1 to become 1.8 to 1. Would you expect the level of working capital to increase or to decrease? Why?

12-14 Suppose you work for a small local department store that manages its own accounts receivable with a private charge card. Your boss has told you to improve the average collection period from 30 to 20 days. How would you go about this? What are the risks in your proposal that might affect the company negatively?

12-15 Distinguish between operating management and financial management.

12-16 What two measures of operating performance are combined to give return on total assets as defined in this chapter?

12-17 "Trading on the equity means exchanging bonds for stock." Do you agree? Explain.

12-18 "Borrowing is a double-edged sword." Do you agree? Explain.

12-19 Why are companies with heavy debt in relation to ownership capital in greater danger when business conditions deteriorate?

12-20 "The tax law discriminates against preferred stock and in favor of debt." Explain.

12-21 "Any company that has income before interest and taxes greater than its interest expense is a relatively safe investment for creditors." Do you agree? Explain.

12-22 What causes the "dilution" in diluted EPS?

12-23 How does the accounting for unusual or nonrecurring items differ from the accounting for extraordinary items?

12-24 "Separate reporting of the results of discontinued operations aids predicting future net income." Do you agree? Explain.

12-25 Suppose you want to compare the financial statements of **Colgate-Palmolive** and **Procter & Gamble**. What concerns might you have in comparing ratios for the two companies?

12-26 "A company with a high dividend payout ratio is a better investment than a company with a low dividend payout ratio." Do you agree? Explain.

Critical Thinking Questions

▶▶ OBJECTIVE 4

12-27 EVA
Your CEO has heard a lot about EVA as a management tool. This officer understands that the basic concept is to calculate an estimate of true economic profit by subtracting an appropriate charge for the firm's cost of capital from its operating profit. However, the CEO wonders why focusing on EVA is any better than focusing on ROE. Can you help explain the concept?

▶▶ OBJECTIVE 7

12-28 Assessing Value
Your accounting teacher has been talking about how important accounting numbers are in valuing a firm, and yet many of the people you know who invest are always talking about growth as the important measure. Who is right?

▶▶ OBJECTIVE 7

12-29 Investment Advice on the Internet
You belong to a stock investment club that is evaluating new stock acquisitions. One of the club members arrives at the meeting and suggests that the group should consider investing in a company she read about on an investment blog that she follows on the Internet. She says that the blog has examples of investments recommended there that have doubled in value in just a few months. What do you think?

▶▶ OBJECTIVE 7

12-30 Which P-E?
Your investment advisor called to suggest buying ABC Company and noted that its P-E was only 20 and the rest of the companies in its industry had P-Es of around 28. You looked in the *Wall Street Journal* and found it reported a P-E of 32 for ABC Company and an average P-E of around 30. How can you make sense of this?

Exercises

12-31 Common-Size Statements

Following are income statements for **Lowe's** and **The Home Depot** for the years ended February 3, 2012, and January 29, 2012, respectively:

▶▶ **OBJECTIVE 2**

	Lowe's (in millions)
Net sales	$50,208
Cost of sales	32,858
Gross profit	17,350
Selling, general, and administrative	12,593
Depreciation	1,480
Interest, net	371
Total operating expenses	14,444
Pretax earnings	2,906
Income tax provision	1,067
Net earnings	$ 1,839

	The Home Depot (in millions)
Net sales	$70,395
Cost of sales	46,133
Gross profit	24,262
Selling, general, and administrative	16,028
Depreciation and amortization	1,573
Total operating expenses	17,601
Operating income	6,661
Interest and investment income	(13)
Interest expense	606
Other	—
Interest and other, net	593
Earnings before provision for income taxes	6,068
Provision for income taxes	2,185
Net earnings	$ 3,883

1. The companies do not use exactly the same account titles. Align the accounts across the two companies in the manner you believe to be most appropriate. Then prepare common-size income statements for Lowe's and The Home Depot.
2. Compare the two companies by using the common-size statements.

12-32 Computation of Ratios

▶▶ **OBJECTIVES 3, 4**

Merck & Co., Inc., the global pharmaceutical company, included the income statements and balance sheets in Exhibit 12-12 in its 2011 annual report. Additional information includes the following:

- Average common shares outstanding of 3,071 million in 2011
- Market price per share of $37.70 at December 30, 2011, the last trading day before its fiscal year-end of December 31, 2011
- Dividends of $1.56 per share were paid on common stock during 2011
- Interest expense in 2011 was $749 million

Compute the following ratios for 2011:

1. Current ratio
2. Quick ratio (use current assets – inventories as the numerator)
3. Average collection period (assume all sales are on credit)
4. Total-debt-to-total-assets (define total debt as total liabilities)
5. Total-debt-to-equity (define total debt as total liabilities)
6. Return on common stockholders' equity
7. Gross profit rate
8. Return on sales
9. Total asset turnover
10. Return on assets (defined as EBIT divided by average total assets)
11. EPS (basic)
12. P-E ratio
13. Dividend-yield ratio (for common stock)
14. Dividend-payout ratio (for common stock)
15. Market-to-book value

Note that Merck has noncontrolling interests and the financial statements provide information about both the total enterprise and about Merck after the noncontrolling interests. You will have to make some choices about which numbers to use in calculating ratios. As an example, Return on Sales can only be calculated for the whole enterprise, but return on common stockholders' equity should be calculated for the Merck common shareholder after the effect of noncontrolling interests.

EXHIBIT 12-12

Merck & Co., Inc., and Subsidiaries

($ in millions, except per share data)

CONSOLIDATED BALANCE SHEETS		
	December 31	
	2011	**2010**
Assets		
Current assets		
Cash and cash equivalents	$ 13,531	$ 10,900
Short-term investments	1,441	1,301
Accounts receivable, net	8,261	7,344
Inventories	6,254	5,868
Deferred income taxes and other current assets	3,694	3,651
Total current assets	33,181	29,064
Investments	3,458	2,175
Property, plant, and equipment (at cost)		
Land	623	658
Buildings	12,733	11,945
Machinery, equipment, and office furnishings	16,919	15,894
Construction in progress	2,198	2,066
	32,473	30,563
Accumulated depreciation	(16,176)	(13,481)
Net property, plant, and equipment	16,297	17,082
Goodwill	12,155	12,378
Other intangibles, net	34,302	39,456
Other assets	5,735	5,626
Total assets	$105,128	$105,781

EXHIBIT 12-12 (Continued)

Merck & Co., Inc., and Subsidiaries

($ in millions, except per share data)

CONSOLIDATED BALANCE SHEETS

	December 31	
	2011	**2010**
Liabilities and shareholders' equity		
Current liabilities		
Loans payable and current portion of long-term debt	$ 1,990	$ 2,400
Trade accounts payable	2,462	2,308
Accrued and other current liabilities	9,731	8,514
Income taxes payable	781	1,243
Dividends payable	1,281	1,176
Total current liabilities	16,245	15,641
Long-term debt	15,525	15,482
Deferred income taxes and noncurrent liabilities	16,415	17,853
Stockholders' equity		
Common stock, $.50 par value		
Authorized—6,500,000,000 shares		
Issued—3,576,948,356 in 2011 and 2010	1,788	1,788
Other paid-in capital	40,663	40,701
Accumulated other comprehensive loss	(3,132)	(3,216)
Retained earnings	38,990	37,536
Treasury stock, at cost		
536,109,713 shares in 2011;		
494,841,533 shares in 2010	(23,792)	(22,433)
Total Merck & Co., Inc. stockholders' equity	54,517	54,376
Noncontrolling interests	2,426	2,429
Total equity	56,943	56,805
Total liabilities and stockholders' equity	$105,128	$105,781

CONSOLIDATED STATEMENTS OF EARNINGS

	For the Years Ended December 31	
	2011	**2010**
Sales	$48,047	$45,987
Costs, expenses, and other		
Materials and production	16,871	18,396
Marketing and administrative	13,733	13,125
Research and development	8,467	11,111
Restructuring costs	1,306	985
Equity income from affiliates	(610)	(587)
Other (income) expense, net	946	1,304
	40,713	44,334
Income before taxes	7,334	1,653
Taxes on income	942	671
Net income	6,392	982
Less: Net income attributable to noncontrolling interests	120	121
Net income attributable to Merck & Co., Inc.	$ 6,272	$ 861

▶▶ OBJECTIVE 3

12-33 Common Stock Ratios and Book Value

The Ebert Corporation has outstanding 550,000 shares of 9% preferred stock with a $100 par value and has issued 12 million shares of $1 par value common stock. The current market price of the common stock is $30 per share, and the latest annual dividend is $2.00 per common share. Common treasury stock consists of 500,000 shares costing $9 million. The company has $150 million of additional paid-in capital, $20 million of retained earnings, and $12 million of investments in affiliated companies at the end of the year. Net income for the current year is $25 million.

Compute the following:

1. Total stockholders' equity
2. Common stock P-E ratio
3. Common stock dividend-yield percentage
4. Common stock dividend-payout percentage
5. Book value per share of common stock

▶▶ OBJECTIVE 4

12-34 Rate-of-Return Computations

1. Aki Company reported a 5% EBIT-to-sales ratio, a 10% rate of return on total assets, and ¥2 billion in average total assets. Compute (a) EBIT, (b) total sales, and (c) total asset turnover.
2. Dublin Corporation reported €1,000 million of sales, €56 million of EBIT, and a total asset turnover of four times. Compute (a) average total assets, (b) the EBIT-to-sales ratio, and (c) the rate of return on total assets.
3. Compare the two companies based on the ratios computed.

▶▶ OBJECTIVE 4

12-35 Return on Assets

The Home Depot, Inc., is the leading retailer in the home improvement industry and ranks among the largest retailers in the United States. Some data from the company's financial statements for the years ended January 29, 2012, and February 3, 2008, follow ($ in millions):

	2012	2008
Sales	$70,395	$77,349
Earnings before interest and taxes	6,674	7,316
Interest expense	606	696
Provision for taxes	2,185	2,410
Net income	3,883	4,395
Property, plant, and equipment, net	24,448	27,476
Average total assets	40,322	48,294
Average stockholders' equity	18,394	21,372

1. Compute The Home Depot's EBIT-to-sales ratio for the years ended January 29, 2012, and February 3, 2008.
2. Compute the total asset turnover for the years ended January 29, 2012, and February 3, 2008.
3. Show how these two ratios determine the return on total assets.
4. Comment on the changes over the 4 years from 2008 to 2012.

▶▶ OBJECTIVE 4

12-36 Trading on the Equity

In all years under consideration Bayol Company has assets of $600 million, bonds payable of $300 million, and stockholders' equity of $300 million. The bonds bear interest at 10% per annum. Carmody Company, which is in the same industry, has assets of $600 million and stockholders' equity of $600 million in each year. Prepare a comparative tabulation of Carmody Company and Bayol Company for each of the 3 years. Show income before interest, interest, net income, ROA, and ROE. The income before interest for both companies was as follows: year 1, $60 million; year 2, $30 million; and year 3, $90 million. Ignore income taxes. Show all monetary amounts in millions of dollars. Comment on the results.

12-37 Using Debt or Equity

▶▶ OBJECTIVE 4

The O'Hare Corporation is trying to decide whether to raise additional capital of $100 million through a new issue of 9% long-term debt or of 6% preferred stock. The income tax rate is 40%. Compute net income less preferred dividends for these alternatives. Assume income before interest expense and taxes is $20 million. Show all dollar amounts in thousands. What is the after-tax cost of capital for debt and for preferred stock expressed in percentages? Comment on the comparison. Compute the interest-coverage ratio for the first year.

12-38 Debt versus Preferred Stock

▶▶ OBJECTIVE 4

In 20X0, Hamilton Corporation had earnings before taxes and interest of $4,247 million. Long-term debt was $12,000 million. The company had no preferred stock outstanding, although 10 million shares were authorized.

Suppose $6,000 million of preferred stock with a dividend rate of 10% had been issued instead of $6,000 million of the long-term debt. The debt had an effective interest rate of 6%. Assume the income tax rate is 40%.

Compute net income and net income attributable to common shareholders under (a) the current situation with $12,000 million of long-term debt and no preferred stock, and (b) the assumed situation with $6,000 million of preferred stock and $6,000 million of long-term debt.

12-39 Earnings per Share

▶▶ OBJECTIVE 5

As of December 31, 2011, JPMorgan Chase & Co. was one of the largest banking institutions in the United States with $2.3 trillion in assets, $183.6 billion in stockholders' equity, and operations in more than 60 countries. For the year ended December 31, 2011, JPMorgan Chase had net income of $18,976 million and paid preferred dividends of $1,408 million. An average of 3,900 million common shares were outstanding during the year.

1. Compute JPMorgan Chase's basic earnings per common share in 2011.
2. Suppose all preferred stock was convertible into 336 million shares of common stock. Compute diluted earnings per common share.

12-40 EPS and Interest-Coverage Ratio Computations

▶▶ OBJECTIVE 5

Baltimore Shipping Company has outstanding 500,000 shares of common stock, $5 million of 8% preferred stock, and $8 million of 10% bonds payable. Its income tax rate is 40%.

1. Assume the company has $6 million of income before interest and taxes. Compute (a) EPS, and (b) number of times bond interest has been earned.
2. Assume $3 million of income before interest and taxes, and make the same computations.
3. Comment on the relative changes of income before interest and taxes, EPS, and times interest earned.

12-41 Nonrecurring Items

▶▶ OBJECTIVE 6

La-Z-Boy Incorporated is a manufacturer, marketer, and retailer of upholstery products and a marketer of imported and manufactured wood furniture products. The following excerpt is taken from the income statement included in La-Z-Boy's 2009 annual report. All dollar amounts are in thousands.

	Fiscal Year Ended		
	4/25/2009	4/26/2008	4/28/2007
Sales	$1,226,674	$1,450,941	$1,621,460
Total cost of sales	887,907	1,056,713	1,193,105
Gross profit	338,767	394,228	428,355
Selling, general, and administrative	375,011	399,470	388,738
Restructuring	2,642	3,078	7,662
Write-down of long-lived assets	7,503	—	—
Write-down of intangibles	47,677	8,426	—
Operating income (loss)	$ (94,066)	$ (16,746)	$ 31,955

1. What line items shown in the excerpts from La-Z-Boy's income statement do you consider to be unusual or nonrecurring items? Defend your response.
2. Adjust operating income (loss) as reported to "recurring operating income" in each of the 3 years represented.
3. Comment on the trends in sales and operating income.

▶▶ OBJECTIVES 3, 4

12-42 Interpretation of Changes in Ratios

Consider each of the following as an independent case:

a. Increase in dividend payout ratio
b. Decrease in interest coverage
c. Increase in return on sales
d. Increase in the P-E ratio
e. Increase in receivables collection period
f. Increase in current ratio

Required

1. From the point of view of a manager of the company, indicate which of these items indicates good news and which indicates bad news. Explain your reasoning for each.
2. Would any of these items be viewed differently by an investor than by a manager? If so, which ones? Why?

MyAccountingLab **Problems**

▶▶ OBJECTIVES 2, 4

12-43 Common-Size Statements

(Alternate is 12-51.) Price-Break and Low-Cost are both discount store chains. Condensed income statements and balance sheets for the two companies are shown in Exhibit 12-13. Amounts are in thousands.

Required

1. Prepare common-size statements for Price-Break and Low-Cost for 20X9.
2. Compare the financial performance for 20X9 and financial position at the end of 20X9 for Price-Break with the performance and position of Low-Cost. Use only the statements prepared in requirement 1.
3. Calculate and compare ROE for the two firms.

▶▶ OBJECTIVES 3, 4

12-44 Financial Ratios

(Alternate is 12-46.) This problem uses the same data as problem 12-43, but it can be solved independently. Price-Break and Low-Cost are both discount store chains. Condensed income statements and balance sheets for the two companies are shown in Exhibit 12-13. Amounts are in thousands.

Additional information follows:

- Cash dividends per share: Price-Break, $2.10; Low-Cost, $1.50
- Market price per share: Price-Break, $50; Low-Cost, $35
- Average shares outstanding for 20X9: Price-Break, 15 million; Low-Cost, 8 million

1. Compute the following ratios for both companies for 20X9: (a) current, (b) quick, (c) accounts receivable turnover, (d) inventory turnover, (e) total-debt-to-total-assets, (f) total-debt-to-total-equity, (g) ROE, (h) gross profit rate, (i) return on sales, (j) total asset turnover, (k) pretax return on assets, (l) EPS, (m) P-E, (n) dividend-yield, and (o) dividend-payout. Total debt includes all liabilities. Assume all sales are on credit.
2. Compare the liquidity, solvency, profitability, market price, and dividend ratios of Price-Break with those of Low-Cost.

INCOME STATEMENTS

	Price-Break	Low-Cost
	Year Ended December 31, 20X9	
Sales	$905,600	$491,750
Cost of sales	602,360	301,910
Gross profit	303,240	189,840
Operating expenses	184,130	147,160
Operating income	119,110	42,680
Other revenue (expense)	(21,930)	6,270
Pretax income	97,180	48,950
Income tax expense	38,870	19,580
Net income	$ 58,310	$ 29,370

BALANCE SHEETS

	Price-Break		Low-Cost	
	December 31		December 31	
	20X9	20X8	20X9	20X8
Assets				
Current assets				
Cash	$ 9,100	$ 10,700	$ 8,200	$ 6,900
Marketable securities	8,300	8,300	4,100	3,800
Accounts receivable	36,700	37,100	21,300	20,500
Inventories	155,600	149,400	105,100	106,600
Prepaid expenses	17,100	16,900	8,800	8,400
Total current assets	226,800	222,400	147,500	146,200
Property and equipment, net	461,800	452,300	287,600	273,500
Other assets	14,700	13,900	28,600	27,100
Total assets	$703,300	$688,600	$463,700	$446,800
Liabilities and stockholders' equity				
Liabilities				
Current liabilities (summarized)	$ 91,600	$ 93,700	$ 61,300	$ 58,800
Long-term debt	156,700	156,700	21,000	21,000
Total liabilities	248,300	250,400	82,300	79,800
Stockholders' equity	455,000	438,200	381,400	367,000
Total liabilities and stockholders' equity	$703,300	$688,600	$463,700	$446,800

12-45 Trend Analysis

▶▶ OBJECTIVE 2

Reuters describes Minnesota Mining and Manufacturing Company (3M) as a diversified technology company with a global presence in the following industries: industrial and transportation; health care; safety, security, and protection services; consumer and office; display and graphics; and electro and communications. The income statements and balance sheets (slightly modified) for the years ended December 31, 2011, and December 31, 2010, are in Exhibit 12-14.

1. Prepare an income statement and balance sheet for 3M that has two columns, one showing the dollar amount of change between 2010 and 2011 and the other showing the percentage of change.

2. Identify and discuss the most significant changes between 2010 and 2011.

▶▶ OBJECTIVES 3, 4

12-46 Financial Ratios

(Alternate is 12-44.) This problem uses the same data as 12-45, but it can be solved independently. **3M** was incorporated in 1929 and has grown to be one of the largest companies in the industrial conglomerates industry. The income statements and balance sheets (slightly modified) for the years ended December 31, 2011, and December 31, 2010, are in Exhibit 12-14. 3M paid a dividend of $2.20 per share in 2011. The market price per share on December 31, 2011, was $81.73.

Compute the following ratios for 3M for the year ending December 31, 2011: (a) current, (b) quick, (c) average collection period, (d) total-debt-to-total-assets, (e) total-debt-to-total-equity, (f) ROE, (g) return on sales, (h) total asset turnover, (i) return on total assets (computed as earnings before interest expense and taxes divided by average total assets), (j) basic EPS (this number is given in Exhibit 12-14 but show how it was derived), (k) P-E, (l) dividend yield, (m) dividend payout, and (n) market-to-book. Total debt includes all liabilities. Assume all sales are on credit.

▶▶ OBJECTIVES 2, 3

12-47 Time-Series Analysis

The **3M** balance sheets in Exhibit 12-14 show goodwill of $6,820 million in 2010 and $7,047 million in 2011.

1. Goodwill increased $227 million or 3.3% from 2010 to 2011. What does this increase tell you about the activities of 3M during the year ended December 31, 2011?
2. Suppose you calculated various ratios for 3M for the year ended December 31, 2011. If you worked problem 12-46 you actually calculated many ratios. This problem does not require use of specific computations. However, you might review problem 12-46 as a reminder of the ratios that might be impacted. Assume you have been asked to compute these same ratios for 2010. Would the increase in goodwill and the activities implied by that increase complicate the comparison of ratios over the 2 years in question? If so, why?

EXHIBIT 12-14

Minnesota Mining and Manufacturing Company (3M) and Subsidiaries

($ in millions, except per share data)

CONSOLIDATED STATEMENT OF INCOME		
	Years Ended December 31	
	2011	**2010**
Net sales	$29,611	$26,662
Operating expenses		
Cost of goods sold	15,693	13,831
Selling, general, and administrative expenses	6,170	5,479
Research, development, and related expenses	1,570	1,434
Total operating expenses	23,433	20,744
Operating income	6,178	5,918
Interest income and expense		
Interest expense	186	201
Interest income	(39)	(38)
Total	147	163
Income before income taxes	6,031	5,755
Provision for income taxes	1,674	1,592
Net income including noncontrolling interest	$ 4,357	$ 4,163
Less: Net income attributable to noncontrolling interest	74	78
Net income attributable to 3M	$ 4,283	$ 4,085
Weighted-average 3M common shares outstanding—basic	708.5	713.7
EPS attributable to 3M common shareholders—basic	$ 6.05	$ 5.72
Weighted-average 3M common shares outstanding—diluted	719.0	725.5
EPS—diluted	$ 5.96	$ 5.63

CONSOLIDATED BALANCE SHEET

At December 31	2011	2010
Assets		
Current assets		
Cash and cash equivalents	$ 2,219	$ 3,377
Marketable securities—current	1,461	1,101
Accounts receivable—net	3,867	3,615
Inventories	3,416	3,155
Other current assets	1,277	967
Total current assets	12,240	12,215
Marketable securities—noncurrent	896	540
Investments	155	146
Property, plant, and equipment—net	7,666	7,279
Goodwill	7,047	6,820
Intangible assets—net	1,916	1,820
Prepaid pension benefits	40	74
Other assets	1,656	1,262
Total assets	$31,616	$30,156
Liabilities and Stockholders' Equity		
Current liabilities		
Short-term borrowings and current portion of long-term debt	$ 682	$ 1,269
Accounts payable	1,643	1,662
Accrued payroll	676	778
Accrued income taxes	355	358
Other current liabilities	2,085	2,022
Total current liabilities	5,441	6,089
Long-term debt	4,484	4,183
Pension and postretirement benefits	3,972	2,013
Other liabilities	1,857	1,854
Total liabilities	15,754	14,139
Stockholders' equity		
Common stock, par value $.01 per share		
Shares outstanding—2011: 694,970,041		
Shares outstanding—2010: 711,977,608	9	9
Additional paid-in-capital	3,767	3,468
Retained earnings	28,348	25,995
Treasury stock	(11,679)	(10,266)
Accumulated other comprehensive income (loss)	(5,025)	(3,543)
Total 3M Company shareholders' equity	15,420	15,663
Noncontrolling interest	442	354
Total equity	15,862	16,017
Total liabilities and stockholders' equity	$31,616	$30,156

12-48 Trend Analysis and Common-Size Statements

Ryan Company furnished the condensed data shown in Exhibit 12-15.

1. Prepare a trend analysis for Ryan's income statements and balance sheets that compares 20X3 with 20X2. Your analysis should show both the dollar amount and the percentage change between 20X2 and 20X3.
2. Prepare common-size income statements for 20X2 and 20X3 and common-size balance sheets for December 31, 20X3, and December 31, 20X2, for Ryan Company.
3. Comment on Ryan Company's financial performance and position for 20X3 compared with 20X2.

12-49 Financial Ratios

Consider the data for Ryan Company in Exhibit 12-15. Assume all sales are on credit.

1. Compute the following ratios for the years 20X2 and 20X3:
   a. Percentage of net income to stockholders' equity (ROE)
   b. Gross profit rate
   c. Percent of net income to sales
   d. Ratio of total debt to stockholders' equity (define total debt as total liabilities)
   e. Inventory turnover
   f. Current ratio
   g. Average collection period for accounts receivable

EXHIBIT 12-15

Ryan Company

Balance Sheets and Income Statements ($ in thousands)

	December 31		
	20X3	**20X2**	**20X1**
Cash	$ 30	$ 25	$ 20
Accounts receivable	90	70	50
Merchandise inventory	80	70	60
Prepaid expenses	10	10	10
Land	30	30	30
Building	70	75	80
Equipment	60	50	40
Total assets	$370	$330	$290
Accounts payable	$ 50	$ 40	$ 30
Taxes payable	20	15	10
Accrued expenses payable	15	10	5
Long-term debt	45	45	45
Paid-in capital	150	150	150
Retained earnings	90	70	50
Total liabilities and stockholders' equity	$370	$330	$290

	Year Ended December 31	
	20X3	**20X2**
Sales (all on credit)	$800	$750
Cost of goods sold	435	410
Operating expenses	305	295
Pretax income	60	45
Income taxes	20	15
Net income	$ 40	$ 30

2. For each of the following items, indicate whether the change from 20X2 to 20X3 for Ryan Company seems to be favorable or unfavorable, and identify the ratios you computed previously that most directly support your answer. The first two items that follow are given as an example.
   a. Return to owners, favorable, a
   b. Gross profit rate basically unchanged, b (increased from 45.3% to 45.6%, could answer favorable)
   c. Ability to pay current debts on time
   d. Collectibility of receivables
   e. Risks of insolvency
   f. Salability of merchandise
   g. Return on sales
   h. Overall accomplishment
   i. Coordination of buying and selling functions
   j. Screening of risks in granting credit to customers

12-50 Computation of Financial Ratios

The financial statements of the Ito Company are shown in Exhibit 12-16.
Compute the following for the 20X2 financial statements.

1. Return on total assets (computed using EBIT in the numerator).
2. Divide your answer to requirement 1 into two components: EBIT-to-sales and total asset turnover.
3. After-tax rate of return on total assets. Be sure to add the after-tax interest expense to net income.

▶▶ **OBJECTIVES 3, 4**

EXHIBIT 12-16

The Ito Company

(¥ in millions)

BALANCE SHEETS		
	December 31	
	20X2	**20X1**
Assets		
Current assets		
Cash	¥ 3,000	¥ 2,000
Short-term investments	—	1,000
Receivables, net	5,000	4,000
Inventories at cost	11,000	8,000
Prepayments	1,000	1,000
Total current assets	¥20,000	¥16,000
Plant and equipment, net	22,000	23,000
Total assets	¥42,000	¥39,000
Liabilities and Stockholders' Equity		
Current liabilities		
Accounts payable	¥10,000	¥ 6,000
Accrued expenses payable	500	500
Income taxes payable	1,500	1,500
Total current liabilities	¥12,000	¥ 8,000
8% bonds payable	¥10,000	¥10,000
Stockholders' equity		
Preferred stock, 12%, par value $100 per share	¥ 5,000	¥ 5,000
Common stock, $5 par value	4,000	4,000
Premium on common stock	8,000	8,000
Retained earnings	2,000	3,000
Reserve for plant expansion	1,000	1,000
Total stockholders' equity	¥20,000	¥21,000
Total liabilities and stockholders' equity	¥42,000	¥39,000

EXHIBIT 12-16
(Continued)

The Ito Company
(¥ in millions)

STATEMENT OF INCOME AND RECONCILIATION OF RETAINED EARNINGS		
		Year Ended **December 31, 20X2**
Sales (all on credit)		¥44,000
Cost of goods sold		32,000
Gross profit on sales		¥12,000
Other operating expenses		
Selling expenses	¥5,000	
Administrative expenses	2,000	
Depreciation	1,000	8,000
Operating income		¥ 4,000
Interest expense		800
Income before income taxes		¥ 3,200
Income taxes at 40%		¥ 1,280
Net income		¥ 1,920
Dividends on preferred stock		600
Net income for common stockholders		¥ 1,320
Dividends on common stock		2,320
Net income retained		¥ (1,000)
Retained earnings, December 31, 20X1		3,000
Retained earnings, December 31, 20X2		¥ 2,000

4. Rate of return on total stockholders' equity including returns to both common and preferred stockholders. Did the preferred and common stockholders benefit from the existence of debt? Explain fully.
5. Rate of return on common stockholders' equity. This ratio is the amount of net income available for the common stockholders, divided by total stockholders' equity less the par value of preferred stock. Did the common stockholders benefit from the existence of preferred stock? Explain fully.
6. Calculate inventory turnover. How would Ito have been helped if it had been able to maintain the level of inventory from 20X1?

12-51 Common-Size Statements
(Alternate is 12-43.) Exhibit 12-17 contains the income statements and balance sheets of The Hershey Company for the years ended December 31, 2011, and December 31, 2010. Hershey is a manufacturer of chocolate and sugar confectionery products. The company's principal product groups include chocolate and confectionery products; food and beverage enhancers, such as baking ingredients, toppings, and beverages; and gum and mint refreshment products.

1. Prepare common-size statements for Hershey for 2011 and 2010.
2. Comment on the changes in component percentages from 2011 to 2010.

▶▶ OBJECTIVES 3, 4

12-52 Liquidity Ratios
Exhibit 12-17 contains the income statements and balance sheets of The Hershey Company, manufacturer of such well-known products as Hershey's chocolate bars, Reese's peanut butter cups, Almond Joy candy bars, and York peppermint patties.

1. Compute the following ratios for 2011: (a) current, (b) average collection period, and (c) inventory turnover. Assume all sales are on credit.
2. Assess Hershey's liquidity compared with the following averages for the food processing industry as provided by Reuters and with ratios computed for Tootsie Roll, a competitor in the candy manufacturing, marketing, sales, and distribution industry. Reuters provides the following overview of the food processing industry. The industry consists of "companies engaged in processing and packaging produce, meats, fish, animal feeds, fruit juices and dairy

products. The industry includes, grain milling, crop cleaning, grading and packaging, animal slaughtering and packaging operations, seafood processing, freezing, canning operations, juice, coffee, tea, dairy and all other food manufacturers, including pet foods."

	Reuters Averages (as of August 31, 2012)	Tootsie Roll (year ended December 31, 2011)
Current ratio	1.38 times	3.64 times
Average collection period	19.1 days*	27.4 days
Inventory turnover	5.89 times	5.69 times

*Reuters reports Receivable Turnover as 19.15 times per year. (365 ÷ 19.15) = 19.1 days.

CONSOLIDATED BALANCE SHEETS		
	2011	**2010**
Assets		
Current assets:		
Cash and cash equivalents	$ 693,686	$ 884,642
Accounts receivable—trade	399,499	390,061
Inventories	648,953	533,622
Deferred income taxes	136,861	55,760
Prepaid expenses and other	167,559	141,132
Total current assets	2,046,558	2,005,217
Property, plant, and equipment, net	1,559,717	1,437,702
Goodwill	516,745	524,134
Other intangibles	111,913	123,080
Deferred income taxes	38,544	21,387
Other assets	138,722	161,212
Total assets	$4,412,199	$4,272,732
Liabilities and Stockholders' Equity		
Current liabilities:		
Accounts payable	$ 420,017	$ 410,655
Accrued liabilities	612,186	593,308
Accrued income taxes	1,899	9,402
Short-term debt	42,080	24,088
Current portion of long-term debt	97,593	261,392
Total current liabilities	1,173,775	1,298,845
Long-term debt	1,748,500	1,541,825
Other long-term liabilities	617,276	494,461
Total liabilities	3,539,551	3,335,131
Stockholders' equity:		
Common stock, shares issued: 299,269,702 in 2011 and 299,195,325 in 2010	299,269	299,195
Class B Common stock, shares issued: 60,632,042 in 2011 and 60,706,419 in 2010	60,632	60,706
Additional paid-in-capital	490,817	434,865
Retained earnings	4,699,597	4,374,718
Treasury—Common stock shares, at cost: 134,695,826 in 2011 and 132,871,512 in 2010	(4,258,962)	(4,052,101)
Accumulated other comprehensive loss	(442,331)	(215,067)
The Hershey Company stockholders' equity	849,022	902,316
Noncontrolling interests in subsidiaries	23,626	35,285
Total stockholders' equity	872,648	937,601
Total liabilities and stockholders' equity	$4,412,199	$4,272,732

EXHIBIT 12-17

The Hershey Company
Years Ended December 31, 2011, and December 31, 2010 ($ in thousands, except per share data)

EXHIBIT 12-17
(Continued)

The Hershey Company
Years Ended December 31, 2011, and December 31, 2010 ($ in thousands, except per share data)

CONSOLIDATED STATEMENT OF OPERATIONS

	For Years Ended	
	December 31, 2011	December 31, 2010
Net sales	$6,080,788	$5,671,009
Costs and expenses:		
Cost of sales	3,548,896	3,255,801
Selling, marketing, and administrative	1,477,750	1,426,477
Business realignment and impairment charges, net	(886)	83,433
Total costs and expenses	5,025,760	4,765,711
Income before interest and income taxes	1,055,028	905,298
Interest expense, net	92,183	96,434
Income before income taxes	962,845	808,864
Provision for income taxes	333,883	299,065
Net income	$ 628,962	$ 509,799
Net income per common share—Basic—Class B Common stock	$ 2.58	$ 2.08
Net income per common share—Diluted—Class B Common stock	$ 2.56	$ 2.07
Net income per common share—Basic—Common stock	$ 2.85	$ 2.29
Net income per common share—Diluted—Common stock	$ 2.74	$ 2.21

▶▶ **OBJECTIVES 3, 4**

12-53 Solvency Ratios

Exhibit 12-17 contains the income statements and balance sheets of The Hershey Company for the years ended December 31, 2011, and December 31, 2010. Hershey manufactures and sells products under more than 80 brand names.

1. Compute the following ratios for 2011: (a) total-debt-to-total-assets, and (b) total-debt-to-total-equity. To be consistent with the source of industry data used in the problem, define total debt as short-term debt and long-term debt (including the current portion) only. This definition is not the one we have used in the text, so it is worth emphasizing that it does not include items such as accounts payable and accrued liabilities; only the items specified.
2. Assess Hershey's solvency compared with the following industry averages for the food processing industry as provided by Reuters and with ratios computed for Tootsie Roll, a competitor in the candy manufacturing, marketing, sales, and distribution industry. See a description of the food processing industry in problem 12-52.

	Reuters Averages (as of August 31, 2012)	Tootsie Roll (year ended December 31, 2011)
Total-debt-to-total-assets	Not available	0.0%*
Total-debt-to-total-shareholders' equity	46.05%	0.0%*

*Tootsie Roll has no debt in its capital structure! In fact, total liabilities are only 22.4% of total assets.

▶▶ **OBJECTIVES 3, 4**

12-54 Profitability Ratios

Exhibit 12-17 contains income statements and balance sheets of The Hershey Company. For more than 100 years, The Hershey Company has enjoyed a position as one of North America's largest manufacturers of quality chocolate and confectionery products. Today, The Hershey Company and its subsidiaries export to approximately 70 countries worldwide.

1. Compute the following ratios for 2011: (a) ROE, (b) gross profit rate, (c) return on sales, (d) total asset turnover, (e) ROA (with after-tax net income in the numerator), and (f) financial leverage ratio. Note that to be consistent with the industry averages used in the problem, return on sales and ROA are computed with after-tax net income, not EBIT in the numerator.
2. Assess Hershey's profitability in 2011 compared with the following industry averages for the food processing industry as provided by Reuters and with ratios computed for Tootsie Roll, a competitor in the candy manufacturing, marketing, sales, and distribution industry. See a description of the food processing industry in problem 12-52.

	Reuters Averages (as of August 31, 2012)	Tootsie Roll (year ended December 31, 2011)
Return on stockholders' equity	19.08%	6.59%
Gross profit rate	38.75%	31.2%
Return on sales (Net income ÷ Sales)	5.91%	8.3%
Total asset turnover	1.11 times	0.62 times
Return on assets (Net income ÷ Assets)	8.16%	5.12%
Financial leverage ratio	Not available	1.29

12-55 Market Price and Dividend Ratios

>> OBJECTIVES **3, 4, 7**

Exhibit 12-17 contains income statements and balance sheets of The Hershey Company. The following information applies to Hershey's common stock, excluding the Class B shares, which are not publicly traded. In 2011, Hershey paid cash dividends of $1.38 per common share, the market price at December 31, 2011, was $61.78 per share, and basic EPS was $2.85.

1. Compute the following ratios for 2011: (a) P-E, (b) dividend-yield, (c) dividend-payout, and (d) market-to-book value.
2. Assess Hershey's market price and dividend ratios for 2011 compared with the following industry averages for the food processing industry as provided by Reuters and with ratios computed for Tootsie Roll, a competitor in the candy manufacturing, marketing, sales, and distribution industry. See a description of the food processing industry in problem 12-52.

	Reuters Averages (as of August 31, 2012)	Tootsie Roll (for year ended December 31, 2011)
Price-earnings	34.83	30.24
Dividend-yield	1.61%	1.40%
Dividend-payout	46.44%	42.11%
Market-to-book value	5.86	1.98

12-56 Income Ratios and Asset Turnover

>> OBJECTIVES **3, 4**

The following data are derived from the 2011, 2010, and 2009 annual reports of The Coca-Cola Corporation. Dollar amounts are in millions.

	2011	2010	2009
Rate of return on stockholders' equity	27.1%	38.1%	27.5%
EBIT-to-sales ratio	25.5%	42.6%	30.0%
Total asset turnover (Sales ÷ Average total assets)	.61	.58	.69
Average total assets	$76,448	$50,796	$44,595
Interest expense	$ 417	$ 733	$ 355
Income tax expense	$ 2,805	$ 2,384	$ 2,040

1. Complete the following condensed income statements for 2011 and 2009. Round to the nearest million.

	2011	2009
Sales	$?	$?
Expenses other than interest and taxes	?	?
EBIT	$?	$?
Interest expense	?	?
Pretax income	$?	$?
Income tax expense	?	?
Net income	$?	$?

2. Compute the following for 2011 and 2009:
   a. Return on total assets (computed as EBIT to average total assets)
   b. Net income-to-sales ratio
   c. Average stockholders' equity
3. Compare the ratios for 2011 with those for 2009.

▶▶ OBJECTIVES 2, 3

12-57 Segment Disclosures

According to its 2011 annual report, CVS Caremark and its subsidiaries are the largest provider of pharmacy health care in the United States, filling or managing more than one billion prescriptions annually. The company achieves this volume of prescriptions through a combination of its pharmacy benefit management, mail order, and specialty pharmacy division, Caremark Pharmacy Services; its more than 7,300 retail drugstores; its retail-based health clinic subsidiary, MinuteClinic; and its online pharmacy, CVS.com. It organizes its business into three reportable business segments, the Pharmacy Services segment, the Retail Pharmacy segment, and the Corporate segment. The Pharmacy Services and Retail Pharmacy segments are the operating units. The Corporate segment does not generate revenue. Rather, it provides management and administrative services, such as human resources, legal, compliance, information technology, and finance, to the operating segments. The following information is from CVS Caremark's 2011 annual report. Intersegment eliminations relate to intersegment revenues that occur when a Pharmacy Services segment customer uses a Retail Pharmacy segment store to purchase covered products. When this occurs, both segments record the revenue on a stand-alone basis.

	Pharmacy Services Segment	Retail Pharmacy Segment	Corporate Segment	Intersegment Eliminations	Consolidated Totals CVS Caremark
2011 (Dollars in millions)					
Net revenues	$58,874	$59,599	—	$(11,373)	$107,100
Gross profit	3,279	17,468	—	(186)	20,561
Operating profit	2,220	4,912	(616)	(186)	6,330

1. Compute the gross profit rate for (a) the Pharmacy Services segment, (b) the Retail Pharmacy segment, and (c) CVS Caremark.
2. Compute the operating profit rate for (a) the Pharmacy Services segment, (b) the Retail Pharmacy segment, and (c) CVS Caremark.
3. Do both segments contribute equally to the profitability of CVS Caremark? Explain.

12-58 Income Ratios and Asset Turnover

▶▶ **OBJECTIVE 4**

Lehane Company included the following data in its 20X2 annual report to stockholders (amounts in millions except for percentages):

Net income	$ 5,920
Total assets	
Beginning of year	$23,744
End of year	$29,192
Net income as a percentage	
of Total revenue	46%
Average stockholders' equity	51%

Using this data, compute the following values for 20X2:

1. Net income as a percentage of average total assets
2. Total revenues
3. Average stockholders' equity
4. Total asset turnover, using two different approaches

12-59 Industry Identification

▶▶ **OBJECTIVES 2, 3**

Exhibit 12-18 presents common-size financial statements and selected ratio values for seven companies from the following industries:

1. Petroleum (exploration, refining, and distribution)
2. Grocery
3. Airline
4. Pharmaceutical
5. Semi-conductor manufacturing
6. Utility
7. Packaged food products manufacturing

Use your knowledge of general business practices to match the industries to the company data.

12-60 Choosing Potential Investments in the Oil Industry

▶▶ **OBJECTIVE 7**

Exhibit 12-19 on page 595 presents some financial information for Chevron (CVX.N) and ExxonMobil (XOM.N). Which do you believe is the preferred investment based on this information gathered in August 2012? Be prepared to defend your answer.

12-61 Choosing Potential Investments in the Retail Industry

▶▶ **OBJECTIVE 7**

Exhibit 12-20 on pages 596–597 presents some financial information for Wal-Mart (WMT), Kohl's (KSS), JCPenney (JCP), and Target (TGT). Which do you believe is the preferred investment based on this information gathered in August 2012? Be prepared to defend your answer.

EXHIBIT 12-18

Common-Size Statements in Seven Industries

(Columns May Not Add Due to Rounding)

	A	B	C	D	E	F	G
	%	%	%	%	%	%	%
Balance sheet							
Cash and marketable securities	21.35	5.93	23.35	2.19	2.33	1.95	12.60
Current receivables	8.07	9.84	3.38	2.95	10.45	3.11	1.46
Inventories	3.94	4.25	7.38	14.82	8.19	2.14	1.42
Other current assets	5.40	2.61	5.07	2.78	2.06	2.73	4.74
Total current assets	38.76	22.63	39.18	22.74	23.03	9.93	20.22
Net property, plant, and equipment	11.95	56.95	34.59	60.87	26.80	64.13	77.16
Other noncurrent assets	49.29	20.42	26.23	16.39	50.17	25.94	2.62
Total assets	100.00	100.00	100.00	100.00	100.00	100.00	100.00
Current liabilities	24.30	19.87	15.42	25.73	32.45	8.19	19.61
Long-term liabilities	23.75	26.37	7.51	35.46	54.32	52.27	45.77
Stockholders' equity	51.95	53.76	77.07	38.81	13.23	39.54	34.62
Total liabilities and stockholders' equity	100.00	100.00	100.00	100.00	100.00	100.00	100.00
Income statement							
Revenue	100.00	100.00	100.00	100.00	100.00	100.00	100.00
Cost of sales	16.80	70.40	44.54	71.62	58.14	63.38	77.93
Gross profit	83.20	29.60	55.46	28.38	41.86	36.62	22.07
Selling, general, and administrative	30.10	2.10	14.52	24.16	26.63	17.60	17.99
R&D	16.45	0.00	15.22	0.00	0.00	0.00	0.00
Interest expense	0.00	0.00	0.00	0.81	2.41	5.61	0.95
Other expenses (income)	16.46	11.76	5.27	0.00	0.09	(1.57)	0.59
Income taxes	3.41	6.97	6.37	1.22	3.78	4.66	0.91
Net income	16.78	8.77	14.08	2.19	8.95	10.32	1.63
Ratio							
Current ratio	1.59	1.14	2.54	0.88	0.71	1.21	1.03
Long-term debt as % of equity*	13.84	7.02	4.83	81.04	81.00	63.13	73.92
ROA† (%)	7.16	15.44	9.95	5.49	10.27	2.65	4.00
ROE (%)	13.22	29.23	12.93	14.30	57.78	6.46	7.94
Inventory turnover (times per year)	1.68	31.60	4.71	11.72	8.19	7.80	NM

*Note that this is the ratio of long-term-debt-to-equity, not long-term-liabilities-to-equity.

†Computed as (After-tax net income ÷ Average total assets).

NM indicates not meaningful.

EXHIBIT 12-19

Comparison of Investments in Oil Companies

Chevron (CVX.N) and ExxonMobil (XOM.N)

PRICE AND VALUATION

Ticker Symbol	Current Price August 29, 2012	52-Week Range	Beta	Latest Annual EPS (TTM*)	Price-Earnings (TTM)
CVX.N	$111.80	$86.68–$113.87	0.80	$13.43	8.33
XOM.N	$87.90	$67.93–$88.91	0.53	$ 9.52	9.23

Ticker Symbol	Price/Sales (TTM)	Price/Book (MRQ†)	Price/Cash Flow (TTM)	Analyst Rating
CVX.N	0.89	1.69	5.52	1.95
XOM.N	0.81	2.49	6.39	2.29

GROWTH RATES AND DIVIDENDS

Ticker Symbol	Latest Annual Revenue (mil) (TTM)	1-yr Revenue Growth	5-yr Revenue Growth	Latest Annual EPS (TTM)	1-yr EPS Growth	5-yr EPS Growth
CVX.N	$247,730	23.80%	3.84%	$13.43	41.78%	11.50%
XOM.N	$498,355	26.93%	5.19%	$ 9.52	35.41%	4.95%

Ticker Symbol	Latest Annual Dividend/Share	Dividend Yield	5-yr Dividend Growth Rate
CVX.N	$3.30	3.22%	8.98%
XOM.N	$1.98	2.59%	7.64%

FINANCIAL STRENGTH

Ticker Symbol	Total Debt/Equity (MRQ)	Long-term Debt/Equity (MRQ)	Current Ratio (MRQ)	Quick Ratio (MRQ)
CVX.N	7.87%	7.59%	1.72	1.50
XOM.N	9.57%	5.45%	1.04	0.82

EFFICIENCY

Ticker Symbol	Inventory Turnover (TTM)	Receivable Turnover (TTM)	Total Asset Turnover (TTM)	Revenue/Employee (000s) (TTM)	Income/Employee (000s) (TTM)
CVX.N	21.96	10.74	1.18	$4,061.1	$438.4
XOM.N	20.25	14.43	1.52	$6,070.1	$582.8

PROFITABILITY

Ticker Symbol	Gross Margin (TTM)	Operating Margin (TTM)	Pretax Margin (TTM)	After-tax Profit Margin (TTM)
CVX.N	33.23%	19.27%	19.27%	10.79%
XOM.N	26.05%	15.94%	15.94%	9.60%

MANAGEMENT EFFECTIVENESS

Ticker Symbol	Return on Assets (TTM)	5-yr Avg. Return on Assets	Return on Equity (TTM)	5-yr Avg. Return on Equity
CVX.N	12.70%	11.99%	21.68%	21.72%
XOM.N	14.59%	14.19%	28.33%	28.20%

Data as of August 30, 2012.
*TTM is Trailing Twelve Months.
†MRQ is Most Recent Quarter.
Source: Reuters (www.reuters.com)

EXHIBIT 12-20

Comparison of Retailers

Wal-Mart (WMT), Kohl's (KSS), JCPenney (JCP), and Target (TGT)

PRICE AND VALUATION

Ticker Symbol	Current Price August 29, 2012	52-Week Range	Beta	Latest Annual EPS (TTM)	Price-Earnings (TTM)
WMT	$72.77	$49.94–$75.24	0.31	$4.75	15.32
KSS	$52.30	$42.14–$56.66	0.84	$4.23	12.36
JCP	$26.23	$19.06–$43.18	1.81	–$2.50	n/a
TGT	$64.26	$47.25–$64.99	0.88	$4.37	14.70

Ticker Symbol	Price/Sales (TTM)	Price/Book (MRQ)	Price/Cash Flow (TTM)	Analyst Rating
WMT	0.53	3.50	9.72	2.38
KSS	0.67	2.03	6.71	2.21
JCP	0.37	1.56	n/a	2.73
TGT	0.59	2.64	8.24	2.16

GROWTH RATES AND DIVIDENDS

Ticker Symbol	Latest Annual Revenue (mil) (TTM)	1-yr Revenue Growth	5-yr Revenue Growth	Latest Annual EPS (TTM)	1-yr EPS Growth	5-yr EPS Growth
WMT	$460,709	5.95%	5.11%	$4.75	8.47%	9.19%
KSS	$ 18,841	2.25%	3.81%	$4.23	17.65%	5.39%
JCP	$ 15,585	–2.81%	–2.81%	–$2.50	–144.02%	n/a
TGT	$ 71,336	3.67%	3.27%	$4.37	6.98%	5.95%

Ticker Symbol	Latest Annual Dividend/Share (TTM)	Dividend Yield	5-yr Dividend Growth Rate
WMT	$1.525	2.18	16.86%
KSS	$1.14	2.45	n/a
JCP	$0.60	n/a	2.13%
TGT	$1.20	2.24	20.11%

FINANCIAL STRENGTH

Ticker Symbol	Total Debt/Equity (MRQ)	Long-term Debt/Equity (MRQ)	Current Ratio (MRQ)	Quick Ratio (MRQ)
WMT	77.72%	62.86%	0.82	0.23
KSS	68.39%	66.87%	1.70	0.37
JCP	85.83%	79.02%	1.91	0.70
TGT	116.46%	95.80%	1.23	0.65

EFFICIENCY

Ticker Symbol	Inventory Turnover (TTM)	Receivable Turnover (TTM)	Total Asset Turnover (TTM)	Revenue/Employee (000s) (TTM)	Income/Employee (000s) (TTM)
WMT	8.71	86.68	2.37	$209.4	$ 7.7
KSS	3.58	not provided	1.36	$628.0	$35.3
JCP	3.13	89.83	1.34	$ 98.0	$–3.4
TGT	6.32	12.67	1.54	$195.4	$ 8.0

EXHIBIT 12-20
(Continued)

Comparison of Retailers

Wal-Mart (WMT), Kohl's (KSS), JCPenney (JCP), and Target (TGT)

	PROFITABILITY			
Ticker Symbol	Gross Margin (TTM)	Operating Margin (TTM)	Pretax Margin (TTM)	After-tax Profit Margin (TTM)
WMT	24.89%	5.94%	5.48%	3.69%
KSS	37.32%	10.60%	8.94%	5.63%
JCP	34.11%	–4.19%	–5.64%	–3.46%
TGT	30.63%	6.22%	6.22%	4.12%

	MANAGEMENT EFFECTIVENESS			
Ticker Symbol	Return on Assets (TTM)	5-yr Avg. Return on Assets	Return on Equity (TTM)	5-yr Avg. Return on Equity
WMT	8.73%	8.74%	23.58%	21.37%
KSS	7.63%	8.28%	15.98%	15.14%
JCP	–4.64%	3.35%	–12.90%	9.00%
TGT	6.63%	6.12%	18.95%	17.73%

Data as of August 30, 2012.
Source: Reuters (www.reuters.com)

12-62 EVA at Briggs & Stratton

▶▶ OBJECTIVE 4

Briggs & Stratton Corporation is the world's largest maker of air-cooled gasoline engines for outdoor power equipment. The company's engines are used by the lawn and garden equipment industry. According to the MD&A in the 2011 annual report, "Management believes that the value of Briggs & Stratton is enhanced if the capital invested in the company's operations yields a cash return that is greater than the cost of capital."

The following data are from Briggs & Stratton's 2011 annual report (thousands of dollars):

	2011	2010
Net Income	$ 24,355	$ 36,615
Shareholder's investment	737,943	650,577

Dividends paid were $.44 in both 2010 and 2011. There were no share repurchases in 2010 or 2011.

1. Comment on the statement from the 10-K relative to the concept of EVA and in light of the data provided. What additional information would be required to actually evaluate EVA for Briggs and Stratton.
2. Did Briggs & Stratton's overall performance improve from 2010 to 2011? Explain your assessment of the change in performance and relate it to the concept of favorable or unfavorable EVA.

12-63 Comparing EVA for Two Companies

▶▶ OBJECTIVE 4

In November 20X9, the following relationships held for two companies in the medical devices industry. Which would you expect to have the larger EVA? Why?

	Company A	Company B
Share price	$87.75	$88.00
EPS	$ 2.45	$ 2.46
P-E	35.82	35.77
PEG ratio	2.5	2.4
Book value per share	$ 5.69	$ 4.60
Shares outstanding (billions)	2.3	1.1

▸▸ OBJECTIVE 1

12-64 MD&A and Ethics

If certain conditions are met, the SEC requires companies to disclose information about future events that are reasonably likely to materially affect the firms' operations. Many companies are understandably reluctant to disclose such information. After all, positive predictions may not materialize and negative predictions may unduly alarm investors. What ethical considerations should a company's managers consider when deciding what prospective information to disclose in the MD&A section of the annual report?

Collaborative Learning Exercise

▸▸ OBJECTIVES 1, 3, 4

12-65 Operating Return on Total Assets

Form groups of four to six students. Each student should choose an industry (a different industry for each student in the group) and pick two companies in that industry. Compute the following for each of the companies:

1. EBIT-to-sales
2. Total asset turnover
3. Return on total assets

Get together as a group and list the industries and the three ratios for each company in the industry. Examine how the ratios differ between the two companies within each industry compared with the differences between industries. As a group, prepare two lists of possible explanations for the differences in ratios. The first list should explain why ratios of two companies within the same industry might differ. The second list should explain why ratios differ by industry.

Analyzing and Interpreting Financial Statements

▸▸ OBJECTIVES 1, 3, 4

12-66 Financial Statement Research

Choose two companies in each of two industries.

Calculate the ROA, ROE, and return on sales for each of the companies. Compare and contrast the two companies in each industry and the averages for each industry.

▸▸ OBJECTIVES 1,2,3,4

12-67 Analyzing Starbucks' Annual Report

Use the financial statements and notes of Starbucks for the year ended October 2, 2011, and respond to the questions that follow. The financial statements are accessible through the Starbucks Web site at www.starbucks.com or on the SEC's EDGAR database at www.sec.gov.

1. Calculate ROE for the year ended October 2, 2011. Compare it with the value for the year ended October 3, 2010.
2. Calculate the current ratio for the year ended October 2, 2011, and compare it with the value for the year ended October 3, 2010.
3. Calculate total-debt-to-total-assets for the year ended October 2, 2011. Compare it with the value for the year ended October 3, 2010. Define total debt as total liabilities for purposes of this problem.

▸▸ OBJECTIVES 1,2,3,4

12-68 Analyzing Financial Statements Using the Internet

Go to www.amazon.com to locate Amazon.com's home page. Select Investor Relations at the bottom of the page. Click on SEC Filings in the left navigation menu and locate the most recent 10-K. Answer the following questions about Amazon:

1. What is Amazon's dividend policy?
2. Where does Amazon report geographic segment information? What segments exist? What information does Amazon provide on a segment basis? Which segment is the largest? Do the segments contribute equally to Amazon's operating income?
3. Calculate Amazon's total-debt-to-total-assets, total-debt-to-equity, and long-term-debt-to-equity ratios for the last 2 fiscal years. For purposes of the first two ratios, define total debt as total liabilities. What is the trend? What does this suggest about Amazon's financing policy?

Glossary

accelerated depreciation   Any depreciation method that writes off depreciable value more quickly than does the straight-line method (p. 347).

account   A summary record of the changes in a particular asset, liability, or owners' equity (p. 11).

account format   A classified balance sheet with the assets on the left (p. 157).

account payable   A liability that results from a purchase of goods or services on open account (p. 13).

accounting   The process of identifying, recording, and summarizing economic information and reporting it to decision makers (p. 3).

accounting controls   The methods and procedures for authorizing transactions, safeguarding assets, and ensuring the accuracy of the financial records (p. 259).

accounting system   The series of steps an organization uses to record financial data and convert them into informative financial statements (p. 6).

accounts receivable (trade receivables, receivables)   Amounts owed to a company by customers as a result of the company's delivering goods or services and extending credit in the ordinary course of business (p. 50).

accounts receivable turnover   Credit sales divided by average accounts receivable for the period during which the sales are made (p. 256).

accrual basis   Accounting method in which accountants record revenue as a company earns it and expenses as the company incurs them—regardless of when cash changes hands (p. 52).

accrue   To accumulate a receivable (asset) or payable (liability) during a given period, even though no explicit transaction occurs, and to record a corresponding revenue or expense (p. 142).

accumulated deficit   A more descriptive term for retained earnings when the accumulated net losses plus dividends exceed accumulated net income (p. 63).

accumulated depreciation (allowance for depreciation)   The cumulative sum of all depreciation recognized since the date of acquisition of an asset (p. 105).

accumulated other comprehensive income (AOCI)   Stockholders' equity account that contains a cumulative total of all items classified as other comprehensive income (p. 63).

adjustments (adjusting entries)   End-of-period entries that assign the financial effects of implicit transactions to the appropriate time periods (p. 142).

administrative controls   All methods and procedures that facilitate management planning and control of operations (p. 259).

affiliated company   A company that has 20%–50% of its voting shares owned by another company (p. 501).

aging of accounts receivable method   An approach to estimating bad debt expense and uncollectible accounts that considers the composition of year-end accounts receivable based on the age of the debt (p. 254).

allowance for uncollectible accounts (allowance for doubtful accounts, allowance for bad debts)   A contra asset account that measures the amount of receivables estimated to be uncollectible (p. 250).

allowance method   A method of accounting for bad debt losses that uses (1) estimates of the amount of sales or receivables that will ultimately be uncollectible, and (2) a contra account that contains the estimated uncollectible amount to be deducted from the total accounts receivable (p. 250).

American Institute of Certified Public Accountants (AICPA)   The principal professional association of CPAs (p. 26).

amortization   When referring to long-lived assets, it usually means the allocation of the costs of intangible assets to the periods that benefit from these assets (p. 342).

annual report   A document prepared by management and distributed to current and potential investors to inform them about the company's past performance and future prospects (p. 7).

articles of incorporation (corporate charter)   Documents a company must file with the secretary of state at the time at which it incorporates (p. 452).

assets   Economic resources that a company expects to help generate future cash inflows or help reduce future cash outflows (p. 9).

audit   An examination of a company's transactions and the resulting financial statements (p. 25).

audit committee   A committee of the board of directors that oversees the internal accounting controls, financial statements, and financial affairs of the corporation (p. 263).

auditor   A person or firm who examines the information used by managers to prepare the financial statements and attests to the credibility of those statements (p. 25).

auditor's opinion (independent opinion)   A report describing the scope and results of an audit. Companies include the opinion with the financial statements in their annual reports (p. 25).

authorized shares   The maximum number of shares of stock that a company can legally issue under the articles of incorporation (p. 453).

available-for-sale securities   Investments in equity or debt securities that are not classified as trading securities or held-to-maturity securities (p. 495).

bad debt expense   The loss that arises from uncollectible accounts (p. 248).

bad debt recoveries   Accounts receivable that were previously written off as uncollectible but then collected at a later date (p. 250).

balance   A numerical total that is the net result of all activity recorded in an account as of a particular point in time. In a T-account the balance is the difference between the total left-side and right-side amounts in the T-account at any particular time. The balance in a general ledger account at the end of an accounting period is computed as the beginning balance in the account, plus the amount of the increases in the account during the period, minus the amount of the decreases (p. 92).

balance sheet equation   Assets = Liabilities + Owners' equity (p. 9)

balance sheet (statement of financial position)   A financial statement that shows the financial status of an organization at a particular instant in time (p. 9).

bankruptcy   When a company seeks court protection from its creditors under federal law (p. 189).

bargain purchase option   A provision that states that the lessee can purchase the asset from the lessor at the end of the lease for substantially less than the asset's expected fair value (p. 408).

basket purchase (lump-sum purchase)   The acquisition of two or more assets for a lump-sum cost (p. 344).

benchmark comparisons   Comparisons of a company's financial ratios with general rules of thumb or "best practices" (p. 551).

board of directors   A body elected by the shareholders to represent them. It is responsible for appointing and monitoring the managers, among other duties (p. 22).

bond discount (discount on bonds)   The excess of face amount over the proceeds on issuance of a bond (p. 396).

bond premium (premium on bonds)   The excess of the proceeds from issuance over the face amount of a bond (p. 396).

bonds   Formal certificates of debt that include (1) a promise to pay interest in cash at a specified annual rate, plus (2) a promise to pay the principal of the bond at a specific maturity date (p. 394).

book of original entry   Another name for the general journal (p. 96).

book value (net book value, carrying amount, carrying value)   The balance of an account shown on the books minus the value of any associated contra accounts. For example, the book value of equipment is its acquisition cost minus accumulated depreciation (p. 105).

book value per share of common stock   Total common stockholders' equity divided by the number of common shares outstanding (p. 467).

call premium   The amount by which the redemption price of a callable bond exceeds face value (p. 395).

call price (redemption price)   The price at which an issuer can buy back a callable preferred stock or bond. The price is typically above the par value (p. 458).

callable   A characteristic of bonds or preferred stock that gives the issuer the right to purchase the bonds or stock back from the owner at a fixed price (p. 458).

callable bonds   Bonds subject to redemption before maturity at the option of the issuer (p. 395).

capital lease (finance lease)   A lease that transfers most risks and benefits of ownership to the lessee (p. 408).

capitalization (capital structure)   The total long-term financing of a company, consisting of long-term debt and stockholders' equity (p. 557).

capitalize   To record the purchase price of an asset in a long-term asset account, recognizing that it will have benefits lasting more than a year (p. 342).

cash basis   Accounting method that recognizes revenue when a company receives cash and recognizes expenses when it pays cash (p. 52).

cash discounts   Reductions in the amount owed by customers due to prompt payment (p. 244).

cash dividends   Distributions of cash to stockholders that reduce retained earnings (p. 61).

cash equivalents   Highly liquid short-term investments that a company can easily and quickly convert into cash, such as money market funds and Treasury bills (p. 190).

cash flows from financing activities   The section of the statement of cash flows that helps users understand management's financing decisions (p. 190).

cash flows from investing activities   The section of the statement of cash flows that helps users understand management's investing decisions (p. 191).

cash flows from operating activities   The first major section of the cash flow statement. It helps users evaluate the cash impact of management's operating decisions (p. 190).

certificates of deposit   Short-term obligations of banks (p. 494).

certified public accountant (CPA)   In the United States, a person earns this designation by meeting standards of both knowledge and integrity set by a State Board of Accountancy. Only CPAs can issue official opinions on financial statements in the United States (p. 25).

charge   A word often used instead of debit (p. 95).

chart of accounts   A numbered or coded list of all account titles (p. 96).

chief executive officer (CEO)   The top manager in an organization (p. 22).

classified balance sheet   A balance sheet that groups the accounts into subcategories to help readers quickly gain a perspective on the company's financial position and to draw attention to certain accounts or groups of accounts (p. 156).

close the books   To transfer the balances in all revenue and expense accounts to retained earnings, which resets the revenue and expense accounts to zero so that they are ready to record the next period's transactions (p. 110).

closing entries   Journal entries that transfer balances in the "temporary" stockholders' equity accounts (revenue and expense accounts) to the "permanent" stockholders' equity account, Retained Earnings (p. 110).

commercial paper   A short-term debt contract issued by prominent companies that borrow directly from investors (p. 389).

common stock   Par value of the stock purchased by common shareholders of a corporation (p. 20).

common stockholders   The owners who have a "residual" ownership in the corporation (p. 21).

common-size statements   Financial statements in which components are expressed as relative percentages (p. 542).

comparability   A characteristic of information produced when all companies use similar concepts and measurements and use them consistently (p. 71).

compensating balances   The required minimum balances a company must keep on deposit designed to partially compensate the bank for providing a loan to the company (p. 258).

completed contract method   Method of recognizing revenue on long-term contracts that delays recognition of both revenue and related expenses until completion of the contract (p. 242).

component depreciation   A depreciation approach required by IFRS where each component of a property, plant, and equipment asset must be depreciated separately if the component cost comprises a significant portion of the total cost (p. 349).

component percentages Elements of financial statements that express each component as a percentage of the total (p. 545).

compound annual growth rate (CAGR) Year-over-year growth rate over a specified period of time (p. 542).

compound entry A transaction that affects more than two accounts (p. 13).

compound interest The interest rate multiplied by a changing principal amount. The principal amount increases each period by the amount of accrued but unpaid interest (p. 423).

comprehensive income Net income plus other comprehensive income that includes all changes in equity except those arising from transactions with stockholders (p. 497).

confirmatory value A quality of information that allows it to confirm or contradict existing expectations (p. 71).

conservatism Selecting methods of measurement that anticipate expenses and liabilities and defer recognition of revenues and assets, yielding lower net income, lower assets, and lower stockholders' equity (p. 150).

consistency Using the same accounting policies and procedures from period to period (p. 71).

consolidated financial statements The financial statements that result when the financial records of two or more separate legal entities are combined into a single set of statements (p. 492).

contingent liability A potential liability that depends on a future event arising out of a past transaction (p. 419).

contra account A separate but related account that offsets or is a deduction from a companion account. An example is accumulated depreciation (p. 105).

contra asset A contra account whose companion account is an asset. A contra asset account has a credit balance. We deduct the balance in the contra asset from an asset account (p. 105).

convertible A characteristic of bonds or preferred stock that gives the owner the option to exchange the bonds or shares of preferred stock for a prespecified number of shares of common stock (p. 458).

convertible bonds Bonds that may, at the holder's option, be exchanged for other securities, usually for a preset number of shares of the issuing company's common stock (p. 395).

copyrights Exclusive rights to reproduce and sell a book, musical composition, film, or similar creative item (p. 362).

corporate proxy A written authority granted by individual shareholders to others (usually members of corporate management) to cast the shareholders' votes (p. 452).

corporation A business organization that is created by individual state laws (p. 17).

correcting entry A journal entry that cancels a previous erroneous entry and adds the correct amounts to the correct accounts (p. 116).

cost of goods available for sale Sum of opening inventory for the period plus purchases during the period (p. 288).

cost of goods sold (cost of sales, cost of revenue) The original acquisition cost of the inventory that a company sells to customers during the reporting period (p. 51).

cost valuation Process of assigning a specific value from the historical-cost records to each item in ending inventory (p. 286).

cost-effectiveness constraint Requirement that standard setting bodies choose rules whose decision-making benefits exceed the costs of providing the information (p. 72).

credit An entry or balance on the right side of any account (p. 95).

creditor A person or entity to whom a company owes money (p. 14).

cross-referencing The process of using numbering, dating, and/or some other form of identification to relate each general ledger posting to the appropriate journal entry (p. 99).

cross-sectional comparisons Comparisons of a company's financial ratios with the ratios of other companies or with industry averages (p. 551).

cumulative A characteristic of preferred stock that requires that undeclared dividends accumulate and the company must pay them before it can pay any dividends to common stockholders (p. 456).

current assets Cash and other assets that a company expects to convert to cash, sell, or consume during the next 12 months or within the normal operating cycle if longer than 1 year (p. 156).

current liabilities Liabilities that come due within the next year or within the normal operating cycle if longer than 1 year. Typically, we expect current liabilities to be paid using assets classified as current (p. 156).

current ratio (working capital ratio) Current assets divided by current liabilities (p. 159).

current replacement cost What it would cost a company to buy an inventory item today (p. 300).

cutoff error Failure to record transactions in the correct time period (p. 303).

data processing The procedures used to record, analyze, store, and report on chosen activities (p. 119).

date of record The date that determines which shareholders will receive a cash dividend (p. 455).

days to collect accounts receivable (average collection period) 365 divided by accounts receivable turnover (p. 257).

debenture A debt security with a general claim against all assets, instead of a specific claim against particular assets (p. 394).

debit An entry or balance on the left side of any account (p. 95).

debt-to-equity ratio Total liabilities divided by total shareholders' equity (p. 420).

debt-to-total-assets ratio Total liabilities divided by total assets (p. 420).

declaration date The date the board of directors formally announces that it will pay a cash dividend. On this date, the dividend becomes a liability (p. 455).

deferred income tax asset An asset arising because the difference between GAAP reporting and tax laws requires companies to pay taxes to the tax authorities before they record income tax expense on the income statement (p. 416).

deferred income tax liability An obligation arising because the difference between GAAP reporting and tax laws requires companies to record income tax expense on the income statement before they are obligated to make payment to the tax authorities (p. 416).

defined benefit pension plan A pension plan where the employer guarantees the employee a specific amount of retirement pay based on factors such as pay earned during final years and total years of service (p. 414).

defined contribution pension plan A pension plan where the employer makes annual contributions directly into a fund belonging to the employee, according to a plan document. The employee's retirement benefit depends on the amount in the fund at retirement (p. 414).

depletion The process of allocating the cost of natural resources to the periods that benefit from their use (p. 342).

depreciable value (depreciable base, allocation base) The cost a company allocates as depreciation over the total useful life of an asset. It is the difference between the total acquisition cost and the estimated residual value (p. 345).

depreciation The systematic allocation of the acquisition cost of long-lived assets to the expense accounts of the particular accounting periods that benefit from the use of the assets (p. 54).

depreciation schedule The list of depreciation amounts for each period of an asset's useful life (p. 346).

dilution Reduction in stockholders' equity per share or EPS that arises from changes among shareholders' proportional interests (p. 469).

direct method A method for computing cash flows from operating activities that subtracts operating cash disbursements from operating cash collections to arrive at cash flows from operations (p. 199).

discontinued operations A component of the business that is distinguishable from the rest of the entity, both operationally and for financial reporting purposes, that a company disposes of or makes plans to dispose of. The results are reported separately, net of tax, on the income statement (p. 564).

discount amortization The spreading of bond discount over the life of the bonds as interest expense (p. 401).

discount rates Interest rates used to compute present values (p. 424).

discounted values Another name for present values (p. 424).

discounting The process of finding the present value (p. 424).

dividend arrearages (dividends in arrears) Accumulated unpaid dividends on preferred stock (p. 456).

dividend-payout ratio Common dividends per share divided by earnings per share (p. 68).

dividend-yield ratio Common dividends per share divided by market price per share (p. 68).

double-declining-balance (DDB) method A common form of accelerated depreciation. It is computed by doubling the straight-line rate and multiplying the resulting DDB rate by the asset's beginning net book value (p. 347).

double-entry system The method usually followed for recording transactions, whereby every transaction affects at least two accounts (p. 92).

early extinguishment When a company chooses to redeem its own bonds before maturity (p. 406).

earnings multiple Another name for the P-E ratio (p. 66).

earnings per share (EPS) Basic EPS is net income divided by the weighted-average number of common shares outstanding during the period over which the net income is measured (p. 65).

EBIT Earnings before interest and taxes (p. 555).

EBIT-to-sales A variation of return on sales computed as earnings before interest and taxes divided by sales (p. 556).

Economic Value Added (EVA) Measure of the residual wealth of a company after deducting its cost of capital from operating profit (p. 559).

effective interest amortization (compound interest method) A method of amortization of bond discounts and premiums whereby each period bears a total interest expense equal to the net liability at the beginning of the period multiplied by the market interest rate in effect when the debt was issued (p. 401).

entity An organization or a section of an organization that stands apart from other organizations and individuals as a separate economic unit (p. 10).

equity method Accounting for an investment at acquisition cost adjusted for the investor's share of dividends and earnings or losses of the investee after the date of investment. Used by investors that have significant influence over, but do not control, the investee (p. 501).

exercise price (strike price) The predetermined price that an employee must pay to purchase a share of stock in a stock option plan (p. 460).

expenditures Purchases of goods or services, whether for cash or credit (p. 342).

expenses Decreases in net assets as a result of consuming or giving up resources in the process of providing products or services to a customer. Expenses decrease owners' equity (p. 48).

explicit transactions Observable events such as cash receipts and disbursements, credit purchases, and credit sales that trigger the majority of day-to-day routine journal entries (p. 142).

extraordinary items Items that are both unusual in nature and infrequent in occurrence that are shown separately, net of tax, on the income statement (p. 564).

F.O.B. destination Seller pays freight costs from the shipping point of the seller to the receiving point of the buyer (p. 290).

F.O.B. shipping point Buyer pays freight costs from the shipping point of the seller to the receiving point of the buyer (p. 290).

face amount (face value) The loan principal or the amount that a borrower promises to repay at a specific maturity date (p. 394).

fair value The value of an asset based on the price for which a company could sell the asset to an independent third party (p. 344).

faithful representation A quality of information that ensures that it captures the economic substance of the transactions, events, or circumstances it describes. It requires information to be complete, neutral, and free from material errors (p. 71).

FASB Accounting Standards Codification A compilation of all standards and other elements of U.S. GAAP into a single searchable database that is organized by topic to make it easy to research financial reporting issues (p. 23).

financial accounting The field of accounting that serves external decision makers, such as stockholders, suppliers, banks, and government agencies (p. 7).

Financial Accounting Standards Board (FASB) The independent private sector body that is responsible for establishing GAAP in the United States (p. 23).

Financial Accounting Standards (U.S. GAAP) The set of GAAP that applies to financial reporting in the United States (p. 23).

financial leverage ratio Ratio of average total assets divided by average total common stockholders' equity. Indicates the proportion of total assets financed by common stockholders relative to those financed by creditors and preferred stockholders (p. 557).

financial management Decisions concerned with where the company gets cash and how it uses that cash to its benefit (p. 555).

financial statement analysis Using financial data to assess some aspect of a company's performance (p. 534).

financing activities A company's transactions that obtain resources by borrowing from creditors or selling shares of stock and use resources to repay creditors or provide a return to shareholders (p. 191).

finished goods inventory The accumulated costs of manufacture for goods that are complete and ready for sale (p. 316).

firm-specific risk The risk that the firm will not repay the loan or will not pay the interest on time (p. 398).

first-in, first-out (FIFO) This method of accounting for inventory assigns the cost of the earliest acquired units to cost of goods sold (p. 294).

fiscal year The year established for accounting purposes, which may differ from the calendar year (p. 47).

Form 10-K A document that U.S. companies file annually with the Securities and Exchange Commission. It contains the companies' financial statements (p. 7).

franchises (licenses) Legal contracts that allow the buyer the right to sell a product or service in accordance with specified conditions (p. 363).

free cash flow Generally defined as net cash flow from operations less capital expenditures (p. 211).

freight in (inward transportation) An additional cost of the goods acquired during the period, which is often shown in the purchases section of an income statement (p. 290).

future value The amount accumulated, including principal and interest (p. 423).

general journal A complete chronological record of an organization's transactions and how each transaction affects the balances in particular accounts (p. 92).

general ledger The collection of all ledger accounts that supports an organization's financial statements (p. 92).

generally accepted accounting principles (GAAP) The term that applies to all the broad concepts and detailed practices to be followed in preparing and distributing financial statements. It includes all the conventions, rules, and procedures that together comprise acceptable accounting practice (p. 23).

generally accepted auditing standards (GAAS) Standards issued by the Public Company Accounting Oversight Board that prescribe the minimum steps that an auditor must take in examining the transactions and financial statements and issuing an auditor's opinion (p. 27).

going concern (continuity) A convention that assumes that an entity will persist indefinitely (p. 72).

goodwill The excess of the amount paid for an acquired company over the fair value of its identifiable net assets (p. 364).

Governmental Accounting Standards Board (GASB) The agency that regulates disclosures for governmental organizations in the United States (p. 31).

gross profit (gross margin) The excess of sales revenue over the cost of the inventory that was sold (p. 164).

gross profit percentage (gross margin percentage) Gross profit (sales revenue – cost of goods sold) divided by sales revenue (p. 166).

gross sales The total amount of sales before deducting returns, allowances, and discounts (p. 242).

held-to-maturity securities Debt securities that the investor purchases with the intent to hold them until maturity (p. 494).

holding gain (inventory profit) Increase in the replacement cost of the inventory held during the current period (p. 311).

impaired When an asset ceases to have economic value to the company at least as large as the book value of the asset (p. 358).

impairment of goodwill Reductions of the goodwill account because the value of the goodwill falls below its current carrying amount. The decrease in value is charged to expense (p. 516).

implicit interest (imputed interest) An interest expense that is not explicitly stated in a loan agreement (p. 407).

implicit transactions Events, such as the passage of time, that do not generate source documents or any visible evidence that the event actually occurred. We do not recognize such events in the accounting records until the end of an accounting period (p. 142).

improvement (betterment, capital improvement) An expenditure that increases the future benefits provided by an existing fixed asset by decreasing its operating cost, increasing its rate of output, improving its safety, reducing its rate of pollution, or prolonging its useful life (p. 353).

imputed interest rate The market interest rate that equates the proceeds from a loan with the present value of the loan payments (p. 407).

income (profits, earnings) The excess of revenues over expenses (p. 48).

income before income tax (earnings before income tax, pretax income) Income before the deduction of income tax expense (p. 149).

income statement (statement of earnings, statement of operations) A report of all revenues and expenses pertaining to a specific time period (p. 57).

indirect method A method for computing cash flows from operating activities that adjusts the previously calculated accrual net income from the income statement to reflect only those income statement activities that involve actual cash receipts and cash disbursements (p. 199).

inflation premium The extra interest that investors require because the general price level may increase between now and the time they receive their money (p. 398).

intangible assets Assets that lack physical substance. They consist of contractual rights, legal rights, or economic benefits. Examples are patents, trademarks, and copyrights (p. 340).

interest The cost the borrower pays the lender to use the principal (p. 422).

interest rate A specified percentage of the principal. It is used to compute the amount of interest (p. 423).

interest-coverage ratio (times-interest-earned ratio) Pretax income plus interest expense divided by interest expense (p. 421).

interim periods The time spans established for accounting purposes that are less than a year (p. 47).

internal control system (internal controls) Checks and balances that ensure all company actions are proper and are consistent with top management's goals and objectives (p. 259).

International Accounting Standards Board (IASB) An international body established to develop, in the public interest, a single set of high-quality, understandable, and enforceable global accounting standards (p. 24).

International Auditing and Assurance Standards Board (IAASB) A body established by the International Federation of Accountants that is working to standardize audit regulation around the globe (p. 27).

International Financial Reporting Standards (IFRS) The set of GAAP that applies to companies reporting in more than 100 countries around the world (p. 23).

inventory Goods held by a company for the purpose of sale to customers (p. 12).

inventory shrinkage Losses of inventory from theft, breakage, or loss (p. 286).

inventory turnover The cost of goods sold divided by the average inventory held during a given period (p. 305).

investing activities Transactions that acquire or dispose of long-lived assets or acquire or dispose of securities held for investment purposes that are not cash equivalents (p. 191).

invoice A bill from the seller to a buyer indicating the number of items shipped, their price, and any additional costs (such as shipping), along with payment terms, if any (p. 389).

issued shares The aggregate number of shares sold to the public (p. 453).

journal entry An analysis of the effects of a transaction on the various accounts, usually accompanied by an explanation (p. 97).

journalizing The process of entering transactions into the general journal (p. 97).

last-in, first-out (LIFO) This inventory method assigns the cost of the most recently acquired units to cost of goods sold (p. 295).

lease A contract whereby an owner (lessor) grants the use of property to a second party (lessee) in exchange for regular payments (p. 408).

leasehold The right to use a fixed asset for a specified period of time beyond 1 year (p. 364).

leasehold improvement Investments by a lessee to add new materials or improvements to a leased property that become part of the leased property and revert to the lessor at the end of the lease (p. 364).

ledger account A listing of all the increases and decreases in a particular account (p. 92).

lessee The party who has the right to use leased property and makes lease payments to the lessor (p. 408).

lessor The owner of property who grants usage rights to the lessee (p. 408).

liabilities Economic obligations of the organization to outsiders, or claims against its assets by outsiders (p. 9).

LIBOR London Interbank Offering Rate, a fluctuating interest rate for loans between banks in London (p. 399).

LIFO layer (LIFO increment) A separately identifiable addition to LIFO inventory at an identifiable cost level (p. 312).

LIFO liquidation A decrease in the physical amount in inventory causing old, low LIFO inventory acquisition costs to become the cost of goods sold, resulting in a high gross profit (p. 312).

LIFO reserve The difference between a company's inventory valued at LIFO and what it would be under FIFO (p. 313).

limited liability A feature of the corporate form of organization whereby corporate creditors (such as banks or suppliers) ordinarily have claims against the corporate assets only, not against the personal assets of the owners (p. 17).

line of credit An agreement with a bank to provide short-term loans up to some predetermined maximum, without significant additional credit checking or other time-consuming procedures (p. 389).

liquidating value The amount a company needs to pay to all preferred stockholders, in addition to any dividends in arrears, before it distributes any assets to common stockholders if the company is liquidated (p. 457).

liquidation Converting assets to cash and paying off outside claims (p. 394).

liquidity An entity's ability to meet its near-term financial obligations with cash and near-cash assets as those obligations become due (p. 159).

long-lived asset An asset that a company expects to use for more than 1 year (p. 11).

long-term-debt-to-total-capital ratio Total long-term debt divided by total shareholders' equity plus total long-term debt (p. 420).

long-term liabilities Obligations that come due more than 1 year after the balance sheet date (p. 388).

long-term solvency An organization's ability to generate enough cash to repay long-term debts as they mature (p. 535).

lower-of-cost-or-market method (LCM) A comparison of the current market price of inventory with its historical cost derived under whichever inventory method the company has adopted. LCM requires reporting the lower of the two as the inventory value (p. 299).

maintenance The routine recurring costs of activities such as oiling, polishing, painting, and adjusting that are necessary to keep a fixed asset in operating condition (p. 353).

management accounting The field of accounting that serves internal decision makers, such as top executives, department heads, college deans, hospital administrators, and people at other management levels within an organization (p. 7).

management discussion and analysis (MD&A) A section of the annual report and 10-K, the content of which is dictated by the SEC, that concentrates on explaining the major changes in operating results, liquidity, and capital resources (p. 541).

market method Method of accounting that reports short-term investments in publicly traded securities in the balance sheet at their fair values. For trading securities changes in market value are included in net income; for available-for-sale securities changes in fair value are included in other comprehensive income (p. 495).

market rate The rate available on investments in similar bonds at a moment in time (p. 396).

market-to-book ratio Market value per share divided by book value per share (p. 475).

marketable securities Notes, bonds, or stocks that can readily be sold on stock exchanges or over-the-counter markets (p. 494).

matching The recording of expenses in the same time period that we recognize the related revenues (p. 53).

materiality A convention that asserts that an item should be included in a financial statement if its omission or misstatement would tend to mislead the reader of the financial statements under consideration (p. 73).

Modified Accelerated Cost Recovery System (MACRS) The underlying basis for computing depreciation for tax purposes (p. 350).

monetary assets Assets that are fixed in terms of units of currency and easily convertible into cash (p. 344).

mortgage bond A form of long-term debt that is secured by the pledge of specific property (p. 394).

moving-average cost method Average cost method used in conjunction with the perpetual inventory system (p. 296).

multiple-step income statement An income statement that contains one or more subtotals that highlight significant relationships (p. 163).

negotiable Legal financial contracts that can be transferred from one lender to another (p. 394).

net assets Assets less liabilities (p. 10).

net income (net earnings) The remainder after deducting all expenses from revenues (p. 57).

net loss The difference between revenues and expenses when expenses exceed revenues (p. 57).

net realizable value The net amount the company expects to receive when it sells the inventory (p. 299).

net sales The total amount of sales after deducting returns, allowances, and discounts (p. 242).

nominal interest rate (contractual rate, coupon rate, stated rate) A contractual rate of interest paid on bonds (p. 394).

noncontrolling interests The claims of nonmajority shareholders in the assets and earnings of a company whose accounts are consolidated into the accounts of the major shareholder (p. 511).

nonmonetary assets Assets that are less liquid than monetary assets and whose price in terms of units of currency is more susceptible to change over time (p. 344).

nonoperating revenues and expenses Revenues and expenses that are not directly related to the mainstream of a firm's operations (p. 164).

nonrecurring items (unusual items) An income statement item that is either unusual in nature or infrequent in occurrence but not both. These items are not expected to happen often for a given firm (p. 563).

notes payable Promissory notes that are evidence of a debt and state the terms of payment (p. 9).

objective of financial reporting To provide information that is useful to present and potential investors and creditors and others in making investment, credit, and similar resource allocation decisions (p. 70).

open account Buying or selling on credit, usually by just an "authorized signature" of the buyer (p. 13).

operating activities Transactions that affect the purchase, processing, and selling of a company's products and services (p. 190).

operating cycle (cash cycle) The time elapsing between the acquisition of goods and services in exchange for cash and the subsequent sale of products to customers, who in turn pay for their purchases with cash (p. 47).

operating expenses A group of recurring expenses that pertain to the firm's routine, ongoing operations (p. 164).

operating income (operating profit, income from operations) Gross profit less all operating expenses (p. 164).

operating lease Leases that should not be recognized as liabilities on the balance sheet, but should be accounted for by the lessee as ordinary rent expenses (p. 409).

operating management Decisions concerned with the day-to-day activities that generate revenues and expenses (p. 555).

ordinary annuity A series of equal cash flows that take place at the end of successive periods of equal length (p. 427).

other comprehensive income (OCI) Changes in stockholders' equity that do not result from net income (net loss) or transactions with shareholders (p. 63).

other postretirement benefits Non-pension benefits provided to retired workers, such as life and health insurance (p. 413).

outstanding shares Issued shares held by the stockholders (p. 453).

owners' equity The owners' claims on an organization's assets, or total assets less total liabilities (p. 9).

paid-in capital The total capital investment in a corporation by its owners, both at and subsequent to the inception of the business (p. 19).

paid-in capital in excess of par value (additional paid-in capital) When issuing stock, the excess of the total amount the company receives for the stock over the par value of the shares (p. 20).

par value (stated value) The nominal dollar amount printed on stock certificates (p. 20).

parent company A company owning more than 50% of the voting shares of another company, called the subsidiary company (p. 504).

participating A characteristic of preferred stock that allows holders of shares to participate in the growth of the company because they share in growing dividends (p. 458).

partnership A form of organization that joins two or more individuals together as co-owners (p. 17).

patents Grants made by the federal government to an inventor, bestowing (in the United States) the exclusive right to produce and sell a given product, or to use a process, for up to 20 years (p. 362).

payment date The date a company pays cash dividends (p. 455).

pensions Payments to former employees after they retire (p. 413).

percentage of accounts receivable method An approach to estimating bad debt expense and uncollectible accounts that bases estimates of uncollectible accounts on the historical percentage of ending accounts receivable that subsequently prove to be uncollectible (p. 253).

percentage of completion method Method of recognizing revenue on long-term contracts as production occurs, rather than waiting until the final product is delivered. The company must also recognize the associated expenses (p. 241).

percentage of sales method An approach to estimating bad debt expense and uncollectible accounts based on the historical relationship between credit sales and uncollectible accounts adjusted for current economic conditions (p. 253).

period costs Expenses supporting a company's operations for a given period. We record these expenses in the time period in which the company incurs them (p. 53).

periodic inventory system An inventory system that computes the cost of goods sold and an updated inventory balance only at the end of an accounting period when the company takes a physical count of inventory (p. 288).

periodicity convention Related to the information characteristic of timeliness, this convention requires that a company break up its economic activity into artificial time periods that will provide timely information to users (p. 73).

permanent differences Differences between net income and taxable income that arise because some revenue or expense items are recognized for either tax or financial reporting purposes, but not for both (p. 416).

perpetual inventory system An inventory system that keeps a continuous record of both inventories on hand and cost of goods sold that helps managers control inventory levels and prepare interim financial statements (p. 286).

physical count The process of identifying, counting, and assigning a specific cost to all items in inventory (p. 286).

posting The transferring of amounts from the general journal to the appropriate accounts in the general ledger (p. 98).

predictive value A quality of information that allows it to help users form their expectations about the future (p. 71).

preemptive rights The right of stockholders to acquire a proportional amount of any new issues of capital stock (p. 452).

preferred stock Stock that offers the stockholder different rights and preferential treatment relative to common stockholders (p. 456).

present value (PV) The value today of a future cash inflow or outflow (p. 424).

pretax and pre-interest return on total assets A version of ROA defined as earnings before interest and taxes divided by average total assets (p. 555).

price-earnings (P-E) ratio Market price per share of common stock divided by earnings per share of common stock (p. 66).

price-earnings growth (PEG) ratio Price-earnings ratio divided by the earnings growth rate (p. 570).

principal The amount borrowed or the amount to be repaid (p. 422).

private accountants Accountants who work for businesses, government agencies, and other nonprofit organizations (p. 25).

private placements Bonds issued by corporations when money is borrowed directly from a financial institution. The general public does not hold or trade such bonds (p. 394).

privately owned (closely held, unlisted) A corporation owned by a family, a small group of shareholders, or a single individual, in which shares of ownership are not publicly sold (p. 18).

pro forma statements A set of projected financial statements or other estimates of predicted results (p. 535).

product costs Costs that are linked with revenues and are charged as expenses when the related revenue is recognized (p. 53).

profitability The ability of a company to provide investors with a particular rate of return on their investment (p. 166).

promissory note A written promise to repay principal plus interest at specific future dates (p. 389).

protective covenant (covenant) A provision in a bond that restricts the ability of the borrower to take certain actions or gives the lender the ability to force early payment under certain conditions (p. 395).

provisions Liabilities of uncertain timing or amount (p. 393).

public accountants Accountants who offer services to the general public on a fee basis (p. 25).

Public Company Accounting Oversight Board (PCAOB) An agency that regulates many aspects of public accounting and sets standards for audit procedures in the United States (p. 27).

publicly traded stock Shares in the ownership of a company that are sold to the public (p. 7).

purchase order A source document that specifies the items ordered and the price to be paid by the ordering company (p. 389).

quick ratio (acid test ratio) Variation of the current ratio that removes less liquid assets from the numerator. Perhaps the most common version of this ratio is (current assets − inventory) ÷ current liabilities (p. 161).

rate of return The return per dollar invested. (p.166)

rate of return on common stockholders' equity (rate of return on equity, ROE, ROCE) Net income less preferred dividends divided by average common equity (p. 474).

raw material inventory The cost of materials held for use in the manufacturing of a product (p. 315).

real interest rate The return that investors demand because they are delaying their consumption (p. 398).

receiving report A source document that specifies the items received by the company and the condition of the items (p. 389).

reconcile a bank statement To verify that the bank balance for cash is in agreement with the accounting records (p. 259).

recoverability test The first step in the asset impairment review process under U.S. GAAP. The test compares the sum of the expected future net cash flows from the use of the asset plus its expected future disposal value with the current carrying value of the asset (p. 359).

recoverable amount Under IFRS, the higher of (1) fair value minus the cost to sell, and (2) the value in use, calculated as the present value of expected future net cash flows (p. 360).

registered public accounting firm An accounting firm that registers with the PCAOB and therefore is allowed to audit companies with publicly traded stock in the United States (p. 27).

relevance The capability of information to make a difference to the decision maker (p. 71).

reliability A quality of information that assures decision makers that the information captures the conditions or events it purports to represent (p. 73).

repairs The occasional costs of restoring a fixed asset to its ordinary operating condition after breakdowns, accidents, or damage (p. 353).

report format A classified balance sheet with the assets at the top (p. 157).

reserve A restriction of dividend-declaring power as denoted by a specific subdivision of retained earnings (p. 473).

residual value (terminal value, disposal value, salvage value, scrap value) The amount a company expects to receive from sale or disposal of a long-lived asset at the end of its useful life (p. 345).

restricted retained earnings (appropriated retained earnings) Any part of retained earnings that companies may not reduce by dividend declarations (p. 473).

restricted stock Stock awarded to employees with certain constraints. These constraints typically prohibit employees from selling the stock until it vests and require employees to forfeit the stock if they leave the company prior to the end of the vesting period (p. 461).

restructuring A significant makeover of part of the company typically involving the closing of plants, firing of employees, and relocation of activities (p. 419).

retailer A company that sells items directly to the public—to individual buyers (p. 304).

retained earnings (retained income) Total cumulative owners' equity generated by income or profits (p. 48).

return on assets ratio (ROA) Net income divided by average total assets (p. 167).

return on common stockholders' equity ratio (ROE or ROCE) Net income divided by invested capital (measured by average common stockholders' equity) (p. 167).

return on sales ratio (profit margin ratio) Net income divided by sales (p. 166).

revenue (sales, sales revenue) The increase in net assets resulting from selling products or services. Revenues increase owners' equity (p. 48).

revenue recognition Criteria for determining whether to record revenue in the financial statements of a given accounting period. To be recognized, revenues must be earned and realized or realizable (p. 52).

reverse stock split A decrease rather than an increase in the number of shares outstanding without changing the total amount of owners' equity (p. 462).

sales allowance (purchase allowance) Reduction of the original selling price (p. 242).

sales returns (purchase returns) Merchandise returned by the customer (p. 242).

Sarbanes-Oxley Act The source of most government regulation of the accounting profession in the United States (p. 27).

Securities and Exchange Commission (SEC) The government agency responsible for regulating capital markets in the United States (p. 7).

short-term debt securities Primarily government- and business-issued notes and bonds with maturities of 1 year or less. May also include certificates of deposit, commercial paper, and U.S. Treasury obligations (p. 494).

short-term equity securities Securities representing ownership interests in other corporations such as common or preferred stock that are held with the intention to liquidate within 1 year (p. 494).

short-term investment A temporary investment of otherwise idle cash in marketable securities (p. 494).

short-term liquidity An organization's ability to meet current payments, such as interest, wages, and taxes, as they become due (p. 535).

simple entry A journal entry for a transaction that affects only two accounts (p. 100).

simple interest The interest rate multiplied by an unchanging principal amount (p. 423).

single-step income statement An income statement that groups all revenues together and then lists and deducts all expenses without reporting any intermediate subtotals (p. 163).

sinking fund A pool of cash or securities set aside for meeting certain obligations (p. 395).

sinking fund bonds Bonds that require the issuer to make annual payments to a sinking fund (p. 395).

sole proprietorship A business with a single owner (p. 17).

source documents The original records supporting any transaction (p. 96).

specific identification method This inventory method concentrates on physically linking the particular items sold with the cost of goods sold that a company reports (p. 294).

specific write-off method (direct write-off method) A method of accounting for bad debt losses that assumes all sales are fully collectible until proven otherwise (p. 249).

stable monetary unit A monetary unit that is not expected to change in value significantly over time. For example, the dollar in the United States, the yen in Japan, and the euro in the European Union (p. 73).

statement of cash flows (cash flow statement) One of the basic financial statements that reports the cash receipts and cash payments of an entity during a particular period and classifies them as financing, investing, and operating cash flows (p. 189).

statement of stockholders' equity (statement of shareholders' equity) A statement that shows all changes during the year in each stockholders' equity account (p. 63).

stock certificate Formal evidence of ownership shares in a corporation (p. 18).

stock dividend Distribution of additional shares to existing shareholders without additional consideration provided by the stockholders. The par value, if any, of the stock is not adjusted (p. 463).

stock options Rights to purchase a specific number of shares of a corporation's capital stock at a predetermined price for a specific time period (p. 460).

stock split Distribution of additional shares to existing stockholders without any additional consideration provided by the stockholders to the firm. The par value, if any, of the stock is adjusted (p. 462).

stockholders' equity (shareholders' equity) Owners' equity of a corporation. The excess of assets over liabilities of a corporation (p. 19).

straight-line depreciation A method that spreads the depreciable value evenly over the useful life of an asset (p. 346).

subordinated debentures Debt securities whose holders have claims against only the assets that remain after satisfying the claims of other, more senior general creditors (p. 394).

subsidiary A corporation owned or controlled by a parent company through the ownership of more than 50% of the voting stock (p. 504).

T-account Device used to portray the individual ledger accounts in the general ledger. Each T-account takes the form of the capital letter T and represents an individual ledger account. We accumulate the transactions that affect a particular ledger account within the related T-account (p. 92).

tangible assets (fixed assets, plant assets) Physical items that can be seen and touched, such as land, buildings, and equipment (p. 340).

tax rate The percentage of taxable income paid to the government (p. 416).

temporary differences Differences between net income and taxable income that arise because some revenue and expense items are recognized at different times for tax purposes than for financial reporting purposes (p. 416).

tender offer A public invitation to all stockholders of a particular class of stock to offer their shares for sale at a specified price, during a specified time, subject to certain conditions (p. 469).

time-series comparisons Comparisons of a company's financial ratios with its own historical ratios (p. 551).

timeliness A characteristic of information that requires information to reach decision makers while it can still influence their decisions (p. 71).

total asset turnover A ratio that measures the sales a company is able to generate for each dollar invested in assets. Computed as: Sales divided by average total assets (p. 556).

trade discounts Reductions to the gross selling price for a particular class of customers (p. 243).

trademarks Distinctive identifications of a manufactured product or of a service, taking the form of a name, a sign, a slogan, a logo, or an emblem (p. 363).

trading on the equity (financial leverage, leveraging, gearing) Using interest-bearing debt to enhance the rate of return on common stockholders' equity (p. 557).

trading securities Short-term investments in equity or debt securities that management intends to resell shortly for short-term profits (p. 494).

transaction Any event that affects the financial position of an entity and that an accountant can reliably record in monetary terms (p. 10).

treasury stock A company's own stock that it has purchased and holds for later use (p. 454).

trend analysis An analysis technique that compares financial trends and changes from one year to the next and identifies patterns that have occurred in the past (p. 537).

trial balance A list of all the accounts in the general ledger together with their balances (p. 96).

turnover Sales or sales revenue (p. 165).

U.S. Treasury obligations Interest-bearing notes, bonds, and bills issued by the federal government (p. 494).

uncollectible accounts (bad debts) Receivables determined to be uncollectible because customers are unable or unwilling to pay their debts (p. 248).

understandability A characteristic of information that requires information to be presented clearly and concisely (p. 71).

underwriters A group of investment bankers that buys an entire bond or stock issue from a corporation and then sells the securities to the general investing public (p. 399).

unearned revenue (revenue received in advance, deferred revenue) Represents cash received from customers who pay in advance for goods or services to be delivered at a future date (p. 144).

units-of-production depreciation (activity method) A depreciation method based on units of service or units of production when physical wear and tear is the dominating influence on the useful life of the asset (p. 347).

unrealized gain (loss) The gain (loss) recognized when the market price of a trading or available-for-sale investment security increases (decreases) (p. 495).

useful life (service life) The shorter of the physical life or the economic life of an asset (p. 345).

verifiability A characteristic of information that can be checked to ensure it is correct (p. 71).

vested options Options that the holders have the power to exercise (p. 460).

warranty A promise to repair or replace a defective product, usually for problems that arise within a specified period of time or usage (p. 392).

weighted-average cost method Average cost method used in conjunction with the periodic inventory system (p. 296).

wholesaler A company that sells in large quantities to retail companies instead of individuals (p. 304).

work in process inventory The cost incurred for partially completed items, including raw materials, labor, and other costs (p. 315).

working capital (net working capital, net current assets) The excess of current assets over current liabilities (p. 157).

write-down A reduction in the recorded historical cost of an item in response to a decline in value (p. 300).

XBRL eXtensible Business Reporting Language, an XML-based computer language that allows easy comparisons across companies (p. 119).

yield to maturity The interest rate at which all contractual cash flows for interest and principal have a present value equal to the current price of the bond (p. 398).

zero coupon bond A bond or note that pays no cash interest payments during its life (p. 406).

Index

COMPANY INDEX

A

B

Photo Credits